Get Connected.

Interactive Presentations

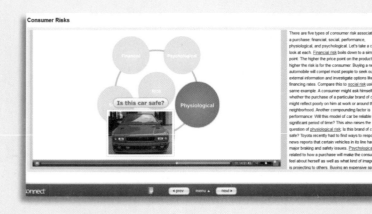

Connect Marketing's **Interactive Presentations** teach each chapter's core learning objectives and concepts through an engaging, hands-on presentation, bringing the text content to life. Interactive Presentations harness the full power of technology to truly engage and appeal to all learning styles. nteractive Presentations are ideal in all class formats—online, face-to-face, or hybrid.

Intelligent Response Technology

Connect Marketing's Interactive Applications offer students a variety of tools to help engage students in application level thinking about the core contents. Interactive Application exercises include: Drag and Drops, Case Analyses, Sequencing, Video Cases, and Decision Generators, which are all autogradable. After completing an activity, students receive immediate feedback and can track their progress through a personalized report, while instructors are provided detailed results on how each student in their course is performing.

Get Engaged.

eBooks

Connect Plus includes a media-rich eBook that allows you to share your notes with your students. Your students can insert and review their own notes, highlight the text, search for specific information, and interact with media resources. Using an eBook with *Connect Plus* gives your students a complete digital solution that allows them to access their materials from any computer.

Lecture Capture

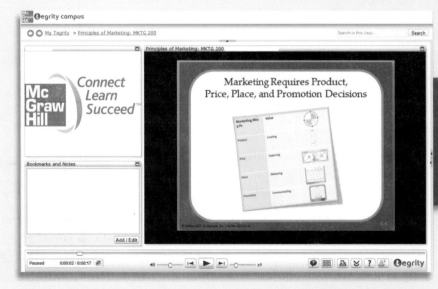

Make your classes available anytime, anywhere. With simple, one-click recording, students can search for a word or phrase and be taken to the exact place in your lecture that they need to review.

Marketing

Marketing is the activity, set of institutions, and processes for creating, *capturing,* communicating, delivering, and exchanging offerings that have value for customers, clients, partners, and society at large.

*The definition of marketing,
the American Marketing Association,*

mhhe.com/gr

Marketing

Fourth Edition

Dhruv Grewal, Ph.D.
Babson College

Michael Levy, Ph.D.
Babson College

McGraw-Hill
Irwin

**McGraw-Hill
Irwin**

MARKETING, FOURTH EDITION

Published by McGraw-Hill/Irwin, a business unit of The McGraw-Hill Companies, Inc., 1221 Avenue of the Americas, New York, NY, 10020. Copyright © 2014 by The McGraw-Hill Companies, Inc. All rights reserved. Printed in the United States of America. Previous editions © 2012, 2010, and 2008. No part of this publication may be reproduced or distributed in any form or by any means, or stored in a database or retrieval system, without the prior written consent of The McGraw-Hill Companies, Inc., including, but not limited to, in any network or other electronic storage or transmission, or broadcast for distance learning.

Some ancillaries, including electronic and print components, may not be available to customers outside the United States.

This book is printed on acid-free paper.

1 2 3 4 5 6 7 8 9 0 DOW/DOW 1 0 9 8 7 6 5 4 3

ISBN   978-0-07-802900-4

MHID   0-07-802900-7

Senior Vice President, Products & Markets: *Kurt L. Strand*
Vice President, General Manager, Products & Markets: *Brent Gordon*
Vice President, Content Production & Technology Services: *Kimberly Meriwether David*
Managing Director: *Paul Ducham*
Executive Brand Manager: *Sankha Basu*
Executive Director of Development: *Ann Torbert*
Senior Development Editor: *Kelly L. Delso*
Marketing Manager: *Donielle Xu*
Lead Project Manager: *Christine A. Vaughan*
Senior Buyer: *Carol A. Bielski*
Senior Designer: *Matt Diamond*
Interior Designer: *Cara Hawthorne*
Cover Designer: *Pam Verros*
Lead Content Licensing Specialist: *Keri Johnson*
Photo Researcher: *Mike Hruby*
Senior Media Project Manager: *Susan Lombardi*
Media Project Manager: *Joyce J. Chappetto*
Typeface: *10/12 Palatino*
Compositor: *Aptara, Inc.*
Printer: *R. R. Donnelley*

All credits appearing on page or at the end of the book are considered to be an extension of the copyright page.

Library of Congress Cataloging-in-Publication Data

Grewal, Dhruv.
    Marketing / Dhruv Grewal, Ph.D., Babson College, Michael Levy, Ph.D., Babson
    College.—Fourth Edition.
       pages cm
    Includes index.
    ISBN-13: 978-0-07-802900-4 (alk. paper)
    ISBN-10: 0-07-802900-7 (alk. paper)
    1. Marketing. I. Levy, Michael, 1950- II. Title.
  HF5415.G6753 2014
  658.8—dc23

                                        2012044583

The Internet addresses listed in the text were accurate at the time of publication. The inclusion of a website does not indicate an endorsement by the authors or McGraw-Hill, and McGraw-Hill does not guarantee the accuracy of the information presented at these sites.

www.mhhe.com

To our families for their never-ending support.

To my wife Diana and my children, Lauren and Alex.

–Dhruv Grewal

To my wife Marcia and daughter Eva.

–Michael Levy

about the authors

Authors Michael Levy (left) and Dhruv Grewal (right).

Dhruv Grewal

Dhruv Grewal Ph.D. (Virginia Tech) is the Toyota Chair in Commerce and Electronic Business and a professor of marketing at Babson College. He was awarded the 2012 Lifetime Achievement Award in Pricing (AMA Retailing & Pricing SIG), the 2010 AMS Cutco/Vector Distinguished Educator Award, the 2010 Lifetime Achievement Award in Retailing (AMA Retailing SIG), and in 2005 the Lifetime Achievement in Behavioral Pricing Award (Fordham University, November 2005). He is a Distinguished Fellow of the Academy of Marketing Science. He was ranked first in the marketing field in terms of publications in the top-six marketing journals during the 1991–1998 period and again for the 2000–2007 period. He has served as VP, research and conferences, American Marketing Association Academic Council (1999–2001), and as VP, development for the Academy of Marketing Science (2000–2002). He was co-editor of *Journal of Retailing* from 2001 to 2007. He co-chaired the 1993 Academy of Marketing Science Conference, the 1998 Winter American Marketing Association Conference, the 2001 AMA doctoral consortium, and the American Marketing Association 2006 Summer Educators Conference.

He has published over 100 articles in journals such as the *Journal of Retailing, Journal of Marketing, Journal of Consumer Research, Journal of Marketing Research*, and *Journal of the Academy of Marketing Science,* as well as other journals. He currently serves on numerous editorial review boards, such as the *Journal of Retailing, Journal of Marketing, Journal of the Academy of Marketing Science, Journal of Interactive Marketing, Journal of Business Research*, and *Journal of Public Policy & Marketing.*

He has won a number of awards for his teaching: 2005 Sherwin-Williams Distinguished Teaching Award, Society for Marketing Advances; 2003 American Marketing Association Award for Innovative Excellence in Marketing Education; 1999 Academy of Marketing Science Great Teachers in Marketing Award; Executive MBA Teaching Excellence Award (1998); School of Business Teaching Excellence Awards (1993, 1999); and Virginia Tech Certificate of Recognition for Outstanding Teaching (1989).

He has taught executive seminars and courses and worked on research projects with numerous firms, such as ExxonMobil, Dell, IRI, TJX, Radio Shack, Telcordia, Khimetriks, Profit-Logic, Monsanto, McKinsey, Ericsson, Council of Insurance Agents & Brokers (CIAB), Met-Life, AT&T, Motorola, Nextel, FP&L, Lucent, Sabre, Goodyear Tire & Rubber Company, Sherwin Williams, Esso International, Asahi, and numerous law firms. He has taught seminars in the United States, Europe, and Asia.

Michael Levy

Michael Levy Ph.D. (Ohio State University) is the Charles Clarke Reynolds Professor of Marketing and director of the Retail Supply Chain Institute at Babson College. He received his Ph.D. in business administration from The Ohio State University and his undergraduate and M.S. degrees in business administration from the University of Colorado at Boulder. He taught at Southern Methodist University before joining the faculty as professor and chair of the marketing department at the University of Miami.

Professor Levy was recognized for 25 years of dedicated service to the editorial review board of the *Journal of Retailing* in 2011. He won the McGraw-Hill Corporate Achievement Award for Grewal-Levy *Marketing 2e* with *Connect* in the category of excellence in content and analytics (2010), Revision of the Year for *Marketing 2e* (Grewal/Levy) from McGraw-Hill/Irwin (2010), the Babson Faculty Scholarship Award (2009), and the Distinguished Service Award, *Journal of Retailing* (2009) (at winter AMA). He was rated as one of the best researchers in marketing in a survey published in *Marketing Educator* (Summer 1997.) He has developed a strong stream of research in retailing, business logistics, financial retailing strategy, pricing, and sales management. He has published over 50 articles in leading marketing and logistics journals, including the *Journal of Retailing, Journal of Marketing, Journal of the Academy of Marketing Science*, and *Journal of Marketing Research*. He currently serves on the editorial review boards of the *Journal of Retailing, International Journal of Logistics Management, International Journal of Logistics and Materials Management*, and *European Business Review*. He is co-author of *Retailing Management*, 8e (2012), the best-selling college-level retailing text in the world. Professor Levy was co-editor of the *Journal of Retailing* from 2001 to 2007. He co-chaired the 1993 Academy of Marketing Science conference and the 2006 summer AMA conference.

Professor Levy has worked in retailing and related disciplines throughout his professional life. Prior to his academic career, he worked for several retailers and a housewares distributor in Colorado. He has performed research projects with many retailers and retail technology firms, including Accenture, Federated Department Stores, Khimetrics (SAP), Mervyn's, Neiman Marcus, ProfitLogic (Oracle), Zale Corporation, and numerous law firms.

Building From Experience

Marketing, **Fourth Edition,** builds from Dhruv Grewal's and Michael Levy's experiences in the classroom and in the marketplace and interacting with marketing instructors and students. Six essential features that the Fourth Edition is built upon are highlighted below:

Learning Orientation: Each chapter features Learning Objectives at the outset (icons that relate the learning objectives to the chapter content); Check Yourself questions at the end of each section; and a Summing Up review of the learning objectives, Marketing Application questions, and Quiz Yourself questions at the end of the chapter.

Student Focused: The text content is engaging and provides illustrations that are highly relevant to students. The content is presented in a visual fashion to facilitate learning.

State-of-the-Art Instructor's Resources: The monthly newsletter continues to gain rave reviews. Each newsletter highlights 10–12 current marketing applications and provides appropriate discussion questions and answers and links to interesting ads and videos. Additionally, it provides PowerPoint slides on this content and have also organized the newsletter by chapter for ease of use and archiving purposes. This will enable instructors to deliver state-of-the-art marketing content on a daily basis.

Applying Concepts: Comprehensive frameworks that organize key concepts are presented in each chapter. These frameworks integrate essential marketing concepts and content with emerging concepts and content.

Interactive Technology: Interactive Toolkits, Interactive Presentations, Applications, and LearnSmart, all based in *Connect* make *Marketing,* Fourth Edition the most comprehensive and usable marketing book (augmented by its ancillaries) in the marketplace.

Assessment: To aid in self-assessment of how they are doing, students can use Check Yourself questions at the end of each section, Quiz Yourself questions at chapter end, Practice Quizzes on the book's student Web site, instructor-created quizzes on *Connect,* or the continuous learning and assessment provided by LearnSmart.

New to the Fourth Edition

Some exciting new additions in the Fourth Edition include:

1. New! Chapter 3 covers social and mobile marketing. The chapter starts with a discussion of a recognized leader in the social media space, Dell, and then circles back to discuss Dell in the concluding case study. This new chapter centers on five learning objectives:

   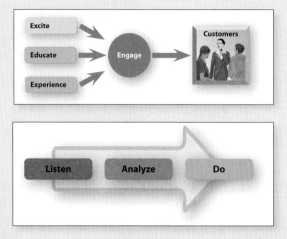

   - Describe the 4E framework of social media marketing. This new framework explains how excitement, education, experience, and engagement are needed for successful social media marketing.
   - Understand the types of social media.
   - Understand the types of mobile applications.
   - Recognize and understand the three components of a social media strategy: listen, analyze, and do.
   - Understand the methods for marketing oneself using social media.

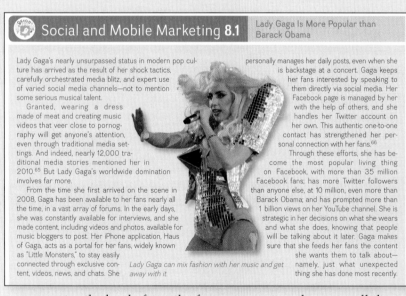

Social and Mobile Marketing 8.1 — Lady Gaga Is More Popular than Barack Obama

Lady Gaga's nearly unsurpassed status in modern pop culture has arrived as the result of her shock tactics, carefully orchestrated media blitz, and expert use of varied social media channels—not to mention some serious musical talent.

Granted, wearing a dress made of meat and creating music videos that veer close to pornography will get anyone's attention, even through traditional media settings. And indeed, nearly 12,000 traditional media stories mentioned her in 2010.[65] But Lady Gaga's worldwide domination involves far more.

From the time she first arrived on the scene in 2008, Gaga has been available to her fans nearly all the time, in a vast array of forums. In the early days, she was constantly available for interviews, and she made content, including videos and photos, available for music bloggers to post. Her iPhone application, Haus of Gaga, acts as a portal for her fans, widely known as "Little Monsters," to stay easily connected through exclusive content, videos, news, and chats. She

personally manages her daily posts, even when she is backstage at a concert. Gaga keeps her fans interested by speaking to them directly via social media. Her Facebook page is managed by her with the help of others, and she handles her Twitter account on her own. This authentic one-to-one contact has strengthened her personal connection with her fans.[66]

Through these efforts, she has become the most popular living thing on Facebook, with more than 35 million Facebook fans; has more Twitter followers than anyone else, at 10 million, even more than Barack Obama; and has prompted more than 1 billion views on her YouTube channel. She is strategic in her decisions on what she wears and what she does, knowing that people will be talking about it later. Gaga makes sure that she feeds her fans the content she wants them to talk about—namely, just what unexpected thing she has done most recently.

Lady Gaga can mix fashion with her music and get away with it.

2. Considering the importance of social and mobile marketing, each chapter includes a relevant box or related material beyond the information included in the new chapter.

3. The book highlights the American Marketing Association's definition of marketing: "Marketing is the activity, set of institutions, and processes for creating, capturing, communicating, delivering, and exchanging offerings that have value for customers, clients, partners, and society at large." The strategic thrust of this definition of marketing—as value creation—permeates the book, from the frozen yogurt on the cover all the way to the final summary at the end. For example, Chapter 1 centers on one of the most popular activities for a hot summer day: eating frozen desserts. The chapter opener talks about how a number of food chains, including Red Mango, an increasingly popular frozen yogurt destination, have created value for their customers. A new video describes how Red Mango creates value. Finally, the chapter concludes with a new case study highlighting the wars between Pinkberry and Red Mango, to remind students of the links with the chapter opener and the cover concept.

4. Further emphasizing the importance of value, each chapter of this text includes at least one Adding Value box that highlights how a particular firm has added value for its customers. Many of these boxes are new to this edition.

5. Substantive changes to Chapter 8, Segmentation, Targeting, and Positioning, ensure that students can understand exactly how firms create their value proposition; the chapter also provides a step-by-step description of perceptual maps.

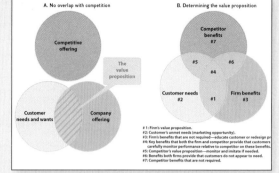

6. In a streamlined Chapter 4, all ethical dilemma vignettes have been moved to an appendix to improve the readability of the chapter. This edition continues to emphasize the importance of ethics and societal issues with Ethical and Societal Dilemma boxes included throughout the text.

7. Each chapter offers key learning objectives at the start; learning objective numbered icons then appear adjacent to the appropriate material in the chapter. The same objectives also are reviewed at the end of each chapter and link the material to the online connect and learning tools on *Connect Marketing*, such as various toolkits and LearnSmart. These online tools greatly facilitate student learning.

8. As the U.S. economy continues to move toward a service economy, this text adapts accordingly, by offering additional service examples woven throughout the text. Many examples are highlighted as Superior Service boxes in each chapter. In addition, the text offers a complete chapter devoted to services (Chapter 13).

9. All chapter-opener examples are new. The illustrations have been carefully chosen to resonate with college students and increase their engagement with marketing content. The end-of-chapter case studies are either new or have been updated. For example, the Chapter 5 case pertains to Seventh Generation's environmentally friendly cleaning products and its long-term goals in the marketing environment.

12. Marketing practitioners and scholars have recognized the need to incorporate marketing metrics into their planning processes. A number of marketing metrics (e.g., customer lifetime value, return on investment) are discussed. Some metrics, such as break-even analysis and customer lifetime value, have been combined with related online tools that instructors can use to demonstrate the concepts, and students can then use the tools to practice these concepts.

13. In Chapter 16, a new discussion details how a firm's channel and supply chain management drive its success. Additional channel concepts are discussed, including channel conflict and push versus pull strategies. Top franchise operations are highlighted in a new exhibit.

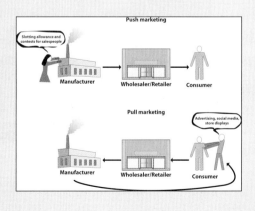

Marketing, Fourth Edition, thus reflects not only the current trends in the marketplace but also the needs of both instructors and students. During the writing and revising of this book, as well as earlier editions, the authors have sought the advice and expertise of hundreds of marketing and educational professionals and have taken their guidance to heart. They are grateful to the hundreds of individuals who participated in the focus groups, surveys, and personal conversations that helped mold this book, and they hope that you enjoy the results.

More Teaching

 **McGraw-Hill *Connect Marketing***

Less Managing. More Teaching. Greater Learning.

McGraw-Hill *Connect Marketing* is an online assignment and assessment solution that connects students with the tools and resources they need to achieve success.

McGraw-Hill *Connect Marketing* helps prepare students for their future by prompting them to complete homework in preparation for class, master concepts, and review for exams.

Sales Promotion: Getting a Good Deal

Business-to-business sales promotion techniques

Consumer sales promotion techniques

1 of 1   1 - Sales Promotion: Getting a Good

Product Placements

Product placements show products in television shows and movies.

3 of 6   3 - Product Placements

Interactive Presentations

Specific to this textbook, the interactive presentations in *Connect* are engaging, online, professional presentations covering the same learning objectives and concepts directly from the chapters. Interactive presentations teach students the core learning objectives in a multimedia format, bringing the content of the course to life. Instructors can assign this content for a grade, meaning students come to class with better knowledge of chapter material. Interactive presentations are a great prep tool for students—and when students are better prepared, they are more engaged and more participative in class.

Greater Learning

Adapt

McGraw-Hill's LearnSmart is an adaptive learning system designed to help students learn faster, study more efficiently, and retain more knowledge for greater success.

Empower

LearnSmart is the premier learning system designed to effectively assess a student's knowledge of course content through a series of adaptive questions, intelligently pinpointing concepts the student does not understand and mapping out a personalized study plan for success. LearnSmart prepares students, allowing instructors to focus valuable class time on higher-level concepts.

Enable

LearnSmart adaptively assesses students' skill levels to determine which topics students have mastered and which require further practice by way of a personalized learning assessment. It offers at-a-glance views of student strengths and weaknesses and prepares students for up-coming lectures or exams, while providing instructors with comprehensive reports of student performance by individual, topic, or learning objective to help gauge for student learning.

Interactive Learning

Connect Interactive Applications

Engaging students beyond simply reading and recall, students practice key concepts by *applying* them with these textbook-specific interactive exercises in every chapter.

Critical thinking makes for a higher level of learning. Each interactive application is designed to reinforce key topics and further increase student understanding. Students walk away from interactive applications with more practice and better understanding than simply reading the chapter. All interactive applications are automatically scored and entered into the instructor gradebook.

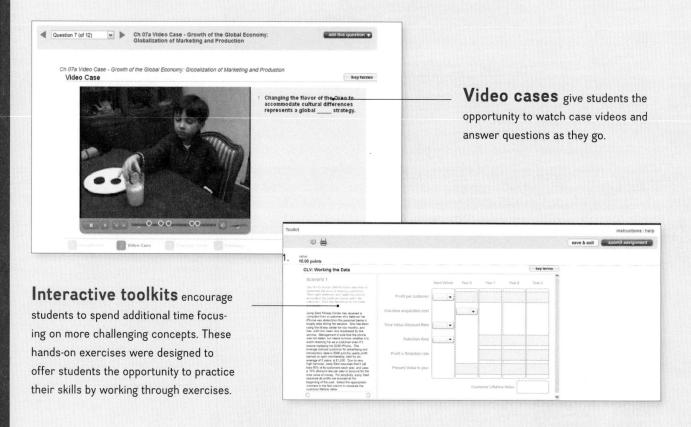

Video cases give students the opportunity to watch case videos and answer questions as they go.

Interactive toolkits encourage students to spend additional time focusing on more challenging concepts. These hands-on exercises were designed to offer students the opportunity to practice their skills by working through exercises.

Decision generators require students to make real business decisions based on specific real world scenarios and cases.

Self-assessments allow students to evaluate skills and assess personal progress.

Case analyses encourage students to read though a case, choose the best answer, and determine if they agree with the strategy that is generated based on their choices. This exercise allows students to demonstrate analytical and critical-thinking skills.

Applying Concepts

Online Learning Center (www.mhhe.com/grewal4e)

The Online Learning Center helps students use *Marketing*, fourth edition, effectively.

Some features on the website are:

- **Self-quizzes** – quizzes focusing on key concepts and providing immediate feedback offer students the opportunity to determine their level of understanding.

- **Marketer's Showdown** – nine cases focusing on up-to-the-minute issues in the music, automotive, and soft drink industries. These cases are designed to allow students to analyze the marketing problem, choose a proposed solution, and then watch their proposal debated by marketing professionals. After the debate, students have the opportunity to change their plan or stick to their guns, then see the outcome of their decisions.

Student-Focused Features

Chapter Opening Vignettes focusing on well-known companies draw students into a discussion about some of the challenges these companies face.

Check Yourself

Questions positioned throughout the chapter after key points allow students to stop and think about what they have learned.

CHECK YOURSELF

1. What are the various components of a marketing strategy?
2. List the four macro strategies that can help a firm develop a sustainable competitive advantage.

THE MARKETING PLAN

LO2 Describe t
a marketi

Effective marketing doesn't just happen. Firms like Nike and adidas carefully plan their marketing strategies to react to changes in the environment, the competition, and their customers by creating a marketing plan. A **marketing plan** is a written document composed of an analysis of the current marketing situation, opportuni-

Real-World Examples

are used to illustrate concepts throughout the text. The authors give students the opportunity to think about how concepts are used in their everyday life. This is shown through various boxed elements:

- **Adding Value** – illustrate how companies add value not only in providing products and services, but in making contributions to society.

- **Ethical & Societal Dilemmas** – emphasize the role of marketing in society.

- **Social and Mobile Marketing** – discuss how social media are used in marketing products.

- **Superior Service** – highlight the emerging role of the service industry.

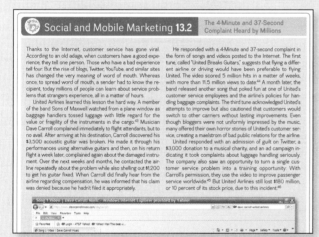

End-of-Chapter Materials

include summary sections organized by chapter learning objective, designed to revisit and reinforce key concepts. Key Terms include definitions and page references for the chapter, and a master list of key terms with definitions can be found at the back of the text. Marketing Applications ask students to consider what they have learned in the chapter to answer essay-style questions. Quiz Yourself questions allow students to test their knowledge by answering chapter-specific questions and checking their skill level against the answer key provided in the back of the text. Net Savvy activities encourage students to go to the Web to research and/or write about a particular company or current practices. End-of-chapter cases are designed to help students develop analytical, critical thinking, and technology skills.

Marketing Applications

Each chapter concludes with eight to eleven Marketing Applications. These essay-style questions determine whether students have grasped the concepts covered in each chapter by asking them to apply what they have learned to marketing scenarios that are relevant to their lives.

Innovative Instructor Resources

Do More

McGraw-Hill Higher Education and Blackboard have teamed up. What does this mean for you?

1. **Your life, simplified.** Now you and your students can access McGraw-Hill's *Connect* right from within your Blackboard course—all with one single sign-on. Say goodbye to the days of logging in to multiple applications.

2. **Deep integration of content and tools.** Not only do you get single sign-on with *Connect*, but you also get deep integration of McGraw-Hill content and content engines right in Blackboard. Whether you're choosing a book for your course or building *Connect* assignments, all the tools you need are right where you want them—inside of Blackboard.

3. **Seamless gradebooks.** Are you tired of keeping multiple gradebooks and manually synchronizing grades into Blackboard? We thought so. When a student completes an integrated *Connect* assignment, the grade for that assignment automatically (and instantly) feeds your Blackboard grade center.

4. **A solution for everyone.** Whether your institution is already using Blackboard or you just want to try Blackboard on your own, we have a solution for you. McGraw-Hill and Blackboard can now offer you easy access to industry leading technology and content, whether your campus hosts it, or we do. Be sure to ask your local McGraw-Hill representative for details.

Student progress tracking

Connect keeps instructors informed about how each student, section, and class is performing, allowing for more productive use of lecture and office hours. The progress-tracking function enables instructors to:

- view scored work immediately and track individual or group performance with assignment and grade reports.

- access an instant view of student or class performance relative to learning objectives.

- collect data and generate reports required by many accreditation organizations, such as AACSB.

Click a subcategory to view **section** details

expand all | collapse all   export to excel 🖾   🖨

AACSB	# questions	# times submitted	# students submitted	category score
▼ AACSB: Analytic	15	2727	25/25	46.11%
Cumulative Quiz-Chapters 1,2,3 (Graded)	6	450	25/25	14.27%
Homework-Chapter 3 Part 2 (Graded)	6	1512	25/25	63.17%
Homework-Chapter 3 Part 1 (Graded)	3	765	25/25	59.2%
▶ AACSB: Reflective Thinking	26	4995	25/25	39.65%

Bloom's	# questions	# times submitted	# students submitted	category score
▼ Bloom's: Analysis	21	4074	25/25	28.42%
Cumulative Quiz-Chapters 1,2,3 (Graded)	7	525	25/25	13.96%
Homework-Chapter 3 Part 2 (Graded)	7	1764	25/25	41.74%
Homework-Chapter 3 Part 1 (Graded)	7	1785	25/25	24.99%
▶ Bloom's: Application	1	255	25/25	58.43%
▶ Bloom's: Comprehension	7	1239	25/25	58.0%
▶ Bloom's: Knowledge	12	2154	25/25	43.39%

McGraw-Hill *Connect Plus Marketing*

McGraw-Hill reinvents the textbook learning experience for the modern student with *Connect Plus Marketing*. A seamless integration of an e-book and *Connect*, *Connect Plus Marketing* provides all of the *Connect* features plus the following:

- An integrated e-book, allowing for anytime, anywhere online access to the textbook.

- Dynamic links between the problems or questions assigned to students and the location in the e-book where that problem or question is covered.

- Powerful search function to pinpoint and connect key concepts in a snap.

In short, *Connect Marketing* offers instructors and students powerful tools and features that optimize time and energy, enabling instructors to focus on course content, teaching, and student learning. Offering a wealth of content resources for instructors and students, this state-of-the-art interactive system supports instructors in preparing students for the world that awaits with adaptive engaging textbook-specific online content.

For more information about *Connect,* go to **connect.mcgraw-hill.com**, or contact your local McGraw-Hill sales representative.

CourseSmart LearnSmart. Choose Smart.

CourseSmart is a new way for faculty to find and review e-textbooks. It's also a great option for students who are interested in accessing their course materials digitally and saving money.

CourseSmart offers thousands of the most commonly adopted textbooks across hundreds of courses from a wide variety of higher education publishers. It is the only place for faculty to review and compare the full text of a textbook online, providing immediate access without the environmental impact of requesting a print exam copy.

With the CourseSmart e-textbook, students can save up to 45 percent off the cost of a print book, reduce their impact on the environment, and access powerful Web tools for learning. CourseSmart is an online e-textbook, which means users access and view their textbook online when connected to the Internet. Students can also print sections of the book for maximum portability. CourseSmart e-textbooks are available in one standard online reader with full text search, notes, and highlighting, and e-mail tools for sharing notes between classmates. For more information on CourseSmart, go to **http://www.coursesmart.com**.

Traditional Instructor Resources

Online Learning Center for Instructors
www.mhhe.com/grewal4e

The Online Learning Center offers instructors a one-stop, secure site for essential course materials, allowing instructors to save prep time before class. The instructor's site offers:

- Instructor's Manual
- PowerPoint Presentations
- Test bank/EZ Test
- Newsletters
- Marketer's Showdown

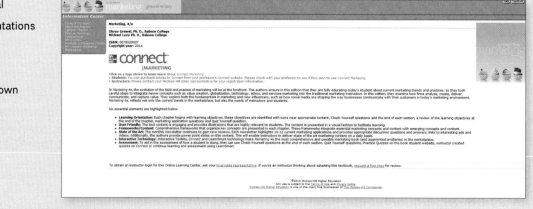

Instructor's Resource CD (IRCD):

This CD contains the Instructor's Manual containing everything an instructor needs to prepare a lecture, including lecture outlines, discussion questions, and links to each chapter's PowerPoint slides, test bank and computerized test bank (including multiple choice, short answer, essay, and application questions), and PowerPoint slides (including exhibits and images from the text as well as additional lecture support materials). The Online Learning Center contains a basic version of the media-enhanced PowerPoint presentations that are found on the IRCD. The media-enhanced version has video and commercials embedded into the presentations and makes for an engaging and interesting classroom lecture.

Video DVD:

A selection of 18 case videos, including 8 brand new videos for this edition, that tie directly to the material covered in the text. Based on feedback received from contact with over 100 instructors, these videos are five to six minutes in length each, instead of the usual 12- to 15-minute videos in many other supplement packages. The shorter videos are much easier for instructors to implement in their courses.

Monthly Newsletter

Each month instructors using *Marketing*, Fourth Edition will receive a newsletter which includes many of the hottest topics in marketing today. Each newsletter contains 8–10 articles, videos, and podcasts on the latest happenings in the marketing discipline, with abstracts and a guide that explains where the information can be implemented in an instructor's course. The content of the newsletter is also posted at **www.grewallevymarketing.com.** This website provides faculty and students with an opportunity to read the various abstracts, post comments, and search by topic or chapter.

Marketing Plan Pro

Marketing Plan Pro is the most widely used marketing plan software program in the industry, and it includes everything students need to create professional, complete, and accurate marketing plans. Marketing Plan Pro can be packaged with *Marketing*, Fourth Edition for a nominal fee.

Responding to Learning Needs

CREATE

Instructors can now tailor their teaching resources to match the way they teach! With McGraw-Hill Create, **www.mcgrawhillcreate.com**, instructors can easily rearrange chapters, combine material from other content sources, and quickly upload and integrate their own content, like course syllabus or teaching notes. Find the right content in Create by searching through thousands of leading McGraw-Hill textbooks. Arrange the material to fit your teaching style. Order a Create book and receive a complimentary print review copy in 3–5 business days or a complimentary electronic review copy (eComp) via e-mail within an one hour. Go to **www.mcgrawhillcreate.com** today and register.

Tegrity Campus: Lectures 24/7

Tegrity Campus is a service that makes class time available 24/7 by automatically capturing every lecture in a searchable format for students to review when they study and complete assignments. With a simple one-click start-and-stop process, you capture all computer screens and corresponding audio. Students can replay any part of any class with easy-to-use browser-based viewing on a PC or Mac.

Educators know that the more students can see, hear, and experience class resources, the better they learn. In fact, studies prove it. With patented Tegrity "search anything" technology, students instantly recall key class moments for replay online, or on iPods and mobile devices. Instructors can help turn all their students' study time into learning moments immediately supported by their lecture.

To learn more about Tegrity, watch a 2-minute Flash demo at **http://tegritycampus .mhhe.com.**

Assurance of Learning Ready

Many educational institutions today are focused on the notion of assurance of learning, an important element of some accreditation standards. *Marketing* is designed specifically to support instructors' assurance of learning initiatives with a simple, yet powerful solution.

Each test bank question for *Marketing* maps to a specific chapter learning outcome/objective listed in the text. Instructors can use our test bank software, EZ Test and EZ Test Online, or *Connect Marketing* to easily query for learning outcomes/objectives that directly relate to the learning objectives for their course. Instructors can then use the reporting features of EZ Test to aggregate student results in similar fashion, making the collection and presentation of assurance of learning data simple and easy.

AACSB Statement

The McGraw-Hill Companies is a proud corporate member of AACSB International. Understanding the importance and value of AACSB accreditation, *Marketing*, Fourth Edition, recognizes the curricula guidelines detailed in the AACSB standards for business accreditation by connecting selected questions in the text and the test bank to the six general knowledge and skill guidelines in the AACSB standards.

The statements contained in *Marketing*, Fourth Edition, are provided only as a guide for the users of this textbook. The AACSB leaves content coverage and assessment within the purview of individual schools, the mission of the school, and the faculty. While *Marketing*, Fourth Edition, and the teaching package make no claim of any specific AACSB qualification or evaluation, we have within *Marketing*, Fourth Edition, labeled selected questions found throughout the supplementary materials according to the six general knowledge and skills areas.

McGraw-Hill Customer Care Contact Information

At McGraw-Hill, we understand that getting the most from new technology can be challenging. That's why our services don't stop after you purchase our products. You can e-mail our product specialists 24 hours a day to get product training online. Or you can search our knowledge bank of frequently asked questions on our support website. For customer support, call **800-331-5094**, e-mail **hmsupport@mcgraw-hill.com**, or visit **www.mhhe.com/support**. One of our technical support analysts will be able to assist you in a timely fashion.

acknowledgments

We would like to acknowledge the considerable contributions of Elisabeth Nevins Caswell, Scott Motyka (Babson College), Kate Woodworth, and Laurie Covens for their help throughout the development of this edition of *Marketing*.

We wish to express our sincere appreciation to Leroy Robinson of University of Houston–Clear Lake for preparing the instructor's manual and the PowerPoint slides, Melissa Martin of George Mason Community College for the test bank, and Kelly Luchtman for the video production. The support, expertise, and occasional coercion from our executive editor Sankha Basu, and development editor Kelly Delso are greatly appreciated. The book would also never have come together without the editorial and production staff at McGraw-Hill/Irwin: Donielle Xu, marketing manager; Christine Vaughan, lead project manager; Matt Diamond, designer; Keri Johnson, lead content licensing specialist; Mike Hruby, photo researcher; Sue Lombardi and Joyce Chappetto, media project managers; and Carol Bielski, senior buyer.

Our colleagues in industry have been invaluable in providing us with case, video, advertising, and photo materials.

Over the years, we have had the opportunity to work with many talented and insightful colleagues. We have benefited from our research and discussions with them. Some of these colleagues are: Ross Petty, Danna Greenberg, Kate McKone-Sweet, Nancy Dlott, and Anne Roggeveen (Babson College); Larry D. Compeau (Clarkson University); Rajesh Chandrashekaran (Fairleigh Dickinson University); Jeanne S. Munger (University of Southern Maine); Arun Sharma, A. Parasuraman, R. Krishnan, Howard Marmorstein, Anuj Mehrotra, and Michael Tsiros (all from University of Miami); Rob Palmatier (University of Washington); Praveen Kopalle, Scott Neslin, and Kusum Ailawadi (Dartmouth); Robert Peterson (University of Texas at Austin); Don Lehmann (Columbia); Ruth Bolton, Steve Brown, and Terry Bristol (Arizona State University); Julie Baker and William Cron (Texas Christian University); Venkatesh Shankar, and Manjit Yadav (Texas A&M); Jerry Gotlieb (University of Western Kentucky); Hooman Estelami (Fordham University); Rajiv Dant and Ken Evans (University of Oklahoma); Monika Kukar Kinney and Kent Monroe (University of Richmond); Ronnie Goodstein (Georgetown); Anthony Miyazaki and Walfried Lassar (Florida International University); Gopal Iyer (Durham University) and Tamara Mangleburg (Florida Atlantic University); David Hardesty (University of Kentucky); M. Joseph Sirgy, Julie Ozanne, and Ed Fern (Virginia Tech); Merrie Brucks and Ajith Kumar (University of Arizona); Valerie Folkes (University of Southern California); Carolyn Costley (University of Waikato); William Dodds (Ft. Lewis College); Ramon Avila (Ball State University); Douglas M. Lambert and Walter Zinn (The Ohio State University); Joan Lindsey-Mullikin and Norm Borin (Cal Poly San Luis Obispo); Abhijit Biswas, Abhijit Guha, and Sujay Dutta (Wayne State University); Wagner Kamakura (Duke); Raj Srivastava (Emory); Cheryl Nikata (University of Illinois, Chicago); K. Sivakumar (Lehigh University); Namwoon Kim (Hong Kong Polytechnic University); Raj Suri (Drexel); Jean-Charles Chebat (HEC Montreal); Thomas Rudolph (St. Gallen University); Zhen Zhu (Suffolk University); A. C. Samli (University of North Florida); Adam Rapp (University of Alabama); Lauren S. Beitelspacher (Portland State University); Nancy M. Puccinelli (Oxford University); Keith Wilcox (Columbia); Ko de Ruyter, Martin Wetzels, and Dominik Mahr (Maastricht University); and Jens Nordfält (Stockholm School of Economics).

For their contributions to the first edition of *Marketing,* we gratefully acknowledge:

Dennis Arnett
Texas Tech University

Laurie Babin
University of Louisiana at Monroe

Ainsworth Bailey
University of Toledo

Joyce Banjac
Myers University

Harvey Bauman
Lees McRae College

Oleta Beard
University of Washington

Sandy Becker
Rutgers Business School

Ellen Benowitz
Mercer County Community College

Gary Benton
Western Kentucky University

Joseph Ben-Ur
University of Houston at Victoria

Patricia Bernson
County College of Morris

Harriette Bettis-Outland
University of West Florida

Parimal Bhagat
Indiana University of Pennsylvania

Jan Bingen
Little Priest Tribal College

John Bishop
University of South Alabama–Mobile

Nancy Bloom
Nassau Community College

Claire Bolfing
James Madison University

Karen Bowman
University of California

Tom Boyd
California State University–Fullerton

Nancy Boykin
Tarleton State University

Cathy Brenan
Northland Community and Technical College

Martin Bressler
Houston Baptist University

Claudia Bridges
California State University

Greg Broekemier
University of Nebraska Kearney

Gary Brunswick
Northern Michigan University

John Buzza
Monmouth University

Rae Caloura
Johnson & Wales University

Michaelle Cameron
St. Edwards University

Lindell Chew
Linn University of Missouri

Dorene Ciletti
Duquesne University

Terry Clark
Southern Illinois University–Carbondale

Joyce Claterbos
University of Kansas

Gloria Cockerell
Collin County College

Paul Cohen
Florida Atlantic University

Mark E. Collins
University of Tennessee

Clare Comm
University of Massachusetts, Lowell

Sherry Cook
Southwest Missouri State University

Stan Cort
Case Western Reserve University

Keith Cox
University of Houston

Ian Cross
Bentley College

Geoffrey Crosslin
Kalamazoo Valley Community College

Joseph DeFilippe
Suffolk County Community College

George Deitz
University of Memphis

Kathleen DeNisco
Erie Community College

Tilokie Depoo
Monroe College

Monique Doll
Macomb Community College

Kimberly Donahue
Indiana University–Purdue University at Indianapolis

Jim D'Orazio
Cleveland State University

James Downing
University of Illinois–Chicago

Michael Drafke
College of DuPage

Leon Dube
Texas A & M University

Colleen Dunn
Bucks County Community College

John Eaton
Arizona State University–Tempe

Nancy Evans
New River Community College

Keith Fabes
Berkeley College

Tina Facca
John Carroll University

Joyce Fairchild
Northern Virginia Community College

David J. Faulds
University of Louisville

Larry Feick
University of Pittsburgh

Karen Flaherty
Oklahoma State University–Stillwater

Leisa Flynn
Florida State University

William Foxx
Auburn University

Douglas Friedman
Penn State University

Stanley Garfunkel
Queensborough Community College

S. J. Garner
Eastern Kentucky University

David Gerth
Nashville State Community College

Peggy Gilbert
Missouri State University

Kelly Gillerlain
Tidewater Community College

Jana Goodrich
Penn State Behrend

Robin Grambling
University of Texas at El Paso

Kimberly D. Grantham
University of Georgia

James I. Gray
Florida Atlantic University

Kelly Gredone
Bucks County Community College

Michael Greenwood
Mount Wachusett Community College

Barbara Gross
California State University–Northridge

David Grossman
Florida Southern College

Hugh Guffey
Auburn University

Reetika Gupta
Lehigh University

John Hafer
University of Nebraska at Omaha

Allan Hall
Western Kentucky University

Joan Hall
Macomb Community College

Clark Hallpike
Elgin Community College

James E. Hansen
University of Akron

Dorothy Harpool
Wichita State University

Lynn Harris
Shippensburg University

Linda Hefferin
Elgin Community College

Lewis Hershey
Fayetteville State University

Tom Hickman
Loyola University

Robbie Hillsman
University of Tennessee–Martin

Nathan Himelstein
Essex County College

Adrienne Hinds
*Northern Virginia Community
College at Annandale*

John Hobbs
University of Oklahoma

Don Hoffer
Miami University

Ronald Hoverstad
University of the Pacific

Kris Hovespian
Ashland University

James Hunt
*University of North Carolina
Wilmington*

Shane Hunt
Arkansas State University

Julie Huntley
Oral Roberts University

Sean Jasso
University of California–Riverside

Doug Johansen
University of North Florida

Candy Johnson
Holyoke Community College

Keith Jones
North Carolina A&T University

Janice Karlen
CUNY–Laguardia Community College

Eric J. Karson
Villanova University

Imran Khan
University of South Alabama–Mobile

Todd Korol
Monroe Community College

Dennis Lee Kovach
Community College of Allegheny County

Dmitri Kuksov
Washington University–St Louis

Jeff Kulick
George Mason University

Michelle Kunz
Morehead State University

John Kuzma
Minnesota State University at Mankato

Sandie Lakin
Hesser College

Timothy Landry
University of Oklahoma

Don Larson
Ohio State University

Felicia Lassk
Northeastern University

J. Ford Laumer
Auburn University

Kenneth Lawrence
New Jersey IT

Rebecca Legleiter
Tulsa CC Southeast Campus

Hillary Leonard
University of Rhode Island

Natasha Lindsey
University of North Alabama

Paul Londrigan
Mott Community College

Terry Lowe
Heartland Community College

Dolly Loyd
University of Southern Mississippi

Harold Lucius
Rowan University

Alicia Lupinacci
Tarrant Community College

Stanley Madden
Baylor University

Lynda Maddox
George Washington University

Cesar Maloles
California State University, East Bay

Karl Mann
Tennessee Tech University

Cathy Martin
University of Akron

Carolyn Massiah
University of Central Florida

Tamara Masters
Brigham Young University

Erika Matulich
University of Tampa

Bob Mayer
Mesa State College

Nancy McClure
University of Central Oklahoma

Mohan Menon
University of South Alabama

Michelle Meyer
Joliet Junior College

Ivor Mitchell
University of Nevada Reno

Mark Mitchell
University of South Carolina

Steven Moff
Pennsylvania College of Technology

Rex Moody
University of Colorado

Rex Moody
Central Washington University at Ellensburg

Farrokh Moshiri
University of California–Riverside

Dorothy Mulcahy
Bridgewater State College

James Munch
Wright State University–Dayton

Suzanne Murray
Piedmont Technical College

James E. Murrow
Drury University

Noreen Nackenson
Nassau Community College

Sandra Blake Neis
Borough of Manhattan Community College

John Newbold
Sam Houston State University

Keith Niedermeier
University of Pennsylvania

Martin Nunlee
Syracuse University

Hudson Nwakanma
Florida A & M University

Lois Olson
San Diego State University

Karen Overton
Houston Community College

Deborah L. Owens
University of Akron

Esther Page-Wood
Western Michigan University

Richard Pascarelli
Adelphi University

Michael Pearson
Loyola University

Jerry Peerbolte
University of Arkansas–Fort Smith

Glenn Perser
Houston Community College

Diane Persky
Yeshiva University

Susan Peters
California State Polytechnic University at Pomona

Renee Pfeifer-Luckett
University of Wisconsin at Whitewater

Gary Pieske
Minnesota State Community and Technical College

Jeff Podoshen
Temple University

Carmen Powers
Monroe Community College

Mike Preis
University of Illinois–Champaign

Rosemary Ramsey
Wright State University

Srikumar Rao
Long Island University

Kristen Regine
Johnston & Wales University

Joseph Reihing
Nassau Community College

William Rice
California State University–Fresno

Patricia Richards
Westchester Community College

Eric Rios
Eastern University

Janet Robinson
Mount St. Mary's College

Heidi Rottier
Bradley University

Juanita Roxas
California State Polytechnic University

Donald Roy
Middle Tennessee State University

Shikhar Sarin
Boise State University

Carl Saxby
University of Southern Indiana

Diana Scales
Tennessee State University

James Schindler
Columbia Southern University

Jeffrey Schmidt
University of Oklahoma–Norman

Laura Shallow
St. Xavier University

Rob Simon
University of Nebraska–Lincoln

Erin Sims
Devry University at Pomona

Lois J. Smith
University of Wisconsin

Brent Sorenson
University of Minnesota–Crookston

James Spiers
Arizona State University–Tempe

Geoffrey Stewart
University of Louisiana

John Striebich
Monroe Community College

Randy Stuart
Kennesaw State University

James Swanson
Kishwaukee College

James Swartz
California State Polytechnic University

Robert R. Tangsrud, Jr.
University of North Dakota

Steve Taylor
Illinois State University

Sharon Thach
Tennessee State University

Mary Tharp
University of Texas at San Antonio

Frank Tobolski
Lake in the Hills

Louis A. Tucci
College of New Jersey

Ven Venkatesan
University of Rhode Island at Kingston

Deirdre Verne
Westchester Community College

Steve Vitucci
Tarleton University Central Texas

Keith Wade
Webber International University

Wakiuru Wamwara-Mbugua
Wright State University–Dayton

Bryan Watkins
Dominican University, Priory Campus

Ron Weir
East Tennessee State University

Ludmilla Wells
Florida Gulf Coast University

Thomas Whipple
Cleveland State University

Tom Whitman
Mary Washington College

Kathleen Williamson
University of Houston–Clear Lake

Phillip Wilson
Midwestern State University

Doug Witt
Brigham Young University

Kim Wong
Albuquerque Tech Institute

Brent Wren
University of Alabama–Huntsville

Alex Wu
California State University–Long Beach

Poh-Lin Yeoh
Bentley College

Marketing, Second Edition benefited from the reviews, focus groups, and individual discussions with many leading scholars and teachers of marketing. Together, these reviewers spent hundreds of hours reading, discussing, and critiquing the manuscript.

We gratefully acknowledge:

Maria Aria
Camden County College

Dennis Arnett
Texas Tech University

Gerard Athaide
Loyola College of Maryland

Aysen Bakir
Illinois State University

Hannah Bell-Lombardo
Bryant University

Amit Bhatnagar
University of Wisconsin, Milwaukee

Linda Calderone
SUNY, Farmingdale

Nathaniel Calloway
University of Maryland, University College

Carlos Castillo
University of Minnesota, Duluth

Eve Caudill
Winona State University

Carmina Cavazos
University of Saint Thomas

Melissa Clark
University of North Alabama

Brent Cunningham
Jacksonville State University

Charlene Davis
Trinity University

Joseph Defilippe
Suffolk County Community College, Brentwood

Alan Friedenthal
Kingsborough Community College

George Goerner
Mohawk Valley Community College

Tom Greene
Eastern Washington University

Don Hanson
Bryant University

Jeffrey Harper
Texas Tech University

Charlane Held
Onondaga Community College

Jonathan Hibbard
Boston University

Craig Hollingshead
Texas A&M University, Kingsville

Donna Hope
Nassau Community College

Carol Johanek
Washington University, St. Louis

Maria Johnson
Macomb Commity College, Clinton Township

Rajiv Kashyap
William Paterson University

Josette Katz
Atlantic Cape Community College

Garland Keesling
Towson University

Marilyn Lavin
University of Wisconsin, Whitewater

Freddy Lee
California State University, Los Angeles

Guy Lochiatto
Massachusetts Bay Community College

Paul Londrigan
Mott Community College

Moutusi Maity
University of Wisconsin, Whitewater

Dennis Menezes
University of Louisville, Louisville

Linda Morable
Richland College

Brian Murray
Jefferson Community College

John Newbold
Sam Houston State University

Daniel Onyeagba
Argosy University, Atlanta

Terry Paul
Ohio State University, Columbus

Renee Pfeifer-Luckett
University of Wisconsin, Whitewater

Frank Alan Philpot
George Mason University

Susan Price
California Polytechnic State University

Lori Radulovich
Baldwin-Wallace College

Bruce Ramsey
Franklin University

Tom Rossi
Broome Community College

Linda Salisbury
Boston College

Nick Sarantakes
Austin Community College

Dwight Scherban
Central Connecticut State University

Dan Sherrell
University of Memphis

Karen Smith
Columbia Southern University

Randy Stuart
Kennesaw State University

Sue Taylor
Southwestern Illinois College

Sue Umashankar
University of Arizona

Deborah Utter
Boston University

Bronis Verhage
Georgia State University

Suzanne Walchli
University of the Pacific

Ludmilla Wells
Florida Gulf Coast University

Douglas Witt
Brigham Young University, Provo

Courtney Worsham
University of South Carolina

Joseph Yasaian
McIntosh College

Paschalina Ziamou
Bernard M. Baruch College

We would like to thank the following reviewers for their thoughtful consideration and helpful contributions to the third edition.

We gratefully acknowledge:

Wendi Achey
Northampton Community College

Praveen Aggarwal
University of Minnesota Duluth

Timothy W. Aurand
Northern Illinois University

Claudia Mendelson Bridges
California State University, Sacramento

Glen H. Brodowsky
California State University, San Marcos

Alan J. Bush
University of Memphis

Catherine Campbell
University of Maryland

Clayton L. Daughtrey
Metropolitan State College of Denver

Michael Dore
University of Oregon

Monique Doll
Macomb Community College

Kimberly Ann Donahue
Indiana University

Kellie Emrich
Cuyahoga Community College

Todd Korol
Monroe Community College

Ann T. Kuzma
Minnesota State University, Mankato

Melissa Martin
George Mason University

Carolyn A. Massiah
University of Central Florida

Maria McConnnell
Lorain County Community College

Melissa Moore
Mississippi State University

Farrokh Moshiri
University of California, Riverside

Suzy Murray
Piedmont Technical College

Beng Ong
California State University, Fresno

Ann Renee Root
Florida Atlantic University

Jeffrey B. Schmidt
University of Oklahoma

Philip Shum
William Paterson University

Lisa Simon
California Polytechnic State University, San Luis Obispo

Rob Simon
University of Nebraska, Lincoln

Lauren Ruth Skinner
University of Alabama at Birmingham

Julie Z. Sneath
University of South Alabama

John Striebich
Monroe Community College

Deirdre Verne
Westchester Community College

Letty Workman
Utah Valley University

We would like to thank all the professors who were instrumental in guiding our revision of the fourth edition through their reviews of not only the text, but also *Connect* and other ancillary materials

Ivan Abel
St. John's University

Wendi Achey
Northampton Community College

Praveen Aggarwal
University of Minnesota Duluth

Keanon Alderson
California Baptist University

Rosalyn Amaro
Florida State College at Jacksonville

Maria Aria
Camden County College

Jill S. Attaway
Illinois State University

Michelle Barnhart
Oregon State University

Robert Belenger
Bristol Community College

Tom Bilyeu
Southwestern Illinois College

Mark Blake
York College of Pennsylvania

Maurice Bode
Delgado Community College

Jean M. Brown
University of Alabama in Huntsville

Gary Brunswick
Northern Michigan University

Desislava Budeva
Ramapo College of New Jersey

Melissa Burnett
Missouri State university

Susan Carder
Northern Arizona University

Ella Carter
Bowie State University

Debi Cartwright
Truman State University

Haozhe Chen
East Carolina University

Angeline Close
The University of Texas at Ausin

Kathleen Ferris-Costa
Bridgewater State University

Kevin Coulson
Emporia State University

Brent Cunningham
Jacksonville State University

Beth Deinert
Southeast Community College

David DiRusso
Millersville University

Michael Dotson
Appalachian State University

Colleen Dunn
Bucks County Community College

Diane Edmondson
Middle Tennessee State University

Burcak Ertimur
Fairleigh Dickinson University

David J. Faulds
University of Louisville

Amy Feest
Tunxis Community College

Troy A. Festervand
Middle Tennessee State University

Paul Fombelle
Northeastern University

John Fraedrich
Southern Illinois University-Carbondale

Theresa E. Frame
Horry Georgetown Technical College

Sheila Fry
Champlain College

Jerome Gafford
Univeristy of North Alabama

Tao (Tony) Gao
Northeastern University

Lance Gentry
Colorado State University-Pueblo

Nabarun Ghose
The University of Findlay

Connie Golden
Lakeland Community College

Lisa Goolsby
Southern Adventist University

Deborah M. Gray
Central Michigan University

Susan Greer
Horry-Georgetown Technical College

Cynthia Grether
Delta College

Mike Griffith
Lone Star College-Kingwood

Barbara Gross
California State University, Northridge

Chiquan Guo
The University of Texas-Pan American

Jamey Halleck
Marshall University

Richard Hanna
Northeastern University

David Eric Hansen
Texas Southern University

Jeffrey Harper
Texas Tech University

Perry Hidalgo
Gwinnett Technical College

Diane Holtzman
Richard Stockton College of New Jersey

Monica Hodis
St. John Fisher College

Donna Hope
Nassau Community College

Gorman Houston
University of Alabama

Erika Hovland
Temple University

Vince Howe
University of North Carolina, Wilmington

Miriam Huddleston
Harford Community College

James B. Hunt
University of North Carolina, Wilmington

Eva Hyatt
Appalachian State University

Roxanne Jackson
Vance-Granville Community College

Grace Jebakumari Johnson
University of Wisconsin Milwaukee

Victoria Jones
University of North Carolina, Wilmington

Sungwoo Jung
Columbus State University

Vishal Kashyap
Xavier University

Mark Kay
Montclair State University

Sylvia Keyes
Bridgewater State University

Tina Kiesler
California State University, Northridge

Brian Kinard
University of North Carolina, Wilmington

John Kinnett
Columbus State University

Peter Knight
University of Wisconsin Parkside

Michael W. Kroff
Montana State University

Ann T. Kuzma
Minnesota State University, Mankato

Theodore Labay
Bishop State Community College

Donald W. Larson
The Ohio State University

James R. Lashley
Bowie State University

E. Scott Lathrop
Whitman School of Management, Syracuse University

Debra Laverie
Texas Tech University

Cary LeBlanc
Assumption College

David M. Lee
Sam Houston State University

Andrea Licari
St. John's University

Junsang Lim
Virginia State University

Bryan D. Little
Marshall University

Ruth Lumb
Minnesota State University Moorhead

Guy Lochiatto
MassBay Community College

Anne Weidemanis Magi
University of South Florida

Datha Damron-Martinez
Truman State University

David Matthews
SUNY Adirondack (Adirondack Community College)

Fredric Mayerson
Kingsborough Community College

Myke McMullen
Long Beach Community College

Rajiv Mehta
New Jersey Institute of Technology

Sanjay S. Mehta
Sam Houston State University

Jeffrey Meier
Fox Valley Technical College

Michael Mejza
University of Nevada Las Vegas

Robert Meyer
Parkland College

Elizabeth Miller
Boston College

Iris Mohr
St. John's University

Josefer Montes
Walla Walla University

Dorothy J. Mulcahy
Bridgewater State University

Jay Mulki
Northestern University–Boston

Benjamin Muller
Portland Community College

Gergana Nenkov
Boston College

John Newbold
Sam Houston State University

Hudson Nwakanma
Florida A&M University

Matt O'Hern
University of Oregon

Richard B. Osborn
York College of Pennsylvania

Rodney Oudan
Worcester State University

Lauren Paisley
Genesee Community College

Mahatapa Palit
Borough of Manhattan Community College

Janet Parish
Texas A&M University

Raymond A. Parkins, Jr.
Florida State College at Jacksonville

Ed Petkus
Ramapo College of New Jersey

Julie M. Pharr
Tennessee Tech University

Rajani Ganesh Pillai
North Dakota State University

Sampath Ranganathan
University of Wisconsin–Green Bay

Mohammed Rawwas
University of Northern Iowa

Virginia Reilly
Ocean County College

John E. Robbins
Winthrop University

Ann R. Root
Florida Atlantic University

Robert Rouwenhorst
University of Iowa

Donald P. Roy
Middle Tennessee State University

Alberto Rubio-Sanchez
University of the Incarnate Word

Catherine Ruggieri
St. John's University, New York

Doreen Sams
Georgia College & State University

Robin Schallie
Fox Valley Technical College

Douglas Scott
State College of Florida

Christine Seel
Delaware Valley College

Daaim Shabazz
Florida A&M University

Abhay Shah
Colorado State University–Pueblo

Rick Shannon
Western Kentucky University

Kenneth Shaw
State University of New York, Oswego

Robert Simon
University of Nebraska-Lincoln

Peter D. Simonson
North Dakota State University

David Smith
Bemidji State University

Dennis Spector
Naugatuck Valley Community College

Vernon R. Stauble
San Bernardino Valley College

Susan Steiz
Norwalk Community College

Geoffrey Stewart
University of Louisiana

Karen L. Stewart
Richard Stockton College of New Jersey

Susan Stone
Shippensburg University of Pennsylvania

Ray Stroup, Jr.
University of Louisiana at Lafayette

James Swenson
Minnesota State Universisty Moorhead

Steven Taylor
Illinois State University

Ramendra Thakur
University of Louisiana–Lafayette

Norman Thiel
Walla Walla University

Dennis Tootelian
California State University, Sacramento

Philip Trocchia
University of South Florida St. Petersburg

Sven Tuzovic
Pacific Lutheran University

Leo Vasquez
San Bernardino Valley College, San Bernardino

Franck Vigneron
California State University Northridge

Doug Wilson
University of Oregon–Lundquist College of Business

Roger Wilson
Fairmont State University

Doug Witt
Brigham Young University

Mike Wittmann
The University of Southern Mississippi

Van R. Wood
Virginia Commonwealth University

Ashley Wright
Spartanburg Community College

Ge Xiao
Wilkes University

Jefrey R. Woodall
York College of Pennsylvania

Elle Wu
Louisiana State University

Jim Zemanek
East Carolina University

Kim Wong
Central New Mexico Community College

Charles Wyckoff
Riverside Community College

Lin Zhang
Truman State University

We express our thanks to all faculty who have contributed to the development of digital learning content:

Barbara Black
University of Miami

Melissa Martin
George Mason University

John Striebech
Monroe Community College

Donna Haeger,
Monroe Community College

Leroy Robinson
University of Houston, Clear Lake

Lois Olson
San Diego State University

Todd Korol
Monroe Community College

Lauren Spinner Beitelspacher
University of Alabama, Birmingham

We'd also like to thank the team at Hurix: Sumesh Yoganath, Namrata Gunjal, and Ashwin Srivastav for their contributions.

brief contents

table of contents

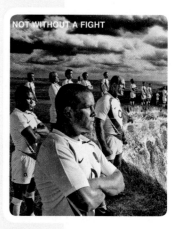

SECTION 7 Value Communication 545

Marketing

Fourth Edition

Assessing the Marketplace

Section One, Assessing the Marketplace, contains four chapters. Following an introduction to marketing in Chapter 1, Chapter 2 focuses on how a firm develops its marketing strategy and a marketing plan. A central theme of that chapter is how firms can effectively create, capture, deliver, and communicate value to their customers. Chapter 3 is devoted to understanding how one can develop social and mobile marketing strategies. Chapter 4 focuses attention on marketing ethics. An ethical decision framework is developed and presented, and the key ethical concepts are linked back to the marketing plan introduced in Chapter 2. Finally, Chapter 5, Analyzing the Marketing Environment, focuses on how marketers can systematically uncover and evaluate opportunities.

SECTION 1

CHAPTER 1

Overview of Marketing

I t's nearing the end of the spring semester, and it's a hot day. Leaving the sweltering classroom, you and your friends decide to go grab a frozen dessert. But now the hard negotiations really begin: ice cream or frozen yogurt? Ben & Jerry's or Red Mango? Someone wants coconut-based instead of milk-based ice cream. Another friend insists it's time for everyone to try gelato. Each of these frozen desserts offers a cool treat, and various companies provide multiple options. So what's the difference among them, and what makes customers loyal to one choice over another?

Let's think about the options available for your frozen dessert indulgence: ice cream, frozen custard, gelato, frozen yogurt, sherbet, sorbet, water ice, single-serving desserts such as popsicles, milkshakes, and blended treats that combine frozen dairy products with bits of cookies or candies.[1] In addition to their wide variety of flavors, they also come in reduced-fat, soy, coconut, organic, fairtrade, probiotic, nutrition-enhanced, and gluten-free versions.

In the grocery store, Unilever and Nestlé/Dreyer's are the undisputed leaders of the frozen dessert market. The former manufactures or distributes Breyer's, Ben & Jerry's, Good Humor, Klondike, and Popsicle;[2] the latter is responsible for Häagen-Dazs, Skinny Cow, and Edy's, as well as Dreyer's and Nestlé brands. Frozen yogurt sales are a relatively small, but growing, part of the $25 billion frozen dessert market. This growth trend has spawned intense competition among existing frozen yogurt shops, as well as inspired new brands to set up shop.

To build and maintain a loyal customer base, each frozen dessert brand must distinguish itself from its competitors by offering products, services, and ambiance that are so appealing that customers shun competitors. Since it opened in 2007, for example, Red Mango has attracted loyal fans devoted to its tart-flavored yogurt, which contains probiotics and thus promises to aid digestion. Stores offer a limited number of exotic flavors, many of which are seasonal, and a wide array of high-end toppings.[3] The minimalism in the flavor choices is part of the company's brand image, as reflected in the stark, bright store layouts. That is, this popular new chain offers consistency across its products and its store images, even as it promises that customers can eat healthy, low-fat, hormone-free milk products, and still indulge in unusual yogurt flavors and interesting toppings.[4]

Red Mango's tart-flavored yogurt contains probiotics and thus promises to aid digestion. By the way, it tastes great!

From the moment the Vermont-based Ben & Jerry's opened its doors in 1978, offering super-premium ice cream, sorbet, and frozen yogurt, it committed to operating in a way that would contribute to the quality of life, both locally and globally.[7] Through the Ben & Jerry Foundation, the company funds community-oriented projects. Its politics are even reflected in its flavor names: In September 2009, "Chubby Hubby" took on a name change to "Hubby Hubby," in honor of Vermont's decision to permit same-sex marriages.

As these examples show, newcomers must constantly try to find a foothold in the market. Already established businesses must grow and change their product offerings and corporate citizenry to keep pace with customer needs and tastes. Red Mango stresses health and style; TCBY gives customers more choices and more control over portions; Ben & Jerry's takes a stand on social issues. Yet what's common to both new and established frozen dessert brands is their traditional approach to marketing: Each company succeeds because it provides good value to its customers.

In contrast, the more traditional dessert idea offered by TCBY allows consumers to help themselves to yogurt flavors like cake batter, red velvet cake, and peanut butter, and then pile on candy, cookies, fruit, sauces, and sprinkles.[5] Because the stores calculate the costs of each dessert by weight rather than by serving size, customers feel free to create towering frozen creations that they might have felt awkward ordering. It also results in a higher per-serving cost.[6]

LO1 Define the role of marketing in organizations.

WHAT IS MARKETING?

Unlike other subjects you may have studied, marketing already is very familiar to you. You start your day by agreeing to do the dishes in exchange for a freshly made cup of coffee. Then you fill up your car with gas. You attend a class that you have chosen and paid for. After class, you pick up lunch (and maybe a frozen dessert) at the cafeteria, which you eat while reading a book on your iPad. Then you leave campus to have your hair cut and take in a movie. On your bus ride back to school, you pass the time by buying a few songs from Apple's iTunes. In each case, you have acted as the buyer and made a decision about whether you should part with your time and/or money to receive a particular service or product. If, after you return home, you decide to sell some clothes you don't wear much anymore on eBay, you have become a seller. And in each of these transactions, you were engaged in marketing.

The American Marketing Association states that "**marketing** is the activity, set of institutions, and processes for creating, *capturing*, communicating, delivering, and exchanging offerings that have value for customers, clients, partners, and society at large."[8] What does this definition really mean? Good marketing is not a random activity; it requires thoughtful planning with an emphasis on the ethical implications of any of those decisions on society in general. Firms develop a **marketing plan**

EXHIBIT 1.1 Core Aspects of Marketing

Marketing helps create value.

Marketing occurs in many settings.

Marketing is about satisfying customer needs and wants.

Marketing

Marketing can be performed by both individuals and organizations.

Marketing entails an exchange.

Marketing requires product, price, place, and promotion decisions.

(Chapter 2) that specifies the marketing activities for a specific period of time. The marketing plan also is broken down into various components—how the product or service will be conceived or designed, how much it should cost, where and how it will be promoted, and how it will get to the consumer. In any exchange, the parties to the transaction should be satisfied. In our previous example, you should be satisfied or even delighted with the song you downloaded, and Apple should be satisfied with the amount of money it received from you. Thus, the core aspects of marketing are found in Exhibit 1.1. Let's see how these core aspects look in practice.

Marketing Is about Satisfying Customer Needs and Wants

Understanding the marketplace, and especially consumer needs and wants, is fundamental to marketing success. In the broadest terms, the marketplace refers to the world of trade. More narrowly, however, the marketplace can be segmented or divided into groups of people who are pertinent to an organization for particular reasons. For example, the marketplace for soft drinks may include most people in the world, but as Pepsi and Coke battle each other worldwide, they divide the global population into a host of categories: men versus women, calorie-conscious or not, people who prefer carbonated versus noncarbonated drinks, and multiple categories of flavor preferences, among others.[9] If you manufacture a beverage with zero

Coke and Pepsi are constantly battling to be number one.

Purchasing a Taylor Swift song from the iTunes store entails an exchange. The customer gets the song, and Apple gets money and information.

calories, you want to know for which marketplace segments your product is most relevant, then make sure that you build a marketing strategy that targets those groups. Certain diet- and health-conscious customers may prefer Diet Coke or Diet Pepsi; others may opt for bottled water products like Dasani or Aquafina.

Although marketers would prefer to sell their products and services to everyone, it is not practical to do so. Because marketing costs money, good marketers carefully seek out potential customers who have both an interest in the product and an ability to buy it. For example, most people need some form of transportation, and many people probably would like to own the new hybrid from Lexus. Starting at more than $110,000, the Lexus LS 600h L is one of the most sophisticated hybrid cars on the market. But Lexus is not actually interested in everyone who wants an LS 600h L, because not everyone can afford to spend that much on a car. Instead, Lexus defines its viable target market as those consumers who want and can afford such a product.[10] Although not all companies focus on such a specific, and wealthy, target, all marketers are interested in finding the buyers who are most likely to be interested in their offerings.

Marketing Entails an Exchange

Marketing is about an **exchange**—the trade of things of value between the buyer and the seller so that each is better off as a result. As depicted in Exhibit 1.2, sellers provide products or services, then communicate and facilitate the delivery of their offering to consumers. Buyers complete the exchange by giving money and information to the seller. Suppose you learn about a new Taylor Swift album by hearing one of her songs on XM Satellite radio. The same day, a friend tweets on her Twitter account that she loves the new album, and you visit the Taylor Swift Facebook fan page, which is full of recommendations. From there, you click into the iTunes Store, where you can purchase the song you heard, multiple songs, or the entire new album. You begin with the song you heard, which you continue to love after hearing it several times. Therefore, you go back to iTunes and take advantage of its offer to complete the album by downloading the rest of the songs to your iTunes library. Your billing

EXHIBIT 1.2   Exchange: The Underpinning of Seller–Buyer Relationships

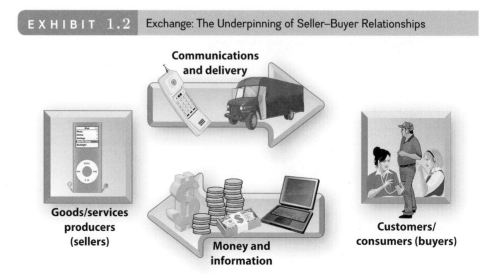

Communications and delivery

Goods/services producers (sellers)

Money and information

Customers/consumers (buyers)

EXHIBIT 1.3   The Marketing Mix

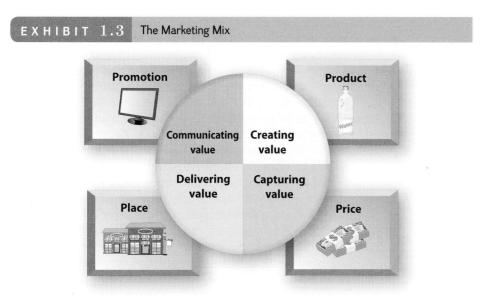

information is already in the company's system, so you do not have to enter your credit card number or other information. Furthermore, iTunes creates a record of your purchase, which it uses, together with your other purchase trends, to create personalized recommendations of other albums or songs that you might like. Thus, Apple uses the valuable information you provide to facilitate future exchanges and solidify its relationship with you.

Marketing Requires Product, Price, Place, and Promotion Decisions

Marketing traditionally has been divided into a set of four interrelated decisions and consequent actions known as the **marketing mix**, or **four Ps**: product, price, place, and promotion (as defined in Exhibit 1.3).[11] The four Ps are the controllable set of decisions/activities that the firm uses to respond to the wants of its target markets. But what does each of these activities in the marketing mix entail?

Product: Creating Value Although marketing is a multifaceted function, its fundamental purpose is to create value by developing a variety of offerings, including *goods*, *services*, and *ideas*, to satisfy customer needs.[12] Take, for example, a frozen dessert. Not too long ago, consumers perceived milk-based ice cream as their primary option. But as we recognized in the chapter opener, numerous other options have evolved, including frozen yogurt, coconut-based frozen desserts, sorbets, and even liquid nitrogen–frozen concoctions.[13] Coconut-based frozen desserts are

Non-dairy options to ice cream are gaining popularity, for example coconut milk frozen desserts and sorbets.

extremely popular dessert options for folks with milk allergies; sorbets and sherbets appeal to people who like something lighter to cleanse their palates. The dessert is a *good*, the *service* might involve your enjoyment of it in a yogurt shop, and there might even be an *idea* driving your experience—that frozen yogurt desserts can be healthy for you too.

Goods are items that you can physically touch. Nike shoes, Pepsi-Cola, Budweiser, Kraft cheese, Tide, an iPad, and countless other products are examples of goods. As we describe at the start of Chapter 2, Nike primarily makes shoes but also adds value to its products by, for example, offering custom designs under its Nike ID brand that increase their fashionable appeal and enlisting popular celebrities such as Rafael Nadal to add their names to the designs.

Unlike goods, **services** are intangible customer benefits that are produced by people or machines and cannot be separated from the producer. When people buy tickets—whether for airline travel, a sporting event, or the theater—they are paying not for the physical ticket stub but of course for the experience they gain. Hotels, insurance agencies, and spas similarly provide services. Getting money from your bank, whether through an ATM or from a teller, is another example of using a service. In this case, cash machines usually add value to the banking experience because they are conveniently located, fast, and easy to use. Many offerings in the market combine goods and services.[14] When you go to an optical center, you get your eyes examined (a service) and purchase new contact lenses (a good). If you enjoy Sting, you can attend a concert that can be provided only at that particular time and place (a service) and that gives you the chance to purchase a Sting concert T-shirt (a good). If you manage to get your shirt signed by Sting himself, you obtain a customized good that puts the finishing touch on and even extends a satisfying service experience.

Rafael Nadal adds value to the Nike brand.

A Sting concert is a service, but a Sting T-shirt purchased at the concert is a product.

Superior Service 1.1   Skiing Industry Offers Service Enhancements

Black-diamond ski runs are not for everyone. But Breckenridge Ski Resort in Colorado still wants your business no matter what your ski level. Breckenridge has invested heavily in amenities off the slopes. Forty-five percent of its runs are intermediate or beginner trails for the less intrepid skier, and a lavish new 88-unit condo hotel, One Ski Hill Place, caters to all kinds of skiers. Whether you want a studio or a four-bedroom apartment, your unit will include a full kitchen, iPod docs, and laundry machines. Off-slope recreation includes a two-lane bowling alley, two indoor swimming pools, and a private movie theater.

This is today's competitive edge on the slopes. Targeting non-skiers, occasional skiers, and the 4-year-olds who are tomorrow's skiers, the ski resort industry has ramped up with newer and more exciting rounds of value-added service enhancements that have nothing to do with cutting wait times or adding more challenging trails. This trend is focused on life off the slopes, with the emphasis on downtime, away from the runs.[15] Like Breckenridge, other resorts are offering spa facilities, bistros that serve up elk tacos and locally brewed ales, balloon rides, and, for children, hotel scavenger hunts and mountaineering classes. By extending a resort's appeal to new segments of the market, these new services ensure that everyone in the family can find something they want to do—even those who tire after just one or two runs down the bunny slopes.

Vail, one of the nation's largest ski resorts, has transformed itself from a traditional, functional ski town into a little piece of the Alps. Its new Four Seasons Resort resembles a Swiss village, with wooden balconies and peaked roofs. The 121 rooms inside the chalet offer gas fireplaces, DVD players, and free-standing oval tubs. For those returning weary after a day on the slopes, there is sushi service in the lobby, beside a glowing fireplace, or massage therapy in the 13-room on-site spa.

Such amenities offer an added draw for companies and business groups seeking a conference venue. Big cities traditionally offer the facilities that can accommodate large meetings, but now ski resorts are targeting this market too. Those that have undertaken extensive off-slope development can promise a blend of spectacular mountaintop scenery and recreational activities for the conference traveler who wants to relax between meetings.[16]

Ski resorts are constantly increasing the amenities offered to their patrons.

One of the most extensive expansions will require congressional action. The Canyons Resort in Utah has proposed development of a two-mile, European-style gondola system that would connect seven Wasatch Mountain ski resorts near Salt Lake City. The resulting valley-to-valley experience could move 1,000 people each hour between the slopes.[17] Four members of Utah's congressional delegation have proposed passage of the Wasatch Range Recreation Access Enhancement Act, which would permit the sale of 30 acres of national forest to develop the "SkiLink" between Canyons Resort and Solitude Mountain Resort.[18] The managing director of this resort calls the project "like nothing else in the U.S." and promises, "It certainly will drive destination visits, and winter tourism."

By offering improved access to more slopes, this project hopes to enhance its service offering in terms of expanding both the product and place. Critics, however, including the Department of Agriculture, cite the environmental risks of such a project to Salt Lake City's watershed and object to what they fear will become an "arms race" among Wasatch area resorts that will compete to become part of the treetop gondola network. In the case of this proposed development, an exciting new product may for its critics simply be in the wrong place.

Although much of their appeal relies on another P—place—ski slopes worldwide also have been striving to provide their customers with a better product, which in this case means more amenities and great customer service, as Superior Service 1.1 relates.

Ideas include concepts, opinions, and philosophies; intellectual concepts such as these also can be marketed. Groups promoting bicycle safety go to schools, give talks, and sponsor bike helmet poster contests for the members of their primary market: children. Then their secondary target market segment, parents and siblings, gets involved through their interactions with the young contest participants. The exchange of value occurs when the children listen to the sponsors' presentation and wear their helmets while bicycling, which means they have adopted, or become "purchasers," of the safety idea that the group marketed.

Price: Capturing Value Everything has a price, though it doesn't always have to be monetary. Price, therefore, is everything the buyer gives up—money, time, energy—in exchange for the product.[19] Marketers must determine the price of a product carefully on the basis of the potential buyer's belief about its value. For example, United Airlines can take you from New York to Denver. The price you pay for that service depends on how far in advance you book the ticket, the time of year, and whether you want to fly coach or business class. If you value the convenience of buying your ticket at the last minute for a ski trip between Christmas and New Year's Day and you want to fly business class, you can expect to pay four or five times as much as you would for the cheapest available ticket. That is, you have traded off a lower price for convenience. For marketers, the key to determining prices is figuring out how much customers are willing to pay so that they are satisfied with the purchase and the seller achieves a reasonable profit.

Place: Delivering the Value Proposition The third P, place, represents all the activities necessary to get the product to the right customer when that customer wants it. For the ski resorts in the Superior Service 1.1 box, their place proposition is pretty well predefined: Skiers have to get to Vail or Breckenridge to ski. But the described effort to link multiple resorts, which would make it easier for consumers to access multiple slopes, represents an attempt to improve delivery on this aspect of marketing.

Place more commonly deals specifically with retailing and marketing channel management. *Marketing channel management,* also known as *supply chain management,* is the set of approaches and techniques that firms employ to efficiently and effectively integrate their suppliers, manufacturers, warehouses, stores, and other firms involved in the transaction (e.g., transportation companies) into a seamless value chain in which merchandise is produced and distributed in the right quantities, to the right locations, and at the right time, while minimizing systemwide costs and satisfying the service levels required by the customers. Many marketing students initially overlook the importance of marketing channel management, because a lot of these activities are behind the scenes. But without a strong and efficient marketing channel system, merchandise isn't available when customers want it. Then customers are disappointed, and sales and profits suffer.

In the frozen desserts domain, for example, marketing channel considerations have pushed a growing number of businesses to adopt multiple convenient locations and self-service delivery systems. Rather than requiring a large, free-standing store, TCBY or Yogurtini have set up smaller kiosk-type storefronts. In these more conveniently located places (which also require fewer staff and therefore reduce costs for the company), consumers get to choose exactly what to put on their desserts. As a consequence, the company does not have to determine the right amounts or variations to offer; the customer makes that decision.[20]

Promotion: Communicating the Value Proposition Even the best products and services will go unsold if marketers cannot communicate their value to customers.

Dishing It Out

Do-it-yourself is a hot idea in the frozen-yogurt business. Here's a look at what customers bring to the counter at self-serve chain Yogurtini

Average ounces in an order
14

Average check size
$5.46

CHECK-OUT

Top three flavors
classic vanila, birthday-cake batter and signature blueberry tartini

Most popular toppings
strawberries and M&Ms

Social and Mobile Marketing **1.1** | Facebook Networks the Web[21]

Facebook would prefer it if you checked your account daily (or even hourly). Its nearly 1 billion users, more than half of whom do log in daily, spend an average of 55 minutes per day on the site. It is the second most frequently visited site in the United States. Facebook also is expanding the network in which it operates by making it easier for users to share information outside of Facebook.

Social plug-ins are those "Like" buttons you see on a business's website that encourage a social experience outside of Facebook. Social plug-ins make it easier for the user to share content from other websites with friends with a single click; if users like the content, whether an article, a restaurant, or a band, this preference gets shared automatically on their Facebook newsfeed. Friends in turn can link easily to the liked site, such that the system benefits both the external company and Facebook—and users. Companies thus place "Like" buttons on their web pages to drive more traffic to Facebook, and then enjoy more return traffic from Facebook to their own web pages.

Around 2.5 million websites contain "Like" buttons, but 10,000 more get added every day. And users like the "Like" button too. Only 13 percent of users ever write reviews on websites, but a much higher percentage of people are willing to click "Like." It is easy, and it gives Facebook users a simple way to communicate with friends and possibly extend their social influence.

Businesses can use Facebook users' information to target potential customers. For example, Yelp can use your preferences to give you personalized information on restaurants or music venues, because Yelp can access songs that you "like" on Pandora, and also the restaurants that you "like" on Yelp.com. Even IMBD, the comprehensive site for movie lovers, is getting in on the game, gathering Facebook users' favorite movies and television shows. By getting to know all those 1 billion users, Facebook offers incredibly relevant and increasingly useful information to advertisers—which is why its annual advertising revenues of more than $1 billion continue to grow.

Promotion is communication by a marketer that informs, persuades, and reminds potential buyers about a product or service to influence their opinions and elicit a response. Promotion generally can enhance a product's or service's value, as happened for Calvin Klein fragrances. The company's provocative advertising has helped create an image that says more than "Use this product and you will smell good." Rather, the promotion sells youth, style, and sex appeal. Social and Mobile Marketing 1.1 considers how Facebook communicates its value by encouraging networks of users and businesses, beyond its site.

Calvin Klein is known for selling youth, fun, and sex appeal in its fragrance promotions. In this photo, ck one models dance to the sounds of DJ Ruckus as they live in a billboard shaped like a giant ck one bottle overlooking the streets of Times Square in New York City.

EXHIBIT 1.4	Marketing Can Be Performed by Both Individuals and Organizations

Marketing Can Be Performed by Both Individuals and Organizations

Marketing Can Be Performed by Both Individuals and Organizations

Imagine how complicated the world would be if you had to buy everything you consumed directly from producers or manufacturers. You would have to go from farm to farm buying your food and then from manufacturer to manufacturer to purchase the table, plates, and utensils you needed to eat that food. Fortunately, marketing intermediaries, such as retailers, accumulate merchandise from producers in large amounts and then sell it to you in smaller amounts. The process by which businesses sell to consumers is known as **B2C (business-to-consumer) marketing**, whereas the process of selling merchandise or services from one business to another is called **B2B (business-to-business) marketing**. With the advent of various Internet auction sites (e.g., eBay) and social media, consumers have started marketing their products and services to other consumers. This third category, in which consumers sell to other consumers, is **C2C marketing**. These marketing transactions are illustrated in Exhibit 1.4.

Individuals can also undertake activities to market themselves. When you apply for a job, for instance, the research you do about the firm, the résumé and cover letter you submit with your application, and the way you dress for an interview and conduct yourself during it are all forms of marketing activities. Accountants, lawyers, financial planners, physicians, and other professional service providers also constantly market their services one way or another.

Marketing Impacts Various Stakeholders

Most people think of marketing as a way to facilitate the sale of products or services to customers or clients. But marketing can also impact several other stakeholders (e.g., supply chain partners, society at large). Partners in the supply chain include wholesalers, retailers, or other intermediaries, such as transportation or warehousing companies. All of these entities are involved in marketing to one another. Manufacturers sell merchandise to retailers, but the retailers often have to convince manufacturers to sell to them. After many years of not carrying Ralph Lauren products, JCPenney has co-introduced a line of clothing and home furnishings called American Living, sold exclusively at JCPenney, that does not bear the Ralph Lauren name.

Marketing also can aim to benefit an entire industry or society at large. The dairy industry has used a very successful, award-winning campaign with its slogan "Got Milk," aimed at different target segments. This campaign has not only created high levels of awareness about the benefits of drinking milk but also increased milk consumption in various target segments, perhaps in response to the use of various celebrities, from David Beckham and Alex Rodriguez to Hayden Panettiere and Demi Lovato. This campaign benefits the entire dairy industry and promotes the health benefits of drinking milk to society at large.

The dairy industry's "Got Milk" ad campaign has created high levels of awareness about the benefits of drinking milk and has increased milk consumption by using celebrities like soccer star David Beckham and singer/songwriter/actress Demi Lovato.

Marketing Helps Create Value

Marketing didn't get to its current prominence among individuals, corporations, and society at large overnight. To understand how marketing has evolved into its present-day, integral business function of creating value, let's look for a moment at some of the milestones in marketing's short history (see Exhibit 1.5).

Production-Oriented Era Around the turn of the twentieth century, most firms were production oriented and believed that a good product would sell itself. Henry Ford, the founder of Ford Motor Co., once famously remarked, "Customers can have any color they want so long as it's black." Manufacturers were concerned

EXHIBIT 1.5 Marketing Evolution: Production, Sales, Marketing, and Value

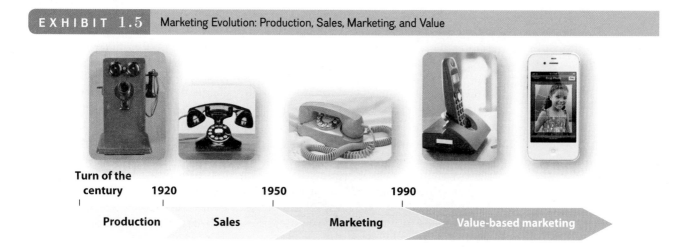

Turn of the century | 1920 | 1950 | 1990

Production | Sales | Marketing | Value-based marketing

with product innovation, not with satisfying the needs of individual consumers, and retail stores typically were considered places to hold the merchandise until a consumer wanted it.

Sales-Oriented Era Between 1920 and 1950, production and distribution techniques became more sophisticated, and the Great Depression and World War II conditioned customers to consume less or manufacture items themselves, so they planted victory gardens instead of buying produce. As a result, manufacturers had the capacity to produce more than customers really wanted or were able to buy. Firms found an answer to their overproduction in becoming sales oriented; they depended on heavy doses of personal selling and advertising.

Market-Oriented Era After World War II, soldiers returned home, got new jobs, and started families. At the same time, manufacturers turned from focusing on the war effort toward making consumer products. Suburban communities, featuring cars in every garage, sprouted up around the country, and the new suburban fixture, the shopping center, began to replace cities' central business districts as the hub of retail activity and a place to just hang out. Some products, once in limited supply because of World War II, became plentiful. And the United States entered a buyers' market—the customer became king! When consumers again had choices, they were able to make purchasing decisions on the basis of factors such as quality, convenience, and price. Manufacturers and retailers thus began to focus on what consumers wanted and needed before they designed, made, or attempted to sell their products and services. It was during this period that firms discovered marketing.

Value-Based Marketing Era Most successful firms today are market oriented.[22] That means they generally have transcended a production or selling orientation and attempt to discover and satisfy their customers' needs and wants. Before the turn of the twenty-first century, better marketing firms recognized that there was more to good marketing than simply discovering and providing what consumers wanted and needed; to compete successfully, they would have to give their customers greater value than their competitors did (the importance of value is appropriately incorporated into the AMA definition of marketing discussed earlier).

In deciding whether to stay at a Sheraton, potential customers trade off the benefits they will receive with the money it will cost them.

Value reflects the relationship of benefits to costs, or what you *get* for what you *give*.[23] In a marketing context, customers seek a fair return in goods and/or services for their hard-earned money and scarce time. They want products or services that meet their specific needs or wants *and* that are offered at a price that they believe is a good value. A creative way to provide value to customers is to engage in **value cocreation**.[24] In this case, customers can act as collaborators to create the product or service. When clients work with their investment advisors, they cocreate their investment portfolios; when Nike allows customers to custom design their sneakers, they are cocreating. Adding Value 1.1 examines how jean makers and retailers have added value to what was once apparel worn for working.

Adding Value **1.1**   Jeans—From Bronco to Boardroom

When blue jeans first hit the market in 1873,[25] they were workingman's wear: rugged cotton pants with metal rivets at stress points to help prevent rips. The pants, created by tailor Jacob Davis and a dry goods businessman named Loeb "Levi" Strauss, were an instant success, flying off the shelves at the then-exorbitant cost of $1 per pair. Today, blue jeans still fly off the shelves, but at substantially higher prices and with so many different styles and details that they are appropriate casual and businesswear for both men and women. In fact, blue jeans show up at formal occasions without raising eyebrows. The evolution of jeans—and how they have managed to remain a wardrobe staple for over a century despite changes in fashion—illustrates how customer perception can increase or undermine the value of a product.

In the 1930s, movie cowboys popularized jeans, creating a market among "urban cowboys" who aspired to a rugged look but wanted comfortable clothing. In the 1950s, jeans-clad movie idol James Dean became the symbol of adolescent rebellion,[26] and teenagers donned them to symbolize the departure from their parents' values. Throughout the 1960s and early 1970s, jeans acquired embroidery, flared bottoms, beads, and paint and began appearing with tie-dyed patterns to match the fashions of the day. They also acquired rips and frays, signs of wear that would soon evolve into fashionable styling on even brand-new jeans. Late in the 1970s, designers caught denim fever, and costly versions appeared with tags bearing names such as Jordache, Vidal Sassoon, Gloria Vanderbilt, Gucci, and Calvin Klein.[27] Using new styles and finishes, these designers revitalized the jeans market throughout the 1980s, turning the $1 workingman's pants into a garment that retailed from $200 to $2000. Even the originals had a new value: A pair of 1850 Levi's 501s sold on eBay for $60,000.

Designer jeans for men became popular, and consumers began paying more attention to the tops, shoes, and accessories they wore with their jeans. This interest led to new value for garments to go with jeans: jeweled shirts, denim vests and jackets, and shoes, from designer heels to basic ballet flats. Meanwhile, the old standby—basic blue jeans from Levi's, Lee's, or Wrangler's—continued to find a solid customer base with a price point in the comfortable double digits for most.

But then the fashion pendulum swung again. Whereas jeans in the 1950s signaled youth and rebellion, they were viewed as pants for parents by teenagers coming of age in the 1990s. Jeans were only acceptable to teens if they looked vintage or second-hand. Levi Strauss & Company, which had remained the preeminent jeans producer despite losing its patent in the late nineteenth century, began closing factories.

The industry has reacted in a variety of ways to rekindle a sense of consumer value.[28] Specialty brands such as Diesel, 7 for All Mankind, Citizens of Humanity, Lucky Jeans, and True Religion have entered the market, positioning themselves as hip or edgy. Some brands, like True Religion, have maintained prices as demand has waned, hoping to perpetuate an aura of prestige for their Western-inspired jeans; others have dropped prices, seeking to attract more budget-conscious consumers who want fashionable jeans. Levi Strauss's Signature line is available exclu-

Everyone wears jeans everywhere and for every occasion, including Drew Barrymore.

sively at Walmart for less than $20 a pair. Other designers have brought back retro styles or hired supermodels to generate renewed interest in their products. Some stores also offer organic and green products for environmentally conscious consumers, which are more expensive than their traditionally made counterparts. And PyjamaJeans, touted as "jeans you sleep in," have made strange and remarkable inroads into the market as well.[29]

Efforts to keep denim king also have enjoyed the contributions of political and business leaders who wear blue jeans in certain venues to impart their own updated image. Russia's president Dmitry Medvedev matched jeans with a blazer and buttoned shirt for dinner with President Obama.[30] These trends build on some of the traditional associations with jeans to project an image of a "new" executive: someone who is confident, creative, and willing to dig in and get the job done. The badge of rebellion has transformed into a symbol of power. Today, the uniform of the laborer is even appearing in some of the last bastions of conservative dress: country clubs.[31]

Jeans are still jeans—cotton twill pants that are most commonly dyed indigo blue. But now they are worn by men, women, and children. They appear at the White House, the coffee shop, and in the fields. They may sport platinum rivets or strategically placed holes, be purchased ready to wear or tailored for an individual fit. Brands and styles sell for various prices, reflecting the value that each offering provides.

In the next section, we explore the notion of value-based marketing further. Specifically, we look at various options for attracting customers by providing them with better value than the competition does. Then we discuss how firms compete on the basis of value. Finally, we examine how firms transform the value concept into their value-driven activities.

CHECK YOURSELF

1. What is the definition of marketing?
2. Marketing is about satisfying _____and _____.
3. What are the four components of the marketing mix?
4. Who can perform marketing?
5. What are the various eras of marketing?

LO2 Describe how marketers create value for a product or service.

How Do Marketing Firms Become More Value Driven?

Firms become value driven by focusing on four activities. First, they share information about their customers and competitors across their own organization and even with other firms, such as the manufacturers and transportation companies that help them get their product or service to the marketplace. Second, they strive to balance their customers' benefits and costs. Third, they concentrate on building relationships with customers. Fourth, they need to take advantage of new technologies and connect with their customers using social and mobile media.

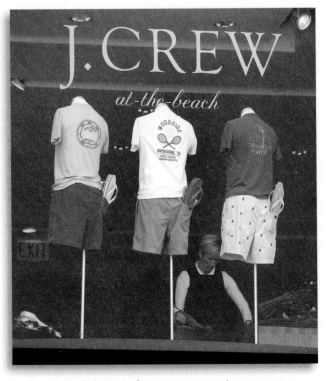

Collecting and sharing information among departments at J.Crew is important for its success.

Sharing Information In a value-based, marketing-oriented firm, marketers share information about customers and competitors (see Chapter 9, Marketing Research) and integrate it across the firm's various departments. The fashion designers for J.Crew, for instance, collect purchase information and research customer trends to determine what their customers will want to wear in the next few weeks; simultaneously, the logisticians—those persons in charge of getting the merchandise to the stores—use the same purchase history to forecast sales and allocate appropriate merchandise to individual stores. Sharing and coordinating such information represents a critical success factor for any firm. Imagine what might happen if J.Crew's advertising department were to plan a special promotion but not share its sales projections with those people in charge of creating the merchandise or getting it to stores.

Balancing Benefits with Costs Value-oriented marketers constantly measure the benefits that customers perceive against the cost of their offerings. They use available customer data to find opportunities to better satisfy their customers' needs, keep costs down, and develop long-term loyalties. For example, IKEA does not have highly paid salespeople to sell its furniture, but its simple designs mean customers can easily choose a product and assemble it themselves.

Building Relationships with Customers

During the past couple of decades, marketers have begun to develop a **relational orientation** as they have realized that they need to think about their customers in terms of relationships rather than transactions.[32] To build relationships, firms focus on the lifetime profitability of the relationship, not how much money is made during each transaction. Thus, Apple makes its new innovations compatible with existing products to encourage consumers to maintain a long-term relationship with the company across all their electronic needs.

Furniture retailer IKEA focuses on what its customers value—low prices and great design.

This relationship approach uses a process known as **customer relationship management (CRM)**, a business philosophy and set of strategies, programs, and systems that focus on identifying and building loyalty among the firm's most valued customers.[33] Firms that employ CRM systematically collect information about their customers' needs and then use that information to target their best customers with the products, services, and special promotions that appear most important to them.

Now that we've examined what marketing is and how it creates value, let's consider how it fits into the world of commerce, as well as into society in general.

Connecting with Customers Using Social and Mobile Media

Marketers are steadily embracing new technologies, such as social and mobile media, to allow them to connect better with their customers and thereby serve

Apple makes its new products compatible with existing ones to maintain a long-term relationship with its customers.

Marketers connect with customers by using social and mobile media.

their needs more effectively. Businesses take social and mobile media seriously, including these advanced tools in the development of their marketing strategies. Approximately three-quarters of U.S. companies now use social media tools for marketing purposes, and 46 percent of Internet users worldwide interact with social media on a daily basis.[34] The explosive growth of mobile phones in India and China means that more than 77 percent of the world's population subscribes to mobile services.[35]

Yet even with this astounding penetration, only 10 percent of the world's population uses Facebook—which means 90 percent still have not signed up. The United States and United Kingdom may be approaching saturation, but there is still huge growth potential for social networks. Before users can sign up for Facebook though, they need access to high-speed Internet.[36] Other countries continue to experience higher Facebook growth rates as they gain greater Internet access and as Facebook becomes available in more languages (around 70 currently). Brazil and Russia have only about 40 percent Internet penetration, and only 33 percent of Chinese people and less than 7 percent of consumers in India have access to the Internet. Furthermore, on a worldwide basis,[37]

- Facebook has almost 1 billion users.
- The average Facebook user spends more than 55 minutes per day there.
- The average user has 130 Facebook friends.
- 20 million Facebook users "like" fan pages per day.
- 60 million status updates occur each day on Facebook.
- Approximately 250 million photos get uploaded to Facebook every day.
- Twitter has 190 million users, who generate an average of 200 million tweets every day.
- Twitter handles more than 800,000 daily search queries.
- LinkedIn has more than 135 million professional users.
- Approximately 2 million companies have LinkedIn pages.
- Over 3 billion videos are streamed every day on YouTube.
- Every minute, 48 hours' worth of video gets uploaded to YouTube.
- Foursquare, the mobile social network, hosts more than 7 million users, with 25,000 new users joining every day.
- Foursquare averages 2 million check-ins daily; the average user checks in three to four times.
- Internet users worldwide spend more hours per week with social media than with any other online pursuit.

Beyond social media sites, online travel agencies such as Expedia, Travelocity, Orbitz, Priceline, and Kayak have become the first place that users go to book travel arrangements: 46 percent of online hotel bookings take place through one of these portals.[38] Customers who book hotels using travel agencies become loyal to the agency that gives them the lowest prices, rather than to any particular hotel brand. So hotels are using social media and mobile applications to lure customers back to their specific brands by engaging in conversations with them on Facebook and allowing fans of the page to book their hotel reservations through Facebook. Some hotel chains have mobile applications that allow customers to make changes to their reservations, shift check-in and check-out times, and add amenities or services to their stays. The hotels know a lot about their customers, because they collect information about their previous visits, including the type of room they stayed in, their preferences (from pillows to drinks consumed from the minibar), and the type of room service they prefer.

Several restaurant chains are exploiting location-based social media applications, such as Foursquare, Gowalla, Scvngr, and Loopt. These customers tend to be more loyal and can help spread the word to others about the restaurant.[39] Using location-based applications on mobile phones, restaurants connect with their customers immediately; customers using these apps visit restaurants nearly twice as often as those who don't. The result is that users are driving the way brands and stores are interacting with social media.

Buffalo Wild Wings suggests that its diners check in to its locations using their phones. The target customers for this chain are young and tech savvy, and with its in-house games and sports broadcasts, Buffalo Wild Wings is uniquely situated to encourage customers to connect and bring their friends along. It offers contests and encourages frequent visits to win. Customers can earn free chicken wings or soft drinks within their first three visits. Other contests encourage patrons to upload photos of the crowd's reaction to a big play. Moreover, customers can develop their own challenges from their bar stools. Approximately 10,000 people participated in 33,000 challenges, and 5000 rewards were given out in the first week of Buffalo Wild Wings' contests using location-based applications.[40]

CHECK YOURSELF

1. Does providing a good value mean selling at a low price?
2. What are the benefits of long-term relationships with customers?
3. How are marketers connecting with customers using social and mobile media?

WHY IS MARKETING IMPORTANT?

LO3 Understand why marketing is important, both within and outside the firm.

Marketing once was only an afterthought to production. Early marketing philosophy went something like this: "We've made it; now how do we get rid of it?" However, marketing not only has shifted its focus dramatically, it also has evolved into a major business function that crosses all areas of a firm or organization, as illustrated in Exhibit 1.6. Marketing advises production about how much of the company's product to make and then tells logistics when to ship it. It creates long-lasting, mutually valuable relationships between the company and the firms from which it buys.[41] It identifies those elements that local customers value and makes it possible for the firm to expand globally. Marketing has had a significant impact on consumers as well. Without marketing, it would be difficult for any of us to learn about new products and services. Understanding marketing can even help you find a job after you finish school.

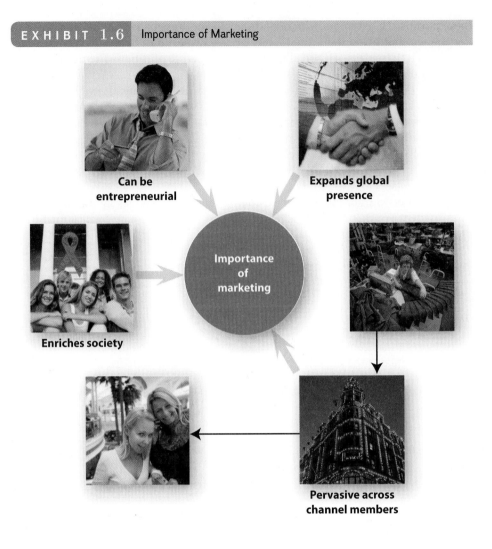

EXHIBIT 1.6   Importance of Marketing

Can be
entrepreneurial

Expands global
presence

Enriches society

Importance
of
marketing

Pervasive across
channel members

Marketing Expands Firms' Global Presence

A generation ago, Coca-Cola was available in many nations, but Levi's and most other U.S. brands weren't. Blue jeans were primarily an American product—made in the United States for the U.S. market. But today most jeans, including those of Levi Strauss & Co., are made in places other than the United States and are available nearly everywhere. Thanks to MTV and other global entertainment venues, cheap foreign travel, and the Internet, you share many of your consumption behaviors with college students in countries all over the globe. The best fashions, music, and even food trends disseminate rapidly around the world. Take a look at your next shopping bag. Whatever it contains, you will find goods from many countries—produce from Mexico, jeans from Japan, electronics from Korea. Global manufacturers and retailers continue to make inroads into the U.S. market. The Dutch grocery store giant Ahold is among the top five grocery store chains in the United States, though you may never have heard of it because it operates under names such as Stop & Shop, GIANT, and Peapod in the United States.[42] As marketing helps expand firms' global presence, it also enhances global career opportunities for marketing professionals.

Marketing Is Pervasive across Marketing Channel Members

Firms do not work in isolation. Manufacturers buy raw materials and components from suppliers, which they sell to wholesalers, retailers, or other businesses after

EXHIBIT 1.7   Supply Chain

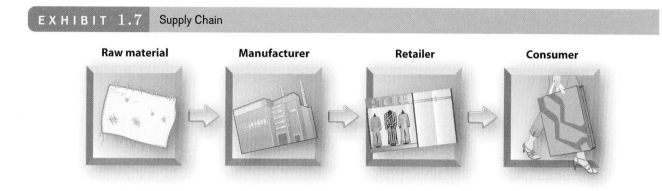

Raw material   **Manufacturer**   **Retailer**   **Consumer**

they have turned the materials into products (see Exhibit 1.7). Every time materials or products are bought or sold, they are transported to a different location, which sometimes requires that they be stored in a warehouse operated by yet another organization. Such a group of firms that make and deliver a given set of goods and services is known as a **supply chain** or a **marketing channel**. All the various channel members (e.g., suppliers, manufacturers, wholesalers, and retailers) of the supply chain are firms that are likely to provide career opportunities to marketing professionals.

Effectively managing supply chain relationships often has a marked impact on a firm's ability to satisfy the consumer, which results in increased profitability for all parties. Consider Levi Strauss & Co. and its close relationship with its major retailers. Not too many years ago, only about 40 percent of orders from the jeans manufacturer to its retailers arrived on time, which made it very difficult for retailers to keep all sizes in stock and therefore keep customers, who are generally not satisfied with anything less than the correct size, happy. Today, Levi's uses an automatic inventory replenishment system through which it manages the retailers' inventory itself. When a customer buys a pair of jeans, the information is transferred directly from the retailer to Levi's, which then determines which items the retailer needs to reorder and automatically ships the merchandise. The

Levi Strauss & Co. helps retailers manage their inventory so they don't run out of stock.

relationship benefits all parties: Retailers don't have to worry about keeping their stores stocked in jeans and save money because they don't have to invest as much money in inventory. Because Levi's has control of the jeans inventory, it can be assured that it won't lose sales because its retailers have let their inventory run down. Finally, customers benefit by having the merchandise when they want it—a good value.

Marketing Enriches Society

Should marketing focus on factors other than financial profitability—such as good corporate citizenry? Many of America's best-known corporations seem to think so, because they have undertaken various marketing activities in this direction, such as developing greener products, making healthier food options and safer products, and improving their supply chains to reduce their carbon footprint. At a more macro level, firms are making socially responsible activities an integral component of everything they do.

Socially responsible firms recognize that including a strong social orientation in business is a sound strategy that is in both its own and its customers' best interest. It shows the consumer marketplace that the firm will be around for the long run and can be trusted with their business. In a volatile market, investors view firms that operate with high levels of corporate responsibility and ethics as safe investments. Similarly, firms have come to realize that good corporate citizenship through socially responsible actions should be a priority because it will help their bottom line in the long run.[43] In a world in which consumers constantly hear about negative examples of ethics, the need for companies to live up to their ethical promises becomes even more important; Ethical & Societal Dilemma 1.1 outlines the challenges companies face when they attempt to go green.

Marketing Can Be Entrepreneurial

Whereas marketing plays a major role in the success of large corporations, it also is at the center of the successes of numerous new ventures initiated by **entrepreneurs**, or people who organize, operate, and assume the risk of a business venture.[44] Key to the success of many such entrepreneurs is that they launch ventures that aim to satisfy unfilled needs. Some examples of successful ventures (and their founders) that understood their customers and added value include

When you think of Oprah Winfrey, think big: Harpo Productions, Inc.; O, The Oprah Magazine; O at Home magazine; Harpo Films; the Oxygen television network; not to mention her philanthropic work with the Oprah Winfrey Foundation.

- Ben & Jerry's (Ben Cohen and Jerry Greenfield)
- Bose (Amar Bose)
- Amazon (Jeff Bezos)
- Netflix (Reed Hastings)
- The Oxygen Network (Oprah Winfrey)

An extraordinary entrepreneur and marketer, Oprah Winfrey was a self-made billionaire before she turned 50 years of age. Winfrey went from being the youngest person and first African-American woman to anchor news at WTVF-TV in Nashville, Tennessee, to being only the third woman in history to head her own production studio. Under the Oprah banner are a variety of successful endeavors, including Harpo Films, Oprah's Book Club, Oprah.com, the Oxygen television network, and OWN (the Oprah Winfrey Network). In addition to producing two of the highest-rated talk shows ever

Ethical and Societal Dilemma 1.1 Going Green

The Ben & Jerry's ice cream brand was built on more than fabulous flavors. With every double scoop of Chunky Monkey, owners Ben Cohen and Jerry Greenfield were also inviting customers to help make the world better. They donated 7.5 percent of profits to charity, paid employees a living wage and good benefits, and bought their Brazil nuts from a cooperative of indigenous Amazon farmers.[45] Combining a delicious ice cream with this socially responsible focus on the "triple bottom line" of profits, people, and planet appealed to consumers and investors alike.

It also drew suitors. In 2000, the corporate giant Unilever purchased Ben & Jerry's at a purchase price that Cohen and Greenfield could not reject. Doing so would have deprived their shareholders of a fair profit. Facing questions about whether the ice cream company's social responsibility mission would survive, Unilever took steps to preserve some of the promises and features of the original brand. Although it was forced to drop the "all-natural" label from packaging and began using processed ingredients, like partially hydrogenated soybean oil, it has attempted to shift its procurement practices to fair-trade sources. Charitable donations from its foundation total $1.8 million annually. These activities continue because the corporation views them as good business practices. But Unilever has set forth no permanent commitment to broad social responsibility goals.

Corporations that want to factor social responsibility explicitly into their bottom-line calculations also can undergo a certification process to become a B Corp, or benefit corporation.[46] The standards for this classification include bylaws that require a business to consider the impact of its actions on its workforce, the community, and the environment. Procter & Gamble (P&G) has staked its claim and commitment to environmental sustainability and social responsibility by retooling its

Going green is certainly in.

business practices—without donning an outside seal of approval. Other companies use the Green Seal® stamp to certify that their manufacturing processes meet environmental standards. Procter & Gamble's Professional Green Guarantee instead is a company-specific promise that all its products, packaging, and operations are environmentally and humanly safe.[47]

In a recent sustainability overview, P&G stated that its goal was "to touch and improve lives, now and for generations to come."[48] It has enlisted both suppliers and social responsibility experts in pursuit of those goals. Its first annual Supplier Environmental Scorecard rated the 310 suppliers that agreed to participate, according to their emissions and resource consumption.[49] Thus far, P&G's self-set goals appear within reach: It has reduced its nonrenewable energy consumption by 16 percent, cut landfill-bound waste by 57 percent, decreased carbon emissions by 12 percent, and lowered water consumption by 22 percent.

Consider for example P&G's new renewable packaging for Pantene Nature Fusion. By switching to bottles made of plant-based plastic, the production of the shampoo involves 70 percent less greenhouse gas emissions. Made of sugar cane, this next-generation packaging also sucks CO_2 out of landfilled or recycled plastic, yielding an overall carbon emission reduction of 170 percent for this product.[50] Who wouldn't want to participate in such positive changes for the planet? Each consumer who buys Pantene, with its upbeat matrix of green and blue leaves on the white plastic bottle, gains the promise of being part of the solution.

Since these firms recognize the benefit of becoming more socially responsible, and their activities resonate with their customers, then why don't all firms make enriching society a core value and major activity?

---

on television, *The Oprah Winfrey Show* and *Dr. Phil*, Harpo Studios has produced films such as *Beloved*. Oprah's philanthropic contributions are vast and varied. Through the Oprah Winfrey Foundation and Oprah's Angel Network, people worldwide have raised more $80 million for scholarships, schools, women's shelters, and youth centers.[51] Although her signature televised talk show has ended, her influence persists.

Great and distinguished entrepreneurs have visions of how certain combinations of products and services can satisfy unfilled needs. They find and understand a marketing opportunity (i.e., the unfilled need), conduct a thorough examination of the marketplace, and develop and communicate the value of their product and services to potential consumers.

CHECK YOURSELF

1. List five functions that illustrate the importance of marketing.
2. A firm doing the right thing emphasizes the importance of marketing to
    _____.

Summing Up

LO1 Define the role of marketing in organizations.

Marketing is the activity, set of institutions, and processes for creating, capturing, communicating, delivering, and exchanging offerings that have value for customers, clients, partners, and society at large. Marketing strives to *create value* in many ways. If marketers are to succeed, their customers must believe that the firm's products and services are valuable; that is, they are worth more to the customers than they cost. Another important and closely related marketing role is to capture value of a product or service based on potential buyers' beliefs about its value. Marketers also enhance the value of products and services through various forms of *communication*, such as advertising and personal selling. Through communications, marketers educate and inform customers about the benefits of their products and services and thereby increase their perceived value. Marketers facilitate the *delivery of value* by making sure the right products and services are available when, where, and in the quantities their customers want. Better marketers are not concerned about just one transaction with their customers. They recognize the value of loyal customers and strive to develop *long-term relationships* with them.

LO2 Describe how marketers create value for a product or service.

Value represents the relationship of benefits to costs. Firms can improve their value by increasing benefits, reducing costs, or both. The best firms integrate a value orientation into everything they do. If an activity doesn't increase benefits or reduce costs, it probably shouldn't occur. Firms become value driven by finding out as much as they can about their customers

and those customers' needs and wants. They share this information with their partners, both up and down the supply chain, so the entire chain collectively can focus on the customer. The key to true value-based marketing is the ability to design products and services that achieve precisely the right balance between benefits and costs. Value-based marketers aren't necessarily worried about how much money they will make on the next sale. Instead, they are concerned with developing a lasting relationship with their customers so those customers return again and again.

LO3 Understand why marketing is important, both within and outside the firm.

Successful firms integrate marketing throughout their organizations so that marketing activities coordinate with other functional areas such as product design, production, logistics, and human resources, enabling them to get the right product to the right customers at the right time. Marketing helps facilitate the smooth flow of goods through the supply chain, all the way from raw materials to the consumer. From a personal perspective, the marketing function facilitates your buying process and can support your career goals. Marketing also can be important for society through its embrace of solid, ethical business practices. Firms "do the right thing" when they sponsor charitable events, seek to reduce environmental impacts, and avoid unethical practices; such efforts endear the firm to customers. Finally, marketing is a cornerstone of entrepreneurialism. Not only have many great companies been founded by outstanding marketers, but an entrepreneurial spirit pervades the marketing decisions of firms of all sizes.

Key Terms

- B2C (business-to-consumer), 12
- B2B (business-to-business), 12
- C2C (consumer-to-consumer), 12
- customer relationship management (CRM), 17
- entrepreneur, 22

- exchange, 6
- goods, 8
- ideas, 9
- marketing, 4
- marketing channel, 21
- marketing mix (four Ps), 7

- marketing plan, 4
- relational orientation, 17
- services, 8
- supply chain, 21
- value, 14
- value cocreation, 14

Marketing Applications

1. Do you know the difference between needs and wants? When companies that sell frozen desserts develop their marketing strategy, do they concentrate on satisfying their customers' needs or wants? What about a utility company, such as the local power company? A humanitarian agency, such as Doctors without Borders?

2. People can apply marketing principles to finding a job. If the person looking for a job is the product, describe the other three Ps.

3. One of your friends was recently watching TV and saw an advertisement that she liked. She said, "Wow, that was great marketing!" Was the ad in fact marketing?

4. Mercedes-Benz manufactures the Smart Car, which sells for around $16,000, and the SL 65 AMG 2-door Roadster for over $100,000. Is Mercedes providing the target markets for these cars with a good value? Explain why.

5. Assume you have been hired into the marketing department of a major consumer products manufacturer, such as Nike. You are having lunch with some new colleagues in other departments—finance, manufacturing, and logistics. They are arguing that the company could save millions of dollars if it just got rid of the marketing department. Develop an argument that would persuade them otherwise.

6. Why do marketers like P&G find it important to embrace societal needs and ethical business practices? Provide an example of a societal need or ethical business practice that P&G is addressing.

Quiz Yourself

www.mhhe.com/grewal4e

1. The "Got Milk" advertising campaign was designed to help market a(n):
   a. individual
   b. firm
   c. industry
   d. organization

2. Henry Ford's statement, "Customers can have any color they want so long as it's black," typified the _____ era of marketing.

   a. production
   b. sales
   c. marketing
   d. value-based

(Answers to these two questions can be found on page 647.)

Go to www.mhhe.com/grewal4e to practice by answering an additional 11 questions.

Net Savvy

1. Visit Apple (www.apple.com). What value does Apple provide customers? What are the advantages to people from using Apple to buy music or to rent/buy videos?

2. Go to www.facebook.com/facebook/info and newsroom.fb.com. What is Facebook's mission? How could a marketer use Facebook, and what other social media tools could they use? What are the drawbacks a marketer might face when using Facebook?

Chapter Case Study

THE YOGURT WARS: PINKBERRY VS. RED MANGO

connect

For two decades prior to the turn of the twenty-first century, frozen yogurt was a popular treat. Then production dropped 45 percent, sales slumped,[52] and the frozen yogurt craze seemed to be at an end. In 2005 however, scientific evidence emerged regarding the health benefits of yogurt, and frozen yogurt rocketed to a new popularity because customers—primarily women—had a healthy, "guilt-free" alternative to ice cream.[53]

Pinkberry, which opened that year in California, attracted such large crowds that parking fines for customers hit $175,000 in the first month.[54] Its rival Red Mango, founded in South Korea in 2002, began serving customers on U.S. soil in Los Angeles in 2007.[55] Since then, the two chains have battled for the largest serving of the lucrative frozen yogurt market, with new challengers popping up on virtually every street corner. In this midst of this increasing competition, both Pinkberry and Red Mango must look for new ways to create value for their customers.

SWIRLY GOODNESS AT PINKBERRY

Pinkberry's first shop was immediately profitable. The company grew quickly in the Los Angeles area and, within a matter of months, had expanded into New York City. That first year, the trendy yogurt shops gained an important friend and supporter: Howard Schultz, CEO of Starbucks. With his history of success maintaining the Starbucks brand during periods of explosive growth, Schultz was a valuable advisor. Pinkberry has opened stores in 20 U.S. states, as well as numerous and far-flung countries such as the U.K., Russia, Morocco, and the United Arab Emirates.

The most promising new markets may be abroad. The company has stores in 13 foreign countries,[56] with plans to open even more stores overseas. Foreign stores differ from U.S. outlets, in that both flavors and toppings reflect local preferences. Customers in the Middle East have options for dates and pistachios; Asian customers can enjoy green-tea flavored yogurt.

Even while creating value for customers in overseas markets, Pinkberry is holding on to its brand image, which includes a modern store design and a visually appealing product that also conveys a sense of play. This feeling of playfulness, accomplished by giving the yogurt a personality and a seasonally appropriate wardrobe that includes shredded coconut earmuffs, is intended to remind customers of childhood summers.[57] The brand's tagline, "Swirly Goodness," also helps convey Pinkberry's unique combination of creativity, taste, and healthfulness. Pinkberry further distinguishes itself with endorsements from celebrity athletes, musicians, and fashion designers and by relying on another signature Schultz touch: customer interaction with the product through individual customization, together with interactions among customers and staff. Product "groupies" bond with one another through an interactive website, Twitter, and Facebook.

RED MANGO®–TREAT YOURSELF WELL®

Red Mango expanded from one store to 60 in the United States during its first two years and soon thereafter moved its headquarters to Dallas.[58] The company's five-year plan includes aggressive growth, including many new store openings in the same cities targeted by Pinkberry. In 2012, Red Mango Inc. is expanding into Mexico and a number of other countries in the Americas. Like its chief rival, Red Mango offers a limited number of unusual flavors with fresh fruit toppings and yogurt containing probiotics to aid digestion. The tagline, "Treat Yourself Well," suggests both the yogurt's nutritional benefits and a sense of indulgence. Store designs are bright, colorful, and inviting.

So how does Red Mango distinguish itself from Pinkberry and create value for customers? Red Mango Inc. founder Dan Kim claims his product has a creamier taste than that of its chief rival, and the chain has introduced new flavors, as well as smoothies, teas, and chocolates (iced and artisan hot) to help create a distinct brand. The company added fresh fruit parfaits and "spoonable smoothies," which take frozen yogurt from healthy treat option to nutritious meal choice.[59] Red Mango is also experimenting with the "do-it-yourself" movement, giving customers the opportunity to create their own combinations of flavors and toppings from an expanded array of offerings.

To help build customer loyalty and a sense of community, Red Mango has launched a loyalty program. Members earn Mango points with every qualified purchase, ultimately earning coupons redeemable for free and discounted products. They also receive event information and special promotions.

Red Mango is constantly embracing new yogurt flavors.

SUSTAINING VALUE IN A CHANGING MARKET

Even as these companies compete and try to grow successfully, they must be aware of changes in the market that could undermine their efforts. Stores that have traditionally sold ice cream, such as Cold Stone Creamery, are adding frozen yogurt to their menus. Established chains like TCBY are adding tart yogurt, the signature taste of both Pinkberry and Red Mango, to their traditional offerings. And just as fast-food chains jumped on the coffee bandwagon with lattes and frozen coffee drinks, more traditional stores are now ramping up their frozen yogurt options. Meanwhile, consumer tastes can change—frozen yogurt shops in the northeastern United States, for example, may notice store traffic drop significantly as the weather turns cold. These are just a few of the challenges marketers face as they strive to bring value to customers and companies.

Questions

1. What are the similarities and differences in the ways Red Mango and Pinkberry create value for their customers?

2. What is Pinkberry doing to add value for international customers?

3. Visit the websites for Pinkberry and Cold Stone Creamery. What differences do you notice in the colors and pictures used on the sites? Are there differences in how the products are described? How do these differences communicate the value messages being communicated by the different companies?

4. Do you like self-serve options such as the ones Red Mango is offering in some stores? Why or why not?

NOT WITHOUT A FIGHT

CHAPTER 2

Developing Marketing Strategies and a Marketing Plan

I n athletic competitions, the goal is clear: Win! For companies that design, produce, and sell athletic equipment to help runners, players, and competitors achieve their best performance, the idea of victory is similar. However, the competition that takes place between companies aiming to appeal most to their valuable customers—whoever they are—is a little more complicated than who crosses a finish line first.

When it comes to Nike and adidas, for example, the competitive contest spans a wealth of product lines, target markets, and marketing approaches. Thus, the firms must carefully and precisely determine the marketing strategies and plans that they use to appeal to customers and ensure their survival and success.

Created by runners in Oregon, Nike began in the early 1970s as an American company, focused mainly on the American market.[1] Its first running shoes featured a then-innovative

design with a waffle-patterned sole. The customers were mainly elite runners, determined to find the lightest shoe they could. But as *Forrest Gump* recounted, running also was gaining popularity among casual athletes, and just like Forrest, many members of this community sported Nikes on their feet.

By 1984, the company had gone public, and it had found Michael Jordan. And thus the entire market—and the very concept of sponsorship—changed forever. The Air Jordan line of basketball shoes turned Nike into a massive success, with broad appeal to sports fans of virtually all ages and profiles. Nike continues to affiliate with high-profile, elite basketball players, including 48 NBA All-Stars, such as Dwayne Wade, Kobe Bryant, and LeBron James.[2]

Basketball shoes may be the most well-known site for the brand's famous swoosh logo, but Nike also has branched into other related sectors. For example, it

adidas spokesperson and NBA star Dwight Howard at a Adidas Crazy Light Challenge event in Tokyo, Japan.

owns Cole-Haan, which makes dress and casual street shoes.[3] It produces other components of athletic uniforms for both professionals (e.g., team jerseys) and casual buyers (e.g., tracksuits, gym bags). It also purchased Umbro, another sports brand that has appealed mainly to soccer enthusiasts in the past.

This purchase of Umbro suggests that Nike is taking on its main competitor, adidas, directly in a market that previously had been dominated by adidas. As a European company, started in Germany in the early twentieth century, adidas began by designing mainly soccer (or in Europe, football) shoes, as well as some track and field footwear.

Today it has spread into other sports, though its focus on international sponsorships of the Olympic Games and the World Cup continues to reflect its origins. Yet it also seems determined to challenge Nike's dominance on the basketball court. With young stars such as Derrick Rose and Dwight Howard as spokespeople, adidas has initiated an advertising offensive, mocking Nike's shoes as

heavier, less technologically advanced, and bland.[4] It also purchased a third competitor in the market, Reebok, in 2005, in a clear effort to gain U.S. market share.

Although their primary markets continue to differ, Nike and adidas are involved in a turf war in more and more segments. Faced with the resulting challenges, they have struggled to enhance their reputations for innovation, while also keeping their costs low. For example, Nike introduced its iPod-focused partnership with Apple. With the Nike + sensor inserted in their shoes, runners can program their iPods to play a collection of songs that matches their distance or time goals.[5] The sensor also keeps track of their speed and distance, and Nike saves the data and provides platforms for social interactions among runners in the same area. Not to be outdone, adidas has moved to introduce the micro-A smart shoe, whose sensors determine the athlete's performance, together with the environmental conditions, then adjust the cushioning and airflow in the shoe to match the conditions.

To produce these high-tech versions of their footwear, both companies outsource production to countries other than their home base.[6] Nike suffered a major public relations scandal in the 1990s when activists uncovered human rights abuses in some Nike factories. Since then, it has worked actively to improve its reputation, led the way in mandating regulations for overseas factories, and donated heavily to philanthropic causes. Although its move to international production is more recent, adidas regards its presence in less developed areas as an inroad to consumers in these markets; its sponsorship of the Beijing Olympics also represented its strong push for dominance in China.

Nike maintains a strong lead in this race: It commands approximately 33 percent of the worldwide market, whereas adidas owns only 22 percent.[7] A count in recent Olympic track and field trials showed that Nike was sponsoring nearly 60 percent of the U.S. athletes present, while adidas shoes appeared on less than 13 percent of these elite feet.[8] But this competition is less a 100-yard dash than a super-marathon. When it comes to their race for market share, Nike and adidas have miles to go, and a strong competitor is always in their sights.

In this chapter, we start by discussing a *marketing strategy*, which outlines the specific actions a firm intends to implement to appeal to potential customers. Then we discuss how to do a *marketing plan*, which provides a blueprint for implementing the marketing strategy. The chapter concludes with a discussion of strategies firms use to grow. Appendix 2A explains how to write a marketing plan and provides an annotated example.

WHAT IS A MARKETING STRATEGY?

LO1 Define a marketing strategy.

A marketing strategy identifies (1) a firm's target market(s), (2) a related marketing mix—its four Ps—and (3) the bases on which the firm plans to build a sustainable competitive advantage. A sustainable competitive advantage is an advantage over the competition that is not easily copied and thus can be maintained over a long period of time. A competitive advantage acts like a wall that the firm has built around its position in a market. This wall makes it hard for outside competitors to contact customers inside—otherwise known as the marketer's target market. Of course, if the marketer has built a wall around an attractive market, competitors will attempt to break down the wall. Over time, advantages will erode because of these competitive forces, but by building high, thick walls, marketers can sustain their advantage, minimize competitive pressure, and boost profits for a longer time. Thus, establishing a sustainable competitive advantage is key to long-term financial performance.

For Nike, its thickest wall is from its strong brand, based on years of technological breakthroughs, which has created a loyal customer base. These customers know the Nike swoosh well and consider the brand as a first option when they need running, basketball, or even just casual athletic shoes. This appeal reflects Nike's careful targeting and marketing mix implementation. In terms of the four Ps, Nike is constantly trying to come up with new versions of its relatively basic product, namely, shoes and related apparel. To sell these varied products, it relies on multiple channels: online, in dedicated Nike stores and superstores, and through independent retailers such as FootLocker. Its pricing spans a broad range, from lower end, simpler options for casual shoes to the most expensive, technically sophisticated, highly reputed lines associated with big name athletes. And these popular athletes are central to its promotion efforts. Thus it remains dominant in most athletic fields, and it feels confident about expanding further.

There are four macro, or overarching, strategies that focus on aspects of the marketing mix to create and deliver value and to develop sustainable competitive advantages, as we depict in Exhibit 2.1:[9]

- **Customer excellence:** Focuses on retaining loyal customers and excellent customer service.
- **Operational excellence:** Achieved through efficient operations and excellent supply chain and human resource management.
- **Product excellence:** Having products with high perceived value and effective branding and positioning.
- **Locational excellence:** Having a good physical location and Internet presence.

Customer Excellence

Customer excellence is achieved when a firm develops value-based strategies for retaining loyal customers and provides outstanding customer service.

Retaining Loyal Customers Sometimes, the methods a firm uses to maintain a sustainable competitive advantage help attract and maintain loyal customers. For instance, having a strong brand, unique merchandise, and superior customer service all help solidify a loyal customer base. In addition, having loyal customers is, in and of itself, an important method of sustaining an advantage over competitors.

EXHIBIT 2.1 Macro Strategies for Developing Customer Value

Loyalty is more than simply preferring to purchase from one firm instead of another.[10] It means that customers are reluctant to patronize competitive firms. Loyal customers buy Nike apparel for all their sporting and casual endeavors, even if adidas goes on sale or opens a new store right around the corner from their house.

More and more firms thus realize the value of achieving customer excellence through focusing their strategy on retaining loyal customers. Nike doesn't think in terms of selling a single pair of fashionable shoes for $100; instead, it focuses on satisfying the customer who buys track shoes for herself, Cole-Haan dress shoes for her spouse, soccer shoes for her daughter, and basketball shoes for her son. Conservatively, she might buy five pairs of shoes every year for 20 years. She is not a $100 customer; combining all purchases for her family over the years, she is at least a $10,000 shoe customer—and that doesn't even count the shorts, shirts, and socks she adds on to her purchases. Viewing customers with a lifetime value perspective, rather than on a transaction-by-transaction basis, is key to modern customer retention programs.[11] We will examine how the lifetime value of a customer is calculated in Chapter 10, Appendix 10A.

Marketers also use several methods to build customer loyalty. One way involves developing a clear and precise positioning strategy. With its long history in the sport, adidas is clearly positioned as a provider of soccer cleats, far more so than Nike. That positioning helps explain why Nike might have bought Umbro. But Nike also left the Umbro brand name alone, so that it could continue to appeal to players of one of the fastest growing sports in the world.

Another method of achieving customer loyalty creates an emotional attachment through loyalty programs. These loyalty programs, which constitute part of an overall customer relationship management (CRM) program, prevail in many industries, from airlines to hotels to movie theaters to retail stores. With such programs, firms can identify members through the loyalty card or membership information the consumer provides when he or she makes a purchase. Using that purchase information, analysts determine which types of merchandise certain groups of customers are buying and thereby tailor their offering to meet the needs of their loyal customers better. For instance, by analyzing their databases, banks develop profiles of customers who have defected in the past and use that information to identify customers who may defect in the future. Once it identifies these customers, the firm can implement special retention programs to keep them.

Superior Service 2.1 Customer Service at Singapore Airlines

As most U.S.-based airlines race for the bottom, in terms of both cost and customer service, Singapore Airlines continues to maintain its industry-leading levels of customer satisfaction on its international flights.[12] The airline's commitment to excellence has been an important part of its brand strategy since the company's inception.

In its early days, Singapore Airlines faced stiff competition. So the airline elected to position itself as a leader in technology, innovation, quality, and customer service. Over the ensuing decades, it has remained committed to that strategy, introducing such customer-friendly services as hot meals, free alcoholic and nonalcoholic drinks, scented hot towels, video-on-demand for all travelers, and personal entertainment systems. When other airlines imitate its ideas, Singapore Airlines develops new ones, such as a centralized, all-in-one business panel with in-seat power supply and USB ports; a 15.4-inch LCD screen in its video systems; and a seat that folds out fully to a flat bed for business class.[13]

Although the airline's cabin crew consists of both men and women, they are referred to as Singapore Girl—an iconic image of the company that was created in 1972 and still persists. The women dress in a signature sarong, created by a French haute-couture designer. All crew members receive rigorous training to ensure they maintain a peaceful and elegant cabin ambiance and caring service.[14]

But to address economic realities in the air travel market, as well as the growth of the Asian market, it has planned the launch of a budget-oriented spin-off airline, Scoot, in 2011. This lower cost option will focus on shorter routes, such as between Singapore and China. Even with a low-cost approach though, Scoot will continue to offer many of the services that have made Singapore Airlines so successful—a new approach described as "like luxury budget" that allows consumers to choose which options they prefer from a wider range of offerings.[15]

Staying ahead of the competition requires continual investment in innovation, a price Singapore Airlines is willing to pay to earn the significant rewards, in the form of a loyal and

Singapore Airlines continues to provide new and innovative customer service offerings to stay ahead of its competition

motivated staff and return customers. To remain competitive, the airline's financial structure accommodates innovation without passing any exorbitant costs on to consumers. With that kind of business sense, it's no wonder Singapore Airlines remains profitable even as other airlines struggle to survive.

Customer Service Marketers also may build sustainable competitive advantage by offering excellent customer service,[16] though consistency in this area can prove difficult. Customer service is provided by employees, and invariably, humans are less consistent than machines. On every visit, for example, Starbucks must attempt to ensure that every single barista greets customers in a friendly way and makes drinks consistently. But what happens when a barista comes to work in a bad mood or simply forgets to add nutmeg to a drink? Firms that offer good customer service must instill its importance in their employees over a long period of time so that it becomes part of the organizational culture.

Although it may take considerable time and effort to build a reputation for customer service, once a marketer has earned a good service reputation, it can sustain this advantage for a long time, because a competitor is hard pressed to develop a comparable reputation. Superior Service 2.1 describes the superb customer service at Singapore Airlines.

Operational Excellence

Firms achieve **operational excellence**, the second way to achieve a sustainable competitive advantage, through their efficient operations, excellent supply chain management, and strong relationships with their suppliers.

All marketers strive for efficient operations to get their customers the merchandise they want, when they want it, in the required quantities, and at a lower delivered cost than that of their competitors. By so doing, they ensure good value to their customers, earn profitability for themselves, and satisfy their customers' needs. In addition, efficient operations enable firms either to provide their consumers with lower-priced merchandise or, even if their prices are not lower than those of the competition, to use the additional margin they earn to attract customers away from competitors by offering even better service, merchandise assortments, or visual presentations.

Firms achieve efficiencies by developing sophisticated distribution and information systems as well as strong relationships with vendors. Like customer relationships, vendor relations must be developed over the long term and generally cannot be easily offset by a competitor.[17] Furthermore, firms with strong relationships may gain exclusive rights to (1) sell merchandise in a particular region, (2) obtain special terms of purchase that are not available to competitors, or (3) receive popular merchandise that may be in short supply.

The supply chain for Netflix represented a remarkable innovation when the company first started: With its high-tech distribution centers, it got movies to most of its subscribers overnight. Its current streaming services expand its offering even further, allowing subscribers to access various movies and television shows immediately through gaming devices (e.g., Wii), tablets (e.g., iPad), Internet-enabled televisions, or computers. Its supply chain thus continues to evolve and become increasingly efficient. The case study at the end of this chapter provides additional information about the methods Netflix has used to become a dominant player in the movie rental industry—as well as some of the challenges it has faced recently.

Netflix customers can receive videos instantly via the iPad, TV, or computer.

Product Excellence

Product excellence, the third way to achieve a sustainable competitive advantage, occurs by providing products with high perceived value and effective branding and positioning. Some firms have difficulty developing a competitive advantage through their merchandise and service offerings, especially if competitors can deliver similar products or services easily. However, others have been able to maintain their sustainable competitive advantage by investing in their brand itself; positioning their product or service using a clear, distinctive brand image; and constantly reinforcing that image through their merchandise, service, and promotion. For instance, *BusinessWeek*'s top global brands—such as Coca-Cola, IBM, Microsoft, Google, GE, McDonalds, Intel, Apple, Disney, and HP—are all leaders in their respective industries, at least in part because they have strong brands and a clear position in the marketplace.[18]

For 3M, innovation is the central rule of its corporate culture. Although it ranks 84th worldwide in terms of its R&D spending at $1.3 billion, it ranks 3rd in the world in innovation reputation.[19] The company is well known for developing the first audio tapes, Scotchgard, Post-It Notes, and so on, and customers know they can turn to 3M to solve their needs. For example, for all those people who store their digital photographs on their computer and never print them, 3M offers Post-It Photo Papers that can be stuck to any surface for others to see.

Locational Excellence

Location is particularly important for retailers and service providers. Many say, "The three most important things in retailing are location, location, location." For example, most people will not walk or drive very far when looking to buy a cup of coffee. A competitive advantage based on location is sustainable because it is not easily duplicated. Starbucks has developed a strong competitive advantage with its location selection. The high density of stores it has established in some markets makes it very difficult for a competitor to enter that market and find good locations. Of course, when McDonald's entered the fancy coffee drink battle, it did not need to worry too much about finding new locations; its stores already appear nearly everywhere!

Multiple Sources of Advantage

In most cases, a single strategy, such as low prices or excellent service, is not sufficient to build a sustainable competitive advantage. Firms require multiple approaches to build a "wall" around their position that stands as high as possible. For example, Southwest Airlines consistently has positioned itself as a carrier that provides good service at a good value—customers get to their destination on time for a reasonable price without having to pay extra for checked luggage. At the same time, its customers know not to have extraordinary expectations, unlike those they might develop when they purchase a ticket from Singapore Airlines. They don't expect food service or seat assignments. But they do expect—and even more important, get—on-time flights that are reasonably priced. By developing its unique capabilities in several areas, Southwest has built very high wall around its position as the value player in the airline industry, which has resulted in a huge cadre of loyal customers.

CHECK YOURSELF

1. What are the various components of a marketing strategy?
2. List the four macro strategies that can help a firm develop a sustainable competitive advantage.

THE MARKETING PLAN

 **L02** Describe the elements of a marketing plan.

Effective marketing doesn't just happen. Firms like Nike and adidas carefully plan their marketing strategies to react to changes in the environment, the competition, and their customers by creating a marketing plan. A marketing plan is a written document composed of an analysis of the current marketing situation, opportunities and threats for the firm, marketing objectives and strategy specified in terms of the four Ps, action programs, and projected or pro-forma income (and other financial) statements.[20] The three major phases of the marketing plan are planning, implementation, and control.[21]

Although most people do not have a written plan that outlines what they are planning to accomplish in the next year, and how they expect to do it, firms do need such a document. It is important that everyone involved in implementing the plan knows what the overall objectives for the firm are and how they are going to be met. Other stakeholders, such as investors and potential investors, also want to know what the firm plans to do. A written marketing plan provides a reference point for evaluating whether or not the firm has met its objectives.

EXHIBIT 2.2   The Marketing Plan

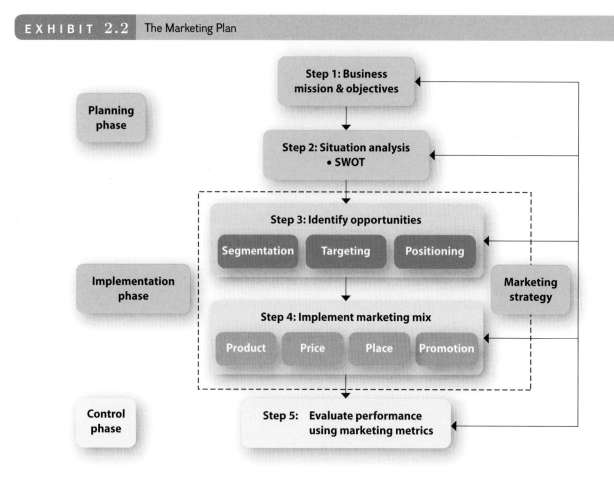

A marketing plan entails five steps, depicted in Exhibit 2.2. In Step 1 of the **planning phase**, marketing executives, in conjunction with other top managers, define the mission and/or vision of the business. For the second step, they evaluate the situation by assessing how various players, both in and outside the organization, affect the firm's potential for success (Step 2). In the **implementation phase**, marketing managers identify and evaluate different opportunities by engaging in a process known as segmentation, targeting, and positioning (STP) (Step 3). They then are responsible for implementing the marketing mix using the four Ps (Step 4). Finally, the **control phase** entails evaluating the performance of the marketing strategy using marketing metrics and taking any necessary corrective actions (Step 5).

As indicated in Exhibit 2.2, it is not always necessary to go through the entire process for every evaluation (Step 5). For instance, a firm could evaluate its performance in Step 5, then go directly to Step 2 to conduct a situation audit without redefining its overall mission.

We first discuss each step involved in developing a marketing plan. Then we consider ways of analyzing a marketing situation, as well as identifying and evaluating marketing opportunities. We also examine some specific strategies marketers use to grow a business. Finally, we consider how the implementation of the marketing mix increases customer value. A sample marketing plan is provided in Appendix 2A, following this chapter.

Step 1: Define the Business Mission

The **mission statement**, a broad description of a firm's objectives and the scope of activities it plans to undertake,[22] attempts to answer two main questions: What type of business are we? What do we need to do to accomplish our goals and objectives? These fundamental business questions must be answered at the highest corporate levels before marketing executives can get involved. Most firms want to maximize stockholders' wealth by increasing the value of the firms' stock and paying dividends.[23] Let's look at Nike and adidas.

- **Nike's Mission Statement:** "To bring inspiration and innovation to every athlete* in the world," and then with its asterisk, defines an athlete by quoting one of its founders: "If you have a body, you are an athlete."[24]

- **adidas's Mission Statement:** "The adidas group strives to be the global leader in the sporting goods industry with brands built on a passion for sport and a sporting lifestyle."[25]

For both of these firms, marketing is primarily responsible for enhancing the value of the company's offering for its customers and other constituents, whether in pursuit of a profit or not. Another key goal or objective often embedded in a mission statement relates to how the firm is building its sustainable competitive advantage.

However, owners of small, privately held firms frequently have other objectives, such as achieving a specific level of income and avoiding risks. Nonprofit organizations instead have nonmonetary objectives like Teach for America:

- **Teach for America's** mission is to build the movement to eliminate educational inequity by enlisting our nation's most promising future leaders in the effort.[26]

Step 2: Conduct a Situation Analysis

After developing its mission, a firm should perform a **situation analysis**, using a **SWOT** analysis that assesses both the internal environment with regard to its **S**trengths and **W**eaknesses and the external environment in terms of its **O**pportunities and **T**hreats. In addition, it should assess the opportunities and uncertainties of the marketplace due to changes in **C**ultural, **D**emographic, **S**ocial, **T**echnological, **E**conomic, and **P**olitical forces (CDSTEP). These factors are

LO3 Analyze a marketing situation using SWOT analysis.

Teach for America helps provide education to all kids.

EXHIBIT 2.3		Examples of Elements in a SWOT Analysis	
		Environment	**Evaluation**
		Positive	*Negative*
Nike	**Internal**	**Strengths** Strong brand Strong celebrity endorsers Innovative products	**Weakness** Overreliance on footwear
	External	**Opportunity** Emerging countries Other fashion segments	**Threats** Cheaper imports Imitation products Retail becoming price competitive
adidas	**Internal**	**Strengths** Strong brand Portfolio of brands Strong global presence	**Weakness** Management of numerous brands
	External	**Opportunity** Emerging countries	**Threats** Cheaper imports Imitation products Recessionary forces

discussed in more detail in Chapter 4. With this information, firms can anticipate and interpret change, so they can allocate appropriate resources.

Consider how Nike might conduct a SWOT analysis, as outlined in Exhibit 2.3. We focus on Nike here, but we also recognize that its marketing managers might find it helpful to perform parallel analyses for competitors, such as adidas. Because a company's strengths (Exhibit 2.3, upper left) refer to the positive internal attributes of the firm, in this example we might include Nike's great brand recognition and the visibility of the celebrities who wear its products. Furthermore, its introduction of the Nike + iPod was the first of its kind, continuing the innovative tradition that has marked Nike since it first came up with waffle-soled running shoes. Its name recognition makes consumers more likely to try out these innovations when they appear on the market—especially when they see their favorite athlete wearing similar apparel on the court or in the field.

Yet every firm has its weaknesses, and Nike is no exception. Weaknesses (Exhibit 2.3, upper right) are negative attributes of the firm. Nike relies heavily—perhaps even too heavily—on its athletic shoe lines, especially for running and basketball. The NBA lockout for the 2012 season put undue stress on its sales in this segment. Not only would players and teams stop buying, but as the old saying goes, "Out of sight, out of mind." If the players are not on the court, their fans aren't thinking about them, and then sales will suffer.[27] In response to the popular emergence of other options, such as "toning" and "barefoot" models, Nike has largely suggested they are fads that will not last, stressing instead its traditional athletic shoe models.[28]

Keke Palmer is wearing her Nikes at a Nickelodeon event.

Opportunities (Exhibit 2.3, lower left) pertain to positive aspects of the external environment. Among Nike's opportunities, it appears determined to pursue dominance in other, sometime niche, sports markets. For the Olympic Games, it introduced footwear for less familiar sports, including fencing, wrestling, and equestrian events.[29] This goal also aligns with another notable opportunity for Nike, that is, growth in global markets. It sells products in 170 countries worldwide, through independent distributors, Nike stores, the website, and licenses.[30] It aims to expand further, and it has devoted significant resources to improving its prominence among European football players and fans.[31]

Nike's strengths include its innovative product tradition. It was the first to introduce the Nike+ iPod, a sensor that when inserted into shoes gives the runner instant feedback on factors such as running time, distance, pace, and calories burned.

Finally, threats (Exhibit 2.3, lower right) represent the negative aspects of the company's external environment. For example, its widespread market dominance makes Nike the primary target for all its competitors,[32] from adidas to New Balance to Li Ning, China's largest shoe maker. All of these firms want to take market share from Nike, which means it must constantly be a little bit on the defensive. Furthermore, a perpetual threat for any apparel company is staying fashionable, as Nike itself acknowledges: "We must . . . respond to trends and shifts in consumer preferences by adjusting the mix of existing product offerings, developing new products, styles and categories, and influencing sports and fitness preferences through aggressive marketing. Failure to respond in a timely and adequate manner could have a material adverse effect on our sales and profitability. This is a continuing risk."[33]

Step 3: Identifying and Evaluating Opportunities Using STP (Segmentation, Targeting, and Positioning)

LO4 Describe how a firm chooses which consumer group(s) to pursue with its marketing efforts.

After completing the situation audit, the next step is to identify and evaluate opportunities for increasing sales and profits using **STP** (segmentation, targeting, and positioning). With STP, the firm first divides the marketplace into subgroups or segments, determines which of those segments it should pursue or target, and finally decides how it should position its products and services to best meet the needs of those chosen targets (more details on the STP process can be found in Chapter 8).

Segmentation   Many types of customers appear in any market, and most firms cannot satisfy everyone's needs. For instance, among Internet users, some do research online, some shop, some look for entertainment, and many do all three. Each of these groups might be a **market segment** consisting of consumers who respond similarly to a firm's marketing efforts. The process of dividing the market into groups of customers with different needs, wants, or characteristics—who therefore might appreciate products or services geared especially for them—is called **market segmentation**.

Let's look at Hertz, the car rental company. The example in Exhibit 2.4 reveals that some of the segments that Hertz targets includes its Fun Collection, including the Corvette ZHZ and Chevrolet Camaro, to single people and couples wanting to have a bit of fun. Its Prestige Collection, which features the Cadillac Escalade and Infiniti QX56, targets business customers and families

EXHIBIT 2.4	Hertz Market Segmentation				
	Segment 1	Segment 2	Segment 3	Segment 4	Segment 5
Segments	Single people and couples wanting to have a bit of fun	Business customers and families who prefer a luxurious ride	Environmentally conscious customers	Families	Commercial customers
	Fun Collection	Prestige Collection	Green Collection	SUV/Minivan & crossover	Commercial Van/Truck
Cars Offered	Corvette ZHZ	Infiniti QX56	Toyota Prius	Toyota Rav 4	
	Chevrolet Camaro	Cadillac Escalade	Ford Fusion	Ford Explorer	Ford Cargo Van

Hertz targets several markets. Its "Fun Collection" (left) appeals to single people and couples wanting to have fun; while its "Prestige Collection" (right) appeals to its business customers and families who prefer a luxurious ride.

who prefer a luxurious ride. With its Green collection of cars such as the Toyota Prius and Ford Fusion, Hertz appeals to environmentally conscious customers, and with its SUV/Minivan collection, it brings in families. It also offers commercial vans for service customers.[34] Thus, Hertz uses a variety of demographics—gender, age, income, interests—to identify customers who might want the Fun, Prestige, Green, and SUV/Minivan collections, but it also applies psychological or behavioral factors, such as a preference for style or a need to move possessions across town, to identify likely consumers of the Fun Collection and its commercial vans.

Nike targets different segments, such as women's fitness, golf, and running.

Going back to our Nike example, let's look at how they segment their customers based on how the products are used and gender. Nike focuses on the following segments: running, basketball, football (soccer), men's training, women's training, action sports, sportswear, and golf.

Targeting After a firm has identified the various market segments it might pursue, it evaluates each segment's attractiveness and decides which to pursue using a process known as **target marketing** or **targeting**. For example, Hertz realizes that its primary appeal for the SUV/Minivan collection centers on young families, so the bulk of its marketing efforts for this business is directed toward that group.

Soft drink manufacturers also divide their massive markets into submarkets or segments. Coca-Cola, for instance, makes several different types of Coke, including regular, Coke II, and Cherry Coke. Among its diet colas, it targets Coke Zero to men and Diet Coke to women, because men prefer not to be associated with diets. It also markets Sprite to those who don't like dark colas, Fruitopia and Minute Maid for more health-conscious consumers, and Dasani bottled water for purists.

Positioning Finally, when the firm decides which segments to pursue, it must determine how it wants to be positioned within those segments. **Market positioning** involves the process of defining the marketing mix variables so that target customers have a clear, distinctive, desirable understanding of what the product does or represents in comparison with competing products. Hertz positions itself as a quality car (and truck) rental company that is the first choice for each of its target segments. In its marketing communications, it stresses that customers will get peace of mind when they rent from Hertz, the market leader in the car rental business, and be able to enjoy their journey (e.g., leisure consumers) and reduce travel time (e.g., business consumers).[35]

To segment the coffee drinker market, Starbucks uses a variety of methods, including geography (e.g., college campuses versus shopping/business districts) and benefits (e.g., drinkers of caffeinated versus decaffeinated products). After determining which of those segments represent effective targets, Starbucks positions itself as a firm that develops a variety of products that match the wants and needs of the different market segments—espresso drinks, coffees, teas, bottled drinks, pastries, and cooler foods.

Social and Mobile Marketing 2.1   Truly Mobile Pizza[36]

The pizza delivery business has always been mobile in one sense, but Pizza Hut is making sure that it spreads into mobile commerce as well. This first-mover introduced its mobile website in 2007, an iPhone application in 2009, and apps for the iPad, Android, and Windows Mobile 7 in 2010.

The decision to go mobile was based on a few insights that Pizza Hut gleaned from its market research. In particular, if it did not offer mobile access quickly, its competitors might be first to do so in the competitive pizza delivery market. The Pizza Hut app lets customers order food through a user-friendly experience, but it also makes sure to identify the closest store locations for delivery or pick-up service.

Without much information about who the consumers who would use the app were, Pizza Hut anticipated more orders from college-aged men, who do not like to cook and want their food on demand, but also are not willing to stop a video game to take the time to order food through more traditional channels. The assumption seemed reasonable—but it also was dead wrong. Further market research, based on the introduction of the app, has shown that there are just as many pizza connoisseurs with iPhones who are older than 55 as there are 13–24-year-olds ordering the pies.

Pizza Hut's mobile app makes ordering pizza a piece of cake.

After identifying its target segments, a firm must evaluate each of its strategic opportunities. A method of examining which segments to pursue is described in the Growth Strategies section later in the chapter. Firms typically are most successful when they focus on opportunities that build on their strengths relative to those of their competition. In Step 4 of the marketing plan, the firm implements its marketing mix and allocates resources to different products and services.

For example, Pizza Hut decided to jump on changing consumer desires for rapid access to its offering by constantly expanding its mobile applications, but it also found its positioning as a convenient option appealing to more markets than it even expected, as Social and Mobile Media 2.1 reveals.

LO5 Outline the implementation of the marketing mix as a means to increase customer value.

Step 4: Implement Marketing Mix and Allocate Resources

When the firm has identified and evaluated different growth opportunities by performing an STP analysis, the real action begins. It has decided what to do, how to do it, and how many resources should be allocated to it. In the fourth step of the

Adding Value 2.1 Innovation at 3M

When a company pours billions of dollars into research and development, a struggling economy is a serious problem. If profits fall, who has money for innovation, right? Not for 3M. This longtime innovator cites a multipronged mission that includes satisfying customers with "innovative technology and superior quality, value, and service," as well as earning "the admiration of all those associated with 3M worldwide" (among other goals).[37] Its product offering spans an incredible range of categories, from health care to highway safety to office and pet care products to fly fishing equipment to solar film.[38]

Because it remains constantly committed to providing useful, new solutions to its customers, 3M continues to reinvest a significant percentage of its revenues to research.[39] Furthermore, in line with 3M's commitment to "value and develop our employees' diverse talents, initiative, and leadership," it allows its researchers to spend time pursuing their own interests—some of science's most important discoveries occur during unrelated research, after all. Thus when industrial architects asked 3M for some ideas for lighting their studios, it put one of its creative designers on the project. The result, the nine-foot Hoop Light, won 3M design awards at interior design international competitions, rather than just industrial contracts.[40]

But these creative researchers cannot do it all on their own. An obvious but still rather uncommon approach to matching product development with customer needs is to involve customers in the process of innovation.[41] Corporate clients in particular are experts in their businesses; they know their customers' demands better than anyone. By interacting with these expert customers and combining their needs with its own broad range of technical expertise and infrastructure, 3M produces novel solutions to difficult challenges.

Many of these interactions take place at the company's customer innovation centers, where visitors outline their business goals for 3M experts and tour the manufacturer's core technologies. Exposure to these technologies, 3M has learned, helps stimulate creative ideas about ways to combine or adapt existing science in one sector to provide solutions in another. A new technology in aerospace, for example, could lead to a breakthrough in healthcare. These innovation centers are so successful that 3M has opened nearly two dozen, and companies like Hershey and Pitney Bowes are following suit.

---

planning process, marketers implement the actual marketing mix—product, price, promotion, and place—for each product and service on the basis of what they believe their target markets will value. At the same time, marketers make important decisions about how they will allocate their scarce resources to their various products and services.

Product and Value Creation **Products**, which include services, constitute the first of the four Ps. Because the key to the success of any marketing program is the creation of value, firms attempt to develop products and services that customers perceive as valuable enough to buy. Dyson fans and fan heaters draw in and redirect surrounding air without potentially dangerous or fast spinning blades or visible heating elements. Although more expensive than conventional fans and space heaters, these sculpturally beautiful appliances are perceived by consumers to be a valuable alternative to products that haven't significantly changed since the early 1900s.

Remember the example of 3M and its research and development efforts? Adding Value 2.1 further details how 3M creates value for its customers.

Price and Value Capture Recall that the second element of the marketing mix is price. As part of the exchange process, a firm provides a product or a service, or some combination thereof, and in return, it gets

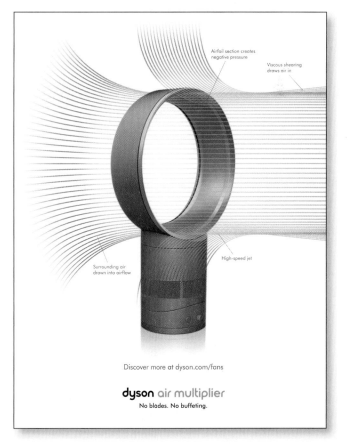

Airfoil section creates negative pressure

Viscous shearing draws air in

Surrounding air drawn into airflow

High-speed jet

Discover more at dyson.com/fans

dyson air multiplier
No blades. No buffeting.

Dyson creates value with its innovative products.

The Home Plus Virtual Stores have created a whole new way of providing the third P, place, and value delivery.

money. Value-based marketing requires that firms charge a price that customers perceive as giving them a good value for the product they receive. Clearly, it is important for a firm to have a clear focus in terms of what products to sell, where to buy them, and what methods to use in selling them. But pricing is the only activity that actually brings in money and therefore influences revenues. If a price is set too high, it will not generate much volume. If a price is set too low, it may result in lower-than-optimal margins and profits. Therefore, price should be based on the value that the customer perceives. Dyson fans can retail for $150 or more while conventional fans retail for around $25. Customers thus can decide just what they want from their fan and choose the one at the price they prefer.

Place and Value Delivery For the third P, place, the firm must be able, after it has created value through a product and/or service, to make the product or service readily accessible when and where the customer wants it. Recently, Tesco took an innovative step along these lines when it opened HomePlus virtual stores in several South Korean subway stations. Busy urban consumers were struggling to find the time to get to a grocery store, so HomePlus reinvented the placement of grocery stores. The virtual stores in subway stations look like grocery stores—except that they are just LCD screens! The virtual markets allow customers to shop with just their smartphones and their items will be delivered to their doorstep.[42]

Promotion and Value Communication The fourth and last P of the marketing mix is promotion. Marketers communicate the value of their offering, or the value proposition, to their customers through a variety of media including television, radio, magazines, sales forces, and the Internet. A relatively new promotion channel relies on daily deal websites such as Groupon or LivingSocial to get the word out. Many smaller companies find that these sites give them greater name recognition than they ever could have achieved on their own.

But when a well-known company uses the sites, the effect is even more remarkable. For example, Whole Foods offered a certificate for $20 worth of goods at a cost of only $10 on LivingSocial.com. Consumers snatched up the deal at a rate of 115,000 per hour.[43] Whole Foods capped the offer at 1 million deals, so it exposed itself to costs of around $10–15 million (if we include the fees it had to pay to LivingSocial to post the deal) in this attempt to get more grocery shoppers to visit its stores.

Step 5: Evaluate Performance Using Marketing Metrics

The final step in the planning process includes evaluating the results of the strategy and implementation program using marketing metrics. A **metric** is a measuring system that quantifies a trend, dynamic, or characteristic. Metrics are used to explain why things happened and also to project the future. They make it possible to compare results across regions, strategic business units (SBUs), product lines, and time periods. The firm can determine why it achieved or did not achieve its performance goals with the help of these metrics. Understanding the causes of the performance, regardless of whether that performance exceeded, met, or fell below the firm's goals, enables firms to make appropriate adjustments.

Typically, managers begin by reviewing the implementation programs, and their analysis may indicate that the strategy (or even the mission statement) needs to be reconsidered. Problems can arise both when firms successfully implement poor strategies and when they poorly implement good strategies.

Who Is Accountable for Performance? At each level of an organization, the business unit and its manager should be held accountable only for the revenues, expenses, and profits that they can control. Thus, expenses that affect several levels of the organization (such as the labor and capital expenses associated with operating a corporate headquarters) shouldn't be arbitrarily assigned to lower levels. In the case of a store, for example, it may be appropriate to evaluate performance objectives based on sales, sales associate productivity, and energy costs. If the corporate office lowers prices to get rid of merchandise and therefore profits suffer, then it's not fair to assess a store manager's performance based on the resulting decline in store profit.

Performance evaluations are used to pinpoint problem areas. Reasons performance may be above or below planned levels must be examined. If a manager's performance is below planned levels, was it because the sales force didn't do an adequate job, because the economy took a downward turn, because competition successfully implemented a new strategy, or because the managers involved in setting the objectives aren't very good at making estimates? The manager should only be held accountable in the case of the inadequate sales force job or setting inappropriate forecasts.

When it appears that actual performance is going to be below the plan because of circumstances beyond the manager's control, the firm can still take action to minimize the harm. For our chapter exemplar Nike, two situations have arisen recently over which the firm had little control—a global recession and a scandal involving a spokesperson. Many consumers cut their spending on things like apparel in the modern recession. And the Tiger Woods infidelity scandal left Nike in an awkward position. According to researchers at Carnegie Mellon University, for the 10 years prior to the scandal, Woods's endorsement had earned Nike's golf ball division approximately $60 million in additional profits. In the year following widespread media reports of his infidelity, Nike lost approximately 105,000 customers and $1.3 million in profit.[44]

In remarkable cases such as this, marketing managers must ask themselves several relevant questions: How quickly were

Tiger Woods is back.

plans adjusted? How rapidly and appropriately were pricing and promotional policies modified? In short, did I react to salvage an adverse situation, or did my reactions worsen the situation? For the Woods scandal, it appears that marketing managers made the right decision by keeping him as an endorser, despite their short-term losses. The same researchers estimate that "even in the midst of the scandal, the overall profit was greater by $1.6 million for Nike with Tiger Woods than without him."[45]

Performance Objectives and Metrics   Many factors contribute to a firm's overall performance, which makes it hard to find a single metric to evaluate performance. One approach is to compare a firm's performance over time or to competing firms, using common financial metrics such as sales and profits. Another method of assessing performance is to view the firm's products or services as a portfolio. Depending on the firm's relative performance, the profits from some products or services are used to fuel growth for others.

Financial Performance Metrics   Some commonly used metrics to assess performance include revenues, or sales, and profits. For instance, sales are a global measure of a firm's activity level. However, a manager could easily increase sales by lowering prices, but the profit realized on that merchandise (gross margin) would suffer as a result. An attempt to maximize one metric may lower another. Managers must therefore understand how their actions affect multiple performance metrics. It's usually unwise to use only one metric because it rarely tells the whole story.

In addition to assessing the absolute level of sales and profits, a firm may wish to measure the relative level of sales and profits. For example, a relative metric of sales or profits is its increase or decrease over the prior year. In addition, a firm may compare its growth in sales or profits relative to other benchmark companies (e.g., Coke may compare itself to Pepsi).

The metrics used to evaluate a firm vary depending on (1) the level of the organization at which the decision is made and (2) the resources the manager controls. For example, while the top executives of a firm have control over all of the firm's resources and resulting expenses, a regional sales manager only has control over the sales and expenses generated by his or her salespeople.

Let's look at Nike's sales revenue and profits (after taxes) and compare them with those of adidas (Exhibit 2.5).

Furthermore, as the corporate consciousness of the importance of social responsibility grows, firms are starting to report corporate social responsibility metrics in major areas, such as their impact on the environment, their ability to diversify their workforce, energy conservation initiatives, and their policies on protecting the human rights of their employees and the employees of their suppliers. Ethical and Societal Dilemma 2.1 examines how Starbucks is working to tackle important societal issues.

EXHIBIT 2.5	Performance Metrics: Nike vs. adidas			
		2010	**2011**	**% Change**
Nike	Net Sales	$19.0B	$20.9B	9.5%
	Net Profit	$ 1.9B	$ 2.1B	10%
	Net Profit/Net Sales	10%	10%	0%
Adidas	Net Sales	€ 12.0B	€13.3B	10.1%
	Net Profit	€894M	€ 1.01B	13%
	Net Profit/Net Sales	7.4%	7.6%	0.2%

Ethical and Societal Dilemma 2.1[46]   Starbucks Working to Make the Earth a Better Place

To ensure it adds value to the broader society that makes up its macroenvironment, Starbucks rates its own corporate social responsibility performance in five categories: ethical sourcing, environment, community, wellness, and diversity. Its brand equity improves in response to its proactive efforts along these socially responsible dimensions; customers feel good about their buying experience; and Starbucks develops stronger relationships with suppliers, both locally and globally.

With regard to its focus on ethical sourcing and sustainable coffee production, Starbucks maintains its C.A.F.E. (Coffee and Farmer Equity) program. The C.A.F.E. guidelines include a scorecard that rates coffee farmers according to their product quality, economic accountability, social responsibility, and environmental leadership. Third parties evaluate whether suppliers meet Starbucks' standards under the C.A.F.E. program. In just a few years, suppliers from 13 different countries had gained C.A.F.E. approval. In turn, Starbucks continues to increase the amount of coffee that it purchases from verified suppliers, from 77 percent in the early 2000s to 81 percent in 2009 to 84 percent by 2010—on its way to its goal of having "100% of our coffee certified or verified by an independent third party."

On a more local level, Starbucks sometimes experiences opposition from local communities that believe its stores will ruin the historical ambiance of an area. To take the needs of local communities into consideration, Starbucks attempts to address historic preservation, environmental, infrastructure, job, and urban revitalization concerns. For example, in La Mesa, California, Starbucks overcame opposition by supporting local events and businesses. In addition, it formed a joint venture with Johnson Development Corporation (JDC) to develop urban coffee opportunities. By opening in diverse urban areas, Starbucks helps stimulate economic growth in the areas by creating jobs, using local suppliers, and attracting other retailers to the area.

Starbucks has also launched a program that focuses on the needs of the more than 1 billion people globally who lack access to safe drinking water. On World Water Day, Starbucks sponsors three-mile walks in many cities, as well as a virtual online walk, to symbolize and raise awareness about the average length that women and children walk to get drinking water each day. Starbucks' Ethos Water brand contributes 5 cents for each bottle of water sold in Starbucks stores to humanitarian water programs around the world, in countries such as

On World Water Day, Starbucks sponsored walks to symbolize and raise awareness about the average length that women and children walk to get drinking water each day.

Bangladesh, Ethiopia, and Kenya. Thus far, it has contributed more than $6 million to help solve the world's water crisis, thereby aiding approximately 420,000 people who lack consistent access.[47]

Lack of water is not the only health worry facing people across the world. By posting nutrition information in its stores, Starbucks attempts to aid in the effort to reduce the prevalence of obesity and diabetes among its consumers. According to one report, communicating this information has prompted Starbucks customers to lower their calorie intake, but not their purchase amounts.

To address the health and welfare of its own employees (whom the company calls "partners"), Starbucks not only offers generous health benefits to both full- and part-time workers but also has undertaken a Thrive Wellness Initiative (TWI).[48] The stated purpose of TWI is to care for the well-being of employees. For example, the newest portion of the TWI is Kinetix, a program that offers classes on nutrition and exercise, as well as eight weeks of sessions with a personal trainer.

Finally, just as it expects its coffee producers to engage in environmentally friendly practices, Starbucks itself attempts to use renewable energy and reduce its negative impact on the environment. Furniture and fixtures in stores are made of sustainable building materials. As a member of the Sustainable Packaging Coalition, Starbucks also works to replace conventional packaging with green alternatives.

LO6 Summarize portfolio analysis and its use to evaluate marketing performance.

Portfolio Analysis In portfolio analysis, management evaluates the firm's various products and businesses—its "portfolio"—and allocates resources according to which products are expected to be the most profitable for the firm in the future. Portfolio analysis is typically performed at the **strategic business unit (SBU)** or **product line** level of the firm, though managers also can use it to analyze brands or even individual items. An SBU is a division of the firm itself that can be managed and operated somewhat independently from other divisions and may have a different mission or objectives. For example, Goodyear is one of the largest tire firms in the world, selling its products on six continents in over 180 countries and with sales of approximately $18 billion. Its four SBUs are organized by geography: North America, Europe, Middle East, Africa, Latin America, and Asia/Pacific.[49]

A product line, in contrast, is a group of products that consumers may use together or perceive as similar in some way. One line of product for Goodyear could be car, van, SUV, and light truck while another line could be racing tires or aviation tires.

One of the most popular portfolio analysis methods, developed by the Boston Consulting Group (BCG), requires that firms classify all their products or services into a two-by-two matrix, as depicted in Exhibit 2.6.[50] The circles represent brands, and their sizes are in direct proportion to the brands' annual sales. The horizontal axis represents the relative market share.

In general, **market share** is the percentage of a market accounted for by a specific entity,[51] and is used to establish the product's strength in a particular market. It is usually discussed in units, revenue, or sales. A special type of market share metric, **relative market share**, is used in this application because it provides managers with a product's relative strength, compared with that of the largest firm in the industry.[52] The vertical axis is the **market growth rate**, or the annual rate of growth of the specific market in which the product competes. Market growth rate thus measures how attractive a particular market is. Each quadrant in the matrix has been named on the basis of the amount of resources it generates for and requires from the firm.

Stars Stars (upper left quadrant) occur in high-growth markets and are high market share products. That is, stars often require a heavy resource investment in such

EXHIBIT 2.6 Boston Consulting Group Matrix

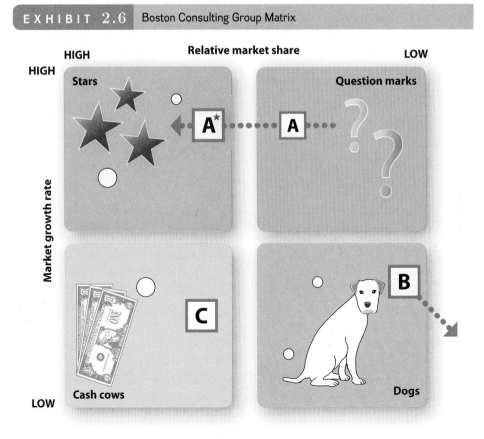

things as promotions and new production facilities to fuel their rapid growth. As their market growth slows, stars will migrate from heavy users of resources to heavy generators of resources and become cash cows.

Cash Cows Cash cows (lower left quadrant) are in low-growth markets but are high market share products. Because these products have already received heavy investments to develop their high market share, they have excess resources that can be spun off to those products that need it. For example, the firm may decide to use the excess resources generated by Brand C to fund products in the question mark quadrant.

Question Marks Question marks (upper right quadrant) appear in high-growth markets but have relatively low market shares; thus, they are often the most managerially intensive products in that they require significant resources to maintain and potentially increase their market share. Managers must decide whether to infuse question marks with resources generated by the cash cows, so that they can become stars, or withdraw resources and eventually phase out the products. Brand A, for instance, is currently a question mark, but by infusing it with resources, the firm hopes to turn it into a star.

Dogs Dogs (lower right quadrant) are in low-growth markets and have relatively low market shares. Although they may generate enough resources to sustain themselves, dogs are not destined for "stardom" and should be phased out unless they are needed to complement or boost the sales of another product or for competitive purposes. In the case depicted in Exhibit 2.6, the company has decided to stop making Brand B.

Now let's look at Apple and some of its products.[53] The four that we will focus our attention on are:

- iPhone
- iPod
- iMac Desktop
- iPad

Goodyear, one of the largest tire firms in the world, organizes its strategic business units by geography.

In which Boston Consulting quadrant do these two products fit?

Let's consider each of these products and place them into the BCG matrix based on these data. The iPhone is clearly a star—a high growth rate (87 percent). In fact, by the end of 2011, Apple returned to its position as the top selling smartphone in the industry, with 16.2 million units sold in their fourth quarter alone, making its relative market share 100 percent.[54]

Apple's iPod is a different story. With a staggering absolute market share consistently above 75 percent, its relative market share is also 100 percent, and with more than 300 million iPods sold in a little over 10 years, it is definitely an important product for Apple. Unfortunately, the MP3 market is contracting (the market shrank by 10 percent from 2010 to 2011). Combine the lack of growth with a large relative market share, and it is likely that the iPod is a cash cow for Apple.[55]

Although popular with graphic designers, the growth rate of the Mac Desktop has slowed to a pitiful 4 percent. Given that it also has a small relative market share in the desktop market, the iMac can be tentatively classified as a dog. Should Apple get rid of the iMac? For at least two reasons, this is probably a bad idea. First, it risks alienating graphic designers and other Apple loyalists who depend on the iMac. Since these customers may also enjoy other Apple products, their dissatisfaction might adversely affect sales of these other products. Second, discontinuing the iMac would leave a gaping hole in its portfolio, and would therefore hurt its brand image as a computer company.

Then we have the iPad with an incredible sales growth rate from 2010 to 2011 of 333 percent, and sales of approximately 55 million units as of early 2012. In 2010, its absolute market share was 95.5 percent, making it the market leader with a relative market share of 100 percent. However, it is also experiencing increasing competition from Android tablets and the Kindle Fire. Looking at 2011 as a whole, the iPad captured 66.6 percent of the tablet market (2 out of every 3 tablets sold was an iPad). But by the end of 2011 its absolute market share had dropped to 57 percent.[56] Where on the BCG matrix would you classify the iPad? Would you argue that a 57 percent absolute market share places it in the star category, or would you be more conservative and put it as a question mark, citing the steady erosion of absolute market share? Will Apple be able to continue to grow and maintain its market share leader position by releasing a new version of the iPad?

Although quite useful for conceptualizing the relative performance of products or services and using this information to allocate resources, the BCG approach and others like it are often difficult to implement in practice. In particular, it is difficult to measure both relative market share and industry growth. Furthermore, other measures easily could serve as substitutes to represent a product's competitive position and the market's relative attractiveness. Another issue for marketers is the potential self-fulfilling prophecy of placing a product or service into a quadrant. As we have shown in our Apple iPad example, whether it is classified as a star or a question mark has profound implications on how it is treated and supported within the firm. Question marks require more marketing and production support.

Because of these limitations, many firms have tempered their use of matrix approaches to achieve a more balanced approach to evaluating products and services and allocating their resources. Instead of assigning allocation decisions to the top levels of the organization, many firms start at lower management levels and employ checks and balances to force managers at each level of the organizational hierarchy to negotiate with those above and below them to reach their final decisions.

Strategic Planning Is Not Sequential

The planning process in Exhibit 2.2 suggests that managers follow a set sequence when they make strategic decisions. Namely, after they've defined the business mission, they perform the situation analysis, identify strategic opportunities, evaluate alternatives, set objectives, allocate resources, develop the implementation plan, and, finally, evaluate their performance and make adjustments. But actual planning processes can move back and forth among these steps. For example, a situation analysis may uncover a logical alternative, even though this alternative might not be included in the mission statement, which would mean that the mission statement would need to be revised. The development of the implementation plan also might reveal that insufficient resources have been allocated to a particular product for it to achieve its objective. In that case, the firm would need to either change the objective or increase the resources; alternatively, the marketer might consider not investing in the product at all.

Now that we have gone through the steps of the marketing plan, let's look at some growth strategies that have been responsible for making many marketing firms successful.

CHECK YOURSELF

1. What are the five steps in creating a marketing plan?
2. What tool helps a marketer conduct a situation analysis?
3. What is STP?
4. What do the four quadrants of the portfolio analysis represent?

GROWTH STRATEGIES

LO7 Describe how firms grow their business.

Firms consider pursuing various market segments as part of their overall growth strategies, which may include the four major strategies in Exhibit 2.7.[57] The rows distinguish those opportunities a firm possesses in its current markets from

EXHIBIT 2.7 Market/Product and Services Strategies

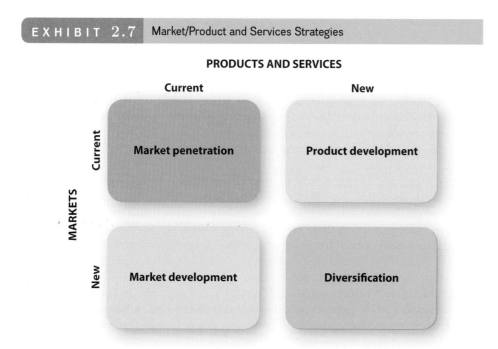

PRODUCTS AND SERVICES

	Current	New
MARKETS — Current	Market penetration	Product development
MARKETS — New	Market development	Diversification

To increase market penetration with its young target audience, MTV produces reality shows like "America's Best Dance Crew."

those it has in new markets, whereas the columns distinguish between the firm's current marketing offering and that of a new opportunity. Let's consider each of them in detail.

Market Penetration

A **market penetration strategy** employs the existing marketing mix and focuses the firm's efforts on existing customers. Such a growth strategy might be achieved by attracting new consumers to the firm's current target market or encouraging current customers to patronize the firm more often or buy more merchandise on each visit. A market penetration strategy generally requires greater marketing efforts, such as increased advertising and additional sales and promotions, or intensified distribution efforts in geographic areas in which the product or service already is sold.

To penetrate its target market, TV network MTV found that it needed new ways to engage its viewers. The young audience to which MTV traditionally appeals consists of text-messaging, video-gaming multitaskers who no longer accept plain video programming on their televisions. Thus, the network is working hard to develop additional strategies and outlets to retain viewers, as well as to encourage them to spend more time interacting with its content. MTV discovered that interactions with the audience through alternative channels increase ratings for its shows. Therefore, in addition to producing and airing reality shows such as *America's Best Dance Crew* and *Jersey Shore*, MTV has partnered with a video game producer Yoostar to offer "Yoostar on MTV" for Xbox 360. The game provides a massive library of constantly updated shows, music videos, and recordings of live events. Using the green screen technology contained in the game, fans of these shows can insert themselves into scenes they've already seen their more famous teen peers undergo. Of course, the game also allows them to upload their completed performance to Facebook, Twitter, or a Yoostar dedicated website.[58] On MTV's website, dedicated forums, blogs, and activities for each show also encourage viewers to connect with characters in their shows. Not only can viewers talk about the characters as if they were friends, but they can buy the products they wear and download the music played during the show.[59]

Market Development

A **market development strategy** employs the existing marketing offering to reach new market segments, whether domestic or international. International expansion generally is riskier than domestic expansion because firms must deal with differences in government regulations, cultural traditions, supply chains, and language. However, many U.S. firms, including MTV, enjoy a competitive advantage in global markets—such as Mexico, Latin America, Europe, China, and Japan—because, especially among young people, U.S. culture is widely emulated for consumer products.

For example, because of rising prosperity worldwide and rapidly increasing access to cable television that offers U.S. programming, fashion trends from the United States have spread to young people in emerging countries. Since its founding in 1981, MTV has expanded well beyond the United States, with niche sites in more than 20 countries, including the United Kingdom, Japan, Brazil, and India. It is available in 562 million households in 161 countries and 33 languages.[60] And thus, the global MTV generation prefers soft drinks to tea, athletic shoes to sandals, French fries to rice, and credit cards to cash. To achieve such growth, MTV

MTV's Real World Las Vegas *cast members: Heather Marter, Dustin Zito, Naomi Defensor, and Jasmine Reynaud.*

leveraged its existing media content but also delivers culturally relevant content using local DJs and show formats.

Product Development

The third growth strategy option, a **product development strategy**, offers a new product or service to a firm's current target market. Consider MTV's dynamic line-up: The network constantly develops new pilots and show concepts to increase the amount of time viewers can spend watching MTV. For example, each version of *The Real World* reality series, and new series such as *Ridiculousness* and *Friendzone* all represent new programs designed to attract and retain existing viewers. Along with its new TV series, MTV develops new online products to engage consumers through more than 25 niche blogs, as well as a website that it uses to dominate a greater share of viewers' minds and time. These various MTV-branded niche sites pertain to social, political, and environmental issues that appeal to different segments in its target market. The sites further encourage viewers to get involved in real-world issues (not *The Real World* issues) through mobile technologies. By visiting the sites, MTV promises that consumers can share mobile content, educate themselves, and take action on important issues.[61]

Diversification

A **diversification strategy**, the last of the growth strategies from Exhibit 2.7, introduces a new product or service to a market segment that currently is not served. Diversification opportunities may be either related or unrelated. In a **related diversification** opportunity, the current target market and/or marketing mix shares something in common with the new opportunity.[62] In other words, the firm might be able to purchase from existing vendors, use the same distribution and/or management information system, or advertise in the same newspapers to target markets that are similar to their current consumers. MTV has pursued related diversification by introducing TV series that focus on more positive social messages, instead of on wealth, celebrities, and excessive youth culture (e.g., *The Hills, My Super Sweet 16*). In series such as *I Used to Be Fat* and *Made*, recognizable and seemingly similar teens still appeal to viewers and provide a healthy dose of drama. However, the plotlines of these shows focus on how people overcome adversity or struggle with everyday challenges to attain some level of happiness.[63]

In contrast, in an **unrelated diversification**, the new business lacks any common elements with the present business. Unrelated diversifications do not capitalize on either core strengths associated with markets or with products. Thus, they would be viewed as very risky. Revisiting our example of the technology innovation company 3M, however, we find an excellent and successful example of unrelated diversification strategies: What began as a sandpaper products company now markets its products in six major business segments, from consumer office supplies to orthodontic technologies.[64]

CHECK YOURSELF

1. What are the four growth strategies?
2. What type of strategy is growing the business from existing customers?
3. Which strategy is the riskiest?

Summing Up

LO1 Define a marketing strategy.

A marketing strategy identifies (1) a firm's target markets(s), (2) a related marketing mix (four Ps), and (3) the bases on which the firm plans to build a sustainable competitive advantage. Firms use four macro strategies to build their sustainable competitive advantage. Customer excellence focuses on retaining loyal customers and excellent customer service. Operational excellence is achieved through efficient operations and excellent supply chain and human resource management. Product excellence entails having products with high perceived value and effective branding and positioning. Finally, locational excellence entails having a good physical location and Internet presence.

LO2 Describe the elements of a marketing plan.

A marketing plan is composed of an analysis of the current marketing situation, its objectives, the strategy for the four Ps, and appropriate financial statements. A marketing plan represents the output of a three-phase process: planning, implementation, and control. The planning phase requires that managers define the firm's mission and vision and assess the firm's current situation. It helps answer the questions, "What business are we in now, and what do we intend to be in the future?" In the second phase, implementation, the firm specifies, in more operational terms, how it plans to implement its mission and vision. Specifically, to which customer groups does it wish to direct its marketing efforts, and how does it use its marketing mix to provide good value? Finally, in the control phase, the firm must evaluate its performance using appropriate metrics to determine what worked, what didn't, and how performance can be improved in the future.

LO3 Analyze a marketing situation using SWOT analysis.

SWOT stands for strengths, weaknesses, opportunities, and threats. A SWOT analysis occurs during the second step in the strategic planning process, the situation analysis. By analyzing what the firm is good at (its strengths), where it could improve (its weaknesses), where in the marketplace it might excel (its opportunities), and what is happening in the marketplace that could harm the firm (its threats), managers can assess their firm's situation accurately and plan its strategy accordingly.

LO4 Describe how a firm chooses which consumer group(s) to pursue with its marketing efforts.

Once a firm identifies different marketing opportunities, it must determine which are the best to pursue. To accomplish this task, marketers go through a segmentation, targeting, and positioning (STP) process. Firms segment various markets by dividing the total market into those groups of customers with different needs, wants, or characteristics who therefore might appreciate products or services geared especially toward them. After identifying the different segments, the firm goes after, or targets, certain groups on the basis of the firm's perceived ability to satisfy the needs of those groups better than competitors and do so profitably. To complete the STP process, firms position their products or services according to the marketing mix variables so that target customers have a clear, distinctive, and desirable understanding of what the product or service does or represents relative to competing products or services.

LO5 Outline the implementation of the marketing mix as a means to increase customer value.

The marketing mix consists of the four Ps—product, price, promotion, and place—and each P contributes to customer value. To provide value, the firm must offer a mix of products and services at prices their target markets will view as indicating good value. Thus, firms make trade-offs between the first two

Ps, product and price, to give customers the best value. The third P, promotion, informs customers and helps them form a positive image about the firm and its products and services. The last P, place, adds value by getting the appropriate products and services to customers when they want them and in the quantities they need.

LO6 Summarize portfolio analysis and its use to evaluate marketing performance.

Portfolio analysis is a management tool used to evaluate the firm's various products and businesses—its "portfolio"—and allocate resources according to which products are expected to be the most profitable for the firm in the future. A popular portfolio analysis tool developed by the Boston Consulting Group classifies all products into four categories. The first, stars, are in high-growth markets and have high market shares. The second, cash cows, are in low-growth markets, but have high market share. These products generate excess resources that can be spun off to products that need them. The third category, question marks, are in high-growth markets, but have relatively low market shares. These products often utilize the excess resources generated by the cash cows. The final category, dogs, are in low-growth markets and have relatively low market shares. These products are often phased out.

LO7 Describe how firms grow their business.

Firms use four basic growth strategies: market penetration, market development, product development, and diversification. A market penetration strategy directs the firm's efforts toward existing customers and uses the present marketing mix. In other words, it attempts to get current customers to buy more. In a market development strategy, the firm uses its current marketing mix to appeal to new market segments, as might occur in international expansion. A product development growth strategy involves offering a new product or service to the firm's current target market. Finally, a diversification strategy takes place when a firm introduces a new product or service to a new customer segment. Sometimes a diversification strategy relates to the firm's current business, such as when a women's clothing manufacturer starts making and selling men's clothes, but a more risky strategy is when a firm diversifies into a completely unrelated business.

Key Terms

- control phase, 36
- customer excellence, 31
- diversification strategy, 54
- implementation phase, 36
- location, 35
- market development strategy, 52
- market growth rate, 48
- market penetration strategy, 52
- market positioning, 41
- market segment, 39

- market segmentation, 39
- market share, 48
- marketing plan, 35
- marketing strategy, 31
- metric, 45
- mission statement, 36
- operational excellence, 34
- planning phase, 36
- product development strategy, 53
- product excellence, 34
- product line, 48

- products, 43
- related diversification, 54
- relative market share, 48
- situation analysis, 37
- STP, 39
- strategic business unit (SBU), 48
- sustainable competitive advantage, 31
- target marketing/targeting, 41
- unrelated diversification, 54

Marketing Applications

1. How have Nike and adidas created sustainable competitive advantages for themselves?

2. Perform a SWOT analysis for the company that made your favorite shoes.

3. How does adidas segment its market? Describe the primary target markets for adidas. How does it position its various offerings so that it appeals to these different target markets?

4. How does Hertz add value for business customers through the implementation of the four Ps?

5. Of the four growth strategies described in the chapter, which is the most risky? Which is the easiest to implement? Why?

6. Choose three companies. You believe the first builds customer value through product excellence, the second through operational excellence, and the third through customer excellence. Justify your answer.

7. You are on the job market and have received offers from three very different firms. Develop a marketing plan to help market yourself to prospective employers.

 www.mhhe.com/grewal4e

Quiz Yourself

1. Suppose Macy's announced it would severely cut back its inventory levels. For clothing manufacturers supplying Macy's this would represent a(n):
   a. weakness
   b. opportunity
   c. situational selling problem
   d. threat
   e. strategic business promotion efficiency

2. Carla, a manager of a local bookstore, in response to increased competition from devices such as the Kindle book reader, has been directed by her regional marketing manager to cut prices on seasonal items, run an ad in the local paper, and tell distributors to reduce deliveries for the next month. Which stage of the strategic marketing planning process is Carla engaged in?
   a. evaluate performance
   b. define the business mission
   c. situation analysis
   d. implement marketing mix and resources
   e. identify and evaluate opportunities

(Answers to these two questions can be found on page 647.)

Go to www.mhhe.com/grewal4e to practice an additional 11 questions.

Toolkit

SWOT ANALYSIS

Assume you are a marketing analyst for a major company and are trying to conduct a situation analysis using SWOT analysis. Use the toolkit provided at www.mhhe.com/grewal4e, and complete the SWOT grids for each company using the appropriate items.

Net Savvy

1. The mission statement for Quaker Oats cites its origins, "inspired by the power and wholesome goodness of the amazing oat." Frito-Lay looks a little more to the present, citing its mission "To be the world's favorite snack and always within arm's reach." These different perspectives also reflect the quite different positioning adopted by each company. Visit the websites of each and review the descriptions of the company, its mission, and its values. Now consider what it means when you learn that both brands are owned by PepsiCo. What is PepsiCo's mission statement? Do you believe these two disparate mission statements reflect what the firms do and how they are portrayed in the media? Justify your answer.

2. More and more firms seem to be entering the dating service industry. Visit www.eharmony.com and tour its website to find the types of activities and methods such companies use to help match compatible couples. Then visit www.okcupid.com and do the same. What are the similarities and differences of these two online dating services? Pick one and perform a SWOT analysis for it.

Chapter Case Study

THE NETFLIX ROLLERCOASTER[65]

The letter arrived in millions of e-mailboxes simultaneously. Reed Hastings, the CEO of Netflix, announced in excited tones the latest innovation by the company that had revolutionized the movie rental industry. But the response was not quite what he, or Netflix shareholders, had expected. The series of events offers a clear lesson in how a failure to plan strategy changes sufficiently can backfire on even the most successful of companies.

THE ORIGINAL OFFER: 1998–2008

The origin story goes that Hastings came up with the idea for Netflix after being charged late fees for keeping a rental movie after its due date. Instead, Netflix would have no late fees; users could keep the movies as long as they wanted. With no brick-and-mortar stores, Netflix relied on the Internet to take customer orders and the mail system to deliver the discs. The company's millions of subscribers—it counted 1 million in 2002, more than 5 million in 2006, and 14 million in 2010—could choose from several flat-rate monthly subscription options and keep up to eight movies out at a time. Customers returned videos using a pre-paid and pre-addressed envelope. Then Netflix automatically mailed the next video on the customer's video queue, and customers could change and update their queues as often as they wanted.

The growing number of customers, along with growing profits, made Netflix's management and stockholders quite happy. Observers praised it as a top company, a great investment, and a stellar example of how innovation could drive profits and growth.

AND THE HITS KEEP COMING: 2008–2010

Netflix was innovative, and its careful analysis of the surroundings suggested some serious threats. First, several competitors had entered the market to compete directly with Netflix. Blockbuster, which enjoyed great name recognition, added mail delivery services to its existing brick-and-mortar stores. Redbox came onto the scene, allowing patrons to borrow first-run, popular movies from conveniently located boxes for just $1 per day.

Second, reports from the U.S. Postal Service indicated an impending problem for Netflix. Due to budget overruns and deficits, the Post Office noted the possibility that it would need to shut down hundreds of local branches. It also started talking about the possibility of halting Saturday service. These threats were significant for Netflix, which relied heavily on the U.S.P.S. to help it get its red envelopes into customers' mailboxes quickly.

Third, it realized that some cable companies and satellite operators were doing more with pay-per-view options. Not limited to special events or boxing matches, this model was being applied to movies, immediately after their video release.

In response, Netflix started down a new path: Customers could view unlimited streaming of movies and TV shows, still for the same monthly fee they were paying for receiving discs in the mail. The new offering was a nearly instant hit, picked up and enjoyed by most of its subscribers. This response encouraged Netflix to expand the option. In addition to streaming through their computers, users could use platforms that would deliver its titles to the Nintendo Wii, Xbox 360, PlayStation 3, and TiVo. Hardware options from Panasonic, Insignia, and Seagate soon joined, though even these were outshone when Netflix also introduced an iPad application.

OOOPS, MY BAD: 2010–2011

Perhaps unsurprisingly, Netflix soon realized it was leaving money on the table by providing both mail and streaming service for the same price it had previously been charging for just the mail service. It was offering more value; it reasoned that it could charge a higher price.

It started by launching a streaming-only plan for $7.99 per month in November 2010. At the same time, it increased the cost of each of its DVD plans by $1 each. If customers wanted both, they could sign up for the streaming plan and add DVDs for $2. Netflix anticipated that most users would drop the mail service, because so many consumers seemed heading toward streaming.

That prediction was not quite accurate. Users still wanted to open their mailboxes to find the red envelopes. In addition, the selection of titles for the mail service was significantly greater than that available through streaming, so customers still found value in it. By July 2011, Netflix announced another new pricing plan. For unlimited streaming, and no discs, customers paid $7.99 per month. For one-disc-at-a-time (the most basic mail plan), and no streaming, customers would pay $7.99 per month. If they wanted both, they paid $15.98. The new pricing would come into effect on September 1, 2011.

Customers were furious. For many of them, the new plan represented an approximately 60 percent price hike. Netflix had anticipated some backlash—it predicted that some customers would even drop the service. But approximately 1 million people did, and the negative press about the company, especially in social media, was intense. On Netflix's own blog, more than 12,000 comments were posted in response to the announcement, and readers would be hard pressed to find one with a positive tone. But investors considered the price move a smart one, and Netflix's stock prices rose.

There were no such silver linings for Netflix's next misstep. At around midnight on Sunday, September 18, 2011, Hastings posted a new announcement to the company blog, entitled "An Explanation and Some Reflections." The text has become somewhat infamous, and the wording is remarkable enough to call for some extensive quotes. The letter began: "I messed up. I owe everyone an explanation." Hastings apologized for not communicating enough about the price change, and he accused himself of sliding "into arrogance based on past success."

Then he explained his solution to the mess:

> . . . we realized that streaming and DVD by mail are becoming two quite different businesses, with very different cost structures, different benefits that need to be marketed differently, and we need to let each grow and operate independently. It's hard for me to write this after over 10 years of mailing DVDs with pride, but we think it is necessary and best: In a few weeks, we will rename our DVD by mail service to "Qwikster."

> We chose the name Qwikster because it refers to quick delivery. We will keep the name "Netflix" for streaming.

> Qwikster will be the same website and DVD service that everyone is used to. It is just a new name, and DVD members will go to qwikster.com to access their DVD queues and choose movies. One improvement we will make at launch is to add a video games upgrade option. . . . Another advantage of separate websites is simplicity for our members. Each website will be focused on just one thing (DVDs or streaming) and will be even easier to use. A negative of the renaming and separation is that the Qwikster.com and Netflix.com websites will not be integrated. So if you subscribe to both services, and if you need to change your credit card or email address, you would need to do it in two places. Similarly, if you rate or review a movie on Qwikster, it doesn't show up on Netflix, and vice-versa.

> There are no pricing changes (we're done with that!). Members who subscribe to both services will have two entries on their credit card statements, one for Qwikster and one for Netflix. The total will be the same as the current charges.

So in addition to paying more, customers in 2011 would need to visit two separate Internet sites to manage their movies, rather than just handling streaming and mail services on Netflix.com. They also would have to reset their preferences on the new site. And they would have to deal with the name "Qwikster"—something that their comments indicated that they universally hated.

By October 10, 2011, in a simple, brief post, Hastings reversed the split. Both services would stay with Netflix, though the price increase would remain in place. But the damage had been done. More customers had left, and Netflix's stock price had plummeted. Observers waited anxiously to see what the 2011 fourth quarter reports would show. The Netflix blog entries went back to promoting new content. Reed Hastings stayed quiet—at least for the moment.

Questions

1. Explain Netflix's marketing strategy. Can it sustain its competitive advantage? Why or why not?
2. How has their strategic change and rapid reversal affected their customers? Do you believe this situation is a short-term public relations nightmare or a long-term reversal of fortune?
3. Perform a SWOT analysis for Netflix. What are its biggest threats and which opportunities should it pursue?
4. What is the best way for Netflix to grow its business? Justify your answer.

Writing a Marketing Plan

Have a plan. Follow the plan, and you'll be surprised how successful you can be. Most people don't have a plan. That's why it's easy to beat most folks.

—Paul "Bear" Bryant, football coach, University of Alabama

WHY WRITE A MARKETING PLAN?[1]

As a student, you likely plan out much in your life—where to meet for dinner, how much time to spend studying for exams, which courses to take next semester, how to get home for winter break, and so on. Plans enable us to figure out where we want to go and how we might get there.

For a firm, the goal is not much different. Any company that wants to succeed (which means any firm whatsoever) needs to plan for a variety of contingencies, and marketing represents one of the most significant. A marketing plan—which we defined in Chapter 2 as a written document composed of an analysis of the current marketing situation, opportunities and threats for the firm, marketing objectives and strategy specified in terms of the four Ps, action programs, and projected or proforma income (and other financial) statements—enables marketing personnel and the firm as a whole to understand their own actions, the market in which they operate, their future direction, and the means to obtain support for new initiatives.[2]

Because these elements—internal activities, external environments, goals, and forms of support—differ for every firm, the marketing plan is different for each firm as well. However, several guidelines apply to marketing plans in general; this appendix summarizes those points and offers an annotated example.

MARKETING PLAN VERSUS BUSINESS PLAN

Of course, firms consider more than marketing when they make plans and therefore commonly develop business plans as well. Yet as this book highlights, marketing constitutes such an important element of business that business plans and marketing plans coincide in many ways.[3] Both marketing and business plans generally encompass

1. Executive summary.
2. Company overview.
3. Objectives or goals, usually according to strategic plan and focus.
4. Situation analysis.
5. Customer segmentation, target marketing, and positioning analysis.
6. Marketing strategy.
7. Financial projections.
8. Implementation plan.
9. Evaluation and control metrics.
10. Appendix

However, a business plan also includes details about R&D and operations, and both may feature details about other key topics, depending on the focus of the company and the plan.

STRUCTURE OF A MARKETING PLAN

This section briefly describes each of the elements of a marketing plan.[4]

Executive Summary

The executive summary essentially tells the reader why he or she is reading this marketing plan—what changes require consideration, what new products need discussion, and so forth—and suggests possible actions to take in response to the information the plan contains.

Company Overview

In this section, the plan provides a brief description of the company, including perhaps its mission statement, background, and competitive advantages.

Objectives/Goals

This section offers more specifics about why readers are reading the marketing plan. What does the company want to achieve, both overall and with this particular marketing plan?

Situation Analysis

Recall from Chapter 2 that a situation analysis generally relies on SWOT considerations; therefore, this section describes the strengths, weaknesses, opportunities, and threats facing the company.

STP Analysis

The analysis proceeds by assessing the market in which the company functions, the products it currently offers or plans to offer in the future, and the characteristics of current or potential customers.

Marketing Strategy

The marketing strategy may be very specific, especially if the plan pertains to, for example, a stable product in a familiar market, or it may be somewhat open to varied possibilities, such as when the firm plans to enter a new market with an innovative product.

Financial Projections

On the basis of the knowledge already obtained, the marketing plan should provide possible developments and returns on the marketing investments outlined in the marketing strategy.

Implementation Plan

This portion of the marketing plan includes the timing of promotional activities, when monitoring will take place, and how expansions likely will proceed.

Evaluation and Control Metrics

The firm must have a means of assessing the marketing plan's recommendations; the marketing plan therefore must indicate the methods for undertaking this assessment, whether quantitatively or qualitatively.

Appendix

The final section(s) offers additional information that might be of benefit, such as a list of key personnel, data limitations that may influence the findings, and suggestions of the plan, relevant legislation, and so forth.

INFORMATION SOURCES[5]

When writing a marketing plan, you likely can turn to a variety of your firm's in-house information sources, including annual reports, previous marketing plans, published mission statements, and so on. In addition, various sources offer suggestions and examples that may provide you with direction and ideas. A reference librarian can help you find many of these sources, which likely are available through your university's library system.

- Knowthis.com—"a knowledge source for marketing"
  http://www.knowthis.com/tutorials/principles-of-marketing/
  how-to-write-a-marketing-plan/21.htm.
- Encyclopedia of American Industries—introduces industry structure; arranged by SIC and NAICS codes.
- Standard & Poor's NetAdvantage—surveys of more than 50 different industries, with financial data about companies in each industry.
- Investext Plus—brokerage house reports.
- IBISWorld—market research on thousands of industries; classified by NAICS code.
- Statistical Abstract of the United States—a vast variety of statistics on a wealth of topics.
- U.S. Bureau of the Census—detailed statistical data gathered every 10 years on all aspects of the U.S. population.
- County Business Patterns: U.S. Bureau of the Census—payroll and employee numbers for most NAICS codes.
- Consumer Expenditure Study: U.S. Bureau of Labor Statistics—income and expenditures by household, classified by various demographics.

- LifeStyle Market Analyst—lifestyle information about geographic areas, lifestyle interest groups, and age and income groups.
- Mediamark Reporter—information about demographics, lifestyles, product and brand usage, and advertising media preferences.
- Scarborough Arbitron—local market consumer information for various media in 75 local markets for consumer retail shopping behavior, product consumption, media usage, lifestyle behavior, and demographics.
- Simmons Study of Media and Markets—products and consumer characteristics; various media audiences and their characteristics.
- Sourcebook America—demographic data, including population, spending potential index, income, race, and *Tapestry* data, presented by state, county, DMA, and zip code, as well as business data by county and zip code.
- Rand McNally Commercial Atlas and Marketing Guide—maps and tables showing demographic, industrial, transportation, railroad, airline, and hospital data.
- "Survey of Buying Power," Sales and Marketing Management—current state, county, city, and town estimates of population by age, retail sales by store group, effective buying income, and buying power index.
- Annual & 10-K reports from *Thomson One Banker, Edgar,* and *LexisNexis*— business descriptions, product listings, distribution channels, possible impact of regulations and lawsuits, and discussions of strategic issues.
- MarketResearch.com Academic—market research reports on a variety of consumer products.
- Mintel Reports Database—market research reports focusing on consumer products, lifestyles, retailing, and international travel industry.

LINGUISTIC AND VISUAL SUGGESTIONS

Again, recall that all marketing plans differ, because all firms differ. However, just as rules exist that dictate what makes for good writing, some rules or guidelines apply to all well-written marketing plans.

- Maintain a professional attitude in the writing and presentation.
- Keep descriptions and summaries concise. Get to the point.
- Use standard, edited English.
- Proofread the entire plan multiple times to catch grammatical, spelling, or other such errors that could dampen the professionalism of the writing.
- Adopt a businesslike tone; avoid flowery or jargon-filled writing.
- Employ direct, rather than passive, and present, rather than past, tense whenever possible (e.g., "We plan to achieve 30 percent growth in two years" rather than "The plan was that 30 percent growth would be achieved by the firm within two years").
- Be positive.
- Avoid meaningless superlatives (e.g., "Our goal is tremendous growth").
- Be specific; use quantitative information whenever possible.
- Insert graphics to convey important concepts succinctly, including photos, graphs, illustrations, and charts.
- Avoid using so many visual elements that they clutter the plan.
- Lay out the plan clearly and logically.

- Organize sections logically, using multiple levels of headings, distinguished clearly by font differences (e.g., bold for first-level heads, italics for second-level heads).
- Consider the use of bullet points or numbered lists to emphasize important points.
- Exploit modern technology (e.g., graphics software, page layout software, laser printers) to ensure the plan looks professional.
- Adopt an appropriate font to make the text easy to read and visually appealing—avoid using anything smaller than 10-point font at a minimum.
- Avoid unusual or decorative fonts; stick with a common serif type to make the text easy to read.
- Consider binding the report with an attractive cover and clear title page.
- Generally aim for a plan that consists of 15–30 pages.

PEOPLEAHEAD MARKETING PLAN ILLUSTRATION[6]

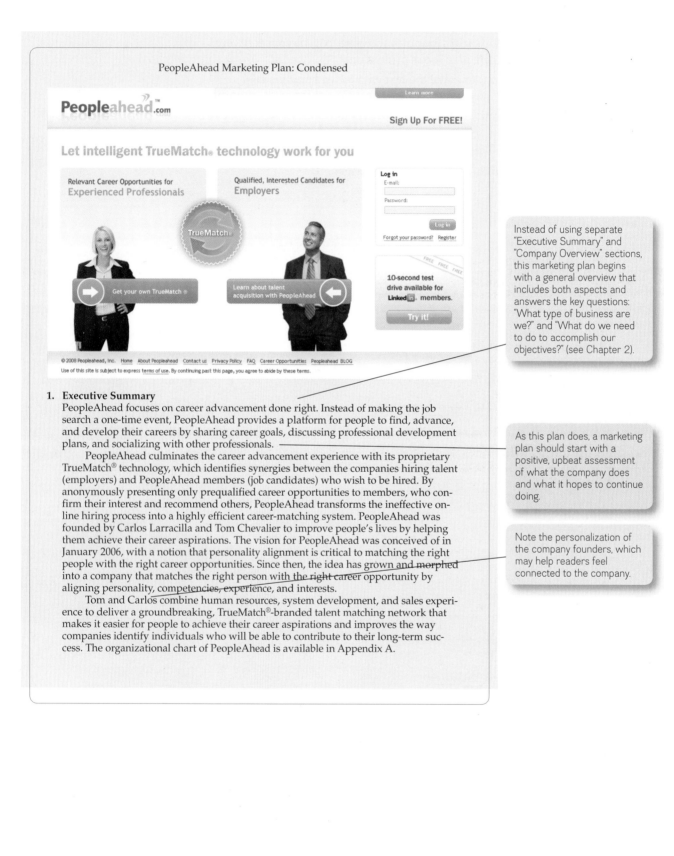

PeopleAhead Marketing Plan: Condensed

Instead of using separate "Executive Summary" and "Company Overview" sections, this marketing plan begins with a general overview that includes both aspects and answers the key questions: "What type of business are we?" and "What do we need to do to accomplish our objectives?" (see Chapter 2).

1. Executive Summary

PeopleAhead focuses on career advancement done right. Instead of making the job search a one-time event, PeopleAhead provides a platform for people to find, advance, and develop their careers by sharing career goals, discussing professional development plans, and socializing with other professionals.

As this plan does, a marketing plan should start with a positive, upbeat assessment of what the company does and what it hopes to continue doing.

PeopleAhead culminates the career advancement experience with its proprietary TrueMatch® technology, which identifies synergies between the companies hiring talent (employers) and PeopleAhead members (job candidates) who wish to be hired. By anonymously presenting only prequalified career opportunities to members, who confirm their interest and recommend others, PeopleAhead transforms the ineffective online hiring process into a highly efficient career-matching system. PeopleAhead was founded by Carlos Larracilla and Tom Chevalier to improve people's lives by helping them achieve their career aspirations. The vision for PeopleAhead was conceived of in January 2006, with a notion that personality alignment is critical to matching the right people with the right career opportunities. Since then, the idea has grown and morphed into a company that matches the right person with the right career opportunity by aligning personality, competencies, experience, and interests.

Note the personalization of the company founders, which may help readers feel connected to the company.

Tom and Carlos combine human resources, system development, and sales experience to deliver a groundbreaking, TrueMatch®-branded talent matching network that makes it easier for people to achieve their career aspirations and improves the way companies identify individuals who will be able to contribute to their long-term success. The organizational chart of PeopleAhead is available in Appendix A.

2. Strategic Objectives

2.1. Mission

PeopleAhead's mission is to help individuals with career advancement and improve the human capital in companies. The site will act as a networking platform for professionals and career matching as opposed to job and resume-posting searches.

> The paragraph provides a general outline of the firm's objectives; the bulleted list offers more specific goals, and the subsequent sections go into more detail about the various factors that may influence these objectives.

2.2. Goals:

- Use brand-matching technology: TrueMatch®
- Build critical mass of users.
- Drive traffic to the Web site through marketing blitzes.
- Utilize word-of-mouth advertising from satisfied users.

2.3. Business Summary

- **Business customers:** This group provides PeopleAhead's revenues. Customers purchase contact information about the Top Ten PROfiles gleaned from the individual member base that have been sorted and ranked by the TrueMatch® technology. PeopleAhead will focus on small and medium businesses (see Market Segmentation section), because these entities are underserved by large competitors in the online recruitment market, and because research shows that this demographic has a less efficient recruitment process that would benefit most readily from PeopleAhead's services. Within this segment, customers include HR managers who are responsible for the sourcing of candidates, functional area managers who require new talent for their team, and executives whose business objectives rely on human capital and efficiency of operations.

> By referring to another section, the plan makes clear where it is heading and enables readers to cross-reference the information.

- **Individual members:** This group does not pay for services but is the main source of data points for PeopleAhead's TrueMatch® system. PeopleAhead will focus on building a base of individual members who range from recent graduates to individuals with 5–7 years of continuous employment. Ideal members are those who are currently employed or will be graduating within nine months and are "poised" to make a career change. These individuals can utilize the services to the fullest extent and are valuable candidates for business customers.

> The plan acknowledges both a general, potential target market and the ideal targets.

2.4. Competitive Advantage

- **TrueMatch® offers a branded technology,** marketed to both business customers and individual candidates for its "black box" value proposition, which establishes PeopleAhead as the category leader for recruitment-matching software. This technology provides a point of differentiation from competitors, which may have technically similar matching software but constantly need to reinforce their marketing messages with explanations of their value proposition.
- **For individual candidates,** PeopleAhead will be the favored career advancement platform online, where individuals enthusiastically create a history and have connections (invited friends, coworkers, and mentors) in place that will make PeopleAhead a staple among their favorite Web sites. PeopleAhead delivers TrueMatch® career opportunities, professional development plans that let people establish a professional record, and valuable career advancement tools, including automatic position feedback, "recommend-a-friend," and team-based career networking.
- **For business customers,** PeopleAhead makes online sourcing and qualification of candidates quick and efficient by prequalifying potential candidates, seeking recommendations for hard-to-find individuals, and delivering only the Top 10 most highly

> As Chapter 2 suggests, the plan notes PeopleAhead's sustainable competitive advantage as part of its overall mission statement.

qualified candidates who have preconfirmed interest in the available position. PeopleAhead will be the most effective candidate-company matching platform available in the market, delivering prequalified, preconfirmed candidates.

In discussing both the external market and the internal advantages of PeopleAhead, the plan carefully distinguishes between individual job candidates and businesses, thus differentiating the focus and objectives according to this segmentation.

3. Situation Analysis—Online Recruitment

Online recruitment is the system whereby companies use the Web to locate and qualify prospective candidates for available positions. The methods employed by online recruitment service providers to serve this market range from resume aggregation to assessment test application to linking strategies. However, the common underlying objective is to locate candidates who would not be found by traditional recruitment methods and use computing power to qualify candidates quickly and with more accuracy than would be possible manually.

3.1. Industry Analysis

Large online recruitment Web sites make this a tedious process by requiring companies to search through many resumes manually to find the right candidate. Other sites solicit recommendations for positions. However, resumes are often "enhanced," such that almost all candidates appear qualified, and information found in the resume or provided through a recommendation is simply not sufficient to make an educated hiring decision. Companies need more information and intelligent tools that make this screening process more accurate.

3.1.1. Market Size:

The market size for both member segments in 2005 was as follows:

Figures provide a visually attractive break in the text and summarize a lot of information in an easy-to-read format.

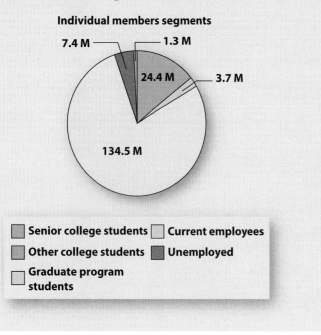

Individual members segments

7.4 M — 1.3 M

24.4 M — 3.7 M

134.5 M

- ▨ Senior college students   ▨ Current employees
- ▨ Other college students   ▨ Unemployed
- ▨ Graduate program students

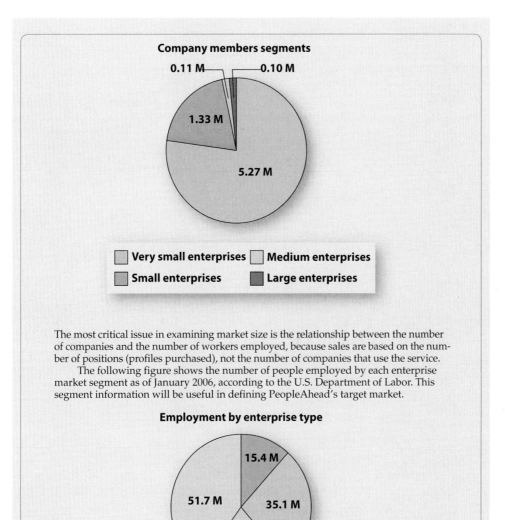

Company members segments

0.11 M — 0.10 M

1.33 M

5.27 M

▨ Very small enterprises	▢ Medium enterprises
▨ Small enterprises	▨ Large enterprises

The most critical issue in examining market size is the relationship between the number of companies and the number of workers employed, because sales are based on the number of positions (profiles purchased), not the number of companies that use the service.

The following figure shows the number of people employed by each enterprise market segment as of January 2006, according to the U.S. Department of Labor. This segment information will be useful in defining PeopleAhead's target market.

Employment by enterprise type

15.4 M

51.7 M   35.1 M

27.3 M

▨ Very small enterprises	▢ Medium enterprises
▢ Small enterprises	▢ Large enterprises

3.1.2. Market Growth

PeopleAhead will operate in the online recruitment market. The growth of this industry is subject to two primary constraints: U.S. economic health and online recruitment advertisement adoption rates. Understanding these constraints will help identify PeopleAhead's opportunity. General indicators suggest the U.S. economy (GDP) will grow at an average annual rate of 4% for the next decade.[7] Online recruitment advertising is expected to grow by 35% per year to reach $7.6 billion by 2010.[8] Not only is the market expanding, but it is exhibiting rapid adoption by new entities, as the following graph shows.[9]

> Another visually attractive graph summarizes complicated information easily. The use of high-quality color can add a professional feel to a marketing plan.

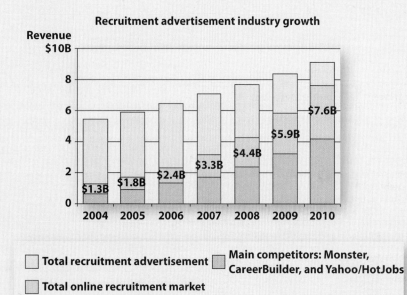

Recruitment advertisement industry growth

Legend:
- ☐ Total recruitment advertisement
- ▨ Main competitors: Monster, CareerBuilder, and Yahoo/HotJobs
- ▨ Total online recruitment market

3.1.3. Market Needs

- **The right person for the right position:** The right employee for one company or position is not the same for all others. Not only must companies locate intelligent individuals with relevant experience, but they also prefer people who are aligned with the position requirements in terms of personality, competencies, and fit with the company culture.

- **Prescreening qualification tools:** Increasing the number of candidates through on-line recruitment can be advantageous, but it can also be a hindrance. When sourcing candidates, recruiters need tools that help them qualify applicants.

- **Time savings:** Companies need to complete the online sourcing and qualification of candidates quickly. Leaving positions unfilled can cause critical performance gaps to emerge within the company.

Before engaging in a firm-specific SWOT analysis (see Chapter 2), this marketing plan assesses the external market environment further and thus establishes a basis for the subsequent SWOT analysis.

3.1.4. Market Trends

The methods by which online recruitment service providers deliver candidates has been undergoing a migration from resume aggregation and search services like Monster and CareerBuilder to new Web 2.0 methodologies that include passive recruitment, "meta tagging," and social networking.

The underlying objective of these Web 2.0 services is to allow individuals to remain on a few, trusted Web sites while enabling companies to access those individuals for financial purposes. In parallel, the focus is moving from aggregation of unique visitors toward engaging existing users more intensively. Internet users are growing familiar with sites that encourage socializing, collaborating, and distributing private information online to help improve network benefits and need to be engaged to maintain contact.

3.2. SWOT Analysis

Using a table and bullet points, the plan summarizes a lot of information succinctly and clearly.

	Positive	Negative
Internal	**STRENGTHS**	**WEAKNESSES**
	• Industry best practices: The networking model used by PeopleAhead draws on the industry accepted best practices contact protocols drawn from multiple industries, including online feedback, recruitment, and social networking and offline professional networking. TrueMatch® software aligns business objectives with appropriate candidates. • Team expertise: The combined talents of the founders include human resources, system development, sales, and marketing. • Web development expertise: PeopleAhead has partnered with an award-winning European software development provider. This company provides quality usually reserved for high-budget projects, at terms that are favorable for a start-up company.	• Absence of industry "influentials": As a start-up, PeopleAhead does not currently have resources to attract influential industry managers. • Inability to guarantee critical mass: As is true of many Internet companies, the business must solve the "chicken and egg" puzzle to build critical mass. • Verifying efficiency of matching capabilities: In theory, the system has an absolute guarantee of effectivity; computations make decisions rather than humans. However, the matching capabilities must be verified as accurate to gain widespread acceptance. • Broad target market: Because PeopleAhead is targeting a wide range of businesses, the product being developed has not been "customized" ideally for each segment.
External	**OPPORTUNITIES** • Service gap: Recruiters are not pleased with current online recruitment vendors. • Industry gap: Job turnover is every 3.5 years per person. • Demand for productive candidates. • Online recruitment advertising: Growing by 35% per year, to reach $7.6 billion by 2010.[10]	**THREATS** • Convergence: Existing competitors may form strategic alliances and establish powerful positions before PeopleAhead can establish itself. • Inability to protect model: Very little intellectual property created by Web sites is protected by law. Although PeopleAhead will

Note that the analysis uses outside sources to support its claims.

(continued)

External   OPPORTUNITIES
- Fragmented business models: Online recruitment is fragmented by recruitment methodology: active (people who need jobs), passive (people who are not looking but would move if enticed), poised (people unsatisfied with jobs they have), and network (finding people of interest based on who or what they know).

THREATS
pursue aggressive IP protection strategies, the model could be copied or mimicked by competitors.
- Inadequate differentiation: Inability to explain our differentiation would relegate PeopleAhead to (unfair) comparisons with competitors. Without differentiation, PeopleAhead will not be able to create scale through network effects.

3.3. Competition

Most online recruitment Web sites compete in the active recruitment market, including Monster, CareerBuilder, and Yahoo/HotJobs. The pervasive segment includes job seekers who actively look for jobs, post their resumes, and search for jobs on company Web sites. Most active recruiters offer free services to users and charge companies on a fee basis. Companies can post jobs and search for candidate resumes in the database (average fee for local searches is $500 and nationwide is $1,000). In this first-generation online recruitment business model, competitors face the challenge to make the process more user-friendly and reduce the effort required to make these sites deliver results.

- **Monster:** Monster.com is the sixteenth most visited Web site in the United States, with more than 43 million professionals in its viewer base. Monster earns revenue from job postings, access to its resume database, and advertisements on Web sites of partner companies.

- **Careerbuilder:** Careerbuilder.com has experienced 75% growth for the past five years. This job post/resume search company uses its media ownership to attract passive candidates from partner Web sites. It achieves growth through affiliate partnerships that host job searches on affiliated Web pages, such as Google, MSN, AOL, *USA Today*, Earthlink, BellSouth, and CNN. Job posting is the primary activity, sold together with or separately from resume searches.

- **Passive recruitment:** The second generation of online recruitment locates candidates who are not necessarily looking for jobs but who could be convinced to move to a new position if the right opportunity was presented. The most recognized competitors in this category include Jobster, LinkedIn, and H3 (Appendix B).

3.4. Company Analysis

PeopleAhead's mission is simple: improve people's lives through career advancement. PeopleAhead recognizes that career advancement means many things to many people and provides a fresh perspective on career networking that is flexible yet powerful:

- **Users are not alone:** Finding a job is not easy. Why search solo? PeopleAhead unites groups of friends, coworkers, and mentors to create natural, team-based career discovery.

- **Job posting is not natural:** People spend countless hours searching job listings and posting resumes, only to be overlooked because their writing style or resume format does not match an overburdened recruiter's preference. Good people, not resumes, make great companies. PeopleAhead's TrueMatch technology matches the right people with the right position. No posting, no applying—just good, quality matches.

If PeopleAhead chooses to adopt a competitor-based pricing strategy (see Chapter 13), detailed information about how other recruitment firms work will be mandatory.

Information about competitors' revenues, customers, growth, and so forth often is available publicly through a variety of sources.

For information that may not belong in the main text, an appendix offers an effective means to provide detail without distracting readers.

This section offers the "product" component of the market/product/customer analysis. Because PeopleAhead's product is mostly a service (see Chapter 12), it focuses on some intangible features of its offering.

- **Professionals being professionals:** There is a place online for social networking, pet networking, and music networking. So why is there no outlet for career networking online—the activity that consumes the majority of our professional lives? People-Ahead is a place where professionals share their experiences, achievements, and objectives with other professionals that care and can be found by employers who value their professionalism.

The last—and some would say most important—piece of the analysis puzzle: customers.

3.5. Customer Analysis

PeopleAhead's R&D efforts show that the impetus to improve recruitment effectivity is pervasive and that unmet needs revolve around a few core issues: the ability to find qualified talent, establishing a fit between the candidate and the company culture, verifying the candidate's career progression, and working quickly and cost effectively. The following customer characteristics represent ideal attributes that align with PeopleAhead's service offering. This information might be used in conjunction with the Marketing Strategy.

3.5.1. Business Customer

- **Industry:** Because companies that value human capital are more likely to take a chance on a start-up that promotes professional development, the broadly defined professional services industry, including insurance, banking, and consulting, is the primary focus.
- **Functional area:** PeopleAhead's system identifies "people" people, so positions that require human interaction are more aligned with system capabilities than those with stringent skill requirements, sets such as programming or accounting.
- **Size:** Large businesses (>1000 employees) have high volume requirements and demand vendors with proven track records; small businesses (<25 employees) hire fewer people and may not justify acquisition costs. PeopleAhead aligns best with medium-sized customers.
- **Hiring need:** PeopleAhead serves two types of searches very well: those with too many applicants and those with too few applicants. By drawing applicants that most systems overlook and delivering only the most qualified applicants, the system assures the right candidate is identified quickly.

Although the introduction to this appendix and the plan's organization suggest that analyses of competitors, products, and customers are separate, as this plan shows, a firm usually cannot address one without considering the other. Here, in the "customer" section, the plan notes what its competitors fail to do and therefore why it offers a more valuable service.

3.5.2. Individual Member

- **Background:** People who value professional development and are familiar with computer networking technologies; most are likely college educated, motivated by career success, and aware of their professional competencies/deficiencies.
- **Situation:** Members should have a professional development plan to share with others who can help them achieve their objectives—likely people who are inquisitive about their professional future and not content with their current situation. The common industry terminology for this group of people is "poised candidates."
- **Outlook:** Proactive people who research, plan, self-educate, and talk about their career. Probably the clearest example of proactivity is a student who devotes time, effort, and financial resources toward career advancement.

Understanding a target customer is not just about numbers. PeopleAhead tries to consider what customers think and feel when searching for jobs too.

4. Marketing Strategy

4.1. Market Segmentation

4.1.1. Business Customers

- **Small enterprises.** Businesses with 10–99 employees. Companies with fewer than 10 employees are categorized as "Very Small Enterprises" and will not be a primary target market.
- **Medium enterprises.** Businesses with 100–1,000 employees.

4.1.2. Individual Members

- **Senior college students.** Students in the process of searching for a first career.
- **Graduate program students.** Mid-career candidates searching for new career opportunities, such as internships, part-time during enrollment, or full-time after graduation.
- **Current employees.** Persons who are currently employed but are poised to locate better career opportunities.
- **Unemployed.** Persons searching for jobs not included in previous segments.

4.2. Target Market

PeopleAhead plans to focus resources on small to medium enterprises (SMEs) in the New England metro market, including Boston, Providence, Hartford, Stamford, Norwalk, Worcester, and Springfield. Online recruitment companies compete for national recruitment spending, but most job seekers are locally based, so market penetration is possible by covering a single geographical location. By maintaining this focus, PeopleAhead will be better equipped to build a critical mass of users that represent the job-seeking population and thus improve both users' and customers' experience, customer service, and the use of financial resources.

4.3. User Positioning

To the proactive professional, PeopleAhead is career advancement done right—providing a platform to discover, plan, and advance careers by uniting friends, coworkers, and mentors with companies searching for the right talent.

5. Marketing Mix

5.1. Products/Services Offered

The first planned offering is **group profiling;** users self-associate with groups to share development plans. Access to groupings is permission based and similar to social networking. Members will be able to share professional experiences with people they know. Group profiling may prompt "voyeur" networking, such that members join to view the profiles of the people they know.

PeopleAhead will then open **group profiling to business customers,** who will be granted access to groups of members to target people they want to hire.

The next added feature will be **user feedback** on professional development plans. PeopleAhead will track data from successful member profile matches to provide feedback for members who have not been matched successfully.

The plan continues with the same segmentation throughout. Here the plan discusses targeting and what makes each segment attractive.

By already identifying key markets in the previous section, the plan provides a foundation for a more specific targeting statement in this section.

The final step in the STP process: Positioning for the segmented, targeted market.

PeopleAhead's mission

Given its own section in this plan, a discussion of the marketing mix constitutes a key element of the strategic planning process (see Chapter 2).

According to well-known marketing concepts, the marketing mix consists of the four Ps: product (service here), price, place (distribution here), and promotion.

The product (service) offering must establish the value for consumers: Why should they expend effort or resources to obtain the offering?

5.2. Price

In addition to a basic pricing schedule, PeopleAhead will offer bulk pricing and contract pricing to business customers to satisfy unique customer needs. The pricing model is expected to remain constant, but customer feedback will be analyzed to ensure alignment with their requirements.

Continuing the new customer acquisition plan, PeopleAhead will encourage new trials by offering promotional pricing to new customers.

5.3. Distribution

- **PeopleAhead Challenge:** The PeopleAhead Challenge will act as a primary user acquisition strategy. Selection will be focused on successful target segments demanded by customers.
- **Direct sales:** Direct customer contact is the preferred method of communication during the first six months. Telesales is the anticipated eventual sales model, due to reduced costs and quicker customer sales cycle, but it limits intimacy between the customer and PeopleAhead. During the initial stages, intimacy and excellent customer service are more highly desired than reduced cost, and direct sales achieves that objective.
- **Industry events:** Attendance at HR industry and recruitment events will supplement direct sales efforts.
- **Challenge groups:** Word-of-mouth distribution by PeopleAhead members.

5.4. Promotion

- **Public profiling:** When the product is ready, with proper precautions for protecting competitive advantages, PeopleAhead can increase its Web presence. Strategies include contributing articles to recruitment publishers, writing op/ed pieces, public profiling of the founders on Web sites like LinkedIn, Ziggs, and zoominfo, and blogging.
- **Blogger community testimonials:** Influential users of blogs will be invited to try the system and be granted "exclusive" access to the inner workings of the site. A subsequent linking blitz will put opinion pieces in front of recruiters, job seekers, and the investment community.
- **Strategic alliances:** PeopleAhead offers a product that complements the services offered by many large organizations. Partner opportunities exist with
  a. Universities, colleges, academic institutions
  b. Professional associations, clubs, industry affiliation groups
  c. Online associations, groups, blogs
  d. Professional services firms, outplacement firms, and executive search firms

Strategic alliances serve multiple purposes: They can help PeopleAhead increase public exposure, increase the user base, expand product offerings, and increase revenue opportunities. These benefits will be considered and partnerships proposed prior to the official launch. For strategic purposes, PeopleAhead prefers to focus on product development in the near term (3 months) and then reassess potential alliances after system efficacy has been proven.

> Making the product (service) available where and when consumers want it may seem somewhat easier for PeopleAhead because of the vast development of the Internet; however, the firm still needs to consider how it can ensure people know where and how to access its offering.

> The plan offers a specific time frame, which recognizes the potential need to make changes in the future, as the market dictates.

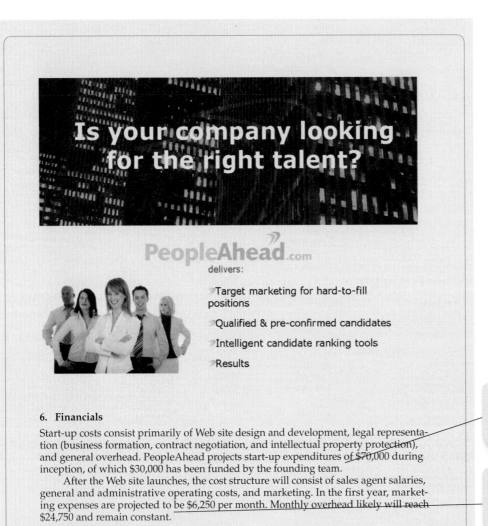

Is your company looking for the right talent?

PeopleAhead.com

delivers:

➤ Target marketing for hard-to-fill positions

➤ Qualified & pre-confirmed candidates

➤ Intelligent candidate ranking tools

➤ Results

6. Financials

Start-up costs consist primarily of Web site design and development, legal representation (business formation, contract negotiation, and intellectual property protection), and general overhead. PeopleAhead projects start-up expenditures of $70,000 during inception, of which $30,000 has been funded by the founding team.

After the Web site launches, the cost structure will consist of sales agent salaries, general and administrative operating costs, and marketing. In the first year, marketing expenses are projected to be $6,250 per month. Monthly overhead likely will reach $24,750 and remain constant.

A.   Projected Income Statement

Pro Forma Income Statement

	Year 1	Year 2	Year 3	Year 4	Year 5
Sales	$56,453	$2,683,665	$8,170,655	$16,312,843	$30,921,013
Gross Margin	$54,194	$2,316,318	$7,383,829	$14,780,329	$28,244,172
Gross Margin %	96.00%	86.31%	90.37%	90.61%	91.34%
Net Profit	($156,906)	$717,403	$3,356,768	$7,035,155	$14,180,041

The marketing plan needs to identify not only costs but also potential revenues to cover those costs.

Certain assumptions or marketing research form the basis for its estimation of start-up costs.

This section contains a lot of numbers in a small space; the graphs and tables help depict those numbers clearly and visually.

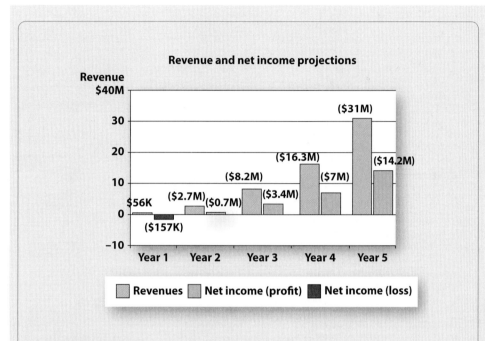

Revenue and net income projections

7. **Implementation Plan**

The launch of PeopleAhead will use a phased approach, beginning with building brand awareness. Brand awareness should be developed through the founders' visible presence at professional events, online searches, membership in professional associations, networking, and strategic alliances. This visibility will help gain investment capital.

7.1. Objective—Growth

- During the first six months of commercial availability, the primary objective is to expand both the user and customer base to maintain a 100:1 user to customer ratio.

  - **Business customers:** Sign 24 regular customers and 72 occasional customers. Execute 117 position matches.

  - **Individual members:** Convert 10,000 people to PeopleAhead members.

7.2. Marketing Objectives—Growth

- **PeopleAhead Challenge:** Pursue groups that were effective during beta trial and represent a cohesive set of profiles. Expand and refine the Challenge to reflect lessons learned.

- **Increase member networking activity:** Increase user numbers through networking initiated by existing members. Improve user experience to promote networking.

- **Increase profile completeness:** Increase user engagement with platform.

- **Generate traffic.**

- **Public relations campaign (PR):** Increase awareness of PeopleAhead brand through concentrated PR efforts directed at the target market of customers and users.

> This plan divides the objectives into three categories: overall objective, marketing, and financial. Although this is a marketing plan, it must also include other aspects that influence marketing, such as financial status.

7.3. Financial Objectives

- **Efficient marketing expenditures:** 9,000 target users (10,000 year-end total – 1,000 during beta) × $5.00 target acquisition cost = $45,000 budget.
- **Revenue:** $482.50 per position × 117 positions = $56,452.50 revenue.

7.4. Key Success Factors:

- **Economical marketing to relevant constituents:** PeopleAhead needs to establish communication (distribution) channels that pinpoint relevant constituents in a manner consistent with mission values. Limited by resources, chosen channels must aggregate many relevant eyes with free, minimal, or deferred costs involved.

- **Crafting of brand identity:** The contrast between PeopleAhead and competitors lies not only in product differentiation but also in the company's mission statement and delivery. One-time job search is available from thousands of online recruitment sources. Social networking has been covered from diverse angles, attracting many different audiences. The challenge is to associate www.PeopleAhead.com and True-Match technology with "career advancement done right." The goal is to become the only company that a person thinks of for long-term career discovery, advancement, and development.

- **Efficient value delivery:** The base of customers (both individual and business) needs to receive the proposed value in a timely manner, with consideration given to quality versus quantity of results, alignment with existing objectives, and overall experience with the PeopleAhead brand.

- **Critical mass of business customers and individual users:** The matching process requires that both customers and users exist in the system from the outset of commercialization. This need brings to the forefront the "chicken and egg" scenario; establishing either customers or users requires the other constituent to exist already. The exact number that constitutes "critical mass" ranges from 100 users per position to 10 users per position, depending on compatibility between each constituency.

- **System effectivity:** The ability of PeopleAhead's TrueMatch software to provide relevant candidate recommendations is critical. The effectiveness of the software depends on the algorithms that match users with positions and the networking protocol that initiates recommendations between users and the people they know. Proposing an inappropriate match could jeopardize the credibility of the system.

- **Intellectual property (IP) strategy:** PeopleAhead is engaged in two primary segments of online enterprise: online recruitment and social networking. Existing competitors have made many efforts to protect their methodologies through U.S. patents. However, precedent has not been established for the legal assertions made by these companies. As a result, PeopleAhead will assume an offensive IP strategy, consisting of diligent IP infringement review, patent application where appropriate, and aggressive trade secret protection of best practices.

- **Financial support:** The founders' investment is sufficient to form the business core and take delivery of PeopleAhead's Web site and software. Financial support will be required to fund operations, execute the IP strategy, and secure customers and users to meet financial targets. Without funding, PeopleAhead will not be able to proceed beyond the product development stage.

- **Sales process:** PeopleAhead's business model requires the acquisition of both business customers who have available positions and users who will be matched with

> By offering quantitative, direct goals, PeopleAhead ensures that it can measure its progress toward those goals.

those positions. These two constituents may be reached through different sales processes without overlap.

8. Evaluation & Control

PeopleAhead will evaluate user profiles to identify sets of profiles that are valuable to new business customers, which will aid in the selection of subsequent target market customers.

8.1. Business Customers

Face-to-face meetings, phone conversations, and e-mail survey contacts with people from a range of industries, company sizes, and functional areas provide a means to (1) build relationships with prospective customers, (2) understand customer needs, and (3) ensure alignment between PeopleAhead's product and customers' recruitment preferences. A summary of the key findings is listed here:

- **Employee fit:** Will the applicant fit our corporate culture? Will the applicant fit with the team we're considering? Will the applicants' competencies fit with the position requirements?
- **Pay for performance:** Objections to recruitment services focus not on price (though it is a consideration) but rather on lack of performance.
- **Unqualified applicants:** Many people who want a job apply, whether they are qualified or not. Recruiters then must scan resumes and weed out unqualified applicants instead of getting to know the qualified applicants.
- **Hard costs vs. soft costs:** Most companies track the recruitment costs of hiring providers, but few measure the time costs of hiring, opportunity costs of hiring the wrong employee, or productivity costs of leaving a position unfilled. Recruitment performance must be easy to measure. Value selling is difficult in the human resources departments.
- **Valuable recommendations:** Most recruiters use online recruitment as a necessary but ineffective means of candidate sourcing, secondary to recommendations. Recommendations include the recommender's judgment of the candidate's fit with the available position.

8.2. Individual Members

Periodic surveys of various prospective users of online recruitment services indicate (1) current services, (2) methods that work well, and (3) biggest problems with online recruitment providers. The following is a qualitative summary of the key findings:

- **Willingness to try:** Careers are important to people; they are averse to spending time uploading resume information to online recruitment Web sites only because of the lack of perceived value. They will spend time when the career opportunities are perceived as valuable.
- **Frustration:** Job seekers are frustrated with available online recruitment providers. Networking is the favored method for career advancement.
- **Lack of differentiation:** Regardless of the qualifications a job seeker possesses, it is difficult to make them evident in a traditional resume.
- **Motivation shift over time:** Early professionals are motivated by financial rewards. Mid-career professionals recommend people because it helps the people they know. Late-career professionals hope to improve their own job search opportunities.

Appendix A. Organizational Chart of PeopleAhead

Appendix B. Competition: Passive Recruiters

The evaluation section retains the segmentation scheme established previously between business customers and individual members.

Additional useful information that might clutter the plan should appear in an appendix, but is not included in this illustration.

CHAPTER 3

Social and Mobile Marketing

Social media have revolutionized how companies communicate with, listen to, and learn from their customers. The volume of information generated can be a powerful tool for improving all business operations, including product design, technical support, and customer service. Few companies have mastered this transformational potential better than Dell, one of the world's largest providers of fast-evolving breakthrough IT solutions for home and business. Today, the company is viewed as one of the top social media brands worldwide.[1]

The company has always valued consumer input, according to founder and CEO Michael Dell: "One of Dell's founding principles was really about listening and learning from our customers, and being able to take that feedback to improve."[2] Now social media channels like Facebook and Twitter have vastly accelerated that learning curve.[3] Dell still offers traditional online support forums, which post questions and answers for different user groups and by topic. A link to Dell's mobile phone app also helps users stay connected on the road.

Dell's multiple, highly developed social media channels differ qualitatively as well. They give the company and its customers the immediacy of instant chat and conversations. Through Facebook, LinkedIn, Twitter, and Google+, as well as Dell's flagship blog Direct2Dell.com and a host of other blogs, it has vastly diversified its marketing channels to target each different audience. In addition to customer support, the new media provide company and product news and food for thought to its customers about digital business and digital life. In turn, they enable the company to monitor and learn from fast-shifting user conversations.[4]

How does a company draw meaning about its products from the thousands of Facebook, Twitter, and other social media interactions that occur daily? Listening and analysis—or social media monitoring—is key, enabling companies to identify salient customer input and trends. For example, with its social media monitoring partner Radian6, Dell conducts a form of market research called "sentiment analysis" to gather, categorize, and interpret vast volumes of online customer discussions. The Radian6 coupling of text analysis and high-volume digital content gathering technologies means Dell can monitor approximately 25,000 conversations a day.[5]

LEARNING OBJECTIVES

LO1 Describe the 4E framework of social media marketing.

LO2 Understand the types of social media.

LO3 Understand the types of mobile applications.

LO4 Recognize and understand the three components of a social media strategy.

LO5 Understand the methods for marketing yourself using social media.

Dell gathers and monitors these online chats and posts, and engages in other discussions from its new Social Media Listening Command Center. The staff includes 70 trained employees who follow and respond to social media conversations in 11 languages. All tweets, Facebook posts, and other comments that warrant a Dell response are answered within 24 hours.[6]

And Dell is not just listening online. At its annual consumer advisory meetings, key bloggers and other digital opinion leaders sit around a table with Dell leadership and staff in open-ended discussions about company products, services, and processes. One blogger last year described herself and other Dell users as "an army of resources" that Dell should continue to "mobilize."[7] And that's clearly Dell's strategic intent. In its aggressive integration of social media, Dell has made the customer a critical partner in the design and evolution of its products and services.

LO1 Describe the 4E framework of social media marketing.

THE 4E FRAMEWORK FOR SOCIAL MEDIA

As we will see throughout the book and as we saw in the chapter opener, social media is becoming an integral component of any integrated marketing communications strategy. The term **social media** refers to content distributed through online and mobile technologies to facilitate interpersonal interactions. These media utilize various firms that offer services or tools to help consumers and firms build connections. Through these connections, marketers and customers share information of all forms—from their thoughts about products or images, to uploaded pictures, music, and videos.

The diffusion of technology used to bring us social media has been accelerating since the Internet came on the scene in the mid- to late-1990s, as depicted in Exhibit 3.1. The ideas were exciting, but ultimately, there was little to engage people. After the "crisis" of Y2K at the turn of the twentieth century, when computers failed to implode as a result of their inability to change their internal clocks to the new century, and after the bursting of the dot-com bubble, social media got a bit more serious and professional. Sites recognized that they had to offer surfers

EXHIBIT 3.1   Technology Evolution over the Life of the Social Web

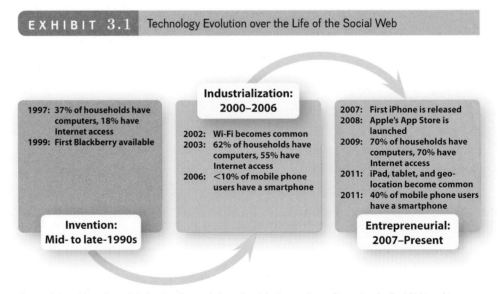

1997: 37% of households have computers, 18% have Internet access
1999: First Blackberry available

Invention:
Mid- to late-1990s

Industrialization:
2000–2006

2002: Wi-Fi becomes common
2003: 62% of households have computers, 55% have Internet access
2006: <10% of mobile phone users have a smartphone

2007: First iPhone is released
2008: Apple's App Store is launched
2009: 70% of households have computers, 70% have Internet access
2011: iPad, tablet, and geo-location become common
2011: 40% of mobile phone users have a smartphone

Entrepreneurial:
2007–Present

Source: Adapted from: Coca-Cola Retailing Research Council and the Integer Group, "Assessing the Social Networking Landscape," in *Untangling the Social Web: Insights for Users, Brands, and Retailers*, January 2012.

something exciting, educational, or experiential if they were to keep them coming back. Today, we have entered the entrepreneurial era, in which companies work to find ways to earn profits from the ways that consumers use and enjoy social media.

The changes and advances in social, mobile, and online technologies have created a perfect storm, forcing firms to change how they communicate with their customers. Traditional ways to market their products, using brick-and-mortar stores, traditional mass media (e.g., print, television, radio), and other sales promotional vehicles (e.g., mail, telemarketing) are no longer sufficient for many firms. The presence of social, mobile, and online marketing is steadily expanding relative to these more traditional forms of integrated marketing communication (IMC).

The changing role of traditional media, sales promotions, and retail, coupled with the new media of social, mobile, and online, has led to a different way of thinking about the objectives of marketing communications using the 4E framework (see Exhibit 3.2):

- Excite customers with relevant offers.
- Educate them about the offering.
- Help them Experience products, whether directly or indirectly.
- Give them an opportunity to Engage with their social network.

Today, multi-tasking is a way of life.

Excite the Customer

Marketers use many kinds of social media–related offers to excite customers, including mobile applications and games to get the customers excited about an idea, product, brand, or company. Firms actively use social networks like Facebook and Google+ to communicate deals that are likely to excite consumers, such as a Groupon price promotion that is communicated through the social networks of already interested consumers.

To excite customers, an offer must be relevant to its targeted customer. Relevancy can be achieved by providing personalized offers, which are determined through insights and information obtained from customer relationship management and/or loyalty programs. To obtain these insights and information, the firm might use online analytic tools such as Google analytics or a listening system such as those provided by Radian6, described in the chapter opener and later in this chapter.

EXHIBIT 3.2   The 4E Framework for Social Media

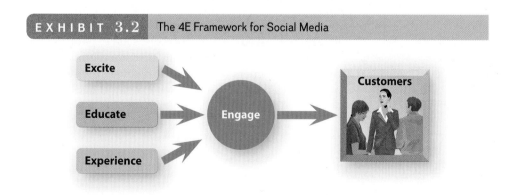

EXHIBIT 3.3	Illustrative Social Media Campaigns
Campaign	**Description**
True Blood	To get fans excited for its most recent season of *True Blood*, HBO released a Facebook app called "Immortalize Yourself." The app allowed vampire lovers and avid fans to break through the barrier of the television, by inserting images of themselves and their friends into *True Blood* video clips. As science fiction fans have long dreamed, they could appear to be actually part of the action—fangs and all.
Heinz	Modern consumers often feel that they lack the time or ability to remember when they should send greeting cards or check in with a sick friend. Instead, they send birthday wishes via Facebook. Therefore, the condiment company expanded the notion by developing a Facebook campaign that allowed users to pay $3 to send a sick friend a can of tomato or chicken soup, inscribed with the friend's name with the greeting "Get Well Soon." How thoughtful did they look—simply by clicking a button!
Volkswagen	A lot of companies ask customers to "like" their site. Although clicking the Facebook thumbs-up icon is easy, Volkswagen decided to make it exciting as well. Customers in the Netherlands who visited Facebook and voted for their favorite classic car—the T1 or the Beetle—were entered automatically into a drawing for a "Fanwagen." This special edition of the winning car model was fully loaded with social media features, including the ability to view Facebook news feeds in the car and display a relationship status on the license plate.
Flair	The fashion magazine *Flair* took the popular question, "Where did you find that fabulous item?" and turned it into the Fashion Tag Facebook app. People have long looked to others, especially relevant members of a social group, for fashion inspiration. With the Fashion Tag app, users can ask about where to find the great looks, including both clothing and accessories, featured in friends' pictures.
Intel–Toshiba	Movies are great, but they would be better if the characters would just listen to the advice viewers give them! Intel and Toshiba understand; they developed the interactive movie, *The Inside Experience*, starring Emmy Rossum. The actress posted clues about her abducted character's whereabouts on Facebook, Twitter, and YouTube, and viewers worked together to solve the central mystery of the film and thus save her character. Anyone who had ever complained about an unbelievable plot twist or disappointing ending had his or her own chance to determine how the show would end.

Source: Adapted from "Like This, Follow That: It's the 10 Best Social Media Campaigns of the Year," *Ad Age*, December 12, 2011.

In some cases location-based software and applications help bring the offer to the customers when they are in the process of making a purchase decision. For instance, Staples may provide a loyal customer a relevant coupon based on previous purchases through his or her mobile phone, while they are in the store—a very relevant and hopefully exciting experience. Exhibit 3.3 highlights some illustrative and successful social media campaigns because they are exciting and relevant to their audiences.

Educate the Customer

An imperative of well-designed social media marketing offers is that they have a clear call to action: To draw customers through their computers, tablets, and mobile devices into online websites or traditional retail stores. When potential customers arrive at the websites or stores, the marketer has a golden opportunity to educate them about its value proposition and communicate the offered benefits. Some of this information may be new, but in some cases, education is all about reminding people about what they already know. Therefore, by engaging in appropriate education, marketers are expanding the overlap of the benefits that they provide with the benefits that customers require. In this sense, the second E of the 4E framework constitutes a method to develop a sustainable competitive advantage.

Several social media tools are critical in helping marketers educate their potential customers, such as blogs and blogging tools (e.g., WordPress and Twitter), HubSpot (all-in-one marketing software), YouTube and

Staples excites its customers by giving them instant rewards through his or her mobile phone, while they are in the store.

Adding Value 3.1   Educating Customers Using HubSpot[8]

Today's marketers reach customers via a new set of inbound marketing tools that includes blogging, tweeting, websites, search engine optimization and analytics. However, effectively using these disconnected strategies requires time and technical savvy. To simplify matters, HubSpot helps its clients post content on websites, Twitter, and other social media platforms, and tracks the results with its proprietary software.

Canadian Mountain Holidays Heli-Skiing & Summer Adventures (CMH) provides helicopter transport, lodging and guides for ski, snowboard, and hiking vacations. The adventure company had tried out a number of web-based tactics but found their approaches cumbersome and inefficient. Furthermore, without data capture, they had no ability to analyze the effectiveness of their efforts. However, after using HubSpot's analytics to help them coordinate and disseminate their social media messages and then analyze the results for three years, CMH documented a 387 percent increase in traffic from social marketing and a 772 percent increase in leads.

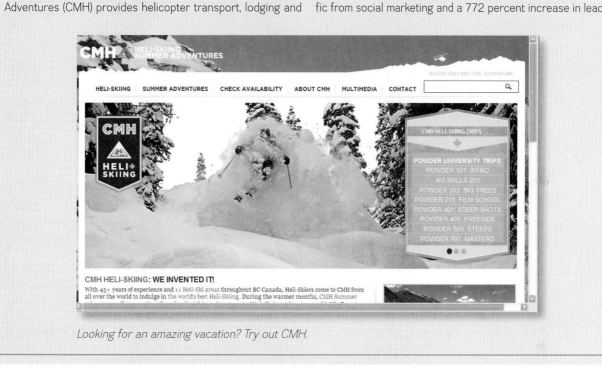

Looking for an amazing vacation? Try out CMH.

Google+, as well as some lesser known options, such as Roost or Schedulicity. Adding Value 3.1 highlights how HubSpot can be used to better educate one's customers.

Experience the Product or Service

Although most of the top videos on YouTube are funny, silly, or otherwise entertaining, the site's most useful contributions may be the vivid information it provides about a firm's goods and services—how they work, how to use them, and where they can be obtained. YouTube and similar sites can come relatively close to simulating real experiences. Such benefits are very common for products that have long been sold online—so much so that we might forget that it used to be difficult to assess these products before buying them. But today, consumers can download a chapter of a new book onto their tablet before buying it. They can try out a software option for a month before buying it. They often can listen to a few seconds or even an entire song before purchasing from iTunes. The diffusion of such products has expanded to feature a wealth of new channels and media options.

For other offerings, such as services, social media again offer experience-based information that was not previously available unless consumers bought and tried the product or service. Need help choosing a new nail polish color or applying a new makeup trend? Check blogs such as Temptalia (http://www.temptalia.com/category/tutorials), which offers both advice and tutorials. Relied too long on clip-on ties? Head over to Tie-a-Tie (http://www.tie-a-tie.net/) to find pictures, videos, and step-by-step instructions on how to manage a Windsor, Pratt, or bow-tie knot, as well as advice on what to wear to an interview.

Home Depot has long been a source for do-it-yourselfers (DIYers). But if eager customers forget what the salesclerk said about installing a newly purchased water heater, they can check the retailer's website (http://www6.homedepot.com/how-to/index.html) to get detailed, in-depth instructions. They also will find a section that enables them to chat with other users who might have run into similar problems in their own installation projects.

Nikon's Digital Learning Center (see http://www.flickr.com/groups/nikon-digitallearningcenter/; http://www.flickr.com/Nikon) provides Flickr members with "tutorials, practical photography tips and advice from Nikon photo professionals to assist them in taking the photos they've always dreamed of capturing."[9] Beyond just providing static photography tips that could be found in a book, Nikon created a two-way dialogue with customers, inviting professional photographers to provide instruction and host question-and-answer sessions, and encouraging users to post their own photos. The more than 64,000 members of the learning center thus learn from others' experiences, even as they create their own.

Engage the Customer

In a sense, the first three Es set the stage for the last one: engaging the customer. With engagement comes action, the potential for a relationship, and possibly even loyalty and commitment. Through social media tools such as blogging and microblogging, customers actively engage with firms and their own social networks. Such engagement can be negative or positive. Positively engaged consumers tend to be more profitable consumers, purchasing 20 to 40 percent more than less engaged customers.[10]

On the other hand, Dave Carroll, a traveling musician whose guitar was roughly handled by United baggage handlers, was also closely engaged (in a negative manner) with the company and other users. He spent considerable time and effort to release three songs and their videos, just to convince others that they should not fly United.

But that story also offers an example of positive engagement. Carroll's music, face, and story gained international recognition as an example of how just one social media user could have a huge negative influence on a giant company. To leverage this fame, Carroll has established a website and blog, where he talks about his experiences. His book offers automatic links to copies of his famous United songs with every purchase. In this sense, Carroll is trying to move beyond the excitement and education he initially elicited from other consumers. Now he wants to engage those same people as consumers—of his book.

Next we'll look at the role of various social media tools in shaping the 4E framework for social media.

CHECK YOURSELF

1. What are the 4 Es?
2. What social media elements work best for each of the 4 Es?

CATEGORIES OF SOCIAL MEDIA

L02 Understand the types of social media.

Consider your own Facebook site. Are all your real-life friends your online friends too? Do you actually know all the friends registered on your online site? In all likelihood, you host online friends you've never met, and your circle of virtual friends may be larger than the number of people you see regularly or talk to personally. Accordingly, the audience for marketers could be bigger on social media sites than through other, more traditional forms of media. Such a huge potential audience has gotten the attention of marketers.

Marketers rely on the three types of social media: social network sites, media-sharing sites, and thought-sharing sites (or blogs) (see Exhibit 3.4) to achieve three objectives. First, members promote themselves to gain more friends. Second, the sites promote to get more members. Third, outside companies promote their products and services to appeal to the potential consumers that are active on the sites.

Social Network Sites

Social network sites are an excellent way for marketers to create *excitement*, the first of the 4 Es. People can interact with friends (e.g., Facebook) or business acquaintances (e.g., LinkedIn). Although the amount of time people spend on such

---

EXHIBIT 3.4   Types of Social Media

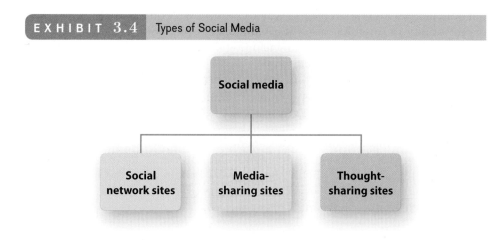

EXHIBIT 3.5 | Length of Time Using Social Networking Sites Daily

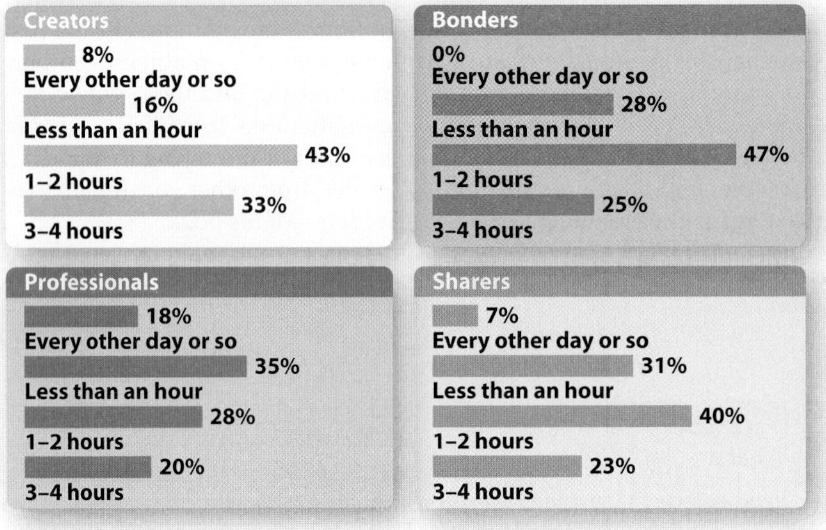

Creators
- 8% Every other day or so
- 16% Less than an hour
- 43% 1–2 hours
- 33% 3–4 hours

Bonders
- 0% Every other day or so
- 28% Less than an hour
- 47% 1–2 hours
- 25% 3–4 hours

Professionals
- 18% Every other day or so
- 35% Less than an hour
- 28% 1–2 hours
- 20% 3–4 hours

Sharers
- 7% Every other day or so
- 31% Less than an hour
- 40% 1–2 hours
- 23% 3–4 hours

Source: Coca-Cola Retailing Research Council and the Integer Group, "Social Networking Personas: A Look at Consumer and Shopper Mind Sets," in *Untangling the Social Web: Insights for Users, Brands, and Retailers,* March 2012.

sites varies, research indicates that they are widely used.[11] Specifically, Exhibit 3.5 shows how much social networks are used by different types of consumers based on their motivations and habits. Note that the vast majority of people in this study use social network sites between one and four hours every day!

- **Creators,** those hip, cool contributors, sit at the cutting edge and plan to stay there. Social media give them new ways to post and share their creative, clever ideas.

- **Bonders** are social butterflies who use social media to enhance and expand their relationships, which they consider all-important in their lives.

- **Professionals,** who are constantly on the go and busy, want to appear efficient, with everything together, so they use social media to demonstrate just how smart they are.

- **Sharers** really want to help others, and the best way to do so is by being constantly well informed so that they can provide genuine insights to others.

All four segments use various types of social networking, as the following sections detail.

Facebook On this well-known social network platform, more than 800 million active users give companies a forum for interacting with their fans. Thus Facebook not only assures individual users a way to connect with others but gives marketers the ability to carefully target their audience. Companies have access to the same features that regular users do, including a "wall" where they can post company updates, photos, and videos or participate in a discussion board. Through this form of free exposure, the company can post content and information regarding products, events, news, or promotions that might be exciting to their customers. Only the fans of their page generally have access to such information, so the company can specifically target its fans.

Successful companies on Facebook attempt to excite their customers regularly. On the fan page for the discount clothing retailer Forever 21, for example,[12] when a fan clicks to indicate that he or she "likes" a certain post, the message gets relayed to a news feed. Then every friend of that user sees what he or she likes, creating an exciting and huge multiplier effect.[13]

Coca-Cola on Facebook: 50 million people like Coca-Cola on Facebook.

Another, albeit more controversial example, was when Burger King launched a Facebook campaign in which customers could earn a free Whopper if they delisted 10 friends from their account. The so-called "Whopper Sacrifice" was intended to show what someone would give up for a Whopper, and the campaign attracted the participation of more than 200,000 active users. After a "Whopper Sacrifice," the ex-friends received notification, which was also published on the Facebook "mini-feed" and thus helped spread the word even more quickly. As the campaign caught on though, Facebook disabled it. Thus, the Facebook page for Burger King read: "Facebook has disabled Whopper Sacrifice after your love for the Whopper sandwich proved to be stronger than 233,906 friendships." By affecting 233,906 people, who were either defriended or actually did the defriending, Burger King created a notable form of excitement—despite being shut down quickly.[14]

Display advertising with Facebook ads targets specific groups of people, according to their profile information, browsing histories, and other preferences. If online users reveal an interest in ski equipment or Burton snowboards, marketers can target both groups. Thus, Facebook offers a variation on more traditional forms of promotion, with the promise of more accurate targeting and segmentation. But being effective and relevant on Facebook is not simply a matter of shifting an offline ad into social network sites, as Adding Value 3.2 recognizes.

LinkedIn A professional, instead of casual or friendship-based site, LinkedIn allows users to share their professional lives. With more than 150 million users, it is a place where users can post their résumés, network with other professionals, and search for jobs.[15] It is *not* the place where you will see games such as Mafia Wars or FarmVille; instead, users post to question-and-answer forums, do job searches, and post personal intellectual property, such as presentations they have given.

The professional networking benefits of LinkedIn are particularly beneficial for small business owners. More than 12 million of LinkedIn's users are small business owners, making it an excellent resource for entrepreneurs to network with

Adding Value 3.2   Effective Friending

The use of social networking in marketing is so new that inexperienced marketers have launched poorly conceived Facebook campaigns with the hope that any strategy that includes social media is "good enough." But good enough is rarely sufficient in a competitive marketplace, and some brands have hurt their images by launching campaigns that are out of step with social media culture.

When a group of industry professionals discussed the ingredients necessary to attract positive attention from Facebook's 800 million users,[16] they agreed that a successful campaign must tell a story. Ideally, the story should involve and engage users in the plotline. Equally important, these creative heavyweights highlighted the need to connect the campaign to the real world, as Heinz did with its campaign that allowed users to send personalized cans of soup to sick friends (recall Exhibit 3.3).

Making good use of consumer data available on Facebook can also improve campaign success by giving marketers the ability to hone in on target audiences and track consumer response. After months of flat reactions to a Facebook promotion of its environmentally friendly cleaners, Clorox launched new initiatives designed to educate people about and increase sales of its Green Works products. The campaign targeted only those women whose Facebook profiles featured the words "clean" or "green."[17] At the same time, Clorox aimed to enhance the experience of other potential users by inviting consumers to nominate green heroes in their community to receive a $15,000 grant. In yet another effort, Clorox offered a $3-off coupon to people who connected to the Green Works web page. The result was a record-breaking engagement rate for the company, demonstrating that social media, when used properly, can be a valuable marketing tool.

Clorox's Facebook promotion is designed to educate people about and increase sales of its Green Works products.

like-minded firms, identify the best vendors, or build brand reputation by participating in LinkedIn's professional association groups. With more than 150,000 company profiles on LinkedIn, it also offers a great place to prospect for new business customers and keep an eye on and get key information about competitors.[18]

Google+   The launch of Google+ represents an attempt to compete with the excitement of Facebook. Its effect on social media and gaming communities was nearly immediate. Within six weeks of its launch, Google+ had added 16 games to its lineup, including Angry Birds and Zynga Poker. The goal was to excite users who love to play, especially games that let them interact with one another—the people who made such a massive success out of Facebook's FarmVille game.[19] If Google+ can attract players effectively, it hopes they never go back to Facebook. With this tactic, Google+ attracted more than 20 million unique visitors within weeks of its launch. But advertisers, users, and gaming companies continue to watch closely to discover how the Google+ network will fare. Are users going to be loyal to Google+, or are they just signing on to check out the newest thing from an Internet giant?[20]

Google+ is Google's answer to Facebook.

Superior Service 3.1 highlights how social network tools help small businesses expand by teaching their customers about what they can provide.

Media—Sharing Sites

The World Wide Web has the ability to connect people more easily and in more ways than have ever been possible before. Media-sharing sites explicitly rely on this capability to enable users to share content they have generated, from videos on YouTube to pictures on Flickr and so on. In terms of the 4E framework, companies use such sites to highlight how consumers can *experience* their goods or services, as well as encourage consumers to *engage* with the firm, its other social media outlets, and other consumers.

YouTube   On this video-sharing social media platform, users upload, share, and view videos. This medium gives companies a chance to express themselves in a different way than they have in the past. YouTube videos also show up in Google searches, making it an appealing vehicle for retailers.[21] The site's demographics indicate visitors are affluent, of the age range most appealing to retailers, and racially reflective of the wider U.S. population.[22]

YouTube also provides an effective medium for hosting contests and posting instructional videos. The Home Depot attracts more than 4,400 viewers with an array of videos detailing new products available in stores, as well as instructional do-it-yourself videos, like "How To Tips for Mowing Your Lawn" or "How To Repair a Toilet."[23] These videos maintain the core identity of the Home Depot brand while also adding value for consumers, who learn useful ways to improve their homes. As a good example of IMC, Home Depot reinforces its brand image and makes itself more relevant to the consumer's life.

Companies can broadcast from their own channel, that is, a YouTube site that contains content relevant only to the company's own products.[24] For example, Home Shopping Network (HSN) offers consumers an interesting vehicle to utilize the 4E framework—*excite, educate, experience,* and *engage*—using a multichannel strategy with its television channel as its central focus. As competition in this field has increased, HSN has added to its communication arsenal an e-commerce site, and

Superior Service 3.1 | Social Networks Help Small Businesses Grow

Any small business, especially a new one, comes right up against the bottom line. A skeletal staff and tight budgets may make it tough to take on a new task, like social media management. When it comes to traditional small businesses, like the neighborhood plumber, Facebook or other social network outlets may seem irrelevant. Word of mouth has always worked for referrals, so why change now? Yet some small business owners have found that social networks are an essential tool to reach customers and put their products on the map.

Specializing in luxury watches like Cartier and Rolex that sell for about $4,000 each, Melrose Jewelers has used social networks to connect with its primary customer base: young, upwardly mobile consumers who are technologically savvy. Its social media activity, including Facebook (with 100,000 likes), a blog, and YouTube, increased sales by 71 percent the first year. One Facebook campaign, a personality quiz that helped customers decide which watch best suited them, attracted $100,000 in sales. Facebook's customer testimonials also helped build credibility with older customers.[25]

The owners of Yeti Coolers specialize in building a rugged cooler that defies all the elements outdoors. Once they began using Facebook and YouTube, fishermen, beach-goers, and others responded. With a Facebook page that soon logged 15,000 likes and fans uploading YouTube videos of lakeside fun around the cooler, Yeti Coolers built a community of customers devoted to its product.[26]

Negri Electronics, a high-end cell phone vendor, uses Google+ for customer communication. Google+ "circles" enable the owner to send specialized messages to each customer group. Google+ also has made Web searching more social, because the +1 feature allows the owner to prioritize web pages for "circle" members. The owner of Mansfield Fine Furniture disagrees, though. After six months in business, he has about a dozen customers who have purchased his pieces, which range in price from $500 to $5,000 each. He finds Facebook still yields a more robust customer response, because Google+ is not yet widely used.[27]

Social networks, with the right management tools, can help a small business grow its customer base. Now, about that plumber, what can social networks do for him or her?

Products promoted on Home Shopping Network (HSN) are available on its dedicated YouTube channel almost immediately after they appear on television.

Facebook and MySpace pages. But perhaps the most powerful tool it has added is its dedicated YouTube channel, which it exploits to reach target shoppers in an exciting way that maximizes the value of its media content. Products promoted on HSN, such as Tori Spelling's jewelry line,[28] are available on YouTube almost immediately after they appear on television. Then HSN marketers can use the information gathered from YouTube to target its direct mail campaigns. For example, it could send jewelry promotions to households that viewed the YouTube video clip for a necklace from the Tori Spelling Collection. Consumer responses get monitored 24/7 and measured against hourly sales goals. There's thus never a dull moment.

Flickr and Other Photo Sites

Whereas YouTube allows users to share videos, Flickr, Picasa, TwitPic, Photobucket, and Imgur allow them to share photos. They tend to be less popular as marketing tools, yet some innovative companies have found ways to engage with customers, such as by hosting picture posting competitions or using photos to communicate core tenets and values.[29]

The U.K. brand Innocent, known for selling pure 100 percent fruit smoothies, uses Flickr to communicate its quirky brand image. Its photo posting competitions, such as the Funny Shaped Fruit Competition (http://www.flickr.com/groups/funnyshapedfruit/), provide significant entertainment value. But it also uses Flickr for more serious purposes, such as to post photos related to its Big Knit charity promotion.[30]

Thought—Sharing Sites

Thought-sharing sites consist of different types of blogs: corporate, professional, personal, and micro. In terms of the 4E framework, blogs are particularly effective at *educating* and *engaging* users, and in many cases enhance their *experience* with the products and services being discussed.

Blogs Once upon a time, confined to a journal or diary in a person's room, the **blog** (from "web log") on the Internet has allowed us to make our thoughts open to the world through thought-sharing websites. For corporations, the comment section allows marketing managers to create a two-way dialogue directly with the end users. The wide availability of free blogging tools such as WordPress, Blogger, and TypePad, which enable non–technically oriented people to create their own blogs, has made blogging a very popular pastime. In 2009 Technorati estimated that 200 million English language blogs existed, and by February of 2012, that number had grown to 450 million.[31]

Companies have responded to this interest and now have several ways to include blogging in their social media marketing strategy. Blogs provide firms the opportunity to *educate* their customers about their offerings, and to *engage* them by responding to their communications, both positive and negative. The reach that marketers have to their customers from blogs can be categorized by the level of control they offer. **Corporate blogs**, which are created by the companies themselves, have the highest level of control, because to a large degree, they can control the content posted on them. Of course, blogs also allow customers to respond to posts, so the content can never be completely controlled, but marketing managers have a good opportunity to pepper their blogs with the messages they wish their customers to see. The best corporate blogs illustrate the importance of engaging customers around the core brand tenets without being overly concerned with a hard sell.

Starbucks (http://mystarbucksidea.force.com/apex/ideaHome) uses its blog for new product development by generating new product and *experience* ideas from its customers. The popular regional grocery store chain Wegman's (http://www.wegmans.com/blog/) blogs to generate loyalty and generate sales by sharing employees' ideas about entertaining, nutrition, and recipes. General Electric (http://www.gereports.com/) *educates* customers through its blog by telling entertaining stories geared at getting customers to realize it sells more than just light bulbs.[32]

From a marketing perspective, **professional blogs** are those written by people who review and give recommendations on products and services. Marketers often offer free products or provide modest remuneration to top-rated professional bloggers, in the hopes of getting a good product review. Marketers have less control over professional bloggers than they do their own corporate blogs. But consumers seem to trust professional bloggers' reviews much more than corporate blogs and other more traditional media, like advertising. Such trust may be fleeting, however, as more consumers realize that professional bloggers are often compensated for positive reviews. "Mommy Blogs," a particularly popular type of professional blog, feature advice and

Innocent uses Flickr to post photos for its Big Knit charity promotion.

Adding Value 3.3   Never Say Never Once Social Media Catches Fire

Teen idol Justin Bieber was just a boy who liked to sing when his mother uploaded some of their homemade videos onto YouTube in 2007. Within a year, the 13-year-old Canadian had been discovered, signed a contract with the record producer Usher, and was well on his way to a blockbuster career. In 2010, he performed for President Obama. His "Baby" video registered the most views on YouTube, with more than 408 million downloads.[33] His phenomenal success worldwide points to the power of social media—especially for anyone trying to reach a global market of adolescent girls.

Bieber's vast social media platform reaches millions of followers worldwide, including around 40 million fans on his Facebook site, and more than 21,000 new members join every day. His music on MySpace has registered more than 108 million plays.[34] Yet Bieber's success was not, at first, guaranteed. When music producer Scooter Braun spotted him on YouTube and took his videos to the record companies, they declined. But Braun believed in his young client's boy-next-door-look and convincing R&B sound. So he decided to continue the YouTube uploads of Bieber performing in any venue they could find.[35] By the time Bieber surpassed 10 million YouTube views, he had also started working with Usher. *My World*, his first album, pushed Bieber's YouTube numbers past 100 million views.[36]

He and his management team never looked back. In 2011, Bieber broke YouTube records by reaching 2 billion views.[37] Twitter helped build so much buzz that one New York concert had to be cancelled after 5,000 fans suddenly swarmed the venue in a kind of flash mob.[38] Bieber also has over 14 million Twitter followers; his account represents 3 percent of the total traffic on Twitter,[39] where his fan clubs thrive. One of biggest began in Australia and soon had 90,000 followers tweeting from @JBSource. Besieged by media requests, the singer granted the two girls leading that club his only interview, rather than meet with the major media. The interview became the most watched video of Bieber's tour. Teenagers want to see Bieber meet and talk with someone like them, Braun later explained, not look for information on a dot-com news site.[40]

The Bieber team also has continued to use social media to promote his records and concerts. When the song "Never Say Never" was released, a web video campaign registered 2.8 million views and 400,000 personalized videos, logging more audience engagement than ever before.[41] In perhaps the perfect convergence of a product, a marketing medium, and the moment, Justin Bieber has ridden social media all the way to the top. Whatever you might think of his singing, it makes for great marketing, especially in the age of instantaneous connection.

DISSECTING JUSTIN BIEBER

myspace
108 MILLION PLAYS

You Tube
2 BILLION VIEWS

facebook
37 MILLION LIKES

twitter
14 MILLION FOLLOWERS

When justin says
"Night Girls"
29,612 girls reply

1994	Justin Drew Bieber (pronounced / ˈdʒʌstɪn ˈbiːbər/) is born
2007	Justin's mother posts a video on YouTube of Justin singing 'So Sick' by Ne-Yo
2008	Justin is signed by Usher
2009	Sings for U.S President Barack Obama
2010	'Baby' is the most viewed (and disliked) Youtube video of the year (with 408 million views)
2010	Justin is accounted for 3% of all Twitter traffic
2010	"justin bieber syphilis" hits #1 on google trends
2010	Justin becomes Proactiv spokesperson
2011	Is the first to reach 2 billion views on Youtube

Crisp

product recommendations from one mother to many others. Dooce, written by Heather Armstrong, has more than 1.5 million mommy followers.[42]

Finally, **personal blogs** are written by people that receive no products or remuneration for their efforts. Thus, of the various types of blogs, marketers have the lowest level of control over this type. However, personal blogs are useful for monitoring what is going on in the marketplace and for responding to customer complaints or compliments.

Microblogs As the name implies, a **microblog** differs from a traditional blog in size—short sentences, short videos, or individual images. On the most popular microblogging site, Twitter, users are limited to 140-character messages. Twitter provides another option for companies to *educate* their customers by providing corporate and product information, and to *engage* them by providing a platform for two-way communications. Even companies that may have once resisted social media are now realizing that Twitter offers an important communications channel.

As much as Twitter can help build a firm's brand image though, it can also tarnish it instantly. Firms have to watch out for hacked Twitter accounts or ill-considered tweets. And Twitter can also act as an international, rapidly spread complaint forum.[43]

A central problem for companies is ownership of relevant Twitter handles and responsibility for outgoing Twitter communication. If Twitter control is shared by a lot of people, the message usually gets muddled. But if only one or two people are in charge, the need to respond to the vast number of incoming tweets might become overwhelming. Different companies thus manage their Twitter strategies in various ways.

Whole Foods tries to develop a broader engagement with customers by interacting with its 2.1 million Twitter followers. It instituted a weekly Twitter chat, for an hour every Thursday, during which Whole Foods representatives discuss topics such as holiday menu planning and healthy eating. Many Whole Foods stores also have their own Twitter accounts to answer questions directly related to their stores.

In contrast, Best Buy hires an army of specialists to manage its Twitter accounts: not just the main account @Best Buy, but also @BestBuy_Deals, @GeekSquad, and @BestBuyNews. The specialists who work Best Buy's help desk also will answer questions through Twitter, at @Twelpforce. Users who tweet the help desk receive an almost instant response from one of Best Buy's 3,000 employees who have signed up to participate on the task force, which further helps showcase the broad spectrum of expertise available through Best Buy.[44]

For small companies with limited marketing budgets, the use of tweeted promotional messages are particularly appealing. A local bakery tweeted, "Two new scones: Lemon Blueberry and Chorizo Cheddar!" and received responses from 400 Twitter followers—a huge captive audience for a local entity.

Of course, some of the most famous Twitter users are celebrities, who have their own brands to manage and marketing goals to reach. Think about how teen idol Justin Bieber and his management team have relied on Twitter and other social media to reach his target audience, as we describe in Adding Value 3.3.

GOING MOBILE AND SOCIAL

LO3 Understand the types of mobile applications.

Although 97 percent of consumers access social media through their computers, 37 percent access these media via their mobile phones, 3 percent through iPads, and 2 percent through e-readers.[45] Also, of the more than 100 million people that have smartphones in the U.S., approximately half of them make purchases on these devices. Thus, mobile marketing is significant and growing. In this huge market, consumers generally are younger and wealthier than others who own

Ethical and Societal Dilemma 3.1   Internet vs. Brick-and-Mortar Stores

Smartphone price check apps help consumers save money by using a scanned bar code, search query, or photo and spoken product name to search multiple merchants for the best price for a particular item. The results tend to favor online merchants, which don't have to bear the cost of brick-and-mortar stores. But Amazon took price checking a step further: Just in time for holiday shopping, the company sliced off an additional 5 percent for shoppers using Amazon's Price Check app in a physical store.[46] The app only revealed Amazon's price, and the discount, which applied to toys, electronics, and DVDs, could be used for up to three items at a maximum savings of $5 per item.

Retailers complained that the app rewarded consumers for using brick-and-mortar stores as showrooms where shoppers could experience an item in a comfortable environment, learn about it from sales staff, decide to buy it, and then receive a discount for purchasing it online—oftentimes while the customer was still in the store. Although the discount didn't apply to books, it triggered outrage and a call for an Amazon boycott from bookstores already hurt by the Internet retailer's low prices and ability to avoid collecting state sales tax.[47] Critics called the promotion predatory and claimed Amazon was compromising the personality and economic stability of communities.

Retailers compete for customers, particularly during the holiday season, and Amazon's promotion helped shoppers save money. But should Amazon have considered the "showroom" effect on brick-and-mortar stores? On a broader scale, how aggressive can a marketer be before triggering backlash that can harm the company's reputation?

older-model mobile phones (or none at all). For example, more than 50 percent of mobile retail consumers earn at least $75,000 annually. In terms of the 4E framework, mobile marketing is particularly useful for creating *excitement* with consumers at the time of sale as we now explain. Several applications have been developed to better market goods and services to these attractive consumers. We briefly discuss a few types: price check apps, fashion apps, and location apps.

Price Check Apps When out shopping, smartphone users no longer have to go from store to store or stop home to go online and compare prices. Using a price checking app, such as at Amazon, or Stylish Girl, customers can scan a product in a store and instantly compare the prices online to see whether a better deal is available. Although price checking can encourage competition, as we discuss in Ethical and Societal Dilemma 3.1, companies can stray into grey ethical areas depending on how they promote their apps.

Realizing that online price checking could be damaging to business, retailers are responding in kind. Lowe's arms its employees with smartphones to help them instantly search the in-store and nearby inventories and place orders online if products are out of stock, to ensure that no customer ever leaves empty handed.[48] Target is working with vendors to create exclusive in-store items, to match online retailer pricing, and to develop a subscription-based online pricing strategy that gives regular buyers special discounts.[49]

Fashion Apps The consumers who are most likely to use mobile media also are likely to buy from technology and fashion-oriented firms, whether they are fashion or technology retailers, sell fashion magazine content, or brand information. Style.com offers a mobile application for people to access the same content available on the *Style* magazine website, including blogs, reviews, couture shows, and video feeds.[50] Other apps provide a more in-depth look at a particular brand. Louis Vuitton's NOWNESS app combines magazine content with brand promotion. Pose is not brand-specific; instead, this photo-sharing app shares various style and fashion views and tips. Pinterest allows people to "pin" merchandise, services, recipes, or ideas onto a virtual bulletin board. For instance, Pinterest users can "pin" clothing and accessories that match their personal taste; while others can browse their pinboards to discover new things and make comments. Marketers therefore can receive unlimited exposure to their products and services as like-minded people share pinned items and services.

Location-Based "Gamified" Apps Smartphone owners are increasingly using location-based apps. Customers can download several free apps that use the GPS function of their phone to share what they are doing, where they are, and when they're doing it. Companies use these apps to build loyalty by making patronage a game, a process known as gamification.

Users of FourSquare can check in at their favorite restaurants and stores, sharing their location on Facebook. They can compete with other users for the title of "Mayor" by achieving the most number of check-ins at a retail location in a 60-day period. Another spin on location-based gamification is SCVNGR. This app takes location-based gaming and direct sales to the next level. Users logging onto the app will be provided with a list of stores near them participating in SCVNGR. By completing challenges at these stores, ranging from simply checking in to "bumping phones" with other SCVNGR users at the establishment to making a portrait of the person sitting across from them out of food and taking a picture of it, users accrue points that unlock in-app badges and real-world coupons such as free coffee. Another interesting app is Snapette, which focuses on shoes and bags and aims to help customers find the merchandise they want according to their immediate location.

In the past two decades, marketers have developed websites and other methods to communicate information about and to sell their goods and services. Their quest for new ways to improve, integrate, and enhance these outcomes has resulted in a confluence of social, mobile, and online marketing. Exhibit 3.6 is a

Users of FourSquare can check in at their favorite restaurants and stores, sharing their location on Facebook.

EXHIBIT 3.6	Firms' Use of Social and Mobile Tools from the 4E Lens			
	Excite	**Educate**	**Experience**	**Engage**
Social networks	◇ ◇			
Media-sharing sites			◇ ◇	◇ ◇
Thought-sharing sites		◇ ◇	◇	◇ ◇
Mobile applications	◇ ◇			◇

brief summary of how these forces and their manifestations align with our 4E framework. It highlights how social network and mobile applications and the associated relevant offers are ideal for stimulating *excitement* in the offers. In particular, mobile location-based apps are exciting because they provide customers with highly relevant offers when they are in close proximity to the retailer or service provider or they can even be used to provide competitive offers. Media-sharing sites (e.g., YouTube and Flickr) are excellent social media tools that provide customers visual *experiences* of customers or professionals who are using these goods and services. They also provide customers an opportunity to *engage* with the firms as well as their own social network by posting their own experiences (i.e., uploading videos), as well as sharing their thoughts (blogs and Twitter posts). Finally, thought-sharing sites, like blogs, are excellent for providing customer *education*, as was highlighted by how HubSpot adds value for their clients.

CHECK YOURSELF

1. What is an example of a social network, a media-sharing site, a thought-sharing site, and a mobile application?

2. On which of the 4e dimensions do social networks, media-sharing sites, thought-sharing sites, and mobile applications excel?

LO4 Recognize and understand the three components of a social media strategy.

HOW DO FIRMS ENGAGE THEIR CUSTOMERS USING SOCIAL MEDIA?

Now that we have an understanding of the various social and mobile media that are at the firm's disposal, it is important to determine how firms should go about engaging customers through social and mobile media. The three-stage process found in Exhibit 3.7 is **listen** to what customers have to say, **analyze** the information available through various touch points, and finally implement (or **do**) social media tactics to excite customers.

Listen

From a market research point of view, companies can learn a lot about their customers by listening (and monitoring) what they say on their social networks, blogs, review sites, etc. Customers appear willing to provide their opinions about just about anything including their interests, and purchases—both their own and those of their friends. Writing blogs and providing opinions via polls about such diverse topics as BOTOX treatments, ASICS running sneakers, or a particular play of an NFL team during the playoffs all constitute new ways that customers communicate with one another—and with marketers who are paying attention.

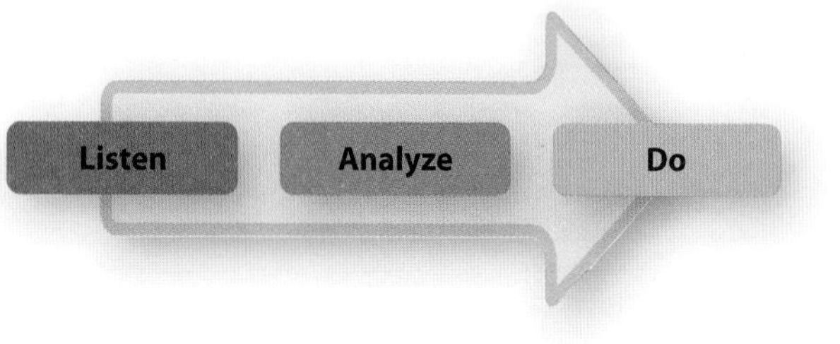

Marketers can analyze the content found on sites like Facebook, Twitter, online blogs, and reviews to assess the favorableness or unfavorableness of the sentiments, using a technique known as **sentiment analysis**. Sentiment analysis allows marketers to analyze data from these sources to collect consumer comments about companies and their products. The data are then analyzed to distill customer attitudes and preferences, including reactions to specific products

EXHIBIT 3.7 Social Media Engagement Process

Listen   Analyze   Do

and IMC campaigns. Scouring millions of sites with sentiment analysis techniques provides new insights into what consumers really think. Companies plugged into such real-time information and insights can become more nimble, allowing for numerous quick changes, such as in a product roll-out, a new advertising campaign, or reacting to customer complaints.

There are several companies that specialize in monitoring social media.[51] For example, Radian6 offers social media listening and engagement tools to help its clients such as Dell, GE, Kodak, Microsoft, and PepsiCo connect with its customers.[52] Using sentiment analysis techniques, it processes a constant stream of online consumer opinion from blogs, Facebook, and other networking sites, including 400 million Twitter tweets a day. The Radian6 tools for managing consumer sentiment data allow companies to identify opinion trends that might warrant an online corporate response. For instance, Radian6 may identify negative consumer sentiment and then provides services to help their client respond. Reacting to attitudes uncovered in sentiment analysis allows companies to counteract negative opinions, maybe influence those perceptions, and perhaps win customer loyalty.[53]

As an example of how a firm like Radian6 can help its clients engage their customers, consider the New York–based nonprofit Let's Get Ready that helps low-income high school students get into college.[54] When it decided to compete for Chase American Giving Awards funding, Let's Get Ready needed broader support. Radian6 helped the organization find Web-based conversations among individuals and groups who might share its educational mission. It further helped Let's Get Ready reach out to potential supporters, share information about its work, and ask for votes. The campaign worked: Let's Get Ready placed second, winning $500,000 for free SAT preparation and college admission counseling to motivated students. Sentiment analysis thus is fundamentally transforming how companies interact with and engage their customers.

Analyze

Fortunately, the companies that help facilitate listening also provide analytic tools to assess what customers are saying about the firm and its competitors. There are three main categories of analysis used for understanding data collected from social media.[55]

Radian6 analyzes customer sentiment for its customers, which enables them to identify opinion trends that might warrant an online corporate response.

First, it is important to determine the amount of traffic using their sites, visiting their blogs, or tweeting about them. Measures used for this purpose include hits (i.e., total requests for a page), visits to a particular site or page, unique visitors to the site, and page views (i.e., the number of times any pages gets viewed by any visitor).

Second, while knowing how many people are using a firm's social media is important, it is even more critical to learn who those visitors are, what they are doing, and what engages and excites them. To analyze these factors, social media marketers use metrics such as the bounce rate, which refers to the percentage of times a visitor leaves the site almost immediately, such as after viewing only one page. Analyzing which pages are the most frequent entry and exit locations provide direction on how to make a website more effective. In addition, following visitors' click paths shows how users proceed through the information—not unlike how grocery stores try to track the way shoppers move through their aisles. A firm can use this information to provide users with an easier navigation experience through the site so they can more quickly find what they are looking for. The data analysis can also reveal conversion rates, a measure that indicates what percentage of visitors or potential customers act as the marketer hopes, whether by clicking, buying, or donating. Click paths and conversion rates can also reveal what users might have wanted, but not found, on the site.

Third, some companies want to analyze data that comes from other sites, such as measuring where people have come from to get to the company's site. Did they search through Google or Amazon? Did they receive a referral from a friend? Which keywords did they use to find the firm? Firms can use keyword analysis to determine what keywords people use to search on the Internet for their products and services. With this information, they can refine their websites by choosing keywords to use on their site that their customers use. Then they can assess the ROI of the investment made by improving the site. This would be done by calculating the incremental profit increase divided by the investment on the site improvement. For social media, it is more challenging to determine ROI than for more traditional IMC applications, because the revenue generated by social media is often not directly related to the expenditure. So, instead of traditional ROI measures, firms often examine questions like: Does having more Twitter followers correlate with having higher sales? Do Facebook fans of the company buy more than nonfans? [56]

These analyses require well-trained marketing managers, marketing analytic software, and perhaps some help with consulting specialists (e.g., IBM, SAS, PriceWaterhouse). But almost everyone seems to be turning to Google Analytics these days, because it offers a sophisticated, in-depth form of analysis, all for free. Not only does Google Analytics track the elements that are shown in Exhibit 3.8, but it also is highly customizable.[57]

Do

Even the greatest analysis has little use if firms fail to implement what they have learned from analyzing their social and mobile media activity. That is, social media may be all about relationships, but ultimately, firms need to use their connections to increase their business.[58] They might launch a new Facebook campaign, actively blog, or provide mobile offers.

When Facebook first introduced its new Page format, many users balked, complaining about having to reformat all their posts. But Macy's jumped on the chance to refresh its image among its Facebook followers, tell a better story, and develop a testing lab for new promotions and offers. On Pinterest, Macy's also is testing communication tactics that might enable it to piggyback on women's posts about things that inspire them. If one user notes her dream of a beach vacation, Macy's might contact her with an offer for bathing suits—even in the dead of winter. In a recent marketing research survey, the retailer discovered—to its surprise—that 40 percent of the responses came through mobile devices. If customers are

EXHIBIT 3.8	Analytics	
Type of Analytic	How It's Used	Competitors Offering Similar Analytics
Content	Understand what's popular and what's not on a firm's website, including page load times and site navigation.	Adobe SiteCatlyst, Clickstream, Coremetrics, IBM SurfAid, Mtracking, VisiStat
Social	Track effectiveness of social media programs, including information on social media referred conversion rates and engagement metrics.	Facebook Insights, Twitter Web Analytics, Webtrends
Mobile	Track website access from mobile devices, track which ads direct people to a firm's app, understand what mobile platform performs best.	AppClix, Bango, Flurry, Localytics, Medialets, Webtrends
Conversion	Moving beyond page views and visitor counts, conversion analytics measures sales, downloads, video plays, or any other action important to a firm.	Clicktale, KeyMetric, Latitude
Advertising	Track the effectiveness of social, mobile, search and display ads, divide ad effectiveness by device, platform, or type.	AdTech, MediaMelon MediaCloud, Metronome, Snoobi, YieldMetrics,

Source: http://www.google.com/analytics/features/index.html.

responding to surveys through their smartphones, what might they do with mobile promotions?[59] Macy's aims to find out.

Although Macy's appears to have undertaken a broad-based approach, deciding which tactics to employ and when is key. The social media marketer needs to act like an orchestra conductor, waving a wand to make sure that hundreds of "musicians," playing a variety of instruments, come together to create some beautiful music. A well-developed marketing strategy involves a host of social and mobile tools, working in conjunction with the firm's traditional IMC tactics, to move the consumer up the purchase decision hierarchy from awareness to purchase to loyalty.

To illustrate how firms might go about undertaking such campaigns, consider the steps involved in developing and implementing a Facebook marketing campaign (Exhibit 3.9).[60] These steps are not unlike the steps used in any integrated

EXHIBIT 3.9   How to Do a Social Media Marketing Campaign

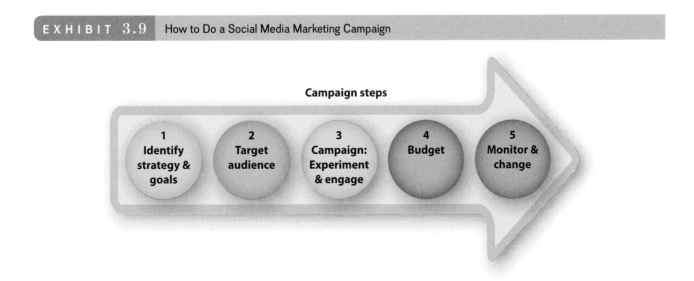

Campaign steps

1 Identify strategy & goals

2 Target audience

3 Campaign: Experiment & engage

4 Budget

5 Monitor & change

EXHIBIT 3.10   Example Facebook Targeting Choices

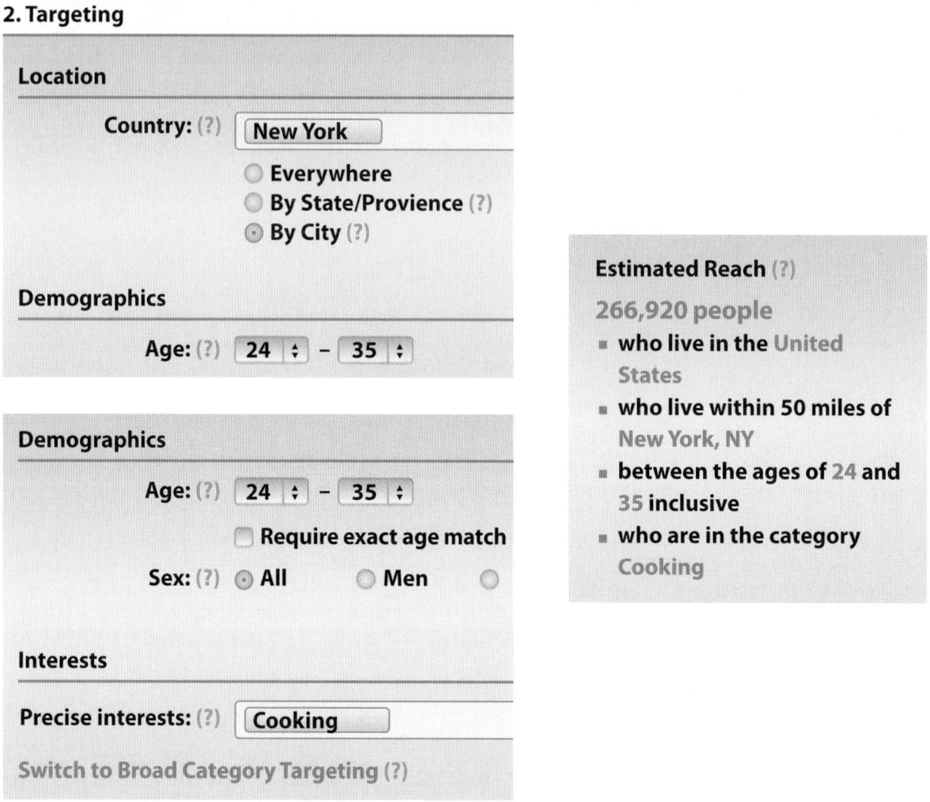

2. Targeting

Location

Country: (?)   [New York]

- ○ Everywhere
- ○ By State/Provience (?)
- ◉ By City (?)

Demographics

Age: (?) [24 ⬍] – [35 ⬍]

Estimated Reach (?)

266,920 people

- who live in the United States
- who live within 50 miles of New York, NY
- between the ages of 24 and 35 inclusive
- who are in the category Cooking

Demographics

Age: (?) [24 ⬍] – [35 ⬍]

☐ Require exact age match

Sex: (?) ◉ All   ○ Men   ○

Interests

Precise interests: (?)   [Cooking]

Switch to Broad Category Targeting (?)

Source: From http://www.facebook.com/business/ads/. Reprinted with permission.

marketing communications (IMC) program. (See Chapters 18 and 19 for more details.) Assume a marketer was developing a Facebook marketing campaign for a new product that they have designed.

1. **Identify strategy and goals.** The firm has to determine exactly what it hopes to promote and achieve through its campaign. Does it want to increase awareness of the product? Are they hoping more potential customers might visit and like their Facebook page? Is their focus mainly on increasing sales of the product? Depending on what they aim to achieve, they might focus on developing a Facebook page, creating a Facebook app, or hosting a Facebook event.

2. **Identify target audience.** The next step is to determine whom they are are targeting. As Exhibit 3.10 shows, Facebook enables the firm to perform targeting that is based on location, language, education, gender, profession, age, relationship status, likes/dislikes, and friends or connections. The marketer's aim is to find a big enough audience to reach those who might adopt their product without being so big that they end up trying to appeal to someone way outside of their target audience.

3. **Develop the campaign: experiment and engage.** Now that the firm knows who it is targeting, the next step is to develop the communication, including the copy and images. Here again, the process is not very different from any other IMC campaign. There should be a call to action that is clear and compelling. Strong, eye-catching images and designs are important. And the campaign must appeal to the right customers. However, an aspect that is more critical with social media than other forms of IMC is that the images

Adding Value 3.4 — Applebee's Listens, Analyzes, and Does Social Media

National brands are recognizing the need to create specific social media pages tailored to local audiences. Applebee's has tried to be true to its "Eating good in the neighborhood" tagline by maintaining a local focus and encouraging franchisees to stay connected to their local communities. Social media has been instrumental in providing franchisees further opportunities to do so. However, with 2,000 restaurants and 44 franchisees, executives were worried that all of the different messages could potentially dilute the brand or differ from Applebee's corporate-driven initiatives. Therefore, the company hired Expion to help manage its social engagement initiatives across franchises and to extend social media development from the brand to the store level. Franchisees are allowed, and encouraged, to develop their own local social media pages. However, each franchisee must go through an approval process, run by corporate headquarters, to post comments and post photos before they appear online. Reviews are usually approved (or denied) within several hours.

In addition, corporate headquarters can send out mass updates, like new menu items or promotional initiatives, which appear to customers as if they are coming from the local store. If customers post negative comments, local and regional managers are alerted immediately.

The new system appears to be paying off: Its Facebook fans have jumped in number from 180,000 to more than 1,000,000. For now, Applebee's is mostly focusing on Facebook content rather than building YouTube or Twitter sites. The goal is to focus on one component of social media, to sufficiently build credibility and trust before trying to reach customers through multiple social media outlets.[61] In this sense, listening entails more than just asking questions and putting the response data into a spreadsheet. It also involves entering into social engagement initiatives by joining various conversations, making judgments about the data, and then applying the lessons provided by those data to improve further listening activities.[62]

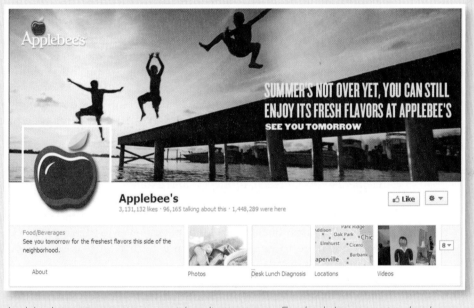

Applebee's is concentrating its social media strategy on Facebook. Its new system has been so successful that its Facebook fans have jumped from 180,000 to over a million.

and messages need to be updated almost constantly. Because people expect changing content online, it would be inappropriate to run the same campaign for several months, as the firm might if they were advertising on television, for example.

4. **Develop the budget.** Budgeting is key. Facebook allows advertisers to set a daily budget: Once their costs (usually per click) reach a certain level, the ad disappears for the rest of the day. Of course, this option can be risky if the firm is getting great feedback, and all of a sudden, a compelling ad disappears. Therefore, similar to the campaign content, budgets demand nearly

constant review. For example, if a competitor lowers its price significantly, it might be necessary to follow suit to avoid being excluded from customers' consideration sets.

5. **Monitor and change.** The final step is to review the success of the campaign and make changes as necessary. Facebook's Ad Manager offers various metrics and reports, such as number of clicks on ads, audience demographics, and ad performance for specific time periods.

Adding Value 3.4 examines how Applebee's <u>listens</u> to its customers, <u>analyzes</u> the information it has collected, and implements (<u>does</u>) a social media program.

LO5 Understand the methods for marketing yourself using social media.

MANAGING YOUR INDIVIDUAL BRAND VALUE IN A SOCIAL MEDIA WORLD

The branding concepts examined in Chapter 11 apply in unique ways in the social media world, in which context people engage in self-branding in new and exciting ways. Recall that brands attempt to build awareness, aim to develop loyalty, and exert an impact. If one applies these concepts to individual brand equity, one might think of individual brand management in some of the following ways.

Measures of individual social media effectiveness or equity use metrics such as **social reach**, which refers to how many people a person influences (e.g., number of individuals in the person's social networks such as Facebook and LinkedIn); **influence**, which is the extent to which the person influences others (e.g., how much do the people in a person's network read that person's content); and **extended network**, or the influence of the person's extended network, that is, the cumulative number of members (10,000) = 100 members each having 100 members of their own.

Several firms have developed metrics to assess a person's social impact (e.g., Klout, PeerIndex, Twitalyzer, and Kred). For example, Klout combines these three elements—social reach, influence, and extended network—to define a Klout score that can range from 0 to 100. The average score earned by regular people that aren't either celebrities or heavily involved in social media, such as bloggers, is around 20. Justin Bieber is the only person ever to earn a perfect 100. But a person does not have to be a star to earn a high Klout score, as Social and Mobile Marketing 3.1 details.

Although Klout offers a good general view of social influence, various other options exist for more specific or detailed analyses, such as PeerIndex (http://www.peerindex.net), Tweetlevel (http://tweetlevel.edelman.com/), Twitalyzer (http://twitalyzer.com/), How Sociable (http://www.howsociable.com/), Postrank (http://www.postrank.com/), or TwitterGrader (http://twittergrader.com/).[63] Links shared through Twitter or Facebook also affect search rankings on search engines such as Google or Bing, such that greater influence increases the chances that people can find a more influential source of information or fashion.[64]

In a sense, social media are like high school:[65] In both places, people self-select into groups or cliques. Many people define their self-worth based on how many "friends" they can count. People's expressions and actions determine their reputation—whether negatively or positively. The environment can be either inclusive or exclusive—and sometimes both. Users seek out others, both as individuals and as groups. Wallflowers get ignored; fun, active, exciting contributors attract attention.

Social and Mobile Marketing 3.1   Gaining Clout through Klout

Getting into the coolest parties in town used to require attaining stardom or at least socialite status. But today, technology geeks might be found rubbing elbows with movie stars, if their social influence online is strong enough. For major events such as Fashion's Night Out, bloggers and tweeters receive invitations to get into the party early, so they will start the virtual buzz flowing. In Miami, the top social media guests even have access to a VIP area, protected from other partygoers.

The challenge for event planners is how best to identify the bloggers who exert the greatest influence. For that, they turn to Klout. Analyzing data from 13 different online networks, Klout's services can identify how people react to content that any blogger or tweeter puts online. The resulting Klout scores are public knowledge, so everyone knows just how influential each invitee might be. Klout also differentiates the dedicated bloggers with huge fan followings from casual posters who blog just for the fun of it.[66]

In the former group, influential commentators are reaping the benefits, including invitations to parties they likely never dreamed of attending, reservations at the best restaurants, and special treatment nearly everywhere they go. Jason Bin, the founder of Niche Media, has a sky-high Klout score and more than 100,000 Twitter followers; for companies, he's even more appealing as a guest than many celebrities. Even without thousands of followers, social media commentators can provoke a dedicated following that earns them a high Klout score—which makes them just the type of people who should start expecting more invitations in their inboxes.

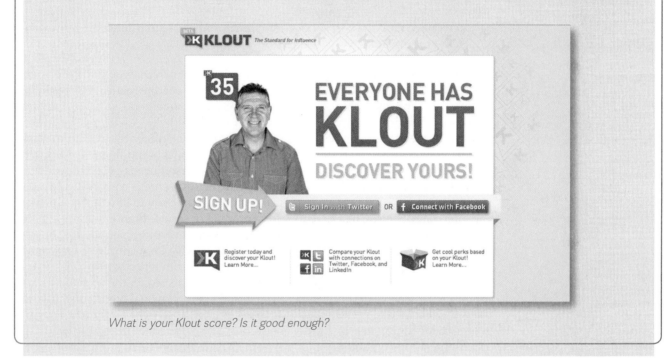

What is your Klout score? Is it good enough?

But remember, "No matter how brilliant and talented you are, you won't be sufficiently appreciated . . . until the broader public recognizes you."[67] Thus, beyond creating an online presence, people with true influence also make use of networks of contacts they make in various realms, give presentations and speeches, publish books and articles as well as blogs, submit themselves for prestigious awards, and try to get on television or other national news outlets.

Even if a person's goal is not necessarily to become the premier expert on a particular topic, social influence can have significant effects on other elements of his or her life, such as hiring success.[68] Employers can check these social presence scores or impact factors, along with other sources of information, to assess how well connected, creative, and active a potential hire is. This source is particularly critical for the rapidly expanding field of social media jobs for marketers.

A student who graduates with a marketing degree likely has a good foundation for one of the following social media jobs:[69]

1. *Social media strategist.* In this quite high paying social media job, people create social media marketing campaigns, then measure the results, using an effective strategic plan.

2. *Community manager.* These positions are responsible for handling corporate forums and blogs, increasing traffic to the site, and broadening their company's community.

3. *Blogger.* These highly sought-after jobs provide great flexibility and freedom. By posting articles on relevant websites, bloggers can earn $35–$75 hourly.

4. *Social media marketing specialist.* These well-paid professionals distribute promotional channels using a range of social media channels, which requires strong online marketing skills.

5. *Search engine marketing associate.* Focusing on search engines, these online marketers rely on their knowledge of optimization techniques to increase the organic search rankings for a website.

6. *Online customer service representative.* Customers like to provide feedback, often online, and the best service companies make sure that someone is on hand to respond.

Regardless of the exact job title, social media jobs are increasing. On the Monster.com job search site for example, the number of social media–related jobs recently jumped by approximately 75 percent.[70] They also offer good salaries and the promise of continued growth, as Exhibit 3.11 shows.

Getting such jobs implies that candidates truly have influence, and these social media impact scores offer some idea about what personal branding really means.[71] First, influence by itself has little impact. Rather, a person needs to leverage his or her personal brand to induce some action, whether that entails convincing friends to support a cause the person likes or convincing a company to hire that person for an internship. Second, just as it does for a product or service brand, building a personal brand takes time, as well as consistent effort. It would be impossible to become really influential by exhibiting a flurry of activity for a couple of days, and then taking a month-long break. Third, there is a big difference between being active and being influential. Simply retweeting comments from other creators is insufficient to achieve true influence. To be influential, a personal brand must follow the 4Es: You need to excite, educate, give experience, and engage your followers.

Moreover, just like any other marketing tactic, personal branding needs to take ethical considerations under advisement. For example, we might think carefully about the spread of metrics especially amid reports about the ways they are being used, perhaps without people's knowledge. For example, at the Palms Casino Resort Hotel, clerks check the Klout scores of guests as they check in and then offer upgrades to those with the highest scores.[72] Is that great marketing, or an ethically questionable exploitation?

The importance of such scores also implies the potential for abuse. What if firms "game" the system, such that the only search engine results you see are those that have developed influence because the companies have paid legions of followers to tweet about their offering?[73] Are you really getting the best choices then?

On a more personal note, it has been pretty well established that embarrassing pictures on Facebook can be detrimental to your future career. But what about just basic posts and influence efforts? Despite the benefits of building your social influence, the more information available about you online, the more information potential employers and others have. One study even suggests that human resource managers should assess social media sources to determine if a potential hire is agreeable (pleasant in interactions, or caustic in humor?), emotionally stable (did

EXHIBIT 3.11 | Social Media Jobs Salary Guide

Source: From Onward Search, Digital Marketing and Creative Staffing Agency, www.onwardsearch.com. Reprinted with permission.

SALARY RANGES
by City / Job Title

	Blogger / Social Media COPYWRITER	Social Media SPECIALIST	Online Community MANAGER	Public Relations / Brand MANAGER	Social Media STRATEGIST	Social Media Marketing MANAGER
1 New York, New York	22k-60k	46k - 71k	54k - 79k	49k - 90k	55k - 103k	73k - 116k
2 San Jose, California	22k-60k	47k - 72k	54k - 80k	50k - 91k	56k - 104k	74k - 117k
3 San Francisco, California	21k-59k	45k - 70k	53k - 78k	48k - 88k	54k - 102k	72k - 114k
4 Los Angeles, California	18k-49k	38k - 59k	44k - 65k	41k - 74k	46k - 85k	61k - 96k
5 Boston, Massachusetts	20k-55k	42k - 65k	49k - 73k	45k - 82k	51k - 95k	67k - 106k
6 Washington, DC	20k-54k	42k - 65k	49k - 72k	45k - 82k	50k - 94k	67k - 106k
7 Baltimore, Maryland	17k-47k	36k - 56k	42k - 63k	39k - 71k	44k - 82k	58k - 92k
8 Chicago, Illinois	18k-50k	39k - 60k	45k - 67k	41k - 76k	46k - 87k	62k - 98k
9 Seattle, Washington	16k-43k	33k - 51k	39k - 57k	35k - 65k	40k - 74k	53k - 84k
10 Philadelphia, Pennsylvania	16k-44k	34k - 52k	39k - 58k	36k - 66k	41k - 76k	54k - 85k
11 Atlanta, Georgia	19k-51k	40k - 61k	46k - 68k	42k - 77k	47k - 88k	63k - 99k
12 Dallas, Texas	17k-47k	36k - 56k	42k - 62k	38k - 70k	43k - 81k	57k - 91k
13 Minneapolis, Minnesota	16k-44k	34k - 52k	39k - 58k	36k - 66k	41k - 76k	54k - 85k
14 Miami, Florida	16k-45k	35k - 54k	41k - 60k	37k - 68k	42k - 79k	56k - 88k
15 Austin, Texas	15k-42k	32k - 50k	38k - 55k	34k - 63k	39k - 72k	51k - 81k
16 San Diego, California	17k-46k	36k - 55k	42k - 61k	38k - 70k	43k - 80k	57k - 90k
17 Denver, Colorado	15k-43k	33k - 51k	39k - 57k	35k - 64k	40k - 74k	53k - 83k
18 Detroit, Michigan	16k-45k	41k - 77k	40k - 59k	37k - 67k	37k - 90k	55k - 87k
19 Houston, Texas	17k-46k	36k - 55k	41k - 61k	38k - 69k	43k - 80k	57k - 90k
20 Phoenix, Arizona	14k-39k	30k - 47k	36k - 52k	32k - 59k	36k - 68k	48k - 77k

Salary ranges represent the 25% and 75% percentile for each job title in each city as obtained from Indeed.com.

Source: From Onward Search, Digital Marketing and Creative Staffing Agency, www.onwardsearch.com. Reprinted with permission.

an interpersonal fight go viral?), or conscientious.[74] Such information also is available for use in legal cases.[75] You thus may be liable for everything you do to enhance your social influence. So think before you post, tweet, or blog: Is this something you want to answer for in court, or even just in the court of public opinion?

CHECK YOURSELF

1. What are the three steps in developing social media engagement strategies?
2. How do firms examine customer sentiments?
3. What are the steps in developing a social media campaign?
4. Why might it be important to develop a personal social media presence?

Summing Up

LO1 Describe the 4E framework of social media marketing.

The 4E framework recognizes that marketers must: **e**xcite customers with relevant offers; **e**ducate them about the offering; help them **e**xperience products, whether directly or indirectly; and give them an opportunity to **e**ngage.

LO2 Understand the types of social media.

Users of social media employ them to promote themselves or their products and services. They do so through three main categories: social networking sites (e.g., Facebook, LinkedIn), media-sharing sites (e.g., YouTube), and thought-sharing sites (e.g., blogs, Twitter).

LO3 Understand the types of mobile applications.

As mobile users increase in number and diversity, the applications developed to appeal to them are spreading as well. For now, most of these apps constitute three broad categories: price checking apps, location-based apps, and fashion apps. However, many applications span more than one category.

LO4 Recognize and understand the three components of a social media strategy.

Firms engage with customers through social and mobile media using a three-step process. First, they listen to the customer using techniques like sentiment analysis. Second, they analyze the data collected in the first step using metrics like bounce rates, click paths, and conversion rates. Finally, they use this information to develop tactics to engage their customers.

LO5 Understand the methods for marketing yourself using social media.

To market themselves, people need to ensure they reach a large number of people, that they influence those people, and that the network of people that they influence is also influential. Several firms, such as Klout, have devised metrics to assess one's social network impact. Having a social network presence is becoming increasingly important in finding certain types of marketing jobs. But on a cautionary note, it is important for people to carefully choose how they are portrayed in social media because once something is posted, it is there for all to see, including potential employers.

Key Terms

- blog, 93
- bonders, 88
- bounce rate, 100
- click paths, 100
- conversion rates, 100
- corporate blogs, 93
- creators, 88
- extended network, 104
- gamification, 97
- hits, 100
- influence, 104
- keyword analysis, 100
- microblog, 95
- page views, 100
- personal blogs, 95
- professional blogs, 93
- professionals, 88
- sentiment analysis, 98
- sharers, 88
- social media, 82
- social reach, 104

Marketing Applications

1. Evaluate Dell's social media strategy using the 4E framework.

2. Using the components of the 4E framework, outline how an entrepreneur marketing T-shirts can augment or enhance his or her marketing mix efforts.

3. Suppose an herbal tea company introduced a new product called mint-enhanced tea—mint and lemon herbal tea. How should it go about creating excitement using various social and mobile media tools?

4. If you were marketing a new sneaker, what sort of mobile applications might enhance your marketing efforts?

5. Assume you work for a large consumer packaged goods firm which has discovered that its latest line of snack foods is moving very slowly off store shelves. Recommend a strategy for listening to what consumers are saying on blogs, review sites, and the firm's website. Describe how your strategy might provide insights into consumers' sentiments about the new product line.

6. If you were assessing the effectiveness of your social media marketing campaign, would sentiment analysis be helpful?

7. As an intern for Dunkin' Donuts, you have been asked to develop a social media campaign for a new glazed muffin. The objective of the campaign is to increase awareness and trial of the new line of muffins. How would you go about putting such a campaign together?

8. What is your Klout score? Do you believe it is "high enough" for what you are planning to do after graduation? How would you go about increasing your score?

Quiz Yourself

www.mhhe.com/grewal4e

1. Reebok is actively offering online coupons on Facebook. It is likely trying to:
   a. excite the consumer
   b. educate the consumer
   c. provide experience to their consumers
   d. allow customers to engage with the firm

2. YouTube is one of the most well-known:
   a. social network sites
   b. media-sharing sites
   c. thought-sharing sites
   d. mobile apps

(Answers to these two questions can be found on page 647.)

Go to www.mhhe.com/grewal4e to practice an additional 11 questions.

Net Savvy

1. Go to http://www.facebook.com/business and learn about how to build pages, ads, sponsored stories, and take advantage of mobile applications. What are some of the steps that Facebook suggests a person consider when marketing using ads?

2. Go to http://www.radian6.com/about-us/ and check out its top case studies. How do these case studies provide insights into how listening and analytic systems can help firms improve their social media marketing?

Chapter Case Study

SOCIAL MEDIA GIVE DELL A DIRECT CONNECTION TO ITS CUSTOMERS

Michael Dell was 19 years of age when he launched his company in 1984, with $1,000 and a vision of how technology should be designed, manufactured, and sold.[76] That vision put customer relationships at the forefront of Dell's core business model, under a simple mantra: "Be direct."[77] The company rolled out its first computers with a

McGraw Hill connect

risk-free return policy.[78] Taking its products directly to the consumer, with the launch of its Dell.com website in March 1996, Dell was generating $1 million a day in sales within six months of going online. The site linked customers to technical assistance through online chat, telephone, and e-mail access points. Bolstered by its comprehensive online support service, Dell.com was generating $40 million a day in revenue in 2000, making it one of the highest-volume e-commerce sites in the world.[79]

But a few years later, Dell fundamentally changed its interaction with customers by making a major commitment to social media. By fully exploiting the potential of Facebook, Twitter, and other social media channels, the company has developed the capacity to engage them even more directly. One of the first corporate social media adopters, Dell is now a leader in the use of social media to transform company performance.[80]

Dell.com is still a customer support workhorse, with all the traditional online marketing strengths. Customers have access to an exhaustive online sales catalog, which complements Dell's worldwide presence through retailers.[81] The website offers product support, technical assistance with downloads, the Windows operating systems, and a multitude of other issues.[82] Online user forums help strengthen the customer relationship, offering Q+A discussions about disk drives, mobile devices, and other topics, as well as more specialized discussions for distinct groups, like new buyers trying to select the right product, small business owners, or those with a special interest, like digital entertainment.[83]

But Dell's social media channels offer the customer a radically different experience. And they provide the company with invaluable customer reactions—both positive and negative—to new products, proposed ad campaigns, service problems, and other aspects of its technology business.

On Facebook, Dell speaks to a variety of market segments, with separate pages for home and business users, small and medium businesses, and large corporate users, along with separate entry points for Dell in Malaysia, Australia, and other countries. A Facebook search in the United States brings the user to Dell's Marketplace, a trendy-looking page that opens to ads and a display of the products currently being promoted.

Links offer users a variety of options. Dell Support plugs users into Dell's online forums, while also showing a scrolling series of live posts offering conversation entry points on questions like how to burn a CD.[84] The Dell Wall feels familiar to any Facebook user. It promotes Dell events and new service offerings. The Buzz Room provides a selection of breaking news from the major media, on topics like Entrepreneurship, Product News, and Mobility, with each page also streaming a relevant Twitter feed.[85]

Other links move in a hipper direction. The Lounge is an edgy Facebook wall, with news of Dell's XPS13 Ultrabook event in Brooklyn, New York, and an online "social media salary guide."[86] The Social Shop offers "the scoop on how real people use and rate their computers," with links to topics like gaming, music, and cloud computing.[87] The Ask Rev link serves up weekly YouTube-like video updates from Dell staffers under a banner that reads "You've got questions. I know stuff."[88]

Twitter gives Dell an entirely different stream of conversations with users. Its main Twitter page[89] links to Dell's multiple Twitter accounts. DellHomeUS announces product launches and gives consumers other product news.[90] Other accounts serve IT professionals at large corporations worldwide (DellEnterprise);[91] customers needing product support (DellCares), with separate Twitter feeds in multiple languages;[92] users who want the headlines from Direct2Dell, Dell's official corporate blog (Direct2Dell);[93] and those who want to tweet directly with Michael Dell (MichaelDell).[94] To boost sales, the company's Dell Outlet site offers flash promotions through Twitter.[95]

Dell.com's blogs facilitate active dialogue between user-subscribers and company leaders. These include Direct2Dell, the company's flagship blog;[96] DellShares, providing investor updates;[97] and DellSoftwareNews, which discusses software products, pricing, and licensing.[98] Working professionals who access Dell through LinkedIn find product updates, recent blog posts, and direct links to Dell managers.[99] Through Google+, Dell offers product news and updates but also invites users to join the group conversations, or "circles," that interest them.[100] Dell has also come up with the ultimate digital suggestion box: IdeaStorm.com, which facilitates crowd-sourced suggestions, inviting customers to collaborate and prioritize product and service improvements.[101]

These multiple channels give Dell an unprecedented ability to build a positive sense of its brand while also gathering insight from thousands of users who personally text, post, and tweet their comments daily, in real time. The corporate learning that Dell derives from that enormous information flow is made possible through the powerful social media infrastructure it has built.

By some estimates, the company has invested tens of millions of dollars in the development of its robust social media platform, considered by many to be a national model.[102] Through its partnership with Radian6, the social media monitoring company, Dell catalogs and analyzes 25,000 user conversations daily.[103] That analysis is critical, notes Karen Quintos, Dell's chief marketing officer: "It's only when you step back from individual problems that patterns emerge that help a company understand the root causes of problems."[104] The nerve center for Dell's operations is the company's new Social Media Listening Command Center, which provides almost instantaneous support in 11 languages to Dell customers around the world.[105] Members of Dell's trained social media staff conduct the listening operation behind a panel of sliding blue glass doors, as they face a bank of digital flat screens alive with data.

"Listening works, even if you can't resolve every issue," says Maribel Sierra, Dell's director of global social media and communities, "because customers appreciate that you listen to their ideas and concerns." That social media connection—the unfiltered conversation between a Dell employee and the customer—has a powerful impact on customer loyalty, brand, and more.[106] Annual training updates and Dell's global social media policy guide all listening conducted by members of Dell's social media staff. They must protect Dell confidential information and personal customer information. Disclosing that they work for Dell is required during every social media contact with someone online. They must adhere to all legal and Dell conduct code requirements. Responding to customer needs is the bottom line.[107]

But Manish Mehta, Dell's VP of social media and community, has stressed that the command center is not intended to simply listen or even just triage, but to remain vigilant, identifying key discussions early, so that employees worldwide can be given the tools to respond.[108] According to a Forrester report, that approach has enabled Dell customer support to reach 46 percent more users, and has produced additional tangible results, including quicker response times; improved issue recognition, mitigation, and management; enhanced coordination and response consistency; and an early warning system to avoid faulty product launches.[109]

Dell also reaches offline to deepen the impact of its social media listening, inviting brand supporters and detractors encountered online to attend its annual consumer advisory meetings. While some companies shun social media critics, fearing that unhappy customers will spread their wrath, Dell seeks to engage with them, reporting that its customer service teams can convert a detractor to a promoter about 30 percent of the time. The company also nurtures influential brand loyalists through special online recognition and invitations to test new products or host online chats.[110]

From its earliest days, Dell has been driven by the potential to engage with its customers. With a corporate culture that has fully embraced social media connectivity,[111] today's Dell is leveraging more powerful interactions with consumers to improve products and services, retain loyal customers, and increase revenues.[112]

Questions

1. What social and mobile media tools are Dell's people using?

2. Evaluate Dell's social media marketing strategy using the 4E framework.

3. Assess their listening capabilities and how they respond to insights gained by their social media command center.

CHAPTER 4

Marketing Ethics

There is so much to like about fish as a key ingredient to a balanced diet. It is relatively lower in saturated fats, it contains essential omega-3 acids and high levels of protein, and it encourages brain development—hence its reputation as brain food. But as more and more consumers turn to fish as an increasing part of their diet, the practices associated with providing those fish meet more and more ethical challenges.

A primary concern is overfishing. Predictions based on current production levels suggest that oceans will be essentially devoid of fish by 2048.[1] Thus fisheries have moved on to alternative tactics to meet demand, including fish farming and the pursuit of alternatives to some of the most popular, and thus most overfished, breeds. To make these alternatives more appealing, some producers simply rename an existing breed. A lot more people are willing to order orange roughy from a waiter than ask for slimehead—the original common name of this fish.[2] Others go less ethical routes and substitute an unknown or less popular fish for similar tasting options, without consumers' knowledge or agreement.

LEARNING OBJECTIVES

LO1 Identify the ethical values marketers should embrace.

LO2 Distinguish between ethics and social responsibility.

LO3 Identify the four steps in ethical decision making.

LO4 Describe how ethics can be integrated into a firm's marketing strategy.

LO5 Describe the ways in which corporate social responsibility programs help various stakeholders.

In Florida for example, grouper sandwiches are a popular local delicacy. But an investigation in dozens of restaurants, in which investigators actually took samples from their plates and tested the DNA of the fish they had been served, revealed only three were actually grouper.[3]

A more recent exposé by the *Boston Globe* showed that the same type of fraud was rampant in Boston-area restaurants.[4] The summary report noted that "consumers routinely and unwittingly overpay for less desirable, sometimes undesirable, species—or buy seafood that is simply not what it is advertised to be. In many cases, the fish was caught thousands of miles away and frozen, not hauled in by local fishermen, as the menu claimed. It may be perfectly palatable—just not what the customer ordered."

The regulations on fish labeling and naming remain relatively flexible, meaning that in many cases, the restaurants are not breaking any laws. And investigators in all these instances admit that sometimes the restaurants serving the wrong fish simply don't know the difference. But other scenarios clearly show an intent to defraud, as fish sellers and restaurants enjoy the benefits of increased demand and higher profit margins when they lie about what is in the fish. The outcome damages consumers, who do not get what they paid for. But it also threatens fishermen, who struggle to sell legitimate catches for reasonable prices, and innocent restaurants, whose reputations come under fire.

In a sense, this ethical scandal began with a sincere attempt to solve the problem. Increased fishing resulted from the desire to improve healthy diets. Relabeling might have represented an effort to encourage diners to try less endangered, more plentiful fish options and avoid overfishing endangered populations. But when consumers are forced to ask, "Is this grouper really grouper, or is it 'grouper'?" then the situation has become unethical. The result remains an ongoing ethical crisis for consumers—and the fish they eat.

Which is the more important corporate objective: making a profit or obtaining and keeping customers?[5] Although firms cannot stay in business without earning a profit, using profit as the sole guiding light for corporate action can lead to short-term decisions that cause the firm to lose customers in the long run. The balancing act may turn out to be the quest to place the company on the firmest footing possible.

This question leads into the primary ethical dilemma facing managers, that is, how to balance shareholder interests with the needs of society. In our opening example, overall societal health can benefit from greater access to fish as part of a healthy diet. But in attempting to provide this benefit, many producers have focused more on earning profits, rather than ensuring they are transparent in their labeling and sales practices. How might a better balance arise in this setting?

Perhaps the fishing industry could take a cue from the European toy industry. New regulations enforced by the European Union places the responsibility for content and safety on toy producers, importers, and distributors.[6] They are responsible to document that the products in any toys imported into the EU contain no dangerous materials, avoid potential allergens, and cannot cause choking risks.

In one month, Mattel recalled more than 20 million potentially dangerous products.

Or maybe that's the wrong place to look; in the United States, new regulations similarly have been designed to prevent the sort of massive toy recalls that Mattel had to undertake when hundreds of millions of its most popular toys—including Barbie dolls, Matchbox cars, and Laughing Elmo—turned up to be safety risks.[7] In the process, manufacturers, regulators, retailers, parents, and various other groups have been battling over the definition of "children's products."[8] Is a stuffed bear with a Valentine's Day theme a product for children or one for adults?

As these examples show, sometimes the ethical dilemma has as much to do with defining our terms as with what the products contain. But even if the question seems to be one of terminology, if customers believe they can no longer trust a company or that the company is not acting responsibly, they will no longer support that company by purchasing its products or services or investing in its stock. For marketers, the firm's ability to build and maintain consumer trust by conducting ethical, transparent, clear transactions must be of paramount importance.

In this chapter, we start by examining what marketing ethics is and why behaving ethically is so important to successful marketing and to long-term profits. We then discuss how firms can create an ethical climate among employees and how their individual behavior can affect the ability of the firm to act ethically. To help you make ethical marketing decisions,

we provide a framework for ethical decision making and then examine some ethical issues within the context of the marketing plan (from Chapter 2). Finally, we present some scenarios that highlight typical ethical challenges marketing managers often must face.

THE SCOPE OF MARKETING ETHICS

Business ethics refers to the moral or ethical dilemmas that might arise in a business setting. **Marketing ethics**, in contrast, examines those ethical problems that are specific to the domain of marketing. Firms' attempts to apply sound ethical principles must be a continuous and dynamic process.[9] The nearby cartoon illustrates the importance of making good ethical decisions. Because the marketing profession is often singled out among business disciplines as the root cause of a host of ethical lapses (e.g., unethical advertising, the promotion of shoddy products), anyone involved in marketing must recognize the ethical implications of their actions. These can involve societal issues, such as the sale of products or services that may damage the environment; global issues, such as the use of child labor (see Chapter 8 as well); and individual consumer issues, such as deceptive advertising[10] or the marketing of dangerous products.[11]

ETHICAL ISSUES ASSOCIATED WITH MARKETING DECISIONS

Unlike other business functions such as accounting or finance, people in marketing interact directly with the public. Because they are in the public eye, it should not be surprising that marketing and sales professionals sometimes rank poorly in ratings of the most trusted professions. In a recent Gallup survey, most professions were rated much higher than advertising or sales professions—lobbyists came in last, and car salespeople fared only slightly better, about the same as congresspeople[12] (see Exhibit 4.1.) For marketers, who depend on the long-term trust of their customers, this low ranking is very disappointing.

Yet there is some good news too.[13] Although many consumers remain highly skeptical of business, and especially of marketing, the marketing function interacts with a vast number of entities outside the firm on a regular basis. Therefore, it has a tremendous opportunity to build public trust. Creating an ethical climate that establishes the health and well-being of consumers as the firm's number one priority just makes good business sense.

EXHIBIT 4.1   Attitudes about Ethical Standards of Various Professions

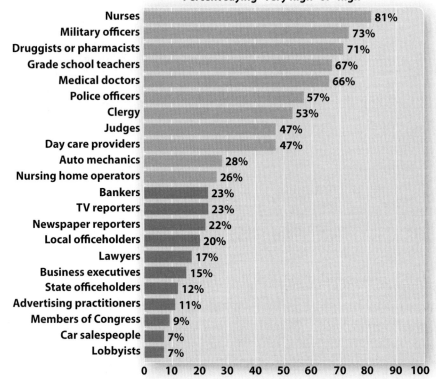

Percent saying "very high" or "high"

Profession	Percent
Nurses	81%
Military officers	73%
Druggists or pharmacists	71%
Grade school teachers	67%
Medical doctors	66%
Police officers	57%
Clergy	53%
Judges	47%
Day care providers	47%
Auto mechanics	28%
Nursing home operators	26%
Bankers	23%
TV reporters	23%
Newspaper reporters	22%
Local officeholders	20%
Lawyers	17%
Business executives	15%
State officeholders	12%
Advertising practitioners	11%
Members of Congress	9%
Car salespeople	7%
Lobbyists	7%

Source: From Honesty/Ethics in Professions, http://www.gallup.com/poll/1654/honesty-ethics-professions.aspx. Reprinted with permission.

Creating an Ethical Climate in the Workplace

The process of creating a strong **ethical climate** within a marketing firm (or in the marketing division of any firm) includes having a set of values that guides decision making and behavior, like Johnson & Johnson's Credo. General Robert Wood Johnson wrote and published the first "Credo" for Johnson & Johnson (J&J) in 1943[14]—a one-page document outlining the firm's commitments and responsibilities to its various stakeholders. The J&J Credo can be summarized as follows:

> We believe our first responsibility is to doctors, nurses, patients, mothers, fathers, and all others who use our products and services. We are responsible to our employees. We must respect their dignity and recognize their merit. Compensation must be fair and adequate and working conditions clean, orderly, and safe. We are responsible to the communities in which we live and work and to the world community as well. Our final responsibility is to our stockholders. When we operate according to these principles, the stockholders should realize a fair return.

Today, J&J continues to follow this credo in its daily business practices, as was evidenced by the infamous Tylenol recall. In the 1980s, seven people taking Tylenol died of cyanide poisoning. Without worrying initially about whether the poison got into the products during production or on the shelf, J&J immediately and voluntarily withdrew all Tylenol from the market until it could ensure its products' safety.

Even more recently, J&J responded to new limits on acetaminophen dosages (the active ingredient in Tylenol) by reassuring consumers that they were safe—

as long as they followed the dosage instructions on the packaging.[15] In advertising communications that touted Tylenol as "the safest brand of pain reliever you can choose," J&J also was careful to remind people that taking more than the recommended dosage could cause them serious liver damage.

But not all firms operate according to the principles in J&J's credo. For instance, Merck & Co. withdrew its highly successful drug Vioxx from the marketplace in 2004 because of evidence that it increased the chance of heart attacks and strokes in patients taking the drug.[16] The move came at least four years after studies showed that patients taking Vioxx had an increased incidence of cardiovascular problems compared to an older drug. Although Merck continued to monitor these ongoing studies, it did not act nor did it initiate new studies. In another pharmaceutical example, AstraZeneca, the maker of the schizophrenia drug Seroquel, faced sanctions and fines for misrepresenting the appropriate uses of the drug to medical practitioners. Eventually, AstraZeneca agreed to pay $520 million to settle the claims of its unethical, "off-label" marketing efforts.[17] Would Merck and AstraZeneca have performed more ethically had they been working with J&J's credo for ethical behavior?[18]

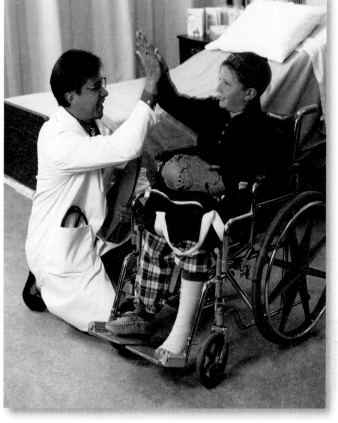

Nurses and doctors are among the most trusted professionals.

Everyone within a firm must share the same understanding of its ethical values and how they translate into the business activities of the firm. They also need to share a consistent language to discuss them. Once the values are understood, the firm must develop explicit rules and implicit understandings that govern all the firm's transactions. Top management must commit to establishing an ethical climate, and employees throughout the firm must be dedicated to that climate, because the roots of ethical conflict often are the competing values of individuals. Each individual holds his or her own set of values, and sometimes those values result in inner turmoil or even conflicts between employees. For instance, a salesperson may believe that it is important to make a sale because her family depends on her for support, but at the same time, she may feel that the product she is selling is not appropriate for a particular customer. Once the rules are in place, there must be a system of controls that helps resolve such dilemmas and rewards appropriate behavior—that is, behavior consistent with the firm's values—and punishes inappropriate behavior.

Johnson & Johnson, makers of Tylenol, continues to act in accordance with its original 1943 "credo" to be responsible to everyone who use its products and services.

Among the most important controls is policing potential violations of human rights and child labor laws. Many firms have had to publicly defend themselves against allegations of human rights, child labor, or other abuses involving the factories and countries in which their goods are made.[19] Fewer imported goods are produced in sweatshop conditions today, though. Some firms even are proactive in enforcing the labor practices of their suppliers. Limited Brands was one of the first U.S. apparel manufacturers to develop and implement policies requiring observance by vendors and their subcontractors and suppliers of core labor standards as a condition of doing business. Among other things, this requirement

Adding Value 4.1   It Isn't Easy to Sell to Walmart[20]

Walmart is known for its low prices, and for driving its vendors nearly to tears to get them. Now it is pressuring its vendors to supply it with environmentally friendly merchandise with labels to prove it. In the future, merchandise sold at Walmart will have the environmental equivalent of nutrition labels, providing information on the product's carbon footprint, the amount of water and air pollution used to produce it, and other environmental issues. To measure how a vendor's products are doing, it has developed a sustainability index that simultaneously takes several issues into consideration.

Walmart is also requiring its top 200 factories to become 20 percent more energy-efficient by 2012—a feat that many experts believe may be impossible, even with Walmart's help. Initial results are promising, however. For example, Jiangsu Redbud Dyeing Technology in China has cut coal consumption by one-tenth and is attempting to cut its toxic emissions to zero.

Walmart hasn't always been touted as a good corporate citizen. In the 1990s, it came to light that workers at some factories producing clothing for Walmart were subjected to inhumane conditions. More recently, two governmental organizations accused Walmart of buying from 15 factories that engage in abuse and labor violations, including child labor, 19-hour shifts, and below-subsistence wages. It and other companies have also been accused of dumping hazardous waste in Oklahoma City.

Some wonder why Walmart is attempting to position itself as the retail industry's sustainability leader. Certainly initiatives that show that it is a good corporate citizen enhance its image. But it expects it to be good for business as well. Its customers, especially those born from 1980 to 2000, are increasingly concerned about how the products they use impact the environment and the people that produce them. Also, Walmart believes that many of these initiatives will help streamline supply chain processes and therefore provide additional financial benefits to its suppliers and customers.

ensures that each supplier pays minimum wages and benefits; limits overtime to local industry standards; does not use prisoners, forced labor, or child labor; and provides a healthy and safe environment.[21] Many other companies that produce or sell goods made in low-wage countries conduct similar self-policing. Self-policing allows companies to avoid painful public revelations. Adding Value 4.1 examines how Walmart is pushing its vendors to be environmentally responsible.

Like companies that develop and apply their ethical codes, many professions, including the marketing profession, also have their own codes of ethics that firms and individuals in the profession agree to abide by. The generally accepted code in marketing, developed by the American Marketing Association, flows from universal norms of conduct to the specific values to which marketers should aspire.[22] It indicates that the basic ethical values marketers should aspire to are honesty, responsibility, fairness, respect, openness, and citizenship. Each subarea within marketing, such as marketing research, advertising, pricing, and so forth, has its own code of ethics that deals with the specific issues that arise when conducting business in those areas.

Now let's examine the ethical role of the individuals within the firm and how individuals contribute to the firm's ethical climate.

The Influence of Personal Ethics

LO1 Identify the ethical values marketers should embrace.

Every firm is made up of individuals, each with his or her own needs and desires. Let's start by looking at why people may make *un*ethical decisions and how firms can establish a process for decision making that ensures they choose ethical alternatives instead.

Why People Act Unethically Every individual is a product of his or her culture, upbringing, genes, and various other influences. In spite of these factors, people continue to grow emotionally in their understanding of what is and is not ethical behavior. As a six-year-old child, you might have thought nothing of taking your brother's toy and bonking him on the head with it. As an adult, you probably have outgrown this behavior. But all of us vary in the way we view more complex situations, depending on our ethical understandings.

Consider product recalls of toys, for example. How can certain manufacturers engage in such egregious behavior as using lead paint on toys marketed toward young children? What makes people take actions that create so much harm? Are all the individuals who contributed to that behavior just plain immoral? These simple questions have complex answers.

As another example, imagine that a brand manager for a car company discovers from conversations with a member of the development team that the hot new energy-efficient hybrid model that is set to go into full production shortly has a potentially dangerous design flaw. There are two options for the brand manager: delay production and remedy the design flaw, which pushes production off schedule, delays revenue, and may result in layoffs and loss of the manager's bonus; or stay on schedule, put the flawed design into production, achieve planned revenues and bonus, and hope it does not result in injuries to consumers and loss of revenue for the firm due to recalls later on. This type of dilemma occurs nearly every day in thousands of different business environments.

When asked in a survey whether they had seen any unethical behavior among their colleagues, chief marketing officers responded that they had observed employees participating in high pressure, misleading, or deceptive sales tactics (45 percent); misrepresenting company earnings, sales, and/or revenues (35 percent); withholding or destroying information that could hurt company sales or image (32 percent); and conducting false or misleading advertising (31 percent).[23] Did all the marketers in these situations view their actions as unethical? Probably not. There may have been extenuating circumstances. In marketing, managers often face the choice of doing what is beneficial for them and possibly the firm in the short run and doing what is right and beneficial for the firm and society in the long run.

For instance, a manager might feel confident that earnings will increase in the next few months and therefore believe it benefits himself, his branch, and his employees to exaggerate current earnings just a little. Another manager might feel considerable pressure to increase sales in a retail store, so she brings in some new merchandise, marks it at an artificially high price, and then immediately puts it on sale, deceiving consumers

What is the "real" price? Did the manager bring the T-shirts in at an artificially high level and then immediately mark them down?

into thinking they are getting a good deal because they viewed the initial price as the "real" price. These decisions may have been justifiable at the time, but they have serious consequences for the company.

To avoid such dire consequences, the short-term goals of each employee must be aligned with the long-term goals of the firm. In our hybrid car example, the brand manager's short-term drive to receive a bonus conflicted with the firm's long-term aim of providing consumers with safe, reliable cars. To align personal and corporate goals, firms need to have a strong ethical climate, explicit rules for governing transactions including a code of ethics, and a system for rewarding and punishing inappropriate behavior.

In the next section, we add the concept of corporate social responsibility to our discussion of ethics.

 LO2 Distinguish between ethics and social responsibility.

Ethics and Corporate Social Responsibility

Although no single, established definition of the concept exists,[24] **corporate social responsibility** generally entails voluntary actions taken by a company to address the ethical, social, and environmental impacts of its business operations and the concerns of its stakeholders. The AMA's definition refers to it as the serious consideration of "the impact of the company's actions and operating in a way that balances short-term profit needs with society's long-term needs, thus ensuring the company's survival in a healthy environment."[25] This notion goes beyond the individual ethics that we've discussed so far, but for a company to act in a socially responsible manner, the employees of the company must also first maintain high ethical standards and recognize how their individual decisions lead to optimal collective actions of the firm. Firms with strong ethical climates tend to be more socially responsible.

However, it is important to distinguish between ethical business practices and corporate social responsibility programs. Ideally, firms should implement programs that are socially responsible, <u>and</u> its employees should act in an ethically responsible manner. (See Exhibit 4.2, upper left quadrant.) Dannon yogurt, for example, has long supported internal research into healthy eating, which supports its ethical commitment to bring "health food to as many people as possible."[26] It is also socially responsible, in that it donates food and money to the hunger-relief

EXHIBIT 4.2 Ethics versus Social Responsibility

Ethics versus Social Responsibility

	Socially Responsible	**Socially Irresponsible**
Ethical	Both ethical and socially responsible	Ethical firm not involved with the larger community
Unethical	Questionable firm practices, yet donates a lot to the community	Neither ethical nor socially responsible

charity Feeding America, encourages employees to volunteer in their communities, holds annual "Children's Day" outreach programs, and reduces its environmental footprints.

Being socially responsible generally means going above and beyond the norms of corporate ethical behavior. For example, a firm's employees may conduct their activities in an ethically acceptable manner, but the firm may still not be considered socially responsible because their activities have little or no impact on anyone other than their closest stakeholders: their customers, employees, and stockholders (Exhibit 4.2, upper right quadrant).

Employees at some firms that are perceived as socially responsible can nevertheless take actions that are viewed as unethical (Exhibit 4.2, lower left quadrant). For instance, a firm might be considered socially responsible because it makes generous donations to charities but is simultaneously involved in questionable sales practices. After the 2010 oil spill in the Gulf of Mexico, BP committed to donating millions of dollars to help economically impacted states promote tourism.[27] Ethically, how do we characterize a firm that obtains its profits through illicit actions but then donates a large percentage of those profits to charity? The worst situation, of course, is when firms behave both unethically and in a socially unacceptable manner (Exhibit 4.2, lower right quadrant).

Consumers and investors increasingly appear to want to purchase products and services from and invest in companies that act in socially responsible ways. They also may be willing to pay more if they can be assured the companies

Dannon is both ethical and socially responsible. It has an ethical commitment to make healthy food. It is socially responsible since it is involved in many activities and charities that help people.

Oil spills are a major catastrophe for all parties.

Adding Value **4.2**   The Barefoot Entrepreneur[28]

Blake Mycoskie doesn't just want his customers to buy his shoes; he wants to turn them into benefactors. In this innovative approach to marketing, his company, TOMS Shoes, does not just engage in charitable acts; the charitable acts are the company. There is no separating TOMS from the social responsibility it embraces.

In 2006, Mycoskie started manufacturing a revised version of a traditional Argentinean shoe called alpargatas and selling them to consumers outside their generally impoverished source nation. The combination of the comfortable shoes and the extreme poverty he observed led to a simple code: "You buy a pair of TOMS, and I give a pair to a child on your behalf. One for One."

His Shoe Drops, during which Mycoskie brings thousands of pairs of shoes to poorer children in underdeveloped nations, have led to the distribution of literally millions of pairs of shoes: The millionth pair was given away in September 2010. As the company has grown, it also has added lines of vegan and recycled shoes. Most recently, it expanded into sunglasses, where the One for One philosophy dictates that for every pair sold, TOMS provides eye care, such as medicine treatment, glasses, or surgery, to someone else in the world at risk of losing his or her sight.

Each year, TOMS also hosts "One Day Without Shoes," a campaign to raise awareness about how difficult it can be to function, even in developed nations, without shoes. In the 2010 iteration, one-quarter of a million people participated, leaving their shoes at home for the entire day. The company also partners with groups such as Insight Argentina, an

When you buy a pair of TOMS shoes, they give a pair to a child in need.

organization offering volunteer activities in Argentina to help that area address its most pressing social issues.

Detractors argue that by shipping in the shoes to be donated, TOMS may do some harm, by reducing demand for locally produced products. But since TOMS has given away more than 1 million pairs of shoes, that means consumers have bought just as many—at an average price of $55 per pair. Clearly, the value they find in these cloth shoes goes well beyond the simple linen and canvas parts that go into making them.

truly are ethical.[29] According to a recent poll conducted by *Time Magazine*, even in economically constrained settings, 38 percent of U.S. consumers actively tried to purchase from companies they considered responsible. The magazine thus cites the rise of the "ethical consumer" and the evolution of the social contract "between many Americans and businesses about what goes into making the products we buy."[30]

With such ethical consumers making up more and more of the market, many large companies have recognized that they must be perceived as socially responsible by their stakeholders to earn their business. Other companies began their operations with such a commitment, as Adding Value 4.2 describes.

We cannot expect every member of a firm to always act ethically. However, a framework for ethical decision making can help move people to work toward common ethical goals.

 LO3 Identify the four steps in ethical decision making.

A Framework for Ethical Decision Making

Exhibit 4.3 outlines a simple framework for ethical decision making. Let's consider each of the steps.

Step 1: Identify Issues The first step is to identify the issue. For illustrative purposes, we'll investigate the use (or misuse) of data collected from consumers by a marketing research firm. One of the issues that might arise is the way the data are collected. For instance, are the respondents told about the real purpose of the

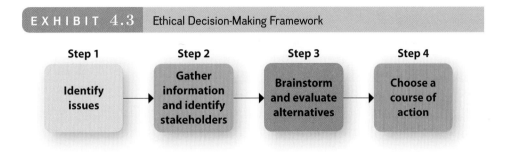

EXHIBIT 4.3 Ethical Decision-Making Framework

Step 1 — Identify issues → **Step 2** — Gather information and identify stakeholders → **Step 3** — Brainstorm and evaluate alternatives → **Step 4** — Choose a course of action

study? Another issue might be whether the results are going to be used in a way that might mislead or even harm the public, such as selling the information to a firm to use in soliciting the respondents.

Step 2: Gather Information and Identify Stakeholders In this step, the firm focuses on gathering facts that are important to the ethical issue, including all relevant legal information. To get a complete picture, the firm must identify all the individuals and groups that have a stake in how the issue is resolved.

Stakeholders typically include the firm's employees and retired employees, suppliers, the government, customer groups, stockholders, and members of the community in which the firm operates. Beyond these, many firms now also analyze the needs of the industry and the global community, as well as "one-off" stakeholders, such as future generations, and the natural environment itself. In describing its sustainability and transparency efforts, for example, the electronics firm Philips notes that it tries to communicate with and consider "anyone with an interest in Philips."[31]

Step 3: Brainstorm Alternatives After the marketing firm has identified the stakeholders and their issues and gathered the available data, all parties relevant to the decision should come together to brainstorm any alternative courses of action. In our example, these might include halting the market research project, making responses anonymous, instituting training on the AMA Code of Ethics for all researchers, and so forth. Management then reviews and refines these alternatives, leading to the final step.

Step 4: Choose a Course of Action The objective of this last step is to weigh the various alternatives and choose a course of action that generates the best solution for the stakeholders using ethical practices. Management will rank the alternatives in order of preference, clearly establishing the advantages and disadvantages of each. It is also crucial to investigate any potential legal issues associated with each alternative. Of course, any illegal activity should immediately be rejected.

To choose the appropriate course of action, marketing managers will evaluate each alternative using a process something like the sample ethical decision-making metric in Exhibit 4.4. The marketer's task here is to ensure that he or she has applied all relevant decision-making criteria and to assess his or her level of confidence that the decision being made meets those stated criteria. If the marketer isn't confident about the decision, he or she should reexamine the other alternatives. Using Exhibit 4.4, you can gauge your own ethical response. If your scores tend to be in the green area (1 and 2), then the situation is not an ethically troubling situation for you. If, in contrast, your scores tend to be in the red area (6 and 7), it is ethically troubling and you know it. If your scores are scattered or in the yellow area, you need to step back and reflect on how you wish to proceed. Appendix 4A at the end of the chapter presents a series of ethical scenarios designed to assist you in developing your skills at identifying ethical issues. Use Exhibit 4.4 to help you evaluate these scenarios.

| EXHIBIT 4.4 | Ethical Decision-Making Metric |

Test	Decision						
	Yes		May be			No	
	1	2	3	4	5	6	7
The Publicity Test Would I want to see this action that I'm about to take described on the front page of the local paper or in a national magazine?							
The Moral Mentor Test Would the person I admire the most engage in this activity?							
The Admired Observer Test Would I want the person I admire most to see me doing this?							
The Transparency Test Could I give a clear explanation for the action I'm contemplating, including an honest and transparent account of all my motives, that would satisfy a fair and dispassionate moral judge?							
The Person in the Mirror Test Will I be able to look at myself in the mirror and respect the person I see there?							
The Golden Rule Test Would I like to be on the receiving end of this action and all its potential consequences?							

Source: Adapted from Tom Morris, *The Art of Achievement: Mastering the 7 Cs of Success in Business and in Life* (Kansas City, MO: Andrew McMeel Publishing, 2002). http://edbrenegar.typepad.com/leading_questions/2005/05/real_life_leade.html.

In using such an ethical metric or framework, decision makers must consider the relevant ethical issues, evaluate the alternatives, and then choose a course of action that will help them avoid serious ethical lapses.

Next, let's illustrate how the ethical decision-making metric in Exhibit 4.4 can be used to make ethical business decisions.

Myra Jansen, the head cook at Lincoln High School in Anytown, USA, has had enough. Reports showing that children rarely eat enough vegetables have combined with studies that indicate school kids have a limited amount of time to eat their lunches. The combination has led to increasing obesity rates and troublesome reports about the long-term effects. Jansen has therefore decided that the tater-tots and hotdogs are out. Vegetables and healthy proteins are in.

The problem, of course, is getting the kids to eat raw vegetables, plant proteins, and lean meat. For many teenagers, recommending that they eat healthy food at lunch is akin to calling detention a play date. But Myra has a plan: She's going to reformulate various menu items using different ingredients, and just never tell the students. Thus the regular hot dogs will be replaced with turkey or soy dogs. The tater-tots will contain the more nutrient-dense sweet potatoes instead of the vitamin-deficient regular spuds they used to be made out of. She is convinced she can make such switches for most of the menu items, and none of the children need to know.

Most of the kitchen staff is onboard with the idea and even have suggested other possible menu switches that would benefit the students by ensuring that they received a well-balanced meal at school. School board members, when appraised of the idea, got very excited and praised Myra for her innovative thinking.

But the community liaison for the school, whose job it is to communicate with parents and other members of the community, is not so sure. Salim Jones is nervous about how students will react when they learn that they have been deceived. He also has two small children of his own, one of whom has a severe wheat allergy. Thus the Joneses are extremely cautious about eating out, always asking for a detailed, specific list of ingredients for anything they order.

Using his training in ethical decision making, Salim sits down to evaluate his alternatives, beginning with identifying possible options available to the school district, as well as the various stakeholders that might be impacted by the decision. He comes up with the following list:

1. Switch out the food without telling students.
2. Leave menus as they are.
3. Switch out the food ingredients but also tell students exactly what is in each item in the cafeteria.

To make a clear recommendation to the board about what would be the best ethical choice, Salim decides to evaluate each alternative using a series of questions similar to those in Exhibit 4.4.

Question 1: Would I want to see this action described on the front page of the local paper? The school board's reaction caused Salim to think that the larger community would appreciate the effort to improve students' health. Thus, option 1 appears best for these stakeholders, and possibly for society, which may reduce the prevalence of obesity among these students. However, he shudders to think about how angry students might be if they learned they had been tricked. They also likely are accustomed to their menu as it is, and therefore, they would prefer option 2.

Question 2: Would the person I admire most engage in this activity, and would I want him or her seeing me engage in this activity? For most of his life, Salim has held up Mahatma Gandhi as his ideal for how to act in the world. For Mahatma Gandhi, truth was an absolute concept, not something that could be changed depending on the situation. Therefore, Salim believes Mahatma Gandhi would strongly disapprove of option 1. However, Mahatma Gandhi also worried about the ethics of eating and took care to avoid food choices that had negative effects on society, so he might reject option 2 as well.

Question 3: Can I give a clear explanation for my action, including an honest account of my motives? In thinking about his children, Salim realizes that he is prioritizing their needs, more so than the needs of other children, such as those who struggle with weight issues. That is, he worries that his daughter might unknowingly be exposed to wheat in a school cafeteria, so he prefers option 3.

Question 4: Will I be able to look at myself in the mirror and respect what I see? By bringing up the ethics of this decision, even when it seems as if everyone else has agreed with it, Salim feels confident that he has taken the right first step. The option chosen is still important, but it is a group decision, and Salim thinks he is doing his part.

Question 5: Would I want to be on the receiving end of this action and its consequences? Salim struggles most with this question. He remembers the kind of junk foods he chose when he was in college, and the 20 pounds he put on as a result. He wishes now that his parents had given him rules to follow about what to eat at school. But he also remembers how rebellious he was and knows that he probably would not have followed those rules. And at the same time, he hates the idea that someone could give him food to eat with falsified ingredients.

On the basis of this exercise, Salim decides that he wants to recommend option 3 to the school board. When he does so, Myra Jansen protests loudly: "This is ridiculous! I know better what kids should be eating, and I know too that some community liaison has no idea what they are willing to eat. You've got to trick them to get them to eat right." Another school board member agrees, noting, "They're just kids. They don't necessarily have the same rights as adults, so we are allowed to decide what's best for them. And hiding the healthy ingredients to get the kids to eat healthy foods is what's best."

So what does the school board decide?

CHECK YOURSELF

1. Identify the stages in the ethical decision-making framework.

LO4 Describe how ethics can be integrated into a firm's marketing strategy.

INTEGRATING ETHICS INTO MARKETING STRATEGY

Ethical decision making is not a simple process, though it can get easier as decision makers within the firm become accustomed to thinking about the ethical implications of their actions from a strategic perspective. In this section, we examine how ethical decision making can be integrated into the marketing plan introduced in Chapter 2. The questions vary at each stage of the strategic marketing planning process. For instance, in the planning stage, the firm will decide what level of commitment to its ethical policies and standards it is willing to declare publicly. In the implementation stage, the tone of the questions switches from "can we?" serve the market with the firm's products or services in an ethically responsible manner to "should we?" be engaging in particular marketing practices. The key task in the control phase is to ensure that all potential ethical issues raised during the planning process have been addressed and that all employees of the firm have acted ethically. Let's take a closer look at how ethics can be integrated at each stage of the strategic marketing planning process.

Planning Phase

Marketers can introduce ethics at the beginning of the planning process simply by including ethical statements in the firm's mission or vision statements (recall our discussion of various mission statements in Chapter 2). Johnson & Johnson has its Credo; other firms use mission statements that include both ethical and social responsibility precepts for shaping the organization. For instance, the mission statement for natural skin care company Burt's Bees is to "create natural, Earth-friendly personal care products formulated to help you maximize your well-being and that of the world around you,"[32] which reflects not only what is good for its customers, but for society in general.

For General Electric, the complexity of its organization and the wealth of ethical issues it faces necessitated an entire booklet, "The Spirit and the Letter." This booklet outlines not only a statement of integrity from the CEO and a code of conduct, but also detailed policies for dealing with everything from international competition laws to security and crisis management to insider trading. In addition, GE publishes an annual citizenship report to determine the scope of its

Since 1982, Newman's Own has given over $280 million to charities like Newman's Hole in the Wall Gang camps for children with life-threatening diseases.

impacts, "produced for the benefit of all stakeholders, including GE employees—the people whose actions define GE every day."[33]

During the planning stage, ethical mission statements can take on another role as a means to guide a firm's SWOT analysis. Newman's Own, for example, has what most would consider a simple but powerful purpose: The company would sell salad dressing (initially; it expanded later to many other product lines) and use the proceeds to benefit charities. This simple idea began in Paul Newman's basement, when he and a friend produced a batch of salad dressing to give as holiday gifts. When they also decided to check with a local grocer to see if it would be interested in the product, they found they could sell 10,000 bottles in two weeks. Thus Newman's Own, a nonprofit organization, quickly grew to include dozens of products. Today, Newman's Own and Newman's Own Organic products are sold in 15 countries and include dozens of lines, from coffee to popcorn to dog food. Profits from Newman's Own—over $280 million since 1982—have been donated to thousands of charities, especially Newman's Hole in the Wall Gang camps for children with life-threatening diseases.[34]

The unique mission of the company and the entrepreneurial flair of the founders made this nonprofit a smashing, ongoing success. Employees of Newman's Own have the great satisfaction of giving back to society, various charities benefit from the donations, and customers enjoy good food with a clear conscience.

Implementation Phase

In the implementation phase of the marketing strategy, when firms are identifying potential markets and ways to deliver the 4Ps to them, firms must consider several ethical issues. Sometimes a firm's choice of target market and how they pursue it can lead to charges of unethical behavior. For instance, Molson Brewery launched a Facebook campaign targeted toward college students in which it asked them to post party pictures, which it would use to identify the "top party school." This effort not only encouraged underage, illegal drinking but also deeply irritated universities across both Canada and the United States, which had little interest in being thus identified. Although these student groups might have been responsive to the firm's efforts, it did not represent an appropriate target market. Marketing through social media has some particular ethical concerns associated with it, as Social and Mobile Marketing 4.1 shows.

Once the strategy is implemented, controls must be in place to be certain that the firm has actually done what it has set out to do. These activities take place in the next phase of the strategic marketing planning process.

Social and Mobile Marketing 4.1   Who Tweeted Me to Buy a Ford Fiesta?[35]

Auto manufacturers have long paid celebrities to be spokespeople for their lines of vehicles. But maybe customers really want to hear from people like themselves, rather than a celebrity paid millions of dollars to promote a car. Although car companies can save a lot of money by paying normal people less than they pay celebrities, they do not want just anyone to promote their products. They want social media gurus or popular Twitter and blog figures with legions of followers.

Marketing campaigns by Lexus, Ford, and LandRover all promote their products socially on the web. Ford recruited 100 people with strong online followings to test drive the Ford Focus and then talk about their experiences online. Ford previously had been successful with its Ford Fiesta campaign, in which anyone who test drove the newly introduced car posted YouTube videos, Flickr photos, and Twitter tweets— adding up to more than 7 million views on YouTube and 4 million mentions on Twitter. As a result, over 130,000 people visited the Ford Fiesta website, 83 percent of whom had never owned a Ford before. The campaign certainly received a lot of attention, though the actual sales conversion has not been disclosed.

Influential online informants also can have negative influences though. Even if a firm pays a blogger or tweeter, no rule can force them to write positive reviews. But the likelihood is that a paid blogger will be more positive than an unpaid, disinterested reviewer. Thus the Federal Trade Commission (FTC) has created guidelines for blogging and tweeting, saying that those who post messages must disclose any compensation they may have received for talking about the product. They also must disclose if there is a connection, such as an employee/employer relationship, between the endorser and the marketer of the product that might affect how people evaluate the endorsement.

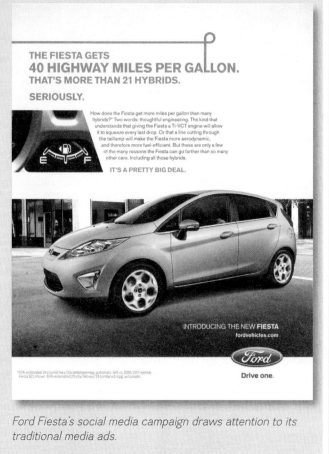

Ford Fiesta's social media campaign draws attention to its traditional media ads.

Are these FTC guidelines strong enough to let potential customers know that the message being received through social media is a paid form of promotion, not unlike an ad on TV?

Control Phase

During the control phase of the strategic marketing planning process, managers must be evaluated on their actions from an ethical perspective. Systems must be in place to check whether each potentially ethical issue raised in the planning process was actually successfully addressed. Systems used in the control phase must also react to change. The emergence of new technologies and new markets ensures that new ethical issues continually arise. Social and Mobile Marketing 4.2 uncovers many of these new privacy issues.

Many firms have emergency response plans in place just in case they ever encounter a situation similar to the Tylenol tampering emergency or an industrial accident at a manufacturing plant. Ethics thus remains an ongoing crucial component of the strategic marketing planning process and should be incorporated into all the firm's decision making down the road.

Social and Mobile Marketing 4.2 — Check-Ins and Facebook Photos Can Be Dangerous

The rise of social media has been a boon for many marketers: When consumers "like" a brand on Facebook, tweet about a consumption experience on Twitter, and check in on Foursquare, they are providing the company free marketing. But they are also giving criminals and unethical marketers an easy means to take advantage of them. Thus the vast benefits of social media combine some threats to consumers.

Consider these examples: On your commute in to work each day, you might pay for your train fare with a monthly transit card that identifies you as the specific user. Say you are running a bit late one day and decide to blame the trains, instead of admitting you slept in late. Conceivably, your boss could check the data gathered when you swiped your card and confront you with the fact that you didn't even get on the train until 9:15. Or your mother could check to see that you got on at a different stop than usual and ask where exactly you spent the night.

These possibilities may seem harmful to your reputation or pride more than anything else. However, when people post their vacation plans or softball schedules on Facebook, they also inform potential burglars exactly when they will be away from their homes. Checking in on Foursquare gives criminals an immediate indication; if you check in at a restaurant, chances are you will not be home for another couple of hours. To highlight this issue, the mashup website Please Rob Me

(www.pleaserobme.com) randomly taps people's posts on Facebook and Twitter to identify those who have clearly broadcast that they are not at home.

Now imagine that an unscrupulous marketer fails to protect information about the items you have bought from it. With just a few clicks of a mouse and some technology savvy, criminals know not only when your house will be empty but also exactly what kinds of valuables they might steal when they break in.

Many users have grown more aware of such concerns and work to avoid such obvious releases of their information. But smartphone cameras stamp each photo taken with latitude and longitude information. Thus, even if you never mention the location of your favorite haunts, stalkers can obtain information about the places where you are likely to be based on the photos you have posted on Facebook, especially if they are uploaded in real time.

The need for a new kind of privacy is thus a critical issue for marketers and consumers alike. Ethical marketers must find a way to collect the priceless data that customers make available through social media while avoiding collecting details that violate people's right to **locational privacy**—defined as a person's ability to move normally in public spaces with the expectation that his or her location will not be recorded for subsequent use.[36]

CHECK YOURSELF

1. What ethical questions should a marketing manager consider at each stage of the marketing plan?

CORPORATE SOCIAL RESPONSIBILITY

LO5 Describe the ways in which corporate social responsibility programs help various stakeholders.

In 1906, Upton Sinclair published *The Jungle*, his novel exposing the horrific conditions in U.S. meat-packing plants, which prompted President Theodore Roosevelt and Congress to force meat companies to take responsibility for the safety of their products. The notion of societal marketing and corporate social responsibility has changed significantly since then, and recent decades have seen its prevalence increase rapidly. Today, companies are undertaking a wide range of corporate social responsibility initiatives, such as establishing corporate charitable foundations, supporting and associating with existing nonprofit groups, supporting minority activities, and following responsible marketing, sales, and production practices. Social responsibility is even one of the key

EXHIBIT 4.5	Top 20 Admired Companies and Illustrative CSR Programs

Rank	Company	Illustration of CSR Program
1	Apple	Actively working to reduce carbon footprint: http://www.apple.com/environment/
2	Google	Google.org funds for pro-profit entrepreneurship in Africa, Google China Social Innovation Cup for College Students
3	Berkshire Hathaway	Donates billions of dollars to the Bill and Melinda Gates Foundation
4	Southwest Airlines	Employees donate volunteer hours to Ronald McDonald Houses throughout the U.S.
5	Procter & Gamble	Live, Learn, and Thrive improves the lives of children worldwide.
6	Coca-Cola	Spent $102 million through The Coca-Cola Campaign focusing on water stewardship, healthy and active lifestyles, community recycling, and education
7	Amazon.com	Developed nonprofit Simple Pay Donation system to help nonprofits raise money easily
8	FedEx	Delivered 440 tons of relief supplies at no charge to Hurricane Katrina victims
9	Microsoft	Developed a system with the American Red Cross for vital information on people's welfare in a disaster's aftermath
10	McDonald's	99% of fish come from MSC-fisheries, transitioning to sustainable food and packaging sources, Ronald McDonald House charities
11	Walmart Stores	Green strategy to reduce packaging and use energy efficient lighting
12	IBM	KidSmart Early Learning, Smarter Cities Challenge, MentorPlace, TryScience programs
13	General Electric	Ecomagination campaign, GE Volunteers Foundation
14	Walt Disney	Disney's Planet Challenge, worldwide animal and conservation fund
15	3M	Pollution Prevention Pays (3Ps) program focuses on conserving resources
16	Starbucks	Develops ecologically friendly growing practices, LEED certified stores
17	Johnson & Johnson	Funds nonprofits that fight AIDS/HIV around the world
18	Singapore Airlines	Provided air travel for Australian social workers to Dhaka in Bangladesh for a project to prevent hearing loss in textile workers at no charge
19	BMW	Light Up Hope and BMW Children's Safety programs
20	American Express	Partners with National Trust for Historic Preservation through the WMF to preserve sites in the U.S and worldwide.

Source: From *Fortune Magazine,* March 19, 2012, "World's Most Admired Companies." Copyright © 2012 Time Inc. Used under license.

measures that *Fortune* magazine uses to create its list of the most admired companies (see Exhibit 4.5).

One of *Fortune*'s most admired companies, McDonald's, concentrates its sustainability efforts in several areas.[37] Some specific highlights include:

- Nutrition and well-being. It promotes awareness of fruit, vegetable, and low-fat or fat-free dairy options for children through advertising and promotions. For example, McDonald's France and Italy introduced "free fruit" campaigns, during which fruit bags were given free with every Happy Meal on selected days.

- Sustainable supply chain. It is committed to sourcing all of its food and packaging from sustainable sources, with an initial focus on beef, poultry, coffee, palm oil, fish, and fiber.

- Environmental responsibility. It has developed better, more reliable energy-related metrics which are used to measure energy savings. It is

EXHIBIT 4.6 McDonald's Global Sustainability Scorecard

Source: http://www.aboutmcdonalds.com/mcd/sustainability/2011_sustainability_scorecard.html.

implementing energy-efficient lighting, occupancy sensors, and energy-efficient equipment.

- Community. It supports the Ronald McDonald House charities by, for instance, having raised $170 million during McHappy Day/Give a Hand events since 2002.

McDonald's Global Sustainability Scorecard is found in Exhibit 4.6.

Some economists and social commentators suggest that CSR is unnecessary, that the goal of any corporation in a capitalist economy is single and simple: Make money.[38] How does it benefit the company or its shareholders if a company worries about such unquantifiable issues as being a good citizen? But the fallout from the recent global economic crisis seems to have pushed economists to repudiate this school of thought.

When companies embrace CSR, they appeal not only to their shareholders, but to their key stakeholders (Exhibit 4.7), including their own employees, consumers, the marketplace, and society at large. Thus the insurance provider Aflac differentiates its

EXHIBIT 4.7 Key CSR Stakeholders

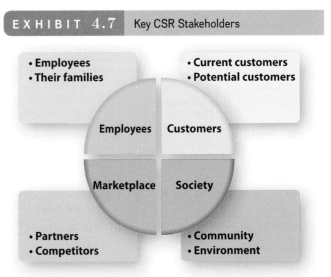

- Employees
- Their families

- Current customers
- Potential customers

Employees   Customers

Marketplace   Society

- Partners
- Competitors

- Community
- Environment

goal, "to be a profitable company," from its calling "to be an ethical partner to our stakeholders—one that plays by the rules and demonstrates leadership in the arena of business ethics."[39]

Let's consider each of these stakeholder categories to understand the meaning and effects of corporate social responsibility in the modern marketing arena, as well as how CSR ultimately can benefit the firm that undertakes it.

Employees Perhaps the most basic corporate social responsibility to employees is to ensure a safe working environment, free of threats to their physical safety, health, or well-being. In some cases though, this basic level of safety seems insufficient to achieve responsibility to workers. Aflac regards its pay-for-performance structure a key element of its responsibility to its employees, with the notion that everyone, from call center operators to the CEO, faces the same compensation standards. In this sense, it ensures equality of treatment and fairness in compensation. In doing so, Aflac earns a reputation as a good place to work and increases the number of people who apply for jobs there. These happy employees also should provide better service to customers, which in turn ensures better outcomes for the firm.

In addition to focusing on employees, more and more firms realize that happy employee families make happy and productive employees. Consequently, firms are focusing their efforts on outreach programs aimed at their employees' families.

Customers Especially as changes in the marketing environment emerge, firms must consider the effects on the customers who currently patronize them and future customers whom they are targeting. Corporate social responsibility programs must take such shifts and trends into account and react to them quickly. A few of the trends that are receiving the most attention include respecting and protecting privacy in an electronic world and ensuring the healthiness of products, especially those aimed at children. Moreover, CSR often increases consumer awareness of the firm, which can lead to better brand equity and sales in the long run.

America on the Move (AOM) has helped launch a variety of initiatives to help develop a healthier way of life through an active lifestyle, such as walking an extra 2,000 steps and eating 100 fewer calories every day.[40] Pepsi has cooperated with AOM to improve many of its products and their labels, such as reducing the saturated fat in its Frito-Lay's Ruffles.[41] The goal of such programs is to increase consumer awareness of the need to eat healthier choices. These efforts ultimately benefit consumers too, who not only gain additional consumption choices but also suffer less risk of the dangers associated with pollution or unhealthy foods.

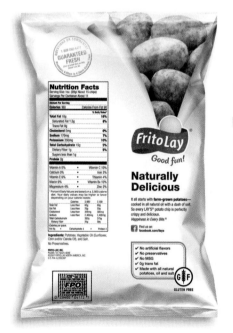

Pepsi cooperated with AOM to improve many of its products, such as reducing the saturated fat in its Frito-Lay's Ruffles.

Marketplace When one firm in the industry leads the way toward CSR, its partners and competitors often have no choice but to follow— or run the risk of not doing business or being left behind. To address issues such as global warming, water scarcity, and energy, GE uses a program it calls ecomagination, which encompasses a business strategy comprised of four commitments: to double investments in clean R&D, increase revenues from ecomagination products, reduce greenhouse gas emissions, and inform the public about these issues.[42] When confronted with such initiatives, other energy companies are forced to make a decision: continue as they have been doing, or adopt more responsible practices themselves. In either case, the initiating firm enjoys an advantage by gaining a reputation for being on the cutting edge of CSR efforts.

Society Firms expend considerable time and energy engaging in activities aimed at improving the overall community and the physical environment. According to a McKinsey & Co. survey, 95 percent of CEOs believe that society increasingly expects companies to take on public responsibilities.[43] That is, in a broad sense, companies cannot ignore societal demands that they act responsibly. A firm that fails to do so causes damage to all the preceding stakeholders, as well as itself. Perhaps the most famous recent example is BP, which failed to offer adequate protections to the workers on the Deep Horizon deep sea oil rig, ensure that consumers could enjoy waters free of oil contamination, or live up to marketplace standards for safety. As a result, society as a whole suffered, as did BP's corporate reputation, profits, and outlook for the future.

CHECK YOURSELF

1. How has corporate social responsibility evolved since the turn of the twenty-first century?
2. Provide examples of each of the stakeholders that firms should consider in their corporate social responsibility efforts.

GE is the industry leader in CSR with its ecomagination program.

Summing Up

LO1 Identify the ethical values marketers should embrace.

Being a part of an ethically responsible firm should be important to every employee, but it is particularly important to marketers, because they interact most directly with customers and suppliers, which offers a multitude of ethical questions and opportunities. AMA's Code of Ethics indicates that the basic ethical values marketers should aspire to are honesty, responsibility, fairness, respect, openness, and citizenship.

LO2 Distinguish between ethics and social responsibility.

Individuals and firms can (and should) act ethically, but the outcome of their acts may not affect society in general. An ethical act may only affect the firm's immediate stakeholders, such as its employees, customers, and suppliers. To be socially responsible, a firm also must take actions that benefit the community in a larger sense, such as helping people who have been affected by a natural disaster like a hurricane.

LO3 Identify the four steps in ethical decision making.

First, firms can include ethics and social responsibility in their corporate mission. Second, they should institute policies and procedures to ensure that everyone working for the firm is acting in an ethically responsible manner. Third, firms can model their ethical policies after a well-established code of ethics like the one provided by the American Marketing Association. Fourth, when making ethically sensitive decisions, firms can utilize a metric such as the ethical decision-making metric shown in Exhibit 4.4.

LO4 Describe how ethics can be integrated into a firm's marketing strategy.

Ethical and socially responsible considerations should be integrated into the firm's mission statement, as long as top management follows through and commits to supporting a strong ethical climate within the organization. When considering their marketing strategy, firms should ask not only "can we implement a certain policy?" but also "should we do it?" Finally, in the control phase, marketers must determine whether they truly have acted in an ethical and socially responsible manner. If not, they should make changes to the marketing strategy.

LO5 Describe the ways in which corporate social responsibility programs help various stakeholders.

To answer this question, we first have to identify the various stakeholders of a company, namely, customers, employees, the marketplace, and society. CSR benefits these stakeholders as follows:

- Customers: When companies adopt CSR, customers know that they can trust the firms to provide healthy, ethically acceptable products and services. Many customers also feel better about buying from a company that engages in responsible practices, which provides them with the additional value of feeling good about buying from that company.

- Employees: A firm committed to CSR likely treats its employees with decency and respect. For many employees (especially members of Generation Y), working for an irresponsible firm would be antithetical to their own morals and values.

- Marketplace: An industry improves its practices, and avoids scandals, when it ensures that the participating firms act responsibly and appropriately in all areas.

- Society: This stakeholder is local, national, or global communities. The benefits of CSR in all cases are numerous—cleaner air and water, aid to the underprivileged, and healthier product options all can result from CSR by companies.

Key Terms

- business ethics, 115
- corporate social responsibility, 120
- ethical climate, 116
- locational privacy, 129
- marketing ethics, 115

Marketing Applications

1. Why are marketers likely to be faced with more ethical dilemmas than members of other functional areas, like finance, accounting, or real estate?

2. Develop an argument for why a cosmetics manufacturer should build and maintain an ethical climate.

3. A clothing company gives generously to charities and sponsors donation drives to help lower-income teen girls get reasonably priced prom dresses. It also locates its manufacturing plants in countries with few labor laws, such that it does not know if children are working in its factories, and works to prevent union activity among its employees in the United States. Evaluate this company from an ethical and social responsibility perspective.

4. Based on the evaluation you developed for question 3, provide responses to the ethical decision-making metric from Exhibit 4.4. Provide a rationale for your score for each question.

5. A company that makes granola and other "healthy" snacks has the following mission statement: "Our goal is to profitably sell good-tasting, healthy products and to better society." Although its products are organic, they also are relatively high in sugar and calories. The company gives a small portion of its profits to the United Way. Evaluate its mission statement.

6. A health inspector found some rodent droppings in one batch of granola made by this same company (in question 6). What should the company do? Base your decision on the ethical decision-making metric in Exhibit 4.4.

7. Choose a company that you believe is particularly socially responsible. How do you justify your choice? What counterarguments might someone make to suggest that your chosen company is not responsible? Consider all key stakeholders in developing both sides of the argument.

Quiz Yourself

www.mhhe.com/ grewal4e

1. Johnson & Johnson's 1943 "credo" was considered radical at the time because it:
    a. parodied the Communist Manifesto.
    b. proposed socialized medicine.
    c. put customers first.
    d. was issued by a general.
    e. sought to undermine American capitalism.

2. The Harvest County school board is concerned about deteriorating school facilities, combined with a shrinking budget. The board began by studying the issue, and then identified parents, children, teachers, staff, and taxpayers as groups who have a vested interest in solving the problem. The school board has listened to each group's concerns. In the ethical decision-making framework, its next action should be to:
    a. identify issues of concern to lawmakers
    b. assess impact of its actions beyond the classroom
    c. engage in brainstorming and evaluate alternatives
    d. choose a course of action
    e. all of these

(Answers to these two questions can be found on page 647.)

Go to www.mhhe.com/grewal4e to practice an additional 11 questions.

Net Savvy

1. Perhaps no subdiscipline of marketing receives more scrutiny regarding ethical compliance than direct marketing, a form of nonstore retailing in which customers are exposed to and purchase merchandise or services through an impersonal medium such as telephone, mail, or the Internet.[44] Ethical issues in direct marketing cover a broad spectrum because this means of selling is conducted

through all forms of communication. The Direct Marketing Association (DMA) takes ethics very seriously and has numerous programs to ensure its member organizations comply with its Code of Ethics. Go to the website for the Direct Marketing Association (http://www.the-dma.org/). Click on "Advocacy." List the different ways that the DMA is involved in assisting consumers and the industry to create a more ethical marketplace.

2. An increasing number of firms are stating their strong commitment to corporate social responsibility initiatives. The Corporate Social Responsibility Newswire Service keeps track of these various initiatives and posts stories on its website about what various corporations are doing. Go to http://www.csrwire.com/ and choose one story. Write a description of the corporation and the initiative.

Chapter Case Study

WHOSE SIDE ARE YOU ON?[45]

connect

Lauren Smith was recently hired by a large architecture and engineering firm as an assistant account manager in the government contracts division. The firm specializes in building hospitals, schools, and other large-scale projects. Lauren is excited to learn that she will be part of the marketing team that presents the firm's proposals to the clients. In this case the clients are primarily federal and state governmental agencies. The presentations are elaborate, often costing $50,000 or more to prepare. But the projects can be worth millions to the firm, so the investment is worth it. The firm has a solid record for building quality projects, on time, and the majority of the time within budget. The firm also has an impressive track record, being awarded government contracts an incredible 85 percent of the time. No other firm in the industry comes close to this record.

The first project Lauren is assigned to is an enormous project to design a new military hospital complex. The team leader, Brian Jenkins, has stressed how crucial it is for the firm to land this contract. He hints that if the team is successful the members will be well compensated. In fact, Lauren heard that the members of the winning team for the last contract this size each received a $10,000 bonus.

Not long after the project commences, Brian invites Lauren to have lunch so they can get to know each other better. During lunch, a man approaches Brian and asks if he has received the information. The man says that he knows that with this information the firm is a sure winner. He also reminds Brian that he is due a bonus for getting such crucial information. After he leaves Brian explains that the man is George Miller, who was the former head of the division awarding the hospital contract. George has been helping Brian by talking to the decision team and getting information relevant to the bid. Brian explains that the information George has gathered about the internal discussions among the buying team will be what makes their proposal a clear winner, obviously good news for the team since a winning bid means bonuses are almost assured.

After lunch Lauren looks at the firm's ethics manual that she was given just last week at a new employee orientation. Lobbying without disclosure and paying for insider information are clearly discussed as unethical practices in the manual. Yet Brian seemed perfectly comfortable discussing George's role with Lauren.

Lauren decides she should check with another team member about the use of insider information, so she asks Sue Garcia. Sue tells Lauren that this kind of thing happens all the time. She jokes that most of the people in the division have at one time or another worked for the government. They all still know people in the various agencies. As far as Sue is concerned, friends will talk and that is not illegal, so there is no problem. It's a win–win situation: the government will get its building, the firm its funding, and the employees their bonuses.

Lauren realizes that with her overdue credit card bill and her needed car repairs, the bonus money would really help out. Besides, she is the most junior

Should Lauren go to the company's ethics officer and report what she knows about the use of insider information?

member of the team. If all the others are comfortable with this practice, why should she be concerned? After all, it is just friends talking, isn't it?

Questions

1. Using the framework for ethical decision making presented in the chapter (Exhibit 4.3), analyze Lauren's dilemma. Should she go to the company's ethics officer and report what she knows about the use of insider information?

2. Do you feel that Lauren, as the most junior member of the team, has less of an ethical duty than more senior members of the team do? Why or why not?

3. If you were the ethics officer for this firm, would you address the belief among employees that it is acceptable to discuss a pending proposal with members of the decision team? If so, how? If you would not discuss this belief, why not?

Understanding 4A Ethics Using Scenarios

n this appendix, we present nine ethical scenarios designed to assist you in developing your skills at identifying ethical issues. There is no one right answer to the dilemmas below, just as there will be no correct answers to many of the ethical situations you will face throughout your career. Instead, these scenarios can help you develop your sensitivity toward ethical issues, as well as your ethical reasoning skills. As mentioned throughout the chapter, Exhibit 4.4 provides an ethical decision-making metric to assist you in evaluating the following and all such ethical dilemmas you may face.

Scenario 1: R.J. Reynolds: Promotions to the Youth Market

Tobacco giant R.J. Reynolds sent a set of coasters featuring its cigarette brands and recipes for mixed drinks with high alcohol content to young adults, via direct mail, on their 21st birthdays (the legal age for alcohol consumption). The alcohol brands in the recipes included Jack Daniels, Southern Comfort, and Finlandia Vodka. The reverse side of the coaster read, "Go 'til Daybreak, and Make Sure You're Sittin'." The campaign, called "Drinks on Us," clearly promoted abusive and excessive drinking. This campaign was eventually stopped because the cigarette company did not have permission to use the alcohol brands.

The FDA (Federal Drug Administration) has been given the authority to regulate tobacco, including banning certain products, limiting nicotine and blocking labels such as "low tar" and "light" that could wrongly imply certain products are less harmful.[46] The law doesn't let the FDA ban nicotine or tobacco entirely. A committee has been formed to study several issues, including dissolvable tobacco products, product changes, and standards, and report back to the FDA. Of particular interest is the increase in the share of smokers using menthol cigarettes from 31 to almost 34 percent in four years, with more pronounced increases among young smokers. It also showed that among black smokers, 82.6 percent used menthol cigarettes, compared with 32.3 percent for Hispanic smokers and 23.8 percent for white smokers.[47] A ban on cigarettes with flavors like clove, chocolate, or fruit took effect in 2009, because they are believed to appeal to youth.

After graduation, you have an offer to work in either marketing or sales at R.J. Reynolds, the tobacco company that sells many popular brands of cigarettes. The pay and benefits are very competitive. The job market is tight, and if you don't get a job right away, you will have to live with your parents. Should you take the job?

Scenario 2: Car Manufacturer Gives Bribes for Contracts

A car and truck manufacturer just found out that two of its overseas business units have been engaging in bribery over a ten-year period of time. The company paid $56 million in bribes to more than 20 countries to gain government contracts for their vehicles.[48] The company is now paying millions in criminal and civil charges because of its violation of the Foreign Corrupt Practices Act (FCPA), and it admits to earning more than $50 million in profits based on its corrupt transactions. The car company recorded the bribe payments as "commissions," "special discounts," or "necessary payments." Should the manufacturer discontinue its operations with the countries that were unlawfully bribed to buy its cars? Are financial fines sufficient to repair the problem? How can companies be sure the commissions they earn are true commissions and not a bribe?

Scenario 3: Retailers Lack Ethical Guidelines

Renata has been working at Peavy's Bridal for less than a year now. Her sales figures have never been competitive with those of her coworkers, and the sales manager has called her in for several meetings to discuss her inability to close the sale. Things look desperate; in the last meeting, the sales manager told her that if she did not meet her quota next month, the company would likely have to fire her.

In considering how she might improve her methods and sales, Renata turned to another salesperson, namely, the one with the most experience in the store. Marilyn has been with Peavy's for nearly 30 years, and she virtually always gets the sale. But how?

"Let me tell you something sweetie," Marilyn tells her. "Every bride-to-be wants one thing: to look beautiful on her wedding day, so everyone gasps when they first see her. And hey, the husband is going to think she looks great. But let's be honest here—not everyone is all that beautiful. So you have to convince them that they look great in one, and only one, dress. And that dress had better be the most expensive one they try, or they won't believe you anyway! And then you have to show them how much better they look with a veil. And some shoes. And a tiara . . . you get the picture! I mean, they need all that stuff anyway, so why shouldn't we make them feel good while they're here and let them buy from us?"

Should she follow Marilyn's advice and save her job?

Scenario 4: Giving Credit Where Credit Isn't Due

A catalog retailer that carries home and children's items, such as children's furniture, clothing, and toys, was seeking a way to reach a new audience and stop the declining sales and revenue trends it was suffering. A market research firm hired by the cataloger identified a new but potentially risky market: lower-income single parents. The new market seemed attractive because of the large number of single parents, but most of these homes were severely constrained in terms of their monetary resources.

The research firm proposed that the cataloger offer a generous credit policy that would allow consumers to purchase up to $500 worth of merchandise on credit without a credit check, provided they signed up for direct payment of their credit account from a checking account. Because these were high-risk consumers, the credit accounts would carry extremely high interest rates. The research firm believed that even with losses, enough accounts would be paid off to make the venture extremely profitable for the catalog retailer.

Should the cataloger pursue this new strategy?

Scenario 5: The Jeweler's Tarnished Image

Sparkle Gem Jewelers, a family-owned and -operated costume jewelry manufacturing business, traditionally sold its products only to wholesalers. Recently however, Sparkle Gem was approached by the charismatic Barb Stephens, who convinced the owners to begin selling through a network of distributors she had organized. The distributors recruited individuals to host "jewelry parties" in their homes. Sparkle Gem's owners, the Billing family, has been thrilled with the revenue generated by these home parties and started making plans for the expansion of the distributor network.

However, Mrs. Billing just received a letter from a jewelry party customer, who expressed sympathy for her loss. Mrs. Billing was concerned and contacted the letter writer, who told her that Barb Stephens had come to the jewelry party at her church and told the story of Sparkle Gem. According to Stephens's story, Mrs. Billing was a young widow struggling to keep her business together after her husband had died on a missionary trip. The writer had purchased $200 worth of jewelry at the party and told Mrs. Billing that she hoped it helped. Mrs. Billing was stunned. She and her very-much-alive husband had just celebrated their 50th wedding anniversary.

What should Mrs. Billing do now?

Scenario 6: No Wonder It's So Good

Enjoy Cola is a new product produced by ABC Beverage and marketed with the slogan "Relax with Enjoy." Unlike other colas on the market, Enjoy does not contain caffeine and therefore is positioned as the perfect beverage to end the day or for a slow-paced weekend, and as a means to help consumers relax and unwind. The market response has been tremendous, and sales of Enjoy have been growing rapidly, especially among women.

ABC Beverage decided not to list on the ingredients label that Enjoy contains a small amount of alcohol because it is not required to do so by the government unless the alcohol content is more than 1 percent.

Mia Rodriguez, the marketing director for Enjoy, only recently learned that Enjoy contains small amounts of alcohol and is troubled about ABC's failure to disclose this information on the ingredients list. She worries about the impact of this omission on consumers who have alcohol sensitivities or those who shouldn't be consuming alcohol, such as pregnant women and recovering alcoholics.

What should Rodriguez do? What would you do in her position?

Scenario 7: Bright Baby's Bright Idea

Bartok Manufacturing produces a line of infant toys under the "Bright Baby" brand label. The Consumer Product Safety Commission (CPSC) recently issued a recall order for the Bright Baby car seat gym, a very popular product. According to the CPSC, the gym contains small parts that present a choking hazard. The CEO of Bartok Manufacturing, Bill Bartok, called an executive meeting to determine the firm's strategy in response to the recall.

Mike Henderson, Bartok's CFO, stated that the recall could cost as much as $1 million in lost revenue from the Bright Baby line. Noting that there had been no deaths or injuries from the product, just the potential for injury, Henderson proposed that the remaining inventory of car seat gyms be sold in regions where there are no rules such as the CPSC's. Sue Tyler, the marketing director for Bartok, recommended that the product be repackaged and sold under a different brand name so that the Bright Baby name would not be associated with the product. Bartok, though a bit leery of the plan, agreed to go along with it to avoid the monetary losses.

What would you have recommended to the CEO?

Scenario 8: Money from Mailing Lists[49]

Sports Nostalgia Emporium sells autographed sports memorabilia online. Recently, the director of marketing, John Mangold, started using a mailing list he had purchased from Marketing Metrix, a marketing research firm that sells consumer information. Mangold relies on such purchased mailing lists to grow the company and sends printed catalogs to thousands of people each month. The mailing lists he gets from Marketing Metrix are much more effective than other mailing lists and generate almost twice as much revenue.

In a recent conversation with a sales representative from Marketing Metrix, Mangold discovered the reason its lists were so effective: Marketing Metrix tracks the online behavior of consumers and uses that information to create targeted lists. The mailing lists that Mangold has been using consist of consumers who visited the websites of Sports Nostalgia Emporium's competitors. Based on what he can discern, Mangold believes that these consumers are not aware that someone is collecting information about their online behavior, along with their names and addresses, and selling it to other firms.

Should Mangold continue to use the Marketing Metrix mailing list? If so, should he tell his new customers how he got their names and addresses? Do consumers need to give consent before firms can collect information about their behavior?

Scenario 9: The Blogging CEO[50]

David Burdick is the CEO of ACME Bubblegum, a successful public company. As one of the cofounders of the company, Burdick has enjoyed speaking and writing about the success of ACME Bubblegum for several years. Typically, he speaks at conferences or directly to the press, but recently, he has been blogging about his firm anonymously. Specifically, he defended a recent advertising campaign that was unpopular among consumers and pointedly attacked one of ACME

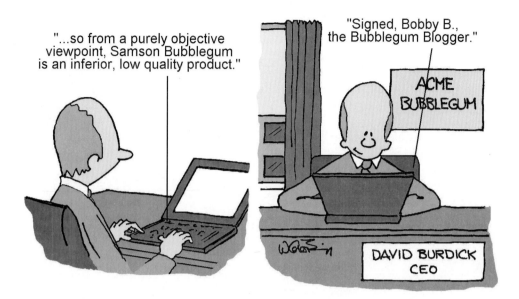

Bubblegum's competitors. Burdick deeply enjoys his anonymous blogging and believes that none of his readers actually know that he works for ACME Bubblegum.

Should Burdick be allowed to praise his company's performance anonymously online? Should he be allowed to attack his competitors without disclosing his relationship with the company? How would you feel if the CEO of a company at which you shopped was secretly writing criticisms of his or her competition? How would you feel if you knew a writer for your favorite blog was actually closely involved in a company that the blog community discussed?

THE COOL HUNTER

ROAMING THE USA AND THE GLOBE, SO YOU'RE IN THE KNOW

Home
News
Architecture
Design
Travel
Fashion
Lifestyle
Music
Art
Amazing Places
Ads
Kids
Stores
Events
Bars
Food
House
Transportation
Offices
Treelife

HOT PICK

Google™ Custom Search

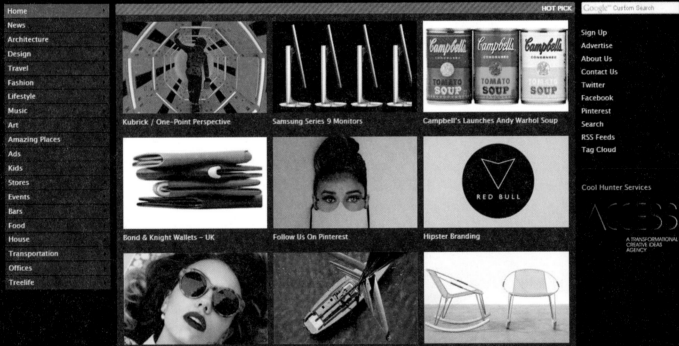

Kubrick / One-Point Perspective

Samsung Series 9 Monitors

Campbell's Launches Andy Warhol Soup

Bond & Knight Wallets – UK

Follow Us On Pinterest

Hipster Branding

Colab Eyewear – ELKE KRAMER

Sign Up To Our Free Newsletter

Made by Tait – Melbourne

Sign Up
Advertise
About Us
Contact Us
Twitter
Facebook
Pinterest
Search
RSS Feeds
Tag Cloud

Cool Hunter Services

ACCESS

A TRANSFORMATIONAL
CREATIVE IDEAS
AGENCY

CHAPTER 5

Analyzing the Marketing Environment

When it comes to being cool, no one wants to be left behind. Adolescents beg their parents (or save money themselves) to buy the latest music, and their parents take care never to be seen in last season's fashions. But the drive for coolness is not limited just to consumers. Many businesses also need to stay on the cutting edge, without being left behind, to stay current in their environment.

To help them, services such as The Cool Hunter and Trend Hunters collect, summarize, and describe the latest and greatest ideas in various realms. Imagine a construction firm that needs to know what kinds of materials people will want in their homes. It can visit the "Architecture" page on The Cool Hunter website to realize that more and more modern homes feature curved glass exterior walls.[1] If customers want them, then construction firms, designers, and architects had better learn how to make them.

The Cool Hunter (or TCH, for those in the know) functions not only as a resource for other firms but also as its own example of how to analyze and respond to the marketing environment. For example, on a recent Lifestyle page, it noted the seemingly constantly growing interest in getting "back" to nature, especially among people who live in urban settings. Thus the site offers glamour shots of trees and plant life, bringing a sense of nature to visitors' computer screens.[2]

Yet the site also rejects the notion that it is simply a trendspotter. Rather, TCH promises that its goal is to be the authority on all things cool. Of course, readers of the site can also contract with its affiliated creative agency, ACCESS, to have it create a new campaign or run an event.

In contrast, Trend Hunters specifically and exclusively targets brands that want more information about what is happening in their environment. It relies on contributions by thousands of trend hunters, each of whom writes up a short description of the trends he or she has noticed. Although some of the most prolific hunters are employed by the company, thousands more post for the "fame, glory, pride" of having their posts published and, they hope, featured on a front page of the site.[3]

The site takes responsibility for filtering the massive number of trends posted. Using crowd filtering, it condenses the 120,000 micro-trends posted by its approximately 80,000 trend hunters into 40,000 of the best micro-trends. Then its professional staff identifies around 1,200 insights that it provides to its professional clients, which they can use to anticipate and predict the shifts in their markets.

LEARNING OBJECTIVES

LO1 Outline how customers, the company, competitors, and corporate partners affect marketing strategy.

LO2 Explain why marketers must consider their macroenvironment when they make decisions.

LO3 Describe the differences among the various generational cohorts.

LO4 Identify various social trends that impact marketing.

For example, Trend Hunters has noted how one obvious and literal element of the marketing environment, billboards, has changed radically. Consumers and passersby no longer notice most billboards; instead, according to Trend Hunters, the best bet is to create shocking, attention-grabbing, in-your-face versions. One featured example makes the post of the billboard look like a fork, with a piece of steak on the end, to advertise a beef producer. While the visual image is arresting, the trend does not stop there: During rush hours (7:00–10:00 a.m. and 4:00–7:00 p.m.), it also sprays a beef scent into the air.[4]

As another example of this trend, Trend Hunters highlights guerilla advertising, such as a social awareness campaign that draws chalk outlines of bodies on sidewalks, within which are listed statistics and information about homelessness in that city.[5] In another effort, guerilla gardeners plant tiny gardens inside unpaved potholes, to bring commuters' attention to street conditions and, perhaps, the need to obey speed limits.[6]

Despite their different targets and aims, both these sites reflect a similar drive: the need to know what is cool, trendy, and hot in the surrounding market. This need is nearly universal, which explains why marketers spend so much time and effort analyzing their marketing environments.

LO1 Outline how customers, the company, competitors, and corporate partners affect marketing strategy.

A MARKETING ENVIRONMENT ANALYSIS FRAMEWORK

As our opening of this chapter has illustrated, marketers continue to find changes in what their customers demand or expect and adapt their product and service offerings accordingly. By paying close attention to customer needs and continuously monitoring the business environment in which the company operates, a good marketer can identify potential opportunities.

Exhibit 5.1 illustrates factors that affect the marketing environment. The centerpiece, as always, is consumers. Consumers may be influenced directly by the

EXHIBIT 5.1   Understanding the Marketing Environment

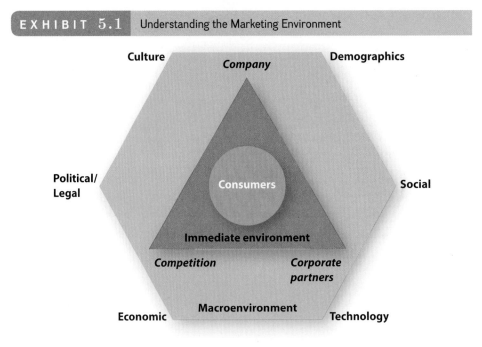

immediate actions of the focal company, the company's competitors, or corporate partners that work with the firm to make and supply products and services to consumers. The firm, and therefore consumers indirectly, is influenced by the macroenvironment, which includes various impacts of culture, demographics, and social, technological, economic, and political/legal factors. We discuss each of these components in detail in this chapter and suggest how they might interrelate.

Because the consumer is the center of all marketing efforts, value-based marketing aims to provide greater value to consumers than competitors offer. Therefore, the marketing firm must consider the entire business process, all from a consumer's point of view.[7] Consumers' needs and wants, as well as their ability to purchase, depend on a host of factors that change and evolve over time. Firms use various tools to keep track of competitors' activities and consumer trends, including sites such as The Cool Hunters and Trend Hunters, and they rely on various methods to communicate with their corporate partners. Furthermore, they monitor their macroenvironment to determine how such factors influence consumers and how they should respond to them. Sometimes, a firm can even anticipate trends.

THE IMMEDIATE ENVIRONMENT

Exhibit 5.2 illustrates the factors that affect consumers' immediate environment: the company's capabilities, competitors, and corporate partners.

Company Capabilities

In the immediate environment, the first factor that affects the consumer is the firm itself. Successful marketing firms focus on satisfying customer needs that match their core competencies. The primary strength of Pepsi is the manufacture, distribution, and promotion of carbonated beverages, but it has also successfully leveraged its core competency in the bottled water arena with its Aquafina brand, after recognizing the marketplace trend toward and consumer desire for bottled water. Marketers can use an analysis of the external environment, like the SWOT analysis described in Chapter 2, to categorize an opportunity as either attractive or unattractive. If it appears attractive, they can assess it in terms of their existing competencies.

EXHIBIT 5.2   Understanding the Immediate Environment

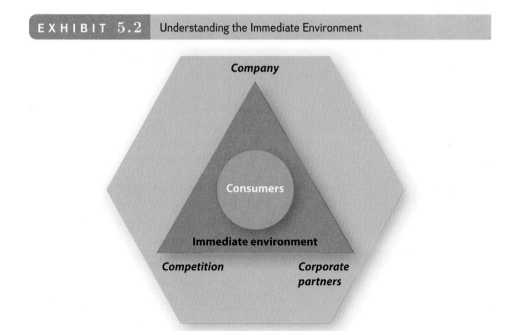

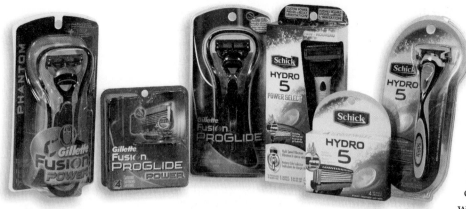

Gillette and Schick are actively engaged in fierce competition for the razor market.

Competitors

Competition also significantly affects consumers in the immediate environment. It is therefore critical that marketers understand their firm's competitors, including their strengths, weaknesses, and likely reactions to the marketing activities that their own firm undertakes. No one would want to get caught in the war between the two razor giants, Gillette Co. and Energizer USA, which makes Schick razors, as each manufacturer works to add ever more blades to its disposable razors.[8] Gillette accused Schick of engaging in false and misleading advertising when ads claimed that its Hydro razor would hydrate skin. Schick's parent company countered with the complaint that Gillette's Fusion ProGlide Razor ads attempt to deceive when they assert that the blades are "Gillette's thinnest blades ever." All these efforts represent the companies' recognition of what their closest competitor is doing, as well as their attempts to halt tactics they consider damaging. But at the same time, each razor company touts its benefits over its competitors, because the ultimate goal, of course, is to appeal to consumers.

Corporate Partners

Few firms operate in isolation. For example, automobile manufacturers collaborate with suppliers of sheet metal, tire manufacturers, component part makers, unions, transport companies, and dealerships to produce and market their automobiles successfully. Parties that work with the focal firm are its corporate partners.

Nau works with its corporate partners to develop a socially responsible strategy.

Consider an example that demonstrates the role these partners play and how they work with the firm to create a single, efficient manufacturing system. Unlike most outdoor clothing manufacturers that use synthetic nonrenewable materials, Nau makes outdoor and ski clothing from renewable sources such as corn and recycled plastic bottles. It was founded by a team of entrepreneurs who left companies such as Nike and Patagonia. To develop clothing from sustainable materials that were rugged and beautiful, these founders turned to manufacturing partners around the world to develop new fabrics, such as PLA (polyactic acid), a fast-wicking biopolymer made from corn. To complement the new fabrics, the company uses only organic cotton and wool from "happy sheep," provided by partners in the ranching industry that embrace animal-friendly practices. Thus, not only does Nau represent the cutting-edge of sustainability and green business; it also clearly demonstrates how "going green" can prompt companies to work more closely with their partners to innovate.[9] Its collaborative attitude has gotten Nau a mention on a trend-spotting site similar to those mentioned in the chapter's opening vignette.[10]

CHECK YOURSELF

1. What are the components of the immediate environment?

MACROENVIRONMENTAL FACTORS

 L02 Explain why marketers must consider their macroenvironment when they make decisions.

In addition to understanding their customers, the company itself, their competition, and their corporate partners, marketers must understand the **macroenvironmental factors** that operate in the external environment, namely, the culture, demographics, social issues, technological advances, economic situation, and political/regulatory environment, or CDSTEP, as shown in Exhibit 5.3.

EXHIBIT 5.3   The Macroenvironment

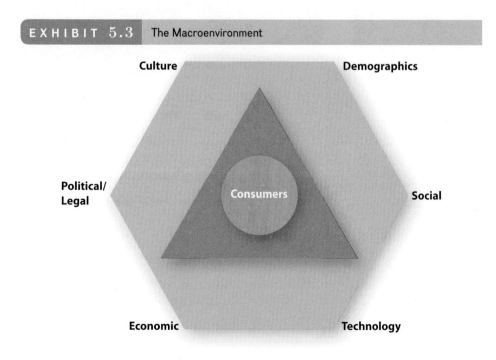

Culture

We broadly define **culture** as the shared meanings, beliefs, morals, values, and customs of a group of people.[11] Transmitted by words, literature, and institutions, culture gets passed down from generation to generation and learned over time. You participate in many cultures: Your family has a cultural heritage, so perhaps your mealtime traditions include eating rugelach, a traditional Jewish pastry, or sharing corned beef and cabbage to celebrate your Irish ancestry on St. Patrick's Day. Your school or workplace also shares its own common culture. In a broader sense, you also participate in the cultural aspects of the town and country in which you live. The challenge for marketers is to have products or services identifiable by and relevant to a particular group of people. Our various cultures influence what, why, how, where, and when we buy. Two dimensions of culture that marketers must take into account as they develop their marketing strategies are the culture of the country and that of a region within a country.

Country Culture The visible nuances of a country's culture, such as artifacts, behavior, dress, symbols, physical settings, ceremonies, language differences, colors and tastes, and food preferences, are easy to spot. But the subtler aspects of **country culture** generally are trickier to identify and navigate. Sometimes the best answer is to establish a universal appeal within the specific identities of country culture. BMW's Mini and other global automobile manufacturers have successfully bridged the cultural gap by producing advertising that appeals to the same target market across countries. The pictures and copy are the same. The only thing that changes is the language.

Regional Culture The region in which people live in a particular country has its own **regional culture** that affects many aspects of people's life, for instance, the way they might refer to a particular product category. In the soft drink market,

Some firms like BMW's Mini have successfully bridged the cultural gap by producing advertising that appeals to the same target market across countries.

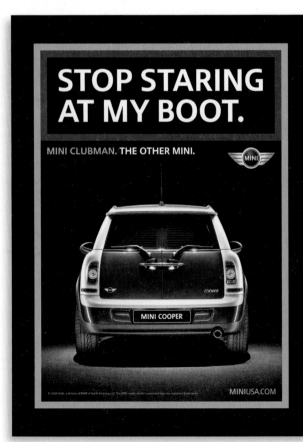

38 percent of Americans refer to carbonated beverages as "soda," whereas another 38 percent call them "pop," and an additional 19 percent call any such beverage a "Coke," even when it is Pepsi.[12] Eat lunch in Indiana, and you'll have the best luck ordering a "pop" from the Midwesterner who owns the restaurant, but if you then head to Atlanta for dinner, you'd better order your "Coke," regardless of the brand you prefer. Head to Massachusetts, and the term is "soda," but if you move to Texas, you might be asked if you'd like a Dr Pepper—a generic term for carbonated beverages in the Lone Star state because it was first formulated there in 1885.[13] Imagine the difficulty these firms have in developing promotional materials that transcend these regional differences.

Demographics

Demographics indicate the characteristics of human populations and segments, especially those used to identify consumer markets. Typical demographics such as age—which includes generational cohorts—gender, race, and income are readily available from market research firms like Symphony/Information Resources Inc. Many firms undertake their own market research as well. For example, with its ExtraCard loyalty program, CVS collects massive amounts of data about shoppers who visit all its stores. It uses this information to target offers for, say, cosmetics to young female shoppers. But it also uses these data to benefit its communities. When the data gathered show that consumers—especially elderly customers of the pharmacy chain—are not refilling their prescriptions at the expected rate, CVS proactively interacts with these at-risk populations to encourage adherence to their medical plans.[14]

Demographics thus provide an easily understood "snapshot" of the typical consumer in a specific target market, as the next few sections detail.

Generational Cohorts Consumers in a **generational cohort**—a group of people of the same generation—have similar purchase behaviors because they have shared experiences and are in the same stage of life. For instance, Baby Boomers (people born after World War II, 1946–1964) and Generation Yers (people born between 1977 and 2000) both gravitate toward products and services that foster a casual lifestyle; however, they tend to do so for different reasons. The aging Baby Boomers, who grew up with jeans and khakis and brought casual dressing into the business arena, are often trying to maintain their youth. Yers, in contrast, typically wear jeans for status.

LO3 Describe the differences among the various generational cohorts.

Applying age as a basis to identify consumers is quite useful to marketers, as long as it is used in conjunction with other consumer characteristics. For example, most media are characterized by the consumers who use it.[15] Age groups can identify appropriate magazine and television shows in which firms should advertise, as well as lists for direct mail and telemarketing campaigns. Age is also useful for identifying the best social media outlets (e.g., Twitter, Facebook). Although there are many ways to cut the generational pie, we discuss four major groups, as listed in Exhibit 5.4.

EXHIBIT 5.4 Generational Cohorts

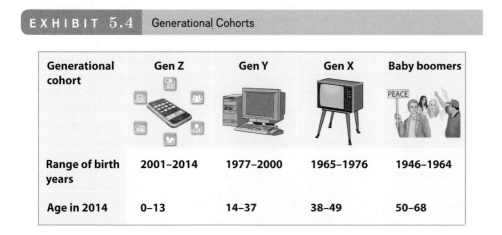

Generational cohort	Gen Z	Gen Y	Gen X	Baby boomers
Range of birth years	2001–2014	1977–2000	1965–1976	1946–1964
Age in 2014	0–13	14–37	38–49	50–68

Generation Z Generation Z is also known as the Digital Natives, because people in this group were born into a world that already was full of electronic gadgets and digital technologies, such as the Internet and social networks.[16] These technologies are being developed and adopted at an unprecedented rate. Whereas it took 38 years for the radio to be adopted by 50 million people and 13 years for television, it only took 2 years for the same number of consumers to sign up for Facebook. Because of the technologies available to them, these digital natives will be more globally connected than previous generations. They thus might have a better appreciation for diverse cultures, but Gen Z consumers also were also born into a world confronted by both national and international terrorism, often facilitated by technology, and widespread environmental concerns.

Generation Z children are being raised by and have a lot in common with their Generation X parents, whom we discuss later. Gen Z and their parents increasingly watch the same television channels, such as Nickelodeon, especially when it shows "nostalgic" shows that the parents remember and the children enjoy anew. Both groups also like video games, leading the industry to develop family-oriented games on communal consoles, such as the Nintendo Wii. Finally, because Gen Z kids still go shopping with their parents, they are developing an affinity for the same brands, prompting retailers such as The Gap (GapKids, babyGap) and JCrew (Crewcuts) to develop special product lines to accommodate their demands. But at a certain point, such accommodation might cross the line into exploitation, as Ethical and Societal Dilemma 5.1 suggests.

Tweens are always connected.

Generation Y Generation Y, also called Millennials, includes more than 60 million members in the United States alone, born between 1977 and 2000. Children of the Baby Boomers, this group is the biggest cohort since the original postwar World War II boom. It also varies the most in age, ranging from teenagers to adults who have their own families.[17] Now that Gen Y is entering the workplace, it is becoming apparent that its members have different expectations and requirements than those of other cohorts. Gen Y puts a strong emphasis on balancing work and life—these young adults want a good job, but they also want to live in a location that supports their lifestyle. They also consider marriage secondary, and not obviously necessary, to being good parents themselves.[18]

The younger edge of this group (often referred to as "tweens") has never lived without the Internet or easy access to cell phones, which makes them technologically savvy. As a result, these Gen Yers look and consume rather similarly across countries. They have similar lifestyles, music, and entertainment. MTV and CNN are available in most developed countries. It is difficult to tell the difference in appearance between Gen Ys in the United States and other developed countries, based solely on their "uniforms" of jeans, sneakers, and T-shirts.

Generation X The next group, Generation X (Xers), includes those born between 1965 and 1976 and represents some 41 million Americans. Vastly unlike their Baby Boomer parents, Xers are the first generation of latchkey children (those who grew up in homes in which both parents worked), and 50 percent of them have divorced parents. This influence has led them to act like "helicopter parents" with their own children, working to shield their offspring from any threats or disappointment.[19] Unlike most previous generations, they are unlikely to enjoy greater economic prosperity than their parents.[20]

Although fewer in number than Generation Y or Baby Boomers,[21] Gen Xers possess considerable spending power because they tend to get married later and buy houses later in life. They're much less interested in shopping than their parents and far more cynical, which tends to make them astute consumers. They demand

Ethical and Societal Dilemma 5.1   The Next Target: Infants?

By the time a child is three years old, he or she can recognize an average of 100 brand logos.[22] Marketers can make use of this information to ensure that their logos and advertising communication are prominent on packaging, as well as on the toys themselves, to ensure that children demand their brand from gift-giving parents.

The influence does not stop with toys, though. More and more companies are placing advertisements in schools and on buses.[23] And even though Facebook and similar sites officially require users to be at least 13 years of age, recent reports suggest that nearly 8 million Facebook visitors actually are younger than 12.[24] Although initially, most social media sites adopted this age restriction so that they could avoid meeting regulations associated with youthful users, it appears they are switching tactics in response to this widespread usage among young "digital natives." Facebook has hired several lobbyists to encourage Congress to change the rules, including the 1998 Children's Online Privacy Protection Act.[25]

For Facebook and similar sites, inviting children to join offers two main advantages. First, it encourages their brand loyalty to the site itself. If a child creates a Facebook profile at the age of 10, she is unlikely to take it down by the time she is 15 or 18 or 26 years old. Second, by making the concept of sharing information more familiar to users from a very young age, Facebook helps encourage the type of behaviors it needs from consumers for it to survive. If digital natives have few expectations

Is expanding demographic target markets to ever younger children a boon for marketers? Or is it rather a danger to children?

of privacy but instead share all their preferences online, advertisers enjoy greater access to their ideas and thoughts.

Brands can then use this information to market their own products to children. As the following exhibit shows, the makers of sugary drinks have done so extensively. Despite concerns about childhood obesity and the ethicality of marketing nutritionally void foods to children, no laws prevent brands from hosting Facebook pages or creating a Twitter account to appeal to children.

Of course, access also potentially extends to sexual predators and others who might do harm to children. Some findings suggest that at least 1 million children get harassed or bullied through Facebook each year.[27] Thus the question becomes: Is expanding demographic target markets to ever younger children a boon for marketers? Or is it rather a danger to children?

Ranking of Brand Followers[26]

Brand	Number of Facebook Fans	Number of Twitter Followers
Coke (regular)	30,747,955	3,000,026
Red Bull	20,462,113	223,494
Monster Energy Drink	11,238,533	75,485
Dr Pepper	9,680,095	43,810
Mountain Dew	5,517,588	39,917
Pepsi (regular)	4,449,173	89,371
Sprite	3,740,522	15,397
Gatorade	3,704,295	329,616
Vitamin Water	2,539,549	13,884
Lipton Brisk Iced Tea	849,800	26,625

Note: Data as of June 15, 2011.

convenience and tend to be less likely to believe advertising claims or what salespeople tell them. Because of their experience as children of working parents, who had little time to shop, Xers developed shopping savvy at an early age and knew how to make shopping decisions by the time they were teenagers. As a result, they grew more knowledgeable about products and more risk averse than other generational cohorts.

Baby Boomers   After World War II, the birth rate in the United States rose sharply, resulting in a group known as the **Baby Boomers**, the 78 million Americans born between 1946 and 1964. Now that the oldest Boomers are collecting Social Security, it is clear that this cohort will be the largest population of 50-plus consumers the United States has ever seen. Although the Baby Boomer generation spans 18 years, experts agree that its members share several traits that set them apart from those born before World War II. First, they are individualistic. Second, leisure time represents a high priority for them. Third, they believe that they will always be able to take care of themselves, partly evinced by their feeling of economic security, even though they are a little careless about the way they spend their money. Fourth, they have an obsession with maintaining their youth. Fifth and finally, they will always love rock 'n roll.

The move from suits and ties to jeans and T-shirts in business is a direct result of Baby Boomers imposing their values on the workplace as they have moved into upper management positions.[28] Boomers, who wore tie-dyed shirts, ripped jeans, and long hair in their younger days, have pushed their casual lifestyles into the workplace and virtually every aspect with which they are associated. Recognizing the opportunity, Levi-Strauss developed its Dockers line of casual shirts and khakis.

Food companies have also targeted Baby Boomers with healthier options for cereals, frozen entrees, and snacks that have no cholesterol, low fat, and no sugar. General Mills has added extra calcium to Yoplait Original yogurt in an attempt to help women increase their daily calcium requirements.[29] It has reduced the sodium in products like Cheerios, Progresso soups, and its Chex Snack Mix line. Finally, General Mills has created a new version of Total cereal containing omega-3 fatty acids, which are good for heart health.

Retailers also recognize the immense buying power of the aging Baby Boomers, so they cater directly to them with larger fonts in signage, staff available to read the small print on product packaging, and seating options in stores.[30] They note that their older customers, even the ones with moderate incomes, are more focused on quality than price and make decisions on what merchandise to carry accordingly. Finally, and perhaps surprisingly, Baby Boomers are heavy Internet users and tend to do research before purchasing online.

Income   Income distribution in the United States has grown more polarized—the highest-income groups are growing, whereas many middle- and lower-income groups' real purchasing power keeps declining. Although the trend of wealthy

No matter how old they get, Baby Boomers will always love rock 'n roll.

households outpacing both poor and middle classes is worldwide, it is particularly prominent in the United States. The average annual income of the richest 1–10 percent of the population is $164,647; the median income in the United States was $49,445 in 2010. And the poorest 10 percent of the population earned an average of only $5,800. Furthermore, the number of people who earn less than the poverty line ($22,314 for a family of four in 2010) continues to grow.[31] The wealthiest 1 percent control 34.6 percent of Americans' total net worth; the bottom 90 percent control only 26.9 percent in comparison.[32] The increase in wealthy families may be due to the maturing of the general population, the increase in dual-income households, and the higher overall level of education. It also may prompt some ethical concerns about the distribution of wealth. However, the broad range in incomes creates marketing opportunities at both the high and low ends of the market.

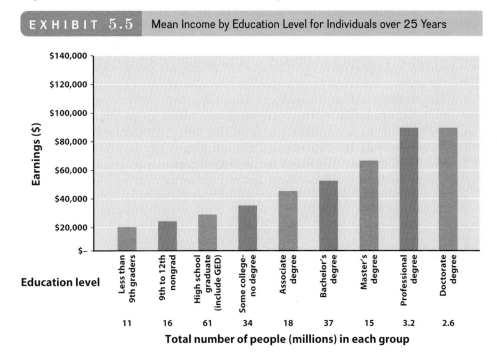

The Fuel Cell Car and Experiment Kit appeals to an affluent customer at specialty retailer, Hammacher Schlemmer.

Although some marketers choose to target only affluent population segments, others have had great success delivering value to middle- and low-income earners. Consider, for example, the toys presented by the specialty retailer Hammacher Schlemmer versus the mass appeal of Walmart's toy sections. Toy buyers at Walmart are looking for inexpensive products; those at Hammacher Schlemmer go to great lengths to find unusual toys like the Fuel Cell Car and Experiment Kit, pictured, or the Gigantic Inflatable Climbing Iceberg.[33]

Another aspect of the income demographic relates to the concept of value. Why are customers searching for value more today than in recent decades? During the first three decades after World War II, most American families experienced real income growth, but starting in the late 1970s and continuing through to today, that growth has stagnated. Family incomes have stayed slightly ahead of inflation (the general rate of price increases), but their health care costs, property taxes, and tuition bills have risen much faster than inflation.

Education Studies show that higher levels of education lead to better jobs and higher incomes.[34] (See Exhibit 5.5.) According the U.S. Bureau of Labor Statistics,

---

EXHIBIT 5.5 Mean Income by Education Level for Individuals over 25 Years

Earnings ($) — y-axis: $-, $20,000, $40,000, $60,000, $80,000, $100,000, $120,000, $140,000

Education level	Total number of people (millions) in each group
Less than 9th graders	11
9th to 12th nongrad	16
High school graduate (include GED)	61
Some college-no degree	34
Associate degree	18
Bachelor's degree	37
Master's degree	15
Professional degree	3.2
Doctorate degree	2.6

employment that requires a college or secondary degree accounts for nearly half of all projected job growth in the near future. Moreover, average annual earnings are higher for those with degrees than for those without. Those who did not graduate from high school have an average annual salary of about $23,000; high school grads earn around $32,500; those with a bachelor's degree earn nearly $54,000.[35]

For some products, marketers can combine education level with other data like occupation and income and obtain pretty accurate predictions of purchase behavior. For instance, a full-time college student with a part-time job may have relatively little personal income but will spend his or her disposable dollars differently than would a high school graduate who works in a factory and earns a similar income. College students tend to play sports and go to nightclubs, whereas high school graduates are more likely watch sports and go to bars. Marketers need to be quite cognizant of the interaction among education, income, and occupation.

Thousands of people line up for the start of the Nike Women's Marathon in San Francisco.

Gender Years ago, gender roles appeared clear, but those male/female roles have been blurred. This shift in attitude and behavior affects the way many firms design and promote their products and services. More firms are careful about gender neutrality in positioning their products and attempt to transcend gender boundaries, especially through increased interactions with their customers. On the basis of its research with men for example, the children's stroller company Bugaboo International designed a high-tech, black-and-chrome contraption with dirt bike tires.

Rather than rely on stereotypical feminine appeals, Nike also has recognized the increasing numbers of women who engage in physically challenging activities. For the annual Women's Marathon in San Francisco, Nike registered 20,000 competitors in just three weeks. In addition to encouraging women to take up the challenge, with the tagline "Run to Be," Nike provides special events for women along the course, such as a "chocolate mile," pedicure stations, and free massages—though it also notes that men are welcome to participate. Every participant also receives a "finisher's" necklace from Tiffany & Co.[36]

Ethnicity[37] Because of immigration and increasing birth rates among various ethnic and racial groups, the United States continues to grow more diverse. Approximately 80 percent of all population growth in the next 20 years is expected to come from African American, Hispanic, and Asian communities. Minorities now represent approximately one-quarter of the population; by 2050, they will represent about 50 percent, and nearly 30 percent of the population will be Hispanic.[38] The United Nations also estimates that approximately 1 million people per year will immigrate from less developed nations to the United States over the next 40 years.[39] Many foreign-born Americans and recent immigrants tend to concentrate in a handful of metropolitan areas, such as New York, Los Angeles, San Francisco, and Chicago.

Among the different groups, Hispanic buying power is projected to reach $1.3 trillion in 2015, a cumulative increase of around 25 percent compared with 2010.[40] The 50 million Hispanic consumers in the United States have increasing influences on mainstream U.S. culture, as Superior Service 5.1 highlights. Many families have been in the United States for multiple generations, and the consumer behavior of these highly acculturated Hispanics differs little from that of other groups of Americans. For example,

The Hispanic market is so large in some areas of the United States that marketers develop entire marketing programs just to meet Hispanics' needs.

Adding Value 5.1   Clever Thrift, or Middle-Class Hoarding?

A $400 grocery tab reduced to $6. Discounts and coupons combined to make the purchases of some staples absolutely free. And garages are filled to the ceiling with nonperishable products. These are the signs of extreme couponing.

As presented most notably on the reality show *Extreme Couponing*, extreme coupon shoppers refuse ever to pay full price. Devoting hours to their planning and coupon clipping, they carefully time their purchases to ensure they only buy items when they go on sale. Then they combine the sale with a coupon or combine multiple coupons for the same item. When they find a good deal, they buy as much as they possibly can and stock up at home, which means they won't need to buy those items again for months.[47]

The effort to get everything at extremely low prices, or even for free, can get a little uncomfortable to watch though. The couponers featured on the show load up multiple carts, driving shoppers lined up behind them, as well as the checkout clerks, into near panic. Then they lug all their purchases home to stash throughout their homes. Some of these extreme shoppers admit to being driven by a sense of fear. Even if they lose their jobs, there are hundreds of jars of peanut butter in their basement, so they won't starve.

The practice requires a middle-class, suburban lifestyle to start though. People living in apartments in the city cannot store the bulk quantities required. Even for consumers in the suburbs, inventory costs might become a concern, just as they are for retailers. If a consumer is fortunate enough to have a spare bedroom that no one is using, it's easy to fill it with groceries. But not everyone has that luxury.[48]

Furthermore, extreme couponers create bottlenecks in store check-out lines, cause stock-outs, and create inventory and supply chain problems for many retailers, especially grocers. In addition to increases in coupon enthusiasts, retailers

Couponers haven't died; they've morphed into a new species on steroids called Extreme Couponers.

are also noticing an increase in fraudulent coupons and coupon misuse. In response, some stores have updated their coupon policies. Target's restated policy prevents customers from combining two buy-one-get-one-free coupons to get both items for free. Rite-Aid restricts the number of coupons customers can use for a specific item. Walgreens updated its current coupon policy to give management the right to limit the number of coupons consumers can use.[49]

expectations of what constitutes a good deal have changed rapidly over the past several years, which means marketers need some new ideas about how to appeal to them.[50]

Health and Wellness Concerns   Health concerns, especially those pertaining to children, are prevalent, critical, and widespread. In the past 20 years, child obesity has doubled and teenage obesity tripled in the United States, leading to skyrocketing rates of high blood pressure, high cholesterol, early signs of heart disease, and Type 2 diabetes among children. The U.S. Centers for Disease Control and Prevention also estimate that approximately one-third of U.S. adults are obese, and the incidence of diabetes has reached 8.3 percent—with much higher rates for people still undiagnosed or classified as having "prediabetes."[51] It is also increasing at alarming rates in other countries and among consumers who adopt more Western diets.

New advertising guidelines therefore require marketers to produce food in reasonably proportioned sizes. Advertised food items must provide basic nutrients, have less than 30 percent of their total calories from fat, and include no added sweeteners. The advertising also cannot be aired during children's programming, and companies cannot link unhealthy foods with cartoon and celebrity figures.

The practice of yoga is growing as more consumers embrace a healthy lifestyle.

For example, Burger King no longer uses SpongeBob SquarePants to promote burgers and fries.[52]

As the same time, consumers' interest in improving their health has opened up several new markets and niches focused on healthy living. For example, consumer spending on yoga classes, mats, and clothing has increased consistently, leading to a 9.5 percent sales jump between 2006 and 2011.[53] Yoga studios actually combine multiple modern trends: As the economy sours, people face increasing stress, which they hope to reduce through yoga. In addition, yoga studios are relatively inexpensive to open and operate, so entrepreneurs and consumers appreciate the value for the money they offer. And of course, Americans remain consistently on the lookout for exercise mechanisms that can help them shed pounds and match media images of athletic prowess. Thus competition is growing in this industry, and some studios have begun combine their basic yoga classes with additional offers to attract clients, such as food services, acupuncture, or massages.[54]

Greener Consumers Green marketing involves a strategic effort by firms to supply customers with environmentally friendly merchandise.[55] Many consumers, concerned about everything from the purity of air and water to the safety of beef and salmon, believe that each person can make a difference in the environment. For example, nearly half of U.S. adults now recycle their soda bottles and newspapers, and European consumers are even more green. Germans are required by law to recycle bottles, and the European Union does not allow beef raised on artificial growth hormones to be imported. Demand for green-oriented products has been a boon to the firms that supply them (the case at the end of this chapter discusses a primary example). Marketers encourage consumers to replace older versions of washing machines and dishwashers with water- and energy-saving models and to invest in phosphate-free laundry powder and mercury-free and rechargeable batteries. New markets emerge for recycled building products, packaging, paper goods, and even sweaters and sneakers, as well as for more efficient appliances, lighting, and heating and cooling systems in homes and offices. Jumping on the "Green" bandwagon, Frito-Lay's SunChip line of snack foods uses solar power at one of its eight production facilities to harness the sun's energy to produce its products.[56] Adding Value 5.2 offers another example of how a company can get creative in responding to consumer demands for green options.

These green products and initiatives suggest a complicated business model. Are they good for business? Some green options are more expensive than traditional products and initiatives. Are consumers interested in or willing to pay the higher prices for green products? Are firms really interested in improving the environment? Or are they disingenuously marketing products or services as environmentally friendly, with the goal of gaining public approval and sales, rather than actually improving the environment? This type of exploitation is common enough that it even has produced a new term: **greenwashing**. Consumers need to question whether a firm is spending significantly more money and time advertising being green and operating with consideration for the environment, rather than actually spending these resources on environmentally sound practices.

Adding Value 5.2 Puma Sacks the Box

When is a shoebox not a shoebox? For the running shoe company Puma, the answer is when it becomes a Clever Little Bag.

More than a decade ago, Puma launched a social and environmental sustainability campaign that included several green initiatives. The company's long-term commitment to green business practices has produced several innovations, including its methods of sourcing raw materials from Cotton made in Africa—a project that promotes sustainable cotton farming in Africa—and opening the first carbon-neutral headquarters in the industry. Puma's most recent advance replaces traditional shoeboxes with a reusable bag/box combination that protects shoes, from the factory door to the customer's closet.[57]

Created by industrial designer Yves Béhar, the bag is the solution selected from 2000 ideas and approximately 40 prototypes.[58] The design uses 65 percent less paper than a box; it also reduces manufacturing consumption of water, diesel, and energy by 60 percent. Carbon emissions thus fell by 10,000 tons annually, and because the box and bag constitute one unit, the company has eliminated the need for a shopping bag for purchased shoes. The innovation also earned Puma several international design awards, as well as widespread praise for its sustainability.[59]

The benefits of the Clever Little Bag don't stop there. The new package design weighs less than traditional shoe boxes, which reduces shipping costs and saves hundreds of thousands of gallons of fuel each year. PUMA also switched from polyethylene to greener materials for its apparel shopping bags and gave its T-shirts an extra fold to decrease packaging size. These efforts keep 29 million plastic bags from becoming postconsumer waste and reduce both fuel consumption and CO_2 emissions during transport. PUMA intends to employ 100 percent sustainable materials in its packaging by 2015.

Consumer reaction to the new packaging, however, is mixed. Some detractors point out that it still contains most of a box, albeit without a top, while others wonder why nearly two years were needed to develop a solution already employed by the British Shoe Corporation. "A good example of greenwash," commented one consumer, and another found it "sad . . . that companies don't think of these small things and big consequences before putting products on the market."[60] These comments clearly indicate the challenges corporations face when publicizing their sustainability messages.

Privacy Concerns More and more consumers worldwide sense a loss of privacy. At the same time that the Internet has created an explosion of accessibility to consumer information, improvements in computer storage facilities and the manipulation of information have led to more and better security and credit check services. Yet controversies still erupt, and some observers suggest hackers are just getting more effective. In 2011, for example, multiple multinational corporations suffered security breaches, including the defense contractor Lockheed Martin, NASA, the Fox Network, and Sony. In the latter case, a group of hackers stole the personal information of 102 million PlayStation users.[61]

The Federal Trade Commission (FTC), responding to consumer outcries regarding unwanted telephone solicitations, has registered the phone numbers of more than 200 million phone numbers in the Do Not Call Registry. This action was designed to protect consumers against intrusions that Congress determined to be particularly invasive.[62] Unfortunately, the Do Not Call Registry may have eliminated many honest telemarketers, leaving the wires open for the crooked groups who often use nontraceable recordings to reach potential customers at home. In the end, most companies are moving resources away from telephone campaigns and refocusing them elsewhere.

A Time-Poor Society Reaching a target market has always been a major challenge, but it is made even more complicated by several trends that increase the difficulty of grabbing those markets' attention. In the majority of families, both parents work, and the kids are busier than ever. Since 1973, the median number of hours that people say they work has jumped from 41 to 49 a week. During that same period, reported leisure time has dropped from 26 to 19 hours a week.[63] Among younger consumers, the trend is to cope with a lack of leisure time by multitasking—watching television or listening to music while talking on the telephone or doing homework. Their divided attention simply cannot focus as well on advertisements that appear in those media.

Superior Service 5.2   Grocery Retailers Help Time-Poor Consumers

Traditional methods of shopping for and preparing food have always been time-consuming. Restaurants, and particularly fast-food restaurants, have helped lighten this burdensome task for decades. But as consumers become more time-pressed and as traditional grocery stores are feeling increased competition from superstores like Walmart and Target and warehouse stores like Costco and Sam's Club, some grocery retailers are developing innovative methods of helping consumers put food on their families' tables.

Through its Signature Café line for example, Safeway provides entrees, side dishes, sandwiches, and pizzas—offerings popular enough that it has earned approximately $100 million in sales of these items each year since introducing them.[64] Even Walgreens, a chain not traditionally known for fresh food items, is slowly introducing fresh foods to its stores. In a somewhat different approach, Walgreens has decided to initiate its program in "food deserts"—that is, urban neighborhoods traditionally underserved when it comes to fresh fruit and vegetable options.[65]

Walgreens also is rolling out another new program to help customers get all their necessary tasks done in a day. With its Web Pickup service, customers in selected markets can shop online, then pick up their orders in around an hour at their local store.[66]

Whole Foods already provides ready-made meals, but it also began to worry about the efficiency with which customers

Self-checkout lanes speed the shopping process, but do they improve customer service?

could get in and out of stores when they were in a hurry. So this chain streamlined the checkout process by organizing checkout lines like a bank. One line is formed, and customers are helped at the next available register.

Marketers must respond to the challenge of getting consumers' attention by adjusting. Noting that many viewers of cooking shows spent little time cooking themselves, the Bravo television network partnered with the Healthy Choice line to sell *Top Chef* branded frozen dinners in grocery stores. Consumers can purchase meals similar to those prepared on the show, like barbecued steak with red potatoes or roasted chicken Marsala with mushrooms. On the Bravo website of course, they also can try their hand at cooking themselves, maybe on the weekends, by ordering a related line of knives, aprons, cookbooks and other equipment.[67]

Retailers are doing their part by making their products available to customers whenever and wherever they want. For instance, many retailers have become full-fledged multichannel retailers that offer stores, catalogs, and Internet shopping options. In addition, retailers like Office Depot and Walgreens have extended their hours of operation so that their customers can shop during hours they aren't working. Automated processes like self-checkout lanes and electronic kiosks speed the shopping process and provide customers with product and ordering information. Grocery stores and home improvement centers have been particularly aggressive in developing strategies to help time-poor customers, as Superior Service 5.2 describes.

To find and develop such methods to make life easier for consumers in the time-poor society, marketers often rely on technology, another macroenvironmental factor and the topic of the next section.

Technological Advances

Technological advances have accelerated during the past decade, improving the value of both products and services. Consumers have constant access to the

Social and Mobile Marketing 5.1 — Foursquare's Promise and Facebook's Response

The location-based mobile platform Foursquare not only awards badges to frequent customers to reflect their status in certain locations, but it also helps people find the locations their friends are frequenting and gives them helpful tips about local bars, restaurants, parks, museums, grocery stores, and movie theaters—such as where to park or what not to order. For the 250,000 companies that appear on the platform,[68] Foursquare also provides an effective means to attract, appeal to, and retain loyal customers.

A Foursquare user who checks in to a local restaurant, for example, accumulates points and rewards, in the form of badges. These badges earn the user discounts and coupons on future visits to the restaurant, as long as he or she keeps checking in at the site. The more a user visits, the more incentives she or he receives. To up the ante even more, customers can earn additional points for bringing along a friend on their next visit and getting that friend to check in at the same time. The social aspects of Foursquare go still further: Users often leave reviews of the venues they visit and then plan ahead to determine the places they will go next, according to what other similar users have said about a location.

For the companies, these uses provide remarkable insights into target markets.[69] They know who is visiting when, how often, and with whom. Finally, because the concept is based on rewarding frequent visitors, companies know they are devoting their best efforts to their best, most loyal customers.

By gathering the vast information from all its users, both consumers and sellers, Foursquare can issue on-target recommendations of other places to go. Did you visit a coffee shop on Elm Street? Foursquare thinks you might find the tea house on Oak Lane interesting as well. If another fellow fan of the local pizza joint also tends to check in at the movie theater down the street, Foursquare can suggest you might like it too.

But Foursquare isn't the only game in town. Facebook also allows users to check in at locations and has the advantage of a much larger social network—more than 800 million users, compared with Foursquare's 10 million or so.[70] Thus Facebook fans can tag friends who are with them, to show how many people are showing up at a particular location. This tool means Facebook can learn about its users and the places they or their friends like to go to. Marketers then can use this information to learn more about their customers, including the places they prefer and how those preferences align with their other interests—as communicated by their Facebook profile.

Internet everywhere through services like WiFi, 3G, and 4G. Smartphones using the Apple, RIM, Android, and Symbian operating systems allow for greater computing, data storage, and communication. Tablet computers, starting with the iPad, have extended mobile computing even further by offering a larger mobile interface in environments that traditionally limited access.

These examples of advanced technology make consumers increasingly dependent on the help they can provide, especially in terms of making decisions and communicating with others. Thus Netflix suggests which movies we should watch, Pandora outlines the music we should listen to, and Amazon tells us what we should read. Near field communication technology takes payments, coupons, and loyalty card data from customers as they walk by the scanner. The next wave of mobile applications is likely to involve wireless payments, such that customers' phones also serve as "m-wallets."

From the firm's perspective, the technology called RFID (radio frequency identification device) enables it to track an item from the moment it was manufactured, through the distribution system, to the retail store, and into the hands of the final consumer. Because they are able to determine exactly how much of each product is at a given point in the supply chain, retailers can also communicate with their suppliers and collaboratively plan to meet their inventory needs.

As Social and Mobile Marketing 5.1 shows, mobile devices enhance the customer's experience, by making it easier to interact with the manufacturer or retailer or other customers, and they add a new channel of access, which makes customers more loyal and more likely to spend more with a particular retailer. Walgreens' applications, in addition to the Web Pickup service we described previously, allow customers to order prescriptions or review their prescription history, check the in-store inventories, and print photos. Steve Madden, the footwear retailer, attracts more than 10 percent of its web traffic from mobile devices—which earns it more than $1 million in mobile sales annually. Furthermore, these shoppers spend an average of seven minutes on Steve Madden's mobile site.[71] Whereas customers view an average of seven web pages during online visits, they browse only four or five pages in a mobile setting.

Mobile applications are not just about shopping with a phone. By 2015, people will access the web more often through smartphones than through laptops and desktops combined. But mobile experiences cannot be identical to web experiences, because the interface is different, and thus the way users employ the sites differ. In particular, the smaller screen on mobile devices means that less information must convey the same brand image.

Economic Situation

Marketers monitor the general economic situation, both in their home country and abroad, because it affects the way consumers buy merchandise and spend money. Some major factors that influence the state of an economy include the rate of inflation, foreign currency exchange rates, and interest rates.

Inflation refers to the persistent increase in the prices of goods and services. Increasing prices cause the purchasing power of the dollar to decline; in other words, the dollar buys less than it used to.

In a similar fashion, foreign currency fluctuations can influence consumer spending. For instance, in the summer of 2002, the euro was valued at slightly less than US$1. By the middle of 2011, it was worth $1.35, but only after it had risen to an all-time high of $1.60 in 2008.[72] As the euro becomes more expensive compared with the dollar, merchandise made in Europe and other countries tied to the euro becomes more costly to Americans, whereas products made in the United States cost less for European consumers. In contrast, the current European financial crisis indicates shrinking value of the euro relative to the U.S. dollar, in which case Europeans might buy fewer American goods.

This crisis that is shaking European economies and the Euro Zone as a whole has several other potential impacts on the U.S. economy. European consumers purchase approximately 22 percent of U.S. exports, a rate that could easily drop if Greece, Italy, and other at-risk economies fail. In addition, global financial markets are closely connected, such that when one falls, everyone suffers.[73]

Finally, interest rates represent the cost of borrowing money. When customers borrow money from a bank, they agree to pay back the loan, plus the interest that accrues. The interest, in effect, is the cost to the customers or the fee the bank charges those customers for borrowing the money. Likewise, if a customer opens a savings account at a bank, he or she will earn interest on the amount saved, which means the interest becomes the fee the consumer gets for "loaning" the money to the bank. If the interest rate goes up, consumers have an incentive to save more, because they earn more for loaning the bank their money; when interest rates go down, however, consumers generally borrow more.

Tourists from other countries flock to the United States to shop because the value of the dollar is low compared to their own currency.

How do these three important economic factors—inflation, foreign currency fluctuations, and interest rates—affect firms' ability to market goods and services? Shifts in the three economic factors make marketing easier for some and harder for others. For instance, when inflation increases, consumers probably don't buy less food, but they may shift their expenditures from expensive steaks to less expensive hamburgers. Grocery stores and inexpensive restaurants win, but expensive restaurants lose. Consumers also buy less discretionary merchandise, though off-price and discount retailers often gain ground at the expense of their full-price competitors. Similarly, the sale of expensive jewelry, fancy cars, and extravagant vacations decrease, but the sale of low-cost luxuries, such as personal care products and home entertainment, tends to increase.

Political/Regulatory Environment

The **political/regulatory environment** comprises political parties, government organizations, and legislation and laws. Organizations must fully understand and comply with any legislation regarding fair competition, consumer protection, or industry-specific regulation. Since the turn of the century, the government has enacted laws that promote both fair trade and competition by prohibiting the formation of monopolies or alliances that would damage a competitive marketplace, fostering fair pricing practices for all suppliers and consumers.

The government enacts laws focused on insuring that companies compete fairly with one another. Although enacted in the early part of the twentieth century, they remain the backbone of U.S. legislation protecting competition in commerce. These laws include the 1890 Sherman Antitrust Act that prohibits monopolies and other activities that would restrain trade or competition and makes fair trade within a free market a national goal; the 1914 Clayton Act that supports the Sherman Act by prohibiting the combination of two or more competing corporations through pooling ownership of stock and restricting pricing policies such as price discrimination, exclusive dealing, and tying clauses to different buyers; and the 1936 Robison-Patman Act that specifically outlaws price discrimination toward wholesalers, retailers, or other producers and requires sellers to make ancillary services or allowances available to all buyers on proportionately equal terms. These laws have been specifically used to increase competition, such as the deregulation of the telephone and energy industries, in which massive conglomerates like Ma Bell, the nickname for AT&T, were broken into smaller, competing companies.

If Greece's economy continues to erode, what will be its impact on the value of the U.S. dollar vis a vie the euro?

Legislation has also been enacted to protect consumers in a variety of ways. First, regulations require marketers to abstain from false or misleading advertising practices that might mislead consumers, such as claims that a medication can cure a disease when in fact it causes other health risks. Second, manufacturers are required to refrain from using any harmful or hazardous materials (e.g., lead in toys) that might place a consumer at risk. Third, organizations must adhere to fair and reasonable business practices when they communicate with consumers. For example, they must employ reasonable debt collection methods and disclose any finance charges, and they are limited with regard to their telemarketing and e-mail solicitation activities. A summary of the most significant legislation affecting marketing interests appears in Exhibit 5.6.

Responding to the Environment

As the examples throughout this chapter show, many companies engage in tactics and marketing strategies that attempt to respond to multiple developments in the wider environment. For example, responding to pressures from the Federal Communications Commission (political and regulatory environment), the economic status of consumers (economic situation), increasing access to faster broadband capabilities (technological advances), and calls for greater social responsibility (social trends), 14 cable companies agreed to provide low-cost Internet access to impoverished families.[74] This remarkable agreement allows the cable companies to promote their social responsibility. But it also ensures that families whose children

EXHIBIT 5.6   Consumer Protection Legislation

Year	Law	Description
1906	Federal Food and Drug Act	Created the Food and Drug Administration. Prohibited the manufacture or sale of adulterated or fraudulently labeled food and drug products.
1914	Federal Trade Commission	Established the Federal Trade Commission (FTC) to regulate unfair competitive practices and practices that deceive or are unfair to consumers.
1966	Fair Packaging and Labeling Act	Regulates packaging and labeling of consumer goods; requires manufacturers to state the contents of the package, who made it, and the amounts contained within.
1966	Child Protection Act	Prohibits the sale of harmful toys and components to children. Sets the standard for child-resistant packaging.
1967	Federal Cigarette Labeling and Advertising Act	Requires cigarette packages to display this warning: "Warning: The Surgeon General Has Determined that Cigarette Smoking Is Dangerous to Your Health."
1972	Consumer Product Safety Act	Created the Consumer Product Safety Commission, which has the authority to regulate safety standards for consumer products.
1990	Children's Television Act	Limits the number of commercials shown during children's programming.
1990	Nutrition Labeling and Education Act	Requires food manufacturers to display nutritional contents on product labels.
1995	Telemarketing Sales Rule	Regulates fraudulent activities conducted over the telephone. Violators are subject to fines and actions enforced by the FTC.
2003	Controlling the Assault of Non-Solicited Pornography and Marketing Act of 2003 (CAN-SPAM Act)	Prohibits misleading commercial e-mail, particularly misleading subject and from lines.
2003	Amendment to the Telemarketing Sales Rule	Establishes a National Do Not Call Registry, requiring telemarketers to abstain from calling consumers who opt to be placed on the list.
2003	Do Not Spam Law	Laws created to reduce spam or unwarranted e-mails.
2010	Financial Reform Law	Created the Consumer Financial Protection Bureau whose aim will be to enforce appropriate consumer-oriented regulations on a number of financial firms, such as banks, mortgage businesses, and payday and student lenders. It also sent up the Financial Services Oversight Council to act as an early warning system.

are eligible for free lunch programs can gain access to the services, opportunities, and options available only online.

We noted the remarkable growth in health and wellness markets, including yoga, previously. Lululemon was one company that was quick to notice the trend and respond with great success. Its yoga pants average $98 per pair—a high price point in the market—but its image as a small, niche brand with a yoga-centric philosophy has helped it succeed.[75]

In a constantly changing marketing environment, the marketers that succeed are the ones that respond quickly, accurately, and sensitively to their consumers.

CHECK YOURSELF

1. What are the six key macroenvironmental factors?
2. Differentiate between country culture and regional culture.
3. Identify the different generational cohorts.
4. What are some important social trends shaping consumer values and shopping behavior?

Summing Up

LO1 **Outline how customers, the company, competitors, and corporate partners affect marketing strategy.**

Everything a firm does should revolve around the customer; without the customer, nothing gets sold. Firms must discover their customers' wants and needs and then be able to provide a valuable product or service that will satisfy those wants or needs. If there were only one firm and many customers, a marketer's life would be a piece of cake. But because this situation rarely occurs, firms must monitor their competitors to discover how they might be appealing to their customers. Without competitive intelligence, a firm's customers might soon belong to its competitors. Though life certainly would be easier without competitors, it would be difficult, if not impossible, without corporate partners. Good marketing firms or departments work closely with suppliers, marketing research firms, consultants, and transportation firms to coordinate the extensive process of discovering what customers want and finally getting it to them when and where they want it. Each of these activities—discovering customer needs, studying competitors' actions, and working with corporate partners—helps add value to firms' products and services.

LO2 **Explain why marketers must consider their macroenvironment when they make decisions.**

What are the chances that a fast-food hamburger restaurant would be successful in a predominantly Hindu neighborhood? Not good. Marketers must be sensitive to such cultural issues to be successful, and they must also consider customer demographics—age, income, market size, education, gender, and ethnicity—to identify specific customer target groups. In any society, major social trends influence the way people live. In no other time in history has technology moved so rapidly and had such a pervasive influence on the way we live. Not only do marketers help identify and develop technologies for practical, everyday uses, but technological advances help marketers provide consumers with more products and services more quickly and efficiently. The general state of the economy influences how people spend their discretionary income. When the economy is healthy, marketing success comes relatively easily. But when the economy gets bumpy, only well-honed marketing skills can yield long-term successes. Naturally, all firms must abide by the law, and many legal issues affect marketing directly. These laws pertain to competitive practices and protecting consumers from unfair or dangerous products.

LO3 **Describe the differences among the various generational cohorts.**

Generational cohorts are groups of consumers of the same generation. They are likely to have similar purchase and consumption behaviors due to their shared experiences and stages of life. The four main types include Gen Z (born 2001–2014), Gen Y (born 1977–2000), Gen X (1965–1976), and Baby Boomers (1946–1964). Each of these segments exhibits different consumption patterns, attitudes toward the world, and preferences with regard to marketing efforts.

LO4 **Identify various social trends that impact marketing.**

Social trends have a tremendous impact on what consumers purchase and consume. Understanding these trends—such as thrift, health and wellness, green marketing, privacy issues, and the time-poor society—can help marketers serve their customers better.

Key Terms

- Baby Boomers, 154
- country culture, 150
- culture, 150
- demographics, 151
- Digital Natives, 152
- foreign currency fluctuations, 164
- Generation X, 152
- Generation Y, 152
- Generation Z, 152
- generational cohort, 151
- green marketing, 160
- greenwashing, 160
- inflation, 164
- interest rates, 164
- macroenvironmental factors, 149
- Millennials, 152
- political/regulatory environment, 165
- regional culture, 150

Marketing Applications

1. Assume you are going to open a new store selling fitness products. Describe it. Who are your competitors? What would you do to monitor your competitors' actions? Who are your customers? What are you going to do to appeal to them? What are your social responsibilities, and how will you meet them?

2. In which generational cohort do you belong? What about your parents? How do you approach buying a computer differently than your parents would? What about buying an outfit to wear to a party? How can firms use their knowledge of generational cohorts to market their products and services better?

3. How can firms use customer demographics like income, market size, education, and ethnicity to market to their customers better?

4. Identify some of the ethnicity changes in the United States. Describe how they might affect the marketing practices of (a) a radio station in Texas, (b) food retailers in cities, and (c) a home furnishing store in New York City.

5. Identify some recent technological innovations in the marketplace and describe how they have affected consumers' everyday activities.

6. Why should a T-shirt shop in the United States care about the value of the Hong Kong dollar?

7. Time-poor consumers have adopted various approaches to "buy" themselves more time, such as (a) voluntarily simplifying their complex lives, (b) using new technologies for greater empowerment and control, (c) using their time productively when traveling or commuting, and (d) multitasking. Identify and describe some products and services that consumers use to implement each of these strategies.

8. Identify a company that you believe does a particularly good job of marketing to different cultural groups. Justify your answer.

 www.mhhe.com/ grewal4e

Quiz Yourself

1. Recently, Jason, one of the few Americans who has not registered with the Do Not Call Registry, received a call from a marketer suggesting Jason needed additional insurance since he had just become a father and changed jobs. Jason was shocked and very concerned about:
   a. his financial situation
   b. his lack of privacy
   c. the marketer's lack of cultural awareness
   d. his telephone bill
   e. his technological comfort

2. Many American consumers are purchasing hybrid automobiles even though they are more expensive when compared to compact conventional cars. Automobile marketers recognize that these consumers:
   a. value contributing to a greener environment
   b. are economically irrational
   c. are responding to global corporate pressure for social responsibility
   d. would prefer an SUV
   e. all of the above

(Answers to these two questions can be found on page 647.)

Go to www.mhhe.com/grewal4e to practice an additional 11 questions.

Net Savvy

1. Seventh Generation is the leading brand of non-toxic, environmentally safe household products in the United States. Visit its website (http://www.seventhgeneration.com) and review the philosophy behind the business. Next, review the site to identify the products the company offers. Briefly summarize some of the consumer trends you think are reflected. Describe the ways in which Seventh Generation's products address the wants and needs of its customers.

2. Visit The Cool Hunter (http://www.thecoolhunter.net) and identify examples that would provide marketers insights regarding social trends.

A NEXT-GENERATION CLEANSER[76]

Taking an Iroquois directive—"In our every deliberation, we must consider the impact of our decisions on the next seven generations"—the consumer product company Seventh Generation has applied a distinctly modern sensibility to derive a long-term approach to the marketing environment. Although its mission statement might be focused on future generations, its efforts to appeal to current consumers are always responsive to their immediate demands.

From its start in Vermont in 1988, Seventh Generation has grown to become a national brand with over $150 million in revenues. Its growth has been sparked largely by consumer desires to buy more sustainable, environmentally safe, green products. Approximately 73 percent of consumers in a recent survey indicated that they thought it was important to buy green offerings, and consumer demand for products in a wide range of categories continues to grow.[77]

But even as more categories appear to offer promising green opportunities for marketers, the primary purchase area continues to be groceries and household products—exactly the space that Seventh Generation dominates. As it has gained brand recognition and trust, it also has proactively altered its market. That is, Seventh Generation does not simply wait for customers to request options. It creates entirely new categories.

Seventh Generation dominates the environmentally friendly cleaning products market in the United States.

With a new line of detergents, Seventh Generation began promoting the idea that perhaps chemical brighteners—common to virtually all commercially available detergents, even those that avoid dyes or fragrances—are not necessary. The company took care not to suggest these chemicals were dangerous. It just says they're unnecessary, and for consumers interested in environmental concerns, that may be enough.

Previously, household magazines such as *Good Housekeeping* or *Real Simple* might rank the best detergent, the best dishwashing soap, and the best surface cleaner. But the entry of companies such as Seventh Generation has created new categories: best green detergent, best green dishwashing soap, and best green cleaner. Seventh Generation products consistently emerge victorious in these new category contests.[78]

In addition, to maintain its brand recognition, it uses extensive, multimedia marketing initiatives. In print ads, it highlights the environmentally friendly contents of its laundry detergent. It provides free samples to active bloggers, along with blacklights so these consumers can test their own clothes to see the residues left by other detergents. Dozens have posted the results of their own in-home experiments.[79]

Yet its products also cost more, which offers a significant challenge in a recessionary economy. Many consumer product companies are touting their downmarket brands, even as Seventh Generation introduces a 4× concentrated laundry detergent that costs significantly more. The new derivation avoids all volatile organic compounds and relies on enzymes to get clothes clean.[80] That may be appealing to some consumers, but can they afford to pay for expensive enzymes included in every load of laundry?

Questions

1. What consumer trends does Seventh Generation respond to most effectively?
2. Which consumer trends might it be missing?

Understanding the Marketplace

The three chapters in Section Two, Understanding the Marketplace, focus on three levels of marketing: to individual consumers; from business to business; and on the global playing field. Chapter 6, Consumer Behavior, discusses why individual consumers purchase products and services. The consumer decision process is highlighted. Chapter 7, Business-to-Business Marketing, explores the whys and hows of business-to-business buying. Finally, Chapter 8, Global Marketing, focuses on global markets. Thus, the three chapters in Section Two move from creating value for the individual consumer, to creating value for the firm or business, to creating value on the global level.

SECTION 2

Understanding the Marketplace

The three chapters in Section Two, Understanding the Marketplace, focus on three levels of marketing: to individual consumers; from business to business; and on the global playing field. Chapter 6, Consumer Behavior, discusses why individual consumers purchase products and services. The consumer decision process is highlighted. Chapter 7, Business-to-Business Marketing, explores the whys and hows of business-to-business buying. Finally, Chapter 8, Global Marketing, focuses on global markets. Thus, the three chapters in Section Two move from creating value for the individual consumer, to creating value for the firm or business, to creating value on the global level.

SECTION 2

CHAPTER 6

Consumer Behavior

As first-year students arrive on college campuses to begin the fall semester, they often are greeted by smiling upper-class students, offering to help them locate their rooms or unload their cars.[1] Other experienced students are on hand to assist newcomers with the purchase of a laptop or to invite them to one of the highlights of back-to-school week, a combined party and late-night shopping excursion. Thoughtful people helping rookies settle in? Maybe.

These goodwill ambassadors are also student marketers, paid by companies such as American Eagle Outfitters, Hewlett-Packard, and Red Bull, to hawk products on campus and through social networks. Even the first big college party is a marketing event in this case, sponsored by Target. Bused by the retail giant to a local superstore, first-year students dance to music spun by a DJ, collect free samples of junk food, and win prizes such as refrigerators and cases of soda—all while shopping for more room furnishings for their dorms.

Using students to promote goods to their peers and classmates gives manufacturers the credibility of word-of-mouth advertising and direct contact with a market segment worth about $36 billion a year. Students promoting the brand and those experiencing it for the first time can become fans and spread the word to their families and high school friends. They can also form a habit and continue purchasing the same brand of toothpaste, smartphone, or jeans as they build their careers and families. This potential to attract new consumers and influence their lifetime shopping behavior, just by marketing to college students, is so significant that two companies that seemingly should function as competitors, Ford Motor Company and Zipcar, have joined forces to take advantage of the opportunities.[2]

A Zipcar, available by the hour for a low rental fee, theoretically might eliminate a student's need to own a car. It thus might steal a customer from Ford. But a Zipcar rental also may be an opportunity for a young driver to test a car model and become comfortable driving it. This familiarity can translate, over time, into a purchase or even repeat purchases. This logic motivated Ford to provide Zipcar with up to 1,000 Ford Focus sedans for use on 250 U.S. college and

LEARNING OBJECTIVES

LO1 Articulate the steps in the consumer buying process.

LO2 Describe the difference between functional and psychological needs.

LO3 Describe factors that affect information search.

LO4 Discuss postpurchase outcomes.

LO5 List the factors that affect the consumer decision process.

LO6 Describe how involvement influences the consumer decision process.

The Zipcar/Ford alliance is designed to appeal to college students and get them hooked on Ford products.

university campuses.[3] With its advanced technology features and fuel efficiency, the Focus is particularly alluring to younger drivers. But Ford further sweetened the deal for students by offering $10 off Zipcar's annual membership fee and a $1 per hour discount on the hourly rental fee for students renting a Ford. Zipcar is also purchasing a few Ford Escape sport utility vehicles, which will be available at discounted fees too.

The alliance helps Ford tap into the spending that college students allow themselves. It also gives them a relatively low-cost way to control the early driving experiences of future car buyers, because the deal means that more than half of all Zipcar vehicles available on U.S. campuses will be Fords. The manufacturer's 20 or so rivals are left to divvy up the remains. The relationship helps Zipcar by increasing its presence on college campuses, but also by increasing the number of U.S. cars it can advertise as being in the company's fleet.

As these events and developments show, companies such as Target, Zipcar, and Ford recognize the value of reaching young buyers to shape both their current and future consumer behavior. By using peer-to-peer endorsements and other approaches that resonate with college students, these companies are creating life-long customers, whose behaviors will continue to benefit the firms.

We are all consumers, and we take this status for granted. But we are also complex and irrational creatures who cannot always explain our own choices and actions. This inability makes the vitally important job of marketing managers even more difficult, in that they must be able to explain consumers' behavior to give marketers as clear an understanding of their customers as possible.

To understand consumer behavior, we must ask *why* people buy goods or services. Using principles and theories from sociology and psychology, marketers have been able to decipher many consumer choices and develop basic strategies for dealing with consumers' behavior. Generally, people buy one product or service instead of another because they perceive it to be the better value for them; that is, the ratio of benefits to costs is higher for the product or service than for any other.[4]

However, "benefits" can be subtle and less than rationally assessed, as we shall see. Consider Katie Smith, who is considering a dress purchase for a job interview. She requires something fashionable but professional looking, and doesn't want to spend a lot of money. In making the decision about where she should buy the dress, Katie asks herself:

- Which alternative gives me the best overall value—the most appropriate, yet fashionable dress at the lowest price?

- Which alternative is the best investment—the dress that I can get the most use of?

Because Katie might have several different reasons to choose a particular store or dress, it is critical for companies like Ann Taylor or Macy's to key in on the specific benefits that are most important to her. Other factors that might influence Katie go beyond her conscious awareness, which means that the retailers need to be even more well-versed in her decision process than she is.[5] Only then can they create a marketing mix that will satisfy Katie.

In this chapter, we explore the process that consumers go through when they buy products and services. Then we discuss the psychological, social, and situational factors that influence this consumer decision process. Throughout the chapter, we emphasize what firms can do to influence consumers to purchase their products and services.

LO1 Articulate the steps in the consumer buying process.

THE CONSUMER DECISION PROCESS

The consumer decision process model represents the steps that consumers go through before, during, and after making purchases.[6] Because marketers often find it difficult to determine how consumers make their purchasing decisions, it is useful for us to break down the process into a series of steps and examine each individually, as in Exhibit 6.1.

Need Recognition

The consumer decision process begins when consumers recognize they have an unsatisfied need, and they would like to go from their actual, needy state to a different, desired state. The greater the discrepancy between these two states, the greater the **need recognition** will be. For example, your stomach tells you that you are hungry, and you would rather not have that particular feeling. If you are only a little hungry, you may pass it off and decide to eat later. But if your stomach is growling and you cannot concentrate, the *need*—the difference between your actual (hungry) state and your desired (not hungry) state—is greater, and you'll want to eat immediately to get to your desired state. Furthermore, your hunger conceivably could be satisfied by a nice healthy salad, but what you really want is a bowl of ice cream. *Wants* are goods or services that are not necessarily needed but are desired.[7] Regardless of

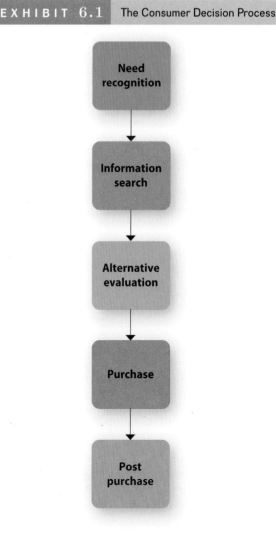

EXHIBIT 6.1   The Consumer Decision Process

- Need recognition
- Information search
- Alternative evaluation
- Purchase
- Post purchase

the level of your hunger, your desire for ice cream will never be satisfied by any type of salad. Consumer needs like these can be classified as functional, psychological, or both.[8]

Functional Needs **Functional needs** pertain to the performance of a product or service. For years, BMW has made functionally superior motorcycles. BMW's K1600 model has an inline-six cylinder motor, something previously available only in BMW automobiles, combined with a stiff aluminum frame. Thus it offers remarkable power on a lightweight bike, enabling it to outperform both the best luxury touring bikes in terms of comfort and serious sporty motorcycles in terms of speed.

Does this motorcycle satisfy functional or psychological needs?

Psychological Needs **Psychological needs** pertain to the personal gratification consumers associate with a product and/or service.[9] Shoes, for instance, provide a functional need—to keep feet clean and protect them from the elements. So why would anyone pay more than $1000 for shoes that may do neither? Because they seek to satisfy psychological needs. Christian Louboutin's shoes, with their signature red sole, may be the hottest shoe on the market.[10] Sarah Jessica Parker sports several pairs in *Sex and the City* and in real life; BMW even featured the shoe in a commercial. Virtually every modern fashion icon, including Penelope Cruz, Catherine Deneuve, Lady Gaga, Ashley Olsen, Beyoncé, and Angelina Jolie, have been photographed wearing Louboutin shoes. And yet a black python-and-lace shoe with a 14-cm heel is not a particularly practical means of spending $1500. As a result of all the media attention though, there is a strong demand for Louboutin shoes by women who love exciting (and expensive) shoes.

These examples highlight that the vast majority of goods and services are likely to satisfy both functional and psychological needs, albeit to different degrees. Whereas the functional characteristics of BMW K1600 are its main selling point, it also maintains a fashionable appeal for bikers and comes in several colors to match buyers' aesthetic preferences. In contrast, Christian Louboutin shoes satisfy psychological needs that overshadow the functional needs, though they still ultimately serve the function of a shoe.

Consider another, slightly more realistic example: You can get a $15 haircut at SuperCuts or spend $80 or more to get basically the same thing at an upscale salon. Are the two haircuts objectively different? The answer might vary depending on which you believe represents a good haircut and a good value: One person might value getting a really good deal; another might enjoy the extra attention and amenities associated with a fancy salon.

A key to successful marketing is determining the correct balance of functional and psychological needs that best appeals to the firm's target markets. Marriott is carefully balancing this fine line. In the modern economic environment, Marriott is focusing on what matters most to guests. Many hotel consumers just step on the newspapers delivered to their doors, without ever picking them up to read. The various Marriott brands—including Courtyard, Residence Inn, Fairfield Inn, and the

Do Christian Louboutin's shoes satisfy functional or psychological needs?

Mariott focuses on what is really important to its customers. But they save money by switching from Haagen-Dazs to Edy's brand ice cream.

Ritz-Carlton—therefore have discontinued deliveries of approximately 50,000 papers daily. The cost savings enable Marriott to avoid massive layoffs, which supports its core value of taking care of employees and thereby encouraging them to treat customers well. The switch to Edy's brand ice cream, instead of Haagen-Dazs, saves money and facilitates employees' jobs, because the less dense dessert is easier to scoop. Yet even as it cuts costs, Marriott recognizes the need to attract more customers, so it offers free nights and discounted rates, including $85 in Medan, Indonesia, and $120 at a casino and beach resort in Curaçao.

Search for Information

The second step, after a consumer recognizes a need, is to search for information about the various options that exist to satisfy that need. The length and intensity of the search are based on the degree of perceived risk associated with purchasing the product or service. If the way your hair is cut is important to your appearance and self-image, you may engage in an involved search for the right salon and stylist. Alternatively, an athlete looking for a short "buzz" cut might go to the closest, most convenient, and cheapest barber shop. Regardless of the required search level, there are two key types of information search: internal and external.

Internal Search for Information In an **internal search for information**, the buyer examines his or her own memory and knowledge about the product or service, gathered through past experiences. For example, every time Katie wants to eat salad for lunch, she and her friends go to Sweet Tomatoes, but if she's craving dessert, she heads straight to The Cheesecake Factory. In making these choices, she relies on her memory of past experiences when she has eaten at these restaurant chains.

External Search for Information In an **external search for information**, the buyer seeks information outside his or her personal knowledge base to help make the buying decision. Consumers might fill in their personal knowledge gaps by talking with friends, family, or a salesperson. They can also scour commercial media for unsponsored and (it is hoped) unbiased information, such as that available through *Consumer Reports*, or peruse sponsored media such as magazines, television, or radio. Sometimes consumers get commercial exposures to products or services without really knowing it. New media such as

Adding Value 6.1   How Fashion Blogs Sell Clothes

Sweatpants and T-shirts used to dominate fashion on college campuses. Now students and young professionals are upgrading their wardrobes, seeking ways to stay current with the rapid change in trends while expressing individuality through how they dress.[11] Where do they find their inspiration?

The time-honored approaches are to page through a fashion magazine, keep an eye on how peers dress, or consult with a friend. Now blogs are replacing magazines and expanding style choices, literally putting the world of fashion at a customer's fingertips. These blogs combine the sense of reliability that comes from peer-to-peer advice with the rapid access to information that today's shoppers have come to expect. The result is a marketing channel that is exerting increasing influence over consumer behavior.[12]

Fashion blogs use the Internet to connect designers and styles to the shoppers who are most likely to buy them, but they feature two distinct differences from passive websites: editors who control what appears on the site and contributors who post comments on what they see. One popular blog written by college women, College Fashion, provides fashion tips on subjects ranging from the must-have updates for a fall wardrobe to the top designers for teens and twenty-somethings.[13] Quizzes help site visitors decide which colors would suit their mood on a given day or which celebrity most inspires their style.[14] Clearly the editor's sense of style helps build followers, but the blog also creates a sense of community, providing a place where fashion-conscious young women can contribute their own point of view or proudly announce a new purchase.

At the other end of the fashion blog spectrum are professional sites, such as Refinery29, which offers separate editions for New York, Los Angeles, Chicago, San Francisco, and Washington DC. Multiple editors juggle blogs about various topics of interest, including diet tips and hair and makeup trends. As an added feature, the site goes beyond a discussion format, providing a members-only shopping site with exclusive offers from popular names in fashion, beauty, and decor. In addition to being able to peruse the site to see what's new, members receive e-mails announcing hot designers, stores, and websites.

Marketers are recognizing the value of these blogs to reach customers. Like College Fashion, Refinery29 and its competitor, FabSugar, host advertisements—yet another way for retailers to reach target markets. FabSugar, which contains

Professional fashion blogs such as Refinery 29 offer a members'—only shopping site, as well as tips on diet, hair and makeup trends.

posts on fashion, entertainment, sex and culture, food, money, pets, and even pregnancy and parenting, is considered one of the top 20 most influential fashion blogs.[15] With projected revenues of $8 million in its sixth year of business, Refinery29's blog demonstrates the ability of this marketing channel to generate both followers and sales.[16]

blogs are steadily becoming a major source of external information to consumers, as Adding Value 6.1 notes.

The Internet provides more information than that contained in blogs though.[17] For example, while watching an episode of CW's *Gossip Girl*, Katie saw the character Vanessa wearing a fantastic outfit consisting of a peasant blouse and leggings. She pulled her laptop over, went to Google and searched for "Shop the Look" and "Gossip Girl." She found a number of websites that carry news items and pictures of the characters. These websites also identify the prices for the various items worn by its characters. A long list of items included both the blouse and the leggings. The blouse was designed by Joie and available for sale for $248, and the leggings by LnA cost $105.[18] But Katie is also a savvy shopper, so she searched "lna leggings" on Google and found that through the company's site, she could get a cropped version on sale for only $45.[19] Satisfied with that purchase, she began flipping through a magazine and saw Reese Witherspoon wearing a pair of jeans she loved. This time, she navigated her mouse directly to www.MyTrueFit.com, which featured those very jeans, designed by 7 for All Mankind, on its homepage.[20] Katie entered her measurements and style preferences, and the website returned recommendations of jeans that would be a good fit for her.

All these types of search are examples of external searches for information. Katie used the television show's dedicated site to find a style she liked; she referred to a magazine for additional style tips; and she found jeans that will be a perfect fit for her using the web. All these events took place without Katie leaving her home to go to the store or try on dozens of pairs of pants.

Factors Affecting Consumers' Search Processes It is important for marketers to understand the many factors that affect consumers' search processes. Among them are the following three factors.

LO3 Describe factors that affect information search.

The Perceived Benefits versus Perceived Costs of Search Is it worth the time and effort to search for information about a product or service? For instance, most families spend a lot of time researching the housing market in their preferred area before they make a purchase because homes are a very expensive and important purchase with significant safety and enjoyment implications. They likely spend much less time researching which inexpensive dollhouse to buy for the youngest member of the family.

The Locus of Control People who have an internal locus of control believe they have some control over the outcomes of their actions, in which case they generally engage in more search activities. With an external locus of control, consumers believe that fate or other external factors control all outcomes. In that case, they believe it doesn't matter how much information they gather; if they make a wise decision, it isn't to their credit, and if they make a poor one, it isn't their fault. People who do a lot of research before purchasing individual stocks have an internal locus of control; those who purchase mutual funds are more likely to believe that they can't predict the market and probably have an external locus of control. These beliefs have widespread effects. For example, when people believe that they can choose their own consumption goals (internal locus of control), they work harder to achieve them than if those goals feel imposed upon them (external locus of control).[21]

You can find the clothing worn by Gossip Girl *characters online.*

Actual or Perceived Risk Five types of risk associated with purchase decisions can delay or discourage a purchase: performance, financial, social, physiological, and psychological. The higher the risk, the more likely the consumer is to engage in an extended search.

Performance risk involves the perceived danger inherent in a poorly performing product or service. An example of performance risk is the possibility that Katie Smith's new interview dress is prone to shrinking when dry cleaned.

Financial risk is risk associated with a monetary outlay and includes the initial cost of the purchase, as well as the costs of using the item or service.[22] Katie is not only concerned that her new dress will provide her with the professional appearance she is seeking, but also that the cost of dry cleaning will not be exorbitant. Retailers recognize buying professional apparel can be a financial burden and therefore offer guarantees that the products they sell will perform as expected. Their suppliers are also well aware that dry cleaning is expensive and can limit the life of the garment, so many offer easy-to-care-for washable fabrics.

Social risk involves the fears that consumers suffer when they worry others might not regard their purchases positively. When buying a dress, consumers like Katie consider what their friends would like. Alternatively, because this job interview is so important, Katie might make a conscious effort to assert a distinctive identity or make a statement by buying a unique, more stylish, and possibly more expensive dress than her friends would typically buy.

Physiological risk could also be called **safety risk**. Whereas performance risk involves what might happen if a product does not perform as expected, physiological (or safety) risk refers to the fear of an actual harm should the product not perform properly. Although physiological risk is typically not an issue with apparel, it can be an important issue when buying other products, such as a car. External agencies and government bodies publish safety ratings for cars to help assuage this risk. Consumers compare the safety records of their various choices, because they recognize the real danger to their well-being if the automobile they purchase fails to perform a basic task, such as stopping when the driver steps on the brakes or protecting the passengers in the cabin even if the car flips.

Another major physiological risk pertains to growing concerns about health risks associated with the food and beverages we consume. McDonald's has come under a lot of associated scrutiny recently, especially in response to *Supersize Me* and related media (see Ethical and Societal Dilemma 6.1).

Finally, **psychological risks** are those risks associated with the way people will feel if the product or service does not convey the right image. Katie Smith, thinking of her dress purchase, read several fashion magazines and sought her friends' opinions because she wanted people to think she looked great in the dress, and she wanted to get the job!

Recent research suggests that psychological risks might help explain why consumers enjoy "supersizing" their menu options. Especially when consumers feel powerless or more vulnerable, they equate larger sizes—whether in televisions, houses, or menu items—with improved status. That is, consumers who feel powerless choose bigger food portions to gain a sense of status.[23]

Evaluation of Alternatives

Once a consumer has recognized a problem and explored the possible options, he or she must sift through the choices available and evaluate the alternatives. Alternative evaluation often occurs while the consumer is engaged in the process of information search. For example, Katie Smith would rule out various stores because she knows they won't carry the style she needs for the job interview. Once in the store, she would try on lots of dresses and eliminate those that don't fit, don't look good on her, or aren't appropriate attire for the occasion. Consumers forgo alternative evaluations altogether when buying habitual (convenience) products; you'll rarely catch a loyal Pepsi drinker buying Coca-Cola.

Attribute Sets Research has shown that a consumer's mind organizes and categorizes alternatives to aid his or her decision process. **Universal sets** include all

Ethical and Societal Dilemma 6.1   The Obesity Epidemic and Fast Foods

Filmmaker Morgan Spurlock has shown us that a steady fast-food diet can be downright dangerous. Thirty days of eating nothing but McDonald's hamburgers, fries, and shakes turned Spurlock—who started the experiment as a healthy 32-year-old man—into an overweight, depressed, and dysfunctional guy with soaring cholesterol levels and liver trouble.

Today, 42 percent of low-income women in the United States are obese,[24] and there is a growing consensus that an overreliance on fast food and junk food has contributed significantly to this health problem. Although marketing is certainly a major factor in attracting customers to McDonald's and other fast-food restaurants, health experts also have shown that multiple other factors also drive obesity-promoting habits.[25]

In particular, working moms with little time to cook appreciate the convenience of fast foods. Families on a tight budget like these low-cost menus. And the fast-food industry has learned to cater to America's taste for foods high in sugar, salt, and fat, which turn into near-addictive desires. Combine those high-calorie habits with a sedentary or car-dependent lifestyle that rarely includes exercise, and you have a prescription for obesity.

The problem is especially serious among children. One Harvard School of Public Health physician noted that children aged 2 to 19 years consume 7 trillion calories through sugar-sweetened beverages a year, fueling a $24 billion industry for kids.[26] It's just one major factor in the 17 percent obesity rate among U.S. youth.

Efforts to revise food labels so that they clearly tell consumers whether a meal or a supermarket item contains unhealthy ingredients have been blocked successfully by the food industry. But McDonald's—the focus of significant pressures from both health advocates and parents, as well as the defendant in at least one lawsuit alleging that its high-fat menu caused obesity-related health damage to two children (*Pelman v. McDonald's Corp.*, 237 F. Supp. 2d 512 [S.D.N.Y. January 22, 2003])—has decided to change some of its ways.

The company has announced a planned 20 percent reduction in the calorie count of its Happy Meals. But it declined to voluntarily jettison the toys that come along with the Happy Meal, a marketing hook that has long made this item one of the most popular on the kids' menu. Lawmakers and parents seeking to break the childhood link between toys and fast food have demanded that such toy giveaways be banned. San Francisco was the first city to enforce such

In the film Super Size Me, *filmmaker Morgan Spurlock ate nothing but McDonald's food for thirty days. He gained weight, became depressed, and developed high cholesterol and liver trouble.*

a law; in response, the restaurant chain chose to charge a dime for each toy, so that it could comply with the regulation but still make the toys easily accessible to its youthful customers.[27] McDonald's also has rejected calls to eliminate French fries altogether, along with its traditional soda. But the company says it will include apple slices with every order and reduce salt content by 2015.

Some critics are not impressed. Changes like a one-ounce reduction in French fries won't help kids much. But McDonald's small concessions should generate huge publicity for the company.

---

possible choices for a product category, but because it would be unwieldy for a person to recall all possible alternatives for every purchase decision, marketers tend to focus on only a subset of choices. One important subset is **retrieval sets**, which are those brands or stores that can be readily brought forth from memory. Another is a consumer's **evoked set**, which comprises the alternative brands or stores that the consumer states he or she would consider when making a purchase decision. If a firm can get its brand or store into a consumer's evoked set, it has increased the likelihood of purchase and therefore reduced search time because the consumer will think specifically of that brand when considering choices.

Katie Smith knows that there are a lot of apparel stores (universal set). However, only some have the style that she is looking for, such as Macy's, Ann Taylor, The Gap, and Banana Republic (retrieval set). She recalls that Ann Taylor is where her mother shops and The Gap is a favorite of her younger sister. But she is sure that Banana Republic and Macy's carry business attire she would like, so only those stores are in her evoked set.

When consumers begin to evaluate different alternatives, they often base their evaluations on a set of important attributes or evaluative criteria. Evaluative criteria consist of salient, or important, attributes about a particular product. For example, when Katie is looking for her dress, she might consider things like the selling price, fit, materials and construction quality, reputation of the brand, and the service support that the retailer offers. At times, however, it becomes difficult to evaluate different brands or stores because there are so many choices,[28] especially when those choices involve aspects of the garment that are difficult to evaluate, such as materials and construction quality.

Consumers utilize several shortcuts to simplify the potentially complicated decision process: determinant attributes and consumer decision rules. Determinant attributes are product or service features that are important to the buyer and on which competing brands or stores are perceived to differ.[29] Because many important and desirable criteria are equal among the various choices, consumers look for something special—a determinant attribute—to differentiate one brand or store from another. Determinant attributes may appear perfectly rational, such as health and nutrition claims offered by certain foods and beverages, or they may be more subtle and psychologically based, such as the red soles on a pair of Christian Louboutin heels. Ethical and Societal Dilemma 6.2 highlights the use of determinant attributes describing food and beverages marketed as natural when in fact they are not.

Consumer Decision Rules Consumer decision rules are the set of criteria that consumers use consciously or subconsciously to quickly and efficiently select

Ann Taylor is part of the retrieval set of stores available to women for business apparel, but Banana Republic is in the evoked set for young women looking for business apparel.

Ethical and Societal Dilemma 6.2 — Wearing the "Healthy" Label: Natural and Organic Foods

With competition for shelf space always at a premium, today's supermarket aisles are more crowded than ever. Much of the new competition comes from natural and organic foods, which comprised more than 4 percent of the $673 billion U.S. food industry in 2010.[30]

For a consumer facing a dizzying array of choices, these natural foods offer a unique appeal: They promise to improve personal and planetary health. Organic and natural food companies claim that their foods are safer and more nutritious because they are produced with only natural ingredients.

Consumers generally believe that these claims mean the food contains no artificial or highly processed ingredients.[31] Yet Snapple's "natural" bottled iced tea contains high-fructose corn syrup, a highly processed, and recently controversial, form of sugar. In California, most organic strawberry farmers use seeds and plants from nurseries that are not organic, including growers producing fruit for Driscoll Strawberry Associates, the largest berry distributor in the world.[32] The farmers argue that once their plants bear fruit, they halt their use of chemical pesticides and herbicides, so the berries themselves are still organic. These companies thus might be contradicting consumer expectations, but they are not actually violating federal requirements.

The U.S. Department of Agriculture (USDA) regulates the production of organic foods. Products bearing the "USDA Organic" label must be grown using organic, not conventional, farming methods.[33] That regulation means using natural fertilizers, such as manure or compost; beneficial insects or birds to control insects, rather than chemical insecticides; and crop rotation or other manual methods to control weeds, rather than chemical herbicides. Animals raised for meat production must be given organic feed and access to the outdoors, rather than antibiotics, growth hormones, and other medications.

Yet the USDA's National Organic Program (NOP) regulations do not explicitly govern the production of seeds and planting stock. Advocates who want to see sustainable production methods used throughout the food-growing process have called on the USDA to outlaw the use of chemical fumigants, including methyl bromide, a widely

used pesticide and soil sterilizer known to deplete the ozone layer.[34] Furthermore, the NOP regulations have not been updated since 2002; they allow conventional agricultural stock to be used whenever organically grown seeds and plants are not "commercially available."

Nor does the USDA regulate the production of foods labeled "natural," except for meats and poultry,[35] which must be minimally processed and free of artificial colors, flavors, sweeteners, preservatives, and ingredients. No such specifics govern other foods that choose to carry the "natural" label rather than an organic claim.

For the consumer, the organic and natural food experience is also about perception. Some shoppers may believe these foods deliver healthful benefits, but studies also reveal that simply identifying a grocery item as a "health food" may affect their eating experience. Students given snacks labeled "health bars" reported feeling hungry afterward and craving foods they enjoyed more. In another study, respondents widely perceived "that 'healthy' isn't going to meet enjoyment goals," which likely reflects consumers' assumption that "healthy foods won't taste good."[36]

How healthy is Snapple?

from among several alternatives. These rules are typically either compensatory or noncompensatory.

Compensatory A compensatory decision rule assumes that the consumer, when evaluating alternatives, trades off one characteristic against another, such that good characteristics compensate for bad characteristics.[37] For instance, Hanna Jackson is looking to buy breakfast cereal and is considering several factors such

EXHIBIT 6.2	Compensatory Purchasing Multi-Attribute Model for Buying Cereal				
	Taste	Calories	Natural /Organic Claims	Price	Overall Score
Importance Weight	0.4	0.1	0.3	0.2	
Cheerios	10	8	6	8	8.2
Post	8	9	8	3	7.1
Kashi	6	8	10	5	7.2

as taste, calories, price, and natural/organic claims. But even if the cereal is priced a little higher than Hanna was planning to spend, a superb overall rating offsets, or compensates for, the higher price.

Although Hanna probably would not go through the formal process of making the purchasing decision based on the **multi-attribute model** described in Exhibit 6.2, this exhibit illustrates how a compensatory model would work.[38] Hanna assigns weights to the importance of each factor. These weights must add up to 1.0. So, for instance, taste is the most important, with a weight of .4, and calories are least important, with a weight of .1. She assigns weights to how well each of the cereals might perform, with 1 being very poor and 10 being very good. Hanna thinks Cheerios has the best taste, so she assigns it a 10. Then she multiplies each performance rating by its importance rating to get an overall score for each cereal. The rating for Cheerios in this example is the highest of the three cereals $[(.4 \times 10) + (.1 \times 8) + (.3 \times 6) + (.2 \times 8) = 8.2]$. This multi-attribute model allows the trade-off between the various factors to be incorporated explicitly into a consumer's purchase decision.

Noncompensatory Sometimes however, consumers use a **noncompensatory decision rule**, in which they choose a product or service on the basis of one characteristic or one subset of a characteristic, regardless of the values of its other attributes.[39] Thus, though Cheerios received the highest overall score of 8.2, Hanna might still pick Kashi because she is particularly sensitive to claims of natural or organic contents, and this brand earned the highest score on this attribute (i.e., a 10).

Once a consumer has considered the possible alternatives and evaluated the pros and cons of each, he or she can move toward a purchase decision. Social and Mobile Marketing 6.1 illustrates how social networks help consumers choose among alternatives.

Social and Mobile Marketing 6.1 · Shopping Online with Friends[40]

At one time, you needed to convince friends to get in the car and go shopping with you to get their opinion on an item you were considering for purchase. Thanks to the Internet though, social shopping has become far easier and more user friendly, because consumers can bring along friends without anyone ever leaving their home. Applications, such as a technology called ShopTogether owned by Buy.com, allow for collaborations among friends on a retailer's site.

E-retailers with ShopTogether let customers bring their friends to the e-retailer so they can shop together. According to the company that produces ShopTogether, retailers using this technology find that shoppers place 25 percent more items in their carts, spend 400 percent more time on the site, and increase their order value by 50 percent. Other estimates indicate retailers also achieve a 15 percent increase in online sales and much higher conversion rates—that is, the number of browsing customers who become actual purchasing customers.

On the MAC beauty products website for example, the retailer allows customer to scan, browse independently, or see what friends are viewing, as well as show friends some items, chat with those friends, and then save the favorite items in a list. An instant messaging program allows up to four people to join in, each of whom can easily add products to the chat conversation to show others what they prefer. Other retailers using the ShopTogether technology include GNC, Mattel, and Charlotte Russe.

The teen apparel e-retailer Wet Seal uses Sesh.com, a sophisticated technology that shoppers can use to discuss products in a chat window. Friends also can write notes to others in the various sections and use a "pen" to draw on the site. One person controls the navigation at a time, guiding the others through the site as they discuss the products together.

Facebook's Stucck application even allows users to go beyond retailers' websites and post side-by-side comparisons of multiple product options they're "stuck" between in their decision. Then their social media contacts can vote on which option the consumer should choose. The application of course makes it easy for consumers to click quickly to a site to buy the favored choice.

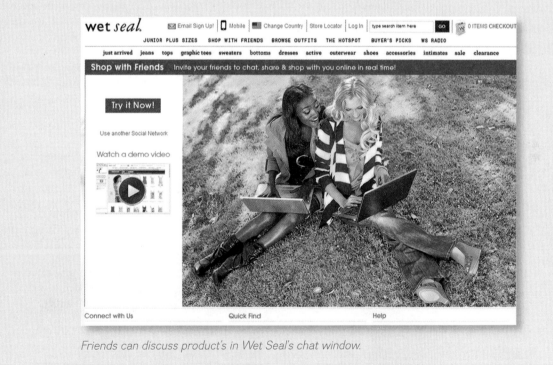

Friends can discuss product's in Wet Seal's chat window.

Purchase and Consumption

After evaluating the alternatives, customers are ready to buy. However, they don't always patronize the store or purchase the brand or item on which they had originally decided. It may not be available at the retail store, for example. Retailers therefore turn to the **conversion rate** to measure how well they have converted purchase intentions into purchases. One method of measuring the conversion rate is the number of real or virtual abandoned carts in the retailer's store or website.

Retailers use various tactics to increase the chances that customers will convert their positive evaluations into purchases. They can reduce the number of abandoned carts by making it easier to purchase merchandise. Most important, they should have plenty of stock on hand of the merchandise that customers want. They can also reduce the actual wait time to buy merchandise by opening more checkout lanes and placing them conveniently inside the store. To reduce perceived wait times, they might install digital displays to entertain customers waiting in line.[41]

For different types of companies, the conversion rate also refers to rentals (e.g., Netflix) or to outright purchases (e.g., haute couture), though some of these lines appear to be blurring as consumers seek new ways to access the items they want. At Rent the Runway, fashion- and budget-conscious shoppers gain temporary possession of the latest fashions from big names, including Badgley Mischka, Kate Spade, and Vera Wang. As if they were dealing with movies on DVDs, members rent haute couture dresses, handbags, jewelry, and even wedding gowns; pay anywhere between $50 and $400 for their chosen items; receive the glam wear in the mail within a few days; and then return the items after their fabulous affair has ended.[42] At the same time, Warner Bros. is working on a new idea to get movie renters to start buying more of its offerings. It purchased Flixster, the movie buff website, and initiated UltraViolet, a movie storage service that enables viewers to purchase a movie once and then access it on any of their connected devices (e.g., computer, tablet, smartphone, web-ready television).[43]

But conversion rates still tend to be lower for consumers using an Internet channel, because they are able to look at products and throw them in their cart, but still delay their purchase decision. To encourage customers to make purchase decisions, Zappos.com and Overstock.com create urgency by alerting customers when an item they have put it in their shopping cart is almost sold out. Other sites, such as Gilt, offer items for specified 36-hour periods or until they run out, and Neiman Marcus runs two-hour, online-only sales. Many retailers send reminder e-mails to visitors about items in carts they have abandoned.[44]

LO4 Discuss postpurchase outcomes.

Postpurchase

The final step of the consumer decision process is postpurchase behavior. Marketers are particularly interested in postpurchase behavior because it entails actual rather than potential customers. Satisfied customers, whom marketers hope to create, become loyal, purchase again, and spread positive word of mouth, so

Gilt.com encourages customers to buy now by offering a limited number of items for short time period.

EXHIBIT 6.3 Postpurchase Outcomes

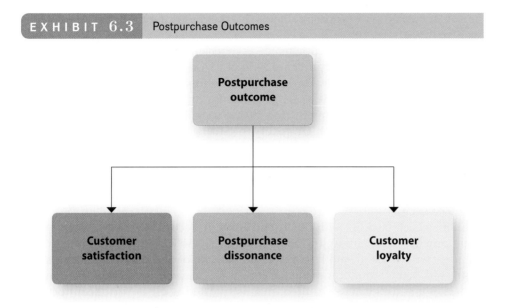

they are quite important. There are three possible positive postpurchase outcomes as illustrated in Exhibit 6.3: customer satisfaction, postpurchase cognitive dissonance, and customer loyalty (or disloyalty).

Customer Satisfaction Setting unrealistically high consumer expectations of the product through advertising, personal selling, or other types of promotion may lead to higher initial sales, but it eventually will result in dissatisfaction if the product fails to achieve high performance expectations (for a related discussion about communication gaps, see Chapter 13). This failure can lead to dissatisfied customers and the potential for negative word of mouth.[45] Setting customer expectations too low is an equally dangerous strategy. Many retailers don't "put their best foot forward." For instance, no matter how good the merchandise and service may be, if a store is not clean and appealing from the entrance, customers are not likely to enter.

Marketers can take several steps to ensure postpurchase satisfaction though, such as to:

- Build realistic expectations, not too high and not too low.
- Demonstrate correct product use—improper usage can cause dissatisfaction.
- Stand behind the product or service by providing money-back guarantees and warranties.
- Encourage customer feedback, which cuts down on negative word of mouth and helps marketers adjust their offerings.
- Periodically make contact with customers and thank them for their support. This contact reminds customers that the marketer cares about their business and wants them to be satisfied. It also provides an opportunity to correct any problems. Customers appreciate human contact, though it is more expensive for marketers than e-mail or postal mail contacts.

Postpurchase Cognitive Dissonance **Postpurchase cognitive dissonance** is an internal conflict that arises from an inconsistency between two beliefs, or between beliefs and behavior. For example, you might have buyer's remorse after purchasing an expensive TV because you question after all whether a high-price TV is appreciably better quality than a similar size TV at a lower price—or whether you need a television at all, considering your ability to stream content through your computer. Thus, postpurchase cognitive dissonance generally occurs when a consumer questions the appropriateness of a purchase after his or her decision has been made.

Postpurchase cognitive dissonance is especially likely for products that are expensive, are infrequently purchased, do not work as intended, and are associated with high levels of risk. Marketers direct efforts at consumers after the purchase is made to address this issue.[46] General Electric sends a letter to purchasers of its appliances, positively reinforcing the message that the customer made a wise decision by mentioning the high quality that went into the product's design and production. Some clothing manufacturers include a tag on their garments to offer the reassurance that because of their special manufacturing process, perhaps designed to provide a soft, vintage appearance, there may be variations in color that have no effect on the quality of the item. After a pang of dissonance, satisfaction may then set in.

Let's check back in with our friend Katie to recognize these effects. When Katie purchased her interview dress at Macy's, she tried it on for some of her friends. Her boyfriend said he loved it, but several of her girlfriends seemed less impressed. Katie thought it made her look more mature. Because of these mixed signals, some dissonance resulted and manifested itself as an uncomfortable, unsettled feeling. To reduce the dissonance, Katie could:

- Take back the dress.
- Pay attention to positive information, such as looking up ads and articles about this particular dress designer.
- Seek more positive feedback from friends.
- Seek negative information about dresses made by designers not selected.

After a while, satisfaction with her experience probably will result.

Customer Loyalty In the postpurchase stage of the decision-making process, marketers attempt to solidify a loyal relationship with their customers. They want customers to be satisfied with their purchase and buy from the same company again. Loyal customers will buy only certain brands and shop at certain stores, and they include no other firms in their evoked set. As we explained in Chapter 2, such customers are therefore very valuable to firms, and marketers have designed customer relationship management (CRM) programs specifically to retain them.

Undesirable Consumer Behavior Although firms want satisfied, loyal customers, sometimes they fail to attain them. Passive consumers are those who don't repeat purchase or recommend the product to others. More serious and potentially damaging, however, is negative consumer behavior, such as negative word of mouth and rumors.

Stores collect customer information for their CRM programs from customer credit cards.

Negative word of mouth occurs when consumers spread negative information about a product, service, or store to others. When customers' expectations are met or even exceeded, they often don't tell anyone about it. But when consumers believe that they have been treated unfairly in some way, they usually want to complain, often to many people. The Internet has provided an effective method of spreading negative word of mouth to millions of people instantaneously through personal blogs, Twitter, and corporate websites. To lessen the impact of negative word of mouth, firms provide customer service representatives—whether online, on the phone, or in stores—to handle and respond to complaints. Many companies also allow customers to post comments and complaints to proprietary social media sites.

Whirlpool posts both good and bad comments on Twitter. It believes that posting negative comments opens up discussions and emphasizes the proactive measures the company is taking to remedy service or product failures.

For example, Whirlpool set up Facebook pages for its appliance brands, Maytag, KitchenAid, and Whirlpool. Customers may share their thoughts on these sites, without fear that their negative feedback will be deleted from the site. Whirlpool believes that it should "keep the bad" to open up discussions and emphasize the proactive measures the company is taking to remedy service or product failures.[47] If a customer believes that positive action will be taken as a result of the complaint, he or she is less likely to complain to family and friends or through the Internet. (A detailed example of word of mouth appears in Chapter 13.)

CHECK YOURSELF

1. Name the five stages in the consumer decision process.
2. What is the difference between a need and a want?
3. Distinguish between functional and psychological needs.
4. What are the various types of perceived risk?
5. What are the differences between compensatory and noncompensatory decision rules?

FACTORS INFLUENCING THE CONSUMER DECISION PROCESS

LO5 List the factors that affect the consumer decision process.

The consumer decision process can be influenced by several factors, as illustrated in Exhibit 6.4. First are the elements of the marketing mix, which we discuss throughout this book. Second are psychological factors, which are influences internal to the customer, such as motives, attitudes, perception, and learning. Third, social factors, such as family, reference groups, and culture, also influence the decision process. Fourth, there are situational factors, such as the specific purchase situation, a particular shopping situation, or temporal state (the time of day), that affect the decision process.

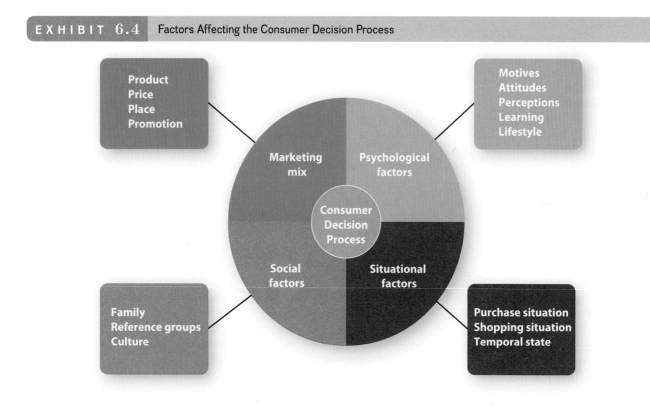

EXHIBIT 6.4 Factors Affecting the Consumer Decision Process

Every decision people make as consumers will take them through some form of the consumer decision process. But, like life itself, this process does not exist in a vacuum.

Psychological Factors

Although marketers can influence purchase decisions, a host of psychological factors affect the way people receive marketers' messages. Among them are motives, attitudes, perception, learning, and lifestyle. In this section, we examine how such psychological factors can influence the consumer decision process.[48]

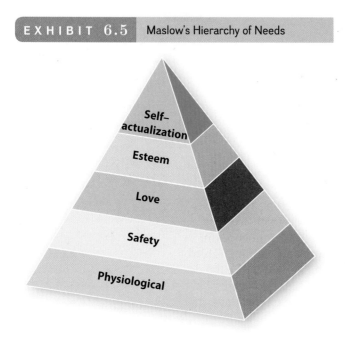

EXHIBIT 6.5 Maslow's Hierarchy of Needs

Motives In Chapter 1, we argued that marketing is all about satisfying customer needs and wants. When a need, such as thirst, or a want, such as a Diet Pepsi, is not satisfied, it motivates us, or drives us, to get satisfaction. So, a **motive** is a need or want that is strong enough to cause the person to seek satisfaction.

People have several types of motives. One of the best known paradigms for explaining these motive types was developed by Abraham Maslow more than 30 years ago, called **Maslow's Hierarchy of Needs.**[49] Maslow categorized five groups of needs, namely, physiological (e.g., food, water, shelter), safety (e.g., secure employment, health), love (e.g., friendship, family), esteem (e.g., confidence, respect), and self-actualization (people engage in personal growth activities and attempt to meet their intellectual, aesthetic, creative, and other such needs). The pyramid in Exhibit 6.5 demonstrates the theoretical progression of those needs.

Physiological needs deal with the basic biological necessities of life—food, drink, rest, and shelter. Although for most people in developed countries these basic needs are generally met, there are those in both developed and less-developed countries who are less fortunate. However, everyone remains concerned with meeting these basic needs.[50] Marketers seize every opportunity to convert these needs into wants by reminding us to eat at Taco Bell, drink milk, sleep on a Beautyrest mattress, and stay at a Marriott.

Safety needs pertain to protection and physical well-being. The marketplace is full of products and services that are designed to make you safer, such as airbags in cars and burglar alarms in homes, or healthier, such as vitamins and organic meats and vegetables.

Love needs relate to our interactions with others. Haircuts and makeup make you look more attractive, and deodorants prevent odor. Greeting cards help you express your feelings toward others.

Esteem needs allow people to satisfy their inner desires. Yoga, meditation, health clubs, and many books appeal to people's desires to grow or maintain a happy, satisfied outlook on life.

Finally, **self-actualization** occurs when you feel completely satisfied with your life and how you live.

Taco Bell satisfies physiological needs.

Ads for crime prevention satisfy safety needs.

Yoga satisifies esteem needs by helping people satisy their inner desires.

Which categories of Maslow's hierarchy of needs do these magazines fulfill?

You don't care what others think. You drive a Ford Fusion because it suits the person you are, not because some celebrity endorses it or because you want others to think better of you.

Which of these needs applies when a consumer purchases a magazine? Magazines such as *Weight Watchers*, for instance, help satisfy physiological needs like how to eat healthy but also esteem needs like how to be happy with one's life.[51] Magazines such as *Family Circle* provide tips on how to make the home a safer place to live, and magazines such as *Weddings* help satisfy love and belonging needs, because they provide instructions on how to prepare gracious invitations for friends and family, for example. Many of these magazines fulfill several needs simultaneously, of course. Good marketers add value to their products or services by nudging people up the needs hierarchy and offering information on as many of the pyramid of needs as they can.

Attitude　We have attitudes about almost everything. For instance, we like this class, but we don't like the instructor. We like where we live, but we don't like the weather. An **attitude** is a person's enduring evaluation of his or her feelings about and behavioral tendencies toward an object or idea. Attitudes are learned and long lasting, and they might develop over a long period of time, though they can also abruptly change. For instance, you might like your instructor for much of the semester—until she returns your first exam. The one thing attitudes have in common for everyone is their ability to influence our decisions and actions.

An attitude consists of three components. The **cognitive component** reflects a person's belief system, or what we believe to be true; the **affective component** involves emotions, or what we feel about the issue at hand, including our like or dislike of something; and the **behavioral component** pertains to the actions we undertake based on what we know and feel. For example, Matt and Lisa Martinez see an advertisement for the latest *Pirates of the Caribbean* movie, showing Johnny Depp dueling with Geoffrey Rush. The ad lists quotes from different movie critics who call it a great and exciting film. Matt and Lisa therefore come to believe that the critics must be correct and that the new *Pirates of the Caribbean* will be a good movie (cognitive component). Later they catch an interview with Johnny Depp, who talks about making the movie and his enjoyment playing Captain Jack Sparrow. Therefore, Matt and Lisa start to believe the movie will be fun and engaging, because they appreciate action adventures and also have enjoyed previous Johnny Depp films (affective component). After weighing their various options—which include various other movies, other entertainment options like attending a concert instead, or just staying home—Matt and Lisa decide to go see the movie (behavioral component).

Ideally, agreement exists among these three components. But when there is incongruence among the three—if Matt and Lisa read positive reviews and like action films but do not find Johnny Depp an appealing actor—cognitive dissonance might occur. Matt and Lisa might decide their reviews and their liking of action films will outweigh their dislike of Johnny Depp and go see the movie. If they then find the movie unenjoyable, because Johnny Depp is the primary star, they may feel foolish for having "wasted" their money.

Such dissonance is a terrible feeling, which people try to avoid, often by convincing themselves that the decision was a good one in some way.[52] In this example, Matt and Lisa might focus on the special effects and the romantic elements of the movie while mentally glossing over the parts that featured the actor they did not enjoy. In this way, they can convince themselves that the parts they liked were good enough to counterbalance the part they didn't like, and thus, they make their movie-going experience a positive event overall.

Although attitudes are pervasive and usually slow to change, the important fact from a marketer's point of view is that they can be influenced and perhaps changed through persuasive communications and personal experience. Marketing communication—through salespeople, advertisements, free samples, or other such methods—can attempt to change what people believe to be true about a product or service (cognitive) or how they feel toward it (affective). If the marketer is successful, the cognitive and affective components work in concert to affect behavior. Continuing with our example, suppose that prior to viewing the movie ad, Matt and Lisa thought that *Cowboys & Aliens* would be the next movie they would go see, but they had heard good things about *Pirates of the Caribbean*. The ad positively influenced the cognitive component of their attitude toward *Pirates of the Caribbean*, making it consistent with their affective component.

Based on positive review (cognitive component) and positive feelings (affective component), many people went to see the latest Pirates of the Caribbean *movie (behavioral component) and came away with a positive attitude.*

Perception Another psychological factor, **perception**, is the process by which we select, organize, and interpret information to form a meaningful picture of the world. Perception in marketing influences our acquisition and consumption of goods and services through our tendency to assign meaning to such things as color, symbols, taste, and packaging. Culture, tradition, and our overall upbringing determine our perception of the world. For instance, Lisa Martinez has always wanted an apartment in the Back Bay neighborhood of Boston because her favorite aunt had one, and they had a great time visiting for Thanksgiving one year. However, from his past experiences, Matt has a different perception. Matt thinks Back Bay apartments are small, expensive, and impractical for a couple thinking about having children—though they would be convenient for single people who work in downtown Boston. The city of Boston has worked hard in recent years to overcome the long-standing negative perceptual bias that Matt and many others hold by working with developers to create larger, modern, and more affordable apartments and using promotion to reposition the perception of apartments in the Back Bay for young couples.[53]

Learning **Learning** refers to a change in a person's thought process or behavior that arises from experience and takes place throughout the consumer decision process. For instance, after Katie Smith recognized that she needed a dress for her job interview, she started looking for ads and searching for reviews and articles on the Internet. She learned from each new piece of information, so her thoughts about the look she wanted in a dress were different from those before she had read anything. She liked what she learned about the clothing line from Macy's. She learned from her search, and it became part of her memory to be used in the future, possibly so she could recommend the store to her friends.

Learning affects both attitudes and perceptions. Throughout the buying process, Katie's attitudes shifted. The cognitive component came into play for her when she learned Macy's had one of the most extensive collections of career apparel. Once she was in the store and tried on some dresses, she realized how much she liked the way she looked and felt in them, which involved the affective component. Then she purchased it, which involved the behavioral component. Each time she was exposed to information about the store or the dresses, she learned something different that affected her perception. Before she tried them on, Katie hadn't realized how easy it would be to find exactly what she was looking for; thus, her perception of Macy's line of dresses changed through learning.

Lifestyle **Lifestyle** refers to the way consumers spend their time and money to live. For many consumers, the question of whether the product or service fits with their actual lifestyle, which may be fairly sedentary, or their perceived lifestyle, which might be outdoorsy, is an important one. Some of the many consumers sporting North Face jackets certainly need the high-tech, cold weather gear because they are planning their next hike up Mount Rainier and want to be sure they have sufficient protection against the elements. Others, however, simply like the image that the jacket conveys—the image that they might be leaving for their own mountain-climbing expedition any day now—even if the closest they have come has been shoveling their driveway.

A person's perceptions and ability to learn are affected by their social experiences, which we discuss next.

Social Factors

The consumer decision process is influenced from within by psychological factors, but also by the external, social environment, which consists of the customer's family, reference groups, and culture.[54] (Refer back to Exhibit 6.4.)

Family Many purchase decisions are made about products or services that the entire family will consume or use. Thus, firms must consider how families make purchase decisions and understand how various family members might influence these decisions.

When families make purchase decisions, they often consider the needs of all the family members. In choosing a restaurant, for example, all the family members may participate in the decision making. In other situations, however, different members of the family may take on the purchasing role. For example, the husband and teenage child may look through car magazines and *Consumer Reports* to search for information about a new car. But once they arrive at the dealership, the husband and wife, not the child, decide which model and color to buy, and the wife negotiates the final deal.[55]

Children and adolescents play an increasingly important role in family buying decisions. Kids in the United States spend over $200 billion a year on personal items such as snacks, soft drinks, entertainment, and apparel. They directly influence the purchase of another $300 billion worth of items such as food, snacks, beverages, toys, health and beauty aids, clothing, accessories, gifts, and school supplies. Their indirect influence on family spending is even higher—$600 billion for items such as recreation, vacations, technology, and even the family car.[56] Even grandparents contribute to the economic impact of children in the United States. It is estimated that grandparents spend $52 billion dollars on purchases for grandchildren.[57]

Influencing a group that holds this much spending power is vitally important. Traditional food retailers are already caught in a squeeze between Walmart, which lures low-end customers, and specialty retailers like Whole Foods, which target the high end. Knowing how children influence food buying decisions is a strategic opportunity for traditional supermarkets and their suppliers to exploit. Currently, the age cohorts referred to as Gen X and Millennials (remember from Chapter 5 that these groups were born anywhere between 1966 and

Children influence parents' purchasing decisions.

1994) tend to shop at Target, Kmart, and Walmart more and spend more at those stores than other generational groups.[58] Getting this group to prefer one store, chain, or product over another can make a difference in the bottom line, as well as in the chances for survival in a difficult marketplace.

Reference Groups A **reference group** is one or more persons whom an individual uses as a basis for comparison regarding beliefs, feelings, and behaviors. A consumer might have various reference groups, including family, friends, coworkers, or famous people the consumer would like to emulate. These reference groups affect buying decisions by (1) offering information, (2) providing rewards for specific purchasing behaviors, and (3) enhancing a consumer's self-image.

Reference groups provide information to consumers directly through conversation or indirectly through observation. For example, Katie received valuable information from a friend about where she should shop for her interview dress. On another occasion, she heard a favorite cousin who is a fashionista praising the virtues of shopping at Macy's, which solidified her decision to go there.

Some reference groups also influence behaviors by rewarding behavior that meets with their approval or chastising behavior that doesn't. For example, smokers are often criticized or even ostracized by their friends and made to smoke outside or in restricted areas.

Consumers can identify and affiliate with reference groups to create, enhance, or maintain their self-image. Customers who want to be seen as "earthy" might buy Birkenstock sandals, whereas those wanting to be seen as "high fashion" might buy Christian Louboutin shoes, as we discussed previously in this chapter. If they purchase a gift for someone else and that gift conflicts with their self-image, they also seek to reestablish their preferred affiliation quickly, by purchasing something more in line with their identity.[59]

Some stores, like Abercrombie & Fitch, play on these forms of influence and hire sales associates they hope will serve as a reference group for customers who shop there. These "cool," attractive, and somewhat aloof employees are encouraged to wear the latest store apparel—thereby serving as living mannequins to emulate.[60]

Culture We defined **culture** in Chapter 5 as the shared meanings, beliefs, morals, values, and customs of a group of people. As the basis of the social factors that impact your buying decisions, the culture or cultures in which you participate are not markedly different from your reference groups. That is, your cultural group might be as small as your reference group at school or as large as the country in which you live or the religion to which you belong. Like reference groups, cultures influence consumer behavior. For instance, the culture at Katie's college is rather fashion conscious. This influences, to some extent, the way she spends, how she dresses, and where she shops.

Situational Factors

Psychological and social factors typically influence the consumer decision process the same way each time. For example, your motivation to quench your thirst usually drives you to drink a Coke or a Pepsi, and your reference group at the workplace coerces you to wear appropriate attire. But sometimes, **situational factors,** or factors specific to the situation, override, or at least influence, psychological and social issues. These situational factors are related to the purchase and shopping situation, as well as to temporal states.[61]

Famous people, like Sarah Jessica Parker, can be part of your reference group, influencing your purchases.

Purchase Situation Customers may be predisposed to purchase certain products or services because of some underlying psychological trait or social factor, but these factors may change in certain purchase situations. For instance, Samantha Crumb considers herself a thrifty, cautious shopper—someone who likes to get a good deal. But her best friend is getting married, and she wants to buy the couple a silver tray. If the tray were for herself, she would probably go to Crate & Barrel or possibly even Walmart. But since it is for her best friend, she went to Tiffany & Co. Why? To purchase something fitting for the special occasion of a wedding.

Shopping Situation Consumers might be ready to purchase a product or service but be completely derailed once they arrive in the store. Marketers use several techniques to influence consumers at this choice stage of the decision process. Consider the following techniques.

Store Atmosphere Some retailers and service providers have developed unique images that are based at least in part on their internal environment, also known as their atmospherics.[62] Research has shown that, if used in concert with other aspects of a retailer's strategy, music, scent, lighting, and even color can positively influence the decision process.[63] Restaurants such as Outback Steakhouse and The Cheesecake Factory have developed internal environments that are not only pleasant but also consistent with their food and service.

Some Wegmans and Whole Foods stores have built bars and restaurants inside their stores, where customers can stop and relax, have a glass of wine or a bite to eat, but still get their shopping done for the week. Whole Foods has cutting edge culinary centers that offer cooking classes in over 30 stores. Other grocery store chains are following suit; the Brewers Yard Kroger in Ohio has a band play in the store on Friday nights. Still other grocery stores offer flat-screen televisions, comfortable chairs, free Wi-Fi hotspots, in-store cooking classes, or wine tasting events to create interactive atmospheres that will appeal to customers.[64]

Salespeople Well-trained sales personnel can influence the sale at the point of purchase by educating consumers about product attributes, pointing out the advantages of one item over another, and encouraging multiple purchases. The salesperson at Tiffany & Co., for instance, explained to Samantha why one platter was better than another and suggested some serving pieces to go with it.

The Cheesecake Factory has developed atmospherics that are not only pleasant, but consistent with their image, menu, and service.

Jordan's Furniture, a New England–based chain, has worked hard to make furniture shopping fun by offering in-store entertainment and food outlets. But after going through all the effort to make the store atmospheres inviting, Jordan's also realized that the quality of its salespeople could mean all the difference between a consumer just visiting the store for fun or making a purchase. It therefore initiated an extensive training program for its entire sales staff to guarantee that salespeople were knowledgeable about anything and everything customers may want to know. The regular training modules take place during workshops at the individual stores, usually before hours over three consecutive days. The sessions focus on various topics, including the differences between solid wood and veneers or the introduction of a new fabric line by a certain manufacturer.

In-store demonstrations entice people to buy.

Crowding Customers can feel crowded because there are too many people, too much merchandise, or lines that are too long. If there are too many people in a store, some people become distracted and may even leave.[65] Others have difficulty purchasing if the merchandise is packed too closely together. This issue is a particular problem for shoppers with mobility disabilities.

In-Store Demonstrations The taste and smell of new food items may attract people to try something they normally wouldn't. Similarly, some fashion retailers offer "trunk shows," during which their vendors show their whole line of merchandise on a certain day. During these well-advertised events, customers are often enticed to purchase that day because they get special assistance from the salespeople and can order merchandise that the retailer otherwise does not carry.

Promotions Retailers employ various promotional vehicles to influence customers once they have arrived in the store. An unadvertised price promotion can alter a person's preconceived buying plan. Multi-item discounts, such as "buy 1, get 1 free" sales, are popular means to get people to buy more than they normally would.[66] Because many people regard clipping coupons from the newspaper as too much trouble, some stores make coupons available in the store, on the Internet, or on their cell phones. Another form of promotion is offering a "free" gift with the purchase of a good or service. This type of promotion is particularly popular with cosmetics.

Packaging It is difficult to make a product stand out in the crowd when it competes for shelf space with several other brands. This problem is particularly difficult for consumer packaged goods, such as groceries and health and beauty products (see Adding Value 6.2). Marketers therefore spend millions of dollars designing and updating their packages to be more appealing and eye catching.[67]

Temporal State Our state of mind at any particular time can alter our preconceived notions of what we are going to purchase. For instance, some people are "morning people," whereas others function better at night. A purchase situation may thus have different appeal levels depending on the time of day and the type of person the consumer is. Mood swings can alter consumer behavior.[68] Suppose Samantha received a parking ticket just prior to shopping at Tiffany & Co. It is likely that she would be less receptive to the salesperson's influence than if she came into the store in a good mood. Her bad mood might even cause her to have a less positive postpurchase feeling about the store. Since retailers can't affect what happens outside the store very much, they should do everything possible to make sure their customers have a positive shopping experience once they are in the store.

The factors that affect the consumer decision process—the marketing mix, psychological factors, social factors, and situational factors—are all impacted by the level of consumer involvement, the subject of the next section.

Adding Value 6.2   Judging a Product by Its Cover[69]

In stores, customers spend just 3 to 10 seconds standing in front of products as they decide whether to buy them. Regardless of the significant time and money put into marketing products in places outside store walls, customers evaluate most products based mainly on their appearance in the store. That means that packaging is tremendously important.

Packaging must sell itself to the customer, over and above any competitors on the shelf. Redesigned packages offer the excitement of exhibiting something new, but they also might alienate customers who find them unfamiliar. Yet increasing the visibility of any package on the shelf helps increase sales— which may be why Pringles keeps packaging its chips in tubes that differ greatly from the formless bags further down the aisle.

But not all product packaging can, or should, remain the same, the way Pringles has. Doublemint Gum undertook its first packaging redesign in 2006—nearly a century after its 1914 product launch. The move was designed to help the chewing gum appeal to a younger audience, even while it maintained its loyal base of older consumers. Another aging brand, Kraft's Macaroni & Cheese, similarly redesigned its packaging, which it launched originally in 1937.

For Nonni's Biscotti, the most recent package redesign involved adding a window to the front of the box, so customers could see the texture of the baked treats. The biscotti, stacked vertically instead of horizontally, now help give a grander impression of the product. Furthermore, by adding decorative touches to make the packaging more visually appealing, Nonni's could encourage customers to leave the box right on their countertops, easily accessible to snackers.

Nonni's redesigned its biscotti packages to include a window so customers could see the products.

CHECK YOURSELF

1. What are some examples of specific needs suggested by Maslow's Hierarchy of Needs?
2. Which social factors likely have the most influence on (a) the purchase of a new outfit for a job interview and (b) the choice of a college to attend?
3. List some of the tactics stores can use to influence consumers' decision processes.

LO6 Describe how involvement influences the consumer decision process.

INVOLVEMENT AND CONSUMER BUYING DECISIONS

Consumers make two types of buying decisions depending on their level of involvement: extended problem solving; and limited problem solving, which includes impulse buying and habitual decision making. **Involvement** is the consumer's degree of interest in the product or service.[70] Consumers may have different levels of involvement for the same type of product. One consumer behavior theory, the elaboration likelihood model, illustrated in Exhibit 6.6, proposes that high- and low-involvement consumers process different aspects of a message or advertisement.

EXHIBIT 6.6 Elaboration Likelihood Model

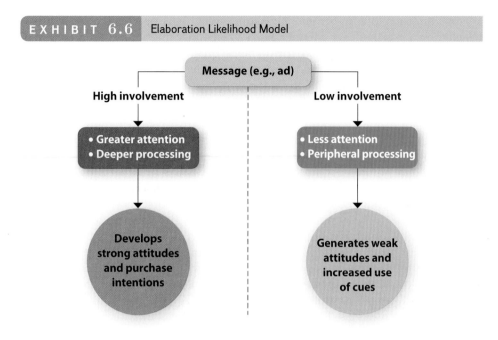

Message (e.g., ad)

High involvement

- Greater attention
- Deeper processing

Develops strong attitudes and purchase intentions

Low involvement

- Less attention
- Peripheral processing

Generates weak attitudes and increased use of cues

If both types of consumers viewed ads for career dresses, the high-involvement consumer (e.g., Katie, who is researching buying a dress for a job interview) will scrutinize all the information provided (price, fabric quality, construction) and process the key elements of the message more deeply. As an involved consumer, Katie likely ends up judging the ad as truthful and forming a favorable impression of the product, or else she regards the message as superficial and develops negative product impressions (i.e., her research suggests the product is not as good as it is being portrayed).

What type of buying decision does each of these products represent?

In contrast, a low-involvement consumer will likely process the same advertisement in a less thorough manner. Such a consumer might pay less attention to the key elements of the message (price, fabric quality, construction) and focus on heuristic elements such as brand name (Macy's I·N·C) or the presence of a celebrity endorser. The impressions of the low-involvement consumer are likely to be more superficial.

Extended Problem Solving

The buying process begins when consumers recognize that they have an unsatisfied need. Katie Smith recognized her need to buy a new dress for a job interview. She sought information by asking for advice from her friends, reading fashion magazines, and conducting research online. She visited several stores to determine which had the best options for her. Finally, after considerable time and effort analyzing her alternatives, Katie purchased a dress at Macy's. This process is an example of **extended problem solving**, which is common when the customer perceives that the purchase decision entails a lot of risk. The potential risks associated with Katie's decision to buy the dress include financial (did I pay too much?) and social (will my potential employer and friends think I look professional?) risks. To reduce her perceived risk, Katie spent a lot of effort searching for information before she actually made her purchase.

Picking up a hamburger at a drive-through fast-food restaurant like In-N-Out Burger requires little thought. It is a habitual decision.

Limited Problem Solving

Limited problem solving occurs during a purchase decision that calls for, at most, a moderate amount of effort and time. Customers engage in this type of buying process when they have had some prior experience with the product or service and the perceived risk is moderate. Limited problem solving usually relies on past experience more than on external information. For many people, an apparel purchase, even a dress for a job interview, could require limited effort.

A common type of limited problem solving is **impulse buying**, a buying decision made by customers on the spot when they see the merchandise.[71] When Katie went to the grocery store to do her weekly shopping, she saw a display case of popcorn and Dr Pepper near the checkout counter. Knowing that some of her friends were coming over to watch a movie, she stocked up. The popcorn and soda were an impulse purchase. Katie didn't go through the entire decision process; instead, she recognized her need and jumped directly to purchase without spending any time searching for additional information or evaluating alternatives. The grocery store facilitated this impulse purchase by providing easily accessible cues (i.e., by offering the popcorn and soda in a prominent display, at a great location in the store, and at a reasonable price).

Some purchases require even less thought. **Habitual decision making** describes a purchase decision process in which consumers engage in little conscious effort. On her way home from the grocery store, for example, Katie drove past an In-N-Out Burger and swung into the drive-through for a cheeseburger and Diet Coke. She did not ponder the potential benefits of going to Wendy's instead for lunch. Rather, she simply reacted to the cue provided by the sign and engaged in habitual decision making. Marketers strive to attract and maintain habitual purchasers by creating strong brands and store loyalty (see Chapters 11 and 12) because these customers don't even consider alternative brands or stores.

CHECK YOURSELF

1. How do low- versus high-involvement consumers process the information in an advertisement?
2. What is the difference between extended versus limited problem solving?

Summing Up

LO1 Articulate the steps in the consumer buying process.

The consumer buying process consists of five main steps: First, during need recognition, consumers simply realize they have an unsatisfied need or want that they hope to address. Second, they begin to search for information to determine how to satisfy that need. Third, during the alternative evaluation stage, they assess the various options available to them to determine which is the best for their purposes. Fourth, the purchase stage involves obtaining and using the product. Fifth and finally, consumers enter the postpurchase stage, during which they determine whether they are satisfied or dissatisfied with their choice.

LO2 Describe the difference between functional and psychological needs.

Functional needs pertain to the performance of a product or service. Psychological needs pertain to the personal gratification consumers associate with a product and/or service.

LO3 Describe factors that affect information search.

The information search that people undertake varies depending on both external and internal factors. Among the former, the type of product or service dictates whether people can make an easy, quick decision or instead must undertake significant research to find the best purchase option. A person's perceptions of the benefits versus the costs of the search also determine how much effort they undertake. These perceptions often relate closely to their perception of the risk involved in their purchase. Finally, people's locus of control, whether external or internal, strongly influences their information search actions.

LO4 Discuss postpurchase outcomes.

Marketers hope that after their purchase, consumers are satisfied and pleased with their purchase, which can lead to customer loyalty, a positive postpurchase outcome. However, consumers also may suffer postpurchase dissonance, or buyer's remorse.

LO5 List the factors that affect the consumer decision process.

The elements of the marketing mix (product, place, promotion, and price) have significant effects, of course. In addition, social factors, such as family and culture, influence not only what a consumer buys but also how a consumer goes about making a purchase decision. The psychological factors that influence purchase decisions include motives (which can be higher or lower on the hierarchy of needs), attitudes, perceptions, learning, and lifestyle. Finally, the specific factors that mark the purchase situation, like the store setting or even the time of day, can alter people's decision process.

LO6 Describe how involvement influences the consumer decision process.

More involved consumers, who are more interested or invested in the product or service they are considering, tend to engage in extended problem solving. They gather lots of information, scrutinize it carefully, and then make their decisions with caution, to minimize any risk they may confront. In contrast, less involved consumers often engage in limited problem solving, undertake impulse purchases, or rely on habit to make their purchase decisions.

Key Terms

- affective component, 192
- attitude, 192
- behavioral component, 192
- cognitive component, 192
- compensatory decision rule, 183
- consumer decision rules, 182
- conversion rate, 185
- culture, 195
- determinant attributes, 182
- esteem needs, 191
- evaluative criteria, 182
- evoked set, 181
- extended problem solving, 200
- external locus of control, 179
- external search for information, 177
- financial risk, 180

- functional needs, 176
- habitual decision making, 200
- impulse buying, 200
- internal locus of control, 179
- internal search for information, 177
- involvement, 198
- learning, 193
- lifestyle, 194
- limited problem solving, 200
- love needs, 191
- Maslow's Hierarchy of needs, 190
- motive, 190
- multi-attribute model, 184
- need recognition, 175
- negative word of mouth, 188

- noncompensatory decision rule, 184
- perception, 193
- performance risk, 179
- physiological needs, 191
- physiological risk, 180
- postpurchase cognitive dissonance, 187
- psychological needs, 176
- psychological risk, 180
- reference group, 195
- retrieval sets, 181
- safety needs, 191
- safety risk, 180
- self-actualization, 191
- situational factors, 195
- social risk, 180
- universal sets, 180

Marketing Applications

1. Does buying Kashi cereal satisfy a consumer's functional or psychological need? How might this information help a Kashi brand manager better promote the product?

2. When consumers buy a new notebook, what sort (internal vs. external) of information search would they conduct? If you were a marketing manager for Sony, how would you use this information?

3. Explain the factors that affect the amount of time and effort that a consumer might take when choosing an oral surgeon to get his or her wisdom teeth removed. How would your answer change if the consumer were looking for a dentist to get a cleaning? How should the office manager for a dental practice use this information?

4. When evaluating different alternatives for a Saturday night outing at a fine restaurant, explain the difference between the universal set, the retrieval set, and the evoked set. From which set of alternatives will the consumer most likely choose the restaurant?

5. What can retailers do to make sure they have satisfied customers after the sale is complete?

6. Tazo makes a blend of exotic green teas, spearmint, and rare herbs into a tea called Zen. Using Maslow's hierarchy of needs, explain which need(s) are being fulfilled by this tea.

7. Identify and describe the three social factors that influence the consumer decision process. Provide an example of how each of these might influence

the purchase of the necessary products and services for a camping trip by the whole family.

8. Trek has designed a new off-road bicycle designed to stand up to the rugged conditions of trail riding. Develop a theme for an advertising strategy that ensures all three components of attitude are positively covered.

9. What can a marketer do to positively influence a situation in which a consumer is ready to buy but has not yet done so?

10. You were recently hired by a multichannel retailer that promotes itself as an American firm selling only American-made goods. The products featured in advertising and in catalogs tell stories of the firms that produced the goods in the United States. The sales response to the firm's Made in America position has been incredible because it resonates with their customers' values. As a result, growth has been impressive. One day while speaking to a vendor, you find out a shipment of merchandise will be delayed since the product is coming from overseas and is late. A few days later you hear a similar story. As it turns out, the firm just barely earns the Made in the USA label. Though technically the products meet a standard to be classified as American made, you worry that the firm is not being truthful to its customers. You decide to write a letter to the VP of marketing detailing your concerns. What would you put in the letter?

1. Laura has a nearly new economy car but wants a sports car. If she decides to purchase a sports car, she will be primarily fulfilling _____ needs.
   a. functional
   b. postpurchase
   c. safety
   d. psychological
   e. functional and psychological

2. When Maya decided to buy a new computer, she thought about all the brands she could recall seeing advertised, but she would only consider those brands she could buy at her local electronics store. This represents Maya's _____ set.
   a. universal
   b. retrieval
   c. evoked
   d. deterministic
   e. behavioral

(Answers to these two questions can be found on page 647.)

Go to www.mhhe.com/grewal4e to practice an additional 11 questions.

Tool Kit

Jill is trying to decide, once and for all, which soft drink company is her favorite. She has created a chart to help her decide. She has rated Coca-Cola, Pepsi-Cola, and Jones Soda in terms of price, taste, variety, and packaging. She has also assessed how important each of these four attributes is in terms of her evaluations.

Please use the toolkit provided at www.mhhe.com/grewal4e to determine which cola Jill will choose using a compensatory model. Which cola would she choose using a noncompensatory model? If you were Jill, which model would you use, the compensatory or the noncompensatory? Why?

Net Savvy

1. Visit the Shopkick site (www.shopkick.com), click "About" at the bottom, and describe the benefits it offers consumers. How are these offers likely to influence consumers' behavior? What kinds of need appeals does this company make to encourage shoppers to join?

2. Customers use a variety of methods to provide feedback to companies about their experiences. Planetfeedback.com was developed as one such venue. Visit its website (www.planetfeedback.com) and identify the types of feedback that customers can provide. Look over the feedback for Verizon by typing "Verizon" in the company search space. Summarize some of the most recent comments. What is the ratio of positive to negative comments about Verizon during the last year or so? Describe the effect these comments might have on customer perceptions of Verizon.

Chapter Case Study

THE DIET BATTLE: WEIGHT WATCHERS, JENNY CRAIG, AND SLIM-FAST[72]

Want to lose weight? For about 71 million Americans and approximately 73 percent of all U.S. women, the answer is yes,[73] and for weight loss companies, that's the right answer. The weight loss industry, worth over $60 billion in 2010,[74] is growing steadily because lifestyles and food choices keep working against people's desire to lose weight. Many Americans spend their days sitting in front of a computer and their evenings sitting in front of a television. Restaurant meals, prepared foods, and high-fat/high-sugar snacks have replaced home-cooked meals, whole grains, and fresh produce. Exercise is limited to clicking a mouse or turning an ignition key. These habits are fattening (both literally and figuratively)

Mc Graw Hill connect

the profits for the weight loss industry, as well as expanding belt sizes. By the time we factor in diet pills, specially packaged weight-loss meals and snacks, diet programs, and the whole range of products and services promising bathing-suit bodies, we've got a highly lucrative market.

Three recognized diet aid behemoths, Weight Watchers, Jenny Craig, and Slim-Fast, share a substantial piece of the pie. These companies stress flexibility to fit a wide range of lifestyles and showcase success stories. But they approach dieting differently in their quest for new members.

THE BIG THREE

Founded in 1963, Weight Watchers International now boasts groups in more than 30 countries worldwide. The program teaches portion control and the basics of good nutrition, allowing members to select their own foods. A point system, based on nutritional value, encourages members to select healthy foods, exercise appropriately, and control portions.[75] Dieters record meals and snacks in a paper or electronic journal. Although members can follow the Weight Watchers regimen without support, the company notes that the most successful members are those who weigh in at weekly group sessions and attend meetings. Weight Watchers members can prepare their own food, dine out, or purchase Weight Watchers–prepared or –endorsed dinners, snacks, and desserts at most grocery stores. To further support dieters in making healthy food choices, Weight Watchers recently changed its point system, increasing the number of points for fat content and reducing them for fiber.[76]

Recently rated the top weight loss program by Consumer Reports Health, Jenny Craig promises a unique and comprehensive plan for food, body, and mind.[77] Members eat meals and snacks prepared and packaged by Jenny Craig, supplemented by fresh fruits and vegetables. Jenny Craig's offerings provide portion control and accommodate busy schedules by reducing meal prep time. Members meet weekly on a one-on-one basis with a personal counselor and are encouraged to develop an exercise program. Like Weight Watchers, Jenny Craig offers customized programs for men and teenagers and for those who prefer to lose weight on their own rather than travel to a center. Jenny Craig lapped Weight Watchers and other diet programs in the Consumer Reports Health ranking because of members' success in weight loss, the duration of time they remained committed to the program, and the nutritional value of the foods.[78]

Slim-Fast, which ranked second in the Consumer Reports Health ratings, offers dieters a combination of three small and healthy snacks, two meal-replacement shakes, and one 500-calorie meal daily.[79] By eating six small meals daily, dieters maintain steady glucose levels, and the plan ensures adequate intakes of carbohydrates, protein, and fiber.[80]

Other diet programs abound, but even when people lose weight on these regimens, the losses tend to be temporary, because the diets are based on unsustainable eating patterns, such as eliminating major food groups (e.g., no carbohydrates). Two of the big diet companies also offer social reinforcement and flexibility, which appears to help people remain committed to their weight-loss programs.

DEFINING THE DIFFERENCE

Perhaps the most significant difference among Jenny Craig, Slim-Fast, and Weight Watchers is the amount of effort required. Jenny Craig dieters don't have to think about what they eat; everything is prepared for them. Dieters on the Weight Watchers plan must learn how to make the right choices from among the foods that surround them in their daily lives. Slim-Fast combines both ease and education, but it provides fewer choices for controlled meals than Jenny Craig does. Each program competes heavily for members, particularly in the early months of the year, when Americans return to the scales after indulging over the holidays.

The diet giants are locked in another battle as well, this one targeted at men.[81] Although a completely different program isn't necessary—both genders need to cut calories and increase exercise to lose weight—marketing specifically to men has the power to bring in new members.

While the Weight Watchers' programs are identical for men and women, the men's website is tailored to their interests and concerns, focusing more on working out and less on the eating plan. The men's site also mentions the link between obesity and erectile dysfunction, implying that a man's sex life might improve if he loses weight.

Jenny Craig's men's program also is very similar to its women's program, but tweaked, to accommodate differences in food cravings and issues with portion control. Men on this program, Jenny Craig promises, can still have a beer and fries once in a while. To further entice men to its program, Jenny Craig uses Jason Alexander, the actor who played George Costanza on the television series *Seinfeld*, as a spokesperson.

The Slim-Fast program tends to appeal to men because they like to lose weight on their own rather than participating in group meetings.[82] The company has used male celebrities, including a former New York mayor, to sell its products.

TECHNOLOGY SUPPORT FOR DIETERS

Dieters have a variety of electronic devices to help track food consumption and exercise. Using any Internet-ready device, Weight Watchers members can check points values for foods, including meals at popular restaurants, and add snacks or meals to their daily journal. Similar services and applications for fitness training are available via cell phone applications. Using a camera-equipped cell phone, for example, dieters can photograph a meal and send the picture to a registered dietitian, who replies with recommendations for modifying portions or food choices. Theoretically this approach is more honest than keeping a food diary, because dieters may be tempted not to record full amounts. These services require additional fees though.

To entice men in its program, Jenny Craig uses Jason Alexander, the actor who played George Costanza on the TV series Seinfeld, *as a spokesperson (pictured with another Jenny Craig spokesperson, Valerie Bertanelli, teenage TV star from the late 70s of* One Day at a Time *and* Touched by an Angel.

Questions

1. Trace how you might go through the steps in the consumer decision process if you were thinking of going on a diet and using any of these diet programs.

2. How have Weight Watchers, Slim-Fast, and Jenny Craig created value?

3. Identify the determinant attributes that set the Weight Watchers, Slim-Fast, and Jenny Craig programs apart. Use those attributes to develop a compensatory purchasing model similar to the one in Exhibit 6.2.

4. How can Weight Watchers, Slim-Fast, and Jenny Craig increase the probability of customer satisfaction?

5. Which factors examined in this chapter might have the most impact on consumers' propensity to go on a diet and choose one of these diet programs?

Business-to-Business Marketing

If you are like most people, jeans are a staple of your wardrobe. However, when you pull on a pair, you probably don't wonder about where they were made, how much material they contain, or the impact they have on the environment. But for Levi Strauss & Co., one of the oldest names in jeans, these questions remain important to the company's long-term survival.[1]

In particular, Levi's is a major consumer of cotton: A single pair of its 501 jeans uses nearly two pounds of cotton,[2] and the vast majority of all Levi's products are made with cotton. Cotton needs water to grow, and jeans continue to require water throughout their lifecycle, whether as part of the stone-wash softening process or in the laundry. By the time your latest pair of jeans has reached the end of its lifecycle, it will have used more than 900 gallons of water.[3]

A decade ago, this water consumption was of less concern. But changes in rainfall patterns caused by global climate change are directly tying Levi's future to water: Less water means less moisture for cotton crops, and less cotton means Levi's will either have to incorporate more synthetics into its clothing—a significant change to its brand—or pay more for scarce raw materials. If the company pays more, the increased prices will be passed along to customers, possibly resulting in Levi's loyalists moving to other brands. A third alternative, reducing the cost of other garment materials such as buttons and zippers, affects both the brand and quality standards, though it can help control the end cost charged to consumers.

To address these challenges, Levi's is working with suppliers to implement more sustainable water use and other environmental practices, as well as more responsible practices with regard to workers throughout its supply chain. These partnerships are challenging to instigate and oversee, because cotton is raised in more than 100 countries and grown primarily on small, family-owned farms.[4] Levi's began, more than 20 years ago, by creating a Terms of Engagement code of conduct that spells out what the company requires from its business partners in terms of social, ethical, legal, and environmental practices and employment standards. The agreement covers such issues as working ages, health and safety, and child labor, as well as wages, benefits, and disciplinary practices.[5]

The company has also partnered with other large consumers of cotton, including IKEA, adidas, and The Gap;

LEARNING OBJECTIVES

LO1 Describe the ways in which business-to-business (B2B) firms segment their markets.

LO2 List the steps in the B2B buying process.

LO3 Identify the roles within the buying center.

LO4 Describe the different types of organizational cultures.

LO5 Detail different buying situations.

environmental organizations such as the World Wildlife Federation; and a cotton industry association to study growing practices that reduce water and pesticide use. In one such study, conducted on a farm in India, cotton plants using a new drip irrigation system were taller and bore more flowers than those using traditional methods. The drip system reduced water use by about 70 percent and shortened the duration of electricity use for the system from three days to three hours. It also distributed fertilizer more evenly. Levi Strauss, IKEA, and adidas thus agreed to set aggressive goals for increasing the amount of this "better cotton" in their products. In addition, Levi Strauss has introduced a line of stone-washed denim that does not use water.

In conjunction with other members of the apparel industry and outdoor-wear makers like Target, Nike, Patagonia, and REI, Levi's has adopted a software tool, the Eco Index, that helps clothing manufacturers determine the environmental and human impact of their products.[6] These efforts go beyond water use to include every step of the garment's life cycle—from raw material production to disposal—and help companies make the most responsible decisions when sourcing and distributing their wares.

Whether working with small farm owners in foreign countries or major retailers in the United States, Levi's efforts to be a responsible consumer have one thing in common: They involve business-to-business relationships among companies.

Business-to-business (B2B) marketing refers to the process of buying and selling goods or services to be used in the production of other goods and services, for consumption by the buying organization and/or resale by wholesalers and retailers. Therefore, a typical B2B marketing transaction involves manufacturers (e.g., Levi's, Siemens, IBM, Ford) selling to wholesalers that, in turn, sell products as retailers. B2B transactions can also involve service firms (e.g., UPS, Oracle, Accenture) that market their services to other businesses but not to the ultimate consumer (e.g., you). The distinction between a B2B and a business-to-consumer (B2C) transaction is not the product or service itself; rather, it is the ultimate user of that product or service. Another key distinction is that B2B transactions tend to be more complex and involve multiple members of both the buying organization (e.g., buyers, marketing team, product developers) and the selling organization (e.g., sellers, R&D support team), whereas B2C often entails a simple transaction between the retailer and the individual consumer.

The demand for B2B sales is often derived from B2C sales in the same supply chain. More specifically, **derived demand** reflects the link between consumers' demand for a company's output and the company's purchase of necessary inputs to manufacture or assemble that particular output. For example, if more customers want to purchase staplers (a B2C transaction), a company that produces them must purchase more metal from its supplier to make additional staplers (a B2B transaction).

Similar to organizations that sell directly to final consumers in B2C transactions, B2B firms focus on serving specific types of customer markets by creating value for those customers.[7] For example, Intel created and produces processors that are critical to the speed of many modern computers sold by Dell or Compaq, as well as smart televisions with the Sony brand name and, in the future, Android phones marketed by Google.[8] Also like B2C firms, many B2B companies find it more productive to focus their efforts on key industries or market segments. Siemens has identified core sectors, including health care, energy, technology, and software, that might benefit from its expertise. Through its market leadership in the field of water treatment, Siemens provides technology that enables its customers, whether corporate or civic, to provide emergency water supplies, institute water treatment processes, and adopt wastewater reuse systems.[9]

In this chapter, we look at the different types of B2B markets and examine the B2B buying process, with an eye toward how it differs from the B2C buying

Siemens serves multiple B2B target markets.

process we discussed in Chapter 6. Several factors influence the B2B buying process, and we discuss these as well.

B2B MARKETS

The most visible types of B2B transactions are those where manufacturers and service providers sell to other businesses. However, resellers, institutions, and governments also may be involved in B2B transactions. Therefore, in the next sections, we describe each of these B2B organizations (see Exhibit 7.1).

LO1 Describe the ways in which business-to-business (B2B) firms segment their markets.

EXHIBIT 7.1 | B2B Markets

```
              Resellers
                 │
                 ▼
Manufacturers/  B2B
Service     → Markets ←  Institutions
providers
                 ▲
                 │
            Government
```

Manufacturers and Service Providers

Manufacturers buy raw materials, components, and parts that allow them to make and market their own goods and ancillary services. For example, the German-based Volkswagen Group, the largest auto manufacturer in Europe, owns and distributes the Audi, Bentley, Bugatti, Lamborghini, Seat, Skoda, Scania VW, and VW Commercial Vehicles brands.[10] Whereas formerly, purchasing agents spent 70 percent of their time searching for, analyzing, validating, and forwarding information about parts and components, today they can use VWSupplyGroup.com to communicate with suppliers for all transactions, from procurement to logistics.

The system is used by 45,600 suppliers, who were engaged in transactions worth 2.13 billion Euros (or nearly US $3 billion) in 2010.[11] Purchasing agents receive product descriptions directly from suppliers online, which means search processes that used to take two hours now require about nine minutes. Users of the system receive alerts of potential parts shortages before they occur and thus can focus on efficiencies instead of redundant paperwork.

IBM provided the consulting services necessary to design the Volkswagen Group's system. IBM, which was once a major manufacturer of computers and related products, now generates over 90 percent of its profits from its software, consulting, and financing businesses—all of which are considered services. Like Volkswagen Group, it requires a host of B2B products and services to support these businesses. For instance, the airlines that IBM consultants and service providers rely on to shuttle them around the globe, also utilize a mix of products like airplanes and fuel, as well as consulting, legal, and other services.

Resellers

Resellers are marketing intermediaries that resell manufactured products without significantly altering their form. For instance, **wholesalers** and **distributors** buy Xerox products and sell them to retailers (B2B transaction), then retailers in turn resell those Xerox products to the ultimate consumer (B2C transaction). Alternatively, these retailers may buy directly from Xerox. Thus, wholesalers,

German-based Volkswagen Group communicates directly with suppliers to acquire parts and components for its cars like this Bentley.

Adding Value 7.1   Buying for Value

Off-price retailers like T.J. Maxx and Marshall's offer an obvious value to customers in the form of lower prices for brand-name merchandise. But these retailers provide an important service to manufacturers as well by supplying an opportunity to reach consumers from a broader spectrum of household incomes than typical retailers, and a way to sell the manufactures' excess merchandise.[12]

Contrary to widespread assumptions that T.J. Maxx and Marshall's parent company, TJX, purchases seconds and whatever other stores cannot sell,[13] the company buys directly from 10,000 manufacturers worldwide, the same manufacturers who sell to department and specialty stores. Nor are the rumors that T.J. Maxx and Marshall's sell merchandise from a previous year or season true. Instead, says the CEO of TJX, the vast majority of merchandise available at T.J. Maxx and Marshall's is from the same season and year for which it was designed. The quality is also the same, which makes sense because the manufacturers would have no desire to compromise their brand by selling "off-price." The only difference between the upscale fashion, health, beauty, and food items found at department and specialty stores and merchandise at Marshall's and T.J. Maxx is the price.[14]

This B2B relationship works well for both parties. High-fashion brands are willing to sell to TJX because the company never advertises specific brand names, thus protecting the high-end image of the brand and avoiding a confrontation with the brand's regularly priced department store customers. In addition, TJX, unlike department stores, does not return unsold clothing to the manufacturer. Rather, it takes merchandise returned by department and specialty stores off the manufacturer's hands, quickly selling these items to T.J. Maxx and Marshall's customers. This arrangement works well for both parties: Designers and manufacturers find buyers for merchandise, and TJX profits from the ultimate sale. Both companies see the positive results of their relationship on their bottom line. It also works well for shoppers, who can take advantage of current season fashions sold at a discount.[15] Through this buying process, TJX works with its partners to ensure end customers are satisfied. Its efforts appear successful; as one blogger recommended, "Buy with confidence, ladies."[16]

T.J. Maxx has a special relationship with its vendors that allows it to pass savings on to its customers.

distributors, and retailers are all resellers. Retailers represent resellers and engage in B2B transactions when they buy merchandise for their stores, fixtures, capital investments, leasing locations, and financing operations. Adding Value 7.1 highlights how T.J. Maxx buyers work with their partners to buy merchandise for their stores.

Social and Mobile Marketing 7.1   iPads Go to Work

Since being introduced in 2010, iPads have rocketed into widespread use for gaming, online access, music, videos, and e-mail. Tech-savvy business executives and educators also have noted some advantages of these devices that could make them useful at work, as well as at play. Tablet computers weigh less and cost less than laptop computers. Uploaded e-books can be more up to date and are less expensive than physical textbooks.[17] And in both the classroom and the workplace, the use of iPads extends the enthusiastic adoption of technology that is already occurring naturally in social contexts.

These devices, educators have learned, go beyond delivery of course materials, by saving additional funds for schools and increasing the value for students. Students can watch videos or tutorials, take notes, or use interactive programs that demonstrate particular skills. They can scroll effortlessly through documents or between texts to reach a section relevant to the current class discussion. Part-time and distance students can communicate more readily with their classmates, potentially enhancing collaboration and team-based learning.[18] Visual learners, children with autism spectrum disorders or learning disabilities, and students who have grown up using electronic devices in various facets of their lives all can benefit from the interactive nature of iPads. And all students benefit from developing comfort with technology, a vital skill set in tomorrow's workforce.

The iPad is finding fans in the workplace as well. Executives, staff members, and clients at companies as diverse as Wells Fargo Bank, the business management software developer SAP, and Daimler's Mercedes-Benz have adopted the device. Airplane pilots have begun replacing paper binders full of flight manuals, navigation charts, and other materials with iPads.[19] Siemens Energy has equipped some of its wind turbine service technicians with iPads so that they have convenient access to manuals, checklists, and cameras, even from atop a 300-foot tower. Thus iPad's manufacturer Apple claims that 80 percent of *Fortune* 100 companies are either using the device or have launched pilot projects to try it.[20]

Whether in the classroom or in the workplace, iPads are not without their disadvantages. Schools may save money in textbook costs but will need funding for repairs and wireless

80 percent of Fortune *100 companies are either using the iPad or have launched pilot projects to try it.*

infrastructure. Tablets may enhance learning, but they cannot replace teachers or peer-to-peer interactions. Academic and business users find that the virtual keyboard is challenging for composing longer text, sharing applications is burdensome, and multitasking is impossible. Some companies are put off by iPad security breaches; others reject Apple's traditional focus on the consumer market, often at the expense of business sales.[21] Despite these challenges though, the iPad has gained a strong foothold in both the classroom and the workplace.[22]

Institutions

Institutions, such as hospitals, educational organizations, and religious organizations, also purchase all kinds of goods and services. A public school system might have a $40 million annual budget for textbooks alone, which gives it significant buying power and enables it to take advantage of bulk discounts. However, if each school makes its own purchasing decisions, the system as a whole cannot leverage its combined buying power. Public institutions also engage in B2B relationships to fulfill their needs for capital construction, equipment, supplies, food, and janitorial services. For example, as Social and Mobile Marketing 7.1 highlights, iPads are playing increasing roles in educational institutions and businesses, which suggests that institutions need to start making purchasing decisions about them too.

Government

In most countries, the central government is one of the largest purchasers of goods and services. For example, the U.S. federal government spends about $3.7 trillion annually on procuring goods and services.[23] If you add in the amount state and local governments spend, these numbers reach staggering proportions. Specifically, with its estimated outlay of over $600 billion dollars for fiscal year 2011, the Pentagon represents a spending force to be reckoned with,[24] especially when it comes to aerospace and defense (A&D) manufacturers, some of the Pentagon's greatest suppliers of products. Policy Studies Inc. (PSI), for instance, offers consulting, technology, and outsourced services to government agencies involved in criminal justice, health care, and human services. One of its most visible services is its child support enforcement programs for state and local government agencies.[25]

The U.S. government spends over $5 billion a year on aerospace and defense for everything from nuts and bolts to this F-14 Tomcat jetfighter.

CHECK YOURSELF

1. What are the various B2B markets?

THE BUSINESS—TO—BUSINESS BUYING PROCESS

LO2 List the steps in the B2B buying process.

The B2B buying process (Exhibit 7.2) parallels the B2C process, though it differs in many ways. Both start with need recognition, but the information search and alternative evaluation steps are more formal and structured in the B2B process. Typically, B2B buyers specify their needs in writing and ask potential suppliers to submit formal proposals, whereas B2C buying decisions are usually made by individuals or families and do not need formal proposals. Thus, for an individual to buy a tablet computer, all that is required is a trip to the store or a few minutes online and perhaps some preliminary research about iPads versus competitors.

For a school district to buy 1,000 tablet computers, however, it must complete requisition forms, accept bids from manufacturers, and obtain approval for the expenditure. The final decision rests with a committee, as is the case for most B2B buying decisions, which often demand a great deal of consideration. Finally, in B2C buying situations, customers evaluate their purchase decision and sometimes experience postpurchase dissonance. However, formal performance evaluations of the vendor and the products sold generally do not occur, as they do in the B2B setting. Let's examine all six stages in the context of a school district buying tablets for middle school students as a resource.

EXHIBIT 7.2 Business-to-Business Buying Process

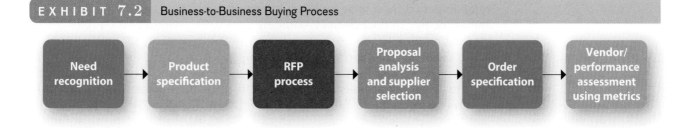

Need recognition → Product specification → RFP process → Proposal analysis and supplier selection → Order specification → Vendor/performance assessment using metrics

The first step in the B2B decision process is to recognize that the middle schools need to purchase 1,000 tablets.

Stage 1: Need Recognition

In the first stage of the B2B buying process, the buying organization recognizes, through either internal or external sources, that it has an unfilled need. The Salt Lake City, Utah, school district wants to introduce computer tablets into its middle-school resource programs to help build literacy and matching skills for students. A group of educators has reviewed pedagogical literature that describes how these devices can help students learn better, because they can directly interact with the materials rather than only hearing information or seeing it on a whiteboard. Using this information, they have convinced the school board to provide sufficient funding. They are ready to purchase 1000 tablets.

Stage 2: Product Specification

After recognizing the need and considering alternative solutions, including laptop computers, the school district wrote a list of potential specifications that vendors might use to develop their proposals. The school's specifications include screen size, battery life, processor speed, how the device connects to the Internet, and delivery date. In addition, the district has requested that a bundle of educational apps be preloaded on the tablets, that all other apps be removed, and that each tablet come equipped with a screen protector, power cord, cover, stand, keyboard, and headphones. The school district has also requested a three-year service contract that includes replacement within 24 hours for any tablets that are returned to the vendor for servicing.

Stage 3: RFP Process

The **request for proposals (RFP)** is a common process through which organizations invite alternative vendors or suppliers to bid on supplying their required components or specifications. The purchasing company may simply post its RFP needs on its website or work through various B2B web portals or inform their preferred vendors directly.[26] Because the school district likely does not have a preferred vendor, it issues an RFP and invites various tablet suppliers, technology companies, and other interested parties to bid on the contract.

Smaller companies may lack the ability to attract broad attention to their requests, so they might turn to a **web portal**, an Internet site whose purpose is to be a major starting point for users when they connect to the web. Although there are general portals such as Yahoo or MSN, B2B partners connect to specialized or niche portals to participate in online information exchanges and transactions. These exchanges help streamline procurement or distribution processes. Portals can provide tremendous cost savings because they eliminate periodic negotiations and routine paperwork, and they offer the means to form a supply chain that can respond quickly to the buyer's needs.

Small to medium-sized companies looking for skilled service workers also can use portals like Guru.com, started to help freelance professionals connect with companies that need their services, whether those services entail graphic design and cartooning or finance and accounting advice. Currently, 724,000 professionals list their offerings on this service-oriented professional exchange, and more than 30,000 companies regularly visit the site to post work orders. Guru.com thus provides value to both companies and freelancers by offering not only a site for finding each other but also dispute resolution, escrow for payments, and a means to rate freelancer quality.[27]

Stage 4: Proposal Analysis, Vendor Negotiation, and Selection

The buying organization, in conjunction with its critical decision makers, evaluates all the proposals it receives in response to its RFP. Thus the school district reviews all proposals it receives, together with the school board, representatives from the teachers' union, and perhaps interested parents. Many firms narrow the process to a few suppliers, often those with which they have existing relationships, and discuss key terms of the sale, such as price, quality, delivery, and financing. Some firms have a policy that requires them to negotiate with several suppliers, particularly if the product or service represents a critical component or aspect of the business. This policy keeps suppliers on their toes; they know that the buying firm can always shift a greater portion of its business to an alternative supplier if it offers better terms.

The school district evaluates proposals on the basis of the amount of experience the vendor has with tablet computers and similar technology products, because it wants to make sure that its investment is reliable in the short-term and flexible enough to accommodate new apps or updates. In addition, the district wants to be sure the technology will remain relevant in the longer term and not become obsolete. The vendor's ability to meet its specifications also is important, because if a battery needs to recharge in the middle of the school day, for example, a student may not have access to the device and may thus fall behind classmates. The vendor's financial position also provides an important indication of whether the vendor will be able to stay in business.

Stage 5: Order Specification

In the fifth stage, the firm places its order with its preferred supplier (or suppliers). The order includes a detailed description of the goods, prices, delivery dates, and, in some cases, penalties for noncompliance. The supplier then sends an acknowledgement that it has received the order and fills it by the specified date. In the case of the school's tablets, the terms are clearly laid out regarding when and how the vendor is expected to perform any preventive maintenance, who the contact person is for any problems with delivery or the tablets themselves, and under what circumstances the vendor will be expected to provide a replacement for a malfunctioning tablet. Issues like maintenance and replacement are important to the school, because it cannot afford to keep an inventory of extra tablets on hand.

Stage 6: Vendor Performance Assessment Using Metrics

Just as in the consumer buying process, firms analyze their vendors' performance so they can make decisions about their future purchases. The difference is that in a B2B setting, this analysis is typically more formal and objective. Let's consider how the school district might evaluate the tablet vendor's performance, as in Exhibit 7.3,

EXHIBIT 7.3	Evaluating a Vendor's Performance		
(1) Key Issues	(2) Importance Score	(3) Vendor's Performance	(4) Importance × Performance (2) × (3)
Customer Service	.40	5	2.0
Issue Resolution	.20	4	0.8
Delivery	.10	5	0.5
Quality	.30	3	0.9
Total	1.0		4.2

using the following metrics: delivery (based on promised delivery date), quality, customer service, and issue resolution.

1. The buying team develops a list of issues that it believes are important to consider in the vendor evaluation.

2. To determine the importance of each issue (column 1), the buying team assigns an importance score to each (column 2). The more important the issue, the higher its score, but the importance scores must add up to 1. In this case, the buying team believes that customer service and quality are most important, whereas the issue resolution and delivery are comparatively less important.

3. In the third column, the buying team assigns numbers that reflect its judgments about how well the vendor performs. Using a five-point scale, where 1 equals "poor performance" and 5 equals "excellent performance," the school district decides that the tablet vendor performs quite well on all issues except product quality.

4. To calculate an overall performance score in the fourth column, the team combines the importance of each issue and the vendor's performance scores by multiplying them. Because the tablet vendor performed well on the most important issues, when we add the importance/performance scores in column 4, we find that the overall evaluation is pretty good—4.2 on a five-point scale.

CHECK YOURSELF

1. Identify the stages in the B2B buying process.
2. How do you perform a vendor analysis?

L03 Identify the roles within the buying center.

THE BUYING CENTER

In most large organizations, several people are responsible for buying decisions. These **buying center** participants can range from employees who have a formal role in purchasing decisions (i.e., the purchasing or procurement department) to members of the design team that is specifying the particular equipment or raw material needed to employees who will be using a new machine that is being ordered. All these employees are likely to play different roles in the buying process, which vendors must understand and adapt to in their marketing and sales efforts.

We can categorize six different buying roles within a typical buying center (see Exhibit 7.4). One or more people may take on a certain role, or one person may take on more than one of the following roles: (1) "**initiator**, the person who first suggests buying the particular product or service; (2) **influencer**, the person whose views influence other members of the buying center in making the final decision; (3) **decider**, the person who ultimately determines any part of or the entire buying decision—whether to buy, what to buy, how to buy, or where to buy; (4) **buyer**, the person who handles the paperwork of the actual purchase; (5) **user**, the person who consumes or uses the product or service; and (6) **gatekeeper**, the person who controls information or access, or both, to decision makers and influencers."[28]

To illustrate how a buying center operates, consider purchases made by a hospital. Where do hospitals obtain their x-ray machines, syringes, and bedpans? Why are some medical procedures covered in whole or in part by insurance, whereas others are not? Why might your doctor recommend one type of allergy medication instead of another?

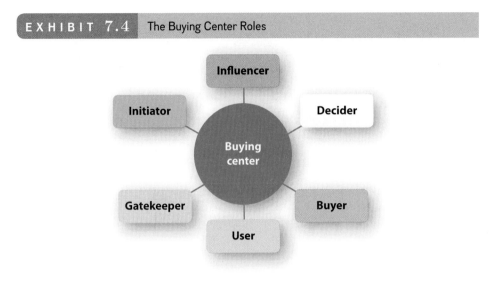

EXHIBIT 7.4   The Buying Center Roles

The Initiator—Your Doctor When you seek treatment from your physician, he or she initiates the buying process by determining the products and services that will best address and treat your illness or injury. For example, say that you fell backward off your snowboard and, in trying to catch yourself, shattered your elbow. You require surgery to mend the affected area, which includes the insertion of several screws to hold the bones in place. Your doctor promptly notifies the hospital to schedule a time for the procedure and specifies the brand of screws she wants on hand for your surgery.

The Influencer—The Medical Device Supplier, the Pharmacy For years, your doctor has been using ElbowMed screws, a slightly higher-priced screw. Her first introduction to ElbowMed screws came from the company's sales representative, who visited her office to demonstrate how ElbowMed screws were far superior to those of its competition. Your doctor recognized ElbowMed as a good value. Armed with empirical data and case studies, ElbowMed's sales rep effectively influenced your doctor's decision to use that screw.

The Decider—The Hospital Even though your doctor requested ElbowMed screws, the hospital ultimately is responsible for deciding whether to buy ElbowMed screws. The hospital supplies the operating room, instrumentation, and surgical supplies, and therefore, the hospital administrators must weigh a variety of factors to determine if the ElbowMed screw is not only best for the patients but also involves a cost that is reimbursable by various insurance providers.

From an ethical perspective, what information should pharmaceutical sales representatives provide to doctors?

The Buyer The actual buyer of the screw will likely be the hospital's materials manager, who is charged with buying and maintaining inventory for the hospital in the most cost-effective manner. Whereas ElbowMed screws are specific to your type of procedure, other items, such as gauze and sutures, may be purchased through a group purchasing organization (GPO), which obtains better prices through volume buying.

The User—The Patient Ultimately though, the buying process for this procedure will be greatly affected by the user, namely, you and your broken elbow. If you are uncomfortable with the procedure or have read about alternative procedures that you prefer, you may decide that ElbowMed screws are not the best treatment.

Ethical and Societal Dilemma 7.1   Is It Business or Bribery?

In some parts of the world, accepting money, offering expensive gifts, or distributing payments to government and business officials to influence business decisions is considered an acceptable business practice.[29] In the United States though, these practices are considered unethical and illegal. As the world moves to a more global economy, pressure is mounting to level the playing field by eliminating bribery. Yet countries that have traditionally relied on business bribery argue that criminalizing this activity will negatively affect their ability to compete.[30] How do executives doing business on an international scale respond when a behavior that could earn them a lucrative contract in one country could earn them jail time in another?

Whenever businesses cooperate with one another or companies intersect with governments, the opportunity exists for bribery. An extravagant gift or economic incentive may mean one contractor lands a lucrative contract. A private exchange of money between an executive and a public official may result in the official driving a new car while the executive's company bypasses a restriction that could hinder its growth. These types of interactions occur behind closed doors and between two people, yet they can have significant repercussions, including unsafe infrastructure, bridges, and buildings, if they occur in the context of large business transactions. Increasingly, the world's economies thus are pushing for an end to foreign bribery.

One tactic they are using is a public report by Transparency International that compares corruption rates of countries and industries.[31] This investigation reveals unexpected trends, such as evidence that bribes passing from one business to another are almost as common as bribes slipped to public officials. By highlighting those business sectors or countries perceived as the worst offenders, the Bribery Index also aims to bring about change, whether through embarrassment or economic repercussions that result when companies refuse to do business in corrupt economies. Finally, this report highlights suggestions for reducing corruption and incentives for improvement.

The 2011 Transparency International Bribery Index, as summarized in the graph, reveals that all the world's 28 largest economies engage in bribery; China and Russia emerged as those most likely to be using money and gifts to influence decisions. Although these figures are relatively unchanged from the 2008 report, both countries have recently begun enforcing legal repercussions for companies and individuals that engage in international business bribery.

The report also highlights positive results of reduced corruption: A business survey conducted in Europe found that two-thirds of respondents believe that a company with a reputation for ethical behavior enjoys a commercial advantage.[32] Findings such as these, along with improved transparency added to business practices, international anti-corruption standards, monitoring and enforcement of anti-corruption business policies and laws, and empowerment of whistleblowers, may also help reduce international bribery rates.

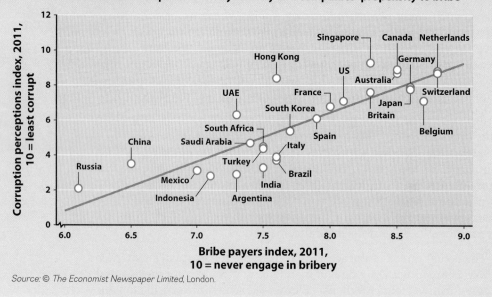

Perceived corruption levels by country and companies' propensity to bribe

Source: © The Economist Newspaper Limited, London.

The Gatekeeper—The Insurance Company Your insurer may believe that ElbowMed screws are too expensive and that other screws deliver equally effective results and therefore refuse to reimburse the hospital in full or in part for the use of the screws.

In the end, the final purchase decision must take into consideration every single buying center participant. Ethical and Societal Dilemma 7.1 examines the unethical, illegal, but also international practice of influencing the influencers through expensive gifts and payments.

EXHIBIT 7.5   Organizational Buying Culture

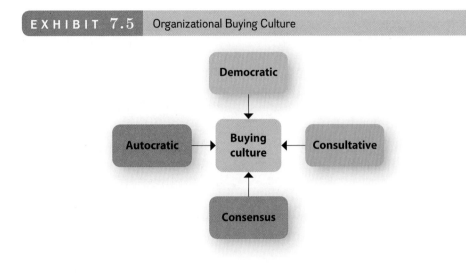

Organizational Culture

A firm's **organizational culture** reflects the set of values, traditions, and customs that guide its employees' behavior. The firm's culture often comprises a set of unspoken guidelines that employees share with one another through various work situations. For example, Walmart buyers are not allowed to accept even the smallest gift from a vendor, not even a cup of coffee. This rule highlights its overall corporate culture: It is a low-cost operator whose buyers must base their decisions only on the products' and vendors' merits.

Organizational culture can have a profound influence on purchasing decisions, and corporate buying center cultures thus might be divided into four general types: autocratic, democratic, consultative, and consensus (as illustrated in Exhibit 7.5). Knowing which buying center culture is prevalent in a given organization helps the seller decide how to approach that particular client, how and to whom to deliver pertinent information, and to whom to make sales presentations.

In an **autocratic buying center**, though there may be multiple participants, one person makes the decision alone, whereas the majority rules in a **democratic buying center**. **Consultative buying centers** use one person to make a decision but solicit input from others before doing so. Finally, in a **consensus buying center**, all members of the team must reach a collective agreement that they can support a particular purchase.[33]

Cultures act like living, breathing entities that change and grow, just as organizations do. Even within some companies, culture may vary by geography, by division, or by functional department. Whether you are a member of the buying center or a supplier trying to sell to it, it is extremely important to understand its culture and the roles of the key players in the buying process. Not knowing the roles of the key players could waste a lot of time and could even alienate the real decision maker.

Building B2B Relationships

In B2B contexts, there are a multitude of ways to enhance relationships, and these methods seem to be advancing and evolving by the minute. For example, blogs and social media can build awareness, provide search engine results, educate potential and existing clients about products or services, and warm up a seemingly cold corporate culture.[34] An expert who offers advice and knowledge about products increases brand awareness, and a blog is a great medium for this information. Web analytics, such as traffic on the website and the number of comments, can offer tangible evaluations, but a better measure is how often the blog gets mentioned elsewhere, the media attention it receives, and the interaction, involvement, intimacy, and influence that it promotes.

LO4 Describe the different types of organizational cultures.

Social and Mobile Marketing 7.2   Making the Most of LinkedIn

Business-to-business (B2B) marketing may seem relatively impersonal, but even in formalized, standardized buying situations, personal relationships count. Thus social media, with a bit of a tweak, play a key role in this setting, just as well as they do in consumer contexts. Perhaps the best example is LinkedIn, the social media site for business professionals. Launched in 2003, the site has been attracting roughly 1 million members weekly. As of March 2011, its worldwide membership surpassed the 100 million mark. The site is available in six languages and 200 countries, which means that it can help B2B interactions overcome geographical boundaries.[35]

In particular, LinkedIn can boast that executives from all the *Fortune* 500 companies have memberships on its site. Accordingly, its promise for networking, whether individually or for the company, is virtually unsurpassed. Such networking entails several key groups:[36]

- Customers and prospective customers. LinkedIn allows a firm or its representatives to introduce themselves to possible buyers, using a credible and easily accessible format. The Q&A option on LinkedIn pages also allows customers to ask questions and suppliers to demonstrate their expertise.

- Investors. The LinkedIn page offers tangible evidence of the firm's existence and its promise, which is critical information for outsiders who might be willing to invest in its development.

- Suppliers. By starting their own group on LinkedIn, B2B buyers might better identify which suppliers in the market are best matched with their needs and most interested in providing the resources they need.

- Employees and prospective employees. LinkedIn is a great source for finding employees who are diligent, professional, interested, and qualified. Furthermore, if

LinkedIn is perhaps the best social media site for networking with business professionals.

a firm retains its links to former employees, it can gain a good source of referrals—assuming those employees left on good terms.

- Analysts. The job of an analyst is to find detailed information about a company and then recommend it, or not, to the market. LinkedIn gives firms a means to provide that information in a credible but still firm-controlled context.

The site also provides sophisticated analytics for keeping track of all these networking opportunities. Users can see who visited their pages, which descriptions they viewed, and even compare their LinkedIn performance against competitors' pages.[37]

The Linkedin.com social network is mainly used for professional networking in the B2B marketplace (see Social and Mobile Marketing 7.2). Twitter, the micro-blogging site, is also valuable for B2B marketers, because they can communicate with other businesses as often as they want. Companies like HootSuite make it easier for companies using Twitter to manage their followers, update their posts, track analytics, and even schedule tweets, just as they would to manage a traditional marketing campaign.[38]

The majority of B2B marketers use white papers for their marketing efforts, and the majority of B2B buyers regularly read them prior to making a purchase.[39] When executives confront an unfulfilled business need, they normally turn to white papers. Their B2B partner may have a technologically advanced solution, but buyers have to understand the solution before they can consider a purchase. A good white paper provides information about the industry and its challenges in an educational context, rather than a promotional sense, to avoid seeming like

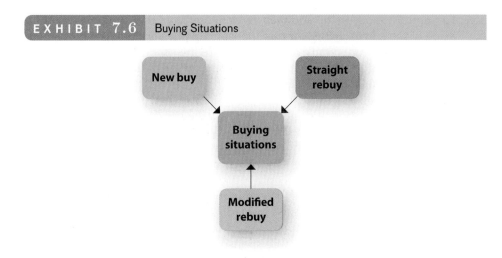

EXHIBIT 7.6 Buying Situations

simply propaganda. That is, the goal of white papers is to provide valuable information that a businessperson can easily understand and that will help the company address its problems with new solutions.

THE BUYING SITUATION

LO5 Detail different buying situations.

The type of buying situation also affects the B2B decision process. Most B2B buying situations can be categorized into three types: new buys, modified rebuys, and straight rebuys. (See Exhibit 7.6.) To illustrate the nuances among these three buying situations, consider how colleges and universities develop relationships with some of their suppliers. Most universities negotiate with sports apparel manufacturers, such as Nike, Reebok, and New Balance, to establish purchasing agreements for their sports teams. Those with successful sports teams have been very successful in managing these relationships, to the benefit of both the team and the company.[40] Large universities that win national championships, such as the University of Alabama or USC, can solicit sponsorships in exchange for free athletic equipment, whereas less popular teams or smaller schools typically must

Schools like the University of Alabama negotiate with sports apparel manufacturers, such as Nike, to get free athletic equipment. The manufacturers, in turn, get to sell apparel with the university logo.

accept an upfront sponsorship and then agree to buy from that vendor for a specified period of time. In exchange for this sponsorship, the vendors gain the right to sell apparel with the university logo and require the school's team to purchase only their equipment. Many apparel companies make a significant portion of their revenue through sponsorship deals that grant them the right to sell apparel with popular university logos.

In a **new buy** situation, a customer purchases a good or service for the first time,[41] which means the buying decision is likely to be quite involved because the buyer or the buying organization does not have any experience with the item. In the B2B context, the buying center is likely to proceed through all six steps in the buying process and involve many people in the buying decision. Typical new buys might range from capital equipment to components that the firm previously made itself but now has decided to purchase instead. For example, a small college might need to decide which apparel company to approach for a sponsorship. For smaller colleges, finding a company that will sponsor multiple sports teams—such as women's soccer as well as men's basketball—is a priority, though it also must balance other considerations, such as the length of the contract. Some vendors offer perks to attract new buyers; New Balance offers teams that sign up for long-term contracts custom fittings for their players' shoes. Each season, a sales team from New Balance visits the school and custom fits each player to achieve the best fit possible.

With another sort of example, Adding Value 7.2 highlights how Hubspot helps buyers become more informed about products before engaging in the B2B buying process.

Another example of a new buy occurs in the fashion industry, where runway shows offer wholesale buyers an opportunity to inspect new lines of clothing and place orders. Designer sales often occur during private meetings with buyers, both before and after runway shows. Buyers meet with the designers, discuss the line, and observe a model wearing the clothing. The buyer's challenge then is to determine which items will sell best in the retail stores he or she represents while trying to imagine what the item will look like in regular, as opposed to model, sizes. Buyers must also negotiate purchases for orders that may not be delivered for as much as six months. Buyers can suggest modifications to make the clothing more or less expensive, or more comfortable for their customers. Buyers and designers recognize the significant value of this relationship, which occasionally prompts buyers to purchase a few items from a designer, even if those items do not exactly fit the store's core customers' tastes. Doing so ensures that the buyer will have access to the designer's collection for the next season.[42]

In a **modified rebuy**, the buyer has purchased a similar product in the past but has decided to change some specifications, such as the desired price, quality level, customer service level, options, or so forth. Current vendors are likely to have an advantage in acquiring the sale in a modified rebuy situation, as long as the reason for the modification is not dissatisfaction with the vendor or its products. The Ohio State University's sports department might ask adidas to modify the specifications for its basketball shoes after noticing some improvements made to the adidas shoes used by the University of Michigan.

Straight rebuys occur when the buyer or buying organization simply buys additional units of products that had previously been purchased. Many B2B purchases are likely to fall in the straight rebuy category. For example, sports teams need to repurchase a tremendous amount of equipment that is not covered by apparel sponsorships, such as tape for athletes' ankles or weights for the weight room. The purchase of bottled water also typically involves a straight rebuy from an existing supplier.

These varied types of buying situations call for very different marketing and selling strategies. The most complex and difficult is the new buy, because it requires the buying organization to make changes in its current practices and

Adding Value 7.2 · Getting the Message Out with Inbound Marketing[43]

Search engines, company web pages, social media sites, and the blogosphere have transformed the way businesses learn about and shop for products and services. Unlike a decade ago, when a prospective customer had little knowledge of a vendor's products at first contact, today's customers have searched the Internet using relevant keywords and reviewed company websites by the time they speak with a vendor. As a result, they are well-informed and seriously interested in a purchase, adding new efficiency to B2B transactions. But this development only works if companies have the marketing savvy to use today's technology to their advantage.

Two entrepreneurs noticed that small companies and start-ups without the skills to use these tools effectively get lost in the "noise," even if prospective customers are searching for vendors in their niche. Furthermore, companies that enlist marketing firms are disadvantaged if those firms rely solely on traditional best practices, such as print advertising, telemarketing, and trade shows. To help these businesses, the two launched a software marketing program, HubSpot, designed to help companies transform their marketing approach. The idea was to abandon intrusive "outbound marketing," which people are increasingly able to screen out, and replace it with "inbound marketing." Inbound marketing, defined as any marketing tactic that relies on earning customer interest rather than buying it, is built on the understanding that Facebook, Twitter, online user reviews, smartphones, blogs, and websites are the true force behind the way actors in today's marketplace actually learn and shop.

HubSpot's software contains easy-to-use tools that help companies get noticed, convert website visitors to customers, and analyze the effectiveness of marketing efforts across channels. Among the tools in the first category, for example, is a keyword grader that helps companies create content and a list of relevant keywords to improve search engine odds and ranking. Using the lead conversion tools, marketers without technical skills can create landing pages with customizable lead capture forms, auto-response e-mails, and thank-you pages. These tools can also be used to send customized e-mails to new leads on a self-selected schedule. The marketing analytics tools allow HubSpot's customers to track competitors, evaluate the impact of a blog, and compare the effectiveness of all marketing channels to provide important insight into the behaviors of customers and the value of each channel to the bottom line.

HubSpot's approach has been successful for both the founders and their customers. The company, launched in June 2006, reached 3,500 customers in four years and is the second fastest growing software-as-a-service (SAS) company in history.

One customer, the nonprofit National Institute for Fitness and Sport (NIFS), wanted to increase its visibility with corporate and retirement fitness centers. After experiencing difficulty driving traffic to the company website—and after an expensive marketing company campaign proved ineffective—NIFS turned to HubSpot. The results were increases in traffic and leads by more than 200 percent and an increase in social media traffic of 16 percent. According to NIFS's director of media, the fitness company "picked up a number of requests for proposals from businesses that never would have paid attention to us initially because we were able to raise where we sit in the search engines."[44]

Companies such as HubSpot are taking advantage of changes that have already occurred in the marketplace to reduce costs and improve the effectiveness of marketing. As technology evolves and more business and individual shoppers use online information to make their purchasing decisions, businesses will have to adapt their marketing strategies to encompass new technologies and new shopping behaviors.

HubSpot helps its customers get noticed on the Internet.

purchases. As a result, several members of the buying center will likely become involved, and the level of their involvement will be more intense than in the case of modified and straight rebuys. In new buying situations, buying center members also typically spend more time at each stage of the B2B buying process, similar to the extended decision-making process that consumers use in the B2C process. In comparison, in modified rebuys, the buyers spend less time at each stage of the B2B buying process, similar to limited decision making in the B2C process (see Chapter 6).

In straight rebuys, however, the buyer is often the only member of the buying center involved in the process. Like a consumer's habitual purchase, straight rebuys often enable the buyer to recognize the firm's need and go directly to the fifth step in the B2B buying process, skipping the product specification, RFP process, and proposal analysis and supplier selection steps.

Thus, in various ways, B2B marketing both differs from and mirrors the consumer behavior (B2C) process we detailed in Chapter 6. The differences in the six stages of the buying process make sense in view of the many unique factors that come into play. The constitution of the buying center (initiator, influencer, decider, buyer, user, and gatekeeper), the culture of the purchasing firm (autocratic, democratic, consultative, or consensus), and the context of the buying situation (new buy, modified rebuy, straight rebuy) all influence the B2B buying process in various ways, which means that sellers must be constantly aware of these factors if they want to be successful in their sales attempts. Finally, just as it has done seemingly everywhere we look, the Internet has radically changed some elements of the B2B world, increasing the frequency of both private electronic exchanges and auctions.

CHECK YOURSELF

1. What factors affect the B2B buying process?
2. What are the six different buying roles?
3. What is the difference between new buy, rebuy, and modified rebuy?

Summing Up

LO1 Describe the ways in which business-to-business (B2B) firms segment their markets.

All firms want to divide the market into groups of customers with different needs, wants, or characteristics who therefore might appreciate products or services geared especially toward them. On a broad level, B2B firms divide the market into four types: manufacturers or service providers, resellers, institutions, and government. Manufacturers and service providers purchase materials to make their products and components, and offer expertise to help run their businesses, such as computer and telephone systems. Resellers are primarily wholesalers, distributors, or retailers that sell the unchanged products. Institutions include nonprofit organizations such as hospitals, schools, or churches. Finally, governments purchase all types of goods and services, but in the United States, defense is among the largest expenditures.

LO2 List the steps in the B2B buying process.

Similar to the B2C buying process, the B2B process consists of several stages: need recognition; product specification; the RFP process; proposal analysis, vendor negotiation, and selection; order specification; and vendor performance assessment using metrics. The B2B process tends to be more formalized and structured than the customer buying process.

LO3 Identify the roles within the buying center.

The initiator first suggests the purchase. The influencer affects important people's perceptions and final decisions. The decider ultimately determines at least some of the buying decision—whether, what, how, or where to buy. The buyer handles the details of the actual purchase. The user consumes or employs the product or service. The gatekeeper controls information and access to decision makers and influencers.

In B2B situations, it is likely that several people, organized into a buying center, will be involved in making the purchase decision. The vendor must understand the relationships among the participants of the buying center to be effective. A firm's organizational culture can also influence the decision process. For instance, if a firm is trying to sell to a young, high-tech computer component manufacturer, it might be well advised to send sales people who are fluent in technology-speak and can easily relate to the customer.

LO4 Describe the different types of organizational cultures.

Firm culture consists of unspoken guidelines that employees share through various work situations. They generally can be classified as autocratic, such that one person makes most decisions; democratic, where the majority rules; consultative, in which one person makes decisions based on the input of others; or consensus, which requires all members of the team to reach collective agreement.

LO5 Detail different buying situations.

The buying process depends to a great extent on the situation. If a firm is purchasing a product or service for the first time (i.e., new buy), the process is much more involved than if it is engaging in a straight rebuy of the same item again. A modified rebuy falls somewhere in the middle, such that the buyer wants essentially the same thing but with slightly different terms or features.

Key Terms

- autocratic buying center, 219
- business-to-business (B2B) marketing, 208
- buyer, 216
- buying center, 216
- consensus buying center, 219
- consultative buying center, 219
- decider, 216
- democratic buying center, 219
- derived demand, 208
- distributors, 210
- gatekeeper, 216
- influencer, 216
- initiator, 216
- modified rebuy, 222
- new buy, 222
- organizational culture, 219
- request for proposals (RFP), 214
- resellers, 210
- straight rebuy, 222
- user, 216
- web portal, 214
- wholesalers, 210

Marketing Applications

1. Provide an example of each of the four types of B2B organizations.

2. What are the major differences between the consumer buying process discussed in Chapter 6 and the B2B buying process discussed in this chapter? Use buying a desktop for personal use versus buying over 100 desktops for a firm to illustrate the key points.

3. Assume you have written this textbook and are going to attempt to sell it to your school. Identify the six members of the buying center. What role would each play in the decision process? Rank them in terms of how much influence they would have on the decision, with 1 being most influential and 6 being least influential. Will this ranking be different in other situations?

4. Now provide an example of the three types of buying situations that the bookstore at your school might face when buying textbooks.

5. Mazda is trying to assess the performance of two manufacturers that could supply music systems for its vehicles. Using the information in the

table below, determine which manufacturer Mazda should use.

Performance Evaluation of Brands

Issues	Importance Weights	Manufacturer A's Performance	Manufacturer B's Performance
Sound	0.4	5	3
Cost	0.3	2	4
Delivery time	0.1	2	2
Brand cachet	0.2	5	1
Total	1		

6. Describe the organizational culture at your school or job. How would knowledge of this particular organization's culture help a B2B salesperson sell products or services to the organization?

7. You have just started to work in the purchasing office of a major pharmaceutical firm. The purchasing manager has asked you to assist in writing an RFP for a major purchase. The manager gives you a sheet detailing the specifications for the RFP. While reading the specifications, you realize that they have been written to be extremely favorable to one bidder. How should you handle this situation?

---

www.mhhe.com/grewal4e

Quiz Yourself

1. After posting an RFP for telecommunication equipment, the University of Central Florida received six proposals from qualified vendors. Next, UCF will:
   a. recognize obstacles that must be circumvented
   b. re-evaluate the firm's needs
   c. give one vendor a purchase order
   d. conduct vendor analysis
   e. evaluate the proposals and narrow the choice to a few suppliers

2. Whenever Kim, a textbook publisher's representative, calls on the business faculty at Major University, her first stop is to chat with Frank, the business department secretary. From Frank, Kim learns which professors have left or are new, and what courses will be taught next semester. Frank also helps Kim to make appointments to see professors to discuss textbook choices. Frank acts as the _____ in the business department buying center.
   a. buyer
   b. initiator
   c. influencer
   d. user
   e. gatekeeper

(Answers to these two questions can be found on page 647.)

Go to www.mhhe.com/grewal4e to practice an additional 11 questions.

Toolkit

B2B VENDOR ANALYSIS

Help David evaluate two software vendors. He has created a chart to help him decide which one to pick. He has rated the two vendors on brand strength, timeliness of deliveries, product quality, and ease of ordering. His firm is generally most interested in quality and then in timeliness. Reputation is somewhat important. The ease of ordering is least important. Please use the toolkit provided at http://www.mhhe.com/grewal4e to specify the importance weights and help David pick the best software vendor.

Net Savvy

1. Ballymaloe Country Relish is an Irish delicacy, sold in fine food stores throughout Ireland. For consumers outside Ireland, it also lists various sellers in different countries. Visit ballymaloecountryrelish.ie, click on "Where Can I Buy," and find the most convenient source for you personally. Why does Ballymaloe offer such information and direct links to other retailers? What benefits does doing so provide the relish maker, the retailer, and customers?

2. Siemens worked with the custom motorcycle manufacturer Orange County Chopper to build the Smart Chopper—the first electric motorcycle. Visit http://www.usa.siemens.com/smartchopper/ to learn about the specifications and details of this new form of chopper. How is Siemens using this innovation to improve its relationships with its business customers? What other outcomes might this services provider expect from its efforts?

Chapter Case Study

UPS: FROM SHIPPING TO SUPPLY CHAIN[45]

OVERVIEW

In 1907, an enterprising teenager borrowed $100 to start a business running errands, delivering packages, carrying notes or bags, and even ferrying food from restaurants to customers. Messengers traveled on foot or, when the trip was longer, by bicycle. More than a century later, that young man's business has morphed into United Parcel Service (UPS), a $45.3 billion company that serves 220 countries and territories, employs more than 400,000 people,[46] and includes UPS Air Cargo, UPS Mail Innovations, Mail Boxes Etc., Inc., and UPS Freight, as well as a supply-chain financing company, global management consulting firm, and logistics and supply chain solutions services.[47]

During its 100+ year span, as technology and demands have changed, the company has upgraded its delivery methods by adding trucks, ocean and train delivery, and even its own jet cargo fleet. Although its fleet of trucks might not be quite as environmentally friendly as a bicycle, UPS carefully manages its delivery dispatches in an attempt to minimize both fuel use and emissions. It is incorporating electric vehicles into its delivery fleet, saving 126,000 gallons of diesel fuel every year,[48] and moving from fuel-burning vehicles to biodiesel blends.[49] In the air, the company adopts a "continuous descent approach" for its carriers, which reportedly reduces pollutants by as much as 34 percent compared with traditional, step-like airplane descents.[50]

UPS uses environmentally friendly hybrid electric vehicles for some of its fleet.

UPS also has expanded into international markets and developed systems to help track the more than 15.1 million packages that pass through its corporate hands each day. This expertise prompted UPS's most recent transition: from a global package and information delivery company to a facilitator of global commerce, capable of providing supply chain solutions to customers.

Through acquisitions and restructuring, the company has added logistics and distribution, consulting, mail, e-commerce, financial services, and international trade management to its portfolio of client services. UPS believes that these new services help customers focus on their own core competencies while protecting UPS from competitors. Building a business line based on information technology rather than fuel use also helps improve the company's environmental profile and build a profit stream protected from rising fuel costs.[51]

COMPETITIVE CHALLENGES

Both FedEx and the United States Postal Service (USPS) are constantly on the lookout for ways to attract business away from UPS. Threatened by drops in regular mail volume, which has largely resulted from increased Internet use, the USPS introduced a flat-rate box, based on size rather than package weight.[52] This move was designed to attract the package shipping business of companies such as Amazon and eBay, which must ship often heavy materials constantly to consumers. Similar to UPS, FedEx has expanded its service offerings, but its expansion has focused on copying services (FedEx Kinko's), along with virtually real-time tracking of ground, freight, and express shipments. FedEx is UPS's greatest competitor, with $39.3 billion in revenue and more than 290,000 employees.[53]

ADDING VALUE FOR BUSINESS CUSTOMERS

The expansion of its business offerings enables UPS to handle a vast array of its client company's operations, including storage, assembly, and repair of merchandise. It even provides customer service functions that demand minimal client involvement. For example, for the French pet food company Royal Canin, UPS employees mix, pack, and ship all sold dog and cat food. In addition to cutting the product delivery time, this model eliminates Royal Canin's need for a U.S. warehouse.

For Toshiba, UPS not only transports broken computers but also fixes and ships them back to their original owners, usually within 24 hours! This approach relieves Toshiba of the need to run repair facilities when its core competency is computer production and design. It also gets a repaired machine back to customers more quickly. And when there is a problem, UPS offers perhaps the most valuable service for both Toshiba and its customers, that is, a scapegoat. As the former CEO of UPS Michael Eskew noted, "Customers wanted one throat to choke when the pressure was on to deliver. We offered them UPS's throat."[54]

These supportive relationships entail not just profits but also an element of UPS's approach to environmental and social sustainability. The company has worked over the past decade to use more environmentally responsible packaging, reduce water use, support community disaster relief programs, provide charitable contributions, and contribute to employee development, as well as to undertake initiatives to reduce carbon emissions. As part of these efforts, the company is working with business customers and other stakeholders to improve accountability for resource use. These relationships ensure that all business partners are focused on balancing environmental concerns and profits and providing value to the communities and individuals who help make them successful.

SPREADING THE WORD

UPS's sustainability efforts are far-reaching. Recognizing that different audiences interpret sustainability in different ways, UPS has worked with nonprofit groups and nongovernmental organizations to better understand stakeholder expectations. As a result of these conversations, UPS is developing new sustainability programs that will provide direction for competitors and other transportation companies and seeking ways to participate in public policy issues that enhance the environmental and social responsibility of businesses.

Furthermore, advertisements directed to its targeted demographic go beyond the conventional methods of television and print media. For example, a recent mobile ad campaign piggybacked on *The New York Times'* BlackBerry application.[55] Using BlackBerries for delivery helped focus messaging on the right audience, because BlackBerry users tend to be businesspeople. If they clicked on a banner that invited users to see how UPS could improve operations for its business customers, the consumers connected to a landing page that featured case studies, videos, and an option to receive additional information.

Questions

1. Describe how you would expect firms to interact with UPS. Use the steps in the B2B buying process discussed in the chapter to facilitate your discussion.

2. Manufacturers, resellers, government, and autioneers on eBay all have alternative delivery options. Describe some ways that UPS provides greater value to these various types of customers than its competitors can. (It might help to review its website at http://www.UPS.com.)

CHAPTER 8

Global Marketing

From the Maharaja Mac in India to the Prosperity Burger prepared especially for the Chinese New Year celebrations, McDonald's has built a global fast-food empire under its golden arches. Only 31 percent of McDonald's revenue now comes from sales in the United States, and most of its international growth has come from the surging economies of Brazil, Russia, China, and India.[1] A pioneer in overseas franchising, McDonald's has spared no effort in its attempts to penetrate foreign markets. In China, it recently announced that within four years, it plans to open one new outlet daily to meet its immediate goal of 2,000 stores.[2] In Brazil, it created Latin America's first environmentally certified fast-food restaurant. A vast market defined by stark cultural differences, India has required a more modest approach that would allow McDonald's to develop its real estate and supply infrastructure, train its local workforce and management at its famed Hamburger University, and adjust the menu for vegetarian customers.[3] Although the McAloo Tikki Burger has been a great success, the company has opened just 210 restaurants in India since 1996.

LEARNING OBJECTIVES

LO1 Describe the components of a country market assessment.

LO2 Understand the marketing opportunities in BRIC countries.

LO3 Identify the various market entry strategies.

LO4 Highlight the similarities and differences between a domestic marketing strategy and a global marketing strategy.

But McDonald's growth strategy relies on more than just added locations. In crowded cities, with real estate prices too high to build drive-through restaurants, the company has hired droves of motorbike drivers to bring Big Macs to customers. This nimble delivery approach is now a mainstay in cities from Beijing to Kuwait City. Online ordering will be next, though the challenge will be to reduce the cost of call centers to support this new distribution model.[4]

Despite growth in these rapidly transitioning economies, Europe still generates the bulk of foreign sales for McDonald's. Most new growth comes from Russia, where the company has 245 locations and controls 70 percent of the booming fast-food business. Even as fast-food competitors face potential market saturation in the United States, Russian demand for quick burgers appears to be insatiable.[5] Driving this Russian appetite has been the growth of a newly affluent middle class, with money to spend to dine out. Infrastructure development in Russia also has been a boon, as cities open malls with food courts, highways are constructed with drive-through locations, and specialty suppliers of frozen food and packaging have appeared.

In the early years of Russian expansion, few private businesses existed to supply all the ingredients McDonald's needed to produce Big Macs and fries. The company solved the problem by building an enormous food processing plant outside Moscow. But it also worked to cultivate relationships with local Russian vendors and contractors, to which it eventually could outsource its supply chain. Today, a grower who began selling cucumbers to McDonald's in 1990 has become the Pickle King of Russia, dominating the processed foods market.[6]

Increasing globalization affects not only massive U.S. corporations that actively search out new markets but also small and medium-sized businesses that increasingly depend on goods produced globally to deliver their products and services. Few people really think about how globalization affects their daily lives, but just take a minute to read the labels on the clothing you are wearing right now. Chances are that most of the items, even if they carry U.S. brand names, were manufactured in another part of the world.

In the United States, the market has evolved from a system of regional marketplaces to national markets to geographically regional markets (e.g., Canada and the United States together) to international markets and finally to global markets. **Globalization** refers to the processes by which goods, services, capital, people, information, and ideas flow across national borders. Global markets are the result of several fundamental changes, such as reductions or eliminations of trade barriers by country governments, the decreasing concerns of distance and time with regard to moving products and ideas across countries, the standardization of laws across borders, and globally integrated production processes.[7]

Each of these fundamental changes has paved the way for marketing to flourish in other countries. The elimination of trade barriers and other governmental actions, for instance, allows goods and ideas to move quickly and efficiently around the world, which in turn facilitates the quick delivery of goods to better meet the needs of global consumers.

As a consequence, consumers have easy access to global products and services. When we walk into a toy store, we expect to find Legos from Denmark. In the local sporting goods store, we anticipate finding running shoes made in China by the German firm, adidas. In the grocery store, we demand out-of-season

How do Legos get from their manufacturer in Denmark to a toy store near your home?

Build it. **LEGO**

produce like blueberries from Chile in January. Or consider how a $12 digital camera for your keychain, made in Taiwan, could be produced, transported halfway around the world, and sold for so little money at your local Target. These are the questions we will be examining in this chapter.

We begin by looking at how firms assess the potential of a given market, with particular attention to the BRIC countries (Brazil, Russia, India, and China.) Then we examine how firms make decisions to go global, and choose how and what they will sell globally. Then we explore how to build the marketing mix for global products.

ASSESSING GLOBAL MARKETS

LO1 Describe the components of a country market assessment.

Because different countries, with their different stages of globalization, offer marketers a variety of opportunities, firms must assess the viability of various potential market entries. As illustrated in Exhibit 8.1, we examine four sets of criteria necessary to assess a country's market: economic analysis, infrastructure and technological analysis, government actions or inactions, and sociocultural analysis. Information about these four areas offers marketers a more complete picture of a country's potential as a market for products and services.

Economic Analysis Using Metrics

The greater the wealth of people in a country, generally, the better the opportunity a firm will have in that particular country. A firm conducting an economic analysis of a country market must look at three major economic factors using well-established metrics: the general economic environment, the market size and population growth rate, and real income.

Evaluating the General Economic Environment In general, healthy economies provide better opportunities for global marketing expansions, and there are several ways a firm can use metrics to measure the relative health of a particular country's economy. Each way offers a slightly different view, and some may be more useful for some products and services than for others.

To determine the market potential for its particular product or service, a firm should use as many metrics as it can obtain. One metric is the relative level of imports and exports. The United States, for example, suffers a trade deficit, which means that the country imports more goods than it exports.[8] For U.S. marketers,

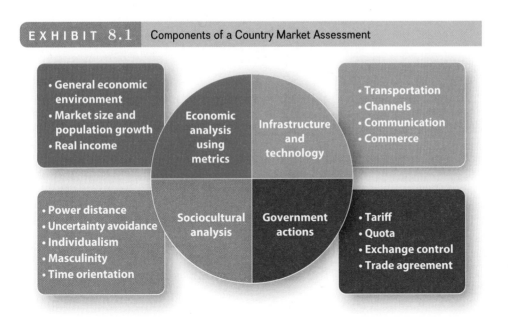

EXHIBIT 8.1 Components of a Country Market Assessment

- General economic environment
- Market size and population growth
- Real income

Economic analysis using metrics

Infrastructure and technology

- Transportation
- Channels
- Communication
- Commerce

- Power distance
- Uncertainty avoidance
- Individualism
- Masculinity
- Time orientation

Sociocultural analysis

Government actions

- Tariff
- Quota
- Exchange control
- Trade agreement

this deficit can signal the potential for greater competition at home from foreign producers. Firms would prefer to manufacture in a country that has a trade surplus, or a higher level of exports than imports, because it signals a greater opportunity to export products to more markets.

The most common way to gauge the size and market potential of an economy, and therefore the potential the country has for global marketing, is to use standardized metrics of output. Gross domestic product (GDP), the most widely used of these metrics, is defined as the market value of the goods and services produced by a country in a year. Gross national income (GNI) consists of GDP plus the net income earned from investments abroad (minus any payments made to nonresidents who contribute to the domestic economy). In other words, U.S. firms that invest or maintain operations abroad count their income from those operations in the GNI but not the GDP.[9]

Another frequently used metric of an overall economy is the purchasing power parity (PPP), a theory that states that if the exchange rates of two countries are in equilibrium, a product purchased in one will cost the same in the other, if expressed in the same currency.[10] A novel metric that employs PPP to assess the relative economic buying power among nations is *The Economist*'s Big Mac Index, which suggests that exchange rates should adjust to equalize the cost of a basket of goods and services, wherever it is bought around the world. Using McDonald's Big Mac as the market basket, Exhibit 8.2 shows that the cheapest burger is in India, where it costs $1.89, compared with an average American price of $4.07. In Brazil, the same burger costs $6.16. This index thus implies that the Indian rupee is 53 percent undervalued, whereas the Brazilian real is 52 percent overvalued, in comparison with the U.S. dollar.[11]

These various metrics help marketers understand the relative wealth of a particular country, though they may not give a full picture of the economic health of a country, because they are based solely on material output. Nor is a weak dollar always a bad thing. For U.S. exporters, a weak dollar means greater demand for

EXHIBIT 8.2   Big Mac Index

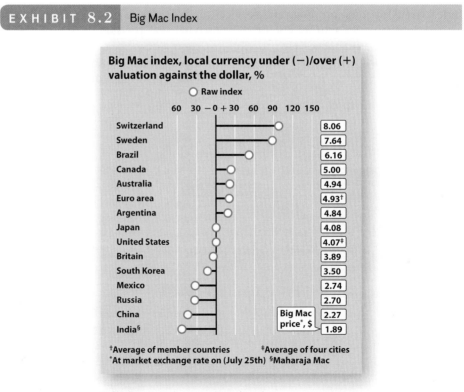

their products in foreign countries, because they can sell at a lower price.[12] Although an understanding of the macroeconomic environment is crucial for managers facing a market entry decision, of equal importance is the understanding of economic metrics of market size and population growth rate.

Evaluating Market Size and Population Growth Rate Global population has been growing dramatically since the turn of the twentieth century, at least. From a marketing perspective, however, growth has never been equally dispersed. Today, less developed nations, by and large, are experiencing rapid population growth, while many developed countries are experiencing either zero or negative population growth. The countries with the highest purchasing power today may become less attractive in the future for many products and services because of stagnated growth. And as we discussed previously, the BRIC countries are likely to be the source of most market growth.

In response, consumer goods companies are paying close attention to the strong demand in BRIC nations. Thus Procter & Gamble, which enjoys a strong advantage in the Chinese market, also is expanding aggressively into India and Brazil (as well as sub-Saharan Africa).[13] With 1.33 billion people, China offers such promise that international companies such as PepsiCo and Coca-Cola cannot afford not to focus their efforts there. Each company plans to invest more than $2.5 billion immediately in China, with the goal of achieving at least double-digit annual growth. Pepsi also plans to build a research and development center for its Asian products to ensure that it correctly targets this new consumer market. In some cases, the companies will sell the same products in China and in the United States; in other situations, they are creating new products to meet Chinese consumers' tastes. The "Minute Maid Pulpy Super Milky" combines fruit juice, milk powder, whey protein, and coconut bits. Pepsi offers cucumber-flavored and crispy prawn–flavored potato chips.[14]

"Minute Maid Pulpy Super Milky" combines fruit juice, milk powder, whey protein, and coconut bits for the Chinese market.

Another aspect related to market size and population growth pertains to the distribution of the population within a particular region; namely, is the population located primarily in rural or urban areas? This distinction determines where and how products and services can be delivered. Long supply chains, in which goods pass through many hands, are often necessary to reach rural populations in less developed countries and therefore add to the products' cost. As we noted previously, India's 1.16 billion people live overwhelmingly in rural areas, though the population is moving toward urban areas to meet the demands of the growing industrial and service centers located in major cities such as Bangalore and New Delhi. This population shift, perhaps not surprisingly, is accompanied by rapid growth in the middle class. Furthermore, relatively careful banking policies and minimal dependence on exports have helped protect India from the global financial crisis. The business impacts of these combined trends of increasing urbanization, a growing middle class, a degree of protectionism by the central government, and a youthful populace make India an absolutely enormous market for consumer goods.

In the capital of India, New Delhi, crowded streets traditionally were filled with horse-drawn carts, bicycles, scooters, and taxis. Yet the growing Indian middle class is demanding more products previously available only to the wealthy. Therefore, the Nano, the world's cheapest car, has begun to appear, jockeying for position with the multitude of other vehicles. The Nano costs only about 100,000 rupees ($2000). It weighs less than half a Honda Accord, and it gets 56 miles per gallon. It can even achieve a top speed of 60 miles per hour, though it needs 23 seconds to reach that speed from a standstill. During the 16-day prebooking period, the manufacturer received orders for 203,000 of the tiny car.[15]

Developed for the Indian market, the Nano is the world's cheapest car—about $2,000.

Similarly, the prevalence of cell phones has grown with the emerging Indian middle class. Fifteen years ago, the country hosted only 5 million total telecom connections, and that number included ground lines. Today, there are more than 752 million.[16] The rapid growth rates of industries create significant opportunities for global companies to sell products. In the telecommunications industry, for example, sellers of accessories such as ringtones and new batteries are enjoying a greatly expanded market. In general, India's economy is expected to continue to outpace world growth.

Evaluating Real Income   Firms can make adjustments to an existing product or change the price to meet the unique needs of a particular country market. Such shifts are particularly common for low-priced consumer goods. For instance, Procter & Gamble developed a single-use shampoo packet for consumers in less developed nations that cannot afford an entire bottle at one time. To increase consumption of Coca-Cola in rural India, the company lowered its price to the equivalent of about 10 cents per bottle; Cadbury International introduced the Dairy Milk Shots for the equivalent of about 4 cents.[17] Textbook publishers sell paperback versions of U.S. books for a fraction of its U.S. price to countries where students would not be able to otherwise afford a text. But pricing adjustments aren't only for inexpensive products. Fashion and jewelry manufacturers also make downward adjustments to their prices in countries where the incomes of their target markets cannot support higher prices.

To adjust for India's lower income, Cadbury International sells its Dairy Milk Shots for the equivalent of about four cents.

Even as multinationals battle for dominance in emerging economies, local marketers also are becoming increasingly price competitive in selling their wares, as the example of India's Tata Motors and its Nano shows. Local marketers already have strong familiarity with their markets, existing distribution channels, and good name recognition. These smaller firms can often exhibit greater flexibility in their pricing to hold on to market share. The best outcome for everyone involved is not

just a higher share of an existing market but rather the ongoing development of the market for everyone.[18]

Analyzing Infrastructure and Technological Capabilities

The next component of any market assessment is an infrastructure and technological analysis. **Infrastructure** is defined as the basic facilities, services, and installations needed for a community or society to function, such as transportation and communications systems, water and power lines, and public institutions like schools, post offices, and prisons.

Marketers are especially concerned with four key elements of a country's infrastructure: transportation, distribution channels, communications, and commerce. First, there must be a system to transport goods throughout the various markets and to consumers in geographically dispersed marketplaces—trains, roads, refrigeration. Second, distribution channels must exist to deliver products in a timely manner and at a reasonable cost. Third, the communications system, particularly media access, must be sufficiently developed to allow consumers to find information about the products and services available in the marketplace. Fourth, the commercial infrastructure, which consists of the legal, banking, and regulatory systems, allows markets to function. In the next section, we focus on how issues pertaining to the political and legal structures of a country can affect the risk that marketers face in operating in a given country.

Analyzing Government Actions

Governmental actions, as well as the actions of nongovernmental political groups, can significantly influence firms' ability to sell goods and services, because they often result in laws or other regulations that either promote the growth of the global market or close off the country and inhibit growth. These issues include tariffs, quotas, exchange controls, and trade agreements. (See Exhibit 8.3.)

Tariffs A **tariff** (also called a **duty**) is a tax levied on a good imported into a country. In most cases, tariffs are intended to make imported goods more expensive and thus less competitive with domestic products,[19] which in turn protects domestic industries from foreign competition. In other cases, tariffs might be imposed to penalize another country for trade practices that the home country views as unfair. When China entered the World Trade Organization, it agreed to

EXHIBIT 8.3   Government Actions

a "safeguard" provision imposed by the United States, which stated that U.S. companies harmed by Chinese imports could ask for protection from a "surge" of Chinese alternatives.

Quotas A **quota** designates the maximum quantity of a product that may be brought into a country during a specified time period. The United States, for instance, allows 1.2 million tons of sugar to be imported (the quota) without a tariff because the country generally consumes more than it produces.[20] It then monitors consumption closely to protect domestic sugar farmers. If demand exceeds supply, it increases the quota.

Tariffs and quotas can have fundamental and potentially devastating impacts on a firm's ability to sell products in another country. Tariffs artificially raise prices and therefore lower demand, and quotas reduce the availability of imported merchandise. Conversely, tariffs and quotas benefit domestically made products because they reduce foreign competition.

Exchange Control **Exchange control** refers to the regulation of a country's currency **exchange rate**, the measure of how much one currency is worth in relation to another.[21] A designated agency in each country, often the central bank, sets the rules for currency exchange, though in the United States, the Federal Reserve sets the currency exchange rates. In recent years, the value of the U.S. dollar has changed significantly compared with other important world currencies. When the dollar falls, it has a twofold effect on U.S. firms' ability to conduct global business. For firms that depend on imports of finished products, raw materials that they fabricate into other products, or services from other countries, the cost of doing business goes up dramatically. At the same time, buyers in other countries find the costs of U.S. goods and services much lower than they were before.

Trade agreements impact the global marketing environment. Here, Uraguayan president, Jose Mujica, delivers a speech during a press conference after the Mercosur Extraordinary Summit at Planalto Palace in Brasilia, Brazil on July 31, 2012.

EXHIBIT 8.4	Trade Agreements
Name	**Countries**
European Union	There are 27 member countries of the EU: Austria, Belgium, Bulgaria, Cyprus, Czech Republic, Denmark, Estonia, Finland, France, Germany, Greece, Hungary, Ireland, Italy, Latvia, Lithuania, Luxembourg, Malta, Netherlands, Poland, Portugal, Romania, Slovakia, Slovenia, Spain, Sweden, and the United Kingdom.[22] There are five official candidate countries to join the EU: Croatia, Macedonia, Turkey, Iceland, and Montenegro.
NAFTA	United States, Canada, and Mexico.
CAFTA	United States, Costa Rica, the Dominican Republic, El Salvador, Guatemala, Honduras, and Nicaragua.
Mercosur	Full members: Argentina, Brazil, Paraguay, Uruguay, and Venezuela.
ASEAN	Brunei Darussalam, Cambodia, Indonesia, Laos, Malaysia, Myanmar, Philippines, Singapore, Thailand, and Vietnam.

Trade Agreements Marketers must consider the **trade agreements** to which a particular country is a signatory or the **trading bloc** to which it belongs. A trade agreement is an intergovernmental agreement designed to manage and promote trade activities for a specific region, and a trading bloc consists of those countries that have signed the particular trade agreement.[23] Some major trade agreements cover two-thirds of the world's international trade: the European Union (EU), the North American Free Trade Agreement (NAFTA), Central America Free Trade Agreement (CAFTA), Mercosur, and the Association of Southeast Asian Nations (ASEAN).[24] These trade agreements are summarized in Exhibit 8.4. The EU represents the highest level of integration across individual nations, whereas the other agreements vary in their integration levels.

The European Union has resulted in lowering trade barriers and strengthening global relationships among member nations.

IKEA in France.

Analyzing Sociocultural Factors

Understanding another country's culture is crucial to the success of any global marketing initiative. Culture, or the shared meanings, beliefs, morals, values, and customs of a group of people, exists on two levels: visible artifacts (e.g., behavior, dress, symbols, physical settings, ceremonies) and underlying values (thought processes, beliefs, and assumptions).[25] Visible artifacts are easy to recognize, but businesses often find it more difficult to understand the underlying values of a culture and appropriately adapt their marketing strategies to them.[26]

For example, IKEA stores across the globe are open seven days a week—except in France. French law prevents retailers from selling on Sundays, and when IKEA tried to challenge the law by keeping one of its stores open, it provoked a lawsuit from a French workers' union. Although IKEA would love to sell over the whole weekend, when it earns approximately one-quarter of its weekly revenues, neither the workers' unions nor French consumers are likely to change their ways any time soon; leaving Sunday as a day of relaxation constitutes a fundamental foundation of French culture.[27] For the Swiss, a similar prohibition against Sunday retailing may soon fall to the wayside though. If stores remain closed, Switzerland will continue to lose tourism revenues, because most foreign visitors, who tend to visit on the weekend, are accustomed to shopping on Sundays. Opening retail stores on Sundays could mean increased consumption and wages for workers who work more hours, as well as employment for more people. But the loss of a day traditionally designated for family time and relaxation might be something the country cannot abide.[28] There may be no completely right answer to this dilemma, but global marketers clearly must be aware of the regulations and cultural norms of the countries they enter.

One important cultural classification scheme that firms can use is Geert Hofstede's cultural dimensions concept, which sheds more light on these underlying values. Hofstede believes cultures differ on five dimensions:[29]

1. **Power distance:** Willingness to accept social inequality as natural.
2. **Uncertainty avoidance:** The extent to which the society relies on orderliness, consistency, structure, and formalized procedures to address situations that arise in daily life.
3. **Individualism:** Perceived obligation to and dependence on groups.
4. **Masculinity:** The extent to which dominant values are male oriented. A lower masculinity ranking indicates that men and women are treated equally in all aspects of society; a higher masculinity ranking suggests that men dominate in positions of power.
5. **Time orientation:** Short- versus long-term orientation. A country that tends to have a long-term orientation values long-term commitments and is willing to accept a longer time horizon for, say, the success of a new product introduction.

To illustrate two of the five dimensions, consider the data and graph in Exhibit 8.5. Power distance is on the vertical axis and individualism is on the horizontal axis. Several Latin American countries, including Brazil, cluster high on power distance but low on individualism; the United States, Australia, Canada,

EXHIBIT 8.5	Country Clusters

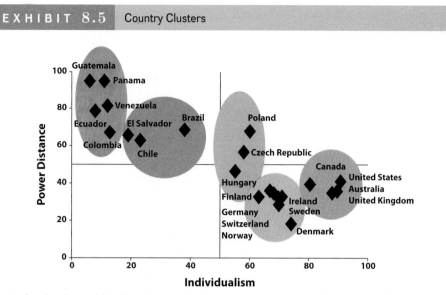

Source: Based on data available at http://www.geert-hofstede.com. Data from: Geert Hofstede, *Culture's Consequences,* 2nd ed. (Thousand Oaks, CA: Sage, 2001), Reprinted with permission of Geert Hofstede.

and the United Kingdom, in contrast, cluster high on individualism but low on power distance. Using this information, firms should expect that if they design a marketing campaign that stresses equality and individualism, it will be well accepted in English-speaking countries, all other factors being equal, but not be as well received in Latin American countries.

We also find that China scores very high on its time orientation but low in individualism; India has medium to high levels on all five dimensions; and Russia posts notably high uncertainty avoidance and power distance scores. Hofstede is careful to warn that these scores are informative only in a comparative sense, but marketers clearly can use them to design strategies for the varied, promising, BRIC growth markets.[30]

Another means of classifying cultures distinguishes them according to the importance of verbal communication.[31] In the United States and most European countries, business relationships are governed by what is said and written down, often through formal contracts. In countries such as China and South Korea, however, most relationships rely on nonverbal cues, so that the situation or context means much more than mere words. For instance, business relationships in China often are formalized by just a handshake, and trust and honor are often more important than legal arrangements.

Overall, culture affects every aspect of consumer behavior: why people buy, who is in charge of buying decisions, and how, when, and where people shop. After marketing managers have completed the four parts of the market assessment, they are better able to make informed decisions about whether a particular country possesses the necessary characteristics to be considered a potential market for the firm's products and services. In the next section, we detail the market entry decision process, beginning with a discussion of the various ways firms might enter a new global market. Adding Value 8.1 gets the discussion started with one illustrative example.

The Appeal of the BRIC Countries

Changes in technology, especially communications, have been a driving force for growth in global markets for decades. The telegraph, radio, television, computer,

L02 Understand the marketing opportunities in BRIC countries.

Adding Value 8.1   Brightening Smiles across the Globe

Known best for its toothpaste, the Colgate-Palmolive Company provides oral, personal, and home care products and pet nutrition products to consumers around the globe.[32] Colgate's strategic plan includes international growth, and the company has built brand loyalty and market share in emerging markets, as well as a global leadership position for the sales of toothpaste and toothbrushes. The roots of this success lie in Colgate's commitment to understanding local tastes, educating consumers about the importance of better oral hygiene, developing relationships with dental professionals, and supporting communities.

In India, for example, Colgate researchers spent two days in a rural village studying the habits and values of inhabitants. The main insight: Mothers hoped desperately for better lives for their children. The resulting campaign stressed the health implications of good oral care habits and offered opportunities for scholarships. In other countries, similar interactions with locals have spawned ideas for new products, including a highly energy efficient toothbrush manufacturing plant in China that adheres to the highest standards of environmental protection. Visits with storeowners in rural Russia led to new packaging options for use in small, crowded shops.

In addition to consumers and store owners, Colgate builds bonds with dental professionals, who are in a position to endorse the brand and provide product samples. These relationships have prompted significant numbers of dentists and hygienists in Brazil, India, and China to recommend Colgate over any other brand to patients. In the United States, Colgate is creating new ties with hygienists by providing oral health education tools and inviting their participation in the company's oral health advisory board.

Colgate's commitment to community support stems from its global values of caring, continuous improvement, and global teamwork. In the United Kingdom, the company teamed with the international retailer Tesco in a customizable "Share a Smile" program that benefits local communities. A partnership in the African country of Malawi promoted healthy oral care habits.

By paying close attention to the unique sociocultural characteristics of various countries and honing its global product strategies, Colgate is able to compete successfully in global and emerging markets, despite the aggressive competition in consumer product markets and the challenging economic conditions worldwide.

Using Bollywood actors Shahid Kapoor and Genelia D'Souza, Colgate promotes Max Fresh as part of its international growth strategy which is based on building brand loyatly and market share in emerging markets like India.

and Internet have increasingly connected distant parts of the world. Today, communication is instantaneous. Sounds and images from across the globe are delivered to TV sets, radios, and computers in real time, which enables receivers in all parts of the world to observe how others live, work, and play.

Perhaps the greatest change facing the global community in recent years has been the growth and expansion of four countries that together have come to be known as the BRIC countries: Brazil, Russia, India, and China. Let's examine each in turn.

Brazil[33]   Long a regional powerhouse, Brazil's ability to weather, and even thrive, during the most recent economic storm has transformed it into a global contender.

In which of the BRIC countries do each of these classic structures reside?

Currently, Brazil is the world's seventh largest economy, but predicted growth rates indicate it will move into the fifth spot within a few years. This growth has been aided by a large, literate population and the impositions of social programs that have allowed more than half of the 190 million Brazilians to enter the middle class. This large South American democracy welcomes foreign investors.

Russia[34] The relations between the United States and Russia are a little more complicated than for Brazil. Since the fall of the former Soviet Union, Russia has undergone multiple up- and downturns in its economy. However, its overall growth prospects appear promising, especially as a consumer market. Long denied access to consumer goods, the well-educated population exhibits strong demand for U.S. products and brands. In particular, the 60 million Russian Internet users are growing at a rate of approximately 15 percent annually. Russia is likely to become Europe's largest online market in the next few years. The country also is negotiating to enter the WTO to improve trade relations with other countries. Russia still faces an aging population and low birth rates. If these trends persist, Russia's population could

Like other countries in which McDonald's thrives, Brazil has a strong and growing middle class.

decline by one-third in the next half-century. At the same time, corruption is widespread creating ethical dilemmas for firms trying to market their goods and services.

India[35] With more than 1.1 billion people, or approximately 15 percent of the world's population, together with expanding middle and upper classes, India is one of the world's fastest growing markets. With a median age of 25 years, India has one of the youngest populations in the world. Its young inhabitants increasingly are adopting global attitudes while living in growing urban centers and shopping at large malls. The well-educated modern generation is largely fluent in English, and the highly skilled workforce holds great attraction for firms that hope to expand using local talent, especially in technical fields.

India's retail environment is still dominated by millions of small stores, and lacks modern supply chain management facilities and systems.[36] Recent changes by the Indian government, however, have the potential to significantly modernize the retail landscape. Foreign retailers that carry multiple brands, like Walmart, are now allowed to own up to 51 percent of joint ventures in India, whereas previously these retailers were permitted only to enter into wholesale joint ventures. Also, retailers that carry only their own brand, like Nike, can now own 100 percent of their Indian businesses, whereas in the past they were only allowed to own up to 51 percent of a partnership with an Indian company.

China[37] For most of the twentieth century, China experienced foreign occupation, civil unrest, major famine, and a

The retail landscape in India is changing. Consumers, particularly young ones, are attracted to large modern malls.

Relaxed Indian governmental restrictions now allow foreign retailers that carry their own brand, like Levi's, to own 100 percent of their Indian businesses.

Ethical and Societal Dilemma 8.1   Can Social Networking and Censorship Coexist?

By Facebook CEO Mark Zuckerberg's own admission, Facebook grew exponentially for years without a strategic plan for international growth.[38] As the company has matured, however, Facebook has refocused its attention on developing a strategy for China. But attempting to combine the inherent openness of social networking with China's censorship rules present significant challenges. Add in local competitors and human rights advocacy groups concerned with government backlash against users, and Facebook may be looking at the same fate that has befallen other Western technology companies trying to expand to the East—including such marketing geniuses as Google, eBay, and Twitter.[39]

Successful entry into the Chinese market requires a particular blend of timing, skill, cultural understanding, and political savvy, and these factors may not be quite in alignment for Facebook yet. The timing may be wrong, because China's autocratic leaders have enforced greater controls on social networking and blogging in response to the Arab Spring uprisings. Nor do Facebook executives appear to have a full grasp of the political and cultural nuances of business in China, despite a good track record of respecting local cultural values, such as when it agreed to block content about Nazism in Germany or drawings of Muhammad in Pakistan. And even if Facebook were to navigate these challenges safely, China has a strong, enduring preference for companies owned and run by its own people.

Zuckerberg can (and does) claim that his company will employ diplomacy in China, but censorship issues are highly complex. For instance, how would Facebook respond to retaliation against users who criticize the government?[40] For Google, whose mission statement simply advises, "Don't Be Evil," such questions became all too pertinent when hackers in China

CEO Mark Zuckerberg (center) claims that Facebook will employ diplomacy in China, but censorship issues are highly complex.

gained access to the e-mail accounts of prominent human rights activists. When Western companies have cooperated with the Chinese government, some operations have led to the imprisonment of online activists.

Censorship has global repercussions too. Blocking a comment generated by someone outside of China, such that readers within China cannot see it, will affect access globally. But the question is about more than whether users can enjoy all the fun of Facebook. When a post on Facebook can lead to jail time, it becomes a question of basic human rights.

strict one-party Communist regime. However, since 1978, China's leadership, while maintaining communist political ideals, has embraced market-oriented economic development, which has led to startlingly rapid gains. For many Chinese, recent developments have dramatically improved their living standards and their levels of personal freedom. Increasing liberalization in the economy has prompted a large increase in China's gross domestic product (GDP); it is now the second-largest economy and the third-largest market for U.S. exports. The U.S. ambassador to China, Gary Locke, has noted: "Everyone that has exported to China reports that what may have started off small builds over time, such that we've seen phenomenal increases in U.S. exports from the United States to China. In fact exports were up some 32 percent last year alone."[41] It makes an excellent target for consumer goods, assuming they can be produced at the right price.

Yet the country continues to suffer from drastically unequal economic distribution, which has led to a significant migrant workforce who subsist on part-time, low paying jobs. These workers were hit hard by the global financial crisis, which reduced demand for Chinese exports for the first time in years. Furthermore, actual growth of the 1.3 billion-strong Chinese population slowed as a result of government population controls which limit each family to one child. Although China's median age is slightly younger than that of the United States currently, at 34.1 years, the application of the one-child policy means that China is one of the most rapidly aging countries in the world.

Even as vast numbers of U.S. companies actively target the massive Chinese market or explore options for entering it, Ethical and Societal Dilemma 8.1 highlights some challenges that one famous potential entrant faces before it makes this choice.

CHECK YOURSELF

1. What metrics can help analyze the economic environment of a country?
2. What types of government actions should we be concerned about as we evaluate a country?
3. What are five important cultural dimensions?
4. Why are each of the BRIC countries viewed as potential candidates for global expansion?

LO3 Identify the various market entry strategies.

CHOOSING A GLOBAL ENTRY STRATEGY

When a firm has concluded its assessment analysis of the most viable markets for its products and services, it must then conduct an internal assessment of its capabilities. As we discussed in Chapter 2, this analysis includes an assessment of the firm's access to capital, the current markets it serves, its manufacturing capacity, its proprietary assets, and the commitment of its management to the proposed strategy. These factors ultimately contribute to the success or failure of a market expansion strategy, whether at home or in a foreign market. After these internal market assessments, it is time for the firm to choose its entry strategy.

A firm can choose from many approaches when it decides to enter a new market, which vary according to the level of risk the firm is willing to take. Many firms actually follow a progression in which they begin with less risky strategies to enter their first foreign markets and move to increasingly risky strategies as they gain confidence in their abilities and more control over their operations, as illustrated in Exhibit 8.6. We examine these different approaches that marketers take when entering global markets, beginning with the least risky.

EXHIBIT 8.6   Global Entry Strategies

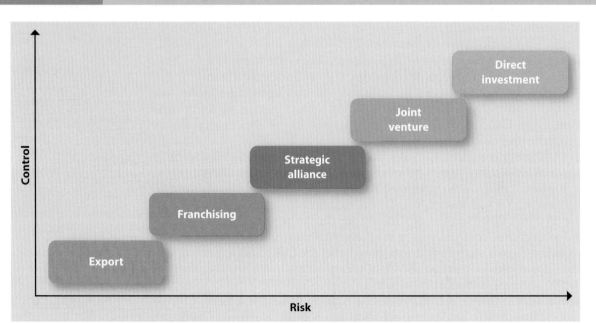

Exporting

Exporting means producing goods in one country and selling them in another. This entry strategy requires the least financial risk but also allows for only a limited return to the exporting firm. Global expansion often begins when a firm receives an order for its product or service from another country, in which case it faces little risk because it has no investment in people, capital equipment, buildings, or infrastructure.[42] By the same token, it is difficult to achieve economies of scale when everything has to be shipped internationally. The Swiss watchmaker Rolex sells relatively small numbers of expensive watches all over the world. Because its transportation costs are relatively small compared with the cost of the watches, the best way for it to service any market is to export from Switzerland.

Franchising

Franchising is a contractual agreement between a firm, the **franchisor**, and another firm or individual, the **franchisee**. A franchising contract allows the franchisee to operate a business—a retail product or service firm or a B2B provider—using the name and business format developed and supported by the franchisor. Many of the best-known retailers in the United States are also successful global franchisors, including McDonald's, Pizza Hut, Starbucks, Domino's Pizza, KFC, and Holiday Inn, all of which have found that global franchising entails lower risks and requires less investment than does opening units owned wholly by the firm. However, when it engages in franchising, the firm has limited control over the market operations in the foreign country, its potential profit is reduced because it must be split with the franchisee, and, once the franchise is established, there is always the threat that the franchisee will break away and operate as a competitor under a different name.

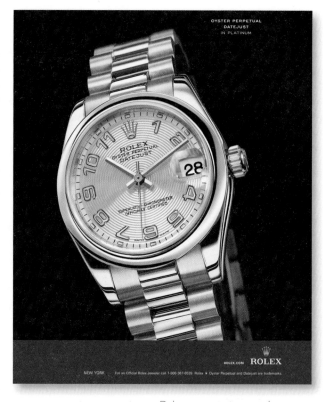

Rolex exports its watches to countries all over the world from its factory in Switzerland.

KFC and Pizza Hut are successful global franchisors.

Strategic Alliance

Strategic alliances refer to collaborative relationships between independent firms, though the partnering firms do not create an equity partnership; that is, they do not invest in one another. Therefore, when Cisco Systems Inc. of San Jose, California, and Tata Consultancy Services of Mumbai, India, entered into their strategic alliance, they both continued to develop market-ready infrastructure and network solutions for customers, but they relied on each other to provide the training and skills that one or the other might have lacked. At the same time, Cisco maintains alliances with various other companies, including Microsoft, Nokia, IBM, and Accenture.

Joint Venture

A **joint venture** is formed when a firm entering a market pools its resources with those of a local firm. As a consequence, ownership, control, and profits are shared. In addition to sharing financial burdens, a local partner offers the foreign entrant greater understanding of the market and access to resources such as vendors and real estate.

Some countries require joint ownership of firms entering their domestic markets, as is the case with the new regulations affecting multi-line retailers entering India, although many of these restrictions are loosening as a result of WTO negotiations and ever-increasing globalization pressures. Problems with this entry approach can arise when the partners disagree or if the government places restrictions on the firm's ability to move its profits out of the foreign country and back to its home country.

In some cases, joint ventures span several markets, as when the Japanese electronics superstar Sony teamed up with the Swedish communication firm Ericsson. A truly global venture, its central management was located in London, and it maintained R&D facilities in India, the United States, Sweden, Japan, China, Germany, and the United Kingdom. The widespread success of this venture ultimately led Sony to pursue complete ownership of the Sony Ericsson mobile handset line.[43]

The joint venture between Sony and Ericsson was so successful that Sony purchased the Ericsson mobile handset line.

Direct Investment

Direct investment requires a firm to maintain 100 percent ownership of its plants, operation facilities, and offices in a foreign country, often through the formation of wholly owned subsidiaries. This entry strategy requires the highest level of investment and exposes the firm to significant risks, including the loss of its operating and/or initial investments. This risk helps explain why Sony and Ericsson worked together on a joint venture for more than a decade before agreeing to make the Sony Ericsson line a wholly owned subsidiary of Sony. A dramatic economic downturn caused by a natural disaster, war, political instability, or changes in the country's laws can increase a foreign entrant's risk considerably. Many firms believe that in certain markets, these potential risks are outweighed by the high potential returns. With this strategy, none of the potential profits must be shared with other firms. In addition to the high potential returns, direct investment offers the firm complete control over its operations in the foreign country.

As we noted, each of these entry strategies entails different levels of risk and rewards for the foreign entrant. But even after a firm has determined how much risk it is willing to take, and therefore how it will enter a new global market, it still must establish its marketing strategy, as we discuss in the next section.

CHECK YOURSELF

1. Which entry strategy has the least risk and why?
2. Which entry strategy has the most risk and why?

CHOOSING A GLOBAL MARKETING STRATEGY

 LO4 Highlight the similarities and differences between a domestic marketing strategy and a global marketing strategy.

Just like any other marketing strategy, a global marketing strategy includes two components: determining the target markets to pursue and developing a marketing mix that will sustain a competitive advantage over time. In this section, we examine marketing strategy as it relates specifically to global markets.

Target Market: Segmentation, Targeting, and Positioning

Global segmentation, targeting, and positioning (STP) are more complicated than domestic STP for several reasons. First, firms considering a global expansion have much more difficulty understanding the cultural nuances of other countries. Second, subcultures within each country also must be considered. Third, consumers often view products and their role as consumers differently in different countries.[44] A product, service, or even a retailer often must be positioned differently in different markets.

Ford has introduced the Figo to first-time value-driven owners in India.

For example, Ford has enjoyed U.S. success with its "venerable" F-Series trucks for many years,[45] but this vehicle is not as appealing to the Indian market, where small cars are more popular. So Ford targeted India's small-car market segment with a new model, the Figo. This small vehicle's technology and architecture were proven in other markets in advance, and its features derived from consumer research and testing on India's roads. Many small-car buyers are first-time automobile owners, so the model also focuses on value for money, offering fuel efficiency, low maintenance costs, and technology enhancements that improve ride and handling on

Proctor & Gamble targeted moms on a global basis with their "Proud Sponsor of Moms" campaign, which ran during the 2012 Summer Olympics.

India's rough roads and crowded streets.[46] Within 15 months of introducing this model, Ford announced it had sold 100,000 Figos in India and planned to expand its Figo exports to 50 additional developing countries.[47] Ford also focuses on other market segments in India with models such as the Ikon, designed to appeal to upwardly mobile urban men looking to purchase an affordable luxury car, and the Fusion, which incorporates the benefits of a sedan and a utility vehicle and targets young families.[48]

Ford's segmentation, targeting, and positioning strategy thus have been successful in India. But the company must continually monitor economic and social trends to protect its position within the market and adjust its products and marketing strategies to meet the changing needs of global markets. In this sense, global marketing is no different from local or national marketing.

Segments and target markets can and should be defined by more than just geography. For example, when Yahoo determines its segmentation and positioning strategies, it relies on research into a segment familiar throughout the world: moms. By working with a global market research firm, Yahoo investigates how moms in Russia, Colombia, China, the United States, Mexico, India, the United Kingdom, Argentina, and France understand and use social media and other modern technologies. This study of "global moms" also aims to determine how digital technology affects family interactions, such as mealtimes, special occasions, and scheduling.[49] Looking on with great interest is the global product brand Procter & Gamble, which ran a global "Proud Sponsor of Moms" campaign during the 2012 Summer Olympics.[50]

When any firm identifies its positioning within the market, it then must decide how to implement its marketing strategies using the marketing mix. Just as firms adjust their products and services to meet the needs of national target markets, they must alter their marketing mix to serve the needs of global markets.

The Global Marketing Mix

During the early stages of globalization, in the 1950s and 1960s, large U.S. firms were uniquely positioned in the global marketplace because they had the skills necessary to develop, promote, and market brand name consumer products. In the 1970s and 1980s however, Japanese firms dominated the global marketplace because they could exploit their skills in production, materials management, and new product development. Today, retailers such as Zara, financial services firms such as Citicorp, and software firms such as Microsoft are dominating the newest stage of globalization by exploiting their technological skills, while Asian and South and Central American countries dominate the manufacturing of consumer products.[51] In the following, we explore the four Ps (product, price, promotion, and place) from a global perspective.

Global Product or Service Strategies There are three potential global product strategies:

- Sell the same product or service in both the home country market and the host country.
- Sell a product or service similar to that sold in home country but include minor adaptations.
- Sell totally new products or services.

The strategy a firm chooses depends on the needs of the target market. The level of economic development, as well as differences in product and technical standards, helps determine the need for and level of product adaptation. Cultural differences such as food preferences, language, and religion also play a role in product strategy planning.

Russia, one of the largest "new" markets in the world, is notable for its past development, including its long-standing embrace of communism. Consumption was limited, with few foreign options available. However, as this BRIC country moves toward a market-based economy, consumers are happily learning to spend the money they have, even though average monthly income levels hover at around $650. As the retail market expands rapidly, companies closely examine these latest consumers. They have disposable income, because they generally live mortgage free; receive heavily subsidized electricity and gas; have very little debt (because credit was not available under communism); and have little interest in saving, because history has taught them that they were likely to lose any pensions they might have saved. Yet the shift to a market economy also has been marked by terrible levels of corruption, unnecessary bureaucracy, significant income disparity, bribery, and uncertain legislation.[52] (For further discussion of a country moving from a communist to a market economy, see the case study at the end of this chapter.)

In such varied cultural settings, bringing even the simplest consumer goods to new markets can be challenging. For example, Campbell discovered that though Russia and China are two of the largest markets for soup in the world, cooks in those countries have unique demands. Chinese consumers drink 320 billion bowls of soup each year, and Russian buyers consume 32 billion servings, compared with only 14 billion bowls of soup served in the United States.

Campbell's research found that Russians eat a lot of soup, and they want time-saving preparation help. So it developed broths to enable cooks to prepare soups with their own flair.

However, Chinese cooks generally refuse to resort to canned soup; though the average Chinese consumer eats soup five times each week, he or she also takes great pride in preparing it personally with fresh ingredients. In contrast, Russian consumers, though they demand very high quality in their soups, had grown tired of spending hours preparing their homemade broths. To identify opportunities in these markets, Campbell sent teams of social anthropologists to study how Chinese and Russian cooks prepare and consume soup. When it faced further hurdles, it entered into a joint venture with the Swire soup company in China. But its efforts in Russia never panned out, forcing Campbell to withdraw after around four years. That is, even with extensive, devoted efforts by an industry giant, global marketing remains a challenge.[53]

The level of economic development affects the global product strategy. Consumers in the United States prefer larger motorcycles with more amenities, like the Honda Goldwing on the left with the air bag deploying. Motorcycles in India are generally smaller.

The level of economic development also affects the global product strategy because it relates directly to consumer behavior. Consumers in developed countries tend to demand more attributes in their products than do consumers in less developed countries. In the United States, Honda does not offer its line of "urban" motorcycles, available in Mexico, China, and India, because the product line resembles a motor scooter more than a motorcycle, which does not tend to appeal to American consumers. Motorcycles sold in the United States have more horsepower and bigger frames and come with an array of options that are not offered in other countries.

Referred to as **glocalization**, some firms also standardize their products globally but use different promotional campaigns to sell them. The original Pringles potato chip product remains the same globally, as do the images and themes of the promotional campaign, with limited language adaptations for the local markets, though English is used whenever possible. However, the company changes Pringles' flavors in different countries, including paprika-flavored chips sold in Italy and Germany.[54]

Global expansion can move in various directions. In **reverse innovation**, for example, companies initially develop products for niche or underdeveloped markets, and then expand them into their original or home markets. For example, General Electric realized that adapting medical diagnostic equipment that had been developed in the United States to sell it in India was ineffective. Few Indian medical providers had sufficient resources to pay $20,000 for the massive machinery. Therefore, GE undertook innovation specific to the Indian market to develop a battery-operated, portable EKG (electrocardiogram) machine for $500. Then it realized that the small, affordable machines would appeal as well to U.S. emergency medical personnel in the field and therefore globalized its offer.[55]

Firms also can just take an existing product and market it "as is" in all foreign markets. Ford Motor Co., for example, envisions a "world" car that will sell everywhere, as we discuss in Adding Value 8.2.

Spain's fashion retailer Zara is priced higher in the United States than in Spain because it ships its merchandise to the United States from Spain by air.

Global Pricing Strategies Determining the selling price in the global marketplace is an extremely difficult task.[56] Many countries still have rules governing the competitive marketplace, including those that affect pricing. For example, in parts of Europe, including Belgium, Italy, Spain, Greece, and France, sales are allowed only twice a year, in January and June or July. In most European countries, retailers can't sell below cost, and in others they can't advertise reduced prices in advance of sales or discount items until they have been on the shelves more than a month. For firms such as Walmart and other discounters, these restrictions threaten their core competitive positioning as the lowest-cost provider in the market. Other issues, such as tariffs, quotas, antidumping laws, and currency exchange policies, can also affect pricing decisions.[57]

Adding Value 8.2   Is One World Car Enough for All of Us?[58]

Virginia Woolf famously wrote, "A rose is a rose is a rose." But in the world of global marketing, that line has never seemed to hold particularly true. Is a car the same as a car the same as a car, the world over?

Previous developments would suggest not. Consider, for example, our discussion of the Nano, the 1300-pound mini-car that has enjoyed great success in India. Or recall how Ford had to give up on the idea of moving F-150 trucks overseas. In the United States, where car buyers love huge SUVs, roads have plenty of room for several cars side by side, and the car culture is well developed, so bigger is often thought of as better. In other areas of the world, huge automobiles are unlikely to prompt much excitement.

Ford CEO Alan Mulally seems determined to find a car that everyone will appreciate, whether they live in New Delhi, New York, or Newfoundland. He chose the name "Fiesta," despite some concerns that the previous iteration of this name was an unpopular, unattractive subcompact in the 1970s. Yet the name also is recognizable, and it does not suffer from any negative translations or connotations in various languages (e.g.,

Volkswagen's Bora model sounded too much like "boring" in English, so it changed the name to Jetta). Therefore, whatever market it appeared in, the one-world car would be the Fiesta.

This choice offers several benefits for the automaker; in particular, it saves on some of its marketing costs. That is, Ford needs only one logo for the Fiesta, and perhaps even one set of marketing communications in various international markets. In addition, it prevents consumer confusion, which is common in an online world when a company uses the same name for different lines. For example, the Ford Fusion is a sedan in Europe but an SUV in the United States. An online shopper who clicks on the wrong link would be terribly confused.

The universal Fiesta first entered the European market and soon became the top-selling small car on that continent. A few years later, Ford rolled out the same car in the United States after investing heavily in determining which features would appeal across the board. For example, it attempted to make the Fiesta aesthetically pleasing across cultures, without increasing costs. Within a year, the Fiesta was the top ranking affordable small car in the U.S. market too.

The Ford Fiesta is designed to be sold similiarly throughout the world. This ad from the U.K. could easily be used in the U.S.

Competitive factors influence global pricing in the same way they do home country pricing, but because a firm's products or services may not have the same positioning in the global marketplace as they do in their home country, market prices must be adjusted to reflect the local pricing structure. Spain's fashion retailer Zara, for instance, is relatively inexpensive in the EU but is priced about 40 percent

Rising fuel costs are changing the way that companies do business. In the past, U.S. companies would outsource manufacturing, obtain materials from all across the world, and then ship the goods to the final destination.

For example, Tesla Motors used to manufacture 1000-pound automobile battery packs in Thailand, ship them to Britain for installation, and then ship the nearly assembled cars to the United States. This model made sense when fuel prices ranged around $10 per barrel, but now that the price has risen by more than tenfold, transportation costs overwhelm such supply chains. Moving goods is very expensive, and many items, especially those with smaller margins (e.g., food), have simply become too expensive to transport. If they were available and the transportation costs were passed on to consumers, avocados from South Africa would cost a U.S. grocery shopper as much as a rib eye steak.

In the new economy, locating factories close to both the suppliers of components and final consumers to reduce the transportation costs is catching on. The result is also a boon for consumers, in that they have ready access to the supply lines from which they gather their purchases. But for many companies, existing supply chains mean that they still rely on massive container ships. Shipping a 40-foot container on a ship sailing from Shanghai to the United States today costs $8,000 compared with $3,000 a decade ago, and it moves slower too, in an attempt to save fuel.

Just-in-time (JIT) systems aim to have components arrive at the exact time they are needed, in an effort to minimize warehousing costs. But modern companies may be forced to buy whichever components are available in the vicinity of their place of need, rather than buying the cheapest products in the world. Furthermore, the recall of millions of vehicles by the world's most famous JIT practitioner Toyota raised some questions about the potential downsides to JIT. If the goal is to meet production deadlines at all costs, is the result an unsafe product?

Finally, due to outsourcing, the United States may have lost significant production skills. However, the advantages of closer production and decreased transportation costs may mean that more companies, especially those specializing in heavy goods (e.g., furniture companies IKEA and La-Z-Boy) will be turning to increased domestic production in the various places they sell products. In all these developments, the question becomes whether the greater service, safety, and satisfaction that localized sourcing might provide can offset the cost benefits of global sourcing.

higher in the United States, putting it right in the middle of its moderately priced competition.[60] Zara is dedicated to keeping production in Spain, but it also must get its fashions to the United States quickly, so it incurs additional transportation expenses, which it passes on to its North American customers. Finally, as we discussed previously in this chapter, currency fluctuations impact global pricing strategies.

Global Distribution Strategies Global distribution networks form complex value chains that involve middlemen, exporters, importers, and different transportation systems. These additional middlemen typically add cost and ultimately increase the final selling price of a product. As a result of these cost factors, constant pressure exists to simplify distribution channels wherever possible.

The number of firms with which the seller needs to deal to get its merchandise to the consumer determines the complexity of a channel. In most developing countries, manufacturers must go through many different types of distribution channels to get their products to end users, who often lack adequate transportation to shop at central shopping areas or large malls. Therefore, consumers shop near their homes at small, family-owned retail outlets. To reach these small retail outlets, most of which are located far from major rail stations or roads, marketers have devised a variety of creative solutions. Unilever's strategy in India is a prime example of how a global company can adapt its distribution network to fit local conditions. Unilever trained 45,000 Indian women to serve as distributors, who in turn extended Unilever's reach to nearly 100,000 villages and their 3 million residents, all across India. The program generates $250 million each year just in villages that otherwise would be too costly to serve.[61] For examples of other new distribution strategies, consider Superior Service 8.1.

Global Communication Strategies The major challenge in developing a global communication strategy is identifying the elements that need to be adapted to be effective in the global marketplace. For instance, literacy levels vary dramatically across the globe. Consider again the BRIC nations: In India, approximately 39 percent of the adult population is illiterate (and for Indian women, the illiteracy rate surpasses 50 percent), compared with 11 percent in Brazil, 7.8 percent in China, and less than 1 percent in Russia.[62] Media availability also varies widely; some countries offer only state-controlled media. Advertising regulations differ too. In an attempt at standardization, the EU recently recommended common guidelines for its member countries regarding advertising to children and is currently initiating a multiphase ban on "junk food" advertising.[63]

Differences in language, customs, and culture also complicate marketers' ability to communicate with customers in various countries. Language can be particularly vexing for advertisers. For example, in the United Kingdom, a thong is only a sandal, whereas in the United States, it can also be an undergarment. To avoid the potential embarrassment that language confusion can cause, firms spend millions of dollars to develop brand names that have no preexisting meaning in any known language, such as Accenture (a management consulting firm) or Avaya (a subsidiary of Lucent Technologies, formerly Bell Labs).

Within many countries there are multiple variants on a language or more than one language. For example, China has three main languages; the written forms produce meaning through the characters used but the spoken forms depend on tone and pronunciation. Some firms choose names that sound similar to their English-language names, such as Nike, whose Chinese brand name is pronounced "nai ke." Others focus on the meanings of the characters, such that Citibank is known as *hui qi yinhang*, which means "star-spangled banner bank." Still other firms, such as Mercedes-Benz, have adapted their names for each language: *peng zee* in Cantonese for Hong Kong, *peng chi* in Mandarin for Taiwan, and *ben chi* in Mandarin for mainland China. Naming is a constant challenge in China, especially to avoid the threat that a brand name evokes unwanted connotations, such as when Microsoft realized that the sound of its search engine name, Bing, meant "virus" in China—not the best image for an online company![64]

Even with all these differences, many products and services serve the same needs and wants globally with little or no adaptation in their form or message. Firms with global appeal can run global advertising campaigns and simply translate the wording in the advertisements and product labeling. Furthermore, as

Nike's Chinese brand name is pronounced "nai ke," which is very similar to the English pronunciation, and means "Enduring and Persevering."

Social and Mobile Marketing 8.1   Lady Gaga Is More Popular than Barack Obama

Lady Gaga's nearly unsurpassed status in modern pop culture has arrived as the result of her shock tactics, carefully orchestrated media blitz, and expert use of varied social media channels—not to mention some serious musical talent.

Granted, wearing a dress made of meat and creating music videos that veer close to pornography will get anyone's attention, even through traditional media settings. And indeed, nearly 12,000 traditional media stories mentioned her in 2010.[65] But Lady Gaga's worldwide domination involves far more.

From the time she first arrived on the scene in 2008, Gaga has been available to her fans nearly all the time, in a vast array of forums. In the early days, she was constantly available for interviews, and she made content, including videos and photos, available for music bloggers to post. Her iPhone application, Haus of Gaga, acts as a portal for her fans, widely known as "Little Monsters," to stay easily connected through exclusive content, videos, news, and chats. She

Lady Gaga can mix fashion with her music and get away with it.

personally manages her daily posts, even when she is backstage at a concert. Gaga keeps her fans interested by speaking to them directly via social media. Her Facebook page is managed by her with the help of others, and she handles her Twitter account on her own. This authentic one-to-one contact has strengthened her personal connection with her fans.[66]

Through these efforts, she has become the most popular living thing on Facebook, with more than 35 million Facebook fans; has more Twitter followers than anyone else, at 10 million, even more than Barack Obama; and has prompted more than 1 billion views on her YouTube channel. She is strategic in her decisions on what she wears and what she does, knowing that people will be talking about it later. Gaga makes sure that she feeds her fans the content she wants them to talk about—namely, just what unexpected thing she has done most recently.

Social and Mobile Marketing 8.1 highlights, social networks grant various brands, including Lady Gaga, access to a global market.

Other products require a more localized approach because of cultural and religious differences. In a classic advertisement for Longines watches, a woman's bare arm and hand appear, with a watch on her wrist. The advertisement was considered too risqué for Muslim countries, where women's bare arms are never displayed in public, but the company simply changed the advertisement to show a gloved arm and hand wearing the same watch.

Even among English speakers there can be significant differences in the effectiveness of advertising campaigns. Take the popular "What Happens in Vegas Stays in Vegas" advertising campaign, which has been very successful and spawned numerous copycat slogans in the United States. Essentially, the U.S. mass market thought the provocative campaign pushed the envelope, but just far enough to be entertaining. However, when the Las Vegas tourism group extended its advertising to the United Kingdom, it found that the ad campaign was not nearly as effective. After conducting focus groups, the group found that British consumers did not find the advertisements edgy enough for their more irreverent British tastes. In response, the advertising agency began studying British slang and phrases to find ways to make the campaign even sexier and more provocative.[67]

CHECK YOURSELF

1. What are the components of a global marketing strategy?
2. What are the three global product strategies?

Summing Up

LO1 Describe the components of a country market assessment.

First, firms must assess the general economic environment. For instance, countries with a trade surplus, strong domestic and national products, growing populations, and income growth generally are relatively more favorable prospects. Second, firms should assess a country's infrastructure. To be successful in a particular country, the firm must have access to adequate transportation, distribution channels, and communications. Third, firms must determine whether the proposed country has a political and legal environment that favors business. Fourth, firms should be cognizant of the cultural and sociological differences between their home and host countries and adapt to those differences to ensure successful business relationships.

LO2 Understand the marketing opportunities in BRIC countries.

Technology, particularly in the communication field, has facilitated the growth of global markets. Firms can communicate with their suppliers and customers instantaneously, easily take advantage of production efficiencies in other countries, and bring together parts and finished goods from all over the globe. Four countries that provide tremendous marketing opportunities are the BRIC nations—Brazil, Russia, India and China. These countries have large populations that are increasingly interested in the latest goods and services.

LO3 Identify the various market entry strategies.

Firms have several options for entering a new country, each with a different level of risk and involvement. Direct investment is the most risky but potentially the most lucrative. Firms that engage in a joint venture with other firms already operating in the host country share the risk and obtain knowledge about the market and how to do business there. A strategic alliance is similar to a joint venture, but the relationship is not as formal. A less risky method of entering a new market is franchising, in which, as in domestic franchise agreements, the franchisor allows the franchisee to operate a business using its name and strategy in return for a fee. The least risky method of entering another country is simply exporting.

LO4 Highlight the similarities and differences between a domestic marketing strategy and a global marketing strategy.

The essence of a global marketing strategy is no different from that of a domestic strategy. The firm starts by identifying its target markets, chooses specific markets to pursue, and crafts a strategy to meet the needs of those markets. However, additional issues make global expansion more problematic. For instance, should the product or service be altered to fit the new market better? Does the firm need to change the way it prices its products in different countries? What is the best way to get the product or service to the new customers? How should the firm publicize its product or service offering in various countries?

Key Terms

- direct investment, 248
- duty, 237
- exchange control, 238
- exchange rate, 238
- exporting, 247
- franchisee, 247
- franchising, 247
- franchisor, 247
- globalization, 232
- glocalization, 252
- gross domestic product (GDP), 234
- gross national income (GNI), 234
- infrastructure, 237
- joint venture, 248
- purchasing power parity (PPP), 234
- quota, 238
- reverse innovation, 252
- strategic alliance, 248
- tariff, 237
- trade agreements, 239
- trade deficit, 233
- trade surplus, 234
- trading bloc, 239

Marketing Applications

1. What is globalization? Why is it important for marketers to understand what globalization entails?

2. Moots is a high-end bicycle manufacturer located in Steamboat Springs, Colorado. Assume the company is considering entering the Brazilian, Chinese, and Indian markets. When conducting its market assessment, what economic factors should Moots consider to make its decision? Which market do you expect will be more lucrative for Moots? Why?

3. Now consider the political, economic, and legal systems of China, India, and Brazil. Explain why you think one country might be more hospitable to Moots than the others.

4. Colgate sells its products in many countries throughout the world. How would you expect its market position to differ in various countries, compared with that in the United States? Consider various areas across the globe in formulating your answer.

5. CITGO, the petroleum company owned by the Venezuelan government, sells its products throughout the world. Do you anticipate that its market positioning and advertising differ in different countries? Why or why not?

6. What are the benefits of being able to offer a globally standardized product? What types of products easily lend themselves to global standardization?

7. Compare and contrast Ford's global marketing strategy for Figo and Fiesta.

Quiz Yourself

www.mhhe.com/
grewal4e

1. Geert Hofstede's cultural dimensions concept focuses on five dimensions of _____ in a country.
   a. symbols
   b. underlying values
   c. ceremonies
   d. dress
   e. visible artifacts

2. NCD company wants to expand into the Mexican market. They have financial resources, want to control business operations, and have had considerable success marketing to Hispanics in the United States. NCD will likely use _____ to expand into the Mexican market.
   a. franchising
   b. exporting
   c. a joint venture
   d. direct investment
   e. a strategic alliance

(Answers to these two questions can be found on page 647.)

Go to www.mhhe.com/grewal4e to practice an additional 11 questions.

Net Savvy

1. For many small businesses, the idea of entering a foreign market is intimidating. The U.S. government and most state governments now offer assistance designed specifically for small-business owners. Visit the website of the Massachusetts Export Center at http://www.mass.gov/export/ and examine the types of services it provides. Click on the Export Statistics link. To what five countries did Massachusetts export the most? Are you surprised?

2. Adidas is a global brand, yet it alters its promotions to meet local tastes. Go to www.addidas.co.uk/shop and visit the U.K. site. Now click on the U.S. or Canadian sites. How are these websites different?

Chapter Case Study

RACING TO CAPTURE CHINA'S LUXURY CAR MARKET

China's car market dates back just three decades, yet the Asian giant is well on its way to surpassing the United States as the world's most lucrative and strategically important auto market. Government investment in infrastructure, including the development of roads and bridges, has helped the nascent car industry, and sales growth in the overall market has soared by 30 percent annually for several years. Last year, Chinese consumers bought 2.2 million vehicles more than United States drivers purchased, and more than 60 percent of them were foreign-origin brands, produced in China through joint ventures.[68]

Perhaps the fiercest arena of competition is China's luxury car market, projected to become the world's largest within five to seven years.[69] The dominant players include Audi and BMW, as well as Mercedes-Benz and Buick. Audi has reported 61 percent increases in Chinese sales; BMW sales in China, Hong Kong, and Taiwan were projected to rise by 85.3 percent over their previous rates.[70]

Yet these figures are not the whole story: China is a challenging market to penetrate, especially because of its continent-wide geographic area, complex cultural diversity, and growing gaps (both economic and social) between poorer rural regions and the booming cities on the coastline. Furthermore, prevailing stereotypes and images of particular car brands are rooted in history, and no foreign carmaker can safely ignore these strong opinions and ideas.[71] Some foreign companies, such as Audi, have eased the path by entering into joint ventures.

Audi was the earliest entrant into the Chinese prestige car market, when its German owner, Volkswagen, struck a joint venture agreement with the Chinese carmaker Yiqi in 1988. By the time BMW opened a plant in China in 2003, Audi had secured a place on the central government's authorized purchase list, and its A6 line had become the de facto car of choice for Chinese bureaucrats. The company captured so much of China's government-car market that it has given

The Chinese luxury car market, dominated by BMW, Audi, Mercedes-Benz, and Buick, is projected to become the world's largest.

rise to the stereotype that the sleek looking A6—invariably with dark, tinted windows—must be carrying a party technocrat whenever it appears on city streets.

Audi has done well with this market segment. A basic Audi A6 costs 355,000 renminbi, or $56,000. Its key competitor, the BMW 5, is more expensive, at 428,000 renminbi, or $67,520. Audi's sales to the government accounts for approximately 20 percent of its Chinese revenues, and it sold 227,938 cars in China in 2010, more than twice the number that it sold in the United States.[72]

Not to be outdone, U.S. carmakers have worked to establish effective brand perceptions and reputations, largely based on improving stereotyping about the car's "face." The American-made Buick seemed "damaged" at the start of the twenty-first century because of the car's longstanding popularity and association with older retirees, but in China, it played on unique historical connections to help ignite demand by reminding car buyers that China's last emperor and its one-time premier Zhou Enlai both drove Buicks. Thus the brand gained a strong position as a top-tier luxury carmaker. Its 2010 Chinese sales were more than triple its revenue in the United States.[73] But for Mercedes-Benz, such stereotyping has persisted. Whereas most U.S. consumers view both these automobiles as cars for people with established wealth, the Mercedes in China may be for the wealthy, but it is still associated with older, retired drivers.[74]

The most dynamic market niche for luxury cars reflects a rising class of young, affluent entrepreneurs with flashy buying habits. BMW, the world's top-selling luxury car brand,[75] has vigorously targeted these brash new drivers with exotic marketing campaigns. The Munich-based automaker began offering test drives and cross-country expeditions with its high-end X5 SUV in the deserts of Inner Mongolia and along Silk Road, enticing thrill-bound luxury car customers.[76] Their campaign showcases new technology, and it has helped build brand loyalty: China is BMW's third-largest market.[77]

Yet its targeting strategy has also left behind some negative Chinese attitudes that link BMW to careless, nouveau riche drivers. That stereotype grew after young BMW drivers, in separate incidents, were charged in fatal accidents. When a young woman intentionally ran over an indigent man after he dented her BMW X5, then settled out of court for $11,000, the story helped fan the tensions between China's rich and poor. In the cross-fire, BMW was tagged with a reputation for catering to the arrogant and the reckless. That tag now extends to other BMW drivers; government officials who show up in a BMW, rather than the typical, less expensive Audi, run the risk of being accused of corruption.[78]

In a push to innovate and perhaps revive a broader appeal, BMW has launched a strategic alliance with Toyota, focused on sustainable technologies. The companies will collaborate on diesel engines, which dominate Europe's fuel-efficient car market. They also have agreed to develop a next-generation lithium battery, a key component of laptops and electric cars.[79]

Other examples of market expansion by luxury carmakers include ventures into some of China's less developed cities. These second- and third-tier locations provide access to a new class of potential buyers, that is, affluent consumers who live farther from the major metropolitan centers. Major cities such as Beijing and Shanghai are limiting car purchases, because their streets cannot handle more traffic, but smaller cities in outlying provinces offer promising alternative markets.

Its early entrance into the market, through a joint venture with a Chinese carmaker, allowed Audi to become deeply entrenched in the government's purchasing system. But with BMW courting wealthier young drivers, the competition between these two foreign automakers is heating up. Strategic partnerships will continue to play a key role in shaping new opportunities, though limits on car registration in some major cities may shift those opportunities to other geographic segments. Amid all these dynamics, Chinese brand attitudes will continue to determine the buying decisions of drivers in the world's largest car market.

Questions

1. Assess China as a potential market for luxury cars. If you worked for a luxury car manufacturer, such as Volvo, would you enter or attempt to increase your presence in China? What entry strategy would you use? Why?

2. Drivers in China approach the luxury car market with a set of strong associations that influence their perceptions of the foreign brands currently available in the marketplace. Multiple factors affect those consumer attitudes, including history, class, and social status. Why are these attitudes so entrenched in China, and why do they play such a critical role in shaping car customer preferences?

3. Both Audi and BMW have allied with other companies to target particular market segments. Assess the relative strength of these two very different positioning strategies.

4. BMW has successfully targeted China's affluent, young car drivers, but the brand's success in that market has also provoked public backlash. What drives such public hostility to the brand, and how serious a problem is it? What marketing approach, if any, should the company undertake in response?

Targeting the Marketplace

Section Three, Targeting the Marketplace, contains two chapters. Chapter 9 focuses on segmentation, targeting, and positioning. In this chapter, we examine how firms segment the marketplace, then pick a target market, and finally position their goods/services in line with their customers' needs and wants. Chapter 10 on marketing research identifies the various tools, techniques, and metrics that marketers use to uncover customers' needs and wants and to ensure that they create goods and services that provide value to their target markets.

SECTION 3

CHAPTER 9

Segmentation, Targeting, and Positioning

Known for its highly watched fashion shows, "Angel" models, and assortment of sexy intimate apparel and sleepwear, Victoria's Secret has reached annual net sales of more than $4 billion and opened more than 1,000 stores.[1] Most of the undergarments that Victoria's Secret sells attempt to conjure romance and seduction, which means they are likely to involve discretionary expenses. Yet women need bras and panties, so the offerings also represent basic necessities.

Determining who its customers are, and then balancing the discrepancies between their needs versus wants is part of what makes Victoria's Secret so successful. Given the changes in the economy, the company introduced lower-priced offerings while simultaneously reducing inventory.[2] The chain's "Everyday" line of bras retail for $29.50, about half the price of other styles. Its popular Seven-Way bra functions well with various clothing silhouettes, so that women do not need to purchase separate bras to wear with T-shirts, strapless tops, racer-back shirts, sheer clothing, and so on. After discontinuing it briefly to encourage sales of the various alternatives, Victoria's Secret was quick to expand the line, such that women could buy multiuse bras across various product lines, including its BioFit and Showstopper selections.[3]

Moving beyond these long-running offerings, Victoria's Secret Pink product line, launched in 2004, is designed to appeal to younger shoppers with brightly colored sweatshirts, T-shirts, pajamas, pillows and bedding, sandals, and swimwear, as well as undergarments.[4] The Wear Everywhere bra costs $32 for a package of two, and rather than going for glamorous or sexy, Pink clothing is intended to be comfortable and cute.

The Pink line also aims to expand the reach of Victoria's Secret through cobranding. Pink offers merchandise imprinted with the logos and names of most major U.S. colleges and universities (though it stumbled when it mistakenly printed the University of Michigan slogan, "Hail to the Victors," beneath the Spartan logo of rival Michigan State University).[5] With these options, the brand may attract more male consumers, who enjoy purchasing gifts for their significant others that are both feminine and indicative of support for a favorite National Football League or Major League Baseball team.[6]

LEARNING OBJECTIVES

LO1 Outline the different methods of segmenting a market.

LO2 Describe how firms determine whether a segment is attractive and therefore worth pursuing.

LO3 Articulate the differences among targeting strategies: undifferentiated, differentiated, concentrated, or micromarketing.

LO4 Determine the value proposition.

LO5 Define positioning, and describe how firms do it.

Even with these extensions though, Victoria's Secret remains true to its core offering: appealing to women who are more concerned with curves than cost. Its Miraculous push-up bra promises to add two cup sizes to a wearer's bust. And its annual fashion show is a widely anticipated event that features top models sporting ornate, handmade wings (to invoke the image of angels), along with minuscule lingerie. There is nothing cozy or price-conscious on display on the runway. Instead, Miranda Kerr hoisted a heavy, clam-shaped set of wings, surrounding her diamond-encrusted bra worth $2.5 million.[7]

Using price points to segment its market; customizing color, fabrics, and styles to appeal to various target audiences; associating its brand with supermodels, baseball and football teams, and colleges; reaching different shoppers through different stores and assortments; and promoting products through multiple selling channels all help Victoria's Secret, and its varied customers, feel quite in the pink.

In Chapter 1, we learned that marketing is about satisfying consumers' wants and needs. Chapter 2 noted how companies analyze their markets to determine the different kinds of products and services people want. But it is not sufficient just to produce such an offering. Firms must also position their offerings in the minds of customers in their target market in such a way that these consumers understand why the thing the company is providing meets their needs better than other, competitive offerings.

This process requires a marketing plan, as we discussed in Chapter 2. As you should recall, the third step of this plan is identifying and evaluating opportunities by performing an STP (segmentation, targeting, and positioning) analysis. This chapter focuses on that very analysis.

LO1 Outline the different methods of segmenting a market.

THE SEGMENTATION, TARGETING, AND POSITIONING PROCESS

In this chapter, we discuss how a firm conducts a market segmentation or STP analysis (see Exhibit 9.1). We first outline a firm's overall strategy and objectives, methods of segmenting the market, and which segments are worth pursuing. Then we discuss how to choose a target market or markets by evaluating each segment's attractiveness and, on the basis of this evaluation, choose which segment or segments to pursue. Finally, we describe how a firm develops its positioning strategy.

Although the STP process in Exhibit 9.1 implies that the decision making is linear, this need not be the case. For instance, a firm could start with a strategy but then modify it as it gathers more information about various segments' attractiveness.

Step 1: Establish Overall Strategy or Objectives

The first step in the segmentation process is to articulate the vision or objectives of the company's marketing strategy clearly. The segmentation strategy must be consistent with and derived from the firm's mission and objectives, as well as its current situation—its strengths, weaknesses, opportunities, and threats (SWOT). Coca-Cola's objective, for instance, is to increase sales in a mature industry. The company knows its strengths are its brand name and its

Coke Zero targets health-conscious men.

ability to place new products on retailers' shelves, but its primary weakness is that it may not have a product line for newer market segments. Identifying this potentially large and profitable market segment, before many of its mainstream competitors can do so, offers a great opportunity. However, following through on that opportunity could lead to a significant threat: competitive retaliation. Coca-Cola's recent choice to pursue health-conscious men with products such as Coke Zero is consistent with its overall strategy and objectives. (See the case study at the end of this chapter for more discussion of Coke's strategy.)

Now let's take a look at methods for segmenting a market.

Step 2: Segmentation Methods

The second step in the segmentation process is to use a particular method or combination of methods to segment the market. This step also develops descriptions of the different segments, which helps firms better understand the customer profiles in each segment. With this information, they can distinguish customer similarities within a segment and dissimilarities across segments. Marketers use geographic, demographic, psychographic, benefits, and behavioral segmentation methods, as Exhibit 9.2 details.

Soft-drink marketers, for instance, divide the carbonated beverage landscape into caffeinated or decaffeinated, regular (with sugar) or diet, and cola versus something else. This segmentation method is based on the *benefits* that consumers derive from the products.

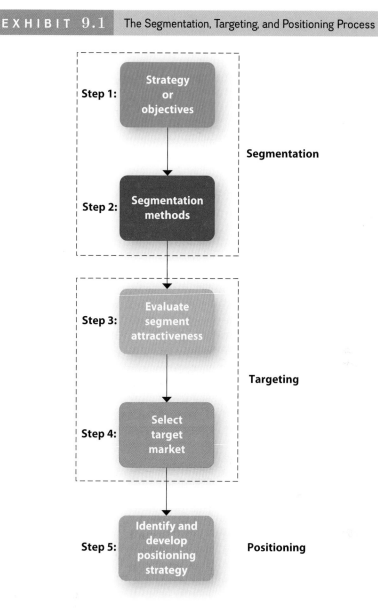

EXHIBIT 9.1   The Segmentation, Targeting, and Positioning Process

Step 1: Strategy or objectives

Step 2: Segmentation methods

Segmentation

Step 3: Evaluate segment attractiveness

Step 4: Select target market

Targeting

Step 5: Identify and develop positioning strategy

Positioning

EXHIBIT 9.2   Methods for Describing Market Segments

Segmentation Method	Sample Segments
Geographic	Continent: North America, Asia, Europe, Africa Within U.S.: Pacific, mountain, central, south, mid-Atlantic, northeast
Demographic	Age, gender, income
Psychographic	Lifestyle, self-concept, self-values
Benefits	Convenience, economy, prestige
Behavioral	Occasion, loyalty

Geographic Segmentation **Geographic segmentation** organizes customers into groups on the basis of where they live. Thus, a market could be grouped by country, region (northeast, southeast), or areas within a region (state, city, neighborhoods, zip codes). Not surprisingly, geographic segmentation is most useful for companies whose products satisfy needs that vary by region.

Firms can provide the same basic goods or services to all segments even if they market globally or nationally, but better marketers make adjustments to meet the needs of smaller geographic groups.[8] A national grocery store chain like Safeway or Kroger runs similar stores with similar assortments in various locations across the United States. Within those similar stores though, a significant percentage of the assortment of goods will vary by region, city, or even neighborhood, depending on the different needs of the customers who surround each location.

Demographic Segmentation **Demographic segmentation** groups consumers according to easily measured, objective characteristics such as age, gender, income, and education. These variables represent the most common means to define segments, because they are easy to identify and because demographically segmented markets are easy to reach. Kellogg's uses age segmentation for its breakfast cereals: Cocoa Krispies and Fruit Loops are for kids; Special K and All-Bran are for adults. It also tends to adopt a gender-based segmentation, such that marketing communications about Special K almost exclusively appeal to women.

Gender plays a very important role in how most firms market products and services.[9] For instance, TV viewing habits vary significantly between men and women. Men tend to channel surf—switching quickly from channel to channel—and watch prime-time shows that are action oriented and feature physically attractive cast members. Women, in contrast, tend to view shows to which they can personally relate through the situational plot or characters and those recommended by friends. A company like Gillette, which sells razors for both men and women, therefore considers the gender appeal of various shows when it buys advertising time on television.

However, demographics may not be useful for defining the target segments for other companies. They are poor predictors of the users of activewear, such as jogging suits and athletic shoes. At one time, firms like Nike assumed that activewear would be purchased exclusively by young, active people, but the health and fitness trend has led people of all ages to buy such merchandise. And even relatively inactive consumers of all ages, incomes, and education find activewear more comfortable than traditional street clothes.

Rethinking some stereotypical ideas about who is buying thus has become a relatively common trend among firms that once thought their target market was well defined. Adding Value 9.1 highlights how Skechers has broadened its appeal by aiming marketing communications at various segments of potential consumers.

Psychographic Segmentation Of the various methods for segmenting, or breaking down, the market, **psychographics** is the one that delves into how consumers actually describe themselves. Usually marketers determine (through demographics, buying patterns, or usage) into which segment an individual consumer falls. Psychographics studies how people self-select, as it were, based on the characteristics of how they choose to occupy their time (behavior) and what underlying psychological reasons determine those choices.[10] For example, a person might have a strong need for inclusion or belonging, which motivates him or her to seek out activities that involve others, which in turn influences the products he or she buys to fit in with the group. Determining psychographics

Adding Value 9.1   Skechers Broadening Its Appeal

In its earliest days, Skechers was mostly a lifestyle brand, with hip styles and vibrant designs that appealed to young trendsetters and hipsters, both men and women. When its Shape-Up line arrived in 2010, it offered promises that even if they were a little older and perhaps not quite as in shape as Christina Aguilera, women could improve muscle tone in their legs and buttocks by wearing the rocker-shaped shoe. It began running advertisements in *AARP the Magazine*, as well as in *Cosmopolitan* and *GQ*.[11] It hired Kris Jenner as a spokesperson, along with her daughter Kim Kardashian. This success among older women prompted further extensions, including Shape-Ups for men and girls.[12]

Skechers has expanded into more athletic arenas, to market itself as an alternative for sports, not just lifestyle. Joe Montana appears in televised ads, and the 2012 Super Bowl featured a prominent commercial with Mark Cuban, the outspoken owner of the Dallas Mavericks, introducing Skechers' latest GOrun line of shoes.[13]

The comparison of its Super Bowl commercials is telling. Whereas in 2011, the ad featured Kim Kardashian, which prominently focused on her physique, the 2012 version puts a small dog in sneakers. Thus the company is trying to appeal to multiple segments.

Skechers creates shoes that appeal to several target markets, including kids.

involves knowing and understanding three components: self-values, self-concept, and lifestyles.

Self-values are goals for life, not just the goals one wants to accomplish in a day. They are the overriding desires that drive how a person lives his or her life. Examples might be the need for self-respect, self-fulfillment, or a specific sense of belonging. This motivation causes people to develop self-images of how they want to be and then images of a way of life that will help them arrive at these ultimate goals. From a marketing point of view, self-values help determine the benefits the target market may be looking for from a product. The underlying, fundamental, personal need that pushes a person to seek out certain products or brands stems from his or her desire to fulfill a self-value.

People's self-image, or **self-concept**, is the image people ideally have of themselves.[14] For instance, a person who has a goal to belong may see, or want to see, himself as a fun-loving, gregarious type whom people wish to be around. Marketers often make use of this particular self-concept through communications that show their products being used by groups of laughing people

Marketers like Benetton want their ads to appeal to people's self-concepts: "I'm like them (or I want to be like them), so I should buy their products."

who are having a good time. The connection emerges between the group fun and the product being shown and connotes a lifestyle that many consumers seek.

Lifestyles, the third component of people's psychographic makeup, are the way we live.[15] If values provide an end goal and self-concept is the way one sees oneself in the context of that goal, lifestyles are how we live our lives to achieve goals.

One of the most storied lifestyles in American legend is the Harley way of life. The open road, wind in your hair, rebelling against conventions—the image nearly always depicted men like Dennis Hopper in *Easy Rider*. But the notions of freedom, rebellion, and standing out from a crowd vastly appeal to all sorts of people. In response, Harley-Davidson has shifted its STP methods to define four main target markets: core (white men older than 35 years), young adults (both genders, 18–34 years), women (white and older than 35 years), and diverse (men and women, African American and Hispanic, older than 35 years).[16]

For women, for example, it encourages lifestyle events such as Garage Parties, women's-only social gatherings hosted in the evenings at dealerships to teach women the basics of motorcycling. The company publication *We Ride* focuses solely on female Hogs, and the HD-1 Customization website offers a separate process for women to build their cycles to match their build, power preferences, and color desires.[17]

The most widely used tool to support such psychographic segmentation efforts is **Value and Lifestyle Survey, VALS™**, owned and operated by Strategic Business Insights (SBI).[18] Consumers can be classified into the eight segments shown in Exhibit 9.3 based on their answers to the questionnaire (http://www.strategicbusinessinsights.com/vals/presurvey.shtml). The vertical dimension of the VALS framework indicates level of resources, including income, education, health, energy level, and degree of innovativeness. The upper segments have more resources and are more innovative than those on the bottom.

Using lifestyle segmentation, Harley-Davidson has four main target markets: On the left is its core segment consisting of white men older than 35 years. On the right are white women older than 35 years.

The horizontal dimension shows the segments' primary psychological motivation for buying. Consumers buy products and services because of their primary motivations—that is, how they see themselves in the world and how that self-image governs their activities. The three primary motivations of U.S. consumers are ideals, achievement, and self-expression. People who are primarily motivated by ideals are guided by knowledge and principles. Those who are motivated by achievement look for products and services that demonstrate success to their peers. Consumers who are primarily motivated by self-expression desire social or physical activity, variety, and risk.

VALS also enables firms to identify target segments and their underlying motivations. It shows correlations between psychology and lifestyle choices. For instance, a European luxury automobile manufacturer used VALS to identify online, mobile applications that would appeal to affluent, early-adopter consumers within the next five years.[19] The VALS analysis enabled the company to prioritize the most promising applications to develop. In another case, VALS was used to help a medical center identify customers most interested and able to afford cosmetic surgery. Based on the underlying motivations of its target customers, the center and its ad agency developed an ad campaign so successful that it had to be pulled early to avoid overbooking at the surgical center.

Firms are finding that psychographic segmentation schemes like VALS are often more useful for predicting consumer behavior than are demographics. This

EXHIBIT 9.3   VALS Framework

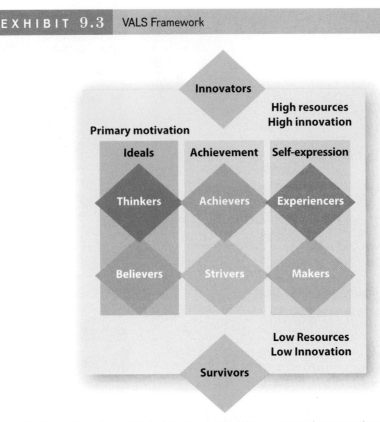

Source: Reprinted with permission of Strategic Business Insights (SBI); www.strategicbusinessinsights.com/VALS.

is because people who share demographics often have very different psychological traits. Take, for example, Jack and John, both 30-year-old, married, college graduates. Demographically, they are the same, but Jack is risk-averse and John is a risk taker. Jack is socially conscious and John is focused on himself. Lumping Jack and John together as a target does not make sense, because the ways they think and act are totally different from each other.

There are limitations to using psychographic segmentation, however. Psychographics are more expensive as a means to identify potential customers. With demographics, for example, a firm like Nike can easily identify its customers

It is just as easy to identify Thinkers (left) as it is Makers (right). A person is given the VALS questionnaire and the VALS program at SRIC-BI runs the answers through the computer for scoring to determine the VALS type.

as, say, men or women and then direct its marketing strategies to each group differently. The problem is that not all men are alike, as we saw with Jack and John. Women are not all alike either! To identify VALS Thinkers or Makers, companies use the VALS questionnaire in surveys or focus groups. Then VALS provides segment descriptions, linkages with consumer product and media data, communication styles, and zip code locations.[21]

Benefit Segmentation **Benefit segmentation** groups consumers on the basis of the benefits they derive from products or services. Because marketing is all about satisfying consumers' needs and wants, dividing the market into segments whose needs and wants are best satisfied by the product benefits can be a very powerful tool.[22] It is effective and also relatively easy to portray a product's or service's benefits in the firm's communication strategies. Social and Mobile Marketing 9.1 describes how Heinz is using social media to convey the specific benefits of its new balsamic vinegar ketchup.

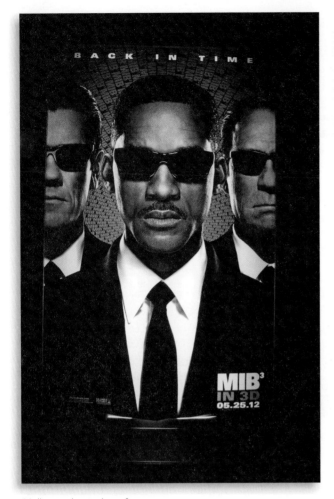

Hollywood uses benefit segmentation to segment moviegoers. Fans of Men in Black *go because they love action movies.*

Airlines use a loyalty segmentation strategy to attract frequent fliers. It costs less for frequent flyer members with more miles to have access to airlines' elite lounges.

Hollywood in particular is a constant and effective practitioner of benefit segmentation. Although all movies may seem to provide the same service—entertainment for a couple of hours—film producers know that people visit the theater or rent films to obtain a vast variety of benefits, and market them accordingly. Need a laugh? Try the latest comedy from Adam Sandler or Melissa McCarthy. Want to cry and then feel warm and fuzzy? Go to a romantic movie starring Katherine Heigl, for by the time you leave the theater, you are likely to feel quite happy, because the lead characters will have faced obstacles, overcome them, and ultimately found love.

Behavioral Segmentation **Behavioral segmentation** divides customers into groups on the basis of how they use the product or service. Some common behavioral measures include occasion and loyalty.

Occasion Behavioral segmentation based on when a product or service is purchased or consumed is called **occasion segmentation**. Men's Wearhouse uses this type of segmentation to develop its merchandise selection and its promotions. Sometimes men need a suit for their everyday work, but other suits are expressly for special occasions, like a prom or a wedding. Snack food companies like Frito-Lay also make and promote snacks for various occasions—individual servings of potato chips for a snack on the run, but 16-ounce bags for parties.

Loyalty Firms have long known that it pays to retain loyal customers. Loyal customers are those who feel so strongly that the firm can meet their relevant needs best that any competitors are virtually excluded from their consideration; that is, these customers buy almost exclusively from the firm. These loyal customers are the most profitable in the long term.[23] In light of the high cost of finding new customers and the profitability of loyal customers, today's companies are using **loyalty segmentation** and investing in retention and loyalty initiatives to retain their most profitable customers.

Airlines definitely believe that not all customers are created equal. At United Airlines, customers who have flown the most miles with the company, the "Premier Executive 1K," receive guaranteed reservations even on sold-out flights, priority check-in, special seating priorities, dedicated reservation services and priority waitlist status.[24] According to Hollywood, flying 10 million miles, like George Clooney's character in *Up in the Air*, even gets you a dedicated customer service line.[25] None of these special services are available to the occasional flyer.

Using Multiple Segmentation Methods Although all segmentation methods are useful, each has its unique advantages and disadvantages. For example, segmenting by demographics and geography is easy because information about who the customers are and where they are located is readily available, but these characteristics don't help marketers determine their customers' needs. Knowing what benefits customers are seeking or how the product or service fits a particular lifestyle is important for designing an overall marketing strategy, but such segmentation schemes present a problem for marketers attempting to identify specifically which customers are seeking these benefits. Thus, firms often employ a combination of segmentation methods, using demographics and geography to identify and target marketing communications to their customers, then using benefits or lifestyles to design the product or service and the substance of the marketing message.

One very popular mixture of segmentation schemes is geodemographic segmentation. Based on the adage "birds of a feather flock together," **geodemographic segmentation** uses a combination of geographic, demographic, and lifestyle characteristics to classify consumers. Consumers in the same neighborhoods tend to buy the same types of cars, appliances, and apparel and shop at the same types of retailers. Two of the most widely used tools for geodemographic segmentation are PRIZM (Potential Rating Index by Zip Market), developed by Nielsen Claritas (www.mybestsegments.com), and ESRI's (www.esri.com) Tapestry. Using detailed demographic data and information about the consumption and media habits of people who live in each U.S. block tract (zip code + 4), PRIZM can identify 66 geodemographic segments or neighborhoods. Each block group then can be analyzed and sorted by more than 60 characteristics, including income, home value, occupation, education, household type, age, and several key lifestyle variables. The information in Exhibit 9.4 describes two PRIZM clusters.

EXHIBIT 9.4   PRIZM Clusters

Segment Name	Bohemian Mix	Big Sky Families
Segment Number	16	33
Demographics traits:		
Urbanicity:	Urban	Rural
Median household income:	$55,665	$57,074
Age ranges:	<55	25–44
Presence of kids:	Family mix	HH w/kids
Homeownership:	Renters	Mostly owners
Employment levels:	White collar, Mix	Blue collar, Service, Mix
Education levels:	College grad	Some college
Ethnic diversity:	White, Black, Asian, Hispanic	White
Lifestyle traits:		
	Shop at Express, 3mo	Own horse
	Own/lease new Volkswagen	Buy children's clothes, 6mos
	Go Snowboarding, 1yr	Own satellite dish
Food & drink:		
	Drink Corona Extra beer, 1wk	Use baby foods, 1wk
	Buy from Au Bon Pain, 1mo	Buy from family restaurant, child decides, 6mo
	Buy from Dunkin Donuts, 1mo	Buy from Hardee's, 1mo
Media usage:		
	Read *The New Yorker*, last issue	Read *Hunting*, last issue
	Visit Internet Movie Database (imdb.com), 1mo	Visit nascar.com, 1mo
	Write a blog online, 1mo	Watch The Disney Channel, 1wk

Source: Reprinted with permission of The Nielsen Company.

Geodemographic segmentation can be particularly useful for retailers because customers typically patronize stores close to their neighborhood. Thus, retailers can use geodemographic segmentation to tailor each store's assortment to the preferences of the local community. If a toy store discovers that one of its stores is surrounded by Big Sky Families, it might adjust its offering to include less expensive toys. This kind of segmentation is also useful for finding new locations; retailers identify their "best" locations and determine what types of people live in the area surrounding those stores, according to the geodemographic clusters. They can then find other potential locations where similar segments reside.

CHECK YOURSELF

1. What are the various segmentation methods?

LO2 Describe how firms determine whether a segment is attractive and therefore worth pursuing.

Step 3: Evaluate Segment Attractiveness

The third step in the segmentation process involves evaluating the attractiveness of the various segments. To undertake this evaluation, marketers first must determine whether the segment is worth pursuing, using several descriptive criteria: Is the segment identifiable, substantial, reachable, responsive, and profitable (see Exhibit 9.5)?

Identifiable Firms must be able to identify who is within their market to be able to design products or services to meet their needs. It is equally important to ensure that the segments are distinct from one another, because too much overlap between segments means that distinct marketing strategies aren't necessary to meet segment members' needs. Thus, Conde Nast is able to identify its market for *Modern Bride* magazine by purchasing mailing lists of people that have bridal registries. It also knows that *Modern Bride* customers tend to be distinct from those who subscribe to *GQ*.

Substantial Once the firm has identified its potential target markets, it needs to measure their size. If a market is too small or its buying power insignificant, it won't generate sufficient profits or be able to support the marketing mix activities. As China's economy started growing, there were not enough middle-class car

EXHIBIT 9.5   Evaluation of Segment Attractiveness

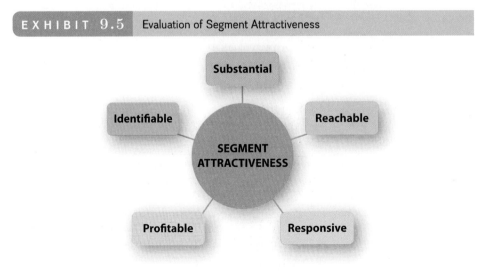

buyers to push foreign automakers to design an entry-level vehicle. It was only after that number reached substantial numbers that it became worthwhile for them to market to these identified consumers.

Can General Motors compete with other luxury car companies for the very lucrative luxury car segment?

Reachable The best product or service cannot have any impact, no matter how identifiable or substantial the target market is, if that market cannot be reached (or accessed) through persuasive communications and product distribution. The consumer must know the product or service exists, understand what it can do for him or her, and recognize how to buy it. If Victoria's Secret fails to tell women that it is offering some less luxurious, more affordable options, shoppers will just walk right past the store and buy basic bras from the Macy's store in the same mall, for example.

Responsive For a segmentation strategy to be successful, the customers in the segment must react similarly and positively to the firm's offering. If, through the firm's distinctive competencies, it cannot provide products or services to that segment, it should not target it. For instance, General Motors (GM) has introduced a line of cars to the large and very lucrative luxury car segment. People in this market typically purchase Porsches, BMWs, Audis, and Lexuses. In contrast, GM has been somewhat successful competing for the middle-priced family-oriented car and light truck segments. Thus, though the luxury car segment meets all the other criteria for a successful segment, GM took a big risk in attempting to pursue this market.

Profitable Marketers must also focus their assessments on the potential profitability of each segment, both current and future. Some key factors to keep in mind in this analysis include market growth (current size and expected growth rate), market competitiveness (number of competitors, entry barriers, product substitutes), and market access (ease of developing or accessing distribution channels and brand familiarity). Some straightforward calculations can help illustrate the profitability of a segment:[26]

Segment profitability = (Segment size × Segment adoption percentage × Purchase behavior × Profit margin percentage) − Fixed costs

where

Segment size = Number of people in the segment

Segment adoption percentage = Percentage of customers in the segment who are likely to adopt the product/service

Purchase behavior = Purchase price × number of times the customer would buy the product/service in a year

Profit margin percentage = (Selling price − variable costs) ÷ selling price

Fixed costs = Advertising expenditure, rent, utilities, insurance, and administrative salaries for managers

To illustrate how a business might determine a segment's profitability, consider Camillo's start-up lawn service. He is trying to determine whether to target homeowners or businesses in a small Midwestern town. Exhibit 9.6 estimates the profitability of the two segments. The homeowner segment is much larger than the business segment, but there are already several lawn services with established customers. There is much less competition in the business segment.

EXHIBIT 9.6   Profitability of Two Market Segments for Camillo's Lawn Service

	Homeowners	Businesses
Segment size	75,000	1,000
Segment adoption percentage	1%	20%
Purchase behavior Purchase price Frequency of purchase	$100 12 times	$500 20 times
Profit margin percentage	60%	80%
Fixed costs	$400,000	$1,000,000
Segment profit	$140,000	$600,000

So, the segment adoption rate for the homeowner segment is only 1 percent, compared with 20 percent for the business segment. Camillo can charge a much higher price to businesses, and they utilize lawn services more frequently. The profit margin for the business segment is higher as well because Camillo can use large equipment to cut the grass and therefore save on variable labor costs. However, the fixed costs for purchasing and maintaining the large equipment are much higher for the business segment. Furthermore, he needs to spend more money obtaining and maintaining the business customers, whereas he would use less expensive door-to-door flyers to reach household customers. On the basis of these informed predictions, Camillo decides the business segment is more profitable for his lawn service.

This analysis provides an estimate of the profitability of two segments at one point in time. It is also useful to evaluate the profitability of a segment over the lifetime of one of its typical customers, as Social and Mobile Marketing 9.2 highlights in a different context, namely, the modern music business.

To address such issues, marketers consider factors such as how long the customer will remain loyal to the firm, the defection rate (percentage of customers who switch on a yearly basis), the costs of replacing lost customers (advertising, promotion), whether customers will buy more or more expensive merchandise in the future, and other such factors. We explicitly address the lifetime value of customers in the appendix following the next chapter.

Now that we've evaluated each segment's attractiveness (Step 3), we can select the target markets to pursue (Step 4).

Step 4: Select Target Market

LO3 Articulate the differences among targeting strategies: undifferentiated, differentiated, concentrated, or micromarketing.

The fourth step in the STP process is to select a target market. The key factor likely to affect this decision is the marketer's ability to pursue such an opportunity or target segment. Thus, as we mentioned in Chapter 2, a firm assesses both the attractiveness of the target market (opportunities and threats based on the SWOT analysis and the profitability of the segment) and its own competencies (strengths and weaknesses based on SWOT analysis) very carefully.

Determining how to select target markets is not always straightforward. Exhibit 9.7 illustrates several targeting strategies, which we discuss in more detail next.

Undifferentiated Targeting Strategy, or Mass Marketing When everyone might be considered a potential user of its product, a firm uses an **undifferentiated targeting strategy**. (See Exhibit 9.7.) Clearly, such a targeting strategy focuses on the similarities in needs of the customers as opposed to the differences. If the product

Social and Mobile Marketing 9.2

Spinning Records Takes on a Totally New Meaning[27]

The music business has long been a microcosm that demonstrates changing technology. From record albums to eight-tracks to CDs to digital downloads, its history summarizes the history of changing customer demand and reinventions of the offerings. And that history shows no signs of changing as the industry once again leads the way in shifting its approach by reimagining what it means to sell to customers.

The industry keeps learning the lesson that major record labels are unnecessary if a band can attract fans on its own. But that can be challenging as a band gets started, so companies such as Topspin offer assistance. With Topspin web applications, bands have a route to upload and sell recordings, along with tickets to shows and merchandise. The company handles the accounting and customer contact details, while also offering detailed advice and suggestions about how best to build a fan base.

Perhaps the most notable of Topspin's recommendations is the notion that bands should reject the $.99 single download model popularized by iTunes. Rather than encouraging fans to buy one single for less than a dollar, bands should give away their product for free, in the hope of encouraging those fans to buy a $15 T-shirt, a $50 deluxe set of recordings, or even a $100 concert ticket.

Whereas the recent trend has been to unbundle music—that is, rather than buying the entire album, consumers can pick and choose which singles they prefer—Topspin encourage "rebundling." Thus it combines free digital downloads with offers for physical products like posters, as well as services such as ticket sales. The average value of transactions on the Topspin website, even when the music is available for free, is $26. If the measure includes sales when customers bought tickets, the average jumps to $88.

The chief executive of Topspin summarizes the idea succinctly:

> You are talking to your fans so you probably know what they want but if you're not sure, ask them! Create something of value for them. It could be as simple as a T-shirt or vinyl or as elaborate as a box set or an in-person experience. But remember not everyone has the same level of fandom or depth of pocketbook. Every day there are people coming to your website who are just entering the "Awareness" phase and there's nothing you're going to do to get them to open their wallet for you. Offer something free, something in the $10 price range, something in the $25 price range, something in the $50 price range, and something in the superfan price range. It turns out the Internet isn't about "going digital" after all, it's about consumer choice. Give your fans a valuable product that fits their budget and level of fandom and they will be happy to support you.

Another digital firm takes a different approach to help musicians evaluate the attractiveness of their fans and potential customers. With the FanTrail application, those musicians set up an easily accessible site for fans. The sites include features such as LoveMail—a function that allows the artist to record a message that gets sent automatically to registered fans' smartphones. Then with the LoveMeter function, that same artist can determine just how active each fan is, measured in terms of purchases and check-ins at concerts. The messages can be precisely targeted, based on fans' location or LoveMeter ranking, which allows artists to reward their biggest, most loyal fans with invitations to secret shows, advance ticket sales, and so forth.

Ian Rogers, CEO of Topspin believes that if you give customers a valuable product, even if it is free music at first, they will be happy and support you as your fandom and depth of pocketbook increases.

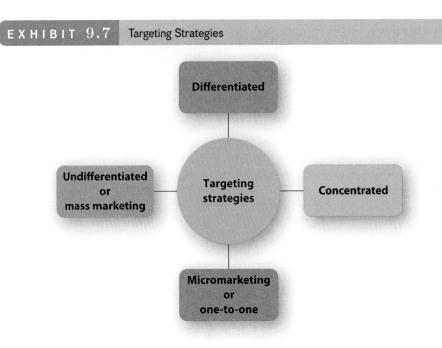

EXHIBIT 9.7   Targeting Strategies

Differentiated

Targeting strategies

Undifferentiated or mass marketing

Concentrated

Micromarketing or one-to-one

or service is perceived to provide similar benefits to most consumers, there simply is little need to develop separate strategies for different groups.

Although not a common strategy in today's complex marketplace, an undifferentiated strategy is used for many basic commodities, such as salt or sugar. However, even those firms that offer salt and sugar now are trying to differentiate their products. Similarly, everyone with a car needs gasoline. Yet gasoline companies have vigorously moved from an undifferentiated strategy to a differentiated one by targeting their offerings to low-, medium-, and high-octane gasoline users.

Conde Nast has more than 20 niche magazines focused on different aspects of life.

Differentiated Targeting Strategy Firms using a **differentiated targeting strategy** target several market segments with a different offering for each (see again Exhibit 9.2). Conde Nast has more than 20 niche magazines focused on different aspects of life—from *Vogue* for fashionistas to *Bon Appetit* for foodies to *GQ* for fashion-conscious men to *The New Yorker* for literature lovers to *Golf Digest* for those who walk the links.

Firms embrace differentiated targeting because it helps them obtain a bigger share of the market and increase the market for their products overall. Readers of *Golf Digest* probably are unlike readers of *Architectural Digest* in their interests, as well as in their demographics, such as gender, age, and income. Providing products or services that appeal to multiple segments helps diversify the business and therefore lowers the company's (in this case, Conde Nast's) overall risk. Even if one magazine suffers a circulation decline, the impact on the firm's profitability can be offset by revenue from another publication that continues to do well. But a differentiated strategy is likely to be more costly for the firm.

Concentrated Targeting Strategy When an organization selects a single, primary target market and focuses all its energies on providing a product to fit that market's needs, it is using a **concentrated targeting strategy**. Entrepreneurial start-up ventures often benefit from using a concentrated strategy, which allows them to employ their limited resources more efficiently. Newton Running, for instance, has concentrated its targeting strategy to runners—but not all runners. It focuses only on those who prefer to land on their forefeet while running, a style that recently has been suggested as more natural, efficient, and less injury-prone than the style encouraged by more traditional running shoes with their heel-first construction and substantial cushioning. In comparison, though it also is known for its running shoes, Nike uses a differentiated targeting strategy (recall the opening vignette about Nike in Chapter 2). It makes shoes for segments that include basketball and football players and skateboarders, as well as fashion-conscious white-collar workers with its subsidiary brand Cole-Haan.

Micromarketing[28] Take a look at your collection of belts. Have you ever had one made to match your exact specifications? (If you're interested, try www.leathergoodsconnection.com.) When a firm tailors a product or service to suit an individual customer's wants or needs, it is undertaking an extreme form of segmentation called **micromarketing** or **one-to-one marketing**.

Such small producers and service providers generally can tailor their offerings to individual customers more easily. But it is far more difficult for larger companies to achieve this degree of segmentation. Major players like Dell (computers) and Lands' End (shirts) tried to capitalize on Internet technologies to offer custom products. Lands' End let customers choose from a variety of options in the fabric, type of collar, sleeve, shape, and based on the customer's specific measurements—but it halted this service when it could not manage to achieve profitable sales. Dell still allows customers to choose the size, color, and speed of their laptops, though it has backed off its promotions and limits the choice of software included. These adjustments demonstrate the difficulty of micromarketing; Superior Service 9.1 on page 283 suggests a way to make it work.

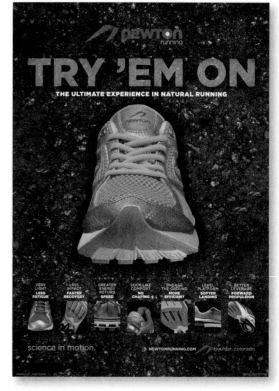

Newton Running has concentrated its targeting strategy on runners that seek to land on the forefront.

The Internet clearly helps facilitate such a segmentation strategy.[29] Companies can cater to very small segments, sometimes as small as one customer at a time, relatively efficiently and inexpensively (e.g., mortgage and insurance sites provide personalized quotes). An Internet-based company can offer one-to-one service more inexpensively than can other venues, such as retail stores or telephone-based businesses. For example, frequent fliers of American Airlines can check prices and choose special services online at a fraction of the cost that the company would incur for a phone consultation with a ticket agent.

The Internet also simplifies customer identification. **Cookies**, or small text files a website stores in a visitor's browser, provide a unique identification of each potential customer who visits and details how the customer has searched the site. Marketers also can ask visitors to fill out an online registration form. Using such information, the company can make a variety of recommendations to customers. Amazon.com is renowned for the algorithms it uses to provide recommendations for related products to customers as they browse the site, which match customer profiles to those of other customers. The marketing strategy therefore is customized in real time, using known and accurate data about the customer. Staples offers merchandise at different prices in different parts of the country—simply by asking customers to enter their zip codes.

Customers can even do the work themselves, both to create items for themselves and to find the perfect gifts for others.[30] Mars' M&Ms site (www.mymms.com) lets customers customize their own M&M's with personalized greetings, including messages for birthday parties, sporting events, graduations, and weddings—as well as wedding proposals! Both online and in stores, Build-A-Bear lets young (or not so young) customers design their very own stuffed furry friend,

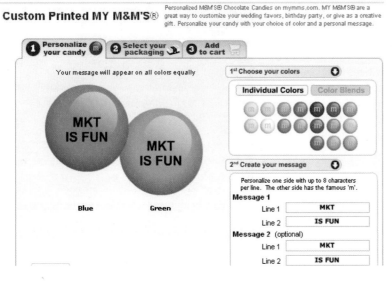

www.mymms.com allows customers to customize their candy.

with unique clothes, accessories, sounds, and the name printed on its birth certificate.

Some consumers appreciate such custom-made goods and services because they are made especially for them, which means they'll meet the person's needs exactly. If a tailor measures you first and then sews a suit that fits your shoulders, hips, and leg length exactly, it probably will fit better than an off-the-rack suit that you pick up at a department store. But such products and services are typically more expensive than ready-made offerings and often take longer to obtain. You can purchase a dress shirt in your size at Macy's and wear it out of the store. Ordering a tailored shirt from an online site that allows you to enter in your measurements might take five to six weeks to receive delivery. And if you visited an old-fashioned tailor, the processes of measuring you, ordering the material, and sewing the pants might take several months—at a much higher cost.

LO4 Determine the value proposition.

Step 5: Develop Positioning Strategy

The last step in developing a market segmentation strategy is positioning. Market positioning involves a process of defining the marketing mix variables so that target customers have a clear, distinctive, desirable understanding of what the product does or represents in comparison with competing products.

The positioning strategy can help communicate the firm's or the product's **value proposition**, which communicates the customer benefits to be received from a product or service and thereby provides reasons for wanting to purchase it.

Build-A-Bear lets customers design their own stuffed furry friend with unique clothes, accessories, sounds, and the name printed on its birth certificate.

Superior Service 9.1 With or Without You: Specified Service[31]

With the effective use of technology, a customer service exchange can occur without any human interaction. This promise and the development of automated customer service offers benefits and harms, to both consumers and service providers.

For customers, the do-it-yourself component of customer self-service is convenient and appealing. Consumers can visit kiosks, websites, or chat rooms to find quick solutions to mundane problems.

For the service providers, greater technology means lower costs, because they can hire fewer workers to respond to customer complaints and questions. In addition, they can provide more consistent service, no longer depending on the inherently variable human component.

Yet technology cannot solve advanced customer service problems or provide empathy to consumers in the midst of a service crisis. When consumers need the complex problem-solving skills that only a human can provide, the limitations of technology-based responses are frustrating. By the time they reach a human customer service representation, their expectations have jumped exponentially: They want perfect, expert assistance. Thus firms must give them more professional, highly trained service representatives. The increased expectations also enhance opportunities for service failures, to the detriment of the firm.

Zappos.com seems to have found a good balance that meets the specific needs of each individual customer who contacts the site. It uses automated technology to handle approximately 75 percent of its customer service transactions. But it also prides itself on hiring and training the best employees available to handle customer service. The other 25 percent of calls that go to a human respondent constitute powerful and influential customer service interactions. By effectively navigating these customer service issues, Zappos has built remarkable brand loyalty and a strong reputation as a customer service leader.

Although Zappos handles 75 percent of its service transactions through automated technology, the other 25 percent get the TLC of a highly trained customer service representative.

To visualize the value proposition, examine the Circles for a Successful Value Proposition framework in Exhibit 9.8A.[32] The first circle represents the customer needs and wants, the second circle represents the benefits that the company provides (i.e., their capabilities), and the final circle represents the benefits provided by competitors. The best situation is if a firm's product or service offering overlaps with customer needs and wants but suffers no overlap with competitors' offerings (Exhibit 9.8A). The shaded portion reflects the value proposition, or the intersection of what the customer needs and wants with what the firm can offer. Unfortunately, even if the situation depicted in Exhibit 9.8A existed, the product or service then would be successful, so it likely would not be sustainable, because competitors would attempt to copy the important product or service attributes and therefore begin to encroach on the firm's value proposition. Maintaining a unique value proposition can be sustained in the long term only in monopoly situations or possibly monopolistic competition situations.

EXHIBIT 9.8   Circles for a Successful Value Proposition

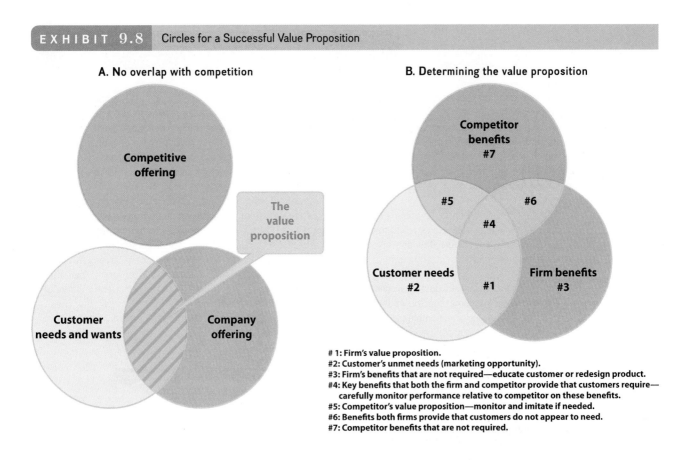

A. No overlap with competition

Competitive offering

Customer needs and wants

Company offering

The value proposition

B. Determining the value proposition

Competitor benefits #7

#5   #6

#4

Customer needs #2   #1   Firm benefits #3

1: Firm's value proposition.
#2: Customer's unmet needs (marketing opportunity).
#3: Firm's benefits that are not required—educate customer or redesign product.
#4: Key benefits that both the firm and competitor provide that customers require—
     carefully monitor performance relative to competitor on these benefits.
#5: Competitor's value proposition—monitor and imitate if needed.
#6: Benefits both firms provide that customers do not appear to need.
#7: Competitor benefits that are not required.

In Exhibit 9.8B, the intersection of customer needs, the benefits provided by our focal firm, and the benefits provided by a competing firm reveal seven specific spaces where a product or service might be located. Let's look at each one in turn, using the offerings of the airline industry as hypothetical examples to understand each space.

Space 1. Representing the firm's value proposition, this space reveals which customer needs are effectively met by the benefits that the firm provides but not by the benefits provided by competitors. That is, there is no overlap between competitors. When airline customers prefer a cattle-call approach to seating, which allows them to choose their own seats on the plane as long as they get an early check-in, they turn to Southwest, and Southwest alone, for their flights.

Space 2. These customer needs are unmet. It represents an important marketing opportunity, in that the firm could create new products or augment existing services to satisfy these needs better. A direct route between two cities that currently are not connected by any airline represents a prime example of such a space.

Space 3. Customers express little need or desire for these company benefits. The firm thus has several options. It might educate customers about the importance and benefits that it provides with this space, to encourage customers to develop a sense of their need. Alternatively, it could reengineer its approach to stop providing these unwanted benefits, which likely would enable it to save money. For example, when airlines realized that passengers cared little about the appearance of a piece of lettuce underneath the in-flight sandwiches they were served, they saved millions of dollars they had previously spent on unwanted produce.

Space 4. These needs are being met by the benefits of the firm, as well as by competitors. Many customers make frequent trips between major cities, like New York and Washington, DC, and many airlines offer multiple direct flights each day between these hubs. Each firm therefore works to compete effectively, such as by offering convenient flight times or striving to increase its on-time rates, to make it easier for customers to compare firms on these specific features.

Space 5. This space constitutes the competitor's value proposition: The needs of customers that are met by benefits a competitor provides, but not by the benefits provided by our focal firm. For example, only a few airlines host separate lounges for their best customers; a lower cost airline cannot compete in this space. However, if more and more customers start to make demands for these benefits, the focal firm needs to carefully monitor developments and match some benefits if possible.

Space 6. Although both the focal firm and its competitors provide these benefits, they somehow are not meeting customer needs. The stringent security screening requirements aim to increase passenger safety, but they also represent a significant inconvenience that many fliers associate with airlines, rather than federal regulators. Expending significant efforts to educate customers by the focal firm about these needs would also benefit competitors, so they likely are lower in the priority list of spending.

Space 7. Finally, some competitor benefits are either undesired or unnecessary among customers. Similar to Space 3, the competitor could invest money to educate customers about the importance of these benefits and highlight their needs through advertising and promotional campaigns. If so, the focal firm should recognize that this need is moving to Space 5. Alternatively, the competitor could reengineer its products to eliminate these benefits, in which case it requires no response from the focal firm.

Regardless of their existing space though, firms must constantly and closely monitor their competitors' offerings. If competitors offer features that the firm does not, it is important to determine their importance to customers. Important attributes should be considered for inclusion into the firm's offering—or else they will provide a unique value proposition for competitors.

In Exhibit 9.9, we highlight the elements of developing and communicating a firm's value proposition. The main value proposition components are:

1. Target market
2. Offering name or brand
3. Product/service category or concept
4. Unique point of difference/benefits

What are the value propositions for Gatorade and 7UP?

EXHIBIT 9.9 Value Proposition Statement Key Elements

	Gatorade	7-Up
Target market:	To athletes around the world	To non-cola consumers
Offering name or brand:	Gatorade	7-Up
Product/service category or concept:	is the sports drink	is a non-caffeinated soft drink
Unique point of difference/ benefits:	representing the heart, hustle, and soul of athleticism and gives the fuel for working muscles, fluid for hydration, and electrolytes to help replace what is lost in sweat before, during, and after activity to get the most out of your body.	that is light, refreshing, lemon-lime flavored and has a crisp, bubbly, and clean taste.

Let's focus on a couple of well-known products, Gatorade and 7-Up, and their potential value propositions (brackets added to separate the value proposition components):

- **Gatorade:**[33] To [athletes around the world] [Gatorade] is the [sports drink] that [represents the heart, hustle, and soul of athleticism and gives the fuel for working muscles, fluid for hydration, and electrolytes to help replace what is lost in sweat before, during, and after activity to get the most out of your body].

- **7-Up:**[34] To [non-cola consumers] [7-Up] is a [non-caffeinated soft drink] that [is light, refreshing, lemon-lime flavored, and has a crisp, bubbly, and clean taste].

L05 Define positioning, and describe how firms do it.

Positioning Methods

Firms position products and services based on different methods such as the value proposition, salient attributes, symbols, and competition.

The positioning strategy can help communicate the firm's or the product's value proposition, the unique value that a product or service provides to its customers, and how it is better than and different from those of competitors. Firms thus position their products and services according to value and salient attributes. **Value** is a popular positioning method because the relationship of price to quality is among the most important considerations for consumers when they make a purchase decision.

Remember that value does not necessarily mean low priced. The watchmaker Patek Philippe uses the advertising tagline, "You never actually own a Patek Philippe. You merely take care of it for the next generation," to encourage buyers to consider its arm candy an investment.[35] The long-running campaign takes on added effectiveness in the modern economic downturn, especially as a way to market a luxury brand in a necessity-focused economy. Other brands that rely on a similar idea of luxury value include Hermes, Chanel, and Mercedes-Benz.

Another common positioning strategy focuses on the product attributes that are most important to the target market. Volvo, the car company traditionally positioned for the safety-conscious driver, wants to stretch its safety image to one focused on driving performance and excitement. The company expects the positioning adjustment to be a long and concentrated effort, because so many of Volvo's boxier vehicles remain on the road today, which reinforces its more conservative image. Volvo's goal is not to abandon the safety notions associated with the brand but rather to expand its image to compete with other top luxury brands.[36]

French retailer Hermes is positioned as a luxury brand, which makes its customers less price-sensitive for its products like this handmade Birkin bag which retails for $9,000.

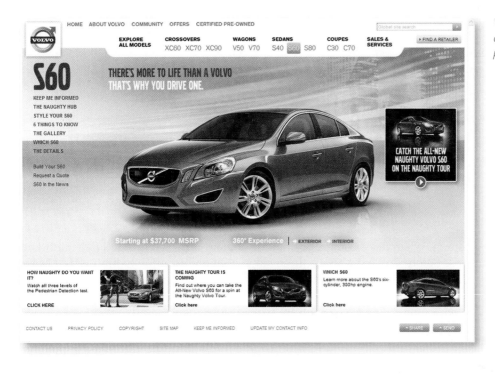

A well-known symbol can also be used as a positioning tool. What comes to mind when you think of Colonel Sanders, the Jolly Green Giant, the Gerber Baby, or Tony the Tiger? Or consider the Texaco star, the Nike swoosh, or the Ralph Lauren polo player. These symbols are so strong and well known that they create a position for the brand that distinguishes it from its competition. Many such symbols are registered trademarks that are legally protected by the companies that developed them.

Firms can choose to position their products or services against a specific competitor or an entire product/service classification. For instance, 7-Up positioned its product as "the Uncola" to differentiate it from caramel-colored cola beverages like Pepsi and Coke. Goodrich tires were promoted as "the other guys," or the ones without the blimp, to set them apart from Goodyear tires.

Marketers must be careful, however, that they don't position their product too closely to their competition. If, for instance, their package or logo looks too much like a competitor's, they might be opening themselves up to a trademark infringement lawsuit. Many private-label and store brands have been challenged for using packaging that appears confusingly similar to that of the national brand leaders in a category. Similarly, McDonald's sues anyone who uses the "Mc" prefix, including McSleep Inns and McDental Services, even though in the latter case there was little possibility that consumers would believe the fast-food restaurant company would branch out into dental services.

Positioning Using Perceptual Mapping

Now that we have identified the various methods by which firms position their products and services, we discuss the actual steps they go through to establish that

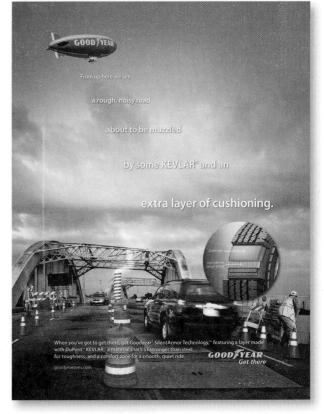

Goodrich positions its tires as the ones without the blimp to set them apart from Goodyear.

Gatorade with football player Jason Taylor (left) and POWERade with soccer player David Beckham (right) are positioned to compete for target markets in Exhibit 9.10.

position. When developing a positioning strategy, firms go through five important steps. Before you read about these steps, though, examine Exhibit 9.10 (Charts A–D), a hypothetical perceptual map of the soft drink industry. A **perceptual map** displays, in two or more dimensions, the position of products or brands in the consumer's mind. We have chosen two dimensions for illustrative purposes: strong versus light taste (vertical) and fun versus healthy (horizontal). Also, though this industry is quite complex, we have simplified the diagram to include only a few players in the market. The position of each brand is denoted by a small circle, and the numbered circles denote consumers' **ideal points**—where a particular market segment's ideal product would lie on the map. The larger the numbered circle, the larger the market size.

To derive a perceptual map such as shown in Exhibit 9.10, marketers follow six steps.

1. **Determine consumers' perceptions and evaluations of the product or service in relation to competitors'.** Marketers determine their brand's position by asking consumers a series of questions about their and competitors' products. For instance, they might ask how the consumer uses the existing product or services, what items the consumer regards as alternative sources to satisfy his or her needs, what the person likes or dislikes about the brand in relation to competitors, and what might make that person choose one brand over another. Exhibit 9.10A depicts the six products using two dimensions (light taste–sweet taste; and less natural–healthy).

2. **Identify the market's ideal points and size.** On a perceptual map, marketers can represent the size of current and potential markets. For example, Exhibit 9.10B uses different sized ovals that correspond to the market size. Ideal point 1 represents the largest market, so if the firm does not

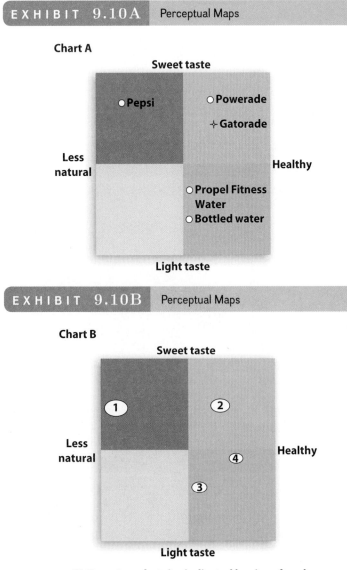

EXHIBIT 9.10A   Perceptual Maps

Chart A

Sweet taste

○ Pepsi   ○ **Powerade**

              ⊹ **Gatorade**

Less natural   **Healthy**

                    ○ **Propel Fitness Water**
                    ○ **Bottled water**

Light taste

EXHIBIT 9.10B   Perceptual Maps

Chart B

Sweet taste

① 1   ② 2

Less natural   ④ 4   **Healthy**

          ③ 3

Light taste

◯ **Target market size indicated by size of oval**

already have a product positioned close to this point, it should consider an introduction. Point 3 is the smallest market, so there are relatively few customers who want a healthy, light tasting drink. This is not to suggest that this market should be ignored; however, the company might want to consider a niche, rather than mass, market strategy for this group of consumers.

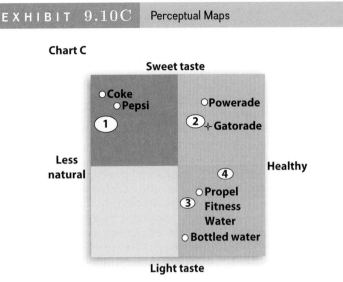

EXHIBIT 9.10C Perceptual Maps

3. **Identify competitors' positions.** When the firm understands how its customers view its brand relative to competitors', it must study how those same competitors position themselves. For instance, POWERade positions itself closely to Gatorade, which means they appear next to each other on the perceptual map and appeal to target market 2 (see Exhibit 9.10C). They are also often found next to each other on store shelves, are similarly priced, and are viewed by customers as sports drinks. Gatorade also knows that its sports drink is perceived to be more like POWERade than like its own Propel Fitness Water (located near target market 3) or Coke (target market 1).

4. **Determine consumer preferences.** The firm knows what the consumer thinks of the products or services in the marketplace and their positions relative to one another. Now it must find out what the consumer really wants, that is, determine the "ideal" product or service that appeals to each market. For example, a huge market exists for traditional Gatorade, and that market is shared by POWERade. Gatorade also recognizes a market, depicted as the ideal product for segment 4 on the perceptual map, of consumers who would prefer a less sweet, less calorie-laden drink that offers the same rejuvenating properties as Gatorade. Currently, no product is adequately serving market 4.

5. **Select the position.** Continuing with the Gatorade example, the company has some choices to appeal to the "less sweet sports drink" target market 4. It could develop a new product to meet the needs of market 4 (see Exhibit 9.10D, option 1). Alternatively, it could adjust or reposition its marketing approach—its product and promotion—to sell original Gatorade to market 4 (option 2). Finally, it could ignore what target market 4 really wants and hope that consumers will be attracted to the original Gatorade because it is closer to their ideal product than anything else on the market.

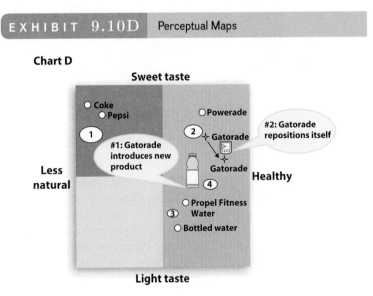

EXHIBIT 9.10D Perceptual Maps

6. **Monitor the positioning strategy.** Markets are not stagnant. Consumers' tastes shift, and competitors react to those shifts. Attempting to maintain the same position year after year can spell disaster for any company. Thus, firms must always view the first three steps of the positioning process as ongoing, with adjustments made in step four as necessary.

Adding Value 9.2   Striving to Encourage the Strivers to Stay[37]

The InterContinental Hotels Group owns several well-known brands, including the Holiday Inn and Crowne Plaza hotel chains. It conducted a $1 billion overhaul of the Holiday Inn brand—only to realize that the Crowne Plaza image was outdated, unfocused, and apparently unappealing to customers. In particular, it identified a target market of young travelers, or "strivers," whose needs Crowne Plaza was not meeting.

Using a combination of promotions and advertisements aimed directly at this target market, Crowne Plaza has worked to highlight its key attractions and events likely to captivate their interest. For example, noting that young travelers are highly likely to book their rooms online and through mobile applications, Crowne Plaza allows people to book same-day reservations through their Android, Blackberry, or iPhone applications.

Beyond age and usage, strivers are interesting in terms of their international character. Richard Solomons, the chief executive of the InterContinental Group, noted the chain's recognition that "there is a big customer base in China that wants a brand that gives them the comfort of being part of an international group but is designed in our China office, by our China team, for our Chinese customers." This group also has specific demands for service, including spaces for entertaining for both business and social contacts in their hotels. By including such spaces in the designs of Crowne Plaza hotels, the brand appeals directly to such customers, without doing anything that would damage its image among strivers from other cultures.

The turbulent state of the hotel industry also suggests that Crowne Plaza will need to reconsider some of its offerings, including whether to shut down underperforming sites. Careful marketing research has suggested that segmentation will increase as customers express increasingly specific preferences and demands.

At the same time, there are some appeals that seem almost universal. All the redesigned hotels therefore will feature a pancake-making machine, available for customers' use any time of the day. It may seem like just a pancake, but it's also fun, different, and playful, and that's exactly the image Crowne Plaza is pursuing.

Repositioning isn't easy! But Crowne Plaza is attempting to reposition itself with an exciting image to appeal to young travelers.

Despite the apparent simplicity of this presentation, marketers should recognize that changing their firm's positioning is never an easy task. Some firms might try to change their image in response to a shift in the target market, such as when Skechers realized that older consumers wanted hip lifestyle shoes too. Crowne Plaza has attempted to reposition itself in the other direction, namely, to gain a more vital, exciting image among younger travelers, as Adding Value 9.2 describes.

CHECK YOURSELF

1. What is a perceptual map?
2. Identify the six positioning steps.

Summing Up

 Outline the different methods of segmenting a market.

There is really no one "best" method to segment a market. Firms choose from various methods on the basis of the type of product/service they offer and their goals for the segmentation strategy. For instance, if the firm wants to identify its customers easily, demographic or geographic segmentation likely will work best. But if it is trying to dig deeper into why customers might buy its offering, then psychographic, geodemographic, benefits, or behavioral segmentation (occasion and loyalty) work best. Typically, a combination of several segmentation methods is most effective.

Describe how firms determine whether a segment is attractive and therefore worth pursuing.

Marketers use several criteria to assess a segment's attractiveness. First, the customer should be identifiable—companies must know what types of people are in the market so they can direct their efforts appropriately. Second, the market must be substantial enough to be worth pursuing. If relatively few people appear in a segment, it is probably not cost-effective to direct special marketing mix efforts toward them. Third, the market must be reachable—the firm must be able to reach the segment through effective communications and distribution. Fourth, the firm must be responsive to the needs of customers in a segment. It must be able to deliver a product or service that the segment will embrace. Finally, the segment must be profitable, both in the near term and over the lifetime of the customer.

Articulate the differences among targeting strategies: undifferentiated, differentiated, concentrated, or micromarketing.

Firms use a targeting strategy after they have identified its segments. An undifferentiated strategy uses no targeting at all and works only for products or services that most consumers consider to be commodities. The difference between a differentiated and a concentrated strategy is that the differentiated approach targets multiple segments, whereas the concentrated targets only one. Larger firms with multiple product/service offerings generally use a differentiated strategy; smaller firms or those with a limited product/service offering often use a concentrated strategy. Firms that employ a micromarketing or one-to-one marketing strategy tailor their product/service offering to each customer—that is, it is custom made. In the past, micromarketing was reserved primarily for artisans, tailors, or other craftspeople who would make items exactly as the customer wanted. Recently, however, larger manufacturers and retailers have begun experimenting with custom-made merchandise as well. Service providers, in contrast, are largely accustomed to customizing their offering.

Determine the value proposition.

A firm's value proposition communicates the customer benefits to be received from a product or service and thereby provides reasons for wanting to purchase it. It consists of the attributes of a product or service that are desired by the target market, but not available from competitors. Firms could attempt to offer attributes that are important to its customers, whether or not they are offered by competitors. For attributes that are not important to its customers, it should either educate its customers about the importance of those attributes, deemphasize them, or not offer those product or service attributes.

Define positioning, and describe how firms do it.

Positioning is the "P" in the STP (segmentation, targeting, and positioning) process. It refers to how customers think about a product, service, or brand in the market relative to competitors' offerings. Firms position their products and services according to several criteria. Some focus on their offering's value—customers get a lot for what the product or service costs. Others determine the most important attributes for customers and position their offering on the basis of those attributes. Symbols can also be used for positioning, though few products or services are associated with symbols that are compelling enough to drive people to buy. Finally, one of the most common positioning methods relies on the favorable comparison of the firm's offering with the products or services marketed by competitors. When developing a positioning strategy and a perceptual map, firms go through six steps. First, they determine consumers' perceptions and evaluations of the product or service in relation to competitors. Second, they identify the market's ideal points and market sizes for those products or services. Third, they identify competitors' positions. Fourth, they determine consumer preferences. Fifth, they select the position. Finally, they monitor the positioning strategy.

Key Terms

- behavioral segmentation, 274
- benefit segmentation, 273
- concentrated targeting strategy, 280
- cookies, 281
- demographic segmentation, 268
- differentiated targeting strategy, 280
- geodemographic segmentation, 275
- geographic segmentation, 268
- ideal point, 288
- lifestyles, 270
- loyalty segmentation, 274
- micromarketing, 281
- occasion segmentation, 274
- one-to-one marketing, 281
- perceptual map, 288
- psychographics, 268
- self-concept, 269
- self-values, 269
- undifferentiated targeting strategy (mass marketing), 278
- value, 286
- Value and Lifestyle Survey (VALS), 270
- value proposition, 282

Marketing Applications

1. What segmentation methods would you suggest for a small entrepreneur starting her own business selling gourmet chocolates? Justify why you would recommend those methods.

2. You have been asked to identify various segments in the market and then a potential targeting strategy. Describe the segments for a pet supply store, and then justify the best targeting strategy to use.

3. How and why would a retailer use micromarketing?

4. You have been asked to evaluate the attractiveness of a group of identified potential market segments. What criteria will you use to evaluate those segments? Why are these appropriate criteria?

5. A small-business owner is trying to evaluate the profitability of different segments. What are the key factors you would recommend she consider? Over what period of time would you recommend she evaluate?

6. Think about the various soft drinks that you know (e.g., Coca-Cola, Pepsi, 7-Up, Gatorade, Powerade). How do those various brands position themselves in the market?

7. Put yourself in the position of an entrepreneur who is developing a new product to introduce into the market. Briefly describe the product. Then, develop the segmentation, targeting, and positioning strategy for marketing the new product. Be sure to discuss (a) the overall strategy, (b) characteristics of the target market, (c) why that target market is attractive, and (d) the positioning strategy. Provide justifications for your decisions.

8. Think of a specific company or organization that uses various types of promotional material to market its offerings. The web, magazine ads, newspaper ads, catalogs, newspaper inserts, direct mail pieces, and flyers might all be sources for a variety of promotional materials. Locate two or three

CHECK YOURSELF

1. What is a perceptual map?
2. Identify the six positioning steps.

Summing Up

LO1 **Outline the different methods of segmenting a market.**

There is really no one "best" method to segment a market. Firms choose from various methods on the basis of the type of product/service they offer and their goals for the segmentation strategy. For instance, if the firm wants to identify its customers easily, demographic or geographic segmentation likely will work best. But if it is trying to dig deeper into why customers might buy its offering, then psychographic, geodemographic, benefits, or behavioral segmentation (occasion and loyalty) work best. Typically, a combination of several segmentation methods is most effective.

LO2 **Describe how firms determine whether a segment is attractive and therefore worth pursuing.**

Marketers use several criteria to assess a segment's attractiveness. First, the customer should be identifiable—companies must know what types of people are in the market so they can direct their efforts appropriately. Second, the market must be substantial enough to be worth pursuing. If relatively few people appear in a segment, it is probably not cost-effective to direct special marketing mix efforts toward them. Third, the market must be reachable—the firm must be able to reach the segment through effective communications and distribution. Fourth, the firm must be responsive to the needs of customers in a segment. It must be able to deliver a product or service that the segment will embrace. Finally, the segment must be profitable, both in the near term and over the lifetime of the customer.

LO3 **Articulate the differences among targeting strategies: undifferentiated, differentiated, concentrated, or micromarketing.**

Firms use a targeting strategy after they have identified its segments. An undifferentiated strategy uses no targeting at all and works only for products or services that most consumers consider to be commodities. The difference between a differentiated and a concentrated strategy is that the differentiated approach targets multiple segments, whereas the concentrated targets only one. Larger firms with multiple product/service offerings generally use a differentiated strategy; smaller firms or those with a limited product/service offering often use a concentrated strategy. Firms that employ a micromarketing or one-to-one marketing strategy tailor their product/service offering to each customer—that is, it is custom made. In the past, micromarketing was reserved primarily for artisans, tailors, or other craftspeople who would make items exactly as the customer wanted. Recently, however, larger manufacturers and retailers have begun experimenting with custom-made merchandise as well. Service providers, in contrast, are largely accustomed to customizing their offering.

LO4 **Determine the value proposition.**

A firm's value proposition communicates the customer benefits to be received from a product or service and thereby provides reasons for wanting to purchase it. It consists of the attributes of a product or service that are desired by the target market, but not available from competitors. Firms could attempt to offer attributes that are important to its customers, whether or not they are offered by competitors. For attributes that are not important to its customers, it should either educate its customers about the importance of those attributes, deemphasize them, or not offer those product or service attributes.

LO5 **Define positioning, and describe how firms do it.**

Positioning is the "P" in the STP (segmentation, targeting, and positioning) process. It refers to how customers think about a product, service, or brand in the market relative to competitors' offerings. Firms position their products and services according to several criteria. Some focus on their offering's value—customers get a lot for what the product or service costs. Others determine the most important attributes for customers and position their offering on the basis of those attributes. Symbols can also be used for positioning, though few products or services are associated with symbols that are compelling enough to drive people to buy. Finally, one of the most common positioning methods relies on the favorable comparison of the firm's offering with the products or services marketed by competitors. When developing a positioning strategy and a perceptual map, firms go through six steps. First, they determine consumers' perceptions and evaluations of the product or service in relation to competitors. Second, they identify the market's ideal points and market sizes for those products or services. Third, they identify competitors' positions. Fourth, they determine consumer preferences. Fifth, they select the position. Finally, they monitor the positioning strategy.

Key Terms

- behavioral segmentation, 274
- benefit segmentation, 273
- concentrated targeting strategy, 280
- cookies, 281
- demographic segmentation, 268
- differentiated targeting strategy, 280
- geodemographic segmentation, 275
- geographic segmentation, 268
- ideal point, 288
- lifestyles, 270
- loyalty segmentation, 274
- micromarketing, 281
- occasion segmentation, 274
- one-to-one marketing, 281
- perceptual map, 288
- psychographics, 268
- self-concept, 269
- self-values, 269
- undifferentiated targeting strategy (mass marketing), 278
- value, 286
- Value and Lifestyle Survey (VALS), 270
- value proposition, 282

Marketing Applications

1. What segmentation methods would you suggest for a small entrepreneur starting her own business selling gourmet chocolates? Justify why you would recommend those methods.

2. You have been asked to identify various segments in the market and then a potential targeting strategy. Describe the segments for a pet supply store, and then justify the best targeting strategy to use.

3. How and why would a retailer use micromarketing?

4. You have been asked to evaluate the attractiveness of a group of identified potential market segments. What criteria will you use to evaluate those segments? Why are these appropriate criteria?

5. A small-business owner is trying to evaluate the profitability of different segments. What are the key factors you would recommend she consider? Over what period of time would you recommend she evaluate?

6. Think about the various soft drinks that you know (e.g., Coca-Cola, Pepsi, 7-Up, Gatorade, Powerade). How do those various brands position themselves in the market?

7. Put yourself in the position of an entrepreneur who is developing a new product to introduce into the market. Briefly describe the product. Then, develop the segmentation, targeting, and positioning strategy for marketing the new product. Be sure to discuss (a) the overall strategy, (b) characteristics of the target market, (c) why that target market is attractive, and (d) the positioning strategy. Provide justifications for your decisions.

8. Think of a specific company or organization that uses various types of promotional material to market its offerings. The web, magazine ads, newspaper ads, catalogs, newspaper inserts, direct mail pieces, and flyers might all be sources for a variety of promotional materials. Locate two or three

promotional pieces for the company and use them as a basis to analyze the segments being targeted. Describe the methods used for segmenting the market reflected in these materials, and describe characteristics of the target market according to the materials. Be sure to include a copy of all the materials used in the analysis.

9. You have been hired recently by a large bank in its credit card marketing division. The bank has relationships with a large number of colleges and prints a wide variety of credit cards featuring college logos, images, and the like. You have been asked to oversee the implementation of a new program targeting the freshman class at the schools with which the bank has a relationship. The bank has already purchased the names and home addresses of the incoming freshman class. You have been told that no credit checks will be required for these cards as long as the student is over 18 years of age. The bank plans a first day of school marketing blitz that includes free hats, T-shirts, and book promotions, as well as free pizza, if the students simply fill out an application. Do you think it is a good idea to target this program to these new students?

Quiz Yourself

www.mhhe.com/grewal4e

1. NASCAR redirected its marketing efforts when a survey indicated that almost 50 percent of race fans were female. This is an example of _____ segmentation.
   a. geographic
   b. psychographic
   c. demographic
   d. benefits
   e. behavioral

2. Within a perceptual map, a(n) _____ represents where a particular market segment's desired product would lie.
   a. point of parity
   b. strategic target

   c. PRIZM cluster
   d. ideal point
   e. benefit centroid

   (Answers to these two questions can be found on page 647.)

   Go to www.mhhe.com/grewal4e to practice an additional 11 questions.

Toolkit

MARKET POSITION MAP ANALYSIS

Assume you are a brand manager for a major manufacturer. You have identified a number of market segments and are trying to understand how its products are positioned relative to other manufacturers'. Use the toolkit provided at www.mhhe.com/grewal4e to conduct a market position analysis.

Net Savvy

1. Go to the Nielsen Claritas' website (www.mybestsegments.com). Click on the tab that says "ZIP Code Look-Up," then enter your zip code to learn which segments are the top five in your zip code. Follow the links for each of the five most common PRIZM segments to obtain a segment description. Write up a summary of your results. Discuss the extent to which you believe these are accurate descriptions of the main segments of people who reside in your zip code.

2. Go to the VALS website (http://www.strategicbusinessinsights.com/vals/presurvey.shtml), and click on the link to complete the VALS survey. After you submit your responses, a screen will display your primary and secondary VALS types. Click on the colored names of each segment to get additional information about them, and print out your results. Assess the extent to which these results reflect your lifestyle, and identify which characteristics accurately reflect your interests and activities and which do not.

Chapter Case Study

COCA-COLA

Back in 1886, an Atlanta pharmacist created a caramel-colored liquid and brought it down the street to Jacobs' Pharmacy, where it was mixed with carbonated water and sold for five cents a glass.[38] The beverage caught on, and sales took off from the initial average of nine drinks a day,[39] to today's total of 1.7 billion Coke-owned beverages consumed daily. The success spawned bottling plants, six-pack cartons, international distribution . . . and imitators. For example, Pepsi followed in 1902 and today is a $29 billion conglomerate with vast holdings.[40]

Both companies spent decades marketing a single brand, Coke or Pepsi. But over the course of the twentieth century, they both expanded their product lines by introducing drink alternatives such as Fanta, Sprite, TAB, Fresca, and Diet Coke (Coca-Cola), along with Diet Pepsi and Mountain Dew. The relatively simple segmentation that these offerings suggested has since grown increasingly complex and sophisticated, especially as the competitors have expanded their international sales into hundreds of diverse country markets. Although they face a number of smaller competitors, the primary focus in this mature market is to take customers away from its main rival, or else find a way to encourage existing customers to drink more cola—both challenging tasks. For Coca-Cola, the best solution is to pursue extensive product development for new and different market segments.[41]

MARKET SEGMENTATION STRATEGY

In a tightening, competitive consumer market, Coke has developed unique products for various specific market segments. Because these unique products appeal to specific groups, Coke has been able to increase its sales without cannibalizing the sales of its other products. In addition to the products already mentioned, for example, the company launched caffeine-free versions of both Coke and Diet Coke to appeal to cola drinkers who wanted to cut back on their caffeine intake but preferred colas to lemon-lime–flavored drinks. By introducing these decaffeinated versions of traditional sodas, Coca-Cola increased the number of sodas it sold each day, without hurting sales, because the consumers targeted by these products already had been avoiding or minimizing cola consumption to reduce their caffeine intake.

DIETERS SEGMENT

As more Americans expressed concerns about their weight, Coca-Cola began by introducing Diet Coke, which became the number one selling diet soft drink in the United States within a year of hitting shelves. In 1986, Diet Cherry Coke joined the brand, followed by Diet Coke with Lemon. Diet Coke with Vanilla and Diet Coke with Lime followed quickly, along with Diet Black Cherry Vanilla Coke. Then new trends in the market led diet-conscious consumers to pay more attention to their overall health, not just calorie content. Thus the company introduced Diet Coke Plus—the familiar version of the beverage but with added vitamins and minerals.

"REAL MEN" SEGMENT

Women hoping to drop a dress size may turn to diet sodas, but "real men" don't want to be caught with a "girly" diet drink. Coca-Cola had a response for them too: the high-profile launch of Coke Zero, which consistently avoided the dreaded word "diet."[42] The successful introduction instead has relied on advertising featuring such masculine images as James Bond to target men through its packaging, promotions, and image. By appealing to men between the ages of 18 to 34 years who wanted to drink a low-calorie cola but would prefer not be seen buying or

Coca-Cola introduced Diet Coke Plus to appeal to a segment of cola drinkers that wants some added nutrients like vitamins B6 and B12.

sipping Diet Coke, Coca-Cola increased its sales of Coke-branded products by one-third.[43]

THE DIY SEGMENT

Soda fountain sales have remained an important part of Coke's business since the company's inception. To boost its cola sales in restaurants, Coke combined the soda fountain concept with the "do it yourself" trend to offer customers up to 104 individualized flavor choices in a new machine.[44] The Freestyle machine was created by the designers of Ferrari race cars. Size-controlled shots of concentrated flavors get released into carbonated water mid-stream, so the drink is mixed in the air; special technology keeps one consumer's beverage from picking up the flavors from the last drink poured. The Freestyle also allows moms to have a Diet Coke with Lime, while dads sip their Coke Zero with Lime and the kids select between a Caffeine-Free Vanilla Coke or a Caffeine-Free Diet Cherry Vanilla Coke.

MARKETING VALUE TO SEGMENTS

A successful new product introduction needs to combine an innovative product with a marketing campaign that communicates the value of that new product to the targeted segment. The Coke Zero launch provides a perfect illustration of this point. Coca-Cola designed a campaign supported by advertisements on television and radio, in print, on outdoor billboards, and online, as well as widespread sampling programs and opportunities.[45] Television commercials for Coke Zero show male athletes like Pittsburg Steeler Troy Polamalu in a remake of the popular "Mean Joe Greene" commercial.[46] Others play on jokes about gender roles and modern relationships by promising that Coke Zero is like enjoying the benefits of having a "girlfriend without the drama." The ongoing media strategy has been to expose as many men as possible to the new product, with a significant bulk of the media budget spent on outdoor advertising.

RESULTS OF COCA-COLA'S SEGMENTATION EFFORTS

By using gender to segment the diet cola market, Coca-Cola was able to customize the advertising for Coca-Cola Zero to appeal to men, whereas Diet Coke ads could concentrate on women. In turn, Coke gained closer connections for its different products with each product's targeted market segment, and Coke Zero became one of the most successful launches in the company's long history.[47] The Freestyle dispenser began in only a few test markets, but in stores in which it was available, the machine bumped up beverage sales by 10 percent at a time when fountain sales on the whole were slipping. In response, several national restaurant chains, including Five Guys and Burger King, decided to roll out Freestyle machines in all their franchises.[48]

Through its efforts to identify and target such specific market segments, Coca-Cola has grown its stable of consumer brands to more than 450 products.[49] Coca-Cola remains the most valuable brand, but Diet Coke and Coca-Cola Zero are not weak siblings: They have joined it as billion-dollar products in their own right.

Questions

1. Which types of segmentation strategies does Coca-Cola use to categorize the cola beverage market?
2. Are these types effective in this market? Provide support for your answer.

CHAPTER 10

Marketing Research

When used in games and movies, virtual reality allows people to participate in scenarios they might never encounter in daily life. Special 3D glasses and realistically rendered images create the sensation of "being there"—whether "there" is in the midst of a military operation, climbing Mt. Everest, or playing a challenging game of tennis. When applied to marketing research, this same technology provides manufacturers with valuable information about how consumers are likely to respond to new products and product displays. Used properly, virtual shopping tools provide more accurate information about customer behaviors than traditional research methods and are more efficient than field testing.[1]

Virtual store testing is not especially new. Companies such as Procter & Gamble (P&G) have been using these tools to conduct market research for more than a decade.[2] But as the technology has evolved, P&G's reliance on it to create, test, and improve package designs, shelf displays, and store layouts has increased.[3] Today, more than three-quarters of global manufacturers' business initiatives rely on virtual solution tools.

For P&G, virtual reality centers on life-sized, 3D images of new products as they might appear on a retailer's shelves, which helps create a fully interactive world. As consumers peruse the shelves, sophisticated software analyzes their reactions, providing insight into common responses to packaging and messaging. Product development teams use this information to make improvements early in the design process, which in turn increases the speed to market, reduces the number of costly physical prototypes, and maximizes the chances of success when the product actually goes live.

The technology also allows P&G to create virtual store environments for analyzing product placement strategies. Marketing researchers supply retailers with information and customer feedback from these tests to help them improve customer satisfaction and build sales. The approach can be used for a single product, such as a new type of fabric refresher aimed at sports enthusiasts. Or it can be used to research an entire line of new products in a private environment, which enables an innovating firm to protect its strategic marketing decisions from snooping competitors.[4]

LEARNING OBJECTIVES

LO1 Identify the five steps in the marketing research process.

LO2 Describe the various secondary data sources.

LO3 Describe the various primary data collection techniques.

LO4 Summarize the differences between secondary data and primary data.

LO5 Examine the circumstances in which collecting information on consumers is ethical.

Today's refinements in virtual reality for marketing research are making the software easier to use for both business decision makers and communicators. The technology has also evolved to provide remarkably realistic graphics and interactivity, which improve insights into consumer responses.[5] Such advanced forms of market research are helping firms like Procter & Gamble understand how to serve its customers and business partners better. And better service means better profits.

As the P&G example shows, **marketing research** is a prerequisite of successful decision making. It consists of a set of techniques and principles for systematically collecting, recording, analyzing, and interpreting data that can aid decision makers involved in marketing goods, services, or ideas.[6] When marketing managers attempt to develop their strategies, marketing research can provide valuable information that will help them make segmentation, positioning, product, place, price, and promotion decisions.

Firms invest billions of dollars in marketing research every year. The largest U.S.-based marketing research firm, the ACNielsen Company, earns annual worldwide revenues of almost $5 billion.[7] Why do marketers find this research valuable? First, it helps reduce some of the uncertainty under which they currently operate. Successful managers know when research might help their decision making and then take appropriate steps to acquire the information they need. Second, marketing research provides a crucial link between firms and their environments, which enables them to be customer oriented because they build their strategies by using customer input and continual feedback. Third, by constantly monitoring their competitors, firms can anticipate and respond quickly to competitive moves.

If you think market research is applicable only to corporate or retailing ventures though, think again. Not-for-profit organizations and governments also use research to serve their constituencies better. The political sector has been slicing and dicing the voting public for decades to determine relevant messages for different demographics. Politicians desperately want to understand who makes up the voting public to determine how to reach them. But not only do they want to know your political views; they also want to understand your media habits, such as what magazines you subscribe to, so they can target you more effectively.

To do so, they rely on the five-step marketing research process we outline in this chapter. We also discuss some of the ethical implications of using the information that these databases can collect. In Appendix 10A, we detail the concept of customer lifetime value (CLV), a popular marketing metric to determine a customer's value to a firm.

THE MARKETING RESEARCH PROCESS

Managers consider several factors before embarking on a marketing research project. First, will the research be useful; will it provide insights beyond what the managers already know and reduce uncertainty associated with the project? Second, is top management committed to the project and willing to abide by the results of the research? Related to both of these questions is the value of the research. Marketing research can be very expensive, and if the results won't be useful or management does not abide by the findings, it represents a waste of money. Third, should the marketing research project be small or large? A project might involve a simple analysis of data that the firm already has, or it could be an in-depth assessment that costs hundreds of thousands of dollars and takes months to complete.

The marketing research process itself consists of five steps (see Exhibit 10.1). Although we present the stages of the marketing research process in a step-by-step progression, of course research does not always, or even usually, happen that way. Researchers go back and forth from one step to another as the need arises. For example, marketers may establish a specific research objective, which they follow with data collection and preliminary analysis. If they uncover new information during the collection step or if the findings of the analysis spotlight new research needs, they might redefine their objectives and begin again from a new starting point. Another important requirement before embarking on a research project is to plan the entire project in advance. By planning the entire research process prior to starting the project, researchers can avoid unnecessary alterations to the research plan as they move through the process.

LO1 Identify the five steps in the marketing research process.

Marketing Research Process Step 1: Defining Objectives and Research Needs

Because research is both expensive and time-consuming, it is important to establish in advance exactly what problem needs to be solved. To do so, marketers must clearly define the objectives of their marketing research project.

Consider the following scenario: McDonald's wants a better understanding of its customers' experience. It also needs to understand how customers view the experience at Wendy's, a main competitor. Finally, McDonald's hopes to gain some insight into how it should set a price for and market its latest combo meal of a hamburger, fries, and drink. Any one of these questions could initiate a research project. The complexity of the project that the company eventually undertakes depends on how much time and resources it has available, as well as the amount of in-depth knowledge it needs.

Researchers assess the value of a project through a careful comparison of the benefits of answering some of their questions and the costs associated with conducting the research. When researchers have determined what information they need to address a particular problem or issue, the next step is to design a research project to meet those objectives.

Marketing Research Process Step 2: Designing the Research

The second step in the marketing research project involves design. In this step, researchers identify the type of data needed and determine the research necessary to collect it. Recall that the objectives of the project drive the type of data needed, as outlined in Step 1.

Let's look at how this second step works, using the McDonald's customer experience. McDonald's needs to ask its customers about their McDonald's experience. However, because people don't always tell the whole truth in surveys, the company also may want to observe customers to see how they actually

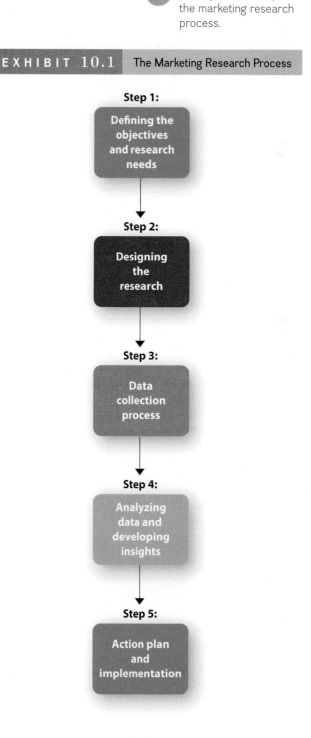

EXHIBIT 10.1 The Marketing Research Process

Step 1:
Defining the objectives and research needs

Step 2:
Designing the research

Step 3:
Data collection process

Step 4:
Analyzing data and developing insights

Step 5:
Action plan and implementation

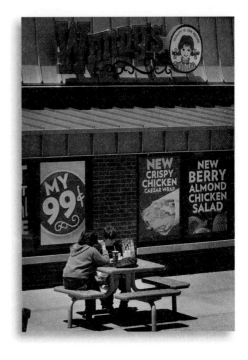

If McDonald's were to do research to better understand its customers' experience, it would study both the McDonald's experience and that of its major competitors, like Wendy's.

enter the stores, interact with employees, and consume the product. The project's design might begin with available data, such as information that shows people with children often come into the restaurants at lunchtime and order Happy Meals. Then McDonald's market researchers can start to ask customers specific questions about their McDonald's experience.

Marketing Research Process Step 3: Data Collection Process

Data collection begins only after the research design process. Based on the design of the project, data can be collected from secondary or primary data sources. **Secondary data** are pieces of information that have been collected prior to the start of the focal research project. Secondary data include both external and internal data sources. **Primary data**, in contrast, are those data collected to address specific research needs. Some common primary data collection methods include focus groups, in-depth interviews, and surveys.

For our hypothetical fast food scenario, McDonald's may decide to get relevant secondary data from external providers such as National Purchase Diary Panel and ACNielsen. The data might include the prices of different ingredients, sales figures, growth or decline in the category, and advertising and promotional

McDonald's assesses its customers' market experience by examining available data, and then asks customers about their experience with products like Happy Meals.

spending. McDonald's is likely to gather pertinent data about sales from its franchisees. However, it also wants competitor data, overall food consumption data, and other information about the quick service restaurant category, which it likely obtains from appropriate syndicated data providers. Based on the data, it might decide to follow up with some primary data using a survey.

No company can ask every customer their opinions or observe every customer, so researchers must choose a group of customers who represent the customers of interest, or a **sample**, and then generalize their opinions to describe all customers with the same characteristics. They may choose the sample participants at random to represent the entire customer market. Or they may choose to select the sample on the basis of some characteristic, such as whether they have children, so they can research the experience associated with buying a Happy Meal.

Marketing researchers use various methods of asking questions to measure the issues they are tackling. In our hypothetical McDonald's scenario, assume the research team has developed a questionnaire (see Exhibit 10.2), using a few different types of questions. Section A measures the customer's experience in McDonald's, Section B measures the customer's experience in Wendy's, Section C measures the customer's habits at McDonald's, and Section D measures customer demographics.[8]

EXHIBIT 10.2   A Hypothetical Fast Food Survey

Please take a few minutes to tell us about your experience at McDonald's and Wendy's. For each question, please respond by checking the box that applies or writing your response in the space provided.

Please Evaluate Your Experience at McDonald's

A. McDonald's	Strongly Disagree 1	Disagree 2	Neither Agree or Disagree 3	Agree 4	Strongly Agree 5
McDonald's food tastes good	❏	❏	❏	☑	❏
McDonald's is clean	❏	❏	❏	☑	❏
McDonald's has low prices	❏	❏	❏	☑	❏

B. Wendy's	Strongly Disagree 1	Disagree 2	Neither Agree or Disagree 3	Agree 4	Strongly Agree 5
Wendy's food tastes good	❏	❏	❏	☑	❏
Wendy's is clean	❏	❏	❏	☑	❏
Wendy's has low prices	❏	❏	❏	☑	❏

C. McDonald's

	Never	1–2 times	3–4 times	More than 5 times
In the last month, how many times have you been to McDonald's?	❏	❏	❏	☑
On average, how much do you spend each visit at McDonald's?	$_____			
What is your favorite item at McDonald's?	_____			

D. Please tell us about yourself

	under 16	17–24	25–35	36+
What is your age?	❏	❏	❏	❏
What is your gender?	Male ❏	Female ❏		

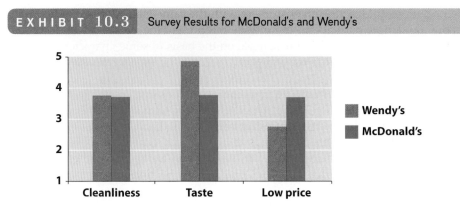

EXHIBIT 10.3   Survey Results for McDonald's and Wendy's

- ■ Wendy's
- ■ McDonald's

Marketing Research Process
Step 4: Analyzing Data and Developing Insights

The next step in the marketing research process—analyzing and interpreting the data—should be both thorough and methodical. To generate meaningful information, researchers analyze and make use of the collected data. In this context, **data** can be defined as raw numbers or other factual information that, on their own, have limited value to marketers. However, when the data are interpreted, they become **information**, which results from organizing, analyzing, and interpreting data and putting them into a form that is useful to marketing decision makers. For example, a checkout scanner in the grocery store collects sales data about individual consumer purchases. Not until those data are categorized and examined do they provide information about which products and services were purchased together or how an in-store promotional activity translated into sales.

For the McDonald's example, we can summarize the results of the survey (from Exhibit 10.2) in Exhibit 10.3. Both McDonald's and Wendy's scored the same on the cleanliness of their restaurants, but McDonald's had lower prices, whereas Wendy's food tasted better. McDonald's thus may want to improve the taste of its food, though without raising prices too much, to compete more effectively with Wendy's.

Marketing Research Process
Step 5: Action Plan and Implementation

In the final phase in the marketing research process, the analyst prepares the results and presents them to the appropriate decision makers, who undertake appropriate marketing strategies. A typical marketing research presentation includes an executive summary, the body of the report (which discusses the research objectives, methodology used, and detailed findings), the conclusions, the limitations, and appropriate supplemental tables, figures, and appendixes.[9]

McDonald's marketing research will show how to better compete against Wendy's.

In the McDonald's hypothetical scenario, according to the research findings, the company is doing fine in terms of cleanliness (comparable to its competitors) and is perceived to have lower prices, but the taste of its food could be improved. Using this analysis and the related insights gained, McDonald's might consider hiring some gourmet chefs as consultants to improve the menu and offerings.[10] It then could highlight its efforts to improve the taste of the food and the additional offerings available in restaurants through marketing communications and promotions. McDonald's also should consider undertaking additional pricing research to determine if its lower prices enhance sales and profits, or if it could increase its prices and still compete effectively with Wendy's.

Now let's take a closer look at sources of secondary and primary data.

SECONDARY DATA

LO2 Describe the various secondary data sources.

A marketing research project often begins with a review of the relevant secondary data. Secondary data might come from free or very inexpensive external sources, such as census data, information from trade associations, and reports published in magazines. Although readily accessible, these inexpensive sources may not be specific or timely enough to solve the marketer's research needs and objectives. Firms also can purchase more specific or applicable secondary data from specialized research firms. Finally, secondary sources can be accessed through internal sources, including the company's sales invoices, customer lists, and other reports generated by the company itself.

In political settings, such secondary data can be critical for candidates running for office. Both major political parties thus have developed proprietary databases that contain vast information about voters, broken down by demographic and geographic information. Before a local politician, canvasser, or poll taker even knocks on doors in a neighborhood, he or she likely knows which houses are inhabited by retirees, who has a subscription to *The Wall Street Journal* or *The New York Times*, for whom the residents said they voted in the last election, or whether they served in the military. All these traits can give hints about the voters' likely concerns, which a good politician can address immediately upon knocking on the door. Such research also can dictate tactics for designing broader campaign materials, or zero in on very specific issues. One gubernatorial candidate in Illinois successfully targeted suburban neighborhoods that housed lots of pets and their owners by running advertisements in which he criticized his opponent's vote for legislation that made it easier for shelters to euthanize strays.[11]

Secondary data is useful to politicians so they know who they are talking to before they knock on their door.

Inexpensive External Secondary Data

Some sources of external secondary data can be quickly accessed at a relatively low cost. The U.S. Census Bureau (www.census.gov), for example, provides data about businesses by county and zip code. If you wanted to open a new location of a business you are already operating, these data may help you determine the size of your potential market.

Often, however, inexpensive data sources are not adequate to meet researchers' needs. Because the data initially were acquired for some purpose other than the research question at hand, they may not be completely relevant or timely. The U.S. Census is a great source of demographic data about a particular market area, and it can be easily accessed at a low cost. However, the data are collected only at the beginning of every decade, so they quickly become outdated. Right now, firms are fortunate because the 2010 Census is relatively current and up-to-date. If an entrepreneur

EXHIBIT 10.4	Syndicated Data Providers and Some of Their Services
Name	**Services Provided**
ACNielsen (www.acnielsen.com)	With its *Market Measurement Services*, the company tracks the sales of consumer packaged goods, gathered at the point of sale in retail stores of all types and sizes.
SymphonyIRI Group (www.symphonyiri.com)	*InfoScan* store tracking provides detailed information about sales, share, distribution, pricing, and promotion across a wide variety of retail channels and accounts.
J.D. Power and Associates (www.jdpower.com)	Widely known for its automotive ratings, it produces quality and customer satisfaction research for a variety of industries.
Mediamark Research Inc. (www.mediamark.com)	Supplies multimedia audience research pertaining to media and marketing planning for advertised brands.
National Purchase Diary Panel (www.npd.com)	Based on detailed records consumers keep about their purchases (i.e., a diary), it provides information about product movement and consumer behavior in a variety of industries.
NOP World (www.nopworld.com)	The *mKids US* research study tracks mobile telephone ownership and usage, brand affinities, and entertainment habits of American youth between 12 and 19 years of age.
Research and Markets (www.researchandmarkets.com)	Promotes itself as a "one-stop shop" for market research and data from most leading publishers, consultants, and analysts.
Roper Center for Public Opinion Research (www.ropercenter.uconn.edu)	The *General Social Survey* is one of the nation's longest running surveys of social, cultural, and political indicators.
Simmons Market Research Bureau (www.smrb.com)	Reports on the products American consumers buy, the brands they prefer, and their lifestyles, attitudes, and media preferences.
Yankelovich (www.yankelovich.com)	The *MONITOR* tracks consumer attitudes, values, and lifestyles shaping the American marketplace.

wanted to open a retail flooring store in 2014 though, the data would already be four years old, and the housing market might be much stronger than it was in 2010. Researchers must also pay careful attention to how other sources of inexpensive secondary data were collected. Despite the great deal of data available on the Internet, easy access does not ensure that the data are trustworthy.

Firms like Kellogg's use scanner data to assess the success of new products like its Special K Popcorn Chips.

Syndicated External Secondary Data

Although the secondary data described previously are either free or inexpensively obtained, marketers can purchase external secondary data called **syndicated data**, which are available for a fee from commercial research firms such as SymphonyIRI Group, the National Purchase Diary Panel, and ACNielsen. Exhibit 10.4 contains information about various firms that provide syndicated data.

Consumer packaged goods firms that sell to wholesalers often lack the means to gather pertinent data directly from the retailers that sell their products to consumers, which makes syndicated data a valuable resource for them. Some syndicated data providers also offer information about shifting brand preferences and product usage in households, which they gather from scanner data and consumer panels.

Scanner data are used in quantitative research obtained from scanner readings of UPC labels at check-out counters. Whenever you go into your local grocery store, your purchases are rung up using scanner systems. The data from these purchases are likely to be acquired by leading marketing research firms, such as SymphonyIRI or

Syndicated external secondary data are obtained from scanner data obtained from scanner readings of UPC codes at check-out counters (left) and from panel data collected from consumers that electronically record their purchases (right).

ACNielsen, which use this information to help leading consumer packaged goods firms (e.g., Kellogg's, Pepsi, Kraft) assess what is happening in the marketplace. For example, a firm can use scanner data to determine what would happen to its sales if it reduced the price of its least popular product by 10 percent in a given month. In the test market in which it lowers the price, do sales increase, decrease, or stay the same?

Panel data are information collected from a group of consumers, organized into panels, over time. Data collected from panelists often include their records of what they have purchased (i.e., secondary data), as well as their responses to survey questions that the client gives to the panel firm to ask the panelists (i.e., primary data). Secondary panel data thus might show that when Diet Pepsi is offered at a deep discount, 80 percent of usual Diet Coke consumers switch to Diet Pepsi. Primary panel data could give insights into what they think of each option. We discuss how marketing researchers use scanner and panel data to answer specific research questions further in the primary data section.

Overall though, both panel and scanner data provide firms with a comprehensive picture of what consumers are buying or not buying. The key difference between scanner research and panel research is how the data get aggregated. Scanner research typically focuses on weekly consumption of a particular product at a given unit of analysis (e.g., individual store, chain, region); panel research focuses on the total weekly consumption by a particular person or household. Both types are valuable, and Adding Value 10.1 describes just how SymphonyIRI provides them to its customers.

Internal Secondary Data

Internally, companies also generate a tremendous amount of secondary data from their day-to-day operations. One of the most valuable resources such firms have at

Adding Value 10.1   SymphonyIRI and the Value of Information

SymphonyIRI was previously known as Information Resources Inc. Regardless of its name though, the company has long provided market research and analytical services for the consumer packaged goods, health care, and retail industries. Ninety-five percent of the *Fortune* Global 500 in the consumer packaged goods and retail industries use SymphonyIRI market research to make their business decisions.[12] For its clients—which include Anheuser-Busch, ConAgra, CVS, Johnson & Johnson, and PepsiCo—SymphonyIRI collects, monitors, and manages a variety of data in some of the most active research markets in the world, including the United States and Europe.

SymphonyIRI tracks a host of data to deliver detailed findings that are designed to grow and enhance clients' operations. To identify trends in private-label sales, for instance, it collects sales data from the scanners at the checkout from almost 95,000 retail stores throughout the United States and Europe,[13] then cross-references these data with data collected from a panel of 70,000 households that SymphonyIRI has armed with personal scanners to track their household purchases.

For example, in a report tracking the increase in private-label brands (see Chapter 11) in the consumer packaged goods industry, SymphonyIRI summarizes how consumer attitudes have changed. If a grocery store chooses to offer its own brand of detergent, it must engage in competition with various branded detergents, such as Tide, Cheer, and All. In the past, private-label products often were positioned as more affordable versions of popular brands and tended to target and attract price-conscious consumers. However, according to SymphonyIRI's findings, recent trends indicate private-label sales are growing across consumer segments, especially as middle-class consumers look for ways to conserve costs in struggling global economies.[14]

Another report highlights the market researcher's findings about the types of trips modern shoppers make and how that determines what they buy. With data that hold interest for both manufacturers and retailers, SymphonyIRI shows that consumer packaged goods shoppers take four types of trips: quick, pantry stock-up, special purpose, or fill-in. The first two account for nearly two-thirds of grocery shoppers' purchases, which means that marketers need to find ways to appeal to people moving fast, as well as those seeking bargains to fill their shelves at home. SymphonyIRI also suggests low-cost, high-value solutions for retailers and manufacturers that can best appeal to these various kinds of shoppers.[15]

Symphony IRI provides market research and analytical services to the consumer packaged goods, health care, and retail industries.

their disposal is their rich cache of customer information and purchase history. However, it can be difficult to make sense of the millions and even billions of pieces of individual data, which are stored in large computer files called **data warehouses**. For this reason, firms find it necessary to use data mining techniques to extract valuable information from their databases.

Data mining uses a variety of statistical analysis tools to uncover previously unknown patterns in the data or relationships among variables. Some retailers try to customize their product and service offerings to match the needs of their customers. For instance, the U.K. grocer Tesco uses its loyalty card to collect massive amounts of information about its individual customers. Every time a loyalty card member buys something, the card is scanned, and the store captures key purchase data, specific to that member. But these specific data are basically useless until Tesco mines and analyzes them to identify three income groups: upscale, middle income, and less affluent. With this mined information, Tesco has been able to create appealing private-label product offerings for each group, according to their preferences, and began targeting promotions to each customer according to his or her income classification. Since 2000, Tesco's market share has grown by more than 20 percent.[16]

Marketers use data mining techniques to determine what items people buy at the same time so they can be promoted and displayed together.

Data mining can also enable a home improvement retailer such as Lowe's to learn that 25 percent of the time its customers buy a garden hose, they also purchase a sprinkler. With such information, the retailer may decide to put the garden hoses next to the sprinklers in the store. Outside the retail realm, an investment firm might use statistical techniques to group clients according to their income, age, type of securities purchased, and prior investment experience. This categorization identifies different segments to which the firm can offer valuable packages that meet their specific needs. The firm also can tailor separate marketing programs to each of these segments. Data mining thus can be useful for a broad range of situations and organizations. By analyzing the enormous amount of information that it possesses about its customers, companies have developed statistical models that help identify when a customer is dissatisfied with his or her service. Once the company identifies an unhappy customer, it can follow up and

Tesco's automated payment system uses a handheld device that allows consumers to scan items as they shop. This device allows customers to keep track of the cost of their shopping as they progress through the store.

Superior Service 10.1   Harrah's

As one of the largest casino operators in the world, Harrah's Entertainment runs more than 50 casinos, spread across four continents, under a variety of brand names, including Caesar's Palace, Horseshoe, and Harrah's. Its facilities typically include hotel and convention space, restaurants, and entertainment facilities.[17] But the company runs another type of facility as well, one that few gamers likely would find as entertaining: It collects a vast amount of data about its millions of customers' preferences and gaming activities. Specifically, Harrah's tracks thousands of details about each visitor, from how much they gamble on each visit to whether they like NASCAR racing.

When Harrah's assigned managers to analyze the data, it found what it considered some surprising information. Conventional wisdom in the gambling industry states that "high rollers" are the most important customers, whereas Harrah's found that the most profitable customers were average, middle-aged working people who gambled only $100–$500 per trip but also visited several times per year.[18]

Next, Harrah's studied these most profitable visitors and found that they were not interested in typical casino incentives, such as free rooms or meals. Instead, what these loyal customers wanted was better service. From this research, Harrah's created its Total Rewards loyalty card program, which classifies four tiers of players—Gold, Platinum, Diamond, and Seven Stars—according to their playing level. Each segment also consists of approximately 90 different groups, based on geography, demographics, psychographics, and usage patterns.

In the Total Rewards program, customers can earn reward credits toward future vacations, sporting events, and merchandise. They also get more of what they want, namely, better service through shorter waits in line. While competing casino operators are trying to lure customers by adding amenities like luxury spas, upscale shopping centers, and fabulous shows, Harrah's is garnering a very loyal following by catering to those who prefer to drop by for an hour after work to play the slots. Total Gold customers must stand in regular lines at the reception desk and restaurants, whereas Total Platinum customers are directed to shorter lines, and the ultra-privileged Total Diamond customers bypass most lines altogether. The company has also made sure that its entire four-tier promotion remains very conspicuous, which makes

customers more interested in rising to the higher tiers. Harrah's use of marketing research thus, in an unavoidable pun, has really paid off big![19]

When Harrah's analyzed its customer data, it found that its most profitable customers weren't the "high rollers" as they had thought. Instead, they were, average middle-aged working people who gambled only $100–500 per trip, but visited several times per year.

proactively address that customer's issues. By mining customer data and information, the company also reduced its churn levels. **Churn** is the number of participants who discontinue use of a service, divided by the average number of total participants. With this knowledge, the company can focus on what it does best. The purpose of converting data to information is to describe, explain, predict, and/or evaluate a particular situation, as Harrah's does in Superior Service 10.1.

Overall, firms hope to use data mining to generate customer-based analytics that they can apply to their strategic decision making, and thereby make good customers better, and make better customers their best. Firms can also use secondary data to assess the profitability of their customers by determining the customer lifetime value (CLV). We offer more details about calculating CLV in Appendix 10A.

CHECK YOURSELF

1. What is the difference between internal and external secondary research?

PRIMARY DATA COLLECTION TECHNIQUES

LO3 Describe the various primary data collection techniques.

In many cases, the information researchers need is available only through primary data, or data collected to address specific research needs. Depending on the nature of the research problem, the primary data collection method can employ a *qualitative* or a *quantitative* research method.

As its name implies, **qualitative research** is used to understand the phenomenon of interest through broad open-ended responses. It provides initial information that helps the researcher more clearly formulate the research objectives. Qualitative research is more informal than quantitative research methods and includes observation, following social media sites, in-depth interviews, focus groups, and projective techniques (see Exhibit 10.5, left side).

Once the firm has gained insights from doing qualitative research, it is likely to engage in **quantitative research**, which are structured responses that can be statistically tested. Quantitative research provides information needed to confirm insights and hypotheses generated via qualitative research or secondary data and helps managers pursue appropriate courses of action. Formal studies such as specific experiments, scanner and panel data, or some combination of these are quantitative in nature. (See Exhibit 10.5, right side.) We now examine each of these primary data collection techniques in order.

Observation

Observation entails examining purchase and consumption behaviors through personal or video camera scrutiny. For example, researchers might observe customers while they shop or when they go about their daily lives, during which processes they use a variety of products. Observation can last for a very brief period of time (e.g., two hours watching teenagers shop for clothing in the mall), or it may take days or weeks (e.g., researchers live with families to observe their use of products). When consumers are unable to articulate their experiences, observation research becomes particularly useful; how else could researchers determine which educational toys babies choose to play with or confirm details of the buying process that consumers might not be able to recall accurately?

Observation may be the best method, and sometimes the only way, to determine how consumers might use a product, and therefore be useful for designing and marketing them. By watching women wash their hair in a rural town in China, Procter &

EXHIBIT 10.5 Qualitative versus Quantitative Data Collection

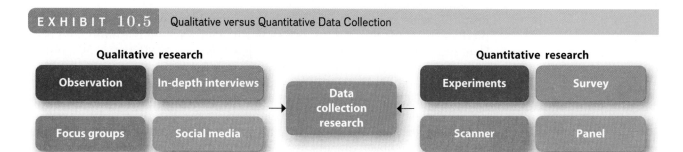

Qualitative research | Quantitative research

Observation   In-depth interviews   →   Data collection research   ←   Experiments   Survey

Focus groups   Social media   Scanner   Panel

By watching women in rural China wash their hair, Procter & Gamble learned that even their poorest customers wanted beautiful hair, but it has to be packaged affordably.

Gamble recognized the fallacy of its assumption that the poorest consumers were only interested in functionality of a product—how to get hair clean. One woman struggled to find ways to wash her long hair effectively, even in the face of severe water shortages, rather than cut off what she considered the source of her beauty. Based on their research, P&G has added value by selling Rejoice shampoo inexpensively ($1.50) to a market that was using alternative options such as laundry detergent. Other observations pushed P&G to develop a more skin-sensitive laundry detergent after noting how many people in developing markets wash their clothes by hand.[20]

These insights might be helpful, both for the company that gathers them and for consumers who ultimately benefit from better products. But Ethical and Societal Dilemma 10.1 also raises a key question: Should people be informed that they are being watched?

Social Media

Social media sites are a booming source of data for marketers. Marketers have realized that social media can provide valuable information that could aid their marketing research and strategy endeavors. In particular, contributors to social media sites rarely are shy about providing their opinions about the firm's own products or its competitors' offerings. If companies can monitor, gather, and mine these vast social media data, they can learn a lot about their customers' likes, dislikes, and preferences. They then might cross-reference such social media commentary with consumers' past purchases to derive a better sense of what they want. Customers also appear keen to submit their opinions about their friends' purchases, interests, polls, and blogs.

Blogs in particular represent valuable sources of marketing research insights. Marketers are paying attention to online reviews about everything from restaurants to running shoes to recycling.[21] On the Videogum blog, the bylined writers invite constant commentary from a community of readers, who go by the collective nickname "Monsters." Their reviews are tongue-in-cheek and a little mischievous, but they also offer justifications and reasons for why the movie *Drive* was one of the best of the year, and then why its star Ryan Gosling also qualifies as one of the 10 best actors.[22] The Truth About Cars blog is known for its unflinchingly objective reviews of various makes and models, as well as discussions about the industry as a whole, marketing tactics, and global competition, among other topics.[23]

Part of what makes blogs so valuable is also what makes them challenging for firms. Bloggers are usually, but not always, unaffiliated with the companies that produce the items they review, which means they have no reason to hold back from negative commentary. When ConAgra tried a hidden camera experiment with a group of food bloggers, it suffered significant backlash throughout the blogosphere. It invited the writers to a dinner, supposedly with a gourmet chef, then fed them a frozen lasagna meal to gauge their responses. Not only did the victims of the prank find it less than funny, they also blasted ConAgra for exposing them, without their permission, to the preservatives and processed ingredients contained in the frozen dinners.[24]

Ethical and Societal Dilemma **10.1**   Watching Consumers

How does sitting in a mall or standing in a store checking out the people in the corner add up to bona fide market research? Well, for Paco Underhill and his company Envirosell, that's just another day on the job.

Envirosell's wide-ranging projects encompass firms in a broad variety of industries. According to its mission statement, Envirosell focuses "on how people, products and spaces interrelate. Our research environments, once rooted in bricks and mortar retail, now span to cover spaces as huge and chaotic as train stations and airports. We've worked in libraries, doctor offices, model homes, showrooms, and every kind of food service imaginable. Our clients are merchants, consumer goods manufacturers, banks, trade associations, not for profits, government agencies and the full spectrum of design, advertising and marketing agencies."[25]

For Staples, for example, it observed consumers in 12 stores, videotaping their movements through the stores for eight hours each research day, as a means to better understand how consumers actually shopped around the various departments to gather products, view signs, and interact with sales associates. Envirosell researchers also conduct interviews with shoppers. On the basis of the results of these studies, Staples rolled out a new store format that focuses on solving customer problems by combining service with self-service rather than just selling individual items. Staples' sales associates can now provide a higher level of service in those areas that demand it, and the new store format gives customers the tools to be self-sufficient if they choose to browse on their own.

Using observational research, marketing research can identify information that would not be accessible to them through more traditional marketing research means—a respondent to a simple questionnaire or people involved in an interview proba-

bly would not be able to provide insightful information about the patterns they follow when walking through a store or a mall. But the method also extends into people's homes. For example, the Swiss sensory firm Givaudan conducted observational research with Chinese consumers to determine how they cook and consume chicken. The research team followed a volunteer, Mrs. Wu, as she shopped in the local market for the exact chicken she wanted butchered to take home. It then entered her home, observed as she cooked it (until she shooed them out of the kitchen so she could arrange the final dish), and sat with the family as they ate. The researchers noted each ingredient Mrs. Wu used, the exact methods she applied to create the meal, and even how the family disposed of the bones. (For your information, in China, it is considered perfectly acceptable to spit out bones onto the tablecloth.)

As a summary of their report notes, their research confirmed that "consuming chicken in China involves an array of sensory experiences—visual, olfactory, gustatory and tactile— so profoundly different from Western experience that an understanding of chicken flavor cannot be understood without referencing Chinese culture as its source."[26] As we discussed in Chapter 8, similar insights also helped Campbell Soup expand its presence in China.

In most cases, researchers obtain consent from the consumers they are watching and videotaping; in other cases though, they do not. The ethical dilemma for marketing researchers centers around whether to use observational techniques in which the subjects are not informed that they are being studied, like viewing customers in a mall or a retail store. Observing uninformed consumers very well may lead to important insights that would not otherwise be discovered. But do the results justify the methodology?

By videotaping customers' movements in a store, it can better understand how consumers actually shopped around the various departments to gather products, view signs, and interact with sales associates.

When Kraft considered the launch of its South Beach product line, it created a virtual community of women who wanted to lose weight and "health and wellness" opinion leaders.

Another creative use of social media for market research involves building online communities for companies. When it considered the launch of its South Beach product line, Kraft hired Communispace to create a virtual community of target consumers: 150 women who wanted to lose weight and 150 "health and wellness" opinion leaders. The participants openly shared their frustrations and difficulties managing their weight, because the community environment prompted them to sense that everyone else on the site struggled with similar issues and concerns. By monitoring the community, Kraft learned that it would need to educate consumers about the South Beach Diet and would need to offer products that could address cravings throughout the day, not just at mealtimes. Six months after the line's introduction, Kraft had earned profits of $100 million.[27]

Noting these various opportunities and market research sources online, many companies—including Ford Motor Co., PepsiCo, Coca-Cola, and Southwest Airlines—have added "heads of social media" to their management teams. These managers take responsibility for scanning the web for blogs, postings, tweets, or Facebook posts in which customers mention their experience with a brand. By staying abreast of this continuous stream of information, companies can gather the most up-to-date news about their company, products, and services, as well as their competitors. These social media searches allow companies to learn about customers' perceptions and resolve customer complaints they may never have heard about through other channels.[28]

The data gathered through the searches also undergo careful analyses: Are customer sentiments generally positive, negative, or neutral? What sort of intensity or interest levels do they imply? How many customers are talking about the firm's products, and how many focus instead on competitors'? This data analysis is understandably challenging, considering the amount of data available online. However, monitoring consumer sentiments has grown easier with the development of social media monitoring platforms.

Radian6 is steadily becoming one of the most sought-after firms for monitoring customers using **sentiment mining**. Using social media sites like Facebook, Twitter, and online blogs, Radian6 and other firms collect consumer comments about companies and their products. The data are then analyzed to distill customer attitudes toward and preferences for products and advertising campaigns. Scouring millions of sites by combining automated online search tools with text analysis techniques, sentiment mining yields qualitative data that provide new insight into what consumers really think. Companies plugged into this real-time information can become more nimble, allowing for quick changes in a product roll-out or a new advertising campaign. Some companies take it a step further, by joining the online conversation with customers, a process called *social engagement*.[29]

In—Depth Interviews

In an **in-depth interview**, trained researchers ask questions, listen to and record the answers, and then pose additional questions to clarify or expand on a particular issue. For instance, in addition to simply watching teenagers shop for apparel, interviewers might stop them one at a time in the mall to ask them a few questions, such as: "We noticed that you went into and came out of Abercrombie & Fitch very quickly without buying anything. Why was that?" If the subject responds that no one had bothered to wait on her, the interviewer might ask a follow-up question like, "Oh? Has that happened to you before?" or "Do you expect more sales assistance there?"

In-depth interviews provide insights that help managers better understand the nature of their industry, as well as important trends and consumer preferences, which can be invaluable for developing marketing strategies. Specifically, they can establish a historical context for the phenomenon of interest, particularly when they include industry experts or experienced consumers. They also can communicate how people really feel about a product or service at the individual level. Finally, marketers can use the results of in-depth interviews to develop surveys.

In-depth interviews are, however, relatively expensive and time consuming. Each interview could cost $200 or more, depending on the length of the interaction and the characteristics of the people included in the sample. If the sample must feature medical doctors, for example, the costs of getting sufficient interviews will be much higher than the costs associated with intercepting teenagers in a mall.

Although relatively expensive, in-depth interviews can reveal information that would be difficult to obtain with other methods.

Focus Group Interviews

In **focus group interviews**, a small group of persons (usually 8 to 12) come together for an intensive discussion about a particular topic. Using an unstructured method of inquiry, a trained moderator guides the conversation, according to a predetermined, general outline of topics of interest. Researchers usually record the interactions by video- or audiotape so they can carefully comb through the interviews later (or feature them in advertisements, as Domino's did in advertisements designed to reposition their pizza)[30] to catch any patterns of verbal or nonverbal responses. In particular, focus groups gather qualitative data about initial reactions to a new or existing product or service, opinions about different competitive offerings, or reactions to marketing stimuli, like a new ad campaign or point-of-purchase display materials.[31]

Campbell's Soup learned from focus groups that women want a nutritious soup that contains ingredients they would use if they made it from scratch. This information helped them develop their Select Harvest line.

To obtain new information to help it continue its innovative success derived from its introduction of low sodium choices, Campbell's Soup conducted extensive focus groups with female shoppers who indicated they would buy ready-to-eat soups. The groups clearly revealed the women's top priorities: a nutritious soup that contained the ingredients they would use if they made soup. They wanted, for example, white meat chicken, fresh vegetables, and sea salt. In addition, focus group participants were equally clear about what they did *not* want, like high fructose corn syrup, MSG, and other stuff whose names they could not even pronounce.[32] The resulting Select Harvest product line showcases the 100 percent natural, flavorful, and healthful ingredients, including vegetables and whole grains. The packaging also reflects the focus groups' preferences, using a simple, clean design that highlights the short list of ingredients. In its first year on the market, the line generated $202 million in sales.[33]

Innovative ideas stemming from marketing research and focus groups are not limited to new products though. The U.S.

Superior Service 10.2   The USPS Sample Showcase

Shuttered post offices. No more one-day delivery. The threat of ending Saturday service. The financial struggles of the U.S. Postal Service (USPS), including annual deficits of $8.5 billion,[34] have been widely discussed, and the continued expansion of digital communication suggests that customers are not likely to turn back to traditional mail anytime soon. In addition to its cost-cutting measures, the USPS thus is working to reinvent key aspects of its operations, including enhanced services for manufacturers that want to distribute their product samples.

The USPS has long distributed samples, especially for consumer packaged goods (CPG) companies and retailers.[35] Yet the sample distribution market began to suffer from higher distribution costs, driven by rising postal rates and freight costs. The USPS could no longer rely on its distinctive capability to deliver physical products into consumers' hands; it needed a new source for a sustainable competitive advantage. To develop a new sample distribution concept that would excite both consumers and retailers, the USPS hired Great Lakes Marketing and gave it the task of finding a way to reduce the per unit cost for CPG manufacturers but still make the product samples interesting to potential customers.

In interviews with retailers, other delivery services, and key industry experts, the USPS had learned that single-product distribution would no longer be viable: It was simply too costly to deliver one manufacturer's product to each postal customer. Combining samples from a group of companies into a single delivery batch seemed preferable, in that it would allow manufacturers to share the costs.[36] But would batching appeal to consumers?

In focus groups conducted in Bethesda, Maryland; Seattle, Washington; and Nashville, Tennessee, participants who identified themselves as their households' primary decision makers offered some remarkable input. In addition to reporting their sincere enthusiasm about sampling, these focus group members noted that they considered mailbox delivery far more convenient than in-store sample distribution. They would love to receive a mailed, bundled sample offering![37]

The focus group findings were compelling enough that the USPS distributed its first round of the bundled Sample Showcase soon thereafter.[38] Each package contains samples from 12 individual companies, including familiar names such as Secret and Starbucks, as well as some less well-known CPG manufacturers, such as Gum Soft-Picks, an oral healthcare company.[39] In addition, the USPS hired an online sample management company to identify 200,000 target households that would opt-in to online recruiting and join targeted purchase lists.

Follow-up surveys with consumers have confirmed the focus group attitudes: A month after the first delivery, 25,418 respondents recalled receiving the samples. Of those, 98.4 percent noted that the mix of products "appealed" to them, and 97.3 percent agreed that with the statement that "Sample Showcase is for someone like me."[40] Furthermore, retailers continue to regard sample distributions as a means to distinguish their brands from "the clutter" in the marketplace. In particular, smaller companies have found that including their products in the same box with high-visibility offerings boosts their own brand recognition.[41]

Focus group findings led USPS to offer Sample Showcase—a package containing samples from 12 individual companies.

Postal Service also has used them to improve its service offering, as Superior Service 10.2 describes.

The growth of online technology, as well as computer and video capabilities, have provided tremendous benefits for focus group research, which now often takes place online. For example, eFocusGroups offers a secure site as a platform for companies to listen in on focus groups and even interact with consumers, without anyone having to travel. The client company not only saves costs but also gains access to a broader range of potential customers who live in various neighborhoods, states, or even countries. Because eFocusGroups automatically records all the online interactions, the company also has a detailed, verbatim transcript of consumers' comments and responses.[42] However, these online focus groups rarely include video feeds, so companies lose some important information that can be gleaned from body language.

CHECK YOURSELF

1. What are the types of qualitative research?

Survey Research

Arguably the most popular type of quantitative primary collection method is a **survey**—a systematic means of collecting information from people using a questionnaire. A **questionnaire** is a form that features a set of questions designed to gather information from respondents and thereby accomplish the researchers' objectives. Individual questions on a questionnaire can be either unstructured or structured. **Unstructured questions** are open ended and allow respondents to answer in their own words. An unstructured question like, "What are the most important characteristics for choosing a brand of shampoo?" yields an unstructured response. However, the same question could be posed to respondents in a structured format by providing a fixed set of response categories, such as price, fragrance, ability to clean, or dandruff control, and then asking respondents to rate the importance of each. **Structured questions** thus are closed-ended questions for which a discrete set of response alternatives, or specific answers, is provided for respondents to evaluate (see Exhibit 10.6).

Survey research uses questionnaires to collect primary data. Questions can be either unstructured or structured.

Developing a questionnaire is part art and part science. The questions must be carefully designed to address the specific set of research questions. Moreover, for a questionnaire to produce meaningful results, its questions cannot be misleading in any fashion (e.g., open to multiple interpretations), and they must address only one issue at a time. They also must be worded in vocabulary that will be familiar and comfortable to those being surveyed. The questions should be sequenced appropriately: general questions first, more specific questions next,

EXHIBIT 10.6   Structured versus Unstructured Response

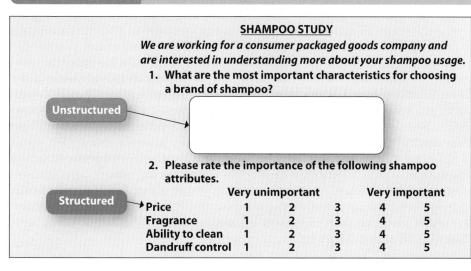

SHAMPOO STUDY
We are working for a consumer packaged goods company and are interested in understanding more about your shampoo usage.

1. **What are the most important characteristics for choosing a brand of shampoo?**

Unstructured

2. **Please rate the importance of the following shampoo attributes.**

	Very unimportant			Very important	
Structured → Price	1	2	3	4	5
Fragrance	1	2	3	4	5
Ability to clean	1	2	3	4	5
Dandruff control	1	2	3	4	5

EXHIBIT 10.7	What Not to Do When Designing a Questionnaire	
Issue	**Good question**	**Bad question**
Avoid questions the respondent cannot easily or accurately answer.	When was the last time you went to the grocery store?	How much money did you spend on groceries last month?
Avoid sensitive questions unless they are absolutely necessary.	Do you take vitamins?	Do you dye your gray hair?
Avoid double-barreled questions, which refer to more than one issue with only one set of responses.	1. Do you like to shop for clothing? 2. Do you like to shop for food?	Do you like to shop for clothing and food?
Avoid leading questions, which steer respondents to a particular response, irrespective of their true beliefs.	Please rate how safe you believe a BMW is on a scale of 1 to 10, with 1 being not safe and 10 being very safe.	BMW is the safest car on the road, right?
Avoid one-sided questions that present only one side of the issue.	To what extent do you believe fast food contributes to adult obesity using a five-point scale? 1: Does not contribute, 5: Main cause	Fast food is responsible for adult obesity: Agree/Disagree

Source: Adapted from A. Parasuraman, Dhruv Grewal, and R. Krishnan, *Marketing Research*, 2nd ed. (Boston: Houghton Mifflin, 2007), Ch. 10.

and demographic questions at the end. Finally, the layout and appearance of the questionnaire must be professional and easy to follow, with appropriate instructions in suitable places. For some tips on what *not* to do when designing a questionnaire, see Exhibit 10.7.[43]

Similar to focus groups, marketing surveys can be conducted either online or offline, but online marketing surveys offer researchers the chance to develop a database quickly with many responses, whereas offline marketing surveys provide a more direct approach that includes interactions with the target market. Web surveys have steadily grown as a percentage of all quantitative surveys. Online surveys have a lot to offer marketers with tight deadlines and small budgets.[44]

In particular, the response rates for online surveys are relatively high. Typical response rates run from 1 to 2 percent for mail and 10 to 15 percent for phone surveys. For online surveys, in contrast, the response rate can reach 30 to 35 percent, or even higher in business-to-business research. It also is inexpensive. An average 20-minute phone interview can cost $30 to $40, compared with $7 to $10 for an online interview. Costs likely will continue to fall as users become more familiar with the online survey process. Results are processed and received quickly. Reports and summaries can be developed in real time and delivered directly to managers in simple, easy-to-digest reports, complete with color, graphics, and charts. Traditional phone or mail surveys require laborious data collection, tabulation, summary, and distribution before anyone can grasp their results.

Diverse online survey software, such as Qualtrics, Surveymonkey, and Zoomerang, makes it very easy to draft an online survey, using questions from existing survey libraries. A survey link can be sent easily in an e-mail to potential respondents or panelists, as well as posted on specific sites that are likely to attract the target audience or people who are willing to perform online work (e.g., Amazon's Mechanical Turk Site).

Panel and Scanner—Based Research

As discussed previously, panel and scanner research can be either secondary or primary. In this section, we consider the use of a panel to collect primary data. Walmart's U.K. subsidiary Asda uses an 18,000-customer panel, which it calls "Pulse of the Nation," to help determine which products to carry. Asda sends e-mails to each participant with product images and descriptions of potential new products. The customers' responses indicate whether they think each product should be carried in stores. As an incentive to participate, Asda enters respondents automatically into a drawing for free prizes.[45]

Walmart's U.K. subsidiary Asda uses an 18,000-customer panel, which it calls "Pulse of the Nation," to help determine which products to carry.

Experimental Research

Experimental research (an **experiment**) is a type of quantitative research that systematically manipulates one or more variables to determine which variables have a causal effect on other variables. For example, in our earlier scenario, one thing the hypothetical McDonald's research team was trying to determine was the most profitable price for a new menu combo item (hamburger, fries, and drink). Assume that the fixed cost of developing the item is $300,000 and the variable cost, which is primarily composed of the cost of the food itself, is $2.00. McDonald's puts the item on the menu at four different prices in four different markets. (See Exhibit 10.8.) In general, the more expensive the item, the less it will sell. But by running this experiment, the restaurant chain determines that the most profitable price is the second least expensive ($5.00). These findings suggest some people may have believed the most expensive item ($7.00) was too expensive, so they refused to buy it. The least expensive item ($4.00) sold fairly well, but McDonald's did not make as much money on each item sold. In this experiment, the changes in price likely caused the changes in quantities sold and therefore affected the restaurant's profitability.

EXHIBIT 10.8	Hypothetical Pricing Experiment for McDonald's				
	1	2	3	4	5
Market	Unit Price	Market Demand at Price (in Units)	Total Revenue (Col. 1 × Col. 2)	Total Cost of Units Sold ($300,000 Fixed Cost + $2.00 Variable Cost)	Total Profits (Col. 3 / Col. 4)
1	$4	200,000	$800,000	700,000	$100,000
2	5	150,000	$750,000	600,000	$150,000
3	6	100,000	$600,000	500,000	$100,000
4	7	50,000	$350,000	400,000	($50,000)

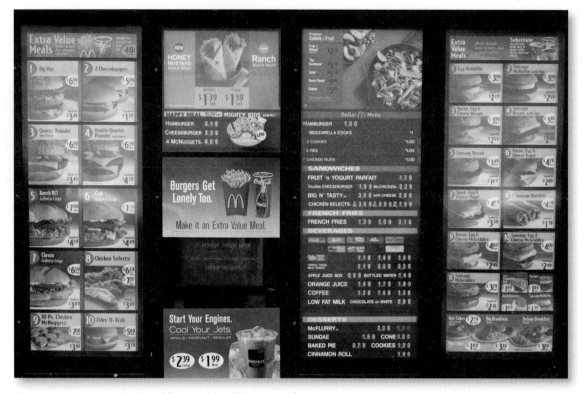

Using an experiment, McDonald's would "test" the price of new menu items to determine which is the most profitable.

LO4 Summarize the differences between secondary data and primary data.

Advantages and Disadvantages of Primary and Secondary Research

Now that we have discussed the various secondary and primary data collection methods, think back over our discussion and ask yourself what seem to be the best applications of each and when you would want to go to secondary sources or use primary collection methods. We can see that both primary data and secondary data have certain inherent and distinct advantages and disadvantages. For a summary of the advantages and disadvantages of each type of research, see Exhibit 10.9.

EXHIBIT 10.9 Advantages and Disadvantages of Secondary and Primary Data

Type	Examples	Advantages	Disadvantages
Secondary research	❏ Census data ❏ Sales invoices ❏ Internet information ❏ Books ❏ Journal articles ❏ Syndicated data	❏ Saves time in collecting data because they are readily available ❏ Free or inexpensive (except for syndicated data)	❏ May not be precisely relevant to information needs ❏ Information may not be timely ❏ Sources may not be original, and therefore usefulness is an issue ❏ Methodologies for collecting data may not be appropriate ❏ Data sources may be biased
Primary research	❏ Observed consumer behavior ❏ Focus group interviews ❏ Surveys ❏ Experiments	❏ Specific to the immediate data needs and topic at hand ❏ Offers behavioral insights generally not available from secondary research	❏ Costly ❏ Time consuming ❏ Requires more sophisticated training and experience to design study and collect data

EMERGING TECHNOLOGY AND THE ETHICS OF USING CUSTOMER INFORMATION

LO5 Examine the circumstances in which collecting information on consumers is ethical.

As we noted in Chapter 4, upholding strong business ethics requires more than a token nod to ethics in the mission statement. A strong ethical orientation must be an integral part of a firm's marketing strategy and decision making. In Chapter 4, we discussed how marketers have a duty to understand and address the concerns of the various stakeholders in the firm.

It is particularly important for marketers to adhere to ethical practices when conducting marketing research. The American Marketing Association provides three guidelines for conducting marketing research: (1) It prohibits selling or fundraising under the guise of conducting research, (2) it supports maintaining research integrity by avoiding misrepresentation or the omission of pertinent research data, and (3) it encourages the fair treatment of clients and suppliers.[46] Numerous codes of conduct written by various marketing research societies all reinforce the duty of researchers to respect the rights of the subjects in the course of their research. The bottom line: Marketing research should be used only to produce unbiased, factual information.

As technology continues to advance though, the potential threats to consumers' personal information grow in number and intensity. Marketing researchers must be vigilant to avoid abusing their access to these data. Security breaches at some of the United States' largest retailers, banks, credit-reporting services, and peer-to-peer networks have shown just how easily stored data can be abused.[47] From charitable giving to medical records to Internet tracking, consumers are more anxious than ever about preserving their fundamental right to privacy. They also demand increasing control over the information that has been collected about them.

Many firms therefore voluntarily notify their customers that any information provided to them will be kept confidential and not given or sold to any other firm. Several organizations, including the Center for Democracy & Technology (CDT) and the Electronic Privacy Information Center (EPIC), have emerged as watchdogs over data mining of consumer information. In addition, national and state governments in the United States play a big part in protecting privacy. Companies are legally required to disclose their privacy practices to customers on an annual basis, for example.[48]

But laws have yet to catch up with advances in other areas, including social media, neuromarketing, and facial recognition software. As we noted previously in this chapter, social media have grown into an important resource for marketing researchers because consumers are so willing and likely to share their attitudes and opinions there. In this case, protecting consumers' privacy is mainly up to the consumer.

In contrast, consumers have little control over facial recognition software that allows companies to detect demographic information based on their appearances. For example, digital billboards embedded with such software can identify passersby and then display ads targeted to them, based on their age, gender, and attention level.[49] The resulting communication is precisely targeted, which should make the advertisement more interesting to the consumer walking by—though it also could lead to embarrassing encounters. Imagine, for example, a teenager with skin problems having a billboard loudly broadcast an acne product ad as he walks by!

On Facebook, facial detection software applied to photographs eliminates the need for users to continue to tag the same people multiple times. It also stores all users' biometric data. **Biometric data** include one or more physical traits such as facial characteristics, iris scans, or fingerprints. Facebookers can turn off the facial detection function, but their biometric data is still collected. In Germany, with its strict privacy laws, regulators have demanded that Facebook stop collecting any biometric data.

Going even deeper than using biometric data, *neuromarketing* claims the ability to read consumers' minds, using wireless electroencephalogram (EEG) scanners that measure the involuntary brainwaves that occur when they view a product, advertisement, or brand images. Such insights would be invaluable for marketers, to discover what truly appeals to consumers. For example, do people love the iPad because of its functionality, or is the true source of its appeal the curves of the tablet, which appeal to a primal preference in humans?[50] But as anyone who has ever seen a science fiction movie can imagine, the potential for abuses of such tools are immense. And a key question remains: Do any consumers want marketers reading their brain waves and marketing goods and services to them in a manner that bypasses their conscious thoughts? One firm, NeuroFocus, used neuromarketing techniques with several global firms to garner customer information that would be difficult, if not impossible, to obtain using more traditional research methods (see Exhibit 10.10).

EXHIBIT 10.10   Findings from Neuromarketing Studies by NeuroFocus

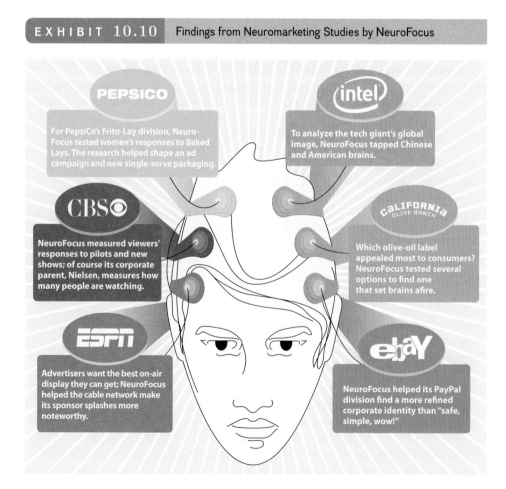

CHECK YOURSELF

1. Under what circumstances is it ethical to use consumer information in marketing research?
2. What challenges do technological advances pose for the ethics of marketing research?

Summing Up

LO1 Identify the five steps in the marketing research process.

The first step is to define objectives and research needs, which sounds so simple that managers often gloss over it. But this step is crucial to the success of any research project because, quite basically, the research must answer those questions that are important for making decisions. In the second step, designing the research project, researchers identify the type of data that is needed, whether primary or secondary, on the basis of the objectives of the project from Step 1, and then determine the type of research that enables them to collect those data. The third step involves deciding on the data collection process and collecting the data. The process usually starts with qualitative research methods such as observation, in-depth interviews, or focus groups. The information gleaned from the qualitative research is then used in quantitative research, which may include a survey, an experiment, or the use of scanner and panel data. The fourth step is to analyze and interpret the data and develop insights. The fifth and final step is to develop an action plan and implementation. Although these steps appear to progress linearly, researchers often work backward and forward throughout the process as they learn at each step.

LO2 Describe the various secondary data sources.

External secondary data comprise information that has been collected from outside sources, such as the U.S. Census, the Internet, books, articles, trade associations, or syndicated data services. Internal secondary data can also be derived from internal company records such as sales, customer lists, and other company reports.

LO3 Describe the various primary data collection techniques.

Primary data are collected to address specific research needs. Techniques used for primary qualitative research include observation, social media, in-depth interviews, and focus groups. Techniques used for primary quantitative research include surveys (both offline and online), scanner, panel, and experiments.

LO4 Summarize the differences between secondary data and primary data.

Compared with primary research, secondary research is quicker, easier, and generally less expensive. The ability to use secondary data also requires less methodological expertise. However, because secondary research is collected for reasons other than those pertaining to the specific problem at hand, the information may be dated, biased, or simply not specific enough to answer the research questions. Primary research, in contrast, can be designed to answer very specific questions, but it also tends to be more expensive and time-consuming.

LO5 Examine the circumstances in which collecting information on consumers is ethical.

Marketing researchers should gain permission to collect information on consumers, and it should be for the sole purpose of conducting marketing research endeavors. Information should not be collected under the guise of marketing research when the intent is to sell products or to fundraise. In addition, marketers must take responsibility for protecting any information they collect.

Key Terms

- biometric data, 320
- churn, 308
- data, 302
- data mining, 307
- data warehouses, 307
- experiment, 317
- experimental research, 317
- focus group interview, 313
- in-depth interview, 312

- information, 302
- marketing research, 298
- observation, 309
- panel data, 305
- primary data, 300
- qualitative research, 309
- quantitative research, 309
- questionnaire, 315
- sample, 300

- sentiment mining, 312
- scanner data, 304
- secondary data, 300
- structured questions, 315
- survey, 315
- syndicated data, 304
- unstructured questions, 315

Marketing Applications

1. A large hardware store collects data about what its customers buy and stores these data in a data warehouse. If you were the store's buyer for lawn equipment, what would you want to know from the data warehouse that would help you be a more successful buyer?

2. Identify a not-for-profit organization that might use marketing research, and describe one example of a meaningful research project that it might conduct. Discuss the steps it should undertake in this project.

3. Marketing researchers do not always go through the steps in the marketing research process in sequential order. Provide an example of a research project that might not follow this sequence.

4. A sunglasses retailer is trying to determine if there is a significant market for its merchandise in a specific mall location where it is considering opening a store. Would it be most likely to use primary or secondary data, or a combination of the two, to answer this question?

5. A consumer package goods company (e.g., Pepsi) has just developed a new beverage. The company needs to estimate the demand for such a new product. What sources of syndicated data could it explore?

6. A bank manager notices that by the time customers get to the teller, they seem irritated and impatient. She wants to investigate the problem further, so she hires you to design a research project to figure out what is bothering the customers. The bank wants two studies: (a) several focus groups of their customers and (b) an online survey of 500 customers. Which study is qualitative, and which is quantitative?

7. PomWonderful has developed a coffee-flavored pomegranate beverage, and it wants to determine if it should begin to market it throughout the United States. The company used two separate studies to help develop the advertising campaign:

   - A focus group to identify the appropriate advertising message for the new beverage.

   - A survey to assess the effectiveness of the advertising campaign for the new PomWonderful beverage.

   Which study was qualitative and which was quantitative? What other studies would you recommend PomWonderful undertake?

8. Suppose your university wants to modify its course scheduling procedures to better serve students. What are some secondary sources of information that might be used to conduct research into this topic? Describe how these sources might be used. Describe a method you could use to gather primary research data about the topic. Would you recommend a specific order in obtaining each of these types of data? Explain your answer.

9. Marshall is planning to launch a new sandwich shop and is trying to decide what features and what prices would entice consumers. He sends a request for proposal to four marketing research vendors, and three respond, as described in the table on next page.

   Which vendor should Marshall use? Explain your rationale for picking this vendor over the others.

Vendor A	Vendor B	Vendor C
The vendor that Marshall has used in the past estimates it can get the job done for $200,000 and in two months. The vendor plans to do a telephone-based survey analysis and use secondary data from the U.S. Census.	Marshall's key competitor has used this vendor, which claims that it can get the job done for $150,000 and in one month. This vendor plans to do a telephone-based survey analysis and use secondary data. During a discussion pertaining to its price and time estimates, the vendor indicates it will draw on insights it has learned from a recent report prepared for one of Marshall's competitors.	This well-known vendor has recently started to focus on the restaurant industry. It quotes a price of $180,000 and a time of one month. The vendor plans to conduct a web-based survey analysis and use secondary data.

Quiz Yourself

www.mhhe.com/grewal4e

1. Through analysis of sales data, Price-Cutters retail store found that customers who bought peanut butter also tended to buy bananas. Price-Cutters was engaged in:
   a. syndicated surveying
   b. focus group analysis
   c. behavioral analysis
   d. data mining
   e. structured sampling

2. Martin has hired a market research company to bring together a small group of soft drink consumers and get feedback on the three new advertising slogans his firm is considering. The market research firm might conduct a(n) _____ to provide the information Martin has requested.
   a. industry survey
   b. experiment
   c. focus group
   d. observational study
   e. data mining analysis

   (Answers to these two questions can be found on page 647.)
   Go to www.mhhe.com/grewal4e to practice an additional 11 questions.

Net Savvy

1. Go to the website for the marketing research company, SymphonyIRI (www.symphonyiri.com). Click on "News and Events," and click on one of the recent press releases. What research question was SymphonyIRI addressing? What type of research did SymphonyIRI conduct, and what insights did it develop for its clients?

2. The epinions.com website (www.epinions.com) is a clearinghouse for consumer reviews about different products and services. Think of a particular business with which you are familiar, and then review the ratings and comments for that business on the epinions website. Discuss the extent to which this site might be useful to a marketer for that company who needs to gather market research about the company and its competitors. Identify the type of research this process involves—secondary or primary?

Chapter Case Study

AUTOTRADER.COM: HOW RESEARCH SEPARATES FACT FROM FICTION

Imagine you are responsible for making next year's media buys for a large automobile dealership. You have your choice among traditional media, like television and newspaper advertising, and Internet-based channels, like social networking sites and automotive sites. How do you decide which types of advertising are most likely to build sales? How can you determine if an approach that works for a dealership in one city will work in another?

The online automobile dealer AutoTrader.com recognizes that convincing car dealers, associations, and manufacturers to advertise on its site requires proof that their media dollars will be well spent. To provide that proof, it offers the numbers that it collects from its website, which show that it hosts more than 3 million vehicle listings from 40,000 dealers and 250,000 private owners and more than 14 million qualified buyers each month.[51] But these basic quantitative details cannot prove that advertising on the site actually leads to sales. To accomplish that goal, AutoTrader.com also conducts market research to help dealers understand how people shop for cars and how the site can deliver those customers as an integral part of the car-shopping process.[52]

Many media buyers assume that the most accurate measure of the success of an online advertisement is click-through rates, that is, the number of clicks on an ad, divided by the number of times the ad gets shown. Although this measure indicates how many times an advertisement is viewed, it does not provide a reliable metric for the ad's impact on customer behavior, especially when it comes to making the final purchase decision. Car dealers also hold their own beliefs about their customers' behavior, which may be inaccurate but still determine their advertising choices. Therefore, to attract advertising dollars, AutoTrader.com needed to provide hard data, coming directly from the source—that is, the dealers and customers themselves.

Therefore, the marketing research performed by AutoTrader.com mainly serves to demonstrate the value of the Internet for selling vehicles.[53] In a survey of recent car buyers, the company found that 71 percent of respondents consulted the Internet to facilitate their new or used car purchase. Most of these buyers reported that the Internet was the single most influential source behind their ultimate purchase choice, that it was the most helpful source of information, and that social media sites played only a small role in their final decision. The study also helped quantify other metrics surrounding car shopping behavior, such as the average length of time consumers spend shopping for a car and how much of that time involved Internet browsing versus visiting dealerships. The result—that buyers spend more than half their shopping time online—helped substantiate the value of advertising on AutoTrader.com. This finding was strengthened by further data showing that independent sites like AutoTrader were used more frequently than dealer or manufacturer sites.

Going even a step further, AutoTrader.com sought to connect advertising on its site to dealership visits, which represent the main goal of advertising on AutoTrader.com by car dealers. Marketing researchers first determined what dealers believed about their customers' behavior, using surveys. Then they gathered information from customers as they left dealerships, to find out the truth. To ensure accuracy and applicability, these researchers solicited customers of dealerships located in diverse markets, selling a variety brands, and operating as both franchises and independently. The results debunked a lot of conventional wisdom (see Exhibit 10.11). For example, newspaper advertising was less effective than dealers had imagined, but Internet advertising played a more significant role in driving walk-in traffic.

While this information might be true based on an average across national dealerships, some dealers believed it was not the case at their particular business. To help convince these skeptics, AutoTrader.com launched hundreds of mini–research studies, including phone interviews with car buyers from individual stores. The results that emerged were remarkably similar to the national study, though some differences reflected geographic locations of the dealership.

Armed with this research, you are now confident that you understand the behavior of car buyers well enough to make your media buy. But can you be completely sure that marketing research accurately predicts customer behavior?

EXHIBIT 10.11	Reality vs. Dealer's Perception

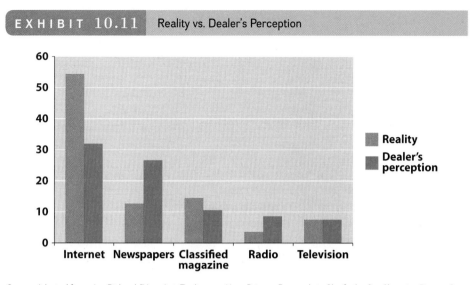

Source: Adapted from: Joe Richard, "How AutoTrader.com. Uses Primary Research to Clarify the Car-Shopping Process," *Quirk's Marketing Research Review*, July 2011, p. 36, http://www.quirks.com/articles/2011/20110704.aspx.

Probably not, because human behavior depends on a vast array of factors, many of which cannot be measured. But marketing research can help you ensure that your advertising dollars are spent wisely and in ways that seem most likely to increase sales.

Questions

1. What are the objectives of AutoTrader.com's marketing research? How have its research projects contributed to the firm's ability to meet these objectives?

2. What methods has AutoTrader.com used to collect data about the effectiveness of dealer advertisements displayed on its site?

Using Secondary Data to Assess Customer Lifetime Value (CLV)

10A

This appendix examines how secondary data from customer transactions can help determine the value of a customer over time. Specifically, **customer lifetime value (CLV)** refers to the expected financial contribution from a particular customer to the firm's profits over the course of their entire relationship[1]

To estimate CLV, firms use past behaviors to forecast future purchases, the gross margin from these purchases, and the costs associated with servicing the customers. Some costs associated with maintaining customer relationships include communicating with customers through advertising, personal selling, or other promotional vehicles to acquire their business initially and then retain them over time.

Measures of customer lifetime value typically apply to a group or segment of customers and use available secondary data. A basic formula for CLV,[2] with the assumption that revenues and profits arrive at the start of the year, is as follows:

To implement this CLV formula, we must answer the following questions:

1. How many years (t) can we expect to do business with a customer? The total number of years is denoted by T.

2. What can we expect the annual profits to be from an individual customer or an average customer? These profits are based on sales minus the costs of merchandise and the costs of serving and retaining the customer.

3. What is the retention rate, that is, the average percentage of customers who continue to purchase from the firm from one time period to another? A 90 percent retention rate means that if we have 100 customers in the first year, we will have 90 at the beginning of the second year.

4. What is the discount rate (i)? The discount rate is based on the idea that a dollar is worth less in the future than it is today, so the

$$CLV = \frac{\sum_{t=1}^{T}[\text{profit at t} \times \text{retention rate}^{t-1}]}{(1 + i)^{t-1}} - \text{acquisition costs}$$

company can use it to adjust future profits and determine a customer's value today for the customer's purchases in the future. For example, if the discount rate is 10 percent, $100 in profits at the beginning of year 2 are worth only $90.91(100/(1 + .1)) at the beginning of year 1.

Consider Gregory Missoni, a fairly new client of Very Clean Cleaners who switched from his other dry cleaner because Very Clean sent him $100 worth of coupons in a direct mailing.

Very Clean Cleaners should consider a customer's lifetime value to determine its service levels.

Greg just picked up his $200 shirt from Very Clean and found that the dry cleaner had broken a brown button and replaced it with a white button. When he complained, the clerk acted as if it were no big deal. Greg explained to the clerk that it was a very expensive shirt that deserved more careful handling, then asked to speak with the manager. At this point, how important is it that the manager makes sure Greg is satisfied, so that he will continue to bring his dry cleaning to Very Clean Cleaners? To answer this question, the manager uses the following information:

- It cost Very Clean $100 to acquire Greg as a customer. Thus, the acquisition cost is $100.
- Very Clean expects Greg to remain a client for 5 years (time horizon T = 5 years).
- Very Clean expects to make a $1,000 profit each year from Greg's dry cleaning.
- On average, 10 percent of customers defect to another cleaner each year. Therefore, the expected retention rate is 90 percent.
- The discount rate is 10 percent per year (i in this illustration). For simplicity, Very Clean assumes all profits are accrued at the beginning of the year.

Applying the formula, such that CLV equals the profits from years 1–5, less the acquisition costs, we obtain:

$$\text{CLV} = \underbrace{\frac{\$1{,}000 \times (.90)^0}{(1 + .1)^0}}_{\textbf{Year 1}} + \underbrace{\frac{\$1{,}000 \times (.90)^1}{(1 + .1)^1}}_{\textbf{Year 2}} + \underbrace{\frac{\$1{,}000 \times (.90)^2}{(1 + .1)^2}}_{\textbf{Year 3}}$$

$$\underbrace{\frac{\$1{,}000 \times (.90)^3}{(1 + .1)^3}}_{\textbf{Year 4}} + \underbrace{\frac{\$1{,}000 \times (.90)^4}{(1 + .1)^4}}_{\textbf{Year 5}} - \$100$$

Or

$$\text{CLV} = \$1{,}000 + \$818.2 + \$669.4 + \$547.7 + \$448.1 - \$100 = \$3{,}383.40$$

Let's see how the formula works. The expected profit from Greg is $1,000 per year. Very Clean assumes profits accrue at the beginning of the year, so the profits for the first year equal $1,000; they are not affected by the retention rate or the discount rate.

However, the retention and discount rates have effects on the profits for the subsequent time periods. In the second year, the retention rate, which Very Clean determined was 90 percent (i.e., 90 percent of customers continue to do business with it) modifies profits, such that expected profits in the second year equal $1,000 × 90% = $900. Moreover, the discount rate is applied such that the profits received in the second year are worth less than if they had been received in the first year. Therefore, the $900 received at the beginning of the second year must be divided by 1.1, which is equivalent to $818.20.

Using similar calculations for the third year, the expected profits adjusted for retention are $1,000 × .9 × .9 = $810. The discount rate then reduces the profit to $810 ÷ 1.1^2 = $669.40 in today's dollars. (Note that the discount rate is squared because it refers to two years in the future.) After calculating the adjusted and discounted profits for the fourth and fifth years in similar fashion, we realize the sum of estimated discounted profits for five years is $3,483.40. However, we still must subtract the $100 spent to acquire Greg, which provides a CLV of $3,383.40.

According to this analysis, it would be a good idea for the manager to take a long-term perspective when evaluating how to respond to Greg's complaint about his button. Greg cannot be viewed as a $2.50 customer, as he would be if Very Clean determined his value based on the cost of laundering his shirt, nor should he be viewed as a $200 customer, based on the cost of the shirt. He actually is worth a lot more than that.

For illustrative purposes, we have simplified the CLV calculations in this example. We assumed that the average profits remain constant at $1,000. But firms usually expect profits to grow over time, or else grow, level off, and then perhaps decline. Retention costs, such as special promotions used to keep Greg coming back, also do not appear in our illustration, though such additional costs would reduce annual profits and CLV. Finally, we assume a five-year time horizon; the CLV obviously would differ for longer or shorter periods. For an infinite time horizon, with first period payments upfront, the formula becomes fairly simple:[3]

$$CLV = profits \times \left[1 + \frac{\text{retention rate}}{(\$1 + \text{discount rate} + \text{retention rate})}\right]$$

$$- \text{acquisition costs}$$

$$= \$1,000 \times \left[1 + \frac{.9}{(1 + .1 - .9)}\right] - \$100$$

$$= \$1,000 \times (1 + 4.5) - \$100$$

$$= \$5,500 - \$100 = \$5,400$$

This illustration thus explains how firms can use secondary data to calculate CLV; it further demonstrates the importance of knowing a customer's lifetime value when executing marketing tactics and strategies. Several customer lifetime value problems can be accessed at www.mhhe.com/grewal4e.

CHAPTER 11

Product, Branding, and Packaging Decisions

As a major player in the highly fragmented sports apparel industry, Under Armour (UA) has gained fame by branding its line of performance clothing as the toughest and most competitive available. Its products combine innovative sports apparel technology with space-age materials, but its reputation for toughness mainly comes from the national ad campaigns that UA runs, featuring heart-pounding images that help build its brand:

- Olympic skiing champion Lindsey Vonn training while running up against a sheet of freezing, face-biting wind.

- A prowling hunter landing arrows in the bull's eye of a target.

- Athletes pounding the competition, vowing to "protect this house"—that is, defend their home turf.

The message? Use our gear, and you will reach your maximum performance goal.

Founder Kevin Plank has always competed to win. He launched the company while he was still in college.

A University of Maryland football player, Plank was fed up with peeling off sweat-soaked T-shirts after every practice. In his search for a better shirt, he came up with a polyester blend that wicks away moisture, which also helps keep sweating players cool. Next, UA expanded this shirt technology to develop ColdGear garments that insulate players from the cold.[1]

Similar combinations of innovation and new product lines have continued to make UA a tough competitor, even against well-established behemoths such as Nike and Adidas. As a $1.4 billion powerhouse, UA controls 3 percent of the U.S. performance clothing market, nearly half of Nike's share.[2] The company produces both men's and women's apparel, including shirts, shorts, and underwear. Newer product lines include sports apparel for youth, footwear, and a line of hunting and fishing gear. In 2011, UA released a shirt with a removable "bug," or compressed sensor, that electronically monitors wearers' blood pressure and heart rate.[3]

But expanding the brand has faced some hurdles as well. The shoe line UA launched with its introduction of football cleats in 2006 has been slow to gain any ground. It continues to drive though, producing a memorable ad to spotlight its patented lightweight, cushioning foam and HeatGear sweat-wicking material in the upper shoe.[4] In "The Footsteps" ad, UA featured major NFL names, including the Baltimore Ravens' tough guy Ray Lewis, the Heisman Trophy winner Cam Newton, and the New England Patriots' famous quarterback Tom Brady, all tearing up the turf in UA's cleats.

Under Armour also struggled with its entry into women's sports apparel, a key industry growth sector. Applying male-oriented designs to the women's line did not work, leading UA to withdraw from the market after its initial foray. After UA developed a line designed by women though, their product started to move, and today generates 25 percent of the company's revenue. To continue this momentum, UA started an ad campaign featuring Vonn that has helped spark the brand's image, especially among active young women.[5]

Targeting new market segments to expand their brand is a challenge for all companies. Succesful companies like Under Armour thrive against competition, but just how far can the brand reach?

As a key element of a firm's marketing mix (the four Ps), product strategies are central to the creation of value for the consumer. A **product** is anything that is of value to a consumer and can be offered through a voluntary marketing exchange. In addition to goods, such as soft drinks, or services, such as a stay in a hotel, products might be places (e.g., Six Flags theme parks), ideas (e.g., "stop smoking"), organizations (e.g., MADD), people (e.g., Oprah Winfrey), or communities (e.g., Facebook.com) that create value for consumers in their respective competitive marketing arenas.

This chapter begins with a discussion of the complexity and types of products. Next we examine how firms adjust their product lines to meet and respond to changing market conditions. Then we turn our attention to branding—why are brands valuable to the firm, and what are the different branding strategies firms use? We also never want to underestimate the value of a product's package and label. These elements should send a strong message from the shelf: Buy me! The final section of this chapter examines packaging and labeling issues.

LO1 Describe the components of a product.

COMPLEXITY AND TYPES OF PRODUCTS

Complexity of Products

There is more to a product than its physical characteristics or its basic service function. Marketers involved with the development, design, and sale of products think of them in an interrelated fashion, as depicted in Exhibit 11.1. At the center is the **core customer value**, which defines the basic-problem solving benefits that consumers are seeking. When Mars manufactures M&Ms, Snickers, and other confectionary products, or when Trek designs bicycles, each company's core question is, What are customers looking for? With Mars, is it a sweet, great tasting snack, or is it an energy boost? With Trek, is the bike being used for basic green transportation (a cruiser), or is it for speed and excitement (a road, hybrid, or mountain bike)?

Marketers convert core customer value into an **actual product**. Attributes such as the brand name, features/design, quality level, and packaging are important, but the level of their importance varies, depending on the product. The Trek Madon 6 Series, for instance, is positioned as "the most exquisitely engineered bicycle ever made."[6] It features a carbon frame that is light, stiff, and comfortable; an advanced shifting system; and other high-tech features. Not only is it beautiful to look at, but customers can choose from three different fits—pro, performance, and touring.

EXHIBIT 11.1	Product Complexity

Actual product

Brand name   Packaging
Quality level   Features/Design

Core
customer
value

Associated services

Financing
Product warranty
Product support

The **associated services** in Exhibit 11.1, also referred to as the **augmented product**, include the nonphysical aspects of the product, such as product warranties, financing, product support, and after-sale service. The amount of associated services also varies with the product. The associated services for a package of M&Ms may include only a customer complaint line, which means they are relatively less important than the associated services for a Trek bicycle. The frame of the Madon 6 Series bicycle is guaranteed for the lifetime of the original owner. Trek only sells its bikes in shops that have the expertise to service them properly. Every possible consumer question is answered on Trek's comprehensive website. Trek even has a financing program that allows customers to purchase a new bike on credit.

When developing or changing a product, marketers start with the core customer value to determine what their potential customers are seeking. Then they make the actual physical product and add associated services to round out the offering.

Types of Products

LO2 Identify the types of consumer products.

Marketers consider the types of products they are designing and selling, because these types affect how they will promote, price, and distribute their products. There are two primary categories of products and services that reflect who buys them: consumers or businesses. Chapter 7 discussed products for businesses. Here we discuss consumer products.

Consumer products are products and services used by people for their personal use. Marketers further classify consumer products by the way they are used and how they are purchased.

Specialty Products/Services **Specialty products/services** are those for which customers express such a strong preference that they will expend considerable effort to search for the best suppliers. Road bike enthusiasts, like those interested in the Trek Madone 6 Series, devote lots of time and effort to selecting just the right one. Other examples might include luxury cars, legal or medical professionals, or designer apparel.

Shopping Products/Services **Shopping products/services** are products or services for which consumers will spend a fair amount of time comparing alternatives, such as furniture, apparel, fragrances, appliances, and travel alternatives. When

A medical professional is a specialty service. Apparel is a shopping product. Soda is a convenience product. Insurance is an unsought service.

people need new sneakers, for instance, they often go from store to store shopping—trying shoes on, comparing alternatives, and chatting with salespeople.

Convenience products/services **Convenience products/services** are those products or services for which the consumer is not willing to spend any effort to evaluate prior to purchase. They are frequently purchased commodity items, usually bought with very little thought, such as common beverages, bread, or soap.

Unsought products/services **Unsought products/services** are products consumers either do not normally think of buying or do not know about at all. Because of their very nature, these products require lots of marketing effort and various forms of promotion. When new-to-the-world products, as GPS systems once were, are first introduced, they are unsought products. Do you have cold hands and don't know what to do about it? You must not have heard yet of HeatMax HotHands Hand Warmers, air-activated packets that provide warmth for up to 10 hours. Do you have an internship in a less developed country and your regular insurance cannot give you the coverage you may need in case of an emergency? You now can turn to a Medex insurance policy.

CHECK YOURSELF

1. Explain the three components of a product.
2. What are the four types of consumer products?

EXHIBIT 11.2	Abbreviated List of Kellogg's Product Mix		
Product Lines			
Ready-to-Eat Cereal	Toaster Pastries and Wholesome Portable Breakfast Snacks	Cookies and Crackers	Natural, Organic, and Frozen
Kellogg's Corn Flakes	Nutri-Grain	Cheez-It	Eggo
All-Bran	Special K	Keebler	Morningstar Farms
Apple Jacks	Kashi	Townhouse	Kashi
Cocoa Krispies	Pop-Tarts	Club	
Frosted Mini-Wheats	Bear Naked	Famous Amos	
Mueslix		Fudge Shoppe	
Kellogg's Raisin Bran		Murray	
Froot Loops			
Kashi			
Special K			
Rice Krispies			

Source: Kellogg's 2010 annual report, http://annualreport2010.kelloggcompany.com/innovation.htm.

PRODUCT MIX AND PRODUCT LINE DECISIONS

LO3 Explain the difference between a product mix's breadth and a product line's depth.

The complete set of all products and services offered by a firm is called its **product mix.** An abbreviated version of Kellogg's product mix appears in Exhibit 11.2. The product mix typically consists of various **product lines**, which are groups of associated items that consumers tend to use together or think of as part of a group of similar products or services. Kellogg's product lines include ready-to-eat cereal; toaster pastries and wholesome portable breakfast snacks; cookies and crackers; and natural, organic, and frozen items.

The product mix reflects the breadth and depth of the company's product lines. A firm's product mix **breadth** represents a count of the number of product lines offered by the firm; Kellogg's has four, as indicated by the four columns in Exhibit 11.2. Product line **depth**, in contrast, equals the number of products within a product line. Within Kellogg's breakfast snack product line, for example, it offers Nutri-Grain, Special K, and Kashi bars, as well as Pop-Tarts.

Kellogg's offers four product lines (breadth), and multiple products within each product line (depth).

However, adding unlimited numbers of new products can have adverse consequences. Too much breadth in the product mix becomes costly to maintain, and too many brands may weaken the firm's reputation.[7] In the past several years, for example, Revlon undertook a significant restructuring. It introduced a new line, Vital Radiance, aimed at women over the age of 45 years. But this line cut into the sales of its other brands and harmed its reputation among younger consumers, so Revlon eliminated the Vital Radiance line, to refocus on those products and markets that were doing well.[8]

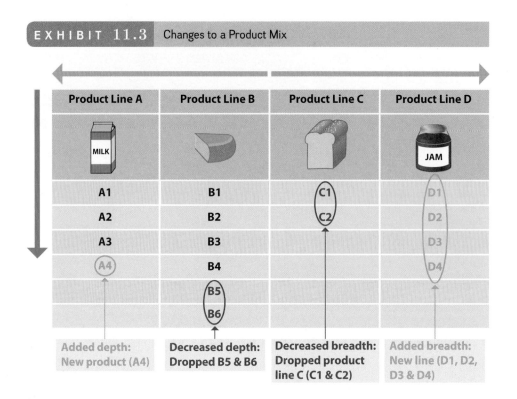

EXHIBIT 11.3   Changes to a Product Mix

Product Line A	Product Line B	Product Line C	Product Line D
MILK			JAM
A1	B1	C1	D1
A2	B2	C2	D2
A3	B3		D3
A4	B4		D4
	B5		
	B6		
Added depth: New product (A4)	**Decreased depth:** Dropped B5 & B6	**Decreased breadth:** Dropped product line C (C1 & C2)	**Added breadth:** New line (D1, D2, D3 & D4)

To increase Tide's depth of assortment, P&G introduced Tide Basic, but soon deleted it because it believed it was undermining the Tide brand.

To increase product line breadth, a firm may add a new line of jam products to complement their bread line.

So why do firms change their product mix's breadth or depth?[9]

Increase Depth Firms might add items to address changing consumer preferences or to preempt competitors while boosting sales (see addition of product A4 in Exhibit 11.3). A service provider like a bank typically offers consumer accounts as one of its product lines. To increase depth in this line, it frequently adds new types of accounts. Bank of America thus added an eChecking account to appeal to online users, as another alternative to its traditional high-balance Advantage with Tiered Interest Checking option or its CampusEdge Checking for college students.[10] Social and Mobile Marketing 11.1 describes another extension in a product market, as Axe expands its fragrance product line to create a version for women.

Decrease Depth From time to time, it is also necessary to delete products within a product line to realign the firm's resources (see deletion of products B5 and B6 in Exhibit 11.3). The decision is never taken lightly. Generally, substantial investments have been made to develop and manufacture the products. Yet firms often must prune their product lines to eliminate unprofitable or low margin items and refocus their marketing efforts on their more profitable items. Procter & Gamble (P&G) introduced Tide Basic as an extension of its Tide line—probably the best known detergent brand and a product that enjoys a reputation as an innovative, high-end brand. Tide Basic was priced 20 percent cheaper than regular Tide, but P&G deleted the extension less than a year after introducing it, worried that an inexpensive, less effective version simply undermined its brand, rather than offering an appealing alternative.[11]

Decrease Breadth Sometimes it is necessary to delete entire product lines to address changing market conditions or meet internal strategic priorities (e.g., deleting product line C in Exhibit 11.3). Thus, the firm drops their line of bread and focuses their attention on their dairy products—milk and cheese (product lines A and B).

Increase Breadth Firms often add new product lines to capture new or evolving markets and increase sales (e.g., product line D in Exhibit 11.3). The firm adds a whole new line of jam products. Jam is a complementary product to their bread line.

Social and Mobile Marketing 11.1

Axe Brands' "Anarchy" Fragrance and Graphic Novel

Axe body spray already owned 75 percent of the men's fragrance market, so when its owner, Unilever, wanted to grow the brand, it needed to expand its product depth. Thus came Axe Anarchy, a new scent offered in both male and female versions, to exploit the promise of irresistible sexuality that has proven so successful thus far.

In a decade's worth of controversial Axe commercials, average guys drew very attractive women to them, simply by spraying themselves with the scent. The Anarchy message is even more edgy. As the name suggests, the product promises the notion of sexual energy that goes slightly out of control. An early commercial depicts a chaotic series of events, including a car pile-up, in which a man and a woman remain oblivious to the havoc but gravitate toward each other until they are just inches apart. "Unleash the chaos," the screen recommends, as the video cuts to shots of the two actors spraying themselves. "New Axe Anarchy for him and for her."[12]

Noting its youthful target market, Unilever also wanted to ensure that the advertising medium for Anarchy fit the brand extension, so the company unleashed an interactive digital campaign in the form of an online graphic novel. The serialized, comic book fantasy about the chaotic exploits of the "Anarchy Girls" would evolve in real time, in response to viewer input. The author and X-Men creator Scott Lobdell was hired to create the narrative, in collaboration with any of the 2.3 million fans who registered on YouTube, Facebook, Twitter, and Axe's other social channels to help shape the story.[13]

The marketing subtext was clear: Break the narrative and also break through sexually, which seemed to offer a potent message for young women. But some observers remain unconvinced that Axe's bold, crowd-sourced digital venture will help the brand make the cross-over into the women's body spray market. Could graphic novels, with their traditionally young male audience, really connect with young women?[14] Would Axe's explosive brand expansion strategy actually alienate the very audience that built its body spray brand, that is, average-guy male teens trying to attract a special girl? Would advertising to girls make Axe lose credibility among boys?

To promote the Axe Anarchy fragrance to young men and women, Unilever created a comic book fantasy about "Anarchy Girls," available in real time on You Tube and other social media.

CHECK YOURSELF

1. What is the difference between product mix breadth and product line depth?
2. Why change product mix breadth?
3. Why change product line depth?

Kate Spade is positioned to appeal to young, fun-loving, urban professionals.

BRANDING

A company lives or dies based on brand awareness. Consumers cannot buy products that they don't know exist. Even if the overall brand name is familiar, it won't help sales of individual products unless consumers know what products are available under that name. When an editor at *Mademoiselle*, known for her style, started the Kate Spade brand in 1993, it was quickly a hit as women snapped up the chance to look as if they had just stepped off the pages of a fashion magazine. But after Neiman Marcus bought the company, it failed to maintain the cutting-edge, fashion-forward brand image, and Kate Spade gained an unfortunate reputation for angular bags carried by suburban moms. Fortunately, its name got a boost when Liz Claiborne purchased it from Neiman Marcus and diligently repositioned the purses to appeal to young, fun-loving, urban professionals who appreciate great design, want to appear neat and polished, and enjoy being the most interesting person in the room. Thus Kate Spade is now Liz Claiborne's best performing brand, outpacing such consumer favorites as Juicy Couture, Mexx Europe, and Lucky Brand.[15]

Branding also provides a way for a firm to differentiate its product offerings from those of its competitors. Both Snapple and Tropicana make and sell fruit drinks, yet consumers may choose one over the other because of the associations that the brands invoke. Pioneer televisions use plasma panels manufactured by Panasonic, and yet the brand still enjoys a unique reputation, distinct and perceived by many to be better than Panasonic's.[16] As we discuss in more detail subsequently, brand names, logos, symbols, characters, slogans, jingles, and even distinctive packages constitute the various brand elements firms use,[17] which they usually choose to be easy for consumers to recognize and remember. Most consumers know the Nike swoosh and would recognize it even if the word Nike did not appear on the product or in an advertisement. Exhibit 11.4 summarizes some of these brand elements.

LO4 Identify the advantages that brands provide firms and consumers.

Value of Branding for the Customer

Brands add value to merchandise and services, for both consumers and sellers, beyond physical and functional characteristics or the pure act of performing the service.[18] Let's examine some ways in which brands add value for both customers and the firm.

Brands Facilitate Purchases Brands are often easily recognized by consumers, and because they signify a certain quality level and contain familiar attributes, brands help consumers make quick decisions, especially about their purchases.[19] The cola market is a particularly strong example of this benefit. Some people think cola is cola, such that one brand is not too different from another. But branding has made it easy for Pepsi drinkers to find the familiar logo on the store shelf and more likely that they simply buy one of Pepsi's other products, should they decide to switch to a diet soda or a flavored version. From promotions, past purchases, or information from friends and family, they recognize the offering before they even read any text on the label, and they likely possess a perception of the brand's level

EXHIBIT 11.4	What Makes a Brand?
Brand Element	**Description**
Brand name	The spoken component of branding, it can describe the product or service/product characteristics and/or be composed of words invented or derived from colloquial or contemporary language. Examples include Comfort Inn (suggests product characteristics), Apple (no association with the product), or Zillow.com (invented term).
URLs (uniform resource locators) or domain names	The location of pages on the Internet, which often substitutes for the firm's name, such as Yahoo! and Amazon.
Logos and symbols	Logos are visual branding elements that stand for corporate names or trademarks. Symbols are logos without words. Examples include the Nike swoosh and the Mercedes star.
Characters	Brand symbols that could be human, animal, or animated. Examples include the Pillsbury Doughboy and the Keebler Elves.
Slogans	Short phrases used to describe the brand or persuade consumers about some characteristics of the brand. Examples include State Farm's "Like A Good Neighbor" and Dunkin Donuts' "America Runs On Dunkin."
Jingles/Sounds	Audio messages about the brand that are composed of words or distinctive music. Examples are Intel's four-note sound signature that accompanies the "Intel Inside" slogan.

Source: Adapted From Kevin Lane Keller, *Strategic Brand Management*, 3rd ed. (Upper Saddle River, NJ: Prentice Hall, 2007).

of quality, how it tastes, whether it is a good value, and, most important, whether they like it and want to buy it. Brands enable customers to differentiate one firm or product from another. Without branding, how could we easily tell the difference between Coca-Cola and Pepsi before tasting them?

Brands Establish Loyalty Over time and with continued use, consumers learn to trust certain brands. They know, for example, that they wouldn't consider switching brands and, in some cases, feel a strong affinity to certain brands. Amazon.com has a loyal following because its reputation for service prompts customers to turn to it first. A customer whose $500 Playstation3 was apparently stolen during delivery received another Playstation3, without even having to pay additional shipping costs. Amazon lost $500, plus shipping, on a mistake that was not its fault, but it also gained a reputation for service with this customer, who would not only buy more electronics from Amazon but also tell everyone he could think of about this extraordinary example of customer service and choose Amazon's brand extension into the Kindle offerings before similar options provided by other brands.[20]

Brands Protect from Competition and Price Competition Strong brands are somewhat protected from competition from other firms and price competition. Because such brands are more established in the market and have a more loyal customer base, neither competitive pressures on price nor retail-level competition is as threatening to the firm. Lacoste is widely known for its golf shirts. Although many similar brands are available and some retailers offer their own brands, Lacoste is perceived to be of superior quality, garners a certain status among its users, and therefore can command a premium price.

Brands Are Assets For firms, brands are also assets that can be legally protected through trademarks and copyrights and thus constitute a unique form of ownership. Firms sometimes have to fight to ensure their brand names are not being used, directly or indirectly, by others. The term "Footsyroll" is literally different

Tootsie Roll Industries, makers of Tootsie Roll candies, claims that the Footzyroll brand of shoes is so similar-sounding that it has the potential of significantly diluting its brand.

 LO5 Explain the various components of brand equity.

from the brand name Tootsie Roll, but the similarity is enough that the candy company brought suit against the new shoe line. The Footsyroll brand refers to comfortable, ballet-type shoes that women can roll up and stick in their purses to wear instead of heels at the end of the day. But Tootsie Roll claims that the similar-sounding term does more than describe the product; it also creates confusion and implies that the candy company has some association with the shoes—with significant potential for brand dilution.[21]

Brands Impact Market Value Having well-known brands can have a direct impact on the company's bottom line. The value of a company is its overall monetary worth, comprising a vast number of assets. The value of the brand, just one of these assets, refers to the earning potential of the brand over the next 12 months.[22] The world's 10 most valuable brands for 2011 appear in Exhibit 11.5—though currently all the brands are U.S.-based firms, that is not the case every year.

Brand Equity for the Owner

The value of a brand translates into **brand equity**, or the set of assets and liabilities linked to a brand that add to or subtract from the value provided by the product or service.[23] Like the physical possessions of a firm, brands are assets a firm can build, manage, and harness over time to increase its revenue, profitability, and overall value. For example, firms spend millions of dollars on promotion, advertising, and other marketing efforts throughout a brand's life cycle. Sometimes this spending comes close to crossing ethical lines, as Ethical and Societal Dilemma 11.1 describes. However, marketing expenditures allocated carefully can result in greater brand recognition, awareness, perceived value, and consumer loyalty for the brand, which all enhance the brand's overall equity.

How do we know how "good" a brand is, or how much equity it has? Experts look at four aspects of a brand to determine its equity: brand awareness, perceived value, brand associations, and brand loyalty.

Coca-Cola is the most valuable brand in the world.

Ethical and Societal Dilemma 11.1   "Video Girl" Barbie Brings Girls to Foursquare

Barbie, the dress-up toy that taught generations of girls what nurses and airline stewardesses look like, has now become a Video Girl with implications for the online generation. As Mattel's gushing, hot-pink YouTube video explains, the new Barbie Video Girl doll "is kind of amazing."[24] She has a tiny video camera in her necklace, an LCD screen on her back, and editing software tucked inside. The new Barbie can record up to 25 minutes of video that "you can download to your computer with a pink USB cable."

And the Video Girl doesn't stop there. She's a "celebrity" Foursquare user that can stay in touch with fans through the location-based social networking website by uploading clues for the Barbie Video Scavenger Hunt.[25] It's the perfect game for Foursquare, which encourages smartphone users to gather and share information while browsing in restaurants and shops. Now girls who aspire to be like Barbie Video Girls can check in as well and perhaps win the scavenger hunt. But is that what parents want?

At New York City's Barbie Fashion Night Out (FNO), a fan scans a QR code of a Barbie wearing Alexis Bittar jewelry. Barbie invited FNO-goers to shop her closet via city-wide scavenger hunt.

Mattel's initiative blurs the line between play and advertising, though such confusion is nothing new in an industry that uses children's television shows and movies as marketing vehicles.[26] Spurred by the success of *Transformers: Revenge of the Fallen* and *Hot Wheels: Battle Force 5*, toy companies are investing heavily in content. Hasbro launched a cable channel, The Hub, to target 6–12-year-old viewers.[27] Mattel requires new toy designers to focus on offerings that can be branded simultaneously through a television show, feature film, or game.[28] In 2010, Disney announced that its movie financing would be prioritized according to toy merchandising potentials.[29]

Groups such as the Coalition for a Commercial-Free Childhood object to this conflation of play and purchasing, especially as the industry reaches into children's lives with everywhere, anytime digital and mobile formats. A recent Federal Trade Commission proposal aims to protect children from unauthorized use of cookies and other online tracking mechanisms. But such limits do nothing to stop Virtual Girl Barbie from moving playtime online.

Brand Awareness **Brand awareness** measures how many consumers in a market are familiar with the brand and what it stands for and have an opinion about it. The more aware or familiar they are, the easier their decision-making process is, which improves the chances of purchase. Familiarity matters most for products that are

EXHIBIT 11.5	The World's Ten Most Valuable Brands		
2011 Rank	**Brand**	**Country of Ownership**	**2011 Brand Value ($ Billions)**
1	Coca-Cola	U.S.	71.8
2	IBM	U.S.	69.9
3	Microsoft	U.S.	59.1
4	Google	U.S.	55.3
5	GE	U.S.	42.8
6	McDonald's	U.S.	35.6
7	Intel	U.S.	35.2
8	Apple	U.S.	33.5
9	Disney	U.S.	29.0
10	Hewlett-Packard	U.S.	28.5

Source: From interbrand.com, http://www.interbrand.com/best_global_brands.aspx. Reprinted with permission.

bought without much thought, such as soap or chewing gum, but brand awareness is also critical for infrequently purchased items or those the consumer has never purchased before. If the consumer recognizes the brand, it probably has attributes that make it valuable.[30] For those who have never purchased a Toyota, the simple awareness that it exists can help facilitate a purchase. Marketers create brand awareness through repeated exposures of the various brand elements (brand name, logo, symbol, character, packaging, or slogan) in the firm's communications to consumers through advertising, publicity, or other methods (see Chapters 18–20). Certain brands gain such predominance in a particular product market over time that they become synonymous with the product itself; that is, the brand name starts being used as the generic product category. Examples include Kleenex tissue, Clorox bleach, Band-Aid adhesive bandages, and Rollerblade skates. Companies must be vigilant in protecting their brand names, because if they are used so generically, over time, the brand itself can lose its trademark status.

Perceived Value The **perceived value** of a brand is the relationship between a product's or service's benefits and its cost. Customers usually determine the offering's value in relationship to that of its close competitors. If they believe a less expensive brand is about the same quality as a premium brand, the perceived value of that cheaper choice is high. Merchandise sold by Target and Kohl's is not always of the highest quality, nor is the apparel the most fashion-forward. But not every customer needs to show up at school looking like they came from a fashion show runway. At the same time, these retailers hire high-fashion designers to create reasonably priced lines to feature in their stores—as Target did with Isaac Mizrahi and Missoni, to create well-designed pieces at Target-level prices.[31]

Brand Associations **Brand associations** reflect the mental links that consumers make between a brand and its key product attributes, such as a logo, slogan, or famous personality. These brand associations often result from a firm's advertising and promotional efforts. Toyota's hybrid car, the Prius, is known for being economical, a good value, stylish, and good for the environment. But firms also attempt to create specific associations with positive consumer emotions, such as fun, friendship, good feelings, family gatherings, and parties. State Farm Insurance thus uses the slogan "like a good neighbor, State Farm is there." Hallmark Cards associates its brand with helping people show they care with quality: "When you care enough to send the very best." Furthermore, the programs on Hallmark television channel are always consistent with the brand's wholesome family image.[32]

Brand Loyalty **Brand loyalty** occurs when a consumer buys the same brand's product or service repeatedly over time rather than buy from multiple suppliers within the same category.[33] Therefore, brand loyal customers are an important source of value for firms. First, firms such as airlines, hotels, long-distance telephone providers, credit card companies, and retailers reward loyal consumers with loyalty or customer relationship management (CRM) programs, such as points customers can redeem for extra discounts or free services, advance notice of sale items, and invitations to special events sponsored by the company. Second, the marketing costs of reaching loyal consumers are much lower because the firm does not have to spend money on advertising and promotion campaigns to attract these customers. Loyal consumers simply do not need persuasion or an extra push to buy the firm's brands. Third, loyal customers tend to praise the virtues of their favorite products, retailers, or services to others. This positive word of mouth reaches potential customers and reinforces the perceived value of current customers, all at no cost to the firm. Fourth, a high level of brand loyalty insulates the firm from competition because, as we noted in Chapter 2, brand loyal customers do not switch to competitors' brands, even when provided with a variety of incentives.

CHECK YOURSELF

1. How do brands create value for the customer and the firm?
2. What are the components of brand equity?

BRANDING STRATEGIES

LO6 Determine the various types of branding strategies used by firms.

Firms institute a variety of brand-related strategies to create and manage key brand assets, such as the decision to own the brands, establishing a branding policy, extending the brand name to other products and markets, cooperatively using the brand name with that of another firm, and licensing the brand to other firms.

Brand Ownership

Brands can be owned by any firm in the supply chain, whether manufacturers, wholesalers, or retailers. There are two basic brand ownership strategies: manufacturer brands and retailer/store brands, as Exhibit 11.6 shows. Additionally, the brands can be marketed using a common/family name or as individual brands.

EXHIBIT 11.6	Who Owns the Brand?

		Who Owns the Brand?	
		Manufacturer/National Brand	Retailer/Store Brand
Common Name or Not?	Family Brands	Kellogg's family line	Kroger's line
	Individual Brands	Kellogg's individual brand	Kroger's individual brand

Manufacturer Brands **Manufacturer brands**, also known as **national brands**, are owned and managed by the manufacturer. Some famous manufacturer brands are Nike, Coca-Cola, KitchenAid, and Sony. With these brands, the manufacturer develops the merchandise, produces it to ensure consistent quality, and invests in a marketing program to establish an appealing brand image. The majority of the brands marketed in the United States are manufacturer brands, and manufacturing firms spend millions of dollars each year to promote their brands. For example, recently Procter & Gamble spent $3.1 billion on U.S. advertising, more than any other company.[34] By owning their brands, manufacturers retain more control over their marketing strategy, are able to choose the appropriate market segments and positioning for the brand, and can build the brand and thereby create their own brand equity.

Retailer/Store Brands **Retailer/store brands**, also called **private-label brands**, are products developed by retailers. In some cases, retailers manufacture their own products, whereas in other cases they develop the design and specifications for their retailer/store brands and then contract with manufacturers to produce those products. Some national brand manufacturers work with retailers to develop a special version of its standard merchandise offering to be sold exclusively by the retailer.

In the past, sales of store brands were limited. But in recent years, as the size of retail firms has increased through growth and consolidation, more retailers have the scale economies to develop private-label merchandise and use this merchandise to establish a distinctive identity. In addition, manufacturers are more willing to accommodate the needs of retailers and develop co-brands for them. Store brands now account for almost 20 percent of the purchases in North America and close to 30 percent in Europe.[35] Kroger's private label accounts for 27 percent of its sales, and Costco and Trader Joe's both have based their brand identities around their store brands.

Naming Brands and Product Lines

Although there is no simple way to decide how to name a brand or a product line, the more the products vary in their usage or performance, the more likely it is that the firm should use individual brands. For example, General Motors utilizes several different individual brands (Cadillac, Chevrolet, GMC), each catering to very different target markets and meeting different needs. Hyundai, on the other hand, utilizes only one brand since usage and level of performance are relatively homogeneous.

Family Brands A firm can use its own corporate name to brand all its product lines and products, so Kellogg's incorporates the company name into the brand name of Kellogg's Rice Krispies (refer back to Exhibit 11.2). When all products are

Kellogg's uses a family branding strategy in which several product lines are sold under one name.

Kellogg's also uses an individual branding strategy since Keebler, Cheez-It, Morningstar, and Famous Amos are all marketed using separate names.

sold under one **family brand**, the individual brands benefit from the overall brand awareness associated with the family name. Kellogg's uses its family brand name prominently on its cereal brands (e.g., Kellogg's Special K, Kellogg's Froot Loops, Kellogg's Rice Krispies).

Individual Brands A firm can use **individual brand** names for each of its products. For example, while Kellogg's makes good use of the corporate branding strategy, it also allows other products, such as Morningstar Farms, Famous Amos cookies, Keebler cookies, and Cheez-Its (Exhibit 11.2), to keep individual identities not readily seen as being under the Kellogg's umbrella.[36]

Brand and Line Extensions[37]

A **brand extension** refers to the use of the same brand name in a different product line. It is an increase in the product mix's breadth.[38] The dental hygiene market, for instance, is full of brand extensions; Colgate and Crest sell toothpaste, toothbrushes, and other dental hygiene products, even though their original product line was just toothpaste. A **line extension** is the use of the same brand name within the same product line, and represents an increase in a product line's depth.

LO7 Distinguish between brand extension and line extension.

There are several advantages to using the same brand name for new products. First, because the brand name is already well established, the firm can spend less in developing consumer brand awareness and brand associations for the new product.[39] Kellogg's has branched out from the cereal company it once was. Its strategy of branding the corporate name into the product name has allowed it to introduce new products quicker and more easily. Kellogg's Eggo Syrup was a natural extension to its product line of breakfast foods.

Second, if either the original brand or the brand extension has strong consumer acceptance, that perception will carry over to the other product. Consumers who had not used the Neutrogena brand before trying the brand extension, Neutrogena Wave power cleanser, might be encouraged to try Neutrogena's core product line of cleansers and moisturizing lotions, especially if their experience with the Wave has been positive.[40]

Third, when brand extensions are used for complementary products, a synergy exists between the two products that can increase overall sales. For example, Frito-Lay markets both chips and dips under its Frito-Lay and Doritos brand names. When people buy the chips, they tend to buy the dips as well.

Lifesavers unsuccessfully attempted a brand extension strategy with its line of soda.

Not all brand extensions are successful, however. Some can dilute brand equity.[41] **Brand dilution** occurs when the brand extension adversely affects consumer perceptions about the attributes the core brand is believed to hold.[42] Here are some examples of unsuccessful brand extensions:[43]

- Cheetos Lip Balm was based on the idea that if you like Cheetos, you would want to wipe it all over your lips.
- Lifesavers Soda did well in prelaunch taste tests, but didn't in subsequent sales.
- Colgate Kitchen Entrees were microwavable frozen dinner entrees that shared the name with the famous toothpaste.
- Bic thought that since people wanted their disposable lighters and razors, they would also want disposable underwear. They were wrong.

To prevent the potentially negative consequences of brand extensions, firms consider the following:

- Marketers should evaluate the fit between the product class of the core brand and that of the extension.[44] If the fit between the product categories is high, consumers will consider the extension credible, and the brand association will be stronger for the extension. Thus, when Starbucks introduced its line of instant coffee, VIA, it made sense to its customers.
- Firms should evaluate consumer perceptions of the attributes of the core brand and seek out similar attributes for the extension because brand-specific associations are very important for extensions.[45] For example, if HP printers were associated with reliability, performance, and value, consumers would expect the same brand-specific attributes in other products that carried the HP brand name.
- Firms should refrain from extending the brand name to too many products and product categories to avoid diluting the brand and damaging brand equity. Donald Trump has been quite successful lending his name to various property, television lines, and Macy's clothing, but was unsuccessful with extending himself to branding steaks.
- Firms should consider whether the brand extension will be distanced from the core brand, especially if the firm wants to use some but not all of the existing brand associations. Marriott has budget hotels, mid-tier, and luxury hotels. Its luxury hotels, including the Ritz-Carlton, Edition, and Renaissance, do not use the name Marriott at all.[46]

Co—branding

Co-branding is the practice of marketing two or more brands together, on the same package, promotion, or store. Co-branding can enhance consumers' perceptions of product quality by signaling "unobservable" product quality through links between the firm's brand and a well-known quality brand. For example, Yum Brands frequently combines two or more of its restaurant chains, including A&W, KFC, Long John Silver's, Pizza Hut, and Taco Bell, into one store space.[47] This co-branding strategy is designed to appeal to diverse market segments and extend the hours in which each restaurant attracts customers. Yet co-branding also creates risks, especially when the customers of each of the brands turn out to be vastly different. For example, the Burger King and Häagen-Dazs co-branding strategy failed because the customer profiles for each brand were too different.[48]

The NBA licenses products like these bobblehead figures of Dallas Mavericks and San Antonio Spurs players to a manufacturer in exchange for a negotiated fee.

Co-branding may also fail when there are disputes or conflicts of interest between the co-brands.

Brand Licensing

Brand licensing is a contractual arrangement between firms, whereby one firm allows another to use its brand name, logo, symbols, and/or characters in exchange for a negotiated fee.[49] Brand licensing is common for toys, apparel, accessories, and entertainment products, such as video games. The firm that provides the right to use its brand (licensor) obtains revenues through royalty payments from the firm that has obtained the right to use the brand (licensee). These royalty payments may take the form of an upfront, lump-sum licensing fee or be based on the dollar value of sales of the licensed merchandise.

One very popular form of licensing is the use of characters created in books and other media. Such entertainment licensing has generated tremendous revenues for movie studios. Disney, for instance, flooded retail stores with products based on *The Princess and the Frog* movie. *Star Wars* memorabilia has continued to be successful since the first film was released in the 1970s. A long-standing staple of licensing has been major league sports teams that play in the NBA, NFL, or NHL, as well as various collegiate sports teams.

Licensing is an effective form of attracting visibility for the brand and thereby building brand equity while also generating additional revenue. There are, however, some risks associated with it. For the licensor, the major risk is the dilution of its brand equity through overexposure of the brand, especially if the brand name and characters are used inappropriately.[50]

Brand Repositioning

Brand repositioning or **rebranding** refers to a strategy in which marketers change a brand's focus to target new markets or realign the brand's core emphasis with changing market preferences.[51] Although repositioning can improve the brand's fit with its target segment or boost the vitality of old brands, it is not without costs

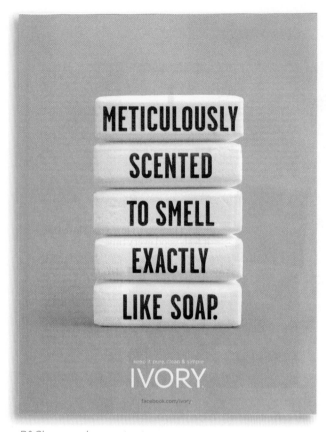

METICULOUSLY SCENTED TO SMELL EXACTLY LIKE SOAP.

keep it pure, clean & simple

IVORY

facebook.com/ivory

P&G's new ad campaign is positioned to appeal to young moms, in addition to keeping its core customers.

and risks. Firms often need to spend tremendous amounts of money to make tangible changes to the product and packages, as well as intangible changes to the brand's image through various forms of promotion. These costs may not be recovered if the repositioned brand and messages are not credible to the consumer or if the firm has mistaken a fad for a long-term market trend.

Yet even when they enjoy the benefits of their well-known name and reputations, brands may find it necessary to reposition, even if that means challenging hundreds of years of tradition. For example, Procter & Gamble's (P&G) Ivory soap brand first appeared in 1879, promoted with an image of purity in white, subdued packaging. The new Ivory comes in brightly colored packages, with cyan, purple, and green splashed across the wrappers and bottles. This new approach nevertheless links to and builds on the brand's well-established position. In humorous televised ads running in select cities with strong markets for the brand, P&G mocks how complicated the use of soap has become today. Unusual soaps made to look like waffles with syrup and sugar contrast against the pure bars that Ivory continues to offer. Yet their repackaging and new advertising push definitely reflect a repositioning. The Ivory brand has long appealed to both men and women, but P&G aims to improve its annual sales of less than $100 million by making a devoted push to appeal to young moms, in addition to keeping core customers.[52]

CHECK YOURSELF

1. What are the differences between manufacturer and private-label brands?
2. What is co-branding?
3. What is the difference between brand extension and line extension?
4. What is brand repositioning?

L08 Indicate the advantages of a product's packaging and labeling strategy.

PACKAGING

Packaging is an important brand element with more tangible or physical benefits than other brand elements. Packages come in different types and offer a variety of benefits to consumers, manufacturers, and retailers. The **primary package** is the one the consumer uses, such as the toothpaste tube. From the primary package, consumers typically seek convenience in terms of storage, use, and consumption.

The **secondary package** is the wrapper or exterior carton that contains the primary package and provides the UPC label used by retail scanners. Consumers can use the secondary package to find additional product information that may not be available on the primary package. Like primary packages, secondary packages add consumer value by facilitating the convenience of carrying, using, and storing the product.

Whether primary or secondary, packaging plays several key roles: It attracts the consumers' attention. It enables products to stand out from their competitors. It offers a promotional tool (e.g., "NEW" and "IMPROVED" promises on labels). Finally, it allows for the same product to appeal to different markets with different sizes, such that convenience stores stock little packages that travelers can buy at the last minute, whereas Costco sells extra large versions of products.

Firms occasionally change or update their packaging as a subtle way of repositioning the product. A change can be used to attract a new target market and/or appear more up to date to its current market. For instance, the Morton Salt umbrella girl has significantly changed since it was first introduced in 1914, but the slogan "when it rains it pours" endures today. Changes also can make consumers feel like they are receiving something tangible in return for paying higher prices, even when the product itself remains untouched. Whether true or not, consumers see new packaging and tend to think that the "new" product may be worth trying. Dr Pepper Snapple Co. has retooled the packages (with a related ad campaign) for Snapple iced teas to tout its blend of "better stuff"—healthy green and tasty black tea leaves.[53]

Some packaging changes are designed to make the product more ecological, such as PepsiCo.'s response to concerns about the waste associated with bottled water. To reduce the amount of plastic it uses, PepsiCo has decreased the weight of its water bottles by 20 percent. The "Eco-Fina" bottle is nearly 50 percent lighter than the version introduced in 2002, which means less plastic in landfills. In a competitive marketplace, a brand that can associate with less harmful impact on the environment often can gain a significant competitive advantage it can use to induce consumers to purchase in good conscience.[54]

Sometimes packaging changes can backfire though, such as when Tropicana changed its packaging to feature a picture of a glass of juice, rather than the familiar straw in an orange. Customers balked, calling the new image "ugly," "stupid," and reminiscent of "a generic bargain brand."[55] The company poorly misjudged its customers' loyalty to its existing brand position, as exemplified by its packaging. For example, before the change, the president of Tropicana North America claimed, "The straw and orange have been there for a long time, but people have not necessarily had a huge connection to them." After suffering tremendous backlash and deciding to rescind its repackaging decision, the same executive

Snapple changed its packages for Snapple iced teas to tout its blend of "better stuff"–healthy and tasty black tea leaves.

admitted, "What we didn't get was the passion this very loyal small group of consumers have."[56]

Many consumers experience "wrap rage"—a great frustration with packaging that makes it seemingly impossible to get at the actual products. So companies are moving away from traditional clamshells, which are the curved plastic package around many electronics goods, because they are so difficult to open. Costco has replaced the clamshells with packaging made of coated paperboard that still requires scissors to open, but is flat and therefore can be opened easily.

Retailers' and manufacturers' priorities for secondary packaging often differ from those of its customers. They want convenience in terms of displaying and selling the product. In addition, secondary packages often get packed into larger cartons, pallets, or containers to facilitate shipment and storage from the manufacturer to the retailer. These shipping packages benefit the manufacturer and the retailer, in that they protect the shipment during transit; aid in loading, unloading, and storage; and allow cost efficiencies due to the larger order and shipment sizes.

Packaging can also be used in a far more subtle way, namely, to help suppliers save costs. For routine purchases, consumers rarely engage in actual decision making but rather just grab their familiar jar of peanut butter from the shelf. In so doing, they likely never notice that Skippy peanut butter jars have gone from containing 18 ounces to just 16.3 ounces—same appearance, same diameter and height of the jar, same price, but a bigger indent in the bottom. Approximately 30 percent of packaged goods similarly have lost content recently, and most of the changes have gone unnoticed by consumers. General Mills even has a department devoted to cost cutting through package redesign or clever content reduction ideas, which it calls the "Holistic Margin Management" department. Because 75 percent of a product's cost may be in the packaging, these savings can represent huge overall savings for the company.[57]

Product Labeling

Labels on products and packages provide information the consumer needs for his or her purchase decision and consumption of the product. In that they identify the product and brand, labels are also an important element of branding and can be used for promotion. The information required on them must comply with general and industry-specific laws and regulations, including the constituents or ingredients contained in the product, where the product was made, directions for use, and/or safety precautions.

Many labeling requirements stem from various laws, including the Federal Trade Commission Act of 1914, the Fair Packaging and Labeling Act of 1967, and the Nutrition Labeling Act of 1990. Several federal agencies, industry groups, and consumer watchdogs carefully monitor product labels. The Food and Drug Administration is the primary federal agency that reviews food and package labels and ensures that the claims made by the manufacturer are true. Ethical and Societal Dilemma 11.2 illustrates the problems associated with the different regulations that apply to various edible products, as well as some associated labeling concerns.

A product label is much more than just a sticker on the package; it is a communication tool. Many of the elements on the label are required by laws and regulations (i.e., ingredients, fat content, sodium content, serving size, calories), but other elements remain within the control of the manufacturer. How manufacturers use labels to communicate the benefits of their products to consumers varies by the product. Many products highlight specific ingredients, vitamin content, or nutrient content (e.g., iron), and country of origin. This focus signals to consumers that the product offers these benefits. The importance of the label as a communication tool should not be underestimated.

Ethical and Societal Dilemma 11.2 — Calories 0, Vitamins 0: How Much Information Can Water Labels Provide?

Water, water everywhere. Especially in developed countries, consumers everywhere can simply turn on the tap, and there it is. And yet firms have been successful in packaging this almost free, natural resource, creating some cachet for it, and selling it.

Bottled water enjoyed double-digit growth, year to year, as U.S. consumers doubled the amount they drank from 1997 to 2007, from 13.4 to 29.3 gallons per year. The popularity and growth of the industry has attracted attention though. Bottled and tap water companies operate under different regulations. Yet many observers and government agencies argue the rules should be the same, with water bottle labeling subject to regulations as detailed as those that the tap water companies experience.

Bottled water, as a food product, currently is regulated by the Food and Drug Administration, so it lists nutrition information and ingredients on the labels (i.e., 0 percent of most nutrients; contents: water). In contrast, municipal water is controlled by the Environmental Protection Agency, which has more authority to enforce quality standards. The result may be misinformed consumers, many of whom believe bottled water is safer and

Would more comprehensive labels on bottled water change your water consumption behavior?

healthier than tap water. And yet according to the U.S. Government Accounting Office (GAO), the FDA lacks the authority to require that water bottlers use certified water quality tests or report those test results. Also, the existing requirements to ensure safe bottled water, both state and federal, are less comprehensive than the rules about safeguarding tap water.[58]

Even without such regulations though, consumers may be changing their attitudes. The bottled water industry recently has experienced flat growth. The cause may be the economic downturn, which has forced consumers to cut costs wherever possible. Environmental concerns may be another factor since bottled water creates significant waste.

Perhaps better labeling of products will mean even less ambiguity about the value of bottled versus tap water, which could offer opportunities for differentiation among bottled water brands that adopt different bottling and labeling methods.[59]

Would more comprehensive labels on bottled water change your water consumption behavior? Is bottled water "better" than tap water? Is buying bottled water an ecologically sound purchase decision?

Summing Up

LO1 Describe the components of a product.

The product itself is important, but so are its associated services, such as support or financing. Other elements combine to produce the core customer value of a product: the brand name, quality level, packaging, and additional features.

LO2 Identify the types of consumer products.

These products tend to be classified into four groups: specialty, shopping, convenience, and unsought products. Each classification involves a different purchase situation and consumer goal.

LO3 Explain the difference between a product mix's breadth and a product line's depth.

Breadth, or variety, entails the number of product lines that a company offers. Depth involves the number of categories within one specific product line.

LO4 Identify the advantages that brands provide firms and consumers.

Brands play important roles in enabling people to make purchase decisions more easily and encouraging customer loyalty. For firms specifically, they also constitute valuable assets and improve a company's bottom line and help protect against competition.

LO5 Explain the various components of brand equity.

Brand equity summarizes the value that a brand adds, or subtracts, from the offering's value. It comprises brand awareness, or how many consumers in the market are familiar with the brand; brand associations, which are the links consumers make between the brand and its image; and brand loyalty, which occurs when a consumer will only buy that brand's offer. Brand equity also encompasses the concept of perceived value, which is a subjective measure that consumers develop to assess the costs of obtaining the brand.

 Determine the various types of branding strategies used by firms.

Firms use a variety of strategies to manage their brands. First, they decide whether to offer manufacturer and/or private-label brands. Second, they have a choice of using an overall corporate brand or a collection of product line or individual brands. Third, to reach new markets or extend their current market, they can extend their current brands to new products. Fourth, firms can co-brand with another brand to create sales and profit synergies for both. Fifth, firms with strong brands have the opportunity to license their brands to other firms. Finally, as the marketplace changes, it is often necessary to reposition a brand.

LO7 **Distinguish between brand extension and line extension.**

Whereas a brand extension uses the same brand name for a new product that gets introduced into new or the same markets, a line extension is simply an increase of an existing product line by the brand.

LO8 **Indicate the advantages of a product's packaging and labeling strategy.**

Similar to brands, packaging and labels help sell the product and facilitate its use. The primary package holds the product, and its label provides product information. The secondary package provides additional consumer information on its label and facilitates transportation and storage for both retailers and their customers. Labels have become increasingly important to consumers because they supply important safety, nutritional, and product usage information.

Key Terms

- actual product, 334
- associated services, 335
- augmented product, 335
- brand association, 344
- brand awareness, 343
- brand dilution, 348
- brand equity, 342
- brand extension, 347
- brand licensing, 349
- brand loyalty, 344
- brand repositioning (rebranding), 349
- breadth, 337

- co-branding, 348
- consumer product, 335
- convenience products/ services, 336
- core customer value, 334
- family brands, 347
- depth, 337
- individual brands, 347
- line extension, 347
- manufacturer brands (national brands), 346
- perceived value, 344
- primary package, 350

- private-label brands, 346
- product, 334
- product lines, 337
- product mix, 337
- retailer/store brands, 346
- secondary package, 350
- shopping products/ services, 335
- specialty products/ services, 335
- unsought products/ services, 336

Marketing Applications

1. LL Bean guarantees that its products will last forever. What features of a pair of pants from LL Bean would be part of the actual product and which would be part of the associated services?

2. Classify each of the following products into either convenience, shopping, specialty, or unsought goods: toothpaste, life insurance, Sharp TV, Eggo waffles, lettuce, Coach handbag, adidas soccer cleats, furniture.

3. Study the following two product mixes. For Product Mix 1: A, B, C and D are the lines; and for Product Mix 2: X, Y and Z are the lines.

A	B	C	D
a1	b1	c1	d1
a2	b2	c2	d2
a3	b3	c2	

Product Mix 1

X	Y	Z
x1	y1	z1
x2	y2	z2
x3	y3	ze
x4	y4	

Product Mix 2

Which mix has more *breadth* and why? Which mix is *deeper* and why?

4. Suppose you are the coffee buyer at Kroger's. There is a strong corporate initiative to increase store label merchandise. Discuss the advantages and disadvantages of offering private-label coffee.

5. Identify a specific brand that has developed a high level of brand equity. What specific aspects of that brand establish its brand equity?

6. Are you loyal to any brands? If so, pick one and explain why you believe you are loyal, beyond that you simply like the brand. If not, pick a brand that you like and explain how you would feel and act differently toward the brand if you were loyal to it.

7. Sears owns several store brands, including DieHard, Kenmore, and Craftsman. Each brand features many models that may appeal to various customer groups. Wouldn't it be easier to just identify them all as Sears? Justify your answer.

8. Do you think all edible items sold in a grocery store should have an ingredient and nutrition label? Consider the perspectives of consumers, the manufacturer, and the store.

9. You are the brand manager for a firm that makes herbs, spices, and other food additives. You have had complaints from some of your retail outlets that they are finding empty bottles of pure vanilla extract stashed around the store. Apparently, due to the high (35 percent) alcohol content of pure vanilla extract, people are grabbing the cute little bottles, having a drink, and getting rid of the evidence. Anecdotal evidence from store employees indicates that the majority of the imbibers are teenagers. The cost of placing a tamper proof cap on the extract is a relatively insignificant percentage of the purchase price, but will make it more difficult to open, particularly for older customers. Also, there has been a significant rise in sales to retailers as a result of the vanilla bean "addicts." What should you do?

Quiz Yourself

www.mhhe.com/grewal4e

1. A university that has separate graduate and undergraduate admission offices recognizes that these are distinct:
   a. brand associations
   b. product/service lines
   c. product mixes
   d. brands
   e. co-brands

2. _____ is the set of assets and liabilities linked to a brand that add to or subtract from the value provided by the product or service.
   a. Brand positioning
   b. Brand licensing
   c. National branding
   d. Brand equity
   e. Brand solvency

(Answers to these two questions can be found on page 648.)

Go to www.mhhe.com/grewal4e to practice an additional 11 questions.

Net Savvy

1. Visit Revlon's website (www.revlon.com). Identify and briefly describe the depth and the breadth of its product lines.

2. Go to Kellogg's website (www.kelloggs.com) and identify a few recently introduced brand extensions to the marketplace. Discuss whether you believe the brand extension examples you provided will benefit or harm the firm.

Chapter Case Study

OPRAH WINFREY, A BRAND UNTO HERSELF

connect

A cultural icon who rose from poverty to become one of the world's most influential entrepreneurs, Oprah Winfrey is many things to many people. Certainly she is an entertainer who comes across as women's most intimate friend and advocate. Winfrey also has inspired and coached an audience of millions on how to "live your best life." But perhaps most of all, Oprah Winfrey is a marketer and the savvy leader of a media empire that has extended her brand worldwide.

Starting with her immensely successful TV program, *The Oprah Winfrey Show*, Winfrey expanded her personal brand through a range of other vehicles, which in any other context would be known as product lines. These lines include her two production companies, Harpo Films and Harpo Studios; *O, The Oprah Magazine*; Oprah.com, her website, which profiles all her ventures; Oprah's Book Club, which some have credited with saving the publishing industry; multiple TV and radio spin-offs; and OWN, the Oprah Winfrey Network, also called her "next chapter."[60] Each element functions as a division of Harpo Productions, her multimedia entertainment company.

Building on Oprah's own compelling story of personal triumph, the Winfrey brand offers multitudes of fans not only an example of self-improvement but also authentic proof, from Winfrey's own life, that anyone can control his or her own destiny. Over the years, Winfrey has chronicled her childhood of poverty and sexual abuse, struggles to control her weight, and the difficulties of being a powerful woman in a highly competitive industry. The revealing details have only strengthened the connection with her viewers, who adore her. The message is compelling and authentic: If I can do it, you can, too.

Viewers believe her. That trust gives Winfrey tremendous influence, and it also translates into a flair for helping other brands connect with her audience. An inveterate shopper, she likes to showcase the products she loves. Her endorsements, offered without compensation, can make little known products into superstars overnight. The month following her episode featuring aromatherapy slippers called Foot Cozys, manufacturer DreamTimes sold 20,000 pairs, up from its usual monthly volume of 3,000. Marketing experts say the Oprah brand, built on the credo of self-improvement and living well, now ranks with the towering brands of Coca-Cola and the Marlboro Man, leaving one observer to admit, "I'm hard-pressed to think of a stronger brand than Oprah."[61] That means that the Oprah brand has been enormously profitable, making Winfrey the wealthiest of America's 400 richest self-made women, with a combined worth of $2.7 billion.[62]

Winfrey began building her public persona long before she gained any national recognition, starting as a local news anchor in Nashville and then a talk-show host in Baltimore. With her move to Chicago in 1984, Winfrey gained increasing attention when her morning program, *AM Chicago*, surpassed the ratings achieved by the then–talk show king Phil Donahue. By 1986, her program was rebranded as *The Oprah Winfrey Show*, and its host was gaining a reputation for offering confessional, straight talk, like a "group therapy session."[63]

Her daily program reigned supreme among talk shows for 25 years, drawing 12 million U.S. viewers at its peak, with more than 4,500 episodes and 30,000 guests. The messages of confronting life's difficult realities and

When you think of Oprah Winfrey, think big: Harpo Productions, Inc.; O, The Oprah Magazine; O at Home Magazine; Harpo Films; and the Oxygen television network; not to mention her philanthropic work with the Oprah Winfrey Foundation.

taking time for self-care remained central in brand extensions, including syndicated spin-offs such as *Dr. Phil* and *Rachael Ray*. Newer shows, usually featuring Winfrey's favored celebrity life coaches, have also increased her brand recognition. On his shows, Dr. Mehmet Oz provides insights into living a "longer, more vibrant life." *In the Bedroom with Dr. Laura Berman* counsels women about how to juggle the pressures of home and work and still feel sexy.[64]

Other extensions focus on different areas. Winfrey has continued to promote her brand and ethos of personal growth in her monthly magazine *O, The Oprah Magazine*, which features Winfrey on every cover and has a circulation of about 2.5 million. Movies produced by Harpo Films also have brought some of the country's most respected actors together with scripts arising from acclaimed books, such as *Tuesdays with Morrie*, featuring Jack Lemmon and based on the best-selling novel by Detroit sportswriter Mitch Albom; *Their Eyes Were Watching God*, based on the Zora Neale Hurston novel and starring Halle Berry; *Beloved*, a film based on Toni Morrison's Pulitzer Prize–winning novel, directed by Jonathan Demme and co-starring Winfrey and Danny Glover; and *The Great Debaters*, which received a Golden Globe nomination and co-starred Denzel Washington and Forest Whitaker. Winfrey also provided backing for the release of *Precious*, an Oscar-winning film based on a novel by Sapphire. Each new introduction celebrated the preservation of human dignity against terrible odds—disabling disease, crippling poverty and abuse, racism.

The latest venture of launching her own cable television network takes Winfrey into new territory, with lots of challenges but also aligned with her brand's promise of controlling one's own destiny. It's not her first risky move: Buoyed by the terrific success of *The Oprah Winfrey Show*, in the late 1980s, Winfrey bolted from both King World Productions, which syndicated the show, and ABC, which produced it. Taking total control through Harpo Productions gave her complete ownership of the brand and syndication fees, estimated at $100 million. That move established the cornerstone of her empire. But the initial launch of OWN was rocky. Early reviews criticized Winfrey for taking the fun out of her programming.[65] *Oprah's Lifeclass*, the flagship show and latest incarnation of Winfrey's personal brand, came off like a series of lectures, preaching that "you are responsible for changing your life and making it better."[66] In contrast, OWN's *The Rosie Show* was entertaining, unpredictable, and simply put, not dull.

With questions mounting, several months after the launch of OWN, Winfrey shuffled her leadership structure and took the top post herself. As always, she was determined to take control of her brand and her company. She would do what she had always exhorted others to do: Live her best life through her own brand.

Questions

1. Visit the company website (http://www.oprah.com/index.html) and identify and describe the different product lines that it markets.

2. How would you describe its product line breadth?

3. Review the different product categories in each of the company's product lines. Which has the greatest depth? Which has the least?

4. How has the company positioned its brand? How does it go about communicating its position?

CHAPTER 12

Developing New Products

When LEGOs first arrived in the United States in the early 1960s, the company had devised a set of principles for the design of the molded stud-and-tube bricks:[1]

- Unlimited play potential
- For girls and for boys
- Fun for every age
- Year-round play
- Healthy, quiet play
- Long hours of play
- Development, imagination, creativity
- The more LEGO, the greater the value
- Extra sets available
- Quality in every detail

Over time, the Danish firm grew to become one of the top toy manufacturers in the world, introducing new sets and variations on its basic theme, including an extensive line of *Star Wars* models (as well as lines related to other popular movie franchises), basic robot technology, and superhero-themed collections. Perhaps unintentionally, it appeared that LEGO had come to violate one of its basic principles, in that its toys appealed widely to boys but not specifically to girls.

LEARNING OBJECTIVES

LO1 Identify the reasons firms create new products.

LO2 Describe the different groups of adopters articulated by the diffusion of innovation theory.

LO3 Describe the various stages involved in developing a new product or service.

LO4 Explain the product life cycle.

Faced with declining profits in the early 2000s, LEGO had determined that the popularity of video and automated games meant it needed to refocus on these areas. It developed LEGO-branded video games to match its *Star Wars* line of building sets. It pushed its website and interactive opportunities. The "My Lego Network" social media site encouraged children to build their own web pages, personalized with pictures of their LEGO creations, music, and sticker compositions.[2]

But these changes caused some members of the LEGO team to worry about the effects on its long-standing traditions. Perhaps the predesigned sets were hindering creativity, rather than encouraging it. Maybe telling kids to go online was not really healthy for long-lasting play. And perhaps product lines focused on pirates, science fiction, and robots were not appealing enough to girls and the ways they like to play.

In additional market research involving in-depth observations of children playing—on their own and as they wished, without any direction or guidance from outside—LEGO gained some notable insights.[3] For example, rather than appealing to children by simplifying its toys, LEGO had made its sets too easy to construct, without room for careful thought or creativity. The observational research showed that children wanted a sense of mastery and accomplishment, not just instant gratification. In addition, its research with girls revealed that they were not uninterested in building. They just wanted to tell stories to go along with their construction—an effort that was undermined by the preset stories in LEGO video games. As a LEGO vice president summarized, "We heard very clear requests from moms and girls for more details and interior building, a brighter color palette, a more realistic figure, role play opportunities and a story line that they would find interesting."[4]

Thus arrived the LEGO Friends, mini-doll figures whose names, back stories, and adventures are up to girls to develop and include in their own narratives.[5] The friends—Mia, Emma, Stephanie, Olivia, and Andrea—live in treehouses, drive convertibles, run a beauty parlor and a bakery, and play with their dogs. The color schemes for all the sets are heavy in pink and purple. Furthermore, the doll figures are slimmer and curvier than the traditional, blocky LEGO figures.

For some parents, these new products that appeal to a new segment of consumers are problematic: The LEGO Friends do not require children to complete the assembly to begin playing, which seemingly could diminish girls' sense of accomplishment. Others suggest that the offerings of beauty parlor and café sets reinforce gender stereotypes, without allowing room for female firefighters or politicians—or space explorers or pirates, for that matter. If the new sets are expressly for girls, does that imply that the old sets were really only for boys?[6]

LEGO insists that it has always tried to appeal to girls through its wide variety of products. And though the final tallies are not in yet on this brand new product, LEGO's legacy suggests it may be on to something big. By focusing on sets, instead of just free-form blocks, LEGO tripled its profits between 2006 and 2010. Three LEGO sets sell every second worldwide.[7] Today, by appealing to girls with an entirely new product, perhaps it can increase that rate to four or five per second.

Few three-letter words are more exciting than "new." It brings forth an image of freshness, adventure, and excitement. Yet "new" also is a complex term when it comes to market offerings, because it might mean adding something new to an existing product, introducing a flavor never offered before, or relying on different packaging that provides added value. But the most exhilarating type of new product is something never seen before. Thousands of patent applications pursue this elusive prize: a successful and truly innovative new product.

Imagine living 200 years ago: You cook meals on a stove fueled by coal or wood; you write out homework by hand (if you are lucky enough to attend school) and by candlelight. To get to school, you hike along unpaved roads to reach a small, cold, basic classroom with just a few classmates, who listen to a lecture from a teacher writing on a blackboard.

Today, you finish your homework on a laptop computer with word processing software that appears to have a mind of its own and can correct your spelling automatically. Your climate-controlled room has ample electric light. While you work on your laptop, you also talk with a friend using the hands-free headset of your wireless phone. As you drive to school in your car, you pick up fast food from a convenient drive-through window while browsing and listening to your personal selection of songs playing through your car speakers, connected wirelessly to your iPod. Your friend calls to discuss a slight change to the homework, so you pull over to grab your BlackBerry, make the necessary change to your assignment, and e-mail it from your smartphone to your professor. When you arrive at school, you sit in a 200-person classroom, where you can plug in your laptop, take notes on your iPad, or digitally record the lecture, right after you check in on Foursquare. The professor adds notes on the day's PowerPoint presentations using her tablet computer. You have already downloaded the PowerPoint presentations and add similar notes through your own laptop. After class, to complete your planning for a last-minute party, you send out a Facebook invitation to your friends and ask for responses to get a headcount. You then text your roommate, telling her to get food and drinks for the right number of people, which she orders through an online grocer that will deliver later in the day.

Our lives are defined by the many new products and services developed through scientific and technological advances and by the added features included in products that we have always used. In this second chapter dealing with the first P in the marketing mix (product), we continue our discussion from the preceding chapter and explore how companies add value to product and service offerings through innovation. We also look at how firms develop new products and services on their own. We conclude the chapter with an examination of how new products and services get adopted by the market and how firms can change their marketing mix as the product or service moves through its life cycle.

WHY DO FIRMS CREATE NEW PRODUCTS?

LO1 Identify the reasons firms create new products.

New market offerings provide value to both firms and customers. But the degree to which they do so depends on how new they really are. When we say a "new product/ service," we don't necessarily mean that the market offer has never existed before—kids have long played with LEGOs, but LEGO Friends are a new version for them. Completely new-to-the-market products represent fewer than 10 percent of all new product introductions each year. It is more useful to think of the degree of newness or innovativeness on a continuum from truly "new-to-the-world"—as WiFi was a few years ago—to "slightly repositioned," such as when Kraft's Capri Sun brand of ready-to-drink beverages were repackaged in a bigger pouch to appeal to teens.

Regardless of where on the continuum a new product lies, firms have to innovate. **Innovation** refers to the process by which ideas get transformed into new offerings, including products, services, processes, and branding concepts that will help firms grow. Without innovation and its resulting new products and services, firms would have only two choices: continue to market current products to current customers or take the same product to another market with similar customers.

LEGO Friends live in treehouses and are designed to appeal to girls.

Moving? Rent Frogbox reusable plastic boxes and spare the landfills.

Although innovation strategies may not always work in the short run—some estimates indicate that only about 3 percent of new products actually succeed—various overriding and long-term reasons compel firms to continue introducing new products and services, as the following sections describe.

Changing Customer Needs

When they add products, services, and processes to their offerings, firms can create and deliver value more effectively by satisfying the changing needs of their current and new customers or by keeping customers from getting bored with the current product or service offering. Sometimes, companies can identify problems and develop products or services that customers never knew they needed. For example, moving can be stressful; among other things, having to buy, build, and dispose of moving boxes is a hassle, expensive, and not very good for the environment. Canadian firm Frogbox rents out reusable plastic moving boxes. It delivers them to the customer, and picks them up at the new address when they are finished. The boxes stack neatly inside each other and don't

Adding Value 12.1   Turning Diaper Changes into Child's Play

Diaper brands face shrinking markets. In most industrialized countries, birth rates are lower than they have been in decades. Furthermore, these fewer parents increasingly note the value of lower cost, store-brand diapers. Then they stick with their choices: 55 percent of diaper purchasers report that they nearly always buy their preferred brand. Facing these tough market dynamics, Huggies, Kimberly-Clark's diaper brand, aimed to introduce a new product to excite, appeal to, and reengage the market of parents of infants.[8]

It knew just where to start—that is, with a consumer study. Huggies quickly recognized that babies around 10 months or so are learning to crawl, starting to walk, and discovering how much fun it is to move around. The parents of these active babies thus had a very particular need: to keep their wild and crazy babies still long enough to get new diapers on them. According to the Huggies study, more than 60 percent of parents reported that their "squirmy" babies frequently scrambled out of reach, making it tough to complete the diaper change.[9]

Thus Huggies developed a clear-cut concept for its new product. Described as a first of its kind,[10] the Little Movers Slip-On diaper features stretchable material on its sides for a snug fit. Looking a little like regular underwear, the slip-ons with legholes offer the same absorbency and leakage protection as regular Huggies diapers, but they are designed specifically to make life easier for scrambling parents.

In online, print, and in-store ad campaigns, Huggies shows how a diaper change with Little Movers can be fun, rather than a battle of wills. Over video of a baby rolling over, a voiceover announces that Huggies' latest product offers parents "a whole new way to change a rolling pin." Then the shot changes to show a series of variations—"the acrobutt" who bends over and peers through her legs, "the streaker" who crawls across the screen naked, and "the booty scoocher," pushing forward on his backside. No fidgety child, whatever the type, will elude a parent armed with a Little Movers diaper. In addition to showing activity that likely resonates with any parents, Huggies has attempted to engage customers by asking them to upload home video of their babies' own "tricky moves" onto its YouTube site. More than 2,000 parents responded almost immediately, with funny videos of their "Jumping Beans" and "Kick n' Roller" babies.[11]

Although the per-diaper price for a Little Movers slip-on averages about 16 percent higher than the price of competing diapers, Kimberly-Clark hopes that simplifying the diaper change for parents is well worth the savings they offer, in terms of the parents' time and perhaps for saving the furniture from an unfortunate accident by a little wild child.

Huggies Little Movers Slip-On diapers are designed to make life easier for parents.

require assembly, eliminating the time-consuming task of building and breaking down boxes. The firm is called Frogbox because it donates 1 percent of sales to frog habitat restoration.[12] Adding to its sustainability efforts, it uses solar energy to power its website and waste-generated biodiesel to fuel its trucks. Adding Value 12.1 examines how Huggies has adapted to consumer needs too.

Market Saturation

The longer a product exists in the marketplace, the more likely it is that the market will become saturated. Without new products or services, the value of the firm

Adding Value 12.2   Carmakers Look for an Edge, Above and Under the Hood

The competition and new partnerships generated by the global car market have yielded a wealth of new product approaches, both above and below the hood, as automakers strive to meet an international aesthetic while also responding to near-universal demand for more fuel-efficient cars. In particular, U.S. carmakers can no longer simply appeal to American tastes, with tailfins, boxy SUVs, and little concern about fuel economy. Car design must meet the demands of drivers overseas. General Motors recently introduced a new concept car, the Chevrolet Tru 140S, an "affordable exotic" model that gets 40 miles per gallon. Another Chevrolet concept, Code 130R, takes elements from the BMW 1 Series, the 1960s Ford Anglia from Europe, and Japanese subcompact car models.

While crafting new looks, GM also is looking for designs that will survive shifting trends. The Cadillac ATS sedan, which aims to compete with the BMW 3 Series, is not nearly as distinctive as classic Cadillac models from the past. But its understated style may enable the ATS to age more gracefully and require fewer, less frequent redesigns. Ford hired European designers to come up with many of its most successful recent models, including the Focus and the Fiesta. These small, quick, sporty cars appeal to the worldwide market. Chrysler's new owner Fiat has added Italian elements to make the U.S. brand appear more global in its design.[13]

Automakers also are relying heavily on new engineering to meet global demand. Tighter fuel efficiency standards and shifting buyer preferences are forcing carmakers to develop lighter, smaller-cylinder cars, more electrics and hybrids, and new turbocharged engines that couple with electric motors.[14] Even luxury cars are becoming lighter. Mercedes-Benz has spent seven years developing the aluminum body of its new SL 550, which is 308 pounds lighter than the previous model yet still offers unparalleled torsion resistance.

Smaller engines are getting a second look too: For the first time in 20 years, Cadillac is offering a four-cylinder engine to deliver fuel efficiency in its ATS. The appeal of these smaller, powerful engines is vast. Ford's new Fusion Hybrid couples a new, lighter lithium ion battery with a lighter four-cylinder engine, to deliver six more miles per gallon in fuel efficiency. Plug-in hybrids are entering the market, including Ford's Fusion Energi, which competes with the Chevy Volt and models influenced by Toyota's Prius.

While re-designing its cars for more European tastes, Fiat-owned Chrysler has revived some of the engineering that made its Dodge Dart compact so efficient. And GM has used its globally successful small-car platform as the basis for both its Chevrolet Sonic subcompact and the Buick Encore crossover. With design oriented to global tastes, and engineering focused on a newer, more efficient bottom line, automakers worldwide are hoping drivers will like what they see.

The Cadillac ATS is less distinctive than earlier models. As a result, its understated style may require fewer redesigns.

will ultimately decline.[15] Imagine, for example, if car companies simply assumed and expected that people would keep their cars until they stopped running. If that were the case, there would be no need to come up with new and innovative models; companies could just stick with the models that sell well. But few consumers actually keep the same car until it stops running. Even those who want to stay with the same make and model often want something new, just to add some variety to their lives. Therefore, car companies revamp their models every year, whether with new features like GPS or a more powerful engine, or by redesigning the entire look of the vehicle. The firms sustain their growth by getting consumers excited by the new looks and new features, prompting many car buyers to exchange their old vehicle years before its functional life is over. Adding Value 12.2 notes some other innovations that carmakers are trying.

Saturated markets can also offer opportunities for a company that is willing to adopt a new process or mentality. At one point in time, mass marketers would not even consider entering a market that they believed would not earn at least $50 million. But General Mills is looking to niche markets for its future growth. Whereas only 1 percent of the U.S. population suffers from celiac disease—a condition that damages the digestive system when sufferers ingest gluten—a much higher percentage of U.S. consumers say they want to reduce or eliminate gluten, a wheat protein, from their diet. As awareness increases, those percentages are growing, such that the U.S. market could be worth up to $6.3 billion. General Mills has created more than 300 gluten-free products, including both variations on its regular offerings, like Chex cereals, and brand new concepts, such as gluten-free desserts and pancake mixes.[16]

Managing Risk through Diversity

Through innovation, firms often create a broader portfolio of products, which help them diversify their risk and enhance firm value better than a single product can.[17] If some products in a portfolio perform poorly, others may do well. Firms with multiple products can better withstand external shocks, including changes in consumer preferences or intensive competitive activity. For this reason, firms like 3M demand that a specific percentage of their sales each year must come from new products introduced within the previous few years. In the cereal aisle, Kellogg's Special K offers many variations of its long-standing basic product, including cereal bars, protein shakes, and even protein water. This diversification enables Special K to enjoy more consistent performance than it would with just one kind of Special K cereal.

Fashion Cycles

In industries that rely on fashion trends and experience short product life cycles—including apparel, arts, books, and software markets—most sales come from new products. For example, a motion picture generates most of its theater, DVD, and cable TV revenues within a year of its release. If the same selection of

The Kellogg's Special K line's risk is lessened by offering many variations of its basic ceral product.

Video games like Madden NFL are "fashionable" because consumers demand new versions. Once they have "beat" the game, they want to be challenged with a new experience.

books were always for sale, with no new titles, there would be no reason to buy more. Consumers of computer software and video games demand new offers because once they have "beat" the game, they want to be challenged by another game or experience the most recent version, as the remarkable sales of successive versions of the Madden NFL game exemplify.[18] In the case of apparel, fashion designers produce entirely new product selections a few times per year.

Improving Business Relationships

New products do not always target end consumers; sometimes they function to improve relationships with suppliers. For example, Kraft, the maker of Capri Sun, found that its lemonade flavor was selling poorly. Through a little market research, it realized that the reason was the placement of the packages in pallets. Because it was placed at the bottom of the stack in pallets, lemonade was the last flavor retailers would sell. By changing and innovating its pallet, Kraft offered chimney stacks for each flavor, enabling the retail stockers to reach whichever flavor they needed easily. Sales of Capri Sun's lemonade improved by 162 percent.[19]

Even if they succeed in innovating and creating new products, new-to-the-world products are not adopted by everyone at the same time. Rather, they diffuse or spread through a population in a process known as *diffusion of innovation.*

To generate sales, apparel fashion designers produce entirely new product selections a few times per year.

CHECK YOURSELF

1. What are the reasons firms innovate?

Apple has released several pioneer products in recent years, including the iPhone.

LO2 Describe the different groups of adopters articulated by the diffusion of innovation theory.

The Green Mountain Coffee K-Cup Packs are one of the top sellling new food and beverage brands.

DIFFUSION OF INNOVATION

The process by which the use of an innovation—whether a product, a service, or a process—spreads throughout a market group, over time and across various categories of adopters, is referred to as **diffusion of innovation**.[20] The theory surrounding diffusion of innovation helps marketers understand the rate at which consumers are likely to adopt a new product or service. It also gives them a means to identify potential markets for their new products or services and predict their potential sales, even before they introduce the innovations.[21]

Truly new product introductions, that is, new-to-the-world products that create new markets, can add tremendous value to firms. These new products, also called **pioneers** or **breakthroughs**, establish a completely new market or radically change both the rules of competition and consumer preferences in a market.[22] The Apple iPod is a pioneer product. Not only did it change the way people listen to music, but it also created an entirely new industry devoted to accessories, such as cases, ear buds, docking stations, and speakers. Although Apple offers many of these accessories itself, other companies have jumped on the bandwagon, ensuring that you can strap your iPod to your arm while on the move or insert it into the base of a desk lamp equipped with speakers to get music and light from your desk. And don't forget: The iPod also launched perhaps the most notable other recent pioneer, the iPhone, along with the innovative iTunes service, the iPod Touch, and even the iPad.[23]

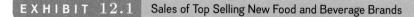

EXHIBIT 12.1   Sales of Top Selling New Food and Beverage Brands

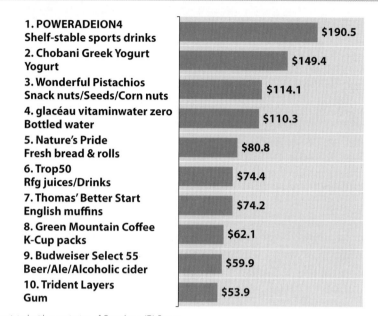

1. POWERADEION4 Shelf-stable sports drinks	$190.5
2. Chobani Greek Yogurt Yogurt	$149.4
3. Wonderful Pistachios Snack nuts/Seeds/Corn nuts	$114.1
4. glacéau vitaminwater zero Bottled water	$110.3
5. Nature's Pride Fresh bread & rolls	$80.8
6. Trop50 Rfg juices/Drinks	$74.4
7. Thomas' Better Start English muffins	$74.2
8. Green Mountain Coffee K-Cup packs	$62.1
9. Budweiser Select 55 Beer/Ale/Alcoholic cider	$59.9
10. Trident Layers Gum	$53.9

Source: Reprinted with permission of Symphony IRI Group.

Pioneers have the advantage of being **first movers**; as the first to create the market or product category, they become readily recognizable to consumers and thus establish a commanding and early market share lead. Studies also have found that market pioneers can command a greater market share over a longer time period than later entrants can.[24] Some recent new entries that have enjoyed such success appear in Exhibit 12.1.

Yet not all pioneers succeed.[25] In many cases, imitators capitalize on the weaknesses of pioneers and subsequently gain advantage in the market. Because pioneering products and brands face the uphill task of establishing the market alone, they pave the way for followers, who can spend less marketing effort creating demand for the product line and focus directly on creating demand for their specific brand. Also, because the pioneer is the first product in the market, it often has a less sophisticated design and may be priced relatively higher, leaving room for better and lower-priced competitive products. A majority of new products are failures: As many as 95 percent of all new consumer goods fail, and products across all markets and industries suffer failure rates of 50 to 80 percent.[26]

An important question to ask is, why is the failure rate for new products so high? One of the main reasons is the failure to assess the market properly by neglecting to do appropriate product testing, targeting the wrong segment, and/or poor positioning.[27] Firms may also overextend their abilities or competencies by venturing into products or services that are inconsistent with their brand image and/or value proposition. We discuss some infamous product failures in Exhibit 12.2.

As the diffusion of innovation curve in Exhibit 12.3 shows, the number of users of an innovative product or service spreads through the population over a period of time and generally follows a bell-shaped curve. A few people buy the product or service at first, then increasingly more buy, and finally fewer people buy as the degree of the diffusion slows. These purchasers can be divided into five groups according to how soon they buy the product after it has been introduced.

Clairol's Touch of Yogurt Shampoo failed because consumers didn't like the idea of washing their hair with yogurt.

EXHIBIT 12.2 Illustrative Product Failures

Product	Concept	Why it failed
New Coke	In response to growing market pressure, Coca-Cola launched a reformulated version of its classic cola in 1985 that was so hated it was pulled from shelves three months later.	Coke underestimated the consumers affinity to the original formulation and their unwillingness to change.
Sony Betamax	In 1975, Sony bet big on the Betamax, one the first ever mass-produced home video recording systems.	Unfortunately, the next year JVC launched the VHS player, ensuing a format-war similar the Blu-Ray and HD-DVD format wars of 2006.
Harley Davidson Perfume	After being successful with lighters and t-shirts bearing the Harley logo, Harley Davidson branched out into its own line of perfumes "associated" with the motorcyle lifestyle.	Although lighters and t-shirts may resonate with the Harley image, customers were not as attracted to smelling like a motorcycle.
Bic Underwear	Bic is well-known for its disposable products: pens, lighters, and razors. Capitalizing on their ability to cross product categories, Bic began producing underwear.	The concept of buying underwear from a company well-known for disposable pens was confusing and off-putting to consumers.
Bottled Water for Pets	Trying to capitalize on the pet pampering craze, makers of *Thirsty Cat!* and *Thirsty Dog!* launched a line of bottled water for cats and dogs. No longer did owners need to give their pet tap water, instead they could give them a "daily pet drink" in flavors such as Crispy Beef, Tangy Fish, and Grilled Chicken.	Although people do indeed desire to pamper their pets, the idea of purchasing bottled water for them never caught on. The associations generated by their flavors, such as "tangy fish" tasting water, probably did not help either.
Frito Lay Lemonade	To Frito Lay, lemonade seemed like a reasonable enough brand extension. After all, the high salt content of corn chips often leads consumers to search out something to quench their thirst.	Associating a salty snack with a supposed "thirst quencher" did not go over well.
Kellogg's Breakfast Mates	Capitalizing on the convenience market, Kellogg's Breakfast Mates launched a line of cereal products in 1998 that came with cereal, spoon, and milk together.	Sometimes a good idea is poorly executed. The milk was usually warm because it did not require refrigeration and the product was not child-friendly, making its appeal very limited.
Apple Newton	Launched in 1993 with a price tag of more than $700, the Apple Newton was one of the first PDAs, which then led the way for the Palm Pilot, BlackBerry, and iPad.	The Newton concept was ahead of its time. Unfortunately due to its bulky size and ridicule by comedians, the Newton only lasted until 1998.
Colgate Kitchen Entrees	Colgate launched a line of frozen dinners. Apparently the idea was that consumers would enjoy eating a Colgate meal and then using Colgate on their tooth brush afterwards.	The association of toothpaste with a chicken stir-fry was something customers did not find appetizing.
Clairol's Touch of Yogurt Shampoo	Shampoo with a "touch of yogurt" to improve hair quality.	Consumers were not enticed with the idea of washing their hair with yogurt, something Clairol should have known after their "Look of Buttermilk" failed in test markets a few years earlier.

Source: DailyFinance.com, Top 25 Biggest Product Flops of All Time. http://www.dailyfinance.com/photos/top-25-biggest-product-flops-of-all-time/3662621.

Innovators

Innovators are those buyers who want to be the first on the block to have the new product or service. These buyers enjoy taking risks and are regarded as highly knowledgeable. You probably know someone who is an innovator—or perhaps you are one for a particular product or service category. For example, the person who stood in line overnight to be sure to get a ticket for the very first showing of the latest superhero movie is an innovator in that context. Firms that invest in the latest technology, either to use in their products or services or to make the firm more efficient, also are considered innovators. Typically, innovators keep themselves very

EXHIBIT 12.3   Diffusion of Innovation Curve

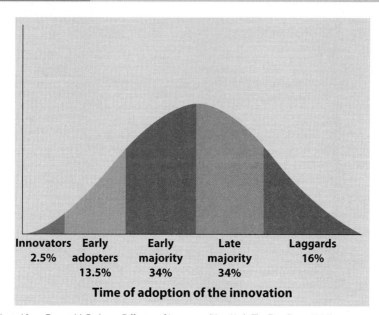

Source: Adapted from Everett M. Rodgers, *Diffusion of Innovation* (New York: The Free Press, 1983).

well informed about the product category by subscribing to trade and specialty magazines, talking to other "experts," visiting product-specific blogs and forums that describe the "coolest new products,"[28] and attending product-related forums, seminars, and special events. Yet innovators represent only about 2.5 percent of the total market for any new product or service.

These innovators are crucial to the success of any new product or service though, because they help the product gain market acceptance. Through talking about and spreading positive word of mouth about the new product, they prove instrumental in bringing in the next adopter category, known as early adopters.[29]

This innovator was the first person to purchase an iPad at this Apple store.

Early Adopters

The second subgroup that begins to use a product or service innovation is **early adopters**. They generally don't like to take as much risk as innovators do but instead wait and purchase the product after careful review. Thus, this market waits for the first reviews of the latest movie before purchasing a ticket, though they likely still go a week or two after it opens. They do not stand in line to grab the first Samsung LED Thin 3D televisions; only after reading the innovators' complaints and praises do they decide whether the new technology is worth the cost.[30] Most of them go ahead and purchase though, because early adopters tend to enjoy novelty and often are regarded as the opinion leaders for particular product categories.

This group, which represents about 13.5 percent of all buyers in the market, spreads the word. As a result, early adopters are crucial for bringing the other three buyer categories to the market. If the early adopter group is relatively small, the number of people who ultimately adopt the innovation likely will also be small.

Early Majority

The **early majority**, which represents approximately 34 percent of the population, is crucial because few new products and services can be profitable until this large group buys them. If the group never becomes large enough, the product or service typically fails.

The early majority group differs in many ways from buyers in the first two stages. Its members don't like to take as much risk and therefore tend to wait until "the bugs" are worked out of a particular product or service. This group probably rents the latest *Pirates of the Caribbean* movie during the first week it comes out on video. Thus, they experience little risk, because all the reviews are in, and their costs are lower because they're renting the movie instead of going to the theater. When early majority customers enter the market, the number of competitors in the marketplace usually also has reached its peak, so these buyers have many different price and quality choices.

When you go see a movie like The Avengers, *are you an early adopter, early majority, majority, late majority, or laggard?*

Late Majority

At 34 percent of the market, the **late majority** is the last group of buyers to enter a new product market. When they do, the product has achieved its full market potential. Perhaps these movie watchers wait until the newest movie is easy to find at the rental store or put it low on their Netflix queue, to be delivered after the other consumers interested in watching it have already seen it. By the time the late majority enters the market, sales tend to level off or may be in decline.

Laggards

Laggards make up roughly 16 percent of the market. These consumers like to avoid change and rely on traditional products until they are no longer available. In some cases, laggards may never adopt a certain product or service. When *Pirates of the Caribbean* eventually shows up on their regular television networks, they are likely to go ahead and watch it.

Using the Diffusion of Innovation Theory

Using the diffusion of innovation theory, firms can predict which types of customers will buy their new product or service immediately after its introduction, as well as later as the product gets more and more accepted by the market. With this knowledge, the firm can develop effective promotion, pricing, and other marketing strategies to push acceptance among each customer group.

When Amazon first introduced its Kindle e-book reader for around $400, it sold out in less than five hours.[31] The Kindle 2 arrived at an initial price of $359. Within six months, Amazon announced a price level below $300, to acknowledge the inroads made by competitors such as Barnes & Noble, Sony, and Apple.[32] Then as the market continued to grow—to approximately 20 million buyers—and Apple's iPad shifted expectations, Amazon plunged ahead with its "iPad killer," the Kindle Fire, priced at just under $200. The plan seems to have been successful; though Amazon does not publish sales numbers, estimates indicate that it sold approximately 6 million Kindle Fire devices within just a few months of its introduction.[33]

However, because different products diffuse at different rates, marketers must work to understand the diffusion curve for each new product and service, as well as the characteristics of the target customers in each stage of the diffusion. For example, the marketing decisions for e-readers are notably different from the parallel decisions for electronic books. When the e-readers first emerged on the market, the price of e-books was a fraction of the price of hardcover versions—a policy that made sense to consumers. But as e-readers have grown increasingly popular and widespread, the price of e-books has become comparable, and in some cases more expensive than, the price of the hardcover versions.[34] Moreover, the speed with which products or services diffuse depends on several characteristics. In the next sections, we'll look at how Apple has responded to Amazon's Kindle and the e-reader and tablet market as a whole with its iPad.

Relative Advantage If a product or service is perceived to be better than substitutes, then the diffusion will be relatively quick. Instead of offering just an e-reader, Apple has developed a multi-purpose "tablet" device (the iPad). When launched, the iPad had several relative advantages, including a touch screen, a vibrant and large color screen, access to various games and apps, and the ability to watch videos and listen to music.[35]

The Chinese version of Web browser Firefox has different features than its Western counterpart.

Compatibility A diffusion process may be faster or slower, depending on various consumer features, including international cultural differences. For example, the Chinese version of web browser Firefox has different features than its Western counterpart because research indicated that Chinese users surf the Internet differently. The Firefox China Edition has more mouse-based controls, like a double-click to close a tab on the browser, as well as a drop-down button on the toolbar for a calculator, screenshot grabber, and image editor.[36] In contrast to Firefox, the iPad is heavily criticized for lack of compatibility. Adobe's Flash, a format that it purports 75 percent of web videos are encoded in, does not work on the iPad. In response to these criticisms, Apple has explained their choice to use HTML5 (over Flash) as being an open source format which they consider the future of the Internet.[37]

Observability When products are easily observed, their benefits or uses are easily communicated to others, which enhances the diffusion process. Consumers seeing their friends using the iPad, seeing the devices on television or on YouTube, or reading about them in the deluge of media coverage surrounding each iPad release may be convinced to purchase one as well. In contrast, since people may not want to talk about their Botox treatments to reduce wrinkles, the use of this product is less easily observed by others and therefore diffused more slowly.

Complexity and Trialability Products that are relatively less complex are also relatively easy to try. These products will generally diffuse more quickly and lead to greater/faster adoption than those that are not so easy to try. For example, most customers who may be interested in purchasing a new tablet know that they can go to any Apple store and immediately try it there in the store. The options for trying a Kindle are a little more complex. Due to the lack of Amazon stores, consumers may not be aware that they can try one at Best Buy. But even the consumers that go to a Best Buy to try one often run into an availability problem—whereas Apple stores may have dozens of iPads for customers to try, electronics stores typically have just a few floor models.

The diffusion of innovation theory thus comes into play in the immediate and long-term aftermath of a new product or service introduction. But before the introduction, firms must actually develop those new offerings. In the next section, we detail the process by which most firms develop new products and services and how they initially introduce them into the market.

CHECK YOURSELF

1. What are the five groups on the diffusion of innovation curve?
2. What factors enhance the diffusion of a good or service?

L03 Describe the various stages involved in developing a new product or service.

HOW FIRMS DEVELOP NEW PRODUCTS

The new product development process begins with the generation of new product ideas and culminates in the launch of a new product and the evaluation of its success. The stages of the new product development process, along with the important objectives of each stage, are summarized in Exhibit 12.4.

Idea Generation

To generate ideas for new products, a firm can use its own internal research and development (R&D) efforts, collaborate with other firms and institutions, license technology from research-intensive firms, brainstorm, research competitors'

EXHIBIT 12.4   The Product Development Process

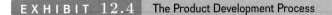

Idea generation	Concept testing	Product development	Market testing	Product launch	Evaluation of results
Development of viable new product ideas.	Testing the new product idea among a set of potential customers.	Development of prototypes and/or the product.	Testing the actual products in a few test markets.	Full-scale commercialization of the product.	Analysis of the performance of the new product and making appropriate modifications.

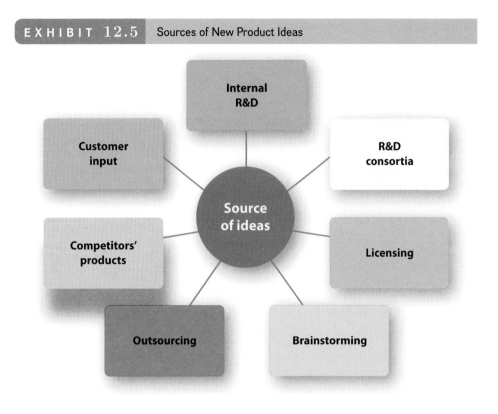

EXHIBIT 12.5   Sources of New Product Ideas

Internal R&D

R&D consortia

Customer input

Source of ideas

Licensing

Competitors' products

Outsourcing

Brainstorming

products and services, and/or conduct consumer research; see Exhibit 12.5. Firms that want to be pioneers rely more extensively on R&D efforts, whereas those that tend to adopt a follower strategy are more likely to scan the market for ideas. Let's look at each of these idea sources.

Internal Research and Development Many firms have their own R&D departments, in which scientists work to solve complex problems and develop new ideas.[38] Historically, firms such as IBM in the computer industry, Black and Decker in the consumer goods industry, 3M in the industrial goods industry, and Merck

From where do you think the idea for a waterproof tablet from Fujitsu was derived? Internal R&R, R&D consortia, licensing, brainstorming, outsourcing, competitor's products, customer input, or a combination?

and Pfizer in the pharmaceuticals industry have relied on R&D development efforts for their new products. In other industries, such as software, music, and motion pictures, product development efforts also tend to come from internal ideas and R&D financial investments.

The product development costs for these firms are quite high, and the resulting new product or service has a good chance of being a technological or market breakthrough. Firms expect such products to generate enough revenue and profits to make the costs of R&D worthwhile. R&D investments generally are considered continuous investments, so firms may lose money on a few new products. In the long run though, these firms are betting that a few extremely successful new products, often known as blockbusters, can generate enough revenues and profits to cover the losses from other introductions that might not fare so well.

Some global firms also are taking an approach called "reverse innovation," as we discussed in Chapter 7. They turn to subsidiaries in less developed markets for new product ideas. From its Shanghai research center, Coca-Cola developed Minute Maid Pulpy, a new juice drink that the corporation has moved into 19 countries and is now worth more than $1 billion. Levi's Denizen brand got its start in India and China, where the company worked on ideas for producing more affordable jeans. In the U.S. market, Denizen jeans sell for about half the cost of a pair of regular Levi's.[39]

R&D Consortia   In recent years, more and more firms have been joining consortia, or groups of other firms and institutions, possibly including government and educational institutions, to explore new ideas or obtain solutions for developing new products. Here, the R&D investments come from the group as a whole, and the participating firms and institutions share the results.

In many cases, the consortia involve pharmaceutical or high-tech members, whose research costs can run into the millions—too much for a single company to bear. The National Institutes of Health (NIH) sponsors medical foundations to conduct research to treat rare diseases. The research then gets disseminated to the medical community, thus encouraging the development of drugs and therapies more quickly and at a lower cost than would be possible if the research were privately funded. The U.S. cable industry has initiated its "CableLabs–Energy Lab" consortium to find ways to improve the energy efficiency of cable set-top boxes and develop more advanced cable services, such as better "sleep" settings, to promote other forms of energy conservation.[40]

Licensing   For many other scientific and technological products, firms buy the rights to use the technology or ideas from other research-intensive firms through a licensing agreement. This approach saves the high costs of in-house R&D, but it means that the firm is banking on a solution that already exists but has not been marketed. Some of the largest recent licensing deals in the pharmaceutical industry are for potential weight-loss solutions. In two separate deals, one worth $1.4 billion and another worth $1.1 billion, two big pharmaceutical firms licensed the marketing rights for new products developed by small biotechnology firms to combat obesity.[41] Yet neither drug had received FDA approval at the time of the deals!

Brainstorming   Firms often engage in brainstorming sessions during which a group works together to generate ideas. One of the key characteristics of a brainstorming session is that no idea can be immediately accepted or rejected. The moderator of the session may channel participants' attention to specific product features and attributes, performance expectations, or packaging. Only at the end of the session do the members vote on the best ideas or combinations of ideas. Those ideas that receive the most votes are carried forward to the next stage of the product development process.

Outsourcing   In some cases, companies have trouble moving through these steps alone, which prompts them to turn to outside firms like IDEO, a design firm based

Balance Body partnered with IDEO to develop a less-intimidating, more-user-friendly reformer to be used with Pilates.

in Palo Alto, California. IDEO offers not new products but rather a stellar service that helps clients generate new product and service ideas in industries such as health care, toys, and computers. IDEO employs anthropologists, graphic designers, engineers, and psychologists whose special skills help foster creativity and innovation. As exercise is becoming more and more popular, companies are looking for ways to capitalize on the beginner's market. Balanced Body is a company that makes and sells reformers to be used with Pilates. A reformer is a device that helps Pilates participants develop good alignment, core strength, and flexibility. When Balanced Body did research and found that people starting Pilates found the reformers that were currently on the market to be too intimidating, they partnered with IDEO to develop a reformer that had better user experience while at the same time maintaining the high-level of functionality their products engender.[42] In an eight-week time period, IDEO created a redesigned model with fewer wheels, while improving functionality and adjustability of the product and at the same time reducing the cost of the machine.[43]

Competitors' Products A new product entry by a competitor may trigger a market opportunity for a firm, which can use reverse engineering to understand the competitor's product and then bring an improved version to market. **Reverse engineering** involves taking apart a product, analyzing it, and creating an improved product that does not infringe on the competitor's patents, if any exist. This copycat approach to new product development is widespread and practiced by even the most research-intensive firms. Copycat consumer goods show up in apparel, grocery and drugstore products, as well as in technologically more complex products like automobiles and computers, as Social and Mobile Marketing 12.1 notes.

Customer Input Listening to the customer in both B2B and B2C markets is essential for successful idea generation.[44] Because customers for B2B products are relatively few, firms can follow their use of products closely and solicit suggestions and ideas to improve those products either by using a formal approach, such as focus groups, interviews, or surveys, or through more informal discussions. The firm's design and development team then works on these suggestions, sometimes in consultation with the customer. This joint effort between the selling firm and the customer significantly increases the probability that the customer eventually will buy the new product.

Social and Mobile Marketing 12.1　　When Microsoft Plays Catch-Up

Microsoft is one of the most innovative companies of all time. After revolutionizing the home computer industry, it set out to be a leader in the information technology home entertainment fields. It seems like not a year ever goes by without something new from the brainchild of Bill Gates.

But one area in which Microsoft has been behind the curve is the search engine market. Google, with its nearly 80 percent market share and massive name recognition, is in no real danger from competitors, including Bing.com, the newest Microsoft offering. But Bing is challenging Yahoo.com for the remainder of the market. Perhaps most important, it is distinguishing itself by providing more frequent updates and feature additions than the other search engines. Consumers benefit overall, because Bing is forcing competitors to improve their offering to keep pace with Microsoft or prevent it from stealing market share from them.

Its efforts have paid off somewhat: Bing now attracts approximately 14 percent of all searches by U.S. users. These gains come mostly at the expense of other competitors, such as Yahoo. Google maintains a remarkably high share. And the costs of its copycat efforts meant that the division responsible for Bing lost $2.56 billion in the most recent fiscal year.[45]

To differentiate itself better, Bing is being promoted as a "decision engine" rather than a search engine. It integrates Foursquare, a location-based phone application, into Bing Maps results. Users can focus in on a particular area, such as South Boston, which means Bing can act like an integrative day planner and list the best things to do in that area. It is working on developing a desktop application, and Bing links seamlessly with Facebook to show users which search outcome their friends like best.[46] Despite Microsoft's problems developing search engines, Bing suggests it intends to stay aggressive in this market.

Customer input in B2C markets comes from a variety of sources. In some cases, consumers may not expressly demand a new product, though their behavior demonstrates their desire for it. After analyzing its sales data, Walmart realized that the majority of its customers always or often buy store brands rather than national brands. So it developed more varied and appealing versions of its Great Value store brand, including all-natural ice cream in innovative flavors like cake batter and mocha mud.[47] Staples also observed how customers use its products in their homes. For example, most people open their mail in the kitchen, but then wait to shred it until they get into their home office. Using this information, Staples designed the Mailmate, a stainless steel shredder that looks like a kitchen appliance and sits on the kitchen counter, to help customers shred their mail instantly after opening it.[48]

Staples observed how customers opened their mail in the kitchen when it developed the Mailmate shredder to look like a kitchen appliance.

Companies also realize that their customers are on the web—writing customer reviews on retailers' websites, talking about their experiences on Yelp.com or Twitter. By monitoring feedback through these online communities, companies can get better ideas about new products or necessary changes to existing ones, as Social and Mobile Marketing 12.2 describes. Many companies also proactively develop their own online communities to focus the conversations around topics in which they are interested.

A particularly successful customer input approach is to analyze **lead users**, those innovative product users who modify existing products according to their own ideas to suit their specific needs.[49] If lead users customize a firm's products, other customers might wish to do so as well. Thus, studying lead users helps the firm understand general market trends that might be just on the horizon. Manufacturers and retailers of fashion products often spot new trends by noticing how innovative trendsetters have altered their clothing and shoes. Designers of high-fashion jeans distress their products in different ways depending on signals they pick

Social and Mobile Marketing 12.2 — From Luxury & Expensive to Fast & Casual

Faced with a severe economic downturn, the luxury chocolatier Godiva set out to determine how its customers were changing too. Godiva's premium products generally had been purchased and gifted only on special occasions. But in a members-only online community, called Chocolate Talk, Godiva asked customers for their insights, in the hope of discovering where and when they buy chocolate—Godiva or any other brand.[50]

The results? People buy Godiva for special occasions for others whom they care about or want to impress, especially during the holiday season and for their birthdays. But true chocolate connoisseurs still expressed their preference for premium chocolate, as opposed to lower end brands. Because Godiva sells in mall boutiques, purchasing the chocolates requires a special trip to the mall—acceptable for a special occasion but not for an impulse treat. Therefore, when chocolate lovers wanted to buy a treat for themselves, they bought premium chocolate from the grocery or drug store where they shopped regularly.

Buying chocolate for themselves and eating it all prompted feelings of guilt in a lot of these community members. Thus Godiva realized that people enjoyed sharing chocolate with co-workers. In this setting, the individually wrapped offerings, such as Lindor Truffles and Ghirardelli Squares, were very appealing.

The company put all these insights together to arrive at a new product concept: premium chocolate, available in regular retail channels such as grocery stores, presented as individually wrapped treats. In so doing, Godiva also was encouraging a new consumer behavior for its customers: casual purchases of luxury Godiva chocolates.

The new Godiva Gems, stand-up bags of individually wrapped truffles, sell for $4.99 at drug stores and grocery stores. The extensive, technology-enabled market research that Godiva undertook in developing this product led to its widespread and great appeal. It already has surpassed Lindt's market share at CVS with 20 percent of the category. Godiva Gems may still sound luxurious, but they are not just for special occasions, nor just for others. They encourage treats for oneself, on a more frequent basis.

Research with Godiva's online community provided the information necessary to develop its new product concept: premium chocolate available in regular retail channels, such as grocery stores.

---

up "on the street." One season, jeans appear with whiskers, the next season they have holes, the next, paint spots.

At the end of the idea-generation stage, the firm should have several ideas that it can take forward to the next stage: concept testing.

Concept Testing

Ideas with potential are developed further into **concepts**, which in this context refer to brief written descriptions of the product; its technology, working principles, and forms; and what customer needs it would satisfy.[51] A concept might also include visual images of what the product would look like.

Concept testing refers to the process in which a concept statement is presented to potential buyers or users to obtain their reactions. These reactions enable the developer to estimate the sales value of the product or service concept, possibly make changes to enhance its sales value, and determine whether the idea is worth further development.[52] If the concept fails to meet customers' expectations, it is doubtful it would succeed if it were to be produced and marketed. Because concept testing occurs very early in the new product introduction process, even before a real product has been made, it helps the firm avoid the costs of unnecessary product development.

These innovative consumers are called lead users *because they modify existing products according to their own ideas to suit their specific needs.*

The concept for an electric scooter might be written as follows:

The product is a lightweight electric scooter that can be easily folded and taken with you inside a building or on public transportation. The scooter weighs 25 pounds. It travels at speeds of up to 15 miles per hour and can go about 12 miles on a single charge. The scooter can be recharged in about two hours from a standard electric outlet. The scooter is easy to ride and has simple controls—just an accelerator button and a brake. It sells for $299.[53]

Concept testing progresses along the research techniques described in Chapter 10. The firm likely starts with exploratory research, such as in-depth interviews or focus groups, to test the concept, after which it can undertake conclusive research through Internet or mall-intercept surveys. Video clips on the Internet might show a virtual prototype and the way it works so that potential customers can evaluate the product or service. In a mall-intercept survey, an interviewer would provide a description of the concept to the respondent and then ask several questions to obtain his or her feedback.

The most important question pertains to the respondent's purchase intentions if the product or service were made available. Marketers also should ask whether the product would satisfy a need that other products currently are not meeting. Depending on the type of product or service, researchers might also ask about the expected frequency of purchase, how much customers would buy, whether they would buy it for themselves or as a gift, when they would buy, and whether the price information (if provided) indicates a good value. In addition, marketers usually collect some information about the customers so they can analyze which consumer segments are likely to be most interested in the product.

Some concepts never make it past concept testing stage, particularly if respondents seem uninterested. Those that do receive high evaluations from potential consumers, however, move on to the next step, product development.

Product Development

Product development or **product design** entails a process of balancing various engineering, manufacturing, marketing, and economic considerations to develop a product's form and features or a service's features. An engineering team develops a product prototype that is based on research findings from the previous concept testing step, as well as their own knowledge about materials and technology. A **prototype** is the first physical form or service description of a new product, still in rough or tentative form, that has the same properties as a new product but is produced through different manufacturing processes—sometimes even crafted individually.[54]

Product prototypes are usually tested through alpha and beta testing. In **alpha testing**, the firm attempts to determine whether the product will perform according to its design and whether it satisfies the need for which it was intended.[55] Rather than use potential consumers, alpha tests occur in the firm's R&D department. For instance, Ben & Jerry's Ice Cream alpha tests all its proposed new flavors on its own (lucky) employees at its corporate headquarters in Vermont.

Many people, consumer groups, and governmental agencies are concerned when alpha testing involves tests on animals, particularly when it comes to pharmaceuticals and cosmetics. Ethical and Societal Dilemma 12.1 discusses these concerns in the United States and the European Union.

Ben & Jerry's Ice Cream uses alpha testing with its own employees to make sure its products have the taste and feel they should.

Ethical and Societal Dilemma 12.1   Should Firms Test on Animals?[56]

Product testing on animals has been a primary issue for animal rights activists for years. As public opposition to animal testing increases, so do many companies' declarations that they "do not test products on animals." However, such statements can be misleading because even though the whole product may not have been tested on animals, the individual ingredients may have been. To help clarify any confusion, companies can apply to the Coalition for Consumer Information on Cosmetics (CCIC), a national group formed by eight animal welfare group members such as the United States Humane Association and the Doris Day Animal League, and be certified as "cruelty free." They then can purchase the trademarked Leaping Bunny Logo from CCIC for use on their labels.

One of the founding principles of The Body Shop, and one that has resonated well with its customers, is that its products are free of animal testing. Another major cosmetics manufacturer, Procter & Gamble, has eliminated animal testing on more than 80 percent of its products. It uses a combination of in vitro testing, computer modeling, and historical data to determine the safety of new products and ingredients. These methods are more expensive than more traditional methods, but P&G claims that the results are better. If performed correctly, new chemicals can either be dropped from consideration or pushed forward in as little as three days compared to the six months previously required for animal testing.

However, animal welfare groups continue to push P&G and other firms to stop the use of animal testing altogether. People

for the Ethical Treatment of Animals (PETA) publicly cites companies it accuses of engaging in animal testing and other activities considered to be inhumane, and praises those that do not. PETA's efforts have caused firms like Hugo Boss, H&M, and Liz Claiborne to stop buying their wool from Australia because some Australian sheep farmers shear their sheep's wool in inhumane ways.

The European Union has passed a ban on animal testing altogether. Beginning in 2009, any cosmetic tested on animals, even in other parts of the world, cannot be sold in the European Union. However, the cosmetics industry is worried that this ban will not only affect their companies' sales but also their customers' ability to find the products they want. The EU cosmetics industry successfully lobbied for an extension on certain areas of toxicity testing to provide more time to find alternatives. The cosmetics industry believes it will be difficult to find alternative testing methods in time, and if they cannot, it will have fewer ingredients to make the products consumers want.

The issues involved in animal testing are complex. At the broadest level, should firms be allowed to develop products that customers want, even if there is some potential harm to the environment or to those animals that share the environment with humans? More specifically, should firms be allowed to test products on animals, even when those products are not specifically designed to improve the health and well-being of their human users? Does the testing that is performed endanger the lives or health of the animals?

Activists of the People for the Ethical Treatment of Animals (PETA) participate in a protest against animal slaughter near a mall where Hermes—the French luxury goods company—has a store in Jakarta, Indonesia. PETA demanded Hermes stop selling exotic animal skin products and released gruesome videos of reptiles being skinned alive in Indonesia.

In contrast, **beta testing** uses potential consumers, who examine the product prototype in a "real use" setting to determine its functionality, performance, potential problems, and other issues specific to its use. The firm might develop several prototype products that it gives to users, then survey those users to determine whether the product worked as intended and identify any issues that need resolution.

Household products manufacturer Kimberly-Clark uses virtual testing in the beta-testing phase of its product development process. The consumer goods company uses a virtual store aisle that mimics a real-life shopping experience by creating a realistic picture of the interior of the store. A retina-tracking device records the movement of a test customer who "shops" the virtual aisle of a store and chooses certain products to investigate further in the virtual simulation. Thus, consumer companies can demonstrate the likely success, or failure, of a product without actually having to produce it for a market and, potentially, expose its secrets to competitors.[57]

Market Testing

The firm has developed its new product or service and tested the prototypes. Now it must test the market for the new product with a trial batch of products. These tests can take two forms: premarket testing or test marketing.

Premarket Tests Firms conduct **premarket tests** before they actually bring a product or service to market to determine how many customers will try and then continue to use the product or service according to a small group of potential consumers. One popular proprietary premarket test version is called Nielsen BASES. During the test, potential customers are exposed to the marketing mix variables, such as the advertising, then surveyed and given a sample of the product to try.[58] After some period of time, during which the potential customers try the product, they are surveyed about whether they would buy/use the product again. This second survey provides an estimation of the probability of a consumer's repeat purchase. From these data, the firm generates a sales estimate for the new product that enables it to decide whether to introduce the product, abandon it, redesign it before introduction, or revise the marketing plan. An early evaluation of this sort—that is, before the product is introduced to the whole market—saves marketers the costs of a nationwide launch if the product fails.

Sometimes firms simulate a product or service introduction, in which case potential customers view the advertising of various currently available products or services along with advertising for the new product or service. They receive money to buy the product or service from a simulated environment, such as a mock web page or store, and respond to a survey after they make their purchases. This test thus can determine the effectiveness of a firm's advertising as well as the expected trial rates for the new product.

Test Marketing A method of determining the success potential of a new product, **test marketing** introduces the offering to a limited geographical area (usually a few cities) prior to a national launch. Test marketing is a strong predictor of product success because the firm can study actual purchase behavior, which is more reliable than a simulated test. A test marketing effort uses all the elements of the marketing mix: It includes promotions like advertising and coupons, just as if the product were being introduced nationally, and the product appears in targeted retail outlets, with appropriate pricing. On the basis of the results of the test marketing, the firm can estimate demand for the entire market.

Test marketing costs more and takes longer than premarket tests, which may provide an advantage to competitors that could get a similar or better product to market first without test marketing. For this reason, some firms might launch new products without extensive consumer testing and rely instead on intuition, instincts, and guts.[59]

The new Nano introduced in India costs about $2,000. It weighs less than a Honda Civic, gets 56 miles per gallon, and takes 23 seconds to get to its top speed of 60 miles per hour.

Product Launch

If the market testing returns with positive results, the firm is ready to introduce the product to the entire market. This most critical step in the new product introduction requires tremendous financial resources and extensive coordination of all aspects of the marketing mix. For example, for Tata Motors' Indian launch of its inexpensive (around $2,000), tiny Nano automobile (which we described in Chapter 8), it had to limit its production to just 500,000 cars per year, though it knew the market would be larger. It simply could not afford to bankroll a wider rollout.[60] For any firm, if the new product launch is a failure, it may be difficult for the product—and perhaps the firm—to recover.

So what does a product launch involve? First, on the basis of the research it has gathered on consumer perceptions, the tests it has conducted, and competitive considerations, the firm confirms its target market (or markets) and decides how the product will be positioned. Then the firm finalizes the remaining marketing mix variables for the new product, including the marketing budget for the first year.[61]

Promotion The test results help the firm determine an appropriate integrated marketing communications strategy.[62] Promotion for new products is required at each link in the supply chain. If the products are not sold and stocked by retailers, no amount of promotion to consumers will sell the products. **Trade promotions**, which are promotions to wholesalers or retailers to get them to purchase the new products, often combine introductory price promotions, special events, and personal selling. **Introductory price promotions** are limited-duration, lower-than-normal prices designed to provide retailers with an incentive to try the products. Manufacturers may run a special event in the form of a special display in a grocery aisle, an introductory celebration, or a party in conjunction with an interesting event like the Academy Awards.

Another outlet for exposing buyers to new products is a **trade show**, which is a temporary concentration of manufacturers that provides retailers the opportunity to view what is available and new in the marketplace. The fashion world's equivalent to trade shows are fashion weeks in which fashion manufacturers meet with retailers and have elaborate runway shows to introduce their new products. Finally, as in many B2B sales situations, personal selling may be the most efficient way to get retailers to purchase their products.

Manufacturers also use promotion to generate demand for new products with consumers. If manufacturers can create demand for the products among consumers, they will go to retailers asking for it (pull demand; see Chapter 19), thus further inducing retailers to carry the products. These promotions are often coupled with short-term price reductions, coupons, or rebates. Sometimes manufacturers promote new products in advance of the product launch to create excitement with potential customers, as well as to measure the likely demand so they have appropriate supply available. Automobile and motorcycle manufacturers, for instance, advertise their new products months before they are available on the dealers' floors.

For products that are somewhat complex or conceptually new, marketers may need to provide for more consumer education about the product's benefits than they would for simpler and more familiar products. The quantum dot technology that is being developed to improve the LCD screens on televisions, computers, and mobile phones is not something that most consumers understand. But marketers can encourage their adoption by highlighting the clearly evident appeal of energy efficiency, longer battery life, and more vibrant color offered by the innovative technology.[63] In addition, technical support staff, like Apple's Geniuses, often must be trained to answer customer questions that may arise immediately after the launch of a new technical innovation.

Place The manufacturer coordinates the delivery and storage of the new products with its retailers to assure that it is available for sale when the customer wants it, at the stores the customer is expecting to find it, and in sufficient quantities to meet demand. Manufacturers work with their retailers on decisions such as:

- Should the merchandise be stored at retailers' distribution centers or distributed directly to stores?
- What initial and fill-in quantities should be shipped?
- Should the manufacturer be involved in reordering decisions?
- Should the merchandise be individually packaged so it is easy to display in the stores?
- Should price stickers be affixed on the merchandise at the factory or at the store?
- Should the manufacturer be involved in the maintenance of the merchandise once in the store?

Price Like the promotion of new products, setting prices is a supply chain–wide decision. Manufacturers must decide at what price they would like products to sell to consumers on the basis of the factors to be discussed in Chapters 14 and 15. They often encourage retailers to sell at a specified price known as the **manufacturer's suggested retail price (MSRP)**. Although retailers often don't abide by the MSRP, manufacturers can withhold benefits such as paying for all or part of a promotion or even refusing to deliver merchandise to noncomplying retailers. It is sometimes easier to start with a higher MSRP and then over time lower it than it is to introduce the new product at a low price and then try to raise the price.

When setting the MSRP, manufacturers also consider the price at which the new products are sold to the retailers. The retailers not only need to make a profit on each sale, but they may also receive a **slotting allowance** from the manufacturer, which is a fee paid simply to get new products into stores or to gain more or better shelf space for their products.

Timing The timing of the launch may be important, depending on the product.[64] Hollywood studios typically release movies targeted toward general audiences (i.e., those rated G or PG) during the summer when children are out of school. New automobile models traditionally are released for sale during September, and fashion products are launched just before the season of the year for which they are intended.

Coca-Cola may never totally outlive its failed New Coke product introduction, but its latest innovation, the Freestyle machine, seems like a good step in that direction. With this introduction, Coke has set out to reinvent the fountain experience and give customers more choice. The result has been a product success for all stakeholders.

For consumers, the Freestyle vending machines offer access to any combination of caffeine, flavor, and calories they prefer. For example, there are 90 different caffeine-free options on every machine!

For supply chain partners, such as restaurants and convenience stores, the Freestyle machines offer high-tech capabilities. Computer software connects every machine to a global supply chain, which enables immediate replenishment and the virtual elimination of out-of-stock situations. It also gives them a new revenue stream.

For Coca-Cola, the Freestyle software tracks exactly what was ordered on each machine. It thus not only knows what machines to refill but also learns about which products customers prefer in which markets. It then can target its advertising ever more precisely, based on totally accurate

preference information that the consumers provide themselves.

For society as a whole, Freestyle machines embody Coca-Cola's "Live Positively" slogan. The cartridges in the machines are LEED gold certified. LEED stands for Leadership in Energy and Environmental Design. LEED certification provides independent, third-party verification that a building, home, community, or product was designed and built using strategies aimed at achieving high performance in key areas of human and environmental health: sustainable site development, water savings, energy efficiency, materials selection and indoor environmental quality.[66] The syrup that goes into beverages poured from the Freestyle machine is highly concentrated, which makes the product 30 percent less bulky than bottled beverages. The outcomes include not just cost savings on shipping for the supply chain but also a reduction in the environmental footprint.

The Coca-Cola vending machine offeres customers any combination of caffeine, flavors, and calories.

Evaluation of Results

After the product has been launched, marketers must undertake a critical post-launch review to determine whether the product and its launch were a success or failure and what additional resources or changes to the marketing mix are needed, if any. Many firms use panel data to improve the probability of success during the test marketing phase of a new product introduction. The consumer panel data is collected by panelists scanning in their receipts using a home scanning device. This information is used to measure individual household first-time trials and repeat purchases. Through such data, market demand can be estimated, so the firm can figure out how best to adjust its marketing mix. Some products never make it out of the introduction stage, especially those that seem almost laughable in retrospect. Bottled water for pets? Harley-Davidson perfume?[67]

For those products that do move on though, firms can measure the success of a new product by three interrelated factors: (1) its satisfaction of technical requirements, such as performance; (2) customer acceptance; and (3) its satisfaction of the firm's financial requirements, such as sales and profits.[68] If the product is not performing sufficiently well, poor customer acceptance will result, which in turn leads to poor financial performance.

The new product development process, when followed rationally and sequentially, helps avoid such domino-type failures. Coca-Cola has learned this recommendation well, as Superior Service 12.1 describes. The product life cycle, discussed in the next section, helps marketers manage their products' marketing mix during and after introduction.

LO4 Explain the product life cycle.

THE PRODUCT LIFE CYCLE

The **product life cycle** defines the stages that products move through as they enter, get established in, and ultimately leave the marketplace. It thereby offers marketers a starting point for their strategy planning. The stages of the life cycle often reflect marketplace trends, such as the healthy lifestyle trend that today places organic and green product categories in their growth stages. Exhibit 12.6 illustrates a typical product life cycle, including the industry sales and profits over time. In their life cycles, products pass through four stages: introduction, growth, maturity, and decline. When the product category first launches, its products initiate the **introduction stage**. In the **growth stage**, the product gains acceptance, demand and sales increase, and more competitors emerge in the product category. In the **maturity stage**, industry sales reach their peak, so firms try to rejuvenate their products by adding new features or repositioning them. If these efforts succeed, the product achieves new life.[69] If not, it goes into **decline** and eventually exits the market.

Not every product follows the same life cycle curve. Many products, such as home appliances, stay in the maturity stage for a very long time. Manufacturers may add features to dishwashers and washing machines, but the mature product category remains essentially the same and seems unlikely to enter the decline stage unless some innovative, superior solution comes along to replace them.

The product life cycle offers a useful tool for managers to analyze the types of strategies that may be required over the life of their products. Even the strategic emphasis of a firm and its marketing mix (four Ps) strategies can be adapted from

EXHIBIT 12.6   Product Life Cycle

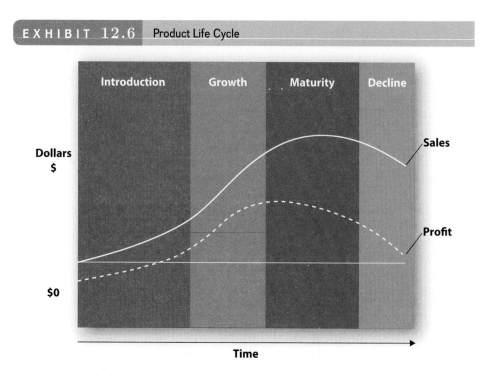

EXHIBIT 12.7	Characteristics of Different Stages of the Product Life Cycle			
	Introduction	Growth	Maturity	Decline
Sales	Low	Rising	Peak	Declining
Profits	Negative or low	Rapidly rising	Peak to declining	Declining
Typical consumers	Innovators	Early adopters and early majority	Late majority	Laggards
Competitors (number of firms and products)	One or few	Few but increasing	High number of competitors and competitive products	Low number of competitors and products

insights about the characteristics of each stage of the cycle, as we summarize in Exhibit 12.7.

Let's look at each of these stages in depth.

Introduction Stage

The introduction stage for a new, innovative product or service usually starts with a single firm, and innovators are the ones to try the new offering. Some new-to-the-world products and services that defined their own product category and industry include the telephone (invented by Alexander Graham Bell in 1876), the transistor semiconductor (Bell Laboratories in 1947), the Walkman portable cassette player (Sony in 1979), the Internet browser (Netscape in 1994), personal digital assistant (Palm in 1996), iTunes (Apple in 2001), Facebook (2004), Blu-Ray (Sony in 2006) and iPad (Apple in 2010). Sensing the viability and commercialization possibilities of some market-creating new product, other firms soon enter the market with similar or improved products at lower prices. The same pattern holds for less innovative products like apparel, music, and even a new soft drink flavor. The introduction stage is characterized by initial losses to the firm due to its high start-up costs and low levels of sales revenue as the product begins to take off. If the product is successful, firms may start seeing profits toward the end of this stage.

Growth Stage

The growth stage of the product life cycle is marked by a growing number of product adopters, rapid growth in industry sales, and increases in both the number of competitors and the number of available product versions.[70] The market becomes more segmented and consumer preferences more varied, which increases the potential for new markets or new uses of the product or service.[71]

Also during the growth stage, firms attempt to reach new consumers by studying their preferences and producing different product variations—varied colors, styles, or features—which enable them to segment the market more precisely. The goal of this segmentation is to ride the rising sales trend and firmly establish the firm's brand, so as not to be outdone by competitors. For example, many food manufacturers are working hard to become the first brand that consumers think of when they consider organic products. Del Monte was the first of the major canned vegetable sellers to go organic, releasing organic versions of its tomatoes, green beans, corn, and sweet peas, along with an organic chicken broth product under its College Inn line. The cans feature bold "organic" banners across the front and promise that no pesticides were used to produce the food items. Even though Del Monte products have been around for over 100 years, in this growth category, the company is a newer entrant in the organic market, so it must work to establish its distinctive appeal.[72]

As firms ride the crest of increasing industry sales, profits in the growth stage also rise because of the economies of scale associated with manufacturing and marketing costs, especially promotion and advertising. At the same time, firms that

Does adding crushed diamonds to hair products enhance their value?

To generate sales in a mature world, Dial Corporation has developed a laundry sheet that includes detergent, fabric softener, and antistatic agents to appeal to a new market segment that wants a premium product while saving money, without cannibalizing its core customer groups.

have not yet established a stronghold in the market, even in narrow segments, may decide to exit in what is referred to as an "industry shakeout."

Maturity Stage

The maturity stage of the product life cycle is characterized by the adoption of the product by the late majority and intense competition for market share among firms. Marketing costs (e.g., promotion, distribution) increase as these firms vigorously defend their market share against competitors. They also face intense competition on price as the average price of the product falls substantially compared with the shifts during the previous two stages of the life cycle. Lower prices and increased marketing costs begin to erode the profit margins for many firms. In the later phases of the maturity stage, the market has become quite saturated, and practically all potential customers for the product have already adopted the product. Such saturated markets are prevalent in developed countries.

In the United States, most consumer packaged goods found in grocery and discount stores are already in the maturity stage. For example, in the well-established hair care product market, consumer goods companies constantly search for innovations to set themselves apart and extend the time in which they maintain their position in the maturity stage. Nivea added actual, ground up diamonds to its Diamond Gloss line. Women who wash and condition their hair with Diamond Gloss products are promised "added brilliance" and "light reflection," making their hair seem shinier and healthier. The crushed up diamonds do nothing to improve hair health, and the company is careful to avoid making that claim. Rather, it promotes the idea that the diamonds themselves, when applied to hair, will make it shine like a diamond would.[73]

As this example shows, firms pursue various strategies during this stage to increase their customer base and/or defend their market share. Other tactics include entry into new markets and market segments and developing new products.

Entry into New Markets or Market Segments   Because the market is saturated at this point, firms may attempt to enter new geographical markets, including international markets (as we discussed in Chapter 8), that may be less saturated. For example, Whirlpool manufactures washing machines for Brazil, China, and India that it prices lower than those it sells in the United States to attract the large consumer base of lower-income consumers in these countries.[74] In many developing economies, the large and growing proportion of middle-class households is just beginning to buy the home, kitchen, and entertainment appliances that have been fairly standard in U.S. households for several decades. In India alone, roughly 487 million middle-class consumers spend over $100 billion a year on a variety of consumer products.[75]

However, even in mature markets, firms may be able to find new market segments. Laundry may be a mundane chore that most people dislike, but it is also a huge marketing opportunity. New product development tends to focus on the detergent delivery methods. So in the United States, where laundry tablets have never been very popular (Americans prefer to pour their liquid detergent and thus control the amount they add to the wash basket), Dial has developed a laundry sheet, similar to the dryer sheets used as fabric softeners. This 3-in-1 product includes laundry detergent, fabric softener, and antistatic agents.[76] It is less expensive than purchasing premium brand versions of the three items. Dial hopes to appeal to a new market segment that

Adding Value 12.3   New Options for Opening Up the Greeting Card Market

As more and more consumers just hit the "send" button to deliver greetings to their friends and families, Hallmark is looking for ways to reposition itself to facilitate this new type of connection. Fear not: It has no plans to abandon traditional paper cards and envelopes. But Hallmark's new product portfolio includes products that grant consumers creative input, greater convenience, and digital options. For example, customizable greeting cards, plates, and interactive storybooks can be personalized for various recipients, and new greeting applications are available for both iPod and iPad users.[77]

The company is also rethinking the very meaning of "greetings," with the notion that any day can—and should—be special. Research has documented the importance of emotional connectedness for people's physical health and longevity, and marketing studies show that that people want to celebrate more of the smaller, often unnoticed moments. As emotion-filled e-mails and text messages seemingly replace more formal ways of saying "I love you," Hallmark needed to meet and resonate with shifting consumer habits and preferences.

The "Life is a Special Occasion" campaign suggests that every day is a good day to send a greeting. Because the campaign moves beyond the idea that cards are only for holidays or birthdays, it encourages consumers to enjoy the value of connecting with loved ones all the time (and for recipients, the unique pleasure of finding a surprise greeting card in the mailbox). For Hallmark, the campaign also increases the reasons and times when people are likely to make a purchase.

Even with these moves though, Hallmark faces significant competition on the digital front. Many applications available for the iPhone, iPad, or Android enable users to send customized "cards" by e-mail or text. A virtual card application from Red Stamp allows consumers to create cards, sent directly from social media sites. Companies such as Sincerely Ink also offer heavy-weight paper printing of customers' personalized, digital cards, to help users mail their greetings the old-fashioned way; even digital natives still like the feel of a physical card.[78] Such nimble product designs may pose the greatest challenge for Hallmark as it moves forward in the digital marketplace.

Hallmark's "Life Is a Special Occasion" campaign moves beyond the idea that cards are only for holidays or birthdays. It encourages consumers to connect with loved ones all the time.

wants a premium product and to save money, without cannibalizing its core customer groups.

Development of New Products

Despite market saturation, firms continually introduce new products with improved features or find new uses for existing products because they need constant innovation and product proliferation to defend market share from intense competition. Firms such as 3M, P&G, and Hewlett-Packard continually introduce new products. Innovations by such firms ensure that they are able to retain or grow their respective market shares. KFC took its expertise with its existing product line consisting of different types of fried chicken and developed Kentucky Grilled Chicken, a relatively innovative product line in an otherwise mature market.[79] And Hallmark, which has been the hallmark name for greeting cards for a long time, is trying a variety of innovations, as Adding Value 12.3 describes.

Decline Stage

Firms with products in the decline stage either position themselves for a niche segment of diehard consumers or those with special needs or they completely exit the market. The few laggards that have not yet tried the product or service enter the market at this stage. Take vinyl long-playing records (LPs) for example. In an age of Internet-downloaded music files, it may seem surprising that vinyl records are still made and sold. Sales of vinyl LPs had long been declining, but they have enjoyed a resurgence in just the past few years as diehard music lovers demand the unique sound of a vinyl record, rather than the digital sound of CDs and music files. Still, the 3.9 million LPs sold in the United States last year pales in comparison with the 1.27 billion digital downloads. The grooves in vinyl records create sound waves that are similar to those of a live performance though, which means they provide a more authentic sound, which in turn means nightclub DJs, discerning music listeners, and collectors will always prefer them.[80]

Aiding this continued demand is the fact that there are simply too many albums of music from the predigital era that are available only on vinyl. It may take many years, maybe even decades, for all the music from earlier generations to be digitized. Until that time, turntable equipment manufacturers, small record-pressing companies such as Music Connection in Manhattan, and new and emerging record companies, such as Premier Crue Music, continue to have a market that demands their LPs.[81]

The Shape of the Product Life Cycle Curve

In theory, the product life cycle curve is bell shaped with regard to sales and profits. In reality, however, each product or service category has its own individual shape; some move more rapidly through their product life cycles than others, depending on how different the category is from offerings currently in the market and how valuable it is to the consumer. New products and services that consumers accept very quickly have higher consumer adoption rates very early in their product life cycles and move faster across the various stages.

For example, DVD players and DVDs moved much faster than VCRs across the life cycle curve and have already reached the maturity stage, likely because consumers who already owned VCRs were accustomed to recording TV shows and playing prerecorded movies and programs. It also was easy to switch VCR customers to DVD technology because DVDs were more durable and had better resolution than videotapes. Finally, prices for DVDs and DVD players dropped more quickly and drastically than did VCR prices, which made the new technology a better value.

Strategies Based on Product Life Cycle: Some Caveats

Although the product life cycle concept provides a starting point for managers to think about the strategy they want to implement during each stage of the life cycle of a product, this tool must be used with care. The most challenging part of applying the product life cycle concept is that managers do not know exactly what shape each product's life cycle will take, so there is no way to know precisely what stage a product is in. If, for example, a product experiences several seasons of declining sales, a manager may decide that it has moved from the growth stage to decline and stop promoting the product. As a result, of course, sales decline further. The manager then believes he or she made the right decision because the product continues to follow a predetermined life cycle. But what if the original sales decline was due to a poor strategy or increased competition—issues that could have been addressed with positive marketing support? In this case, the product life cycle decision became a self-fulfilling prophecy, and a growth product was doomed to an unnecessary decline.[82]

Fortunately, new research, based on the history of dozens of consumer products, suggests that the product life cycle concept is indeed a valid idea, and new analytical tools now provide "rules" for detecting the key turning points in the cycle.[83]

CHECK YOURSELF

1. What are the stages in the product life cycle?
2. How do sales and profits change during the various stages?

Summing Up

LO1 Identify the reasons firms create new products.

Firms need to innovate to respond to changing customer needs, prevent declines in sales from market saturation, diversify their risk, and respond to short product life cycles, especially in industries such as fashion, apparel, arts, books, and software markets, where most sales come from new products. Finally, innovations can help firms improve their business relationships with suppliers.

LO2 Describe the different groups of adopters articulated by the diffusion of innovation theory.

The diffusion of innovation theory can help firms predict which types of customers will buy their products or services immediately upon introduction, as well as later as they gain more acceptance in the market. Innovators are those buyers who want to be the first to have the new product or service. Early adopters do not take as much risk as innovators but instead wait and purchase the product after careful review. The members of the early majority really don't like to take risk and therefore tend to wait until "the bugs" have been worked out of a particular product or service. The late majority are buyers who purchase the product after it has achieved its full market potential. Finally, laggards like to avoid change and rely on traditional products until they are no longer available. Laggards may never adopt a certain product or service.

LO3 Describe the various stages involved in developing a new product or service.

When firms develop new products, they go through several steps. First, they generate ideas for the product or service using several alternative techniques, such as internal research and development, R&D consortia, licensing, brainstorming, tracking competitors' products or services, or working with customers. Second, firms test their concepts by either describing the idea of the new product or service to potential customers or showing them images of what the product would look like. Third, the design process entails determining what the product or service will actually include and provide. Fourth, firms test market their designs. Fifth, if everything goes well in the test market, the product is launched. Sixth, firms must evaluate the new product or service to determine its success.

LO4 Explain the product life cycle.

The product life cycle helps firms make marketing mix decisions on the basis of the product's stage in its life cycle. In the introduction stage, companies attempt to gain a strong foothold in the market quickly by appealing to innovators. During the growth stage, the objective is to establish the brand firmly. When the product reaches the maturity stage, firms compete intensely for market share, and many potential customers already own the product or use the service. Eventually, most products enter the decline phase, during which firms withdraw marketing support and eventually phase out the product. Knowing where a product or service is in its life cycle helps managers determine its specific strategy at any given point in time.

Key Terms

- alpha testing, 378
- beta testing, 380
- concept, 377
- concept testing, 377
- decline stage, 384
- diffusion of innovation, 366
- early adopter, 370
- early majority, 370
- first movers, 367
- growth stage, 384
- innovation, 361

- innovator, 368
- introduction stage, 384
- introductory price promotion, 381
- laggard, 370
- late majority, 370
- lead user, 376
- manufacturer's suggested retail price (MSRP), 382
- maturity stage, 384
- pioneer (breakthrough), 366

- premarket test, 380
- product design, 378
- product development, 378
- product life cycle, 384
- prototype, 378
- reverse engineering, 375
- slotting allowance, 382
- test marketing, 380
- trade promotion, 381
- trade show, 381

Marketing Applications

1. Some people think that a product should be considered "new" only if it is completely new to the market and has never existed before. Describe or give examples of other types of new products.

2. Panasonic's new 3D HD personal camcorder allows users to record live events in three dimensions, instead of two. How quickly do you think this product will diffuse among the U.S. population? Describe the types of people that you expect will be in each of the diffusion of innovation stages.

3. What are the advantages and disadvantages for companies that are the first to introduce products that create new markets?

4. Identify and describe the ways that companies generate new product ideas. Which of these ways involve the customer? How can firms assess the value of the ideas that customers generate?

5. Describe an example of a new product or service that is targeted at the college student market. Using the concept testing discussion in the chapter, describe how you would conduct a concept test for this product or service.

6. How does the Internet help companies gain customer input on their existing and new products?

7. Nature's Path is about to introduce a type of granola and is in the market testing phase of the new product development process. Describe two ways that Nature's Path might conduct initial market testing prior to launching this new product.

8. As a brand manager at Kimberly Clark, you are responsible for marketing its newest Huggies slip-on diaper. How would slotting allowances and trade promotions help promote your product?

9. What type of deodorant do you use? What stage of the product life cycle is it in? Is the deodorant manufacturer's marketing strategy—its four Ps—consistent with the product's stage in its life cycle? Explain.

10. In what stage of the product life cycle is a new model of a PlayStation video game console? Is Sony's marketing strategy—its four Ps—consistent with the product's stage in its life cycle? How is it different from that of the deodorant in the previous question? Explain.

11. You have recently been hired by a cosmetics company in the product development group. The firm's brand is a top-selling, high-end line of cosmetics. The head of the development team has just presented research that shows that "tween" girls, aged 11 to 15, are very interested in cosmetics and have the money to spend. The decision is made to create a line of tween cosmetics based on the existing adult line. As the product moves through development you begin to notice that the team seems to lean toward a very edgy and sexual theme for the line, including naming the various lines "envy," "desire," "prowess," and "fatal attraction." You begin to wonder, is this concept too much for girls in the targeted age group?

Quiz Yourself

1. By the time BMW and Mercedes Benz entered the mini-SUV market, there were many competitors, sales had peaked, and profits were declining. These firms entered the market during the _____ stage of the product life cycle.
   a. introduction
   d. leveling
   c. maturity
   d. growth
   e. decline

2. Lorraine belongs to a national consumer panel created by a market research company. She regularly receives samples of new products from a variety of firms and fills out questionnaires about the products. The national consumer panel Lorraine is part of is engaged in:
   a. premarket testing.
   b. product launch.
   c. test marketing.
   d. product development.
   e. concept testing.

   (Answers to these two questions can be found on page 648.)

   Go to www.mhhe.com/grewal4e to practice an additional 11 questions.

Net Savvy

1. Go to www.inventables.com. Choose two of the products found at the site. What are some potential applications of these ideas?

2. The automotive industry is constantly adding new and different products and technologies to their cars—both above and under the hood. Conduct an Internet or library database search and discuss two innovative new automotive technologies that are changing the industry.

Chapter Case Study

APPLE FURTHER TRANSFORMS THE USER EXPERIENCE WITH IPAD 2 AND 3

Skeptics yawned a bit when Apple rolled out its iPad 2. Reviewers acknowledged that Apple's updated tablet did have two cameras and a gyroscope. But the prelaunch prediction was that the new version was basically the same as the iPad, only thinner, lighter, and twice as fast. Then people began using it, and they discovered once again that Apple had further transformed the digital experience.

WHAT THE IPAD 2 OFFERS

A tablet is meant to be held, not set on your lap or atop a desk. Apple's new iPad—15 percent lighter, just .34 inches thick, with rounded edges, and speedier than ever—is a pleasure to hold. The Motorola Xoom, considered the best Android competitor, felt massive by comparison. And despite the iPad 2's lighter, slimmer dimensions, its battery still held a charge for 10 hours. Like competing tablets, Apple's new iPad featured a camera on the back to record high-definition video, along with a low-resolution front camera for video phone calls. The more expensive models offered online capability, with either AT&T's or Verizon's cellular networks. With a simple $40 adapter, the iPad 2 could be connected to a high-definition television too, making it a great platform for viewing slideshows, presentations, or movies.[84]

But one of the simplest innovations was the one reviewers hailed as "magic." Apple's new SmartCover, a rigid, hinged sheet of polyurethane (or for $70, leather), could be used to prop up the iPad, so the user could watch movies or freely use the on-screen keyboard with both hands. Opening and closing the cover turned the iPad on or off almost instantaneously, saving the average user six minutes a week, according to one reviewer. Given modern consumers' expectations that digital devices will keep getting faster, that time-saver was bound to please.[85]

These descriptions involve the physical aspects. Apple also transformed the overall user experience. With the new speed and ease of iPad 2, Apple had finally made using a digital tablet more like reading a book. No buttons to press, no menus to scroll through. Ratcheting up its competition with other e-readers, Apple had delivered "the swiftness of print." Users could just open the iPad 2 and start reading. E-mail, the news, a novel for their subway ride—everything was instantly available. In terms of Apple's other advantages in the tablet market, users could immediately turn to the 65,000 apps already available for the iPad, not to mention the 290,000 iPhone applications that could also be used on the iPad.[86]

A stable price tag was perhaps its biggest competitive edge. The starting price for the iPad 2 was the same as that for the original iPad: $499, and much less than Samsung's Galaxy Tab or Motorola's Xoom, two tough Android competitors.[87] Within nine months of the iPad 2 launch, Apple had sold 15 million devices, generating $9.5 billion in revenue.

Apple's financial efficiency remains tough to duplicate. Enormous cash reserves, estimated at $60 billion, enable the company to form strategic partnerships with component manufacturers and secure volume discounts. It avoids licensing fees for some high-cost items by having them designed in-house by a company it bought. Revenue from its successful App Store helps subsidize the price of the iPad. And Apple's global network of retail stores eliminates mark-ups by third-party sellers, like Best Buy.[88]

WHAT'S HAPPENING IN THE MARKET

The digital tablet market appears on the verge of an explosion. Forrester Research predicts the market will generate $35 billion in revenue, from the one-third of U.S. adults who will own tablets by 2015.[89] Critics had once questioned whether consumers really would spring for yet one more digital device, but the numbers have proved those skeptics wrong.

User habits also are changing. The digital tablet offers a popular online shopping venue, especially for affluent consumers. Retailers such as Macy's, Abercrombie & Fitch, and The Gap report that their customers who browse their Internet sites with a digital tablet are more likely to complete the purchase than are online shoppers who use computers or smartphones. In addition, those consumers using the new digital tablets to shop tend to buy high-end, high-priced items, typically spending 10 to 20 percent more than other online shoppers.[90] Market research confirms these findings by developing a matching profile of tablet owners: They tend to be wealthier, so the new online format helps retailers tap into a higher-spending market niche.

Thus advertisers began shifting their behavior. Shopping networks and individual retailers now feature videos, slideshows, and "how-to" demonstrations in their catalogs, as they seek to exploit the digital capabilities of the new tablets.

WHAT OTHERS ARE DOING, AND HOW APPLE WILL RESPOND

In almost no time, Apple's iPad 2 faced nearly 100 competitors, vying for a place in the tablet market.[91] Some offered customers a benefit or two that could not be found on the iPad 2, such as the Flash capability provided by the Androids for viewing videos and animation on the Web. Others offer the ability to dictate text, using a program that sends the information into any box that accepts typing. Another popular option is a navigation application that displays turn-by-turn travel directions on GPS-generated maps.[92]

Amazon jumped into the market too with its Kindle Fire, an updated e-reader with digital tablet capabilities, priced at only $199. With competition mounting, observers predicted that Apple would make key changes in its next iPad release. Dedicated forums have been full of discussion about the possible inclusion of Siri, Apple's sophisticated vocal interface, on the iPad 3 (a feature available on iPhone4).[93]

But Apple's biggest move amid these prerelease rumors has been its announcement that it has added digital textbooks to its next iPad—access that Amazon's Kindle and the Nook from Barnes & Noble already offer. Apple's entry into the digital textbook market is fueled by its partnerships with a number of textbook publishers. Apple offers these publishing partners three key capabilities: its iBooks2, an e-book reading application for the iPad; an e-book authoring tool for the iPad, called iBooks Author; and iTunes U, an expanded online commerce platform for digital textbooks. The first slated release would include a trio of high school textbooks: biology, algebra 1, and environmental science.[94]

Proponents suggest that digital textbooks offer students a wealth of benefits, including interactive connections with the information, access to constantly updated study material, lighter backpacks, and lower prices than paperbound textbooks. But some opponents doubt that the promised savings on individual texts will ever fully materialize, because the major cost for traditional publishing has always been taken up by research and writing, not printing and production.[95]

Still, considering that the textbook industry inevitably is undergoing a digital transformation, Apple's collaboration with two of the largest textbook publishers in the United States likely represents a major coup. The maker of the MacBook, the iPhone, the iPod, and the iPad has moved once again to secure a competitive edge.

Questions

1. At what stage in the product life cycle is the iPad?

2. How well has Apple responded to the changing competitive landscape for digital tablets, particularly the emergence of the Androids?

3. Which iPad 2 and iPad 3 features create the most value for users?

4. How will the iPad stack up against the e-textbook options on other digital tablets?

CHAPTER 13

Services: The Intangible Product

Even when online retailers offer great merchandise, the customer service they offer can be a deciding factor in their success. How well personnel respond to the stream of customer inquiries may determine whether the company thrives or takes a nose dive. But relating to customers also can be highly variable; it depends on individual employees. How do you mobilize an entire company to speak with one voice? How can a service firm ensure that employee–customer interactions consistently meet, or exceed, the company's service standards?

Zappos, the Las Vegas–based online clothing and shoe retailer, seems to have the answers to these questions. Valued at more than $1.6 billion, one year after its acquisition by Amazon,[1] Zappos may sell apparel, but it really has built its business on its superb service. The company's core values stress that customer satisfaction is more important than cost cutting; that message permeates every single aspect of its operations. The goal is to "wow" each customer with service that far exceeds expectations.

Of course, costs are something that every company must address. Therefore, Zappos.com uses automated technology to handle approximately 75 percent of its customer service transactions. But the other 25 percent of calls that go to a human respondent constitute powerful and influential customer service interactions, because those human representatives are determined to make the interaction a happy one.[2]

Instilling such values in every worker begins with the interview process. Applicants undergo separate interviews for experience and fit within the company culture. During training, which lasts up to five weeks, all new employees are required to work in the call center. Anyone who thinks the assignment is beneath them is paid for his or her time and shown the door. Trainees are not given a script or a time limit for calls. Instead, during training and once on the job, workers are urged to creatively solve problems, even if customer satisfaction means doing something a little "weird," like buying shoes from a competing retailer for a customer in distress.

That was the solution one worker devised when a woman called, desperate to buy another pair of her favorite Zappos shoes when she discovered, after arriving at her hotel, that she had forgotten to pack them. The

LEARNING OBJECTIVES

LO1 Describe how the marketing of services differs from the marketing of products.

LO2 Discuss the four gaps in the Service Gap Model.

LO3 Examine the five service quality dimensions.

LO4 Explain the zone of tolerance.

LO5 Identify three service recovery strategies.

shoes were no longer in stock, but the employee located a pair near the woman's hotel and had them hand-delivered—and Zappos paid the bill.[3] The customer was astonished.

That approach was totally consistent with Zappos' core values, which suggest that a little "weirdness" may be just the right approach if it helps solve a customer problem. And of course, the company doesn't mind the "wow" stories that such efforts generate for customers to share with all their friends.

Zappos's shopping procedures are also designed to please. Customers are encouraged to order multiple sizes and colors of an item, so they can touch, feel, and try on prospective purchases. Returned goods ship free for up to a year. And Zappos likes to impress customers with speedy delivery. So it ships items faster than its website indicates. Good customers often get upgraded to next- or second-day air shipping at no extra cost.[4]

Employees who meet Zappos's unconventional customer service standards are rewarded. Its most common salaried job, fulfillment center process manager, pays more than $47,500 a year, and the company is ranked eleventh among the country's best places to work.[5]

When retail goes online, delivering the product is just half the battle. Distance complicates service, and how that service gets delivered, whether online or through a call center, can make or break the customer relationship. Zappos offers a model for delivering service excellence, by enlisting workers in the challenge of "wow-ing" each and every customer.

Whereas a **service** is any intangible offering that involves a deed, performance, or effort that cannot be physically possessed,[6] **customer service** specifically refers to human or mechanical activities firms undertake to help satisfy their customers' needs and wants. By providing good customer service, firms add value to their products.

Exhibit 13.1 illustrates the continuum from a pure service to a pure good. Most offerings, like those of Zappos, lie somewhere in the middle and include some service and some good (i.e., a hybrid of the two). Even those firms that are engaged primarily in selling a good, like an apparel store, typically view service as a method to maintain a sustainable competitive advantage. This chapter moves on to take an inclusive view of services as anything from pure service businesses to a business that uses service as a differentiating tool to help it sell physical goods.

Economies of developed countries like the United States have become increasingly dependent on services. Services account for 76 percent of the U.S. gross domestic product (GDP), a much higher percentage than they did 50, 20, or even 10 years ago. In turn, the current list of *Fortune* 500 companies contains more service companies and fewer manufacturers than in previous decades.[7] This dependence and the growth of service-oriented economies in developed countries have emerged for several reasons.

EXHIBIT 13.1   The Service–Product Continuum

| Doctor | Hotel | Dry cleaners | Restaurant | Apparel specialty store | Grocery store |

Service dominant ←   → **Product dominant**

Specialized services like personal training are thriving.

First, it is generally less expensive for firms to manufacture their products in less developed countries. Even if the goods are finished in the United States, some of their components likely were produced elsewhere. In turn, the proportion of service production to goods production in the United States, and other similar economies, has steadily increased over time.

Second, people place a high value on convenience and leisure. For instance, household maintenance activities, which many people performed themselves in the past, have become more popular and quite specialized. Food preparation, lawn maintenance, house cleaning, pet grooming, laundry and dry cleaning, hair care, and automobile maintenance are all often performed by specialists.

Third, as the world has become more complicated, people are demanding more specialized services—everything from plumbers to personal trainers, from massage therapists to tax preparation specialists, from lawyers to travel and leisure specialists and even to health care providers. The aging population in particular has increased the need for health care specialists, including doctors, nurses, and caregivers in assisted living facilities and nursing homes, and many of those consumers want their specialists to provide personalized, dedicated services.

SERVICES MARKETING DIFFERS FROM PRODUCT MARKETING

LO1 Describe how the marketing of services differs from the marketing of products.

The marketing of services differs from product marketing because of the four fundamental differences involved in services: Services are intangible, inseparable, heterogeneous, and perishable.[8] (See Exhibit 13.2.) This section examines these differences and discusses how they affect marketing strategies.

Intangible

As the title of this chapter implies, the most fundamental difference between a product and a service is that services are **intangible**—they cannot be touched, tasted, or seen like a pure product can. When you get a physical examination, you see and hear the doctor, but the service itself is intangible. This intangibility can prove highly challenging to marketers. For instance, it makes it difficult to convey

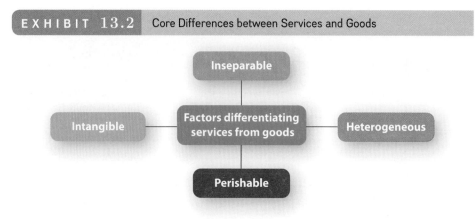

EXHIBIT 13.2 Core Differences between Services and Goods

the benefits of services—try describing whether the experience of visiting your dentist was good or bad and why. Service providers (e.g., physicians, dentists) therefore offer cues to help their customers experience and perceive their service more positively, such as a waiting room stocked with television sets, beverages, and comfortable chairs to create an atmosphere that appeals to the target market.

A service that cannot be shown directly to potential customers also is difficult to promote. Marketers must creatively employ symbols and images to promote and sell services, as Six Flags does in using its advertising to evoke images of happy families and friends enjoying a roller coaster ride. Professional medical services provide appropriate images of personnel doing their jobs in white coats surrounded by high-tech equipment. Educational institutions promote the quality of their services by touting their famous faculty and alumni, as well as their accreditations. They also often use images of happy students sitting spellbound in front of a fascinating professor or going on to lucrative careers of their own.

Because of the intangibility of services, the images that marketers use must reinforce the benefit or value that a service provides. Professional service providers, such as doctors, lawyers, accountants, and consultants, depend heavily on consumers' perceptions of their integrity and trustworthiness, but they also need to market their offerings using promotional campaigns. At one time, lawyers were prohibited from advertising, because such marketing seemingly would undermine the integrity of the profession. The repeal of those laws resulted in much more advertising, some of which may go too far. Critics point to the aggressive promotions some attorneys use to prey on potential clients' vulnerabilities after they have been injured. The lawyers claim instead they are providing a valuable service to society. This ethical debate continues, though the American Bar Association (ABA) has drafted a set of rules that its members must abide by when creating their advertising, such as banning any use of pop-up ads or actors when advertising law services.[9]

For lawyers, the challenge of advertising services creates an ethical dilemma. But some other services have found excellent ways to make their offerings more tangible to their customers, as Adding Value 13.1 notes.

Since it is difficult to show a service, marketers like Six Flags evoke images in its advertising of happy families and friends enjoying a ride at one of its amusement parks.

Adding Value 13.1   Carbonite's Secure Online Back-Up

The prospect of losing data haunts virtually every computer user. And for good reason, especially among business users: The Federal Emergency Management Agency says 40–60 percent of small businesses fail to reopen after they suffer a severe data disruption.[10] To address their fears of data loss or contamination, some users rely on external hard drives or disk storage. But that means they have to remember to perform the back-up, and these options do not provide protection against a fire or other emergencies that destroy that hard drive, along with the computer.

Online back-ups involve backing up the data on remote servers. This provides a more secure, less user-dependent alternative. Carbonite was one of the first entrants into this market. It provides simple, affordable, unlimited online backup for individual home users, as well as small and medium businesses. With these target markets, Carbonite has kept its service, price, and customer support well within the reach of users. The basic yearly rate for a home customer is $59 per computer; a business pays $229 a year to cover all company computers.

Carbonite software runs invisibly on both Macs and PCs,[11] performing back-ups automatically. With customers in more than 100 countries, the company has backed up more than 100 billion files, and recovered nearly 10 billion of them in the past few years.[12] For portable, digital access, the company offers free mobile applications for Blackberry, iPad, iPhone, and Android devices.[13]

To live up to its promise of "hassle-free" service, the company also offers free support by telephone, e-mail, and online live chat. It answers customer inquiries on its Twitter and Facebook sites, which then provide transparent proof of its handling of customer complaints. As for security, Carbonite's system is comparable to the safeguards used by major banks, credit card companies, and online retailers.[14] All files are encrypted with two layers of technology, stored on enterprise-grade servers to protect against mechanical disk failure, and kept in state-of-the-art data centers guarded 24 hours a day, 365 days a year. Personnel must pass through biometric scans and electronic pin coding to enter.

Carbonite thus has firmly established its market position by delivering a reliable, secure, easy-to-use service, combined with reasonable pricing and easily accessible technical support. As the shift to cloud computing intensifies, the company's main advantage may be its focus on staying abreast of user needs and expectations, so it can keep all its customers happy.

Carbonite backs up computer data on remote servers.

Inseparable Production and Consumption

Unlike a pair of jeans that may have been made six months prior to their purchase, halfway around the world, services are produced and consumed at the same time; that is, service and consumption are **inseparable**. When getting a haircut, the customer is not only present but also may participate in the service process. Furthermore, the interaction with the service provider may have an important impact on the customer's perception of the service outcome. If the hair stylist appears to be having fun while cutting hair, it may positively impact the experience.

Because the service is inseparable from its consumption, customers rarely have the opportunity to try the service before they purchase it. And after the service has been performed, it can't be returned. Imagine telling your hair stylist that you want to have the hair around your ears trimmed as a test before doing the entire head. Because the purchase risk in these scenarios can be relatively high, service firms sometimes provide extended warranties and 100 percent satisfaction guarantees.[15] The Choice Hotels chain, for instance, states: "We guarantee total guest satisfaction at Comfort Inn, Comfort Suites, Quality, Sleep Inn, Clarion and MainStay Suites hotels. If you are not satisfied with your accommodations or our service, please advise the front desk of a problem right away."[16]

Heterogeneous

The more humans are needed to provide a service, the more likely there is to be **heterogeneity** or variability in the service's quality. A hair stylist may give bad haircuts in the morning because he or she went out the night before. Yet that stylist still may offer a better service than the undertrained stylist working in the next station over. A restaurant, which offers a mixture of services and products, generally can control its food quality but not the variability in food preparation or delivery. If a consumer has a problem with a product, it can be replaced, redone, destroyed, or, if it is already in the supply chain, recalled. In many cases, the problem can even be fixed before the product gets into consumers' hands. But an inferior service can't be recalled; by the time the firm recognizes a problem, the damage has been done.

Marketers also can use the variable nature of services to their advantage. A micromarketing segmentation strategy can customize a service to meet customers' needs exactly (see Chapter 9). For example, a Massachusetts store called Tech Superpowers specializes in helping new Apple customers set up their new toys and enjoy all their functions—basic services that the Geniuses in Apple stores may tend to ignore. At the center of the store is a Lexus IS300, demonstrating how Apple products can be integrated into the vehicle. A 23-inch monitor in the backseat streams content through from a Mac mini. An iPad is mounted in the dashboard. Better than any verbal explanation, this real-world display appeals to customers by promising the great capabilities they gain with Apple products—as well as how clever the Superpowers can be when it comes to anything Apple.[17]

In an alternative approach, some service providers tackle the variability issue by replacing people with machines. For simple transactions like getting cash, using an ATM is usually quicker and more convenient—and less variable—than waiting in line for a bank teller. Many retailers have installed kiosks with broadband

Tech Superpowers specializes in helping Apple customers set up their new toys to enjoy all their capabilities.

Since services are perishable, service providers like ski areas offer less expensive tickets at night to stimulate demand.

Internet access in their stores. In addition to offering customers the opportunity to order merchandise not available in the store, kiosks can provide routine customer service, freeing employees to deal with more demanding customer requests and problems and reducing service variability. For example, customers can use kiosks to locate merchandise in the store and determine whether specific products, brands, and sizes are available. Kiosks can also be used to automate existing store services, such as gift registry management, rain checks, film drop-off, credit applications, and preordering service for bakeries and delicatessens.

Perishable

Services are **perishable** in that they cannot be stored for use in the future. You can't stockpile your membership at Gold's Gym like you could a six-pack of V-8 juice, for instance. The perishability of services provides both challenges and opportunities to marketers in terms of the critical task of matching demand and supply. As long as the demand for and supply of the service match closely, there is no problem, but unfortunately, this perfect matching rarely occurs. A ski area, for instance, can be open as long as there is snow, even at night, but demand peaks on weekends and holidays, so ski areas often offer less expensive tickets during off-peak periods to stimulate demand. Airlines, cruise ships, movie theaters, and restaurants confront similar challenges and attack them in similar ways.

Certainly, providing great service is not easy, and it requires a diligent effort to analyze the service process piece by piece. In the next section, we examine what is known as the Gaps Model, which is designed to highlight those areas where customers believe they are getting less or poorer service than they should (the gaps) and how these gaps can be closed.

CHECK YOURSELF

1. What are the four marketing elements that distinguish services from products?
2. Why can't we separate firms into just service or just product sellers?

LO2   Discuss the four gaps in
the Service Gap Model.

PROVIDING GREAT SERVICE: THE GAPS MODEL

Customers have certain expectations about how a service should be delivered. When the delivery of that service fails to meet those expectations, a **service gap** results. The Service Gaps Model (Exhibit 13.3) is designed to encourage the systematic examination of all aspects of the service delivery process and prescribes the steps needed to develop an optimal service strategy.[18]

As Exhibit 13.3 shows, there are four service gaps:

1. The **knowledge gap** reflects the difference between customers' expectations and the firm's perception of those customer expectations. Firms can close this gap by determining what customers really want by doing research using marketing metrics such as service quality and the "zone of tolerance."

2. The **standards gap** pertains to the difference between the firm's perceptions of customers' expectations and the service standards it sets. By setting appropriate service standards, training employees to meet and exceed those standards, and measuring service performance, firms can attempt to close this gap.

3. The **delivery gap** is the difference between the firm's service standards and the actual service it provides to customers. This gap can be closed by getting employees to meet or exceed service standards when the service is being delivered by empowering service providers, providing support and incentives, and using technology where appropriate.[19]

4. The **communication gap** refers to the difference between the actual service provided to customers and the service that the firm's promotion program promises. If firms are more realistic about the services they can provide and at the same time manage customer expectations effectively, they generally can close this gap.

As we discuss the four gaps subsequently, we will apply them to the experience that Marcia Kessler had with a motel in Maine. She saw an ad for a package weekend that quoted a very reasonable daily rate and listed the free amenities available at Paradise Motel: free babysitting services, a piano bar with a nightly singer, a free Continental breakfast, a heated swimming pool, and newly decorated rooms. When she booked the room, Marcia discovered that the price advertised was not available during the weekend, and a three-day minimum stay was required. Because of the nice amenities, however, she went ahead. After checking in with a very unpleasant person at the front desk, Marcia and her

---

EXHIBIT 13.3   Service Gaps Model for Improving Service

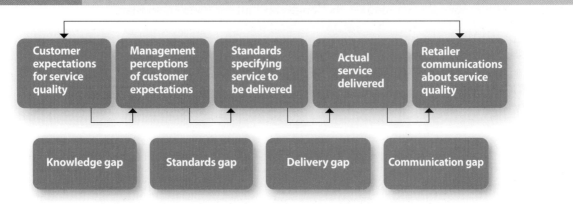

Sources: Michael Levy and Barton Weitz, *Retailing Management*, 8th ed. (Burr Ridge, IL: McGraw-Hill, 2012). Adapted from Valarie Zeithaml, A. Parasuraman, and Leonard Berry, *Delivering Quality Customer Service* (New York: The Free Press, 1990); and Valarie Zeithaml, Leonard Berry, and A. Parasuraman, "Communication and Control Processes in the Delivery of Service Quality," *Journal of Marketing* 52, no. 2 (April 1988), pp. 35–48.

husband found that their room appeared circa-1950 and had not been cleaned. When she complained, all she got was "attitude" from the assistant manager. Resigned to the fact that they were slated to spend the weekend, she decided to go for a swim. Unfortunately, the water was "heated" by Booth Bay and stood at around 50 degrees. No one was using the babysitting services because there were few young children at the resort. It turns out the piano bar singer was the second cousin of the owner, and he couldn't carry a tune, let alone play the piano very well. The Continental breakfast must have come all the way from the Continent, because everything was stale and tasteless. Marcia couldn't wait to get home.

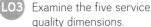

What service gaps did Marcia experience while on vacation at the Paradise Motel in Maine?

The Knowledge Gap: Understanding Customer Expectations

An important early step in providing good service is knowing what the customer wants. It doesn't pay to invest in services that don't improve customer satisfaction.[20] To reduce the knowledge gap, firms must understand customers' expectations. To understand those expectations, firms undertake customer research and increase the interaction and communication between managers and employees.

Customers' expectations are based on their knowledge and experiences.[21] Marcia's expectations were that her room at the motel in Maine would be ready when she got there, the swimming pool would be heated, the singer would be able to sing, and the breakfast would be fresh. Not a lot to expect, but in this extreme example the Paradise was suffering a severe knowledge gap perhaps based on their assumption that being on the ocean in Maine was enough. If the resort never understood her expectations, it is unlikely it would ever be able to meet them.

Expectations vary according to the type of service. Marcia's expectations might have been higher, for instance, if she were staying at a Ritz-Carlton rather than the Paradise Motel. At the Ritz, she might expect employees to know her by name, be aware of her dietary preferences, and have placed fresh fruit of her choice and fresh-cut flowers in her room before she arrived. At the Paradise Motel, she expected easy check-in/checkout, easy access to a major highway, a clean room with a comfortable bed, and a TV, at a bare minimum.

People's expectations also vary depending on the situation. If she had been traveling on business, the Paradise Motel might have been fine (had the room at least been clean and modern), but if she were celebrating her 10th wedding anniversary, she probably would prefer the Ritz. Thus, the service provider needs to not only know and understand the expectations of the customers in its target market but also have some idea of the occasions of service usage.

To help ensure that JetBlue understands customers' expectations, it surveys at least 35 customers from every flight it operates.[22] The airline brings together top executives to discuss what customers are saying and how it should respond. On the basis of its customer feedback, it has changed the way it deals with customers who face delays and cancellations. It also knows which planes have problems with the entertainment system and which airports have the rudest staff.

Evaluating Service Quality Using Well-Established Marketing Metrics To meet or exceed customers' expectations, marketers must determine what those expectations are. Yet because of their intangibility, the **service quality**, or customers' perceptions of how well a service meets or exceeds their expectations, often is difficult for customers to evaluate.[23] Customers generally use five distinct service dimensions to determine overall service quality: reliability, responsiveness, assurance,

LO3 Examine the five service quality dimensions.

EXHIBIT 13.4 Building Blocks of Service Quality

Reliability:
The ability to perform the service dependably and accurately.

Responsiveness:
The willingness to help customers and provide prompt service.

Assurance:
The knowledge of and courtesy by employees and their ability to convey trust and confidence.

Empathy:
The caring, individualized attention provided to customers.

Tangibles:
The appearance of physical facilities, equipment, personnel, and communication materials.

empathy, and tangibles (see Exhibit 13.4). Adding Value 13.2 describes how the Broadmoor Hotel maintains its five-star rating by focusing on these five service characteristics.

If you were to apply the five service dimensions to your own decision-making process, for instance, when you selected a college—which provides you the service of education—you might find results like those in Exhibit 13.5.

If your expectations include an individualized experience at a state-of-the-art institution, perhaps University B is a better alternative for you. But if you are relying heavily on academic performance and career placement from your university experience, then University A might be a better choice in terms of the five service dimensions. If a strong culture and tradition are important to you, University A

EXHIBIT 13.5 Collegiate Service Dimensions

	University A	University B
Reliability	Offers sound curriculum with extensive placement services and internships.	Curriculum covers all the basics but important courses are not always available. Career placement is haphazard at best.
Responsiveness	Slow to respond to application. Very structured visitation policy. Rather inflexible with regard to personal inquiries or additional meetings.	Quick response during application process. Open visitation policy. Offers variety of campus resources to help with decision making.
Assurance	Staff seems very confident in reputation and services.	Informal staff who convey enthusiasm for institution.
Empathy	Seems to process student body as a whole rather than according to individual needs or concerns.	Very interested in providing a unique experience for each student.
Tangibles	Very traditional campus with old-world look and feel. Facilities are manicured. Dorm rooms are large, but bathrooms are a little old.	New campus with modern architecture. Campus is less manicured. Dorm rooms are spacious with newer bathrooms.

Adding Value 13.2   The Broadmoor Manages Service Quality for a Five-Star Rating

Established in 1891 as a gambling casino and transformed into a "grand resort" in 1918, the Broadmoor, in Colorado Springs, Colorado, is one of the world's premier resorts.[24] It has received a record 50 consecutive years of five-star ratings from the *Forbes Travel Guide*. Perry Goodbar, former vice president of marketing for the Broadmoor, emphasizes, "It's the people who truly make this place special. Exceptional service quality begins with exceptional people." Some aspects of its service quality are as follows:

Reliability Every new Broadmoor employee, before ever encountering a customer, attends a two-and-a-half day orientation session and receives an employee handbook. Making and keeping promises to customers is a central part of this orientation. Employees are trained always to give an estimated time for service, whether it be room service, laundry service, or simply how long it will take to be seated at one of the resort's restaurants. When an employee makes a promise, he or she keeps that promise. Employees are trained to never guess if they don't know the answer to a question. Inaccurate information only frustrates customers. When an employee is unable to answer a question accurately, he or she immediately contacts someone who can.

Assurance The Broadmoor conveys trust by empowering its employees. An example of an employee empowerment policy is the service recovery program. If a guest problem arises, employees are given discretionary resources to rectify the problem or present the customer with something special to help mollify them. For example, if a meal is delivered and there's a mistake in the order or how it was prepared, a waiter can offer the guest a free item such as a dessert or, if the service was well below expectations, simply take care of the bill. Managers then review each situation to understand the nature of the problem and help prevent it from occurring again.

Tangibles One of the greatest challenges for the Broadmoor in recent years has been updating rooms built in the early part of the twentieth century to meet the needs of twenty-first century visitors. To accomplish this, it spent millions in improvements, renovating rooms, and adding a new outdoor pool complex.

Empathy One approach used to demonstrate empathy is personalizing communications. Employees are instructed to always address a guest by name, if possible. To accomplish this, employees are trained to listen and observe carefully to determine a guest's name. Subtle sources for this information include convention name tags, luggage ID tags, credit cards, or checks. In addition, all phones within the Broadmoor display a guest's room number and name on a screen.

Responsiveness Every employee is instructed to follow the HEART model of taking care of problems. First, employees must "Hear what a guest has to say." Second, they must "Empathize with them" and then "Apologize for the situation." Fourth, they must "Respond to the guest's needs" by "Taking action and following up."

The Broadmoor in Colorado Springs, Colorado, is known for exceptional service quality.

offers this type of environment. What your expectations are has a lot to do with your perception of how your university falls within these service dimensions.

Marketing research (see Chapter 10) provides a means to better understand consumers' service expectations and their perceptions of service quality. This research can be extensive and expensive, or it can be integrated into a firm's everyday interactions with customers. Today, most service firms have developed voice-of-customer programs and employ ongoing marketing research to assess how well they are meeting their customers' expectations. A systematic **voice-of-customer (VOC) program** collects customer inputs and integrates them into managerial decisions.

 LO4 Explain the zone of tolerance.

An important marketing metric to evaluate how well firms perform on the five service quality dimensions (see again Exhibit 13.4) is the **zone of tolerance**, which refers to the area between customers' expectations regarding their desired service and the minimum level of acceptable service—that is, the difference between what the customer really wants and what he or she will accept before going elsewhere.[25] To define the zone of tolerance, firms ask a series of questions about each service quality dimension that relate to:

• The desired and expected level of service for each dimension, from low to high.

• Customers' perceptions of how well the focal service performs and how well a competitive service performs, from low to high.

• The importance of each service quality dimension.

Exhibit 13.6 illustrates the results of such an analysis for Lou's Local Diner, a family-owned restaurant. The rankings on the left are based on a nine-point scale, on which 1 is low and 9 is high. The length of each box illustrates the zone of tolerance for each service quality dimension. For instance, according to the short length of the reliability box, customers expect a fairly high level of reliability (top of the box) but will accept only a fairly high level of reliability (bottom of the box). On the other end of the scale, customers expect a high level of assurance (top of the box) but will also accept a fairly low level (bottom of the box). This difference is to be expected, because the customers also were asked to assign an important score to the five service quality dimensions so that the total equals 100 percent (see bottom of Exhibit 13.6). Looking at the average importance score, we conclude that

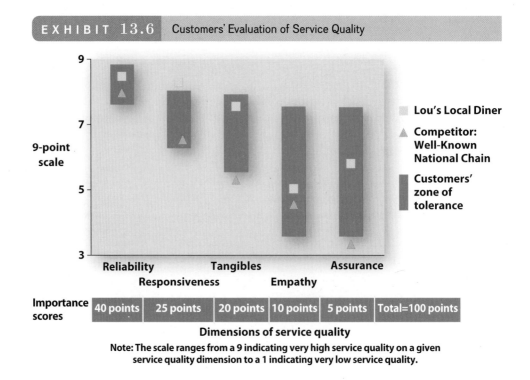

EXHIBIT 13.6   Customers' Evaluation of Service Quality

Note: The scale ranges from a 9 indicating very high service quality on a given service quality dimension to a 1 indicating very low service quality.

reliability is relatively important to these customers, but assurance is not. So customers have a fairly narrow zone of tolerance for service dimensions that are fairly important to them and a wider range of tolerance for those service dimensions that are less important. Also note that Lou's Local Diner always rates higher than its primary competitor, Well-Known National Chain, on each dimension.

Further note that Well-Known National Chain scores below the zone of tolerance on the tangibles dimension, meaning that customers are not willing to accept the way the restaurant looks and smells. Lou's Local Diner, in contrast, performs above the zone of tolerance on the responsiveness dimension—maybe even too well. Lou's may wish to conduct further research to verify which responsiveness aspects it is performing so well, and then consider toning those aspects down. For example, being responsive to customers' desires to have a diner that serves breakfast 24 hours a day can be expensive and may not add any further value to Lou's Diner, because customers would accept more limited times.

Lou's Local Diner always rates higher than its primary competitor, Well-Known National Chain, on each service quality dimension.

A very straightforward and inexpensive method of collecting consumers' perceptions of service quality is to gather them at the time of the sale. Service providers can ask customers how they liked the service—though customers often are reticent to provide negative feedback directly to the person who provided the service—or distribute a simple questionnaire. Regardless of how information is collected, companies must take care not to lose it, which can happen if there is no effective mechanism for filtering it up to the key decision makers. Furthermore, in some cases, customers cannot effectively evaluate the service until several days or weeks later. Automobile dealers, for instance, often call their customers a week after they perform a service like an oil change to assess their service quality.[26]

Another excellent method for assessing customers' expectations is making effective use of customer complaint behavior. Even if complaints are handled effectively to solve customers' problems, the essence of the complaint is too often lost on managers. For instance, an airline established a policy that customer service reps could not discuss any issues involving fees to travel agents with customers. So when a customer calls to complain about these fees, the representative just changes the subject, and management therefore never finds out about the complaint.[27]

Even firms with the best formal research mechanisms in place must put managers on the front lines occasionally to interact directly with the customers. The late Sam Walton, founder of Walmart, participated in and advocated this strategy, which is known as, "management by walking around."[28] Unless the managers who make the service quality decisions know what their service providers are facing on a day-to-day basis, and unless they can talk directly to the customers with whom those service providers interact, any customer service program they create will not be as good as it could be.

The Standards Gap: Setting Service Standards

Getting back to the Paradise Motel in Maine for a moment, suppose because of a number of complaints or because business was falling off it set out to determine customers' service expectations and gained a pretty good idea of them. The next step would be to set its service standards accordingly and develop systems to meet the customers' service expectations. How, for instance, can it make sure that every room is cleaned and ready by an optimum time of day in the eyes of the customers, or that the breakfast is checked for freshness and quality every day?

Service providers, like this housekeeper at a hotel, generally want to do a good job, but they need to be trained to know what exactly a good job entails.

To consistently deliver service that meets customers' expectations, firms must set specific, measurable goals. For instance, for the Paradise Motel, the most efficient process might have been to start cleaning rooms at 8:00 a.m. and finish by 5:00 p.m. But many guests want to sleep late, and new arrivals want to get into their room as soon as they arrive, often before 5:00. So a customer-oriented standard would mandate that the rooms get cleaned between 10:00 a.m. and 2:00 p.m.

Service providers generally want to do a good job, as long as they know what is expected of them.[29] Motel employees should be shown, for instance, exactly how managers expect them to clean a room and what specific tasks they are responsible for performing. In general, more employees will buy into a quality-oriented process if they are involved in setting the goals. For instance, suppose an important employee of the motel objects to disposable plastic cups and suggests actual drinking glasses in the rooms would be classier as well as more ecological. There might be a cost/benefit trade-off to consider here, but if management listens to her and makes the change in this case, it should likely make the employee all the more committed to other tasks involved in cleaning and preparing rooms.

The employees must be thoroughly trained not only to complete their specific tasks but also how to treat guests, and the manager needs to set an example of high service standards, which will permeate throughout the organization. The kind of "attitude" Marcia got, for instance, when she registered a complaint with the assistant manager at the Paradise is not a recipe for generating repeat customers and should not be tolerated. For frontline service employees under stress, however, pleasant interactions with customers do not always come naturally. Although people can be taught specific tasks related to their jobs, this is not easily extended to interpersonal relations. But it is simply not enough to tell employees to "be nice" or "do what customers want." A quality goal should be specific, such as: Greet every customer/guest you encounter with "Good morning/afternoon/evening, Sir or Ma'am." Try to greet customers by name.

In extreme cases, such training becomes even more crucial. From long ticket lines to cancelled flights to lost baggage to safety concerns, customer service incidents are on the rise in the airline industry. (See Social and Mobile Marketing 13.2, later in the chapter, for one such famous incident.) Faced with these mounting complaints, some airlines are attempting to implement better employee training geared toward identifying and defusing potentially explosive situations.

The Delivery Gap: Delivering Service Quality

The delivery gap is where "the rubber meets the road," where the customer directly interacts with the service provider. Even if there are adequate standards in place, the employees are well-trained, and management is committed to meeting or exceeding customers' service expectations, there can still be delivery gaps. It could very well have been that Marcia experienced several delivery gaps at the Paradise Motel. It could have been that the unclean room, the assistant manager's attitude, the unheated swimming pool, the poor piano bar singer, or the stale food resulted from unforeseen or unusual circumstances. While some of these issues such as an unclean room or the "attitude" Marcia encountered should have been avoided, it is possible that the motel had a power outage resulting in the unheated swimming pool, the regular piano bar singer was ill, and the breakfast was stale because of a missed delivery. The maid could not vacuum the room because of the lack of power, and the assistant manager felt assaulted on all sides by these problems. But the result was a lost customer. Even if there are no other gaps, a delivery gap always results in a service failure.

EXHIBIT 13.7 Methods to Reduce Delivery Gaps

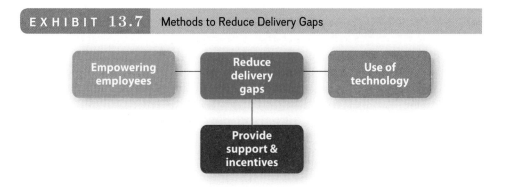

Delivery gaps can be reduced when employees are empowered to spontaneously act in the customers' and the firm's best interests when problems or crises are experienced. Such empowerment might have saved the day for Marcia and the Paradise. Empowerment means employees are supported in their efforts to do their jobs effectively.[30] (See Exhibit 13.7.)

Empowering Service Providers In the service context, **empowerment** means allowing employees to make decisions about how service gets provided to customers. When frontline employees are authorized to make decisions to help their customers, service quality generally improves. Empowerment becomes more important when the service is more individualized. Nordstrom provides an overall objective—satisfy customer needs—and then encourages employees to do whatever is necessary to achieve the objective. For example, a Nordstrom shoe sales associate decided to break up two pairs of shoes, one a size 10 and the other a size 10½, to sell a hard-to-fit customer. Although the other two shoes were unsalable and therefore it made for an unprofitable sale, the customer purchased five other pairs that day and became a loyal Nordstrom customer as a result. Empowering service providers with only a rule like "Use your best judgment" (as Nordstrom does) might cause chaos. At Nordstrom, department managers avoid abuses by coaching and training salespeople to understand what "Use your best judgment" specifically means.

Support and Incentives for Employees To ensure that service is delivered properly, management needs to support the service providers in several ways and give them incentives. This is basic. A service provider's job can often be difficult, especially when customers are unpleasant or less than reasonable. But the service provider cannot be rude or offensive just because the customer is. The old cliché, "Service with a smile," remains the best approach, but for this to work employees must feel supported.

First, managers and coworkers should provide **emotional support** to service providers by demonstrating a concern for their well-being and standing behind their decisions. Because it can be very disconcerting when a waiter is abused by a customer who believes her food was improperly prepared, for instance, restaurant managers must be supportive and help the employee get through his or her emotional reaction to the berating experienced.[31] Such support can extend to empowering the waiter to rectify the situation by giving the customer new food and a free dessert, in which case the manager must understand the waiter's decision, not punish him for giving away too much.

Second, service providers require **instrumental support**—the systems and equipment to deliver the service properly. Many retailers provide state-of-the-art instrumental support for their service providers. In-store kiosks help sales associates provide more detailed and complete product information and enable them to make sales of merchandise that is either not carried in the store or is temporarily out of stock.

Social and Mobile Marketing 13.1   Making Apps Work to Serve[32]

More than 100 million people have smartphones. Approximately half of them make purchases on these devices. Thus nearly 100 percent of companies want to find ways to exploit the potential of this channel. In this huge market, consumers generally are younger and wealthier than others who own older-model mobile phones. For example, more than 50 percent of mobile retail consumers earn at least $75,000 annually.

These statistics also describe the consumers most likely to buy from fashion-oriented companies, whether they sell fashion magazine content, commerce, or brand information. In response, Style.com offers a mobile application for people to access the same content available on the *Style* magazine website, including blogs, reviews, couture shows, and video feeds. Other apps provide a more in-depth look at a particular brand. Louis Vuitton's NOWNESS app combines magazine content with brand promotion. For London's famous Harrods

department store, a mobile app helps consumers navigate the extensive geography of the actual store.

With the Stylish Girl app, customers instead can search a variety of stores, to compare prices and available assortments, while also storing their favorite items from each store in a virtual closet. Pose is a photo-sharing app for style and fashion; Snapette focuses on shoes and bags and aims to help customers find the merchandise they want according to their immediate location.

Even with all of these different types of apps, only a few actually improve the multichannel customer's shopping experience, such as by helping customers regardless of whether they use their smartphones or visit the stores. Such multichannel services represent the best way forward for mobile applications if they hope to get shoppers, and their vast purchasing power, on board.

Third, the support that managers provide must be consistent and coherent throughout the organization. Patients expect physicians to provide great patient care using state-of-the-art procedures and medications, but because they are tied to managed-care systems (health maintenance organizations or HMOs), many doctors must squeeze more people into their office hours and prescribe less optimal, less expensive, courses of treatment. These conflicting goals can be very frustrating to patients.

Finally, a key part of any customer service program is providing rewards to employees for their excellent service. Numerous firms have developed a service reputation by ensuring that their employees are themselves recognized for recognizing the value the firm places on customer service. Travelocity, for example, features employees who champion the customer service experience in a weekly e-mail. Believing that engaged employees are the key to customer satisfaction, it works to create an atmosphere that reinforces the commitment to customers by encouraging employees to nominate colleagues who exemplify its commitment to customers. Through constant feedback about who is serving the customer best, as well as smaller events such as monthly lunches with the CEO for selected employees, Travelocity creates a business environment that recognizes and rewards customer service.[33] The results for Travelocity have been a wealth of awards, such as a top ranking on the Customer Online Respect Survey and a designation as the "World's Leading Travel Internet Site" for several consecutive years.[34]

Use of Technology Technology can also be employed to reduce delivery gaps. Technology has become an increasingly important facilitator of the delivery of services. Using technology to facilitate service delivery can provide many benefits, such as access to a wider variety of services, a greater degree of control by the customer over the services, and the ability to obtain information. Social and Mobile Marketing 13.1 describes one such option. The use of technology also improves the service provider's efficiency and reduces servicing costs; in some cases, it can lead to a competitive advantage over less service-oriented competitors.[35]

Technological advances that help close the delivery gap are expanding. Salons and cosmetics counters use kiosks to show customers how they would look with different beauty products and various hair colors. Stores enable customers to scan price tags and then have a kiosk recommend complementary items. Touchscreen

Which store has better customer service: the one with self-checkout (left), or the store offering a face-to-face interaction with the customer? It depends on whom you ask.

terminals at tables in Chuck E. Cheese let customers order food and play games, from the comfort of their own table.[36] The technological delivery of services can cause problems though. Some customers either do not embrace the idea of replacing a human with a machine for business interactions or have problems using the technology. In other cases, the technology may not perform adequately, such as ATMs that run out of money or are out of order. Supermarket self-checkout devices are too challenging for some customers.

The Communications Gap: Communicating the Service Promise

Poor communication between marketers and their customers can result in a mismatch between an ad campaign's or a salesperson's promises and the service the firm can actually offer. Although firms have difficulty controlling service quality because it can vary from day to day and provider to provider, they have nearly constant control over how they communicate their service package to their customers. This control involves a significant responsibility, as Ethical and Societal Dilemma 13.1 notes.

If a firm promises more than it can deliver, customers' expectations won't be met. An advertisement may lure a customer into a service situation once, but if the service doesn't deliver on the promise, the customer will never return. Dissatisfied customers also are likely to tell others about the underperforming service, using word of mouth or, increasingly, the Internet, which has become an important channel for dissatisfied customers to vent their frustrations.

The communications gap can be reduced by managing customer expectations and by promising only what you can deliver, or possibly even a little less.[37] Suppose you need an operation, and the surgeon explains, "You'll be out of the hospital in five days and back to your normal routine in a month." You have the surgery and feel well enough to leave the hospital three days later. Two weeks after that, you're

Ethical and Societal Dilemma 13.1   Fake Reviews[38]

Yelp, TripAdvisor, and Amazon have all made user ratings and reviews a familiar—and even essential—part of the online toolbox for shoppers and other consumers. From the consumer's perspective, what better preparation could there be for a major purchase than to see what other, objective customers have to say about the product or service under consideration?

For retailers and service professionals, online reviews offer a huge benefit too. For some companies, especially small service providers that cannot afford much marketing, online reviews function as a low-cost form of advertising. A business seeking to meet or exceed customer expectations receives valuable, candid feedback from customers, which it can use to measure how well it is meeting customer expectations. Some firms even use this feedback in their formal voice-of-customer programs to improve company operations.

But who benefits from fake consumer reviews? Seemingly the company might, assuming it does not get caught. But federal regulators are taking action to ensure that such deceptive advertising does not pay, and recent events suggest that companies that fake their reviews often get caught.

VIP Deals, an online retailer that sells leather cases for digital tablets on Amazon, invited its customers to post reviews—and promised that if those reviews were positive, the customer would receive a complete refund. Within weeks, nearly all of the company's 355 online reviews gave the VIP Deals leather case four or five stars. But Amazon guidelines prohibit compensation for customer reviews, and the VIP Deals page soon disappeared.

A leather case for your iPad is one thing. Accurate, truthful information takes on paramount importance for a service like plastic surgery. But Lifestyle Lift seemed to disregard customers' expectations that they could receive truthful information. When unhappy customers started posting too many negative comments on its website, the company launched a coverup, rather than investigating the complaints to help its physicians and staff address the problems. On bogus websites, fictitious posters gave high praise to the company, while also asserting that previously posted complaints had been phony. The state of New York soon filed suit and prompted a $300,000 settlement from Lifestyle Lift.

Crowd-sourced online opinions of consumers have become a major source of information about products and services (recall our discussion of crowd-sourcing in Chapter 11). When that information is authentic, it serves consumers and companies both. But when companies manipulate online reviews, it seems as if all of society is harmed. What—if anything—should be done about it?

---

playing tennis again. Clearly, you will tend to think your surgeon is a genius. However, regardless of the operation's success, if you had to stay in the hospital for 10 days and it took you two months to recover, you would undoubtedly be upset.

A relatively easy way to manage customer expectations is to coordinate how the expectation is created and the way the service is provided. Expectations typically are created through promotions, advertising, or personal selling. Delivery is another function altogether. If a salesperson promises a client that an order can be delivered in one day, and that delivery actually takes a week, the client will be disappointed. However, if the salesperson coordinates the order with those responsible for the service delivery, the client's expectations likely will be met. As we noted in this chapter's opener, Zappos regularly provides better than promised delivery dates to help delight their customers.

Customer expectations can be managed when the service is delivered. Recorded messages tell customers who have phoned a company with a query how many minutes they will have to wait before the next operator is available. Sellers automatically inform online customers of any items that are out of stock. Whether online or in a store, retailers can warn their customers to shop early during a sale because supplies of the sale item are limited. People are generally reasonable when they are warned that some aspect of the service may be below their expectations. They just don't like surprises!

When Amazon first introduced its Prime service, its goal was to build customer loyalty. For $79 per year, membership guaranteed unlimited two-day shipping on all products purchased on the site. The innovation was an immediate success. Millions of Amazon's customers signed up, and they were less likely to purchase from anywhere else.

The program played directly on their consumer psychology: Customers realize that they earn more from the program when they use it more, at no extra cost to them. For example, 10 products purchased on Amazon with two-day shipping likely pay for the $79 membership. If they go on to buy 100 or 1000 products, still for just $79, customers feel like they have put one over on the company. In a sense, they have. Amazon has demonstrated its willingness to lose significant profits to develop its program and build unparalleled customer loyalty.

Over time, Amazon has added many new features to Prime, but the cost remains the same. Estimates suggest that Amazon spends about $90 annually on Prime customers, at a loss of $11 per customer. Such spending has dampened Amazon's profits because of increased operating expenses. But Amazon believes it can offset these losses by increasing demand for its products from Prime customers.

The offering has improved dramatically with the introduction of Amazon's Kindle Fire. Specifically, Amazon now offers a book-lending service for Prime customers who own the Kindle Fire, even though some publishers demand that Amazon pay for the digital copies any and every time a customer borrows a book. For example, the books in the popular *Hunger Games* series sell for $8 wholesale. Amazon plans to buy those titles for Prime customers to borrow. Because analysts estimate that several million Prime customers own a Kindle Fire, the lending service could cost Amazon tens of millions of dollars annually!

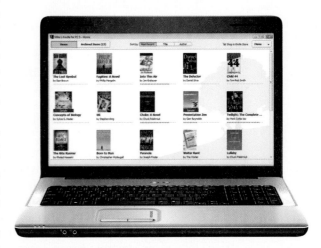

At Amazon.com's Kindle store, Prime customers can borrow books for free.

Service Quality and Customer Satisfaction and Loyalty

Good service quality leads to satisfied and loyal customers. As we discussed in Chapter 6, customers inevitably wind up their purchase decision process by undertaking a postpurchase evaluation. This evaluation after the purchase may produce three outcomes: satisfaction, dissonance, and loyalty (see again Exhibit 6.3 in Chapter 6). Dissonance may just be a passing emotion that is overcome; we will discuss recovery from an actual service failure in the next section. Satisfaction, on the other hand, often leads to loyalty.

Assuming that none of the service gaps that we have discussed above occur, or at least are not too wide, customers should be more or less satisfied. Surveys of customers that ask them to identify the retailer that provides the best customer service thus often show some consistency. A service provider that does a good job one year is likely to keep customers satisfied the next year too, as Exhibit 13.8 shows.

If a firm not only minimizes but eliminates any service gaps, customers are likely to exhibit significant loyalty to that firm—which is what Amazon hopes to achieve with its Amazon Prime service, as Superior Service 13.1 describes. Customers want to

EXHIBIT 13.8	Top Ten Retailers for Customer Service	
Ranking	2010	2011
1.	Zappos	Amazon.com
2.	Amazon.com	L.L.Bean
3.	L.L. Bean	Zappos
4.	Overstock.com	Overstock.com
5.	Lands' End	QVC
6.	JCPenney	Kohl's
7.	Kohl's	Lands' End
8.	QVC	JCPenney
9.	Nordstrom	Newegg
10.	Newegg	Nordstrom

Source: NRF Foundation/American Express, "Consumer Choice Awards," http://www.nrffoundation.com/content/customers-choice-awards. Reprinted with permission of NRF Foundation.

continue receiving such superior service and have no desire to go elsewhere for the offerings it provides them.

CHECK YOURSELF

1. Explain the four service gaps identified by the Gaps Model.
2. List at least two ways to overcome each of the four service gaps.

LO5 Identify three service recovery strategies.

SERVICE RECOVERY

Despite a firm's best efforts, sometimes service providers fail to meet customer expectations. When this happens, the best course of action is to attempt to make amends with the customer and learn from the experience. Of course, it is best to avoid a service failure altogether, but when a failure does occur, the firm has a unique opportunity to demonstrate its customer commitment.[40] Effective service recovery efforts can significantly increase customer satisfaction, purchase intentions, and positive word of mouth, though customers' post-recovery satisfaction levels usually fall lower than their satisfaction level prior to the service failure.[41]

Social and Mobile Marketing 13.2 articulates how social media like YouTube have provided customers with an enormous stage on which to air their dissatisfaction with a product or service. No longer are dissatisfied customers only able to vent their frustrations with a few friends. Today, word of mouth, especially in electronic form, can spread to millions of recipients.

Remember the Paradise Motel in Maine? It could have made amends with Marcia Kessler after its service failures if it had taken some relatively simple, immediate steps: The assistant manager could have apologized for his bad behavior and quickly upgraded her to a suite and/or given her a free night's lodging for a future stay. The motel could also have given her a free lunch or dinner to make up for the bad breakfast. Alternatively, the assistant manager could have asked Marcia how he could resolve the situation and worked with her to come up with an equitable solution. None of these actions would have cost the motel much money.

Had it used the customer lifetime value approach we described in Chapter 10, the motel would have realized that by not taking action, it lost Marcia as a customer forever. Over the next few years, she could have been responsible for several thousand dollars in sales. Instead, Marcia is now likely to spread negative word of mouth about the motel to her friends, family, and through social media like Yelp.com because of its failure to recover. Effective service recovery thus demands (1) listening to the customers and involving them in the service recovery, (2) providing a fair solution, and (3) resolving the problem quickly.[42]

Listening to the Customers and Involving Them in the Service Recovery

Firms often don't find out about service failures until a customer complains. Whether the firm has a formal complaint department or the complaint is offered directly to the service provider, the customer must have the opportunity to air the complaint completely, and the firm must listen carefully to what he or she is saying.

Customers can become very emotional about a service failure, whether the failure is serious (a botched surgical operation) or minor (the wrong change at a restaurant). In many cases, the customer may just want to be heard, and the service provider should give the customer all the time he or she needs to "get it out." The very process of describing a perceived wrong to a sympathetic listener is therapeutic in and of itself. Service providers therefore should welcome the opportunity to

Social and Mobile Marketing 13.2

The 4-Minute and 37-Second Complaint Heard by Millions

Thanks to the Internet, customer service has gone viral. According to an old adage, when customers have a good experience, they tell one person. Those who have a bad experience tell four. But the rise of blogs, Twitter, YouTube, and similar sites has changed the very meaning of word of mouth. Whereas once, to spread word of mouth, a sender had to know the recipient, today millions of people can learn about service problems that strangers experience, all in a matter of hours.

United Airlines learned this lesson the hard way. A member of the band Sons of Maxwell watched from a plane window as baggage handlers tossed luggage with little regard for the value or fragility of the instruments in the cargo.[43] Musician Dave Carroll complained immediately to flight attendants, but to no avail. After arriving at his destination, Carroll discovered his $3,500 acoustic guitar was broken. He made it through his performances using alternative guitars and then, on his return flight a week later, complained again about the damaged instrument. Over the next weeks and months, he contacted the airline repeatedly about the problem while also shelling out $1,200 to get his guitar fixed. When Carroll did finally hear from the airline regarding compensation, he was informed that his claim was denied because he hadn't filed it appropriately.

He responded with a 4-Minute and 37-second complaint in the form of songs and videos posted to the Internet. The first tune, called "United Breaks Guitars," suggests that flying a different airline or driving would have been preferable to flying United. The video scored 5 million hits in a matter of weeks, with more than 11.5 million views to date.[44] A month later, the band released another song that poked fun at one of United's customer service employees and the airline's policies for handling baggage complaints. The third tune acknowledged United's attempts to improve but also cautioned that customers would switch to other carriers without lasting improvements. Even though bloggers were not uniformly impressed by the music, many offered their own horror stories of United's customer service, creating a maelstrom of bad public relations for the airline.

United responded with an admission of guilt on Twitter, a $3,000 donation to a musical charity, and an ad campaign indicating it took complaints about luggage handling seriously. The company also saw an opportunity to turn a single customer service problem into a training opportunity: With Carroll's permission, they use the video to improve passenger service worldwide.[45] But United Airlines still lost $180 million, or 10 percent of its stock price, due to this incident.[46]

Warning to United Airlines: Don't mess with Dave Carroll or his guitar. If you do, he will write a song about you and post it on the Internet.

be that sympathetic ear, listen carefully, and appear (and actually be) anxious to rectify the situation to ensure it doesn't happen again.[47]

When the company and the customer work together, the outcome is often better than either could achieve on their own. This co-creation logic applies especially well to service recovery. A service failure is a negative experience, but when customers participate in its resolution, it results in a more positive outcome than simply listening to their complaint and providing a preapproved set of potential solutions that may satisfy them.

Suppose, for instance, that when you arrived at the airport in San Francisco, your flight had been overbooked, and you were bumped. Of course, good customer service required the ticket agent to listen to your frustration and help provide a fair solution. But the most obvious potential solution from the airline's perspective might not have been the best solution for you. They might have been inclined to put you on the next available flight which would be a red-eye that left at midnight and got you to New York at 6:30 a.m. But if you don't sleep well on planes and you have an important business meeting the next afternoon, the best solution from your perspective would be to have the airline put you up in an airport hotel so you can get a good night's sleep, and then put you on an early morning flight that would get you to New York in time for your meeting, well-rested and ready to go. Thus, by working closely with you to understand your needs, the ticket agent would be able to co-create a great solution to the service failure.

Finding a Fair Solution

Most people realize that mistakes happen. But when they happen, customers want to be treated fairly, whether that means *distributive* or *procedural* fairness.[48] Their perception of what "fair" means is based on their previous experience with other firms, how they have seen other customers treated, material they have read, and stories recounted by their friends.

Distributive Fairness **Distributive fairness** pertains to a customer's perception of the benefits he or she received compared with the costs (inconvenience or loss). Customers want to be compensated a fair amount for a perceived loss that resulted from a service failure. If, for instance, a person arrives at the airport gate and finds her flight is overbooked, she may believe that taking the next flight that day and receiving a travel voucher is adequate compensation for the inconvenience. But if no flights are available until the next day, the traveler may require additional compensation, such as overnight accommodations, meals, and a round-trip ticket to be used at a later date.[49]

The key to distributive fairness, of course, is listening carefully to the customer. One customer, traveling on vacation, may be satisfied with a travel voucher, whereas another may need to get to the destination on time because of a business appointment. Regardless of how the problem is solved, customers typically want tangible restitution—in this case, to get to their destination—not just an apology. If providing tangible restitution isn't possible, the next best thing is to assure the customer that steps are being taken to prevent the failure from recurring.

Procedural Fairness With regard to complaints, **procedural fairness** refers to the perceived fairness of the process used to resolve them. Customers want efficient complaint procedures over whose outcomes they have some influence. Customers tend to believe they have been treated fairly if the service providers follow specific company guidelines. Nevertheless, rigid adherence to rules can have deleterious effects. Have you ever returned an item to a store, even a very inexpensive item, that needed a manager's approval? The process can take several minutes and irritate everyone in the checkout line. Furthermore, most managers' cursory inspection of the item or the situation would not catch a fraudulent return. In a case like this, the procedure the company uses to handle a return probably overshadows any potential positive outcomes. Therefore, as we noted previously, service providers should be empowered with some procedural flexibility to solve customer complaints.

A "no questions asked" return policy has been offered as a customer service by many retailers for years. But because of its high cost as a result of customers abusing the policy, many retailers have modified their return policy.[50] Some large retailers now limit their returns to 90 days, considered a reasonable amount of time for customers to return an item. Others will only grant a store credit based on the lowest selling price for the item if the customer doesn't have a receipt. In addition, for some consumer electronics products that have been opened, customers must pay a 15 percent restocking fee.

Resolving Problems Quickly

The longer it takes to resolve a service failure, the more irritated the customer will become and the more people he or she is likely to tell about the problem. To resolve service failures quickly, firms need clear policies, adequate training for their employees, and empowered employees. Health insurance companies, for instance, have made a concerted effort in recent years to avoid service failures that occur because customers' insurance claims have not been handled quickly or to the customers' satisfaction.

CHECK YOURSELF

1. Why is service recovery so important to companies?
2. What can companies do to recover from a service failure?

Summing Up

LO1 **Describe how the marketing of services differs from the marketing of products.**

Unlike products, services are intangible, inseparable, variable, and perishable. They cannot be seen or touched, which makes it difficult to describe their benefits or promote them. Service providers therefore enhance service delivery with tangible attributes, like a nice atmosphere or price benefits. Services get produced and consumed at the same time, so marketers must work quickly, and they are more variable than products, though service providers attempt to reduce this variability as much as possible. Finally, because consumers cannot stockpile perishable services, marketers often provide incentives to stagger demand.

LO2 **Discuss the four gaps in the Service Gap Model.**

The knowledge gap reflects the difference between customers' expectations and the firm's perception of those customer expectations. Firms need to match customer expectations with actual service through research. The standards gap is the difference between the firm's perceptions of customers' expectations and the service standards it sets. Appropriate service standards and measurements of service performance help close this gap. The delivery gap is the difference between the firm's service standards and the actual service it provides to customers. Closing this gap requires adequate training and empowerment of employees. The communication gap refers to the difference between the actual service provided to customers and the service that the firm's promotion program promises. Firms close the communications gap by managing customer expectations and promising only what they can deliver.

LO3 **Examine the five service quality dimensions.**

First, reliability refers to whether the provider consistently provides an expected level of service. Second, responsiveness means that the provider notes consumers' desires and requests and then addresses them. Third, assurance reflects the service provider's own confidence in its abilities. Fourth, empathy entails the provider's recognition and understanding of consumer needs. Finally, tangibles are the elements that go along with the service, such as the magazines in a doctor's waiting room.

LO4 **Explain the zone of tolerance.**

The area between customers' desired service and the minimum level of service they will accept is the zone of tolerance. It is the difference between what the customer really wants and what he or she will accept before going elsewhere. Firms can assess their customers' zone of tolerance by determining the desired and expected level of service for each service dimension, their perceptions of how well the focal service performs and how well a competitive service performs, and the importance of each service quality dimension.

LO5 **Identify three service recovery strategies.**

In a best-case scenario, the service never fails. But some failures are inevitable and require the firm to make amends to the customer by: (1) listening carefully and involving the customer in the service recovery; (2) finding a fair solution to the problem that compensates the customer for the failure and follows procedures the customer believes are fair; and (3) resolving the problem quickly.

Key Terms

- communication gap, 402
- customer service, 396
- delivery gap, 402
- distributive fairness, 416
- emotional support, 409
- empowerment, 409
- heterogeneity, 400

- inseparable, 399
- instrumental support, 409
- intangible, 397
- knowledge gap, 402
- perishable, 401
- procedural fairness, 416
- service, 396

- service gap, 402
- service quality, 403
- standards gap, 402
- voice-of-customer (VOC) program, 406
- zone of tolerance, 406

Marketing Applications

1. Those companies from which you purchase products and services are not pure sellers of services, nor are they pure sellers of products. What services does a pizza restaurant provide? What goods does the post office provide?

2. You have been sitting in the waiting room of your mechanic's shop for more than an hour. With the knowledge that products are different from services, develop a list of the things the shop manager could do to improve the overall service delivery. Consider how the shop might overcome problems associated with the tangibility, separability, heterogeneity, and perishability of services.

3. You have conducted a zone of tolerance analysis for a local dry cleaners. You find that the lengths of the reliability and responsiveness boxes are much greater than those of the other three service quality dimensions. You also find that the dry cleaners is positioned above the zone box on reliability but below the box on responsiveness. What should you tell the manager to do?

4. Assume you were hired by the local grocery store to help assess their service quality. How would you go about undertaking this project?

5. What should a restaurant server do who is faced with an irate customer who has received undercooked food after a long wait? How can they avoid a service failure by being empowered? What should they do?

6. What types of support and incentives could your university provide advisors to help make them more attentive to students' needs?

7. What technologies do you use that help facilitate your transactions with a specific retailer or service provider? Would you rather use the technology or engage in a face-to-face relationship with a person? How, if at all, would your parents' answer to these two questions be different?

8. A local health club is running a promotional campaign that promises you can lose an inch a month off your waist if you join the club and follow its program. How might this claim cause a communications gap? What should the club do to avoid a service failure?

9. Suppose the health club didn't listen to your advice and ran the promotional campaign as is. A new member has come in to complain that not only did he not lose inches off his waist, he actually gained weight. How should the health club manager proceed?

10. You are hired by a career consulting firm that promises to market new graduates to high-paying employers. The firm provides potential clients with an impressive list of employers. It charges the clients a fee, and then a separate finder's fee if the client gets a position. The firm aggressively markets its services and has a large client base. You learn that the firm simply takes submitted résumés and posts them to a variety of online job search engines. The firm never actually contacts any firms on its clients' behalf. The CEO, himself a recent college grad, tells you that the firm never promises to actually contact potential employers, only that they have access to employers and will distribute clients' résumés. What do you think of the career consulting firm's practices?

1. Yolanda manages a Best Sleep Inn along an interstate highway. She knows from experience that five to 10 last-minute customers will call after 8 p.m. each evening looking for a room and asking the price. Yolanda has empowered her staff to offer discounts when the motel is largely vacant, and to quote the standard price when the motel is close to full. She knows her service is _____, meaning that if no one stays in the room, it generates no revenue that evening.

    a. intangible
    b. inseparable
    c. variable
    d. durable
    e. perishable

2. A _____ gap reflects the difference between firm's perception of customer expectations and firm standards for service to be delivered.

    a. seniority
    b. knowledge
    c. standards
    d. delivery
    e. communication

    (Answers to these two questions can be found on page 648.)

    Go to www.mhhe.com/grewal4e to practice an additional 11 questions.

SERVICES ZONE OF TOLERANCE

Use the Toolkit provided at www.mhhe.com/grewal4e to assess the zone of tolerance for several service providers.

1. What services does JetBlue (www.jetblue.com) offer? Go to JetBlue's website, click on "Flying on Jet Blue." Compare the services of JetBlue and Delta Airlines (www.delta.com). Which would you prefer to fly if the price of a ticket was the same?

2. Go to Zappos' website, www.zappos.com, and examine its customer service offerings. Next, go to Reseller Ratings, www.resellerratings.com, and look up Zappos. Based on these reviews, does Zappos have a service gap? If so, how can they close it?

ZIPCAR: DELIVERING ONLY AS MUCH DRIVING AS YOU WANT

Historically, the expectation that your car will be waiting for you at the curb every morning got hard-wired into many Americans with the growth of the auto industry. But that expectation has gone haywire by now for many city dwellers, who have been frustrated by the soaring costs and parking pressures that confront modern drivers. For them, Zipcar, the world's leading car-sharing company,[51] offers the pleasure of driving without the hassles of ownership.

The Cambridge, Massachusetts–based company rents self-service vehicles by the hour or day to urban residents who prefer to pay for just as much driving as they absolutely need. Car sharing eliminates issues related to parking shortages; overnight parking restrictions; or soaring gas, insurance, and tax bills. That promise resonates well with consumer expectations on many fronts, especially among Zipcar's primary urban customers, the large segments of college students who also enjoy the service, and even suburbanites who just work in the city.

Zipcars are for people who don't need a car all the time, like urbanites and college students.

Still Zipcar CEO Scott Griffith realizes that the company's biggest growth obstacle is Americans' inability to envision life without a car.[52] To push an attitude shift, Zipcar makes the car-sharing experience as easy as possible, with just four simple steps:

1. Join the network.
2. Reserve your car online or from your smartphone.
3. Unlock the car with your Zipcard.
4. Drive away.

Today the car-sharing network has more than 650,000 members and 9,500 vehicles in 13 major metropolitan areas and on 150 college campuses throughout the United States, Canada, and Britain.[53] With so many locations, the company could bring convenient car sharing to a far larger market; it estimates that 10 million residents, business commuters, and university students now live or work just a short walk away from an available Zipcar.[54]

Zipcar is banking on more than shifting attitudes. Emerging trends due to the economic downturn and changing buying habits have helped spur growth. On average, automobiles consume 19 percent of household incomes,[55] yet many cars stand idle for 90 percent of each day. Drivers seeking a less expensive and less wasteful alternative thus might save up to 70 percent on their transportation costs, because an annual Zipcar membership costs just $42, and the average member spends $428 a year.[56]

Zipcar's service model fits in with the emergence of on-demand, pay-per-use options, such as Netflix for movies, iTunes for music, and e-readers for books. Moreover, the popularity of mobile shopping and the growing expectation that they can order anything, anywhere, anytime from their smartphones have made urban young adults and college students two of Zipcar's most fervent member groups. For these "Zipsters," ordering up a set of wheels on the go is far more appealing than being saddled with car payments.

A strong urban public transportation system also helps make car sharing more attractive. That's why Zipcar started off in high-density urban areas such as Boston, New York, and Washington, DC, with their great public transportation systems already in place. Wherever subways and buses work, car sharing can extend the transit system's reach. By locating cars near transit route endpoints, travelers gain an easy extension on subway or bus schedules to their final destinations. Zipcar even offers members an overnight option, for grabbing a car in the evening and returning it the next morning.

Finally, the logic of car sharing works well in settings marked by increased urbanization. According to the United Nations, cities will contain 59 percent of the world's population by 2030.[57] Many of these areas already face congestion, space demands, and environmental threats from crowding too many gas-driven vehicles into a small, population-dense space. Griffith estimates that every Zipcar would replace 15–20 personal cars.[58] Thus some cities work with Zipcar to identify and secure parking spaces close to subway stops and rail stations. New York and Chicago also rent Zipcars for municipal workers so they can shuttle more efficiently across city locations during their workday. Zipcar also provides fleet management services to local, state, and federal agencies.

Car sharing could translate into a $10 billion market globally.[59] Cities in Europe and Asia are well primed for car sharing, by virtue of their strong rail systems, heavy reliance on public transit, and widespread adoption of mobile and wireless technologies. A deal with Spain's largest car-sharing company, Avancar, is a first venture in Zipcar's planned global expansion.[60]

Such growth requires strong logistics, and Zipcar is backed by a corps of fleet managers and vehicle coordinators who track, schedule, and oversee vehicle maintenance; proprietary hardware and software technology that helps it communicate with drivers and track vehicles; and a large fleet that includes hybrid vehicles for fuel efficiency, as well as minivans to appeal to families who want to take a trip to the beach.[61] Zipcar estimates that it processes 2.6 million reservations per year, and its reservation system has almost never failed.[62]

These behind-the-scenes moves aim to make Zipcar's service simple, convenient, and reliable. But failures are inevitable, as one customer's experience showed. The customer went to pick up his designated vehicle at the time and place reserved for him, but he discovered no car there. The Zipcar representative told him that it might be out, being serviced or cleaned, or it could have been delayed by another driver running late. But such excuses did little to alleviate the frustration of being stuck with no transportation.

Learning of his predicament, Zipcar tried but was unable to find another car in close proximity. Therefore, it quickly authorized the customer to take a taxi and promised to reimburse him up to $100. Although the "free ride" did not altogether mitigate the stress and inconvenience of the service failure, Zipcar's response showed him that the company was committed to doing right by him, even if that meant sending business to a competitor, the taxi company.

The considerable dimensions of a global car-sharing market are already emerging. Zipcar's 10-year experience and first-mover status in the market positions it well to compete. But the race to dominate is sure to intensify, especially as traditional car rental companies with great name recognition, such as Hertz and Enterprise, move into the marketplace.[63] Whether Zipcar can maintain its space in this market depends mostly on its ability to meet its own standards for customer service—simplicity, convenience, and reliability—consistently and effectively.

Questions

1. Using the building blocks (five dimensions) of service quality (see Exhibit 13.4), evaluate Zipcar.

2. Compare Zipcar's service quality performance with that of the most recent car rental service (e.g., Avis, Hertz) that you may have used.

3. How well has Zipcar handled service failure situations? What could it do to improve recovery efforts?

Value Capture

CHAPTER 14
Pricing Concepts for Establishing Value

CHAPTER 15
Strategic Pricing Methods

Section Five contains two chapters on pricing dedicated to value capture. Chapter 14 examines the importance of setting the right price, the relationship between price and quantity sold, break-even analysis, the impact of price wars, and how the Internet has changed the way people shop. Chapter 15 looks specifically at how to set prices.

SECTION 5

CHAPTER 14

Pricing Concepts for Establishing Value

P ricing is a key part of the value proposition for any purchase. After all, value reflects the relationship between benefits and costs. And when the economy sours, and consumer income drops, no sticker price escapes sharp scrutiny, especially in the supermarket. Shoppers on a tight budget may still need to buy that gallon of milk every week; but demand is far more elastic for items like candy or soft drinks. For such nonessential products, the challenge comes down to pricing strategy: How do you lure customers back when they're desperate to spend less?

Even corporate giant Coca-Cola has had to grapple with this question. The soda that became shorthand worldwide for a quick, ice-cold drink started out in 1886 as a headache cure called Coca-Cola. By the end of World War II, the popular American brand controlled more than 60 percent of the soft drink market worldwide. Over the years, that dominance gave way to an intense rivalry with Pepsi-Cola; today each company controls about a third of the $75 billion U.S. retail soda market, the other key player being Dr Pepper Snapple Group.[1]

But recent market changes have transformed the soda industry. Health-conscious consumers have abandoned high-sugar sodas; and new alternative beverages—iced teas, bottled waters, and vitamin drinks—now compete for shelf space. U.S. soda consumption has declined, as a result, for six years in a row,[2] and over the last decade, Coke and its rivals have lost well over a third of their sales.[3] Overseas business now generates the bulk of Coca-Cola's revenue growth, much of it coming from Russia and China.[4]

In the search for a pricing strategy to jumpstart flagging U.S. revenues, Coca-Cola has also confronted another problem. Manufacturing costs are up about $700 million a year to cover higher prices for plastic, high-fructose syrup, and fruit.[5]

So Coke's new pricing approach had to reconcile two diverging trends: rising costs and the demand for lower prices. Fortunately, the company had already confronted this problem in Mexico, the world's largest per-capita consumer of Coke. When economic crisis hit and the peso dropped in 1994, Coca-Cola started offering smaller, lower-priced packages to get customers to buy again. Today

LEARNING OBJECTIVES

LO1 List the four pricing orientations.

LO2 Explain the relationship between price and quantity sold.

LO3 Explain price elasticity.

LO4 Describe how to calculate a product's break-even point.

LO5 Indicate the four types of price competitive levels.

Coke fans there have more than 30 package options, from 6.75 ounce containers to three-liter bottles.[6]

In the U.S., Coke traditionally has offered three sizes—20-ounce bottles, two-liter bottles, and cases of 12-ounce cans. Now it has added three smaller package options for consumers looking to spend less. Under this increasingly segmented price-packaging strategy, Coke now comes in a 12.5-ounce bottle for 89 cents and a new 99-cent 16-ounce bottle. The company also cut the price on its eight-pack of 7.5-ounce "mini" cans, hoping that the smaller can originally designed for weight-conscious consumers will also appeal to those on a budget.

Can Coca-Cola boost U.S. revenue and profits while offering reduced-volume options? That seems like a paradox, but the company may have found a strategic "sweet spot." Smaller containers cost less, but consumers pay more per ounce. Those who still want larger bottles and cans will face higher prices. Coca-Cola is hoping that its selection of sizes and prices will ensure that for every fan, Coke is still the real thing.

Although knowing how consumers arrive at their perceptions of value is critical to developing successful pricing strategies, sellers also must consider other factors—which is why developing a good pricing strategy is such a formidable challenge to all firms. Do it right, and the rewards to the firm will be substantial. Do it wrong, and failure will be swift and severe. But even if a pricing strategy is implemented well, consumers, economic conditions, markets, competitors, government regulations, and even a firm's own products change constantly—and that means that a good pricing strategy today may not remain an effective pricing strategy tomorrow.

So much rides on marketers setting the right price that we take two chapters to explain the role of price in the marketing mix. First, in this chapter, we explain what "price" is as a marketing concept, why it is important, how marketers set pricing objectives, and how various factors influence price setting. In the next chapter, we extend this foundation by focusing on specific pricing strategies that capitalize on capturing value.

Imagine that a consumer realizes that to save money on a particular item, she will have to drive an additional 20 miles. She may determine that her time and travel costs are not worth the savings, so even though the price tag is higher at a nearby store, she judges the overall cost of buying the product there to be lower. To include aspects of price such as this, we may define **price** as the overall sacrifice a consumer is willing to make to acquire a specific product or service. This sacrifice necessarily includes the money that must be paid to the seller to acquire the item, but it also may involve other sacrifices, whether nonmonetary, like the value of the time necessary to acquire the product or service, or monetary, like travel costs, taxes, shipping costs, and so forth, all of which the buyer must give up to take possession of the product.[7] It's useful to think of overall price like this to see how the narrower sense of purchase price fits in.

Previously, we have defined *value* as the relationship between the product's benefits and the consumer's costs, which is another way of looking at the same thing. Consumers judge the benefits the product delivers against the sacrifice necessary to obtain it, then make a purchase decision based on this overall judgment of value. Thus, a great but overpriced product can be judged as low in value and may not sell as well as an inferior but well-priced item. In turn, we cannot define price without referring specifically to the product or service associated with it. The key to successful pricing is to match the product or service with the consumer's value perceptions.

In this equation, price also provides information about the quality of products and services. If firms can price their products or services too high, can they price them too low as well? Quite simply, yes. Although price represents the sacrifice consumers make to acquire the product or service, looked at the other way around it also provides helpful signals to consumers. A price set too low may signal low quality, poor performance, or other negative attributes about the product or service. Would you trust your looks to a plastic surgeon advertising rhinoplasty surgery (commonly referred to as a nose job) for only $299.99? We discuss this aspect of price in further detail when we talk about specific pricing strategies in the next chapter, but for now, note that consumers don't necessarily want a low price all the time or for all products. Rather, what they want is high value, which may come with a relatively high or low price, depending on the bundle of benefits the product or service delivers. If the firm wants to deliver value and value is judged by the benefits relative to the cost, then pricing decisions are absolutely critical to the effort to deliver value.

Because price is the only element of the marketing mix that does not generate costs, but instead generates revenue, it is important in its own right. Every other element in the marketing mix may be perfect, but with the wrong price, sales and thus revenue will not accrue. Research has consistently shown that consumers usually rank price as one of the most important factors in their purchase decisions.[8]

Knowing that price is so critical to success, why don't managers put greater emphasis on it as a strategic decision variable? Price is the most challenging of the four Ps to manage, partly because it is often the least understood. Historically, managers have treated price as an afterthought to their marketing strategy, setting prices according to what competitors were charging or, worse yet, adding up their costs and tacking a desired profit on to set the sales price. Prices rarely changed except in response to radical shifts in market conditions. Even today pricing decisions are often relegated to standard rules of thumb that fail to reflect our current understanding of the role of price in the marketing mix.

For example, retailers sometimes use a 100 percent markup rule, otherwise known as "keystoning." That is, they simply double what they paid for the item when they price it for resale (price = wholesale cost × 2). Yet what happens if the store receives a particularly good deal from the manufacturer on an item? If consumers are not sensitive to price changes for the product, should marketers blindly pass this lower price on to consumers? Why lower the price if it will not stimulate more sales? In this case, it might be better for the store not to follow its standard markup practice and instead take the additional profit. Similarly, if the store's cost for an item goes up and consumers are particularly sensitive to price increases for that product, the store might want to set the price at less than double the cost.

As we said, all this is crucial because consumers may use the price of a product or service to judge its quality.[9] Price is a particularly powerful indicator of quality when consumers are less knowledgeable about the product category—a lesson brought home by the movie (based on the book of the same name) *Moneyball*. As the character played by Jonah Hill argues convincingly to Brad Pitt's character, baseball teams often overpay for young, untested talent or big name players, because they don't know how else to set an accurate price.[10]

In a more everyday example of this effect, a research team at Stanford conducted a study in which they gave consumers samples of "different" energy drinks with varying prices, though two of the drinks actually were the same product. These participants paid more or less for the same drink, but "the people who paid discounted prices

Demonstrating that price is often used to judge quality, in the movie Moneyball, *Jonah Hill explains to Brad Pitt's character that baseball teams often overpay for young, untested talent or big name players, because they don't know how else to gauge an appropriate salary.*

Since people use price to judge quality or performance of a product, when a group of people paid less for an energy drink, they were able to solve fewer puzzles than those who paid more.

LO1 List the four pricing orientations.

consistently solved fewer puzzles than the people who paid full price for the drinks."[11] Apparently, consumers believe more expensive products will perform better for them—so strongly that they even display more energy after drinking a more expensive energy booster. In summary, marketers should view pricing decisions as a strategic opportunity to create value rather than as an afterthought to the rest of the marketing mix. Let us now turn to the five basic components of pricing strategies.

THE FIVE CS OF PRICING

Successful pricing strategies are built around the five critical components (the five Cs) of pricing found in Exhibit 14.1.

We examine these components in some detail, because each makes a significant contribution to formulating good pricing policies.[12] To start, the first step is to develop the company's pricing objectives.

Company Objectives

By now, you know that different firms embrace very different goals. These goals should spill down to the pricing strategy, such that the pricing of a company's products and services should support and allow the firm to reach its overall goals. For example, a firm with a primary goal of very high sales growth will likely have a different pricing strategy than a firm with the goal of being a quality leader.

Each firm then embraces objectives that seem to fit with where management thinks the firm needs to go to be successful, in whatever way it defines success. These specific objectives usually reflect how the firm intends to grow. Do managers want it to grow by increasing profits, increasing sales, decreasing competition, or building customer satisfaction?

Company objectives are not as simple as they might first appear. They often can be expressed in slightly different forms that mean very different things. Exhibit 14.2 introduces some common company objectives and corresponding examples of their implications for pricing strategies. These objectives are not always mutually exclusive, because a firm may embrace two or more noncompeting objectives.

Profit Orientation Even though all company methods and objectives may ultimately be oriented toward making a profit, firms implement a **profit orientation** specifically by focusing on target profit pricing, maximizing profits, or target return pricing.

- Firms usually implement **target profit pricing** when they have a particular profit goal as their overriding concern. To meet this targeted profit objective, firms use price to stimulate a certain level of sales at a certain profit per unit.

| EXHIBIT 14.1 | The 5 Cs of Pricing |

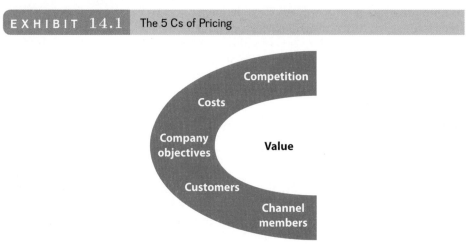

EXHIBIT 14.2	Company Objectives and Pricing Strategy Implications
Company Objective	**Examples of Pricing Strategy Implications**
Profit-oriented	Institute a companywide policy that all products must provide for at least an 18 percent profit margin to reach a particular profit goal for the firm.
Sales-oriented	Set prices very low to generate new sales and take sales away from competitors, even if profits suffer.
Competitor-oriented	To discourage more competitors from entering the market, set prices very low.
Customer-oriented	Target a market segment of consumers who highly value a particular product benefit and set prices relatively high (referred to as premium pricing).

- The **maximizing profits** strategy relies primarily on economic theory. If a firm can accurately specify a mathematical model that captures all the factors required to explain and predict sales and profits, it should be able to identify the price at which its profits are maximized. Of course, the problem with this approach is that actually gathering the data on all these relevant factors and somehow coming up with an accurate mathematical model is an extremely difficult undertaking.

- Other firms are less concerned with the absolute level of profits and more interested in the rate at which their profits are generated relative to their investments. These firms typically turn to **target return pricing** and employ pricing strategies designed to produce a specific return on their investment, usually expressed as a percentage of sales.

Sales Orientation Firms using a **sales orientation** to set prices believe that increasing sales will help the firm more than will increasing profits. Coca-Cola might adopt such an orientation selectively, when it introduces new products that it wants to establish in the market. A new health club might focus on unit sales, dollar sales, or market share and therefore be willing to set a lower membership fee and accept less profit at first to focus on and generate more unit sales. In contrast, a high-end jewelry store might focus on dollar sales and maintain higher prices. The jewelry store relies on its prestige image, as well as the image of its suppliers, to provoke sales. Even though it sells fewer units, it can still generate high dollar sales levels.

Some firms may be more concerned about their overall market share than about dollar sales per se (though these often go hand in hand), because they believe that market share better reflects their success relative to the market conditions than do sales alone. A firm may set low prices to discourage new firms from entering the market, encourage current firms to leave the market, and/or take market share away from competitors—all to gain overall market share. For example, though Apple has sold more than 10 billion songs since the introduction of its iTunes service, it wants to keep increasing its market share, especially as competitors such as Amazon.com make inroads in this arena. Therefore, instead of 99 cents per song—the fixed pricing structure it previously maintained—Apple sets three price tiers (69 cents, 99 cents, and $1.29) for its songs, according to their popularity and recency. The songs that are the most popular cost the most, but by charging less for less popular songs, Apple aims to increase its sales per customer.[13]

Yet adopting a market share objective does not always imply setting low prices. Rarely is the

Philadelphia brand cream cheese dominates its market and is a premium-priced brand.

lowest-price offering the dominant brand in a given market. Heinz ketchup, Philadelphia brand cream cheese, Crest toothpaste, and Nike athletic shoes have all dominated their markets, yet all are premium-priced brands. On the services side, IBM claims market dominance in human resource outsourcing, but again, it is certainly not the lowest price competitor.[14] **Premium pricing** means the firm deliberately prices a product above the prices set for competing products to capture those customers who always shop for the best or for whom price does not matter. Thus, companies can gain market share by offering a high-quality product at a price that is perceived to be fair by its target market as long as they use effective communication and distribution methods to generate high value perceptions among consumers. Although the concept of value is not overtly expressed in sales-oriented strategies, it is at least implicit because, for sales to increase, consumers must see greater value.

Competitor Orientation When firms take a **competitor orientation**, they strategize according to the premise that they should measure themselves primarily against their competition. Some firms focus on **competitive parity**, which means they set prices that are similar to those of their major competitors. Another competitor-oriented strategy, **status quo pricing**, changes prices only to meet those of the competition. For example, when Delta increases its average fares, American Airlines and United often follow with similar increases; if Delta rescinds that increase, its competitors tend to drop their fares too.[15] Value is only implicitly considered in competitor-oriented strategies, but in the sense that competitors may be using value as part of their pricing strategies, copying their strategy might provide value.

Can you tell the difference between the $8,500 and the $320 speakers?

Customer Orientation A **customer orientation** is when a firm sets its pricing strategy based on how it can add value to its products or services. When CarMax promises a "no-haggle" pricing structure, it exhibits a customer orientation because it provides additional value to potential used car buyers by making the process simple and easy.[16]

Firms may offer very high-priced, "state-of-the-art" products or services in full anticipation of limited sales. These offerings are designed to enhance the company's reputation and image and thereby increase the company's value in the minds of consumers. Paradigm, a Canadian speaker manufacturer, produces what many audiophiles consider a high-value product, yet offers speakers priced as low as $320 per pair. However, Paradigm also offers a very high-end speaker, for $8,500 per pair. Although few people will spend $8,500 on a pair of speakers, this "statement" speaker communicates what the company is capable of and can increase the image of the firm and the rest of its products—even that $320 pair of speakers. Setting prices with a close eye to how consumers develop their perceptions of value can often be the most effective pricing strategy, especially if it is supported by consistent advertising and distribution strategies.

After a company has a good grasp on its overall objectives, it must implement pricing strategies that enable it to achieve those objectives. As the second step in this process, the firm should look toward consumer demand to lay the foundation for its pricing strategy.

Customers

When firms have developed their company objectives, they turn to understanding consumers' reactions to different prices. The second C of the five Cs of pricing focuses on the customers. Customers want value, and as you likely recall, price is half of the value equation.

To determine how firms account for consumers' preferences when they develop pricing strategies, we must first lay a foundation of

Adding Value 14.1 Lower Apple Prices in the Premium Price Segment[18]

For years, Apple had a strong reputation for offering high quality at high prices. The first iPhone cost nearly $500—way more than most other phones, but well worth it for Apple aficionados. Mac computers also cost more, but they offered great quality, advanced technology, and better protection from viruses and malware.

Today though, Apple actually undercuts many of its competitors. Although Apple products still appear in the premium price category and continue to offer significant quality, the iPad (at $499) costs less than a comparable Xoom tablet from Motorola ($800). The 11-inch MacBook Air is $999; Samsung's entry into the ultrathin notebook category, the Series 9, instead runs $1,049. Obviously, there are cheaper computers available. But when it comes to matching offerings, Apple is often the least expensive entrant in the premium market.

It is able to do so largely because of its increasing popularity. As more and more consumers adopt Apple products, its increasing scale has enabled the company to buy more supplies for less. For example, it had the resources to enter into a five-year, $1.25 billion deal that gave Apple first dibs on flash memory chips, which are critical for iPods and similar devices. With the supply going first to Apple, its competitors have had to scramble to find and bid for the remaining chips on the

market, which has pushed their costs higher. But rather than increase the prices of its consumer products, Apple has chosen to pass on its supply chain efficiencies to customers in the form of lower prices. With this customer-oriented strategy, it should increase its market share even further, leading to a virtuous cycle that may be hard for any competitors to break.

Although Apple products are considered to be in the premium price category, it continues to price below competition.

traditional economic theory that helps explain how prices are related to demand (consumers' desire for products) and how managers can incorporate this knowledge into their pricing strategies.[17] But first read through Adding Value 14.1, which considers how Apple has leveraged consumers' love for its offerings into a sophisticated pricing strategy.

Demand Curves and Pricing   A **demand curve** shows how many units of a product or service consumers will demand during a specific period of time at different prices. Although we call them "curves," demand curves can be either straight or curved, as Exhibit 14.3 shows. Of course, any demand curve relating demand to

LO2 Explain the relationship between price and quantity sold.

EXHIBIT 14.3   Demand Curve for Teeth Whitening Kits

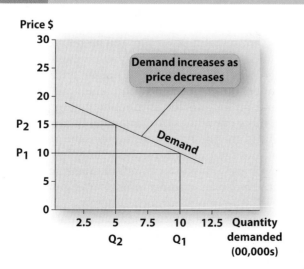

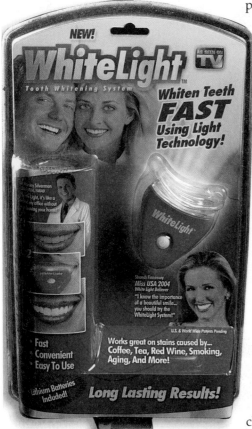

Based on Exhibit 14.3, what is the best price for White Light?

With prestige products like this expensive Faberge egg, the higher the price, the higher the status associated with it, and possibly, the more it will sell.

price assumes that everything else remains unchanged. For the sake of experiment, marketers creating a demand curve assume that the firm will not increase its expenditures on advertising and that the economy will not change in any significant way.

Exhibit 14.3 illustrates a classic downward-sloping demand curve for teeth whitening kits. As price increases, demand for the product or service decreases. In this case, consumers will buy more as the price decreases. As we noted in Adding Value 14.1, Apple expects increasing purchases with lower prices. We can expect a demand curve similar to this one for many, if not most, products and services.

The horizontal axis in Exhibit 14.3 measures the quantity demanded for the teeth whitening kits in units and plots it against the various price possibilities indicated on the vertical axis. Each point on the demand curve then represents the quantity demanded at a specific price. So, in this instance, if the price of a kit is $10 per unit ($P_1$), the demand is 1,000,000 units (Q_1), but if the price were set at $15 ($P_2$), the demand would only be 500,000 units (Q_2). The firm will sell far more teeth whitening kits at $10 each than at $15 each. Why? Because of the greater value this price point offers.

Knowing the demand curve for a product or service enables a firm to examine different prices in terms of the resulting demand and relative to its overall objective. In our preceding example, the retailer will generate a total of $10,000,000 in sales at the $10 price ($10 × 1,000,000 units) and $7,500,000 in sales at the $15 price ($15 × 500,000 units). In this case, given only the two choices of $10 or $15, the $10 price is preferable as long as the firm wants to maximize its sales in terms of dollars and units. But what about a firm that is more interested in profit? To calculate profit, it must consider its costs, which we cover in the next section.

Not all products or services follow the downward-sloping demand curve for all levels of price depicted in Exhibit 14.3 though. Consider **prestige products or services**, which consumers purchase for their status rather than their functionality. The higher the price, the greater the status associated with it and the greater the exclusivity, because fewer people can afford to purchase it. Faberge, the French jeweler known for making jeweled eggs for the Russian Tsar Alexander III, among other exotic items, considers itself so prestigious that it doesn't even have a physical store. It offers its latest jewelry line on its website (www.faberge.com), with prices ranging from $40,000 to $7 million per item. According to Mark Dunhill, Faberge's CEO, "Our customers won't need to appear outside of a store between 10 in the morning and 6 in the evening. They can log on anytime, while sitting on their yacht, their chalet or their country home."[19] But don't expect to go surfing their site: You need to register and make an appointment, and then Faberge will contact you.

With prestige products or services, a higher price may lead to a greater quantity sold, but only up to a certain point. The price demonstrates just how rare, exclusive, and prestigious the product is. When customers value the increase in prestige more than the price differential between the prestige product and other products, the prestige product attains the greater value overall.

However, prestige products can also run into pricing difficulties. The Fender Telecaster and Stratocaster guitars are absolute necessities for any self-respecting guitar hero, but for students just learning or hobbyists, the price of owning a Fender "axe" was simply too much. In response, Fender introduced a separate, budget-priced line of similar guitars under a different brand name, so as not to dilute the prestige of the Fender name. The Squier line, made in Japan with automated manufacturing and less expensive parts, offers a look similar to the famous Fender guitars and performance just a notch below the originals. Today, an American-made

EXHIBIT 14.4 Demand Curve for Caribbean Cruise

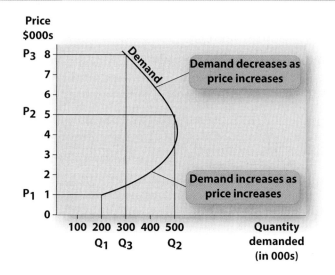

Vintage Hot Rod '62 Fender Stratocaster lists for $2,400, more than 10 times as much as a Squire Bullet Strat model that retails for around $200.[20]

Exhibit 14.4 illustrates a demand curve for another hypothetical prestige service, a Caribbean cruise. As the graph indicates, when the price increases from $1,000 ($P_1$) to $5,000 ($P_2$), the quantity demanded actually increases from 200,000 (Q_1) to 500,000 (Q_2) units. However, when the price increases to $8,000 ($P_3$), the demand then decreases to 300,000 (Q_3) units.

Although the firm likely will earn more profit selling 300,000 cruises at $8,000 each than 500,000 cruises at $5,000 each, we do not know for sure until we bring costs into the picture. However, we do know that more consumers are willing to book the cruise as the price increases initially from $1,000 to $5,000 and that more consumers will choose an alternative vacation as the price increases further from $5,000 to $8,000.

We must consider this notion of consumers' sensitivity to price changes in greater depth.

Price Elasticity of Demand Although we now know something about how consumers react to different price levels, we still need to determine how consumers respond to actual changes in price. These responses vary depending on the product or service. For example, consumers are generally less sensitive to price increases for necessary items, like milk, because they have to purchase the items even if the price climbs. When the price of milk goes up, demand does not fall

John Frusciante of the Red Hot Chilli Peppers uses a Fender Stratocaster.

 Explain price elasticity.

Consumers are less sensitive to the price of milk than to steak. When the price of milk goes up, demand does not fall significantly because people still need to buy milk. However, if the price of steak rises beyond a certain point, people will buy less because they can turn to many substitutes for steak.

significantly because people still need to buy milk. However, if the price of T-bone steaks rises beyond a certain point, people will buy less because they can turn to the many substitutes for this cut of meat. Marketers need to know how consumers will respond to a price increase (or decrease) for a specific product or brand so they can determine whether it makes sense for them to raise or lower prices.

Price elasticity of demand measures how changes in a price affect the quantity of the product demanded. Specifically, it is the ratio of the percentage change in quantity demanded to the percentage change in price.

We can calculate it with the following formula:

$$\text{Price elasticity of demand} = \frac{\%\ \text{Change in quantity demanded}}{\%\ \text{Change in price}}$$

The demand curve provides the information we need to calculate the price elasticity of demand. For instance, what is the price elasticity of demand if we increase the price of our teeth whitening kit from $10 to $15?

$$\%\ \text{Change in quantity demanded} = \frac{(1{,}000{,}000 - 500{,}000)}{1{,}000{,}000} = 50\%,\ \text{and}$$

$$\%\ \text{Change in price} = \frac{(\$10 - \$15)}{10} = -50\%,\ \text{so}$$

$$\text{Price elasticity of demand} = \frac{50\%}{-50\%} = -1.$$

Thus, the price elasticity of demand for our teeth whitening kit is −1.

In general, the market for a product or service is price sensitive (or elastic) when the price elasticity is less than –1, that is, when a 1 percent decrease in price produces more than a 1 percent increase in the quantity sold. In an elastic scenario, relatively small changes in price will generate fairly large changes in the quantity demanded, so if a firm is trying to increase its sales, it can do so by lowering prices. However, raising prices can be problematic in this context, because doing so will lower sales. To refer back to our grocery examples, a retailer can significantly increase its sales of filet mignon by lowering its price, because filets are elastic.

The market for a product is generally viewed as price insensitive (or inelastic) when its price elasticity is greater than –1, that is, when a 1 percent decrease in price results in less than a 1 percent increase in quantity sold. Generally, if a firm must raise prices, it is helpful to do so with inelastic products or services because in such a market, fewer customers will stop buying or reduce their purchases. However, if the products are inelastic, lowering prices will not appreciably increase demand; customers just don't notice or care about the lower price.

Consumers are generally more sensitive to price increases than to price decreases.[21] That is, it is easier to lose current customers with a price increase than it is to gain new customers with a price decrease. Also, the price elasticity of demand usually changes at different points in the demand curve unless the curve is actually a straight line, as in Exhibit 14.3. For instance, a prestige product or service, like our Caribbean cruise example in Exhibit 14.4, enjoys a highly inelastic demand curve up to a certain point, so price increases do not affect sales significantly. But when the price reaches that certain point, consumers start turning to other alternatives because the value of the cruise has finally been reduced by the extremely high price.

When companies believe they cannot raise prices without invoking negative consumer responses, they can turn to different strategies to increase prices without changing the numbers on the price tag. Ethical and Societal Dilemma 14.1 describes one such method that some consumers question.

Factors Influencing Price Elasticity of Demand We have illustrated how price elasticity of demand varies across different products and at different points along a demand curve, as well as how it can change over time. What causes these differences in

Ethical and Societal Dilemma 14.1   The Incredible Shrinking Package[22]

When the costs of raw materials increase, producers have to increases prices or lose profits. But raising prices, especially in the tough economic environment that prompted the higher costs, is a risky proposition. Consumers are struggling too, and finding higher prices for the staples they need to feed their families can cause a lot of anger and frustration. To avoid such a confrontation, manufacturers are turning to a more subtle strategy: Keep prices the same, but reduce package sizes a bit.

Thus cans of corn, once sold in 16 ounce sizes, are now 14.5 ounces. Virtually every product on grocery store shelves shows similar shrinking trends: cereal, crackers, orange juice, diapers, pasta, canned tuna, candy, ketchup . . . the list goes on and on. In some cases, the manufacturers tout the smaller sizes as an added value, such as when smaller package sizes for cookies or ice cream are sold as "healthy" portions, at a higher

price per unit than the larger package sizes.

When customers notice the difference, their reaction is often just what the manufacturers had hoped to avoid—anger and frustration, plus a sense of being tricked or cheated. But the producers are counting on a well-known marketing rule: People tend to be more sensitive to price changes than to quantity changes. Thus if the firm can make the change subtle—such as by leaving the package the same size but filling it less—it knows that few consumers are likely to look closely at the contents. In many cases, they won't even notice, until they start cooking and realize that they don't have enough in the pot to feed everyone around the dinner table.

Coca-Cola has smaller bottles so it can charge more per ounce.

---

the price elasticity of demand? We discuss a few of the more important factors next.

Income Effect The income effect refers to the change in the quantity of a product demanded by consumers due to a change in their income. Generally, as people's income increases, their spending behavior changes: They tend to shift their demand from lower-priced products to higher-priced alternatives. That is, consumers buy hamburger when they're stretching their money but steak when they're flush. Similarly, they may increase the quantity they purchase and splurge on a five-star hotel during their six-day Las Vegas trip rather than three-star lodging over a weekend visit. In turn, when the economy is good and consumers' incomes are rising overall, the price elasticity of steak or hotel rooms may actually drop, even though the price remains constant. Conversely, when incomes drop, consumers turn to less expensive alternatives or purchase less.

Substitution Effect The substitution effect refers to consumers' ability to substitute other products for the focal brand. The greater the availability of substitute products, the higher the price elasticity of demand for any given product will be. For example, there are many close substitutes for the various brands of orange juice. If Tropicana raises its prices, many consumers will turn to Minute Maid, Florida's Natural, or the store brand, because they are more sensitive to price increases when they can easily find lower-priced substitutes. Extremely brand-loyal consumers, however, are willing to pay a higher price, up to a point, because in their minds, Tropicana still offers a better

If there are many close substitues for a product, customers will be sensitive to small price changes, and the product will be highly elastic. If, for instance, Skippy raises its price, many customers will switch to another brand.

value than the competing brands, and they believe the other brands are not adequate substitutes.

Keep in mind that marketing plays a critical role in making consumers brand loyal. And because of this brand loyalty and the lack of what consumers judge to be adequate substitutes, the price elasticity of demand for some brands is very low. For example, Polo/Ralph Lauren sells millions of its classic polo shirts at $85, while shirts of equal quality but without the polo player logo sell for much less. Getting consumers to believe that a particular brand is unique, different, or extraordinary in some way makes other brands seem less substitutable, which in turn increases brand loyalty and decreases the price elasticity of demand.

Cross-Price Elasticity Cross-price elasticity is the percentage change in the quantity of Product A demanded compared with the percentage change in price in Product B. If Product A's price increased, Product B could either increase or decrease, depending on the situation and whether the producs are complementary or substitutes. We refer to products like Blu-ray discs and Blu-ray players as complementary products, which are products whose demands are positively related, such that they rise or fall together. In other words, a percentage increase in the quantity demanded for Product A results in a percentage increase in the quantity demanded for Product B.[23] However, when the price for Blu-ray players dropped, the demand for DVD players went down, so DVD players and Blu-ray players are substitute products because changes in their demand are negatively related. That is, a percentage increase in the quantity demanded for Product A results in a percentage decrease in the quantity demanded for Product B.[24] In addition, on the Internet, shopping bots like TheFind.com and Bizrate.com have made it much easier for people to shop for substitutable products like consumer electronics, which likely has affected the price elasticity of demand for such products.[25]

The way a product or service is marketed to customers can have a profound effect on its price elasticity. Superior Service 14.1 describes how good marketing in the form of great customer service can make customers less sensitive to price. Prior to this point, we have focused on how changes in prices affect how much customers buy. Clearly, knowing how prices affect sales is important, but it cannot give us the whole picture. To know how profitable a pricing strategy will be, we must also consider the third C, costs.

Costs

To make effective pricing decisions, firms must understand their cost structures so they can determine the degree to which their products or services will be profitable at different prices. In general, prices should *not* be based on costs, because consumers make purchase decisions based on their perceived value; they care little about the firm's costs to produce and sell a product or deliver a service. For example, Bank of America (BOA) announced it would charge a monthly fee to some customers to use their debit cards, ostensibly to cover increasing costs. Recognizing they had many choices for banking services and that BOA was no longer providing sufficient value, a significant number took their business elsewhere. Within weeks, BOA rescinded the new fee.[26] Consumers use just the price they must pay and the benefits they may receive to judge value; they will not pay a higher price for an inferior product simply because the firm cannot be as cost efficient as its competitors or because events out of their control drive the cost of raw materials or labor higher.

Bank of America may have had trouble passing its costs on to consumers, but other companies can do so with few negative repercussions. For example, even though deodorant sales have been stagnant for years, revenues shot up recently as a result of a price hike. The "clinical" formula of Secret deodorant costs $8.50 per tube, more than twice as much as the regular version. The reason consumers likely accept this price increase is the value that deodorant offers, in the form of peace of

Superior Service 14.1   Great Service Lowers Price Elasticity

Why can some hotels, doctors, and retailers get away with charging more than their competitors and keep customers coming back for more? In some cases, it is the service. Consider the Ritz-Carlton chain of hotels. When it opens a new hotel, each employee undergoes more than 80 hours of training. About half the staff are transferred from other Ritz hotels to ensure that the new opening maintains the customer service and attention to every detail for which the company is well known.[27]

Every shift, every day, on every Ritz property, a 15-minute meeting acts as a refresher to remind employees to act on one of the 12 "service values" that constitute the company's "gold standard." Employees are empowered to do whatever it takes to solve guest problems. For example, employees are allotted $2,000 per day per guest to solve any problems that a guest may have—without supervisor approval.[28]

To support its performance, the Ritz collects information about guests, from special requests to informal observations. This system is relatively difficult to implement, because observations need to be "actionable" and confirmed by various aspects of the customer's stay. For example, if a customer orders a martini with pearl onions three times, the bartender should enter it into the system as the customer's favorite drink, but if that same customer orders a similar martini only once, it likely is not something worth noting. Employees are constantly trying to "wow" their customers, so any knowledge that helps them to do so in the future provides value to both employees and customers.[29]

Customers likely are accustomed to finding concierge services in such a hotel, but some doctors are expanding the idea to their practices too. For patients tired of waiting for hours to see an overbooked primary care doctor, concierge doctors promise to keep precise appointments, be available 24/7, and give medical tests that the physician, not the insurance company, deems necessary.[30] These doctors also promise to limit their patient load to 600 instead of the usual 2,500 to 3,000. Despite the clear appeal of such offerings, they can cost as much as $25,000 per year. Clearly people who adopt this service are not price sensitive.

We might find the same customers cruising the aisles and loading up on merchandise from specialty department stores, such as Neiman Marcus, Nordstrom, and Saks Fifth Avenue. These stores have great merchandise, some of which is unavailable at other stores in the area. But even more important, they provide outstanding service—service so good that many people don't mind paying relatively high prices. Salespeople get to know their good customers as well as they know their merchandise. Then they do whatever it takes to exceed those customers' expectations. If a store is out of an item that a good customer is requesting, a salesperson in one of these service-oriented stores is likely to not only try to get it from other stores in the same chain but even go to competitors' stores to find the item. For such service, some customers will pay almost any price.

But not everyone who walks in the door gets this level of service. Department stores devote their premier services to their premier customers. Neiman Marcus's top 100,000 customers spend more than $12,000 per year at the store; whereas the average customer spends about $600 per year.[31] Its loyalty program for its best customers offers luxury vehicles like the Lexus ISF for customers who earn 5 million points or spend $5 million—and it grants such rewards every year. Nordstrom and Saks similarly offer their best customers free shipping, vacations, and invitations to special events.

Under what circumstances, if any, would you be willing to pay more for better service?

mind. To avoid the social embarrassment associated with sweat-stained clothing, consumers overlook the higher price.[32]

Although companies incur many different types of costs as a natural part of doing business, there are two primary cost categories: variable and fixed.

Variable Costs **Variable costs** are those costs, primarily labor and materials, that vary with production volume. As a firm produces more or less of a good or service, the total variable costs increase or decrease at the same time. Because each unit of the product produced incurs the same cost, marketers generally express variable costs on a per-unit basis. Consider a bakery like Entenmann's: The majority of the variable costs are the cost of the ingredients, primarily flour. Each time Entenmann's makes a loaf of bread, it incurs the cost of the ingredients.

In the service industry, variable costs are far more complex. A hotel, for instance, incurs certain variable costs each time it rents a room, including the costs associated with the labor and supplies necessary to clean and restock the room. Note that the hotel does not incur these costs if the room is not booked. Suppose that a particular hotel calculates its total variable costs to be $10 per room; each time it rents a room, it incurs another $10 in variable costs. If the hotel rents out 100 rooms on a given night, the total variable cost is $1,000 ($10 per room × 100 rooms).

In either case, however, variable costs tend to change depending on the quantity produced. If Entenmann's makes 100,000 loaves of bread in a month, it would have to pay a higher price for ingredients on a per pound basis than if it were producing a million loaves. Similarly, a very large hotel will be able to get a lower per unit price on most, if not all, the supplies it needs to service the room because it purchases such a large volume. However, as the hotel company continues to grow, it may be forced to add more benefits for its employees or increase wages to attract and keep long-term employees. Such changes will increase its overall variable labor costs and affect the total variable cost of cleaning a room. Thus, though not always the case, variable costs per unit may go up or down (for all units) with significant changes in volume.

Fixed Costs **Fixed costs** are those costs that remain essentially at the same level, regardless of any changes in the volume of production. Typically, these costs include items such as rent, utilities, insurance, administrative salaries (for executives and higher-level managers), and the depreciation of the physical plant and equipment. Across reasonable fluctuations in production volume, these costs remain stable; whether Entenmann's makes 100,000 loaves or a million, the rent it pays for the bakery remains unchanged.

Total Cost Finally, the **total cost** is simply the sum of the variable and fixed costs. For example, in one year, our hypothetical hotel incurred $100,000 in fixed costs. We also know that because the hotel booked 10,000 room nights, its total variable cost is $100,000 (10,000 room nights × $10 per room). Thus, its total cost is $200,000.

Next, we illustrate how to use these costs in simple analyses that can inform managerial decision making about setting prices.

 Describe how to calculate a product's break-even point.

Break-Even Analysis and Decision Making

A useful technique that enables managers to examine the relationships among cost, price, revenue, and profit over different levels of production and sales is called **break-even analysis**. Central to this analysis is the determination of the **break-even point**, or the point at which the number of units sold generates just enough revenue to equal the total costs. At this point, profits are zero. Although profit, which represents the difference between the total cost and the total revenue (total revenue or sales = selling price of each unit sold × number of units sold), can indicate how much money the firm is making or losing at a single period of time, it cannot tell managers how many units a firm must produce and sell before it stops losing money and at least breaks even, which is what the break-even point does.

How do we determine the break-even point? Exhibit 14.5 presents the various cost and revenue information we have discussed in a graphic format. The graph contains three curves (recall that even though they are straight, we still call them

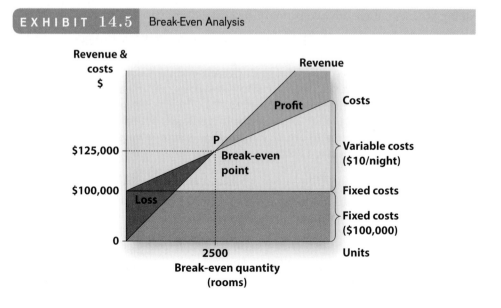

EXHIBIT 14.5   Break-Even Analysis

curves): fixed costs, total costs, and total revenue. The vertical axis measures the revenue or costs in dollars, and the horizontal axis measures the quantity of units sold. The fixed cost curve will always appear as a horizontal line straight across the graph because fixed costs do not change over different levels of volume.

The total cost curve starts where the fixed cost curve intersects the vertical axis at $100,000. When volume is equal to zero (no units are produced or sold), the fixed costs of operating the business remain and cannot be avoided. Thus, the lowest point the total costs can ever reach is equal to the total fixed costs. Beyond that point, the total cost curve increases by the amount of variable costs for each additional unit, which we calculate by multiplying the variable cost per unit by the number of units, or quantity.

Finally, the total revenue curve increases by the price of each additional unit sold. To calculate it, we multiply the price per unit by the number of units sold. The formulas for these calculations are as follows:

$$\text{Total variable cost} = \text{Variable cost per unit} \times \text{Quantity}$$

$$\text{Total cost} = \text{Fixed cost} + \text{Total variable cost}$$

$$\text{Total revenue} = \text{Price} \times \text{Quantity}$$

We again use the hotel example to illustrate these relationships. Recall that the fixed costs are $100,000 and the variable costs are $10/room rented. If the rooms rent for $50 per night, how many rooms must the hotel rent over the course of a year to break even? If we study the graph carefully, we find the break-even point at 2,500, which means that the hotel must rent 2,500 rooms before its revenues equal its costs. If it rents fewer rooms, it loses money (the red area); if it rents more, it makes a profit (the green area). To determine the break-even point in units mathematically, we must introduce one more variable, the **contribution per unit**, which is the price less the variable cost per unit.

In this case,

$$\text{Contribution per unit} = \$50 - \$10 = \$40$$

Therefore, the break-even point becomes

$$\text{Break-even point (units)} = \frac{\text{Fixed costs}}{\text{Contributions per unit}}$$

That is,

$$\text{Break-even point (units)} = \frac{\$100,000}{\$40} = 2,500 \text{ room nights}$$

When the hotel has crossed the break-even point of 2,500 rooms, it will start earning profit at the same rate of the contribution per unit. So if the hotel rents 4,000 rooms—1,500 rooms more than the break-even point—its profit will be $60,000 (1,500 rooms × $40 contribution per unit).

$$\text{Profit} = (\text{Contribution per unit} \times \text{Quantity}) - \text{Fixed Cost}$$
$$\text{Profit} = (\$40 \times 4,000) - \$100,000 = \$60,000$$

Or an alternative formula would be:

$$\text{Profit} = (\text{Price} \times \text{Quantity}) - (\text{Fixed Cost} + (\text{Variable Cost} \times \text{Quantity}))$$
$$\text{Profit} = (\$50 \times 4,000) - (\$100,000 + (\$10 \times 4,000))$$
$$\text{Profit} = \$200,000 - (\$100,000 + \$40,000) = \$60,000$$

Let's extend this simple break-even analysis to show how many units a firm must produce and sell to achieve a target profit. Say the hotel wanted to make $200,000 in profit each year. How many rooms would it have to rent at the current price? In this instance, we need only add the targeted profit to the fixed costs to determine that number:

$$\text{Break-even point (units)} = \frac{(\text{Fixed costs} + \text{Target profit})}{\text{Contributions per unit}}$$

or

$$7{,}500 \text{ rooms} = \frac{(\$100{,}000 + \$200{,}000)}{\$40}$$

Although a break-even analysis cannot actually help managers set prices, it does help them assess their pricing strategies, because it clarifies the conditions in which different prices may make a product or service profitable. It becomes an even more powerful tool when performed on a range of possible prices for comparative purposes. For example, the hotel management could analyze various prices, not just $50, to determine how many hotel rooms it would have to rent at what price to make a $200,000 profit.

Naturally, however, there are limitations to a break-even analysis. First, it is unlikely that a hotel has one specific price that it charges for each and every room, so the price it would use in its break-even analysis probably represents an "average" price that attempts to account for these variances. Second, prices often get reduced as quantity increases because the costs decrease, so firms must perform several break-even analyses at different quantities. Third, a break-even analysis cannot indicate for sure how many rooms will be rented or, in the case of products, how many units will sell at a given price. It only tells the firm what its costs, revenues, and profitability will be given a set price and an assumed quantity. To determine how many units the firm actually will sell, it must bring in the demand estimates we discussed previously.

Mark-Up and Target Return Pricing

In many situations, the manufacturer may want to achieve a standard markup—let's say 10 percent of cost. In our example of the teeth whitening kit, let's assume:

Variable costs per unit are:	$8.00
Fixed costs are:	$1,000,000
Expected sales are:	1,000,000 units

In a hotel, the cost of the physical structure, including the lobby, is fixed—it is incurred even if no rooms are rented. The costs of washing the towels and sheets are variable—the more rooms that are rented, the more the costs.

The teeth whitening kit manufacturer would like to calculate the price at which they would make a 10 percent mark-up. The formula for calculating a target return price based on a mark-up on cost is:

Target return price = (Variable cost + (Fixed cost ÷ Expected unit sales)) × (1 + Target return % [expressed as a decimal])

In this example, this would result in the firm charging $9.90.

Target return price = ($8 + ($1,000,000 ÷ 1,000,000)) × (1 + 0.10)
Target return price = $9.00 × 1.1 = $9.90

Competition

Because the fourth C, competition, has a profound impact on pricing strategies,[33] we use this section to focus on its effect, as well as on how competitors react to certain pricing strategies. There are four levels of competition—monopoly, oligopolistic competition, monopolistic competition, and pure competition—and each has its own set of pricing challenges and opportunities (see Exhibit 14.6).

In a **monopoly**, one firm provides the product or service in a particular industry, which results in less price competition. For example, there is often only one provider of power in each region of the country: Florida Power and Light in most of Florida, NStar in most of Massachusetts, and so forth. Power companies operate more efficiently when there is one service provider, so the government regulates the pricing of utility monopolies to prevent them from raising prices uncontrollably. A monopoly that restricts competition by controlling an industry can be deemed illegal and broken apart by the government.

LO5 Indicate the four types of price competitive levels.

| **EXHIBIT 14.6** | Four Levels of Competition: Can you match each photo to its respective type of competition? |

Less price competition	**More price competition**	
Monopoly One firm controls the market	**Oligopoly** A handful of firms control the market	**Fewer firms**
Monopolistic comp. Many firms selling differentiated products at different prices	**Pure competition** Many firms selling commodities for the same prices	**Many firms**

Ethical and Societal Dilemma 14.2   The Battle of the Books

Price wars have been commonplace in many industries historically (e.g., airlines, fast food). But the fight that is being waged by some vicious combatants is taking the concept to a new and constantly shifting level. Watch out for the booksellers: They're tougher than you think.

On one side of the field is the American Booksellers Association (ABA), a trade group that represents small, independent bookstores. In recent years, it has asked the U.S. Department of Justice to intervene to stop big retailers such as Amazon, Walmart, and Target from engaging in unfair practices—namely, pricing bestselling new releases for as little as $8.98 per book—far below the list prices of around $35.[34]

Amazon earns particular scorn from the ABA for linking its Kindle e-readers to only Kindle book files. That is, anyone who buys a Kindle (and that's a lot of people, as we noted in Superior Service 13.1 from Chapter 13) must purchase all his or her e-books from the Kindle platform on Amazon. In response, the ABA is taking the battle to Amazon's self-publishing sector, such that ABA's IndieCommerce Site will not carry any Amazon-published titles unless those titles also are published "in all available formats."[35]

On the other hand, getting Stephen King's latest thriller or the Steve Jobs biography for less than the list price is deeply appealing to consumers, who are more likely to visit the stores or websites that offer these prices. That consumer behavior is exactly what the retailers are counting on, because if they can get people in stores or to their websites, those buyers are likely to purchase more than just the price-reduced best-seller.[36]

So at what point are price wars problematic? According to the ABA, the precipitous drop in prices represents predatory pricing behavior, designed to drive small book stores out of the market and thus enable the big retailers to do whatever they want, unhindered by competition and creating a monopoly. And yet the expanded availability of electronic versions of books expands the total market. For consumers, the price wars mean less expensive books today. Will they mean less competition and therefore higher prices in the future though?

Even in the face of declining prices, some consumers continue to pay more, because they value other aspects of the offer. The independent booksellers that belong to the ABA may not be able to compete on price, but they can offer personalized service, hard-to-find titles, and a cozy atmosphere that the big retailers can never mimic.[37]

Should large retailers like Amazon, Walmart, and Target be allowed to sell this book about Steve Jobs for less than what independent booksellers pay for it?

When a market is characterized by **oligopolistic competition**, only a few firms dominate. Firms typically change their prices in reaction to competition to avoid upsetting an otherwise stable competitive environment. Examples of oligopolistic markets include the soft drink market and commercial airline travel. Sometimes reactions to prices in oligopolistic markets can result in a **price war**, which occurs when two or more firms compete primarily by lowering their prices. Firm A lowers its prices; Firm B responds by meeting or beating Firm A's new price. Firm A then responds with another new price, and so on. In some cases though, these tactics result in **predatory pricing**, when a firm sets a very low price for one or more of its products with the intent to drive its competition out of business, a possibility exemplified in Ethical and Societal Dilemma 14.2.

Monopolistic competition occurs when there are many firms competing for customers in a given market but their products are differentiated. When so many firms compete, product differentiation rather than strict price competition tends to appeal to consumers. This is the most common form of competition. Hundreds of firms make wristwatches, and thus the market is highly differentiated. Timex sells a durable watch that tells time, has a stop watch, and a sporty design. Swatch watches have more style than a Timex, but if you are really looking for a lot of style, fashion designers such as Armani have their own wrist watches. Timepiece aficionados may opt for the high quality workmanship of a Patek Philippe or a Vacheron Constantin. Depending on the features, style and quality, companies compete in very different markets for the same product. Thus, by differentiating their products using various attributes, prices, brands, etc., they have created unique value propositions in the minds of their customers.

With **pure competition**, there is a large number of sellers of standardized products or commodities that consumers perceive as substitutable, such as grains, gold, meat, spices, or minerals. In such markets, price usually is set according to the laws of supply and demand. For example, wheat is wheat, so it does not matter to a commercial bakery whose wheat it buys. However, the secret to pricing success in a pure competition market is not necessarily to offer the lowest price, because doing so might create a price war and erode profits.

Instead, some firms have brilliantly decommoditized their products. For example, most people feel that all chickens purchased in a grocery are the same. But companies like Tyson's have branded their chickens to move into a monopolistically competitive market.

When a commodity can be differentiated somehow, even if simply by a sticker or logo, there is an opportunity for consumers to identify it as distinct from the rest, and in this case, firms can at least partially extricate their product from a pure competitive market.

Channel Members

Channel members—manufacturers, wholesalers, and retailers—can have different perspectives when it comes to pricing strategies. Consider a manufacturer that is focused on increasing the image and reputation of its brand but working with a retailer that is primarily concerned with increasing its sales. The manufacturer may desire to keep prices higher to convey a better image, whereas the retailer wants lower prices and will accept lower profits to move the product, regardless of consumers' impressions of the brand. Unless channel members carefully communicate their pricing goals and select channel partners that agree with them, conflict will surely arise.

Channels can be very difficult to manage, and distribution outside normal channels does occur. A **gray market** employs irregular but not necessarily illegal methods; generally, it legally circumvents authorized channels of distribution to sell goods at prices lower than those intended by the manufacturer.[38] Many manufacturers of consumer electronics therefore require retailers to sign an agreement that demands certain activities (and prohibits others) before they may become authorized dealers. But if a retailer has too many high-definition TVs in stock, it may sell them at just above its own cost to an unauthorized discount dealer. This move places the merchandise in the market at prices far below what authorized dealers can charge, and in the long term, it may tarnish the image of the manufacturer if the discount dealer fails to provide sufficient return policies, support, service, and so forth.

To discourage this type of gray market distribution, some manufacturers, such as Fujitsu, have resorted to large disclaimers on their websites, packaging, and other communications to warn consumers that the manufacturer's product warranty becomes null and void unless the item has been purchased from an authorized dealer.[39]

CHECK YOURSELF

1. What are the five Cs of pricing?
2. Identify the four types of company objectives.
3. What is the difference between elastic versus inelastic demand?
4. How does one calculate the break-even point in units?

MACRO INFLUENCES ON PRICING

Thus far, we have focused mainly on product- and firm-specific factors—the five Cs—that influence pricing. Now we turn to the broader factors that have a more sweeping effect on pricing in general. In this section, we consider the Internet and various economic factors.

The Internet

The shift among consumers to acquiring more and more products, services, and information online has made them more price sensitive and opened new categories of products to those who could not access them previously. Gourmet foods, books (and now e-books), music, movies, and electronics are just a few of the product categories that present a significant online presence. Because they have gained access to rare cheeses, breads, meats, spices, and confections, consumers are demanding more from their local grocery stores in terms of selection and variety and have become more sensitive about prices. Furthermore, consumers' ability to buy electronics at highly discounted prices online has pushed bricks-and-mortar stores to attempt to focus consumers' attention on prepurchase advice and expertise, consulting services, and after-sales service—and away from price.

The Internet and new mobile apps that encourage showrooming enable consumers to find the best prices for any product quickly, which again increases their price sensitivity and reduces the costs associated with finding lower-price alternatives.[40] **Showrooming** is when customers visit a store to touch, feel, and even discuss a product's features with a sales associate, and then purchase it online from another retailer at a lower price. As such, the visited store essentially becomes a showroom for online shoppers. Showrooming is particularly popular with customers purchasing electronics.

However, the notion that retail prices are lower online may disappear soon. Currently, retailers are required to collect state sales taxes only in states in which they have a physical presence (e.g., a brick-and-mortar store, a distribution center). But proposed legislation would require online retailers to collect sales taxes on all purchases. Some retailers argue that this legislation would level the playing field, so that online retailers could not constantly outcompete them on price, as Exhibit 14.7 summarizes. Others argue that the initiative will just add complexity to the already challenging tax code—while also raising prices overall for consumers.[41]

Another implication of the Internet for prices has been the growth of online auction sites such as eBay. Gone are the days when sellers had to offer their unwanted items to local buyers at "fire sale" prices. Although there certainly are good deals to be had on eBay, many items can fetch a premium price because bidders tend to get caught up in the bidding process. Also, unique and special-interest items, which previously required professional appraisals before their value could be established, now have millions of potential bidders clearly articulating a value for everything from a 2011 Lexus LX9 for $61,200 to an 18-karat gold

EXHIBIT 14.7 | Example Price Comparisons

Price Advantage | Amazon doesn't collect sales tax in Texas and most other states, which some big retailers say gives it an unfair advantage. It does collect the tax in New York and four other states. An online price comparison:

		Target	**Walmart**	**Amazon**	**Amazon**
	CANON POWERSHOT SX13015	IN HOUSTON	IN HOUSTON	IN HOUSTON	IN NEW YORK
		Price: $199.99 Sales tax $16.50 Total Price: $216.49	Price: $199.00 Sales tax $16.42 Total Price: $215.42	Price: $198.99 Sales tax $0 Total Price: $198.99	Price: $198.99 Sales tax $17.66 Total Price: $216.65
	VIZIO M470NV 47-INCH	Price: $999.99 Sales tax $86.66 Total Price: $1,086.65	Price: $998 Sales tax $82.34 Total Price: $1,080.34	Price: $948.00 Sales tax $0 Total Price: $948.00	Price: $948.00 Sales tax $84.14 Total Price: $1,032.14
	PLAYSTATION 3	Price: $299.99 Sales tax $25.91 Total Price: $325.90	Price: $299.99 Sales tax $25.91 Total Price: $324.90	Price: $299.99 Sales tax $0 Total Price: $299.99	Price: $299.99 Sales tax $26.62 Total Price: $326.61

Source: From Miguel Bustillo, "Retailers Push Amazon on Taxes," *The Wall Street Journal*, March 17, 2011. Copyright © 2011 by Dow Jones & Company, Inc. Reproduced with permission of Dow Jones & Company, Inc. via Copyright Clearance Center.

Signature S cell phone for $24,100. Many consumers use eBay's prior auction section to determine the prices at which products have sold in the past and establish a value for new offerings. Social and Mobile Marketing 14.1 describes some eBay pricing strategies for sellers and buyers.

Economic Factors

Two interrelated trends that have merged to impact pricing decisions are the increase in consumers' disposable income and status consciousness. Some consumers appear willing to spend money for products that can convey status in some way. Products once considered only for the very rich, such as Rolex watches and Mercedes-Benz cars, are now owned by more working professionals. Despite a lingering slow worldwide economic situation, luxury goods manufacturers' sales are seeing double-digit increases, fueled in part by unrelenting demand in emerging markets.[42] Although such prestige products are still aimed at the elite, more and more consumers are making a financial leap to attain them.

Stores like H&M have introduced disposable chic to America.

At the same time, however, a countervailing trend finds customers attempting to shop cheap. The popularity of everyday low-price retailers like Walmart and Target, extreme value stores such as Dollar General, and wholesale clubs like Costco attract customers who can afford to shop at department and specialty stores, yet find it is cool to save a buck. Retailers like Old Navy and H&M also have introduced cross-shopping into middle America's shopping habits. In this context, **cross-shopping** is the pattern of buying both premium and low-priced merchandise or patronizing both expensive, status-oriented retailers and price-oriented retailers. These stores offer fashionable merchandise at great values—values so good that if items last for only a few wearings, it

Social and Mobile Marketing 14.1   Pricing on eBay

Researchers have published dozens of papers using eBay as their data source.[43] One research question often investigated is, "What can sellers do to get the highest price?" Here are a few tips:

1. **Set the starting price relatively low.** It is important to start prices relatively low to stimulate interest among potential bidders. For instance, starting a Nikon camera auction at $0.01 resulted in significantly higher final prices than the average price for all camera auctions. In another case, when the seller started an auction for a kitchen sink at $225, it ended without a single bidder. When reauctioned with a starting price of $75, the sink sold for $275. There is one exception to the start-low rule: If the item is somewhat idiosyncratic and therefore might not have many bids, it is best to set the price closer to the item's actual value.[44]

2. **Use reserve prices with caution, especially for low-priced items.** A reserve price in an auction is secret to potential bidders, and is the minimum amount at which a seller will sell an item. Sellers use reserve prices as protection against selling an item too low. Using a reserve price reduces the probability that the auction will end in a sale. In an experiment using relatively low-value Pokémon trading cards, researchers found that auctions utilizing reserves on average resulted in fewer serious bidders per auction and lower final sale prices. However, other research suggests that for items over $25.00, the reserve might push revenues higher when the auctions end in a successful sale.[45]

3. **Use photos to generate bids.** Listings with photos receive much more traffic than listings without photos. More traffic to the listing results in bids, and the more bids, the higher the sale price.[46]

4. **Don't flood the market.** To sell multiples of an item, don't sell them all at the same time. The market appreciates the illusion of scarcity. Items that are scarce or even unique are perceived to be more valuable. Also, spacing out the listings increases the size of the potential market because people float in and out of the market.

5. **Spell-check.** Misspellings decrease the amount of traffic an auction receives. People search for specific words. If those words are spelled wrong, the item won't pop up. One study found that Michael Jordan shirts listed "Micheal" went unsold almost twice as often as those that were spelled correctly. When sold, the misspelled brand names resulted in lower final sale prices.[47]

6. **Hype it up.** It is good to exaggerate a little. For instance, in selling a handbag, say, "Runway special! A must-have for fall!" Also, if the suggested retail price is relatively high, mention it. One study found that auctions that mention the high retail price in an item description sell for 7 percent more on average.[48]

7. **Hold longer auctions.** Longer auctions tend to fetch higher prices. Research shows that three-day and five-day auctions yield approximately the same prices, seven-day auctions are about 24 percent higher, and 10-day auctions 42 percent higher on average.[49]

8. **Don't end auctions when everyone else does.** A study found that auctions ending during peak hours on eBay are actually 9.6 percent less likely to result in a sale. About 35 percent of auctions end between 5 p.m. and 8:59 p.m., when only 25 percent of bids are placed.[50]

9. **Charge for shipping—but not too much.** Bidders don't pay much attention to shipping costs when placing bids. In one study, CDs listed with a starting price of one cent with $3.99 shipping averaged 21 percent higher final sale prices than CDs set with an opening price of $4 and no shipping charge. When the CDs were listed with a $2 starting price and a $6 shipping cost, five of the 20 CDs went unsold.[51]

10. **Avoid negative feedback.** Sellers who have even a few positive feedback reports are more likely than sellers who have no history to receive bids and to have their auctions result in a sale. Positively rated sellers also receive higher bids.[52]

By implementing these sellers' strategies from a buyers' perspective, one might be able to get some good deals. For instance, if an item has lots of bids, it may sell for an artificially high price. It pays to check out items without pictures or with misspelled words since they get fewer bids and therefore usually end up selling for less. Finally, look for short-duration auctions with items at high starting or reserve prices.

doesn't matter to the customers. The net impact of these contradictory trends on prices has been that some prestige items have become more expensive, whereas many other items have become cheaper.

Finally, the economic environment at local, regional, national, and global levels influences pricing. Starting at the top, the growth of the global economy has changed the nature of competition around the world. Many firms maintain a presence in multiple countries—products get designed in one country, the parts are manufactured in another, the final product assembled in a third, and after-sales service is handled by a call center in a fourth. By thinking globally, firms can seek out the most cost-efficient methods of providing goods and services to their customers.

On a more local level, the economy still can influence pricing. Competition, disposable income, and unemployment all may signal the need for different pricing strategies. Rural areas are often subjected to higher prices because it costs more to get products there and because competition is lower. Similarly, retailers often charge higher prices in areas populated by people who have more disposable income and enjoy low unemployment rates. Ironically, other retailers, particularly food retailers, have been known to charge more in low-income urban areas where residents have limited access to transportation outside the area and competition is limited.

By thinking globally, firms can seek out the most cost-efficient methods of providing goods and services to their customers.

CHECK YOURSELF

1. How have the Internet and economic factors affected the way people react to prices?

Summing Up

LO1 List the four pricing orientations.

A profit-oriented pricing strategy focuses on maximizing, or at least reaching a target, profit for the company. A sales orientation instead sets prices with the goal of increasing sales levels. With a competitor-oriented pricing strategy, a firm sets its prices according to what its competitors do. Finally, a customer-oriented strategy determines consumers' perceptions of value and prices accordingly.

LO2 Explain the relationship between price and quantity sold.

Generally, when prices go up, quantity sold goes down. Sometimes, however—particularly with prestige products and services—demand actually increases with price.

LO3 Explain price elasticity.

Changes in price generally affect demand; price elasticity measures the extent of this effect. It is based on the percentage change in quantity divided by the percentage change in price. Depending on the resulting value, a market offering can be identified as elastic, such that the market is very price sensitive, or inelastic, in which case the market cares little about the price.

LO4 Describe how to calculate a product's break-even point.

Because the break-even point occurs when the units sold generate just enough profit to cover the total costs of producing those units, it requires knowledge of the fixed cost, total cost, and total revenue curves. When these curves intersect, the marketer has found the break-even point.

LO5 Indicate the four types of price competitive levels.

In a monopoly setting, either one firm controls the market and sets the price, or many firms compete with differentiated products, rather than on price. Monopolistic competition occurs when there are many firms competing for customers in a given market but their products are differentiated. In an oligopolistic competitive market, a few firms dominate and tend to set prices according to a competitor-oriented strategy. Finally, pure competition means that consumers likely regard the products offered by different companies as basic substitutes, so the firms must work hard to achieve the lowest price point, limited by the laws of supply and demand.

Key Terms

- break-even analysis, 438
- break-even point, 438
- competitive parity, 430
- competitor orientation, 430
- complementary products, 436
- contribution per unit, 439
- cross-price elasticity, 436
- cross-shopping, 445
- customer orientation, 430
- demand curve, 431
- elastic, 434
- fixed costs, 438
- gray market, 443

- income effect, 435
- inelastic, 434
- maximizing profits, 429
- monopoly, 441
- monopolistic competition, 442
- oligopolistic competition, 442
- predatory pricing, 442
- premium pricing, 430
- prestige products or services, 432
- price, 426
- price elasticity of demand, 434

- price war, 442
- profit orientation, 428
- pure competition, 443
- reserve price, 446
- sales orientation, 429
- showrooming, 444
- status quo pricing, 430
- substitute products, 436
- substitution effect, 435
- target profit pricing, 428
- target return pricing, 429
- total cost, 438
- variable costs, 437

Marketing Applications

1. You and your two roommates are starting a pet grooming service to help put yourselves through college. There are two other well-established pet services in your area. Should you set your price higher or lower than that of the competition? Justify your answer.

2. One roommate believes the most important objective in setting prices for the new pet grooming business is to generate a large profit while keeping an eye on your competitors' prices; the other roommate believes it is important to maximize sales and set prices according to what your customers expect to pay. Who is right and why?

3. Assume you have decided to buy an advertisement in the local newspaper to publicize your new pet grooming service. The cost of the ad is $1,000. You have decided to charge $40 for a dog grooming, and your variable costs are $20 for each dog. How many dogs do you have to groom to break even on the cost of the ad? What is your break-even point if you charge $60 per dog?

4. The local newspaper ad isn't helping much; so you decide to post your services on an auction site, where customers can bid for your services. What should the starting price of the auction be?

5. Is there a difference between a $5,900 Loro Piana vicuña sweater and a $150 cashmere sweater from L.L. Bean? Have you ever purchased a higher-priced product or service because you thought the quality was better than that of a similar, lower-priced product or service? What was the product or service? Do you believe you made a rational choice?

6. A soft drink manufacturer opened a new manufacturing plant in the Midwest. The total fixed costs are $100 million. It plans to sell soft drinks for $6.00 for a package of 10 12-ounce cans to retailers. Its variable costs for the ingredients are $4.00 per package. Calculate the break-even volume. What would happen to the break-even point if the fixed costs decreased to $50 million, or the variable costs decreased to $3 due to declines in commodity costs. What would the break-even be if the firm wanted to make $20 million?

7. On your weekly grocery shopping trip, you notice that the price of spaghetti has gone up 50 cents a pound. How will this price increase affect the demand for spaghetti sauce, rice, and Parmesan cheese? Explain your answer in terms of the price elasticity of demand.

8. Zinc Energy Resources Co., a new division of a major battery manufacturing company, recently patented a new battery that uses zinc-air technology. The unit costs for the zinc-air battery are as follows: The battery housing is $8, materials are $6, and direct labor is $6 per unit. Retooling the existing factory facilities to manufacture the zinc-air batteries amounts to an additional $1 million in equipment costs. Annual fixed costs include sales, marketing, and advertising expenses of

$1 million; general and administrative expenses of $1 million; and other fixed costs totaling $2 million. Please answer the following questions.

a. What is the total per-unit variable cost associated with the new battery?

b. What are the total fixed costs for the new battery?

c. If the price for the new battery was set at $35, what would the break-even point be?

9. How do pricing strategies vary across markets that are characterized by monopolistic, oligopolistic, monopolistic competition, and pure competition?

10. Suppose you are in the market for a new Sharp LCD television. You see one advertised at a locally owned store for $300 less than it costs at HHGregg. The salesperson at the local store tells you that the television came from another retailer in the next state that had too many units of that model. Explain who benefits and who is harmed from such a gray market transaction: you, Sharp, HHGregg, the local store?

11. Has the Internet helped lower the price of some types of merchandise? Justify your answer.

Quiz Yourself
www.mhhe.com/grewal4e

1. If a shoe company has $2 million in fixed costs, its average shoe sells for $100 a pair, and variable costs are $60 per unit, how many units does the company need to sell to break even?
   a. 5,000
   b. 10,000
   c. 50,000
   d. 100,000
   e. 500,000

2. Porsche's 918 Spyder is priced at $550,000. The demand for such a prestigious car is likely to be:

   a. cross-price elastic
   b. price inelastic
   c. price elastic
   d. status quo elastic
   e. derived demand inelastic

(Answers to these two questions can be found on page 648.)

Go to www.mhhe.com/grewal4e to practice an additional 11 questions.

Toolkit

BREAK-EVEN ANALYSIS
A shoe manufacturer has recently opened a new manufacturing plant in Asia. The total fixed costs are $50 million. It plans to sell the shoes to retailers for $50, and its variable costs (material and labor) are $25 per pair. Calculate the break-even volume. Now see what would happen to the break-even point if the fixed costs increased to $60 million due to the purchase of new equipment, or the variable costs decreased to $20 due to a new quantity discount provided by the supplier. Please use the toolkit provided at www.mhhe.com/grewal4e to experiment with changes in fixed cost, variable cost, and selling price to see what happens to break-even volume.

Net Savvy

1. Several different pricing models can be found on the Internet. Each model appeals to different customer groups. Go to www.eBay.com and try to buy this book. What pricing options and prices are available? Do you believe that everyone will choose the least expensive option? Why or why not? Now go to www.Amazon.com. Is there more than one price available for this book? If so, what are those prices? Are different versions available? If you had to buy another copy of this book, where would you buy it, and why would you buy it there?

2. Prices can vary, depending on the market being served. Because Dell sells its computers directly to consumers all around the world, the Dell website makes it easy to compare prices for various markets. Go to www.dell.com/home and look at the price of an Inspirion 6200 desktop computer. Next go to http://www.dell.co.uk/, the Dell United Kingdom website, and find the price of the same computer. (If you need to convert currency to U.S. dollars, go to www.xe.com.) How does the price of the desktop computer vary? What would account for these differences in price?

Chapter Case Study

PAYING FOR ALL THOSE PINSTRIPES[53]

When the New York Yankees opened their new $1.5 billion stadium at the start of the 2009 baseball season, the team already had sold 85 percent of its premium seating. But a few hundred of the best seats, closest to the action, remained unsold.

At the time, the highest priced seats, those in the first row, were $2,500 each. To increase sales, in the spring of 2009, the Yanks cut prices 50 percent to $1,250. The $1,000 seats also were reduced to $650. Customers who had purchased tickets at the full price received a refund. The team needed the brand new stadium to be full all the time to give the impression that it was an exciting place to be. Empty premium seats would be an embarrassment to a marquee team like the Yankees.

And then came October 2009, and the Yankees' 27th World Series victory. Even after it had achieved approximately 90 occupancy rates for most of the successful season, the team announced that it would lower prices on many season ticket packages for 2010, including some of the highest priced ones. For example, the first level of nonpremium seats (one level up, behind home plate) would cost $250 per seat per game, a decrease of almost 25 percent from the previous price of $325. The rationale the team gave? The Yankees' general managing partner Hal Steinbrenner was sensitive to the struggling economy and consumer responses, so he would continue to review prices.

The review has persisted as the Yankees have continued their legendary success. In 2011, though the team lost in the first round of the playoffs, fans were able to watch Mariano Rivera reach 602 saves, more than any other pitcher in the history of the game. They also followed Derek Jeter's every swing until he got his 3000th hit in thrilling fashion with a long home run. For Yankee fans, any season without a ring may be a failure, but the excitement throughout the year led to high hopes for the 2012 season.

When they seek out season tickets, these fans will find even more variation in the charged prices. For field-level seats in Section 115, they must pay $210 per game. If they shift down to Section 125, the price drops to $175. In the bleachers though, rates for the lowest priced seats have risen, from $14 to $20. Yet many fans still consider the bleacher seats the best value in the park, offering a better view than some of the more expensive upper deck rows.

But the team's recent successes also mean that not everyone who wants tickets can get them. Season ticket subscriptions continue to be high, and people who want individual tickets for a single game may be out of luck. So even if the Yankees' official site shows that seats in Section 305 cost $40, how much are they really worth to a fan? If buyers cannot snatch up the seats quickly enough, StubHub, the official ticket resale site sanctioned by Major League Baseball, offers an alternative: seats in the same section for $129–$175 a ticket.

And for those who just can't get enough, the Yankees provide other forms of access to the team. In the offseason, fans can purchase behind-the-scenes tours of the Stadium, which includes visits to the dugout, Monument Park (where the Yankees honor their legends, like Ruth and Mantle, as well as 9-11 victims), batting cages, the Yankee Museum, and the clubhouse. For those who want to see their favorite players in the sunshine, tickets to spring training are available for just $17 to $33, though they would have to go to Tampa, Florida, to catch these practice games.

Questions

1. Which seats in Yankee Stadium does the team management price according to a premium pricing plan? Which seats represent value pricing tactics?

2. What environmental factors influence the prices of Yankee tickets?

3. If Yankee Stadium does not sell out, what are the costs to the company? Consider a broad range of costs, not just the price of the unsold seat.

The Art Institute of Chicago – Chicago (Loop)

$9 for Art Museum Admission (Up to $18 Value)

♥ Cultural Pursuits   🎁 Buy it for a friend!

Art involves creativity and a release of inner emotions, unlike Latin, which

$9.00	Deal Has Ended

$18.00	50%	$9.00
Value	Discount	You Save

Over 1,000 bought   00:00:00
Limited availability   Time left to buy

The Fine Print

- Expires Mar 22, 2012
- Limit 10 per person. Not valid for museum membership. Must use promotional value in 1 visit.

And for those who just can't get enough, the Yankees provide other forms of access to the team. In the offseason, fans can purchase behind-the-scenes tours of the Stadium, which includes visits to the dugout, Monument Park (where the Yankees honor their legends, like Ruth and Mantle, as well as 9-11 victims), batting cages, the Yankee Museum, and the clubhouse. For those who want to see their favorite players in the sunshine, tickets to spring training are available for just $17 to $33, though they would have to go to Tampa, Florida, to catch these practice games.

Questions

1. Which seats in Yankee Stadium does the team management price according to a premium pricing plan? Which seats represent value pricing tactics?

2. What environmental factors influence the prices of Yankee tickets?

3. If Yankee Stadium does not sell out, what are the costs to the company? Consider a broad range of costs, not just the price of the unsold seat.

Strategic Pricing Methods

Every day, Groupon alerts its users to several "featured deals."[1] The discounts are organized according to the major U.S. cities that Groupon serves, offered to site users who live in or near those markets. A woman living in New York, for example, receives offers for discounts to nail salons nearby. Economically, the deals are attractive: $10 worth of pizza for $5,[2] a 64 percent discount on a membership to the Chicago Art Institute, or nearly half off interactive cooking classes that culminate with a four-course gourmet meal.[3] They often revolve around social events, like classes or dining out, and encourage access to goods or services that customers may find appealing but have been unwilling to try, whether because they appear frivolous (e.g., spa services) or because of cost (e.g., hot air balloon rides).

Although Groupon searches for deals with companies that demand few fine-print restrictions, the site attaches its own strings to discounts: A minimum number of people must sign up before the promotion takes effect. This caveat motivates users to spread the word, mostly through social networking sites. Without a minimum number of buyers, the discount does not apply, and no one receives the deal.

So far though, maximums have been more of an issue than minimums. The Chicago Art Institute promotion added 5,000 new members, an impressive addition to the 85,000 members the museum had accumulated in the previous 100 years. The owner of the pizza chain offering 50 percent off coupons had 9,000 responses. Business owners, Groupon warns, need to be ready for this kind of interest. Some small businesses cap their offers to avoid overwhelming staff or frustrating customers who may have to wait months for an appointment.

Groupon itself faces an avalanche of interest from site users and businesses. A still struggling economy creates appeal among users, which has triggered growth rates of up to 25 percent in just one month. Groupon has sold more than 22 million deals to its approximately 50 million subscribers,[4] and most of these users are young professionals in their 20s and 30s, a highly desirable target market.

Businesses see Groupon as a cost-effective way to bring in new customers; 120 were lined up for promotions in Chicago, where Groupon launched in 2008, and Groupon has expanded to other cities. Investors are also excited about Groupon's business model because it doesn't involve inventory or shipping (users print Groupon's coupon and bring it to the vendor). Finally, because most offers are intangibles, such as services or classes instead of products or goods, Groupon rarely faces the problems with stock-outs that other group buying sites suffer. Even as it has expanded into "Groupon Goods," it makes clear that the offers are first come, first served.

At a time when retailers are investing their marketing dollars with great care, Groupon's payment structure encourages businesses to sign on. If the promotion is successful, Groupon takes a share of the profits. If it's unsuccessful, neither Groupon nor the company makes money. But even if actual redemption rates are high, many firms question whether Groupon promotions sufficiently generate long-term customers.[5] Many may try the promotion once, and never come back. Worse yet, if the promotion is too successful, and the firm is unable to adequately satisfy demand, customers will become disgruntled, never to return again, and potentially spread negative reviews to their friends and in social media.

The future of the daily deal is unknown. Analysts believe that Groupon and other daily deals will be absorbed by larger online entities, and that companies like Amazon, Google, and Facebook will have a daily deal as part of their marketing strategy. Few daily deals are expected to survive as independent businesses.

Coming up with the "right" price is never easy, as the opening example shows. How might this new option for finding deals cause shifts overall—both in what consumers are willing to pay and in what manufacturers can charge? What kinds of effects might Groupon have on future sales of products and services that customers first find on this deal site? What other members of the market might such price changes affect? To answer such questions, we examine various pricing strategies in this chapter.

Chapter 14 was devoted to examining what "price" is, why it is important, how marketers set pricing objectives, and the factors that influence prices. In this chapter, we extend that foundation by focusing on specific considerations for setting pricing strategies and then discuss a number of pricing strategies. We also examine the implications of various pricing tactics for both consumers and businesses, as well as some of the more important legal and ethical issues associated with pricing.

LO1 Identify three methods that firms use to set their prices.

CONSIDERATIONS FOR SETTING PRICE STRATEGIES

Firms embrace different objectives, face different market conditions, and operate in different manners. Thus, they employ unique pricing strategies that seem best for the particular set of circumstances in which they find themselves. Even a single firm needs different strategies across its products and services and over

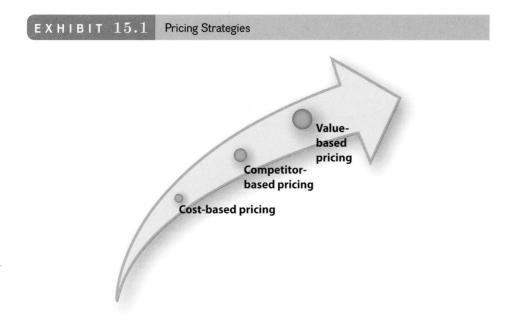

EXHIBIT 15.1   Pricing Strategies

time as market conditions change. The choice of a pricing strategy thus is specific to the product/service and target market. Although firms tend to rely on similar strategies when they can, each product or service requires its own specific strategy, because no two are ever exactly the same in terms of the marketing mix. Three different methods that can help develop pricing strategies—cost-based, competitor-based, and value-based—are discussed in this section (see Exhibit 15.1).

Cost–Based Methods

As their name implies, **cost-based pricing methods** determine the final price to charge by starting with the cost. Relevant costs (e.g., fixed, variable, overhead) and a profit are added. Then this total amount is divided by the total demand to arrive at a cost-plus price. For example, assume the fixed costs to produce an item are $200,000, the variable costs add up to $100,000, and the estimated number of units to be produced is 30,000. Then,

$$(100,000 + 200,000) \div 30,000 = \$10$$

which is the total allocated cost per unit when 30,000 units are produced. If the desired markup is 20 percent, we multiply $10 by 1.20 (i.e., by 100 + 20 = 120 percent) to attain the cost-plus price for this item: $12. This sales price represents a cost-plus-percentage markup.

Cost-based methods do not recognize the role that consumers or competitors' prices play in the marketplace though. Although they are relatively simple, compared with other methods used to set prices, cost-based pricing requires that all costs be identified and calculated on a per-unit basis. Moreover, the process assumes that these costs will not vary much for different levels of production. If they do, the price might need to be raised or lowered according to the production level. Thus, with cost-based pricing, prices are usually set on the basis of estimates of average costs.

Competition–Based Methods

Recall from Chapter 14 that some firms set prices according to their competitors' prices. But even if they do not have a strict competitor orientation, most firms still know that consumers compare the prices of their products with the different product/price combinations that competitors offer. Thus, using a **competition-based pricing method**, they may set their prices to reflect the way they want consumers to interpret their own prices, relative to competitors' offerings. For example, setting a price very close to a competitor's price signals to consumers that the product is similar, whereas setting the price much higher signals greater features, better quality, or some other valued benefit.

Value–Based Methods

Value-based pricing methods include approaches to setting prices that focus on the overall value of the product offering as perceived by the consumer. Consumers determine value by comparing the benefits they expect the product to deliver with the sacrifice they will need to make to acquire the product. Of course, different consumers perceive value differently. So how does a manager use value-based pricing methods? We consider two key approaches.

Improvement Value Method

With the first method, the manager must estimate the improvement value of a new product or service. This **improvement value** represents an estimate of how much more (or less) consumers are willing to pay for a product relative to other comparable products. For example, suppose a major telecommunications company has developed a new cell phone. Using any of a host of research methods—such as consumer surveys—the manager could get customers to assess the new product relative to an existing product and provide an estimate of how much better it is, or its improvement value.

Exhibit 15.2 illustrates how to calculate the improvement value. Consumers evaluate how much better (or worse) the new cell phone is than an existing product on five dimensions: clarity, range, security, battery life, and ease of use. According to the respondents to the survey, the new cell phone has 20 percent more clarity than the comparison phone. These consumers also weight the importance of the five attributes by allocating 100 points among them to indicate their relative importance; for the clarity dimension, this weighting is .40. When the manager multiplies the improvement weight by the relative importance percentage, clarity (20 × .40) emerges with a weighted factor of 8 percent. The marketer repeats the process for each benefit and sums the weighted factors to arrive at an approximation of the improvement value of the new product from customers' point of view. In this illustration, the improvement value is equal to 21 percent, so if the other cell phone costs $100, the firm should be able to charge customers a value-based price as high as $121 ($100 × 1.21).

EXHIBIT 15.2	Improvement Value		
Incremental Benefits	**Improved Value**	**Benefit Weight**	**Weighted Factor**
Clarity	20%	.40	8%
Range	40%	.20	8%
Security	10%	.10	1%
Battery life	5%	.20	1%
Ease of use	30%	.10	3%
Overall		1.00	21%

One way to determine the price of a new product, like a new cell phone model, is to determine the improvement value from the customers' perspective.

Cost of Ownership Method Another value-based method for setting prices determines the total cost of owning the product over its useful life. Using the **cost of ownership method**, consumers may be willing to pay more for a particular product because, over its entire lifetime, it will eventually cost less to own than a cheaper alternative.[6]

Consider, for example, that an energy-efficient fluorescent light bulb costs $3 and is expected to last 6,000 hours. Alternatively, a conventional light bulb costs $1 but its average life is only 1,500 hours. The fluorescent bulb is expected to last four times longer than a conventional bulb, but it only costs three times as much. Using the cost of ownership method, and considering the cost per hour, the fluorescent bulb manufacturer could charge $4 for each bulb, if it wanted to be equivalent to the cost of the conventional bulb. But research also has indicated that many consumers are reluctant to spend $4 for a bulb when they have been used to getting them for $1, so the manufacturer chose to charge only $3.

Implementing Value-based Pricing Methods Although value-based pricing methods can be quite effective, they also necessitate a great deal of consumer research to be implemented successfully. Sellers must know how consumers in different market segments will attach value to the benefits delivered by their products, as Adding Value 15.1 describes. They also must account for changes in consumer attitudes, because the way customers perceive value today may not be the way they perceive it tomorrow.

CHECK YOURSELF

1. What are the three different considerations for setting prices?
2. How can you use value-based methods for setting prices?

Adding Value 15.1   Clearly a Winning Strategy[7]

Would you buy glasses or contact lenses over the Internet? You might for the right price. When Roger Hardy and Michaela Tokarksi founded Clearly Contacts in 2000, their Vancouver basement office had a computer, a phone, and a Ping-Pong table. In a few short years, it has become the world's fastest growing online retailer of eyeglasses and contact lenses. How have they managed it?

While working for a contact lens manufacturer, Hardy realized that the margins were extremely high. He knew there had to be a better, cheaper way for consumers to buy eye-care products, so he defined a new mission: "Saving the World from Overpriced Eyeglasses." In the past, the prescription glasses market has been dominated by opticians. The Clearly Contacts business model instead eliminated any middlemen, automated the order process, and shipped directly to consumers, for prices 50 to 70 percent less than traditional eye-care retailers. Prices range from $38 to $198, great values for designer brands such as Prada, Dior, Armani, and Fendi.

Yet initially, the online company struggled. Although consumers clearly were willing to purchase books or clothes over the Internet, they had reservations about buying eyeglasses online. It is a more complex purchase, with relatively high risk. Consumers also need to change their behavior and do something a little different to complete the purchase. Therefore, to help make the offer more valuable, Clearly Contacts added a Virtual Mirror application, to let customers see how the glasses designs look on their faces, as well as free shipping and liberal payment terms.

Furthermore, the company decided to give 2,000 pairs of designer glasses away for free, if consumers signed up online to get a coupon code. The strategy was to get the high-quality glasses in the hands of consumers and thus dispel concerns about buying them on the Internet. The success of such promotions has led the company to keep up its free offers; new buyers can easily find coupons for their first pair.

As a result of this winning formula, the company has captured about 10 percent of the eyeglasses market and earned a spot on Canada's *Profit* magazine's 100 Top Fastest Growing Companies in Canada. With operations in North America, Europe, and Asia, more than 2 million customers, and revenues of $119 million, it is clearly on its way to becoming the world's largest online optical store.

Would you buy contacts or eyeglasses over the Internet? Maybe if the price were right?

L02 Describe the difference between an everyday low price strategy (EDLP) and a high/low strategy.

PRICING STRATEGIES

In this section, we discuss a number of commonly used price strategies: everyday low pricing, high/low pricing, and new product strategies.[8]

Everyday Low Pricing (EDLP)

With an **everyday low pricing (EDLP)** strategy, companies stress the continuity of their retail prices at a level somewhere between the regular, nonsale price and the deep-discount sale prices their competitors may offer.[9] By reducing consumers' search costs, EDLP adds value; consumers can spend less of their valuable time comparing prices, including sale prices, at different stores. With its EDLP strategy, Walmart communicates to consumers that, for any given group of often-purchased

Social and Mobile Marketing 15.1

Price Check on Aisle . . . Anywhere[10]

Most marketers assume that a Gen X guy and his mom would shop in very different ways. But the benefits offered by the latest mobile phone software are blending those shopping methods by helping consumers of all types shop smarter.

Eric Olson wanted a Blu-ray version of *Heat*, but at Best Buy, where he was shopping before Christmas, the disc cost $26, which seemed high to the 33-year-old consumer. Therefore, while still in Best Buy, he scanned the UPC barcode using his Android smartphone and went on the mobile application ShopSavvy to check the price of the disc at nearby stores. Walmart.com was charging only $19. Eric's mom Carrie Olson also regularly uses a RedLaser application to scan the bar codes of books and DVDs.

Amazon wants both Eric and Carrie to shop its site instead, for everything they need, so its price checking application is not only free to customers, but at times, it even offers them money to use it. In the preholiday shopping season, Amazon promised customers a $5 discount on their order if they scanned a barcode on an item in a competitor's store, then bought that same item from Amazon.[11]

It is nothing new to check on prices online. It is the mobility of these checks that is really advancing the practice—and making some sellers really nervous.

Using a smartphone with the ShopSavvy app, consumers can find out which nearby stores carry the desired product at the lowest prices, as well as which stores are closest to them.

Anyone with a smartphone can use ShopSavvy to find out which nearby stores carry the desired product at the lowest price, as well as which stores are closest to the consumer. Amazon's version only compares prices with the items available on its site, but as the site continues to grow, that includes a lot of items.

ShopSavvy's database instead includes tens of thousands of retailers and millions of store locations, such as Walmart, Target, American Eagle, Best Buy, The Gap, and online-only retailers. Because these technologies rely on the retailers' websites or databases for pricing information, sometimes the details provided are a little out of date, especially if the retailer decides to change the price at the last minute. But 20 million people have downloaded the application, and 10 million of them use it with some frequency—about 20 percent of the total population of smartphone users in the United States.

For Eric and Carrie Olson, the options are nearly endless. But for retailers, especially those that cannot compete very well on price, the options seem to be shrinking fast. If everyone can instantly perform price research, what is a higher priced seller to do?

---

items, its prices will tend to be lower than those of any other company in that market. This claim does not necessarily mean that every item that consumers may purchase will be priced lower at Walmart than anywhere else—in fact, some competitive retailers will offer lower prices on some items. However, for an average purchase, Walmart's prices tend to be lower overall. Social and Mobile Marketing 15.1 reinforces the advantages of offering everyday low prices.

The bottom line is that if sellers want to imply EDLP, odd prices may be appropriate. However, odd prices also can suggest lower quality.[12] Some consumers may perceive higher value because of the low price (especially if quality is less important to them than price), whereas others may infer lower value on the basis of the low-quality image the odd price suggests (especially if price is less important to them than quality).

High/Low Pricing

An alternative to EDLP is a **high/low pricing** strategy, which relies on the promotion of sales, during which

Odd prices signal to consumers that the price is low.

Ethical and Societal Dilemma 15.1   Is It Really 45 Percent Off?[13]

For the truly fashionable—or at least those who consider themselves as members of that group—the trade-off between luxury and affordability can be a tricky one. You want the newest, hottest fashion, but trying to keep up can be exhausting on your wallet. What's a maven to do?

Private sale online sites such as Gilt, RueLaLa, and HauteLook promise a solution. They host limited-time sales of products from high-end fashion brands. A sale starts at a specified time and lasts for 48 hours, or until the sale is sold out. So, if you must have the Nova Armored Baby Beaton handbag from Burberry, you can have it for 45 percent off the list price, or $877 instead of $1,595, as long as you are on Hautelook.com when the sale starts. Brick-and-mortar retailers are following suit with "flash sales," such as when Banana Republic offers 40 percent of its full-priced sweaters but only between 11:00 a.m. and 2:00 p.m. on specific days.

But is it really 40 or 45 percent off, and 45 percent off of what? A reference price like $1,595 gives consumers a cue as to what that specific handbag should be worth. Research shows that the greater the difference between a suggested retail and a sale price, the greater the perceived value. When customers see Sears offering a refrigerator for $1,300 off its original price, that huge number is nearly impossible to ignore. The better the deal, the more consumers will be attracted to buy. But if the retailer inflates the suggested or original price,

the percentage discount and dollars off seem much better than they actually are.

When the private sale sites have been caught inflating the suggested retail prices to show a greater percentage discount, they generally claim that the original prices they list are accurate and come from the manufacturer. Any errors, they argue, are because the manufacturer gave them the wrong price, or else it might be due to employee error. For example, if the suggested retail price of the Burberry bag was actually only $1,100 instead of $1,595, then the bag was only discounted 20 percent. A customer in the heat of the moment may buy the bag because it is reported to be 45 percent off; were it only 20 percent off, she might not have purchased.

In some cases, the complicated coupon, discount, and flash pricing offers make it nearly impossible to determine the extent of the deal without a calculator. Because consumers rarely have the time or energy to calculate exactly what kind of discount they are getting, retailers can play on their excitement when it seems like a great deal.

Should private sale sites and in-store retailers be required to substantiate their reference prices? Which price should they use as the reference price? Is it their responsibility if the manufacturer gives them the wrong pricing information? Do you think they are intentionally misleading their customers?

Walmart uses an everyday low pricing (EDLP) strategy.

prices are temporarily reduced to encourage purchases. A high/low strategy is attractive because it attracts two distinct market segments: those who are not price sensitive and are willing to pay the "high" price and more price-sensitive customers who wait for the "low" sale price. High/low sellers can also create excitement and attract customers through the "get them while they last" atmosphere that occurs during a sale.

Sellers using a high/low pricing strategy often communicate their strategy through the creative use of a **reference price**, which is the price against which buyers compare the actual selling price of the product and that facilitates their evaluation process. The seller labels the reference price as the "regular price" or an "original price." When consumers view the "sale price" and compare it with the provided reference price, their perceptions of the value of the deal will likely increase.[14]

In the advertisement on this page, Sears has provided a reference price, in smaller print and labeled "Reg.," to indicate that $24.99 is the regular price of Lee jeans. In addition, the advertisement highlights the current "sale" price of $21.99. Thus, the reference price suggests to consumers that they are getting a good deal and will save money. However, as Ethical and Societal Dilemma 15.1 notes,

sometimes the veracity of such a reference price is open to challenge.

EDLP and High/Low Strategies Are Influenced by Price–Quality Relationships

In the end, whether consumers prefer sellers offering EDLP or a high/low strategy depends on how those consumers evaluate prices and quality. Some prefer not to expend the time to find the lowest price and favor EDLP as an efficient way to get low, even if not the very lowest, prices. Other consumers may relish the challenge of getting the lowest price or be so price sensitive that they are willing to expend the time and effort to seek out the lowest price every time.

These decisions get even more complicated, in that customers also infer quality based on whether the seller uses an EDLP or a high/low strategy. Some consumers perceive that sellers that use EDLP carry lower-quality goods, whereas high/low pricing sellers tend to carry better-quality items. In part, this perception forms because consumers view the initial high price at a high/low seller as the reference price. They might assume that the higher the reference price, the higher the merchandise quality. For instance, if a sweater at Macy's originally sold for $150, but is now on sale

Sears ad with reference price.

for $50, many consumers would assume that it is higher quality than a similar regular price $50 sweater at JCPenney.[15]

Yet as we noted in Ethical and Societal Dilemma 15.1, some of these references prices might be fake. At JCPenney, the prices listed on price tags rose over the past decade, from an average of $27 to $36. But with access to nearly constant discounts, promotions, and coupons, the price that customers actually paid for each item stayed the same—an average of around $10. The retailer made the discounts seem bigger by increasing the original prices. By putting nearly everything on a steep discount nearly all the time, and spending a lot to communicate the 600 unique promotions it ran each year, JCPenney realized it

Some retailers use an everyday low pricing (EDLP) strategy (left), while others use a high-low pricing strategy (right).

also was discounting its brand. No one believed it offered sufficient quality, because everything was being discounted. Instead, the retailer has begun to apply a three-tiered pricing system across the board: everyday prices, monthly specials, and clearance items. Whether this hybrid approach to pricing will succeed remains to be seen.[16]

 Explain the difference between a price skimming and a market penetration pricing strategy.

New Product Pricing Strategies

Developing pricing strategies for new products is one of the most challenging tasks a manager can undertake. When the new product is similar to what already appears on the market, this job is somewhat easier, because the product's approximate value has already been established and the value-based methods described earlier in this chapter can be employed. But when the new product is truly innovative, or what we call "new to the world," determining consumers' perceptions of its value and pricing it accordingly become far more difficult.

Two distinct new product pricing strategies are discussed next: market penetration pricing and price skimming.

Market Penetration Pricing Firms using a **market penetration strategy** set the initial price low for the introduction of the new product or service. Their objective is to build sales, market share, and profits quickly. The low market penetration price is an incentive to purchase the product immediately. Vendors of security software often adopt such a tactic: By adding their products, such as Microsoft's anti-virus package, to a computer software bundle at no extra charge, providers can increase their market share. They also increase the likelihood that customers will pay to obtain updates of software that is already implanted into their computer. Firms using a market penetration strategy expect the unit cost to drop significantly as the accumulated volume sold increases, an effect known as the **experience curve effect**. With this effect, as sales continue to grow, the costs continue to drop.

In addition to offering the potential to build sales, market share, and profits, penetration pricing discourages competitors from entering the market because the profit margin is relatively low. Furthermore, if the costs to produce the product drop because of the accumulated volume, competitors that enter the market later will face higher unit costs, at least until their volume catches up with the early entrant.

A penetration strategy has its drawbacks. First, the firm must have the capacity to satisfy a rapid rise in demand—or at least be able to add that capacity quickly. Second, low price does not signal high quality. Of course, a price below their expectations decreases the risk for consumers to purchase the product and test its quality for themselves. Third, firms should avoid a penetration pricing strategy if some segments of the market are willing to pay more for the product; otherwise, the firm is just "leaving money on the table."

Price skimming is often used for high demand video games like Call of Duty because fans will pay a higher price to be one of the first to own the newest version.

Price Skimming In many markets, and particularly for new and innovative products or services, innovators and early adopters (see Chapter 12) are willing to pay a higher price to obtain the new product or service. This strategy, known as **price skimming**, appeals to these segments of consumers who are willing to pay the premium price to have the innovation first. This tactic is

particularly common in technology markets, where sellers know that fans of *Call of Duty* will wait in line for hours, desperate to be the first to own the newest version. These innovators are willing to pay the very highest prices to obtain brand-new examples of technology advances, with exciting product enhancements. However, after this high-price market segment becomes saturated and sales begin to slow down, companies generally lower the price to capture (or skim) the next most price sensitive market segment, which is willing to pay a somewhat lower price. For most companies, the price dropping process can continue until the demand for the product has been satisfied, even at the lowest price points.

The spread of new media for movies illustrates a price skimming strategy. As with VCRs in the 1970s and DVD players in the 1990s, consumers were slow to embrace the new, more expensive Blu-Ray discs. But enough early adopters purchased the Blu-Ray discs that manufacturers continued to refine Blu-Ray players to penetrate wider target markets. Consumers are buying the devices at a faster pace than the earlier movie-playing devices. One obvious reason for this sales growth is that prices for high-quality Blu-Ray players have dropped below $80, a steep drop from the $300-plus that retailers charged for debut models.[17]

For price skimming to work though, the product or service must be perceived as breaking new ground in some way, offering consumers new benefits currently unavailable in alternative products. When they believe it will work, firms use skimming strategies for a variety of reasons. Some may start by pricing relatively high to signal high quality to the market. Others may decide to price high at first to limit demand, which gives them time to build their production capacities. Similarly, some firms employ a skimming strategy to try to quickly earn back some of the high research and development investments they made for the new product. Finally, firms employ skimming strategies to test consumers' price sensitivity. A firm that prices too high can always lower the price (recall our discussion in Chapter 12 of Amazon's price decreases for the original Kindle), but if the price is initially set too low, it is almost impossible to raise it without significant consumer resistance.

Furthermore, for a skimming pricing strategy to be successful, competitors cannot be able to enter the market easily; otherwise, price competition will likely force lower prices and undermine the whole strategy. Competitors might be prevented from entering the market through patent protections, their inability to copy the innovation (because it is complex to manufacture, its raw materials are hard to get, or the product relies on proprietary technology), or the high costs of entry.

Skimming strategies also face a significant potential drawback in the relatively high unit costs associated with producing small volumes of products. Therefore, firms must consider the trade-off between earning a higher price and suffering higher production costs. Finally, firms using a skimming strategy for new products must face the consequences of ultimately having to lower the price as demand wanes. Margins suffer, and customers who purchased the product or service at the higher initial price may become irritated when the price falls. Adding Value 15.2 illustrates the use of skimming and penetration pricing strategies in the field of technology products.

CHECK YOURSELF

1. Explain the difference between EDLP and high/low pricing.
2. What pricing strategies should be considered when introducing a new product?

Adding Value 15.2   Cellular All Around: The Market Penetration of Phones[18]

At its initial introduction, the groundbreaking iPhone sold for $599, then dropped slightly in price a few months later. Successive generations have added speed, screen resolution, battery life, new carriers, and Siri, but the prices have dropped from the initial level, as Exhibit 15.3 shows.[19]

The success of the initial version of the iPhone prompted Apple and its initial sole carrier AT&T to bank on low customer turnover and thus expect profits in the long term from mobile data services. But Google, Samsung, LG, and BlackBerry soon introduced touchscreen phones to compete with Apple's iPhone, meaning customers, especially those who did not want to switch carriers, had plenty of options.

Yet Apple's iPhone pricing strategy generally has been successful: Charge the highest prices to the Apple fans who must have the latest version the moment it comes out. Lower prices for the previous generation at the same time. Earn ad-

Apple's iPhone uses a market penetration pricing strategy.

ditional revenues from applications and other services.

Moreover, even if Apple products seem somewhat pricey, in the history of new innovations, they are actually quite reasonable. When telephone service initially became available in the United States for example, it cost the equivalent of around $2000 per month. Thus, only businesses purchased innovations like the telegraph, the typewriter, and the personal computer when they first arrived on the scene. The growth of the smartphone and tablet markets has been different, in that they are driven by consumer purchases, not business users.[20]

Some analysts suggest that Apple will apply a similar pricing strategy to the iPad as well, to combat competitors in the tablet market. It's hard to argue with that recommendation. Thus far, Apple has sold more than 37 million iPhones, and its projections continue to look strong.

EXHIBIT 15.3   iPhone Comparison Chart

How Apple Continually Adds Value to the iPhone				
Generation	Model Name	Key Value-Adding Features	Initial Price For Top Model	Current Price*
1	iPhone	Initial model. Touch screen, 4GB/8GB storage, MP3 player integration	$599	Discontinued
2	iPhone 3G	Added 16GB option, GPS, 3G, white color option	$299	Discontinued
3	iPhone 3GS	Added 32GB option, improved camera from 2MP to 3MP, ability to take videos, faster processor	$299	$0.99
4	iPhone 4	Improved screen resolution, faster processor, added front-facing camera for FaceTime, added support for Verizon network	$299	$99.99
5	iPhone 4S	Added Siri, 64GB option, 1080p HD video recording, faster processor, added support for Sprint netowrk	$399	$399.99

*Prices based on 2 year contract with AT&T as of Feb 29th, 2011

Source: Adapted from: Sam Costello, "iPhone Comparison Chart," *About.com,* http://ipod.about.com/od/decidingwhichipodtobuy/a/iphone_chart.htm.

PRICING TACTICS

It is important to distinguish clearly between pricing strategies and pricing tactics. A **pricing strategy** is a long-term approach to setting prices broadly in an integrative effort (across all the firm's products) based on the five Cs (company objectives, costs, customers, competition, and channel members) of pricing discussed in Chapter 14. **Pricing tactics,** in contrast, offer short-term methods to focus on select components of the five Cs. Generally, a pricing tactic represents either a short-term response to a competitive threat (e.g., lowering price temporarily to meet a competitor's price reduction) or a broadly accepted method of calculating a final price for the customer that is short term in nature. We separate our discussion of pricing tactics into those directed at end consumers and those aimed at intermediaries in a business-to-business (B2B) setting

LO4 Identify tactics used to reduce prices to consumers.

Stores like Aldi use a pricing tactic called leader pricing to build store traffic aggressively pricing and advertising regularly purchased items, often at or just above the store's cost.

Pricing Tactics Aimed at Consumers

When firms sell their products and services directly to consumers, rather than to other businesses, the pricing tactics they use naturally differ. Some of the tactics aimed directly at consumers—such as markdowns, quantity discounts, seasonal discounts, coupons, rebates, leasing, price bundling, leader pricing, and price lining—continue to be important factors.

Markdowns **Markdowns** are the reductions retailers take on the initial selling price of the product or service.[21] An integral component of the high/low pricing strategy we described previously, markdowns enable retailers to get rid of slow-moving or obsolete merchandise, sell seasonal items after the appropriate season, and match competitors' prices on specific merchandise. Retailers must get rid of merchandise that isn't selling, because holding on to such items hurts the retailer's image and ties up money in inventory that could be used more productively elsewhere.

Retailers also use markdowns to promote merchandise and increase sales. Particularly when used in conjunction with promotions, markdowns can increase traffic into the store or onto their websites, which many retailers view as half the battle. Once customers are in the store or on their websites, retailers always hope they will purchase other products at regular prices.

Quantity Discounts for Consumers The most common implementation of a quantity discount at the consumer level is the **size discount**. For example, there are three sizes of General Mills' popular cereal Cheerios: 10-, 15-, and 20-ounce boxes priced at approximately $3.89, $4.49, and $5.99, respectively. The larger the quantity, the less the cost per ounce, which means the manufacturer is providing a quantity discount. The goal of this tactic is to encourage consumers to purchase larger quantities each time they buy. In turn, these consumers are less likely to switch brands and often tend to consume more of the product, depending on the product usage characteristics. Typically, buying a larger package of toilet tissue does not mean consumers will use it faster, but buying a larger box of cereal may encourage them to eat more of it or eat it more often.[22]

Customers get a size discount for buying larger sizes. With Cheerios, the larger the box, the less it costs per ounce.

Seasonal Discounts **Seasonal discounts** are price reductions offered on products and services to stimulate demand during off-peak seasons. You can find hotel rooms, ski lift tickets, snowmobiles, lawn mowers, barbeque grills, vacation packages, flights to certain destinations, and Christmas cards at discounts during their "off" seasons. Some consumers even plan

their buying around these discounts, determined to spend the day after Christmas stocking up on discounted wrapping paper and bows for the following year.

Coupons Coupons offer a discount on the price of specific items when they're purchased. Coupons are issued by manufacturers and retailers in newspapers, on products, on the shelf, at the cash register, over the Internet, and through the mail.[23] Retailers use coupons because they can induce customers to try products for the first time, convert those first-time users to regular users, encourage large purchases, increase usage, and protect market share against competition. However, the impact of coupons on profitability is questionable.

Coupon promotions, like all temporary promotions, may be stealing sales from a future period without any net increase in sales. For instance, if a supermarket runs a coupon promotion on sugar, households may buy a large quantity of sugar and stockpile it for future use. Thus, unless the coupon is used mostly by new buyers, the net impact on sales is negligible, and there will be a negative impact on profits due to the amount of the redeemed coupons and cost of the coupon redemption procedures. In addition, as we discussed in Chapter 5, some consumers engage in "extreme couponing," such that their purchases represent losses for the manufacturer and the retailer selling the products.

Coupons also may annoy, alienate, and confuse consumers and therefore do little to increase store loyalty. Customers see an ad for a supermarket with a headline reading "Double Coupons" but don't realize there might be conditions, such as a minimum purchase required, or that it may only apply to certain manufacturers.

Recognizing these problems, some retailers have reduced coupon usage and cut the number of days in which customers can redeem coupons. Other retailers, like CVS, are making coupons more attractive to loyal customers by customizing their content to be in line with their unique needs. For instance, if a customer typically spends a small amount during each shopping trip, the customer will receive coupons that encourage larger purchases, such as "buy one, get one free." If another customer spends a lot each time she shops, but shops sporadically, that customer will get coupons that expire relatively quickly. Unique coupons will also encourage customers to try new brands within categories that they normally purchase, or products that complement their usual purchases, such as shampoo to customers that purchase hair color.[24]

As discussed in this chapter's opener, Internet sites provide customers with instant coupons. For instance, a customer might go to a Walmart and find a Hot Wheels video game for $29.99. A scan of the bar code on his cell phone to ShopSavvy.com might find the same item across at a Target a mile away for $19.99. Another scan to MyCoupons.com provides a coupon for $10, thus saving the customer $20 in a matter of minutes.

Rebates Rebates provide another form of discounts for consumers off the final selling price. In this case, however, the manufacturer, instead of the retailer, issues the refund as a portion of the purchase price returned to the buyer in the form of cash. Rebates can be even more frustrating than coupons for consumers, but the idea is similar. Whereas a coupon provides instant savings when presented, a rebate promises savings, usually mailed to the consumer at some later date, only if the consumer carefully follows the rules. The "hassle factor" for rebates thus is higher than for coupons. The consumer must first buy the item during a specified time period, then mail in the required documentation—which usually includes the original sales receipt—and finally wait four to six weeks (or more!) for a check to arrive.

Manufacturers generally like rebates because as much as 90 percent of consumers never bother to redeem them. Manufacturers also embrace this form of price reduction because it lets them offer price cuts to consumers directly. With a traditional wholesale price cut from its vendors, retailers can keep the price on the shelf the same and pocket the difference. Rebates can also be rolled out and shut off quickly. That allows manufacturers to fine-tune inventories or respond quickly

Superior Service 15.1 Oh, This Old Porsche? I'm Just Leasing It This Month . . .

A red Ferrari or a turbo Porsche—or how about a Bentley GTC convertible? Members of the Classic Car Club can drive one each week by paying initiation fees and annual dues of $7,000 to $23,000, plus a daily rental. Customers can drive around in an Audi R8 sports car during a vacation and then show up at a business meeting in a Bentley sedan. It is like a ZipCar (see the Chapter 13 case study) for the well-to-do. It is not just luxury cars, however. Consumers are leasing everything from fashion to art, putting hard-to-own luxury items within the reach of more people.[25] The focus on owning luxury products has become less important than having multiple options, limiting financial exposure, and experiencing products that most people cannot afford to own.

Leasing luxury products involves more than just the product. Those firms that do it well also provide excellent service. For example, the Classic Car Club invites members to weekly happy hour events, offers special activities such as driving a race car around a track, and provides reciprocal privileges for renting in locations where the Club does not exist.

The Wardrobe Company leases designer gowns from Dolce & Gabbana, Carolina Herrera, and Behnaz Sarafpour for 15 percent of the retail price. For frequent event attendees, these prices provide quite a deal! Bag, Borrow, or Steal allows its members to rent premium handbags and jewelry. There are also firms that rent art for a house to make it more appealing to potential buyers.

The flexibility and convenience of leasing ensures customers do not have to make big decisions about big products and yet still get to enjoy the experience. In this sense, the service

of providing the lease goods is just as important as the products themselves. Many customers avoid serious investments and their attendant risk, but they still appreciate the experience of carrying a Louis Vuitton bag for a week or driving a different Ferrari each month. Leasing allows these customers to fulfill their psychological needs and gain the extra perks that go along with the products.

Want to impress a date? Lease a car from Classic Car Club.

to competitors without actually cutting prices. Finally, because buyers are required to fill out forms with names, addresses, and other data, rebates become a great way for vendors to build a customer data warehouse. From the retailer's perspective, rebates are more advantageous than coupons since they increase demand in the same way coupons may, but the retailer has no handling costs.

Leasing For some products, discounts, coupons, and rebates may not be sufficient to bring the price to within consumers' reach. With a **lease**, consumers pay a fee to purchase the right to use a product for a specific amount of time. They never own the product, they are just renting it. Leasing products opens up new, less price sensitive, target markets. Some consumers also like leases because they get tired of the product before its useful life is over, and they don't have to worry about selling it, trading it, or throwing it away. Car companies have used leasing options for years to appeal to consumers who plan to keep their cars only for a few years and will want to trade in for a new model sooner rather than later. Other industries are recognizing that what works for Toyotas and Chevy trucks also works for gowns, handbags, art, and luxury cars. As Superior Service 15.1 notes, though consumers lease products, it is the ancillary service that makes it so valuable.

Price Bundling When you signed up for your high-speed Internet connection, did you also get cable TV and telephone? If so, you probably pay less than if you were to get the three services separately. This practice of selling more than one product for a single, lower price is called **price bundling**.[26] Firms bundle products or services together to encourage customers to stock up so they won't purchase competing brands, to encourage trial of a new product, or to provide an incentive to purchase a less desirable product or service to obtain a more desirable one in the same bundle.

Leader Pricing **Leader pricing** is a tactic that attempts to build store traffic by aggressively pricing and advertising a regularly purchased item, often priced at or just above the store's cost. The rationale behind this tactic argues that, while in the store to get the great deal on, say, milk, the consumer will also probably pick up other items, which sell at a higher margin. The higher margins and profits on these other items then will more than cover the lower mark-up on the milk. Imagine the marketing potential of various combinations of products; the store uses leader pricing on cocktail sauce, which gives employees the perfect opportunity to ask, "How about a pound of fresh shrimp to go with the cocktail sauce you're purchasing?" Leader pricing can be illegal under some circumstances though, as discussed subsequently in this chapter.

Coupons offer a discount on the price of specific items when they're purchased.

Price Lining When marketers establish a price floor and a price ceiling for an entire line of similar products and then set a few other price points in between to represent distinct differences in quality, the practice is called **price lining**. Imagine that you need a new dress shirt because you have an important job interview. You go to brooksbrothers.com and find similar looking shirts for $79.50 (non-iron), $135 (classic cotton), and $295 (luxury). Which are you going to buy? Are you going to risk the success of the interview by purchasing the least expensive shirt? Probably not. Will the interviewee be able to tell the difference between the $135 classic cotton and the $295 Sea Island cotton shirt? Probably not. You will probably purchase the middle quality shirt because you don't want to look cheap, but you really can't afford the highest priced shirt.[27]

Business Pricing Tactics and Discounts

 Identify tactics used to reduce prices to businesses.

The pricing tactics employed in B2B settings differ significantly from those used in consumer markets. Among the most prominent are seasonal and cash discounts, allowances, quantity discounts, and uniform delivered versus zone pricing. (See Exhibit 15.4.)

Seasonal Discounts A **seasonal discount** is an additional reduction offered as an incentive to retailers to order merchandise in advance of the normal buying season. For instance, Lennox may offer its air conditioner dealers an additional seasonal discount if they place their orders and receive delivery before April 1, prior to the warm months when air conditioner sales are highest. If it can ship earlier in the season, Lennox can plan its production schedules more easily and lessen its

EXHIBIT 15.4	Business-to-Business Pricing Tactics
Tactic	**Description**
Seasonal discounts	An additional reduction offered as an incentive to retailers to order merchandise in advance of the normal buying season.
Cash discounts	An additional reduction that reduces the invoice cost if the buyer pays the invoice prior to the end of the discount period.
Allowances	Advertising or slotting allowances (additional price reductions) offered in return for specific behaviors. Advertising allowances are offered to retailers if they agree to feature the manufacturer's product in their advertising and promotional efforts. Slotting allowances are offered to get new products into stores or to gain more or better shelf space.
Quantity discounts	Providing a reduced price according to the amount purchased.
Uniform delivered versus zone pricing	Uniform delivered price: shipper charges one rate, no matter where the buyer is located. Zone price: different prices depending on the geographical delivery area.

finished goods inventory. Its dealers, however, must weigh the benefits of a larger profit because of the discount versus the extra cost of carrying the inventory for a longer period of time.

Cash Discounts A **cash discount** reduces the invoice cost if the buyer pays the invoice prior to the end of the discount period. Typically, it is expressed in the form of a percentage, such as "3/10, n/30," or "3%, 10 days, net 30," which means the buyer can take a 3 percent discount on the total amount of the invoice if the bill is paid within 10 days of the invoice date; otherwise the full, or net, amount is due within 30 days. Why do B2B sellers offer cash discounts to customers? By encouraging early payment, they benefit from the time value of money. Getting money earlier rather than later enables the firm to either invest the money to earn a return on it or avoid borrowing money and paying interest on it. In both instances, the firm is better off financially.

Allowances Another pricing tactic that lowers the final cost to channel members is allowances, such as advertising or slotting allowances, offered in return for specific behaviors. An **advertising allowance** offers a price reduction to channel members if they agree to feature the manufacturer's product in their advertising and promotional efforts. Advertising allowances are legal as long they are available to all customers and not structured in such a way that they consistently and obviously favor one or a few buyers over others. **Slotting allowances** are fees paid to retailers simply to get new products into stores or to gain more or better shelf space for their products. Some argue that slotting allowances are unethical because they put small manufacturers that cannot readily afford allowances at a competitive disadvantage. Demanding large slotting allowances could be considered a form of bribery—"paying off" the retailer to get preferential treatment.

Quantity Discounts A **quantity discount** provides a reduced price according to the amount purchased. The more the buyer purchases, the higher the discount and, of course, the greater the value.

A **cumulative quantity discount** uses the amount purchased over a specified time period and usually involves several transactions. This type of discount particularly encourages resellers to maintain their current supplier because the cost to switch must include the loss of the discount. Recall that we noted that automobile dealers must buy the products they hope to sell to consumers from the manufacturer. They often attempt to meet a quota or a sales goal for a specific time period, such as a quarter or a year, because if they meet those quotas, they earn discounts on all the cars they purchased from the manufacturer, in the form of a cumulative quantity discount. For this very reason, you will often find good deals on cars at the end of a quarter or fiscal year. If the dealership can just sell a few more cars to meet its quota, the cumulative quantity discount earned can be substantial, so taking a few hundred dollars less on those last few cars is well worth the opportunity to receive a rebate check worth many times the amount of the losses.

A **noncumulative quantity discount**, though still a quantity discount, is based only on the amount purchased in a single order. It therefore provides the buyer with an incentive to purchase more merchandise immediately. Such larger, less frequent orders can save manufacturers order processing, sales, and transportation expenses. For example, a retail store might get a 40 percent discount off the manufacturer's suggested retail price for placing a $500 order; a 50 percent discount for an order of $501–$4,999; and a 60 percent discount for an order of greater than $5,000.

Uniform Delivered versus Zone Pricing These pricing tactics are specific to shipping, which represents a major cost for many manufacturers. With a **uniform delivered pricing** tactic, the shipper charges one rate, no matter where the buyer is located, which makes things very simple for both the seller and the buyer. **Zone pricing**, however, sets different prices depending on a geographical division of the delivery areas. For example, a manufacturer based in New York City might divide the United States into seven different zones and use different shipping rates for each zone to reflect the average shipping cost for customers located therein. This way, each customer in a zone is charged the same cost for shipping. Zone pricing can be advantageous to the shipper because it reflects the actual shipping charges more closely than uniform delivered pricing can.

CHECK YOURSELF

1. What are some consumer-oriented pricing tactics?
2. What are some B2B-oriented pricing tactics?

LO6 List pricing practices that have the potential to deceive customers.

LEGAL AND ETHICAL ASPECTS OF PRICING

With so many different pricing strategies and tactics, it is no wonder that unscrupulous firms find ample opportunity to engage in pricing practices that can hurt consumers. We now take a look at some of the legal and ethical implications of pricing.

Prices tend to fluctuate naturally and respond to varying market conditions. Thus, though we rarely see firms attempting to control the market in terms of product quality or advertising, they often engage in pricing practices that can unfairly reduce competition or harm consumers directly through fraud and deception. A host of laws and regulations at both the federal and state levels attempt to prevent unfair pricing practices, but some are poorly enforced, and others are difficult to prove.

Deceptive or Illegal Price Advertising

Although it is always illegal and unethical to lie in advertising, a certain amount of "puffery" is typically allowed (see Chapter 19).[28] But price advertisements should never deceive consumers to the point of causing harm. For example, a local car dealer's advertising that it had the "best deals in town" would likely be considered puffery. In contrast, advertising "the lowest prices, guaranteed" makes a very specific claim and, if not true, can be considered deceptive. The European Union takes a more stringent view of puffery than the United States. For example, when U.K.-based Tesco advertised that it was "Britain's Biggest Discounter," the U.K. Advertising Standards Authority forced it to end the campaign. Because differences in the items purchased made it difficult to determine if Tesco really was less expensive than its competitors, such as Aldi or Asda, the Authority ruled that the claim was inherently misleading.[29]

U.K.-based Tesco wasn't allowed to make the claim that is "Britains's Biggest Discounter" because it was considered to be misleading. Such a claim would probably be considered to be puffery in the U.S., and therefore allowed.

Deceptive Reference Prices Previously, we introduced reference prices, which create reference points for the buyer against which to compare the selling price. If the reference price is bona fide, the advertisement is informative. If the reference price has been inflated or is just plain fictitious, however, the advertisement is deceptive and may cause harm to consumers. But it is not easy to determine whether a reference price is bona fide. What standard should be used? If an advertisement specifies a "regular price," just what qualifies as regular? How many units must the store sell at this price for it to be a bona fide regular price—half the stock? A few? Just one? Finally, what if the store offers the item for sale at the regular price but customers do not buy any? Can it still be considered a regular price? In general, if a seller is going to label a price as a regular price, the Better Business Bureau suggests that at least 50 percent of the sales have occurred at that price.[30]

Is this a legitimate sale, or is the retailer using deceptive reference prices?

Loss Leader Pricing As we discussed previously, leader pricing is a legitimate attempt to build store traffic by pricing a regularly purchased item aggressively but still above the store's cost. **Loss leader pricing** takes this tactic one step further by lowering the price *below* the store's cost. No doubt you have seen "buy one, get one free" offers at grocery and discount stores. Unless the markup for the item is 100 percent of the cost, these sales obviously do not generate enough revenue from the sale of one unit to cover the store's cost for both units, which means it has essentially priced the total for both items below cost, unless the manufacturer is absorbing the cost of the promotion to generate volume. In some states, this form of pricing is illegal and considered a form of bait and switch.

Bait and Switch Another form of deceptive price advertising occurs when sellers advertise items for a very low price without the intent to really sell any. This **bait-and-switch** tactic is a deceptive practice because the store lures customers in with a very low price on an item (the bait), only to aggressively pressure these customers into purchasing a higher-priced model (the switch) by disparaging the low-priced item, comparing it unfavorably with the higher-priced model, or professing an inadequate supply of the lower-priced item. Again, the laws against bait-and-switch practices are difficult to enforce because salespeople, simply as a function of their jobs, are always trying to get customers to trade up to a higher-priced model without necessarily deliberately baiting them. The key to proving deception centers on the intent of the seller, which is also difficult to prove.

Predatory Pricing

When a firm sets a very low price for one or more of its products with the intent to drive its competition out of business, it is using **predatory pricing**. Predatory pricing is illegal under both the Sherman Antitrust Act and the Federal Trade Commission Act because it constrains free trade and represents a form of unfair competition. It also tends to promote a concentrated market with a few dominant firms (an oligopoly).

But again, predation is difficult to prove. First, one must demonstrate intent, that is, that the firm intended to drive out its competition or prevent competitors from entering the market. Second, the complainant must prove that the firm charged prices lower than its average cost, an equally difficult task. Recall from Chapter 14 that the American Booksellers Association, which represents independent booksellers, has asked the U.S. Department of Justice to investigate the practice of selling hardcover best-seller books for approximately $9, about $25 less than the suggested retail price.[31] The issue to be resolved by the Justice Department is whether the intent of large stores is to put small stores out of business, or whether they are being highly price competitive on books to bring customers into their stores to buy other, more profitable merchandise.

Another challenging case involves Google's dominance in the search engine market. Advertisers on Google bid on specific keywords; if they win the auction, their product appears first in the paid results section on the search engine. However, Google also includes a "quality handicap" and charges poor quality advertisers more. It claims this tactic ensures that users are more likely to find high quality results from their searches. The algorithm it uses to define quality is confidential though, so some observers allege that Google can manipulate the paid search results in such a way that it undermines competitors' offerings, while promoting its own.[32] The unresolved question is: because of Google's dominance in the search engine market, with its resulting ability to control prices, would its practice of charging more for its "quality handicap" be predatory?

Price Discrimination

There are many forms of price discrimination, but only some of them are considered illegal under the Clayton Act and the Robinson-Patman Act. When firms sell the same product to different resellers (wholesalers, distributors, or retailers) at different prices, it can be considered **price discrimination**; usually, larger firms receive lower prices.

We have already discussed the use of quantity discounts, which is a legitimate method of charging different prices to different customers on the basis of the quantity they purchase. The legality of this tactic stems from the assumption that it costs less to sell and service 1,000 units to one customer than 100 units to 10 customers. But quantity discounts must be available to all customers and not be structured in such a way that they consistently and obviously favor one or a few buyers over others.

The Robinson-Patman Act does not apply to sales to end consumers, at which point many forms of price discrimination occur. For example, students and seniors often receive discounts on food and movie tickets, which is perfectly acceptable under federal law. Those engaged in online auctions like eBay are also practicing a legal form of price discrimination because sellers are selling the

Is this price discrimination illegal?

same item to different buyers at various prices. In addition, to deal ethically with the rising costs of health care, some hospitals offer a "sliding scale" based on income, such that lower-income patients receive discounts or even free medical care, especially for children.[33]

Price Fixing

Price fixing is the practice of colluding with other firms to control prices. Price fixing might be either horizontal or vertical. Whereas horizontal price fixing is clearly illegal under the Sherman Antitrust Act, vertical price fixing falls into a gray area.[34]

Horizontal price fixing occurs when competitors that produce and sell competing products or services collude, or work together, to control prices, effectively taking price out of the decision process for consumers. This practice clearly reduces competition and is illegal. Six South African airlines were accused of colluding to hike the price of fares for flights within the country during the World Cup.[35] The major tobacco companies also have been accused of colluding to fix the prices of cigarettes worldwide.[36] As a general rule of thumb, competing firms should refrain from discussing prices or terms and conditions of sale with competitors. If firms want to know competitors' prices, they can look at a competitor's advertisements, its websites, or its stores.

Vertical price fixing occurs when parties at different levels of the same marketing channel (e.g., manufacturers and retailers) agree to control the prices passed on to consumers. Manufacturers often encourage retailers to sell their merchandise at a specific price, known as the **manufacturer's suggested retail price (MSRP)**. Manufacturers set MSRP prices to reduce retail price competition among retailers, stimulate retailers to provide complementary services, and support the manufacturer's merchandise. Manufacturers enforce MSRPs by withholding benefits such as cooperative advertising or even refusing to deliver merchandise to noncomplying retailers. The Supreme Court has ruled that the ability of a manufacturer to require retailers to sell merchandise at MSRP should be decided on a case-by-case basis, depending on the individual circumstances.[37]

As these legal issues clearly demonstrate, pricing decisions involve many ethical considerations. In determining both their pricing strategies and their pricing tactics, marketers must always balance their goal of inducing customers, through price, to find value and the need to deal honestly and fairly with those same customers. Whether another business or an individual consumer, buyers can be influenced by a variety of pricing methods. It is up to marketers to determine which of these methods works best for the seller, the buyer, and the community.

CHECK YOURSELF

1. What common pricing practices are considered to be illegal or unethical?

Summing Up

LO1 Identify three methods that firms use to set their prices.

The various methods of setting prices have their advantages and disadvantages. The three primary methods are cost-based, competitor-based, and value-based. The cost-based techniques are quick and easy but fail to reflect the competitive environment or consumer demand. Although it is always advisable to be aware of what competitors are doing, using competitor-based pricing should not occur in isolation without considering cost considerations and consumer reactions. Taking a value-based approach to pricing, whether the improvement value or the total cost of ownership approach, in conjunction with these other methods provides a nicely balanced method of setting prices.

LO2 Describe the difference between an everyday low price strategy (EDLP) and a high/low strategy.

An everyday low pricing strategy is maintained when a product's price stays relatively constant at a level that is slightly lower than the regular price from competitors using a high/low strategy, and is less frequently discounted. Customers enjoy an everyday low pricing strategy because they know that the price will always be the about the same and a better price than the competition. High/low pricing strategy starts out with a product at one (higher) price, and then discounts the product. This strategy first attracts a less price sensitive customer that pays the regular price, and then a very price sensitive customer that pays the low price.

LO3 Explain the difference between a price skimming and a market penetration pricing strategy.

When firms use a price skimming strategy, the product or service must be perceived as breaking new ground or customers will not pay more than what they pay for other products. Firms use price skimming to signal high quality, limit demand, recoup their investment quickly, and/or test people's price sensitivity. Moreover, it is easier to price high initially and then lower the price than vice versa. Market penetration, in contrast, helps firms build sales and market share quickly, which may discourage other firms from entering the market. Building demand quickly also typically results in lowered costs as the firm gains experience making the product or delivering the service.

LO4 Identify tactics used to reduce prices to consumers.

Marketers use a variety of tactics to provide lower prices to consumers. The tactics include markdowns, quantity discounts, seasonal discounts, coupons, rebates, leasing, price bundling, leader pricing, and price lining. For example, leader pricing involves retailers pricing certain products or services at very low prices, with the hope that these same customers will also buy other, more profitable items.

LO5 Identify tactics used to reduce prices to businesses.

Seasonal discounts give retailers an incentive to buy prior to the normal selling season, cash discounts prompt them to pay their invoices early, and allowances attempt to get retailers to advertise the manufacturer's product or stock a new product. In addition, quantity discounts can cause retailers to purchase a larger quantity over a specific period of time or with a particular order. Finally, zone pricing bases the cost of shipping the merchandise on the distance between the retailer and the manufacturer—the farther away, the more it costs.

LO6 List pricing practices that have the potential to deceive customers.

There are almost as many ways to get into trouble by setting or changing a price as there are pricing strategies and tactics. Some common legal issues pertain to advertising deceptive prices. Specifically, if a firm compares a reduced price with a "regular" or reference price, it must actually have sold that product or service at the regular price. Bait and switch is another form of deceptive price advertising, where sellers advertise items for a very low price without the intent to really sell any at that price. In many states, advertising the sale of products priced below the retailer's cost also constitutes a form of bait and switch. Collusion among firms to fix prices is always illegal.

Key Terms

- advertising allowance, 469
- bait-and-switch, 471
- cash discount, 469
- competition-based pricing method, 456
- cost-based pricing method, 455
- cost of ownership method, 457
- coupon, 466
- cumulative quantity discount, 469
- everyday low pricing (EDLP), 458
- experience curve effect, 462
- high/low pricing, 459
- horizontal price fixing, 473

- improvement value, 456
- leader pricing, 468
- lease, 467
- loss leader pricing, 471
- manufacturers' suggested retail price (MSRP), 473
- markdowns, 465
- market penetration strategy, 462
- noncumulative quantity discount, 470
- predatory pricing, 472
- price bundling, 468
- price discrimination, 472
- price fixing, 473

- price lining, 468
- price skimming, 462
- pricing strategy, 465
- pricing tactics, 465
- quantity discount, 469
- rebate, 466
- reference price, 460
- seasonal discount, 465
- size discount, 465
- slotting allowances, 469
- uniform delivered pricing, 470
- value-based pricing method, 456
- vertical price fixing, 473
- zone pricing, 470

Marketing Applications

1. Suppose you have been hired as the pricing manager for a drugstore chain that typically adds a fixed percentage onto the cost of each product to arrive at the retail price. Evaluate this technique. What would you do differently?

2. Some high fashion retailers, notably H&M and Zara, sell what some call "disposable fashion"—apparel priced so reasonably low that it can be disposed of after just a few wearings. Here is your dilemma: You have an important job interview and need a new suit. You can buy the suit at one of these stores for $129 or at Brooks Brothers for $500. Of course, the Brooks Brothers suit is of higher quality and will therefore last longer. How would you use the two value-based approaches described in this chapter to determine which suit to buy?

3. A phone manufacturer is determining a price for its product using a cost-based pricing strategy. The fixed costs are $100,000, and the variable costs are $50,000. If 1000 units are produced and the company wants to have a 30 percent markup, what is the price of the phone?

4. Identify two stores at which you shop, one of which uses everyday low pricing and another that uses a high/low pricing strategy. Do you believe that each store's chosen strategy is appropriate for the type of merchandise it sells and the market of

customers to whom it is appealing? Justify your answer.

5. As the product manager for Whirlpool's line of washing machines, you are in charge of pricing new products. Your product team has developed a revolutionary new washing machine that relies on radically new technology and requires very little water to get clothes clean. This technology will likely be difficult for your competition to copy. Should you adopt a skimming or a penetration pricing strategy? Justify your answer.

6. What is the difference between a cumulative and a noncumulative quantity discount?

7. If you worked for a manufacturing firm located in Oregon and shipped merchandise all over the United States, which would be more advantageous, a zone or a uniform delivered pricing policy? Why? What if your firm were located in Kansas—would it make a difference?

8. Coupons and rebates benefit different distribution channel members. Which would you prefer if you were a manufacturer, a retailer, and a consumer? Why?

9. Suppose the president of your university got together with the presidents of all the universities in your athletic conference for lunch. They discussed

what each university was going to charge for tuition the following year. Are they in violation of federal laws? Explain your answer.

10. Imagine that you are the newly hired brand manager for a restaurant that is about to open. Both the local newspaper and a gourmet food magazine recently ran articles about your new head chef, calling her one of the best young chefs in the country. In response to these positive reviews, the company wants to position its brand as a premium, gourmet restaurant. Your boss asks what price you should charge for the chef's signature filet mignon dish. Other restaurants in the area charge around $40 for their own filet offerings. What steps might you undertake to determine what the new price should be?

11. You have been hired by a regional supermarket chain as the candy and snack buyer. Your shelves are dominated by national firms, like Wrigley's and Nabisco. The chain imposes a substantial slotting fee to allow new items to be added to their stock selection. Management reasons that it costs a lot to add and delete items, and besides, these slotting fees are a good source of revenue. A small, minority-operated, local firm produces several potentially interesting snack crackers and a line of gummy candy, all with natural ingredients, added vitamins, reduced sugar, and a competitive price—and they also happen to taste great. You'd love to give the firm a chance, but its managers claim the slotting fee is too high. Should your firm charge slotting fees? Are slotting fees fair to the relevant shareholders—customers, stockholders, vendors?

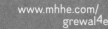

Quiz Yourself

1. Tina is considering upgrading her smartphone for a more advanced version. She asks her friends how much they paid for their smartphones and she also does some research online. When Tina enters AT&T, she has an idea of how much her new smartphone will cost. This is an example of a(n) _____.

   a. improvement price
   b. odd-even price
   c. everyday low price
   d. reference price
   e. cost of ownership price

2. When Apple Inc. introduced its iPhone in 2007, it priced it at $599, considerably higher than either the iPod or competing cellular phones. Apple was probably pursuing a _____ pricing strategy.

   a. market penetration
   b. slotting allowance
   c. price fixing
   d. reference
   e. skimming

   (Answers to these two questions can be found on page 648.)

   Go to www.mhhe.com/grewal4e to practice an additional 11 questions.

Net Savvy

1. Go to www.coupons.com. In which product categories does this website offer coupons? Choose a product from each category.

   • How effective are coupons for selling these types of products? Why?

   • Do any sellers offer rebates through this website? Why or why not?

   • What are the benefits to the seller of using Coupons.com instead of offering coupons in a newspaper?

   • How do you think coupons.com makes money? For example, consider what companies are advertising on the site. Do the same companies who advertise on their site offer coupons?

2. Visit the website for Bag, Borrow, or Steal (www. bagborroworsteal.com) and select handbags. Click on the "Handbags," then choose "Gucci," in the Designer category on the left column, and then "Sort by" Price. What is the difference between Gucci's highest and lowest priced bags? Notice that if a product says "Waitlist," it has already been borrowed, but if it says "Borrow," then it is available for you to borrow. Are the bags that are waitlisted the highest priced or the lowest priced? How would you determine the price it charges to rent a bag?

Chapter Case Study

PRICE WARS IN THE CELLULAR MARKET

Cell phone companies may already have all the available customers. Cellular subscriptions have nearly topped 322 million in the United States—a rate equal to 102 percent of the population. That is, there are more cellular subscriptions than there are people in the United States.[38] Examining how cell phone companies like Verizon Wireless, AT&T, Sprint, and T-Mobile grow once they've run out of potential customers provides a glimpse into the value of strategic pricing.

THE PLAYERS

With 108.7 million subscribers,[39] Verizon leads the pack. The company is a joint venture of Verizon Communications and Vodafone. In addition to cellular phone service, it offers broadband capability through its wireless network, which was the first broadband network available in the United States. Verizon not only boasted the first wireless consumer 3G multimedia service, but today it also hosts the largest 4G LTE network. Furthermore, its international presence spreads across 195 countries, and it provides business solutions to all the firms listed in the *Fortune* 500.

AT&T traces its roots back to 1876 and Alexander Graham Bell's discovery of the telephone. Although it lags behind Verizon in number of subscribers (100.7 million), it earns more revenue. It also claims to have the fastest mobile broadband

EXHIBIT 15.5 U.S. Market Share of Cellular Providers

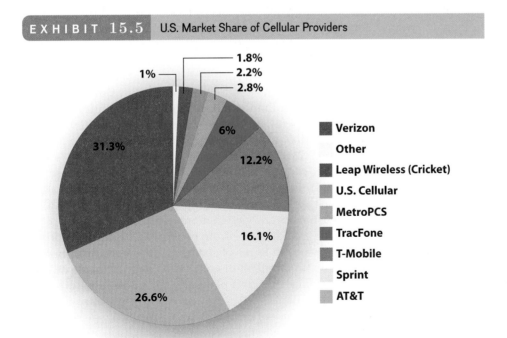

Provider	
■	Verizon
	Other
■	Leap Wireless (Cricket)
	U.S. Cellular
	MetroPCS
■	TracFone
■	T-Mobile
	Sprint
	AT&T

Source: From "Time for Verizon to Buy Sprint?" *CNN Money,* March 23, 2011, http://money.cnn.com/2011/03/23/technology/sprint_verizon/index.htm. Copyright © 2011 Time Inc. Used under license.

network, whose speed is increasing through 4G technology. Moreover, AT&T promises the widest international wireless coverage that offers 99.999 percent reliability. With its WiFi network, the company again claims to be the largest international coverage of any U.S. wireless carrier.[40]

Sprint Nextel holds third place with approximately 55 million customers. The company's most recent innovation is its leading development of the first wireless 4G service.[41] The company merged with Nextel to provide walkie-talkie service in 2004, but running separate networks through the 2G Nextel service and the 3G and 4G Sprint lines has been expensive. Sprint thus plans to decommission its Nextel services by the end of 2013.[42]

T-Mobile USA is owned by Deutsch Telecom and was the subject of several acquisition attempts by competitors, including AT&T and Sprint, throughout 2011 and 2012. With 33.8 million subscribers, T-Mobile relies on its global partner to ensure worldwide coverage. In addition it is a member of the Open Handset Alliance, a collaboration designed to develop the Android platform and provide innovative mobile services more quickly.[43]

MARKET SHARES AND PRICE WARS

As the cost of cell service has continued to decline, customers' bills have remained flat. Increasing prices is not an option for building revenue in this market. With no new customers to attract, the major phone companies have sought instead to increase their share of the market. Accomplishing that goal has meant competing ferociously to attract customers from competitors. But if the companies tried to lure subscribers with reduced rates, they ran the very real risk of causing harm to their economic bottom line. At the same time, the players could not afford to sit on their hands and do nothing, especially as consumers gave up their home phones, leading to contraction in the landline businesses.

The tactics the competitors use are constantly changing. Let's consider what happened at the introduction of 4G services. Verizon offered a data rate of $50 per month for 5GB of usage on the 4G network—less expensive than its $60/month rate for 3G services. Sprint priced its services at $60 per month for unlimited 4G data usage and 5GB of 3G usage.[44] Initially though, 4G coverage has not been universal, which means that customers often wind up reverting to more 3G usage. Thus the best option for each customer depends largely on how much data he or she plans to use each month, which remains a difficult estimate for most users.

Although it may seem as though everyone is using advanced data plans on smartphones and tablets, there remains a market for voice-only options as well. Verizon Wireless cut prices for its unlimited talk and unlimited talk & text plans. The company also lowered costs for its family share plans.[45] AT&T promptly matched Verizon's changes. T-Mobile already had an unlimited talk plan for $60, $10 less than the new prices at AT&T and Verizon. Sprint can claim that its "Everything Data" plans already were cheaper than Verizon's, saving individual users as much as $240 per year and families almost $600.[46]

The goal of cost cuts on voice plans, according to Verizon Wireless's CEO Lowell McAdam, is to get customers enrolled in more expensive unlimited plans, especially for data. Capturing market share from competitors is also important, but it does not offer the same value in terms of generating revenue. Verizon Wireless, for example, may give up $540 million in voice revenue but experience a net gain of $90 million because of changes in data plan sales and because of the healthier margins associated with data plans.[47]

Networks account for only a piece of a wireless company's revenue stream. To access voice, text, or data services, customers need handsets, which are becoming increasingly more sophisticated. But here again, companies are cutting prices on handsets in an effort to attract market share. Suppliers of Apple devices sometimes sell the iPhones for $200 less than they have paid Apple for them, just to lure subscribers to its two-year plans.

The war is far from over, especially in such a rapidly changing, frequently innovating market. Increased broadband use has challenged overburdened networks, and cell phone companies may be forced to invest in their networks to avoid service failures and customer complaints. If voice plans drop further, revenue from data plans may no longer provide the margins cell phone companies need. Some wireless providers may consolidate; others will fade away.

Questions

1. Who are the key players in this industry?
2. If a price war will reduce margins, as the case suggests, why would any company embrace this strategy?
3. On what other strategy elements could the wireless companies compete?
4. What pricing tactics could Verizon use to target consumer customers?
5. What pricing tactics could Verizon use to target business customers?

Value Delivery: Designing the Channel and Supply Chain

CHAPTER 16

Supply Chain and Channel Management

CHAPTER 17

Retailing and Multichannel Marketing

Section Six deals with the value delivery system. It is critical that merchandise is delivered in time to stores to meet customer demand. To achieve this, retailers have initiated many innovative programs with their vendors and developed sophisticated transportation and warehousing systems. We devote two chapters to value delivery. Chapter 16 takes a look at marketing channels and how to manage the supply chain, while Chapter 17 concentrates on retailing and multichannel marketing.

SECTION 6

Supply Chain and Channel Management

When a company saves a dollar by increasing the efficiency of its distribution system, the overall benefits are worth much more than that single dollar. So for example, if a retailer can get its goods to its stores quickly, in the right quantities, and when its customers want them, customers are happy, which ultimately increases sales and profits. At the same time, the retailer can reduce one of its costliest expenses, namely its distribution costs. Also, because of these distribution systems manufacturers that sell products in its stores have a good sense of how much they need to make and when, which reduces their inventory costs. Thus profits rise, and everyone is happy.

That claim is perhaps too simplistic, but when we consider Walmart, the largest retailer in the world, it seems about right. Most of Walmart's power—in terms of setting prices, growing rapidly, and pleasing customers—stems directly from its notable innovations in marketing channel and supply chain management. Its influence has also spread to its vendors, altering the way they manufacture and deliver merchandise.

Walmart's cooperation with the consumer goods giant Procter & Gamble (P&G) is unusual in its scope.

LEARNING OBJECTIVES

LO1 Understand the importance of marketing channels and supply chain management.

LO2 Understand the difference between direct and indirect marketing channels.

LO3 Describe how marketing channels are managed.

LO4 Describe the flow of information and merchandise in the marketing channel.

Software links the two corporations closely, such that the moment Walmart's distribution centers run out of a certain brand or size of a P&G product, P&G initiates a shipment to replenish it. Such cooperation helps P&G plan its production, but it also enables Walmart to track arrivals at its distribution centers and thus coordinate shipments to stores more effectively.

Other innovations (many of which have been copied throughout the retail industry) by Walmart include extensive information systems, to transmit the millions of point-of-sale transactions that take place in its stores everyday; cross-docking to ensure that approximately half the goods that arrive at a distribution center move out to stores within 24 hours; the widespread adoption of bar codes and radio frequency identification tags for keeping track of inventory; and consolidated global sourcing to purchase directly from suppliers rather than relying on third-party procurement services.[1]

Even with its remarkable supply chain successes, Walmart is hesitant to rest on its laurels, so it constantly reviews its supply chain to find new efficiencies. In a recent move, the company has sought out ways to keep its delivery trucks full more often, instead of allowing them to make return trips with empty trailers. Thus, many of the retailer's 6,500 trucks and 55,000 trailers now pick up goods directly from manufacturers, rather than just traveling back and forth from stores to a distribution center (though they still make these trips, of course). As a result, its travel miles have fallen by 100 million miles relative to the past year—simply by reducing the number of trips and avoiding trucks on the move with empty trailers.[2]

In all of these cases, Walmart's superior marketing channel and supply chain management has enabled it to reap the rewards of higher levels of customer service and satisfaction, lower production and transportation costs, and more productive uses of its retail space. Fundamentally, Walmart has a unique ability to link together suppliers, distribution centers, retail outlets, and, ultimately, customers, regardless of their location. As a result, the cost savings achieved by both Walmart and its suppliers benefit their bottom lines. Even more, when those cost savings get passed through, they benefit customers in the form of lower prices which is another reason for them to shop the world's largest retailer.

In this chapter, we discuss the third P, *place*, which includes all activities required to get the right product to the right customer when that customer wants it.[3] Specifically, as we noted in Chapter 1, **marketing channel management**, which also has been called **supply chain management**, refers to a set of approaches and techniques firms employ to efficiently and effectively integrate their suppliers, manufacturers, warehouses, stores, and transportation intermediaries into a seamless operation in which merchandise is produced and distributed in the right quantities, to the right locations, and at the right time, as well as to minimize systemwide costs while satisfying the service levels their customers require.[4] Students of marketing often overlook or underestimate the importance of place in the marketing mix, simply because it happens behind the scenes. Yet marketing channel management adds value, say for customers at Walmart, because it gets the products to them efficiently, quickly and at low cost.

LO1 Understand the importance of marketing channels and supply chain management.

THE IMPORTANCE OF MARKETING CHANNEL/SUPPLY CHAIN MANAGEMENT

So far in this book, we have reviewed the methods companies use to conduct in-depth market research, gain insights into consumer and business behaviors, segment markets, select the best target markets, develop new products and services, and set prices that provide good value. But even if firms execute these activities flawlessly, unless they can secure the placement of products in appropriate outlets in sufficient quantities exactly when customers want them, they are likely to fail. Adding Value 16.1 examines how Goya Foods recognized it needed to do a better job at getting products into stores to satisfy customers' demand, and what it did about it.

Convincing wholesalers and retailers to carry new products can be more difficult than you might think. **Wholesalers** are firms that buy products from manufacturers and resell them to retailers; retailers sell products directly to consumers. For example, PenAgain, a small California-based manufacturer of ergonomic pens and other writing instruments, wanted to put its offerings in Walmart stores, but first it had to get Walmart to buy what it was selling.[5] After a tough selling session, Walmart agreed to give PenAgain a one-month trial in 500 stores, but only if it lowered its costs. PenAgain thus moved production overseas. Walmart provided

Adding Value 16.1   The Beans May Be Slow Cooked, but the Delivery Is Quick[6]

As Goya Foods celebrated its 75th year in business, its top managers were dealing with some very serious growing pains. Selling a wide variety of Hispanic and Latin foods, the company had achieved a dominant market share, was the largest Hispanic-owned company in the United States, and had annual sales of around $1 billion. In specific local and regional markets, demand for its products were substantial—a great success that also came with a notable challenge.

That is, many of the markets that loved Goya products had slightly different preferences, reflecting the diversity of Hispanic consumers in the United States. People of Cuban heritage wanted items made somewhat differently than consumers whose families originated in Mexico, and so on. Thus, the number of unique inventory items or stockkeeping units (SKUs) that Goya provided reached over 1,600. The supply chain network grew more complex. And in all the confusion, service levels, as measured by its in-stock availability, dropped. Quite simply, with all the complexity, buyers were spending too much time manually calculating and determining shipments and inventory levels, leaving them insufficient time or energy to think strategically. Making decisions without sophisticated analytics was not something that Goya could sustain anymore.

For Goya, the solution was to automate the transportation and inventory planning processes, using software that enabled it to keep track of demand, order fulfillment, and replenishment with minimal effort. By automating its

To simplify its supply chain, Goya automated the transportation and inventory planning processes that enabled it to keep track of demand, order fulfillment, and replenishment.

ordering processes, Goya's buyers could work smarter. For example, making sure delivery trucks were more efficiently utilized resulted in millions of dollars in transportation savings. The new system also improved its in-stock availability to 98 percent, which resulted in a proportional increase in sales.

---

no marketing support though, and PenAgain was too small to afford traditional print or television advertising, so it developed a viral marketing program and produced displays to use in the stores. To keep track of sales, it relied on Walmart's Internet-based Retail Link system, though it also hired a firm that sends representatives into stores to check out display placement and customer traffic. Finally, PenAgain agreed to adhere to strict packaging, labeling, and shipping requirements. And remember, for all this effort, its entry in stores was only a test, and a very expensive gamble! But if it could succeed in Walmart stores, PenAgain would be well on its way to prosperity.

In the simplified supply chain in Exhibit 16.1, manufacturers make products and sell them to retailers or wholesalers. The exhibit would be much more complicated if we had included the suppliers of materials to manufacturers and all the manufacturers, wholesalers, and stores in a typical marketing channel.

Exhibit 16.1 represents a typical flow of manufactured goods: Manufacturers ship to a wholesaler or to a retailer's distribution center (e.g., Manufacturer 1 and Manufacturer 3) or directly to stores (Manufacturer 2). In addition, many variations on this supply chain exist. Some retail chains, such as Home Depot or Costco, function as both retailers and wholesalers. They act as retailers when they sell to consumers directly and as wholesalers when they sell to other businesses, like building contractors or restaurant owners. When manufacturers such as Avon sell directly to consumers, they perform both production and retailing activities. When

EXHIBIT 16.1   Simplified Supply Chain

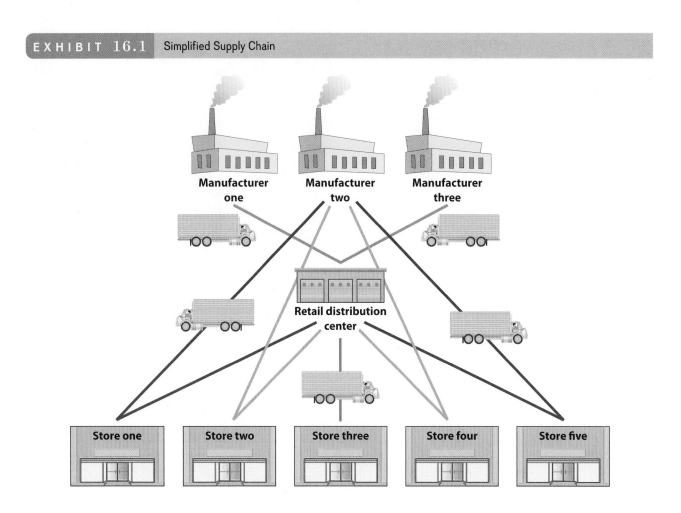

Dell sells computers to a university or business, it becomes a business-to-business (B2B) transaction, but when it sells to students or employees individually, it is a B2C (business-to-consumer) operation.

Marketing Channels Add Value

Why do manufacturers use wholesalers or retailers? Don't these added channel members just cut into their profits? Wouldn't it be cheaper for consumers to buy directly from manufacturers? In a simple agrarian economy, the best supply chain likely does follow a direct route from manufacturer to consumer: The consumer goes to the farm and buys food directly from the farmer. Modern "eat local" environmental campaigns suggest just such a process. But before the consumer can eat a fresh steak procured from a local farm, she needs to cook it. Assuming the consumer doesn't know how to make a stove and lacks the materials to do so, she must rely on a stove maker. The stove maker, which has the necessary knowledge, must buy raw materials and components from various suppliers, make the stove, and then make it available to the consumer. If the stove maker isn't located near the consumer, the stove must be transported to where the consumer has access to it. To make matters even more complicated, the consumer may want to view a choice of stoves, hear about all their features, and have the stove delivered and installed.

How many companies are involved in making and getting a stove to your kitchen?

Each participant in the channel adds value.[7] The components manufacturer helps the stove manufacturer by supplying parts and materials. The stove maker turns the components into the stove. The transportation company gets the stove to the retailer. The retailer stores the stove until the customer wants it, educates the customer about product features, and delivers and installs the stove. At each step, the stove becomes more costly but also more valuable to the consumer.

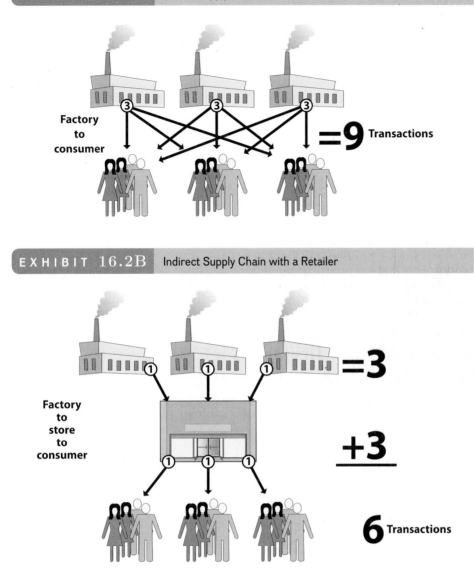

EXHIBIT 16.2A   Direct Supply Chain without a Retailer

Factory to consumer

=9 Transactions

EXHIBIT 16.2B   Indirect Supply Chain with a Retailer

Factory to store to consumer

=3

+3

6 Transactions

Exhibits 16.2A and 16.2B show how using channel partners can provide value overall. Exhibit 16.2A shows three manufacturers, each of which sells directly to three consumers in a system that requires nine transactions. Each transaction costs money—for example, the manufacturer must fill the order, package it, write up the paperwork, and ship it—and each cost is passed on to the customer. Exhibit 16.2B shows the same three manufacturers and consumers, but this time they go through a retailer. The number of transactions falls to six, and as transactions are eliminated, the channel and supply chain becomes more efficient, which adds value for customers by making it more convenient and less expensive to purchase merchandise.

Marketing Channel Management Affects Other Aspects of Marketing

Every marketing decision is affected by and has an effect on marketing channels. When products are designed and manufactured, how and when the critical components reach the factory must be coordinated with production. The sales department must coordinate its delivery promises with the factory or distribution centers. A **distribution center**, a facility for the receipt, storage, and redistribution of goods to company stores or customers, may be operated by retailers, manufacturers, or distribution specialists.[8] Furthermore, advertising and promotion must be coordinated with those departments that control inventory and transportation. There is no faster way to lose credibility with customers than to promise deliveries or run a promotion and then not have the merchandise when the customer expects it.

 LO2 Understand the difference between direct and indirect marketing channels.

DESIGNING MARKETING CHANNELS

When a firm is just starting out or entering a new market, it doesn't typically have the option of designing the "best" marketing channel structure—that is, choosing from whom it buys or to whom it sells. A new sporting goods retailer may not have the option of carrying all the manufacturer lines it wants, because other competing retailers in its market area might carry the same products. On the other side, a small specialty sporting goods apparel manufacturer may not be able to place its products in major stores like Sports Authority, because its line is unproven, and the products might duplicate lines that the retailer already carries. Chapter 17 discusses how manufacturers choose their retailer partners in more depth.

Although there are thus various constraints on marketing channel partners with regard to the design of the "best" channel structure, all marketing channels take the form of a direct channel, an indirect channel, or some combination thereof.

Direct Marketing Channel

As shown in Exhibit 16.3 (left), there are no intermediaries between the buyer and seller in a **direct marketing channel**. Typically the seller is a manufacturer, such as when a carpentry business sells bookcases through its own store and online to individual consumers. The seller also can be an individual, such as when a knitter sells blankets and scarves at craft fairs, on Craigslist, or through eBay. (Recall our discussion of consumer-to-consumer [C2C] transactions in Chapter 1.) When the buyer is another business, such as when Boeing sells planes to JetBlue, the marketing channel still is direct, but in this case, the transaction is a business-to-business one (see Chapter 7).

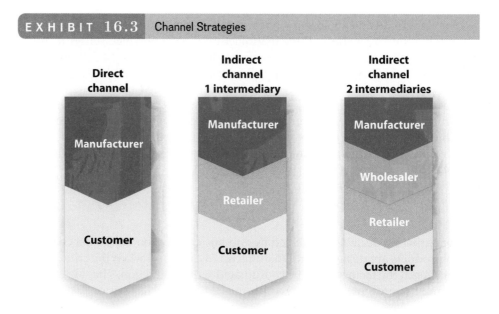

EXHIBIT 16.3   Channel Strategies

Direct channel

Manufacturer

Customer

Indirect channel 1 intermediary

Manufacturer

Retailer

Customer

Indirect channel 2 intermediaries

Manufacturer

Wholesaler

Retailer

Customer

Indirect Marketing Channel

In **indirect marketing channels,** one or more intermediaries work with manufacturers to provide goods and services to customers. In some cases, there may only be one intermediary involved. Automobile manufacturers such as Ford and General Motors often use indirect distribution, such that dealers act as retailers, as shown in Exhibit 16.3 (middle). As shown in Exhibit 16.3 (right), wholesalers are more common when the company does not buy in sufficient quantities to make it cost-effective for the manufacturer to deal directly with them—independent book sellers, wine merchants, or independent drug stores. Wholesalers are also prevalent in less-developed economies where large retailers are rare.

MANAGING THE MARKETING CHANNEL AND SUPPLY CHAIN

LO3 Describe how marketing channels are managed.

Marketing channels and supply chains comprise various buying entities, such as retailers and wholesalers; sellers, such as manufacturers or wholesalers; and facilitators of the exchange, such as transportation companies. Similar to interpersonal interactions, their relationships can range from close working partnerships to one-time arrangements. In almost all cases though, interactions occur because the parties want something from each other: Home Depot wants hammers from Stanley Tool Company; Stanley wants an opportunity to sell its tools to the general public; both companies want UPS to deliver the merchandise.

Each member of the marketing channel also performs a specialized role. If one member believes that another has failed to do its job correctly or efficiently, it can replace that member. So, if Stanley isn't getting good service from UPS, it can switch to FedEx. If Home Depot believes its customers do not perceive Stanley tools as a good value, it may buy from another tool company. Home Depot even could decide to make its own tools or use its own trucks to pick up tools from Stanley. However, any time a marketing channel member is replaced, the function it has performed remains, so someone needs to complete it.[9]

If a marketing channel is to run efficiently, the participating members must cooperate. Often, however, supply chain members have conflicting goals and this may result in channel conflict (Exhibit 16.4). For instance, Stanley wants Home Depot to carry all its tools but not those of its competitors so that Stanley can maximize its sales. But Home Depot carries a mix of tool brands so it can maximize the sales in its tool category. When supply chain members that buy and sell

The Home Depot and Stanley Tool Company have a mutually beneficial partnership. The Home Depot buys tools from Stanley because their customers find value in Stanley products. Stanley sells tools to Home Depot because they have established an excellent market for its products.

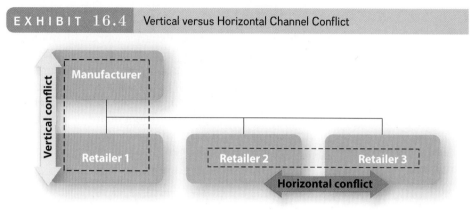

EXHIBIT 16.4   Vertical versus Horizontal Channel Conflict

to one another are not in agreement about their goals, roles, or rewards, **vertical channel conflict** or discord results.

Horizontal channel conflict can also occur when there is disagreement or discord among members at the same level of marketing channel, such as two competing retailers or two competing manufacturers. For instance, if Home Depot and Lowes engage in a price war on Stanley Tools, all three parties are affected. Home Depot and Lowe's make less money because they are both offering lower prices. Stanley Tools may experience increased pressure from Home Depot and Lowe's to recover some of its lost profits by pressuring it to lower its prices to them. Also, other retailers may stop buying Stanley Tools because they cannot afford to get involved in the price war between Home Depot and Lowe's.

Avoiding vertical channel conflicts demands open, honest communication. Buyers and vendors all must understand what drives the other party's business, their roles in the relationship, each firm's strategies, and any problems that might arise over the course of the relationship. As we mentioned in the opening vignette for this chapter, Walmart and Procter & Gamble (P&G) recognize that it is in their common interest to remain profitable business partners. Walmart's customers demand and expect to find P&G products in stores; P&G needs the sales generated through the world's largest retailer. Walmart cannot demand prices so low that P&G cannot make money, and P&G must be flexible enough to accommodate the

Walmart and Procter & Gamble (P&G) recognize that it is in their common interest to remain profitable business partners.

needs of its biggest customer. With a common goal, both firms then have the incentive to cooperate, because they know that by doing so, each will boost its sales.

Common goals also help sustain the relationship when expected benefits fail to arise. If one P&G shipment fails to reach a Walmart store on time, due to an uncontrollable event like a misrouting by the trucking firm, Walmart does not suddenly call off the whole arrangement. Instead, it recognizes the incident as a simple, isolated mistake and maintains the good working relationship, because Walmart knows that both it and P&G are committed to the same goals in the long run.

In this sense, their partnership exhibits both of the non–mutually exclusive ways that exist to manage a marketing channel or supply chain: Coordinate the channel using a vertical marketing system, and develop strong relationships with marketing channel partners—topics we now examine.

Managing the Marketing Channel and Supply Chain through Vertical Marketing Systems

Although conflict is likely in any marketing channel, it is generally more pronounced when the channel members are independent entities. Marketing channels that are more closely aligned, whether by contract or ownership, share common goals and therefore are less prone to conflict.

In an **independent** or **conventional marketing channel**, several independent members—a manufacturer, a wholesaler, and a retailer—each attempts to satisfy its own objectives and maximize its profits, often at the expense of the other members, as we portray in Exhibit 16.5 (left). None of the participants has any control over the others. Using our previous example, the first time Walmart purchases pens from PenAgain, both parties likely try to extract as much profit from the deal as possible. After the deal is consummated, neither party feels any responsibility to the other.

Over time though, Walmart and PenAgain might develop a relationship marked by routinized, automatic transactions, such that Walmart's customers come to expect PenAgain products in stores, and PenAgain depends on Walmart to buy a good portion of its output. This scenario represents the first phase of a **vertical marketing system**, a marketing channel in which the members act as a unified system, as in Exhibit 16.5 (right). Three types of vertical marketing systems—administered, contractual, and corporate—reflect increasing phases of formalization and control. The more formal the vertical marketing system, the less likely conflict will ensue.

EXHIBIT 16.5   Independent versus Vertical Marketing Channels

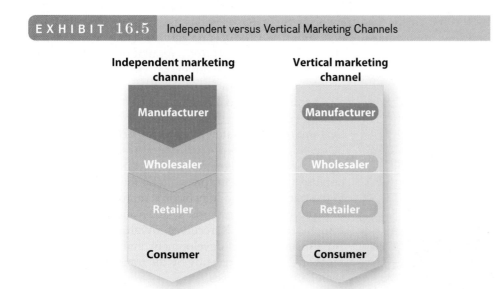

Independent marketing channel

Manufacturer
Wholesaler
Retailer
Consumer

Vertical marketing channel

Manufacturer
Wholesaler
Retailer
Consumer

Administered Vertical Marketing System The Walmart/PenAgain marketing channel relationship offers an example of an **administered vertical marketing system**: There is no common ownership or contractual relationships, but the dominant channel member controls or holds the balance of power. Because of its size and relative power, Walmart imposes controls on PenAgain. **Power** in a marketing channel exists when one firm has the means or ability to dictate the actions of another member at a different level of distribution. A retailer like Walmart exercises its power over suppliers in several ways. With its **reward power**, Walmart offers rewards, often a monetary incentive, if PenAgain will do what Walmart wants it to do. **Coercive power** arises when Walmart threatens to punish or punishes the other channel member for not undertaking certain tasks, such as if it were to delay payment to PenAgain for a late delivery. Walmart may also have **referent power** over PenAgain if the supplier desperately wants to be associated with Walmart, because being known as an important Walmart supplier enables PenAgain to attract other retailers' business. If Walmart exerts **expertise power** over PenAgain, it relies on its expertise with marketing of pens. Because Walmart has vast information about the office supply and back-to-school markets, it can exert **information power** over PenAgain by providing or withholding such important market information. Finally, **legitimate power** is based on getting a channel member, like PenAgain, to behave in a certain way because of a contractual agreement between the two firms. As Walmart deals with PenAgain and its other suppliers, it likely exerts multiple types of power to influence their behaviors. If either party dislikes the way the relationship is going though, it can simply walk away.

Contractual Vertical Marketing System Over time, Walmart and PenAgain may formalize their relationship by entering into contracts that dictate various terms, such as how much Walmart will buy each month and at what price, as well as the penalties for late deliveries. In **contractual vertical marketing systems** like this, independent firms at different levels of the marketing channel join together through contracts to obtain economies of scale and coordination and to reduce conflict.[10]

Franchising is the most common type of contractual vertical marketing system. **Franchising** is a contractual agreement between a franchisor and a franchisee that allows the franchisee to operate a retail outlet using a name and format developed and supported by the franchisor. Exhibit 16.6 lists the United States' top franchise opportunities. These rankings, determined by *Entrepreneur* magazine, are created using a number of objective measures, such as financial strength, stability, growth rate, and size of the franchise system.[11]

In a franchise contract, the franchisee pays a lump sum plus a royalty on all sales in return for the right to operate a business in a specific location. The franchisee also agrees to operate the outlet in accordance with the procedures prescribed by the franchisor. The franchisor typically provides assistance in locating and building the business, developing the products or services sold, management training, and advertising. To maintain the franchisee's reputation, the franchisor also makes sure that all outlets provide the same quality of services and products.

A franchise system combines the entrepreneurial advantages of owning a business with the efficiencies of vertical marketing systems that function under single ownership (i.e., a corporate system, as we discuss next). Franchisees are motivated to make their stores successful because they receive the profits, after they pay the royalty to the franchisor. The franchisor is motivated to develop new products, services, and systems and to promote the franchise because it receives royalties on all sales. Advertising, product development, and system development are all done efficiently by the franchisor, with costs shared by all franchisees.

Hampton Hotels are ranked the number one franchise by Entrepreneur *magazine in 2012.*

EXHIBIT 16.6	Top 10 Franchises for 2012			
Rank	Franchise Name	Number of US Outlets	Number of Non-US Outlets	Startup Costs
1	Hampton Hotels Midprice hotels	1,775	58	$3.75M–13.11M
2	Subway Submarine sandwiches and salads	24,899	11,454	$84.8K–258.8K
3	7-Eleven Inc. Convenience store	6,723	32,880	$30.8K–611.1K
4	Servpro Insurance/disaster restoration and cleaning	1,580	1	$132.05K–180.45K
5	Days Inn Midprice hotels	1,662	203	$202.17K–6.76M
6	McDonald's Hamburgers, chicken, salads	12,546	14,532	$1.07M–1.89M
7	Denny's Inc. 24/7 lowprice restaurant	1,386	92	$1.13M–2.4M
8	H & R Block Tax preparation and electronic filing	4,317	558	$35.51K–136.2K
9	Pizza Hut Inc. Pizza, sandwiches, pasta	7,083	4,570	$295K–2.15M
10	Dunkin' Donuts Coffee shop	6,900	3,120	$368.9K–1.74M

Source: From Entrepreneur's 2012 Franchise 500, http://www.wntrepreneur.com/franchise500/index.html with permission of Entrepreneur Media, Inc. © 2012 by Entrepreneur Media, Inc. All rights reserved.

Corporate Vertical Marketing System In a **corporate vertical marketing system**, the parent company has complete control and can dictate the priorities and objectives of the marketing channel because it owns multiple segments of the channel, such as manufacturing plants, warehouse facilities, and retail outlets. By virtue of its ownership and resulting control, potential conflict among segments of the channel is lessened.

American Apparel, a clothing manufacturer based in Los Angeles, California, represents a corporate vertical marketing system because it manufacturers its own products, rather than having contractual relationships with other firms, and it operates its own retail stores selling T-shirts and other men's and women's sportswear. With this corporate ownership structure, it is able to bring fashion-sensitive items from the idea stage to market in a very short time.

American Apparel represents a corporate vertical marketing system because it manufacturers its own products and operates its own retail stores.

Managing Marketing Channels and Supply Chains through Strategic Relationships

There is more to managing marketing channels and supply chains than simply exercising power over other members in an administered system or establishing a contractual or corporate vertical marketing system. There is also a human side.

In a conventional marketing channel, relationships between members often are based on the argument over the split of the profit pie—if one party gets ahead, the other party falls behind. Sometimes this type of transaction is acceptable if the parties have no interest in a long-term relationship. For instance, if Walmart believes that the PenAgain's ergonomic pens are just a short-term fad, it may only be interested in purchasing once. In that case, it might seek to get the best one-time price, even if it means that PenAgain will make very little money and therefore might not want to sell to Walmart again.

More often than not, however, firms seek a **strategic relationship**, also called a **partnering relationship**, in which the marketing channel members are committed to maintaining the relationship over the long term and investing in opportunities that are mutually beneficial. In a conventional or administered marketing channel, there are significant incentives to establishing a strategic relationship, even without contracts or ownership relationships. Both parties benefit because the size of the profit pie has increased, so both the buyer and the seller increase their sales and profits. These strategic relationships are created explicitly to uncover and exploit joint opportunities, so members depend on and trust each other heavily; share goals and agree on how to accomplish those goals; and are willing to take risks, share confidential information, and make significant investments for the sake of the relationship. Successful strategic relationships require mutual trust, open communication, common goals, interdependence and credible commitments.

Mutual Trust Mutual trust holds a strategic relationship together. Trust is the belief that a partner is honest (i.e., reliable, stands by its word, sincere, fulfills obligations) and benevolent (i.e., concerned about the other party's welfare). When vendors and buyers trust each other, they are more willing to share relevant ideas, clarify goals and problems, and communicate efficiently. Information shared between the parties, such as inventory positions in stores, thus becomes increasingly comprehensive, accurate, and timely.

With trust, there's also less need for the supply chain members to constantly monitor and check up on each other's actions, because each believes the other won't take advantage, even if given the opportunity. Although it is important in all relationships, monitoring supply chain members becomes particularly pertinent when suppliers are located in less-developed countries, where issues such as the use of child labor, poor working conditions, and below-subsistence wages have become a shared responsibility. Ethical and Societal Dilemma 16.1 highlights how Apple has both stumbled in this responsibility and changed its practices to improve its dedication to ethical choices.

Open Communication To share information, develop sales forecasts together, and coordinate deliveries, Walmart and its suppliers maintain open and honest communication. This maintenance may sound easy in principle, but some businesses don't tend to share information with their business partners. But open, honest communication is a key to developing successful relationships, because supply chain members need to understand what is driving each other's business, their roles in the relationship, each firm's strategies, and any problems that arise over the course of the relationship.

Common Goals Supply chain members must have common goals for a successful relationship to develop. Shared goals give both members of the relationship an incentive to pool their strengths and abilities and exploit potential opportunities together. Such commonality also offers an assurance that the other partner won't do anything to hinder the achievement of those goals within the relationship.

Walmart and its suppliers recognize that it is in their common interest to be strategic partners. Walmart needs its suppliers to satisfy its customers, and those manufacturers recognize that if they can keep Walmart happy, they will have more than enough business for years to come. With common goals, both firms have an

Ethical and Societal Dilemma 16.1 Do Customers Care More about the Newest iPhone or about Working Conditions in China?[12]

An iPad user reading a recent issue of *The New York Times* on their tablet might have suffered a strange sense of guilt. The newspaper published reports of labor abuses that seemingly run rampant in the Chinese factories responsible for producing Apple's most popular products. These in-depth reports catalogued a long list of failures: the presence of child workers, more than 12-hour shifts, regular work weeks of longer than 60 hours, workers housed in tiny dormitories with approximately 20 people limited to three rooms, allegations of suicides, and lax safety standards that have led to fatal explosions.

The reports focus mostly on a Foxconn factory in Chengdu, in southwestern China, that manufactures iPhones and iPads. An explosion caused by insufficient ventilation of aluminum dust (created when the cases for the gadgets get polished) in May 2011 killed four workers. A similar explosion followed six months later at another factory. The ensuing investigations by *The New York Times* revealed multiple other violations of the code of conduct that Apple has established for its suppliers.

With this code of conduct, as well as the frequent audits it performs, Apple asserts that it is doing the best that it can to ensure its suppliers live up to reasonable standards and fair labor practices. An anonymous former Apple executive asserts, "There is a genuine, companywide commitment to the code of conduct." Yet abuses continue, as Apple's own corporate responsibility reports reveal. Audits show that several supply companies continue to engage in labor practices that violate the code, with few punishments or changes to the supply chain.

Part of the reason stems from Apple's need for secrecy—once it finds a supply partner that can manufacturer its high-tech gadgets, it wants to maintain that relationship to avoid any leakage of innovation information. So even if a supplier violates the code again and again, Apple is unlikely to switch.

Furthermore, Apple's focus on innovation means that it must work constantly to come up with new ideas and products, which it needs to produce quickly and in sufficient quantities to keep customers happy. This demanding supply chain leaves little room for flexibility. When Apple says it needs 1 million products, say, then its supplier is going to do whatever it takes to get those products ready in time. The code of conduct might ask that factory workers be limited to 60-hour work weeks, but in truth, Apple is asking the factories to keep running all day, every day, to make the order.

To keep its costs low, Apple also offers very slim profit margins to suppliers. In turn, these factories aim to reduce their own costs. Another Apple supplier thus began using a toxic chemical, instead of rubbing alcohol, to polish the screens of iPhones, because the chemical dries faster. But it exposes workers to the threat of paralysis and nerve damage.

The primary reason for these labor abuses may come only at the end of the supply chain—the consumer. A survey of Apple consumers showed that only 2 percent of them recognized labor issues as a concern. In a remarkably succinct summary of the challenge, another anonymous Apple executive asserted, "You can either manufacture in comfortable, worker-friendly factories, or you can reinvent the product every year, and make it better and faster and cheaper, which requires factories that seem harsh by American standards. And right now, customers care more about a new iPhone than working conditions in China."

Although Apple attempts to monitor its channel partners' behavior with regard to labor issues, sometimes abuses fall through the cracks.

incentive to cooperate, because they know that by doing so, both can boost sales. If Walmart needs a special production run of pens to meet demand for back-to-school buyers, PenAgain will work to meet the challenge. If PenAgain has difficulty financing its inventory, it is in Walmart's best interest to help it because they are committed to the same goals in the long run.

Interdependence When supply chain members view their goals and ultimate success as intricately linked, they develop deeper long-term relationships. Interdependence between supply chain members that is based on mutual benefits is key to developing and sustaining the relationship.[13] Walmart's suppliers recognize that without Walmart, their sales would be significantly less. Although certainly the more powerful member of the supply chain, Walmart also recognizes that it can depend on these suppliers to be a dependable source of supply, thus enabling it to have a very efficient marketing channel.

Credible Commitments Successful relationships develop because both parties make credible commitments to, or tangible investments in, the relationship. These commitments go beyond just making the hollow statement, "I want to be your partner"; they involve spending money to improve the products or services provided to the customer and on information technology to improve supply chain efficiency.[14] Walmart works closely with its suppliers to streamline the entire marketing channel. In an early endeavor, it collaborated with P&G to link its distribution centers with the giant consumer packaged goods manufacturer. When a Walmart store sold a particular P&G item, the information flowed directly to P&G's planning and control systems. When the inventory level of P&G's products at Walmart's distribution center got to the point where it needed to reorder, the system automatically alerted P&G to ship more products. This information helped P&G plan its production. Walmart was also able to track when a P&G shipment arrived at one of its distribution warehouses, which enabled it to coordinate its own outbound shipments to stores. Both Walmart and P&G realized savings from the better inventory management and order processing, savings that in turn were passed on to Walmart's consumers through its everyday low prices.

Just like many other elements of marketing, managing the marketing channel can seem like an easy task at first glance: Put the right merchandise in the right place at the right time. But the various elements and actors involved in a marketing channel create its unique and compelling complexities and require that firms work carefully to ensure they are achieving the most efficient and effective chain possible. We now turn our attention to how information and merchandise flows through marketing channels.

CHECK YOURSELF

1. What is the difference between an indirect and a direct marketing channel?
2. What are the differences among the three types of vertical marketing systems?
3. How do firms develop strong strategic partnerships with their marketing channel partners?

LO4 Describe the flow of information and merchandise in the marketing channel.

MAKING INFORMATION FLOW THROUGH MARKETING CHANNELS

Information flows from the customer to stores, to and from distribution centers, possibly to and from wholesalers, to and from product manufacturers, and then on to the producers of any components and the suppliers of raw materials. To simplify our discussion and because information flows are similar in other marketing channel links and B2B channels, we shorten the supply chain in this section to exclude wholesalers, as well as the link from suppliers to manufacturers. Exhibit 16.7 illustrates the flow of information that starts when a customer buys a Sony HDTV at Best Buy. The flow follows these steps:

Flow 1 (Customer to Store): The sales associate at Best Buy scans the Universal Product Code (UPC) tag on the HDTV packaging, and the customer receives a receipt. The UPC tag is the black-and-white bar code found on most merchandise. It contains a 13-digit code that indicates the manufacturer of the

EXHIBIT 16.7 Information Flows

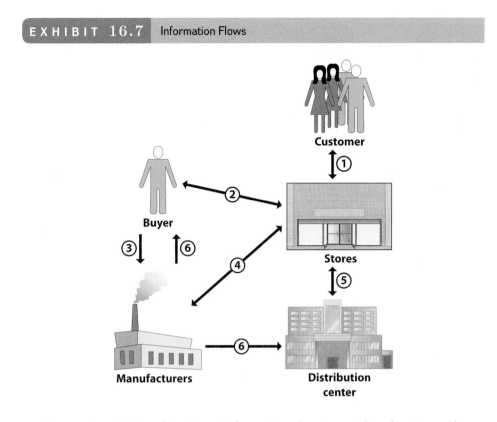

item, a description of the item, information about special packaging, and special promotions.[15] In the future, RFID tags, discussed at the end of this chapter, may replace UPC tags.

Flow 2 (Store to Buyer): The point-of-sale (POS) terminal records the purchase information and electronically sends it to the buyer at Best Buy's corporate office. The sales information is incorporated into an inventory management system and used to monitor and analyze sales and to decide to reorder more HDTVs, change a price, or plan a promotion. Buyers also send information to stores about overall sales for the chain, ways to display the merchandise, upcoming promotions, and so on.

Flow 3 (Buyer to Manufacturer): The purchase information from each Best Buy store is typically aggregated by the retailer as a whole, which creates an order for new merchandise and sends it to Sony. The buyer at Best Buy may also communicate directly with Sony to get information and negotiate prices, shipping dates, promotional events, or other merchandise-related issues. Adding Value 16.2 examines how Neiman Marcus works with its suppliers to expedite a key issue in this flow: U.S. Customs import processes.

Flow 4 (Store to Manufacturer): In some situations, the sales transaction data are sent directly from the store to the manufacturer, and the manufacturer decides when to ship more merchandise to the distribution centers and the stores. In other situations, especially when merchandise is reordered

The flow of information starts when the UPC tag is scanned at the point-of-purchase.

Adding Value 16.2   Neiman Marcus Expedites Shipments through Customs

Neiman Marcus receives most of its apparel, accessories, jewelry, and home products from other countries. Because it deals with fashions that have short product life cycles, good communication with its suppliers is essential.[16]

A major impediment to getting deliveries in a timely manner was the delay caused by U.S. Customs and Border Protection agencies, which demand comprehensive and complicated paperwork before they will allow shipments into the United States. With so much paperwork, incomplete information and errors are common, which kept Neiman Marcus' shipments from arriving on time. The company therefore instituted an Internet-based system that remains in contact with every business partner that touches a shipment, to ensure that the documents are prepared properly for U.S. Customs. Trust is one thing, but this system guarantees that the work gets done correctly. Any missing paperwork prompts an automatic alert to the appropriate business partner, which can then send the required paperwork to U.S. Customs while the shipment is still en route, rather than wait to be notified by Customs after it has arrived. Missing or incorrect documents found by Customs once the shipment has arrived can delay the process even more. This initiative eliminated a full two days from the shipping cycle.

As an added bonus, Neiman Marcus uses the system to comply more closely with import regulations. The duty/tariff laws of different countries vary and can change quickly. To keep up to date with these changes in the more than 60 countries with which it does business, Neiman Marcus requires vendors to guarantee that they will update any tariff changes on the Internet-based system within 24 hours of the country's rule change. Shipments then receive an HTSUS (harmonized tariff schedule of the United States), making it easier for U.S. Customs to identify the import shipments and move them through the clearance process. As a result, Neiman Marcus shipments have a low risk rating and move through Customs much faster than those of many of its competitors.

Changes like these demonstrate the symbiotic nature of relationships along the marketing channel. Retailers with sufficient strength in the marketplace can insist that their vendors adhere to new processes, even if they demand new investments by the vendor. In a recent initiative to address shrinking profits for example, Neiman Marcus asked its vendors to create designer merchandise at a lower price point.[17] The replicas, produced in the same style and same factory as more expensive models, still sport a designer's name but are made from less costly materials. Some suppliers found the request too challenging, but others embraced it, recognizing an opportunity to protect future sales and expand their offerings. As news about these lower-cost designer items spreads across the Internet, Neiman Marcus will learn quickly whether this approach buoys its flagging sales or sends customers to other stores that have retained their luxury brand image.

To facilitate getting merchandise through U.S. Customs, it uses an Internet-based system that remains in contact with every business partner that touches a shipment.

frequently, the ordering process is done automatically, bypassing the buyers. By working together, the retailer and manufacturer can better satisfy customer needs.[18]

Flow 5 (Store to Distribution Center): Stores also communicate with the Best Buy distribution center to coordinate deliveries and check inventory status. When the store inventory drops to a specified level, more HDTVs are shipped to the store, and the shipment information is sent to the Best Buy computer system.

Flow 6 (Manufacturer to Distribution Center and Buyer): When the manufacturer ships the HDTVs to the Best Buy distribution center, it sends an advanced shipping notice to the distribution centers. An **advanced shipping notice (ASN)** is an electronic document that the supplier sends the retailer in advance of a shipment to tell the retailer exactly what to expect in the shipment. The center then makes appointments for trucks to make the delivery at a specific time, date, and loading dock. When the shipment is received at the distribution center, the buyer is notified and authorizes payment to the vendor.

Data Warehouse

Purchase data collected at the point of sale (information flow 2 in Exhibit 16.7) goes into a huge database known as a data warehouse. The information stored in the data warehouse is accessible on various dimensions and levels, as depicted in the data cube in Exhibit 16.8.

As shown on the horizontal axis, data can be accessed according to the level of merchandise aggregation—SKU (item), vendor, category (e.g., dresses), or all merchandise. Along the vertical axis, data can be accessed by level of the company—store, divisions, or the total company. Finally, along the third dimension, data can be accessed by point in time—day, season, or year.

The CEO might be interested in how the corporation is generally doing and could look at the data aggregated by quarter for a merchandise division, a region of the country, or the total corporation. A buyer may be more interested in a particular manufacturer in a certain store on a particular day. Analysts from various levels of the retail operation extract information from the data warehouse to make a plethora of marketing decisions about developing and replenishing merchandise assortments.

EXHIBIT 16.8 Retail Data Warehouse

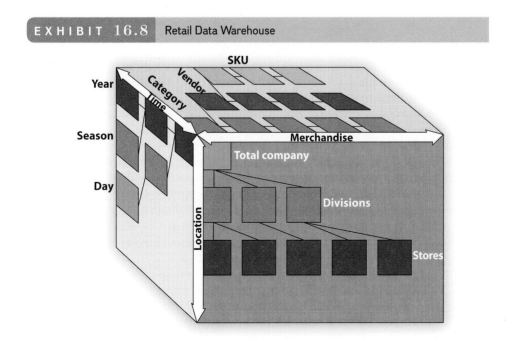

In some cases, manufacturers also have access to this data warehouse. They communicate with retailers using electronic data interchange (EDI) and use supply chain systems known as vendor-managed inventory, which are discussed next.

Electronic Data Interchange

In information flows 3, 4, and 6 in Exhibit 16.7, the retailer and manufacturer exchange business documents through EDI. **Electronic data interchange (EDI)** is the computer-to-computer exchange of business documents from a retailer to a vendor and back. In addition to sales data, purchase orders, invoices, and data about returned merchandise can be transmitted back and forth.

Many retailers now require vendors to provide them with notification of deliveries before they take place using an advanced shipping notice. If the ASN is accurate, the retailer can dispense with opening all the received cartons and checking in merchandise. In addition, EDI enables vendors to transmit information about on-hand inventory status, vendor promotions, and cost changes to the retailer, as well as information about purchase order changes, order status, retail prices, and transportation routings.

Using EDI, suppliers can describe and show pictures of their products, and buyers can issue requests for proposals. The two parties then can electronically negotiate prices and specify how the product will be made and how it should look.

The use of EDI thus provides three main benefits to marketing channel members. First, EDI reduces the **cycle time**, or the time between the decision to place an order and the receipt of merchandise. Information flows quicker using EDI, which means that inventory turnover is higher. Second, EDI improves the overall quality of communications through better recordkeeping, fewer errors in inputting and receiving an order, and less human error in the interpretation of data. Third, the data transmitted by EDI are in a computer-readable format that can be easily analyzed and used for a variety of tasks ranging from evaluating vendor delivery performance to automating reorder processes.

Because of these benefits, many retailers are asking their suppliers to interface with them using EDI. However, small- to medium-sized suppliers and retailers face significant barriers, specifically, cost and the lack of information technology (IT) expertise, to become EDI enabled. However, EDI remains an important component of any vendor-managed inventory system.

Vendor—Managed Inventory

Vendor-managed inventory (VMI) is an approach for improving marketing channel efficiency in which the manufacturer is responsible for maintaining the retailer's inventory levels in each of its stores.[19] By sharing the data in the retailer's data warehouse and communicating that information via EDI, the manufacturer automatically sends merchandise to the retailer's store or distribution center when the inventory at the store reaches a prespecified level.[20]

In ideal conditions, the manufacturer replenishes inventories in quantities that meet the retailer's immediate demand, reducing stockouts with minimal inventory. In addition to better match retail demand to supply, VMI can reduce the vendor's and the retailer's costs. Manufacturer sales people no longer need to spend time generating orders on items that are already in the stores, and their role shifts to selling new items and maintaining relationships. Retail buyers and planners no longer need to monitor inventory levels and place orders.

Frito-Lay and other snack food, candy, and beverage vendors have been involved with VMI in supermarkets for a long time. However, technological advances have increased the sophistication of VMI. The sharing of point-of-sale (POS) transaction data, for instance, allows manufacturers to sell merchandise on consignment; the manufacturer owns the merchandise until it is sold by the retailer, at which time the retailer pays for the merchandise. Consignment selling provides an incentive for the manufacturer to pick stockkeeping units (SKUs) and inventory levels that will minimize inventory and generate sales. Because the manufacturer is bearing the financial cost of owning the inventory, retailers are more willing to allow the manufacturer to be responsible for determining the inventory plan and appropriate assortment for each store.

Although it is a more advanced level of collaboration than simply using EDI and sharing information, retailers cannot use VMI blindly. Whereas the manufacturer coordinates the supply chain for its specific products, it does not know what other actions the retailer is taking that might affect the sales of its products in the future. For example, Pepsi might not know that a supermarket will be having a big promotion in three weeks for a new beverage introduced by Coca-Cola. The supermarket's buyer must monitor the VMI orders and inform Pepsi to cut back on its usual orders.

Push versus Pull Marketing Channels

As illustrated in Exhibit 16.9, the way information is transferred from one party to another in a marketing channel is generally classified as either a pull or a push strategy. In a **push marketing strategy** merchandise is allocated to stores based on previous sales forecasts, which is likely to be a collaborative process between the manufacturer, wholesaler, and retailer. Once a forecast is developed, specified quantities of merchandise are shipped (pushed) to distribution centers and stores at predetermined time intervals. The manufacturer works with wholesalers and retailers to get the products on the shelf by providing incentives such as slotting allowances, contests for salespeople, and other promotional support at all levels of the marketing channel. The goal is to increase demand for the product by providing incentives and focusing one's efforts on wholesalers, retailers, or their sales

EXHIBIT 16.9 Push versus Pull Marketing Strategies

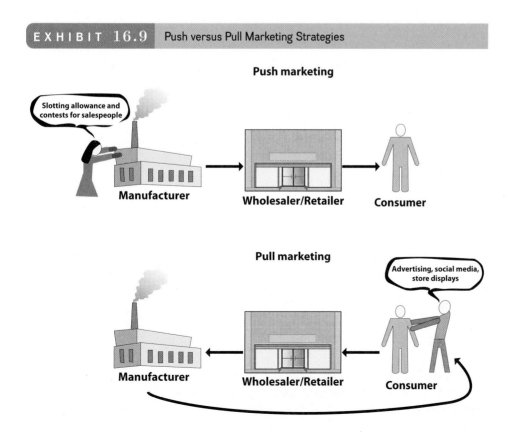

people. These campaigns attempt to motivate the seller to highlight the product, rather than those of competitors, and thereby *push* the product to consumers.

With a **pull marketing strategy**, the amount of merchandise sent to the store is determined based on sales data captured by POS terminals. In essence, customers *pull* the product into the marketing channel by demanding it. Marketers create customer pull-based demand by designing integrative marketing campaigns using several types of media such as advertising, social media, and in-store displays, to create awareness and ultimately demand for the product.

With a pull marketing strategy, there is less likelihood of being overstocked or out of stock because the store orders merchandise as needed on the basis of consumer demand. As a result, a pull strategy increases inventory turnover and is more responsive to changes in customer demand. A pull approach becomes even more efficient than a push approach when demand is uncertain and difficult to forecast because the forecast is based on consumer demand. That is, the stores get just what they need, no more, no less.

Although generally more desirable, a pull approach is not the most effective in all situations. First, a pull approach requires a more costly and sophisticated information system to support it. Second, for some merchandise, retailers do not have the flexibility to adjust inventory levels on the basis of demand. For example, commitments must be made months in advance for fashion and private-label apparel. Because these commitments cannot be easily changed, the merchandise has to be pre-allocated to the stores at the time the orders are formulated. Third, push strategies are efficient for merchandise that has steady, predictable demand, such as milk and eggs, basic men's underwear, and bath towels. Because both pull and push marketing strategies have their advantages, most channel partners use a combination of these approaches.

CHECK YOURSELF

1. What are the marketing channel links associated with each information flow?
2. How do marketing channel members use data warehouses to make decisions?
3. What is EDI and how is it used?
4. Why do some marketing channels use VMI, while others do not?
5. What is the difference between a push and a pull marketing channel?

MAKING MERCHANDISE FLOW THROUGH MARKETING CHANNELS

Exhibit 16.10 illustrates different types of merchandise flows:

1. Sony to Best Buy's distribution centers, or
2. Sony directly to stores.
3. If the merchandise goes through distribution centers, it is then shipped to stores,
4. and then to the customer.

Making merchandise flow involves first deciding if the merchandise is going to go from the manufacturer to a retailer's distribution center or directly on to stores. Once in a distribution center, multiple activities take place before it is shipped on to a store.

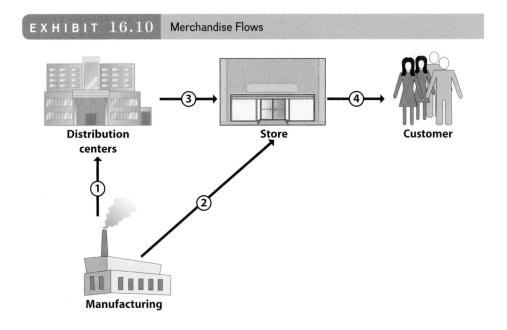

EXHIBIT 16.10 Merchandise Flows

Distribution Centers versus Direct Store Delivery

As indicated in Exhibit 16.10, manufacturers can ship merchandise directly to a retailer's stores—direct store delivery (flow 2)—or to their distribution centers (flow 1). Although manufacturers and retailers may collaborate, the ultimate decision is usually up to the retailer and depends on the characteristics of the merchandise and the nature of demand. To determine which distribution system—distribution centers or direct store delivery—is better, retailers consider the total cost associated with each alternative and the customer service criterion of having the right merchandise at the store when the customer wants to buy it.

There are several advantages to using a distribution center:

- More accurate sales forecasts are possible when retailers combine forecasts for many stores serviced by one distribution center rather than doing a forecast for each store. Consider a set of 50 Target stores, serviced by a single distribution center that each carries Michael Graves toasters. Each store normally stocks 5 units for a total of 250 units in the system. By carrying the item at each store, the retailer must develop individual forecasts, each with the possibility of errors that could result in either too much or too little merchandise. Alternatively, by delivering most of the inventory to a distribution center and feeding the stores merchandise as they need it, the effects of forecast errors for the individual stores are minimized, and less backup inventory is needed to prevent stockouts.

- Distribution centers enable the retailer to carry less merchandise in the individual stores, which results in lower inventory investments systemwide. If the stores get frequent deliveries from the distribution center, they need to carry relatively less extra merchandise as backup stock.

- It is easier to avoid running out of stock or having too much stock in any particular store because merchandise is ordered from the distribution center as needed.

- Retail store space is typically much more expensive than space at a distribution center, and distribution centers are better equipped than stores to prepare merchandise for sale. As a result, many retailers find it cost-effective to store merchandise and get it ready for sale at a distribution center rather than in individual stores.

The use of distribution centers helps reduce stockouts.

But distribution centers aren't appropriate for all retailers. If a retailer has only a few outlets, the expense of a distribution center is probably unwarranted. Also, if many outlets are concentrated in metropolitan areas, merchandise can be consolidated and delivered by the vendor directly to all the stores in one area economically. Direct store delivery gets merchandise to the stores faster and thus is used for perishable goods (meat and produce), items that help create the retailer's image of being the first to sell the latest product (e.g., video games), or fads. Finally, some manufacturers provide direct store delivery for retailers to ensure that their products are on the store's shelves, properly displayed, and fresh. For example, employees delivering Frito-Lay snacks directly to supermarkets replace products that have been on the shelf too long and are stale, replenish products that have been sold, and arrange products so they are neatly displayed.

Superior Service 16.1 examines how Home Depot improved service to its customers by transitioning from direct store delivery to a more integrated use of distribution centers.

The Distribution Center

The distribution center performs the following activities: coordinating inbound transportation; receiving, checking, storing, and cross-docking; getting merchandise "floor ready"; and coordinating outbound transportation. To illustrate these activities being undertaken in a distribution center, we'll continue our example of Sony HDTVs being shipped to a Best Buy distribution center.

Management of Inbound Transportation Traditionally, buyers focused their efforts, when working with vendors, on developing merchandise assortments, negotiating prices, and arranging joint promotions. Now, buyers and planners are much more involved in coordinating the physical flow of merchandise to the stores. **Planners** are employees responsible for the financial planning and analysis of merchandise, and its allocation to stores. The TV buyer has arranged for a truckload of HDTVs to be delivered to its Houston, Texas, distribution center on Monday between 1:00 and 3:00 PM. The buyer also specifies how the merchandise should be placed on pallets for easy unloading.

The truck must arrive within the specified time because the distribution center has all of its 100 receiving docks allocated throughout the day, and much of the merchandise on this particular truck is going to be shipped to stores that evening. Unfortunately, the truck was delayed in a snowstorm. The **dispatcher**—the person who coordinates deliveries to the distribution center—reassigns the truck delivering the HDTVs to a Wednesday morning delivery slot and charges the firm several hundred dollars for missing its delivery time. Although many manufacturers pay transportation expenses, some retailers negotiate with their vendors to absorb this expense. These retailers believe they can lower their net merchandise cost and better control merchandise flow if they negotiate directly with trucking companies and consolidate shipments from many vendors.

Receiving and Checking Using UPC and Radio Frequency Identification (RFID) Device Receiving is the process of recording the receipt of merchandise as it

Superior Service 16.1   Home Depot Transitions to Distribution Centers[21]

The ultimate goal of any supply chain is to improve the customer experience. No store manager wants customers leaving empty-handed because the item they wanted wasn't on the shelves. Nor do they want their employees tied up in a back room, hunting missing stock or coping with a delivery overload.

For the first three decades of its existence, Home Depot didn't worry much about its supply chain. It didn't need to: The company was growing, and its warehouse stores doubled as distribution centers. But as the retailer built stores with smaller footprints in secondary markets, fuel costs rose, and competition began nibbling at its profits, Home Depot execs realized supply chain changes were imperative.

In Home Depot's original supply chain model, more than three-quarters of its inventory was shipped directly from suppliers to stores, with store managers placing 70 percent of orders. As the business evolved, this approach resulted in a bloated, expensive logistics infrastructure that failed to protect stores from stockouts. To correct the situation, Home Depot elected to undergo a massive, rapid, but also long-term supply chain overhaul.

The renovation included the arrival of high-capacity, flow-through distribution centers, called Rapid Deployment Centers (RDCs). The RDCs, supported by new warehousing and transportation systems, serve around 100 stores each, and most of them are highly automated. These RDCs assume responsibility for ordering for stores, which has improved inventory forecasting. However, some bulky items, such as lumber and lawn mowers, continue to ship directly from vendors to stores.

The results have been splendid: double-digit increases in net income from quarter to quarter, notable sales jumps, and significant decreases in the value of inventory held on hand. That is, Home Depot is paying to hold on to less stuff, even as it is selling more. And the company hopes to improve even more.

Today it handles approximately 65 percent of its merchandise through its RDCs, but it aims to improve that level to 75 percent within the next three years.

Home Depot's net income has increased significantly since it switched the majority of its deliveries from going directly to stores to using distribution centers.

---

arrives at a distribution center. **Checking** is the process of going through the goods upon receipt to make sure they arrived undamaged and that the merchandise ordered was the merchandise received.

In the past, checking merchandise was a very labor-intensive and time-consuming process. Today, however, many distribution systems using EDI are designed to minimize, if not eliminate, these processes. The advance shipping notice (ASN) tells the distribution center what should be in each carton. A UPC label or radio frequency identification (RFID) tag on the shipping carton that identifies the carton's contents is scanned and automatically counted as it is being received and checked. **Radio frequency identification (RFID) tags** are tiny computer chips that automatically transmit to a special scanner all the information about a container's contents or individual products. Approximately as large as a pinhead, these RFID tags consist of an antenna and a chip that contains an electronic product code that stores far more information about a product than bar (UPC) codes can. The tags also act as passive tracking devices, signaling their presence over a radio frequency when they pass within a few yards of a special scanner. The tags have long been used in high-cost applications, such as automated highway toll systems and security identification badges.

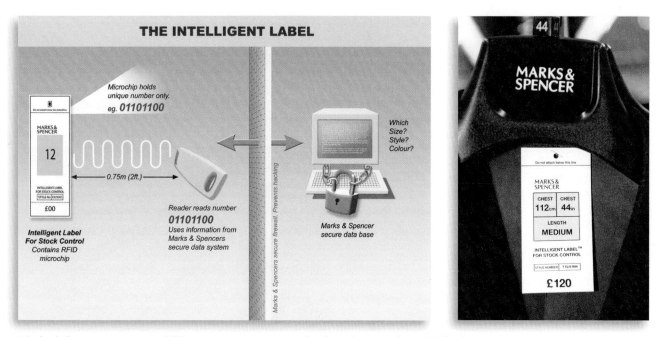

Marks & Spencer expects its RFID system to save time and reduce the cost of spoiled food.

A key advantage of RFID is that it eliminates the need to handle items individually by enabling distribution centers and stores to receive whole truckloads of merchandise without having to check in each carton. Another advantage is that manufacturers and distributors are able to reduce overall inventory thanks to greater supply chain efficiency. Marks & Spencer (U.K.) is replacing bar codes with an RFID system, including tags for the millions of containers that hold food being shipped from suppliers to its stores. It takes a mere five seconds to receive data from 50 containers, an 85 percent improvement over the time it takes to scan bar codes. The savings of time, as well as reduced costs of spoiled food, are expected to make the system's $3 million price tag feasible.[22]

Other prominent retailers taking advantage of this new technology are Bloomingdale's (a division of Macy's), Walmart, Metro AG (Germany) and Walgreens. Macy's is even rolling out item-level RFID, which will enable it to track the precise location of every item, both on its way to and inside the store.[23] In addition, it can ensure that the moment an item sells, it gets replenished on store racks, which should increase the retailer's inventory system accuracy. However, in most of these cases, the retailers ask vendors and manufacturers to attach the RFID chips. In the case of Macy's individual-item RFID initiative, the costs and efforts required will be substantial.

Thus the watchword, for both retailers and manufacturers of consumer products, is still caution. For most supply chain members, long-term investments in RFID technology are still too risky and expensive.

Walmart speeds merchandise from its distribution centers to stores.

Storing and Cross-Docking   After the merchandise is received and checked, it is either stored or cross-docked. When merchandise is stored, the cartons are transported by a conveyor system and forklift trucks to racks that go from the distribution center's floor to its ceiling. Then, when the merchandise is needed in the stores, a forklift driver goes to the rack, picks up the carton, and places it on a conveyor system that routes the carton to the loading dock of a truck going to the store.

Merchandise cartons that are **cross-docked** are prepackaged by the vendor for a specific store. The UPC labels on the carton indicate the store to which it is to be sent. The vendor also may affix price tags to each item in the carton. Because the merchandise is ready for sale, it is placed on a conveyor system that routes it from the unloading dock at which it was received to the loading dock for the truck going to the specific store—thus, the name *cross-docked*. The cartons are routed on the conveyor system automatically by sensors that read the UPC label on the cartons. Cross-docked merchandise is in the distribution center only for a few hours before it is shipped to the stores.

Merchandise sales rate and degree of perishability or fashionability typically determine whether cartons are cross-docked or stored. For instance, because Sony's HDTVs sell so quickly, it is in Best Buy's interest not to store them in a distribution center. Similarly, cross-docking is preferable for fashion apparel or perishable meat or produce.

Getting Merchandise Floor-Ready For some merchandise, additional tasks are undertaken in the distribution center to make the merchandise floor-ready. **Floor-ready merchandise** is merchandise that is ready to be placed on the selling floor. Getting merchandise floor-ready entails ticketing, marking, and, in the case of some apparel, placing garments on hangers (or maybe attaching RFID chips). At Tesco's Fresh & Easy Neighborhood Markets in California, it is essential that products ship in ready-to-sell units so that it has little manipulation or sorting to do at the distribution center or in the stores. To move the store-ready merchandise it receives from suppliers quickly into the store, Tesco demands that products sit on roll cages rather than pallets. Then, store employees can easily wheel them onto the retail floor. The stores' backrooms only have two or three days' worth of backup inventory, and since the stores are relatively small (about 10,000 square feet), it is important to keep inventory levels low and receive lots of small, accurate deliveries from its suppliers—which also helps cut costs.[24]

Tesco makes sure its merchandise is floor-ready before it is shipped to its stores.

Ticketing and marking refers to affixing price and identification labels to the merchandise. It is more efficient for a retailer to perform these activities at a distribution center than in its stores. In a distribution center, an area can be set aside and a process implemented to efficiently add labels and put apparel on hangers. Conversely, getting merchandise floor-ready in stores can block aisles and divert sales people's attention from their customers. An even better approach from the retailer's perspective is to get vendors to ship floor-ready merchandise, thus totally eliminating the expensive, time-consuming ticketing and marking process.

Preparing to Ship Merchandise to a Store At the beginning of the day, the computer system in the distribution center generates a list of items to be shipped to each store on that day. For each item, a pick ticket and shipping label is generated. The **pick ticket** is a document or display on a screen in a forklift truck indicating how much of each item to get from specific storage areas. The forklift driver goes to the storage area, picks up the number of cartons indicated on the pick ticket, places UPC shipping labels on the cartons that indicate the stores to which the items are to be shipped, and puts the cartons on the conveyor system, where they are automatically routed to the loading dock for the truck going to the stores.

Shipping Merchandise to Stores Shipping merchandise to stores from a distribution center has become increasingly complex. Most distribution centers run 50–100 outbound truck routes in one day. To handle this complex transportation problem, the centers use sophisticated routing and scheduling computer systems that consider the locations of the stores, road conditions, and transportation operating constraints to develop the most efficient routes possible. As a result, stores are provided with an accurate estimated time of arrival, and vehicle utilization is maximized.

Inventory Management through Just–In–Time Inventory Systems

Marketing channel management offers the 21st century's answer to a host of distribution problems faced by firms. As recently as the early 1990s, even the most innovative firms needed 15 to 30 days—or even more—to fulfill an order from the warehouse to the customer. The typical order-to-delivery process had several steps: order creation, usually using a telephone, fax, or mail; order processing, using a manual system for credit authorization and assignment to a warehouse; and physical delivery. Things could, and often did, go wrong. Ordered goods were not available. Orders were lost or misplaced. Shipments were misdirected. These mistakes lengthened the time it took to get merchandise to customers and potentially made the entire process more expensive. As Nieman Marcus, profiled in Adding Value 16.2, realized, the traditional ways of doing things were not necessarily the best ways.

Faced with such predicaments, firms began stockpiling inventory at each level of the supply chain (retailers, wholesalers, and manufacturers), but keeping inventory where it is not needed becomes a huge and wasteful expense. If a manufacturer has a huge stock of items stuck in a warehouse, it not only is not earning

To reduce lead time, UPS works with adidas by providing it with special labeling, garments on hangers, and advanced shipping notices.

profits by selling those items but also must pay to maintain and guard that warehouse.

Therefore, more recently, many firms, such as American Apparel, Zara, Mango, and Forever 21, have adopted a practice developed by Toyota in the 1950s (see the Zara case study at the end of this chapter). **Just-in-time inventory systems**, also known as **quick response** (QR) systems in retailing, are inventory management systems that deliver less merchandise on a more frequent basis than traditional inventory systems. The firm gets the merchandise "just-in-time" for it to be used in the manufacture of another product or for sale when the customer wants it. The benefits of a JIT system include reduced lead time, increased product availability, and lower inventory investment.[25]

Reduced Lead Time By eliminating the need for paper transactions the EDI in the JIT system reduces **lead time**, or the amount of time between the recognition that an order needs to be placed and the arrival of the needed merchandise at the seller's store, ready for sale. Because the vendor's computer acquires the data automatically, no manual data entry is required on the recipient's end, which reduces lead time even more and eliminates vendor recording errors. Even better, the shorter lead times further reduce the need for inventory because the shorter the lead time, the easier it is for the retailer to forecast its demand.

Increased Product Availability and Lower Inventory Investment In general, as a firm's ability to satisfy customer demand by having stock on hand increases, so does its inventory investment; that is, it needs to keep more backup inventory in stock. But with JIT, the ability to satisfy demand can actually increase while inventory decreases. Because a firm like American Apparel can make purchase commitments or produce merchandise closer to the time of sale, its own inventory investment is reduced. American Apparel needs less inventory because it's getting less merchandise in each order, but receiving those shipments more often. Since firms using JIT are ordering merchandise to cover shorter-term demand, inventory is even further reduced.

The ability to satisfy customer demand by keeping merchandise in stock also increases in JIT systems as a result of the more frequent shipments. For instance, if an American Apparel store runs low on a medium-sized Kelly T-shirt, its JIT system ensures a shorter lead time than those of more traditional retailers. As a result, it is less likely that the American Apparel store will be out of stock for its customers before the next shirt shipment arrives.

Costs of a JIT System Although firms achieve great benefits from a JIT system, it is not without its costs. The distribution function becomes much more complicated with more frequent deliveries. With greater order frequency also come smaller orders, which are more expensive to transport and more difficult to coordinate. Therefore, JIT systems require a strong commitment by the firm and its vendors to cooperate, share data, and develop systems.

CHECK YOURSELF

1. How does merchandise flow through a typical marketing channel?
2. What activities occur in a distribution center and what technologies facilitate those activities?
3. Why have just-in-time inventory systems become so popular?

Summing Up

LO1 Understand the importance of marketing channels and supply chain management.

Marketing channels allow companies to get their products in the appropriate outlets in sufficient quantities to meet consumer demand. To anticipate this demand, advertising and promotions must be coordinated with the departments that control inventory and transportation. Otherwise, customers would come in seeking a promotion and not find the product.

Without a marketing channel, consumers would be forced to find raw materials, manufacture products, and somehow get them to where they could be used, all on their own. Thus, each marketing channel member adds value to the product by performing one or more of these functions. Marketing channel management also creates value for each firm in the chain and helps bind together many company functions, including manufacturing, inventory management, transportation, advertising, and marketing.

LO2 Understand the difference between direct and indirect marketing channels.

There are ways by which businesses get their goods to consumers. Using a direct marketing channel, a customer can purchase goods from the manufacturer without needing to go through a retailer or intermediary, generally online (e.g., Ascend speakers) or at company stores (e.g., Apple). More commonly, manufacturers choose to offer their goods to consumers through an intermediary, such as a retailer (e.g., Walmart), implementing an indirect marketing channel strategy.

LO3 Describe how marketing channels are managed.

The more closely aligned the marketing channel members are with each other, the less likely there will be significant conflict. An administered marketing channel occurs when a dominant and powerful marketing channel member has control over the other members. In a contractual marketing channel (e.g., franchising), coordination and control are dictated by contractual relationships between members. Corporate marketing channels can operate relatively smoothly because one firm owns the various levels of the chains. Marketing channels also can be effectively managed through strong relationships developed with marketing channel partners. To create such relationships, the partners must trust each other, communicate openly, have compatible goals, realize there is benefit in being interdependent, and be willing to invest in each other's success.

LO4 Describe the flow of information and merchandise in the marketing channel.

Information flow involves: Flow 1 (customer to store), Flow 2 (store to buyer), Flow 3 (buyer to manufacturer), Flow 4 (store to manufacturer), Flow 5 (store to distribution center), and Flow 6 (manufacturer to distribution center and buyer). Merchandise flow involves: Flow 1 (manufacturer to retailer distribution centers), Flow 2 (manufacturer directly to stores), Flow 3 (distribution centers to stores, when shipped first to distribution centers), and Flow 4 (retailer to customer).

Key Terms

- administered vertical marketing system, 492
- advanced shipping notice (ASN), 499
- checking, 505
- coercive power, 492
- consignment, 501
- contractual vertical marketing system, 492
- corporate vertical marketing system, 493
- cross-dock, 507
- cycle time, 500
- direct marketing channel, 488
- dispatcher, 504
- distribution center, 488
- electronic data interchange (EDI), 500
- expertise power, 492
- floor-ready merchandise, 507
- franchising, 492

Marketing Applications

1. Describe marketing channel management by identifying the major activities that it involves. Identify several ways that marketing channel management adds value to a company's offerings, with regard to both consumers and business partners.

2. In what ways can the flow of information be managed in the supply chain? How can the ready flow of information increase a firm's operating efficiencies?

3. Describe how B2B transactions might employ EDI to process purchase information. Considering the information discussed in Chapter 7 about B2B buying situations, determine which buying situation (new task, modified rebuy, or straight rebuy) would most likely align with the use of EDI technology. Justify your answer.

4. What are the differences between the use of a traditional distribution center and one that relies on cross-docking? Discuss the extent to which one is more efficient than the other, being sure to detail your reasoning.

5. Discuss the advantages to a retailer like Tesco of expending the time and effort to get merchandise floor-ready at either the point of manufacture or in the distribution center rather than having retail store staff members do it in the stores. Provide the logic behind your answer.

6. A just-in-time (JIT) inventory system appears to be an important success factor for retailers like American Apparel and Forever 21. Choose a local retailer and examine the advantages and disadvantages of its use of a JIT system. Do you believe it should use JIT? Why?

7. Give an example of a retailer that participates in an independent (conventional) supply chain and one involved in a vertical marketing system. Discuss the advantages and disadvantages of each.

8. For each of the following consumer products, identify the type of vertical marketing system used, and justify your answer: (a) Bertolli pasta sold through grocery stores, (b) Krispy Kreme donuts sold through franchises, and (c) www.polo.com by Ralph Lauren.

9. Why might a big company like Dell want to develop strategic partnerships with locally owned computer stores? Describe what Dell would have to do to maintain such relationships.

10. You are hired as an assistant brand manager for a popular consumer product. One day in an emergency meeting, the brand manager informs the group that there is a problem with one of the suppliers and that he has decided to send you over to the manufacturing facilities to investigate the problem. When you arrive at the plant, you learn that a key supplier has become increasingly unreliable in terms of quality and delivery. You ask the plant manager why the plant doesn't switch suppliers, because it is becoming a major problem for your brand. He informs you that the troubled supplier is his cousin, whose wife has been very ill, and he just can't switch right now. What course of action should you take?

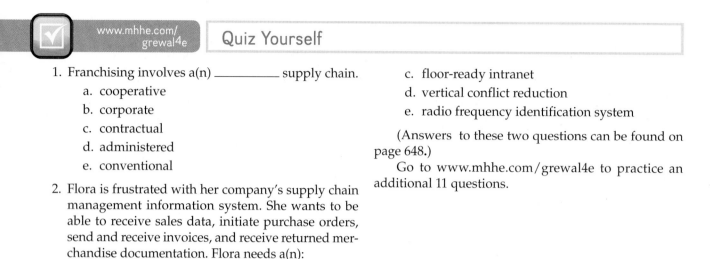

www.mhhe.com/
grewal4e

Quiz Yourself

1. Franchising involves a(n) _____ supply chain.
   a. cooperative
   b. corporate
   c. contractual
   d. administered
   e. conventional

2. Flora is frustrated with her company's supply chain management information system. She wants to be able to receive sales data, initiate purchase orders, send and receive invoices, and receive returned merchandise documentation. Flora needs a(n):
   a. cross-docking distribution center
   b. electronic data interchange

   c. floor-ready intranet
   d. vertical conflict reduction
   e. radio frequency identification system

   (Answers to these two questions can be found on page 648.)
   Go to www.mhhe.com/grewal4e to practice an additional 11 questions.

Net Savvy

1. Zappos.com, an online shoe seller, has received praise for its stellar supply chain management. Go to http://about.zappos.com/zappos-story/fulfillment-facility, read the "In the Beginning," "Looking Ahead," and "Customer Testimonial" sections, and see how a shoe ultimately reaches the customer. How does its distribution center enable Zappos to adhere to its marketing communications message and provide excellent customer service?

2. The case study for this chapter examines how Zara International, a division of Inditex, successfully

manages its supply chain. Visit Inditex's website (www.inditex.com) and go to "Corporate Responsibility," then review the company's commitment to corporate social responsibility, particularly the section that pertains to its Internal Code of Conduct. Considering the discussion in this chapter about strategic relationships, how does Inditex address the factors necessary for mutually beneficial partnerships, according to its code of conduct?

Chapter Case Study

ZARA DELIVERS FAST FASHION[26]

connect

In the fast fashion retail business strategy, supply chain management processes serve to introduce fashionable merchandise rapidly, such that stores can respond immediately to customer demand for merchandise. This was pioneered by Zara, a global specialty apparel chain located in La Coruna, Spain, but it also has been adopted by other retailers, including American Apparel, H&M (headquartered in Sweden), TopShop (U.K.) and Forever 21 (U.S.).

The approach is particularly effective for specialty apparel retailers that target fashion-conscious consumers who simply must have the latest looks—but they want to do so on a very limited budget. These shoppers load up on new fast fashions every few weeks, instead of purchasing a few higher-priced basics every few months.

Zara's competitive advantage in specialty apparel retailing is based on its efficient supply chain that delivers fashionable merchandise to its stores frequently.

To fit with such short cycles and meet customers' demands, the fast fashion process starts with the receipt of timely information from store managers. At Zara, store managers always have their reporting devices literally in hand. These hand-held devices, which are linked directly to the company's corporate office in Spain, enable daily reports on what customers are buying (or not) and what they are asking for but not finding.

For example, customers might want a purple version of a pink shirt that they see on the shop floor. Managers immediately pass the information on to the designers in Spain. Those designers then communicate electronically with the factory that produces fabric for shirts. This factory starts up its automated equipment, which is run by assemblers who live in close proximity to the factory. (The undyed fabric comes from Asia, where Zara finds inexpensive sources, and then bulk fabric ships to Spain and Portugal to be manufactured into apparel.) The robots in the company's 23 highly automated factories start cutting out shirts and mixing purple dye. For final construction, a network of 300 or so small assemblers, located near the factories in Galicia, Spain, and northern Portugal, take responsibility for making the final product. Finally, to ensure timely delivery, the shirts get shipped by truck to stores in Europe and by air express to stores in the rest of the world.

THE BENEFITS OF FAST FASHION FOR ZARA

Zara's main advantage over its competitors, such as The Gap and H&M, has resulted from its highly responsive and tightly organized supply chain. Unlike these competitors, Zara selects factory locations that are in close geographic proximity to the company's headquarters in Spain. Although this approach increases labor costs, compared with outsourced production in lower-cost countries in Asia, it also improves communication, reduces shipping costs and time, and reduces the time before new fashions appear in stores. It also gives Zara the flexibility to modify its operations in one supply chain function to expedite processes in another, such as pricing or tagging. It might hang merchandise on racks in the warehouse so that store employees can move apparel directly from delivery to the sales floor. And it can do all this because it maintains complete control over the entire process.

Furthermore, instead of shipping new products a few times a season, as many of its competitors do, Zara makes deliveries to every one of its stores every few days. The purple shirts would be in stores in two weeks—compared with the several months it would take for most department stores and other specialty apparel stores to accomplish the same feat. Because its fast fashion system also ensures shorter lead times, it's less likely that any Zara store will be out of stock before the next sweater shipment arrives. Limiting the stock in stores even can create a sense of scarcity among its customers. If they don't buy now, the item might not be available next time they visit the store. By producing and shipping in these small quantities, Zara can quickly recover from its (rare) fashion faux pas.

Finally, the efficiency of its supply chain means Zara rarely has to discount merchandise that is not selling. At Zara, the number of items that end up marked down is about half the industry average. Even with these results, Zara still manages to introduce around 10,000 new designs and 40,000 new SKUs each year.

MOVING TOO FAST? THE NEGATIVE EFFECTS OF FAST FASHION

Despite some strong signals of success—including annual growth rates of approximately 20 percent in terms of sales and number of stores—Zara started to outgrow its own strategy. By their very nature, fashion trends change rapidly and constantly, and so must the merchandise on Zara's shop floors. Faced with disappointed customers, some sales managers ordered extra quantities of hot items, to avoid stockouts. Even with this attempt to circumvent the replenishment system, some stores still suffered from stockouts, because they received fewer units than they had ordered when overall demand exceeded inventory levels. For some items, Zara even confronted perhaps the most frustrating scenario in a supply chain: Inventory sat unused, eating up storage costs, at one location, even as another store desperately pleaded for the same inventory to meet its customers' demand.

As noted among the benefits, the company launches as many as 10,000 new styles annually, with a range of colors and sizes, resulting in hundreds of thousands of SKUs in the system. If we add in replenishment orders, which are received twice weekly, Zara's average shipping total reached nearly 2.5 million items per week, all coming from the company's distribution center. Its legendary supply chain efficiency thus was in danger of a clogged artery.

In response, Zara has adopted some new mathematical processes that turn human experience and mountains of data into actionable information. These models factor in store managers' unique requests for merchandise replenishments, together with historical trends in the sales of the same item. Merchandise display practices have been altered, such as removing all sizes of a garment from the sales floor if a popular size is not available. This practice helps reduce customer frustration, in that they never see an item that might not be available in their size. It also diminishes shipping; if the medium size is unavailable, the small and large sizes do not get shipped either. Instead, these remaining sizes head toward the stores that still have all sizes in stock, so they can be available to customers there.

Growth, costs, market demand, and technology advances all can push retail executives to rethink their business processes. But truly savvy managers search for ways to optimize operations, even when business is running smoothly. As Zara learned, current approaches will not necessarily work tomorrow. As the founder of Zara's corporate owner Inditex told the company's first deputy chair and CEO, "Once a month, come here thinking that we are near bankruptcy. You will find a lot of things to change."[27]

Questions

1. How does an individual firm like Zara manage a supply chain? How does it get new products from design to store so quickly?

2. What are some of the ways that Zara's supply chain management system has helped create value for its customers? Provide specific examples.

3. What challenges did Zara's focus on supply chain efficiency create? Are all such systems destined to suffer such "growing pains"?

CHAPTER 17

Retailing and Multichannel Marketing

Begun as a local cable channel in 1982, Home Shopping Network (HSN) offered consumers a central location from which to buy through their televisions.[1] The format for home shopping networks like HSN and QVC has remained the same for years: products loaded with kitsch, hawked by energetic salespeople who promise an incredible deal. As competition in this field increased, HSN tailored its communication strategy to reach more shoppers. For example, HSN.com was one of the top 10 most visited e-commerce sites, and its Facebook, Twitter, and YouTube presence fill out HSN's marketing mix. Today, it carries higher-end brands to appeal to the nearly 90 million households that watch shopping networks.[2]

The television broadcasts are only the first step. The HSN channel simulcasts all its shows on its website, and customers have constant access to related YouTube footage. Across these media, the shopping networks have developed a somewhat lower key sales approach, such that they use a talk show, lifestyle-oriented atmosphere to promise exclusive, branded products, including HSN's exclusive fragrance with Mary J. Blige, *ELLE* magazine–endorsed fashion products, and Emeril Lagasse and Wolfgang Puck lines of kitchenware. Jennifer Lopez recently promoted her Love & Light fragrance.

The reinvention of television shopping makes such retail channels relevant to customers, because they sell lifestyles, as well as the products to attain those lifestyles. An average customer of HSN earns a household income of more than $75,000; for QVC, this average is $200,000! Thus, a viewer who loves reality television and "keeps up with the Kardashians" can easily tune in to QVC to enjoy the K-Dash line, then visit the pop-up store that QVC set up in Rockefeller Center during Fashion Night Out (the kickoff of fashion week).

Although both HSN and QVC are much more than television channels, television is still their core delivery medium. Even in this forum though, the communication has evolved—from pitching products to providing an entertaining, multipronged selling machine. A cooking "show" demonstrates how viewers can make a featured recipe, offers some helpful hints, and then highlights all the pots and kitchenware for sale (which are also available on

LEARNING OBJECTIVES

- **LO1** Discuss the four factors manufacturers should consider as they develop their strategy for working with retailers.
- **LO2** Outline the considerations associated with choosing retail partners.
- **LO3** List the three levels of distribution intensity.
- **LO4** Describe the various types of retailers.
- **LO5** Describe the components of a retail strategy.
- **LO6** Identify the benefits of stores.
- **LO7** Identify the benefits of multichannel retailing.
- **LO8** Detail the challenges of multichannel retailing.

the website, of course). In a not-so-subtle form of product placement, Jamie Oliver, the chef and show host, makes a pasta dish using Barilla pasta, with the brand displayed on screen. Oliver mentions that the pasta is multigrain and a great source of protein, fiber, and omega 3 that also tastes great. In exchange, HSN receives advertising revenue from Barilla.[3]

On YouTube, visitors are affluent and of the age range most appealing to retailers.[4] By reaching 40–50 percent of the company's target market, YouTube gives HSN a way to interact differently with its customers and further increase its share of wallet from its current customers. In addition, these videos show up in Google searches, so it offers an appealing vehicle for retailers. The video format humanizes the connection and provides additional information about products. For example, HSN

has a dedicated channel on YouTube that enables it to control the content and look of its page.[5] The site's tracking capabilities also facilitate a deeper understanding of HSN customers,[6] including which other videos and programs attract their attention.

For consumers, YouTube offers a seamless multichannel experience. Products promoted on HSN, such as Tori Spelling's jewelry line,[7] are available on YouTube almost immediately after they appear on television. Then HSN marketers can use the information gathered from YouTube to target direct mail campaigns. For example, HSN should send jewelry promotions to households that viewed the YouTube video clip for a necklace from the Tori Spelling Collection. Consumer responses get monitored 24/7 and measured against hourly sales goals. There's never a dull moment—it's like the CNN of shopping!

Retailing sits at the end of the supply chain, where marketing meets the consumer. But there is far more to retailing than just manufacturing a product and making it available to its customers. It is primarily the retailer's responsibility to make sure that these customers' expectations are fulfilled.

Retailing is defined as the set of business activities that add value to products and services sold to consumers for their personal or family use. Our definition includes products bought at stores, through catalogs, and over the Internet, as well as services like fast-food restaurants, airlines, and hotels. Some retailers claim they sell at "wholesale" prices, but if they sell to customers for their personal use, they are still retailers, regardless of their prices. Wholesalers (see Chapter 16) buy products from manufacturers and resell them to retailers or industrial or business users.

Retailing today is changing, both in the United States and around the world. Manufacturers no longer rule many supply chains, as they once did. Retailers like Walmart, Carrefour (a French hypermarket), Metro (a German retail conglomerate), Tesco, Schwarz (another German conglomerate), Kroger, Costco, Aldi, Home Depot, and Target[8]—the largest retailers in the world—dictate to their suppliers what should be made, how it should be configured, when it should be delivered, and, to some extent, what it should cost. These retailers are clearly in the driver's seat.

This chapter extends Chapter 16's discussion of supply chain management by examining why and how manufacturers utilize retailers. The manufacturer's strategy depends on its overall market power and how consistent a new product or product line is with current offerings. Consider the following scenarios:

M-A-C will use different criteria for placing products in retail stores than either Coach for Men or Eva's green cosmetics.

- Scenario 1: Cosmetics conglomerate Estée Lauder's subsidiary brand M-A-C is introducing a new line of mascara.

| EXHIBIT 17.1 | Factors for Establishing a Relationship with Retailers |

| Choosing retailing partners | Identifying types of retailers | Developing a retail strategy | Managing a multichannel strategy |

- Scenario 2: Coach, well-known for its women's handbags, has introduced a line of men's leather goods, apparel, gifts, shoes, and other accessories—products not previously in its assortment.

- Scenario 3: Eva, a young entrepreneur, is launching a new line of environmentally friendly (green) cosmetics.

Each of these scenarios is different and requires the manufacturer to consider alternatives for reaching its target markets through retailers.

Exhibit 17.1 illustrates four factors manufacturers consider to establish their strategy for working with retailers.[9] In choosing retail partners, the first factor, manufacturers assess how likely it is for certain retailers to carry their products. Manufacturers also consider where their target customers expect to find the products, because those are exactly the stores in which they want to place their products. The overall size and level of sophistication of the manufacturer will determine how many of the marketing channel functions it performs and how many it will hand off to other channel members. Finally, the type and availability of the product and the image the manufacturer wishes to portray will determine how many retailers within a geographic region will carry the products.

For the second factor, manufacturers identify the types of retailers that would be appropriate to carry their products. Although the choice is often obvious—such as a supermarket for fresh produce—manufacturers may have a choice of retailer types for some products.

As we discussed in Chapter 16, a hallmark of a strong marketing channel is one in which manufacturers and retailers coordinate their efforts. In the third factor, manufacturers and retailers therefore develop their strategy by implementing the four Ps.

Finally, many retailers and some manufacturers use a **multichannel strategy**, which involves selling in more than one channel (e.g., store, catalog, and Internet). The fourth factor therefore consists of examining the circumstances in which sellers may prefer to adopt a particular strategy. Although these factors are listed consecutively, manufacturers may consider them all simultaneously or in a different order.

LO1 Discuss the four factors manufacturers should consider as they develop their strategy for working with retailers.

CHOOSING RETAILING PARTNERS

LO2 Outline the considerations associated with choosing retail partners.

Imagine, as a consumer, trying to buy a new leather jacket without being able to visit a retailer or buy online. You would have to figure out exactly what size, color, and style of jacket you wanted. Then you would need to contact various manufacturers, whether in person, by phone, or over the Internet, and order the jacket. If the jacket fit you reasonably well but not perfectly, you still might need to take it to a tailor to have the sleeves shortened. You wouldn't find this approach to shopping very convenient.

Manufacturers like Coach use retailers such as Macy's to undertake partnerships that create value by pulling together all the actions necessary for the greatest possible customer convenience and satisfaction. The store offers a broad selection of purses, leather jackets, scarves, and other accessories that its buyers have carefully chosen in advance. Customers can see, touch, feel, and try on any item while

Coach partners with retailers to help conveniently deliver its products to satisfied customers.

Most consumer packaged goods companies, such as Pepsi (top), strive for intensive distribution—they want to be everywhere. But cosmetics firms like Estee Lauder (bottom) use an exclusive distribution strategy by limiting their distribution to a few select higher-end retailers in each region.

in the store. They can buy one scarf or leather jacket at a time or buy an outfit that works together. Finally, the store provides a salesperson to help customers coordinate their outfits and a tailor to make the whole thing fit perfectly.

When choosing retail partners, manufacturers look at the basic channel structure, where their target customers expect to find the products, channel member characteristics, and distribution intensity.

Channel Structure

The level of difficulty a manufacturer experiences in getting retailers to purchase its products is determined by the degree to which the channel is vertically integrated, as described in Chapter 16; the degree to which the manufacturer has a strong brand or is otherwise desirable in the market; and the relative power of the manufacturer and retailer.

Scenario 1 represents a corporate vertical marketing system. Because M-A-C is made by Estée Lauder and operates its own stores, when the new mascara line gets introduced, the stores receive the new line automatically with no decision on the part of the retailer. In contrast, Revlon would have a much more difficult time getting CVS to buy a new mascara line, because these supply chain partners are not vertically integrated.

When an established firm like Coach enters a new market with men's leather goods, apparel, gifts, shoes, and other accessories, as is the case in Scenario 2, it cannot place the products with any retailer. It must determine where its customers would expect to find these products and then use its established relationships with women's handbag buyers, the power of its brand, and its overall reputation to leverage its position in this new product area.

Eva (Scenario 3) would have an even more difficult time convincing a retailer to buy and sell her green cosmetics line, because she lacks power in the marketplace—she is small, and her brand is unknown. She would have trouble getting buyers to see her, let alone consider her line. She might face relatively high slotting allowances (Chapter 15) just to get space on retailers' shelves. But like Coach in Scenario 2, Eva should consider where the end customer expects to find her products, as well as some important retailer characteristics.

Customer Expectations

Retailers should also know customer preferences regarding manufacturers. Manufacturers, in contrast, need to know where their target market customers expect to find their products and those of their competitors. As we see in the hypothetical example in Exhibit 17.2, Coach currently sells handbags at stores such as Dillard's, Neiman Marcus, and Marshall's, as well as in its own stores (orange arrows). Its competitor Cole Haan sells at Dillard's and Neiman Marcus (green arrows). A survey of male Coach customers shows that they would expect to find its products at Saks Fifth Avenue, Dillard's, Neiman Marcus, and its own stores (blue box). On the basis of this information, Coach decides to try selling at Saks' Fifth Avenue but to stop selling at Marshall's, to better meet customers' expectations.

Customers generally expect to find certain products at some stores but not at others. For example, Estée Lauder would not choose

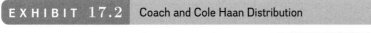

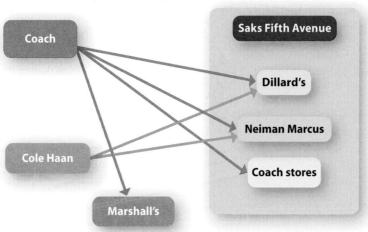

EXHIBIT 17.2 Coach and Cole Haan Distribution

to sell to CVS or Dollar General because its customers would not expect to shop at those stores for high-end cosmetics like Estée Lauder's. Instead, CVS might carry less expensive cosmetic brands, like Revlon and Maybelline, and bargain close-outs probably appear at Dollar General. But male Coach customers definitely expect to find the brand's clothing offerings at major department stores and at Coach stores.

Channel Member Characteristics

Several factors pertaining to the channel members themselves help determine the channel structure. Generally, the larger and more sophisticated the channel member, the less likely that it will use supply chain intermediaries. Eva will probably use a group of independent salespeople to help sell her line of green cosmetics, whereas a large manufacturer like Estée Lauder will use its own sales force that already has existing relationships in the industry. In the same way, an independent grocery store might buy merchandise from a wholesaler, but Walmart, the world's largest grocer, only buys directly from the manufacturer. Larger firms often find that by performing the channel functions themselves, they can gain more control, be more efficient, and save money.

Distribution Intensity

When setting up distribution for the first time, as is the case with Eva's green cosmetics (Scenario 3), or introducing a new product line, as is the case with Coach for men (Scenario 2), firms decide the appropriate level of **distribution intensity**—the number of channel members to use at each level of the marketing channel. Distribution intensity commonly is divided into three levels: intensive, exclusive, and selective.

LO3 List the three levels of distribution intensity.

Intensive Distribution An **intensive distribution** strategy is designed to place products in as many outlets as possible. Most consumer packaged goods companies, such as Pepsi, Procter & Gamble, Kraft, and other nationally branded products found in grocery and discount stores, strive for and often achieve intensive distribution. Pepsi wants its product available everywhere—grocery stores, convenience stores, restaurants, and vending machines. The more exposure the products get, the more they sell.

Exclusive Distribution Manufacturers also might use an **exclusive distribution** policy by granting exclusive geographic territories to one or very few retail customers so no other retailers in the territory can sell a particular brand. Exclusive distribution can benefit manufacturers by assuring them that the most appropriate retailers represent their products. Luxury goods firms such as Coach limit distribution to a few select, higher-end retailers in each region. The company believes that selling its products to full-line discount stores or off-price retailers would weaken its image.

When supply is limited or a firm is just starting out, providing an exclusive territory to one retailer or retail chain helps ensure enough inventory to provide the buying public an adequate selection. By granting exclusive territories, Eva guarantees her retailers will have an adequate supply of her green cosmetics. This guarantee gives these retailers a strong incentive to market her products. The retailers that Eva uses know there will be no competing retailers to cut prices, so their profit margins are protected. This knowledge gives them an incentive to carry more inventory and use extra advertising, personal selling, and sales promotions.

Selective Distribution Between the intensive and exclusive distribution strategies lies **selective distribution**, which relies on a few selected retail customers in a territory to sell products. Like exclusive distribution, selective distribution helps a seller maintain a particular image and control the flow of merchandise into an area. These advantages make this approach attractive to many shopping goods manufacturers. Recall that shopping goods are those products for which consumers are willing to spend time comparing alternatives, such as most apparel items, home items like branded pots and pans or sheets and towels, branded hardware and tools, and consumer electronics. Retailers still have a strong incentive to sell the products but not to the same extent as if they had an exclusive territory.

As we noted in Chapter 16, like any large complicated system, a marketing channel is difficult to manage. Whether the balance of power rests with large retailers like Walmart or with large manufacturers like Procter & Gamble, channel members benefit by working together to develop and implement their channel strategy. In the next section, we explore the different types of retailers with an eye toward which would be most appropriate for each of our scenarios: M-A-C Cosmetics, Coach's products for men, and Eva's new line of environmentally friendly cosmetics.

CHECK YOURSELF

1. What issues should manufacturers consider when choosing retail partners?
2. What are the differences among intensive, exclusive, and selective levels of distribution intensity?

LO4 Describe the various types of retailers.

IDENTIFY TYPES OF RETAILERS

At first glance, identifying the types of retailers that Coach and Eva may wish to pursue when attempting to place their new lines seems straightforward. But the choice is not always easy. Manufacturers need to understand the general characteristics of different types of retailers to determine the best channels for their product. The characteristics of a retailer that are important to a food manufacturer may be quite different than those considered valuable by a cosmetics manufacturer. In the next few sections, we examine the various types of retailers, identify some major players, and discuss some of the issues facing each type (Exhibit 17.3).

EXHIBIT 17.3 Types of Retailers

Food	General merchandise		Service
Supermarket	Full-line discount	Specialty	Auto rental
Supercenter	Category specialist	Department	Health spa
Convenience	Drug	Off-price	Vision center
Warehouse club		Extreme value	Bank

Food Retailers

The food retailing landscape is changing dramatically. Twenty years ago, consumers primarily purchased food at conventional supermarkets. Now conventional supermarkets account for slightly more than half of food sales (not including restaurants). Bankruptcies have closed the doors of many supermarket chains and independent franchises.[10] The fastest growing sectors of the food retail market are supercenters, warehouse clubs, convenience stores, and extreme value food retailers.[11] While full-line discount stores like Walmart and warehouse clubs like Costco are offering more food items, traditional supermarkets are carrying more nonfood items. Many supermarkets offer pharmacies, health care clinics, photo processing centers, banks, and cafés.

The world's largest food retailer, Walmart, has more than $310 billion in sales of supermarket-type merchandise, followed by Carrefour (France), Metro Group (Germany), Tesco (U.K.), Schwartz Group (Germany), and Kroger (U.S.).[12]

Supermarkets A **conventional supermarket** is a self-service retail food store offering groceries, meat, and produce with limited sales of nonfood items, such as health and beauty aids and general merchandise.[13] Perishables including meat, produce, baked goods, and dairy account for approximately 50 percent of supermarket sales and typically have higher margins than packaged goods.[14]

Conventional supermarkets carry about 30,000 individual items or **stock keeping units (SKUs)**. An SKU represents a unique inventory item. **Limited assortment supermarkets** or **extreme value food retailers** such as Save-A-Lot and ALDI stock only 2,000 SKUs.[15] Rather than carry 20 brands of laundry detergent, limited assortment stores offer one or two brands and sizes, one of which is a store brand. By trimming costs, limited assortment supermarkets can offer merchandise at 40 percent lower prices than conventional supermarkets.[16]

Conventional supermarkets thus are under substantial competitive pressure from other types of food retailers, full-line discount chains, supercenters, warehouse clubs, extreme value retailers, convenience stores, online grocers, and restaurants.

Thus to compete successfully against intrusions by other food retailing formats, conventional supermarkets have begun to differentiate their offerings by (1) emphasizing fresh, locally sourced perishables; (2) targeting health-conscious and ethnic consumers with new lines of natural, organic, or culture-specific items; (3) offering more private-label brands; and (4) providing a better in-store experience with a better overall atmosphere, demonstrations, and fun, as Adding Value 17.1 describes.

Adding Value 17.1   How I Met . . . Your Dinner[17]

The supermarket as a social scene has long been a punch line in sitcoms and films, usually involving a nervous new dater knocking over the pyramid of tomatoes, or something similar. But date night at the supermarket has taken on new meaning in the modern era of experience marketing.

As we have noted, conventional supermarkets face extreme pressures on all sides, including price pressures from discount chains (e.g., Walmart, Aldi) and quality pressures from specialty retailers (e.g., Fresh Market, Whole Foods). To attract customers with something different, many stores encourage shoppers to come in, linger, and perhaps meet someone new in the aisles. At weekly socials hosted by some chains, the loudspeakers switch from playing background instrumentals to piping out romantic Luther Vandross and Al Green tunes. Tables set up in common areas encourage prospective dates to get to know each other. The mood is both social and safe, because customers can always claim they are simply making a visit to their local supermarket.

But a lot of supermarket shoppers already have partners, and children too. For them, the live music played on Friday nights provides an excuse to participate in a convenient, efficient date night. Couples can get their shopping done for the week while also enjoying a night out, where they sit in the store's café, share a takeout meal from the deli counter, and listen to the band play.

Thus savvy supermarket chains are reconsidering their design and strategy. Rather than just a place to pick up household products and milk, the store can become "a gathering place for customers to come in and let us entertain them."

To better compete with other food retailing formats, some conventional supermarkets host social events.

Supercenters Supercenters are large stores (185,000 square feet) that combine a supermarket with a full-line discount store. Walmart operates more than 3,000 supercenters in the United States,[18] accounting for the vast majority of total supercenter sales—far outpacing its competitors Meijer, SuperTarget (Target), Fred Meyer (Kroger Co.), and Super Kmart Center (Sears Holding). By offering broad assortments of grocery and general merchandise products under one roof, supercenters provide a one-stop shopping convenience to customers.

Warehouse Clubs Warehouse clubs are large retailers (100,000–150,000 square feet) that offer a limited and irregular assortment of food and general merchandise, little service, and low prices to the general public and small businesses. The largest warehouse club chains are Costco, Sam's Club (Walmart), and BJ's Wholesale Club (operating only on the east coast of the United States). Customers are attracted to these stores because they can stock up on large packs of basics like paper towels, mega-sized packaged groceries such as a quart of ketchup, best-selling books and CDs, fresh meat and produce, and an unpredictable assortment of upscale merchandise and services (e.g., jewelry, electronics, home décor) at lower prices than are available at other retail stores. Typically, members pay an annual fee of around $50, which amounts to significant additional income for the chains.

Although both Coach for Men and Eva's products could be sold in warehouse clubs, these retailers probably are not the best choices. Both product lines will have an upscale image, which is inconsistent with any warehouse club. If, however, either firm has overstock merchandise as a result of overestimating demand or underestimating returned merchandise from retailers, warehouse clubs are a potential outlet.

Convenience Stores Convenience stores provide a limited variety and assortment of merchandise at a convenient location in 3,000–5,000 square foot stores with speedy checkout. They are the modern version of the neighborhood mom-and-pop grocery/general store. Convenience stores enable consumers to make purchases quickly without having to search through a large store and wait in a lengthy checkout line. Convenience store assortments are limited in terms of depth and breadth, and they charge higher prices than supermarkets. Milk, eggs, and bread once represented the majority of their sales, but now most sales come from gasoline and cigarettes.

Convenience stores also face increased competition from other retail formats. In response to these competitive pressures, convenience stores are taking steps to decrease their dependency on gasoline sales by offering fresh food and healthy fast food, tailoring assortments to local markets, and making their stores even more convenient to shop. Finally, convenience stores are adding new services, such as financial service kiosks that give customers the opportunity to cash checks, pay bills, and buy prepaid telephone minutes, theater tickets, and gift cards.

General Merchandise Retailers

The major types of general merchandise retailers are department stores, full-line discount stores, specialty stores, category specialists, home improvement centers, off-price retailers, and extreme value retailers.

Department Stores **Department stores** are retailers that carry a broad variety and deep assortment, offer customer services, and organize their stores into distinct departments for displaying merchandise. The largest department store chains in the United States include Sears, Macy's, Kohl's, JCPenney, and Nordstrom.[19] Department stores would be an excellent retail channel for Coach for Men and Eva's new lines.

To compete and gain better traction among younger consumers, who generally favor smaller specialty stores,[20] many department stores are increasing the amount of exclusive and private-label merchandise they sell. For example, Macy's has introduced exclusive apparel and home lines from celebrities Donald Trump, Jessica Simpson and Martha Stewart.[21] In addition, department stores are becoming true multichannel retailers: At Macy's and Nordstrom, customers can buy or reserve products online, then pick them up in the store.

Full-Line Discount Stores **Full-line discount stores** are retailers that offer a broad variety of merchandise, limited service, and low prices. The largest full-line discount store chains are Walmart, Target, and Kmart (Sears Holding).

Although full-line discount stores typically might carry men's leather goods, accessories, and cosmetics, they are not good options for Coach for Men or Eva's new green cosmetics line. Customers do not expect higher-end products in full-line discount stores. Rather, they are looking for value prices on these items and are willing to compromise on quality or cachet.

Walmart accounts for approximately two-thirds of full-line discount store retail sales in the United States.[22] Target has experienced considerable growth because its stores offer fashionable merchandise at low prices in a pleasant shopping environment. The retailer has developed an image of "cheap chic" by offering limited-edition exclusive apparel and cosmetic lines.

Department stores like Macy's carry a broad variety and deep assortment, offer customer services, and organize their stores into distinct departments for displaying merchandise.

Social and Mobile Marketing 17.1   Buy, Play, and Sell, Wherever You Choose

To become the one-stop shop for video gamers, GameStop not only provides unique in-store experiences but also encourages online interactions by its customers, both among themselves and with its representatives. Gaming enthusiasts thus can hang out at the stores to compete in the latest version of the hottest game, or they can interact online.[23] In these social settings, video game players chat with other gamers, discover codes and tricks in the game, and find passwords that help them achieve higher levels of play.

In this entertainment category—the fastest growing overall—GameStop has continually achieved strong sales increases, including double-digit increases in same-store sales, through its GameStop, EB Games, Electronics Boutique, EBgames.com, and GameStop.com brands. Although the typical video gamer is a 37-year-old man, 72 percent of U.S. households actively participate in gaming, and 42 percent of gamers are women.[24]

A typical video game is used for approximately 80 hours, making it a great value on a cost per hour basis, especially compared with other forms of entertainment. Yet despite this value, new video games are relatively expensive, costing around $60. So GameStop sells used games and equipment

and grants customers credit for used games they trade in to the store. In addition, it has developed the GameStop Network online, which includes four sectors: Kongregate, Jolt, Impulse Driven, and GameStop.

On Kongregate, for example, players can access more than 50,000 free games that they play with others. There are varied ways to connect: chat rooms and forums, competitions in the games, and through the mobile app, Kongregate Arcade. By playing, users also can earn PowerUp Rewards points, which they can redeem on the other GameStop sites for access to paying games and other in-game benefits.[25] On Jolt, they can participate in a social gaming soccer league by joining the *Championship Manager: Rivals* series and providing the decisions for their chosen team.[26] Most of these options also have Facebook links, enabling friends to play through their pages.

Such tactics have made GameStop the largest multichannel video game retailer in the world and led to new innovations as well, such as Spawn Labs, its new streaming technology platform.[27] To get to the gamers, GameStop is ready to go anywhere they are.

Specialty Stores **Specialty stores** concentrate on a limited number of complementary merchandise categories. targeted toward very specific market segments by offering deep but narrow assortments and sales associate expertise. Although such shops are familiar in brick-and-mortar forms, more retailers also are expanding their online specialty profile as well, as Social and Mobile Marketing 17.1 describes.

Estée Lauder's M-A-C line of cosmetics sells in the company's own retail specialty stores, as well as in some department stores. Certain specialty stores would be excellent outlets for the new lines by Coach for Men and Eva. Customers likely expect to find Coach for Men leather goods and accessories in men's apparel or leather stores. Eva's line of green cosmetics would fit nicely in a cosmetics specialty store like Sephora.

Drugstores **Drugstores** are specialty stores that concentrate on pharmaceuticals and health and personal grooming merchandise. Prescription pharmaceuticals represent almost 70 percent of drugstore sales. The largest drugstore chains in the United States are CVS, Walgreens, and Rite Aid—three chains that account for about 38 percent of U.S. drugstore revenue.[28] In this concentrated industry, the top 50 chains also account for 70 percent of revenues.[29]

Although Estée Lauder's new line would not be consistent with the merchandise found in drugstores, Eva's green cosmetics may be a welcome addition. Some drugstores have recognized consumer demand for green products, even though Eva's cosmetics may be priced higher than its competitors. Eva must decide whether her high-end products will suffer a tarnished image if she sells them in drugstores or if drugstores could be a good channel for increasing her brand awareness.

Drugstores face competition from pharmacies in discount stores and pressure to reduce health care costs. The major drugstore chains are offering a wider

Superior Service 17.1 — Making New York a Little Friendlier[30]

At one point, Duane Reade, now a subsidiary of the Walgreen Company, had so fully embraced its minimalist approach to service that one blogger created an entire blog dedicated to hatred for the store, entitled "I Hate Duane Reade: Service from Hell." The stores had messy shelves and aisles and unfriendly employees.

So patrons entering the Duane Reade on Wall Street, near the New York Stock Exchange, must be shocked at what they find on display today: $10 manicures, a hair salon staffed by a dedicated beauty consultant, a juice bar, and sushi chefs, next to typical drugstore products. Medical questions can be answered by the doctor who works there. In this store, the top sellers are now sushi, fresh juice, and bananas—though customers have not changed completely, so rounding out the top five sellers are coffee and Marlboro cigarettes.

With its 256 stores in New York City, Duane Reade already has significant real estate advantages. If it can transform the shopping experience in most of its stores, similar to the way it has on Wall Street, its image seems destined to change as well.

It appears that the company has started paying closer attention to complaints, including those on popular blogs, and decided to change in response.

The change has not been simple though. In 2008, early remodeling efforts divided Duane Reade stores into three sections: "How I look," "How I feel," and "What I need." This strategy prompted a couple of new slogans: "New York living made easy" or "Your City. Your Drugstore."

Then after a host of operational miscues and challenges, it brought in the former president of the successful Canadian supermarket chain Loblaws, which is best known for its immensely successful private label, President's Choice. This high-end line was modeled after the offerings in European grocery stores and spans many product categories, from cookies to mobile phone service to pet insurance. Following this model, Duane Reade has developed a private-label line called Delish, and it hopes it can mimic the success of President's Choice as well. Thus far, the signs are good: Private-label sales at Duane Reade doubled from 2008 to 2010.

assortment of merchandise, as Superior Service 17.1 recognizes. Drugstores also are expanding their role as a fill-in trip destination by carrying products typically found in convenience and grocery stores including fresh produce. The jury is still out, however, regarding how successful this initiative will be because drugstore prices on these items are at par with convenience stores—about 25 percent higher than grocery stores.[31]

Category Specialists Category specialists are big box retailers or category killers that offer a narrow but deep assortment of merchandise. Most category specialists use a predominantly self-service approach, but they offer assistance to customers in some areas of the stores. For example, the office supply store Staples has a warehouse atmosphere with cartons of copy paper stacked on pallets, plus equipment in boxes on shelves. But in some departments, such as computers or electronics and other high-tech products, salespeople staff the display area to answer questions and make suggestions.

By offering a complete assortment in a category at somewhat lower prices than their competition, category specialists can "kill" a category of merchandise for other retailers, which is why they are frequently called category killers. Using their category dominance, these retailers exploit their buying power to negotiate low prices.

Extreme Value Retailers Extreme value retailers are small, full-line discount stores that offer a limited merchandise assortment at very low prices. The largest extreme value retailers are Dollar General and Family Dollar Stores.

Like limited assortment food retailers, extreme value retailers reduce costs and maintain low prices by buying opportunistically from manufacturers with excess merchandise, offering a limited assortment, and operating in low-rent locations. They offer a broad but shallow assortment of household goods, health and beauty aids, and groceries.

Many value retailers target low-income consumers, whose shopping behavior differs from that of typical discount store or warehouse club customers. Although

Dollar General is one of the United States' largest extreme value retailers. It has small full-line discount stores that offer a limited assortment at very low prices.

The outlet mall in San Marco, Texas, has tenants such as Neiman Marcus Last Call, Zegna, Escada, and Salvatore Ferragamo.

these consumers might demand well-known national brands, they often cannot afford to buy large-sized packages. So vendors such as Procter & Gamble often create special, smaller packages for extreme value retailers, often using the reverse innovation approaches we discussed in Chapter 8. Also, higher-income consumers are increasingly patronizing these stores for the thrill of the hunt. Some shoppers regard the extreme value retailers as an opportunity to find some hidden treasure among the household staples.

Extreme value retailers would not be an obvious consumer choice for Coach for Men or Eva's new lines, because these stores are not consistent with the brands' image. But if these manufacturers find themselves in an overstock situation, they could utilize these retailers to reduce inventory. For the same reason, they might use off-price retailers.

Off-Price Retailers Off-price retailers offer an inconsistent assortment of brand name merchandise at a significant discount from the manufacturer's suggested retail price (MSRP). In today's market, these off-price retailers may be brick-and-mortar stores, online outlets, or a combination of both. America's largest off-price retail chains are TJX Companies (which operates TJMaxx, Marshalls, Winners [Canada], HomeGoods, AJWright, and HomeSense [Canada]), Ross Stores, Burlington Coat Factory, Big Lots Inc., Overstock.com, and Bluefly.com.

To be able to sell at prices 20–60 percent lower than the MSRP,[32] most merchandise is bought opportunistically from manufacturers or other retailers with excess inventory at the end of the season. Therefore, customers cannot be confident that the same merchandise or even type of merchandise will be available each time they visit a store or website. The discounts off-price retailers receive from manufacturers reflect what they do not do as well: They do not ask suppliers to help them pay for advertising, make them take back unsold merchandise, charge them for markdowns, or ask them to delay payments.

Services Retailers

The retail firms discussed in the previous sections sell products to consumers.[33] However, **services retailers**, or firms that primarily sell services rather than merchandise, are a large and growing part of

Dry cleaners are retailers that provide services instead of products.

the retail industry. Consider a typical Saturday: After a bagel and cup of coffee at a nearby Peet's Coffee and Tea, you go to the laundromat to wash and dry your clothes, drop a suit off at a dry cleaner, have a prescription filled at a CVS drugstore, and make your way to Jiffy Lube to have your car's oil changed. In a hurry, you drive through a Burger King so you can eat lunch quickly and be on time for your haircut at Supercuts. By midafternoon, you're ready for a workout at your health club. After stopping at home for a change of clothes, you're off to dinner, a movie, and dancing with a friend. Finally, you end your day with a café latte at Starbucks, having interacted with 10 different services retailers during the day.

There are a wide variety of services retailers, along with some national companies that provide these services. These companies are retailers because they sell goods and services to consumers. However, some are not just retailers. For example, airlines, banks, hotels, and insurance and express mail companies sell their services to businesses as well as consumers.

Organizations such as banks, hospitals, health spas, legal clinics, entertainment firms, and universities that offer services to consumers traditionally have not considered themselves retailers. Yet due to increased competition, these organizations are adopting retailing principles to attract customers and satisfy their needs.

Several trends suggest considerable future growth in services retailing. For example, the aging population will increase demand for health care services. Younger people are also spending more time and money on health and fitness. Busy parents in two-income families are willing to pay to have their homes cleaned, lawns maintained, clothes washed and pressed, and meals prepared so they can spend more time with their families.

Now that we've explored the types of stores, we can examine how manufacturers and retailers coordinate their retail strategy using the four Ps.

CHECK YOURSELF

1. What strategies distinguish the different types of food retailers?
2. What strategies distinguish the different types of general merchandise retailers?
3. Are organizations that provide services to consumers retailers?

L05 Describe the components of a retail strategy.

DEVELOPING A RETAIL STRATEGY USING THE FOUR PS

Like other marketers, retailers perform important functions that increase the value of the products and services they sell to consumers. We now examine these functions, classified into the four Ps: product, price, promotion, and place.

Material Girl is a Macy's exclusive co-brand developed by Madonna and her daughter Lourdes.

Product

A typical grocery store carries 30,000 to 40,000 different items; a regional department store might carry as many as 100,000. Providing the right mix of merchandise and services that satisfies the needs of the target market is one of retailers' most fundamental activities. Offering assortments gives customers a choice. To reduce transportation costs and handling, manufacturers typically ship cases of merchandise, such as cartons of mascara or boxes of leather jackets, to retailers. Because customers generally do not want or need to buy more than one of the same item, retailers break up the cases and sell customers the smaller quantities they desire.

Manufacturers don't like to store inventory because their factories and warehouses are typically not available or attractive shopping venues. Consumers don't want to purchase more than they need because storage consumes space. Neither group likes keeping inventory that isn't being used, because doing so ties up money that could be used for something else. Retailers thus provide, in addition to other values to both manufacturers and customers, a storage function, although many retailers are beginning to push their suppliers to hold the inventory until they need it. (Recall our discussion of JIT inventory systems in Chapter 16.)

It is difficult for retailers to distinguish themselves from their competitors through the merchandise they carry because competitors can purchase and sell many of the same popular brands. Thus, many retailers have developed private-label brands (also called store brands), which are products developed and marketed by a retailer and available only from that retailer. For example, if you want a Giani Bernini leather hand bag, you have to go to Macy's.

Retailers often work together with their suppliers to develop an exclusive co-brand. An **exclusive co-brand** is a brand that is developed by a national brand vendor, often in conjunction with a retailer, and is sold exclusively by the retailer. So, for example, Karl Lagerfeld, the internationally famous designer known for working with luxury fashion houses such as Chanel and Fendi, is collaborating with Macy's to design a line aimed at 18- to 30-year-olds who want to move beyond the fast fashion offered by Zara, H&M, Mango, and Forever 21 but cannot quite afford the prices that most designers charge.[34] The Lagerfeld collection at Macy's includes around 45 items that are similar to his more expensive designs but produced with less expensive fabrics and fewer details.

Exclusive co-brands offer a double benefit: They are available at only one retailer, and they provide name recognition similar to that of a national brand. The disadvantage of exclusive co-brands, from the manufacturer's perspective, is that they can be sold by only one retailer, and therefore, the manufacturer's market is limited. From the retailer's perspective, the disadvantage is that it has to share its profits with the national brand manufacturer, whereas with a private-label brand, it does not.

Price

Price helps define the value of both the merchandise and the service, and the general price range of a particular store helps define its image. Although both Saks Fifth Avenue and JCPenney are department stores, their images could not be more different. Thus, when Coach considers which of these firms is most appropriate for its new line for men, it must keep customers' perceived images of these retailers' price–quality relationship in mind. The company does not, for instance, want to attempt to sell its new line at JCPenney if it is positioning the line with a relatively high price.

Price must always be aligned with the other elements of a retailer's strategy: product, promotion, and place. A customer would not expect to pay $600 for a Coach for Men briefcase at a JCPenney store, but she might question the briefcase's quality if its price is significantly less than $600 at Neiman Marcus. As we discovered in Chapters 14 and 15, there is much more to pricing than simply adding a markup onto a product's cost. Manufacturers must consider at what price they will sell the product to retailers so that both the manufacturer and the retailer can make a reasonable profit. At the same time, both the manufacturer and the retailer are concerned about what the customer is willing and expecting to pay.

Given the price of a Coach bag, would you expect to find it in Saks Fifth Avenue or JCPenney?

Promotion

Retailers and manufacturers know that good promotion, both within the retail environments and in the media, can mean the difference between flat sales and a growing consumer base. Advertising in traditional media such as newspapers, magazines, and television continues to be important to get customers into stores. Increasingly, electronic communications are being used for promotions as well. Some traditional approaches, such as direct mail, are being reevaluated by retailers, but many are still finding value in sending catalogs to customers and selected mailing lists. Companies also offer real-time promotions on their websites. For example, CVS.com contains in-store and online coupons that customers can use immediately on the Web site or print to use in the store. Coupons.com similarly offers an array of promotions for many grocery store items. Customers can even follow this vendor on Twitter@Coupons to find even more savings opportunities.

Technology is thus expanding the ways in which retailers can reach customers with their promotional message. For example, customers can access a retailer's Internet site using a variety of devices, ranging from a computer to a mobile phone. Due to the rapid growth of domestic and international broadband access through mobile devices, retailers are investing in **mobile commerce (M-commerce)**— product and service purchases through mobile devices. However, the typical retailer's website is not designed to accommodate a mobile device's small screen and slower download speeds. Various firms, including ESPN, therefore have developed special sites for users to access through mobile devices. In addition, retailers have created specialized applications that enable mobile device users to shop or obtain more merchandise information. Technology innovations will continue to provide growing opportunities for new forms of promotion. Social and Mobile Marketing 17.2 describes the value of mobile applications for customers.

A coordinated effort between the manufacturer and retailer helps guarantee that the customer receives a cohesive message and that both entities maintain their image. For example, Coach for Men might work with its most important retailers to develop advertising and point-of-sale signs. It may even help defray the costs of advertising by paying all or a portion of the advertising's production and media costs, an agreement called **cooperative (co-op) advertising**.

Consumers can access retailers' coupons from their mobile devices.

Social and Mobile Marketing 17.2   Mobile Apps Meet the Physical World[35]

Mobile applications that drive customers into the stores have great value for retailers. But simple gimmicks cannot hold consumers' attention for long—and may even annoy them—such that their retention rate is poor, regardless of the number of downloads. Instead, customers like using applications that are fun, convenient, and helpful in terms of making their tasks easier.

Walgreens' successful mobile application has a simple primary goal: improve convenience for customers. Before customers even get in their cars to go to the store, they can order a prescription refill. The application also includes a feature called "Refill by Scan" that lets customers scan their medication's bar code with their smartphone camera to order their refill. Customers then can change their store pickup locations if needed and select the pickup date and time that is convenient for them. When the prescription is filled, the store sends the customer a text alert. Thus the application drives traffic to the stores by helping them get through the stores more efficiently. More than 1 million people already have opted in for such alerts.

Other retailers turn to Shopkick, a location-based application that partners with the retailers to encourage customers

to check in at the stores by rewarding them with points and coupons. Unlike Foursquare or other location-based applications which estimate your location within 1000 feet, Shopkick communicates with a specific sensor in each store, ensuring you are actually in the store. Customers automatically receive points or "kickbucks" when they enter the store, and retailers know exactly where the customer is. To encourage customers to browse, various location hotspots grant them additional kickbucks when they enter the target area, whether the electronics department or housewares.

The Shopkick app encourages customers to check in at stores by rewarding them with points and coupons.

Some of the biggest names in retailing—including Target, Best Buy, Macy's, Crate & Barrel, and American Eagle—thus pay Shopkick a fee for each customer the application gets inside their doors. Some of that fee goes back to the customer: They earn 75 kickbucks just by entering and can earn more if they purchase products in the store (875 kickbucks are equivalent to a $25 gift certificate). Then they can instantly redeem their kickbucks by downloading the rewards to their smartphones and presenting the downloaded information at the register.

Walgreen's phone app, "Refill by scan," lets customers scan their prescription bar code with their smartphone camera to order their refill.

Store credit cards and gift cards are more subtle forms of promotion that also facilitate shopping. Retailers might offer pricing promotions—such as coupons, rebates, in-store or online discounts, or perhaps buy-one-get-one-free offers—to attract consumers and stimulate sales. These promotions play a very important role in driving traffic to retail locations, increasing average purchase size, and creating opportunities for repeat purchases. But retail promotions also are valuable to customers; they inform customers about what is new and available and how much it costs.

Another type of promotion occurs inside the store, where retailers use displays and signs, placed at the point of purchase (POP) or in strategic areas such as the end of aisles, to inform customers and stimulate purchases of the featured products.

In addition to traditional forms of promotion, many retailers are devoting more resources to their overall retail environment as a means to promote and showcase what the store has to offer. These promotions may take the form of recognizable approaches, such as in-store and window displays, or they may be entirely new experiences designed to help retailers draw customers and add value to the shopping experience. Bass Pro Shops Outdoor World in Lawrenceville, Georgia, offers a

30,000-gallon aquarium stocked with fish for casting demonstrations, an indoor archery range, and a 43-foot climbing wall. These features enhance customers' visual experiences, provide them with educational information, and enhance the store's sales potential by enabling customers to "try before they buy." In addition to adding fun to the shopping experience, these activities help offset the current drop in brick-and-mortar customers engendered by online shopping.

A variety of factors influence whether customers will actually buy once they are in the store. Some of these factors are quite subtle. Consumers' perceptions of value and their subsequent patronage are heavily influenced by their perceptions of the store's "look and feel." Music, color, scent, aisle size, lighting, the availability of seating, and crowding can also significantly affect the overall shopping experience.[36] Therefore, the extent to which stores offer a more pleasant shopping experience fosters a better mood, resulting in greater spending.

Consider the funky C. Wonder emporium for example. This 72,000-square-foot megastore is divided into various "nooks," each with its own personality or feel, including English Town House, Vail Cabin, Palm Springs Modern, and Hollywood Regency. The separate sectors help customers navigate through the vast amount of merchandise available. To grant them control over their experience, C. Wonder's fitting rooms also come equipped with control panels, such that people trying on items can adjust the type and volume of music played, as well as the lighting, to suit their preferences.[37]

Bass Pro Shops Outdoor World in Lawrenceville, Georgia, uses its 43-foot climbing wall as a way to promote its store.

Personal selling and customer service representatives are also part of the overall promotional package. Retailers must provide services that make it easier to buy and use products, and retail associates—whether in the store, on the phone, or on the Internet—provide customers with information about product characteristics and availability. These individuals can also facilitate the sale of products or services that consumers perceive as complicated, risky, or expensive, such as an air conditioning unit, a computer, or a diamond ring. Manufacturers can play an important role in getting retail sales and service associates prepared to sell their products. Eva thus could conduct seminars or Webinars about how to use and sell her new line of green cosmetics and supply printed educational materials to sales associates. Last but not least, sales reps handle the sales transactions.

In some retail firms, salesperson and customer service functions are being augmented, or even replaced, by technology in the form of in-store kiosks, the Internet, or self-checkout lanes. At C. Wonder, microchips embedded in the sales tags of every item help the sales staff keep track of where the merchandise is in the store. They also can check out customers anywhere in the store, using handheld registers, which eliminates the need for customers to head to the checkout counter before they leave.[38]

Traditionally, retailers treated all their customers the same. Today, the most successful retailers concentrate on providing more value to their best customers. The knowledge retailers gain from their store personnel, the Internet browsing and buying activities of customers, and the data they collect on customer shopping habits can be used in customer relationship management (CRM). Using this information, retailers may modify product, price, and/or promotion to attempt to increase their **share of wallet**—the percentage of the customer's purchases made from that particular retailer. For instance, multichannel retailers use consumer information collected from the customers' Internet browsing and buying behavior to send dedicated e-mails to customers promoting specific products or services. Retailers also may offer special discounts to good customers to help them become even more loyal.

Place

Retailers already have realized that convenience is a key ingredient to success, and an important aspect of this success is convenient locations.[39] As the old cliché

To make their locations more convenient, Walgreens has some free-standing stores, not connected to other retailers, so the stores can offer a drive-up window for customers to pick up their prescriptions.

claims, the three most important things in retailing are "location, location, location." Many customers choose stores on the basis of where they are located, which makes great locations a competitive advantage that few rivals can duplicate. For instance, once Starbucks saturates a market by opening in the best locations, Peet's will have difficulty breaking into that same market—where would it put its stores?

In pursuit of better and better locations, retailers are experimenting with different options to reach their target markets. Walgreens has free-standing stores, unconnected to other retailers, so the stores can offer a drive-up window for customers to pick up their prescriptions. Other stores, like Brookstone, have opened stores where they have a captive market—airports. Walmart, Staples, and others are opening smaller stores in urban location to better serve those markets.

LO6 Identify the benefits of stores.

BENEFITS OF STORES FOR CONSUMERS

In this section, we explore the relative advantages of the most traditional retail channels, the bricks-and-mortar store, from consumers' perspective. In the following section, we examine how the addition of the Internet channel has added value to retailers' ability to satisfy their customers' needs.

Browsing Shoppers often have only a general sense of what they want (e.g., a sweater, something for dinner, a gift) but don't know the specific item they want.

At LegoLand in Minneapolis' Mall of America, customers can browse, touch, and feel the product, enjoy personal service, be entertained, and interact with others.

They go to a store to see what is available before making their final decision about what to buy. Although some consumers surf the Web and look through catalogs for ideas, many still prefer browsing in stores. Some also employ both approaches, getting a sense of what's available through catalogs or the Internet, and then going to the store to try on apparel or view the actual object.

Touching and Feeling Products Perhaps the greatest benefit offered by stores is the opportunity for customers to use all five of their senses—touch, smell, taste, vision, and hearing—to examine products.

Personal Service Sales associates have the capability to provide meaningful, personalized information. Salespeople can be particularly helpful when purchasing a complicated product, like consumer electronics, or something the customer doesn't know much about, like raw Japanese selvedge denim jeans.

Cash and Credit Payment Stores are the only channel that accepts cash payments. Some customers prefer to pay with cash because it is easy, resolves the transaction immediately, and does not result in potential interest payments. And, of course, some people don't have a credit card. Some customers also prefer to use their credit card or debit card in person rather than send the payment information electronically via the Internet.

Entertainment and Social Experience In-store shopping can be a stimulating experience for some people, providing a break in their daily routine and enabling them to interact with friends.

Immediate Gratification Stores have the advantage of allowing customers to get the merchandise immediately after paying for it.

Risk Reduction When customers purchase merchandise in stores, the physical presence of the store reduces their perceived risk of buying and increases their confidence that any problems with the merchandise will be corrected.

BENEFITS OF THE INTERNET AND MULTICHANNEL RETAILING

LO7 Identify the benefits of multichannel retailing.

In the previous section, we detailed the relative benefits of stores from the consumers' perspective. In this section, we examine how the addition of the Internet channel to traditional store-based retailers has improved their ability to serve their customers and build a competitive advantage in several ways.

First, the addition of an Internet channel has the potential to offer a greater selection of products. Second, an Internet channel enables retailers to provide customers with more personalized information about products and services. Third, it offers sellers the unique opportunity to collect information about consumer shopping behavior—information that they can use to improve the shopping experience across all channels. Fourth, the Internet channel allows sellers to enter new markets economically.

Deeper and Broader Selection

One benefit of adding the Internet channel is the vast number of alternatives retailers can make available to consumers without crowding their aisles or increasing their square footage. Stores and catalogs are limited by their size. By shopping on the Internet, consumers can easily "visit" and select merchandise from a broader array of retailers. Individual retailers' websites typically offer deeper assortments of merchandise (more colors, brands, and sizes) than are available in stores or catalogs. This expanded offering enables them to satisfy consumer demand for less popular styles, colors, or sizes. Many retailers also offer a broader assortment (more categories) on their websites. Staples.com, for instance, offers soft drinks and cleaning supplies, which are not available in stores, so that its business customers will view it as a one-stop shop.

Personalization

Another benefit of adding the Internet channel is the ability to personalize promotions and services economically, including heightened service or individualized offerings.

Personalized Customer Service Traditional Internet channel approaches for responding to customer questions—such as FAQ (frequently asked questions) pages and offering an 800 number or e-mail address to ask questions—often do not provide the timely information customers are seeking. To improve customer service from an electronic channel, many firms offer live **online chats**, so that customers can click a button at any time and participate in an instant messaging conversation with a customer service representative. This technology also enables firms to send a proactive chat invitation automatically to customers on the site. At Bluefly.com, for example, if a visitor searches for more than three items in

At Bluefly.com, customers can have an instant messaging, e-mail, or voice conversation with a customer service representative.

Ethical and Societal Dilemma 17.1   Protecting Customer Privacy

If you knew someone was following you, tracking your footsteps or peering through your windows, you'd probably feel your privacy was being violated. Yet some Internet retailers are tracking consumers' virtual footprints and observing browsing, shopping, and spending habits. Simultaneously, these retailers are going to great lengths to protect consumer privacy by using advanced security technology to protect personal and financial information for online shoppers. So how do we define privacy in an online environment, and how do we know when privacy has been violated?

This subject comes under extensive debate, because not every individual, culture, or country defines personal privacy the same way. Individuals, for example, may feel that their personal information belongs to them and should not be shared without permission. Alumni associations, in contrast, may feel they have a right to know the whereabouts of their past graduates for fundraising and networking purposes.

Retailers find gathering and analyzing shoppers' online habits can be profitable to them. Cookies can help collect data on how customers navigate through a website, monitoring each mouse click to track characteristics of the products customers considered and what products customers looked at but did not buy.[40] Collecting such information from store or catalog shoppers would be difficult; someone would have to follow customers around the store or observe them browsing catalog pages. One e-commerce marketing company found that consumers are 50 percent more likely to open and click through a targeted e-mail than a generic one and that targeted e-mails generate 50 percent more revenue than generic e-mails.[41] Although some consumers appreciate getting these e-mails, these and similar practices are alarming to privacy and

consumer groups and objectionable to many shoppers. The concerns stem more from the possibility of misuse of personal information than from the way information is currently used.

The situation grows more complicated when viewed on a global scale, because privacy laws differ in other countries. The European Union (EU) and other countries have more stringent consumer privacy laws than does the United States. The EU's policy is that consumers must specifically consent to receiving direct marketing e-mails. This consent is referred to as an opt in. In contrast, personal information in the United States is generally viewed as being in the public domain, and retailers can direct market to consumers unless the consumers explicitly tell retailers not to use their personal information—they must opt out. In both the United States and the EU, direct marketing e-mails must contain opt out information.[42]

The Federal Trade Commission (FTC) continues to develop guidelines that protect consumer privacy online. Suggested practices recommend informing consumers of information collection and use, allowing consumers to opt in or opt out and confirm the accuracy of information, and protecting personal information from theft or tampering. The FTC gives special protection to children under the Children's Online Privacy Protection Act (COPPA). It mandates that commercial websites must secure a parent's permission prior to collecting information from a child under 13 years of age.[43]

However, compliance with guidelines for adult sites is voluntary and therefore often ignored. Consumer advocacy groups are pushing to make the guidelines mandatory. In response, an increasing number of retailers are disclosing their information-gathering practices and allowing consumers to opt in or out.

---

five minutes, thereby demonstrating more than a passing interest, Bluefly will display a pop-up window with a friendly face offering help.[44]

Personalized Offering The interactive nature of the Internet also provides an opportunity for retailers to personalize their offerings for each of their customers, based on customers' behavior. Just as a well-trained salesperson would make recommendations to customers prior to checkout, an interactive webpage can make suggestions to the shopper about items that he or she might like to see based on previous purchases, what other customers who purchased the same item purchased, or common web viewing behavior.

Some multichannel retailers are able to personalize promotions and Internet homepages on the basis of several attributes tied to the shopper's current or previous web sessions, such as the time of day, time zone as determined by a computer's Internet address, and assumed gender.[45] However, some consumers worry about this ability to collect information about purchase histories, personal information, and search behavior on the Internet. How will this information be used in the future? Will it be sold to other firms, or will the consumer receive unwanted promotional materials online or in the mail? To answer these questions, consider Ethical and Societal Dilemma 17.1.

Expand Market Presence

The market for customers that shop in stores is typically limited to consumers living in proximity to those stores. The market for catalogs is limited by the high cost

Adding Value 17.2   Personalization in the Warehouse[46]

Walmart and its wholesale club, Sam's Club, are known best for their mass marketing approaches. They offer something for everyone. But when customers purchase a membership in Sam's Club's eValues program, they also receive customized, targeted offers from the retailer. These "smart" discounts are more appealing than generic promotional campaigns, because they pertain specifically to items the customer already has expressed interest in through past purchases.

Sam's Club relies on sophisticated data mining techniques to collect information from every transaction. This information not only enables it to target customers better but also supports complex evaluations of the best products to carry and which to eliminate.

In turn, Sam's Club develops predictive analytics that estimate what any particular customer will buy in the future. As a simple example, imagine a household that buys newborn baby diapers. During that shopping trip, these customers might receive a coupon for wipes, to encourage immediate purchases. Then later, the family might receive a coupon for the next larger diaper size, to encourage future purchase. Each customer's offers get loaded onto his or her member card, so there is no need to remember to bring discount coupons on the shopping trip.

Sam's Club designates its offers into three categories and ensures that customers receive promotions in each: rewards, incentives for products the customer normally purchases, and cross-category offers for items the customer has never bought. The response rates for the targeted items are impressive. Whereas mass marketing offers usually yield a 1–2 percent response rate and segmented offers increase that rate to 5–6 percent, Sam's Club has achieved a 20–30 percent response rate with its predictive analytics.

With the power of analytics, Sam's Club thus is offering tremendous value to its customers.

---

of printing and mailing them and increasing consumer interest in environmentally friendly practices. By adding the Internet channel, retailers can expand their market without having to build new stores or incur the high cost of additional catalogs. Adding an Internet channel is particularly attractive to retailers with strong brand names but limited locations and distribution. For example, retailers such as Nordstrom's, REI, IKEA, and L.L. Bean are widely known for offering unique, high-quality merchandise. If these retailers only had a store, customers would have to travel vast distances to buy the merchandise they carry.

EFFECTIVE MULTICHANNEL RETAILING

LO8 Detail the challenges of multichannel retailing.

Consumers desire a seamless experience when interacting with multichannel retailers. They want to be recognized by a retailer, whether they interact with a sales associate, the retailer's website, or the retailer's call center by telephone. Customers want to buy a product through the retailer's Internet or catalog channels and pick it up or return it to a local store; find out if a product offered on the Internet channel is available at a local store; and, when unable to find a product in a store, determine if it is available for home delivery through the retailer's Internet channel.

However, providing this seamless experience for customers is not easy for retailers. Because each of the channels is somewhat different, a critical decision facing multichannel retailers is the degree to which they should or are able to integrate the operations of the channels. To determine how much integration is best, each retailer must address issues such as integrated CRM, brand image, pricing, and the supply chain.[47]

Integrated CRM

Effective multichannel operations require an integrated CRM (customer relationship management) system with a centralized customer data warehouse that houses a complete history of each customer's interaction with the retailer, regardless of whether the sale occurred in a store, on the Internet, or on the telephone.[48] Adding Value 17.2 provides an interesting example of how one well-known chain has done so. This information storehouse allows retailers to efficiently handle

Multichannel retailers like Patagonia sell on the Internet (left), in catalogs (right), and in stores (bottom).

complaints, expedite returns, target future promotions, and provide a seamless experience for customers when they interact with the retailer through multiple channels.

Brand Image

Retailers need to provide a consistent brand image across all channels. For example, Patagonia reinforces its image of selling high-quality, environmentally friendly sports equipment in its stores, catalogs, and website. Each of these channels emphasizes function, not fashion, in the descriptions of Patagonia's products. Patagonia's position about taking care of the environment is communicated by carefully lighting its stores and using recycled polyester and organic, rather than pesticide-intensive cotton, in many of its clothes.

Pricing

Pricing represents another difficult decision for a multichannel retailer. Customers expect pricing consistency for the same SKU across channels (excluding shipping charges and sales tax). However, in some cases, retailers need to adjust their pricing strategy because of the competition they face in different channels. For example, Barnes & Noble offers lower prices through its Internet channel (www.bn.com) than in its stores to compete effectively against Amazon.com.

Retailers with stores in multiple markets often set different prices for the same merchandise to compete better with local stores. Customers generally are not aware of these price differences because they are only exposed to the prices in their local markets. However, multichannel retailers may have difficulties sustaining these regional price differences when customers can easily check prices on the Internet.

Supply Chain

Multichannel retailers struggle to provide an integrated shopping experience across all their channels, because unique skills and resources are needed to manage each channel.[49] For example, store-based retail chains operate and manage many stores, each requiring the management of inventory and people. With Internet and catalog operations, inventory and telephone salespeople instead are typically centralized in one or two locations. Also, retail distribution centers (DCs) supporting a store channel are designed to ship many cartons of merchandise to stores. In contrast, the DCs supporting a catalog and Internet channel are designed to ship a few items to individual customers. The difference in shipping orientation for the two types of operations requires a completely different type of distribution center.

Due to these operational differences, many store-based retailers have a separate organization to manage their Internet and catalog operations. But as the multichannel operation matures, retailers tend to integrate all operations under one organization. Both Walmart and JCPenney initially had separate organizations for their Internet channel but subsequently integrated them with stores and catalogs.

CHECK YOURSELF

1. What are the components of a retail strategy?
2. What are the advantages of traditional stores versus Internet-only stores?
3. What challenges do retailers face when marketing their products through multiple channels?

Summing Up

LO1 Discuss the four factors manufacturers should consider as they develop their strategy for working with retailers.

When they initiate the decision process for choosing retail partners, manufacturers determine how likely it is that certain retailers would carry their products and whether target customers expect to find their products for sale at those retail locations. Next, manufacturers need to identify types of retailers that would be appropriate locations for their products. After identifying likely and appropriate retailers, manufacturers work with their retailer partners to develop a strategy that comprises the four Ps. Finally, manufacturers, again with their retail partners, must determine which elements of a multichannel strategy will be effective. Manufacturers often make these decisions simultaneously or in varying orders.

LO2 Outline the considerations associated with choosing retail partners.

Manufacturers often start by noting the basic channel structure, which includes the level of vertical integration, the relative strength of the retailer and the manufacturer, and the strength of the brand. They also consider where their target customers expect to find products, which depends largely on the retailer's image. Channel member characteristics also are important inputs, as is the level of distribution intensity.

LO3 List the three levels of distribution intensity.

Intensive distribution intensity means the product is available virtually everywhere, in as many places as will agree to carry it. In an exclusive distribution intensity strategy, the manufacturer allows only one retailer (or retail chain) in each area to sell its products. Selective distribution is the middle ground option; several retailers carry the products, but not all of them.

LO4 Describe the various types of retailers.

Retailers generally fall into one of three categories: food retailers, general merchandise retailers, or service retailers. Each of the categories consists of various formats, including supermarkets, supercenters, warehouse clubs, convenience stores, department stores, discount stores, specialty retailers, drugstores, category specialists, extreme value retailers, and off-price stores. Although service retailers primarily sell services, if they sell to consumers, they are still retailers. Service retailers span the gambit from universities to automobile oil change shops.

LO5 Describe the components of a retail strategy.

To develop a coordinated strategy—which represents a key goal for an effective channel partnership between retailers and manufacturers—both retailers and manufacturers need to consider all of the four Ps in conjunction: product, place, promotion, and price.

LO6 **Identify the benefits of stores.**

Because consumers often have just a general idea of what they want to purchase, stores' main benefits come from giving shoppers a place to browse. They can touch and feel products, obtain personal services, pay using cash or credit, engage in an entertaining and social experience, receive instant gratification, and reduce their sense of risk.

LO7 **Identify the benefits of multichannel retailing.**

The various types of retail channels—stores, catalogs, and the Internet—all offer their own benefits and limitations, including those related to availability, convenience, and safety, among others. If a retailer adopts a multichannel strategy, it can exploit the benefits and mitigate the limitations of each channel and help expand its overall market presence. Furthermore, a multichannel strategy offers the chance to gain a greater share of customers' wallets and more insight into their buying behaviors.

LO8 **Detail the challenges of multichannel retailing.**

To function in multiple channels, retailers must organize their operations carefully to ensure an integrated customer experience. In particular, they have to have an integrated CRM system, and determine how to maintain a consistent brand image across the various channels, whether to charge the same or different prices, and how best to deliver merchandise to multiple channels.

Key Terms

- big box retailers, 527
- category killers, 527
- category specialists, 527
- cooperative (co-op) advertising, 531
- convenience stores, 524
- conventional supermarket, 523
- cookie, 536
- department stores, 525
- distribution intensity, 521
- drugstores, 526
- exclusive co-brand, 530

- exclusive distribution, 521
- extreme value food retailers, 523
- extreme value retailers, 527
- full-line discount stores, 525
- intensive distribution, 521
- limited assortment supermarkets, 523
- mobile-commerce (M-commerce), 531
- multichannel strategy, 519
- off-price retailers, 528

- online chat, 535
- opt in, 536
- opt out, 536
- retailing, 518
- selective distribution, 522
- services retailers, 529
- share of wallet, 533
- specialty stores, 526
- stock keeping unit (SKU), 523
- supercenters, 524
- warehouse clubs, 524

Marketing Applications

1. Does Reebok pursue an intensive, an exclusive, or a selective distribution intensity strategy? Would you suggest any changes to this strategy?

2. Why don't traditional department stores have the same strong appeal to younger American consumers that they once enjoyed during their heyday in the last half of the twentieth century? Discuss which types of retailers are now competing with department stores.

3. Assume that adidas, the shoe manufacturer, has decided to sell expensive wristwatches for men and women. What factors should it consider when developing its strategy for choosing retail partners?

4. Some argue that retailers can be eliminated from the distribution channel because they only add costs to the final product without creating any value-added services in the process. Do you agree with this perspective? Are consumers likely to make most purchases directly from manufacturers in the near future? Provide justification for your answers.

5. Assume you have been given some money but told that it must be invested in a retailer's stock. In which type of retailer would you choose to invest? Which specific retailer? Provide a rationale for your answers.

6. Provide examples of how manufacturers work with retailers to jointly plan and implement the four Ps.

7. Why have so many bricks-and-mortar retailers adopted a multichannel strategy?

8. You can purchase apparel at a discount store, specialty store, category specialist, off-price retailer, department store, or Internet-only store. From which of these types of stores do you shop? Explain why you prefer one type store over another.

9. Should Eva (a young entrepreneur), launching a new line of environmentally friendly (green) cosmetics, sell through a physical store, catalog, or Internet? Explain two key benefits of each channel for her business.

10. Search the Internet for a product you want to buy. Are there differences in the prices, shipping charges, or return policies among the different retailers offering the product? From which retailer would you buy? Explain the criteria you would use to make the decision.

11. Name a retailer from which you have received personalized service, product, or promotion offerings online. What form of personalization did you receive? Did the personalization influence your purchase decision? Explain why or why not.

Quiz Yourself

www.mhhe.com/grewal4e

1. TJX is an example of a(n)
   a. department store
   b. off-price retailer
   c. discount store
   d. specialty store
   e. extreme value retailer

2. Walmart and Target dominate the _____ industry in the United States.
   a. department store
   b. off-price retailer

   c. discount store
   d. specialty store
   e. category specialist

(Answers to these two questions can be found on page 648.)

Go to www.mhhe.com/grewal4e to practice an additional 11 questions.

Net Savvy

1. How do JCrew.com and Gap.com provide value to their customers beyond the physical products that they sell? Why would a customer purchase online instead of going to the store? Under what circumstances would the customer prefer a store-based experience?

2. Select a familiar multichannel retailer. Evaluate its website in terms of how well it provides value to its customers. Do you believe that offering multiple selling channels to customers enhances their shopping experience? How does it help the retailer? Explain your answer.

Chapter Case Study

TARGET AND ITS NEW GENERATION OF PARTNERSHIPS

The country's second-largest retailer, Minneapolis-based Target has been an innovator in structuring retail partnerships that offer customers something special: fashion-forward housewares and apparel at prices they can afford. In addition to its Target.com website, the company operates nearly 1,800 stores in 49 states, along with 37 distribution centers nationally and a separate headquartered location in India.[50] Apparel and accessories account for approximately 20 percent of Target's annual sales.

connect

Similar to its more standardized rivals Walmart and Kmart, Target offers the vast breadth of a full-line discount store, featuring everything from cosmetics to baby clothes, housewares to electronics. But Target also has uniquely positioned itself through a series of exclusive partnerships with top designers, such as Michael Graves and Isaac Mizrahi, who have collaborated with the retailer to offer limited-edition, distinctive products. Although other retailers also have developed relationships with designers to create exclusive brands—such as Kohl's Simply Vera line from designer Vera Wang, which accounted for 50 percent of its apparel sales in 2010—these competitors have struggled to maintain their lower prices.[51]

Thus, though it is not alone in partnering with designers, Target appears to be the best practitioner of this strategy. The company launched its first retail partnership in 1999 with renowned architect Michael Graves, whose teakettles and toasters were hailed for having brought the word "design" back to the housewares category.[52] Since then, the company has worked with more than 80 design partners who have generally welcomed the chance to reach a mass market with their exclusive labels.[53]

Most of the partnerships have been limited to a specific time, which also has built a sense of urgency and exclusivity around the offers. Target's 2011 holiday offerings featured a number of designer labels: Harajuku Mini kids' clothing from designer Gwen Stefani; hats from Albertuse Swanepoel; and a jewelry line featuring designs by Dana Kellin. Whether time-limited or longer term, such partnerships have consistently offered high-profile labels at moderate prices, helping the retailer boost its bottom line.

Target's collaboration with Missoni made the biggest splash though. The fashion world was stunned when the Italian fashion house agreed to create a collection for Target. The big American retail store is the diametric opposite of the high-end shops that have typically carried Missoni's expensive knitwear and apparel. Target's announcement through Facebook, other social media sites, and a Manhattan pop-up shop for fashion editors, celebrities, and other Missoni clientele helped stoke public excitement.

Of course, such excitement can cause problems as well. Target's website crashed just moments after the Missoni launch, as customers clicked in droves to buy up the designer duds.[54] Although the site remained up when Jason Wu (the designer of Michelle Obama's famous 2008 inaugural gown) released his line, many stores reported nearly immediate stockouts. Customers in a Miami store watched in shock and dismay as one couple swooped in and purchased the entire selection that was on the retail floor.[55]

Now Target has created a new model for retail partnership as a way to offer its shoppers something different. Through a store-inside-a-store initiative that it has dubbed The Shops at Target, the retailer is partnering directly with small specialty shops and boutiques to offer their limited-edition merchandise, from dog biscuits to vintage furniture, at prices ranging from $1.99 to $159.99.

The store-within-a-store, with dedicated space branded by the designer, has already proven a successful strategy elsewhere. Macy's has Ralph Lauren boutiques; Bloomingdale's has Chanel boutiques. JCPenney, a close Target competitor, also hosts Sephora boutiques, MNG by Mango, and other designer brands.[56]

The Shops at Target collaboration is being rolled out as a series of six-week partnerships. For its first round, launched in May 2012, the retailer chose five independently owned specialty shops—The Candy Store; the Cos Bar cosmetic shop; Polka Dog Bakery; the Privet House home accessories shop; and The Webster, a high-end Miami clothing store—all getting their first crack at a national market through Target's nearly 1,800 locations, not to mention its website. Target plans to repeat the program subsequently with new sets of boutiques, but the initial group alone will add nearly 400 new and exclusive products to Target's online and store inventories.[57]

In a separate but parallel development, Target has also announced that Apple will open 25 small retail shops at Target locations around the country.[58] This isn't a first for Apple; it already has some mini-stores at Best Buy locations. So what's the special appeal? Target already sells both iPads and iPods, but the expanded in-store venture can introduce Apple products to new groups of customers, including those who might not be looking for electronics.[59] Full-blown shops for Apple products, with their own décor and personality, should encourage Target shoppers to test out the products. Furthermore, of the vast number of people who enter Target stores every day, many of them will stumble on an Apple shop and be unable to resist playing around with the appealing, fun products. Whether they buy on that shopping trip or on another visit back to Target, Apple thus is likely to expand its sales.

Target shoppers thus have come to expect a steady stream of exclusive new designer brands, along with the constant possibility of finding something unique, even unpredictable, in the next aisle over. Now the big merchandiser is hoping to keep that excitement going with its new specialty-shop partnerships. But just as it was introducing that new retail model, Target was also forced to announce disappointing sales figures and declining profits.[60] The question going forward will be whether Target—the store loyal customers have dubbed "Tarzhay" for its supply of "cheap chic"—can keep its steady customers coming back, while attracting more shoppers with new rounds of boutique surprises.

Questions

1. Assess the role of consumer expectations in Target's success as a major discount retailer.

2. What differentiates Target's new retail partnership model from its longstanding partnerships with top designers? What are the relative strengths of each?

3. What explains Target's ability to attract top designers and high-end specialty shops as retail partners?

4. Given that Apple has long operated its own retail locations, how do you explain its interest in partnering with Target?

5. Using the factors for choosing retail partners outlined in the chapter, do you believe that Eva's line of green cosmetics should attempt to get placement in Target?

6. Develop a strategy for Target to promote Eva's line of green cosmetics as part of its new specialty shop partnership program.

Value Communication

CHAPTER 18
Integrated Marketing Communications

CHAPTER 19
Advertising, Public Relations, and Sales Promotions

CHAPTER 20
Personal Selling and Sales Management

In Section Seven we explore value communication. Today, value communication methods are more complex because of new technologies that have added e-mail, blogs, Internet, and podcasts to the advertising mix that once utilized only radio, television, newspapers, and magazines to relay messages to consumers. Chapter 18 introduces the breadth of integrated marketing communications. Chapter 19 discusses advertising, public relations, and sales promotions. The text concludes with a discussion of personal selling in Chapter 20.

SECTION 7

CHAPTER 18

Integrated Marketing Communications

The incredible expansion of the Internet and online tools has radically changed advertising. More and more, companies spread their messages over all sorts of media—television, print, radio, e-mail, Internet, and so on. To really stand out then, a company may need to go further than ever.

To achieve success in a market, companies invariably must communicate the value of their offerings in diverse, well-rounded ways. When companies promote their brands through multiple channels, they stand a better chance of reaching their customers. Coordination across these platforms is the key to effective multichannel marketing communications. But it is difficult to ensure brand consistency when their radio, television, and print ads each require different types of elements, unique voices, and varying styles. In addition, firms need to integrate their marketing communications even further by incorporating new opportunities to reach customers through social media sites, such as Facebook and Twitter.

A great example of such communications integration appeared during Super Bowl XLVI, when the marketing giant Coca-Cola introduced its integrated marketing event through televised advertising that also drove consumers to its social media marketing channels. As the New York

Giants beat the New England Patriots, the well-known polar bears that serve as Coca-Cola's spokescharacters appeared in a series of commercials featuring updated, live-animation techniques.[1] The bears first appeared in Coke's 1993 Super Bowl commercials. This time around, the technologically remarkable animation showed the bears reacting to actual events during the game. The televised spots also invited viewers to plug into Coke's live-stream YouTube feed to watch the bears react to the game in real time, not just during the commercial breaks.[2]

In addition to nearly half a million views of "Catch," Coca-Cola's halftime commercial, in which a rotund bear gracefully stumbles on the ice to catch a precious bottle of Coke, YouTube registered more than 33,000 views of bears doing a fourth-quarter touchdown dance.[3] Thus Coca-Cola was named the Super Bowl's "brand winner," and three of its ads were rated among the 10 most effective spots for this contest[4]—as ever, the Super Bowl is the world's largest stage for advertisers.[5]

By reaching through the television screen to connect with the approximately 100 million Super Bowl viewers, Coca-Cola integrated its traditional commercials with its live-stream YouTube feed, as well as Twitter and Facebook. The integrated marketing event thus offered consumers

LEARNING OBJECTIVES

LO1 Identify the components of the communication process.

LO2 Explain the four steps in the AIDA model.

LO3 Describe the various integrative communication channels.

LO4 Explain the methods used to allocate the integrated marketing communications (IMC) budget.

LO5 Identify marketing metrics used to measure IMC success.

multiple ways to "interact" with the bears. For example, viewers could exchange their Super Bowl reactions with the bears through Twitter. In a postgame extension, Coke also offered fans of the winning and losing teams a choice of Facebook apps to share video of either a delighted or a dismayed bear, along with a coupon for a free Coke, of course.

The costs were substantial though. Coca-Cola spent more than $10 million just to buy Super Bowl airtime, without even calculating the production costs.[6] Why? A pregame announcement suggests one answer: Coca-Cola produced the multimedia experience for viewers to remind them that popping open an ice-cold Coke is one way to "Open Happiness," a phrase that also serves as the name of the overall campaign.[7]

Furthermore, Coca-Cola's integrated Super Bowl campaign gave it a great way to connect with consumers through their computers, smartphones, and tablet devices. As the boundaries of advertising shift to include digital and social media, the integration of multiple marketing channels is crucial for catching customers wherever they are: in front of the television, typing on their home computer, or on the go. The challenge persists, even for a marketing giant like Coca-Cola.

As the description of Coke's innovative campaign attests, each element of an integrated marketing communication (IMC) strategy must have a well-defined purpose and support and extend the message delivered by all the other elements. (For a description of how another soft drink has used some notably similar elements to create its latest integrated campaign, see the discussion of Tropicana in the next chapter.)

Throughout this book, we have focused our attention on how firms create value by developing products and services. However, consumers are not likely to come flocking to new products and services unless they are aware of them. Therefore, marketers must consider how to communicate the value of a product and/or service—or more specifically, the value proposition—to the target market. A firm must develop a communication strategy to demonstrate the value of its product. We begin our consideration by examining what IMC is, how it has developed, and how it contributes to value creation.

Integrated marketing communications (IMC) represents the Promotion P of the four Ps. It encompasses a variety of communication disciplines—advertising, personal selling, sales promotion, public relations, direct marketing, and online marketing including social media—in combination to provide clarity, consistency, and maximum communicative impact.[8] Instead of consisting of separated marketing communication elements with no unified control, IMC programs regard each of the firm's marketing communications elements as part of a whole, each of which offers a different means to connect with the target audience. This integration of elements provides the firm with the best means to reach the target audience with the desired message, and it enhances the value story by offering a clear and consistent message.

There are three elements in any IMC strategy: the consumer, the channels through which the message is communicated, and the evaluation of the results of the communication. This chapter is organized around these three elements. In the first section, the focus is on consumers, so we examine how consumers receive communications, whether via media or other methods, as well as how the delivery of that communication affects a message's form and contents. The second section examines the various communication channels that make up the components of IMC and how each is used in an overall IMC strategy. The third section considers how the level of complexity in IMC strategies leads marketers to design new ways to measure the results of IMC campaigns.

EXHIBIT 18.1 The Communication Process

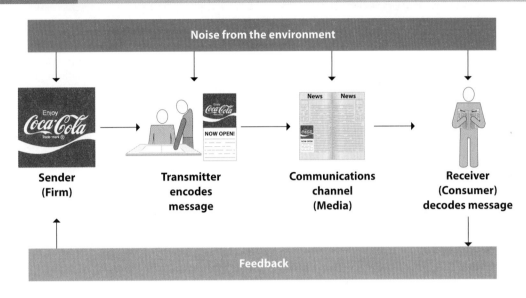

COMMUNICATING WITH CONSUMERS

As the number of communication media has increased, the task of understanding how best to reach target consumers has become far more complex. In this section, we examine a model that describes how communications go from the firm to the consumer and the factors that affect the way the consumer perceives the message. Then we look at how marketing communications influence consumers—from making them aware that a product or service exists to moving them to buy.

The Communication Process

Exhibit 18.1 illustrates the communication process. Let's first define each component and then discuss how they interact.

The Sender The message originates from the **sender**, who must be clearly identified to the intended audience. Recall the case study in Chapter 9, which described how Coca-Cola has introduced new options, including its Freestyle vending machines. To make customers aware of this option, Coke works with retailers and other outlets that host Freestyle, such as Burger King, Kroger, Five Guys Burgers, or Kmart, to send messages about its new machines.

The Transmitter The sender works with a creative department, whether in-house or from a marketing (or advertising) agency, to develop marketing communications to highlight the new beverage. With the assistance of its marketing department, Coca-Cola and its partners might develop flyers, in-store displays, and window banners. The marketing department or external agency receives the information and transforms it for use in its role as the **transmitter**.

Encoding **Encoding** means converting the sender's ideas into a message, which could be verbal, visual, or both. A television commercial could show consumers pouring a new beverage from a Freestyle machine. Billboards

LO1 Identify the components of the communication process.

To make customers aware of Coke's Freestyle vending machines, it works with retailers like Dairy Queen to send messages.

Adding Value 18.1   The Appeal of Scripted Nerds[9]

For several years, television critics have suggested that the success of *American Idol* would change the face of the medium forever: We would no longer find scripted shows, as networks continued to rely on less expensive, highly appealing contests, as well as their cousins, the ubiquitous reality shows. But a recent trend suggests there is still some value to be found, for viewers, networks, and their advertisers, in more traditional forms of entertainment.

The Big Bang Theory has been on the air for five years. But its popularity has never been greater. For a few weeks, it even beat *American Idol* in viewing numbers in their head-to-head competition. Social media tracking for the most recent season also showed that the number of comments about the show, its characters, and their scripted quotes nearly quadrupled compared with the previous year.

Yet *American Idol* still attracts far more social media comments overall. Whereas the 12,000 comments from social media users represented a huge jump for *The Big Bang Theory*, they still paled in comparison with *Idol*'s 110,000 comments per episode. The difference reflects the basic appeals of the varying types of shows and the integrated marketing they comprise. Inherently, reality and contest shows rely on social media connections, because viewers already are online to vote for their favorites. Adding comments in another channel thus is simple.

But fans of *The Big Bang Theory* have plenty to say as well. They claim to feel smarter just from watching a show featuring theoretical physicists, and they enjoy repeated references to Sheldon's "Rock, Paper, Scissors, Lizard, Spock" game. The implications for advertisers are appealing. Even when a show seems to involve only one media channel, it still can attract attention in other realms. In addition, advertisers can communicate with significant numbers of young, hip viewers by buying airtime during various types of shows. Such promise may be particularly appealing for firms whose products do not fit very well with reality shows—and maybe especially those that target a nerd-friendly audience.

Firms can communicate with hip viewers of The Big Bang Theory *through various communication channels.*

showcasing the well-designed machines might highlight their pictures with a message asking, "Have You Tried It Yet?" Although a picture can be worth a thousand words, the most important facet of encoding is not what gets sent but rather what is received. Consumers must receive information that makes them want to try the new machines and to continue to buy from it for the innovation to be successful.

The Communication Channel The **communication channel** is the medium—print, broadcast, the Internet, and so forth—that carries the message. Coca-Cola could transmit through television, radio, and various print advertisements, but it also realizes that the media chosen must be appropriate to connect itself (the sender) with its desired recipients. If the company believes its target market is broad, Coca-Cola might advertise on popular television shows, like *The Big Bang Theory* (see Adding Value 18.1) and *The Voice*. As the opening vignette suggested,

---

Superior Service 18.1   Hiring the Newest Chief Chocolate Officer, with Consumers' Help[10]

In the opening vignette, we described one of the great ad campaigns of the 2012 Super Bowl—an event for which the ad rates reached $3.5 million for 30 seconds of airtime. But 111 million people watched Super Bowl XLV, so this massive audience remains appealing for marketers, including Mars, the makers of M&Ms. It grabbed the opportunity to respond to consumers' frequent question: "Of all the candy spokescharacters—grumpy Red, innocent Yellow, sexy Green—why was there no Brown?"

In an earlier contest that asked consumers to vote for their favorite character, many responded by asking why they could not vote for brown M&Ms. After several years of skipping the Super Bowl, Mars chose to introduce Ms. Brown, the Chief Chocolate Officer, on this grand stage.

This strategic use of the feedback loop paid off well for Mars. The "Just My Shell" ad that introduced Ms. Brown won YouTube's Ad Blitz, a contest in which users vote for their favorite commercials. That earned it prime position on YouTube's homepage. Furthermore, approximately one-third of the votes in the Ad Blitz contest came from tablet devices, which gave Mars significant information about how, when, and where consumers were viewing its ads. That is, even as they watched the ad on their television screens during game time, people were logging on to sites using portable devices, which gave advertisers an additional channel through which to reach them.

Coke is also likely to rely on social media channels to encourage fans to consider this alternative source for some of their favorite beverage flavors.

The Receiver The **receiver** is the person who reads, hears, or sees and processes the information contained in the message and/or advertisement. The sender, of course, hopes that the person receiving it will be the one for whom it was originally intended. Coca-Cola wants its message received and decoded properly by a broad population, including teens, young adults, and families who often visit fast food restaurants. **Decoding** refers to the process by which the receiver interprets the sender's message.

Noise **Noise** is any interference that stems from competing messages, a lack of clarity in the message, or a flaw in the medium. It poses a problem for all communication channels. Coca-Cola may choose to advertise in newspapers that its target market doesn't read, which means the rate at which the message is received by those to whom it has relevance has been slowed considerably. As we have already defined, encoding is what the sender intends to say, and decoding is what the receiver hears. If there is a difference between them, it is probably due to noise.

Feedback Loop The **feedback loop** allows the receiver to communicate with the sender and thereby informs the sender whether the message was received and decoded properly. Feedback can take many forms: a customer's purchase of the item, a complaint or compliment, the redemption of a coupon

The intended receivers of a Coca-Cola Zero ad are male.

or rebate, a tweet about the product on Twitter, and so forth. Superior Service 18.1 describes another kind of feedback that Mars used in a successful IMC campaign for its M&Ms brand. More simply though, if Coca-Cola observes an increase in sales, its managers know that the intended audience received the message.

How Consumers Perceive Communication

The actual communication process is not as simple as the model in Exhibit 18.1 implies. Each receiver may interpret the sender's message differently, and senders

Consumers will perceive this giant billboard differently depending on their level of knowledge and attitude toward the brand.

often adjust their message according to the medium used and the receivers' level of knowledge about the product or service.

Receivers Decode Messages Differently Each receiver decodes a message in his or her own way, which is not necessarily the way the sender intended. Different people shown the same message will often take radically different meanings from it. For example, what does the image above convey to you?

If you are a user of this brand, it may convey satisfaction. If you recently went on a diet and gave up your soda, it may convey dismay or a sense of loss. If you have chosen to be a nonuser, it may convey some disgust. If you are a recently terminated employee, it may convey anger. The sender has little, if any, control over what meaning any individual receiver will take from the message.

Senders Adjust Messages According to the Medium and Receivers' Traits Different media communicate in very different ways, so marketers make adjustments to their messages and media depending on whether they want to communicate with suppliers, shareholders, customers, or the general public, as well as the specific segments of those groups.[11]

Online grocery retailer Peapod adjusted its communication medium and message to attract more customers.

For example, the high-technology firm Analtech sells thin layer chromatography plates to companies that need equipment to determine the ingredients of samples of virtually anything. It is not a particularly easy product to explain and sell to laypeople, even though some purchasers might not have a science degree. Therefore, in addition to traditional marketing through trade shows and scientific conferences, Analtech developed a Monty Python–inspired YouTube video (http://www.ichromatography.com/adventuresofana.html) in which a "witch" overcomes threats to drown her by proving that the ink in the king's decree is actually from the sheriff's pen. It also highlights points in *CSI* episodes when the television detectives rely on its products. With these more broadly popular appeals, Analtech ensures its messages reach and can be received accurately by a wider audience, with less noise than might occur through more scientific appeals.

Senders must adjust messages according to the receivers' traits. LG, for instance, uses the ad on the left to target consumers. The LG ad on the right is targeted to the B2B audience.

The AIDA Model

LO2 Explain the four steps in the AIDA model.

Clearly, IMC is not a straightforward process. After being exposed to a marketing communication, consumers go through several steps before actually buying or taking some other action. There is not always a direct link between a particular marketing communication and a consumer's purchase.

To create effective IMC programs, marketers must understand how marketing communications work. Generally, marketing communications move consumers stepwise through a series of mental stages, for which there are several models. The most common is the **AIDA model** (Exhibit 18.2),[12] which suggests that **A**wareness leads to **I**nterest, which leads to **D**esire, which leads to **A**ction. At each stage, the consumer makes judgments about whether to take the next step in the process.

EXHIBIT 18.2 The AIDA Model

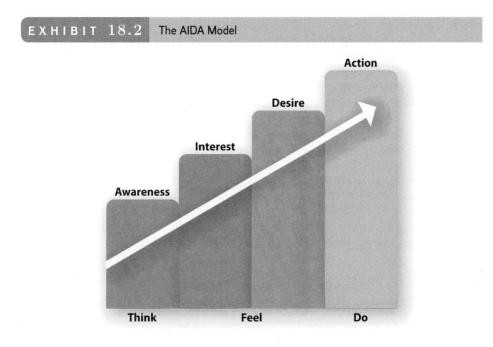

Customers actually have three types of responses, so the AIDA model is also known as the "think, feel, do" model. In making a purchase decision, consumers go through each of the AIDA steps to some degree, but the steps may not always follow the AIDA order. For instance, during an impulse purchase, a consumer may "feel" and "do" before he or she "thinks."

Awareness Even the best marketing communication can be wasted if the sender doesn't gain the attention of the consumer first. **Brand awareness** refers to a potential customer's ability to recognize or recall that the brand name is a particular type of retailer or product/service. Thus, brand awareness is the strength of the link between the brand name and the type of merchandise or service in the minds of customers.

Coca-Cola already has excellent brand awareness and thus might not have to focus as much effort on this step when it wants to introduce a new flavor or its Freestyle machines. In contrast, when Jay-Z wanted to promote his memoir, he needed to exert more effort to get consumers to think of him as an author, rather than a musician, as the case study at the end of this chapter describes.

There are several awareness metrics, including aided recall and top-of-mind awareness. **Aided recall** is when consumers indicate they know the brand when the name is presented to them. **Top-of-mind awareness**, the highest level of awareness, occurs when consumers mention a specific brand name first when they are asked about a product or service. For example, Harley-Davidson has top-of-mind awareness if a consumer responds "Harley" when asked about American-made motorcycles. High top-of-mind awareness means that the brand probably enters the evoked set of brands (see Chapter 6) when customers decide to shop for that particular product or service. Manufacturers, retailers, and service providers build top-of-mind awareness by having memorable names; repeatedly exposing their name to customers through advertising, locations, and sponsorships; and using memorable symbols.

As an excellent example of the latter method, imagine two smaller circles, sitting on opposite sides atop a larger circle. Did you see Mickey Mouse ears? Did you think of Disney? In addition, the company has moved on to images brighter than circles to ensure that its name comes easily to the front of young consumers' minds. Whether individual acts like Miley Cyrus, Selena Gomez, or Demi Lovato or groups such as the KSM, Lemonade Mouth, and Allstar Weekend, Disney starts off its stars with Disney Channel shows, records them on the Disney-owned Hollywood Record label, plays the songs in heavy rotation on Radio Disney and Disney movie soundtracks, organizes concert tours with Disney-owned Buena Vista Concerts, and sells tie-in merchandise throughout Disney stores. Each of these marketing elements reminds the various segments of the target market about both the brand (e.g., "Hannah Montana," "Jonas Brothers") and their owner, Disney. With this multichannel approach, Disney gets the same "product" into more markets than would be possible with a more conservative approach—further building top-of-mind awareness for both Disney and its stars.[13]

Interest Once the consumer is aware that the company or product exists, communication must work to increase his or her interest level. It isn't enough to let people know that the product exists; consumers must be persuaded that it is a product worth investigating. Marketers do so by ensuring that the ad's message includes attributes that are of interest to the target audience. Disney increases interest in an upcoming tour or record by including a mention, whether casual or not, in the stars' television shows. Because the primary target market for the tour is also probably watching the show, the message gets received by the correct recipient.

Desire After the firm has piqued the interest of its target market, the goal of subsequent IMC messages should move the consumer from "I like it" to "I want it." If

When young consumers read the Jonas Brothers' blog, they might beg their parents to buy a concert ticket. The marketing communication drives the customer to take action.

Allstar Weekend appears on *Good Morning America* (on ABC, which is owned by Disney) and talks about their upcoming activity and how great it is going to be, the viewing audience is all the more likely to demand access—in this case, probably parents who hope to score points with their adolescent children by buying the latest album or reserving seats to an upcoming tour.

Action The ultimate goal of any marketing communication is to drive the receiver to action. If the message has caught consumers' attention and made them interested enough to consider the product as a means to satisfy a specific desire of theirs, they likely will act on that interest by either searching for the product or making a purchase. If young consumers read the Jonas Brothers' blog, they might in turn beg their parents to make an actual purchase of a concert ticket or album related to this favorite Disney Channel show.

The Lagged Effect Sometimes consumers don't act immediately after receiving a marketing communication because of the lagged effect—a delayed response to a marketing communication campaign. It generally takes several exposures to an ad before a consumer fully processes its message.[14] In turn, measuring the effect of a current campaign becomes more difficult because of the possible lagged response to a previous one.[15] For example, Toyota's "Prius Goes Plural" campaign promotes its addition of a family-sized (Prius v) and urban version (Prius c) of its popular hybrid car model. The campaign demands consumer participation, by challenging the viewing public to come up with a plural form of the word "Prius" (e.g., Prii, Prien, Priuses), as touted in online banner and television ads, virtual polling booths, and videos. But the Prius v was not slated for release until six months after the campaign started, and the lag time for the Prius c was even longer. Thus the company might never know for sure whether exposure to this marketing communication actually led consumers to check out or purchase the new vehicles.[16]

Now that we've examined various aspects of the communication process, let's look at how specific media are used in an IMC program.

Toyota's "Prius Goes Plural" campaign promotes its addition of a family-sized (Prius v) and urban version (Prius c) of its popular hybrid car model.

CHECK YOURSELF

1. What are the different steps in the communication process?
2. What is the AIDA model?

ELEMENTS OF AN INTEGRATED MARKETING COMMUNICATION STRATEGY

For any communications campaign to succeed, the firm must deliver the right message to the right audience through the right media, with the ultimate goal of profiting from long-term customer relationships rather than just short-term transactions. Reaching the right audience is becoming more difficult, however, as the media environment grows more complicated.[17]

No single channel is necessarily better than another channel; the goal of IMC is to use them in conjunction so that the sum exceeds the total of the individual channels. However, advances in technology have led to a variety of new and traditional media options for consumers, all of which vie for consumers' attention. Print media have also grown and become more specialized. This proliferation of media has led many firms to shift their promotional dollars from advertising to direct marketing, website development, product placements, and other forms of promotion in search of the best way to deliver messages to their target audiences.

We now examine the individual elements of IMC and the way each contributes to a successful IMC campaign (see Exhibit 18.3). The elements can be viewed on two axes: passive and interactive (from the consumer's perspective) and offline and online. Some elements (e.g., advertising, sales promotion, public relations, personal selling, direct and online marketing) are discussed in far more detail in subsequent chapters, so we discuss them only briefly here.

LO3 Describe the various integrative communication channels.

EXHIBIT 18.3   Elements of an IMC Strategy

Note that as the marketer's repertoire of IMC elements has expanded, so too have the ways in which marketers can communicate with their customers. So, for instance, direct marketing appears in all four boxes. Firms have expanded their use of these traditional media (e.g., advertising, public relations and sales promotions) from pure offline approaches to a combination of offline and online.

Advertising

Perhaps the most visible of the IMC components, **advertising**, entails the placement of announcements and persuasive messages in time or space purchased in any of the mass media by business firms, nonprofit organizations, government agencies, and individuals who seek to inform and/or persuade members of a particular target market or audience about their products, services, organizations, or ideas.[18] In Chapter 19, we discuss the purpose of advertising and its various types, but for now, we note that advertising is extremely effective for creating awareness of a product or service and generating interest. Mass advertising can entice consumers into a conversation with marketers, though it does not necessarily require much action by consumers, which places it on the passive end of the spectrum. Traditionally, advertising has been passive and offline (e.g., television, magazines, newspapers; see Exhibit 18.3), though recently there has been a growth in online advertising and interactive features. Advertising thus must break through the clutter of other messages to reach its intended audience. To do so, many advertisers rely on certain images; Ethical and Societal Dilemma 18.1 notes the conflict when advertisers use underweight, skinny models in ads they aim at teenaged consumers.

Public Relations (PR)

Public relations is the organizational function that manages the firm's communications to achieve a variety of objectives, including building and maintaining a positive image, handling or heading off unfavorable stories or events, and maintaining positive relationships with the media. Like advertising, this tactic is relatively passive, in that customers do not have to take any action to receive it. Public relations activities support the other promotional efforts by the firm by generating "free" media attention, as we discuss further in Chapter 19.

Ethical and Societal Dilemma 18.1   Too Skinny

The objective of an integrated marketing communications (IMC) campaign is to build profits by encouraging consumers to purchase more products. But what happens if the campaign leads to harmful behaviors? Companies could claim that shoppers have a choice about the goods they purchase, or assert that marketing only influences brand decisions. But sometimes marketing directed at younger consumers complicates that reasoning, because few children or teens can separate unhealthy body images from the popular fashion looks that surround them.

Advertising models have always tended to be thin. But they have become increasingly so in the past decade or so. The tragic deaths of Ana Carolina Reston and Isabelle Caro—two very thin models suffering from anorexia—led some fashion industry leaders to call for a change. That was nearly a decade ago, and still underage and dangerously thin young girls continue to find work as fashion advertising models. The designers and clothing companies continue to hire girls as young as 14 years of age to walk the runway—a clear child-labor law violation according to critics.[19] Even worse, it continues to reinforce the notion that to be beautiful, women and girls need to starve themselves.

These concerns apply not only to the teenaged girls targeted by such ads but also to the models themselves—young girls who are working long hours, subjected to harsh criticisms and widespread rejection. Most child development research suggests that children younger than 16 years are ill-prepared to deal with such scenarios.

In the United Kingdom, the Advertising Standards Authority (ASA) thus has banned some ads outright for being "socially irresponsible." An ad run by Drop Dead, a British clothing line, prompted the watchdog agency to condemn the brand's image: a shockingly thin model who sends dangerously inappropriate style signals to teenage girls. In its statement, the ASA complained that the young model's "hip, rib and collar bones were highly visible" and noted that she had visible (and unnatural) "hollows in her thighs."[20] Under such pressures, some U.K. companies have begun to respond. The fashion brand Topshop removed an ad from its website after advocates complained that the featured model was dangerously gaunt and thus a negative influence on young shoppers.[21]

In the United States, the Council of Fashion Designers of America (CFDA) also has denounced the hiring of underage models, yet violations continue. Recently, it called on designers and modeling agencies to require identification from models, showing that they were at least 16 years old. It also began educating industry members to recognize early signs of eating disorders, called for the provision of healthy snacks backstage, and banned the use of models under 18 years at fittings or photo shows held after midnight. Despite widespread skepticism that the industry can regulate itself, the National Eating Disorders Association has applauded the CFDA guidelines.

Change thus appears to be coming, but slowly still. Designers such as Tommy Hilfiger and Tory Burch complain that the models who apply with them continue to appear young and thin. "I still see some girls coming in who are really emaciated," Burch said. "It's still a problem." Those concerned about the ultra-thin style promoted by fashion advertising for young girls will be watching, but changing the tone of this communication is more challenging than just checking IDs and offering up a snack.

Promoting products using ultra-thin models sends dangerously inappropriate style signals to teenage girls.

Sales Promotions

Sales promotions are special incentives or excitement-building programs that encourage the purchase of a product or service, such as coupons, rebates, contests, free samples, and point-of-purchase displays. Marketers typically design these incentives for use in conjunction with other advertising or personal selling

tions, like free samples or point-of-purchase dis-
short-term sales. Others, like contests and sweep-
components of firms' CRM programs as a means to
discuss such sales promotions in more detail in

two-way flow of communication between a buyer and a
influence the buyer's purchase decision. Personal selling
settings: face-to-face, video teleconferencing, on the tele-
net. Although consumers don't often interact with profes-
sonal selling represents an important component of many
ally in business-to-business (B2B) settings.
municating directly with a potential customer is quite high
er forms of promotion, but it is simply the best and most effi-
tain products and services. Customers can buy many products
out the help of a salesperson, but salespeople simplify the buy-
viding information and services that save customers time and
sales representatives add significant value, which makes the
loying them worthwhile. We devote Chapter 20 to personal
ement.

has received the greatest increase in aggregate spend-
ting, or marketing that communicates directly with
response or transaction.[22] Direct marketing contains
ew forms of marketing communication initiatives.
ncludes mail and catalogs sent through the mail;
-mail and mobile marketing.
have had a profound effect on direct marketing
n be directed to a specific consumer. Firms use
merchandise and special promotions, confirm
when an order has been shipped. Currently
dheld devices can function as a payment me-
he transaction occurs in much the same way

abases has enabled marketers to identify
s purchase situations, which has contrib-
ting. Marketers have been able to build
creased use of credit and debit cards,
online shopping, all of which require
ion that becomes part of its database.
ases better when they possess such
direct marketing efforts appropri-
how companies are targeting con-
chasing behavior and how the

t their customers so they will be
or example, sends e-mail cou-
iously, mails slick pictures of
have received orders in the
ft-giving occasions, such as
se different forms of direct
on both the interactivity

Whereas once companies bought ads on websites related to the product
(e.g., a healthy drink on the GNC website), more targeted advertising now pr
lar customer rather than all visitors to a particular site.[24] Based on web b
and past purchases, a firm like Target can, for instance, determine with som
curacy who among its customers is pregnant.[25] It can then entice those v
husbands to visit Target or Target.com and buy baby-related products using p
coupons geared directly to them. But how would these customers react if th
ceive these promotions knowing that Target should have no idea that they we
Even worse, what would be the reaction if a targeted promotion was sent to th
unwed teenage mother whose father was unaware of the pregnancy?

Because of the changing ways in which firms are using data collected from t
ers, the Consumer Privacy Bill of Rights was passed, so that consumers can
choose not to be tracked. In particular, consumers now have the following rights

- **Individual Control** Consumers can control what personal data companies co
  how it is used.
- **Transparency** Consumers should be able to easily find and understand the pri
  practices of companies.
- **Context** Companies that collect and use personal data will do so in ways consi
  with how consumers provided the data.
- **Security** The use of personal data will not put consumers at risk.
- **Access and Accuracy** Companies should make efforts to make sure that person
  is accurate and provide access to consumers to correct data that is inaccurate.
- **Focused Collection** The collection of consumers' personal data will be limited an
  stricted by the context of how it was supplied in the first place.
- **Accountability** Companies are responsible to establish systems, train employee
  limit the access of third parties to consumers' personal data. They are responsi
  to consumers and enforcement authorities to assure this takes place.

Are consumers' personal privacy rights being unjustly invaded by firms that pro
with targeted promotions based on their browsing habits? Or are the marketing
gaged in these activities just providing them with helpful information that may r
buying decisions more pleasant and efficient?

Mobile marketing is marketing through wireless handheld dev
cellular telephones.[27] Smartphones have become far more than tools
they offer a kind of mobile computer with the ability to obtain
weather, music, videos, and text messages, as well as purchase
Marketing success rests on integrating marketing communications
ful apps that are consistent with these consumer attitudes toward
In response, firms are steadily improving customers' potential e
their mobile interface. Exhibit 18.4 highlights five successful m
campaigns; the Westin mobile campaign is discussed in more de
Mobile Marketing 18.1.

Online Marketing

We now examine in greater depth several electronic media
blogs, and social media.

Websites Firms have increased their emphasis on communic
ers through their websites. They use their websites to build th
educate customers about their products or services, as well a
purchased. Retailers and some manufacturers sell merc

programs. Many sales promotions, like free samples or point-of-purchase displays, are designed to build short-term sales. Others, like contests and sweepstakes, have become integral components of firms' CRM programs as a means to build customer loyalty. We discuss such sales promotions in more detail in Chapter 19.

Personal Selling

Personal selling is the two-way flow of communication between a buyer and a seller that is designed to influence the buyer's purchase decision. Personal selling can take place in various settings: face-to-face, video teleconferencing, on the telephone, or over the Internet. Although consumers don't often interact with professional sales people, personal selling represents an important component of many IMC programs, especially in business-to-business (B2B) settings.

The cost of communicating directly with a potential customer is quite high compared with other forms of promotion, but it is simply the best and most efficient way to sell certain products and services. Customers can buy many products and services without the help of a salesperson, but salespeople simplify the buying process by providing information and services that save customers time and effort. In many cases, sales representatives add significant value, which makes the added expense of employing them worthwhile. We devote Chapter 20 to personal selling and sales management.

Direct Marketing

The component of IMC that has received the greatest increase in aggregate spending recently is **direct marketing**, or marketing that communicates directly with target customers to generate a response or transaction.[22] Direct marketing contains a variety of traditional and new forms of marketing communication initiatives. Traditional direct marketing includes mail and catalogs sent through the mail; direct marketing also includes e-mail and mobile marketing.

Internet-based technologies have had a profound effect on direct marketing initiatives. E-mail, for instance, can be directed to a specific consumer. Firms use e-mail to inform customers of new merchandise and special promotions, confirm the receipt of an order, and indicate when an order has been shipped. Currently available technologies also mean handheld devices can function as a payment medium: Just tap your cell phone, and the transaction occurs in much the same way it occurs with a credit card.[23]

The increased use of customer databases has enabled marketers to identify and track consumers over time and across purchase situations, which has contributed to the rapid growth of direct marketing. Marketers have been able to build these databases, thanks to consumers' increased use of credit and debit cards, store-specific credit and loyalty cards, and online shopping, all of which require the buyer to give the seller personal information that becomes part of its database. Because firms understand customers' purchases better when they possess such information, they can more easily focus their direct marketing efforts appropriately. Ethical and Societal Dilemma 18.2 details how companies are targeting consumers with promotions based on their purchasing behavior and how the government has reacted to curb potential abuse.

Direct marketing retailers try to carefully target their customers so they will be more receptive to their messages. Omaha Steaks, for example, sends e-mail coupons for items that customers have purchased previously, mails slick pictures of gourmet steaks and meal packages to addresses that have received orders in the past, and calls customers personally during likely gift-giving occasions, such as the holidays, to offer to repeat a previous gift order. These different forms of direct marketing demonstrate how this IMC format can vary on both the interactivity and online/offline dimensions of the matrix.

Ethical and Societal Dilemma 18.2 — The Consumer Privacy Bill of Rights

Whereas once companies bought ads on websites related to the product being promoted (e.g., a healthy drink on the GNC website), more targeted advertising now pursues a particular customer rather than all visitors to a particular site.[24] Based on web browsing activity and past purchases, a firm like Target can, for instance, determine with some degree of accuracy who among its customers is pregnant.[25] It can then entice those women or their husbands to visit Target or Target.com and buy baby-related products using promotions and coupons geared directly to them. But how would these customers react if they were to receive these promotions knowing that Target should have no idea that they were pregnant? Even worse, what would be the reaction if a targeted promotion was sent to the home of an unwed teenage mother whose father was unaware of the pregnancy?

Because of the changing ways in which firms are using data collected from their customers, the Consumer Privacy Bill of Rights was passed, so that consumers can more easily choose not to be tracked. In particular, consumers now have the following rights:[26]

- **Individual Control** Consumers can control what personal data companies collect and how it is used.
- **Transparency** Consumers should be able to easily find and understand the privacy practices of companies.
- **Context** Companies that collect and use personal data will do so in ways consistent with how consumers provided the data.
- **Security** The use of personal data will not put consumers at risk.
- **Access and Accuracy** Companies should make efforts to make sure that personal data is accurate and provide access to consumers to correct data that is inaccurate.
- **Focused Collection** The collection of consumers' personal data will be limited and restricted by the context of how it was supplied in the first place.
- **Accountability** Companies are responsible to establish systems, train employees and limit the access of third parties to consumers' personal data. They are responsible both to consumers and enforcement authorities to assure this takes place.

Are consumers' personal privacy rights being unjustly invaded by firms that provide them with targeted promotions based on their browsing habits? Or are the marketing firms engaged in these activities just providing them with helpful information that may make their buying decisions more pleasant and efficient?

Mobile marketing is marketing through wireless handheld devices, such as cellular telephones.[27] Smartphones have become far more than tools to place calls; they offer a kind of mobile computer with the ability to obtain sports scores, weather, music, videos, and text messages, as well as purchase merchandise. Marketing success rests on integrating marketing communications with fun, useful apps that are consistent with these consumer attitudes toward mobile devices. In response, firms are steadily improving customers' potential experience with their mobile interface. Exhibit 18.4 highlights five successful mobile marketing campaigns; the Westin mobile campaign is discussed in more detail in Social and Mobile Marketing 18.1.

Online Marketing

We now examine in greater depth several electronic media vehicles: websites, blogs, and social media.

Websites Firms have increased their emphasis on communicating with customers through their websites. They use their websites to build their brand image and educate customers about their products or services, as well as where they can be purchased. Retailers and some manufacturers sell merchandise directly to

Social and Mobile Marketing 18.1   Getting Tourists to Tap into Hotel Bookings[28]

It was a rough winter. People living in colder climates suffered through snowstorm after snowstorm, broken up only by freezing temperatures and icy winds. Recognizing that a large group of travelers was likely ready to take a break, Westin Hotels offered an easily accessible, aptly targeted campaign that held out the promise of sunshine.

When miserable cold-weather sufferers opened their Weather Channel app on their mobile devices, to see how long the latest cold snap would last, a banner appeared on their screens. "Tap here to warm up," it invites, nearly irresistibly. When their shivering fingers do so, users find the screens on their phones covered by the image of a layer of frost.

Wiping it away (virtually) leads them to a carousel of glamorous images of pools, palm trees, and beaches that sit right outside Westin hotels in places like Maui, Scottsdale, Cancun, Fort Lauderdale, Puerto Vallarta, and Palm Springs.

The app is appealing: Users get to play a little when wiping away the frost, and the narrative keeps them entertained, as do the pretty pictures. If they are entranced enough, it also allows them to move directly to the Westin reservation page, of course. Furthermore, the precise targeting—the banner ad only appears to people who have actively chosen to check the weather in cold geographies—and opt-in nature of the app means that the visitors are already interested in the promise of a warm vacation.

consumers over the Internet. For example, in addition to selling merchandise, Office Depot's website hosts a Business Resource Center for its business customers that provides advice, product knowledge, and connections to networking contacts in other businesses. It also provides forms that businesses can use to comply with Occupational Safety and Health Act (OSHA) requirements, check job applicant records, estimate cash flow, and develop a sexual harassment policy; posts workshops for running a business; and summarizes local and national business news. By providing this information, Office Depot reinforces its image as an essential source of products, services, and information for small businesses.

Many firms operate websites devoted to community building. These sites offer an opportunity for customers with similar interests to learn about products and services that support their hobbies and share information with others. Visitors

EXHIBIT 18.4   Illustrative Mobile Marketing Campaigns

Companies	Campaign
Dr Pepper HTML5 animation	Using its mobile app, and drawing on its animated television commercials, Dr Pepper presents customers with banner pop-ups of an animated boy enlisting their help in finding his cartoon friends. By using HTML5 animation, Dr Pepper has found a way to keep customers engaged with its ad longer than they normally would.
Herbal Essences Microsoft tags	Herbal Essences launched a mobile campaign to help customers determine the optimal product for their own personal type of hair. In more than 53,000 stores, customers can scan a Microsoft tag with their smartphones that will bring them to a customized site featuring in-depth information on Herbal Essences, including recommendations for hair types and styling tips.
Volkswagen Augmented reality	Volkswagen has put a new twist on an old print campaign concept. Customers could use their Apple devices to take a virtual test drive of the Passat. By placing their iPhone over the print ad, an animated Passat appears on the road. If customers "drive" too close to the edges of the road, the iPhone vibrates, simulating the Lane Assist feature. In Adaptive Lights mode, the animated car's headlights follow the edge of the road.
Kimberly Clark Pull-Ups iPad magazine	Although print media are declining, interest in tablet-oriented magazines is increasing. Pull-ups designed multimedia ads for the iPad version of *Parents* magazine to promote its Go Potty application, in which users can "color" a picture of a mother and child doing "The Potty Dance."
Westin Hotels and Resorts Geo-targeted ads	Customers in cold climates using The Weather Channel app see a small banner ad inviting them to "Tap here to warm up," after which they are invited to "wipe away the frost" from their screens. This brings them to images of Westin Hotels in warm areas, as well as an opportunity to reserve a room or view their reservations at Westin Hotels.

Source: Adapted from Gisele Tsirulnik, "Top 10 Mobile Advertising Campaigns in Q1," *Mobile Marketer,* April 20, 2011, http://www.mobilemarketer.com/cms/news/advertising/9747.html.

Theknot.com builds a community by allowing brides-to-be to post questions and/or comments about issues such as what to do about an overly zealous bachelor party being planned by the best man.

can also post questions seeking information and/or comments about issues, products, and services. For example, at www.theknot.com, a community site targeting couples planning their weddings, a bride-to-be might ask how to handle an overly zealous bachelor party being planned by the best man. Others who have experienced this problem then can post their advice.

Many firms, especially retailers, encourage customers to post reviews of products they have bought or used and even have visitors to their websites rate the quality of the reviews. Research has shown that these online product reviews increase customer loyalty and provide a competitive advantage for sites that offer them.[29]

Blogs A **blog (weblog)** contains periodic posts on a common webpage. A well-received blog can communicate trends, announce special events, create positive word of mouth, connect customers by forming a community, allow the company to respond directly to customers' comments, and develop a long-term relationship with the company. By its very nature, a blog is supposed to be transparent and contain authors' honest observations, which can help customers determine their trust and loyalty levels.

Nowadays, blogs are becoming more interactive as the communication between bloggers and customers has increased. Southwest Airlines' blog, "Nuts about Southwest," is used primarily to connect customers with the company's employees, letting them in on the culture and operations. The corporate contributors include everyone from mechanics to executives to pilots. The blog is also used to announce new product launches and collect information on which to base corporate decisions.[30]

Southwest Airlines' blog, "Nuts about Southwest," is used primarily to connect customers with the company's employees.

In addition, blogs can be linked to other social media such as microblog Twitter. Consider the situation in which Kevin Smith, the popular director of films such as *Clerks* and *Dogma* (and the actor who played Silent Bob in several of his movies), was removed from a Southwest flight because his large size required him to purchase two seats. Smith immediately tweeted about the situation to his more than 1.6 million Twitter followers. Then when he got onto another flight, he followed up with a picture of himself, proclaiming "SouthwestAir! Look how fat I am on your plane! Quick! Throw me off!"[31] Southwest quickly responded on its blog, citing its long-standing rules and concern for other passengers. Consumers' responses were about equally split in support of the airline and Smith.[32]

Social Media **Social media** is media content distributed through social interactions (see Chapter 3). The three most popular facilitators of social media are YouTube, Facebook, and Twitter. In these online sites, consumers review, communicate about, and aggregate information about products, prices, and promotions. These social media also allow users to interact among themselves (e.g., form a community), as well as provide other like-minded consumers (i.e., members of their community) and marketers their thoughts and evaluations about a firm's products or services. Thus, social media help facilitate the consumer decision process (Chapter 6) by encouraging need recognition, information search, alternative evaluation, purchase, and post-purchase reviews.

When Kevin Smith was removed from a Southwest Airlines flight because his large size required him to purchase two seats, he tweeted to his 1.6 million Twitter followers.

CHECK YOURSELF

1. What are the different elements of an IMC program?

PLANNING FOR AND MEASURING IMC SUCCESS

We begin by examining how marketers set strategic goals before implementing any IMC campaign. After they have established those goals, marketers can set the budget for the campaign and choose marketing metrics they will use to evaluate whether it has achieved its strategic objectives.

Goals

As with any strategic undertaking, firms need to understand the outcome they hope to achieve before they begin. These goals can be short-term, such as generating inquiries, increasing awareness, and prompting trial. Or they can be long-term in nature, such as increasing sales, market share, and customer loyalty. Selling beverages is always the primary and long-term goal of Coca-Cola, but in the short term, its polar bear advertising campaign (as described in the opening vignette)

EXHIBIT 18.5	Illustrative Marketing Goals and Related Campaigns			
Company and Campaign	Goals	Target Market	Media Used	Outcome
ASICS Sound Mind, Sound Body	Branch out beyond serious runner market segment and target casual runners.	Even split males and females, age 30–49	Television and print ads, online advertising	12% increase in market share
Columbia Sportswear Company Greater Outdoors	Showcase Columbia's technical innovation ability and overcome perceptions of inferior products.	60% males, age 20–59	Print ads, mobile media, social media, videos, online advertising	1% increase in sales, and +2 point brand awareness increase compared with previous year
GAP Ready for Holiday Cheer	Capture consumers' attention and get them to shop in the store during the holiday season.	Even split males and females, age 20–39	Print inserts, television ads, special website, social media, customizable videos	Kelly Awards Best Inset Winner; sales turned from a 12% decline in the previous year to a 1% increase
Southwest Airlines Grab Your Bag. It's On!	Encourages travelers to fly despite tough economic conditions.	Even split males and females, all ages	Television, radio, print, and in-airport ads	Contributed $99 million in profits
BMW Diesel Reinvented	Overcome the negative image of diesel that most consumers have.	Three segments: idea class, enthusiasts, and environmentally conscious	Print ads, videos	+1,463% year-to-year sales increase

Source: http://www.magazine.org/advertising/case_studies/.

aimed to establish brand awareness and purchase intentions. Some other goals are outlined in Exhibit 18.5.

Such goals, both short- and long-term, should be explicitly defined and measured. They also might change over time, as Superior Service 18.2 describes. Regardless of their measure or changes though, goals constitute part of the overall

Southwest Airlines, "Grab Your Bag. It's On" campaign's goal is to encourage travelers to fly despite tough economic conditions.

Columbia Sportswear Company's "Greater Outdoors" campaign's goal is to showcase Columbia's technical innovation ability and overcome perceptions of inferior products.

Superior Service 18.2 — Changing Priceline by Killing Captain Kirk

When Priceline, the online travel service, started offering a new fixed-price discount, in addition to its longstanding "name your own price" discounts, the company basically had to change the subject. That meant killing the messenger: the over-the-top actor William Shatner. His mouthy, dramatic "The Negotiator" character had personified Priceline's negotiated discount approach for 14 years.[33]

As a global leader in online travel services, Priceline offers online reservations for airline tickets, hotel rooms, rental cars, vacation packages, and cruises. It serves consumers in more than 140 countries, with services available in 41 languages.[34] The company has long offered travelers a way to negotiate low-price discounts, but now it is expanding its offer, and thus redefining its goals, so that it can become known for offering fixed-price options for same-day reservations.

Although it was rapidly becoming the fastest growing part of its hotel business, Priceline also wanted to alert more customers to its new fixed-price Tonight-Only Deals service. To get that new message through, Priceline decided it needed a new approach, especially in its television advertising. According to Priceline's chief marketing officer, Shatner's bawdy parody of a tough guy "negotiator" had so dominated the company's commercial image that it might make it tough for viewers to

pick up on Priceline's new, same-day fixed-pricing. "One of the challenges we face is that Bill is so awesome and so closely associated with Priceline that we needed to grab back consumers' attention," he said.[35]

So Shatner's last ad was a fatal one. In the last Priceline featuring him, Shatner rushed travelers off a bus as it hit a bend in the road, then teetered at the edge of a cliff. Without their vehicle, these riders would need a place to stay the night, so Shatner hands them his mobile phone—just as the bus pitches over into the abyss and crashes in flames. ("It's what he would have wanted," protests one survivor who has taken the time to book a room rather than mourn the lost Negotiator.)

To make its fixed-price discount deals even more accessible to its highly mobile customer base, Priceline developed free apps for Apple's iPad, iPhone, and iPod Touch, as well as for Android devices. A Tonight-Only Deals app is part of its free Hotel Negotiator application.

And what about Shatner? Is the popular celebrity spokesman, who offered Priceline customers laughs as well as great deals, really gone? No! After "killing" his character seven months earlier, Priceline has brought him back as its pitchman.[36]

---

promotional plan, which is usually a subsection of the firm's marketing plan. Another part of the promotional plan is the budget.

Setting and Allocating the IMC Budget

Firms use a variety of methods to plan their marketing communications budgets. Because all the methods of setting a promotional budget have both advantages and disadvantages, no one method should be used in isolation.[37]

The **objective-and-task method** determines the budget required to undertake specific tasks to accomplish communication objectives. To use this method, marketers first establish a set of communication objectives, then determine which media best reach the target market and how much it will cost to run the number and types of communications necessary to achieve the objectives. This process—set objectives, choose media, and determine costs—must be repeated for each product or service. The sum of all the individual communication plan budgets becomes the firm's total marketing communications budget. In addition to the objective-and-task method, various **rule-of-thumb methods** can be used to set budgets (see Exhibit 18.6).

These rule-of-thumb methods use prior sales and communication activities to determine the present communication budget. Although they are easy to implement, they have various limitations, as noted in Exhibit 18.6. Clearly, budgeting is not a simple process. It may take several rounds of negotiations among the various managers, who are each competing for resources for their own areas of responsibility, to devise a final IMC budget.

Measuring Success Using Marketing Metrics

Once a firm has decided how to set its budget for marketing communications and its campaigns have been developed and implemented, it reaches the point that it

LO4 Explain the methods used to allocate the integrated marketing communications (IMC) budget.

LO5 Identify marketing metrics used to measure IMC success.

EXHIBIT 18.6	Rule-of-Thumb Methods	
Method	Definition	Limitations
Competitive parity	The communication budget is set so that the firm's share of communication expenses equals its share of the market.	Does not allow firms to exploit the unique opportunities or problems they confront in a market. If all competitors use this method to set communication budgets, their market shares will stay approximately the same over time.
Percentage-of-sales	The communication budget is a fixed percentage of forecasted sales.	Assumes the same percentage used in the past, or by competitors, is still appropriate for the firm. Does not take into account new plans (e.g., to introduce a new line of products in the current year).
Available budget	Marketers forecast their sales and expenses, excluding communication, during the budgeting period. The difference between the forecast sales and expenses plus desired profit is reserved for the communication budget. That is, the communication budget is the money available after operating costs and profits have been budgeted.	Assumes communication expenses do not stimulate sales and profit.

must measure the success of the campaigns, using various marketing metrics.[38] Each step in the IMC process can be measured to determine how effective it has been in motivating consumers to move to the next step in the buying process. However, recall that the lagged effect influences and complicates marketers' evaluations of a promotion's effectiveness, as well as the best way to allocate marketing communications budgets. Because of the cumulative effect of marketing communications, it may take several exposures before consumers are moved to buy, so firms cannot expect too much too soon. They must invest in the marketing communications campaign with the idea that it may not reach its full potential for some time. In the same way, if firms cut marketing communications expenditures, it may take time before they experience a decrease in sales.

Traditional Media When measuring IMC success, the firm should examine when and how often consumers have been exposed to various marketing communications. Specifically, they use measures of frequency and reach to gauge consumers' exposure to marketing communications. For most products and situations, a single exposure to a communication is hardly enough to generate the desired response. Therefore, marketers measure the **frequency** of exposure—how often the audience is exposed to a communication within a specified period of time. The other measure used to measure consumers' exposure to marketing communications is **reach**, which describes the percentage of the target population exposed to a specific marketing communication, such as an advertisement, at least once.[39] Marketing communications managers usually state their media objectives in terms of **gross rating points (GRP)**, which represents reach multiplied by frequency (GRP = reach × frequency).

This GRP measure can refer to print, radio, or television, but any comparisons require a single medium. Suppose that Kenneth Cole places seven advertisements in *Vogue* magazine, which reaches 50 percent of the "fashion forward" target segment. The total GRP generated by these seven magazine advertisements is 50 reach × 7 advertisements = 350 GRP. Now suppose Kenneth Cole includes 15 television ads as part of the same campaign, run during the program *America's Next Top Model*, which has a rating (reach) of 9.2. The total GRP generated by these 15 advertisements is 138 (9.2 × 15 = 138). However, advertisements typically appear

When calculating the gross rating points (GRP) of America's Next Top Model, the advertiser would multiply the reach times the frequency.

in more than one television program. So, if Kenneth Cole also advertises 12 times during *The Voice*, which earns a rating of 1.8, its GRP would be 1.8 × 12 = 21.6, and the total GRP for both programs would be 138 + 21.6 = 159.6.

Web-Based Media Firms are spending over $26 billion dollars annually on online advertising, which includes paid search, display ads, e-mail, and sponsorships.[40] Although GRP is an adequate measure for television and radio advertisements, assessing the effectiveness of any web-based communication efforts in an IMC campaign generally requires web tracking software to measure how much time viewers spend on particular webpages, the number of pages they view, how many times users click on banner ads, which website they came from, and so on. All these performance metrics can be easily measured and assessed using a variety of software, including Google Analytics.

Facebook also helps companies to see who has been visiting their fan pages, what those people are doing on the fan pages, and who is clicking on their advertisements.[41] By keeping track of who is visiting their fan pages, marketers can better customize the material on their pages by getting to know the people visiting.

Planning, Implementing, and Evaluating IMC Programs— An Illustration of Google Advertising

Imagine a hypothetical upscale sneaker store in New York City, called Transit, that is modeled after vintage New York City subway trains. Transit's target market is young, well-educated, hip men and women aged 17–34 years. The owner's experience indicates the importance of personal selling for this market because they (1) make large purchases, and (2) seek considerable information before making a decision. Thus, Jay Oliver, the owner, spends part of his communication budget on training his sales associates. Oliver has realized his communication budget is considerably less than that of other sneaker stores in the area. He has therefore decided to concentrate his limited budget on a specific segment and use electronic media exclusively in his IMC program.

The IMC program Oliver has developed emphasizes his store's distinctive image and uses his website, social shopping, and some interesting community building techniques. For instance, he has an extensive customer database as part of his CRM system from which he draws information for matching new merchandise with his customers' past purchase behaviors and little personal

Advertisers pay Google to show up in the Sponsored Link section in the right-hand column of this screen grab based on the keywords customers use in their searches.

nuggets of information that he or other sales associates have collected on the customers. He then e-mails specific customers information about new products that he believes they will be interested in. He also encourages customers to use blogs hosted on his website. Customers chat about the "hot" new sneakers, club events, and races. He does everything with a strong sense of style.

To reach new customers, he is using **search engine marketing (SEM)**. In particular, he is using Google AdWords, a search engine marketing tool offered by Google that allows advertisers to show up in the Sponsored Links section of the search results page based on the keywords potential customers use (see the sponsored link section in the right-hand column of the Google screen grab above).

Oliver must determine the best keywords to use for his sponsored link advertising program. Some potential customers might search using the key words, "sneakers," "sneakers in New York City," "athletic shoes," or other such versions. Using Google AdWords, Oliver can assess the effectiveness of his advertising expenditures by measuring the reach, relevance, and return on investment for each of the keywords that potential customers used during their Internet searches.

To estimate reach, Oliver uses the number of **impressions** (the number of times the ad appears in front of the user) and the **click-through rate (CTR)**. To calculate CTR, he takes the number of times a user clicks on an ad and divides it by the number of impressions.[42] For example, if a sponsored link was delivered 100 times and 10 people clicked on it, then the number of impressions is 100, the number of clicks is 10, and the CTR would be 10 percent.

The **relevance** of the ad describes how useful an ad message is to the consumer doing the search. Google provides a measure of relevance through its AdWords system using a quality score. The quality score looks at a variety of factors to measure how relevant a keyword is to an ad's text and to a user's search query. In general, a high quality score means that a keyword will trigger ads in a higher position and at a lower cost-per click.[43] In a search for "sneaker store," the Transit ad showed up fourth, suggesting high relevance.

Using the following formula, Oliver also can determine an ad's **return on investment (ROI)**:

$$\text{ROI} = \frac{\text{Sales revenue} - \text{Advertising cost}}{\text{Advertising cost}}$$

For the two keyword searches in Exhibit 18.7, Oliver finds how much the advertising cost him (Column 3), the sales produced as a result (Column 4), and the

EXHIBIT 18.7	ROI Assessment				
(1) Keyword	(2) Clicks	(3) Cost	(4) Sales	(5) Sales Revenue (Col. 4) − Cost (Col. 3)	(6) ROI = (Col. 5/Col. 3) × 100
Sneaker store	110	$10/day	$35/day	$25	250%
New York City sneakers	40	$25/day	$40/day	$15	60%

EXHIBIT 18.8	Program Effectiveness Results			
Communication Objective	Questions	Before Campaign	6 Months After	One Year After
Awareness (% mentioning store)	What stores sell sneakers?	38%	46%	52%
Knowledge (% giving outstanding rating for sales assistance)	Which stores would you rate outstanding on the following characteristics?	9	17	24
Attitude (% first choice)	On your next shopping trip for sneakers, which store would you visit first?	13	15	19
Visit (% visited store)	Which of the following stores have you been to?	8	15	19

ROI (Column 6). For "sneaker store," the Transit website had a lot more clicks (110) than the clicks received from "New York City sneakers" (40) (see Column 2, Exhibit 18.7). Even though the sales were lower for the keywords "sneaker store" at $35/day, versus $40/day for the keywords "New York City sneakers," the ROI was much greater for the "sneaker store" keyword combination. In the future, Oliver should continue this keyword combination, in addition to producing others that are similar to it, in the hope that he will attain an even greater return on investment.

To evaluate his IMC program, Oliver compares the results of the program with his objectives (Exhibit 18.8). To measure his program's effectiveness, he conducted an inexpensive online survey using the questions in Exhibit 18.8, which shows the survey results for one year.

The results show a steady increase in awareness, knowledge of the store, and choice of the store as a primary source of sneakers. This research provides evidence that the IMC program was conveying the intended message to the target audience.

CHECK YOURSELF

1. Why is the objective-and-task method of setting an IMC budget better than the rule-of-thumb methods?
2. How do firms use GRP to evaluate the effectiveness of traditional media?
3. How would a firm evaluate the effectiveness of its Google advertising?

Summing Up

LO1 Identify the components of the communication process.

The communication process begins with a sender, which provides the message to a transmitter that develops or encodes the message for transmission through a communication channel. When a recipient receives the message, it may have been altered by noise in the environment. To find out, the sender needs to receive some form of feedback from the recipient.

LO2 Explain the four steps in the AIDA model.

Awareness is the first "thinking" step, during which the consumer simply recognizes a brand or product. During the interest step, the consumer starts to "feel" and become intrigued enough to explore the product or brand. This interest then leads to another feeling, namely, desire for the marketed item. Finally, to be successful, marketing communication must prompt an action: a purchase, a commitment, a recommendation, or whatever else the company is trying to get consumers to do.

 Describe the various integrative communication channels.

Advertising has long been the primary channel for marketing communication and is still a constant presence, but other media channels have become more and more prominent. For example, direct marketing media options, particularly online options, have increased in recent years. Outbound direct marketing telephone calls have declined, but Internet-based technologies like e-mail and m-commerce have increased. Public relations also has become increasingly important as other media forms become more expensive and as consumers grow more skeptical of commercial messages. With regard to new and electronic media, the wealth of recent options include websites, corporate blogs, and social media such as YouTube, Facebook, and Twitter.

LO4 Explain the methods used to allocate the integrated marketing communications (IMC) budget.

Various rule-of-thumb methods rely on prior sales and communication activities to determine the best allocation. For example, the competitive parity method sets the budget so that the share of communication expenses equals the firm's share of the market. The percentage-of-sales method, just as it sounds, uses a fixed percentage of sales as the amount of the budget. In contrast, the objective-and-task method establishes specific communication objectives, identifies which media can best attain those objectives, and then determines the related costs to expend.

LO5 Identify marketing metrics used to measure IMC success.

Marketers rely on a mix of traditional and nontraditional measures to determine IMC success. Because potential customers generally need to be exposed to IMC messages several times before they will buy, firms estimate the degree to which customers are exposed to a message by multiplying frequency (the number of times an audience is exposed to a message) by reach (the percentage of the target population exposed to a specific marketing communication). Measuring Internet IMC effectiveness requires different measures, such as click-through tracking that measures how many times users click on banner advertising on websites.

Key Terms

- advertising, 557
- AIDA model, 553
- aided recall, 554
- blog (Weblog), 562
- brand awareness, 554
- click-through rate (CTR), 568
- communication channel, 550
- decoding, 551
- direct marketing, 559
- encoding, 549
- feedback loop, 551
- frequency, 566

- gross rating points (GRP), 566
- impressions, 568
- integrated marketing communications (IMC), 548
- lagged effect, 555
- mobile marketing, 560
- noise, 551
- objective-and-task method, 565
- personal selling, 559
- public relations, 557
- reach, 566
- receiver, 551

- relevance, 568
- return on investment (ROI), 568
- rule-of-thumb methods, 565
- sales promotions, 558
- search engine marketing (SEM), 568
- sender, 549
- social media, 563
- top-of-mind awareness, 554
- transmitter, 549

Marketing Applications

1. Assume that the contemporary apparel company Juicy Couture has embarked on a new IMC strategy. It has chosen to advertise on TV during the NBC Nightly News and in print in *Time* magazine. The message is designed to announce new styles for the season and uses a 17-year-old woman as the model. Evaluate this strategy, and if appropriate propose an alternative.

2. Using the steps in the AIDA model, explain why a potential consumer in question 1 who views Juicy Couture's advertising may not be ready to go out and purchase a new pair of jeans.

3. Suppose a snack company introduces a new product called SumSeeds—sunflower seeds with energy boosters like caffeine, taurine, lysine, and ginseng.

How would you expect this product's IMC program to differ from that for regular sunflower seeds sold as snacks?

4. It's holiday time, and you've decided to purchase a box of chocolates for the person of your choice. Evaluate how Godiva's advertising, personal selling, public relations, and electronic media might influence your purchase decision. How might the relative importance of each of these IMC elements be different if your parents were making the purchase?

5. Suppose you saw your instructor for this course being interviewed on TV about the impact of a big storm on an upcoming holiday's sales. Is this interview part of your college's IMC program? If so, do you believe it benefits the college? How?

6. A retail store places an ad in the local newspaper for yoga wear. The sales of the featured items increase significantly for the next two weeks. Sales in the rest of the sportswear department go up as well. What do you think are the short- and long-term objectives of the ad? Justify your answer.

7. As an intern for Coca-Cola, you have been asked to help with developing an IMC budget. The objective of the IMC strategy is to raise Diet Coke's market share by 2 percent in the United States in the next 18 months. Your manager explains, "It's real simple; just increase the budget 2 percent over last year's." Evaluate your manager's strategy.

8. You were sitting in the school cafeteria yesterday, and a young man from your marketing class, whom you don't know well, asked if he could sit down. He then started telling you about this very cool new Apple product that allows you to record class lectures and play them back on an MP3 player. Although you recognize the merit in the product, you later find out that he works for Apple. Do you believe his action constitutes an ethical IMC strategy? How will it affect your attitude toward Apple and the potential that you will purchase the product?

Quiz Yourself

www.mhhe.com/grewal4e

1. Senders often use cues or heuristics to facilitate _____ in the communication process.
   a. encoding
   b. decoding
   c. recoding
   d. transcoding
   e. feedback

2. Ingrid wants her company to expand its use of public relations. She argues that, as other IMC alternatives become more expensive and _____, public relations should be a larger part of her company's IMC efforts.
   a. online couponing has declined
   b. consumers have become more skeptical of marketing claims

   c. web tracking software has become more sophisticated
   d. gross rating points have become marginalized
   e. commercial speech has become more effective

(Answers to these two questions can be found on page 648.)

Go to www.mhhe.com/grewal4e to practice an additional 11 questions.

Toolkit

RETURN ON MARKETING EXPENDITURES

Suppose Jay Oliver (marketing manager of Transit sneaker store) is considering two search engine marketing (SEM) options to reach out to new customers to market Transit. In particular, he is using Google AdWords, a search engine marketing tool offered by Google that allows firms to show up in searches based on the keywords potential customers use. Transit is targeting young adults age 17–28. The sneaker market is about $500,000,000 sales annually, and the target market is about 35% of that. Their gross margins are 20%. Oliver estimates that Transit will capture a 2% market share of the target market with a $500,000 advertising and keyword budget (option 1) and a 3% market share with a $1,000,000 advertising and keyword budget (option 2). Which marketing plan produces the higher ROI for the year? Please use the toolkit provided at www.mhhe.com/grewal4e to assess the ROI of the two options.

Net Savvy

1. Visit http://www.thephelpsgroup.com and click on the "Work" tab at the top. Compare the IMC for the different companies. What were the goals of the integrated marketing campaign? Which IMC components were used in that particular campaign? How do those components contribute to the success of the IMC campaign in achieving its stated goals?

2. *The Journal of Integrated Marketing Communications,* published annually by graduate students of the Medill School at Northwestern University, attempts to identify best practices and provide "a forum for communications industry professionals and academia to discuss the theory and application of integrated marketing communications." Visit their site and see what suggestions they make. To whom does the site seem targeted?

Chapter Case Study

JAY-Z AND BING: THE CAMPAIGN TO CONVERT JAY-Z DECODERS INTO BING USERS

When Microsoft needed a strategy to boost people's use of its Bing search engine, it found an oddly perfect vehicle in an integrated marketing campaign—one that also has been called a "transmedia event."[44] The ad agency that Microsoft hired proposed that the Bing campaign could work in conjunction with the new campaign for another of its clients: Jay-Z, the rap star and dominating producer, who wanted a global marketing strategy for the publication of his memoir, *Decoded*.

The creative process that led to this innovative marketing campaign—integrated in more ways than one—started with the ad agency, Droga5. It had these two separate mega-clients: Microsoft wanted to drive more users to its search engine, and Jay-Z wanted a way to promote his memoir. Proposing a new kind of synergy, the agency developed a plan to transform each client into the other's promotional vehicle.

Using outdoor advertising, search engines, a broad media strategy, and open source publishing,[45] Droga5 staged a month-long "transmedia" scavenger hunt, before the book was actually released. Jay-Z sent out clues through Facebook, Twitter, and a Bing page that told fans where to look for enormous versions of the individual pages from his book, pasted onto public locations. A facsimile of each of the 320 pages in the book would appear in a real-world location (e.g., New York, Los Angeles, New Orleans, Miami, Detroit, London) that reflected the story being told on that page. For example, a bronze plaque bolted to the wall of the Marcy Avenue apartment building where Jay-Z spent his childhood displayed pages 2 and 3 of *Decoded*, where Jay-Z wrote about the summer of 1978, "when I was nine years old."

Fans plugged the clues that Jay-Z had released into the Bing search engine, to search for the specific locations where they would find pages. The clues could only be decoded (pun intended) through Bing's search and street-mapping interface. Every public posting of a *Decoded* page also featured the URL for Bing.com/Jay-Z, along with the Bing logo.[46] The plan also created a public art project; if a relevant location could not be found, it was conjured up and created.

In turn, the campaign engaged consumers in at least a dozen cities worldwide. The majority of the wall-sized mock-ups of *Decoded* pages appeared on building walls in New York's Bedford-Stuyvesant neighborhood, where Jay-Z grew up. There were installations at subway stops, on a boardwalk in front of a Brooklyn beach, and on the backboard of a basketball hoop in Bedford-Stuyvesant where Jay-Z hung with friends, all in reference to events or moments discussed in the book. Secured through a partnership with the outdoor advertising firm Clear Channel, enormous billboards appeared overnight, often atop dingy, store-fronted buildings, apartment towers, and other cityscapes.[47] Accordingly, fans could "walk through Jay-Z's life"[48]—both virtually through Bing and on the streets he once walked.

In New Orleans, a huge replica of pages 220–21 spread across the Orpheum Theater's roof, describing Jay-Z's reaction to Hurricane Katrina's devastation. In a guitar shop in the Chelsea neighborhood of New York, an electric guitar was imprinted with pages 100–101, which recalled Kurt Cobain and how he "OD'd on fame." In Gleason's Gym in New York City, the pages were imprinted on two punching bags. Imprints also appeared on the stage curtains of the Apollo Theater in Harlem; on plates in The Spotted Pig, one of Jay-Z's favorite restaurants; and on a billboard at a subway stop in Abbey Road in London. Then *Decoded* pages showed up in the lining of custom-made Gucci leather jackets; on the sky-blue, painted bottom of the concrete pool at Miami's Delano Hotel, with an excerpt talking about the rapper's hit, "Big Pimpin"; and on the green felt surface of the pool table at the 40/40 Club, an upscale sports bar he owns.[49]

Over the course of a month, fans tracked down all 320 pages of the book, relying solely on the cues Jay-Z released through social media and their searches for the location on Bing. Bing's street-maps function helped those likely to get lost easily; it also enabled people who lived far from any of the sites to get a virtual visual tour of any neighborhood. Fans posted their photos of the found pages on the dedicated website. Through this collaboration, they assembled the entire memoir, even before any books were available on shelves. The first users to discover each page also became eligible to win a signed copy of the book and enter into a drawing for the grand prize: a trip to Las Vegas to see Jay-Z and Coldplay in concert on New Year's Eve.[50]

In addition to putting up the pages, Clear Channel helped build more buzz by running promotional spots, interviews on its radio stations, and exclusive videos of the performer on its websites. The campaign thus drew coverage in mainstream media as well, including *The New York Times* and *New York Observer*, which headlined its description, "Jay-Z's Book to Be Utterly Inescapable Thanks to Bing, Clear Channel."[51] The campaign was financed by Bing, not by the publisher of *Decoded*.[52]

The Jay-Z–Bing collaboration was clearly innovative. It drew rave reviews for its stunning creativity and novel approaches. But even more important, it was also effective. It converted millions of offline Jay-Z fans and prospective book buyers into online Bing users, and vice versa. In addition to winning two international awards at the Cannes International Festival of Creativity,[53] the campaign pushed Bing onto the global list of the top 10 visited sites for the first time. In numerical terms, it increased visits to the search engine by nearly 12 percent, many of them by new users.[54] Meanwhile, *Decoded* became a national bestseller and sat on that list for 19 consecutive weeks. The performer also picked up around a million new Facebook followers.

The prepublication event thus became a major cultural event. Celebrities like Ryan Seacrest and Snoop Dogg used their own Twitter accounts to get in on the conversation too. Snoop Dogg sent this tweet: "My big homie Jay-Z is hidin' pages of his book all over the world and fans gotta find it on Bing."[55]

The advertising agency's massive, cross-platform campaign to herald the publication of Jay-Z's memoir using the Bing search engine succeeded in reaching and engaging Jay-Z fans globally. Droga5's creative, transmedia campaign to increase the reach and name recognition of the Bing search engine using a connection with a popular musician succeeded in reaching and engaging search engine users worldwide. Thus, this masterfully integrated marketing campaign managed to push two mega-brands forward mainly by bringing them together. There are several postings on YouTube (e.g., http://www.youtube.com/watch?v=XNic4wf8AYg&feature=player_embedded) where you can learn more about the campaign and view some of the pages posted at unusual sites.

Questions

1. What different IMC components did the Jay-Z–Bing campaign use? Were these marketing elements integrated, in the sense defined in this chapter?

2. How might the various interested parties (e.g., Jay-Z, his publisher, Droga5, Clear Channel, Bing) measure the effectiveness of the campaign?

Advertising, Public Relations, and Sales Promotions

I f it ain't broke, don't fix it! This conventional wisdom seems so obvious, and so conventional, that it is the rare company that would go against it. And yet when it comes to their advertising, it seems that more and more companies are going after campaigns that already work well, in an attempt to make them even more successful.

In particular, when competition gets heavy between two dominant players in a market, the result is often new, more aggressive advertising. In the orange juice wars for example, the top-selling brand is PepsiCo's Tropicana, which dominates the domestic orange juice market with approximately $1 billion in annual sales.[1] Despite its existing advantage though, Tropicana wanted to consolidate its lead over Coca-Cola's Simply Orange. Therefore, the brand unleashed a new wave of advertising, with costs of $500–$600 million, in a vigorous attempt to gain even more market share.[2]

For example, Tropicana's "Awake to Alive" campaign in the United Kingdom suggests its juice as a gentle, natural way to start the day, with the tagline, "Tap Into Nature." A family wakens slowly as the soothing voice of an older, British man proffers morning greetings that parallel the phrasing from the beloved

children's book, *Goodnight Moon.* "Good morning, morning," he murmurs, against shots of a city asleep, then "Good morning, sideways world," as a man peers from the sheets at his knocked-over digital alarm clock. "Good morning, ruffled hair," he adds, as a woman rises, rubbing her hair, and "Good morning, sleepyheads, everywhere," he says to the child emerging from blankets. As these sleepy actors begin their days with glasses of juice, the reassuring voice promises, "The Tropicana oranges have been gently picked and squeezed. It's time to wake up."

The commercial suggests that the world wakes up to a brighter morning with Tropicana. The wider campaign added an innovative promotional event in London's Trafalgar Square to reinforce the concept. An enormous, orange-sheathed globe resembling a small sun, lit from within, hung in midair in the famous site, glowing from just before dawn until early evening on a dreary January day.[3] The January launch was purposeful; "At a really dark and slightly miserable time of year," said Peter Charles, Tropicana's U.K. marketing director, "we wanted to bring us a slice of brightness and really make people feel alive."[4]

LEARNING OBJECTIVES

LO1 Describe the steps in designing and executing an advertising campaign.

LO2 Identify three objectives of advertising.

LO3 Describe the different ways that advertisers appeal to consumers.

LO4 Identify the various types of media.

LO5 Identify agencies that regulate advertising.

LO6 Describe the elements of a public relations toolkit.

LO7 Identify the various types of sales promotions.

Indeed, the art installation provided mid-winter London with three hours of additional "daylight."[5] The whimsical structure, with no mention of orange groves, pulp, fruit growers, or any other such links, was suspended from a cable connected to the famous Nelson's Column (which honors Admiral Horatio Nelson, a Napoleonic War hero). Weighing 2.5 tons and emitting 210,000 watts of light,[6] it did look a little like an enormous orange.

A video of the installation's first public unveiling showed a public enchanted by the warm glow arising from Trafalgar Square.[7] For those who live outside the city or could not make it to the Square that day, Tropicana posted two videos of the day-long spectacle (see www.facebook.com/tropicanajuices). Furthermore, PepsiCo gave away free cartons of Tropicana through a link on its Facebook page.

Tropicana's New York City campaign had a very different tone and style—though the advertising concept was similarly emotional, location-driven, and public, as part of people's daily routines. However, these edgy ads, posted in Penn Station and several other well-traveled subway locations, spoke uniquely to Manhattanites.[8]

With a focus on the new "mini-carafe" container, the ads maintained a simple image, but the copy varied for each panel. The nearly two dozen versions, each just a few words, represented excerpts of the private reality of New Yorkers, always in a hurry ("You woke up 30 minutes early and got to work 30 minutes late") and rarely able to get a good night's sleep in the city ("Your alarm clock is roadwork outside your window"). The copy also empathized with the irritations that beset transit riders, like getting stuck on the platform ("Mariachi band only knows one song") or inadvertently hopping on the wrong train ("You could've sworn you read downtown").[9] Still other ads, in a clear nod to the city's singles community, commented on

Tropicana's New York City ad campaign reflects the private reality of its inhabitants.

the occasional embarrassments of Manhattan's dating life ("City of 8 million and you run into that guy" or "One train two ex-boyfriends").

Across these varying, cryptic "thought-bites," the consistent refrain was a reminder—pointing to the new mini-carafe—that Tropicana's juice is "the good part of New York mornings." This amusing, rather intimate tone knowingly teased New Yorkers about their morning complaints. Thus the campaign deftly suggested that Tropicana orange juice really understands, and even is a part of, life in the Big Apple. If a company can take the edge off a wintry, dreary day or make an annoying commute a little entertaining, how can it go wrong?

Advertising is a paid form of communication, delivered through media from an identifiable source, about an organization, product, service, or idea, designed to persuade the receiver to take some action, now or in the future.[10] This definition provides some important distinctions between advertising and other forms of promotion, which we discussed in the previous chapter. First, advertising is not free; someone has paid, with money, trade, or other means, to get the message shown. Second, advertising must be carried by some medium—television, radio, print, the Web, T-shirts, sidewalks, and so on. Third, legally, the source of the message must be known or knowable. Fourth, advertising represents a persuasive form of communication, designed to get the consumer to take some action. That desired action can range from "Don't drink and drive" to "Buy a new Mercedes."

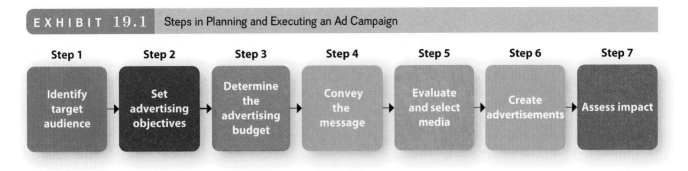

EXHIBIT 19.1 Steps in Planning and Executing an Ad Campaign

Step 1	Step 2	Step 3	Step 4	Step 5	Step 6	Step 7
Identify target audience	Set advertising objectives	Determine the advertising budget	Convey the message	Evaluate and select media	Create advertisements	Assess impact

Some activities that are called advertising really are not, such as word-of-mouth advertising. Even political advertising technically is not advertising because it is not for commercial purposes and thus is not regulated in the same manner as true advertising.

Advertising encompasses an enormous industry and clearly is the most visible form of marketing communications—so much so that many people think of marketing and advertising as synonymous. Global advertising expenditures are almost $500 billion, and almost half that amount is spent in the United States. Although expenditures dropped somewhat during the global downturn, advertising remains virtually everywhere, and predictions are that it will continue to grow.[11]

Yet how many of the advertisements you were exposed to yesterday do you remember today? Probably not more than three or four. As you learned in Chapter 6, perception is a highly selective process. Consumers simply screen out messages that are not relevant to them. When you notice an advertisement, you may not react to it. Even if you react to it, you may not remember it later. Even if you remember the ad, you may not remember the brand or sponsor—or worse yet from the advertiser's point of view, you may remember it as an advertisement for another brand.[12]

To get you to remember their ad and the brand, advertisers must first get your attention. As we discussed in Chapter 17, the increasing number of communication channels and changes in consumers' media usage have made the job of advertisers far more difficult.[13] As our opening example about Tropicana's constant efforts, despite its market leadership, demonstrated, advertisers continually endeavor to use creativity and various media to reach their target markets.

As a consumer, you are exposed only to the end product—the finished advertisement. But many actions must take place before you actually get to see an ad, as the Toolkit available for this chapter will show you (see the end of this chapter, page 602). In this chapter, we examine the ingredients of a successful advertising campaign, from identifying a target audience to creating the actual ad to assessing performance. Although our discussion is generally confined to advertising, much of the process for developing an advertising campaign is applicable to the IMC media vehicles discussed in Chapter 18. We conclude with some regulatory and ethical issues for advertising, then move on to public relations, sales promotions, and their use.

Designing and carrying out a successful advertising program requires much planning and effort. Exhibit 19.1 shows the key steps in the process, each of which helps ensure that the intended message reaches the right audience and has the desired effect. Let's examine each of these steps.

LO1 Describe the steps in designing and executing an advertising campaign.

STEP 1: IDENTIFY TARGET AUDIENCE

The success of an advertising program depends on how well the advertiser can identify its target audience. Firms conduct research to identify their target audience, then use the information they gain to set the tone for the advertising program and help them select the media they will use to deliver the message to that audience.

During this research, firms must keep in mind that their target audience may or may not be the same as current users of the product. For example, adidas knows that NBA fans likely are at least familiar with its offerings, even if they do not currently purchase sports gear from adidas. Thus some advertisements feature Chicago Bulls guard, Derrick Rose, to encourage them to buy more of the brand's products. But teenaged pop music fans might be less likely to pay attention to sporting goods. So in its marketing, adidas also features Katy Perry.[14] Another example of marketing and advertising towards different segments (e.g., consumer vs. business users) is illustrated by Visa and MasterCard, which have different ads and offerings aimed at these segments.

STEP 2: SET ADVERTISING OBJECTIVES

Advertising campaign objectives are derived from the overall objectives of the marketing program and clarify the specific goals that the ads are designed to accomplish. Generally, these objectives appear in the **advertising plan**, a subsection of the firm's overall marketing plan that explicitly analyzes the marketing and advertising situation, identifies the objectives of the advertising campaign, clarifies a specific strategy for accomplishing those objectives, and indicates how the firm can determine whether the campaign was successful.[15] An advertising plan is crucial because it will later serve as the yardstick against which advertising success or failure is measured.

Generally, in advertising to consumers, the objective is a **pull strategy** in which the goal is to get consumers to pull the product into the marketing channel by demanding it. **Push strategies** also exist and are designed to increase demand by focusing on wholesalers, retailers, or salespeople. These campaigns attempt to motivate the seller to highlight the product, rather than the products of competitors, and thereby push the product to consumers. In this chapter, we will focus on pull strategies. Push strategies are examined in Chapters 16, 17, and 20.

All advertising campaigns aim to achieve certain objectives: to inform, persuade, and remind customers. Another way of looking at advertising objectives is to examine an ad's focus. Is the ad designed to stimulate demand for a particular product or service, or more broadly for the institution in general? Also, ads can be used to stimulate demand for a product category or an entire industry, or for a specific brand, firm, or item. Fiat's U.S. ads suggest its efforts to stimulate demand for specific models, with relevant messages in each case, as Adding Value 19.1 shows. We first look at the broad overall objectives: to inform, persuade, and remind. Then we examine advertising objectives based on the focus of the ad: product versus institutional.

LO2 Identify three objectives of advertising.

Informative Advertising

Informative advertising is a communication used to create and build brand awareness, with the ultimate goal of moving the consumer through the buying cycle to a purchase. Such advertising helps determine some important early stages of a product's life cycle (see Chapter 12), particularly when consumers have little information about the specific product or type of product. Retailers often use informative advertising to tell their customers about an upcoming sales event or the arrival of new merchandise.

Persuasive Advertising

When a product has gained a certain level of brand awareness, firms use **persuasive advertising** to motivate consumers to take action. Persuasive advertising generally occurs in the growth and early maturity stages of the product

Adding Value 19.1   Jenny from the Block, or Charlie on House Arrest[16]

As Fiat, the Italian car company that purchased Chrysler, increases its presence in the United States, it wants car buyers to recognize its overall brand name. But it also needs to get people excited about each of the models it will be putting on dealers' floors.

The ad campaign began with Jennifer Lopez, who drove her Fiat 500 through Bronx-related scenery, in line with her well-known claim to be "Jenny from the block." But the ads were more sweet than anything, and Fiat realized that it had faltered by making the car look too "girly."

Although its next ad featured a woman as well, there was nothing sweet about it. Premiering during the Super Bowl, the "Seduction" ad for Fiat's Abarth model—the "bad boy" in its lineup—allowed a nervous-looking fellow to dream of a connection with a striking, tall model, whose scorpion tattoo matched the brand logo. In this campaign, Fiat aimed to capture the spirit of the Abarth, which the firm's chief marketing officer calls "the 'small but wicked' personality of the Fiat." That is, the Jennifer Lopez ad might have helped increase brand awareness, but the Abarth ads offered "a different kind of messaging." The "Seduction" spot originally was not intended for television, but positive feedback on the sexy ad shown online (it received more than 8 million YouTube hits) led Fiat to tap it for the Super Bowl.

The Super Bowl slot was available because the planned ad was not ready. Now that it has emerged, the latest "House Arrest" ad takes the bad boy image even further, by featuring perhaps the most notorious modern celebrity bad boy: Charlie Sheen. His well-publicized, erratic behavior, which prompted his firing from a hit sitcom, has gained him a notable reputation for breaking the rules. But Fiat upends the moral lesson: Sheen races a black Abarth model throughout a mansion, before screeching to a stop and emerging from the car to show off his ankle monitor and claim, "I love being under house arrest." (Notably, the model whom Sheen embraces as he drops his line is the same scorpion-tattooed woman, Catrinel Menghia from the "Seduction" campaign.)

Pleased with its ability to develop specific and unique images of the models, Fiat plans to persist in its advertising plans for the Fiat 500 and the Abarth, separately. The need for consumers to ask for these models has been heightened by failures in other elements of Fiat's marketing campaign, including delayed dealer rollouts and supply chain disruptions. In the meantime, the focus remains on building more awareness of the brand.

Fiat has separate advertising plans for its Fiat 500 and its souped-up, sexy Abarth.

life cycle, when competition is most intense, and attempts to accelerate the market's acceptance of the product. In later stages of the product life cycle, persuasive advertising may be used to reposition an established brand by persuading consumers to change their existing perceptions of the advertised product. Firms like Cover Girl often use persuasive advertising to convince consumers

to take action—switch brands,[17] try a new product, or even continue to buy the advertised product.

Reminder Advertising

Finally, **reminder advertising** is a communication used to remind or prompt repurchases, especially for products that have gained market acceptance and are in the maturity stage of their life cycle. Such advertising certainly appears in traditional media, such as television or print commercials, but it also encompasses other forms of advertising. For example, if you decide to buy tissue paper, do you carefully consider all the options, comparing their sizes, prices, and performance, or do you just grab the first thing you see on the shelf? When your grocery store places a display of Kleenex on the end of the paper products aisle, it relies on your top-of-the-mind awareness of Kleenex, which the manufacturer has achieved through advertising. That is, Kleenex tissue paper maintains a prominent place in people's memories and triggers their response, without them having to put any thought into it. The advertising and the end cap display thus prompt you, and many other consumers, to respond by buying a package, just the response Kleenex hoped to attain.

Focus of Advertisements

An ad campaign's objectives determine each specific ad's focus. The ad can be product-focused, might have an institutional focus, or could have a public service focus. **Product-focused advertisements** inform, persuade, or remind consumers about a specific product or service. The Pepsi Max ad shown here is designed to generate sales for Pepsi Max.

Institutional advertisements inform, persuade, or remind consumers about issues related to places, politics, or an industry. Perhaps the best-known institutional advertising campaign is the long-running "Got Milk?" campaign to encourage milk consumption by appealing to consumers' needs to affiliate with the milk-mustached celebrities shown in the ads.[18] The ads highlight the beneficial properties of milk for building strong bones, which involves a more informative appeal, combined with a mild emotional fear appeal in its assertion that failing to drink milk can lead to medical problems. Its Spanish-language ad campaign, "Toma Leche," similarly touts milk as a "wonder tonic" that fights cavities, sleeplessness, and bone loss. A recent campaign, as exemplified in the ad with Rebecca Romjin and her babies, even promises that drinking milk helps families stay together.[19]

A specific category of institutional advertising is **public service advertisements (PSAs)**. PSAs focus on public welfare; generally they are sponsored by nonprofit institutions, civic groups, religious organizations, trade associations, or political groups.[20] Like product and institutionally focused advertising, PSAs also inform, persuade, or remind consumers, but the focus is for the betterment of society. As such, PSAs represent a form of **social marketing**, defined as the application of marketing principles to a social issue to bring about attitudinal and behavioral change among the general public or a specific population segment.

The "Got Milk" institutional advertising campaign is used to encourage milk consumption by appealing to consumers' needs to affiliate with milk-mustached celebrities like Rebecca Romjin and her two babies.

Although the "Got Milk" campaign is actually sponsored by sellers of milk, it can claim some PSA elements, in that it touts the improvement of people's health through milk consumption. Another recent PSA campaign is sponsored by Yum Brands, the corporation that owns Pizza Hut, Taco Bell, and KFC. To promote hunger relief efforts, Yum has created World Hunger Relief, with a focus on "fighting hunger, not marketing products."[21] The related PSAs, featuring Christina Aguilera, describe ways to help combat hunger, with no mention of purchasing from the fast-food giants. To expand the reach of the PSA campaign, the CEO of Yum Brands, David Novak, appeared in a separate campaign targeted at the business community. PSAs can also be targeted to decrease consumption. For instance, the "Indoor Tanning Is Out" campaign is designed to raise awareness of the increased risk of melanoma, the deadliest form of skin cancer, and decrease usage of tanning salons.[22]

Because PSAs are a special class of advertising, under Federal Communications Commission (FCC) rules, broadcasters must devote a specific amount of free airtime to them. Also, since they often are designed by top advertising agencies for nonprofit clients, PSAs usually are quite creative and stylistically appealing. For example, what is your reaction to the truth public service antismoking campaign summarized in Ethical and Societal Dilemma 19.1?

Regardless of whether the advertising campaign's objective is to inform, persuade, or remind, with a focus on a particular product or the institution in general, each campaign's objectives must be specific and measurable. For a brand awareness campaign, for example, the objective might be to increase brand awareness among the target market by 50 percent within six months. Another campaign's goal may be to persuade 10 percent of a competitor's customers to switch to the advertised brand. Once the advertising campaign's objectives are set, the firm sets the advertising budget.

Ethical and Societal Dilemma 19.1   Getting to the Truth[23]

Smoking is the single biggest preventable cause of death in the world; someone dies from tobacco use every eight seconds.[24] Smoking causes cancers of the lung, throat, and mouth; it also leads to high blood pressure, heart problems, and lung diseases other than cancer. Yet worldwide, one in five teens between the ages of 13 and 15 years smokes, and many of those smokers will reach for their cigarettes for another 15 to 20 years. What can marketers do to help people avoid or quit this hazardous habit?

As part of the historic tobacco settlement between various states' attorneys general and the tobacco industry, The American Legacy Foundation receives over a billion dollars to educate the public about the dangers of smoking. The Foundation uses this money to fund the truth® campaign, the largest national young anti-smoking campaign and the only campaign not controlled by the tobacco industry. The campaign's goal is to tell the truth about the tobacco industry, including health effects, marketing strategies, and manufacturing practices. Focused primarily on youths between the ages of 12 and 17 years, the campaign presents facts and allows teens to make their own decisions rather than telling them what they should or should not do.

The campaign had a direct impact on smoking, accelerating the decline in teen smoking during its first two years. Seven years after truth® was launched, research showed that teens exposed to the campaign had a more accurate perception of the number of their peers who smoke. Considering how much most teens want to fit in with their peers, changing perceptions can help reduce the number of young people who pick up a cigarette.

To reach them, truth® uses videos online and in cinemas, as well as social media, website games, television integration, radio advertising, and live tours. It has employed scare tactics, such as a pile of body bags piled up in front of Philip Morris headquarters.[25] But it also relies on humor, animation, murals at the SXSW music festival, and Broadway-style song and dance routines to communicate the message.

But is humor the right way to communicate about a subject that kills millions of people each year? Is a pile of body bags an effective way to reach young smokers, who don't believe nicotine-related diseases will happen to them? Is this kind of messaging, which tobacco companies claim is abusive to them and their employees, appropriate or fair? How would you feel if you worked for a tobacco company? How would you feel about tobacco advertising if someone in your family had emphysema from smoking?

STEP 3: DETERMINE THE ADVERTISING BUDGET

The various budgeting methods for marketing communication (Chapter 18) also apply to budgeting for advertising. First, firms must consider the role that advertising plays in their attempt to meet their overall promotional objectives. Second, advertising expenditures vary over the course of the product life cycle. Third, the nature of the market and the product influence the size of advertising budgets. The nature of the market also determines the amount of money spent on advertising. For instance, less money is spent on advertising in B2B (business-to-business) marketing contexts than in B2C (business-to-consumer) markets. Personal selling, as we discuss in Chapter 20, likely is more important in B2B markets.

STEP 4: CONVEY THE MESSAGE

In this step, marketers determine what they want to convey about the product or service. First, the firm determines the key message it wants to communicate to the target audience. Second, the firm decides what appeal would most effectively convey the message. We present these decisions sequentially, but in reality, they must be considered simultaneously.

The Message

The message provides the target audience with reasons to respond in the desired way. A logical starting point for deciding on the advertising message is to tout the key benefits of the product or service. The message should communicate its problem-solving ability clearly and in a compelling fashion. In this context, advertisers must remember that products and services solve problems, whether real or perceived. That is, people are not looking for 1/4-inch drill bits; they are looking for 1/4-inch holes to hang a picture on the wall.[26] Because there are many ways to make a 1/4-inch hole, a firm like Black & Decker must convey to consumers that its drill bit is the best way to get that hole.

Another common strategy differentiates a product by establishing its unique benefits. This distinction forms the basis for the **unique selling proposition (USP)** or the value proposition (as discussed in Chapter 9), which is often the common theme or slogan in an advertising campaign. A good USP communicates the unique attributes of the product and thereby becomes a snapshot of the entire campaign. Some of the most famous USPs include the following:

Red Bull . . . Gives You Wings

Ford . . . Built Tough

Oreo . . . Milk's Favorite Cookie

TNT . . . We Know Drama

Kellogg's Corn Flakes® Is The Original and Best™ Cereal

The New York Times . . . All The News That's Fit to Print

Trek . . . We Believe in Bikes

Vail . . . Like Nothing On Earth

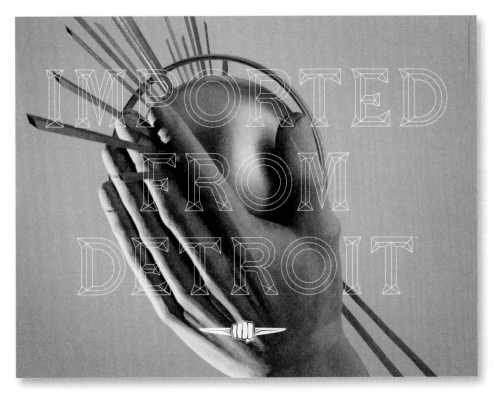

Chrysler's new USP is "Imported from Detroit."

The selling proposition communicated by the advertising must be not only unique to the brand but also meaningful to the consumer. It furthermore must be sustainable over time, even with repetition.

 LO3 Describe the different ways that advertisers appeal to consumers.

The Appeal

According to early theories of rhetoric (the study of the principles and rules of composition), there are three main types of appeals that an argument may use: logos (logical), ethos (ethical), and pathos (emotional). Advertisers similarly use different appeals to portray their product or service and persuade consumers to purchase them, though advertising tends to combine the types of appeals into two categories: informational and emotional.

Informational Appeals **Informational appeals** help consumers make purchase decisions by offering factual information that encourages consumers to evaluate the brand favorably on the basis of the key benefits it provides.[27] Thus Exxon Mobil attempts to explain technical aspects of its products, such as lithium ion batteries, hydrogen technology, biofuels, and CO_2-capture technologies, in an attempt to convince consumers that the company is environmentally friendly, efficient, innovative and responsible.[28] This appeal is well suited to this type of product: By informing consumers about a potential source of its competitive advantage, including tangible features and images of science, the advertising copy directly delivers an informational, persuasive message.

Chevrolet is providing information to prospective consumers by favorably comparing its Equinox FWD to the Toyota Rav4 4×2.

EXHIBIT 19.2	Emotional Appeals in Advertising	
Emotional Appeal	**Company**	**Example**
Fear/Safety	ADT Security	"Breaking into Your Apartment Is Easier than You Think"
Humor	Best Buy	"Game On, Santa"
Happiness	Tropicana	"Awake to Alive"
Love/sex	Axe Body Spray	"Unleash the Chaos"
Comfort	Kleenex	"Softness Worth Sharing"
Nostalgia	Chevrolet	"Chevy Runs Deep"

Emotional Appeals An **emotional appeal** aims to satisfy consumers' emotional desires rather than their utilitarian needs. These appeals therefore focus on feelings about the self.[29] Although the term "emotion" often conveys the image of tears, many other effective appeals are used in advertising. The key to a successful emotional appeal is the use of emotion to create a bond between the consumer and the brand. Exhibit 19.2 shows firms and examples of the most common types of emotional appeals: fear, safety, humor, happiness, love (or sex),[30] comfort, and nostalgia.[31]

STEP 5: EVALUATE AND SELECT MEDIA

The content of an advertisement is tied closely to the characteristics of the media that firms select to carry the message, and vice versa. **Media planning** refers to the process of evaluating and selecting the **media mix**— the combination of the media used and the frequency of advertising in each medium—that will deliver a clear, consistent, compelling message to the intended audience.[32] For example, Macy's may determine that a heavy dose of television, radio, print, and billboards is appropriate for the holiday selling season between Thanksgiving and the end of the year.

Because the **media buy**, the actual purchase of airtime or print pages, is generally the largest expense in the advertising budget, marketers must make their decisions carefully. Television advertising is by far the most expensive. Total U.S. advertising expenditures per medium have remained roughly constant for some time, though some shifts are currently taking place. For example, whereas television advertising is consistent at approximately 45 percent, digital advertising continues to grow and now accounts for 21 percent of spending. Spanish-language media also are growing, but newspaper advertising is rapidly losing share.[33] To characterize these various types of media, we use a dichotomy: mass and niche media.

The emotional appeal of Halle Berry's new perfume is love.

A McDonald's billboard in a specific community, like Mt. Horeb, targets a focused niche market.

LO4 Identify the various types of media.

Mass and Niche Media

Mass media channels include national newspapers, magazines, radio, and television and are ideal for reaching large numbers of anonymous audience members. **Niche media** channels are more focused and generally used to reach narrower segments, often with unique demographic characteristics or interests. Specialty television channels (e.g., Home and Garden TV) and specialty magazines such as *Skateboarder* or *Cosmo Girl* all provide examples of niche media. The Internet provides an opportunity to appeal to the masses through ads on the home page of Internet sites like www.comcast.net or www.yahoo.com or more niched opportunities, such as an American Express business card on *The Wall Street Journal* site (www.wsj.com). In a similar fashion, a billboard advertising McDonald's displays on a major highway would target the masses, but a McDonald's billboard in a specific community would target a more focused niche market.

Choosing the Right Medium

For each class of media, each alternative has specific characteristics that make it suitable for meeting specific objectives (see Exhibit 19.3).[34] For example, consumers use different media for different purposes, to which advertisers should match their messages. Television is used primarily for escapism and entertainment, so most television advertising relies on a mix of visual and auditory techniques.

Communication media also vary in their ability to reach the desired audience. For instance, radio is a good medium for products such as grocery purchases or fast food because many consumers decide what to purchase either on the way to the store or while in the store. Because many people listen to the radio in their cars, it becomes a highly effective means to reach consumers at a crucial point in their decision process. As we discussed in Chapter 18, each medium also varies in its reach and frequency. Advertisers can determine how effective their media mix has been in reaching their target audience by calculating the total GRP (reach × frequency) of the advertising schedule, which we discuss next.

EXHIBIT 19.3	Types of Media Available for Advertising	
Medium	Advantages	Disadvantages
Television	Wide reach. Incorporates sound and video.	High cost. A lot of channel and program options. May increase awareness of competitors' products.
Radio	Relatively inexpensive. Can be selectively targeted. Wide reach.	No video, which limits presentation. Consumers give less focused attention than TV. Exposure periods are short.
Magazines	Very targeted. Subscribers pass along to others.	Relatively inflexible. Takes some time for the magazine to be available.
Newspapers	Flexible. Timely. Able to localize.	Can be expensive in some markets. Advertisements have short life span.
Internet	Can be linked to detailed content. Highly flexible and interactive. Allows for specific targeting.	Becoming cluttered. The ad may be blocked by software on the computer.
Outdoors	Relatively inexpensive. Offers opportunities for repeat exposure.	Is not easily targeted. Has placement problems in some markets. Exposure time is very short.
Direct Marketing	Is highly targeted. Allows for personalization.	Cost can vary depending on type of direct marketing used. Traditional media, like mail, will be more expensive than newer media.

Determining the Advertising Schedule

Another important decision for the media planner is the **advertising schedule**, which specifies the timing and duration of advertising. There are three types of schedules, as Exhibit 19.4 displays:[35]

- A **continuous schedule** runs steadily throughout the year and therefore is suited to products and services that are consumed continually at relatively steady rates and that require a steady level of persuasive and/or reminder advertising. For example, Procter & Gamble advertises its Tide brand of laundry detergent continuously.
- **Flighting** refers to an advertising schedule implemented in spurts, with periods of heavy advertising followed by periods of no advertising. This pattern generally functions for products whose demand fluctuates, such as suntan lotion, which manufacturers may advertise heavily in the months leading up to and during the summer.
- **Pulsing** combines the continuous and flighting schedules by maintaining a base level of advertising but increasing advertising intensity during certain periods. For example, airlines, hotels, and car rental companies might continuously advertise to ensure brand awareness, but might increase the advertising in spikes during certain low demand periods.

STEP 6: CREATE ADVERTISEMENTS

After the advertiser has decided on the message, type of ad, and appeal, its attention shifts to the actual creation of the advertisement. During this step, the message and appeal are translated creatively into words, pictures, colors, and/or music. Often, the execution style for the ad will dictate the type of medium used to deliver the message. To demonstrate an image, advertisers can use television

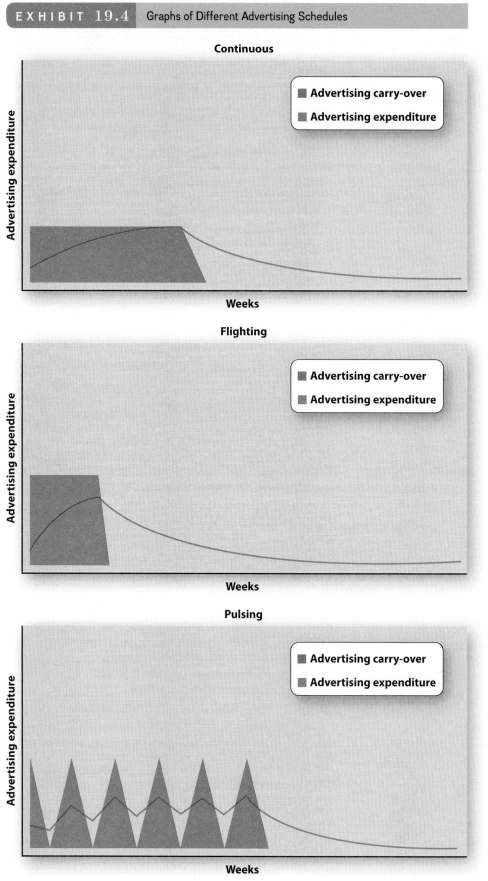

EXHIBIT 19.4   Graphs of Different Advertising Schedules

Source: Reprinted with permission from Brand Science Network, http://www.brandsciencenetwork.com/pages/tv_flighting_pattern_works_best.htm.

and magazines. To promote price, they can use newspapers and radio. To appeal to specific target markets, they can use some of the electronic media vehicles described in Chapter 18. When using multiple media to deliver the same message, however, they must maintain consistency across the execution styles—that is, integrated marketing—so that the different executions deliver a consistent and compelling message to the target audience.

How do advertisers go about creating advertisements? They simultaneously consider the objectives of the ad, the targeted customer segment(s), the product or service's value proposition or the unique selling proposition, and how the ad will be coordinated with other IMC elements.

They then go about creating an ad or the ad campaign. Using the print ad for Duluth Trading Company shown here as an example, the first component that the reader generally notices is the visual, and as such it should be eye-catching. The picture of the shipyard welder denotes tough masculinity. Although it is not always possible to meet all possible objectives with the visual, other important purposes are to identify the subject of the ad, show the product being used and its unique features, create a favorable impression of the product or advertiser, and arouse the readers' interest in the headline, which is generally noticed second.[36]

The **headline** is the large type in an ad that is designed to draw attention. In the Duluth Trading Company ad, the headline, Last Pants Standing, works with the visual to connote toughness and durability. But the **subhead**, an additional smaller headline, provides more information about the pants it is selling, specifically it is the fire hose workpants. Headlines and subheads should be short and use simple words; include the primary product or service benefits, the name of the brand, and an interest-provoking idea. It should ideally contain an action verb and give enough information for learning even if only the headline is read.

The **body copy** represents the main text portion of the ad. It is used to build on the interest generated by the visual and headlines, explains in more depth what the headline and subheads introduced, arouses desire for the product, and provides enough information to move the target consumer to action. In this case, the body copy, "The only pants tough enough for shipyard welder, Mike L," is short, but powerful.

Finally, the ad typically has a number of **brand elements** that identify the sponsor of the ad, typically through a logo (Duluth Trading Company) and a unique selling proposition (not found in this ad). The advertiser must convey its message using compelling visuals, headlines, body copy, and identifying brand elements.

Although creativity plays a major role in the execution stage, advertisers must remain careful not to let their creativity overshadow the message. Whatever the execution style, the advertisement must be able to attract the audience's attention, provide a reason for the audience to spend its time viewing the advertisement, and accomplish what it set out to do. In the end, the execution style must match the medium and objectives.

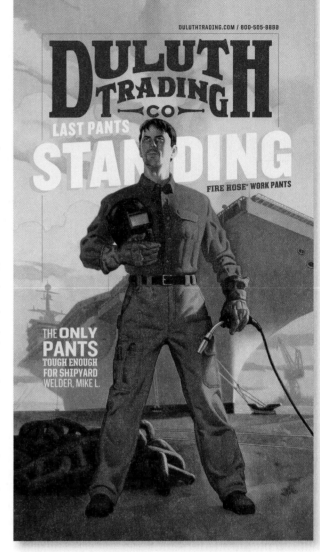

Duluth Trading Company creates powerful ads through simple yet powerful visuals and text.

Ads for the new Ford Fusion emphasize fuel economy as well as interesting technology that it hopes will appeal to young consumers.

Although the Chevy Malibu offers a fuel-efficient hybrid model, it is positioned as a family sedan.

Automobile manufacturers and dealers are among the most active advertisers, and utilize very different messages in their advertising campaigns. Consider, for instance, two well-known car companies that recently introduced new four-door sedan models, each with very different advertising campaigns.

- **Chevrolet Malibu**. Another entry into the hybrid market, the Malibu employs a battery pack and offers good gas mileage. It is also positioned as a family sedan, though the most recent revamping reduced the size of the backseat. Likely advertising outlets include family-oriented magazines and television spots.
- **Ford Fusion**. With a focus on fuel economy, ads for the new Fusion promise its availability with both a hybrid and a conventional engine. Furthermore, it emphasizes Ford's SYNC technology which uses voice recognition to make phone calls, find and play music, and get directions. With these appeals, Ford is focusing largely on social media to get young consumers, who tend to care about technology and environmental concerns, attached to the new model.[37]

At times, though, even when advertisers think they have done their best to appeal to consumers, their actions can backfire, as Ethical and Societal Dilemma 19.2 describes.

STEP 7: ASSESS IMPACT USING MARKETING METRICS

The effectiveness of an advertising campaign must be assessed before, during, and after the campaign has run. **Pretesting** refers to assessments performed before an ad campaign is implemented to ensure that the various elements are working in an integrated fashion and doing what they are intended to do.[38] **Tracking** includes monitoring key indicators, such as daily or weekly sales volume, while the advertisement is running to shed light on any problems with the message or the medium. **Posttesting** is the evaluation of the campaign's impact after it is has been implemented. At this last stage, advertisers assess the sales and/or communication impact of the advertisement or campaign.

Measuring sales impact can be especially challenging because of the many influences other than advertising on consumers' choices, purchase behavior,

Ethical and Societal Dilemma 19.2 — When Makeup Companies Really Do Make Up Models' Faces

Is Julia Roberts really that good looking? Of course, she's beautiful, but the portrayal of her face in advertising has, more likely than not, been given a "Photoshop fix." Airbrushing may be as old as advertising, but improved technology makes the changes nearly imperceptible—can you tell the difference between the normal thickness of an eyelash and the version that Taylor Swift sported in a CoverGirl NatureLeuxe Mousse Mascara ad? Ultimately, the National Advertising Division of the Council of Better Business Bureaus ruled the ad was misleading,[39] prompting the brand to pull the ad.

But in other cases, cosmetics and fashion companies claim that "fixing" elements of appearance is both ubiquitous and expected by consumers. They assert they are not misleading anyone but rather creating a perfect image for their brand. So is it wrong for cosmetic companies to retouch ads, brushing away wrinkles and skin imperfections digitally?[40]

When selling cosmetics, is it ethical to touch up photos of models and celebrities like Julia Roberts to make them even more beautiful?

The U.K. Advertising Standards Agency considers touching up photos in ads to be wrong. That oversight agency banned two separate ads by L'Oreal recently, charging that they were misleading. One ad featured Julia Roberts promoting Teint Miracle, a new Lancome skin product that, according to the company, provides "luminosity to the skin." The other featured the model Christy Turlington, promoting a cosmetic concealer called Eraser that promises to hide wrinkles and skin discoloration. Although the company protested that the ads did not exaggerate their product effectiveness, the U.K. Advertising Standards Agency was not convinced.[41]

Do consumers want realistic images and measured promises, or do they accept and even prefer exaggerated claims and unrealistic images of beauty?

---

and attitudes. These influences include the level of competitors' advertising, economic conditions in the target market, sociocultural changes, in-store merchandise availability and even the weather, all of which can influence consumer purchasing behavior. For instance, the sales resulting from even the best ads can be foiled by a lack of merchandise in the stores or a blizzard. Advertisers must try to identify these influences and isolate those of the particular advertising campaign.

For frequently purchased consumer goods in the maturity stage of the product life cycle such as soda, sales volume offers a good indicator of advertising effectiveness. Because their sales are relatively stable, and if we assume that the other elements of the marketing mix and the environment have not changed, we can attribute changes in sales volume to changes in advertising. Exhibit 19.5 illustrates a hypothetical sales history for Red Bull in a grocery store chain. Using a statistical technique called time-series analysis, sales data from the past is used to forecast the future. The data in Exhibit 19.5 can be decomposed into its basic trend (green), the seasonal influences (red), and the **lift** or additional sales caused by the advertising (orange). In this case, the lift caused by the advertising campaign is substantial.

For other types of goods in other stages of the product life cycle, sales data offer but one of the many indicators that marketers need to examine to determine advertising effectiveness. For instance, in high-growth markets, sales growth alone can be misleading, because the market as a whole is growing. In such a situation, marketers measure sales relative to those of competitors to determine their relative market share. Firms find creative ways to identify advertising effectiveness. For example, digital cable allows them to present a specific advertisement to certain neighborhoods and then track sales by local or regional retailers.

Sales volume is a good indicator of advertising effectiveness for frequently purchased consumer goods in the maturity stage of the product life cycle, such as Red Bull energy drink.

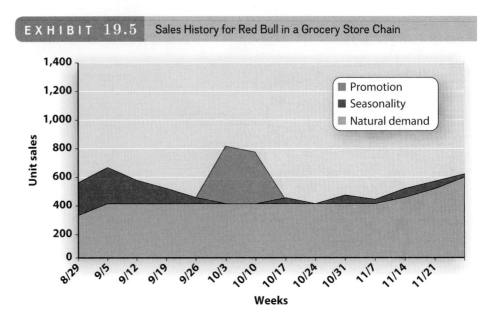

EXHIBIT 19.5   Sales History for Red Bull in a Grocery Store Chain

CHECK YOURSELF

1. What are the steps involved in planning an ad campaign?
2. What is the difference between informational, persuasive, and reminder advertising?
3. What are the pros and cons of the different media types?
4. How can the effectiveness of advertising be evaluated?

LO5 Identify agencies that regulate advertising.

REGULATORY AND ETHICAL ISSUES IN ADVERTISING

In the United States, the regulation of advertising involves a complex mix of formal laws and informal restrictions designed to protect consumers from deceptive practices.[42] Many federal and state laws, as well as a wide range of self-regulatory agencies and agreements, affect advertising (Exhibit 19.6). The primary federal agencies that regulate advertising activities are the Federal Trade Commission

EXHIBIT 19.6   Federal Agencies That Regulate Advertising

Federal Agency	General Purpose	Specific Jurisdiction
Federal Trade Commission (FTC) (established 1914)	Enforces federal consumer protection laws.	Enforces truth in advertising laws; defines deceptive and unfair advertising practices.
Federal Communications Commission (FCC) (1934)	Regulates interstate and international communications by radio, television, wire, satellite, and cable.	Enforces restrictions on broadcasting material that promotes lotteries (with some exceptions); cigarettes, little cigars, or smokeless tobacco products; or that perpetuates a fraud. Also enforces laws that prohibit or limit obscene, indecent, or profane language.
Food and Drug Administration (1930)	Regulates food, dietary supplements, drugs, cosmetics, medical devices (including radiation-emitting devices such as cell phones), biologics (biological issues), and blood products.	Regulates package labeling and inserts, definition of terms such as "light" and "organic," and required disclosure statements (warning labels, dosage requirements, etc.).

(FTC), Federal Communications Commission (FCC), and Food and Drug Administration (FDA). In addition to these agencies, others, such as the Bureau of Alcohol, Tobacco, and Firearms and the U.S. Postal Service, regulate advertising to some degree.

The FTC is the primary enforcement agency for most mass media advertising. Occasionally, it cooperates with other agencies to investigate and enforce regulations on particular advertising practices. For example, when the Smart Choices program logo, which was designed to indicate healthier foods, somehow appeared on boxes of Fruit Loops, the FTC relied on the FDA. The confusion and apparent lack of regulation, along with consumer complaints, led the FDA to issue warning letters that asked manufacturers to review their nutrition labels and claims for accuracy. The program also was suspended while the FDA reviewed the claims that the logos implied.[43]

Is this ad an example of puffery or deception?

Many product categories fall under self-regulatory restrictions or guidelines. For example, advertising to children is regulated primarily through self-regulatory mechanisms designed by the National Association of Broadcasters and the Better Business Bureau's Children's Advertising Review Unit. The only formal regulation of children's advertising appears in the Children's Television Act of 1990, which limits the amount of advertising broadcast during children's viewing hours.[44]

Recently, to make matters even more complicated for advertisers, state attorneys general's offices have begun to inquire into various advertising practices and assert their authority to regulate advertising in their states. The EU also has increased its regulation of advertising for EU member nations. Many of these state and European regulations are more restrictive than existing U.S. federal requirements.

The line between what is legal and illegal is more difficult to discern when it comes to **puffery**, which is the legal exaggeration of praise, stopping just short of deception, lavished on a product. When Match.com claims that it leads to "Better First Dates," it's puffery, because "better" is a subjective measure. But it if claims it produces "More Second Dates," it must be able to back up its numerical, quantitative assertion. Even cartoon bears must follow the rules: Charmin's animated spokescharacters need to be drawn with a few pieces of toilet paper on their rears, instead of none, to ensure that Charmin's claims only extend to leaving less toilet paper behind than other brands (puffery), not eliminating the problem altogether (deception).[45]

How do the courts determine what makes an ad deceptive, rather than simply puffery? The FTC's position is that it "will not pursue cases involving obviously exaggerated or puffing representations, i.e., those that ordinary consumers do not take seriously."[46] In general, the less specific the claim, the less likely it is considered to be deceptive. In the end, puffery is acceptable as long as consumers know that the firm is stretching the truth through exaggeration.[47]

PUBLIC RELATIONS

As you may recall from Chapter 18, **public relations (PR)** involves managing communications and relationships to achieve various objectives, such as building and maintaining a positive image of the firm, handling or heading off unfavorable stories or events, and maintaining positive relationships with the media. In many cases, public relations activities support other promotional efforts by generating "free" media attention and general goodwill.

Designers, for example, vie to have celebrities, especially those nominated for awards, wear their fashions on the red carpet. Their brands offer intangible benefits, not just functional benefits. Events such as the Oscars, with its 35 million annual viewers, provide an unparalleled opportunity to showcase the emotional benefits of the brand and make others want to be a part of it. Thus, the celebrities that designers pursue and offer their items are those that will sell the most or provide the best iconic images. When Fergie wore an Emilio Pucci dress to the Grammys, paired with a Judith Leiber clutch, both brands sent out press releases to make sure everyone knew.[48] The placement of designer apparel at media events benefits both the designer and the celebrity. And neither happens by accident. Public relations people on both sides help orchestrate the events to get the maximum benefit for both parties.

Good PR has always been an important success factor. Yet in recent years, the importance of PR has grown as the cost of other forms of marketing communications has increased. At the same time, the influence of PR has become more powerful as consumers have become increasingly skeptical of marketing claims made in other media.[49] In many instances, consumers view media coverage generated through PR as more credible and objective than any other aspects of an IMC program, because the firm does not "buy" the space in print media or time on radio or television.

Certainly the Chili's restaurant chain conducts plenty of media buys in traditional advertising spaces. But it also has partnered, since 2004, with St. Jude's Research Hospital in one of the most successful examples of **cause-related marketing** (i.e., commercial activity in which businesses and charities form a partnership to market an image, product, or service for their mutual benefit)[50] in history. For several years, the restaurant has offered customers the opportunity to purchase a paper icon, in the shape of a chili, natch, that they may color and hang on restaurant walls. The cause marketing campaign runs in September, which is also National Childhood Cancer Awareness Month. On the last Monday of the month, the restaurant puts its money where its mouth is and donates all its profits on sales during the day to St. Jude. In addition to the relatively common Create-a-Chili paper icons, employees of the restaurants make and sell customized T-shirts and wristbands. Chili's also hosts a dedicated website, www.createapepper.com, where civic-minded consumers can purchase or donate more, as well as buy St. Jude–branded Chili's gift cards.[51]

Chili's partners with St. Jude's Research Hospital in a cause-related marketing program to raise money for the hospital by donating its profits on the last Monday of September.

Part of Red Bull's PR toolkit is its cliff diving event.

Another very popular PR tool is event sponsorship. **Event sponsorship** occurs when corporations support various activities (financially or otherwise), usually in the cultural or sports and entertainment sectors. Some of them are big name events; the titles of most college football playoff games now include the name of their sponsors (e.g., the Allstate Sugar Bowl). Others are slightly less famous; for example, Rollerblade USA, the maker of Rollerblade in-line skates, sponsors Skate-In-School, a program it developed with the National Association for Sport and Physical Education (NAPSE) to promote the inclusion of rollerblading in physical education curricula.

Firms often distribute a PR toolkit to communicate with various audiences. Some toolkit elements are designed to inform specific groups directly, whereas others are created to generate media attention and disseminate information. We depict the various elements of a PR toolkit in Exhibit 19.7.

LO6 Describe the elements of a public relations toolkit.

EXHIBIT 19.7	Elements of a Public Relations Toolkit
PR Element	**Function**
Publications: Brochures, special-purpose single-issue publications such as books	Inform various constituencies about the activities of the organization and highlight specific areas of expertise.
Video and audio: Programs, public service announcements	Highlight the organization or support cause-related marketing efforts.
Annual reports	Give required financial performance data and inform investors and others about the unique activities of the organization.
Media relations: Press kits, news releases, speeches, event sponsorships	Generate news coverage of the organization's activities or products/services.
Electronic media: Websites, e-mail campaigns	Websites can contain all the previously mentioned toolbox elements, while e-mail directs PR efforts to specific target groups.

LO7 Identify the various types of sales promotions.

SALES PROMOTION

Advertising rarely provides the only means to communicate with target customers. As we discussed in Chapter 18, a natural link appears between advertising and sales promotion. **Sales promotions** are special incentives or excitement-building programs that encourage consumers to purchase a particular product or service, typically used in conjunction with other advertising or personal selling programs. Many sales promotions, like free samples or point-of-purchase (POP) displays, attempt to build short-term sales, whereas others, like loyalty programs, contests, and sweepstakes, have become integral components of firms' long-term customer relationship management (CRM) programs, which they use to build customer loyalty.

We present these sales promotions tools next. The tools of any sales promotion can be focused on any channel member—wholesalers, retailers, or end-user consumers. Just as we delineated for advertising, when sales promotions are targeted at channel members, the marketer is employing a push strategy; when it targets consumers themselves, it is using a pull strategy. Some sales promotion tools can be used with either a push or pull strategy. We now consider each of the tools and how they are used.

Types of Sales Promotion

Coupons **Coupons** offer a discount on the price of specific items when they're purchased. Coupons are issued by manufacturers and retailers in newspapers, on products, on the shelf, at the cash register, over the Internet, and through the mail to stimulate demand. Some retailers have linked their coupons directly to their loyalty programs. The drugstore chain CVS tracks customers' purchases when they use their Extra Care loyalty card and gives them coupons that are tailored just for them and their unique needs.[52] If a customer typically spends a small amount during each shopping trip, he or she might receive coupons to encourage larger purchases, such as "buy one, get one free."

Internet sites also provide customers with instant coupons of their choosing. Imagine a customer who visits her local Walmart and finds a Hot Wheels video game for $29.99. By scanning the bar code, using her cell phone, she connects to ShopSavvy.com and finds that same item, at a Target store a mile away, is only $19.99. Another scan and a connection to MyCoupons.com provides her with a $10 coupon—which means she's saved $20 in a matter of minutes and just a few clicks.

Some coupons, whether printed from the Internet or sent to mobile phones, also contain information about the customer who uses it.[53] The bar code may identify the customer, his or her Internet address, Facebook page information, and even the search terms the customer used to find

This sales promotion deal for Payless ShoeSource is a short-term price promotion that encourages customers to buy a second pair of shoes at one-half off.

the coupon in the first place. These new breeds of coupons may look standard, but they offer up a startling amount of data, which promises benefits for advertisers who want to target their marketing more closely. Traditionally, coupons had low redemption rates and were therefore a relatively inexpensive sales promotion tool, but firms like Groupon have resulted in higher redemption rates, increasing their expense.

Deals   A **deal** refers generally to a type of short-term price reduction that can take several forms, such as a "featured price," a price lower than the regular price; a "buy one, get one free" offer; or a certain percentage "more free" offer contained in larger packaging. Another form of a deal involves a special financing arrangement, such as reduced percentage interest rates or extended repayment terms. Deals encourage customers to try a product because they lower the risk for consumers by reducing the cost of the good.

But deals can also alter perceptions of value—a short-term price reduction may signal a different price/quality relationship than would be ideal from the manufacturer's perspective. In addition, as Old Spice learned, offering too many deals can offset likely gains. Its popular "Old Spice Guy" campaign attracted consumer attention through funny television commercials and interactive online campaigns, and sales of Old Spice jumped. But the company offered so many buy one, get one free deals at the same time that the potential profit impact of the great ads was essentially eliminated by the costs of the deals.[54]

Premiums   A **premium** offers an item for free or at a bargain price to reward some type of behavior, such as buying, sampling, or testing. These rewards build goodwill among consumers, who often perceive high value in them. Premiums can be distributed in a variety of ways: They can be included in the product packaging, such as the toys inside cereal boxes; placed visibly on the package, such as a coupon for free milk on a box of Cheerios; handed out in the store; or delivered in the mail, such as the free perfume offers Victoria's Secret mails to customers. Furthermore, premiums can be very effective if they are consistent with the brand's message and image and highly desirable to the target market. However, finding a premium that meets these criteria at a reasonable cost can be a serious challenge.

Contests   A **contest** refers to a brand-sponsored competition that requires some form of skill or effort. ESPN's website hosts a page devoted just to sports-related contests: "Get me to the World Cup sponsored by Sony" or "Player of the month presented by Kia."[55] For the "Get Me to the World Cup" contest, each participant must create and upload a short video demonstrating why he or she should be the one picked to attend the international event. For those who need some help sparking their creativity, ESPN provides some sample videos—including one by Kobe Bryant. Since contests require consumer involvement, they can create a lot of excitement or buzz around a product or service.

Sweepstakes   A form of sales promotion that offers prizes based on a chance drawing of entrants' names, **sweepstakes** do not require the entrant to complete a task other than buying a ticket or filling out a form. For example, fans who purchased movie tickets to see *Dolphin Tale* from the Fandango website were automatically entered into a sweepstakes for a family vacation to St. Petersburg, Florida, where the movie's star Winter—a dolphin fitted with a prosthetic tail—lives. Often the key benefit of sweepstakes is that they encourage current consumers to consume more if the sweepstakes form appears inside the packaging or with the product. Many states, however, specify that no purchase can be required to enter sweepstakes.

Samples   **Sampling** offers potential customers the opportunity to try a product or service before they make a buying decision. Distributing samples is one of the

Axeman, the new personalized gaming experience from AXE, lets users play their own music while earning points to redeem more than 1.2 million dollars in real rewards from Planet AXE.

most costly sales promotion tools but also one of the most effective. Quick service restaurants and grocery stores frequently utilize sampling. For instance, Starbucks provides samples of new products to customers. Costco uses so many samples that customers can have an entire meal. Sometimes trial-size samples come in the mail or are distributed in stores.

Loyalty Programs As part of a sales promotion program, **loyalty programs** are specifically designed to retain customers by offering premiums or other incentives to customers who make multiple purchases over time. Well-designed loyalty programs encourage consumers to increase their engagement and purchases from a given firm. Such sales promotions are growing increasingly popular and are tied to long-term CRM systems. (Loyalty programs are examined in Chapters 2 and 3.) These programs need to be carefully managed as they can be quite costly.

Point-of-Purchase Displays **Point-of-purchase (POP) displays** are merchandise displays located at the point of purchase, such as at the checkout counter in a supermarket. Retailers have long recognized that the most valuable real estate in the store is at the POP (point of purchase) since they increase product visibility and encourage trial. Customers see products like a magazine or a candy bar while they are waiting to pay for their purchases, and impulsively purchase them. In the Internet version of a point-of-purchase display, shoppers are stimulated by special merchandise, price reductions, or complementary products that Internet retailers feature on the checkout screen.

Rebates **Rebates** are a particular type of price reduction in which a portion of the purchase price is returned by the seller to the buyer in the form of cash. Many products, such as consumer electronics, offer significant mail-in rebates that may lower the price of the item significantly. Some companies enjoy the added exposure when they appear on consumer websites like PriceGrabber.com and Nextag.com, where products are sorted by the price, with links to the retailer's website. Firms offer such generous rebates because the likelihood that consumers will actually apply for the rebate is low. The firms garner considerable value from rebates because they attract consumers and therefore stimulate sales, but they may not have to pay off all the rebates offered.

Product Placement When marketers use **product placement**, they pay to have their product included in nontraditional situations, such as in a scene in a movie or television program.[56] By doing so, they increase the visibility of their products. Product placement may be subtly placed, such as when American Idol judges are seen drinking Coca-Cola. On CBS's *The Big Bang Theory*, not only do scenes regularly show the characters working and eating there, but Sheldon also asserts his need to get "access to the Cheesecake Factory walk-in freezer."

A new Bollywood film is taking the approach further though. In the popular roadtrip film *Zindagi Na Milegi Dobara* (*You Only Live Once*), the lead characters get inspired by a Spanish flamenco dancer and proceed through a series of adventures in Seville, Costa Brava, Pamplona, and other locations in Spain. The selection of these locales was made not by the film's writers or its director, but by Turespana, Spain's tourism agency, which helped turn the film into a kind of feature-length tourism guide. The agency also helped promote the film, spending more than $660,000 on television ads. And its investment worked: Indian tourism to Spain increased 65 percent after the film's release.[57] Although other countries have worked with Bollywood too, offering tax breaks or subsidies, no other site has gained so much influence over the production, plot, and promotion of a major Indian film.

The hard part is determining which movies will be successes. For Apple, the challenge is a little less stringent, because U.S. film directors seem to love its sleek white laptops, ear-budded iPods, and ubiquitous iPhones. Thus more than one-third of all top grossing films at the U.S. box office—129 of 374 movies—have included Apple-branded products in the past decade. Recent appearances include both hits and Oscar-nominated offerings, such as *Green Lantern*, *Transformers: Dark of the Moon*, *Rise of the Planet of the Apes*, *Bridesmaids*, *The Girl with the Dragon Tattoo*, and *Diary of a Wimpy Kid*.[58] Matt Damon's *We Bought a Zoo* even featured an extended scene showing how to use the iPhoto app. Apple is also unique in that it claims it does not pay for product placement, nor does it comment on film appearances. An analytics firm that estimates the dollar value of product placements has reported that Apple's five-minute screen time in *Mission Impossible* alone was worth more than $23 million.[59] Apple seemingly can earn those returns without paying for the placements, but not all companies are so lucky.

The Bollywood film Zindagi Na Milegi Dobara *was partially sponsored by Spain's tourism agency. After the film's release Indian tourism to Spain increased 65 percent.*

Using Sales Promotion Tools

Marketers must be careful in their use of sales promotions, especially those that focus on lowering prices. Depending on the item, consumers may stock up when items are offered at a lower price, which simply shifts sales from the future to now and thereby leads to short-run benefits at the expense of long-term sales stability. For instance, using sales promotions like coupons to stimulate sales of household cleaning supplies may cause consumers to stockpile the products and decrease demand for those products in the future. But a similar promotion used with a perishable product like Dannon yogurt should increase its demand at the expense of competitors like Yoplait.

Many firms are also realizing the value of **cross-promoting**, when two or more firms join together to reach a specific target market. To achieve a successful cross-promotion, the two products must appeal to the same target market and together create value for consumers. J. Crew has teamed up with several famous brands, including Belstaff, Levi's, Barbour, Timex, and Sperry Top-Sider, to offer exclusive products in the J.Crew stores and website.[60]

The goal of any sales promotion is to create value for both the consumers and the firm. By understanding the needs of its customers, as well as how best to entice them to purchase or consume a particular product or service, a firm can develop promotional messages and events that are of interest to and achieve the desired response from those customers. Traditionally, the role of sales promotion has been to generate short-term results, whereas the goal of advertising was to generate long-term results. As this chapter demonstrates, though, both sales promotion and advertising can generate both long- and short-term effects. The effective combination of both types of activities leads to impressive results for the firm and the consumers.

CHECK YOURSELF

1. What are various forms of sales promotions?
2. What factors should a firm consider when evaluating a sales promotion?

Summing Up

LO1 Describe the steps in designing and executing an advertising campaign.

Firms (1) identify their target market, (2) set advertising objectives, (3) set the advertising budget, (4) depict their product or service, (5) evaluate and select the media, (6) create the ad, and (7) assess the impact of the ad.

LO2 Identify three objectives of advertising.

All advertising campaigns are designed to inform, persuade, or remind customers. Informative advertising is communication used to create and build brand awareness. Persuasive advertising is communication used to motivate consumers to take action. Finally, reminder advertising is communication used to remind or prompt repurchases.

LO3 Describe the different ways that advertisers appeal to consumers.

Advertising appeals are either informational or emotional. Informational appeals influence purchase decisions with factual information and strong arguments built around relevant key benefits that encourage consumers to evaluate the brand favorably. Emotional appeals indicate how the product satisfies emotional desires rather than utilitarian needs.

LO4 Identify the various types of media.

Firms can use mass media channels like newspapers or television to reach large numbers of anonymous audience members. Niche media, such as cable television and specialty magazines, are generally used to reach narrower segments with unique demographic characteristics or interests. When choosing media, firms must match their objectives to that channel. Also, certain media are better at reaching a particular target audience than others.

LO5 Identify agencies that regulate advertising.

Advertising is regulated by a plethora of federal and state agencies. The most important federal agencies are the FTC, which protects consumers against general deceptive advertising; the FCC, which has jurisdiction over radio, television, wire, satellite, and cable and covers issues regarding the use of tobacco products and objectionable language; and the FDA, which regulates food, dietary supplements, drugs, cosmetics, and medical devices.

LO6 Describe the elements of a public relations toolkit.

A variety of elements compose a firm's public relations toolkit. They include publications, video and audio programs, public service announcements, annual reports, media kits (e.g., press kits), news releases, and electronic media (e.g., websites).

LO7   **Identify the various types of sales promotions.**

Sales promotions are special incentives or excitement-building programs that encourage purchase and include coupons, deals, premiums, contests, sweepstakes, samples, POP displays, rebates, and product placement. They either push sales through the channel, as is the case with contests directed toward retail salespeople, or pull sales through the channel, as coupons and rebates do.

Key Terms

- advertising, 576
- advertising plan, 578
- advertising schedule, 587
- body copy, 589
- brand elements, 589
- cause-related marketing, 594
- contest, 597
- continuous advertising schedule, 587
- coupon, 596
- cross-promoting, 599
- deal, 597
- emotional appeal, 585
- event sponsorship, 595
- flighting advertising schedule, 587
- headline, 589
- informational appeal, 584

- informative advertising, 578
- institutional advertisements, 581
- lift, 591
- loyalty program, 598
- mass media, 586
- media buy, 585
- media mix, 585
- media planning, 585
- niche media, 586
- persuasive advertising, 578
- point-of-purchase (POP) display, 598
- posttesting, 590
- premium, 597
- pretesting, 590
- product placement, 598
- product-focused advertisements, 580

- public relations (PR), 593
- public service advertising (PSA), 581
- puffery, 593
- pull strategy, 578
- pulsing advertising schedule, 587
- push strategy, 578
- rebate, 598
- reminder advertising, 580
- sales promotion, 596
- sampling, 597
- social marketing, 581
- subhead, 589
- sweepstakes, 597
- tracking, 590
- unique selling proposition (USP), 583

Marketing Applications

1. What are the objectives of the Tropicana ad (page 576)? Does the ad have more than one objective? Explain your answer.

2. Using the same ad, explain what kind of appeal it uses.

3. Verizon spends millions of dollars each year on advertising for many different purposes. Provide an example of how it might design an informative ad, a persuasive ad, and a reminder ad.

4. Name a current advertising slogan you believe is particularly effective for developing a unique selling proposition.

5. Bernard's, a local furniture company, target markets to college students with apartments and households of young people purchasing their first furniture items. If you worked for Bernard's, what type of media would you use for your advertising campaign? Justify your answer.

6. Should Bernard's use continuous, pulsing, or flighting for its advertising schedule? Why?

7. Suppose Porsche is introducing a new line of light trucks and has already created the advertising campaign. How would you assess the effectiveness of the campaign?

8. Suppose now that Porsche is planning a sales promotion campaign to augment its advertising campaign for the new line of light trucks. Which push and pull sales promotion tools do you believe would be most effective? Why?

9. Consider all the diet products that are currently advertised on television today, including weight loss supplements, weight loss programs, and fitness equipment. Do you believe that some of these ads overstate what the product or service can actually do? Do you think any of these ads are actually deceptive or puffery?

10. You are invited to your six-year-old niece's birthday party and bring her the new superhero doll being advertised on television. She's thrilled when she unwraps the gift but is in tears a short time later because her new doll is broken. She explains that on TV, the doll flies and does karate kicks, but when she tried to play with the doll this way, it broke. You decide to call the manufacturer, and a representative tells you he is sorry your niece is so upset but that the ad clearly states the doll does not fly. The next time you see the televised ad, you notice very small print at the bottom that states the doll does not fly. You decide to write a letter to the FTC about this practice. What information should you include in your letter?

www.mhhe.com/grewal4e

Quiz Yourself

1. The Got Milk (milk moustaches worn by celebrities) ads are examples of successful:
   a. selective demand strategies
   b. public puffery campaigns
   c. pretracking publicity
   d. product-focused advertisements
   e. institutional advertising campaigns

2. Campbell Soup Company ran a series of radio ads tied to local weather forecasts. Before an impending storm, the ads said, "Time to stock up on Campbell Soup." During the storm, the ads said, "Stay home and stay warm with Campbell Soup." The first ad was _____ advertising, while the second ad was _____ advertising.
   a. informative; persuasive
   b. persuasive; reminder
   c. reminder; persuasive
   d. discussive; informative
   e. institutional; persuasive

(Answers to these two questions can be found on page 648.)

Go to www.mhhe.com/grewal4e to practice an additional 11 questions.

Toolkit

MAKE AN ADVERTISEMENT
Suppose you have been hired to develop a new ad for a product or service to target the college student market. The ad will appear in college student newspapers around the world. Please use the toolkit provided at www.mhhe.com/grewal4e to develop the ad.

Net Savvy

1. Go to the website for the Children's Advertising Review Unit (CARU), one of the major self-regulatory bodies for children's advertising, at www.asrcreviews.org. Click on "CARU" and then "About Us—CARU" and examine the activities of CARU. How does this form of regulation complement the more formal regulation of federal and state agencies? Now look under the News and Publications link. Choose one of the press releases and discuss what action CARU took against the identified company or group. What was the main issue in the case?

2. PR Newswire attempts to provide information for "professional communicators." Visit its website at www.prnewswire.com and explore the "Products and Services" it has to offer. What would you con-sider this organization's primary purpose? To whom does PR Newswire address the advertising appeals on its website?

Chapter Case Study

MAKING MASTERCARD PRICELESS

How do you pay for books, clothing, groceries, or travel? For many consumers, the answer is MasterCard, which has more than 200 million cards in circulation.[61] Yet despite the credit card's popularity, it lags behind its major competitor, Visa, by nearly 100 million cards. It is also outstripped by American Express for both monthly and annual purchases and spending volume. Because MasterCard's primary function is to process transactions between each customer's bank and each merchant's bank, the company must appeal to two customer bases to build market share: the merchants who accept MasterCard for payment and the purchasers who use the card. These audiences are closely related, which implies that a single campaign can target both, likely even for an extended period. However, even the most successful campaigns can grow stale.

In 1997, MasterCard International and the advertising agency McCann Erickson Worldwide launched the emotion-based "Priceless" campaign, which celebrated life's most precious moments with the tagline, "There are some things money can't buy. For everything else, there's MasterCard."[62] The campaign was hugely successful, saving MasterCard from disaster, even in direct competition with the more widely accepted Visa card.[63] However, as consumer values and needs changed and the marketplace evolved, MasterCard faced a new challenge: how to retain customer loyalty and brand identification while reinvigorating its advertising. The solution was the "Priceless Cities" campaign.

EXPANDING SERVICES TO MEET MARKET DEMAND

In 1966, a group of California banks created a member-owned association called the Interbank Card Association. This association grew its services, changing its name to MasterCard in 1979 to reflect a commitment to international growth.[64] As it reached new markets across the globe, MasterCard also focused on technology innovation to help make economic transactions faster, more convenient, and more secure. The company acquired interest in the international credit card EuroCard (known today as Europay International), as well as Cirrus, a worldwide interbank network that links MasterCard, Maestro, and Diner's Club credit, debit, and prepaid cards to an international network of ATMs. The company also added fraud/risk management providers to its network of services.

Today MasterCard's technology platform can handle more than 160 million transactions every hour with a 99.9 percent reliability rate,[65] and the company has issued a contactless, or smart, card that communicates with terminals via radio waves. This payment method does not require a signature and can be a card or key fob that is tapped rather than swiped; it also appears as a smartphone app. To provide even more value to customers, the company has added sophisticated consulting and information services that help merchants gain insight into consumer spending, according to their transaction data and in-depth analyses.[66] These efforts have dovetailed with changes in consumer behavior as shoppers have begun relying more on electronic payment options and less on paper-based currency. In 2006, the company transitioned to a new corporate governance and ownership structure and began trading on the New York Stock Exchange.

PRICELESS REVISITED

MasterCard began its Priceless campaign by identifying its target audience, which in this case focused on consumers. Hoping to persuade shoppers to keep their MasterCard at the top of their wallets, the campaign stressed the relationship between the card and experiences, as opposed to possessions. In early television ads, the narration linked the price of beauty parlor visits and new outfits to the "priceless" expression on an ex-boyfriend's face at a reunion, to create positive self-assessment feelings.[67] In another, the cost of tickets, refreshments, and souvenirs at a game were tied to the "priceless" opportunity for meaningful conversation between father and son, to invoke both happiness and love.[68] The Priceless campaign included various promotions and competitions, in additions to these television spots.

In 2004, Priceless print ads took a new tack, weaving well-known retailers into the ads, together with MasterCard's theme. These retailers—which represented another of MasterCard's target audiences—received value from the prominent placement of their names and product images in the ads. Messaging moved from the general to the specific; an ad showing a teenage rock band playing in a garage that might once have said, "extra-long extension cord, $11; moving them out of the living room: priceless," was modified to indicate that the extension cord was from Radio Shack. The result was a form of symbiotic marketing in which well-known brand names helped attract consumer attention to MasterCard ads, and each brand appeared to be endorsing the other.[69]

MAGIC MOMENTS, PRICELESS CITIES

In July 2011, MasterCard launched an expanded campaign, called Priceless Cities. This campaign, kicked off initially in New York, offers cardholders special experiences in major cities that can be shared with family and friends.[70] Designed to provide busy consumers with memorable opportunities in the realms of sports, music, entertainment, shopping, travel, arts, culture, and dining out, the campaign touted early opening times at the toy store FAO Schwartz, a safari sleepover at the Bronx Zoo, prime tickets to a Yankees game with an ex-Yankee, and VIP dining experiences designed by a famed chef.[71] The idea, says MasterCard's chief marketing officer, is to transform consumers' perception of the card from simply part of a priceless moment to being the force that enables such experiences. In a shaky economy, when most competitors focus on deals and discounts, the MasterCard campaign attracts attention by appealing to emotions rather than wallets and stressing unforgettable experiences rather than cost savings. The campaign forges an additional bond with card users, because it places MasterCard at the center of these memorable social activities.

The ads run in more than 100 countries and air in more than 50 languages and the overall campaign uses print, radio, transit, outdoor advertising, and television. It also includes digital platforms to drive home its message, including a new section of the MasterCard website created specifically for the campaign, as well as social media channels such as Facebook and Twitter. Cardholders register at the site to access special offers; World Elite MasterCard holders get preferred access to the events, as well as special offers.

Marketers must continuously evaluate their campaigns and update them to ensure they are effectively communicating with their customers. New channels like social marketing can change shopping behaviors, creating opportunities that must be considered as part of any marketing strategy. As MasterCard has shown, even the best ideas need new infusions and innovations to keep appealing to their targets.

Questions

1. Why was the original Priceless campaign such a success?

2. Why has MasterCard started to use "Priceless" more actively in its messaging?

Personal Selling and Sales Management

When she was just 31 years of age, Lauren Crampsie landed a top job at Ogilvy & Mather, one of the largest marketing communications companies in the world.[1] In her new position, worldwide chief marketing officer for global operations, Crampsie is responsible for developing the business strategy that will engage clients with Ogilvie & Mather's full range of marketing services, even as she continues to lead the company's North American business development efforts.

Despite her meteoric rise in the eight years since she entered the job force, Crampsie's original career aspirations had nothing to do with marketing. After graduating from Lehigh University, she deferred an acceptance to law school to work as an assistant in broadcast television. Two years later, she joined Ogilvie as a new business coordinator. And then just six years after that, she was the agency's youngest new business director and then the youngest director of business development for all of North America.[2]

The secret to her success? According to her supervisors, the key is Crampsie's track record of bringing new clients—such as IKEA, UPS, and Intercontinental Hotels Group—into the Ogilvie & Mather portfolio.[3] She achieves these integrations largely through her stellar understanding of how to use both new and established marketing channels to give clients the results they want. Furthermore, Crampsie works tirelessly to build relationships with everyone she meets, whether they are CEOs, junior staffers, or just an interesting contact in a social setting. Anyone has the potential to provide her with insight into the culture and business goals of a potential new client. Armed with this knowledge, she carefully considers the unique challenges and needs of prospective clients, then demonstrates how her agency can surmount those obstacles using a combination of creativity and strategic insights.

To build client trust and overcome resistance put up by business prospects, Crampsie uses high-tech tools, including social media, digital strategies, and other marketing innovations. But she never ignores her old-fashioned social and conversational skills either. Her client and staff interactions run the gamut from check-ins on Foursquare to text messages to morning jogs with her staff to face-to-face briefings over coffee to formal cocktail receptions.[4] Combining all these attributes are critical to making a great salesperson—along with trustworthiness, a relentless passion for the company's product or service, and a personality that attracts others, including customers.[5]

Crampsie's approach may seem closely linked to her youth and hipness, but her sales arsenal isn't all that different from that of another successful saleswoman and

LEARNING OBJECTIVES

- **LO1** Describe the value added of personal selling.
- **LO2** Define the steps in the personal selling process.
- **LO3** Describe the key functions involved in managing a sales force.
- **LO4** Describe the ethical and legal issues in personal selling.

68-year old grandmother, Holly Chen. Chen heads a 300,000-member sales force for Amway that earns the former first-grade teacher an estimated $10 million annually.[6] The keys to success, according to Chen, are an ability to use emotion to motivate action and a knack for making friends and forming connections. She agrees that potential relationships are everywhere: standing next to you in line at Starbucks, seated at an adjoining table in a restaurant, embedded in the social networks of people you have already met. Anyone who crosses Chen's path, whether on the street or in cyberspace, is a possible recruit to her legendary sales force. Once recruited, new salespeople reach out to their friends and acquaintances to make a sale, encourage them to join the team, or simply spread the word.

Modern marketing companies like Amway use an arsenal of social media tools to give them a competitive edge much greater than the face-to-face sales interactions of the past. Today, companies that lag in their use of developing direct connections with potential customers through Google, Twitter, Yelp, and so on are overlooking remarkable resources. Not only do these networks offer information that can influence, but they also offer a key path to savvy customers and closed deals.[7] Well-informed customers, who find a wealth of information in their myriad Web interactions, usually have both factual and emotional data about a product or service long before they contact a salesperson. If sellers understand how to use all their interactions while applying and updating the conventional wisdom about how to ensure successful sales, they will be the ones—like Lauren Crampsie and Holly Chen—who achieve success for their customers, their companies, and themselves.

Just like advertising, which we discussed in Chapter 19, personal selling is so important to integrated marketing communications that it deserves its own chapter. Almost everyone is engaged in some form of selling. On a personal level, you sell your ideas or opinions to your friends, family, employers, and professors. Even if you have no interest in personal selling as a career, a strong grounding in the topic will help you in numerous career choices. Consider, for instance, Harry Turk, a very successful labor attorney. He worked his way through college selling sweaters to fraternities across the country. Although he loved his part-time job, Harry decided to become an attorney. When asked whether he misses selling, he said, "I use my selling skills every day. I have to sell new clients on the idea that I'm the best attorney for the job. I have to sell my partners on my legal point of view. I even use selling skills when I'm talking to a judge or jury."

LO1 Describe the value added of personal selling.

THE SCOPE AND NATURE OF PERSONAL SELLING

Personal selling is the two-way flow of communication between a buyer or buyers and a seller, designed to influence the buyer's purchase decision. Personal selling can take place in various situations: face-to-face, via video teleconferencing, on the telephone, or over the Internet, for example. More than 15 million people are employed in sales positions in the United States,[8] including those involved in business-to-business (B2B) transactions—like manufacturers' representatives selling to retailers or other businesses—and those completing business-to-consumer (B2C) transactions, such as retail salespeople, real estate agents, and insurance agents. Salespeople are referred to in many ways: sales representatives or reps, account executives, agents. And as Harry Turk found, most professions rely on personal selling to some degree.

Salespeople don't always get the best coverage in popular media. In Arthur Miller's famous play *Death of a Salesman*, the main character Willie Loman leads a pathetic existence and suffers from the loneliness inherent in being a traveling salesman.[9] The characters in David Mamet's play *Glengarry Glen Ross* portray salespeople as crude, ruthless, and of questionable character. Unfortunately, these powerful Pulitzer Prize–winning pieces of literature weigh heavily on our collective consciousness and often overshadow the millions of hardworking professional salespeople who have fulfilling and rewarding careers and who add value to their firm and provide value for their customers.

Personal Selling as a Career

Personal or professional selling can be a satisfying career for several reasons. First, many people love the lifestyle. Salespeople are typically out on their own. Although they occasionally work with their managers and other colleagues, salespeople tend to be responsible for planning their own day. This flexibility translates into an easier balance between work and family than many office-bound jobs can offer. Many salespeople now can rely on virtual offices, which enable them to communicate from anywhere and at any time with their colleagues and customers. Because salespeople are evaluated primarily on the results they produce, as long as they meet and exceed their goals, they experience little day-to-day supervision. You thus might find a salesperson at the gym in the middle of the day, when few other people are there, because no one keeps track of the length of his or her lunch break.

Second, the variety of the job often attracts people to sales. Every day is different, bringing different clients and customers, often in a variety of places. Their issues and problems and the solutions to those problems all differ and require creativity.[10] For example, when Lauren Crampsie signed The Gap as an account with Ogilvy, she worked with the company's CEO in a boardroom meeting, but she also got a chance to chat with some junior designers from the firm about trends they'd all noticed in nightclubs. Such diversity is a regular feature of personal selling. Especially for outgoing, vivacious personalities, the broad range of client relations can be professionally rewarding, as well as fun.

Third, professional selling and sales management can be a very lucrative career. Sales is among the highest-paying careers for college graduates, and compensation often includes perks, such as the use of a company car or bonuses for high performance. A top performer can have a total compensation package of over $150,000; even lower-level salespeople can make well over $50,000. Although the monetary compensation can be significant, the satisfaction of being involved in interesting, challenging, and creative work is rewarding in and of itself.

Fourth, because salespeople are the frontline emissaries for their firm, they are very visible to management. Furthermore, their performance is fairly straightforward to measure, which means that high-performing salespeople who aspire to management positions are in a good position to get promoted.

Many salespeople now can rely on virtual offices, which enable them to communicate via the Internet with colleagues and customers.

The Value Added by Personal Selling

The benefits for salespeople mean that they are expensive for firms. Experts estimate that the average cost of a single B2B sales call is about $400.[11] So why include them in the marketing channel at all? In response to this question, some firms have turned to the Internet and

Salespeople provide information and advice.

technology to lower the costs of personal selling. (See Social and Mobile Marketing 20.1.) Other firms, especially some retailers, have made the decision not to use a sales force and thus require customers to perform the sales function on their own. But the firms that continue to use personal selling as part of their integrated marketing communications program recognize the value that it adds to their product or service mix. That is, personal selling is worth more than it costs. Personal selling adds value by educating customers and providing advice, saving the customer time, making things easier for customers, and building long-term strategic relationships with customers.[12]

Salespeople Provide Information and Advice Imagine how difficult it would be to buy a custom suit, a house, or a car without the help of a salesperson. UPS wouldn't dream of investing in a new fleet of airplanes without the benefit of Boeing's selling team. Boeing's sales team can provide UPS with the technical aspects of the aircraft, as well as the economic justification for the purchase. If you need formalwear for your friend's upcoming wedding or a school dance, you might find it helpful to solicit the input of a retail sales associate, who can tell you what colors are hot this season, how to tie a bowtie, how each garment tends to fit, what the latest fashions are in formalwear, and how long your dress should be for a function that starts at 6:00 p.m. Certainly you could figure out most of this information on your own, but most customers find value in and are willing to pay for the education and advice that salespeople provide.

Salespeople Save Time and Simplify Buying Time is money! Customers perceive value in time and labor savings. In many grocery and drugstore chains, salespeople employed by the vendor supplying merchandise straighten stock, set

A salesperson's product knowledge and ability to facilitate the sale can make buying a car easy and possibly even enjoyable.

up displays, assess inventory levels, and write orders. In some cases, such as bakeries or soft drink sales, salespeople and truck drivers even bring in the merchandise and stock the shelves. These are all tasks that retail employees would otherwise have to do. To appeal to end customers, manufacturers might send salespeople into stores to provide cooking demonstrations or free samples in the case of grocery stores, or trunk or made-to-measure shows in the case of apparel or shoe retailers. In this case, the vendor increases convenience for both its immediate customer (the retailer) and the end consumer.

Sometimes however, turning over too many tasks to suppliers' salespeople can cause problems. Imagine a grocery store that has turned its inventory management function over to a supplier, like the consumer

Social and Mobile Marketing 20.1 — Personal Selling Goes Virtual

Rising fuel costs, increasing staff productivity, cutbacks in airline service, minimizing carbon footprints, reducing corporate expenditure—these are just some of the reasons for meetings to go virtual. Foremost among them is that the technology has matured to the point that conversing in cyberspace frequently makes more sense than meeting in the same room.[13]

The most advanced of these technologies, telepresence, includes three screens that display life-size images of conference attendees, plus an additional screen for shared work. Resolution on the screens exceeds that of high-definition televisions. Images can be magnified, allowing attendees to view minute product details from across the globe. These systems, which also feature custom lighting and acoustics, cost as much as $350,000. For corporations like Cisco, which has more than 200 telepresence rooms, the investment still represents a savings over travel costs. They aren't alone: The management consulting and technology service firm Accenture estimates its teleconferencing rooms save millions of dollars each year, as well as saving its staff the wear and tear of travel.

Other collaborative technologies involve less financial outlay. Web-meeting services, for example, allow companies to conduct online training, edit documents collaboratively, demonstrate applications, give training or sales presentations, poll attendees, chat online, conduct question and answer sessions, and provide technical support.[14] As long as you have a computer with a web browser and an Internet connection, you can use collaborative tools like wikis or VoIP technology like Skype.

This technology also helps small companies go global. Lisa Kirschner, president of a Chicago-based marketing and graphic design firm, had a hot lead in Italy.[15] But she lacked the resources to meet in person and felt brainstorming via e-mail would be too cumbersome. Taking the risk of investing in web conferencing, which was unheard of in her industry, she secured clients in Italy, Japan, and Britain. The technology has earned her $100,000—one-eighth of her total annual revenue.

Reduced business travel means a slump in the conference business.[16] Increasingly, companies are relying on technology for virtual conferences. One product, Expos2, digitizes the conference. Attendees begin with a screen showing the convention center layout and follow links to exhibits, programs, and live presentations that have interactive functionality. Digital meeting technology isn't intended to replace face-to-face meetings or travel but rather to provide an alternative for companies hoping to optimize their travel budgets. Closing a deal is more likely during an in-person meeting, and business travel to other countries provides important insights into communities and cultures. All transactions benefit from a personal touch. Nevertheless, web-based and conventional videoconferencing technology will have a profound impact on the way companies do business in the coming years.

Salespeople no longer have to meet face-to-face with their customers to make the sale.

packaged goods firm Kraft. The supplier might place competitors' products in disadvantageous shelf positions. Unless the relationship involves significant trust or the grocery has precautionary measures in place, the Kraft sales representative might place plenty of Kraft Thousand Island dressing on the shelf but leave little room for its competitors' products, designating a suboptimal amount of shelf space to Wishbone's Thousand Island offering. Although this relationship benefits Kraft, it may not help the grocer, especially if that retailer earns better margins on the competitors' products. Salespeople certainly can help facilitate a buying situation, but they should never be allowed to take it over.

The same might be said of your own personal shopping. When you go to buy a new car, the salesperson likely will work hard to convince you that you should purchase a specific make or model. Although an automotive salesperson has a significant amount of knowledge about the products and therefore can simplify the car buying process, the final decision must remain up to you, the consumer.

Salespeople Build Relationships As we discussed in Chapter 16, building strong marketing channel relationships is a critical success factor. Who in the organization is better equipped to manage this relationship than the salesperson, the front-line emissary for the firm? The most successful salespeople are those who build strong relationships with their customers—a rule that holds across all sorts of sales. That is, whether you are selling yourself as a job candidate, a product produced by your company, or a concept to a client, your sale is not successful if it leads to just a one-time transaction. Instead, good salespeople of all stripes consistently take a long-term perspective.

Building on the relationship concept introduced in Chapter 16, **relationship selling** refers to a sales philosophy and process that emphasizes a commitment to maintaining the relationship over the long term and investing in opportunities that are mutually beneficial to all parties.[17] Relationship-oriented salespeople work with their customers to find mutually beneficial solutions to their wants and needs. As we described in Chapter 7, colleges often negotiate long-term agreements with apparel companies to supply their sports teams. Similarly, a Lenovo sales team might be working with your university to provide you with the computer support and security you need for all four years you spend working on the school's network or in their computer labs.

LO2 Define the steps in the personal selling process.

THE PERSONAL SELLING PROCESS

Although selling may appear a rather straightforward process, successful salespeople must follow several steps. Depending on the sales situation and the buyer's readiness to purchase, the salesperson may not use every step, and the time required for each step varies with the situation. For example, if a customer goes into The Gap already prepared to purchase some chinos, the selling process will be fairly quick. But if IBM is attempting to sell personal computers for the first time to your university, the process may take several months. With this in mind, let's examine each step of the selling process (Exhibit 20.1).

Step 1: Generate and Qualify Leads

The first step in the selling process is to generate a list of potential customers (**leads**) and assess their potential (**qualify**). Salespeople who already have an established relationship with a customer will skip this step, and it is not used extensively in retail settings. In B2B situations, however, it is important to work continually to find new and potentially profitable customers.

Salespeople can generate and qualify leads in a variety of ways.[18] They might discover potential leads by talking to current customers, doing research on the

EXHIBIT 20.1 The Personal Selling Process

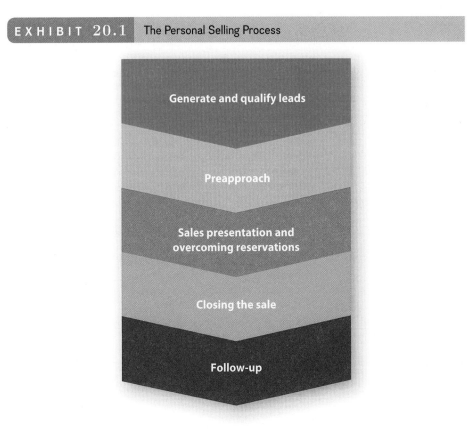

Generate and qualify leads

Preapproach

Sales presentation and overcoming reservations

Closing the sale

Follow-up

Internet, or networking at events such as trade shows, industry conferences, or chamber of commerce meetings. Salespeople can also generate leads through cold calls.

The Internet has been a boon for generating and qualifying leads. Prior to its explosion, it was cumbersome to perform research on products, customers, or competitors. Salespeople would rely on a research staff for this information, and it could take weeks for the research to be completed and sent through the mail.

Trade shows also offer an excellent forum for finding leads. These major events are attended by buyers who choose to be exposed to products and services offered by potential suppliers in an industry. Consumer electronics buyers always make sure that they attend the annual International Consumer Electronics Show (CES) in Las Vegas, the world's largest trade show for consumer technology (www.cesweb.org). The most recent show was attended by 153,000 people (including more than 34,000 international attendees), such as vendors, developers, and suppliers of consumer-technology hardware, content, technology delivery systems, and related products and services. Nearly 3,100 vendor exhibits took up 1.861 million net square feet of exhibit space, showcasing the very latest products and services. Vendors often use CES to introduce new products, including the first camcorder (1981), high-definition television (HDTV, 1998), and Internet protocol television (IP TV, 2005). More than 20,000 new products were launched at the 2012 conference alone.[19] In addition to providing an opportunity for retail buyers to see the latest products, the CES conference program features prominent speakers from the technology sector.[20]

Trade shows, like the International Consumer Eletronics Show in Las Vegas, are an excellent way to generate and qualify leads.

Adding Value 20.1   College Athletics Turn to the Pros for Sales Help

Not that long ago, a few billboards and word of mouth were enough to sell out tickets for a college game. Demand for tickets to college basketball and football games was so high that many schools added seats as fast as they could, and still had to turn fans away. But a dip in the economy, increased demands on leisure time, rising gas prices, and better television technology have combined to diminish ticket sales, leaving colleges with empty seats and a diminishing revenue stream, even as they face other budget constraints.[21] In response, some athletic programs are outsourcing ticket sales to commission-driven experts, in the hopes of bringing fans back to the bleachers.[22]

Ticket marketing companies catering to colleges use the model adopted by professional sports organizations: Sales staff work for commissions and make as many as 100 calls a day to students, alumni, faculty, and anyone else connected to the university. As these callers chat about the team, the school, or college athletics, they listen for clues to customers' personalities and needs, then adjust their sales strategy accordingly. The commission structure ensures the strong motivation of the sales force, which benefits the schools, because every ticket sold promises additional potential income in the form of concessions. Furthermore, filled stadiums significantly improve the public perception of the team, team spirit, and the likelihood of national publicity.

Some ticketing companies also provide related services to help generate revenue. Callers versed in the specifics of the college's athletics program might request donations for athletic scholarships or sport-related programming. Sport marketers with contacts in the world of professional athletics can help schools pull together appropriate fundraising events. They provide research and insights, coordinate print production for programs and signage, assist with challenging media situations, help build sales of apparel and merchandise, and even rent seat cushions for homecoming games.[23] Sophisticated software programs link ticketing, fundraising, and marketing functions to help track interactions, increase ticket sales, and improve the college's brand.[24]

Other athletic departments prefer to hire and manage their own ticket sales staff. This approach gives the school greater control over its brand. It also avoids privacy concerns about sharing university databases with an external seller, which may be too aggressive for the school's educational environment, or running afoul of complex NCAA rules. However, internal sales might not be as effective, considering the competing priorities that confront the athletic department, the limited experience of the sales staff, the prohibitions on commission-based incentives for university employees, and ineffective channels of communication.

More than 100 million fans are available to attend college athletic events. Thus universities want the pros on their team, selling tickets to their events.

Cold calls are a method of prospecting in which salespeople telephone or go to see potential customers without appointments.[25] **Telemarketing** is similar to a cold call, but it always occurs over the telephone. Sometimes professional telemarketing firms, rather than the firm's salespeople, make such calls. Adding Value 20.1 examines how colleges use it to boost attendance at sports events.

However, cold calls and telemarketing have become less popular over time, primarily because their success rate is fairly low. During cold calls, the salesperson

Telemarketing is a type of cold call in which salespeople generate or qualify leads on the telephone.

is not able to establish the potential customer's specific needs ahead of time. Accordingly, these methods can be very expensive. Second, both federal and state governments are regulating the activities of telemarketers. Federal rules prohibit telemarketing to consumers whose names appear on the national Do-Not-Call list, which is maintained by the Federal Trade Commission. Even for those consumers whose names are not on the list, the rules prohibit calling before 8:00 a.m. or after 9:00 p.m. (in the consumer's time zone) or after the consumer has told the telemarketer not to call. Federal rules also prohibit unsolicited fax messages and unsolicited telephone calls, as well as e-mail messages to cell phones.

After salespeople generate leads, they must qualify those leads by determining whether it is worthwhile to pursue them and attempt to turn them into customers. In B2B settings, the costs of preparing and making a presentation are so substantial that the seller must assess a lead's potential. Salespeople consider, for example, whether the potential customer's needs pertain to a product or a service. They should assess whether the lead has the financial resources to pay for the product or service.[26] Clients looking to sell multi-million dollar properties want real estate agents to qualify potential buyers first. Therefore, the sales agents might create a password-protected website that features floor plans and inside views for the shopping convenience of interested buyers. But to obtain the password, the customer must be prequalified as someone who could actually afford to buy the property. Such qualifications save both the agent and the seller the trouble of showing properties to curious people who could never actually afford to buy.

In a retail setting though, qualifying potential customers is both dangerous and potentially illegal. Retail salespeople should never "judge a book by its cover" and assume that a person in the store doesn't fit the store's image or cannot afford to purchase there. Imagine going to an upscale jewelry store to purchase an engagement ring, only to be snubbed because you are dressed in your everyday, casual school clothes.

Step 2: Preapproach and the Use of CRM Systems

The **preapproach** occurs prior to meeting the customer for the first time and extends the qualification of leads procedure described in Step 1. Although the salesperson has learned about the customer during the qualification stage, in this step, he or she must conduct additional research and develop plans for meeting with the customer. Suppose, for example, a management consulting firm wants to sell a bank a new system for finding checking account errors. The consulting firm's salesperson should first find out everything possible about the bank: How many checks does it process? What system is the bank using now? What are the benefits of the consultant's proposed system compared with the competition? The answers to these questions provide the basis for establishing value for the customer.

In the past, this customer information, if it was available at all, was typically included in a manual system that each individual salesperson kept, using a notebook or a series of cards. Today, salespeople often can access all this information immediately and conveniently from their firm's CRM system.

In most cases, these CRM systems have several components. There is a customer database or data warehouse. Whether the salesperson is working for a retail store or manages a selling team for an aerospace contractor, he or she can record transaction information, customer contact information, customer preferences, and market segment information about the customer. Once the data have been analyzed and CRM programs developed, salespeople can help implement the programs.

Having done the additional research, the salesperson establishes goals for meeting with the customer. It is important that he or she knows ahead of time exactly what should be accomplished. For instance, the consulting firm's

Salespeople input customer information into their PDAs to develop a customer database for CRM systems.

These salespeople are role playing. The woman standing at the easel is acting out a simulated buying situation while her colleagues act as the buying group. Afterward they will critique her presentation.

salesperson cannot expect to get a purchase commitment from the bank after just the first visit. But a demonstration of the system and a short presentation about how the system would benefit the customer would be appropriate. It is often a good idea to practice the presentation prior to the meeting, using a technique known as **role playing**, in which the salesperson acts out a simulated buying situation while a colleague or manager acts as the buyer. Afterward, the practice sales presentation can be critiqued and adjustments can be made.

Step 3: Sales Presentation and Overcoming Reservations

The Presentation   Once all the background information has been obtained and the objectives for the meeting are set, the salesperson is ready for a person-to-person meeting. Let's continue with our bank example. During the first part of the meeting, the salesperson needs to get to know the customer, get his or her attention, and create interest in the presentation to follow. The beginning of the presentation may be the most important part of the entire selling process, because it is when the salesperson establishes exactly where the customer is in his or her buying process (Exhibit 20.2). (For a refresher on the B2B buying process, see Chapter 7.)

Suppose, for instance, that the bank is in the first stage of the buying process: need recognition. It would not be prudent for the salesperson to discuss the pros and cons of different potential suppliers, because doing so would assume that the customer already had reached Step 4 (of the B2B buying proess), proposal analysis and customer selection. By asking a series of questions though, the salesperson can assess the bank's need for the product or service and adapt or customize the presentation to match the customer's need and stage in the decision process.[27]

Asking questions is only half the battle; carefully listening to the answers is equally important. Some salespeople, particularly inexperienced ones, believe that to be in control, they must do all the talking. Yet it is impossible to really understand where the customer stands without listening carefully. What if the COO

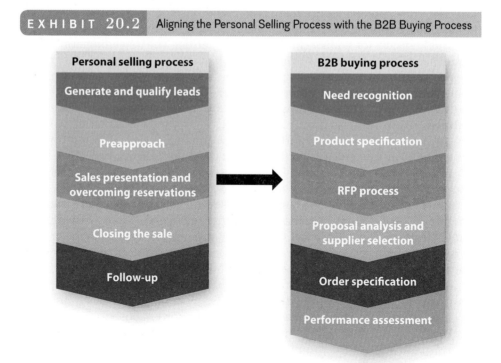

EXHIBIT 20.2   Aligning the Personal Selling Process with the B2B Buying Process

Personal selling process

- Generate and qualify leads
- Preapproach
- Sales presentation and overcoming reservations
- Closing the sale
- Follow-up

B2B buying process

- Need recognition
- Product specification
- RFP process
- Proposal analysis and supplier selection
- Order specification
- Performance assessment

says, "It seems kind of expensive"? If the salesperson isn't listening carefully, he or she won't pick up on the subtle nuances of what the customer is really thinking. In this case, it probably means the COO doesn't see the value in the offering.

When the salesperson has gotten a good feel for where the customer stands, he or she can apply that knowledge to help the customer solve its problem or satisfy its need. The salesperson might begin by explaining the features or characteristics of the system that will reduce checking account errors. It may not be obvious, solely on the basis of these features, however, that the system adds value beyond the bank's current practices. Using the answers to some of the questions the salesperson posed earlier in the meeting, he or she can clarify the product's advantages over current or past practices, as well as the overall benefits of adopting the new system. The salesperson might explain, for instance, that the bank can expect a 20 percent improvement in checking account errors and that, because of the size of the bank and number of checks it processes per year, this improvement would represent $2 million in annual savings. Because the system costs $150,000 per year and will take only three weeks to integrate into the current system, it will add significant and almost immediate value.

Handling Reservations An integral part of the sales presentation is handling reservations or objections that the buyer might have about the product or service. Although reservations can arise during each stage of the selling process, they are very likely to occur during the sales presentation. Customers may raise reservations pertaining to a variety of issues, but they usually relate in some way to value, such as that the price is too high for the level of quality or service.

Good salespeople know the types of reservations buyers are likely to raise. They may know, for instance, that their service is slower than competitors' or that their selection is limited. Although not all reservations can be forestalled, effective salespeople can anticipate and handle some. For example, when the bank COO said the check service seemed expensive, the salesperson was ready with information about how quickly the investment would be recouped.

As in other aspects of the selling process, the best way to handle reservations is to relax and listen, then ask questions to clarify any reservations.[28] For example, the salesperson could respond to the COO's reservation by asking, "How much do you think the bank is losing through checking account errors?" Her answer might open up a conversation about the positive trends in a cost–benefit analysis. Such questions are usually more effective than trying to prove the customer's reservation is not valid, because the latter approach implies the salesperson isn't really listening and could lead to an argument—the last thing a customer usually wants.

Step 4: Closing the Sale

Closing the sale means obtaining a commitment from the customer to make a purchase. Without a successful close, the salesperson goes away empty handed, so many salespeople find this part of the sales process very stressful. Although losing a sale is never pleasant, salespeople who are involved in a relationship with their customers must view any specific sales presentation as part of the progression toward ultimately making the sale or building the relationship. An unsuccessful close on one day may just be a means of laying the groundwork for a successful close during the next meeting. Superior Service 20.1 examines the art of soft-selling.

Although we have presented the selling process as a series of steps, closing the sale rarely follows so neatly. However, good salespeople listen carefully to what potential customers say and pay attention to their body language. By reading these signals, they can achieve an earlier close. Suppose that our hypothetical bank, instead of being in the first step of the buying process, were in the final step of negotiation and selection. An astute salesperson would pick up on these signals and ask for the sale.

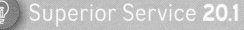

Superior Service 20.1   Soft Selling Works

Ever feel as though a salesperson is trying not to tap her foot or roll his eyes while you decide what flavor ice cream you want? Or ever had a sales associate eagerly assure you an outfit looks great on you, when the mirror tells you differently? If so, those salespeople are making a significant mistake. By focusing on a single transaction, they could be losing repeat customers. Soft selling, or acting as a knowledgeable consultant to help customers solve a problem, is far more likely to result in a completed sale in the present and more business in the future.[29]

The soft sell, also known as consultative or customer-centric sales, involves creating and maintaining a pleasant environment, interacting pleasantly with customers, providing useful information about products, helping customers reach a decision, and selling a product or service that the sales associate believes in. The concept isn't new: In the days of small neighborhood stores, employees greeted shoppers by name, knew their preferences and personalities, and helped customers track down products, even if it meant calling a competitor (remember *Miracle on 34th Street*?). But a focus on profits instead introduced the hard sell, characterized by pressure and hype. Over time, hard selling backfired, driving customers to more pleasant environments for their purchases. Now savvy retailers, returning to the original approach, are building profits, even in the midst of a challenging economy.

Yoforia's frozen yogurt stores provide a good example of soft sales of soft serve. Servers greet customers warmly, suggest samples to help with flavor decisions, and describe what makes the yogurt healthy. The result has been a 40 percent increase in sales over last year. Soft selling has even made it to the Girl Scouts, where parents helping their children hawk Thin Mints and Samoas are making sign-up sheets available in public spaces rather than tracking coworkers to their cubicles.[30]

Consultative selling also works well for larger purchases, and even in situations in which months or years may elapse before a transaction takes place. The idea is to provide prospects with quality information that helps them solve their problems[31]— delivered over lunch or via webinar, blog, white paper, or e-mail. It needn't promote a particular product or service. Rather, the focus should be on reliable content that consumers can use to make a purchase decision. Apple stores have online screenings of new models and the Genius Bar for free technical help.

Training sales associates in consultative selling requires subtlety. Sales associates at The Container Stores are selected for their ability to solve problems and relate to customers. They work for salary and not for commissions. Servers at Yoforia gain sales skills through one-on-one interactions with the store's cofounder Jun Kim, who stresses a good customer experience over making sales. The key to a positive experience is constant communication with customers to determine their needs, then using that information to identify appropriate choices and provide advice. Additional products or services should be suggested only if the customer has indicated a potential need. Ultimately, the goal of soft sales is to keep a customer for life, not just a single transaction.

The Girl Scouts have adopted the soft sell approach by making sign-up sheets available in public spaces rather than tracking coworkers to their cubicles.

Step 5: Follow-Up

> "It ain't over till it's over."
> —Yogi Berra[32]

With relationship selling, it is never really over, even after the sale. The attitudes customers develop after the sale become the basis for how they purchase in the future. The follow-up therefore offers a prime opportunity for a salesperson to solidify the customer relationship through great service quality. Let's apply the five service quality dimensions we discussed in Chapter 13 to the follow-up:[33]

- **Reliability.** The salesperson and the supporting organization must deliver the right product or service on time.

- **Responsiveness.** The salesperson and support group must be ready to deal quickly with any issue, question, or problem that may arise.

- **Assurance.** Customers must be assured through adequate guarantees that their purchase will perform as expected.

- **Empathy.** The salesperson and support group must have a good understanding of the problems and issues faced by their customers. Otherwise, they cannot give them what they want.

- **Tangibles.** Because tangibles reflect the physical characteristics of the seller's business, such as its website, marketing communications, and delivery materials, their influence is more subtle than that of the other four service quality dimensions. That doesn't mean it is any less important. Retail customers are generally more pleased with a purchase if it is carefully wrapped in nice paper instead of being haphazardly thrown into a crumpled plastic bag. The tangibles offer a signal that the product is of high quality, even though the packaging has nothing to do with the product's actual performance.

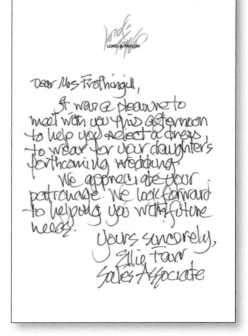

A postsale follow-up letter, call, or e-mail is the first step in initiating a new order and sustaining the relationship.

When customers' expectations are not met, they often complain—about deliveries, the billing amount or process, the product's performance, or after-sale services such as installation or training (recall the Gaps Model from Chapter 13). Effectively handling complaints is critical to the future of the relationship. As we noted in Chapter 13, the best way to handle complaints is to listen to the customer, provide a fair solution to the problem, and resolve the problem quickly.

The best way to nip a postsale problem in the bud is to check with the customer right after he or she takes possession of the product or immediately after the service has been completed. This speed demonstrates responsiveness and empathy. It also shows the customer that the salesperson and the firm care about customer satisfaction. Finally, a postsale follow-up call, e-mail, or letter takes the salesperson back to the first step in the sales process, for initiating a new order and sustaining the relationship.

CHECK YOURSELF

1. Why is personal selling important to an IMC strategy?
2. What are the steps in the personal selling process?

LO3 Describe the key functions involved in managing a sales force.

MANAGING THE SALES FORCE

Like any business activity involving people, the sales force requires management. **Sales management** involves the planning, direction, and control of personal selling activities, including recruiting, selecting, training, motivating, compensating, and evaluating, as they apply to the sales force.

Managing a sales force is a rewarding yet complicated undertaking. In this section, we examine how sales forces can be structured, some of the most important issues in recruiting and selecting salespeople, sales training issues, ways to compensate salespeople, and finally how to supervise and evaluate salespeople.

Sales Force Structure

Imagine the daunting task of putting together a sales force from scratch. Will you hire your own salespeople, or should they be manufacturer's representatives? What will each salesperson's primary duties be: order takers, order getters, sales support? Finally, will they work together in teams? In this section, we examine each of these issues.

Company Sales Force or Manufacturer's Representative A **company sales force** comprises people who are employees of the selling company. **Independent agents**, also known as **manufacturer's representatives**, or "**reps**," are salespeople who sell a manufacturer's products on an extended contract basis but are not employees of the manufacturer. They are compensated by commissions and do not take ownership or physical possession of the merchandise.

Manufacturer's representatives are useful for smaller firms or firms expanding into new markets, because such companies can achieve instant and extensive sales coverage without having to pay full-time personnel. Good sales representatives have many established contacts and can sell multiple products from noncompeting manufacturers during the same sales call. Also, the use of manufacturer's representatives facilitates flexibility; it is much easier to replace a rep than an employee and much easier to expand or contract coverage in a market with a sales rep than with a company sales force.

Company sales forces are more typically used for established product lines. Because the salespeople are company employees, the manufacturer has more control over what they do. If, for example, the manufacturer's strategy is to provide extensive customer service, the sales manager can specify exactly what actions a company sales force must take. In contrast, because manufacturer's representatives are paid on a commission basis, it is difficult to persuade them to take any action that doesn't directly lead to sales.

Order takers process routine orders, reorders, or rebuys for products.

Salesperson Duties Although the life of a professional salesperson is highly varied, salespeople generally play three important roles: order getting, order taking, and sales support.

Order Getting An **order getter** is a salesperson whose primary responsibilities are identifying potential customers and engaging those customers in discussions to attempt to make a sale. An order getter is also responsible for following up with the customer to ensure that the customer is satisfied and to build the relationship. In B2B settings, order getters are primarily involved in new buy and modified new buy situations (see Chapter 7). As a result, they require extensive sales and product knowledge training. The Coca-Cola salesperson who goes to Safeway's headquarters to sell a special promotion of Vanilla Coke is an order getter.

Order Taking An **order taker** is a salesperson whose primary responsibility is to process routine orders, reorders, or rebuys for products. Colgate employs order takers around the globe who go into stores and

Social and Mobile Marketing 20.2   Singing for Sales

Social media has revolutionized buying, such that consumers can learn lots about products and services from sources such as Facebook, Google+, Twitter, Yelp, and LinkedIn. Salespeople therefore have begun exploring creative ways to use social media in their various roles, with the ultimate goal of building sales.

On Broadway, the pop star Ricky Martin is now playing in a revival of *Evita*. He is not a traditional salesperson, yet for his more than 3 million Facebook fans and 5 million Twitter followers, he functions as an order getter.[34] Five days before show tickets went on sale to the public, Martin created a video that showed his Twitter followers how to buy tickets early. These fans snatched up about a half million dollars' worth of tickets.

Real estate agents may not be quite as fabulous as the singer of "Livin' La Vida Loca," but they are crazy about social media. It offers a great way to stay in touch with current and past clients, offer support after the sale, maintain an image of relevance in a changing marketplace, and build a referral network for new business.[35]

A survey of 1,000 sales professionals in the United States, United Kingdom, Brazil, and China revealed that nearly half of them viewed social media as important to their success.[36] Some traditionalists may be hesitant to use social networking sites, which offer no guarantee of control over a brand image as consumers use them to spread their own opinions about a particular company. But by embracing social marketing, as the *Evita* producers did, sellers can turn it into a valuable additional marketing channel. The sites can be used to provide shoppers with the information they crave, including factual advice, expert opinions, and information about special offers. They can be mined for information about consumers' behavior, needs, and stages in the buying process, as well as for finding sales leads and then following up with previous buyers.

distribution centers that already carry Colgate products to check inventory, set up displays, write new orders, and make sure everything is going smoothly.

Sales Support Sales support personnel enhance and help with the overall selling effort. For example, if a Best Buy customer begins to experience computer problems, the company has a Geek Squad door-to-door service, as well as support in the store. Those employees who respond to the customer's technical questions and repair the computer serve to support the overall sales process.

Combination Duties Although some salespeople's primary function may be order getting, order taking, or sales support, others fill a combination of roles, as the creative approach in Social and Mobile Marketing 20.2 suggests. For instance, a computer salesperson at Staples may spend an hour with a customer educating him or her about the pros and cons of various systems and then make the sale. The next customer might simply need a specific printer cartridge. A third customer might bring in a computer and seek advice about an operating system problem. The salesperson was first an order getter, next an order taker, and finally a sales support person.

Some firms use selling teams that combine sales specialists whose primary duties are order getting, order taking, or sales support but who work together to service important accounts. As companies become larger and products more complicated, it is nearly impossible for one person to perform all the necessary sales functions.

Recruiting and Selecting Salespeople

When the firm has determined how the sales force will be structured, it must find and hire salespeople. Although superficially this task may sound as easy as posting the job opening on the Internet or running an ad in a newspaper, it must be performed carefully, because firms don't want to hire the wrong person. Salespeople are very expensive to train. Recall our discussion of Zappos in Chapter 13, a company that considers finding the right people so important that it will pay them to leave after a few weeks if they are not a good fit.

The most important activity in the recruiting process is to determine exactly what the salesperson will be doing and what personal traits and abilities a person should have to do the job well. For instance, the Coca-Cola order getter who goes to Safeway to pitch a new product will typically need significant sales experience, coupled with great communication and analytical skills. Coke's order takers need to be reliable and able to get along with lots of different types of people in the stores, from managers to customers.

Many firms give candidates personality tests, but they stress different personality attributes, depending on the requisite traits for the position and the personality characteristics of their most successful salespeople.[37] For instance, impatience is often a positive characteristic for sales, because it creates a sense of urgency to close the sale. But for very large, complicated sales targeting large institutions, like the bank in our previous example, an impatient salesperson may irritate the decision makers and kill the deal.

When recruiting salespeople, is it better to look for candidates with innate sales ability, or can a good training program make anyone a successful salesperson? In other words, are good salespeople born, or are they made?[38] By a margin of seven to one in a survey of sales and marketing executives, respondents believed that training and supervision are more critical determinants of selling success than the salesperson's inherent personal characteristics.[39] Yet some of those same respondents noted that they knew "born salespeople" and that personal traits are important for successful sales careers. So, it appears that while training is critical, it also helps to possess certain personal traits.

What are those personal traits? Managers and sales experts have identified the following:[40]

- *Personality.* Good salespeople are friendly, sociable, and, in general, like being around people. Customers won't buy from someone they don't like.

- *Optimism.* Good salespeople tend to look at the bright side of things. Optimism also may help them be resilient—the third trait.

- *Resilience.* Good salespeople don't easily take no for an answer. They keep coming back until they get a yes.

- *Self-motivation.* As we have already mentioned, salespeople have lots of freedom to spend their days the way they believe will be most productive. But if the salespeople are not self-motivated to get the job done, it probably won't get done.

- *Empathy.* Empathy is one of the five dimensions of service quality discussed previously in this chapter and in Chapter 13. Good salespeople must care about their customers, their issues, and their problems.

Sales Training

Even people who possess all these personal traits need training. All salespeople benefit from training about selling and negotiation techniques, product and service knowledge, technologies used in the selling process, time and territory management, and company policies and procedures.

Firms use varied delivery methods to train their salespeople, depending on the topic of the training, what type of salesperson is being trained, and the cost versus the value of the training. For instance, an on-the-job training program is excellent for communicating selling and negotiation skills, because managers can observe the sales trainees in real selling situations and provide instant feedback. They can also engage in role-playing exercises in which the salesperson acts out a simulated buying situation and the manager critiques the salesperson's performance.

A much less expensive, but for some purposes equally valuable, training method is the Internet. Online training programs have revolutionized the way training happens in many firms. Firms can provide new product and service knowledge, spread the word about changes in company policies and procedures, and share selling tips in a user-friendly environment that salespeople can access anytime and anywhere. Distance learning sales training programs through teleconferencing enable a group of salespeople to participate with their instructor or manager in a virtual classroom. And testing can occur online as well. Online sales training may never replace the one-on-one interaction of on-the-job training for advanced selling skills, but it is quite effective and efficient for many other aspects of the sales training task.

Motivating and Compensating Salespeople

An important goal for any effective sales manager is to get to know his or her salespeople and determine what motivates them to be effective. Some salespeople prize their freedom and like to be left alone; others want attention and are more productive when they receive accolades for a job well done. Still others are motivated primarily by monetary compensation. Great sales managers determine how best to motivate each of their salespeople according to what is most important to each individual. Although sales managers can emphasize different motivating factors, except in the smallest companies, the methods used to compensate salespeople must be fairly standardized and can be divided into two categories: financial and nonfinancial.

Technology has changed the lives of salespeople and sales training. Companies can conduct distance learning and training through videoconferencing.

Financial Rewards Salespeople's compensation usually has several components. Most salespeople receive at least part of their compensation as a salary, a fixed sum of money paid at regular intervals. Another common financial incentive is a commission, which is money paid as a percentage of the sales volume or profitability. A bonus is a payment made at management's discretion when the salesperson attains certain goals. Bonuses usually are given only periodically, such as at the end of the year. A sales contest is a short-term incentive designed to elicit a specific response from the sales force. Prizes might be cash or other types of financial incentives. For instance, Volkswagen may give a free trip to Germany for the salesperson who sells the most Touaregs.

The bulk of any compensation package is made up of salary, commission, or a combination of the two. The advantage of a salary plan is that salespeople know exactly what they will be paid, and sales managers have more control. Salaried salespeople can be directed to spend a certain percentage of their time handling customer service issues. Under a commission system, however, salespeople have only one objective—make the sale! Thus, a commission system provides the most incentive for the sales force to sell.

Sales contests are a type of financial reward that provides prizes like these or other types of financial incentives.

Nonfinancial Rewards As we have noted, good salespeople are self-motivated. They want to do a good job and make the sale because it makes them feel good. But this good feeling also can be accentuated by recognition from peers and management. For instance, the internal monthly magazine at the cosmetics firm Mary Kay provides an outlet for not only selling advice but also companywide recognition of individual salespeople's accomplishments.[41]

Nonfinancial rewards should have high symbolic value, as plaques, pens, or rings do. Free trips or days off are also effective rewards.

GO FOR THE GOLD
SALES MARATHON

July 1 - October 1

Earn Points for Hitting Sales Goals....
Spend Points on Brand Name Merchandise!

BONUS POINTS AWARDED FOR:

• TOP 3 SALES GENERATORS

• MOST IMPROVED SALES

• 3 OR MORE NEW ACCOUNTS

• CUSTOMER COMPLIMENT

See your manager for more details.

Visit the rewards website to track your points, view your ranking and browse the awards available to spend points on.

Canon   SONY   SAMSUNG   acer   MOVADO   weber

AWARDS NETWORK™
awards worth remembering

Mary Kay gives high-performing salespeople an award that has both high symbolic value and material value—a pink Cadillac.

More important than what the reward is, however, is the way it is operationalized. For instance, an award should be given at a sales meeting and publicized in the company newsletter. It should also be done in good taste, because if the award is perceived as tacky, no one will take it seriously.[42] Mary Kay recognizes salespeople's success with unusually large rewards that have both high symbolic and high material value. More than 100,000 independent beauty consultants and sales directors have earned the use of one of the famous pink Cadillacs, but it is also possible to gain rewards and recognition such as a set of faux pearl earrings within the first week of becoming a consultant.

Evaluating Salespeople by Using Marketing Metrics

Salespeople's evaluation process must be tied to their reward structure. If salespeople do well, they should receive their rewards, in the same way that if you do well on your exams and assignments in a class, you should earn a good grade. However, salespeople should be evaluated and rewarded for only those activities and outcomes that fall under their control. If Macy's makes a unilateral decision to put Diesel jeans in all its stores, after a negotiation with Diesel's corporate headquarters in Italy, the Diesel sales representatives responsible for individual Macy's stores should not receive credit for making the sale, nor should they get all the windfall commission that would ensue from the added sales.

Considering this guiding principle—evaluate and reward salespeople for what they do and not for what they don't do—how should sales managers evaluate salespeople? The answer is never easy, because measures must be tied to performance, and there are many ways to measure performance in a complex job like selling. For example, evaluating performance on the basis of monthly sales alone fails to consider how profitable the sales were, whether any progress was made to build new business that will be realized sometime in the future, or the level of customer service the salesperson provided. Because the sales job is multifaceted with many contributing success factors, sales managers should use multiple measures.[43]

Evaluation measures can be objective or subjective. Sales, profits, and the number of orders represent examples of objective measures. Although each is somewhat useful to managers, such measures do not provide an adequate perspective for a thorough evaluation, because there is no means of comparison with other salespeople. For instance, suppose salesperson A generated $1 million last year, but salesperson B generated $1.5 million. Should salesperson B automatically receive a significantly higher evaluation? Now consider that salesperson B's territory has twice as much potential as salesperson A's. Knowing this, we might suppose that salesperson A has actually done a better job. For this reason, firms use ratios like profit per customer, orders per call, sales per hour, or expenses compared to sales as their objective measures.

Whereas objective measures are quantitative, subjective measures seek to assess salespeople's behavior: what they do and how well they do it. By their very nature, subjective measures reflect one person's opinion about another's performance. Thus, subjective evaluations can be biased and should be used cautiously and only in conjunction with multiple objective measures.

CHECK YOURSELF

1. What do sales managers need to do to successfully manage their sales force?
2. What is the difference between monetary and nonmonetary incentives?

ETHICAL AND LEGAL ISSUES IN PERSONAL SELLING

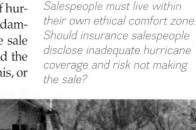

LO4 Describe the ethical and legal issues in personal selling.

Although ethical and legal issues permeate all aspects of marketing, they are particularly important for personal selling. Unlike advertising and other communications with customers, which are planned and executed on a corporate level, personal selling involves a one-to-one, and often face-to-face, encounter with the customer. Thus, sellers' actions are not only highly visible to customers but also to other stakeholders, such as the communities in which they work.

Ethical and legal issues arise in three main areas. First, there is the relationship between the sales manager and the sales force. Second, in some situations, an inconsistency might exist between corporate policy and the salesperson's ethical comfort zone. Third, both ethical and legal issues can arise when the salesperson interacts with the customer, especially if that salesperson or the selling firm collects significant information about the customer. To maintain trustworthy customer relationships, companies must take care that they respect customer privacy and respect the information comfort zone—that is, the amount of information a customer feels comfortable providing.[44]

The Sales Manager and the Sales Force

Like any manager, a sales manager must treat people fairly and equally in everything he or she does. With regard to the sales force, this fairness must include hiring, promotion, supervision, training, assigning duties and quotas, compensation and incentives, and firing.[45] Federal laws cover many of these issues. For instance, equal employment opportunity laws make it unlawful to discriminate against a person in hiring, promotion, or firing because of race, religion, nationality, sex, or age.

The Sales Force and Corporate Policy

Sometimes salespeople face a conflict between what they believe represents ethical selling and what their company asks them to do to make a sale. Suppose an insurance agent, whose compensation is based on commission, sells a homeowner's policy to a family that has just moved to New Orleans, an area prone to flooding as a result of hurricanes. Even though the policy covers hurricane damage, it does not cover water damage from hurricanes. If the salesperson discloses the inadequate coverage, the sale might be lost because additional flood insurance is very expensive. What should the salesperson do? Salespeople must live within their own ethical comfort zone. If this, or any other situation, is morally repugnant to the salesperson, he or she must question the choice to be associated with such a company.[46]

Salespeople must live within their own ethical comfort zone. Should insurance salespeople disclose inadequate hurricane coverage and risk not making the sale?

Salespeople also can be held accountable for illegal actions sanctioned by the employer. If the homeowner asks if the home is above the floodplain or whether water damage from flooding is covered by the policy, and it is company policy to intentionally mislead potential customers, both the salesperson and the insurance dealership could be susceptible to legal action.

The Salesperson and the Customer

As the frontline emissaries for a firm, salespeople have a duty to be ethically and legally correct in all their dealings with their customers. Not only is it the right thing to do, it simply means good business. Long-term relationships can deteriorate quickly if customers believe that they have not been

Perhaps nowhere is ethical selling more hotly debated than in the pharmaceutical industry. Physicians have become accustomed to the perks offered by the pharmaceutical representatives who visit their office and restock their shelves with product samples, extras such as free tickets to Broadway musicals and pens—tons and tons of pens. It's a fine line between buying a prospect's time to demonstrate your wares and bribing him or her to prescribe your firm's drugs.

Promotional budgets for pharmaceuticals have reached $21 billion, with roughly 100,000 people in the sales force. Pharmaceutical companies hand out samples liberally as a central part of their marketing program, to the extent of about $15.9 billion in samples each year. Many patients benefit from these samples; however, most companies only give out samples of their high-priced products. The net result, according to a study by Washington University, becomes that many doctors dispense and prescribe drugs that are not their primary drug of choice.

At the end of the day, many ethical decisions rest on the shoulders of the independent sales representatives. Are they using tactics that promote the best health care options for the

patients, or are they simply pushing their product? On a broader scale, are they inflating medication costs as a result of these selling methods so that, ultimately, the customer cannot afford the prescription anyway?

Are pharmaceutical salespeople promoting the best health care option for the patients, or are they simply pushing their product?

treated in an ethically proper manner. Unfortunately, salespeople sometimes get mixed signals from their managers or simply do not know when their behaviors might be considered unethical or illegal. Formal guidelines can help, but it is also important to integrate these guidelines into training programs in which salespeople can discuss various issues that arise in the field with their peers and managers.[48] Most important, however, is for sales managers to lead by example. If managers are known to cut ethical corners in their dealings with customers, it shouldn't surprise them when their salespeople do the same. Ethical and Societal Dilemma 20.1 considers the ethical issues that pharmaceutical salespeople face.

CHECK YOURSELF

1. What are three areas of personal selling in which ethical and legal issues are more likely to arise?

Summing Up

LO1 Describe the value added of personal selling.

Although the cost of an average B2B sales call is expensive, many firms believe they couldn't do business without their sales forces. Customers can buy many products and services without the help of a salesperson, but in many other cases, it is worth the extra cost built into the price of a product to be educated about the product or get valuable advice. Salespeople

can also simplify the buying process and therefore save the customer time and hassle.

LO2 Define the steps in the personal selling process.

Although we discuss selling in terms of steps, it truly represents a process, and the time spent in each step varies according to the situation. In the first step, the salesperson generates a list of viable customers. During the second step, the preapproach, the salesperson gathers information about the customer and prepares for the presentation. The third step, the sales presentation, consists of a personal meeting between the salesperson and the customer. Through discussion and by asking questions, the salesperson learns where the customer is in the buying process and tailors the discussion around what the firm's product or service can do to meet that customer's needs. During the fourth step, the close, the salesperson asks for the order. Finally, during the follow-up, the salesperson and support staff solidify the long-term relationship by making sure the customer is satisfied with the purchase and addressing any complaints. The follow-up therefore sets the stage for the next purchase.

LO3 Describe the key functions involved in managing a sales force.

The first task of a sales manager, assuming a firm is starting a sales force from scratch, is to determine whether to use a company sales force or manufacturer's representatives. Then sales managers must determine what the primary selling responsibilities will be—order getter, order taker, or sales support. The sales manager recruits and selects salespeople, but because there are all sorts of sales jobs, he or she must determine what it takes to be successful and then go after people with those attributes. In the next step, training, firms can choose between on-the-job and online training. Sales managers are also responsible for motivating and compensating salespeople. Most salespeople appreciate a balance of financial and nonfinancial rewards for doing a good job. Finally, sales managers are responsible for evaluating their salespeople. Normally, salespeople should be evaluated on a combination of objective measures, such as sales per hour, and subjective measures, such as how friendly they appear to customers.

LO4 Describe the ethical and legal issues in personal selling.

Ethical and legal issues arise in three areas in personal selling. First, ethical and legal issues could arise based on how the sales manager interacts with the sales force. Second, there might be inconsistencies between corporate policy and the salesperson's ethical comfort zone. Finally, ethical and legal issues can arise as the salesperson interacts with customers.

Key Terms

- bonus, 623
- closing the sale, 617
- cold calls, 614
- commission, 623
- company sales force, 620
- independent agents, 620
- leads, 612
- manufacturer's representative, 620
- order getter, 620
- order taker, 620
- personal selling, 608
- preapproach, 615
- qualify, 612
- relationship selling, 612
- reps, 620
- role playing, 616
- salary, 623
- sales contest, 623
- sales management, 620
- sales support personnel, 621
- selling teams, 621
- telemarketing, 614
- trade shows, 613

Marketing Applications

1. How has your perception of what it would be like to have a career in sales changed since you read this chapter?

2. "Salespeople just make products cost more." Do you agree or disagree with this statement? Discuss why you've taken that position.

3. Choose an industry or a specific company that you would like to work for as a salesperson. How would you generate and qualify leads?

4. Why is it important for salespeople to be good listeners? To be good at asking questions?

5. Suppose you are a salesperson at a high-end jewelry store. What can you do to ensure that your customers are satisfied? Now imagine you are the store manager of the same store; what can you do in your position to guarantee customers remain happy with the service they receive?

6. Imagine that a time machine has transported you back to 1961. How was a day in the life of a salesperson selling appliances such as washing machines different in 1961 than it is in 2013?

7. What are some of the potentially ethically troubling and illegal situations facing professional salespeople, and how should they deal with them?

8. Why would Gillette use a company sales force, while a small independent manufacturer of organic shaving cream uses manufacturer's representatives?

9. Similar to the way a sales manager evaluates a salesperson, your instructors evaluate your performance to assign you a grade. Choose one of your classes and analyze the advantages and disadvantages of the objective and subjective bases used to evaluate your performance.

10. A customer has the following reservations. How do you respond?
    a. "I really like all the things this copier does, but I don't think it's going to be very reliable. With all those features, something's got to go wrong."
    b. "Your price for this printer is higher than the price I saw advertised on the Internet."

11. Imagine that you have just been hired by the school newspaper to sell ad space. You are asked what you think would be a "fair" compensation package for you. Using the information from the chapter, make a list of all the elements that should be included in your compensation package. How would this compensation package change over time and with continued performance?

12. You have taken a summer job in the windows and doors department of a large home improvement store. During sales training, you learn about the products, how to best address customers' needs and how to sell the customer the best product to fit their needs regardless of price point. One day your manager informs you that you are to recommend Smith Windows to every window customer. Smith Windows are more expensive and don't really provide superior benefit except in limited circumstances. The manager is insistent that you recommend Smith. Not knowing what else to do, you recommend Smith Windows to customers who would have been better served by lower-cost windows. The manager rewards you with a sales award. Later the manager tells you that he received an all-expenses-paid cruise for his family from Smith Windows. What, if anything, should you do with this information?

Quiz Yourself

1. Consumers often ask workers in supermarkets where something is located, only to learn the worker is a vendor stacking and straightening his or her company's products on the store shelves. These manufacturer's sales representatives benefit retailers by _____.
    a. educating them
    b. giving them advice
    c. saving them time and money
    d. adding product lines
    e. increasing marketing costs to the seller

2. Diana went to Kleinfeld's (the retailer on the TLC show, "Say Yes to the Dress") to look at wedding dresses. She had an idea of what she was looking for, but was also interested in feedback from the sales associate. The sales associate, sensing Diana's buying mode, began with the _____ stage of the selling process.
    a. generate leads
    b. preapproach
    c. closing the sale
    d. follow-up
    e. sales presentation

(Answers to these two questions can be found on page 648.)

Go to www.mhhe.com/grewal4e to practice an additional 11 questions.

Net Savvy

1. Go to Salesforce.com's You Tube channel at www.youtube.com/user/salesforce. Watch a few of the short videos and discuss how the tools described would help you as a salesperson.

2. To learn more about careers in sales, go to www.bls.gov/oco/, the website for the Bureau of Labor Statistics. This site contains a wealth of information about careers in all fields. Click on "Sales." Choose any of the sales fields listed, and explore that career field. What experience is necessary to be hired for that job? What is the median salary? What do earners in the highest 10 percent of performance earn? Is job growth anticipated in that field?

Chapter Case Study

ALTA DATA SOLUTIONS: MAKING THE SALE[49]

When Vicki Cambridge reached her office, she had a message from Mike Smith, the regional sales manager, to meet him in his office regarding the Burtell Inc. order. Vicki Cambridge is a senior sales associate for Alta Data Solutions Inc., a firm that markets software and hardware designed for data storage. The Burtell order represents a multimillion-dollar contract for Alta Data Solution and would help Burtell boost its productivity levels and revenue for the region. To prepare for the meeting, Vicki reviews her sales call report notes on the Burtell account.

ALTA DATA SOLUTIONS

Alta Data Solutions provides software and hardware solutions to large firms and has an established track record for delivering an exceptional standard of quality and high levels of customer service. This excellent reputation allows Alta Data Solutions to charge a substantial premium, ranging from 10 to 20 percent above the market leader.

The data storage software services market has been dominated for two decades by this market leader. Alta Data Solutions holds the second position in the marketplace, with a considerably lower but growing market share. Only one other competitor, an aggressive, small, low-price player, holds a significant market share; this provider has made inroads into the market in the past several years through its aggressive sales tactics.

What are the key points Vicki should make in her presentation?

Alta Data Solutions has just built a new facility and hired 50 new software programmers. Therefore, the company must generate new business to meet its higher financial goals; even more important in the short run, it must keep the new programmers working on interesting projects to retain them.

BURTELL INC.

Burtell Inc. is a division of a major U.S.-based consumer products firm. Its purchasing department negotiates contracts for software services and coordinates the interface among a variety of members from different departments. The business environment for consumer products has become highly competitive in recent years, leading to tight budgets and higher levels of scrutiny of the value added by vendors. Competition is fierce, as large numbers of end-user customers are considering vendors that provide the most data analysis with their products.

Burtell Inc. has been consistently buying software development services from the market leader since 1991 and is generally satisfied with its service. A recent change in corporate leadership, however, has increased concerns about its overreliance on one vendor for a particular service. Also, because of the difficult economic climate, the company is concerned about the cost of software services and whether it is necessary to provide such a high service level.

VICKI'S CALL REPORT

A call report is like a diary of sales calls made to a particular client. The notes in Vicki's Burtell file pertaining to the current negotiations began on June 4:

June 4: I contacted Bethany O'Meara, chief purchasing officer at Burtell, to introduce myself to her and get a sense of what their future software needs might be. She told me that the slowed business climate had caused Burtell to institute a program for increased efficiency in operations and that they would be looking to negotiate a new contract for software solutions. She gave me some insights into the technological aspects of their needs.

June 18: Met with Jon Aaronson, head of R&D, to explain our productivity-enhancing solutions. Went into considerable depth explaining how Burtell could service their needs and learned what they were looking for in a provider. I went over some specific product specification issues, but Jon did not seem impressed. But he did ask for a price and told me that the final decision rested with Brad Alexander, the chief financial officer.

July 2: Presented to Bethany O'Meara and Jon Aaronson. They first asked about the price. I gave them a quote of $10 million. They suggested that other services were much cheaper. I explained that our price reflected the latest technology and that the price differential was an investment that could pay for itself several times over through faster communication speeds. I also emphasized our reputation for high-quality customer service. While the presentation appeared to meet their software needs, they did not seem impressed with the overall value. I also sent a copy of the presentation in report form to Brad Alexander and attempted to get an appointment to see him.

July 9: Contacted Jon Aaronson by phone. He told me that we were in contention with three other firms and the debate was heated. He stated that the other firms were also touting their state-of-the-art technology. Discussed a lower price of $7 million. Also encouraged him to visit Alta Data Solutions headquarters to meet with the product manager who oversaw the product development efforts and would manage the implementation of the product. He wasn't interested in making the two-day trip even though it would spotlight our core competencies.

July 15: Received a conference call from Brad Alexander and Jon Aaronson to discuss the price. Brad said the price was still too high and that he could not depreciate that amount over the life of the software and meet target levels of efficiency. He wanted a final quote by August 6.

THE FINAL PITCH

Vicki prepared for her meeting with Mike by going over her notes and market data about the competitors. Mike's voicemail indicated that they would be meeting to put together their best possible proposal.

Questions

Help Vicki prepare her sales presentation.

1. Who should be at the presentation?
2. How should Vicki start the meeting?
3. What are the key points she should make in her presentation?
4. What reservations should she expect? How should she handle them?

actual product The physical attributes of a product including the brand name, features/design, quality level, and packaging.

administered vertical marketing system A *supply chain* system in which there is no common ownership and no contractual relationships, but the dominant channel member controls the channel relationship.

advanced shipping notice (ASN) An electronic document that the supplier sends the retailer in advance of a shipment to tell the retailer exactly what to expect in the shipment.

advertising A paid form of communication from an identifiable source, delivered through a communication channel, and designed to persuade the receiver to take some action, now or in the future.

advertising allowance Tactic of offering a price reduction to channel members if they agree to feature the manufacturer's product in their advertising and promotional efforts.

advertising plan A section of the firm's overall marketing plan that explicitly outlines the objectives of the advertising campaign, how the campaign might accomplish those objectives, and how the firm can determine whether the campaign was successful.

advertising schedule The specification of the timing and duration of advertising.

affective component A component of *attitude* that reflects what a person feels about the issue at hand—his or her like or dislike of something.

AIDA model A common model of the series of mental stages through which consumers move as a result of marketing communications: *A*wareness leads to *I*nterests, which lead to *D*esire, which leads to *A*ction.

aided recall Occurs when consumers recognize a name (e.g., of a brand) that has been presented to them.

alpha testing An attempt by the firm to determine whether a product will perform according to its design and whether it satisfies the need for which it was intended; occurs in the firm's research and development (R&D) department.

associated services (also called augmented product) The non-physical attributes of the product including product warranties, financing, product support, and after-sale service.

attitude A person's enduring evaluation of his or her feelings about and behavioral tendencies toward an object or idea; consists of three components: *cognitive, affective,* and *behavioral.*

augmented product See *associated services.*

autocratic buying center A buying center in which one person makes the decision alone, though there may be multiple participants.

B2B (business-to-business) The process of selling merchandise or services from one business to another.

B2C (business-to-consumers) The process in which businesses sell to consumers.

Baby Boomers Generational cohort of people born after World War II, between 1946 and 1964.

background In an advertisement, the backdrop, which is usually a single color.

bait and switch A deceptive practice of luring customers into the store with a very low advertised price on an item (the bait), only to aggressively pressure them into purchasing a higher-priced model (the switch) by disparaging the low-priced item, comparing it unfavorably with the higher-priced model, or professing an inadequate supply of the lower-priced item.

behavioral component A component of *attitude* that comprises the actions a person takes with regard to the issue at hand.

behavioral segmentation A segmentation method that divides customers into groups based on how they use the product or service. Some common behavioral measures include occasion and loyalty.

benefit segmentation The grouping of consumers on the basis of the benefits they derive from products or services.

beta testing Having potential consumers examine a product prototype in a real-use setting to determine its functionality, performance, potential problems, and other issues specific to its use.

big box retailer Discount stores that offer a narrow but deep assortment of merchandise; see *category killer.*

biometric data Digital scanning of the physiological or behavioral characteristics of individuals as a means of identification.

blog (Weblog) A Web page that contains periodic posts; corporate blogs are a new form of marketing communications.

body copy The main text portion of an ad.

bonder Social butterflies who use social media to enhance and expand their relationships, which they consider all-important in their lives.

bonus A payment made at management's discretion when the salesperson attains certain goals; usually given only periodically, such as at the end of the year.

bounce rate The percentage of times a visitor leaves the website almost immediately, such as after viewing only one page.

boycott A group's refusal to deal commercially with some organization to protest against its policies.

brand The name, term, design, symbol, or any other features that identify one seller's good or service as distinct from those of other sellers.

brand association The mental links that consumers make between a brand and its key product attributes; can involve a logo, slogan, or famous personality.

brand awareness Measures how many consumers in a market are familiar with the brand and what it stands for; created through repeated exposures of the various brand elements (brand name, logo, symbol, character, packaging, or slogan) in the firm's communications to consumers.

brand dilution Occurs when a brand extension adversely affects consumer perceptions about the attributes the core brand is believed to hold.

brand elements Characteristics that identify the sponsor of a specific ad.

brand equity The set of assets and liabilities linked to a brand that add to or subtract from the value provided by the product or service.

brand extension The use of the same brand name for new products being introduced to the same or new markets.

branding In an advertisement, the portion that identifies the sponsor of the ad.

brand licensing A contractual arrangement between firms, whereby one firm allows another to use its brand name, logo, symbols, or characters in exchange for a negotiated fee.

brand loyalty Occurs when a consumer buys the same brand's product or service repeatedly over time rather than buying from multiple suppliers within the same category.

brand personality Refers to a set of human characteristics associated with a brand, which has symbolic or self-expressive meanings for consumers.

brand repositioning (rebranding) A strategy in which marketers change a brand's focus to target new markets or realign the brand's core emphasis with changing market preferences.

breadth Number of product lines offered by a firm; also known as variety.

break-even analysis Technique used to examine the relationships among cost, price, revenue, and profit over different levels of production and sales to determine the *break-even point*.

break-even point The point at which the number of units sold generates just enough revenue to equal the total costs; at this point, profits are zero.

breakthroughs See *pioneers*.

bricks-and-mortar retailer A traditional, physical store.

business ethics Refers to a branch of ethical study that examines ethical rules and principles within a commercial context, the various moral or ethical problems that might arise in a business setting, and any special duties or obligations that apply to persons engaged in commerce.

business-to-business (B2B) marketing The process of buying and selling goods or services to be used in the production of other goods and services, for consumption by the buying organization, or for resale by wholesalers and retailers.

buyer The buying center participant who handles the paperwork of the actual purchase.

buying center The group of people typically responsible for the buying decisions in large organizations.

C2C (consumer-to-consumer) The process in which consumers sell to other consumers.

cannibalization Customers who formerly made purchases through one retail channel switch to a different retail channel without increasing the overall sales to the retailer.

cash discount Tactic of offering a reduction in the invoice cost if the buyer pays the invoice prior to the end of the discount period.

category depth The number of stock keeping units (SKUs) within a category.

category killer A specialist that offers an extensive assortment in a particular category, so overwhelming the category that other retailers have difficulty competing.

category specialist A retailer that offers a narrow variety but a deep assortment of merchandise.

cause-related marketing Commercial activity in which businesses and charities form a partnership to market an image, a

product, or a service for their mutual benefit; a type of promotional campaign.

channel conflict When members of a marketing channel are in disagreement or discord. Channel conflict can occur between members of the same marketing channel (see *vertical channel conflict* or *vertical supply chain conflict*) or between members at the same level of a marketing channel (see *horizontal channel conflict* or *horizontal supply chain conflict*).

checking The process of going through the goods upon receipt to ensure they arrived undamaged and that the merchandise ordered was the merchandise received.

churn The number of consumers who stop using a product or service, divided by the average number of consumers of that product or service.

click path Shows how users proceed through the information on a website—not unlike how grocery stores try to track the way shoppers move through their aisles.

click-through rate (CTR) The number of times a user clicks on an online ad divided by the number of impressions.

click-through tracking A way to measure how many times users click on banner advertising on websites.

clinical trial Medical test of the safety and efficacy of a new drug or treatment with human subjects.

close-out retailers Stores that offer an inconsistent assortment of low priced, brand name merchandise.

closing the sale Obtaining a commitment from the customer to make a purchase.

co-branding The practice of marketing two or more brands together, on the same package or promotion.

coercive power Threatening or punishing the other channel member for not undertaking certain tasks. Delaying payment for late delivery would be an example.

cognitive component A component of *attitude* that reflects what a person believes to be true.

cold calls A method of prospecting in which salespeople telephone or go to see potential customers without appointments.

collaborative planning, forecasting, and replenishment (CPFR) An inventory management system that uses an electronic data interchange (EDI) through which a retailer sends sales information to a manufacturer.

commercial speech A message with an economic motivation, that is, to promote a product or service, to persuade someone to purchase, and so on.

commission Compensation or financial incentive for salespeople based on a fixed percentage of their sales.

communication channel The medium—print, broadcast, the Internet—that carries the message.

communication gap A type of *service gap*; refers to the difference between the actual service provided to customers and the service that the firm's promotion program promises.

company sales force Comprised of people who are employees of the selling company and are engaged in the selling process.

compensatory decision rule At work when the consumer is evaluating alternatives and trades off one characteristic against another, such that good characteristics compensate for bad ones.

competitive intelligence (CI) Used by firms to collect and synthesize information about their position with respect to their rivals; enables companies to anticipate market developments rather than merely react to them.

competitive parity A firm's strategy of setting prices that are similar to those of major competitors.

competitor orientation A company objective based on the premise that the firm should measure itself primarily against its competition.

competitor-based pricing A strategy that involves pricing below, at, or above competitors' offerings.

competitor-based pricing method An approach that attempts to reflect how the firm wants consumers to interpret its products relative to the competitors' offerings; for example, setting a price close to a competitor's price signals to consumers that the product is similar, whereas setting the price much higher signals greater features, better quality, or some other valued benefit.

complementary products Products whose demand curves are positively related, such that they rise or fall together; a percentage increase in demand for one results in a percentage increase in demand for the other.

concentrated targeting strategy A marketing strategy of selecting a single, primary target market and focusing all energies on providing a product to fit that market's needs.

concept testing The process in which a concept statement that describes a product or a service is presented to potential buyers or users to obtain their reactions.

concepts Brief written descriptions of a product or service; its technology, working principles, and forms; and what customer needs it would satisfy.

conclusive research Provides the information needed to confirm preliminary insights, which managers can use to pursue appropriate courses of action.

consensus buying center A buying center in which all members of the team must reach a collective agreement that they can support a particular purchase.

consignment Part of a VMI (vendor managed inventory) program whereby the manufacturer owns the merchandise until it is sold by the retailer.

consultative buying center A buying center in which one person makes the decision but he or she solicits input from others before doing so.

consumer decision rules The set of criteria that consumers use consciously or subconsciously to quickly and efficiently select from among several alternatives.

consumer product Products and services used by people for their personal use.

contest A brand-sponsored competition that requires some form of skill or effort.

continuous advertising schedule Runs steadily throughout the year and therefore is suited to products and services that are consumed continually at relatively steady rates and that require a steady level of persuasive or reminder advertising.

contractual vertical marketing system A system in which independent firms at different levels of the supply chain join together through contracts to obtain economies of scale and coordination and to reduce conflict.

contribution per unit Equals the price less the variable cost per unit. Variable used to determine the break-even point in units.

control phase The part of the strategic marketing planning process when managers evaluate the performance of the marketing strategy and take any necessary corrective actions.

convenience goods/services Those for which the consumer is not willing to spend any effort to evaluate prior to purchase.

convenience store Type of retailer that provides a limited number of items at a convenient location in a small store with speedy checkout.

conventional supermarket Type of retailer that offers groceries, meat, and produce with limited sales of nonfood items, such as health and beauty aids and general merchandise, in a self-service format.

conversion rates Percentage of consumers who buy a product after viewing it.

cookie Computer program, installed on hard drives, that provides identifying information.

cooperative (co-op) advertising An agreement between a manufacturer and retailer in which the manufacturer agrees to defray some advertising costs.

copycat brands Mimic a manufacturer's brand in appearance but generally with lower quality and prices.

core customer value The basic problem solving benefits that consumers are seeking.

corporate blog A website created by a company and often used to educate customers.

corporate brand (family brand) The use of a firm's own corporate name to brand all of its product lines and products.

corporate social responsibility Refers to the voluntary actions taken by a company to address the ethical, social, and environmental impacts of its business operations and the concerns of its stakeholders.

corporate vertical marketing system A system in which the parent company has complete control and can dictate the priorities and objectives of the supply chain; it may own facilities such as manufacturing plants, warehouse facilities, retail outlets, and design studios.

cost of ownership method A value-based method for setting prices that determines the total cost of owning the product over its useful life.

cost-based pricing A pricing strategy that involves first determining the costs of producing or providing a product and then adding a fixed amount above that total to arrive at the selling price.

cost-based pricing method An approach that determines the final price to charge by starting with the cost, without recognizing the role that consumers or competitors' prices play in the marketplace.

countertrade Trade between two countries where goods are traded for other goods and not for hard currency.

country culture Entails easy-to-spot visible nuances that are particular to a country, such as dress, symbols, ceremonies, language, colors, and food preferences, and more subtle aspects, which are trickier to identify.

coupon Provides a stated discount to consumers on the final selling price of a specific item; the retailer handles the discount.

cross-dock In a distribution center, merchandise that is ready for sale and is placed on a conveyor system that routes it from the unloading dock at which it was received to the loading dock for the truck going to a specific store for delivery.

cross-docking distribution center A distribution center to which vendors ship merchandise prepackaged and ready for sale. The merchandise goes to a staging area rather than into storage. When all the merchandise going to a particular store has arrived in the staging area, it is loaded onto a truck, and away it goes. Thus, merchandise goes from the receiving dock to the shipping dock—cross dock.

cross-price elasticity The percentage change in demand for product A that occurs in response to a percentage change in price of product B; see *complementary products*.

cross-promoting Efforts of two or more firms joining together to reach a specific target market.

cross-shopping The pattern of buying both premium and low-priced merchandise or patronizing both expensive, status-oriented retailers and price-oriented retailers.

cultural imperialism The belief that one's own culture is superior to that of other nations; can take the form of an active, formal policy or a more subtle general attitude.

culture The set of values, guiding beliefs, understandings, and ways of doing things shared by members of a society; exists on two levels: visible artifacts (e.g., behavior, dress, symbols, physical settings, ceremonies) and underlying values (thought processes, beliefs, and assumptions).

cumulative quantity discount Pricing tactic that offers a discount based on the amount purchased over a specified period and usually involves several transactions; encourages resellers to maintain their current supplier because the cost to switch must include the loss of the discount.

customer excellence Involves a focus on retaining loyal customers and excellent customer service.

customer lifetime value The expected financial contribution from a particular customer to the firm's profits over the course of their entire relationship.

customer orientation A company objective based on the premise that the firm should measure itself primarily according to whether it meets its customers' needs.

customer relationship management (CRM) A business philosophy and set of strategies, programs, and systems that focus on identifying and building loyalty among the firm's most valued customers.

customer service Specifically refers to human or mechanical activities firms undertake to help satisfy their customers' needs and wants.

cycle time The time between the decision to place an order and the receipt of merchandise.

data Raw numbers or facts.

data mining The use of a variety of statistical analysis tools to uncover previously unknown patterns in the data stored in databases or relationships among variables.

data warehouses Large computer files that store millions and even billions of pieces of individual data.

deal A type of short-term price reduction that can take several forms, such as a "featured price," a price lower than the regular price; a "buy one, get one free" offer; or a certain percentage "more free" offer contained in larger packaging; can involve a special financing arrangement, such as reduced percentage interest rates or extended repayment terms.

deceptive advertising A representation, omission, act, or practice in an advertisement that is likely to mislead consumers acting reasonably under the circumstances.

decider The buying center participant who ultimately determines any part of or the entire buying decision—whether to buy, what to buy, how to buy, or where to buy.

decision heuristics Mental shortcuts that help consumers narrow down choices; examples include price, brand, and product presentation.

decline stage Stage of the product life cycle when sales decline and the product eventually exits the market.

decoding The process by which the receiver interprets the sender's message.

delivery gap A type of *service gap;* the difference between the firm's service standards and the actual service it provides to customers.

demand curve Shows how many units of a product or service consumers will demand during a specific period at different prices.

democratic buying center A buying center in which the majority rules in making decisions.

demographic segmentation The grouping of consumers according to easily measured, objective characteristics such as age, gender, income, and education.

demographics Information about the characteristics of human populations and segments, especially those used to identify consumer markets such as by age, gender, income, and education.

department store A retailer that carries many different types of merchandise (broad variety) and lots of items within each type (deep assortment); offers some customer services; and is organized into separate departments to display its merchandise.

depth The number of categories within a product line.

derived demand The linkage between consumers' demand for a company's output and its purchase of necessary inputs to manufacture or assemble that particular output.

determinant attributes Product or service features that are important to the buyer and on which competing brands or stores are perceived to differ.

differentiated targeting strategy A strategy through which a firm targets several market segments with a different offering for each.

diffusion of innovation The process by which the use of an innovation, whether a product or a service, spreads throughout a market group over time and over various categories of adopters.

Digital Native Also known as *Generation Z,* people in this group were born into a world that already was full of electronic gadgets and digital technologies, such as the Internet and social networks.

direct investment When a firm maintains 100 percent ownership of its plants, operation facilities, and offices in a foreign country, often through the formation of wholly owned subsidiaries.

direct marketing Sales and promotional techniques that deliver promotional materials individually.

direct marketing channel The manufacturer sells directly to the buyer.

discount To offer for sale or sell at a reduced price.

discount store A type of retailer that offers a broad variety of merchandise, limited service, and low prices.

disintermediation A manufacturer sells directly to consumers and bypasses retailers.

dispatcher The person who coordinates deliveries to distribution centers.

distribution center A facility for the receipt, storage, and redistribution of goods to company stores or customers; may be operated by retailers, manufacturers, or distribution specialists.

distribution intensity The number of supply chain members to use at each level of the supply chain.

distributive fairness Pertains to a customer's perception of the benefits he or she received compared with the costs (inconvenience or loss) that resulted from a service failure.

distributor A type of reseller or marketing intermediary that resells manufactured products without significantly altering their form. Distributors often buy from manufacturers and sell to other businesses like retailers in a B2B transaction.

diversification strategy A growth strategy whereby a firm introduces a new product or service to a market segment that it does not currently serve.

drugstore A specialty store that concentrates on health and personal grooming merchandise, though pharmaceuticals may represent more than 60 percent of its sales.

dumping The practice of selling a good in a foreign market at a price that is lower than its domestic price or below its cost.

duty See *tariff.*

early adopters The second group of consumers in the diffusion of innovation model, after *innovators,* to use a product or service innovation; generally don't like to take as much risk as innovators but instead wait and purchase the product after careful review.

early majority A group of consumers in the diffusion of innovation model that represents approximately 34 percent of the population; members don't like to take much risk and therefore tend to wait until bugs are worked out of a particular product or service; few new products and services can be profitable until this large group buys them.

economic situation Macroeconomic factor that affects the way consumers buy merchandise and spend money, both in a marketer's home country and abroad; see *inflation, foreign currency fluctuations,* and *interest rates.*

elastic Refers to a market for a product or service that is price sensitive; that is, relatively small changes in price will generate fairly large changes in the quantity demanded.

electronic data interchange (EDI) The computer-to-computer exchange of business documents from a retailer to a vendor and back.

emotional appeal Aims to satisfy consumers' emotional desires rather than their utilitarian needs.

emotional support Concern for others' well-being and support of their decisions in a job setting.

employment marketing Marketing programs to attract applicants to the hiring firm.

empowerment In context of service delivery, means allowing employees to make decisions about how service is provided to customers.

encoding The process of converting the sender's ideas into a message, which could be verbal, visual, or both.

English auction Goods and services are simply sold to the highest bidder.

entrepreneur A person who organizes, operates, and assumes the risk of a new business venture.

environmental concerns Include, but are not limited to, the excessive use of natural resources and energy, refuse from manufacturing processes, excess trash created by consumer goods packages, and hard-to-dispose-of products like tires, cell phones, and computer monitors.

esteem needs Needs that enable people to fulfill inner desires.

ethical climate The set of values within a marketing firm, or in the marketing division of any firm, that guide decision making and behavior.

evaluative criteria Consist of a set of salient, or important, attributes about a particular product.

event sponsorship Popular PR tool; occurs when corporations support various activities (financially or otherwise), usually in the cultural or sports and entertainment sectors.

everyday low pricing (EDLP) A strategy companies use to emphasize the continuity of their retail prices at a level somewhere between the regular, nonsale price and the deep-discount sale prices their competitors may offer.

evoked set Comprises the alternative brands or stores that the consumer states he or she would consider when making a purchase decision.

exchange The trade of things of value between the buyer and the seller so that each is better off as a result.

exchange control Refers to the regulation of a country's currency *exchange rate.*

exchange rate The measure of how much one currency is worth in relation to another.

exclusive co-brand Developed by national brand vendor and retailer and sold only by that retailer.

exclusive distribution Strategy in which only selected retailers can sell a manufacturer's brand.

exclusive geographic territories Territories granted to one or very few retail customers by a manufacturer using an exclusive distribution strategy; no other customers can sell a particular brand in these territories.

experience curve effect Refers to the drop in unit cost as the accumulated volume sold increases; as sales continue to grow, the costs continue to drop, allowing even further reductions in the price.

experiment See *experimental research.*

experimental research (experiment) A type of conclusive and quantitative research that systematically manipulates one or more variables to determine which variables have a causal effect on another variable.

expertise power When a channel member uses its expertise as leverage to influence the actions of another channel member.

expertise power A type of marketing channel power that occurs if the channel member exerting the power has expertise that the other channel member wants or needs and can therefore get them to do what they want.

exploratory research Attempts to begin to understand the phenomenon of interest; also provides initial information when the problem lacks any clear definition.

exporting Producing goods in one country and selling them in another.

extended network In social media, it is the total number of people a person or entity reaches or has influence over.

extended problem solving A purchase decision process during which the consumer devotes considerable time and effort to analyzing alternatives; often occurs when the consumer perceives that the purchase decision entails a lot of risk.

external locus of control Refers to when consumers believe that fate or other external factors control all outcomes.

external reference price A higher price to which the consumer can compare the selling price to evaluate the purchase.

external search for information Occurs when the buyer seeks information outside his or her personal knowledge base to help make the buying decision.

external secondary data Data collected from sources outside of the firm.

extranet A collaborative network that uses Internet technology to link businesses with their suppliers, customers, or other businesses.

extreme value food retailer See *limited assortment supermarkets*.

extreme value retailer A general merchandise discount store found in lower-income urban or rural areas.

factory outlets Outlet stores owned by manufacturers.

family brand A firm's own corporate name used to brand its product lines and products.

feedback loop Allows the receiver to communicate with the sender and thereby informs the sender whether the message was received and decoded properly.

financial risk Risk associated with a monetary outlay; includes the initial cost of the purchase, as well as the costs of using the item or service.

first movers Product pioneers that are the first to create a market or product category, making them readily recognizable to consumers and thus establishing a commanding and early market share lead.

fixed costs Those costs that remain essentially at the same level, regardless of any changes in the volume of production.

flighting advertising schedule An advertising schedule implemented in spurts, with periods of heavy advertising followed by periods of no advertising.

floor-ready merchandise Merchandise that is ready to be placed on the selling floor immediately.

focus group interview A research technique in which a small group of persons (usually 8 to 12) comes together for an intensive discussion about a particular topic, with the conversation guided by a trained moderator using an unstructured method of inquiry.

foreground In an advertisement, everything that appears on top of the *background*.

foreign currency fluctuations Changes in the value of a country's currency relative to the currency of another country; can influence consumer spending.

franchisee See *franchising*.

franchising A contractual agreement between a *franchisor* and a *franchisee* that allows the franchisee to operate a business using a name and format developed and supported by the franchisor.

franchisor See *franchising*.

frequency Measure of how often the audience is exposed to a communication within a specified period of time.

full-line discount stores Retailers that offer low prices, limited service, and a broad variety of merchandise.

functional needs Pertain to the performance of a product or service.

gamification The process of building customer loyalty through the offering of free apps.

gatekeeper The buying center participant who controls information or access to decision makers and influencers.

General Agreement on Tariffs and Trade (GATT) Organization established to lower trade barriers, such as high tariffs on imported goods and restrictions on the number and types of imported products that inhibited the free flow of goods across borders.

Generation X (Gen X) Generational cohort of people born between 1965 and 1976.

Generation Y (Gen Y) Generational cohort of people born between 1977 and 1995; biggest cohort since the original postwar baby boom.

Generation Z (Gen Z) Also known as the *Digital Natives*, because people in this group were born into a world that already was full of electronic gadgets and digital technologies, such as the Internet and social networks.

generational cohort A group of people of the same generation—typically have similar purchase behaviors because they have shared experiences and are in the same stage of life.

generic (house) brand No-frills products offered at a low price without any branding information.

geodemographic segmentation The grouping of consumers on the basis of a combination of geographic, demographic, and lifestyle characteristics.

geographic segmentation The grouping of consumers on the basis of where they live.

global labor issues Includes concerns about working conditions and wages paid to factory workers in developing countries.

globalization Refers to the processes by which goods, services, capital, people, information, and ideas flow across national borders.

globalization of production Also known as *offshoring*; refers to manufacturers' procurement of goods and services from around the globe to take advantage of national differences in the cost and quality of various factors of production (e.g., labor, energy, land, capital).

glocalization The process of firms standardizing their products globally, but using different promotional campaigns to sell them.

goods Items that can be physically touched.

gray market Employs irregular but not necessarily illegal methods; generally, it legally circumvents authorized channels of distribution to sell goods at prices lower than those intended by the manufacturer.

green marketing Involves a strategic effort by firms to supply customers with environmentally friendly merchandise.

green product An ecologically safe product that may be recyclable, biodegradable, more energy-efficient, and/or have better pollution controls.

greenwashing Exploiting a consumer by disingenuously marketing products or services as environmentally friendly, with the goal of gaining public approval and sales.

gross domestic product (GDP) Defined as the market value of the goods and services produced by a country in a year; the most widely used standardized measure of output.

gross national income (GNI) Consists of GDP plus the net income earned from investments abroad (minus any payments made to nonresidents who contribute to the domestic economy).

gross rating points (GRP) Measure used for various media advertising—print, radio, or television; $GRP = reach \times frequency$.

growth stage Stage of the product life cycle when the product gains acceptance, demand and sales increase, and competitors emerge in the product category.

habitual decision making A purchase decision process in which consumers engage with little conscious effort.

headline In an advertisement, large type designed to draw attention.

heterogeneity As it refers to the differences between the marketing of products and services, the delivery of services is more variable.

high/low pricing A *pricing* strategy that relies on the promotion of sales, during which prices are temporarily reduced to encourage purchases.

hit A request for a file made by web browsers and search engines. Hits are commonly misinterpreted as a metric for website success, however the number of hits typically is much larger than the number of people visiting a website.

home improvement center Category specialist that offers home improvement tools for contractors and do-it-yourselfers.

horizontal channel conflict A type of channel conflict in which members at the same level of a marketing channel, for example, two competing retailers or two competing manufacturers, are in disagreement or discord, such as when they are in a price war.

horizontal price fixing Occurs when competitors that produce and sell competing products collude, or work together, to control prices, effectively taking price out of the decision process for consumers.

horizontal supply chain conflict See *horizontal channel conflict*

house brand See *private-label brands.*

human development index (HDI) A composite measure of three indicators of the quality of life in different countries: life expectancy at birth, educational attainment, and whether the average incomes are sufficient to meet the basic needs of life in that country.

ideal point The position at which a particular market segment's ideal product would lie on a *perceptual map.*

ideas Intellectual concepts—thoughts, opinions, and philosophies.

implementation phase The part of the strategic marketing planning process when marketing managers (1) identify and evaluate different opportunities by engaging in segmentation, targeting, and positioning (see *STP*) and (2) implement the marketing mix using the four Ps.

impressions The number of times an advertisement appears in front of the user.

improvement value Represents an estimate of how much more (or less) consumers are willing to pay for a product relative to other comparable products.

impulse buying A buying decision made by customers on the spot when they see the merchandise.

income effect Refers to the change in the quantity of a product demanded by consumers due to a change in their income.

independent agents Salespeople who sell a manufacturer's products on an extended contract basis but are not employees of the manufacturer; also known as *manufacturer's representatives* or *reps.*

independent (conventional) marketing channel A marketing channel in which several independent members—a manufacturer, a wholesaler, and a retailer—each attempts to satisfy its own objectives and maximize its profits, often at the expense of the other members.

independent (conventional) supply chain A loose coalition of several independently owned and operated supply chain members—a manufacturer, a wholesaler, and a retailer—all attempting to satisfy their own objectives and maximize their own profits, often at the expense of the other members.

in-depth interview An exploratory research technique in which trained researchers ask questions, listen to and record the answers, and then pose additional questions to clarify or expand on a particular issue.

indirect marketing channel When one or more intermediaries work with manufacturers to provide goods and services to customers.

individual brands The use of individual brand names for each of a firm's products.

inelastic Refers to a market for a product or service that is price insensitive; that is, relatively small changes in price will not generate large changes in the quantity demanded.

inflation Refers to the persistent increase in the prices of goods and services.

influence In a social media context, the extent to which the person influences others (e.g., how much do the people in a person's network read that person's content).

influencer The buying center participant whose views influence other members of the buying center in making the final decision.

information Organized, analyzed, interpreted data that offer value to marketers.

information power A type of marketing channel power that occurs if the channel member exerting the power has information that the other channel member wants or needs and can therefore get them to do what they want.

information power A type of marketing channel power within an administered vertical marketing system in which one party (e.g., the manufacturer) provides or withholds important information to influence the actions of another party (e.g., the retailer).

informational appeal Used in a promotion to help consumers make purchase decisions by offering factual information and strong arguments built around relevant issues that encourage them to evaluate the brand favorably on the basis of the key benefits it provides.

informative advertising Communication used to create and build brand awareness, with the ultimate goal of moving the consumer through the buying cycle to a purchase.

infrastructure The basic facilities, services, and installations needed for a community or society to function, such as transportation and communications systems, water and power lines, and public institutions like schools, post offices, and prisons.

initiator The buying center participant who first suggests buying the particular product or service.

innovation The process by which ideas are transformed into new products and services that will help firms grow.

innovators Those buyers who want to be the first to have the new product or service.

inseparable A characteristic of a service: it is produced and consumed at the same time; that is, service and consumption are inseparable.

institutional advertisement A type of advertisement that informs, persuades, or reminds consumers about issues related to places, politics, or an industry (e.g. Got Milk? ads).

instrumental support Providing the equipment or systems needed to perform a task in a job setting.

intangible A characteristic of a service; it cannot be touched, tasted, or seen like a pure product can.

integrated marketing communications (IMC) Represents the promotion dimension of the four Ps; encompasses a variety of communication disciplines—general advertising, personal selling, sales promotion, public relations, direct marketing, and electronic media—in combination to provide clarity, consistency, and maximum communicative impact.

intensive distribution A strategy designed to get products into as many outlets as possible.

interest rates These represent the cost of borrowing money.

internal locus of control Refers to when consumers believe they have some control over the outcomes of their actions, in which case they generally engage in more search activities.

internal reference price Price information stored in the consumer's memory that the person uses to assess a current price offering—perhaps the last price he or she paid or what he or she expects to pay.

internal search for information Occurs when the buyer examines his or her own memory and knowledge about the product or service, gathered through past experiences.

internal secondary data Data collected from a firm's own data taken from their day-to-day operations.

International Monetary Fund (IMF) Established with the original General Agreement on Tariffs and Trade (GATT); primary purpose is to promote international monetary cooperation and facilitate the expansion and growth of international trade.

intranet A secure communication system contained within one company, such as between the firm's buyers and distribution centers.

introduction stage Stage of the product life cycle when innovators start buying the product.

introductory price promotion Short-term price discounts designed to encourage trial.

involvement Consumer's interest in a product or service.

irregulars Merchandise with minor construction errors.

joint venture Formed when a firm entering a new market pools its resources with those of a local firm to form a new company in which ownership, control, and profits are shared.

just-in-time (JIT) inventory systems Inventory management systems designed to deliver less merchandise on a more frequent basis than traditional inventory systems; the firm gets the merchandise "just in time" for it to be used in the manufacture of another product, in the case of parts or components, or for sale when the customer wants it, in the case of consumer goods; also known as *quick response (QR) systems* in retailing.

keyword analysis An evaluation of what keywords people use to search on the Internet for their products and services.

knowledge gap A type of *service gap;* reflects the difference between customers' *expectations* and the firm's perception of those expectations.

laggards Consumers who like to avoid change and rely on traditional products until they are no longer available.

lagged effect A delayed response to a marketing communication campaign.

late majority The last group of buyers to enter a new product market; when they do, the product has achieved its full market potential.

lead time The amount of time between the recognition that an order needs to be placed and the arrival of the needed merchandise at the seller's store, ready for sale.

lead users Innovative product users who modify existing products according to their own ideas to suit their specific needs.

leader pricing Consumer pricing tactic that attempts to build store traffic by aggressively pricing and advertising a regularly purchased item, often priced at or just above the store's cost.

leads A list of potential customers.

learning Refers to a change in a person's thought process or behavior that arises from experience and takes place throughout the consumer decision process.

lease A written agreement under which the owner of an item or property allows its use for a specified period of time in exchange for a fee.

legitimate power A type of marketing channel power that occurs if the channel member exerting the power has a contractual agreement with the other channel member that requires the other channel member to behave in a certain way. This type of power occurs in an administered vertical marketing system.

licensed brand An agreement allows one brand to use another's name, image, and/or logo for a fee.

lifestyles A component of *psychographics;* refers to the way a person lives his or her life to achieve goals.

lift Additional sales caused by advertising.

limited assortment supermarkets Retailers that offer only one or two brands or sizes of most products (usually including a store brand) and attempt to achieve great efficiency to lower costs and prices.

limited problem solving Occurs during a purchase decision that calls for, at most, a moderate amount of effort and time.

line extension The use of the same brand name within the same product line and represents an increase in a product line's depth.

locational excellence A method of achieving excellence by having a strong physical location and/or Internet presence.

locational privacy A person's ability to move normally in public spaces with the expectation that his or her location will not be recorded for subsequent use.

logistics management The integration of two or more activities for the purpose of planning, implementing, and controlling the efficient flow of raw materials, in-process inventory, and finished goods from the point of origin to the point of consumption.

loss leader pricing Loss leader pricing takes the tactic of *leader pricing* one step further by lowering the price below the store's cost.

love needs Needs expressed through interactions with others.

loyalty program Specifically designed to retain customers by offering premiums or other incentives to customers who make multiple purchases over time.

loyalty segmentation Strategy of investing in loyalty initiatives to retain the firm's most profitable customers.

macroenvironmental factors Aspects of the external environment that affect a company's business, such as the culture, demographics, social issues, technological advances, economic situation, and political/regulatory environment.

manufacturer brands (national brands) Brands owned and managed by the manufacturer.

manufacturer's representative See *independent agents*.

manufacturer's suggested retail price (MSRP) The price that manufacturers suggest retailers use to sell their merchandise.

markdowns Reductions retailers take on the initial selling price of the product or service.

market development strategy A growth strategy that employs the existing marketing offering to reach new market segments, whether domestic or international.

market growth rate The annual rate of growth of the specific market in which the product competes.

market penetration strategy A growth strategy that employs the existing marketing mix and focuses the firm's efforts on existing customers.

market positioning Involves the process of defining the marketing mix variables so that target customers have a clear, distinctive, desirable understanding of what the product does or represents in comparison with competing products.

market segment A group of consumers who respond similarly to a firm's marketing efforts.

market segmentation The process of dividing the market into groups of customers with different needs, wants, or characteristics—who therefore might appreciate products or services geared especially for them.

market share Percentage of a market accounted for by a specific entity.

marketing An organizational function and a set of processes for creating, *capturing,* communicating, and delivering value to customers and for managing customer relationships in ways that benefit the organization and its stakeholders.

marketing channel The set of institutions that transfer the ownership of and move goods from the point of production to the point of consumption; consists of all the institutions and marketing activities in the marketing process.

marketing channel management Also called supply chain management, refers to a set of approaches and techniques firms employ to efficiently and effectively integrate their suppliers.

marketing ethics Refers to those ethical problems that are specific to the domain of marketing.

marketing information system (MkIS) A set of procedures and methods that apply to the regular, planned collection, analysis, and presentation of information that then may be used in marketing decisions.

marketing mix (four Ps) Product, price, place, and promotion—the controllable set of activities that a firm uses to respond to the wants of its target markets.

marketing plan A written document composed of an analysis of the current marketing situation, opportunities and threats for the firm, marketing objectives and strategy specified in terms of the four Ps, action programs, and projected or pro forma income (and other financial) statements.

marketing research A set of techniques and principles for systematically collecting, recording, analyzing, and interpreting data that can aid decision makers involved in marketing goods, services, or ideas.

marketing strategy A firm's target market, marketing mix, and method of obtaining a sustainable competitive advantage.

Maslow's Hierarchy of Needs A paradigm for classifying people's motives. It argues that when lower-level, more basic needs (physiological and safety) are fulfilled, people turn to satisfying their higher-level human needs (social and personal); see *physiological, safety, social,* and *personal needs*.

mass customization The practice of interacting on a one-to-one basis with many people to create custom-made products or services; providing one-to-one marketing to the masses.

mass media Channels that are ideal for reaching large numbers of anonymous audience members; include national newspapers, magazines, radio, and television.

maturity stage Stage of the product life cycle when industry sales reach their peak, so firms try to rejuvenate their products by adding new features or repositioning them.

maximizing profits A profit strategy that relies primarily on economic theory. If a firm can accurately specify a mathematical model that captures all the factors required to explain and predict sales and profits, it should be able to identify the price at which its profits are maximized.

M-commerce (mobile commerce) Communicating with or selling to consumers through wireless handheld devices such as cellular phones.

media buy The actual purchase of airtime or print pages.

media mix The combination of the media used and the frequency of advertising in each medium.

media planning The process of evaluating and selecting the *media mix* that will deliver a clear, consistent, compelling message to the intended audience.

metric A measuring system that quantifies a trend, dynamic, or characteristic.

microblog Differs from a traditional blog in size. Consists of short sentences, short videos, or individual images. Twitter is an example of a microblog.

micromarketing An extreme form of segmentation that tailors a product or service to suit an individual customer's wants or needs; also called *one-to-one marketing*.

Millennials Consumers born between 1977 and 2000 and the children of the Baby Boomers.

mission statement A broad description of a firm's objectives and the scope of activities it plans to undertake; attempts to answer two main questions: What type of business is it? What does it need to do to accomplish its goals and objectives?

mobile commerce See *M-commerce*.

mobile marketing Marketing through wireless handheld devices.

modified rebuy Refers to when the buyer has purchased a similar product in the past but has decided to change some specifications, such as the desired price, quality level, customer service level, options, or so forth.

monopolistic competition Occurs when there are many firms that sell closely related but not homogeneous products; these products may be viewed as substitutes but are not perfect substitutes.

monopoly One firm provides the product or service in a particular industry.

motive A need or want that is strong enough to cause the person to seek satisfaction.

multi-attribute model A compensatory model of customer decision making based on the notion that customers see a product as a collection of attributes or characteristics. The model uses a weighted average score based on the importance of various attributes and performance on those issues.

multichannel retailers Retailers that sell merchandise in more than one retail channel (e.g., store, catalog, and Internet).

multichannel strategy Selling in more than one channel (e.g., stores, Internet, catalog).

need recognition The beginning of the consumer decision process; occurs when consumers recognize they have an unsatisfied need and want to go from their actual, needy state to a different, desired state.

negative word of mouth Occurs when consumers spread negative information about a product, service, or store to others.

new buy In a B2B setting, a purchase of a good or service for the first time; the buying decision is likely to be quite involved because the buyer or the buying organization does not have any experience with the item.

niche media Channels that are focused and generally used to reach narrow segments, often with unique demographic characteristics or interests.

noise Any interference that stems from competing messages, a lack of clarity in the message, or a flaw in the medium; a problem for all communication channels.

noncommercial speech A message that does not have an economic motivation and therefore is fully protected under the First Amendment.

noncompensatory decision rule At work when consumers choose a product or service on the basis of a subset of its characteristics, regardless of the values of its other attributes.

noncumulative quantity discount Pricing tactic that offers a discount based on only the amount purchased in a single order;

provides the buyer with an incentive to purchase more merchandise immediately.

North American Industry Classification System (NAICS) codes U.S. Bureau of Census classification scheme that categorizes all firms into a hierarchical set of six-digit codes.

objective-and-task method An IMC budgeting method that determines the cost required to undertake specific tasks to accomplish communication objectives; process entails setting objectives, choosing media, and determining costs.

observation An exploratory research method that entails examining purchase and consumption behaviors through personal or video camera scrutiny.

occasion segmentation A type of behavioral segmentation based on when a product or service is purchased or consumed.

odd prices Prices that end in odd numbers, usually 9, such as $3.99.

off-price retailer A type of retailer that offers an inconsistent assortment of merchandise at relatively low prices.

offshoring See *globalization of production*.

oligopolistic competition Occurs when only a few firms dominate a market.

one-to-one marketing See *micromarketing*.

online chat Instant messaging or voice conversation with an online sales representative.

online couponing A promotional Web technique in which consumers print a coupon directly from a site and then redeem the coupon in a store.

online referring A promotional Web technique in which consumers fill out an interest or order form and are referred to an offline dealer or firm that offers the product or service of interest.

operational excellence Involves a firm's focus on efficient operations and excellent supply chain management.

opt in The option giving the consumer complete control over the collection and dissemination of his/her personal information, usually referred to in an Internet setting.

opt out The option whereby the consumer must actively choose to prevent personal information from being used or shared with third parties, usually referred to in an Internet setting.

order getter A salesperson whose primary responsibilities are identifying potential customers and engaging those customers in discussions to attempt to make a sale.

order taker A salesperson whose primary responsibility is to process routine orders or reorders or rebuys for products.

organizational culture Reflects the set of values, traditions, and customs that guide a firm's employees' behavior.

outlet stores Off-price retailers that often stock irregulars, out-of-season merchandise, or overstocks from the parent company.

own brands See *private-label brands*.

page view The number of times an Internet page gets viewed by any visitor.

panel data Information collected from a group of consumers.

panel research A type of quantitative research that involves collecting information from a group of consumers (the panel) over time; data collected may be from a survey or a record of purchases.

perceived value The relationship between a product's or service's benefits and its cost.

perception The process by which people select, organize, and interpret information to form a meaningful picture of the world.

perceptual map Displays, in two or more dimensions, the position of products or brands in the consumer's mind.

performance risk Involves the perceived danger inherent in a poorly performing product or service.

perishability A characteristic of a service: it cannot be stored for use in the future.

personal blog Websites written by people that receive no products or remuneration for their efforts.

personal needs Relate to ways people satisfy their inner desires.

personal selling The two-way flow of communication between a buyer and a seller that is designed to influence the buyer's purchase decision.

persuasive advertising Communication used to motivate consumers to take action.

physiological needs Those relating to the basic biological necessities of life: food, drink, rest, and shelter.

physiological risk The fear of an actual harm should a product not perform properly.

pick ticket A document or display on a screen in a forklift truck indicating how much of each item to get from specific storage areas.

pioneers New product introductions that establish a completely new market or radically change both the rules of competition and consumer preferences in a market; also called *breakthroughs*.

planners In a retailing context, employees who are responsible for the financial planning and analysis of merchandise, and its allocation to stores.

planning phase The part of the strategic marketing planning process when marketing executives, in conjunction with other top managers, (1) define the mission or vision of the business and (2) evaluate the situation by assessing how various players, both in and outside the organization, affect the firm's potential for success.

point-of-purchase (POP) display A merchandise display located at the point of purchase, such as at the checkout counter in a grocery store.

political/regulatory environment Comprises political parties, government organizations, and legislation and laws.

pop-up stores Temporary storefronts that exist for only a limited time and generally focus on a new product or a limited group of products offered by a retailer, manufacturer, or service provider; give consumers a chance to interact with the brand and build brand awareness, but are not designed primarily to sell the product.

postpurchase dissonance The psychologically uncomfortable state produced by an inconsistency between beliefs and behaviors that in turn evokes a motivation to reduce the dissonance; buyers' remorse.

posttesting The evaluation of an IMC campaign's impact after it has been implemented.

power A situation that occurs in a marketing channel in which one member has the means or ability to have control over the actions of another member in a channel at a different level of

distribution, such as if a retailer has power or control over a supplier.

preapproach In the personal selling process, occurs prior to meeting the customer for the first time and extends the qualification of leads procedure; in this step, the salesperson conducts additional research and develops plans for meeting with the customer.

predatory pricing A firm's practice of setting a very low price for one or more of its products with the intent to drive its competition out of business; illegal under both the Sherman Antitrust Act and the Federal Trade Commission Act.

premarket test Conducted before a product or service is brought to market to determine how many customers will try and then continue to use it.

premium An item offered for free or at a bargain price to reward some type of behavior, such as buying, sampling, or testing.

premium brand A branding strategy that offers consumers a private label of comparable or superior quality to a manufacturer brand.

premium pricing A competitor-based pricing method by which the firm deliberately prices a product above the prices set for competing products to capture those consumers who always shop for the best or for whom price does not matter.

prestige products or services Those that consumers purchase for status rather than functionality.

pretesting Assessments performed before an ad campaign is implemented to ensure that the various elements are working in an integrated fashion and doing what they are intended to do.

price The overall sacrifice a consumer is willing to make—money, time, energy—to acquire a specific product or service.

price bundling Consumer pricing tactic of selling more than one product for a single, lower price than what the items would cost sold separately; can be used to sell slow-moving items, to encourage customers to stock up so they won't purchase competing brands, to encourage trial of a new product, or to provide an incentive to purchase a less desirable product or service to obtain a more desirable one in the same bundle.

price discrimination The practice of selling the same product to different resellers (wholesalers, distributors, or retailers) or to the ultimate consumer at different prices; some, but not all, forms of price discrimination are illegal.

price elasticity of demand Measures how changes in a price affect the quantity of the product demanded; specifically, the ratio of the percentage change in quantity demanded to the percentage change in price.

price fixing The practice of colluding with other firms to control prices.

price lining Consumer market pricing tactic of establishing a price floor and a price ceiling for an entire line of similar products and then setting a few other price points in between to represent distinct differences in quality.

price skimming A strategy of selling a new product or service at a high price that *innovators* and *early adopters* are willing to pay in order to obtain it; after the high-price market segment becomes saturated and sales begin to slow down, the firm generally lowers the price to capture (or skim) the next most price sensitive segment.

price war Occurs when two or more firms compete primarily by lowering their prices.

pricing strategy A long-term approach to setting prices for the firms' products.

pricing tactics Short-term methods, in contrast to long-term pricing strategies, used to focus on company objectives, costs, customers, competition, or channel members; can be responses to competitive threats (e.g., lowering price temporarily to meet a competitor's price reduction) or broadly accepted methods of calculating a final price for the customer that is short term in nature.

primary data Data collected to address specific research needs.

primary demand advertising Ads designed to generate demand for the product category or an entire industry.

primary package The packaging the consumer uses, such as the toothpaste tube, from which he or she typically seeks convenience in terms of storage, use, and consumption.

private exchange Occurs when a specific firm, either buyer or seller, invites others to join to participate in online information exchanges and transactions; can help streamline procurement or distribution processes.

private-label brands Brands developed and marketed by a retailer and available only from that retailer; also called *store brands*.

procedural fairness Refers to the customer's perception of the fairness of the process used to resolve complaints about service.

product Anything that is of value to a consumer and can be offered through a voluntary marketing exchange.

product assortment The complete set of all products offered by a firm; also called the *product mix*.

product category An assortment of items that the customer sees as reasonable substitutes for one another.

product design See *product development*.

product development Also called *product design;* entails a process of balancing various engineering, manufacturing, marketing, and economic considerations to develop a product's form and features or a service's features.

product development strategy A growth strategy that offers a new product or service to a firm's current target market.

product excellence Involves a focus on achieving high-quality products; effective branding and positioning is key.

product life cycle Defines the stages that new products move through as they enter, get established in, and ultimately leave the marketplace and thereby offers marketers a starting point for their strategy planning.

product lines Groups of associated items, such as those that consumers use together or think of as part of a group of similar products.

product mix See *product assortment*. The complete set of all products offered by a firm.

product placement Inclusion of a product in nontraditional situations, such as in a scene in a movie or television program.

product-focused advertisements Used to inform, persuade, or remind consumers about a specific product or service.

professional blog Websites written by people who review and give recommendations on products and services.

profit orientation A company objective that can be implemented by focusing on *target profit pricing, maximizing profits,* or *target return pricing.*

projective technique A type of qualitative research in which subjects are provided a scenario and asked to express their thoughts and feelings about it.

prototype The first physical form or service description of a new product, still in rough or tentative form, that has the same properties as a new product but is produced through different manufacturing processes, sometimes even crafted individually.

psychographic segmentation A method of segmenting customers based on how they spend their time and money, what activities they pursue, and their attitudes and opinions about the world in which they live.

psychographics Used in segmentation; delves into how consumers describe themselves; allows people to describe themselves using those characteristics that help them choose how they occupy their time (behavior) and what underlying psychological reasons determine those choices.

psychological needs Pertain to the personal gratification consumers associate with a product or service.

psychological risk Associated with the way people will feel if the product or service does not convey the right image.

public relations The organizational function that manages the firm's communications to achieve a variety of objectives, including building and maintaining a positive image, handling or heading off unfavorable stories or events, and maintaining positive relationships with the media.

public service advertising (PSA) Advertising that focuses on public welfare and generally is sponsored by nonprofit institutions, civic groups, religious organizations, trade associations, or political groups; a form of *social marketing.*

puffery The legal exaggeration of praise, stopping just short of deception, lavished on a product.

pull strategy Designed to get consumers to pull the product into the supply chain by demanding it.

pull supply chain Strategy in which orders for merchandise are generated at the store level on the basis of demand data captured by point-of-sales terminals.

pulsing advertising schedule Combines the continuous and flighting schedules by maintaining a base level of advertising but increasing advertising intensity during certain periods.

purchasing power parity (PPP) A theory that states that if the exchange rates of two countries are in equilibrium, a product purchased in one will cost the same in the other, expressed in the same currency.

pure competition Occurs when different companies sell commodity products that consumers perceive as substitutable; price usually is set according to the laws of supply and demand.

push strategy Designed to increase demand by motivating sellers—wholesalers, distributors, or salespeople—to highlight the product, rather than the products of competitors, and thereby push the product onto consumers.

push supply chain Strategy in which merchandise is allocated to stores on the basis of historical demand, the inventory position at the distribution center, and the stores' needs.

qualify leads The process of assessing the potential of sales leads.

qualitative research Informal research methods, including observation, following social media sites, in-depth interviews, focus groups, and projective techniques.

quantity discount Pricing tactic of offering a reduced price according to the amount purchased; the more the buyer purchases, the higher the discount and, of course, the greater the value.

quantitative research Structured responses that can be statistically tested to confirm insights and hypotheses generated via qualitative research or secondary data.

questionnaire A form that features a set of questions designed to gather information from respondents and thereby accomplish the researchers' objectives; questions can be either unstructured or structured.

quick response An inventory management system used in retailing; merchandise is received just in time for sale when the customer wants it; see *just-in-time (JIT) systems*.

quota Designates the maximum quantity of a product that may be brought into a country during a specified time period.

radio frequency identification (RFID) tags Tiny computer chips that automatically transmit to a special scanner all the information about a container's contents or individual products.

reach Measure of consumers' exposure to marketing communications; the percentage of the target population exposed to a specific marketing communication, such as an advertisement, at least once.

rebate A consumer discount in which a portion of the purchase price is returned to the buyer in cash; the manufacturer, not the retailer, issues the refund.

receiver The person who reads, hears, or sees and processes the information contained in the message or advertisement.

receiving The process of recording the receipt of merchandise as it arrives at a distribution center or store.

recession A temporary depression in economic activity or prosperity.

reference group One or more persons whom an individual uses as a basis for comparison regarding beliefs, feelings, and behaviors.

reference price The price against which buyers compare the actual selling price of the product and that facilitates their evaluation process.

referent power A type of marketing channel power that occurs if one channel member wants to be associated with another channel member. The channel member with whom the others wish to be associated has the power and can get them to do what they want.

regional culture The influence of the area within a country in which people live.

related diversification A growth strategy whereby the current target market and/or marketing mix shares something in common with the new opportunity.

relational orientation A method of building a relationship with customers based on the philosophy that buyers and sellers should develop a long-term relationship.

relationship selling A sales philosophy and process that emphasizes a commitment to maintaining the relationship over the long term and investing in opportunities that are mutually beneficial to all parties.

relative market share A measure of the product's strength in a particular market, defined as the sales of the focal product divided by the sales achieved by the largest firm in the industry.

relevance In the context of search engine marketing (SEM), it is a metric used to determine how useful an advertisement is to the consumer.

reminder advertising Communication used to remind consumers of a product or to prompt repurchases, especially for products that have gained market acceptance and are in the maturity stage of their life cycle.

reps See *independent agents*.

request for proposals (RFP) A process through which buying organizations invite alternative suppliers to bid on supplying their required components.

resellers Marketing intermediaries that resell manufactured products without significantly altering their form.

reserve price The price in an auction that is the minimum amount at which a seller will sell an item.

retailer/store brands Also called private-label brands, are products developed by retailers.

retailing The set of business activities that add value to products and services sold to consumers for their personal or family use; includes products bought at stores, through catalogs, and over the Internet, as well as services like fast-food restaurants, airlines, and hotels.

retrieval set Includes those brands or stores that the consumer can readily bring forth from memory.

return on investment (ROI) The amount of profit divided by the value of the investment. In the case of an advertisement, the ROI is (the sales revenue generated by the ad − the ad's cost) ÷ the ad's cost.

reverse auction The buyer provides specifications to a group of sellers, who then bid down the price until the buyer accepts a specific bid.

reverse engineering Involves taking apart a competitor's product, analyzing it, and creating an improved product that does not infringe on the competitor's patents, if any exist.

reverse innovation When companies initially develop products for niche or underdeveloped markets, and then expand them into their original or home markets.

reward power A type of marketing channel power that occurs when the channel member exerting the power offers rewards to gain power, often a monetary incentive, for getting another channel member to do what it wants it to do.

ritual consumption Refers to a pattern of behaviors tied to life events that affect what and how people consume.

role playing A good technique for practicing the sales presentation prior to meeting with a customer; the salesperson acts out a simulated buying situation while a colleague or manager acts as the buyer.

rule-of-thumb methods Budgeting methods that base the IMC budget on either the firm's share of the market in relation to competition, a fixed percentage of forecasted sales, or what is left after other operating costs and forecasted sales have been budgeted.

safety needs One of the needs in the PSSP hierarchy of needs; pertain to protection and physical well-being.

safety risk See *psychological risk*.

salary Compensation in the form of a fixed sum of money paid at regular intervals.

sales contest A short-term incentive designed to elicit a specific response from the sales force.

sales management Involves the planning, direction, and control of personal selling activities, including recruiting, selecting, training, motivating, compensating, and evaluating, as they apply to the sales force.

sales orientation A company objective based on the belief that increasing sales will help the firm more than will increasing profits.

sales promotions Special incentives or excitement-building programs that encourage the purchase of a product or service, such as coupons, rebates, contests, free samples, and point-of-purchase displays.

sales support personnel Employees who enhance and help with a firm's overall selling effort, such as by responding to the customer's technical questions or facilitating repairs.

sample A group of customers who represent the customers of interest in a research study.

sampling Offers potential customers the opportunity to try a product or service before they make a buying decision.

scanner data A type of syndicated external secondary data used in quantitative research that is obtained from scanner readings of UPC codes at check-out counters.

scanner research A type of quantitative research that uses data obtained from scanner readings of Universal Product Codes (UPCs) at checkout counters.

scenario planning A process that integrates macroenvironmental information in an attempt to understand the potential outcomes of different applications of a firm's marketing mix; enables a firm to predict, monitor, and adapt to the ever-changing future.

search engine marketing (SEM) A type of Web advertising whereby companies pay for keywords that are used to catch consumers' attention while browsing a search engine.

seasonal discount Pricing tactic of offering an additional reduction as an incentive to retailers to order merchandise in advance of the normal buying season.

secondary data Pieces of information that have already been collected from other sources and usually are readily available.

secondary package The wrapper or exterior carton that contains the primary package and provides the UPC label used by retail scanners; can contain additional product information that may not be available on the primary package.

selective demand Demand for a specific brand.

selective demand advertising Ads designed to generate demand for a specific brand, firm, or item.

selective distribution Lies between the intensive and exclusive distribution strategies; uses a few selected customers in a territory.

self-actualization When a person is completely satisfied with his or her life.

self-concept The image a person has of him- or herself; a component of *psychographics*.

self-values Goals for life, not just the goals one wants to accomplish in a day; a component of *psychographics* that refers to overriding desires that drive how a person lives his or her life.

selling teams Combinations of sales specialists whose primary duties are order getting, order taking, or sales support but who work together to service important accounts.

sender The firm from which an IMC message originates; the sender must be clearly identified to the intended audience.

seniors America's fastest-growing generational cohort; people aged 55 to 64 years.

sentiment analysis A technique that allows marketers to analyze data from social media sites to collect consumer comments about companies and their products.

sentiment mining Data gathered by evaluating customer comments posted through social media sites such as Facebook and Twitter.

service Any intangible offering that involves a deed, performance, or effort that cannot be physically possessed; intangible customer benefits that are produced by people or machines and cannot be separated from the producer.

service gap Results when a service fails to meet the expectations that customers have about how it should be delivered.

service quality Customers' perceptions of how well a service meets or exceeds their expectations.

service retailer A firm that primarily sells services rather than merchandise.

share of wallet The percentage of the customer's purchases made from a particular retailer.

sharer A type of consumer that uses social media sites and wants to help by being constantly well informed, so that they can provide genuine insights to others.

shopping products/services Those for which consumers will spend time comparing alternatives, such as apparel, fragrances, and appliances.

showrooming Customers visit a store to touch, feel, and even discuss a product's features with a sales associate, and then purchase it online from another retailer at a lower price.

situation analysis Second step in a marketing plan; uses a SWOT analysis that assesses both the internal environment with regard to its **S**trengths and **W**eaknesses and the external environment in terms of its **O**pportunities and **T**hreats.

situational factors Factors affecting the consumer decision process; those that are specific to the situation that may override, or at least influence, psychological and social issues.

size discount The most common implementation of a quantity discount at the consumer level; the larger the quantity bought, the less the cost per unit (e.g., per ounce).

slotting allowances Fees firms pay to retailers simply to get new products into stores or to gain more or better shelf space for their products.

social marketing The content distributed through online and mobile technologies to facilitate interpersonal interactions.

social media Media content used for social interactions such as YouTube, Facebook, and Twitter.

social reach A metric used to determine to how many people a person influences (e.g., number of individuals in the person's social networks such as Facebook and LinkedIn).

social risk The fears that consumers suffer when they worry others might not regard their purchases positively.

social shoppers Consumers who seek emotional connections through shopping.

social shopping The use of the Internet to communicate about product preferences with other shoppers.

specialty products/services Products or services toward which the customer shows a strong preference and for which he or she will expend considerable effort to search for the best suppliers.

specialty store A type of retailer that concentrates on a limited number of complementary merchandise categories in a relatively small store.

standards gap A type of *service gap;* pertains to the difference between the firm's perceptions of customers' expectations and the service standards it sets.

status quo pricing A competitor-oriented strategy in which a firm changes prices only to meet those of competition.

stock keeping units (SKUs) Individual items within each product category; the smallest unit available for inventory control.

store brands See *private-label brands.*

STP The processes of segmentation, targeting, and positioning that firms use to identify and evaluate opportunities for increasing sales and profits.

straight rebuy Refers to when the buyer or buying organization simply buys additional units of products that have previously been purchased.

strategic alliance A collaborative relationship between independent firms, though the partnering firms do not create an equity partnership; that is, they do not invest in one another.

strategic business unit (SBU) A division of the firm itself that can be managed and operated somewhat independently from other divisions and may have a different mission or objectives.

strategic relationship (partnering relationship) A supply chain relationship that the members are committed to maintaining long term, investing in opportunities that are mutually beneficial; requires mutual trust, open communication, common goals, and credible commitments.

structured questions Closed-ended questions for which a discrete set of response alternatives, or specific answers, is provided for respondents to evaluate.

subhead An additional smaller headline in an ad that provides a great deal of information through the use of short and simple words.

substitute products Products for which changes in demand are negatively related; that is, a percentage increase in the quantity demanded for product A results in a percentage decrease in the quantity demanded for product B.

substitution effect Refers to consumers' ability to substitute other products for the focal brand, thus increasing the price elasticity of demand for the focal brand.

supercenter Large stores combining full-line discount stores with supermarkets in one place.

supply chain The group of firms that make and deliver a given set of goods and services.

supply chain conflict See *channel conflict.*

supply chain management Refers to a set of approaches and techniques firms employ to efficiently and effectively integrate their suppliers, manufacturers, warehouses, stores, and transportation intermediaries into a seamless value chain in which merchandise is produced and distributed in the right quantities, to the right locations, and at the right time, as well as to minimize systemwide costs while satisfying the service levels their customers require.

survey A systematic means of collecting information from people that generally uses a *questionnaire.*

sustainable competitive advantage Something the firm can persistently do better than its competitors.

sweepstakes A form of sales promotion that offers prizes based on a chance drawing of entrants' names.

syndicated data Data available for a fee from commercial research firms such as Information Resources Inc. (IRI), National Purchase Diary Panel, and ACNielsen.

target marketing/targeting The process of evaluating the attractiveness of various segments and then deciding which to pursue as a market.

target profit pricing A pricing strategy implemented by firms when they have a particular profit goal as their overriding concern; uses price to stimulate a certain level of sales at a certain profit per unit.

target return pricing A pricing strategy implemented by firms less concerned with the absolute level of profits and more interested in the rate at which their profits are generated relative to their investments; designed to produce a specific return on investment, usually expressed as a percentage of sales.

tariff A tax levied on a good imported into a country; also called a *duty.*

technological advances Macroenvironmental factor that has greatly contributed to the improvement of the value of both products and services in the past few decades.

telemarketing A method of prospecting in which salespeople telephone potential customers.

test marketing Introduces a new product or service to a limited geographical area (usually a few cities) prior to a national launch.

ticketing and marking Creating price and identification labels and placing them on the merchandise.

top-of-mind awareness A prominent place in people's memories that triggers a response without them having to put any thought into it.

total cost The sum of the *variable* and *fixed costs.*

tracking Includes monitoring key indicators, such as daily or weekly sales volume, while the advertisement is running to shed light on any problems with the message or the medium.

trade agreements Intergovernmental agreements designed to manage and promote trade activities for specific regions.

trade area The geographical area that contains the potential customers of a particular retailer or shopping center.

trade deficit Results when a country imports more goods than it exports.

trade promotion Advertising to wholesalers or retailers to get them to purchase new products, often through special pricing incentives.

trade shows Major events attended by buyers who choose to be exposed to products and services offered by potential suppliers in an industry.

trade surplus Occurs when a country has a higher level of exports than imports.

trading bloc Consists of those countries that have signed a particular trade agreement.

traditional distribution center A warehouse in which merchandise is unloaded from trucks and placed on racks or shelves for storage.

transactional orientation Regards the buyer-seller relationship as a series of individual transactions, so anything that happened before or after the transaction is of little importance.

transmitter An agent or intermediary with which the sender works to develop the marketing communications; for example, a firm's creative department or an advertising agency.

undifferentiated targeting strategy (mass marketing) A marketing strategy a firm can use if the product or service is perceived to provide the same benefits to everyone, with no need to develop separate strategies for different groups.

uniform delivered pricing The shipper charges one rate, no matter where the buyer is located.

unique selling proposition (USP) A strategy of differentiating a product by communicating its unique attributes; often becomes the common theme or slogan in the entire advertising campaign.

Universal Product Code (UPC) The black-and-white bar code found on most merchandise.

universal set Includes all possible choices for a product-category.

unrelated diversification A growth strategy whereby a new business lacks any common elements with the present business.

unsought product/services Products or services consumers either do not normally think of buying or do not know about.

unstructured questions Open-ended questions that allow respondents to answer in their own words.

user The person who consumes or uses the product or service purchased by the buying center.

value Reflects the relationship of benefits to costs, or what the consumer *gets* for what he or she *gives*.

Value and Lifestyle Survey (VALS™) A psychographic tool developed by SRI Consulting Business Intelligence; classifies consumers into eight segments: innovators, thinkers, believers, achievers, strivers, experiencers, makers, or survivors.

value-based pricing A pricing strategy that involves first determining the perceived value of the product from the customer's point of view and then pricing accordingly.

value-based pricing method An approach that focuses on the overall value of the product offering as perceived by consumers, who determine value by comparing the benefits they expect the product to deliver with the sacrifice they will need to make to acquire the product.

value cocreation Customers act as collaborators with a manufacturer or retailer to create the product or service.

value proposition The unique value that a product or service provides to its customers and how it is better than and different from those of competitors.

variability A characteristic of a service: its quality may vary because it is provided by humans.

variable costs Those costs, primarily labor and materials, that vary with production volume.

vendor-managed inventory An approach for improving supply chain efficiency in which the manufacturer is responsible for maintaining the retailer's inventory levels in each of its stores.

vertical channel conflict A type of channel conflict in which members of the same marketing channel, for example, manufacturers, wholesalers, and retailers, are in disagreement or discord.

vertical marketing system A supply chain in which the members act as a unified system; there are three types: *administrated, contractual*, and *corporate*.

vertical price fixing Occurs when parties at different levels of the same marketing channel (e.g., manufacturers and retailers) collude to control the prices passed on to consumers.

vertical supply chain conflict See *vertical channel conflict*.

viral marketing A marketing phenomenon that encourages people to pass along a marketing message to other potential consumers.

viral marketing campaign See *viral marketing*.

virtual community Online networks of people who communicate about specific topics.

voice-of-customer (VOC) program An ongoing marketing research system that collects customer inputs and integrates them into managerial decisions.

warehouse clubs Large retailers with an irregular assortment, low service levels, and low prices that often require membership for shoppers.

Web portal An Internet site whose purpose is to be a major starting point for users when they connect to the Web.

Web tracking software Used to assess how much time viewers spend on particular Web pages and the number of pages they view.

wholesalers Those firms engaged in buying, taking title to, often storing, and physically handling goods in large quantities, then reselling the goods (usually in smaller quantities) to retailers or industrial or business users.

World Bank Group A development bank that provides loans, policy advice, technical assistance, and knowledge-sharing services to low- and middle-income countries in an attempt to reduce poverty in the developing world.

World Trade Organization (WTO) Replaced the GATT in 1994; differs from the GATT in that the WTO is an established institution based in Geneva, Switzerland, instead of simply an agreement; represents the only international organization that deals with the global rules of trade among nations.

zone of tolerance The area between customers' expectations regarding their desired service and the minimum level of acceptable service—that is, the difference between what the customer really wants and what he or she will accept before going elsewhere.

zone pricing The shipper sets different prices depending on a geographical division of the delivery areas.

Quiz Yourself answer key

Chapter 1

1. The "Got Milk" advertising campaign was designed to help market an:

   Answer: (c) industry

2. Henry Ford's statement, "Customers can have any color they want so long as it's black," typified the _____ era of marketing.

   Answer: (d) production

Chapter 2

1. Suppose Macy's announced it would severely cut back its inventory levels. For clothing manufacturers supplying Macy's this would represent a(n):

   Answer: (d) threat

2. Carla, a manager of a local bookstore, in response to increased competition from devices such as the Kindle book reader, has been directed by her regional marketing manager to cut prices on seasonal items, run an ad in the local paper, and tell distributors to reduce deliveries for the next month. Which stage of the strategic marketing planning process is Carla engaged in?

   Answer: (d) implement marketing mix and resources

Chapter 3

1. Reebok is actively offering online coupons on Facebook. It is likely trying to:

   Answer: (a) Excite the consumer

2. YouTube is one of the most well-known:

   Answer: (b) media-sharing sites

Chapter 4

1. Johnson & Johnson's 1943 "Credo" was considered radical at the time because it:

   Answer: (c) put customers first

2. The Harvest County school board is concerned about deteriorating school facilities, combined with a shrinking budget. The board began by studying the issue, and then identified parents, children, teachers, staff, and taxpayers as groups who have a vested interest in solving the problem. The school board has listened to each group's concerns. In the ethical decision-making framework, its next action should be to:

   Answer: (c) engage in brainstorming and evaluate alternatives

Chapter 5

1. Recently, Jason, one of the few Americans who has not registered with the Do Not Call Registry, received a call from a marketer suggesting Jason needed additional insurance since he had just become a father and changed jobs. Jason was shocked and very concerned about:

   Answer: (b) his lack of privacy

2. Many American consumers are purchasing hybrid automobiles even though they are more expensive when compared to compact conventional autos. Automobile marketers recognize these consumers:

   Answer: (a) value contributing to a greener environment

Chapter 6

1. Laura has a nearly new economy car but wants a sports car. If she decides to purchase a sports car, she will be primarily fulfilling _____ needs.

   Answer: (d) psychological

2. When Maya decided to buy a new computer, she thought about all the brands she could recall seeing advertised, but she would only consider those brands she could buy at her local electronics store. This represents Maya's _____ set.

   Answer: (c) evoked

Chapter 7

1. After posting an RFP for telecommunication equipment, University of Central Florida received six proposals from qualified vendors. Next, UCF will:

   Answer: (e) evaluate the proposals and likely narrow the choice to a few suppliers

2. Whenever Kim, a textbook publisher's representative, calls on the business faculty at Major University, her first stop is to chat with Frank, the business department secretary. From Frank, Kim learns which professors have left or are new, and what courses will be taught next semester. Frank also helps Kim to make appointments to see professors to discuss textbook choices. Frank acts as the _____ in the business department buying center.

   Answer: (e) gatekeeper

Chapter 8

1. Geert Hofstede's cultural dimensions concept focuses on five dimensions of _____ in a country.

   Answer: (b) underlying values

2. NCD company wants to expand into the Mexican market. They have financial resources, want to control business operations, and have had considerable success marketing to Hispanics in the United States. NCD will likely use _____ to expand into the Mexican market.

   Answer: (d) direct investment

Chapter 9

1. NASCAR redirected its marketing efforts when a survey indicated that almost 50 percent of race fans were female. This is an example of _____ segmentation.

   Answer: (c) demographic

2. Within a perceptual map, a(n) _____ represents where a particular market segment's desired product would lie.

   Answer: (d) ideal point

Chapter 10

1. Through analysis of sales data, Price-Cutters retail store found that customers who bought peanut butter also tended to buy bananas. Price-Cutters was engaged in:

   Answer: (d) data mining

2. Martin has hired a market research company to bring together a small group of soft drink consumers and get feedback on the three new advertising slogans his firm is considering. The market research firm might conduct a(n) _____ to provide the information Martin has requested.

   Answer: (c) focus group

Chapter 11

1. A university that has separate graduate and undergraduate admission offices recognizes that these are distinct:

   Answer: (b) product/service lines

2. _____ is the set of assets and liabilities linked to a brand that add to or subtract from the value provided by the product or service.

   Answer: (d) Brand equity

Chapter 12

1. By the time BMW and Mercedes Benz entered the mini-SUV market, there were many competitors, sales had peaked, and profits were declining. These firms entered the market during the _____ stage of the product life cycle.

   Answer: (c) maturity

2. Lorraine belongs to a national consumer panel created by a market research company. She regularly receives samples of new products from a variety of firms and fills out questionnaires about the products. The national consumer panel Lorraine is part of is engaged in:

   Answer: (a) premarket testing.

Chapter 13

1. Yolanda manages a Best Sleep Inn along an interstate highway. She knows from experience that five to 10 last-minute customers will call after 8 p.m. each evening looking for a room and asking the price. Yolanda has empowered her staff to offer discounts when the motel is largely vacant, and to quote the standard price when the motel is close to full. She knows her service is _____, meaning that if no one stays in the room, it generates no revenue that evening.

   Answer: (e) perishable

2. A _____ gap reflects the difference between firm's perception of customer expectations and firm standards for service to be delivered.

   Answer: (c) standards

Chapter 14

1. If a shoe company has $2 million in fixed costs, its average shoe sells for $100 a pair, and variable costs are $60 per unit, how many units does the company need to sell to break even?

   Answer: (c) 50,000

2. Porsche's 918 Spyder is priced at $550,000. The demand for such a prestigious car is likely to be:

   Answer: (b) price inelastic

Chapter 15

1. Tina is considering upgrading her smartphone for a more advanced version. She asks her friends how much they paid for their smartphones and she also does some research online. When Tina enters AT&T, she has an idea of how much her new smartphone will cost. This is an example of a(n) _____.

   Answer: (a) improvement value

2. When Apple Inc. introduced their iPhone in 2007, they priced it at $599, considerably higher than either their iPod or competing cellular phones. Apple was probably pursuing a _____ pricing strategy.

   Answer: (e) skimming

Chapter 16

1. Franchising involves a _____ supply chain.

   Answer: (c) contractual

2. Flora is frustrated with her company's supply chain management information system. She wants to be able to receive sales data, initiate purchase orders, send and receive invoices, and receive returned merchandise documentation. Flora needs an:

   Answer: (b) electronic data interchange

Chapter 17

1. TJX is an example of a(n):

   Answer: (b) off-price retailer

2. Walmart and Target dominate the _____ industry in the United States.

   Answer: (c) discount store

Chapter 18

1. Senders often use verbal, visual or both cues to facilitate the _____ in the communication process.

   Answer: (a) encoding

2. Ingrid wants her company to expand its use of public relations. She argues that as other IMC alternatives become more expensive and _____, public relations should be a larger part of her company's IMC efforts.

   Answer: (b) consumers have become more skeptical of marketing claims

Chapter 19

1. The Got Milk ads (milk moustaches worn by celebrities) are examples of a successful:

   Answer: (e) institutional advertising campaign

2. Campbell Soup Company ran a series of radio ads tied to local weather forecasts. Before an impending storm, the ads said, "Time to stock up on Campbell Soup." During the storm, the ads said, "Stay home and stay warm with Campbell Soup." The first ad was _____ advertising, while the second ad was _____ advertising.

   (b) persuasive; reminder

Chapter 20

1. Consumers often ask workers in supermarkets where something is located only to learn the workers are vendors stacking and straightening their companies' products on the store shelves. These manufacturer's sales representatives benefit retailers by _____.

   Answer: (c) saving them time and money

2. Diana went to Kleinfeld's (the retailer on the TLC show, "Say Yes to the Dress") to look at wedding dresses. She had an idea of what she was looking for, but was also interested in feedback from the sales associate. The sales associate, sensing Diana's buying mode, began with the _____ stage of the selling process.

   Answer: (e) sales presentation

Chapter 1

1. Packaged Facts, "Ice Cream and Frozen Desserts in the U.S.: Markets and Opportunities in Retail and Foodservice, 6th ed., January 2010.

2. http://www.unileverusa.com/brands/foodbrands/benandjerrys/.

3. http://www.redmangousa.com/red-mango/.

4. http://www.redmangousa.com/menu/.

5. "Menu _ Nutrition," http://tcby.com/menu-nutrition/soft-serve/.

6. Jaime Levy Pessin, "Yogurt Chains Give Power to the People," *The Wall Street Journal*, August 22, 2011.

7. Packaged Facts, op. cit., p. 135.

8. The American Marketing Association, http://www.marketing-power.com/content4620. Word in italics was added by the authors. Discussions of the latest revision of the AMA's marketing definition are widespread. See Gregory T. Gundlach and William L. Wilkie (2008), "AMA's New Definition of Marketing: Perspective and Commentary on the 2007 Revision," *Journal of Public Policy & Marketing* 28, no. 2 (2008), pp. 259–64; see also the Fall 2007 issue of the *Journal of Public Policy & Marketing* (26, no. 2), which contains eight different perspectives on the new definition.

9. Mike Esterl, "Coke Tailors Its Soda Sizes," *The Wall Street Journal*, September 19, 2011, http://online.wsj.com/article/SB10001424053111903374004576578980270401662.html; Natalie Zmuda, "Diet Coke Blasts Past Pepsi," *Advertising Age*, March 17, 2011, http://adage.com/article/news/diet-coke-blasts-past-pepsi/149453/; Natalie Zmuda, "Can Pepsi's Big Marketing Shake-Up Bring Back Fizz to Its Beverage Brands?" *Advertising Age*, June 20, 2011, http://adage.com/article/news/pepsi-s-marketing-reorg-bring-back-fizz-beverages/228292/.

10. http://www.lexus.com/models/LSh/index.html.

11. The idea of the four Ps was conceptualized by E. Jerome McCarthy, *Basic Marketing: A Managerial Approach* (Homewood, IL: Richard D. Irwin, 1960). Also see Walter van Watershoot and Christophe Van den Bulte, "The 4P Classification of the Marketing Mix Revisited," *Journal of Marketing*, 56 (October 1992), pp. 83–93.

12. Raphael Thomadsen, "Seeking an Expanding Competitor: How Product Line Expansion Can Increase All Firms' Profits," *Journal of Marketing Research* (forthcoming).

13. http://www.nitrodessertstation.com/.

14. Wolfgang Ulaga and Werner Reinartz, "Hybrid Offerings: How Manufacturing Firms Combine Goods and Services Successfully," *Journal of Marketing* 75 (November 2011), pp. 5–23.

15. Elaine Glusac, "From Vail to Gstaad, Lures Beyond the Slopes," December 10, 2010, *The New York Times*, http://travel.nytimes.com/2010/12/12/travel/12openings.html.

16. Dani Sharp, "Business Meeting Facilities at Ski Resorts Add Scenery and Fun to Meetings," *Article Tavern*, June 1, 2011, http://articletavern.com/business/business-meeting-facilities-at-ski-resorts-add-scenery-and-fun-to-meetings.

17. Ryan Alford, "Canyons Resort in Park City Announces New Amenities and Programming for Grand Opening of 2011/2012 Ski Season," *Snowshoe Magazine*, November 23, 2011, http://www.snowshoemag.com/2011/11/23/canyons-resort-in-park-city-announces-new-amenities-and-programming-for-grand-opening-of-20112012-ski-season.

18. Christopher Solomon, "Proposed Gondola Would Link Utah Ski Resorts," *The New York Times*, December 10, 2011, http://intransit.blogs.nytimes.com/2011/12/10/proposed-gondola-would-link-utah-ski-resorts.

19. Anja Lambrecht and Catherine Tucker, "Paying with Money or Effort: Pricing When Customers Anticipate Hassle," *Journal of Marketing Research* (forthcoming).

20. Jaime Levy Pessin, "Yogurt Chains Give Power to the People," *The Wall Street Journal*, August 22, 2011, http://online.wsj.com/article/SB10001424052702303365804576432063658323394.html.

21. Pew Internet and American Life Project, "Social Networking Sites and Our Lives," June 16, 2011, http://pewinternet.org/~/media//Files/Reports/2011/PIP%20-%20Social%20networking%20sites%20and%20our%20lives.pdf; "Statistics," http://www.facebook.com/press/info.php?statistics; Mike Elgan, "Click 'Like' if You Like 'Like'," *BusinessWeek*, May 4, 2011; David Goldman, "Get Ready for some Big Facebook Changes," *CNNMoney.com*, April 21, 2010; Venture Capital Dispatch, "Giving Credits Where Credits Are Due: Facebook to Aid Developers," *The Wall Street Journal*, April 22, 2010; Liz Gannes, "Facebook: The Entire Web Will Be Social," *Gigaom.com*, April 21, 2010; Jessica Vascellaro, "Facebook Wants to Know More Than Just Who Your Friends Are," *The Wall Street Journal*, April 22, 2010; Samuel Axon, "Facebook's Open Graph Personalizes the Web," *Mashable.com*, April 21, 2010; Harry McCracken, "Microsoft Melds Office With Facebook," *Technologizer.com*, April 21, 2010.

22. George S. Day, "Aligning the Organization with the Market," *Marketing Science Institute*, 5, no. 3 (2005), pp. 3–20.

23. Kimmy Wa Chan, Chi Kin (Bennett) Yim, and Simon S.K. Lam, "Is Customer Participation in Value Creation a Double-Edged Sword? Evidence from Professional Financial Services Across Cultures," *Journal of Marketing* 74, no. 3 (May 2010); Dhruv Grewal, Kent B. Monroe, and R. Krishnan, "The Effects of Price Comparison Advertising on Buyers' Perceptions of Acquisition Value and Transaction Value," *Journal of Marketing* 62 (April 1998), pp. 46–60.

24. Anne L. Roggeveen, Michael Tsiros and Dhruv Grewal, "Understanding the Co-Creation Effect: When Does Collaborating with Customers Provide a Lift to Service Recovery?" *Journal of the Academy of Marketing Science* (2011), forthcoming; Sigurd Troye and Magne Supphellen, "Consumer Participation in Coproduction: 'I Made It Myself' Effects on Consumers' Sensory Perceptions and Evaluations of Outcome and Input Product," *Journal of Marketing* (forthcoming); Neeli Bendapudi and Robert P. Leone, "Psychological Implications of Customer Participation in Co-Production," *Journal of Marketing* 67 (January 2003), pp. 14–28.

25. http://www.ideafinder.com/history/inventions/bluejeans.htm.

26. "The History of the Wonderful Fabric, Denim!," DenimBlog.com, February 1, 2010, http://www.denimblog.com/denimblog/the-history-of-the-wonderful-fabric-denim/.

27. http://en.wikipedia.org/wiki/Designer_jeans.

28. "What Denim Brands Are Slipping Into," *Los Angeles Times*, August 14, 2011, http://www.latimes.com/features/image/la-ig-denim-lines-20110814,0,4018416.story.

29. Adam Tschorn, "Is the PyjamaJeans Brand a Sleeping Giant?" *Los Angeles Times*, August 14, 2011, http://latimesblogs.latimes.com/alltherage/2011/08/is-pajamajeans-a-sleeping-giant.html.

30. Christina Binkley, "The Relentless Rise of Power Jeans," *The Wall Street Journal*, November 6, 2009.

31. Christina Binkley, "Admitting Jeans to the Club," *The Wall Street Journal*, May 27, 2010.

32. V. Kumar and Denish Shah., "Can Marketing Lift Stock Prices?" *Sloan Management Review* 52, no. 4 (2011), pp. 24–26; V. Kumar, Eli Jones, Rajkumar Venkatesan, and Robert P. Leone, "Is Market Orientation a Source of Sustainable Competitive Advantage or Simply the Cost of Competing?" *Journal of Marketing* 75 (January 2011), pp. 16–30; Stephen A. Samaha, Robert W. Palmatier, and Rajiv P Dant, "Poisoning Relationships: Perceived Unfairness in Channels of Distribution," *Journal of Marketing* 75 (May 2011), pp. 99–117; Alexander Krasnikov, Satish Jayachandran, and V. Kumar, "The Impact of CRM Implementation on Cost and Profit Efficiencies: Evidence from US Commercial Banking Industry," *Journal of Marketing* 73 (November 2009), pp. 61–76.

33. Krasnikov, Jayachandran, and Kumar, op. cit.; V. Kumar, Denish Shah, and Rajkumar Venkatesan, "Managing Retailer Profitability—One Customer at a Time!" *Journal of Retailing*, 82, no. 4 (2006), pp. 277–94.

34. Randy Schrum, "Social Media 2010, The Fastest Growth Ever," *mycorporatemedia.com*, January 30, 2011; http://www.online-marketing-trends.com/2011/03/50-of-us-users-will-be-facebook-in-2013.html; Jonah Berger and Katherine L Milkman, "What Makes online Content Viral?" *Journal of Marketing Research* (forthcoming).

35. http://mobithinking.com/stats-corner/global-mobile-statistics-2011-all-quality-mobile-marketing-research-mobile-web-stats-su

36. http://thenextweb.com/socialmedia/2011/01/20/could-facebook-reach-one-billion-users-in-2011/

37. "Statistics," http://www.facebook.com/press/info.php?statistics; "Twitter Statistics: Updated Stats for 2011," July 7, 2011, http://www.marketinggum.com/twitter-statistics-2011-updated-stats/; "About Us," http://press.linkedin.com/about; Amy Lee, "YouTube Shares Surprising Statistics on 6th Birthday," *The Huffington Post*, May 25, 2011, http://www.huffingtonpost.com/2011/05/25/youtube-statistics-birthday_n_866707.html.

38. Julie Weed, "Hotels Turn to Social Media to Connect with Travelers," *The New York Times*, April 18, 2011.

39. Elizabeth Olson, "Restaurants Reach Out to Customers with Social Media," *The New York Times*, January 19, 2011.

40. Ibid.

41. Raji Srinivasan, Gary L. Lilien, and Shrihari Sridhar, "Should Firms Spend More on Research and Development and Advertising During Recessions?" *Journal of Marketing* 75 (May 2011), pp. 49–65.

42. http://www.ahold.com.

43. Philip Kotler, "Reinventing Marketing to Manage the Environmental Imperative," *Journal of Marketing* 75 (July 2011), pp. 132–35; Katherine White, Rhiannon MacDonnell, and John H Ellard, "Belief in a Just World: Consumer Intentions and Behaviors Toward Ethical Products," *Journal of Marketing* 76 (January 2012), pp. 103–118.

44. http://dictionary.reference.com/search?q=Entrepreneurship

45. Tina Rosenberg, "A Scorecard for Companies With a Conscience," *The New York Times*, April 11, 2011, http://opinionator.blogs.nytimes.com/2011/04/11/a-scorecard-for-companies-with-a-conscience/.

46. Ibid.

47. "P&G Professional's Green Guarantee," http://www.greenguarantee.com/faqs.htm.

48. "Commitment to Everyday Life," 2011 Sustainability Overview, http://www.pg.com/en_US/downloads/sustainability/reports/PG_2011_Sustainability_Overview.pdf.

49. Jonathan Bardeline, "P&G Scorecard Puts Supply Chain on Notice," *Greenbiz.com*, April 7, 2011, http://www.greenbiz.com/news/2011/04/07/procter-gamble-scorecard-puts-supply-chain-notice.

50. "Commitment to Everyday Life," op. cit.

51. http://www.oprah.com; "Oprah Winfrey," http://en.wikipedia.org/wiki/Oprah_Winfrey.

52. Molly Knight, "Cold Competition," *Shopping Centers Today*, February 2008. Accessed online at http://www.icsc.org/srch/sct/sct0208/RT-Pinkberry.php.

53. Emily Bryson, "Frozen Yogurt Rivalry Heating up in Chicago," Chicago Tribune, July 8, 2011. Accessed online on December 11, 2011 at http://articles.chicagotribune.com/2011-07-08/business/ct-biz-0708-pinkberry-20110708_1_yogurt-war-red-mango-tutti-frutti

54. Leslie Patton, "Pinkberry Looks Abroad to Keep Its Cool," *Bloomberg Businessweek*, April 28, 2011.

55. Ice Cream and Frozen Desserts in the U.S.: Markets and Opportunities in Relation and Foodservice, 6th Edition. Packaged Facts, July 2010, p. 171.

56. http://www.pinkberry.com/storelocations.html.

57. Yolanda Santosa, "The Making of Pinkberry," Brand Packaging, November 2, 2011. Accessed electronically at http://www.brand-packaging.com/Articles/Feature_Articles/BNP_GUID_9-5-2006_A_10000000000001122589.

58. Packaged Facts, January 2010, p. 171.

59. http://www.redmangousa.com/default.html.

Chapter 2

1. "About Nike Inc.," http://nikeinc.com/pages/about-nike-inc.

2. Bob Young, "No NBA? Let the Shoe Wars Begin," *The Arizona Republic*, October 16, 2011, http://www.azcentral.com/sports/suns/articles/2011/10/16/20111016heat-index-nba-lockout-shoe-wars.html.

3. Nike, 10-K report, July 20, 2010.

4. "Sneaker Wars: adidas Puts a Chainsaw to Kobe Bryant's Nikes," http://balljunkie.com/2011/05/27/sneaker-wars-adidas-puts-a-chainshaw-to-kobe-bryants-nikes/.

5. "Nike + iPod," http://www.apple.com/ipod/nike/run.html.

6. "Nike vs. Adidas," http://recomparison.com/comparisons/100305/nike-vs-adidas/.

7. Georgios Dogiamis and Narain Vijayshanker, "adidas: Sprinting Ahead of Nike," white paper, Winter 2009.

8. "Nike Crushes adidas on the Track in Olympic Shoe Wars," http://www.tracktownusa.com/track.item.79/Nike-Crushes-Adidas-on-the-Track-in-Olympic-Shoe-Wars.html

9. Michael Treacy and Fred Wiersema, *The Disciplines of Market Leaders* (Reading, MA: Addison Wesley, 1995). Treacy and Weirsema suggest the first three strategies. We suggest the fourth—locational excellence.

10. Petersen, J. Andrew, Leigh McAlister, David J. Reibstein, Russell S. Winer, V. Kumar and Geoff Atkinson (2009), "Choosing the Right Metrics to Maximize Profitability and Shareholder Value", *Journal of Retailing*, Vol. 85 (1), pp. 95–111.

11. Petersen, Andrew, Leigh McAlister, David J. Reibstein, Russell S. Winer, V. Kumar, and Geoff Atkinson, "Choosing the Right Metrics to Maximize Profitability and Shareholder Value," 2009, *Journal of Retailing*, 85, no. 1, pp. 95-111; V. Kumar, "Tough Times Call for CLV," *The Economist*, March 29, 2009; V. Kumar, *Managing Customers for Profit: Strategies to Increase Profits and Build Loyalty*, Philadelphia: Wharton School Publishing, 2008.

12. "Singapore Airlines Tops Survey for Best Service," *The New York Times*, http://community.nytimes.com/comments/intransit.blogs.nytimes.com/2010/03/31/singapore-airlines-tops-survey-for-best-international-service/

13. Singapore Airlines, http://www.singaporeair.com/en_UK/flying-with-us/.

14. "Singapore Girls: You're a Great Way to Fly," http://www.singaporeair.com/en_UK/flying-with-us/singaporegirl/.

15. Alex Kennedy, "Singapore Airlines Unveils Scoot Budget Carrier," November 1, 2011, http://www.boston.com/business/articles/2011/11/01/singapore_airlines_unveils_scoot_budget_carrier/.

16. Valarie A. Zeithaml, Mary Jo Bitner, and Dwayne D. Gremler, *Services Marketing: Integrating Customer Focus Across the Firm*, 5th ed. (Burr Ridge, IL: McGraw-Irwin, 2009).

17. James R. Stock, Stefanie L. Boyer, and Tracy Harmon, "Research Opportunities in Supply Chain Management," *Journal of the Academy of Marketing Science*, 2010, 38, no. 1, pp. 32-41. Also see articles in special issue edited by: John T. Mentzer and Greg Gundlach, "Exploring the Relationship between Marketing and Supply Chain Management: Introduction to the Special Issue," *Journal of the Academy of Marketing Science*, 2010, 38, no. 1, pp. 1–4.

18. http://www.interbrand.com/en/best-global-brands/Best-Global-Brands-2011.aspx.

19. Glenn Karwoski, "3M Still Tops Among Investors," January 13, 2011, http://tcbmag.blogs.com/innovations/2011/01/3m-still-tops-among-innovators.html.

20. http://www.marketingpower.com/_layouts/Dictionary.aspx?dLetter=M.

21. Donald Lehman and Russell Winer, *Analysis for Marketing Planning*, 7th ed. (Burr Ridge, IL: McGraw-Hill/Irwin, 2008).

22. Andrew Campbell, "Mission Statements," *Long Range Planning*, 30 (1997), pp. 931–933.

23. Alfred Rappaport, *Creating Shareholder Value: The New Standard for Business Performance* (New York: Wiley, 1988).

24. http://help-us.nike.com/app/answers/detail/a_id/113/~/what-is-nike's-mission-statement%3F.

25. http://adidas-group.corporate-publications.com/2010/gb/en/group-management-report-our-group/corporate-mission-statement.html

26. http://www.teachforamerica.org/mission/mission_and_approach.htm.

27. Michael McCarthy, "NBA Lockout Not Good for the Shoes," *USA Today*, November 1, 2011, http://www.usatoday.com/sports/basketball/nba/story/2011-10-30/NBA-lockout-not-good-for-the-shoes/51007210/1.

28. Matt Townsend, "As Nike Scoffs, Toning Shoes Gain Traction," *Bloomberg Business Week*, June 7–13, 2010, pp. 22–24.

29. Eric Siemers, "Nike Takes New Marketing Tack," *Portland Business Journal*, September 12, 2010, http://www.bizjournals.com/portland/stories/2010/09/13/story9.html.

30. Nike 10-K report, July 20, 2010.

31. Russel Parsons, "Nike Beating Official Sponsor adidas in World Cup Stakes," *Marketing Week*, June 24, 2010, p. 7.

32. Eric Siemans, "New Balance TV Spots Target Nike," *Portland Business Journal*, March 7, 2011, http://www.bizjournals.com/portland/blog/2011/03/new-balance-tv-spots-target-nike.html?page=2.

33. Nike 10-K report, July 20, 2010.

34. http://www.hertz.com/rentacar/vehicleguide/index.jsp?targetPage=vehicleGuideHomeView.jsp&countryCode=US&category=Car/Sedan.

35. https://images.hertz.com/pdfs/VMVWeb.pdf; http://www.adweek.com/aw/content_display/creative/new-campaigns/e3i21cea1586dd4edf5d50f9a17e7f18bf3.

36. Peter Johnston, "Share of the Mobile Pie," *Stores*, October 2011.

37. http://solutions.3m.com/wps/portal/3M/en_US/about-3M/information/about/us/

38. http://solutions.3m.com/en_US/; "3M Expands Manufacturing Facility for Solar Film." *Wireless News*, October 16, 2010; Michael

Arndt, "3M's Seven Pillars of Innovation," *Business Week*, May 10, 2006, http://www.businessweek.com/innovate/content/may2006/id20060510_682823.htm.

39. Dana Mattioli, Kris Maher, "At 3M, Innovation Comes in Tweaks and Snips," *The Wall Street Journal*, March 2, 2010.

40. Chuck Salter, "The 9 Passions of 3M's Mauro Porcini," *Fast Company*, October 2011, pp. 128–34.

41. Mary Tripsas, "Seeing Customers as Partners in Invention," *The New York Times*, December 26, 2009.

42. Sandy Smith, "Category Killing, Korea Style," *Stores*, October 2011.

43. Rick Moss, "What Whole Foods Gained from Its LivingSocial Deal," *Forbes*, September 15, 2011, http://www.forbes.com/sites/retailwire/2011/09/15/what-whole-foods-gained-from-its-livingsocial-deal/.

44. Kevin Chung, Timothy Derdenger, and Kannan Srinivasan, "Economic Value of Celebrity Endorsement: Tiger Woods' Impact on Sales of Nike Golf Balls," working paper, Carnegie Mellon University, December 2, 2010. Available at http://www.andrew.cmu.edu/user/derdenge/TWExecutiveSummary.pdf.

45. Ibid., p. 1.

46. "Starbucks Shared Plan: Goals and Progress 2010," http://www.starbucks.com/responsibility/learn-more/goals-and-progress; http://www.starbucks.com/responsibility/sourcing/coffee; "2010 World's Most Ethical Companies," *Ethisphere*, http://ethisphere.com/wme2010/.

47. http://www.ethoswater.com/; http://www.starbucks.com/responsibility/community/ethos-water-fund; http://www.starbucks.com/responsibility/sourcing/coffee.

48. http://www.starbucks.com/responsibility/wellnesshttps://www.webmdhealth.com/starbucks/default.aspx?secure=1.

49. "More Driven: Goodyear 2010 Annual Report." Available at http://www.goodyear.com/investor/pdf/ar/2010ar.pdf.

50. This discussion is adapted from Roger A. Kerin, Steven W. Hartley, and William Rudelius, *Marketing*, 10th ed. (Burr Ridge, IL: McGraw-Hill/Irwin, 2011).

51. Farris et al., *Marketing Metrics: 50+ Metrics Every Executive Should Master*, p. 17.

52. Relative market share = brand's market share ÷ largest competitor's market share. If, for instance, there are only two products in a market, A and B, and product B has 90 percent market share, then A's relative market share is 10 ÷ 90 = 11.1 percent. If, on the other hand, B only has 50 percent market share, then A's relative market share is 10 ÷ 50 = 20 percent. Farris et al., *Marketing Metrics: 50+ Metrics Every Executive Should Master*, p. 19.

53. Apple Inc., "Form 10-K 2011 Annual Report," http://files.shareholder.com/downloads/AAPL/1710549824x0x512287/5a5d7b14-9542-4640-841d-e047ec28bb96/AAPL_10K_FY11_10.26.11.pdf

54. "Strategy Analytics: Apple Becomes World's Largest Smartphone Vendor in Q4 2011," *Business Wire* January 26, 2012, http://www.businesswire.com/news/home/20120126006752/en/Strategy-Analytics-Apple-Worlds-Largest-Smartphone-Vendor

55. Sherilynn Macale, "Apple has Sold 300M iPods, Currently Holds 78% of the Music Player Market," *The Next Web*, October 4, 2011, http://thenextweb.com/apple/2011/10/04/apple-has-sold-300m-ipods-currently-holds-78-of-the-music-player-market/; Chris Smith, "iPad Tablet Market Share Down to 57 Percent," Techradar.com, February 16th 2012, http://www.techradar.com/news/mobile-computing/tablets/ipad-tablet-market-share-down-to-57-per-cent-1064010

56. Joe Wilcox, "iPad Market Share Plunged 20 Percent in Q4 2010," *BetaNews*, February 2011, http://betanews.com/2011/03/10/ipad-market-share-plunged-20-percent-in-q4-2010/; Mohit Agrawal, "Tablets OS Market Share," *Telecom Circle*, October 7, 2011, http://www.telecomcircle.com/2011/10/tablets-os-market-share/

57. Roger Kerin, Vijay Mahajan, and P. Rajan Varadarajan, *Contemporary Perspectives on Strategic Market Planning* (Boston: Allyn & Bacon, 1991), chapter 6; Susan Mudambi, "A Topology of Strategic Choice in Marketing," *International Journal of Market & Distribution Management* (1994), pp. 22–25.

58. http://www.gamestop.com/xbox-360/movies-tv/yoostar-on-mtv/91616.

59. http://www.mtv.com/shows/teen_mom/season_3/series.jhtml.

60. http://www.viacom.com/ourbrands/globalreach/Pages/default.aspx.

61. http://www.stayteen.org/; http://www.mtv.com/mobile/.

62. Thompson, A.A., Margaret A. Peteraf, John E. Gamble and A/J. Strickland. (2012) *Crafting and Executing Strategy,* 18th edition, New York, NY: McGraw-Hill Irwin.

63. http://www.mtv.com/shows/made/series.jhtml; Tim Arango, "Make Room, Cynics; MTV Wants to Do Some Good," *The New York Times,* April 18, 2009; Robert Seidman, "MTV Continues to Diversify Slate with New Scripted Comedies "The Hard Times of RJ Berger" and "Warren the Ape"," tvbythenumbers.com, January 15, 2010.

64. http://solutions.3m.com/wps/portal/3M/en_US/about-3M/information/about/businesses/.

65. http://www.netflix.com; "Netflix," http://en.wikipedia.org/wiki/Netflix#cite_note-QwisterBlogPost-19; Scott Stein, "Netflix on iPad, More to Follow?" *CNET Reviews,* April 1, 2010; Jessie Baker, "Netflix Introduces New Plans and Announces Price Changes," Netflix blog, July 12, 2011, http://blog.netflix.com/2011_07_01_archive.html; Brian Stelter, "Netflix Stock Falls After Change," *The New York Times,* September 15, 2011, http://mediadecoder.blogs.nytimes.com/2011/09/15/price-hike-sends-netflixs-stock-downward/; Reed Hastings, "An Explanation and Some Reflections," Netflix blog, September 18, 2011, http://blog.netflix.com/2011_09_01_archive.html; Elizabeth Harris, "Netflix to Break Business in Two," *The New York Times,* September 19, 2011, http://mediadecoder.blogs.nytimes.com/2011/09/19/netflix-c-e-o-apologizes-for-handling-of-price-increase/; Jenna Wortham and Brian Stelter, "Latest Move Gets Netflix More Wrath," *The New York Times,* September 19, 2011, http://mediadecoder.blogs.nytimes.com/2011/09/19/netflix-strategy-prompts-backlash/; Reed Hastings, "DVDs Will Be Staying at Netflix.com," Netflix blog, October 10, 2011, http://blog.netflix.com/2011_10_01_archive.html.

Appendix 2A

1. This appendix was written by Tom Chevalier, Britt Hackmann, and Elisabeth Nevins Caswell, in conjunction with the textbook authors (Dhruv Grewal and Michael Levy) as the basis of class discussion rather than to illustrate either effective or ineffective marketing practice.

2. http://www.knowthis.com/tutorials/principles-of-marketing/how-to-write-a-marketing-plan.htm (accessed May 16, 2008); see also "Marketing Plan Online," http://www.quickmba.com/marketing/plan/ (accessed May 16, 2008); "Marketing Plan," http://www.businessplans.org/Market.html (accessed May 18, 2008).

3. Roger Kerin, Steven Hartley, and William Rudelius, *Marketing* (New York: McGraw-Hill/Irwin, 2008), p. 53.

4. Ibid., p. 54; http://www.knowthis.com/tutorials/principles-of-marketing/how-to-write-a-marketing-plan.htm (accessed May 16, 2008).

5. This listing of sources largely comes from the Babson College Library Guide, http://www3.babson.edu/Library/research/market-ingplan.cfm, May 12, 2008 (accessed May 15, 2008). Special thanks to Nancy Dlott.

6. This marketing plan presents an abbreviated version of the actual plan for PeopleAhead. Some information has been changed to maintain confidentiality.

7. Publishers' and Advertising Directors' Conference, September 21, 2005.

8. Mintel International Group, "Online Recruitment–US," January 1, 2005, http://www.marketresearch.com (accessed September 1, 2005).

9. Corzen Inc., May 1, 2004, http://www.wantedtech.com/ (accessed May 17, 2004).

10. Mintel International Group, "Online Recruitment–US."

Chapter 3

1. Andrea Edwards, "Dell—a Top Five Social Media Brand—Looking for Fresh Ideas," SAJE . . . Communication, October 12, 2011, http://sajeideas.wordpress.com/2011/10/12/dell-a-top-five-social-media-brand-%E2%80%93-looking-for-fresh-ideas/.

2. Dell.com, "Introducing Dell's Social Media Command Center," http://content.dell.com/us/en/corp/d/videos-en/Documents-dell-social-media-command-center.aspx.aspx,.

3. Edwards, op. cit.

4. Dell.com, "Social Media," http://content.dell.com/us/en/corp/about-dell-social-media.aspx?c=us&l=en&s=corp&-ck=mn.

5. Ed Twittel, "How Dell Really Listens to Its Customers," *ReadWriteEnterprise,* July 22, 2011, http://www.readwriteweb.com/enterprise/2011/07/how-dell-really-listens-to-its.php.

6. Ibid.

7. Susan Payton, "Closing Comments at Dell's 2nd Annual Consumer Advisory Panel," Flickr, http://www.flickr.com/photos/dellphotos/5960769218/in/set-72157627234641908.

8. HubSpot company website, http://www.hubspot.com/internet-marketing-company/; Canadian Mountain Holidays website, http://www.canadiananmountainholidays.com/heli-skiing/trips; http://www.hubspot.com/customer-case-studies/bid/31288/Travel-and-Leisure-Industry-Sucess-Story-CMH-Heli-Skiing-Summer-Adventures.

9. Nikon, press release, August 22, 2007, http://press.nikonusa.com/post/2007/08/22/nikons-new-digital-learning-center-on-flickr-provides-a-first-of-its-kind-interactive-experience-that-assists-everyday-people-in-taking-better-photos/.

10. Chris Barry, Rob Markey, Eric Almquist and Chris Brahm (2011), "Putting Social Media to Work," Bain & Co.

11. Coca-Cola Retailing Research Council and the Integer Group, "Social Networking Personas: A Look at Consumer and Shopper Mind Sets," in *Untangling the Social Web: Insights for Users, Brands, and Retailers,* March 2012, http://www.cokesolutions.com/BusinessSolutions/Studies/Untangling%20the%20Social%20Web_Part%203.pdf.

12. Forever 21 Facebook Fan Page, http://www.facebook.com/#!/Forever21?ref=ts.

13. Ibid.

14. Andrew LaVallee, "Burger King Cancels Facebook Ad Campaign," *The Wall Street Journal,* January 15, 2009.

15. "LinkedIn Announces Fourth Quarter and 2011 Fiscal Year Financial Results," *LinkedIn,* February 9, 2012, http://press.linkedin.com/node/1104.

16. Ann-Christine Diaz, "Facebook 101: Is Your Brand Worth a Like?" *Ad Age Digital,* January 30, 2012.

17. Pam Dyer, "Facebook Advertising Case Study: Clorox Green Works," http://www.pamorama.net/2011/02/26/facebook-advertising-case-study-clorox-green-works/.

18. Guy Kawaski, "Ten Ways for Small Businesses to Use LinkedIn," *LinkedIn Blog,* April 12, 2010, http://blog.linkedin.com/2010/04/12/linkedin-small-business-tips/.

19. Catherine Smith, "Google + Adds Games: Angry Birds, Zynga Poker, and Bejeweled," Huffington Post, August 11, 2011.

20. Ibid.

21. M.P. Mueller, "Small Businesses That Understand Social Media," *The New York Times*, July 11, 2011, http://boss.blogs.nytimes.com/2011/07/11/small-businesses-that-understand-social-media/.

22. Mueller, op. cit.

23. David H. Freedman, "Debating the Merits of Facebook and Google+," *The New York Times*, February 7, 2012, http://boss.blogs.nytimes.com/2012/02/07/debating-the-merits-of-facebook-and-google/.

24. Ross Blum, "Where Have All the Customers Gone?" p. 8.

25. "In The Know," YouTube, Fall 2009 http://www.gstatic.com/youtube/engagement/platform/autoplay/advertise/downloads/YouTube_InTheKnow.pdf.

26. The Home Depot Branded Channel, http://www.youtube.com/user/homedepot?blend=2&ob=4#p/a.

27. "Brand Channels," YouTube, http://www.gstatic.com/youtube/engagement/platform/autoplay/advertise/downloads/YouTube_BrandChannels.pdf.

28. Leah Shafer, "Re-Branding the Dynasty: Tori Spelling's HSN Clips on YouTube," March 25, 2010, http://mediacommons.futureofthebook.org/imr/2010/03/24/re-branding-dynasty-tori-spellings-hsn-clips-youtube.

29. "Brands on Flickr," *Supercollider*, July 12, 2008. http://geoffnorthcott.com/blog/2008/07/brands-on-flickr/.

30. Leah Shafer, "Re-Branding the Dynasty: Tori Spelling's HSN Clips on YouTube," March 25, 2010, http://mediacommons.futureofthebook.org/imr/2010/03/24/re-branding-dynasty-tori-spellings-hsn-clips-youtube.

31. "So How Many Blogs Are There Anyways?" *Hat Trick Associates*, February 1, 2012. http://www.hattrickassociates.com/tag/how-many-blogs-exist/

32. Mark W. Schaefer, "The 10 Best Corporate Blogs in the World," *BusinessGrow.com*, January 1, 2011, http://www.businessesgrow.com/2011/01/05/the-10-best-corporate-blogs-in-the-world/.

33. Ganesh Babu, "Justin Bieber's Social Media Fame [Infographic]," *AXLERATION*, http://www.axleration.com/justin-biebers-social-media-fame-infographic/.

34. Famecount, "Justin Bieber Facebook Statistics," www.famebook.com/facebook/justin-bieber.

35. Eric Goldstein, "Justin Bieber: A Social Media Case Study," *Social Media Today*, June 12, 2011, http://socialmediatoday.com/eric-goldstein/305692/justin-bieber-social-media-case-study.

36. Babu, op. cit.

37. Ibid.

38. Goldstein, op. cit.

39. Babu, op. cit.

40. Goldstein, op. cit.

41. Goldstein, op. cit.

42. "Top 10 Most Influential Mommy Blogs," *Cision Navigator*, May 5, 2011, http://navigator.cision.com/Top-10-Most-Influential-Mommy-Bloggers.aspx.

43. Elizabeth Holmes, "Tweeting Without Fear," *The Wall Street Journal*, December 9, 2011.

44. Ibid.

45. Coca-Cola Retailing Research Council and the Integer Group, "Assessing the Social Networking Landscape," in *Untangling the Social Web: Insights for Users, Brands, and Retailers*, January 2012.

46. Brad Tuttle, "Use Amazon's Price Check App and Save $15 This Saturday," http://moneyland.time.com/2011/12/08/use-amazons-price-check-app-and-save-15-this-saturday/ (accessed April 12, 2012).

47. "Local Bookstores Ask Customers to Boycott Amazon Over New Price Check App Offer," http://www.commondreams.org/headline/2011/12/12-3 (accessed April 12, 2012).

48. Brad Tuttle, "How Smartphones, Price-Check Apps, and Daily-Deals are Changing Black Friday–And the Entire Holiday Season," *Time Magazine Moneyland Blog*, November 25, 2011, http://moneyland.time.com/2011/11/25/how-smartphones-price-check-apps-and-daily-deals-are-changing-black-friday-and-the-entire-holiday-shopping-season/

49. Tom Ryan, "Target Looks to Battle Pricing App, *Retail Wire*, January 24, 2012.

50. Marguerite Darlington, "The History and Future of Mobile's Role in Fashion," FashionablyMarketing.me, November 22, 2011.

51. Katie Van Domelin, "Social Media Monitoring Tools–How to Pick the Right One," July 7, 2010, http://www.convinceandconvert.com/social-media-monitoring/social-media-monitoring-tools-how-to-pick-the-right-one/.

52. "New Radian6 Features Help to Scale 'Social' Across the Enterprise," Radian6 website, November 12, 2011, http://www.radian6.com/wp-content/uploads/2010/12/NovemberRelease.pdf.

53. Radian6 website, http://www.radian6.com/2011.

54. Let's Get Ready website, http://www.letsgetready.org/About/MissionAndVision.

55. Laura S. Quinn and Kyle Andrei, "A Few Good Web Analytics Tools," May 19, 2011, http://www.techsoup.org/learningcenter/internet/page6760.cfm.

56. Christina Warren, "How to Measure Social Media ROI," Ocotber 27, 2009, http://mashable.com/2009/10/27/social-media-roi/.

57. "iNoobs: What Is Google Analytics?" http://inspiredm.com/what-is-google-analytics/. http://www.google.com/analytics/features/index.html; http://www.advanced-web-metrics.com/docs/web-data-sources.pdf; http://mobile.tutsplus.com/articles/marketing/7-solutions-for-tracking-mobile-analytics/; http://www.practicalecommerce.com/articles/3062-10-Web-Analytics-Solutions-for-Ecommerce-Merchants

58. Amy Porterfield, "3 Steps to an Effective Social Media Strategy," *Social Media Examiner*, March 1, 2012, http://www.socialmediaexaminer.com/3-steps-to-an-effective-social-media-strategy/.

59. Sarah Mahoney, "Macy's Gets Face(book) Lift, Expands 'Ecosystem'," *Marketing Daily*, February 29, 2012.

60. Andy Shaw, "How to Create a Facebook Ad Campaign," *Social Media Tips*, September 23, 2011, http://exploringsocialmedia.com/how-to-create-a-facebook-ad-campaign/;

61. Karen Kroll, "Localizing the Message," *Stores News*, September 2011.

62. "Should Social Media Listening Replace Your Asking Consumer Research?"April 6, 2012, http://socialmediatoday.com/neilglassman/485074/should-social-media-listening-replace-your-asking-consumer-research-convo.

63. "What Is the Best Alternative to Klout?" http://www.quora.com/What-is-the-best-alternative-to-Klout.

64. Mark W. Schaefer, "Google and Bing Reveal that Social Influence Bumps Search Engine Results," December 2, 2010, http://www.businessesgrow.com/2010/12/02/google-and-bing-reveal-that-social-influence-bumpdrives-search-engine-results/.

65. Erin Griffith, "Getting Your Klout Out," *AdWeek*, May 17, 2011, http://www.adweek.com/news/advertising-branding/getting-your-klout-out-131629.

66. Dorie Clark, "How to Become a Thought Leader in Six Steps," *Harvard Business Review*, November 9, 2010, http://blogs.hbr.org/cs/2010/11/how_to_become_a_thought_leader.html.

67. Landman, "Are You a V.I.P.? Check Your Klout Score," *The New York Times*, November 18, 2011.

68. "Social Media Career Advice from Leading Marketers," http://www.onwardsearch.com/Social-Media-Career-Advice/; Griffith, op. cit.

69. James Tomerson, "Looking for Job Opportunities in Social Media?" http://www.jobdiagnosis.com/myblog/social-media-jobs.htm.

70. Shan Li, "Employers Are Liking—and Hiring—Social Media Workers," *Los Angeles Times*, September 28, 2011, http://articles.latimes.com/2011/sep/28/business/la-fi-social-media-jobs-20110929.

71. "The Klout Score," http://klout.com/understand/score.

72. Seth Stevenson, "What Your Klout Score Really Means," *Wired*, April 24, 2012, http://www.wired.com/epicenter/2012/04/ff_klout/.

73. Schaefer, op. cit.

74. Kashmir Hill, "Facebook Can Tell You if a Person Is Worth Hiring," *Forbes*, March 5, 2012, http://www.forbes.com/sites/kashmirhill/2012/03/05/facebook-can-tell-you-if-a-person-is-worth-hiring/?partner=yahoo.

75. Barry Murphy, "The Next Governance Frontier: Social Media," *Forbes*, http://www.forbes.com/sites/barrymurphy/2012/02/28/the-next-governance-frontier-social-media/

76. Dell.com, "The History of Dell," http://content.dell.com/us/en/corp/our-story-company-timeline.aspx.

77. Sean McDonald, "Dell – A Leader in Social Media Innovation," Ant'sEyeView.com, February 7, 2011, http://www.antseyeview.com/blog/dell-still-the-leader-in-social-media-innovation/.

78. Dell.com, "History."

79. Dell.com, "History."

80. Chris Barry, Rob Markey, Eric Almquist, and Chris Brahm, "Putting Social Media to Work," Bain Brief, September 12, 2011, http://www.bain.com/publications/articles/putting-social-media-to-work.aspx.

81. Dell.com, "Shop for Home and Office," http://www.dell.com/us/p/

82. Dell.com, http://support.dell.com/support/index.aspx?c=us&l=en&s=dhs&~ck=mn.

83. Dell.com, "Welcome to Home User Support," http://en.community.dell.com/support-forums/default.aspx.

84. Dell,"Dell Support," http://www.facebook.com/dell?ref=ts#!/dell?sk=app_155719871129476.

85. Dell, "Dell Buzz Room," http://apps.facebook.com/dellbuzzroom/?cat=product_news.

86. Dell, "Dell Lounge," http://www.facebook.com/dell?ref=ts#!/DellUniversity.

87. Dell, "Social Shop," http://www.facebook.com/dell?ref=ts#!/dell?sk=app_131112203596270.

88. Dell, "Ask Rev," http://www.facebook.com/dell?ref=ts#!/dell?sk=app_236634689716925.

89. Dell, "Dell," https://twitter.com/#!/search/Dell.

90. Dell, "DellHomeUS," https://twitter.com/#!/DellHomeUS.

91. Dell, "DellEnterprise," https://twitter.com/#!/DellEnterprise.

92. Dell, DellCares," https://twitter.com/#!/DellCares.

93. Dell,"Direct2Dell," https://twitter.com/#!/Direct2Dell.

94. Dell, "Michael Dell," https://twitter.com/#!/MichaelDell.

95. Barry et al., op. cit.

96. Dell.com, "Direct2dell," http://en.community.dell.com/dell-blogs/direct2dell/b/direct2dell/default.aspx.

97. Dell.com, "DellShares," http://en.community.dell.com/dell-blogs/dell-shares/b/dell-shares/default.aspx.

98. Dell.com, "DellSoftwareNews," http://en.community.dell.com/dell-blogs/software/b/software/default.aspx.

99. Dell, http://www.linkedin.com/company/1093?goback=%2Efcs_MDYS_Dell_false_*2_*2_*2_*2_*2_*2_*2_*2_*2_*2_*2_*2&trk=ncsrch_hits.

100. Dell, https://plus.google.com/117161668189080869053/posts#117161668189080869053/postsGoogle+.

101. Chris Barry, Rob Markey, Eric Almquist, and Chris Brahm, "Putting Social Media to Work," Bain Brief, September 12, 2011, http://www.bain.com/publications/articles/putting-social-media-to-work.aspx.

102. Chris Barry, Rob Markey, Eric Almquist, and Chris Brahm, "Putting Social Media to Work," Bain Brief, September 12, 2011, http://www.bain.com/publications/articles/putting-social-media-to-work.aspx.

103. Ed Twittel, "How Dell Really Listens to Its Customers," *ReadWriteEnterprise*, July 22, 2011, http://www.readwriteweb.com/enterprise/2011/07/how-dell-really-listens-to-its.php.

104. Cory Edwards and Dell, "When It Comes to Social Media, How Big Are Your Company's Ears?" *Forbes*, December 6, 2011, http://www.forbes.com/sites/dell/2011/12/06/when-it-comes-to-social-media-how-big-are-your-companys-ears/.

105. Zocalo Group, "Forrester Groundswell Awards: The Dell Listening & Command Center," Empowered, http://groundswell-discussion.com/groundswell/awards2011/detail.php?id=699.

106. Ginger Conlon, "Dell Takes Command of Social Media Listening," Think Customers: The 1to1 Blog, September 9, 2011, http://www.1to1media.com/weblog/2011/09/dell_takes_command_of_social_m.html.

107. Dell.com, "Global Social Media Policy," http://content.dell.com/us/en/corp/d/corp-comm/social-media-policy.aspx.

108. Sean McDonald, "Dell – A Leader in Social Media Innovation," Ant'sEyeView.com, February 7, 2011, http://www.antseyeview.com/blog/dell-still-the-leader-in-social-media-innovation/.

109. Zocalo Group, "Forrester Groundswell Awards: The Dell Listening & Command Center," Empowered, http://groundswell-discussion.com/groundswell/awards2011/detail.php?id=699.

110. Chris Barry, Rob Markey, Eric Almquist, and Chris Brahm, "Putting Social Media to Work," Bain Brief, September 12, 2011, http://www.bain.com/publications/articles/putting-social-media-to-work.aspx.

111. Cory Edwards and Dell, "When It Comes to Social Media, How Big Are Your Company's Ears?" *Forbes*, December 6, 2011, http://www.forbes.com/sites/dell/2011/12/06/when-it-comes-to-social-media-how-big-are-your-companys-ears/.

112. Chris Barry, Rob Markey, Eric Almquist, and Chris Brahm, "Putting Social Media to Work," Bain Brief, September 12, 2011, http://www.bain.com/publications/articles/putting-social-media-to-work.aspx.

Chapter 4

1. *National Geographic*, "Overfishing: Plenty of Fish in the Sea? Not Always," http://ocean.nationalgeographic.com/ocean/critical-issues-overfishing/.

2. Jennifer L. Jacquet and Daniel Pauly, "Trade Secrets: Renaming and Mislabeling of Seafood," *Marine Policy* 32 (2008), pp. 309–18.

3. Stephen Nolgren and Terry Tomalin, "You Order Grouper; What Do You Get?" *St. Petersburg Times*, August 6, 2006, http://www.sptimes.com/2006/08/06/Tampabay/You_order_grouper_wha.shtml.

4. "On the Menu, but Not on Your Plate," *Boston Globe*, October 23, 2011, http://www.boston.com/business/articles/2011/10/23/on_the_menu_but_not_on_your_plate/?cbResetParam=1; Chris Reidy, "Consumer Reports 'Mystery Fish' Story Finds Similar Results to Globe's Investigation into Seafood Mislabeling," *Business Updates*, October 28, 2011, http://www.boston.com/Boston/businessupdates/2011/10/consumer-reports-mystery-fish-story-finds-similar-results-globe-investigation-into-seafood-mislabeling/adaY8Am98dkSNO7MD8W1ZM/index.html. See also "Fish Fraud Expose in Boston Globe Sparks Conversation," http://jacquelinechurch.com/pig-tales-a-fish-friends/2133-fish-fraud-expose-in-boston-globe-sparks-conversation.

5. Theodore Levitt, *Marketing Imagination* (Detroit, MI: The Free Press, 1983).

6. Kevin Peachy, "EU Toy Safety Rules to Be Stricter," *BBC News*, July 7, 2011, http://www.bbc.co.uk/news/business-14012541.

7. "Mattel Apologizes to China for Recall," *The New York Times*, September 21, 2007, http://www.nytimes.com/2007/09/21/business/worldbusiness/21iht-mattel.3.7597386.html (accessed April 21, 2010); "Plenty of Blame to Go Around," *The Economist*, September 29, 2007.

8. Andrew Martin, "Toy Makers Fight for Exemption from Rules," *The New York Times*, September 28, 2010, http://www.nytimes.com/2010/09/29/business/29toys.html.

9. For a detailed compilation of articles that are involved with ethical and societal issues, see: Gregory T. Gundlach, Lauren G. Block, and William W. Wilkie, *Explorations of Marketing in Society* (Mason, OH: Thompson Higher Education, 2007); G. Svensson and G. Wood, "A Model of Business Ethics," *Journal of Business Ethics*, 77, no. 3 (2007), pp. 303–322.

10. Christy Ashley and Hillary A. Leonard, "Betrayed by the Buzz? Covert Content and Consumer–Brand Relationships," *Journal of Public Policy & Marketing* 28, no. 2 (2009), pp. 212–20.

11. Elizabeth S. Moore and Victoria J. Rideout (2007), "The Online Marketing of Food to Children: Is it Just Fun and Games?" *Journal of Public Policy & Marketing*, 26, (2), 202-220; Elizabeth S. Moore (2007), "Perspectives on Food Marketing & Childhood Obesity: Introduction to the Special Section," *Journal of Public Policy & Marketing*, 26(2), 157-161; Elizabeth S. Moore (2007), "Food Marketing Goes Online: A Content Analysis of Websites for Children," in *Obesity in America: Development and Prevention*, Vol. 2, Hiram E. Fitzgerald and Vasiliki Mousouli (eds.), Westport, CT: Praeger, 93-115. William L. Wilkie and Elizabeth S. Moore, "Marketing's Contributions to Society," *Journal of Marketing* 63 (Special Issue, 1999), pp. 198–219.

12. Jeffrey M. Jones, "Nurses Top Honesty and Ethics List for 11th Year," Gallup, December 3, 2010, http://www.gallup.com/poll/145043/nurses-top-honesty-ethics-list-11-year.aspx.

13. http://www.workingvalues.com/Dec06WorkingValuesWhtPpr.pdf.

14. http://www.jnj.com/our_company/our_credo/index.htm.

15. Vanessa O'Connell and Shirley Wang, "J&J Acts Fast on Tylenol," *The Wall Street Journal*, July 9, 2009.

16. Erin Cavusgil, "Merck and Vioxx: An Examination of an Ethical Decision-Making Model," *Journal of Business Ethics*, 76 (2007), pp. 451–61.

17. Jeanne Whalen, "AstraZeneca Sharpens Focus on Ethics," *The Wall Street Journal*, December 3, 2009, http://online.wsj.com/article/SB10001424052748704157304574611724066010600.html; "AstraZeneca Weighs Response to UK Body on Ethics Code Breach," *The Wall Street Journal*, March 9, 2010, http://online.wsj.com/article/BT-CO-20100309-706314.html.

18. For an interesting discussion of why pharmaceutical companies seem to have lost their ethical luster, see Matthew Herper, "Big Pharma: What Went Wrong?" http://www.forbes.com/sites/matthewherper/2011/06/22/big-pharma-what-went-wrong/.

19. "In Brief: Retailers sever ties over child labor," *The Spokesman-Review*, October 31, 2009; George Anderson, "Walmart Says 'No' to Uzbek Cotton Over Child Labor," *Retail Wire*, October 1, 2008; Dan McDougall, "Child Sweatshop Shame Threatens Gap's Ethical Image," *The Observer*, October 28, 2007.

20. Walmart Launches Major Initiative to Make Food Healthier and Healthier Food More Affordable; http://walmartstores.com/pressroom/news/10514.aspx; Stephanie Rosenbloom, "At Walmart, Labeling to Reflect Green Intent," *The New York Times*, July 16, 2009; Stephanie Rosenbloom, "Wal-Mart to Toughen Standards," *The New York Times*, Octobeer 22, 2008; Adam Aston, "Walmart: Making Its Suppliers Go Green," *BusinessWeek*, May 18, 2009.

21. http://www.limitedbrands.com/social_responsibility/labor/labor.jsp; http://www.greenamericatoday.org/.

22. http://www.marketingpower.com/AboutAMA/Pages/Statement%20of%20Ethics.aspx.

23. http://www.cmomagazine.com/info/release/090104_ethics.html. This survey was conducted in 2006; more recent reports suggest that 49 percent of respondents to a 2009 survey reported having seen ethical misconduct overall. See Ethics Resource Center, "2009 National Business Ethics Survey," http://www.ethics.org/nbes/files/nbes-final.pdf.

24. Alexander Dahlsrud lists 37 different definitions! See "How Corporate Social Responsibility Is Defined," *Corporate Social Responsibility and Environmental Management* 15, no. 1 (January/February 2008), pp. 1–13.

25. "Social Responsibility," *AMA Dictionary of Marketing Terms*, http://www.marketingpower.com/_layouts/Dictionary.aspx?dLetter=S.

26. Christopher Marquis, Pooja Shah, Amanda Tolleson, and Bobbi Thomason, "The Dannon Company: Marketing and Corporate Social Responsibility," *Harvard Business School Case 9-410-121*, April 1, 2010.

27. "Restoring the Economy," BP, http://www.bp.com/sectiongenericarticle800.do?categoryId=9036578&contentId=7067597.

28. http://www.toms.com/our-movement; http://www.toms.com/corporate-info/; http://www.insightargentina.org; Christina Binkley, "Charity Gives Shoe Brand Extra Shine," *The Wall Street Journal*, April 1, 2010, http://online.wsj.com/article/SB10001424052702304252704575155903198032336.html.

29. Michael Connor, "Survey: U.S. Consumers Willing to Pay for Corporate Responsibility," *Business Ethics*, March 29, 2010, http://business-ethics.com/2010/03/29/1146-survey-u-s-consumers-willing-to-pay-for-corporate-responsibility/.

30. Richard Stengel, "Doing Well by Doing Good," *Time Magazine*, September 10, 2009, http://www.time.com/time/magazine/article/0,9171,1921591,00.html.

31. "2011 World's Most Ethical Companies," *Ethisphere*, http://ethisphere.com/2011-worlds-most-ethical-companies.

32. http://www.burtsbees.com/c/story/mission-vision/.

33. General Electric, "Sustainable Growth: GE 2010 Citizenship Report," http://www.gecitizenship.com; General Electric, "The Spirit and the Letter," http://integrity.ge.com.

34. Interviews with Nell Newman and Peter Meehan, co-founders of Newman's Own Organic, 2007.

35. Suzanne Vranica, "Tweeting to Sell Cars," *The Wall Street Journal*, November 14, 2010; http://business.ftc.gov/documents/bus71-ftcs-revised-endorsement-guideswhat-people-are-asking; Gary Hoffman, "Selling Cars on Twitter," AOL Autos, August 10, 2010.

36. Andrew J. Blumberg and Peter Eckerdsly, "On Locational Privacy, and How to Avoid Losing It Forever," Electronic Frontier Foundation White Paper, August 2009, http://www.eff.org/wp/locational-privacy.

37. http://www.aboutmcdonalds.com/mcd/sustainability/2011_sustainability_scorecard.html

38. The most famous proponent of this view was Milton Friedman. See for example *Capitalism and Freedom* (Chicago: University of Chicago Press, 2002) or *Free to Choose: A Personal Statement* (Orlando, FL: Harcourt, 1990).

39. Dan Amos, "Aflac's Ethics in Action: Pay for Performance—Keep Stakeholders Informed," January 12, 2009, http://ethisphere.com/aflacs-ethics-in-action-pay-for-performance-keep-stakeholders-informed/

40. James Townsend, "Smart Choice Program Set to Begin," *Functional Ingredients*, June 23, 2009.

41. Frito-Lay, "Straight Talk on Snacking," http://www.fritolay.com/your-health/feature-answers.html; Mike Esterl, "Can This Chip Be Saved?" *The Wall Street Journal*, March 24, 2011, http://online.wsj.com/article/SB100014240527487040502045762184926 08111416.html.

42. http://www.ge.com/news/our_viewpoints/energy_and_climate .html; "GE Launches New Ecomagination Healthcare Products, Opens Renewable Energy HQ," February 2, 2010, http://www .greenbiz.com/news/2010/02/02/ge-launches-new-ecomagination-healthcare-products-opens-renewable-energy-hq#ixzz0lsaVqopP.

43. D.B. Bielak, S. Bonini, and J.M. Oppenheim,"CEOs on Strategy and Social Issues", *McKinsey Quarterly*, 2007, http://www.mckinsey-quarterly.com.

44. http://www.marketingpower.com/_layouts/Dictionary.aspx ?dLetter=D (accessed January 18, 2010).

45. This case was written by Catharine Curran-Kelly (University of Massachusetts at Dartmouth) in conjunction with the textbook authors (Dhruv Grewal and Michael Levy) as the basis of class discussion rather than to illustrate either effective or ineffective marketing practice.

Appendix 4A

46. Michael Felberbaum, "Panel to Examine Menthol Cigarettes' Impact," *Associated Press*, March 29, 2010.

47. Ibid., based on a study by the Substance Abuse and Mental Health Services Administration in November, 2009.

48. Department of Justice, Office of Public Affairs, "Daimler AG and Three Subsidiaries Resolve Foreign Corrupt Practices Act Investigation and Agree to Pay $93.6 Million in Criminal Penalties," press release, April 1, 2010; Michael Connor, "Daimler Agrees to Pay $185 Million to Settle Bribery Charges," *Business Ethics*, March 26, 2010, http://business-ethics.com/2010/03/26/1354-daimler-to-pay_185-million-to-settle-bribery-charges/.

49. Emily Steel, "How Marketers Hone Their Aim Online," *The Wall Street Journal*, June 19, 2007, p. B6.

50. "Mr. Mackey's Offense," *The Wall Street Journal*, July 16, 2007, p. A12.

Chapter 5

1. http://www.thecoolhunter.net/architecture, November 3, 2011.

2. http://www.thecoolhunter.net/lifestyle, September 7, 2011.

3. http://www.trendhunter.com/join.

4. Michael Hines, "Smelly Billboards," http://www.trendhunter.com/trends/steak-scented-billboard.

5. Alex Scott, "Guerilla Socialvertising," http://www.trendhunter .com/trends/alex-seo-crisis-campaign.

6. Katherine Vong, "Guerilla Asphalt Garden," http://www.trend-hunter.com/trends/guerilla-asphalt-gardens.

7. Peter F. Drucker, *The Essential Drucker* (New York: Harper Collins, 2001).

8. Linda Doell, "In Razor vs. Razor, Neither Gillette Nor Schick Gains Edge With Ad Watchdog," March 17, 2011, http://www.daily finance.com/2011/03/17/in-razor-vs-razor-neither-gillette-nor-schick-gains-edge-with/.

9. http://www.nau.com; Chris Dannen, "Wanted: The Light, Recycled Trench," *Fast Company*, November 19, 2010, http://www.fastcompany.com/1703910/wanted-the-light-recycled-trench; Polly Labarre, "Leap of Faith," *Fast Company*, June 2007.

10. http://www.coolhunting.com/style/waterproof-parka-shells.php.

11. Del I. Hawkins, David L. Mothersbaugh, *Consumer Behavior: Building Marketing Strategy*, 11e, Burr Ridge, IL: McGraw-Hill/ Irwin, 2009.; Cateora, Philip and John Graham, *International Marketing*, 13e, Burr Ridge, IL: McGraw-Hill/Irwin, 2006.

12. http://popvssoda.com/.

13. www.drpepper.com.

14. "Corporate Responsibility," http://info.cvscaremark.com/our-company/corporate-responsibility.

15. Geoffrey E. Meredith, Charles D. Schewe, and Janice Karlovich, *Defining Markets, Defining Moments: America's 7 Generational Cohorts, Their Shared Experiences, and Why Businesses Should Care*. New York: Wiley, 2002.

16. "Consumers of Tomorrow: Insights and Observations about Generation Z," Grail Research, June 2010.

17. Suzy Menkes, "Marketing to the Millennials," *The New York Times*, March 2, 2010; Pamela Paul, "Getting Inside Gen Y," *American Demographics* 23, no. 9; Sharon Jayson, "A Detailed Look at the Millenials," *USA Today*, February 23, 2010.

18. Wendy Wang and Paul Taylor, "For Millenials, Parenthood Trumps Marriage," March 9, 2011, http://www.pewsocialtrends .org/2011/03/09/for-millennials-parenthood-trumps-marriage/1/.

19. Brenda Wells, "Truly Understanding Millenials," September 2011, http://www.irmi.com/expert/articles/2011/wells09-insurance-industry-risk-management-insurance-education.aspx.

20. Julia B. Issacs, *Economic Mobility of Families Across Generations*, http://www.economicmobility.org/assets/pdfs/EMP _ES_Across_Generations.pdf.

21. "Baby Boomers, Gen X and Gen Y (Consumer Patterns, Behaviors, Lifestyles and Demographics): How Generations Are Changing the Face of Consumer Goods Market," March 10, 2009, http: //www.smartbrief.com/news/aaaa/industryBW-detail .jsp?id=98D8B421-C1B2-4ADF-BB75-5041373C3BB1.

22. Brian Braiker, "The Next Great American Consumer," *Adweek*, September 26, 2011, http://www.adweek.com/news/advertising-branding/next-great-american-consumer-135207?page=1.

23. Dan Hardy, "To Balance Budgets, Schools Allow Ads," October 16, 2011, http://articles.philly.com/2011-10-16/news/30286428_1 _pennsbury-ads-middle-and-high-school; Tonyaa Wethersby, "Ad on School Busses a Tacky Idea," October 5, 2011, http://jackson-ville.com/opinion/columnists/2011-10-06/story/ads-school-buses-tacky-idea.

24. "That Facebook Friend Might be 10 Years Old, and Other Troubling News," *Consumer Reports*, June 2011, http://www.consumer reports.org/cro/magazine-archive/2011/june/electronics-comput-ers/state-of-the-net/facebook-concerns/index.htm; Matt Richtel and Miguel Helft, "Facebook Users Who Are Underage Raise Concerns," *The New York Times*, March 12, 2011, http://www .nytimes.com/2011/03/12/technology/internet/12underage.html? _r=1&ref=magazine.

25. Emily Bazelon, "Why Facebook Is After Your Kids," *The New York Times*, October 12, 2011, http://www.nytimes.com/2011/10/16 /magazine/why-facebook-is-after-your-kids.html?_r=3.

26. Yale Rudd Center for Food Policy and Obesity, "Sugary Drink Facts," report, October 2011.

27. Ibid.

28. Meredith et al., *Defining Markets, Defining Moments*.

29. Robert Brown and Ruth Washton, "Healthy 50+ Americans: Trends and Opportunities in the Emerging Wellness Market," April 1911, Rockville, MD: Packaged Facts

30. Rieva Lesonsky, "Small Retailers: Don't Ignore Senior Consumers," *Retail Trends*, October 26, 2011.

31. U.S. Census Bureau, "Income, Poverty, and Health Insurance Coverage in the United States, 2010," http://www.census.gov /newsroom/releases/archives/income_wealth/cb11-157.html.

32. Dave Gilson and Carolyn Perot, "It's the Inequality, Stupid," *Mother Jones* (March/April 2011), http://motherjones.com/politics/2011/02 /income-inequality-in-america-chart-graph; OECD, "Growing Unequal? Income Distribution and Poverty in OECD Countries," 2008, http://www.oecd.org/dataoecd/47/2/41528678.pdf.

33. http://www.Hammacher.com.

34. http://www.census.gov/population/www/socdemo/education/cps2009.html; http://www.infoplease.com/ipa/A0883617.html.

35. Bureau of Labor Statistics, "Education Pays," May 4, 2011, http://www.bls.gov/emp/ep_chart_001.htm/.

36. http://inside.nike.com/blogs/nikerunning_events-en_US/?tags=nike_womens_marathon_2010.

37. Tom Pirovano, "U.S. Demographics Are Changing . . . Are Your Marketing Plans Ready?" *NielsenWire*, March 10, 2010, http://blog.nielsen.com/nielsenwire/consumer/u-s-demographics-are-changing-are-your-marketing-plans-ready; "Cents and Sensibility: Why Marketing to Multicultural Consumers Requires a Subtle Touch," *Knowledge@Wharton*, March 10, 2010 http://www.wharton.universia.net/index.cfm?fa=viewArticle&id=1855&language=english; "Ethnic Consumers Hold $282 Billion in Purchasing Power," February 24, 2009, http://news.newamerica-media.org/news/view_article.html?article_id=d4fb122372537fa407312301f85e5446.

38. Jeffrey S. Passel and D'Vera Cohn, "U.S. Population Projections: 2005–2050," Pew Research Center, http://pewhispanic.org/files/reports/85.pdf.

39. Joel Kotkin, "The Changing Demographics of America," *Smithsonian Magazine* (August 2010), http://www.smithsonian-mag.com/specialsections/40th-anniversary/The-Changing-Demographics-of-America.html?c=y&page=2.

40. Julie Jargon, "Pizza Chain Seeks Slice of Bicultural Pie," *WSJ.com*, December 30, 2010.

41. Robert Brown and Ruth Washton "Latino Consumers: Demographic Patterns and Spending Trends among Hispanic Americans," 8th Edition, Rockville, MD: Packaged Facts, January 2011.

42. Richard Westlund, "Finding the Gold in Hispanic Marketing," *Adweek*, July 27, 2010, http://www.adweek.com/sa-article/finding-gold-hispanic-marketing-130612.

43. Todd Wasserman, "Report: Shifting African American Population," *Adweek*, January 12, 2010, http://www.adweek.com/news/advertising-branding/report-shifting-african-american-population-114439; U.S. Census Bureau, "Annual Social and Economic Supplement to the Current Population Survey," http://www.census.gov/population/www/socdemo/race/black.html.

44. Nielsen, "The State of the African-American Consumer," September 2011, p. 5.

45. Leah Ingram, "Suddenly Frugal," http://www.suddenlyfrugal.com/; Brad Tuttle, "Cash Crunch: Why Extreme Thriftiness Stunts Are the Rage," *Time*, April 5, 2010, http://www.time.com/time/magazine/article/0,9171,1975323-2,00.html.

46. Stephanie Clifford and Andrew Martin, "In Time of Scrimping, Fun Stuff Is Still Selling," *The New York Times*, September 23, 2011, http://www.nytimes.com/2011/09/24/business/consumers-cut-back-on-staples-but-splurge-on-indulgences.html?_r=1&ref=consumerbehavior. Brad Tuttle. "Smart Spending: Consumer Phrase of the Day: 'Lipstick Effect'," Time, April 19, 2011,: http://moneyland.time.com/2011/04/19/consumer-phrase-of-the-day-lipstick-effect/#ixzz1flspJeob

http://moneyland.time.com/2011/04/19/consumer-phrase-of-the-day-lipstick-effect/

47. Laura T. Coffey, "Extreme Couponing! How to Get $1,100 of Merchandise for $40," Today.com, April 6, 2011, http://today.msnbc.msn.com/id/42419291/ns/today-money/t/extreme-couponing-how-get-merchandise/#.TtTjYWA79U0.

48. *Extreme Couponing*, http://tlc.discovery.com/videos/extreme-couponing/; Jon Caramanica, "Miles of Aisles, Endless Opportunities to Save," *The New York Times*, April 5, 2011. http://tv.nytimes.com/2011/04/06/arts/television/extreme-couponing-on-tlc-review.html.

49. EJ Schultz, "Retailers Start to Suffer Super-Couponer Fatigue," *Advertising Age*, July 11, 2011.

50. Seth Fiegerman, 'Deal Burnout: Too Many Discounts?" *The Street*, August 8, 2011.

51. Centers for Disease Control and Prevention, "National Diabetes Fact Sheet, 2011," http://www.cdc.gov/diabetes/pubs/pdf/ndfs_2011.pdf.

52. "Guidelines for Marketing Food to Kids Proposed," CSPI Press Release, January 5, 2005.

53. Yoga Buzz, "Yoga Biz Thrives Despite Economy," October 24, 2011, http://blogs.yogajournal.com/yogabuzz/page/2.

54. Catherine Clifford, "Yoga: The Booming Business of Zen," CNNMoney, October 18, 2011, http://money.cnn.com/2011/10/18/smallbusiness/yoga_pilates/.

55. This definition of green marketing draws on work by Jacquelyn A. Ottman, *Green Marketing: Opportunity for Innovation* (Chicago: NTC Publishing, 1997).

56. http://www.sunchips.com/healthier_planet.shtml.

57. "Sustainable Packaging: PUMA's Launches new Green Packaging and Distribution," *Packaging Digest*, April 13, 2010.

58. "PUMA.safe Launches New Sustainable Packaging Designed by Yves Behar,"http://vision.puma.com/us/en/2010/04/puma-launches-new-sustainable-packaging-designed-by-yves-behar/.

59. "The Dieline Awards 2011: Best of Show—Puma Clever Little Bag," http://www.thedieline.com/blog/2011/6/24/the-dieline-awards-2011-best-of-show-puma-clever-little-bag.html ; "PUMA a Winner at Innovation and Design Awards," http://vision.puma.com/us/en/2011/05/puma-a-winner-at-innovation-and-design-awards/.

60. "The New Puma Fusesafe Packaging," YouTube.com, http://www.youtube.com/watch?v=vwRulz8hPKI.

61. Matt Liebowitz, "2011 Set to Be Worst Year Ever for Security Breaches," *Security News Daily*, June 9, 2011, http://www.securitynewsdaily.com/2011-worst-year-ever-security-breaches-0857/.

62. http://www.ftc.gov/opa/2008/04/dncfyi.shtm; http://www.ftc.gov/os/2010/12/101206dncdatabook.pdf.

63. Bureau of Labor Statistics, "American Time Use Survey Summary," http://www.bls.gov/news.release/atus.nr0.htm; Martin Peers, "Buddy, Can You Spare Some Time?" *The Wall Street Journal*, January 26, 2004, pp. B1, B3; additional statistics from Harris Interactive.

64. http://www.safeway.com/ShopStores/Signature-Cafe.page; http://phx.corporate-ir.net/External.File?item=UGFyZW50SUQ9OTQ1MjI8Q2hpbGRJRDOtMXxUeXBlPTM=&t=1; "Safeway CEO Steve Burd Says Fresh, Prepared Food Sales at $100 Million Annually," February 25, 2010, http://freshneasybuzz.blogspot.com/2010/02/safeway-ceo-burd-says-fresh-prepared.html.

65. Doug Sovern, "Walgreens Opens First 'Fresh Food Oasis' in Underserved San Francisco Neighborhood," July 8, 2011, http://sanfrancisco.cbslocal.com/2011/07/08/walgreens-opens-first-fresh-food-oasis-in-underserved-san-francisco-neighborhood/; http://news.walgreens.com/article_display.cfm?article_id=5451.

66. http://news.walgreens.com/article_display.cfm?article_id=5515.

67. http://www.bravotv.com/top-chef/season-9/top-chef-healthy-showdown/healthy-marriage; https://secure.shopbybravo.com/kitchen-utensils-gadgets/index.php?v=bravo_shows_top-chef_kitchen-utensils-and-gadgets&icid=herobanner4_TC-tools_110811

68. "What Is Foursquare?" https://foursquare.com/about. Membership data as of April 2011.

69. Mark Didas, "Market Your Regional Product or Service with Foursquare," http://www.wavespawn.com/market-regional-product-service-foursquare.

70. "About Foursquare," https://foursquare.com/about/; "Facebook Introduces Check-in Feature," CNN.com, August 18, 2010.

71. Marianne Wilson, "Growing Power of Mobile," *Chain Store Age*, December 2010; Deena M.Amato-McCoy, "Focus on: The Mobile Channel," *Chain Store Age*, March 2011.

72. William L. Watts and Lisa Twaronite, "Dollar Sags as Bernanke Cites Growth Risks," *MarketWatch*, July 15, 2008.

73. Catherine Rampell, "The Euro Zone Crisis and the U.S.: A Primer," *The New York Times*, November 14, 2011, http://economix.blogs.nytimes.com/2011/11/14/the-euro-zone-crisis-and-the-u-s-a-primer/.

74. Brendan Greeley, "Providing Internet Access to the Poor," *Bloomberg Businessweek*, November 17, 2011, http://www.businessweek.com/magazine/providing-internet-access-to-the-poor-11172011.html?chan=magazine+technology+channel_news+-+politics+%26amp%3b+policy.

75. Ashley Lutz, "Lululemon Envy Has Retailers From Gap to Nordstrom Chasing Yoga Devotees," *Bloomberg*, September 9, 2011; Ian Austin, "Lululemon Athletica Combines Ayn Rand and Yoga," *The New York Times*, November 27, 2011, http://www.nytimes.com/2011/11/28/business/media/combines-ayn-rand-and-yoga.html.

76. http://www.seventhgeneration.com.

77. "Seventh Gen, Whole Foods Top Green Brands Ranking," *Environmental Leader*, June 10, 2011, http://www.environmental-leader.com/2011/06/10/seventh-gen-whole-foods-top-green-brands-ranking/?graph=full&id=1.

78. "The Best Cleaning Products," *Real Simple*, http://www.realsimple.com/magazine-more/inside-website/daily-finds/best-cleaning-products-00000000033167/page2.html

79. Andrew Adam Newman, "Seventh Generation Highlights Its Chemical-Free Detergent," *The New York Times*, December 29, 2010, http://www.nytimes.com/2010/12/30/business/media/30adco.html; "Seventh Generation Promotes Eco-Friendly Detergents Through Multichannel Marketing Initiative," December 30, 2010, http://www.ricg.com/marketing_articles/digital_marketing/seventh_generation_promotes_eco_friendly_detergents_through_multichannel_marketing_initiative/.

80. Dan D'Ambrosio, "Seventh Generation Looks to Buck Trend in Concentrated Laundry Detergent Market," *Burlington Free Press*, October 13, 2011, http://www.burlingtonfreepress.com/article/20111013/BUSINESS08/111012021/Seventh-Generation-looks-buck-trend-concentrated-laundry-detergent-market.

Chapter 6

1. Natasha Singer, "On Campus, It's One Big Commercial," *The New York Times*, September 10, 2011.

2. Paul Vlasic, "Via Zipcar, Ford Seeks Young Fans," *The New York Times*, August 31, 2011.

3. James R. Healey, "Ford and Zipcar Court College Kids with High-Tech Focus," *USA Today*, August 31, 2011.

4. J. Jeffrey Inman, Russell S. Winer, and Rosella Ferraro, "The Interplay Among Category Characteristics, Customer Characteristics, and Customer Activities on In-Store Decision Making," *Journal of Marketing* 73, no. 5 (September 2009), pp. 19–29.

5. For example, when trying on a dress, Katie might be influenced by the way that same dress looks on a salesperson in the store. See Darren W. Dahl, Jennifer J. Argo, and Andrea C. Morales. "Social Information in the Retail Environment: The Importance of Consumption Alignment, Referent Identity, and Self-Esteem." *Journal of Consumer Research*, (February 2012), in press.

6. For a detailed discussion of customer behavior, see J. Paul Peter and Jerry C. Olson, *Consumer Behavior and Marketing Strategy*, 9th ed. (New York: McGraw-Hill, 2009).

7. Martin R Lautman and Koen Pauwels, "Metrics That Matter: Identifying the Importance of Consumer Wants and Needs," *Journal of Advertising Research*, 49, no. 3 (2009), 339–359.

8. Liz C. Wang, Julie Baker, Judy A. Wagner, and Kirk Wakefield, "Can a Retail Web Site Be Social?" *Journal of Marketing* 71, no. 3 (2007), pp. 143–57; Barry Babin, William Darden, and Mitch Griffin, "Work and/or Fun: Measuring Hedonic and Utilitarian Shopping Value," *Journal of Consumer Research* 20 (March 1994), pp. 644–56.

9. Jing Xu and Norbert Schwarz, "Do We Really Need a Reason to Indulge?" *Journal of Marketing Research* 46, no. 1 (February 2009), pp. 25–36.

10. "Christian Louboutin Styles for the Uptown Girl," http://www.newshoefashion.com/; "Celebrities Who Love Christian Louboutin Shoes," http://fashion.telegraph.co.uk/galleries/TMG8437766/1/Celebrities-who-love-Christian-Louboutin-shoes.html; Cindy Clark, "Christian Louboutin's Red-Soled Shoes Are Red-Hot," *USA Today*, http://www.usatoday.com/life/lifestyle/fashion/2007-12-25-louboutin-shoes_N.htm.

11. Ruth La Ferla, "The Campus as Runway," *The New York Times*, October 12, 2011.

12. http://www.signature9.com/fashion/the-20-million-dollar-fashion-blog-refinery29-projects-400-revenue-growth.

13. http://www.collegefashion.net.

14. "Quiz: Which Celebrity Is Your Style Icon?" http://www.collegefashion.net/inspiration/quiz-which-celebrity-is-your-style-icon/.

15. Ibid.

16. http://www.signature9.com/fashion/the-20-million-dollar-fashion-blog-refinery29-projects-400-revenue-growth.

17. Peng Huang, Nicholas H. Lurie, and Sabyasachi Mitra, "Searching for Experience on the Web: An Empirical Examination of Consumer Behavior for Search and Experience Goods," *Journal of Marketing* 73, no. 2 (March 2009), pp. 55–69.

18. http://store.cwtv.com/detail.php?p=146017&v=cwtv_shows_gossip-girl_character_vanessa&pagemax=all.

19. http://www.lnaclothing.com/WOMENatLNAClothing-CID235.aspx.

20. http://www.mytruefit.com.

21. Ying Zhang, Jing Xu, Zixi Jiang, and Szu-chi Huang. "Been There, Done That: The Impact of Effort Investment on Goal Value and Consumer Motivation." *Journal of Consumer Research*, 38, no. 1 (June 2011), pp. 78-93.

22. Debabrata Talukdar, "Cost of Being Poor: Retail Price and Consumer Price Search Differences Across Inner-City and Suburban Neighborhoods," *Journal of Consumer Research* 35, no. 3 (October 2008), pp. 457–71.

23. David Dubois, Derek D. Rucker, and Adam D. Galinsky. "Super Size Me: Product Size as a Signal of Status," *Journal of Consumer Research*, April 2012, in press.

24. Diane M. Gibson, "Food Stamps and Obesity," *The New York Times*, September 27, 2011, http://www.nytimes.com/roomfordebate/2011/09/27/expand-the-use-of-food-stamps/the-link-between-food-stamps-and-obesity.

25. Jane E. Brody, "Attacking the Obesity Epidemic by First Figuring Out Its Cause," *The New York Times*, September 12, 2011, http://www.nytimes.com/2011/09/13/health/13brody.html?pagewanted=all

26. Ibid.

27. "Burger King Joins McDonald's in Charging for Kids' Meal Toys to Comply with San Francisco Ban," *Washington Post*, December 1, 2011, http://www.washingtonpost.com/business/burger-king-joins-mcdonalds-in-charging-for-kids-meal-toys-to-comply-with-san-francisco-ban/2011/12/01/gIQAlk7kGO_story.html.

28. Benjamin Scheibehenne, Rainer Greifeneder, and Peter M. Todd. "Can There Ever Be Too Many Options? A Meta-Analytic Review of Choice Overload," *Journal of Consumer Research* 37, no. 3 (October 2010), pp. 409–45.

29. The term *determinance* was first coined by James Myers and Mark Alpert nearly three decades ago; http://www.sawtoothsoftware.com/productforms/ssolutions/ss12.shtml.

30. 2011 U.S. Organic Industry Overview, Organic Trade Association, http://www.ota.com/pics/documents/2011OrganicIndustrySurvey.pdf.

31. Ashby Jones, "Is Your Dinner 'All Natural'?," *The Wall Street Journal,* September 20, 2011; "Diet and Nutrition Report," *Consumer Reports,* February 2009, http://www.consumerreports.org/health/healthy-living/diet-nutrition/healthy-foods/grocery-aisle-gotchas/natural/grocery-aisle-gotchas-natural.htm.

32. Rachel Gross, "Farmers Seek to Raise Standards for Berries," *The New York Times,* September 23, 2011, http://www.nytimes.com/2011/09/23/us/farmers-seek-to-raise-standards-for-berries.html?pagewanted=all.

33. Mayo Clinic Staff, "Organic Foods: Are They Safer? More Nutritious?" http://www.mayoclinic.com/health/organic-food/NU00255.

34. Gross, op. cit.

35. Natural and Organic Foods Backgrounder, Food Marketing Institute, http://www.fmi.org/media/bg/natural_organic_foods.pdf.

36. Stacey R. Finkelstein and Ayelet Fishbach, "When Healthy Food Makes You Hungry," *Journal of Consumer Research* 37, no. 3 (October 2010) pp. 357-67.

37. http://www.sawtoothsoftware.com/productforms/ssolutions/ss12.shtml.

38. Julie R. Irwin and Rebecca Walker Naylor, "Ethical Decisions and Response Mode Compatibility: Weighting of Ethical Attributes in Consideration Sets Formed by Excluding Versus Including Product Alternatives," *Journal of Marketing Research* 46, no. 2 (April 2009), pp. 234–46; Richard Lutz, "Changing Brand Attitudes through Modification of Cognitive Structure," *Journal of Consumer Research* 1, no. 1 (1975), pp. 125–36.

39. Caroline Goukens, Siegfried Dewitte, and Luk Warlop, "Me, Myself, and My Choices: The Influence of Private Self-Awareness on Choice," *Journal of Marketing Research* 46, no. 5 (October 2009), pp. 682–92.

40. Emili Vesilind, "MAC Cosmetics launches technology that lets you e-shop with your friends," *LATimes.com,* April 27, 2011; Tyna Werner, "MAC Shop Together – shopping buddies around the world unite!," *weheartthis.com,* May 4, 2011; "Shoping With Friends: The Ultimate Shopping Experience, http://www.janrain.com/blogs/shopping-friends-ultimate-shopping-experience; http://www.decisionstep.com/solutions/social-shopping/shoptogether-friends/; maccosmetics.com; http://www.sesh.com/; http://www.wetseal.com/content.jsp?pageName=ShopWithFriends; "New Shopping App Lets Facebook Friends Help You Decide," The Realtime Report, November 15, 2011, http://therealtimereport.com/2011/11/15/new-shopping-app-lets-facebook-friends-help-you-decide/.

41. Ruby Roy Dholakia and Miao Zhao, "Retail Web Site Interactivity: How Does It Influence Customer Satisfaction and Behavioral Intentions? *International Journal of Retail & Distribution Management,* 37, 2009, pp. 821 - 838

42. "30 Under 30 2011: Where Are They Now?" http://www.inc.com/ss/30-under-30-2011-where-are-they-now#1; http://www.renttherunway.com.

43. Brooks Barnes, "A Bid to Get Film Lovers Not to Rent," *The New York Times,* November 11, 2011, http://www.nytimes.com/2011/11/12/business/media/with-flixster-studios-bet-consumers-will-buy-movies-again.html?_r=2&adxnnl=1&ref=consumerbehavior&adxnnlx=1323184510-oduUDsCsTCg7Ms1Wl7HZTg.

44. Claire Cain Miller, "Closing The Deal At The Virtual Checkout Counter," *New York Times,* October 12, 2009.

45. "Beware of Dissatisfied Consumers: They Like to Blab," *Knowledge@Wharton,* March, 8, 2006, based on the "Retail Customer Dissatisfaction Study 2006" conducted by the Jay H. Baker Retailing Initiative at Wharton and The Verde Group.

46. Goutam Challagalla, R. Venkatesh, and Ajay K. Kohli, "Proactive Postsales Service: When and Why Does It Pay Off?" *Journal of Marketing* 73, no. 2 (March 2009), pp. 70–87.

47. Randall Stross, "Consumer Complaints Made Easy. Maybe Too Easy," *The New York Times,* May 28, 2011, http://www.nytimes.com/2011/05/29/technology/29digi.html.

48. For a more extensive discussion on these factors, see Banwari Mittal, *Consumer Behavior* (Cincinnati, OH: Open Mentis, 2008); Peter and Olson, *Consumer Behavior and Marketing.*

49. A. H. Maslow, *Motivation and Personality* (New York: Harper & Row, 1970).

50. Kelly D. Martin and Ronald Paul Hill. "Life Satisfaction, Self-Determination, and Consumption Adequacy at the Bottom-of-the-Pyramid," *Journal of Consumer Research,* April 2012, in press; Hazel Rose Markus and Barry Schwartz, "Does Choice Mean Freedom and Well-Being?" *Journal of Consumer Research* 37, no. 2 (August 2010), pp. 344–55.

51. Stacy Wood, "The Comfort Food Fallacy: Avoiding Old Favorites in Times of Change," *Journal of Consumer Research* 36, no. 6 (April 2010), pp. 950–63; Stacey Finkelstein and Ayelet Fishbach, "When Healthy Food Makes You Hungry," *Journal of Consumer Research* 37, no. 3 (October 2010), pp. 357–67.

52. Lee, Amir, and Ariely, "In Search of Homo Economicus"; Anish Nagpal and Parthasarathy Krishnamurthy, "Attribute Conflict in Consumer Decision Making: The Role of Task Compatibility," *Journal of Consumer Research* 34, no. 5 (February 2008), pp. 696–705.

53. http://www.bostonbackbay.com/.

54. For more discussion on these factors, see: Mittal, *Consumer Behavior;* Peter and Olson, *Consumer Behavior and Marketing Strategy;* Michael Levy and Barton A. Weitz, *Retailing Management,* 7th ed. (Burr Ridge IL: Irwin/McGraw-Hill, 2009), chapter 4.

55. Juliano Laran, "Goal Management in Sequential Choices: Consumer Choices for Others Are More Indulgent than Personal Choices," *Journal of Consumer Research* 37, no. 2 (August 2010), pp. 304–14.

56. "Retailers Must Understand Modern Family Buying Decisions," http://www.articlesnatch.com/Article/Retailers-Must-Understand-Modern-Family-Buying-Decisions/2437285; http://www.entrepreneur.com/startingabusiness/businessideas/startupkits/article190444.html.

57. "The Power of the Grandparent Economy," http://www.grandparents.com/gp/content/newsoftheday/news/article/the-power-of-the-grandparent-economy.html.

58. Todd Hale, "Mining the U.S. Generation Gaps," *Nielsen Wire,* March 4, 2010, http://blog.nielsen.com/nielsenwire/consumer/mining-the-u-s-generation-gaps/

59. Morgan K. Ward and Susan Bronziarczyk, "It's Not Me, It's You: How Gift Giving Creates Giver Identity Threat as a Function of Social Closeness," *Journal of Consumer Research* 38, no. 1 (June 2011), pp. 164–81.

60. Dahl et al., "Social Information in the Retail Environment," op. cit.

61. For a greater discussion on these factors, see Mittal, *Consumer Behavior;* Peter and Olson, *Consumer Behavior and Marketing Strategy.*

62. The concept of atmospherics was introduced by Philip Kotler, "Atmosphere as a Marketing Tool," *Journal of Retailing,* 49 (Winter 1973), pp. 48–64.

63. Sylvie Morin, Laurette Dubé and Jean-Charles Chebat, "The Role of Pleasant Music in Servicescapes: A Test of the Dual Model of Environmental Perception," *Journal of Retailing,* 83, no. 1 (2007), pp. 115–130.

64. www.wegmans.com; http://wholefoodsmarket.com/stores/cooking-classes/; Tracy Turner, "New Hangout Supermarket," *Columbus Dispatch*, March 20, 2011.

65. Alexander Chernev and Ryan Hamilton, "Assortment Size and Option Attractiveness in Consumer Choice Among Retailers," *Journal of Marketing Research* 46, no. 3 (June 2009), pp. 410–20; Marc-Andre Kamel, Nick Greenspan, and Rudolf Pritzl, "Standardization Is Efficient but Localization Helps Shops to Stand Out," *The Wall Street Journal*, January 21, 2009.

66. Jeffrey Trachtenberg, "Publishers Bundle E-Books to Boost Sales, Promote Authors," *The Wall Street Journal*, February 11, 2011.

67. Pierre Chandon, J. Wesley Hutchinson, Eric T. Bradlow, and Scott H. Young, "Does In-Store Marketing Work? Effects of the Number and Position of Shelf Facings on Brand Attention and Evaluation at the Point of Purchase," *Journal of Marketing* 73, no. 6 (November 2009), pp. 1–17.

68. Dan King and Chris Janiszewski, "Affect-Gating," *Journal of Consumer Research* 38, no. 4 (December 2011), pp. 697–711.

69. Christine Birkner, "Thinking Outside of the Box," *Marketing News*, March 30, 2011.

70. Mittal, *Consumer Behavior*; Peter and Olson, *Consumer Behavior and Marketing Strategy*.

71. Karen M. Stilley, J. Jeffrey Inman, and Kirk L. Wakefield, "Planning to Make Unplanned Purchases? The Role of In "Store Slack in Budget Deviation," *Journal of Consumer Research*, DOI: 10.1086/651567.

72. This case was written by Kate Woodworth in conjunction with Dhruv Grewal and Michael Levy as the basis of class discussion rather than to illustrate either effective or ineffective marketing practices.

73. Lydia Saad, "To Lose Weight, Americans Rely More on Dieting than Exercise," Gallup, November 28, 2011, http://www.gallup.com/poll/150986/lose-weight-americans-rely-dieting-exercise.aspx; Vauhini Vara, "New Gadgets Aim to Help Users Watch Their Weight," *The Wall Street Journal*, May 12, 2005.

74. "U.S. Weight Loss Market Worth $60.9 Billion," May 9, 2011, http://www.prweb.com/releases/2011/5/prweb8393658.htm.

75. All About: Weight Loss and Diet Plans, http://www.aa-lose-weight-loss-diet-plans.com/diet-comparison/weight-watchers-jenny-craig.html.

76. http://www.weightwatchers.com/util/art/index_art.aspx?tabnum=1&art_id=105421&sc=3002.

77. Chris Moran, "Jenny Craig Beats Out Weight Watchers For Top Spot in Consumer Reports Health Ratings," May 10, 2011, http://consumerist.com/2011/05/jenny-craig-beats-out-weight-watchers-for-top-spot-in-consumer-reports-health-ratings.html; http://jennycraig.com/programs/.

78. Jennifer Fermino, "Jenny Craig Is Top Heavy Hitter," *New York Post*, May 10, 2011,http://www.nypost.com/p/news/national/craig_is_top_heavy_hitter_Le5SprctcoGlp93YLL55XJ.

79. http://www.slim-fast.com/plan/.

80. Maura Shenker, "Men's Slim-Fast Diet Health," Livestrong.com, July 20, 2011, http://www.livestrong.com/article/497109-mens-slim-fast-diet-health/.

81. Dave McGinn, "The Changing Face of Male Wight Loss," *The Globe and Mail*, December 23, 2010, http://www.theglobeandmail.com/life/health/the-changing-face-of-male-weight-loss/article1446724/; Jennifer LaRue Huget, "Weight Watchers and Jenny Craig Offer Programs for Men Who Want to Shed Pounds," *The Washington Post*, March 25, 2010; All About, op. cit.; Moran, op. cit.; Fermino, op. cit.

82. http://www.bestdietforme.com/top60dietreviews/SlimFast.htm.

Chapter 7

1. Leslie Kaufman, "Stone Washed Blue Jeans (Minus the Wash), *The New York Times*, November 1, 2011, http://www.nytimes.com/2011/11/02/science/earth/levi-strauss-tries-to-minimize-water-use.html?pagewanted=all.

2. Ibid.

3. Ibid.

4. "Cotton/Raw Materials," http://www.levistrauss.com/sustainability/product/cottonraw-materials.

5. "Worker Rights," http://www.levistrauss.com/sustainability/people/worker-rights.

6. Christina Binkley, "How Green Are Your Jeans?" *The Wall Street Journal, Classroom Edition*, October 2010, http://wsjclassroom.com/cre/articles/10oct_cs_envi_greenjeans.htm.

7. Arun Sharma, R. Krishnan, and Dhruv Grewal, "Value Creation in Markets: A Critical Area of Focus for Business-to-Business Markets," *Industrial Marketing Management*, 30, no. 4 (2001), pp. 391–402.

8. http://www.intel.com/content/www/us/en/homepage.html#.

9. http://www.usa.siemens.com/en/about_us/us_business_groups.htm.

10. http://www.volkswagenag.com/vwag/vwcorp/content/en/brands_and_companies/automotive_and_financial.html; Martin Hofmann, Emily-Sue Sloane, and Elena Malykhina, "VW Revs Its B2B Engine," *Optimize*, March 2004, pp. 22–26.

11. http://www.vwgroupsupply.com/b2bpub/zusammenarbeit/kbp/daten_fakten.html.

12. Jayne O'Donnell, "Behind the Bargains at T.J. Maxx, Marshalls," *USA Today*, October 26, 2011.

13. "The Truth about TJ Maxx," http://www.thebudgetbabe.com/archives/916-The-Truth-about-TJ-Maxx.html.

14. Lydia Dishman, "Is TJ Maxx Poised to Scoop Loehmann's Slice of Designer Pie?" CBS Money Watch, February 2, 2010, http://www.cbsnews.com/8301-505123_162-42440123/is-tj-maxx-poised-to-scoop-loehmanns-slice-of-designer-pie/.

15. "T.J. Maxx: The Right Clothes for the Right Price," http://www.thefashionablehousewife.com/08/2009/tj-maxx-the-right-clothes-for-the-right-price/.

16. The Truth about T.J. Maxx," http://www.thebudgetbabe.com/archives/916-The-Truth-about-TJ-Maxx.html.

17. Stephanie Reitz, "Many US Schools Adding iPads, Trimming Textbooks," Yahoo Finance, September 3, 2011, http://finance.yahoo.com/news/Many-US-schools-adding-iPads-apf-1245885050.html.

18. "Do iPads in Schools Change Behavior?" February 22, 2011, http://www.ipadinschools.com/271/do-ipads-in-school-change-behavior/

19. Nick Wingfield, "Once Wary, Apple Warms Up to Business Market," *The New York Times*, November 15, 2011, http://www.nytimes.com/2011/11/16/technology/businesses-too-have-eyes-for-ipads-and-iphones.html?scp=2&sq=business%20to%20business%20marketing%20&st=cse.

20. Rachel King, "Apple Woos Businesses Despite Security Worries," *Bloomberg Businessweek*, July 7, 2010, http://www.msnbc.msn.com/id/38128833/ns/business-us_business/t/apple-woos-businesses-despite-security-worries/.

21. Ibid.; Reitz, op. cit., "Do iPads in Schools Change Behavior," op. cit.; Wingfield, op.cit.

22. Dawn Kawamoto, "iPad 2 Launch Adds Muscle to Apple's Invasion of Corporate America," *Daily Finance*, March 10, 2011, http://www.dailyfinance.com/2011/03/10/ipad-2-launch-adds-muscle-to-apples-invasion-of-corporate-ameri/; Leander Kahney, "iPad May Replace Computers and Textbooks in Schools, Experts

Predict," Cult of Mac, http://www.cultofmac.com/70112/ipad-may-replace-computers-and-textbooks-in-schools-expert-predicts-appli-in-education/.

23. "Budget of the United States Government: Fiscal Year 2012," Executive Office of the United States: Office of Management and Budget.

24. "Budget of the United States Government: Fiscal Year 2012."

25. http://www.hoovers.com/company/Policy_Studies_Inc/rrjyjxi-1.html.

26. "The Social Media RFP: How to Get the Best Results," January 18, 2010, http://hashtagsocialmedia.com/blog/tag/request-for-proposal.

27. David Whitford, "Hired Guns on the Cheap," *Fortune Small Business*, January 3, 2008.

28. http://www.marketingpower.com/live/mg-dictionary-view435.php. These definitions are provided by www.marketingpower.com (the American Marketing Association's website). We have bolded key terms.

29. Sean Silverthorne, "Business Ethics: Pay the Bribe?" CBS Money Watch, http://www.cbsnews.com/8301-505125_162-31540217/business-ethics-pay-the-bribe/.

30. Stephen H. Unger, "Ethical Aspects of Bribing People in Other Countries," http://www1.cs.columbia.edu/~unger/articles/bribery6-98.html.

31. Transparency International, "Bribe Payers Index 2011," http://bpi.transparency.org/; "International Back Scratching," *The Economist*, November 2, 2011, http://www.economist.com/blogs/dailychart/2011/11/bribe-payers-index.

32. Ernst and Young, "European Fraud Survey 2011: Recovery, regulation and integrity,"http://www.ey.com/GL/en/Services/Assurance/Fraud-Investigation---Dispute-Services/European-fraud-survey-2011--recovery--regulation-and-integrity.

33. http://www.goer.state.ny.us/train/onlinelearning/FTMS/500s1.html.

34. Kimberly Maul, "More b-to-b companies Find that Social Media is an Essential Business Platform," PRweekus.com, June 2009; Ellis Booker, "B-to-B marketers Apply Analytics to Social Media," *BtoB*, April 12, 2010; Elisabeth A. Sullivan, "A Long Slog," *Marketing News*, February 28, 2009.

35. LinkedIn Press Center, "About Us," http://press.linkedin.com/about/.

36. Heidi Cohen, "5 LinkedIn Business Goals," March 25, 2011, http://heidicohen.com/linkedin-business-goals/.

37. Maria Tabaka, "How to Launch a LinkedIn Company Page," *Inc.*, April 17, 2011, http://www.inc.com/how-to-launch-a-linkedin-company-page.html.

38. http://www.hootsuite.com.

39. Daniel B. Honigman, "Make a Statement," *Marketing News*, May 1, 2008.

40. Michael Krause, "How Does Oregon Football Keep Winning? Is It the Uniforms?" *Grantland*, August 30, 2011, http://www.grantland.com/story/_/id/6909937/how-does-oregon-football-keep-winning.

41. Barton A. Weitz, Stephen B. Castleberry, and John F. Tanner, *Selling Building Partnerships*, 6th ed. (Burr Ridge, IL: McGraw-Hill/Irwin, 2005), p. 93.

42. Maggie Hira, "How Does a Fashion Buyer Spend a Workday?" http://www.ehow.com/how-does_4601086_fashion-buyer-spend-workday.html; U.S. Department of Labor, http://www.bls.gov/oco/ocos023.htm; Amanda Fortini, "How the Runway Took Off: A Brief History of the Fashion Show," *Slate Magazine*, February 8, 2006.

43. http://www.hubspot.com

44. http://www.hubspot.com/customer-case-studies/.

45. This case was written by Kate Woodworth in conjunction with Dhruv Grewal and Michael Levy as the basis of class discussion rather than to illustrate either effective or ineffective marketing practices.

46. UPS 2010 Sustainability Report, "Sustainability Is...," http://www.sustainability.ups.com/Sustainability?WT.mc_id=iPros_UPS-Green_45809923&WT.srch=1&gclid=CJzOrZuy16wCFQ1x5QodszUEpw.

47. http://www.ups.com/content/corp/companies/index.html#Customer+Solutions.

48. Laura K. Cowan, "Brown Goes Green: UPS Purchases 100 EV Delivery Trucks for Its Next-Gen California Fleet," *inhabitat*, August 30, 2011, http://inhabitat.com/brown-goes-green-ups-purchases-100-ev-delivery-trucks-for-its-next-gen-california-fleet//.

49. National Biodiesel Board, "UPS Goes Green with Biodiesel Switch," June 6, 2011, http://westernfarmpress.com/management/ups-goes-green-biodiesel-switch.

50. UPS, http://www.community.ups.com/Environment/Innovative+Fleets+and+Facilities.

51. Thomas Friedman agrees with this assessment in his best-selling book *The World Is Flat* (New York: Farrar, Straus and Giroux, 2006), in which he cites UPS's supply chain as a prime example of a global "flattener."

52. Sheldon Liber, "FedEx & UPS Challenged by USPS Flat Rates," August 31, 2009.

53. "FedEx Corp. Reports Higher Fourth Quarter Earnings," June 22, 2011, http://investors.fedex.com/phoenix.zhtml?c=73289&p=irol-newsArticle&ID=1585119&highlight=; FedEx, "What's in a Number?" http://media.fedex.designcdt.com/bythenumbers/; http://about.fedex.designcdt.com/our_company/company_information/fedex_corporation.

54. "Is Insourcing the New In Thing?" June 9, 2008, http://www.geekpreneur.com/is-insourcing-the-new-in-thing

55. Gail Tsirulnik, "UPS Debuts B2B Mobile Campaign Targeting Business Decision Makers," MobileMarketer.com, November 26, 2009, http://www.mobilemarketer.com/cms/news/advertising/4730.html.

Chapter 8

1. "McDonald's Sees Strong Revenue on Global Demand," Associated Press, December 8, 2011, http://www.msnbc.msn.com/id/45596583/ns/business-retail/t/mcdonalds-sees-strong-revenue-global-demand/; Annie Gasparro, "Yum Splits India into Separate Division, Names New International CEO," *The Wall Street Journal*, November 23, 2011, http://online.wsj.com/article/SB10001424052970204443404577054332348348586.html.

2. "McDonald's China Plans to Open a New Store Every Day in Four Years," Huffington Post, September 28, 2011, http://www.huffingtonpost.com/2011/07/29/mcdonalds-china-new-stores_n_913071.html.

3. "McDonald's Best Practices," http://bestpractices.mcdonalds.com/sections/1/case_studies/97; Gasparro, op. cit.

4. Julie Jargon, "For Food Delivery, China Calls McDonald's," *The Wall Street Journal*, December 12, 2011, http://online.wsj.com/article/SB1000142405297020439770457707498215154931 6.html.

5. "McDonald's Sees Strong Revenue," op. cit.; Ravi Krishnani, "McDonald's in Russia – Defeated Communism with a 'Happy' Meal," *Business Today*, http://www.businesstoday-eg.com/case-studies/case-studies/mcdonalds-in-russia-defeated-communism-with-a-happy-meal.html; Press Brief, http://www.mcdpressoffice.eu/downloads/pr/2010/Factsheet_Russia_20yr_Anniversary.pdf.

6. Andrew E. Kramer, "Russia's Evolution, Seen Through Golden Arches," *The New York Times*, February 2, 2010, http://www.nytimes.com/2010/02/02/business/global/02mcdonalds.html.

7. Pierre-Richard Agenor, *Does Globalization Hurt the Poor?* (Washington, DC: World Bank, 2002); "Globalization: Threat or Opportunity," International Monetary Fund, http://www.imf.org/external/np/exr/ib/2000/041200.htm#II.

8. For example, the deficit for the month of October 2011 was $43.5 billion. See http://www.census.gov/indicator/www/ustrade.html.

9. http://www.acdi-cida.gc.ca/CIDAWEB/webcountry.nsf/VLUDocEn/Cameroon-Factsataglance#def.

10. http://siteresources.worldbank.org/DATASTATISTICS/Resources/GNIPC.pdf; Arthur O'Sullivan, Steven Sheffrin, and Steve Perez, *Macroeconomics: Principles and Tools Activebook*, 5th ed. (Upper Saddle River, NJ: Prentice Hall, 2007).

11. *The Economist*, "Currency Comparisons, To Go," July 28, 2011, http://www.economist.com/blogs/dailychart/2011/07/big-mac-index.

12. Justin Dove, "Taking Advantage of Dollar Weakness," *Investor U*, July 28, 2011, http://www.investmentu.com/2011/July/taking-advantage-of-dollar-weakness.html.

13. Jack Neff, "Emerging-Market Growth War Pits Global Brand Giants Against Scrappy Local Rivals," *Ad Age*, June 13, 2011, http://adage.com/article/global-news/global-brand-giants-battle-scrappy-local-rivals/228142/.

14. Jeremiah McWilliams, "Pepsi, Coke in Race to Conquer China," *Atlanta Journal-Constitution*, May 28, 2010.

15. Chris Gaylord, "World's Cheapest Car, Tata Nano, Revs Toward US," *The Christian Science Monitor*, January 15, 2011, http://www.csmonitor.com/Innovation/Horizons/2010/0115/World-s-cheapest-car-Tata-Nano-revs-toward-US; Nandini Lakshman, "Indian Car Buyers Snap Up the Nano," May 6, 2009, http://www.time.com/time/world/article/0,8599,1896414,00.html?iid=sphere-inline-sidebar. Jyoti Thottam and Niljanjana Bhowmick, "Nano Power," *Time*, April 13, 2009.

16. "India," *The CIA World Factbook*, https://www.cia.gov/library/publications/the-world-factbook/geos/in.html.

17. "Coca-Cola Tackles Rural Indian Market," (video) *The Wall Street Journal*, May 3, 2010.

18. Neff, op. cit.

19. David L. Scott, *Wall Street Words: An A to Z Guide to Investment Terms for Today's Investor* (Boston: Houghton Mifflin, 2003).

20. Leslie Josephs, "U.S. Increases Sugar Quota for Second Time," *Wall Street Journal*, June 23, 2011.

21. "Exchange Rate," http://en.wikipedia.org/wiki/Exchange_rate.

22. http://en.wikipedia.org/wiki/European_Union (accessed May 19, 2010); http://www.nationsonline.org/oneworld/europe_map.htm (accessed May 19, 2010).

23. http://ucatlas.ucsc.edu/trade/subtheme_trade_blocs.php.

24. http://www.unescap.org/tid/mtg/postcancun_rterta.pps#1.

25. Johny Johansson, "Global Marketing" (McGraw-Hill: 2008)

26. Philip R. Cateora, Mary C. Gilly, and John L. Graham, *International Marketing*, 15th ed. (New York: McGraw-Hill, 2011); Danielle Medina Walker and Thomas Walker, *Doing Business Internationally: The Guide to Cross-Cultural Success*, 2nd ed. (Princeton, NJ: Trade Management Corporation, 2003).

27. Devorah Lauter, "IKEA Fined for Sunday Opening in France," *Forbes*, April 6, 2008.

28. Stefania Summermatter, "Can Sunday Shopping Help Beat the Crisis," *Swissinfo.ch*, August 1, 2009.

29. For a website dedicated to Hofstede's research, see http://www.geert-hofstede.com/. Some of his more influential publications include Geert Hofstede and Gert Jan Hofstede, *Cultures and Organizations: Software of the Mind* (New York: McGraw-Hill/Irwin, 2004); Geert Hofstede, "Management Scientists Are Human," *Management Science*, 40 (January 1994), pp. 4–13; Geert Hofstede and Michael H. Bond, "The Confucius Connection from Cultural Roots to Economic Growth," *Organizational Dynamics*, 16 (Spring 1988), pp. 4–21. See also Masaaki Kotabe and Kristiaan Helsen, *Global Marketing Management*, 3rd ed. (Hoboken, NJ: John Wiley & Sons, 2004).

30. http://geert-hofstede.com/countries.html.

31. James W. Carey, *Communication as Culture*, Revised edition (New York: Routledge, 2009); Tian Feng and Julian Lowe, "The Influence of National and Organizational Culture on Absorptive Capacity of Chinese Companies," *International Journal of Knowledge, Culture, and Change Management* 7, no. 10 (2007), pp. 9–16.

32. Colgate Palmolive 2010 Annual Report, "Colgate: Global Strategies, Local Strength."

33. "Brazil," U.S. Department of State, November 30, 2011, http://www.state.gov/r/pa/ei/bgn/35640.htm.

34. "Russia," U.S. Department of State, November 2, 2011, http://www.state.gov/r/pa/ei/bgn/3183.htm.

35. "India," U.S. Department of State, November 8, 2011, http://www.state.gov/p/sca/ci/in/.

36. Megha Bahree, "India Unlocks Door for Global Retailers, *Wall Street Journal*, November 25, 2011

37. Gary Locke, "U.S. Trade with China," U.S. Department of State, November 29, 2011, http://www.state.gov/p/eap/ci/ch/index.htm.

38. Jacon Kincaid, "Mark Zuckerberg on Facebook's Strategy for China (And His Wardrobe)," *Tech Crunch*, October 16, 2010, http://techcrunch.com/2010/10/16/mark-zuckerberg-on-face-books-strategy-for-china-and-his-wardrobe/.

39. Normandy Madden, "What Will Facebook Find if it Ventures Into China?" *Ad Age Global*, June 13, 2011, http://adage.com/article/global-news/facebook-find-ventures-china/228068/.

40. Chloe Albanesius, "Human Rights Group Slams Facebook over China Strategy," *PCMag.com*, June 3, 2011, http://www.pcmag.com/article2/0,2817,2386380,00.asp.

41. "China," U.S. Department of State, September 6, 2011, http://www.state.gov/r/pa/ei/bgn/18902.htm.

42. Lance Eliot Brouthers, George Nakos, John Hadjimarcou, and Keith D. Brouthers, "Key Factors for Successful Export Performance for Small Firms," *Journal of International Marketing* 17, no. 3 (2009), pp. 21–38; "Selling Overseas," November 12, 2009, http://www.entrepreneur.com/growyourbusiness/internationalexpansion/article204028.html.

43. http://www.sonyericsson.com/cws/corporate/press/pressreleases/pressreleasedetails/ericssonsshare-20111027.

44. Philip R. Cateora, Mary C. Gilly, and John L. Graham, *International Marketing*, 14th ed. (New York: McGraw-Hill, 2009); Bruce D. Keillor, Michael D'Amico, and Veronica Horton, "Global Consumer Tendencies," *Psychology & Marketing* 18, no. 1 (2001), pp. 1–20.

45. "Top 10 Best-Selling Cars November 2011," http://blogs.cars.com/kickingtires/2011/12/top-10-best-selling-cars-november-2011.html#more.

46. "Figo Drives New Sales Records for Ford in India," April 1, 2010, http://media.ford.com/article_display.cfm?article_id=32342; "Figo Chassis Designed for the Global Market—Tailored for Indian Roads," March 9, 2010, http://www.india.ford.com/servlet/Content Server?pageid=1178851252772&cid=1248869037192&pagename=FIPL%2FDFYArticle%2FWeb-Standalone&theme=default&direction=ltr&c=DFYArticle&site=FIPL.

47. "Ford India Delivers 100,000th Figo: Vehicle Sales up 53 Percent for the Year," July 1, 2011, http://media.ford.com/article_display.cfm?article_id=34894.

48. Michael J. Ureel, "Ford Looks to Improve Market Share, Sales in Emerging Indian Economy," http://media.ford.com/article_display.cfm?article_id=21882&make_id=trust.

49. Jack Neff, "Yahoo Ramps Up Global Study of Moms and Technology," *Ad Age*, November 17, 2011, http://adage.com/article/digital/yahoo-ramps-global-study-moms-tech-starcom/231060/.

50. http://www.pgeverydaysolutions.ca/thankyoumom/helping-moms.jsp.

51. Hill, *Global Business Today*.

52. Lidia Kelly and Maya Dyakina, "Analysis: Russia's Wealth Gap Wounds Putin," *Reuters*, December 20, 2011, http://www.reuters.com/article/2011/12/20/us-russia-inequality-idUSTRE7BJ19Z20111220; Transparency International, http://www.transparency.org/news_room/in_focus/2011.

53. Julie Jargon, "Can M'm, M'm Good Translate?" *The Wall Street Journal*, July 9, 2007, p. A16; Brad Dorfman and Martinne Geller, "Campbell Soup in Joint Venture to Expand in China," *Reuters*, January 12, 2011, http://www.reuters.com/article/2011/01/12/us-campbellsoup-swire-china-idUSTRE70B46620110112; Julie Jargon, "Campbell Soup to Exit Russia," *The Wall Street Journal*, June 29, 2011, http://online.wsj.com/article/SB100014240527023044478045764142024604912 10.html.

54. http://www.pringles.it/.

55. Natalie Zmuda, "P&G, Levi's, GE Innovate by Thinking in Reverse," *Ad Age*, June 13, 2011, http://adage.com/article/global-news/p-g-levi-s-ge-innovate-thinking-reverse/228146/.

56. Silvia Fabiana, Claire Loupias, Fernando Martins, and Roberto Sabbatini (eds.), *Pricing Decisions in the Euro Era: How Firms Set Prices and Why* (Oxford: Oxford University Press, 2007); Gilly et al., *International Marketing*.

57. Fabiana et al., *Pricing Decisions*; Amanda J. Broderick, Gordon E. Greenley, and Rene Dentiste Mueller, "The Behavioural Homogeneity Evaluation Framework: Multi-level Evaluations of Consumer Involvement in International Segmentation," *Journal of International Business Studies*, 38 (2007), pp. 746–763; Terry Clark, Masaaki Kotabe, and Dan Rajaratnam, "Exchange Rate Pass-Through and International Pricing Strategy: A Conceptual Framework and Research Propositions," *Journal of International Business Studies* 30, no. 2 (1999), pp. 249–268.

58. David Kiley, "One World, One Car, One Name," *BusinessWeek*, March 13, 2008, http://www.businessweek.com/magazine/content/08_12/b4076063825013.htm; "2012 Ford Fiesta Review," November 2, 2011, http://usnews.rankingsandreviews.com/cars-trucks/Ford_Fiesta/; http://www.fordvehicles.com/.

59. Larry Rohter, "Shipping Costs Start to Crimp Globalization," *The New York Times*, August 3, 2008, http://www.nytimes.com/2008/08/03/business/worldbusiness/03global.html; William J. Holstein, "How Toyota Manufactured Its Own Fall from Grace," bnet.com, February 9, 2010, http://www.bnet.com/2403-13056_23-391889.html.

60. Sarah Morris, "How Zara Clothes Turned Galacia into a Retail Hotspot,"*Reuters*, October 31, 2011, http://www.reuters.com/article/2011/10/31/spain-retail-galicia-idUSL5E7LV33E20111031.

61. "India: Creating Rural Entrepreneurs," http://www.unilever.com/sustainability/casestudies/economic-development/creating-rural-entrepreneurs.aspx.

62. https://www.cia.gov/library/publications/the-world-factbook/fields/2103.html.

63. Jess Halliday, "Industry Prepares to Fight Junk Food Ad Watershed," Food and Drink Europe.com, January 3, 2008, http://www.foodanddrinkeurope.com/Products-Marketing/Industry-prepares-to-fight-junk-food-ad-watershed.

64. Michael Wines, "Picking Brand Names in Asia Is a Business Itself," *Ad Age*, November 11, 2011, http://www.nytimes.com/interactive/2011/11/12/world/asia/12brands-english-chinese-pdf.html?ref=asia; *Brand Channel*, http://www.brandchannel.com/features_effect.asp?pf_id=274.

65. Simon Owens, "The Secrets of Lady Gaga's Social Media Success," *TNW Media*, March 15, 2011; "Undressing Lady Gaga's Social Strategy," http://www.houseblogger.com/houseblogger/2011/02/undressing-lady-gagas-social-strategy.html.

66. Caitlin Burns, "Lady Gaga and Social Media," http://thesocialrobot.com/2010/03/lady-gaga-and-social-media/.

67. Joan Voight, "How to Customize Your U.S. Branding Effort to Work Around the World," *Adweek*, September 3, 2008.

68. Andrew Jacobs and Adam Century, "In China, Car Brands Evoke an Unexpected Set of Stereotypes," *The New York Times*, November 14, 2011, http://www.nytimes.com/2011/11/15/business/global/in-china-car-brands-evoke-an-unexpected-set-of-stereo-types.html?pagewanted=all.

69. "Rich Chinese Fueling Luxury Car Market Growth," *People's Daily Online*, April 29, 2010, http://english.peopledaily.com.cn/90001/90778/90860/6967022.html.

70. "Audi AG: Strong Sales Figures in China, United Kingdom and United States," *Volkswagen News*, November 7, 2011, http://www.volkswagenag.com/content/vwcorp/info_center/en/news/2011/11/AUDI_AG__Strong_sales_figures_in_China__United_Kingdom_and_United_States.html; "BMW in Record Profits Helped by Strong Sales in China," *BBC News*, March 10, 2011, http://www.bbc.co.uk/news/business-12701854.

71. Jacobs and Century, op. cit.

72. Ibid.

73. Ibid.

74. Derek Kreindler, "Audi, Buick Still Hot In China, While Consumers Avoid Mercedes-Benz, BMW," *AutoGuide.com*, November 17, 2011, http://www.autoguide.com/auto-news/2011/11/audi-buick-still-hot-in-china-while-consumers-avoid-mercedes-benz-bmw.html.

75. Horatiu Boeriu, "July 2011: BMW Maintains Global-Sales Lead Over Rivals Audi, Mercedes," *BMW Blog*, August 9, 2011, http://www.bmwblog.com/2011/08/09/july-2011-bmw-maintains-global-sales-lead-over-rivals-audi-mercedes/.

76. Bloomberg News, "BMW Catching Audi in China by Driving X5 SUV Across Mongolian Desert," July 28, 2011, http://www.bloomberg.com/news/2011-07-27/bmw-catching-audi-in-china-by-driving-x5-suv-across-mongolian-desert-cars.htm.

77. Boeriu, op. cit.

78. Jacobs and Century, op. cit.

79. Hiroko Tabuchi, "An Alliance for BMW and Toyota," *The New York Times*, December 1, 2011, http://www.nytimes.com/2011/12/02/business/global/toyota-and-bmw-in-technology-alliance.html.

Chapter 9

1. LimitedBrands, http://limited.com/brands/vs/index.jsp.

2. "The Designer Collection," http://www.victoriassecret.com/panties/the-victorias-secret-designer-collection?pageAt=all; Elizabeth Holmes, "Victoria's Secret Shifts Focus to Lower-Price Items," *The Wall Street Journal*, August 20, 2009, http://online.wsj.com/article/SB125078611265846741.html.

3. "Multi-Way Bras," http://www.victoriassecret.com/bras/multi-way.

4. http://www.buec.udel.edu/antil/BUAD%20301/BUAD%20301%20Fall%20%2708/Victoria%27s%20Secret%20Pink.pdf.

5. Tim Feran, "How to Insult the Whole State of Michigan," *The Columbus Dispatch*, November 22, 2011, http://www.dispatch.com/content/stories/business/2011/11/22/how-to-insult-the-whole-state-of-michigan.html/

6. http://www.victoriassecret.com/pink/nfl-shop-by-team; "Victoria's Secret PINK and Major League Baseball Properties Announce New Co-Branded Collection," Forbes.com, March 15, 2010, http://www.forbes.com/feeds/prnewswire/2010/03/15/prnewswire201003151254PR_NEWS_USPR_____NY70507.html.

7. "With Wings and Little Else: Behind Victoria's Secret Fashion Show," *The New York Times*, http://www.nytimes.com/slideshow/2011/11/10/fashion/VICTORIAS-SECRET-FASHION--14.html; Christine Whitney, "Where Angels Learn to Tread," *The New*

York Times Magazine, November 10, 2011, http://tmagazine.blogs
.nytimes.com/2011/11/10/where-angels-learn-to-tread/.

8. James Agarwal, Naresh K. Malhotra, and Ruth N. Bolton, "A Cross-National and Cross-Cultural Approach to Global Market Segmentation: An Application Using Consumers' Perceived Service Quality," *Journal of International Marketing* 18, no. 3 (September 2010), pp. 18–40.

9. Alex Sood, "The Lost Boys Found: Marketing to Men through Games," *Fast Company*, March 10, 2011, http://www.fastcompany .com/1737372/the-lost-boys-found-marketing-to-men-through-games; Jeanine Poggi, "Men's Shopping Shrines," *Forbes.com*, September 30, 2008, http://www.forbes.com/2008/09/30 /men-shopping-shrines-forbeslife-cx_jp_0930style.html; Melanie Shortman, "Gender Wars," *American Demographics*, April 2002, p. 22.

10. Banwari, Mittal, *Consumer Behavior* (Cincinnati, OH: Open Mentis, 2008); J. Paul Peter and Jerry C. Olson, *Consumer Behavior and Marketing Strategy*, 8th ed. (New York: McGraw-Hill, 2008); Michael R. Solomon, *Consumer Behavior: Buying, Having, and Being*, 7th Ed. (Upper Saddle River, NJ: Prentice Hall, 2006); Jagdish Sheth, Banwari Mittal, and Bruce I. Newman, *Customer Behavior: Consumer Behavior and Beyond* (Fort Worth, TX: The Dryden Press, 1999).

11. Bill Carter and Tanzina Vega, "In Shift, Ads Try to Entice Over-55 Set," *The New York Times*, May 13, 2011, http://www.nytimes .com/2011/05/14/business/media/14viewers.html?pagewanted =1&_r=2.

12. Augusta Christensen, "No, Skechers, Shape-Ups Are Nothing Like the First Lady's Let's Move Campaign," The Huffington Post, May 13, 2011, http://www.huffingtonpost.com/augusta-christensen /post_2000_b_861499.html.

13. "Mark Cuban 'Buys Into' Skechers," January 10, 2012, http://skx .com/press.jsp.

14. Chi Kin (Bennett) Yim, Kimmy Wa Chan, and Kineta Hung, "Multiple Reference Effects in Service Evaluations: Role of Alternative Attractiveness and Self-Image Congruity," *Journal of Retailing*, 83 no. 1 (2007), pp. 147–157; Tamara Mangleburg, M. Joseph Sirgy, Dhruv Grewal, Danny Axsom, Maria Hatzios, C. B. Claiborne, and Trina Bogle, "The Moderating Effect of Prior Experience in Consumers' Use of User-Image Based versus Utilitarian Cues in Brand Attitude," *Journal of Business & Psychology*, 13 (fall 1998), pp. 101–113; M. Joseph Sirgy et al., "Direct versus Indirect Measures of Self-Image Congruence," *Journal of the Academy of Marketing Science*, 25, no. 3 (1997), pp. 229–241.

15. Mittal, *Consumer Behavior*; Peter and Olson, *Consumer Behavior and Marketing Strategy*; Solomon, *Consumer Behavior: Buying, Having, and Being*; Sheth, Mittal and Newman, *Customer Behavior: Consumer Behavior and Beyond*.

16. James M. Hagerty, "Harley, With Macho Intact, Tries to Court More Women," *The Wall Street Journal*, October 31, 2011, http: //online.wsj.com/article/SB1000142405297020450530457665 55244217556816.html#articleTabs%3Darticle; Harley-Davidson, "Global Customer Focus," http://investor.harley-davidson.com /phoenix.zhtml?c=87981&p=irol-demographics.

17. Harley-Davidson, "Women Riders," http://www.harley-davidson .com/en_US/Content/Pages/women-riders/landing.html.

18. http://www.strategicbusinessinsights.com/vals/store /USconsumers/intro.shtml.

19. http://www.strategicbusinessinsights.com/vals/applications/apps-pos.shtml.

20. John Melloy, "Heinz Facebook Gaffe: 'Where's My Balsamic Ketchup?,'" *Fast Money*, November 14, 2011, http://www.cnbc .com/id/45293583/Heinz_Facebook_Gaffe_Where_s_My_ Balsamic_Ketchup; Andrew Adam Newman, "Ketchup Moves Upmarket, with a Balsamic Tinge," *The New York Times*, October

25, 2011, http://www.nytimes.com/2011/10/26/business/media /ketchup-moves-upmarket-with-a-balsamic-tinge.html? _r=2&ref=consumerbehavior; Brian Steinberg, "Recognition Factor," *Boston Globe*, March 25, 2009; Mary H.J. Farrell, "New Heinz Balsamic Ketchup Available Only on Facebook," *Consumer Reports*, November 16, 2011, http://news.consumerreports.org /home/2011/11/new-heinz-balsamic-ketchup-available-only-on-facebook.html.

21. "Segmentation and Targeting," http://www.kellogg.northwestern .edu/faculty/sterntha/htm/module2/1.html; Michael D. Lam, "Psychographic Demonstration: Segmentation Studies Prepare to Prove Their Worth," *Pharmaceutical Executive*, January 2004.

22. For an interesting take on this issue, see Joseph Jaffe, *Flip the Funnel* (Hoboken, NJ: John Wiley & Sons, 2010).

23. Irit Nitzan and Barak Libai, "Social Effects on Customer Retention," *Journal of Marketing*, 75, no. 6 (November 2011), pp. 24–38; Yuping Liu, "The Long-Term Impact of Loyalty Programs on Consumer Purchase Behavior and Loyalty," *Journal of Marketing* 71, no. 4 (October 2007), pp. 19–35; V. Kumar and Denish Shah, "Building and Sustaining Profitable Customer Loyalty for the 21st Century," *Journal of Retailing*, 80, no. 4 (2004), pp. 317–330.

24. http://www.united.com/page/article/0,6722,1171,00.html.

25. Bryan Alexander, "*Up in the Air* Fantasies: What Does 10 Million Miles Get You?" *Time*, December 22, 2009.

26. Dhruv Grewal, "Marketing Is All About Creating Value: 8 Key Rules," in *Inside the Mind of Textbook Marketing* (Boston, MA: Aspatore Inc., 2003), pp. 79–96.

27. Ben Sisario, "You've Got a Fan Club? Network and Mobilize It," *The New York Times*, March 2, 2011, http://www.nytimes .com/2011/03/03/business/media/03music.html; Ben Sisario, "Online Tools Help Bands Do Business," *The New York Times*, October 2, 2011, http://www.nytimes.com/2011/10/03/business /media/high-tech-tools-help-bands-market-directly-to-fans .html?pagewanted=1; Ian Rogers, "Getting Practical: A Step-by-Step Guide to Building an Online Marketing Plan that Works," *Topspin.com*, February 17, 2011, http://www.topspinmedia .com/2011/02/getting-practical-a-step-by-step-guide-to-building-an-online-marketing-plan-that-works-ians-presentation-from-new-music-seminar-los-angeles-february-2011.

28. Thorsten Blecker, *Mass Customization: Challenges and Solutions* (New York: Springer, 2006); B. Joseph Pine, *Mass Customization: The New Frontier in Business Competition* (Cambridge, MA: Harvard Business School Publishing, 1999); James H. Gilmore and B. Joseph Pine, eds., *Markets of One: Creating Customer-Unique Value through Mass Customization* (Cambridge, MA: Harvard Business School Publishing, 2000).

29. G. R. Iyer, A. D. Miyazaki, D. Grewal, and M. Giordano, "Linking Web-Based Segmentation to Pricing Tactics," *Journal of Product & Brand Management*, 11, no. 5 (2002), pp. 288–302; B. Jaworski and K. Jocz, "Rediscovering the Consumer," *Marketing Management*, September/October 2002, pp. 22–27; L. Rosencrance, "Customers Balk at Variable DVD Pricing," *Computer World*, September 11, 2000, p. 4; M. Stephanek, "None of Your Business: Customer Data Were Once Gold to E-Commerce. Now, Companies Are Paying a Price for Privacy Jitters," *BusinessWeek*, June 26, 2000, p. 78; D. Wessel, "How Technology Tailors Price Tags," *The Wall Street Journal*, June 23, 2001, p. A1.

30. C. Page Moreau, Leff Bonney, and Kelly B Herd, "It's the Thought (and the Effort) That Counts: How Customizing for Others Differs from Customizing for Oneself," *Journal of Marketing* 75, no. 5 (September 2011), pp. 120–33.

31. Keith Wilcox and Sangyoung Song, "Discrepant Fluency in Self-Customization," *Journal of Marketing Research* 48, no. 4 (August 2011), pp. 729–40; Doug Stephens, "The Declining Need for and Escalating Value of Human Service," *Retail Prophet*, September 26, 2011.

32. This circular depiction of value proposition is based on work by John Bers (Vanderbilt University) and adaptation and development of circles of success by Ronald Goodstein (Georgetown University).

33. http://www.gatorade.com/frequently_asked_questions/default .aspx.

34. http://www.drpeppersnapplegroup.com/brands/7up/.

35. Allen Adamson, "Pitch Your Luxury Offering as an 'Investment Brand'," *Forbes*, May 4, 2010, http://www.forbes.com/2010/05/04 /luxury-branding-platinum-brands-bmw-hermes-investment- branding-cmo-network-allen-adamson.html.

36. Stuart Schwartzapfel, "Volvo S80: Playing It Too Safe?" *BusinessWeek*, July 23, 2007; Jean Halliday, "Maloney Wants Volvo Viewed as Both Safe and Luxurious," *Advertising Age*, 75, no. 12 (2004), p. 22.

37. Kris Hudson, "Hotelier Gets Face-Lift to Draw Young Travelers," *The Wall Street Journal*, November 14, 2011, http://online.wsj .com/article/SB10001424052970203537304577032402793 23664.html.

38. http://heritage.coca-cola.com/.

39. "Our Company," http://www.thecoca-colacompany.com/our company/ar/.

40. "The Pepsi Cola Story," http://www.pepsiusa.com/PepsiLegacy _Book.pdf.

41. Betsy McKay, "Zero Is Coke's New Hero," *The Wall Street Journal*, April 17, 2007.

42. Kate Fitzgerald, "Coke Zero," *Advertising Age*, November 12, 2007.

43. "Products," http://www.thecoca-colacompany.com/brands/index .html.

44. "Company and Coca-Cola Highlights," http://www.thecoca-cola company.com/ourcompany/ar/highlights.html?intro=true; Valerie Bauerlein, "Coke Goes High-Tech to Mix Its Sodas," *The Wall Street Journal*, May 10, 2010, http://online.wsj.com/article/SB100 01424052748703612804575222350086054976.html.

45. (No reference material)

46. Various press releases, http://www.thecoca-colacompany.com /dynamic/press_center/2011/07/coke-zero-lap-promotion.html

47. (No reference material)

48. "Five Guys Becomes Largest Chain to Roll Out Coca-Cola Freestyle Nationwide," September 30, 2011, http://www.thecoca- colacompany.com/dynamic/press_center/2011/09/five-guys-and- coca-cola-freestyle.html; "Burger King Restaurants to Launch Coca-Cola Freestyle Across the U.S.," December 6, 2011, http: //www.thecoca-colacompany.com/dynamic/press_center /2011/12/burger-king-to-launch-coca-cola-freestyle.html.

49. "The Chronicle of Coca-Cola," http://www.thecoca-colacompany .com/heritage/chronicle_global_business.html.

Chapter 10

1. In-Store Marketing Institute, "Shaping Retail: The Use of Virtual Store Simulations in Marketing Research and Beyond," http://kelley .iu.edu/cerr/files/09ismi_virtualretailing.pdf, p. 3.

2. Alliston Ackerman, "P&G Shapes the Store," *Consumer Goods Technology*, November 16, 2011, http://consumergoods.edgl.com /case-studies/P-G-Shapes-the-Store75556.

3. Accenture, "Accenture and Procter & Gamble Partner in Delivering Virtual Solutions BPO Services," http://www.accenture.com /SiteCollectionDocuments/PDF/Accenture_CGS_PG_Virtual _Solutions.pdf.

4. Michael Letchford, "Pioneering Virtual Stores with Procter and Gamble," *Insights in Retail*, http://www.insightsinretail.com /virtual-stores/pioneering-virtual-stores-with-procter-and-gamble/.

5. Michael Letchford, "Virtual Shelf–Next Generation Visual Merchandising?" *Insights in Retail*, http://www.insightsinretail .com/visual-merchandising-virtual-shelf/virtual-shelf-a-new- generation-of-visual-merchandising/.

6. A. Parasuraman, Dhruv Grewal, and R. Krishnan, *Marketing Research*, 2nd ed. (Boston: Houghton Mifflin, 2007), p. 9.

7. Jack Honomichl, "The Honomichl Global Top 25 Report," *Marketing News*, August 30, 2011.

8. Detailed illustrations of scales are provided in two books: Gordon C. Bruner, *Marketing Scales Handbook, Volume V: A Compilation of Multi-Item Measures* (Carbondale, IL: GCBII Productions, 2009); William O. Bearden and Richard G. Netemeyer, *Handbook of Marketing Scales: Multi-Item Measures for Marketing and Consumer Behavior Research* (Thousand Oaks, CA: Sage Publications, 1999). Sources for the scales used in the exhibit are: Dhruv Grewal, Gopalkrishnan Iyer, Jerry Gotlieb, and Michael Levy, "Developing a Deeper Understanding of Post-Purchase Perceived Risk and Repeat Purchase Behavioral Intentions in a Service Setting," *Journal of the Academy of Marketing Science* 35, no. 2 (2007), pp. 250–258; Anthony Miyazaki, Dhruv Grewal, and Ronald C. Goodstein, "The Effect of Multiple Extrinsic Cues on Quality Perceptions: A Matter of Consistency," *Journal of Consumer Research* 32 (June 2005), pp. 146–153.

9. For a more thorough discussion of effective written reports, see Parasuraman, Grewal, and Krishnan, *Marketing Research*, Chapter 16.

10. John Cloud, "McDonald's Chef: The Most Influential Cook in America?" *Time Magazine*, February 22, 2010, http://www.time .com/time/magazine/article/0,9171,1963755,00.html.

11. Kristen McQueary, "A Revolution in Canvassing Among Voters," *The New York Times*, November 19, 2011, http://www.nytimes .com/2011/11/20/us/a-revolution-in-canvassing-among-voters .html?scp=2&sq=marketing%20research%20&st=cse.

12. "About," http://symphonyiri.com/About/tabid/59/Default.aspx.

13. "Who We Are," http://iridev.bluebooltlive.com/About/WhoWeAre /tabid/62/Default.aspx.

14. SymphonyIRI, "Special Report: Retail Private Label Brands in Europe—Current and Emerging Trends," December 15, 2011, http://www.symphonyiri.com/Insights/ArticleDetail/tabid/117 /ItemID/1394/View/Details/Default.aspx..

15. SymphonyIRI, "The CPG Basket: Fostering Growth in a Time of Conservation," December 14, 2011, http://www.symphonyiri.com /Insights/ArticleDetail/tabid/117/ItemID/1393/View/Details/Default .aspx.

16. Thomas Davenport, "Realizing the Potential of Retail Analytics," Babson Executive Education, August 2008; Marc-Andre Kamel, Nick Greenspan, and Rudolf Pritzl, "Standardization Is Efficient but Localization Helps Shops to Stand Out," *The Wall Street Journal*, January 21, 2009.

17. http://www.harrahs.com.

18. SAS, "Harrah's Hits Customer Loyalty Jackpot," http://www .sas.com/success/harrahs.html; Sudhir H. Kale and Peter Klugsberger, "Reaping Rewards," *Marketing Management*, July/ August 2007.

19. Charles Higgins, "Harrah's Total Rewards players club initiates at Planet Hollywood on April 1st," *Las Vegas Examiner*, March 28, 2010; Gary Loveman, "Diamonds in the Data Mine," *Harvard Business Review* 81, no. 5 (May 2003), pp. 109–13; http://www .harrahs.com.

20. Jennifer Reingold, "Can P&G Make Money in a Place Where People Make Earn $2 Per Day?" *CNN Money*, January 6, 2011, http://features.blogs.fortune.cnn.com/2011/01/06/can-pg-make- money-in-places-where-people-earn-2-a-day/.

21. Elisabeth A. Sullivan, "Be Sociable," *Marketing News*, January 15, 2008.

22. Harry McCracken, "The Best Blogs of 2011," *Time*, June 6, 2011, http://www.time.com/time/specials/packages/article/0,28804,2075431_2075447_2075479,00.html; http://videogum.com/

23. http://www.thetruthaboutcars.com/.

24. Andrew Adam Nieman, "Bloggers Don't Follow the Script, to ConAgra's Chagrin," *The New York Times*, September 6, 2011, http://www.nytimes.com/2011/09/07/business/media/when-bloggers-dont-follow-the-script-to-conagras-chagrin.html.

25. "History: The Science of Shopping," http://www.envirosell.com/index.php?option=com_content&task=view&id=40&Itemid=45.

26. Michael P. Cook and Hy Mariampolski, "How Culture Helps Marketers Understand Sensory Experiences," *Quirk's Marketing Research Review*, November 2009, p. 26.

27. "Client Story: Kraft," http://www.communispace.com/assets/pdf/C_Cli_casestudy_kraft_final.pdf.

28. Sarah Needleman, "For Companies, a Tweet in Time Can Avert PR Mess," *The Wall Street Journal*, August 3, 2009.

29. Rachael King, "Sentiment Analysis Gives Companies Insight Into Consumer Opinion," *Bloomberg BusinessWeek*, March 1, 2011, http://www.businessweek.com/technology/content/feb2011/tc20110228_366762.htm

30. Ashley Heher, "Our Pizza Didn't Taste Good, Domino's Says in New Ads," *Boston Globe*, January 12, 2010.

31. Richard A. Krueger and Mary Anne Casey, *Focus Groups: A Practical Guide for Applied Research* (Thousand Oaks, CA: Sage Publications, 2009).

32. "Campbell's Select Harvest Soups Top 2009 IRI New Product Pacesetters List: Second Time in Three Years That Campbell's Soups Top List," *MarketWatch*, March 23, 2010, http://www.marketwatch.com/story/campbells-select-harvest-soups-top-2009-iri-new-product-pacesetters-list-2010-03-23?reflink=MW_news_stmp.

33. http://www.campbellsoup.com/select.aspx.

34. Amanda Green, "Smaller Companies Embrace USPS Sampling," *Direct Marketing News*, May 1, 2011, http://www.dmnews.com/smaller-companies-embrace-usps-sampling/article/201336/.

35. Emily Goon, "How Research Helped Develop the USPS's Sample Showcase Program," *Quirk's Marketing Research Review* (December 2011).

36. Ibid.

37. Ibid.

38. "Sample Showcase," http://www.startsampling.com/showcase/howitworks.iphtml

39. Green, op. cit.

40. United States Postal Service, "Getting the Most Out of Sampling," Promotion Marketing Association, Inc., April 2011, http://www.pmalink.org/resource/resmgr/annual_2011_presentations/usps_pma.pdf.

41. Green, op. cit.

42. http://www.e-focusgroups.com/online.html.

43. Adapted from A. Parasuraman, Dhruv Grewal, and R. Krishnan, *Marketing Research*, 2nd ed. (Boston: Houghton Mifflin, 2007), Ch. 10.

44. Floyd J. Fowler, *Survey Research Methods* (Thousand Oaks, CA: Sage Publications, 2009); Don A. Dillman, Glenn Phelps, Robert Tortora, Karen Swift, Julie Kohrell, Jodi Berck, and Benjamin L. Messer, "Response Rate and Measurement Differences in Mixed-Mode Surveys Using Mail, Telephone, Interactive Voice Response (IVR) and the Internet," *Social Science Research* 38 (March 2009), pp. 1–18.

45. https://pulse.asda.com; Joel Warady, "Asda Takes the 'Pulse of the Nation'," *Retail Wire*, July 16, 2009.

46. http://www.marketingpower.com/AboutAMA/Pages/Statement%20of%20Ethics.aspx; http://www.helleniccomserve.com/marketingcodeofethics.html.

47. Federal Trade Commission, "Widespread Data Breaches Uncovered by FTC Probe: FTC Warns of Improper Release of Sensitive Consumer Data on P2P File-Sharing Networks," February 22, 2010, http://www.ftc.gov/opa/2010/02/p2palert.shtm.

48. Cecilia Kang, "Library of Congress plan for Twitter: a big, permanent retweet," *Washington Post*, April 16, 2010; www.cdt.org; Mark Penn, "Did Google Violate Privacy Laws?," www.politicallyillustrated.com, April 2, 2010; Lona M. Farr, "Whose Files Are They Anyway? Privacy Issues for the Fundraising Profession," *International Journal of Nonprofit and Voluntary Sector Marketing*, 7, no. 4 (November 2002), p. 361.

49. Natasha Singer, "Face Recognition Makes the Leap from Sci-Fi," *The New York Times*, November 12, 2011.

50. Adam Penenberg, "NeuroFocus Uses Neuromarketing to Hack Your Brain," *Fast Company*, August 8, 2011, http://www.fastcompany.com/magazine/158/neuromarketing-intel-paypal.

51. http://www.autotrader.com/about/index.jsp.

52. Joe Richards, "How AutoTrader.com Uses Primary Research to Clarify the Car-Shopping Process," *Quirk's Marketing Research Review* (July 2011), p. 36, http://www.quirks.com/articles/2011/20110704.aspx.

53. Bruce Giffin and Joe Richards, "The Role of the Internet in the New and Used Vehicle Purchase Process," Polk View, February 2011, http://www.industryrelations.autotrader.com/downloads/Independent%20Market%20Reports/2011%20Polk%20View%20-%20The%20Role%20of%20the%20Internet%20in%20the%20New%20and%20Used%20Vehicle%20Purchase%20Process.pdf.

Appendix 10A

1. V. Kumar, A. Petersen and R. P. Leone, "How Valuable Is the Word of Mouth?" *Harvard Business Review*, October 2007, pp. 139–146; V. Kumar and Morris George, "Measuring and Maximizing Customer Equity: A Critical Analysis," *Journal of the Academy of Marketing Science*, 35, no. 2 (June 2007), pp. 157–171; V. Kumar, Denish Shah, and Rajkumar Venkatesan, "Managing Retailer Profitability: One Customer at a Time!" *Journal of Retailing*, 82, no. 4 (October 2006), pp. 277–294; V. Kumar, "Profitable Relationships," *Marketing Research: A Magazine of Management and Applications*, 18, no. 3 (Fall 2006), pp. 41–46; V. Kumar, "Customer Lifetime Value: A Databased Approach," *Journal of Relationship Marketing*, 5, no. 2/3 (2006), pp. 7–35; Sunil Gupta, Dominique Hanssens, Bruce Hardie, William Kahn, V. Kumar, Nathaniel Lin, Nalini Ravishanker, and S. Sriram, "Modeling Customer Lifetime Value," *Journal of Service Research*, 9 (November 2006), pp. 139–155; V. Kumar, R. Venkatesan, and Werner Reinartz, "Knowing What to Sell, When and to Whom," *Harvard Business Review*, March, 2006, pp. 131–137; Werner Reinartz, J. Thomas, and V. Kumar, "Balancing Acquisition and Retention Resources to Maximize Profitability," *Journal of Marketing*, 69 (January 2005), pp. 63–79; R. Venkatesan and V. Kumar, "A Customer Lifetime Value Framework for Customer Selection and Resource Allocation Strategy," *Journal of Marketing*, 68 (October 2004), pp. 106–125; V. Kumar and J. Andrew Petersen, "Maximizing ROI or Profitability: Is One Better Than the Other," *Marketing Research: A Magazine of Management and Applications*, 16, no. 3 (Fall 2004), pp. 28–34; V. Kumar, G. Ramani, and T. Bohling, "Customer Lifetime Value Approaches and Best Practice Applications," *Journal of Interactive Marketing* 18, no. 3 (Summer 2004), pp. 60–72; J. Thomas, Werner Reinartz, and V. Kumar, "Getting the Most out of All Your Customers," *Harvard Business Review* (July–August 2004), pp. 116–123; Werner Reinartz and V. Kumar, "The Impact of Customer Relationship

Characteristics on Profitable Lifetime Duration," *Journal of Marketing*, 67 (January 2003), pp. 77–99; Werner Reinartz and V. Kumar, "The Mismanagement of Customer Loyalty," *Harvard Business Review* (July 2002), pp. 86–97; W. Reinartz and V. Kumar, "On the Profitability of Long Lifetime Customers: An Empirical Investigation and Implications for Marketing," *Journal of Marketing*, 64 (October 2000), pp. 17–32.

2. We have made some minor adjustments to the formula suggested by Gupta et al., "Modeling Customer Lifetime Value."

3. Sunil Gupta and Donald R. Lehmann, *Managing Customers as Investments* (Philadelphia, PA: Wharton School Publishing, 2005); Gupta et al.,"Modeling Customer Lifetime Value."

Chapter 11

1. Daniel Roberts, "Under Armour Gets Serious," *Fortune Magazine*, October 26, 2011, http://management.fortune.cnn.com/2011/10/26/under-armour-kevin-plank/.

2. Ibid.

3. Carol Torgan, "Self-Tracking Meets Ready-To-Wear: Make Room in Your Closet for Smart Clothes," *Kinetics*, http://www.caroltorgan.com/self-tracking-smart-clothes/.

4. Elizabeth Olson, "Under Armour Applies Its Muscle to Shoes," *The New York Times*, August 8, 2011, http://www.nytimes.com/2011/08/09/business/media/for-under-armour-a-focus-on-shoes-advertising.html?pagewanted=all.

5. Elizabeth Olson, "Under Armour Wants to Dress Athletic Young Women," *The New York Times*, August 31, 2010, http://www.nytimes.com/2010/09/01/business/media/01adco.html.

6. http://www.trekbikes.com/us/en/bikes/road/madone/6_series/meet_madone/.

7. Sharon Ng, "Cultural Orientation and Brand Dilution: Impact of Motivation Level and Extension Typicality," *Journal of Marketing Research* 47, No. 1 (February 2010), pp. 186–98; Paraskevas C. Argouslidis and George Baltas, "Structure in Product Line Management: The Role of Formalization in Service Elimination Decisions," *Journal of the Academy of Marketing Science*, 35, no. 4 (2007), pp. 475–491; John A. Quelch and David Kenny, "Extend Profits, Not Product Lines," *Harvard Business Review*, September–October 1994, pp. 153–160.

8. Simon Pittman, "Revlon Switches CEO as Pressure Mounts over Performance," *Cosmeticsdesign.com*, September 19, 2006.

9. Michael A. Wiles, Neil A. Morgan, and Lopo L. Rego, "The Effect of Brand Acquisition and Disposal on Stock Returns," *Journal of Marketing* 76, No. 1 (2012), pp. 38–58.

10. "Compare Checking Accounts," https://www.bankofamerica.com/deposits/index.action?body=check_compare.

11. Ellen Byron, "Tide Turns 'Basic' for P&G in Slump," *The Wall Street Journal*, August 6, 2009; Barry Silverstein, "P&G Scrubs Out Tide Basic," *BrandChannel*, June 6, 2010, http://www.brandchannel.com/home/post/2010/06/24/Tide-Basic-Killed.aspx.

12. Andrew Adam Newman, "Axe Adds Fragrance for Women to Its Lineup," *The New York Times*, January 8, 2012, http://www.nytimes.com/2012/01/09/business/media/axe-adds-fragrance-for-women-to-its-lineup.html?_r=1&scp=4&sq=brandi.ng&st=cse.

13. Dianna Dilworth, "Axe Campaign Has Fans Collaboratively Write Graphic Novel Online," *Direct Marketing News*, January 10, 2012, http://www.dmnews.com/axe-campaign-has-fans-collaboratively-write-graphic-novel-online/article/222581/.

14. Todd Wasserman, "Axe Launches Fragrance with a Graphic Novel on YouTube," *Mashable Business*, January 10, 2012, http://mashable.com/2012/01/10/axe-graphic-novel/.

15. Cotton Timberlake, "Kate Spade's Got a Brand New Bag," *Business Week*, February 24, 2011.

16. *Consumer Reports*, "TV Buying Guide: Brands," http://www.consumerreports.org/cro/electronics-computers/tvs-services/tvs/tv-buying-advice/tv-brands/tvs-brands.htm (accessed December 9, 2009).

17. Kevin Lane Keller, *Strategic Brand Management: Building, Measuring, and Managing Brand Equity*, 3rd ed. (Upper Saddle River, NJ: Prentice Hall, 2007).

18. This discussion of the advantages of strong brands is adapted from Keller, *Strategic Brand Management*, pp. 104–112; Elizabeth S. Moore, William L. Wilkie, and Richard J. Lutz, "Passing the Torch: Intergenerational Influences as a Source of Brand Equity," *Journal of Marketing*, 66, no. 2 (2002), p. 17. See also Kevin Lane Keller and Donald R. Lehmann, "Brands and Branding: Research Findings and Future Priorities," *Marketing Science* 25 (November 2006), pp. 740–59.

19. Kevin Lane Keller and Donald R. Lehmann, "Assessing Long-Term Brand Potential," *Journal of Brand Management* 17 (2009), 6–17.

20. Evan Carmichael, "Obsess Over Your Customers—Jeff Bezos," *www.youngentrepreneur.com*, April 7, 2009; http://www.amazon.com/New-Rules-Marketing-PR-Podcasting/dp/0470113456.

21. Parija Kavilanz, "Tootsie Roll to Footsyroll: See Ya in Court!" *CNN Money*, November 18, 2011, http://money.cnn.com/2011/11/18/smallbusiness/tootsie_roll_footzy_roll/index.htm.

22. http://www.interbrand.com/best_global_brands.aspx. The net present value of the earnings over the next 12 months is used to calculate the value.

23. David Aaker, *Brand Portfolio Strategy: Creating Relevance, Differentiation, Energy, Leverage, and Clarity* (New York: Free Press, 2004); David A. Aaker, *Managing Brand Equity* (New York: Free Press, 1991).

24. Jennifer Van Grove, "Barbie Joins Foursquare," *Mashable Business*, July 15, 2010, http://mashable.com/2010/07/15/barbie-joins-foursquare/.

25. "Video Girl Scavenger Hunt: Lights! Barbie! Action!" http://alldolldup.typepad.com/all_dolld_up/2010/07/video-girl-scavenger-hunt-lights-barbie-action.html.

26. Campaign for a Commercial-Free Childhood, "The Commercialization of Childhood," http://www.commercialfreechildhood.org/issues/overview.html.

27. T.L. Stanley, "Mattel, Hasbro Transform Themselves," *BrandWeek*, June 2010, http://login.vnuemedia.com/bw/superbrands/article_toys.html.

28. Claude Brodesser-Akner, "Thanks to a Big Mattel Move, Toys and Movies Come One Step Closer to Being the Exact Same Thing," *New York Magazine*, March 24, 2010, http://nymag.com/daily/entertainment/2010/03/mattel_hollywood_new_movie_syn.html.

29. Claude Brodesser-Akner, "Disney to Hollywood: If It Can't Sell Toys, It Had Better Be Cheap," February 17, 2010, http://nymag.com/daily/entertainment/2010/02/the_middle_is_toast_at_disney.html.

30. Lopo L. Rego, Matthew T. Billett, and Neil A. Morgan, "Consumer-Based Brand Equity and Firm Risk," *Harvard Business Review*, 73, no. 6, November 2009, pp. 47–60; Natalie Mizik and Robert Jacobson, "Valuing Branded Businesses," *Harvard Business Review*, 73, no. 6, November 2009, p. 137–53; Shuba Srinivasan and Seenu Srinivasan, *Brand Equity: Measuring, Analyzing, and Predicting* (Boston: Harvard Business Press, May 8, 2006); David Aaker, *Building Strong Brands* (New York: Simon & Schuster, 2002); David A. Aaker, "Measuring Brand Equity Across Products and Markets," *California Management Review*, 38 (1996), pp. 102–120.

31. Stephanie Clifford, "Demand at Target for Fashion Line Crashes Web Site," *The New York Times*, September 13, 2011, http://www.nytimes.com/2011/09/14/business/demand-at-target-for-fashion-line-crashes-web-site.html. Kara G. Morrison, "Chic on the Cheap," *The Detroit News*, February 15, 2008; http://www.fxmagazine.co.uk/story.asp?storyCode51632.

32. www.hallmarkchannel.com.

33. http://www.marketingpower.com/_layouts/Dictionary.aspx?dLetter=B.

34. "Kantar Media Reports U.S. Advertising Expenditures Increased 6.5 Percent in 2010," March 17, 2011, http://kantarmediana.com/insight-center/news/us-advertising-expenditures-increased-65-percent-2010.

35. Lien Lamey, Barbara Deleersnyder, Marnik G. Dekimpe, and Jan-Benedict E.M. Steenkamp, "How Business Cycles Contribute to Private-Label Success: Evidence from the United States and Europe," *Journal of Marketing* 71 (January 2007), pp. 1–15; PLMA (2009), http://www.plmainternational.com/es/private_label_es2.htm.

36. Kellogg's 2010 annual report, http://annualreport2010.kelloggcompany.com/innovation.htm.

37. The distinction between brand and line extensions is clarified in Barry Silverstein, "Brand Extensions: Risks and Rewards," Brandchannel.com, January 5, 2009.

38. See Thorsen Hennig-Thurau, Mark B. Houson, and Torsten Heitjans, "Conceptualizing and Measuring the Monetary Value of Brand Extensions: The Case of Motion Pictures," *Journal of Marketing* 73, no. 6 (November 2009), pp. 167–83; Rohini Ahluwalia, "How Far Can a Brand Stretch? Understanding the Role of Self-Construal," *Journal of Marketing Research*, 45, no. 3 (2008); Byung Chul Shine, Jongwon Park, and Robert S. Wyer, "Brand Synergy Effects in Multiple Brand Extensions," *Journal of Marketing Research* 44, no. 4 (2007), pp. 663–670; Gochen Wu and Yung-Ghien Yen, "How the Strength of Parent Brand Associations Influences the Interaction Effects of Brand Breadth and Product Similarity with Brand Extension Evaluations," *Journal of Product & Brand Management*, 16, no. 4–5 (2007), pp. 334–341; Franziska Volckner and Henrik Sattler, "Drivers of Brand Extension Success," *Journal of Marketing*, 70, no. 2 (2006), pp. 18–34; Subramanian Balachander and Sanjoy Ghose, "Reciprocal Spillover Effects: A Strategic Benefit of Brand Extensions," *Journal of Marketing*, 67, no. 1 (2003), pp. 4–13; Kalpesh Kaushik Desai and Kevin Lane Keller, "The Effects of Ingredient Branding Strategies on Host Brand Extendibility," *Journal of Marketing*, 66, no. 1 (2002), pp. 73–93; Tom Meyvis and Chris Janiszewski, "When Are Broader Brands Stronger Brands? An Accessibility Perspective on the Success of Brand Extensions," *Journal of Consumer Research*, 31, no. 2 (2004), pp. 346–357.

39. David Aaker, "Brand Extensions: The Good, the Bad, and the Ugly," *Sloan Management Review*, 31 (Summer 1990), pp. 47–56.

40. www.neutrogena.com; Vanitha Swaminathan, Richard J. Fox, and Srinivas K. Reddy, "The Impact of Brand Extension Introduction on Choice," *Journal of Marketing* 65, no. 3 (2001), pp. 1–15.

41. Devon DelVecchio and Daniel C. Smith, "Brand-Extension Price Premiums: The Effects of Perceived Fit and Extension Product Category Risk," *Journal of the Academy of Marketing Science* 33, no. 2 (2005), pp. 184–96; Jennifer Aaker, Susan Fournier, and S. Adam Brasel, "When Good Brands Do Bad," *Journal of Consumer Research*, 31, no. 1 (2004), pp. 1–16.

42. Costas Hadjicharalambous, "A Typology of Brand Extensions: Positioning Cobranding as a Sub-Case of Brand Extensions," *Journal of American Academy of Business* 10, no. 1 (2006), pp. 372–377; H. Sjodin and F. Torn, "When Communication Challenges Brand Associations: A Framework for Understanding Consumer Responses to Brand Image Incongruity," *Journal of Consumer Behaviour* 5, no. 1 (2006), pp. 32–42; C.H. Chen and S.K. Chen, "Brand Dilution Effect of Extension Failure–A Taiwan Study," *Journal of Product and Brand Management* 9, no. 4 (2000), pp. 243–254.

43. Mario Marsicano, "Cheetos Lip Balm & More Bizarre Brand Extensions," *The Wall Street Journal*, July 15, 2009.

44. David A. Aaker and Kevin Lane Keller, "Consumer Evaluations of Brand Extensions," *Journal of Marketing* 54, no. 1 (1990), pp. 27–41.

45. Guoqun Fu, Jiali Ding, and Riliang Qu, "Ownership Effects in Consumers' Brand Extension Evaluations," *Journal of Brand Management* 16 (2009), pp. 221–233; Christoph Burmann, Sabrina Zeplin, and Nicola Riley, "Key Determinants of Internal Brand Management Success: An Exploratory Empirical Analysis," *Journal of Brand Management* 16 (2009), pp. 264–84; Raisa Yakimova and Michael Beverland, "The Brand-Supportive Firm: An Exploration of Organisational Drivers of Brand Updating," *Journal of Brand Management* 12, no. 6 (2005), pp. 445–60.

46. http://www.marriott.com/corporateinfo/glance.mi.

47. Cathy Enz, "Multibranding Strategy: The Case of Yum! Brands," *Cornell Hotel & Restaurant Administration Quarterly*, February 2005.

48. T. Kippenberger, "Co-Branding as a Competitive Weapon," *Strategic Direction* 18, no. 10 (2002), pp. 31–33.

49. Keller, *Strategic Brand Management: Building, Measuring, and Managing Brand Equity*.

50. Keller, *Strategic Brand Management: Building, Measuring, and Managing Brand Equity*.

51. Muzellec, Laurent, and Mary Lambkin, "Corporate Rebranding and the Implications for Brand Architecture Management: The Case of Guinness (Diageo) Ireland," *Journal of Strategic Marketing*, 16, No. 4. (2008), pp. 283–299; Lomax, W., & Mador, M. (2006), "Corporate Re-Branding: from Normative Models to Knowledge Management," *Journal of Brand Management*, 14, no. 1/2, pp. 82–95; Merrilees, B., & Miller, D. (2008), "Principles of Corporate Rebranding," *European Journal of Marketing*, 42, no. 5/6, pp. 537–552; Muzellec, L., and Lambkin, M. (2006), "Corporate Rebranding: Destroying, Transferring or Creating Brand Equity?," *European Journal of Marketing*, 40, no. (7/8), pp. 803-824; Yakimova and Beverland, "The Brand-Supportive Firm"; Stephen Brown, Robert V. Kozinets, and John F. Sherry Jr., "Teaching Old Brands New Tricks: Retro Branding and the Revival of Brand Meaning," *Journal of Marketing*, 67, no. 2 (2003), p. 19.

52. Jane Levere, "Ivory Soap Refreshes Its Ads and Its Look, But Is Resolutely Simple," *The New York Times*, November 7, 2011.

53. Brian Steinberg, "Recognition Factor," *Boston Globe*, March 25, 2009.

54. Valerie Bauerlein, "Pepsi to Pare Plastic for Bottled Water," *The Wall Street Journal*, March 25, 2009.

55. Steve Inskeep, "Consumers Reject New Tropicana Carton," *Morning Edition*, February 23, 2009.

56. Stuart Elliot, "Tropicana Discovers Some Buyers Are Passionate About Packaging," *The New York Times*, February 22, 2009.

57. Chris Serres, "It's True: Food Packages Shrunk Last Year," *Minneapolis Star Tribune*, December 31, 2008.

58. U.S. Government Accounting Office, "Bottled Water: FDA Safety and Consumer Protections Are Often Less Stringent Than Comparable EPA Protections for Tap Water," July 8, 2009.

59. Associated Press, "Stricter Labeling Urged for Bottled Water," *The Wall Street Journal*, July 8, 2008.

60. Susan Berfield, "Brand Oprah Has Some Marketing Lessons," *Bloomberg Businessweek*, May 19, 2011, http://www.businessweek.com/magazine/content/11_22/b4230020001120.htm.

61. Ibid.

62. Clare O'Connor, "Forbes 400: Meet America's Richest Women (And Not Just Oprah and Meg)," *Forbes*, September 22, 2011, http://www.forbes.com/sites/clareoconnor/2011/09/22/forbes-400-meet-americas-richest-women-and-not-just-oprah-and-meg/.

63. Sara Krulwich, "Oprah Winfrey," *The New York Times*, May 25, 2011, http://topics.nytimes.com/top/reference/timestopics/people/w/oprah_winfrey/index.html?scp=1&sq=oprah%20winfrey%20network&st=cse.

64. "The Dr. Oz Show," Oprah Radio, June 3, 2011, http://www.oprah.com/oprahradio/About-Oprah-Radio-Host-Dr-Mehmet-Oz; "The

Dr. Laura Berman Show," Oprah Radio, June 1, 2011, http://www.oprah.com/oprahradio/About-Oprah-Radio-Host-Dr-Laura-Berman.

65. Alessandra Stanley, "Among the Lectures, a Bit of Shtick," *The New York Times*, October 14, 2011, http://www.nytimes.com/2011/10/15/arts/television/the-rosie-show-and-oprahs-life-class-on-own.html.

66. *Oprah's Lifeclass*, Oprah.com, http://www.oprah.com/oprahs-lifeclass/oprahs-lifeclass.html

Chapter 12

1. "LEGO History Timeline," http://aboutus.lego.com/en-us/lego-group/the_lego_history/.

2. http://mln.lego.com/en-us/network/status.aspx?icmp=COUSCreateShareSL100MLN.

3. Brad Wieners, "Lego Is for Girls," *BusinessWeek*, December 14, 2011.

4. Shari Roan, "A New Lego Line for Girls Is Offensive, Critics Say," *Los Angeles Times*, January 23, 2012, http://www.latimes.com/health/boostershots/la-heb-lego-girls-toy-protest-20120123,0,141471.story.

5. http://friends.lego.com/en-us/Products/Default.aspx.

6. Carrie Goldman, "Legos for Girls: Let's Focus the Discussion on the Right Issues," *Portrait of an Adoption*, January 30, 2012, http://www.chicagonow.com/portrait-of-an-adoption/2012/01/legos-for-girls-lets-focus-the-discussion-on-the-right-issues/; Ruth Davis Konigsberg, "Lego Friends for Girls: Have They Stooped to Stereotype?" *Time Magazine*, January 2, 2012, http://ideas.time.com/2012/01/02/lego-friends-for-girls-have-they-stooped-to-stereotype/; "Whether Pink Legos Are Just Building Stereotypes," *NPR*, January 24, 2012, http://www.npr.org/templates/story/story.php?storyId=145705192.

7. Scott Stinson and Hollie Shaw, "Gender Games," *National Post*, January 21, 2012, http://www.nationalpost.com/arts/books/Gender+games/6030953/story.html.

8. Andrew Adam Newman, "Making the Diaper Change Easier for the Changer," *The New York Times*, July 28, 2011, http://www.nytimes.com/2011/07/29/business/media/making-the-diaper-change-easier.html?ref=consumerbehavior.

9. "Huggies Brand Announces a Whole New Way to Change Diapers," July 13, 2011, http://investor.kimberly-clark.com/releasedetail.cfm?releaseid=590910.

10. Ibid.

11. "The Huggies Brand Encourages Parents to Showcase Their Active Babies," *The New York Times*, January 19, 2012, http://markets.on.nytimes.com/research/stocks/news/press_release.asp?docTag=201201190702PR_NEWS_USPRX____CG37939&feedID=600&press_symbol=178330.

12. "Doing the Right Thing," www.frogbox.com/therightthing.php.

13. Phil Patton, "Out of the Melting Pot and Into a Global Market," January 13, 2012, *The New York Times*, http://www.nytimes.com/2012/01/15/automobiles/out-of-the-melting-pot-and-into-a-global-market.html?hp.

14. Paul Stenquist, "A Buffet of Canny Tweaks in Hot Pursuit of Mileage," January 13, 2012, *The New York Times*, http://www.nytimes.com/2012/01/15/automobiles/a-buffet-of-canny-tweaks-in-hot-pursuit-of-mileage.html?pagewanted=all.

15. Koen Pauwels, Jorge Silva-Risso, Shuba Srinivasan, and Dominique M. Hanssens, "New Products, Sales Promotions, and Firm Value: The Case of the Automobile Industry," *Journal of Marketing*, 68, no. 4 (2008), p. 142.

16. Keith O'Brien, "Should We All Go Gluten-Free?" *The New York Times*, November 25, 2011, http://www.nytimes.com/2011/11/27/magazine/Should-We-All-Go-Gluten-Free.html?pagewanted=all.

17. Kalpesh Kaushik Desai and Kevin Lane Keller, "The Effects of Ingredient Branding Strategies on Host Brand Extendibility," *Journal of Marketing*, 66, no. 1 (2002), pp. 73–93.

18. Don Reisinger, "Madden Sales Up 10 Percent Over Last Year," *cnet.com*, September 8, 2011, http://news.cnet.com/8301-13506_3-20103229-17/madden-sales-up-10-percent-over-last-year/.

19. http://www.ideo.com/work/featured/kraft.

20. http://www.marketingpower.com/_layouts/Dictionary.aspx?dLetter=D.

21. Barak Libai, Eitan Muller, and Renana Peres, "The Diffusion of Services," *Journal of Marketing Research* 46 (April 2009), pp. 163–75; Yvonne van Everdingen, Dennis Fok, and Stefan Stemersch, "Modeling Global Spillover of New Product Takeoff," *Journal of Marketing Research* 46 (October 2009), pp. 637–52.

22. Rosabeth Moss Kanter, *SuperCorp: How Vanguard Companies Create Innovation, Profits, Growth, and Social Good* (New York: Crown Business, 2009); Rajesh K. Chandy, Jaideep C. Prabhu, and Kersi D. Antia, "What Will the Future Bring? Dominance, Technology Expectations, and Radical Innovation," *Journal of Marketing*, 67, no. 3 (2003), pp. 1–18; Harald J. van Heerde, Carl F. Mela, and Puneet Manchanda, "The Dynamic Effect of Innovation on Market Structure," *Journal of Marketing Research*, 41, no. 2 (2004), pp. 166–183.

23. http://www.apple.com; Clayton M. Christensen and Michael E. Raynor, *The Innovator's Solution* (Boston: Harvard Business School Press, 2003).

24. James L. Oakley, Adam Duhachek, Subramanian Balachander, and S. Sriram, "Order of Entry and the Moderating Role of Comparison Brands in Brand Extension Evaluation," *Journal of Consumer Research*, 34, no. 5 (2008), pp. 706–712; Fernando F. Suarez and Gianvito Lanzolla, "Considerations for a Stronger First Mover Advantage Theory," *Academy of Management Review*, 33, no. 1 (2008), pp. 269–270; Ralitza Nikolaeva, "The Dynamic Nature of Survival Determinants in E-commerce," *Journal of the Academy of Marketing Science*, 35, no. 4 (2007), pp. 560–571.

25. Matt Haig, *Brand Failures* (London: Kogan Page, 2005); Raji Srinivasan, Gary L. Lilien, and Arvind Rangaswamy, "First in, First out? The Effects of Network Externalities on Pioneer Survival," *Journal of Marketing*, 68, no. 1 (2004), p. 41.

26. K. Tyagi, "New Product Introductions and Failures under Uncertainty," *International Journal of Research in Marketing*, 23, no. 2 (2006), pp. 199–213; Lori Dahm, "Secrets of Success: The Strategies Driving New Product Development at Kraft," *Stagnito's New Products Magazine*, 2 (January 2002), p. 18ff; *BusinessWeek*, "Flops," August 16, 1993, p. 76ff.

27. "Top 10 Reasons for New Product Failure," *The Marketing Fray*, January 7, 2010 (http://www.marketingfray.com/2010/01/top-10-reasons-for-new-product-failure.html)

28. http://smashinghub.com/10-coolest-upcoming-gadgets-of-2011.htm.

29. Jacob Goldenberg, Sangman Han, Donald R. Lehmann, and Jae Weon Hong, "The Role of Hubs in the Adoption Process," *Journal of Marketing* 73 (March 2009), pp. 1–13.

30. "25 Most Promising Products for 2011," http://www.businesspundit.com/25-most-promising-products-for-2011/.

31. Erica Ogg, "ZOMG: Amazon.com Drops Kindle Price 10 Percent," *CNET News*, May 27, 2008.

32. Dylan F. Tweney, "Large-Screen Kindle Won't Mean Squat if Apple Tablet Arrives," *Wired*, May 4, 2009.

33. David Streitfeld, "Will the Kindle Fire Kill E-Readers," *The New York Times*, January 10, 2012, http://bits.blogs.nytimes.com/2012/01/10/will-the-kindle-fire-kill-e-readers/; Julie Bosman, "Table and E-Reader Sales Soar," *The New York Times*, January 22, 2012, http://mediadecoder.blogs.nytimes.com/2012/01/22/tablet-and-e-reader-sales-soar/#.

34. Jeffrey A. Trachtenberg, "E-Book Readers Face Sticker Shock," *The Wall Street Journal*, December 15, 2011.

35. "Kindle vs the iPad," Go4Expert.com, November 3rd, 2010 (http://www.go4expert.com/forums/showthread.php?t=23749)

36. Sarah Perez, "Firefox China Edition: Everything a Local Browser Should Be," *ReadWriteWeb.com*, November 24, 2008.

37. Steve Jobs, "Thoughts on Flash," Apple.com (http://www.apple.com/hotnews/thoughts-on-flash/)

38. L.M. De Luca and K. Atuahene-Gima, "Market Knowledge Dimensions and Cross-Functional Collaboration: Examining the Different Routes to Product Innovation Performance," *Journal of Marketing* 71 (2007), pp. 95–112; Subin Im and John P. Workman Jr., "Market Orientation, Creativity, and New Product Performance in High-Technology Firms," *Journal of Marketing*, 68, no. 2 (2004), p. 114.

39. Natalie Zmuda, "P&G, Levi's, GE Innovate by Thinking in Reverse," *Ad Age*, June 13, 2011, http://adage.com/article/global-news/p-g-levi-s-ge-innovate-thinking-reverse/228146/; "Minute Maid Pulpy Joins Growing List of Billion Dollar Brands for the Coca-Cola Company," press release, February 1, 2011, http://www.thecoca-colacompany.com/dynamic/press_center/2011/02/pulpy-joins-roster-of-billion-dollar-brands.html.

40. Rajani Baburajan, "U.S. Cable Industry Launches CableLabs—Energy Lab within its R&D Consortium," *Green Technology World*, November 21, 2011, http://green.tmcnet.com/topics/green/articles/239182-us-cable-industry-launches-cablelabs-energy-lab-with.htm.

41. Stefan Stremersch and Walter Van Dyck, "Marketing of the Life Sciences: A New Framework and Research Agenda for a Nascent Field," *Journal of Marketing* 73 (July 2009), pp. 4–30; Brady Huggett, John Hodgson, and Riku Lähteenmäki "Public Biotech 2010–The Numbers," *Nature Biotechnology* 29 (2011), pp. 585–91, http://www.nature.com/nbt/journal/v29/n7/fig_tab/nbt.1913_T3.html.

42. "Pilates Allegra 2 Reformer for Balanced Body," IDEO Case Study, 2011.

43. ibid.

44. Pilar Carbonell, Ana I. Rodríguez-Escudero, Devashish Pujari, "Customer Involvement in New Service Development: An Examination of Antecedents and Outcomes," *Journal of Product Innovation Management* 26 (September 2009), pp. 536–50; Glen L. Urban and John R. Hauser, "'Listening In' to Find and Explore New Combinations of Customer Needs," *Journal of Marketing*, 68, no. 2 (2004), p. 72.

45. Steve Lohr, "Can Microsoft Make You 'Bing'?" *The New York Times*, July 30, 2011, http://www.nytimes.com/2011/07/31/technology/with-the-bing-search-engine-microsoft-plays-the-underdog.html?pagewanted=all.

46. Renay San Miguel, "Bing's New Bells and Whistles Could Leave Searchers' Heads Ringing," *TechNewsWorld*, March 29, 2010; Jared Newman, "How Microsoft Plans to Beat Google with Bing," *PCWorld*, August 1, 2011, http://www.pcworld.com/article/237017/how_microsoft_plans_to_beat_google_with_bing.html.

47. Associated Press, "Wal-Mart Adds Products as Store Brands Boom," *Boston Globe*, March 17, 2009; Matthew Boyle, "Wal-Mart Gives Its Store Brand a Makeover," *BusinessWeek*, March 16, 2009.

48. Interview with Jevin Eagle, Executive Vice President of Merchandising and Marketing at Staples, June 18, 2009.

49. Jim Highsmith, *Agile Product Management: Creating Innovative Products* (Boston, Addison-Wesley, 2009); http://www.betterproductdesign.net/tools/user/leaduser.htm; Eric von Hippel, *The Sources of Innovation* (New York: Oxford University Press, 1988); Eric von Hippel, "Successful Industrial Products from Consumers' Ideas," *Journal of Marketing* 42, no. 1 (1978), pp. 39–49.

50. "Godiva Gems and Communispace for B2C Listening," *Communispace*, 2010.

51. Karl T. Ulrich and Steven D. Eppinger, *Product Design and Development*, 4th ed. (Boston: Irwin-McGraw-Hill, 2008).

52. http://www.marketingpower.com.

53. Ulrich and Eppinger, *Product Design and Development*.

54. Min Zhao, Steven Hoeffler, and Darren W. Dahl, "The Role of Imagination-Focused Visualization on New Product Evaluation," *Journal of Marketing Research*, 46 (February 2009), pp. 46–55; http://www.marketingpower.com.

55. Ulrich and Eppinger, *Product Design and Development*.

56. The Humane Society, "Cosmetic and Product Testing," http://www.humanesociety.org/issues/cosmetic_testing/; The Body Shop, "Saying No to Animal Testing," http://www.thebodyshop.com/_en/_ww/values-campaigns/against-animal-testing.aspx; Proctor & Gamble, "Animal Welfare and Alternatives," http://www.pg.com/en_US/sustainability/point_of_view/animal_welfare.shtml; http://www.peta.org; https://secure.peta.org/site/Advocacy?cmd=display&page=UserAction&id=2305.

57. Ellen Byron, "A Virtual View of the Store Aisle," *The Wall Street Journal*, October 3, 2007.

58. http://en-us.nielsen.com/tab/product_families/nielsen_bases.

59. Gernot H. Gessinger, *Materials and Innovative Product Development: From Concept to Market* (Oxford: Elsevier, 2009).

60. Jyoti Thottam Pune and Niljanjana Bhowmick, "Nano Power," *Time*, April 13, 2009.

61. Product Development Management Association, *The PDMA Handbook of New Product Development*, 2nd ed., Kenneth K. Kahn, ed. (New York: John Wiley & Sons, 2004).

62. Christian Homburg, Jan Wieske, and Torsten Bornemann, "Implementing the Marketing Concept at the Employee–Customer Interface: The Role of Customer Need Knowledge," *Journal of Marketing* 73 (July 2009), pp. 64–81; Christian Homburg, Jan Wieseke, & Torsten Bornemann Ashwin W. Joshi and Sanjay Sharma, "Customer Knowledge Development: Antecedents and Impact on New Product Success," *Journal of Marketing*, 68, no. 4 (2004), p. 47.

63. Katherine Bourzac, "Colorful Quantum Dot Displays Coming to Market," *Technology Review*, http://www.technologyreview.com/computing/25460/?a=f.

64. Yuhong Wu, Sridhar Balasubramanian, and Vijay Mahajan, "When Is a Preannounced New Product Likely to Be Delayed?" *Journal of Marketing*, 68, no. 2 (2004), p. 101.

65. "Coca-Cola Freestyle, Best Global Brands 2011," *Interbrand*, 2011.

66. http://www.usgbc.org/DisplayPage.aspx?CMSPageID=1988

67. http://www.walletpop.com/specials/top-25-biggest-product-flops-of-all-time.

68. http://www.pdma.org/.

69. Theodore Levitt, *Marketing Imagination* (New York: The Free Press, 1986).

70. Donald R. Lehmann and Russell S. Winer, *Analysis for Marketing Planning*, 7th ed. (Burr Ridge Il.: McGraw-Hill/Irwin, 2008).

71. Ibid.; Glen L. Urban and John R. Hauser, *Design and Marketing of New Products*, 2nd ed. (Upper Saddle River, NJ: Prentice Hall, 1993), pp. 120–121.

72. http://www.organicearthday.org/DelMonteFoods.htm; http://www.delmonte.com/Products/.

73. http://www.beiersdorf.com/Brands_Innovations/Innovations.html?TG=Brands_Sustainability; http://www.nivea.com/highlights/int_product/show/nhc_diamond_gloss/.

74. "Whirlpool Washing Machines," http://www.scribd.com/doc/13643826/Whirlpool-Washing-Machines; Miriam Jordan and Jonathan Karp, "Machines for the Masses; Whirlpool Aims Cheap Washer at Brazil, India and China; Making Do with Slower Spin," *The Wall Street Journal*, December 9, 2003, p. A19.

75. "The New Global Middle Class: Potentially Profitable—But also Unpredictable," *Knowledge@Wharton*, July 9, 2008; Eric D. Beinhocker, Diana Farrell, and Adil S. Zainulbhai, "Tracking the Growth of India's Middle Class," *McKinsey Quarterly* (August 2007).

76. Ellen Byron, "Purex Tackles Tough Market, Using New Spin," *The Wall Street Journal*, April 28, 2009.

77. Natalie Zmuda and Jennifer Rooney, "Hallmark Breaks Out of Special Occasion Mold," *Advertising Age*, July 6, 2011, http://adage.com/article/cmo-interviews/hallmark-breaks-special-occasion-mold/228558/.

78. Claire Cain Miller, "Smartphone Apps Send Holiday Greetings," *The New York Times*, November 23, 2011, http://www.nytimes.com/2011/11/24/technology/personaltech/this-year-send-holiday-greetings-by-app.html.

79. Noreen O'Leary, "KFC's Grilled Chicken Tops Most-Recalled '09 Launches," *Brandweek*, December 12, 2009; "BrandIndex: Big Spenders on Advertising Get the Most Buzz," *Advertising Age*; Lisa Respers France, "Oprah Coupon Craze Leaves KFC Customers Hungry for More," *CNN.com*, May 8, 2009.

80. Yvonne Zipp, "As Vinyl Records Get Back in the Groove, Kalamazoo Record Stores See Sales Climb," *MLive*, January 15, 2012, http://www.mlive.com/business/west-michigan/index.ssf/2012/01/as_vinyl_records_get_back_in_t.html.

81. Steven Levenstein, "Sony's New USB Turntable Sparks Vinyl Revival," www.inventospot.com, March 14, 2008; http://www.electronichouse.com/article/vinyl_the_classic_format/C155; Roy Bragg, "LP Vinyl Records Are Making a Comeback in Audiophile Circles," *Knight Ridder Tribune Business News*, January 3, 2004 (ProQuest Document ID: 521358371); Susan Adams, "You, the Record Mogul," *Forbes*, October 27, 2003, p. 256ff.

82. Goutam Challagalla, R. Venkatesh, and Ajay Kohli, "Proactive Postsales Service: When and Why Does It Pay Off?" *Journal of Marketing* 73 (March 2009), pp. 70–87; Kevin J. Clancy and Peter C. Krieg, "Product Life Cycle: A Dangerous Idea," *Brandweek*, March 1, 2004, p. 26; Nariman K. Dhalla and Sonia Yuseph, "Forget the Product Life-Cycle Concept," *Harvard Business Review* (January–February 1976), p. 102ff.

83. Peter Golder and Gerard Tellis, "Cascades, Diffusion, and Turning Points in the Product Life Cycle," MSI Report No. 03-120, 2003.

84. David Pogue, "Appeal of iPad 2 Is a Matter of Emotions," *The New York Times*, March 9, 2011, http://www.nytimes.com/2011/03/10/technology/personaltech/10pogue.html.

85. Ibid.; Nick Bilton, "The iPad 2, 5.1 Seconds and Smart Covers," *The New York Times*, March 11, 2011, http://bits.blogs.nytimes.com/2011/03/11/the-ipad-2-5-seconds-and-smart-covers.

86. Ibid.

87. Jenna Wortham, "So Far Rivals Can't Beat iPad's Price," *The New York Times*, March 6, 2011, http://www.nytimes.com/2011/03/07/technology/07tablet.html.

88. Ibid.

89. Ibid.; Dana Mattioli, "Tablets Ultimate buying Machines," *The Wall Street Journal*, September 22, 2011, http://online.wsj.com/article/SB10001424052970204010604576597151983657300.html.

90. Mattiolo, op. cit.

91. Charles Arthur, "iPad to Dominate Tablet Sales Until 2015 As Growth Explodes, says Gartner," *The Guardian*, September 22, 2011, http://www.guardian.co.uk/technology/2011/sep/22/tablet-forecast-gartner-ipad.

92. Pogue, op. cit.

93. "iPad 3 News," January 24, 2012, http://www.ipad-3-news.com/.

94. D.C. Denison, "Textbook Publishers Sign On with Apple to Take Advantage of iPad," *The Boston Globe*, January 26, 2012.

95. "iPad 3 News," op. cit.

Chapter 13

1. Aida Ahmed, "Zappos Ranks No. 11 on List of Best Companies to Work For," *VegasInc*, January 19, 2012, http://www.vegasinc.com/news/2012/jan/19/zappos-ranks-no-11-list-best-companies.

2. Doug Stephens, "The Declining Need for and Escalating Value of Human Service," *Retail Prophet*, September 26, 2011.

3. Armando Roggio, "The Zappos Effect: 5 Great Customer Service Ideas for Smaller Businesses," *Practical Ecommerce*, http://www.practicalecommerce.com/articles/2662-The-Zappos-Effect-5-Great-Customer-Service-Ideas-for-Smaller-Businesses.

4. Janine Popick, "Zappos: A Great Example of Exceeding Expectations," *Vertical Response*, http://blog.verticalresponse.com/verticalresponse_blog/2011/08/zappos-email.html.

5. Ahmed, op. cit.

6. Valarie A. Zeithaml, Mary Jo Bitner, and Dwayne D. Gremler, *Services Marketing: Integrating Customer Focus Across the Firm*, 5th ed. (Burr Ridge, IL: McGraw-Irwin, 2009).

7. Bureau of Economic Analysis, news release, January 27, 2012, http://www.bea.gov/newsreleases/national/gdp/2012/pdf/gdp4q11_adv.pdf; "Fortune 500," *CNNMoney*, May 23, 2011, http://money.cnn.com/magazines/fortune/fortune500/2011/index.html.

8. Zeithaml, Bitner, and Gremler, *Services Marketing*.

9. "Center for Professional Responsibility," http://www.abanet.org/cpr/professionalism/lawyerAd.html.

10. Ramon Ray, "Carbonite Offers Data Peace of Mind: A Solid Solution for Small Biz," *Business Insider*, January 24, 2012, http://www.businessinsider.com/carbonite-offers-data-peace-of-mind-a-solid-solution-for-small-biz-2012-1.

11. David Huber, "Carbonite Inc. (CARB) Online Backup Service," IRA.com, January 26, 2011, http://www.ira.com/carbonite-inc-carb-online-backup.

12. http://www.carbonite.com/en/home/online-backup.

13. Eric A. Taub, "Storing Your Files Inside the Cloud," *The New York Times*, March 2, 2011, http://www.nytimes.com/2011/03/03/technology/personaltech/03basics.html?scp=1&sq=online%20backup%20options%20Eric%20A.%20Taub&st=cse.

14. http://www.carbonite.com/en/home/online-backup.

15. Dhruv Grewal, Michael Levy, Gopal Iyer, and Jerry Gotlieb, "Developing a Deeper Understanding of Post-Purchase Perceived Risk and Repeat Purchase Behavioral Intentions in a Service Setting," *Journal of the Academy of Marketing Science* 35, no. 2 (2007), pp. 250–58; Jerry Gotlieb, Dhruv Grewal, Michael Levy, and Joan Lindsey-Mullikin, "An Examination of Moderators of the Effects of Customers' Evaluation of Employee Courtesy on Attitude toward the Service Firm," *Journal of Applied Social Psychology* 34 (April 2004), pp. 825–47.

16. Choice Hotels, "Special Guest Policies," http://www.choicehotels.com/ires/en-US/html/GuestPolicies.

17. Jesse Serwer, "I.T. with a Personal Touch," *SCT*, September 2011.

18. The discussion of the Gaps Model and its implications draws heavily from Michael Levy and Barton A. Weitz, *Retailing Management*, 7th ed. (Burr Ridge, IL: Irwin/McGraw-Hill, 2009) and also is based on Deon Nel and Leyland Pitt, "Service Quality in a Retail Environment: Closing the Gaps," *Journal of General Management* 18 (Spring 1993), pp. 37–57; Zeithaml, Parasuraman, and Berry, *Delivering Quality Service*; Valerie Zeithaml, Leonard Berry, and A. Parasuraman, "Communication and Control Processes in the Delivery of Service Quality," *Journal of Marketing* 52, no. 2 (April 1988), pp. 35–48.

19. Zhen Zhu, Cheryl Nakata, K. Sivakumar, and Dhruv Grewal, "Self-Service Technology Effectiveness: The Roles of Interactivity, Comparative Information, and Individual Differences on Perceived Control and Interface Evaluation," *Journal of the Academy of Marketing Science* 35, no. 4 (2007), pp. 492–506; Zhen Zhu, Cheryl Nakata, K. Sivakumar, and Dhruv Grewal, "Fix It Or Leave it? Customer Recovery from Self-Service Technology Failures," working paper, 2012, Babson College; Peter C. Verhoef, Katherine N. Lemon, A. Parasuraman, Anne Roggeveen, Michael Tsiros, and Leonard A. Schlesinger, "Customer Experience Creation: Determinants, Dynamics and Management Strategies," *Journal of Retailing* 85, no. 1 (2009), pp. 31–41.

20. Adam Braff and John C. DeVine, "Maintaining the Customer Experience," *The McKinsey Quarterly,* December 2008.

21. J. Aspara and H. Tikkanen, "Interactions of Individuals' Company-Related Attitudes and Their Buying of Companies' Stocks and Products," *Journal of Behavioral Finance* 9 (2008), pp. 85–94; Caroline Goukens, Siegfried Dewitte, and Luk Warlop, "Me, Myself, and My Choices: The Influence of Private Self-Awareness on Choice," *Journal of Marketing Research* 46 (October 2009), pp. 703–14.

22. Kemba J. Dunham, "Beyond Satisfaction," *The Wall Street Journal,* October 30, 2006, p. R4.

23. Zeithaml, Bitner, and Gremler, op. cit.

24. http://www.forbestravelguide.com/five-star-spas.htm; Allison Scott, "New Renovations Add to the Guest and Meeting Experience," *www.release-news.com;* http://www.broadmoor .com/luxury-resort-services.php.

25. Stephen L. Vargo, Kaori Nagao, Yi He, and Fred W. Morgan, "Satisfiers, Dissatisfiers, Criticals, and Neutrals: A Review of Their Relative Effects on Customer (Dis)Satisfaction," *Academy of Marketing Science Review* (January 2007), p. 1.

26. Goutam Challagalla, R. Venkatesh, and Ajay K. Kohli, "Proactive Postsales Service: When and Why Does It Pay Off?" *Journal of Marketing* 73 (March 2009), pp. 70–87.

27. Janelle Barlow, "A Complaint Is a Gift Corner," http://www.tmius .com/2cigcorn.HTML.

28. Michael Bergdahl. *The Retail Revolution: How Wal-Mart Created a Brave New World of Business.* (New York: Metropolitan Books, 2009) and Michael Bergdahl, *The 10 Rules of Sam Walton: Success Secrets for Remarkable Results* (Hoboken, NJ: John Wiley & Sons, 2006).

29. Hazel-Anne Johnson and Paul Spector, "Service With a Smile: Do Emotional Intelligence, Gender, and Autonomy Moderate the Emotional Labor Process?" *Journal of Occupational Health Psychology,* October 2007, pp. 319–33; Merran Toerien and Celia Kitzinger, "Emotional Labour in Action: Navigating Multiple Involvements in the Beauty Salon," *Sociology,* August 2007, pp. 645–62.

30. Michael T. Manion and Joseph Cherian, "Do Services Marketers' Success Measures Match Their Strategies?" *Journal of Services Marketing* 23, no. 7 (2009), pp. 476–86; Alison M. Dean and Al Rainnie, "Frontline Employees' Views on Organizational Factors that Affect the Delivery of Service Quality in Call Centers," *Journal of Services Marketing* 23, no. 5 (2009), pp. 326–37.

31. Jason Colquitt, Jeffery LePine, and Michael Wesson, *Organizational Behavior: Improving Performance and Commitment in the Workplace,* 2nd ed. (Burr Ridge, IL: McGraw-Hill, 2010); Felicitas M. Morhart, Walter Herzog, and Torsten Tomczak, "Brand-Specific Leadership: Turning Employees into Brand Champions," *Journal of Marketing* 73 (September 2009), pp. 122–42.

32. Carmine Gallo, "Bringing Passion to Starbucks, Travelocity," *BusinessWeek,* January 9, 2008.

33. Marguerite Darlington, "The History and Future of Mobile's Role in Fashion," *FashionablyMarketing.me,* November 22, 2011.

34. "Travelocity," http://www.sabre-holdings.com/ourBrands/travelocity .html; "Awards," http://svc.travelocity.com/about/newsroom/awards _main/1,5711,00.html.

35. Suzanne C. Makarem, Susan M. Mudambi, and Jeffrey S. Podoshen, "Satisfaction in Technology-Enabled Service Encounters," *Journal of Services Marketing* 23, no. 1 (2009).

36. Anne Eisenberg, "Thinking of Going Blond? Consult the Kiosk First," *The New York Times,* March 29, 2009; Marianne Wilson, "Digital Dining," *Chain Store Age,* September 2008.

37. Anita Whiting and Naveen Donthu (2009), "Closing the Gap Between Perceived and Actual Waiting Times in a Call Center: Results from a Field Study," *Journal of Services Marketing* 23, no. 5 (2009), pp. 279–328.

38. David Streitfield, "For $2 a Star, an Online Retailer Gets 5-Star Product Reviews," *The New York Times,* January 26, 2012, http:// www.nytimes.com/2012/01/27/technology/for-2-a-star-a-retailer-gets-5-star-reviews.html?_r=2&src=me&ref=general; David Streitfield, "Faking It to Make It: A Beautiful Try," *The New York Times,* January 27, 2012, http://bits.blogs.nytimes.com/2012/01/27/faking-it-to-make-it-a-beautiful-try/?scp=20&sq=customer%20 service&st=cse.

39. Stu Woo, "Amazon 'Primes' Pump for Loyalty," *The Wall Street Journal,* November 14, 2011; Stu Woo and John Letzing, "Amazon's Spending Habit Hurts Profit," *The Wall Street Journal,* February 1, 2012; Brad Stone, "What's in Amazon's Box? Instant Gratification," *BusinessWeek,* November 24, 2010.

40. Christopher Reynolds, "Smashed Guitar, YouTube Song—United is Listening Now," *Los Angeles Times,* July 7, 2009.

41. http://www.youtube.com/watch?v=5YGc4zOqozo; Steve Keenan, "United Broke My Guitar: Song 2," *Times Online,* August 19, 2009.

42. Alison Bonaquro, "United Broke His Guitar and Learned a Lesson," July 10, 2009, http://blog.cmt.com/2009-07-10/united-broke-his-guitar-and-learned-a-lesson/.

43. http://www.economist.com/blogs/gulliver/2009/07/did_dave _carroll_cost_united_1

44. Grewal, Dhruv, Anne Roggeveen and Michael Tsiros, "Compensation as a Service Recovery Strategy: When Does it Work?" *Journal of Retailing* 84, no. 4 (2008), pp. 424–34.

45. Peter C. Verhoef, Katherine N. Lemon, A. Parasuraman, Anne Roggeveen, Michael Tsiros, and Leonard A. Schlesinger (2009), "Customer Experience Creation: Determinants, Dynamics and Management Strategies," *Journal of Retailing,* 85 (1), pp. 31–41; Beibei Dong, Kenneth R. Evans, and Shaoming Zou (2008), "The Effects of Customer Participation in Co-Created Service Recovery," *Journal of the Academy of Marketing Science* 36 (Spring), pp. 123–37; Dhruv Grewal, Anne Roggeveen, and Michael Tsiros (2008), "Compensation as a Service Recovery Strategy: When Does it Work?" *Journal of Retailing* 84 (4), pp. 424–34.

46. Dhruv Grewal, Anne L. Roggeveen, and Michael Tsiros, "The Effect of Compensation on Repurchase Intentions in Service Recovery," *Journal of Retailing* 84, no. 4 (2008), pp. 424–34.

47. Ibid.

48. Yany Grégoire, Thomas M. Tripp, and Renaud Legoux, "When Customer Love Turns into Lasting Hate: The Effects of Relationship Strength and Time on Customer Revenge and Avoidance," *Journal of Marketing* 73 (November 2009), pp. 18–32.

49. Anne L. Roggeveen, Michael Tsiros, and Dhruv Grewal (2012), "Understanding the Co- Creation Effect: When Does Collaborating with Customers Provide a Lift to Service Recovery?" *Journal of the Academy of Marketing Science,* (forthcoming). Dong, B., Evans, K. R., & Zou, S. (2008). "The Effects of Customer Participation in Co-created Service Recovery." *Journal of the Academy of Marketing Science,* 36 (1), 123-137. Grewal, Roggeveen, and Tsiros, "The Effect of Compensation on Repurchase Intentions"; Amy K. Smith, Ruth N. Bolton, and Janet Wagner, "A Model of Customer Satisfaction with Service Encounters Involving Failure and Recovery," *Journal of Marketing Research* 36 (August 1999), pp. 356–72; Scott R. Swanson and Scott W. Kelley, "Attributions and Outcomes of the Service Recovery Process," *Journal of Marketing: Theory and Practice* 9 (Fall 2001), pp. 50–65.

50. Jayne O'Donnell, "Some Retailers Tighten Return Policies," *USA Today,* February 1, 2008.

51. http://www.zipcar.com.

52. April Kilcrease, "A Conversation with Zipcar's CEO Scott Griffith," GigaOM, December 5, 2011, http://gigaom.com/cleantech/a-conversation-with-zipcars-ceo-scott-griffith/.

53. http://www.zipcar.com.

54. United States Securities and Exchange Commission, "Zipcar S-1 Filing," June 1, 2010, http://sec.gov/Archives/edgar/data/1131457 /000095013010001923/ds1.htm.

55. Kilcrease, op. cit.

56. United States Securities and Exchange Commission, op. cit.; JP Morgan SMid Cap Conference, December 11, 2011.

57. United States Securities and Exchange Commission, op. cit.

58. Kilcrease, op. cit.

59. Ibid.

60. United States Securities and Exchange Commission, op. cit

61. http://www.zipcar.com.

62. United States Securities and Exchange Commission, op. cit.

63. Courtney Rubin, "How Will the IPO Market Treat Zipcar?" Inc.com, June 2, 2010, http://www.inc.com/news/articles/2010/06/zipcar-files-for-ipo.html

Chapter 14

1. Mike Esterl, "Coke Tailors Its Soda Sizes," Wall Street Journal, http://online.wsj.com/article/SB10001424053111903374004576578980270401662.html, September 19, 2011.

2. Ibid, Esterl.

3. Douglas A. McIntyre, "The Sodas America No Longer Drinks," 247wallst.com (online), http://247wallst.com/2011/11/18/the-sodas-america-no-longer-drinks/, November 18, 2011.

4. Reuters, "Coca-Cola's Results Are Lifted by Overseas Business," The New York Times, http://www.nytimes.com/2011/07/20/business/coca-colas-results-are-lifted-by-overseas-business.html, July 19, 2011.

5. Ibid, Reuters.

6. Ibid, Esterl.

7. Hooman Estelami, Dhruv Grewal, and Anne L. Roggeveen, "The Effect of Policy Restrictions on Consumer Reactions to Price-Matching Guarantees," Journal of the Academy of Marketing Science, 35, no. 2 (2007), pp. 208–219; Monika Kukar-Kinney and Dhruv Grewal, "Comparison of Consumer Reactions to Price-Matching Guarantees in Internet and Bricks-and-Mortar Retail Environments," Journal of the Academy of Marketing Science, 35, no. 2 (2007), pp. 197–207; Sujay Dutta, Abhijit Biswas, and Dhruv Grewal, "Low Price Signal Default: An Empirical Investigation with Low-Price Guarantees," Journal of the Academy of Marketing Science, 35, no. 1 (2007), pp. 76–88; Kent B. Monroe, Pricing: Making Profitable Decisions, 3rd ed. (New York: McGraw-Hill, 2003); Dhruv Grewal, Kent B. Monroe, and R. Krishnan, "The Effects of Price Comparison Advertising on Buyers' Perceptions of Acquisition Value and Transaction Value," Journal of Marketing, 62 (April 1998), pp. 46–60.

8. Jennifer Frighetto, "U.S. Consumers Place More Importance on Price and Value," ACNielsen, October 28, 2008; Laura Wood, "It's Not Easy Being Green, Part 2," Research and Markets, October 6, 2009; Food Marketing Institute (2003), "American Shoppers Economize, Show Greater Interest in Nutrition and Awareness of Food Safety Issues, According to Trends in the United States: Consumer Attitudes and the Supermarket 2003"; "The New Value Equation," Supermarket News, 50 (June 10, 2002), p. 12.

9. Anthony Miyazaki, Dhruv Grewal, and Ronnie Goodstein, "The Effects of Multiple Extrinsic Cues on Quality Perceptions: A Matter of Consistency," Journal of Consumer Research, 32 (June 2005), pp. 146–153; William B. Dodds, Kent B. Monroe, and Dhruv Grewal, "The Effects of Price, Brand, and Store Information on Buyers' Product Evaluations," Journal of Marketing Research, 28 (August 1991), pp. 307–319.

10. Moneyball, directed by Bennett Miller (2011; Sony Pictures). See also Michael Lewis, Moneyball (New York: W.W. Norton, 2004).

11. Johan Lehrer, "Grape Expectations: What Wine Can Tell Us about the Nature of Reality," Boston Globe, February 24, 2008.

12. Bang-Ning Hwang, Jack Tsai, Hsiao-Cheng Yu, and Shih-Chi Chang, "An Effective Pricing Framework in a Competitive Industry: Management Processes and Implementation Guidelines," Journal of Revenue and Pricing Management (November 2009); Oliver Roll, "Pricing Trends from a Management Perspective," Journal of Revenue and Pricing Management 8 (July 2009), pp. 396–98; Robert J. Dolan, "Note on Marketing Strategy," Harvard Business School (November 2000), pp. 1–17; Dhruv Grewal and Larry D. Compeau, "Pricing and Public Policy: An Overview and a Research Agenda," Journal of Public Policy & Marketing, 18 (Spring 1999), pp. 3–11.

13. Ethan Smith and Yukari Iwatani Kane, "Apples Changes Tune on Music Pricing," The Wall Street Journal, January 7, 2009.

14. "IBM Market Share Leader in Human Resources (HR) Business Transformation Outsourcing, Enterprise Sector," press release.

15. Rebecca Heslin, "Virgin America Joins Airline Fare Sale Stampede," USA Today, January 6, 2010; "Delta Rescinds Fare Increase on Some of Its U.S. Routes," Salt Lake City News, September 11, 2007 (accessed electronically January 3, 2010).

16. http://www.carmax.com/enus/car-dealer/default.html.

17. Nick Wingfield, "Apple's Lower Prices Are All Part of the Plan," The New York Times, October 24, 2011, http://www.nytimes.com/2011/10/24/technology/apples-lower-prices-are-all-part-of-the-plan.html.

18. Monroe, Pricing: Making Profitable Decisions.

19. William Lee Adams, "Would You Buy this $320,000 Brooch Online?" Time, November 9, 2009.

20. Fender Electric Guitars, http://www.fender.com/products/index.php?bodyShape=Stratocaster®&section=guitars.

21. Monroe, Pricing: Making Profitable Decisions. See also Richard B. McKenzie, Why Popcorn Costs So Much at the Movies: And Other Pricing Puzzles (New York: Springer, 2008).

22. Stephanie Clifford and Catherine Rampell, "Food Inflation Kept Hidden in Tinier Bags," The New York Times, March 29, 2011, http://www.nytimes.com/2011/03/29/business/29shrink.html?_r=2&ref=consumerbehavior.

23. http://www.marketingpower.com/_layouts/Dictionary.aspx?dLetter=C.

24. http://www.marketingpower.com/_layouts/Dictionary.aspx?dLetter=S.

25. Joan Lindsey-Mullikin and Dhruv Grewal, "Market Price Variation: The Availability of Internet Market Information," Journal of the Academy of Marketing Science, 34, no. 2 (2006), pp. 236–243.

26. Chris Morran, "Bank Of America Debit Card Fiasco Resulted In 20% Jump In Closed Accounts," The Consumerist, January 23, 2012.

27. Suzanne Marta, "As Ritz Opening Nears, Every Detail Counts," Knight Ridder Tribune Business News, August 6, 2007.

28. Jack Gordon, "Redefining Elegance, Training 44, no. 2 (2007), pp. 14–20.

29. Ibid.

30. Kevin Sack, "Despite Recession, Personalized Health Care Remains in Demand," The New York Times, May 11, 2009; Lori Calabro, "At Your Beck and Call," CFO Magazine, September 1, 2007.

31. Vanessa O'Connell, "Posh Retailers Pile on Perks for Top Customers," The Wall Street Journal, April 26, 2007; "InCircle," http://www.incircle.com/store/catalog/templates/Entry.jhtml?itemId=cat103411&parentId=cat103410&parentId=cat000001&icid=points1.

32. Andrew Adam Newman, "If You're Nervous, Deodorant Makers Have a Product for You," The New York Times, February 17, 2009.

33. Cenk Koça and Jonathan D. Bohlmann, "Segmented Switchers and Retailer Pricing Strategies," Journal of Marketing, 72, no. 3 (2008), pp. 124–142; Ruth N. Bolton and Venkatesh Shankar, "An Empirically Derived Taxonomy of Retailer Pricing and Promotion

Strategies," *Journal of Retailing,* 79, no. 4 (2003), pp. 213–224; Rajiv Lal and Ram Rao, "Supermarket Competition: The Case of Every Day Low Pricing," *Marketing Science,* 16, no. 1 (1997), pp. 60–80.

34. American Booksellers Association, "ABA Asks Department of Justice to Investigate Bestseller Price Wars," October 22, 2009.

35. Judith Rosen, "ABA's IndieCommerce Site Dropping Amazon Publisher Titles," *Publisher's Weekly,* February 8, 2012, http://www.publishersweekly.com/pw/by-topic/industry-news/bookselling/article/50551-aba-s-indiecommerce-site-dropping-amazon-publishing-titles.html.

36. Jeff Jacoby, "Latest Battle in Book Price Wars," *Boston Globe,* October 28, 2009.

37. Jacoby, "Latest Battle"; Michael Bungert, *Termination of Price Wars: A Signaling Approach* (Frankfurt am Main, Springer Verlag, 2003); A. R. Rao, M. E. Bergen, and S. Davis, "How to Fight a Price War," *Harvard Business Review,* 78 (March–April 2000), pp. 107–116.

38. *Merriam-Webster's Dictionary of Law,* 1996.

39. http://www.plasmavision.com/warranty.htm.

40. Uptal Dholakia, Barbara Kahn, Randy Reeves, Aric Rindfleish, David Stewart, and Earl Taylor (2010), "Consumer Behavior in a Multichannel, Multimedia Retailing Environment, *Journal of Interactive Marketing,* forthcoming; P.K. Kannan, Barbara K. Pope, and Sanjay Jain (2009), "Pricing Digital Content Product Lines: A Model and Application for the National Academies Press," *Marketing Science,* forthcoming; Brian Ratchford (2009), "Online Pricing: Review and Directions for Research," *Journal of Interactive Marketing,* 23 (1), 82-90; Koen Pauwels and Allen Weiss (2008), "Moving from Free to Fee: How Online Firms Market to Successfully Change their Business Model," *Journal of Marketing Perspectives,* 19 (2), 139–158.Dhruv Grewal, Gopalkrishnan R. Iyer, R. Krishnan, and Arun Sharma, "The Internet and the Price-Value-Loyalty Chain," *Journal of Business Research,* 56 (May 2003), pp. 391–398.

41. Sandra Block, "Momentum Growing for Sales Taxes on Online Purchases," *USA Today,* February 8, 2012, http://www.usatoday.com/money/perfi/taxes/story/2012-02-08/online-sales-taxes/53015142/1; Michael Mazerov and Steve DelBianco, "Should States Require Online Retailers to Collect Sales Taxes," *The Wall Street Journal,* November 15, 2011, http://online.wsj.com/article/SB10001424052970204528204577007511298359048.html.

42. "Rises on Sale of Luxury Goods," *Wall Street Journal,* February 21, 2012: "New Rich Drive Sales of Luxury Goods," *Wall Street Journal,* February 17, 2012.

43. Kerry Miller, "eBay Sellers Go Back to School: 10 Tips," September 7, 2006.

44. Gillian Ku, Adam D. Galinsky, and J. Keith Murnighan, "Starting Low but Ending High: A Reversal of the Anchoring Effect in Auctions," *Journal of Personality and Social Psychology,* 90, no. 6 (2006), pp. 975–986.

45. Patrick Bajari and Ali Hortacsu, "The Winner's Curse, Reserve Prices and Endogenous Entry: Empirical Insights from eBay Auctions," *Journal of Economics,* 34, no. 2 (2002), p. 329.

46. Barbara Stern and Maria Royne Stafford, "Individual and Social Determinants of Winning Bids in Online Auctions," *Journal of Consumer Behavior,* 5 (July 2006), pp. 43–55.

47. Ku, Galinsky, and Murnighan, "Starting Low but Ending High."

48. Stern and Stafford, "Individual and Social Determinants of Winning Bids in Online Auctions;" Ku, Galinsky, and Murnighan, "Starting Low but Ending High."

49. David Lucking-Reiley, Doug Bryan, Naghi Prasad, and Daniel Reeves, "Pennies from eBay: The Determinants of Price in Online Auctions," *Journal of Industrial Economics,* forthcoming.

50. Uri Simonsohn and Dan Ariely, "eBay's Happy Hour: Non-Rational Herding in Online Auctions," unpublished manuscript.

51. Tanjim Hossain and John Morgan, " . . . Plus Shipping and Handling: Revenue (Non) Equivalence in Field Experiments on eBay," *Advances in Economic Analysis and Policy,* 6, no. 2 (2006), Article 3; eBay, "Tips for Successful Selling," http://pages.ebay.com/help/sell/seller-tips.html.

52. Jeffrey A. Livingston, "How Valuable Is a Good Reputation? A Sample Selection Model of Internet Auctions," *Review of Economics and Statistics,* 87, no. 3 (2005), pp. 453–465; Steven T. Anderson, Daniel Friedman, Garrett H. Daniel, and Nirvikar Singh, "Seller Strategies on eBay," April 2004, UC Santa Cruz Economics Working Paper No. 564.

53. This case was written by Elisabeth Nevins Caswell with the text-book authors, Dhruv Grewal and Michael Levy, as a basis for class discussion rather than to illustrate effective or ineffective marketing practices. See Matthew Futterman, "Yankees Slash Prices to Fill Costly Seats at New Park," *The Wall Street Journal,* April 29, 2009; The Stadium Insider, "Yankees Sneak In a Price Increase On Bleacher Seats For 2010 Partial Plan Season Tickets," November 28, 2009, http://newstadiuminsider.blogspot.com/2009/11/yankees-sneak-in-price-increase-on.html; Tyler Klepner, "Jeter Reaches 3,000 Hit with Home Run," *The New York Times,* July 10, 2011, http://www.nytimes.com/2011/07/10/sports/baseball/jeter-reaches-3000-hits-with-home-run.html; Ian Begley, "Mariano Rivera Sets New Saves Record," *ESPN.com,* September 20, 2011, http://espn.go.com/new-york/mlb/story/_/id/6993396/new-york-yankees-mariano-rivera-sets-mlb-mark-602nd-save; New York Yankees, "Stadium Map and Ticket Prices," http://newyork.yankees.mlb.com/nyy/ballpark/seating_pricing.jsp; New York Yankees, "Spring Training Tickets," http://newyork.yankees.mlb.com/spring_training/home.jsp?c_id=nyy; StubHub, "Los Angeles Angels at New York Yankee Tickets, April 13, 2012," http://www.stubhub.com/new-york-yankees-tickets/yankees-vs-angels-4-13-2012-2009229/.

Chapter 15

1. Mary Pilon, "Finding Group Discounts Online," *The Wall Street Journal,* August 11, 2009.

2. www.groupon.com.

3. http://www.bespokecuisine.com/cooking-parties/index.php.

4. As of January 2011. "Groupon Press Kit," http://www.groupon.com/pages/press-kit.

5. Doug Stephens, "Is the (Daily) Deal Finally Done?" *Retail Wire,* February 2, 2012.

6. Thomas T. Nagle and Reed K. Holden, *The Strategy and Tactics of Pricing,* 3rd ed. (Upper Saddle River, NJ: Pearson, 2002).

7. Independent Equity Research Corp., "Coastal Contacts Inc. Update Report," http://eresearch.ca/profile.asp?companyID=437; Mary Biti, "Clearly a Winning Strategy," http://investors.coastalcontacts.com/mediacoverage.asp?ticker=T.OA&report=show&id=6151&lang=EN&title=null; Eve Lazarus, "Trevor Linden Plays with Clearly Contacts," www.marketingmag.ca/english/news/marketer/article.jsp?content=20100528_164119_13472; "The Timeline," http://investors.coastalcontacts.com/custommessage.asp?ticker=t.oa&message=fifth&title=null.

8. Kristina Shampanier, Nina Mazar, and Dan Ariely, "Zero as a Special Price: The True Value of Free Products," *Marketing Science* 26, no. 6 (2007), pp. 742-57; Sucharita Chandran and Vicki G. Morvitz, "The Price of "Free"-dom: Consumer Sensitivity to Promotions with Negative Contextual Influences," *Journal of Consumer Research* 33, no. 4 (2006), pp. 384–92; E. Shafir and R.H. Thaler, "Invest Now, Drink Later, Spend Never: On the Mental Accounting of Delayed Consumption," *Journal of Economic Psychology* 27 (2006), pp. 694–712; Lisa E. Bolton, Luk Warlop, and Joseph W. Alba, "Consumer Perceptions of Price (Un)

Fairness," *Journal of Consumer Research*, 29 (March 2003), pp. 474–491; Peter R. Darke and Darren W. Dahl, "Fairness and Discounts: The Subjective Value of a Bargain," *Journal of Consumer Psychology*, 13, no. 3 (2003), pp. 328–338; Margaret C. Campbell, "Perceptions of Price Unfairness: Antecedents and Consequences," *Journal of Marketing Research*, 36 (May 1999), pp. 187–199; Sarah Maxwell, "What Makes a Price Increase Seem 'Fair'?" *Pricing Strategy & Practice*, 3, no. 4 (1995), pp. 21–27.

9. Michael Levy and Barton A. Weitz, *Retailing Management*, 8th ed. (Burr Ridge, IL: Irwin/McGraw-Hill, 2012).

10. Geoffrey A. Fowler and Yukari Iwatani Kane, "New Mobile Applications Use Bar-Code Scanners," *The Wall Street Journal*, December 16, 2009; http://shopsavvy.mobi/.

11. Brad Tuttle, "Use Amazon's Price Check App and Save $15," *Time*, December 8, 2011, http://moneyland.time.com/2011/12/08/use-amazons-price-check-app-and-save-15-this-saturday/; Susan Payton, "Amazon Price Check App: Small Business Threat or Sign of the Times?" *Small Business Trends*, December 15, 2011, http://smallbiztrends.com/2011/12/amazon-price-check-app-small-business-threat-or-sign-of-the-times.html.

12. Ibid.

13. Carl Bialik, Elizabeth Holmes, Ray A. Smith, "Many Discounts, Few Deals," *The Wall Street Journal*, December 15, 2010, http://online.wsj.com/article/SB10001424052748704694004576019771942029048.html; Vanessa O'Connell, "It's 50% Off . . . Well, Maybe 35%. How Good Are Deals on Members'-Only Web Sites?" *The Wall Street Journal*, January 16, 2010; http://www.hautelook.com; http://www.gilt.com.

14. Dhruv Grewal, Kent B. Monroe, and R. Krishnan, "The Effects of Price Comparison Advertising on Buyers' Perceptions of Acquisition Value and Transaction Value," *Journal of Marketing*, 62, April 1998, pp. 46–60.

15. Dhruv Grewal and Anne Roggeveen, "Decomposing the Intricate Role of Price, Quality, and Value Relationships," *Legends in Marketing Series: Kent B. Monroe: The Price-Quality-Value Relationship*, Volume 3, Dhruv Grewal and Anne Roggeveen, eds. (New Delhi: Sage Publication, 2010).

16. Stephanie Clifford, "J.C. Penney to Revise Pricing Methods and Limit Promotions," *The New York Times*, January 25, 2012, http://www.nytimes.com/2012/01/26/business/jc-penneys-chief-ron-johnson-announces-plans-to-revamp-stores.html?_r=2.

17. Eric A. Staub, "As Prices Fall, Blu-Ray Players Are Invited Home," *The New York Times*, December 13, 2009.

18. Poornima Gupta, "Apple Returns to Form, Blows Street Targets Away," *Reuters*, January 24, 2012, http://www.reuters.com/article/2012/01/24/us-apple-idUSTRE80N2BQ20120124; Federico Viticci, "Apple Q1 2012 Results," *MacStories*, January 24, 2012, http://www.macstories.net/news/apple-q1-2012-results-46-33-billion-revenue-37-04-million-iphones-15-43-million-ipads-sold/; Sam Costello, "iPhone Comparison Chart," *About.com*, http://ipod.about.com/od/decidingwhichipodtobuy/a/iphone_chart.htm.

19. Sam Costello, "iPhone Comparison Chart," *About.com*, http://ipod.about.com/od/decidingwhichipodtobuy/a/iphone_chart.htm.; Wikipedia.com iPhone Model Comparison Chart Hyperlink: http://en.wikipedia.org/wiki/Iphone#Model_comparison

20. James Suroweicki, "BlackBerry Season," *The New Yorker*, February 13 & 20, 2012, p. 38.

21. This section draws from Levy and Weitz, *Retailing Management*.

22. Sha Yang and Priya Raghubir, "Can Bottles Speak Volumes? The Effect of Package Shape on How Much to Buy," *Journal of Retailing*, 81, no. 4 (2005), pp. 269–281.

23. This section is adapted from Levy and Weitz, *Retailing Management*.

24. Personal communication with Rob Price, VP of Retail Marketing, CVS, June 16, 2009.

25. http://www.leasingluxurylifestyles.com/category/press/; http://bagborroworsteal.com.

26. Marco Bertini and Luc Wathieu, "Research Note: Attention Arousal through Price Partitioning," *Marketing Science* 27, no. 2 (2008), pp. 236–46; Rebecca W. Hamilton and Joydeep Srivastava, "When 2+2 Is Not the Same as 1+3: Variations in Price Sensitivity Across Components of Partitioned Prices," *Journal of Marketing Research* 45, no. 4 (2008), pp. 450–61.

27. http://www.brooksbrothers.com/IWCatSectionView.process?IWAction=Load&Merchant_Id=1&Section_Id=663.

28. Alison Jing Xu and Robert S. Wyer, Jr., "Puffery in Advertisements: The Effects of Media Context, Communication Norms and Consumer Knowledge," *Journal of Consumer Research*, August 2010.

29. "Tesco Rapped Over 'Misleading' Price Claims," *Sky News*, July 29, 2009; www.asa.org.uk/.

30. Joan Lindsey-Mullikin and Ross D. Petty, "Marketing Tactics Discouraging Price Search: Deception and Competition," *Journal of Business Research*, (forthcoming). DOI: 10.1016/j.jbusres.2009.10.003.

31. Maria Sciullo, "Will Price War Hurt Independent Bookstores?" *Pittsburgh Post-Gazette*, October 27, 2009.

32. FairSearch, "Google's Transformation from Gateway to Gatekeeper," white paper, http://www.fairsearch.org/wp-content/uploads/2011/10/Googles-Transformation-from-Gateway-to-Gatekeeper.pdf.

33. Uwe E. Reinhardt, "Ending Hospital Price Discrimination Against the Uninsured," *The New York Times*, January 8, 2010.

34. Daniel M. Garrett, Michelle Burtis and Vandy Howell, "Economics of Antitrust: An Economic Analysis of Resale Price Maintenance, www.GlobalCompetitionReview.com, 2008; Stephen Labaton, "Century-Old Ban Lifted on Minimum Retail Pricing," *The New York Times*, June 29, 2007.

35. "South African Airlines to Be Investigated for Alleged World Cup Price-Fixing, Report DialAFlight," *Business Wire*, February 1, 2010.

36. Tom Bawden, "Bloody Nose for OFT in Row over Tobacco Price-Fixing," *The Independent (London)*, December 13, 2011, http://www.independent.co.uk/news/business/news/bloody-nose-for-oft--in-row-over-tobacco-pricefixing-6276246.html; "The Marlboro Cartel," http://www.smokingate.com/2011/11/30/cartel/.

37. Daniel M. Garrett, Michelle Burtis, and Vandy Howell, "Economics of Antitrust: An Economic Analysis of Resale Price Maintenance, www.GlobalCompetitionReview.com, 2008; Stephen Labaton, "Century-Old Ban Lifted on Minimum Retail Pricing," *The New York Times*, June 29, 2007.

38. "Global Mobile Statistics 2012," February 2012, http://mobithinking.com/mobile-marketing-tools/latest-mobile-stats.

39. http://aboutus.verizonwireless.com/ataglance.html.

40. http://www.att.com/gen/investor-relations?pid=5711.

41. http://www.sprint.com/about/.

42. Roger Cheng, "Sprint Gets the Nextel Monkey Off Its Back," cnet.com, February 8, 2012, http://news.cnet.com/8301-1035_3-57373457-94/sprint-gets-the-nextel-monkey-off-its-back/?tag=mncol;7n.

43. http://www.t-mobile.com/Company/CompanyInfo.aspx?tp=Abt_Tab_CompanyOverview&tsp=Abt_Sub_History.

44. Larry Dignan, "4G Data Plans: Price Wars Already?" ZDNet, December 7, 2010, http://www.zdnet.com/blog/btl/4g-data-plans-price-wars-already/42440.

45. (No reference material)

46. Tim Conneally, "Sprint on the Wireless Price War: We Were Already Cheaper!" betanews.com, January 19, 2010, http://www.betanews.com/article/Sprint-on-the-wireless-price-war-We-were-already-cheaper/1263944727.

47. Olga Kharif, "Verizon Wireless-AT&T 'Price War' May Boost Revenues," *Bloomberg Businessweek*, January 20, 2010.

Chapter 16

1. William B. Cassidy, "Wal-Mart Tightens the Chain," *Journal of Commerce*, January 18, 2010.

2. Chris Burritt, Carol Wolf, and Matthew Boyle, "Wal-Mart Asks Suppliers to Cede Control of Deliveries (Update2)," *Bloomberg Businessweek*, June 1, 2010.

3. This chapter draws from Michael Levy and Barton A. Weitz, *Retailing Management*, 8th ed. (Burr Ridge, IL: McGraw-Hill/Irwin, 2012).

4. (No reference material)

5. Based on Barton A. Weitz, "PenAgain Sells to Walmart," in Michael Levy and Barton A. Weitz, *Retailing Management*, 8th ed. (Burr Ridge, IL: McGraw-Hill/Irwin, 2012), pp. 564–565; http://www. Penagain.com; Gwendolyn Bounds, "The Long Road to Walmart," *The Wall Street Journal*, September 19, 2005, p. R1; Gwendolyn Bounds, "One Mount to Make it," *The Wall Street Journal*, May 30, 2006, p. B1.

6. *SCDigest*, "Supply Chain News: Goya Foods Shows Path to Success for Mid-Market Companies from New Supply Chain Planning Tools," July 13, 2011, http://www.scdigest.com/ontarget/11-07-13-1 .php?cid=4724.

7. Terry L. Esper, Alexander Ellinger, Theodore Stank, Daniel Flint, Mark Moon, "Demand and Supply Integration: a Conceptual Framework of Value Creation through Knowledge Management," *Journal of the Academy of Marketing Science* 38, no. 1 (2010), pp. 5–18.

8. See http://www.marketingpower.com/_layouts/Dictionary.aspx.

9. George E. Stigler, "The Division of Labor Is Limited by the Extent of the Market," *Journal of Political Economy* 59, no. 3 (1951), pp. 185–93.

10. http://www.marketingpower.com/live/mg-dictionary.

11. "*Entrepreneur's* 2012 Franchise 500," http://www.entrepreneur .com/franchise500/index.html.

12. Charles Duhigg and David Barbosa, "In China, Human Costs Are Built into an iPad," *The New York Times*, January 25, 2012, http://www.nytimes.com/2012/01/26/business/ieconomy-apples-ipad-and-the-human-costs-for-workers-in-china.html?pagewanted=1&_r=3&ref=business&src=me&adxnnlx=1331046030-59qBpuAMRNH8OEI6dxh/7g; Melissa J. Anderson, "The Supply Chain Enters the Spotlight," *Evolved Employer*, February 14, 2012, http://www.evolvedemployer.com/2012/02/14/the-supply-chain-enters-the-spotlight/.

13. Lisa Scheer, Fred Miao, and Jason Garrett, "The Effects of Supplier Capabilities on Industrial Customers' Loyalty: the Role of Dependence," *Journal of the Academy of Marketing Science* 38, no. 1 (2010), pp. 90–104; Robert W. Palmatier, Rajiv Dant, and Dhruv Grewal, "A Longitudinal Analysis of Theoretical Perspectives of Interorganizational Relationship Performance," *Journal of Marketing* 71 (October 2007), pp. 172–94; Robert W. Palmatier, Rajiv Dant, Dhruv Grewal, and Kenneth Evans, "A Meta-Analysis on the Antecedents and Consequences of Relationship Marketing Mediators: Insight into Key Moderators," *Journal of Marketing* 70 (October 2006), pp. 136–53.

14. Donna Davis and Susan Golicic, "Gaining Comparative Advantage in Supply Chain Relationships: the Mediating Role of Market-Oriented IT Competence," *Journal of the Academy of Marketing Science* 38, no. 1 (2010), pp. 56–70; Beth Davis-Sramek, Richard Germain, and Karthik Iyer, "Supply Chain Technology: the Role of Environment in Predicting Performance," *Journal of the Academy of Marketing Science* 38, no. 1 (2010), pp. 42–55; Erin Anderson and Barton Weitz, "The Use of Pledges to Build and Sustain Commitment in Distribution Channels," *Journal of Marketing Research* 29 (February 1992), pp. 18–34.

15. http://www.marketingpower.com/_layouts/Dictionary.aspx.

16. Jean Thilmany, "Neiman Marcus Sails through Customs," *Apparel Magazine*, 49, no. 2 (2007).

17. Matthew Waller, Brent Williams, Andrea Tangari, and Scot Burton, "Marketing at the Retail Shelf: an Examination of Moderating Effects of Logistics on SKU Market Share," *Journal of the Academy of Marketing Science* 38, no. 1 (2010), pp. 105–17.

18. Vanessa O'Connell and Peter Latman, "Neiman Enlists Designers in Cost-Cutting Plan," *The Wall Street Journal*, December 10, 2009.

19. http:// http://www.vendormanagedinventory.com.

20. G. P. Kiesmüller and R. A. C. M. Broekmeulen, "The Benefit of VMI Strategies in a Stochastic Multi-Product Serial Two Echelon System," *Computers and Operations Research* 37, no. 2 (2010), pp. 406–16; Dong-Ping Song and John Dinwoodie, "Quantifying the Effectiveness of VMI and Integrated Inventory Management in a Supply Chain with Uncertain Lead-Times and Uncertain Demands," *Production Planning & Control* 19, no. 6 (2008), pp. 590–600; S. P. Nachiappan, A. Gunasekaran, and N. Jawahar, "Knowledge Management System for Operating Parameters in Two-Echelon VMI Supply Chains," *International Journal of Production Research* 45, no. 11 (2007), pp. 2479–2505; Andres Angulo, Heather Nachtmann, and Matthew A. Waller, "Supply Chain Information Sharing in a Vendor Managed Inventory Partnership," *Journal of Business Logistics* 25 (2004), pp. 101–120.

21. "Home Depot Expands Supply Chain Gains," *Journal of Commerce*, September 23, 2011, http://www.joc.com/supply-chain-manage-ment/home-depot-expands-supply-chain-gains-tabs-fidelitone; Jon Kell, "Supply Chain Boosts Net at Home Depot," *The Wall Street Journal*, November 16, 2011, http://online.wsj.com/article/SB100014 24052970204323904577039673053195242.html.

22. http://seekingalpha.com/article/194466-rfid-technology-transforming-food-retailers-like-wal-mart.

23. George Anderson, "Macy's Moves to Item-Level Tracking Using RFID," *Retail Wire*, September 29, 2011.

24. Kevin Scarpati, "Tesco Big Price Drop Helped by Supply Chain Management," *Supply Chain Digital*, September 23, 2011, http://www.supplychaindigital.com/global_logistics/tesco-big-price-drop-helped-by-supply-chain-management; Michael Garry, "Supply Chain Systems Seen Boosting Tesco's U.S. Stores," *Supermarket News*, 55, no. 43 (2007).

25. André Luís Shiguemoto, and Vinícius Amaral Armentano, "A Tabu Search Procedure for Coordinating Production, Inventory and Distribution Routing Problems, *International Transactions in Operational Research* 17, no. 2 (2009), pp. 179–95; Ayse Akbalik, Sekoun Kebe, Bernard Penz, and Najiba Sbihi, "Exact Methods and a Heuristic for the Optimization of an Integrated Replenishment-Storage Planning Problem," *International Transactions in Operational Research*, 15, no. 2 (March 2008), pp. 195–214.

26. Vertica Bhardwaj and Ann Fairhurst, "Fast Fashion: Response to Changes in the Fashion Industry," *International Review of Retail, Distribution and Consumer Research* 20 (February 2010), pp. 165–73; Felipe Caro, Jérémie Gallien, Miguel Díaz Miranda, Javier García Torralbo, Jose Manuel Corrediora Corras, Marcos Montes Vazques, José Antonio Ramos Calamonte, and Juan Correa, "Zara Uses Operations Research to Reengineer Its Global Distribution Process," *Interfaces* 40 (2010), pp. 71–84; Carmen Lopez and Ying Fan, "Case Study: Internationalisation of the Spanish Fashion Brand Zara," *Journal of Fashion Marketing and Management* 13, no. 2 (2009), pp. 279–96; Mark Mulligan, "Spanish Professor Who Uncovers the Detail in Retail; Constant Contact with Corporate Life Is a Valuable Teaching Tool," *Financial Times*, August 18, 2008, p. 12; "Combining Art with Science, Zara Competes with 'Fast Fashion'," *SupplyChainBrain*, February 7, 2008.

27. Zeynep Ton, Elena Corsi, and Vincent Dessain, "Zara: Managing Stores for Fast Fashion," Harvard Business School, March 2011.

Chapter 17

1. Wikipedia, http://en.wikipedia.org/wiki/Home_Shopping_Network; Ross Blum, "Where Have All the Customers Gone?" p. 8.

2. Barbara Thau, "HSN, QVC Makeover: Tacky Baubles Out, Couture In," *CNBC*, August 18, 2010.

3. Suzanne Vranica, "HSN Starts Mixing Ads Into Its Usual Sales Pitches," *The Wall Street Journal*, September 28, 2009.

4. "In The Know," YouTube, Fall 2009 http://www.gstatic.com/youtube/engagement/platform/autoplay/advertise/downloads/YouTube_InTheKnow.pdf; http://www.youtube.com/t/advertising_audience_targeting.

5. "Brand Channels," YouTube, Fall 2009 http://www.gstatic.com/youtube/engagement/platform/autoplay/advertise/downloads/YouTube_BrandChannels.pdf; http://www.youtube.com/t/advertising_brand_channels.

6. "YouTube Insight," YouTube, Fall 2009 http://www.gstatic.com/youtube/engagement/platform/autoplay/advertise/downloads/YouTube_Insight.pdf; http://www.youtube.com/t/advertising_insight.

7. Leah Shafer, "Re-Branding the Dynasty: Tori Spelling's HSN Clips on YouTube," http://mediacommons.futureofthebook.org/imr/2010/03/24/re-branding-dynasty-tori-spellings-hsn-clips-you-tube, March 25, 2010.

8. "Top 10 Global Retailers," http://www.cnbc.com/id/40989307/Top_10_Global_Retailers?slide=11.

9. This chapter draws heavily from Michael Levy and Barton A. Weitz, *Retailing Management*, 8th ed. (Burr Ridge, IL: McGraw-Hill/Irwin, 2012).

10. Patricia Marx, "A Bushel and a Peck," *The New Yorker*, January 16, 2012, pp. 32–36.

11. *Industry Outlook: Food Channel* (Columbus, OH: Retail Forward, July 2008); *Industry Outlook: Food Channel* (Columbus, OH: Retail Forward, April 2007).

12. Mary Holz-Clause and Malinda Geisler, "Grocery Industry," February 2012, http://www.agmrc.org/markets__industries/food/grocery_industry.cfm; "Top 25 Global Retailers 2011, http://supermarketnews.com/top-25-global-retailers-2011.

13. http://www.fmi.org/glossary/?search=Yes&letter=C.

14. "Supermarket Sales by Department," October 2011, http://www.fmi.org/docs/facts_figs/grocerydept.pdf.

15. http://www.tmcnet.com/usubmit/2007/10/13/3012485.htm.

16. http://www.tmcnet.com/usubmit/2007/10/13/3012485.htm.

17. "Supermarket Social Scenes," *Retail Wire*, March 22, 2011.

18. "Walmart Supercenters," http://walmartstores.com/AboutUs/7606.aspx.

19. https://www.deloitte.com/assets/Dcom-Global/Local%20Assets/Documents/Consumer%20Business/dtt_CBT_GPRetailing2012.pdf.

20. Karen Talley, "Department Stores Are In Good Position After 1Q Resurgence," Dow Jones Newswires, May 16, 2011.

21. http://www.walletpop.com/blog/2009/05/14/love-amidst-the-layoffs-macys-parades-its-new-fashion-label/.

22. http://walmartstores.com/sites/annualreport/2011/financials/Walmart_2011_Annual_Report.pdf; Sandra M. Jones, "*Wal-Mart Making Little Plans*," Chicago Tribune, May 14, 2011.

23. Craig Guillot, "Masters of the Game," *Stores*, July 2009; http://www.gamestop.com/gs/tournaments/h3o/default.aspx.

24. "Industry Facts," The Entertainment Software Association, http://www.theesa.com/facts/index.asp.

25. "About Kongregate," http://www.kongregate.com/pages/about.

26. http://joltonline.com/about/.

27. "Corporate Profile," http://phx.corporate-ir.net/phoenix.zhtml?c=130125&p=irol-irhome.

28. Russell Redman, "Industry Outlook: Drug Chains Lifted by Improved Economy," *Chain Drug Review*, May 2, 2011, http://www.chaindrugreview.com/inside-this-issue/news/04-25-2011/industry-outlook-drug-chains-lifted-by-improved-economy.

29. Hoover's, "Drug Stores," http://www.hoovers.com/industry/drug-stores/1532-1.html.

30. Susan Berfield, "Duane Reade's Miracle Makeover," *BusinessWeek*, September 29, 2011.

31. George Anderson, "Are Drugstores Priced Too High to Compete in Grocery?" *Retailwire*, October 7, 2011.

32. http://www.wikinvest.com/industry/Off-price_Retail.

33. This section draws from Michael Levy and Barton A. Weitz, *Retailing Management 9e*, 2015, Burr Ridge Il: McGraw-Hill/Irwin, Chapter 2.

34. Lydia Dishman, "Why Karl Lagerfeld's Collection for Macy's Is the Retailer's Ticket to Profits," *Fortune.com*, July 21, 2011.

35. Sandhya Raman, "Shopkick's CEO Talks Entrepreneurship, Mobile Marketing and the Future," Fiercemobilecontent.com, May 10, 2011; Adam Ostrow, "How Accurate Is Your Smartphone's GPS? [MAP]," Mashable, March 9, 2011; Rimma Kats, "Walgreens: Mobile is Key Component of Multichannel Loyalty Strategy," Mobilecommercedaily.com, March 4, 2011; Jennifer Van Grove, "242 Target Stores Start Offering Shopkick Checkin Rewards," Mashable, November 16, 2010.

36. Nancy M. Pucinelli, Dhruv Grewal, Susan Andrzejewski, Ereni Markos, and Tracy Noga, "The Value of Knowing What Customers Really Want: Interpersonal Accuracy as an Environmental Cue," working paper (2012); Nancy Puccinelli, Ronald C. Goodstein, Dhruv Grewal, Rob Price, Priya Raghubir, and David Stewart, "Customer Experience Management in Retailing: Understanding the Buying Process," *Journal of Retailing* 85 (2009), pp. 15–30.

37. Patricia Marx, "C. Wonder," *The New Yorker*, November 21, 2011, p. 34.

38. Ibid.

39. Kathleen Seiders, Glenn B. Voss, Andrea L. Godfrey, and Dhruv Grewal, "SERVCON: A Multidimensional Scale for Measuring Perceptions of Service Convenience," *Journal of the Academy of Marketing Science* 35, no. 1 (2007), pp. 144–56; Leonard Berry, Kathleen Seiders, and Dhruv Grewal, "Understanding Service Convenience," *Journal of Marketing* 66, no. 3 (July 2002).

40. Randolph E. Bucklin and Catarina Sismeiro, "Click Here for Internet Insight: Advances in Clickstream Data Analysis in Marketing," *Journal of Interactive Marketing* (February 2009), pp. 35–48.

41. Jayne O'Donnell, "Are Retailers Going Too Far Tracking Our Web Habits?" *USA Today*, October 26, 2009.

42. http://www.lsoft.com/resources/optinlaws.asp.

43. http://www.ftc.gov/bcp/edu/pubs/business/ecommerce/bus28.shtm.

44. Kenneth Hein, "Study: Web Research Nets In-Store Sales," *Brandweek*, May 7, 2007.

45. "Sponsored Supplement: Expanding the Reach of Personalization," *Internet Retailer*, March 2010.

46. Susan Reda, "The Personal Touch," *Stores*, January 2011.

47. Jill Avery, Thomas J. Steenburgh, John Deighton, and Mary Caravella, "Adding Bricks to Clicks: The Contingencies Driving Cannibalization and Complementarity in Multichannel Retailing," *SSRN working paper* (2009), http:\\ssrn.com\abstract=961567.

48. J. C. Williams Group, "Organizing for Cross-Channel Retailing," white paper, Toronto, January 2008; IBM Global Business Services, "Customer Centricity Drives Retail's Multichannel Imperative," white paper, Armonk, NY, 2008.

49. Jie Zhang, Paul Farris, John Irvin, Tarun Kushwaha, Thomas Steenburgh, and Barton Weitz, "Crafting Integrated Multichannel Retailing Strategies," *Journal of Interactive Marketing*, 2010.

50. Target.com, "Corporate Overview," http://pressroom.target.com /pr/news/corporate-overview.aspx.

51. Jessica Wohl, "Target Hopes Exclusive Designer Deals Boost Sales," *Reuters*, August 2, 2011.

52. Mary Catherine O'Connor, "Target Shoppers: Say Goodbye to Michael Graves' Budget-Friendly Design," *smartplanet*, February 16, 2012, http://www.smartplanet.com/blog/design-architecture /target-shoppers-say-goodbye-to-michael-graves-budget-friendly-design/4215.

53. Target.com, "Target Unveils New Design Partnership Program," January 13, 2012, http://pressroom.target.com/pr/news/target-unveils-new-design-partnership-221743.aspx.

54. Emanualla Grinberg, "'Missoni for Target' Line Crashes Site," CNN .com, September 13, 2011, http://articles.cnn.com/2011-09-13 /living/living_missoni-for-target-line-creates-black-friday-like-demand_1_missoni-isaac-mizrahi-target-com?_s=PM:LIVING.

55. "Jason Wu for Target Apparel Sells Out in Hours," ABCNews.com, February 6, 2012, http://abcnews.go.com/blogs/business/2012/02 /jason-wu-for-target-sells-out-in-first-morning-2/.

56. Stephanie Clifford, "In a Test, Target Plans to Add an Apple 'Store' Inside 25 Stores," *The New York Times*, January 12, 2101, http:// www.nytimes.com/2012/01/13/business/target-plans-apple-mini-stores.html.

57. Ibid.; Target.com, op. cit.

58. Samantha Murphy, "Apple Mini-Stores Coming to Target," *The Wall Street Journal*, January 13, 2012, http://mashable.com/2012/01/13 /apple-store-target/.

59. Ibid, Clifford.

60. Ibid, Clifford.

Chapter 18

1. Coca-Cola Company, "Treasure Hunt for the 1922 Coca-Cola Polar Bear Ad," October 28, 2011, http://www.coca-colaconversations.com/my_weblog/2011/10/treasure-hunt-for-the-1922-coca-cola-polar-bear-ad.html.

2. Coca-Cola Company, "Live from the Arctic: Coca-Cola Animated Polar Bears to 'Catch' the Big Game on Feb. 5," Press Release, January 26, 2012, http://www.thecoca-colacompany.com/dynamic /press_center/2012/01/coca-cola-polar-bears-to-catch-the-big-game .html.

3. Coca-Cola Company, "The Coca-Cola Polar Bowl–Game Day Moments," http://www.youtube.com/playlist?list=PL0D74B5C94 759942A.

4. Ace Metrix, "Doritos Crashes the Super Bowl Once Again and So Does M&Ms," Press Release, https://www.acemetrix.com/news /press-releases/doritos-crashes-the-super-bowl-once-again-and-so-does-mms/.

5. Ibid.

6. Alan Parker, "Coca-Cola and the Polar Bears," *Toronto Star*, December 1, 2011, http://blogs.canoe.ca/parker/general/coca-cola-and-the-polar-bears/.

7. Coca-Cola Company, "Live from the Arctic," op. cit.

8. Terence A. Shimp, *Advertising Promotion and Other Aspects of Integrated Marketing Communication*, 8th ed. (Mason, OH: South-Western College Publishers, 2008); T. Duncan and C. Caywood, "The Concept, Process, and Evolution of Integrated Marketing Communication," in *Integrated Communication: Synergy of Persuasive Voices*, eds. E. Thorson and J. Moore (Mahwah, NJ: Lawrence Erlbaum Associates, 1996); see also various issues of the *Journal of Integrated Marketing Communications*, http:// jimc.medill.northwestern.edu.

9. Simon Dumenco, "The Show that Beats American Idol: Exploring the Popularity of *The Big Bang Theory*," *Ad Age*, February 24, 2012, http://adage.com/article/mediaworks/inside-exploding-popularity-big-bang-theory/232946/.

10. Stuart Elliott, "M&M's to Unveil New Speaking Role at Super Bowl," *The New York Times*, January 16, 2012; Tim Nudd, "M&M's Wins YouTube's Super Bowl Ad Blitz Contest," *Ad Week*, February 20, 2012, http://www.adweek.com/news/advertising-branding/mms-wins-youtubes-super-bowl-ad-blitz-contest-138418

11. Terence A. Shimp, *Advertising Promotion and Other Aspects of Integrated Marketing Communication*, 8th ed. (Mason, OH: South-Western College Publishers, 2008); Deborah J. MacInnis, Christine Moorman, and Bernard J. Jaworski, "Enhancing and Measuring Consumers' Motivation, Opportunity," *Journal of Marketing*, 55, no. 4 (October 1991), pp. 32–53; Joan Meyers-Levy, "Elaborating on Elaboration: The Distinction between Relational and Item-Specific Elaboration," *Journal of Consumer Research*, 18 (December 1991), pp. 358–367.

12. E. K. Strong, *The Psychology of Selling* (New York: McGraw Hill, 1925).

13. Disney, "Music Stars," http://disney.go.com/characters/#/characters/musicstars/; Belinda Luscombe, "How Disney Builds Stars," *Time*, November 2, 2009.

14. John Philip Jones, "What Makes Advertising Work?" *The Economic Times*, July 24, 2002.

15. http://www.legamedia.net/lx/result/match/0591dfc9787c111b1b2 4dde6d61e43c5/index.php.

16. http://popsop.com/wp-content/uploads/toyota_prius_plural_02. jpg; http://www.youtube.com/watch?v=nUor4gdFoyg&feature=p layer_embedded#!; http://www.saatchi.com/news/archive/prius_ goes_plural_through_new_integrated_campaign.

17. Chris Barrows, "Unauthorized Verses," *Journal of Integrated Marketing Communications*, Evanston: Northwestern University, 2009.

18. American Marketing Association, *Dictionary of Marketing Terms* (Chicago: American Marketing Association, 2008).

19. Eric Wilson, "Checking Models' IDs at the Door," *The New York Times*, February 8, 2012, http://www.nytimes.com/2012/02/09 /fashion/efforts-to-stop-use-of-underage-models-during-new-york-fashion-week.html?pagewanted=all.

20. Ellie Krupnick, "Drop Dead Ads Banned by ASA for Too-Skinny Model," *The Huffington Post*, November 10. 2011, http://www .huffingtonpost.com/2011/11/10/drop-dead-ads-banned-asa _n_1085903.html.

21. David Gianastasio, "Fashion Site Nixes Photo of Freakishly Thin-Looking Model," *AdWeek*, July 13, 2011, http://www.adweek.com /adfreak/fashion-site-nixes-photo-freakishly-thin-looking-model-133367.

22. Teri Evans, "Firms Hold Fast to Snail Mail Marketing," *The Wall Street Journal*, January 12, 2010, http://online.wsj.com/article/SB 10001424052748703481004574646904234860412.html; George E. Belch and Michael A. Belch, *Advertising and Promotion: An Integrated Marketing Communications Perspective* (New York: McGraw-Hill, 2007).

23. Rebecca Lieb, "Q&A: Cindy Krum Cuts Through the Mobile Marketing Alphabet Soup of NFC and RFID," http://econsultancy. com/blog/5608-q-a-cindy-krum-cuts-through-the-mobile-marketing-alphabet-soup-of-nfc-and-rfid, March 16, 2010.

24. Emily Steel, "How Marketers Hone Their Aim Online," *The Wall Street Journal*, June 19, 2007.

25. Charles Duhigg, "How Companies Learn Your Secrets," *New York Times*, February 16, 2012.

26. George Anderson, "White House, Web Giants Address Consumer Privacy Online," *Retail Wire*, February 24, 2012.

27. Akihisa Fujita, "Mobile Marketing in Japan: The Acceleration of Integrated Marketing Communications," *Journal of Integrated Marketing Communications* (2008), pp. 41-46; Mobile update:

http://www.businessinsider.com/henry-blodget-enough-empty-headed-puffery-about-mobile-ads-time-for-analysts-to-stop-jawboning-and-think-2009-10; http://www.informationweek.com/news/security/privacy/showArticle.jhtml?articleID=222300256&subSection=News; http://www.nearbynow.com/info/iphone_platform.html, accessed May 26. 2010.

28. Tanya Irwin, "Weston Invites Customers to 'Warm Up,'" *Marketing Daily*, March 13, 2011, http://www.mediapost.com/publications/article/146572/; Rimma Kats, "Westin Hotels & Resorts Aiming for Increased Bookings Via Geo-Targeted Mobile Ad," *Mobile Commerce Daily*, March 9, 2011, http://www.mobilecommerce-daily.com/2011/03/09/westin-hotels-resorts-aims-for-increased-bookings-via-geo-targeted-mobile-ad; Rimma Kats, "Westin Hotels & Resorts Bolsters Mobile Bookings Via TWC iPad Sponsorship," *Mobile Commerce Daily*, October 24, 2011, http://www.mobilecommercedaily.com/2011/10/24/westin-hotels-resorts-bolsters-mobile-bookings-via-twc-ipad-sponsorship.

29. Yubo Chen, Scott Fay, and Qi Wang, "The Role of Marketing in Social Media: How Online Consumer Reviews Evolve," *Journal of Interactive Marketing* 25, no. 2 (May 2011), pp. 85–94; Bonnie Rochman, "Sweet Spot," *Time*, November 2009.

30. www.blogsouthwest.com.

31. Chris Lee, "Kevin Smith's Southwest Incident Sets Web All A-Twitter," *Los Angeles Times*, February 16, 2010, http://articles.latimes.com/2010/feb/16/entertainment/la-et-kevin-smith16-2010feb16.

32. Christi Day, "Not So Silent Bob," February 14, 2010, http://www.blogsouthwest.com/blog/not-so-silent-bob.

33. Dennis Schaal, "Priceline Unveils New Ad Campaign with Shatner and Kareem," tnooz, February 14, 2011, http://www.tnooz.com/2011/02/14/news/priceline-unveils-new-ad-campaign-with-shatner-naomi-pryce-and-kareem/; Rich Tomaselli, "Priceline Kills the Messenger Because Ads Worked Too Well," *Advertising Age*, January 30, 2010, http://adage.com/article/news/priceline-kills-messenger-ads-worked/232409/.

34. "Priceline.com to Webcast 4th Quarter 2011 Financial Results on February 27th," *The New York Times*, January 30, 2012, http://markets.on.nytimes.com/research/stocks/news/press_release.asp?docTag=201201301601PR_NEWS_USPRX____NY43796&feedID=600&press_symbol=226354.

35. Tomaselli, op. cit.

36. Chris Isidore, "Shorter Returns to Priceline Ads," *CNN Money Tech*, August 15, 2012.

37. This section draws from Michael Levy and Barton A. Weitz, *Retailing Management*, 8th ed. (Burr Ridge, IL: McGraw-Hill/Irwin, 2012).

38. Megan Halscheid, Micheline Sabatté, and Sejal Sura, "Beyond the Last Click: Measuring ROI and Consumer Engagement with Clickstream Analysis," *Journal of Integrated Marketing Communications* (2009), pp. 43–50; Vikram Mahidhar and Christine Cutten, "Navigating the Marketing Measurement Maze," *Journal of Integrated Marketing Communications* (2007), pp. 41–46.

39. http://www.riger.com/know_base/media/understanding.html.

40. "IAB Reports Full-Year Internet Ad Revenues for 2010 Increase 15% to $26 Billion, a New Record," April 13, 2011, http://www.iab.net/about_the_iab/recent_press_releases/press_release_archive/press_release/pr-041311.

41. "Facebook Pages: Insights for your Facebook Page," http://www.facebook.com/help/?search=insights#!/help/?faq=15221.

42. "Marketing and Advertising Using Google," Google 2007.

43. http://publishing2.com/2008/05/27/google-adwords-a-brief-history-of-online-advertising-innovation/.

44. Drew Davis, "Jay-Z's Offline Campaign Leads to Online Action," *Tipping Point Labs*, August 25, 2011, http://tippingpointlabs.com/2011/08/25/jay-zs-offline-campaign-leads-to-online-action/.

45. Teressa Iezzi, "Jay-Zs 'Decoded' Campaign Wins Integrated Grand Prix and Titanium at Cannes," *Fast Company*, June 25, 2011, http://www.fastcocreate.com/1679205/jay-z-decoded-wins-integrated-grand-prix-and-titanium-at-cannes.

46. Ibid.; Andrew Adam Newman, "Find Jay-Z's Memoir at a Bookstore, or on Billboard," *The New York Times*, October 18, 2010, http://www.nytimes.com/2010/10/18/business/media/18adco.html.

47. Newman, op. cit.

48. Droga5, "Bing/Decode Jay-Z Case Study," YouTube, http://www.youtube.com/watch?v=XNic4wf8AYg&feature=player_embedded.

49. http://bing.decodejay-z.com/?fbid=Xbh8cDvdLDY&wom=false.

50. Newman, op. cit.

51. Dan Duray, "Jay-Z's Book to Be Utterly Inescapable, Thanks to Bing, Clear Channel," *New York Observer*, October 18, 2010, http://www.observer.com/2010/10/jayzs-book-to-be-utterly-inescapable-thanks-to-bing-clear-channel/?utm_medium=partial-text&utm_campaign=home.

52. Newman, op. cit.

53. Iezzi, op. cit.

54. Droga5, op. cit.

55. Ibid.

Chapter 19

1. Natalie Zmuda, "Tropicana Goes Back to Nature in New Global Pitch," *Ad Age Global*, February 20, 2012, http://adage.com/article/global-news/tropicana-back-nature-global-pitch/232819/.

2. Stuart Elliott, "Marketing Budgets Rise for Some Giants," *The New York Times*, February 21, 2012, http://www.nytimes.com/2012/02/21/business/media/marketing-budgets-rise-for-some-giants.html.

3. Shirley Brady, "Here Comes the Sun: Tropicana Wakes Up London," *brandchannel.com*, January 24, 2012, http://www.brandchannel.com/home/post/2012/01/24/Tropicana-Wakes-Up-London-012412.aspx.

4. Ibid.

5. Greyworld, "Trafalgar Sun 2012," http://greyworld.org/archives/1108.

6. Ibid.

7. Brady, op. cit.

8. Jeff Greenhouse, "Tropicana Playfully Squeezes the Big Apple with New Ad Campaign," August 4, 2011, http://www.jeffgreenhouse.com/2011/08/04/tropicana-new-york-mornings-campaign/.

9. Jeff Greenhouse, "DDB Squeezes New York for Another Round of Great Tropicana Ads," February 2, 2010, http://www.jeffgreenhouse.com/2012/02/02/ddb-squeezes-new-york-for-another-round-of-great-tropicana-ads/.

10. George E. Belch and Michael A. Belch, *Advertising and Promotion: An Integrated Marketing Communications Perspective* (New York: McGraw-Hill, 2007); Jef I. Richards and Catherine M. Curran, "Oracles on 'Advertising': Searching for a Definition," *Journal of Advertising* 31, no. 2 (Summer 2002), pp. 63–77.

11. Alexandra Bruell, "ZenithOptimedia Forecasts Slow, Steady Growth in Global Ad Spend," *Ad Age*, March 12, 2012, http://adage.com/article/agency-news/zenithoptimedia-forecasts-steady-growth-global-ad-spend/233286/.

12. Dan Zigmond, Sundar Dorai-Raj, Yannet Interian, and Igor Naverniouk, "Measuring Advertising Quality on Television: Deriving Meaningful Metrics from Audience Retention Data," *Journal of Advertising Research* 49, no. 4 (December 2009), pp. 419–28; Robert G. Heath, Agnes C. Nairn, and Paul A. Bottomley, "How Effective is Creativity? Emotive Content in TV Advertising Does Not Increase Attention," *Journal of Advertising Research* 49, no. 4 (December 2009), pp. 450–63; Raymond R. Burke and Thomas K. Srull, "Competitive Interference and Consumer Memory for Advertising," *Journal of Consumer Research*, 15 (June 1988),

pp. 55–68; Kevin Lane Keller, "Memory Factors in Advertising: The Effect of Advertising Retrieval Cues on Brand Evaluation," *Journal of Consumer Research*, 14 (December 1987), pp. 316–333.

13. Markus Pfeiffer and Markus Zinnbauer, "Can Old Media Enhance New Media?: How Traditional Advertising Pays off for an Online Social Network," *Journal of Advertising Research* 50, no. 1 (2010), pp. 42–49; Terry Daugherty, Matthew Eastin, and Laura Bright, "Exploring Consumer Motivations for Creating User-Generated Content," *Journal of Interactive Advertising*, 8, no. 2 (2008); Anthony Bianco, "The Vanishing Mass Market," *BusinessWeek*, July 12, 2004, pp. 61–68.

14. David Griner, "Adidas Fires Up Its Largest Ad Campaign Ever," *AdWeek*, March 16, 2011.

15. William F. Arens, Michael F. Weigold, and Christian Arens, *Contemporary Advertising* 12th ed. (New York: McGraw-Hill, 2008).

16. Stephen Williams, "Fiat Enlists Ultimate Bad Boy for Ads: Charlie Sheen," *Ad Age*, March 1, 2012, http://adage.com/article/adages/fiat-enlists-ultimate-bad-boy-ads-charlie-sheen/233045/.

17. Tulin Erdem, Michael Keane, and Baohong Sun, "The Impact of Advertising on Consumer Price Sensitivity in Experience Goods Markets," *Quantitative Marketing and Economics* 6 (June 2008), pp. 139–76; Xiaojing Yang and Robert E. Smith, "Beyond Attention Effects: Modeling the Persuasive and Emotional Effects of Advertising Creativity," *Marketing Science* 28 (September/October 2009), pp. 935–49; Matthew Shum, "Does Advertising Overcome Brand Loyalty? Evidence from the Breakfast Cereal Market," *Journal of Economics and Management Strategy* 13, no. 2 (2004), pp. 77–85.

18. "Got Milk?" http://www.gotmilk.com.

19. Elaine Wong, "Rebecca Romjin Makes Milk Run," *Brandweek*, January 13, 2010.

20. http://www.marketingpower.com/_layouts/Dictionary.aspx?dLetter=P.

21. Jonathan Blum, "Why Yum Brands Fights Hunger," *Ad Age*, November 1, 2011, http://adage.com/article/goodworks/yum-brands-fights-hunger/230740/.

22. "Jaime's Story," http://www.aad.org/media-resources/public-service-advertisements/jaimes-story.

23. http://www.thetruth.com.

24. truth, "Facts," http://www.thetruth.com/facts/.

25. Alina Tugend, "Cigarette Makers Take Anti-Smoking Ads Personally," *The New York Times*, October 27, 2002.

26. Theodore Leavitt, *The Marketing Imagination* (New York: The Free Press, 1986).

27. Belch and Belch, *Advertising and Promotion: An Integrated Marketing Communications Perspective*.

28. Exxon Mobil, http://www.exxonmobil.com/corporate/news_ad_corpus_clean.aspx.

29. Katherine White and John Peloza, "Self-Benefit Versus Other-Benefit Marketing Appeals: Their Effectiveness in Generating Charitable Support," *Journal of Marketing* 73 (July 2009), pp. 109–124.

30. Darren W. Dahl, Jaideep Sengupta, and Kathleen D. Vohs, "Sex in Advertising: Gender Differences and the Role of Relationship Commitment," *Journal of Consumer Research* 36, no. 2 (2009), pp. 215–31; Jaideep Sengupta and Darren W. Dahl, "Gender-Related Reactions to Gratuitous Sex Appeals in Advertising," *Journal of Consumer Psychology* 18, no. 1 (2008), pp. 62–78.

31. Jack Loftus, "ADT Ad Campaign Scares Homeowners into Buying ADT Security," Gizmodo, http://gizmodo.com/5654365/adt-ad-campaign-scares-homeowners-into-buying-adt-security; Jack Neff, "What the Stylish Garbage Can Is Wearing," *Ad Age*, November 3, 2011, http://adage.com/article/news/marketing-hefty-blackout-designer-kitchen-bags/146880/; Natalie Zmuda, "Best Buy Ups Holiday Spending, Introduces 'Game On, Santa' Campaign," *Ad Age*, November 17, 2011, http://adage.com/article/news/game-buy-ups-holiday-spending/231086/; Andrew Adam Newman, "Axe Adds Fragrance for Women to Its Lineup," *The New York Times*, January 8, 2012, http://www.nytimes.com/2012/01/09/business/media/axe-adds-fragrance-for-women-to-its-lineup.html.

32. AMA Dictionary, http://www.marketingpower.com/_layouts/Dictionary.aspx?dLetter=M

33. Anthony Crupy, "Cable Sports Take a Bite Out of Broadcast Ad Sales," *Adweek*, September 13, 2011, http://www.adweek.com/news/television/cable-sports-take-bite-out-broadcast-ad-sales-134805; John Tejada, "Marketers Flock to Digital Media," *Adweek*, November 30, 2011, http://www.adweek.com/news/advertising-branding/marketers-flock-digital-media-136784.

34. Some illustrative articles look at the effectiveness of given media: Robert Heath, "Emotional Engagement: How Television Builds Big Brands at Low Attention," *Journal of Advertising Research* 49, no. 1 (March 2009), pp. 62–73; Lex van Meurs and Mandy Aristoff, "Split-Second Recognition: What Makes Outdoor Advertising Work?" *Journal of Advertising Research* 49, no. 1 (March 2009), pp. 82–92.

35. Arens, Weigold, and Arens, *Contemporary Advertising*.

36. William F. Arens, David H. Schaefer, Michael F. Weigold, *Advertising, M-Series*, Burr Ridge: Irwin/McGraw-Hill, 2012

37. Stephen Williams, "New Sedans Aim to Break Out of the Pack," *AdAge*, February 20, 2012, http://adage.com/article/news/sedans-aim-break-pack/232794/.

38. Dean M. Krugman, Leonard N. Reid, S. Watson Dunn, and Arnold M. Barban, *Advertising: Its Role in Modern Marketing* (New York: The Dryden Press, 1994), pp. 221–26.

39. David Kiefaber, "Taylor Swift's CoverGirl Ad Is Pulled Over Bogus Eyelashes," *Adweek*, December 23, 2011, http://www.adweek.com/adfreak/taylor-swifts-covergirl-ad-pulled-over-bogus-eye-lashes-137269.

40. David Gianastasio, "Turlington Ads: So Photoshopped They're Misleading?" *Adweek*, July 28, 2011, http://www.adweek.com/adfreak/julia-roberts-christy-turlington-ads-so-photoshopped-theyre-misleading-133731.

41. Tanzina Vega, "British Authority Bans Two Ads by L'Oreal," *The New York Times*, July 27, 2011, http://mediadecoder.blogs.nytimes.com/2011/07/27/british-authority-bans-two-ads-by-loreal/.

42. Herbert Jack Rotfeld and Charles R. Taylor, "The Need for Interdisciplinary Research of Advertising Regulation: A Roadmap for Avoiding Confusion and Errors," *Journal of Advertising* (Winter 2009).

43. Andrea Thompson, "Misleading Food Labels to Get Makeover," *MSNBC.com*, March 15, 2010, http://www.msnbc.msn.com/id/35839186/ns/health-diet_and_nutrition/.

44. Debra Harker, Michael Harker, and Robert Burns, "Tackling Obesity: Developing a Research Agenda for Advertising Researchers," *Journal of Current Issues & Research in Advertising*, 29, no. 2 (2007), pp. 39–51; N. Kapoor and D. P. S. Verma, "Children's Understanding of TV Advertisements: Influence of Age, Sex and Parents," *Vision*, 9, no. 1 (2005), pp. 21–36; Catharine M. Curran and Jef I. Richards, "The Regulation of Children's Advertising in the U.S.," *International Journal of Advertising and Marketing to Children*, 2, no. 2 (2002).

45. Irina Slutsky, "Nine Things You Can't Do in Advertising if You Want to Stay on the Right Side of the Law," *AdAge*, March 7, 2011, http://adage.com/article/news/advertising-regulation-nad-case-rulings-remember/149226/.

46. Bob Hunt, "Truth in Your Advertising: Avoid Puffery?" *Realty Times*, June 20, 2007.

47. Ibid.

48. Christina Binkley, "Which Stars Sell Fashion?" *The Wall Street Journal,* February 4, 2010.

49. Diego Rinallo and Suman Basuroy, "Does Advertising Spending Influence Media Coverage of the Advertiser?" *Journal of Marketing* 73 (November 2009), pp. 33–46; Carl Obermiller and Eric R. Spangenberg, "On the Origin and Distinctness of Skepticism toward Advertising," *Marketing Letters,* 11, no. 4 (2000), p. 311.

50. Jackie Huba, "A Just Cause Creating Emotional Connections with Customers," http://www.inc.com/articles/2003/05/25537.html.

51. http://www.createapepper.com; http://causerelatedmarketing.blogspot.com/2008/03/how-chilis-used-cause-related-marketing.html.

52. Personal communication with Rob Price, VP of Retail Marketing, CVS, June 16, 2009; Carol Angrisani, "CVS Moves to Personalization," *SN: Supermarket News,* 56, no. 2 (March 24, 2008), p. 29.

53. Stephanie Clifford, "Web Coupons Know Lots About You, and They Tell," *New York Times,* April 16, 2010.

54. Jack Neff, "Old Spice Is Killing It on YouTube Again, But Sales Are Down Double-Digits," *AdAge,* August 4, 2011, http://adage.com/article/the-viral-video-chart/spice-killing-youtube-sales/229080/.

55. http://sports.espn.go.com/espn/contests/index.

56. Eva A. van Reijmersdal, Peter C. Neijens, and Edith G. Smit, "A New Branch of Advertising: Reviewing Factors that Influence Reactions to Product Placement," *Journal of Advertising Research* 49, no. 4 (December 2009), pp. 429–49; Pamela Mills Homer, "Product Placement: The Impact of Placement Type and Repetition on Attitude," *Journal of Advertising* (Fall 2009); Elizabeth Cowley and Chris Barron, "When Product Placement Goes Wrong: The Effects of Program Liking and Placement Prominence," *Journal of Advertising* (Spring 2008).

57. Neil Munshi, "Spain's Starring Role in Bollywood Movie a Boon to Tourism," *AdAge,* February 6, 2012, http://adage.com/article/global-news/spain-s-starring-role-bollywood-movie-a-boon-tourism/232511/.

58. Abe Sauer, "Announcing the 2012 Brandcameo Product Placement Award Winners," *brandchannel.com,* February 13, 2012, http://www.brandchannel.com/home/post/2012-Brandcameo-Product-Placement-Awards-021312.aspx#one.

59. Ibid.

60. www.jcrew.com.

61. http://www.cardhub.com/edu/market-share-by-credit-card-network/.

62. http://www.youtube.com/watch?v=3dcxQ2dvqmc.

63. http://marketingpractice.blogspot.com/2006/11/mastercard-priceless.html.

64. http://www.mastercard.com/us/company/en/docs/CorporateOverview_FINAL.pdf.

65. https://www.mastercard.com/us/company/en/docs/CorporateOverview_FINAL.pdf.

66. http://www.mastercardadvisors.com/.

67. http://www.youtube.com/watch?v=3dcxQ2dvqmc.

68. http://www.youtube.com/watch?v=Q_6stXKGuHo.

69. Stuart Elliott, "MasterCard Revamps Print Ads," *The New York Times,* August 11, 2004.

70. Stuart Elliott, "MasterCard Brings `Priceless' to a Pricey Place," *The New York Times,* July 7, 2011; http://www.creditcardeducation.com/news/mastercard-offers-priceless-city-experiences.html.

71. http://newsroom.mastercard.com/press-releases/priceless-new-york-gives-mastercard-cardholders-privileged-access-to-the-citys-preeminent-experiences/.

Chapter 20

1. "Lauren Crampsie Named Worldwide Chief Marketing Officer, Ogilvie & Mather," press release, January 4, 2012, http://www.ogilvy.com/News/Press-Releases/January-2012-Lauren-Crampsie-to-be-new-Ogilvy-Mather-Worldwide-Chief-Marketing-Officer.aspx.

2. Rupal Parekh, "Women to Watch: Lauren Crampsie, Ogilvie," *Ad Age,* May 30, 2011, http://adage.com/article/special-report-women-to-watch/women-watch-lauren-crampsie-ogilvy/227761/.

3. "New Appointments Drive Growth and Multi-Channel Ideas for Ogilvy," press release, June 7, 2010, http://www.ogilvy.com/News/Press-Releases/June-2010-Creative-Marketing-and-Innovation-Appointments-at-Ogilvy-North-America.aspx.

4. "A Day in the Life of Ad Week," http://advertising.yahoo.com/photos/lauren-crampsie-1318018203-slideshow/.

5. Brian Fetherstonhaugh, "The Future of Selling," http://www.slideshare.net/OgilvyWW/the-future-of-sell.

6. "Inside the Amway Selling Machine," February 14, 2012, http://infoseekchina.blogspot.com/2012/02/inside-amway-sales-machine.html.

7. Brian Fetherstonhaugh, "The Future of Selling: It's Social," *Forbes.com,* December 3, 2010, http://www.forbes.com/2010/12/03/future-of-selling-leadership-sales-leadership-ogilvyone.html.

8. Bureau of Labor Statistics, "Employed and Unemployed Persons by Occupation," March 9, 2012, http://www.bls.gov/news.release/empsit.t13.htm.

9. This section draws from Mark W. Johnston and Greg W. Marshall, *Relationship Selling,* 3rd ed. (Burr Ridge, IL: Irwin/McGraw-Hill, 2009); Mark W. Johnston and Greg W. Marshall, *Relationship Selling and Sales Management,* 2nd ed. (Burr Ridge, IL: Irwin/McGraw-Hill, 2007).

10. Geoffrey James, "Selling Gets Complex," *Strategy+Business,* August 27, 2009; Dale Carnegie, *How to Win Friends and Influence People* (New York: Pocket, 1990); Neil Rackham, *SPIN Selling* (New York: McGraw-Hill, 1988).

11. John Fox, "What Is the Real Cost of a B2B Sales Call?" http://www.marketing-playbook.com/sales-marketing-strategy/what-is-the-real-cost-of-a-b2b-sales-call.

12. Bill Stinnett, *Think Like Your Customer* (Burr Ridge, IL: McGraw-Hill, 2004).

13. Al Jury, "The Golden Ratio of Virtual Meetings to Face-to-Face," June 19, 2011, http://virtualteamsblog.com/2011/the-golden-ratio-of-virtual-meetings-to-face-to-face/.

14. Brad Grimes, "Have Web, Don't Travel," http://pcworld.about.com/magazine/1912p030id65174.htm.

15. "Brainstorming Online," *BusinessWeek,* Fall 2005, http://www.businessweek.com/magazine/content/05_38/b3951402.htm.

16. Joe Sharkey, "On the Road—New Meetings Industry Arises After Boom and Bust," *The New York Times,* February 1, 2010.

17. Pam Baker, "Best Sales Practices: Build Lasting Relationships," *CRM Buyer,* January 27, 2009.

18. Mark W. Johnston and Greg W. Marshall, *Relationship Selling,* 2nd ed. (Burr Ridge, IL: Irwin/McGraw-Hill, 2008).

19. Paciolan, http://paciolan.com/.

20. "2012 CES Grows, Excites, and Catalyzes," January 13, 2012, http://www.cesweb.org/news/releaseDetail.asp?id=12284.

21. Steve Berkowitz, "Marketers Reshape How College Teams Sell Tickets," *USA Today,* August 5, 2011, http://www.usatoday.com/sports/college/2011-08-05-college-outsourcing-sports-ticket-sales_n.htm.

22. "Accelerating the Trend Toward Outsourcing Athletic Event Ticket Sales, Two More Universities Partner With IMG College," press release, May 31, 2011, http://www.imgworld.com/news/news/2011/may/accelerating-the-trend-toward-outsourcing-athletic.aspx.

23. IMG College, http://www.imgcollege.com/services/imgc-services .html.

24. Michael Levy and Barton A. Weitz, *Retailing Management,* 8th ed. (New York: McGraw-Hill/Irwin, 2011).

25. Christine Comaford, "Sales Stuck? Try Sticking to a Script," *BusinessWeek,* April 4, 2008.

26. Christine Comaford-Lynch, "A Bad Lead Is Worse Than No Lead at All," *BusinessWeek,* March 26, 2008.

27. Barton A. Weitz, Harish Sujan, and Mita Sujan, "Knowledge, Motivation, and Adaptive Behavior: A Framework for Improving Selling Effectiveness," *Journal of Marketing,* October 1986, pp. 174–91.

28. Robert Keller, "Handling Objections in Today's Tough Environment," *SMM,* March 30, 2009.

29. Jeremy Quittner, "The Art of the Soft Sell," *BWSSmallBiz–Sales,* October 9, 2009.

30. Ibid.; Rachel Emma Silverman, "Selling Girl Scout Cookies at the Office," *The Wall Street Journal,* February 6, 2009.

31. "B2B Sales Pitching: Why Soft Selling Works," http://bx.businessweek.com/how-to-market-your-small-business/view?url=http%3A%2F%2Fblog.verticalresponse.com%2Fverticalresponse_blog%2F2010%2F04%2Fb2b-sales-pitch-educational-selling-vs-the-hard-sell.html.

32. http://www.quotedb.com/quotes/1303.

33. Mark W. Johnston and Greg W. Marshall, *Churchill/Ford/Walker's Sales Force Management,* 9th ed. (Burr Ridge, IL: McGraw-Hill/Irwin, 2009).

34. Barbara Chai, "Social Media Add Twist to Publicity Tango for 'Evita,'" *The Wall Street Journal,* March 4, 2010, http://online.wsj.com/article/SB10001424052970203370604577261692169958110.html.

35. Liz Wolf, "Selling Via Social Network," *Star Tribune* (Twin Cities), March 15, 2012, http://www.startribune.com/business/142829525.html.

36. Fetherstonhaugh, *Forbes,* op. cit.

37. Susan Greco, "Personality Testing for Sales Recruits," *INC.,* March 1, 2009.

38. Johnston and Marshall, *Relationship Selling and Sales Management,* pp. 375–76; Johnston and Marshall, *Churchill/Ford/Walker's Sales Force Management.*

39. Rene Y. Darmon, "Where Do the Best Sales Force Profit Producers Come From?" *Journal of Personal Selling and Sales Management,* 13, no. 3 (1993), pp. 17–29.

40. Julie Chang, "Born to Sell?" *Sales and Marketing Management,* July 2003, p. 36.

41. "Mary Kay: Where's the Money?" http://www.marykay.com; http://www.Marykay.com/lsoulier; "Mary Kay Museum," www.addisontexas.net.

42. Johnston and Marshall, *Relationship Selling and Sales Management.*

43. For a discussion of common measures used to evaluate salespeople, see Johnston and Marshall, *Churchill/Ford/Walker's Sales Force Management.*

44. David H. Holtzman, "Big Business Knows Us Too Well," *BusinessWeek,* June 22, 2007.

45. Johnston and Marshall, *Churchill/Ford/Walker's Sales Force Management.*

46. "Ethical Breach," *Sales & Marketing Management,* July 2004.

47. http://www.thepharmaletter.com/file/370eb820e9e3d7b076deb176fe7fca5f/usas-budget-office-reviews-promotional-spending-for-prescription-drugs.html; http://www.plosmedicine.org/article/info:doi/10.1371/journal.pmed.0050001; Erin Stout, "Doctoring Sales," Salesandmarketing.com, May 2001; "Pushing Pills; Pharmaceuticals," *The Economist,* 366, no. 8311 (February 15, 2003), p. 65; R. Stephen Parker and Charles E. Pettijohn, "Ethical Considerations in the Use of Direct-to-Consumer Advertising and Pharmaceutical Promotions: The Impact on Pharmaceutical Sales and Physicians," *Journal of Business Ethics,* 48, no. 3 (December 2, 2003), p. 279; "Pharmaceutical Sales Ethics: New Reforms or Business as Usual?" press release, July 23, 2004, http://www.medzilla.com/press72304.html; Kate Moore and Jahi Harvey, "Drug Companies Push Pills to Doctors," *MorningJournal.com,* August 7, 2002.

48. Casey Donoho and Timothy Heinze, "The Personal Selling Ethics Scale: Revisions and Expansions for Teaching Sales Ethics" *Journal of Marketing Education* 33, no. 1 (April 2011), pp. 107–22.

49. This case was written by Jeanne Munger in conjunction with the textbook authors Dhruv Grewal and Michael Levy as the basis of class discussion rather than to illustrate either effective or ineffective marketing practice. For a discussion of common measures used to evaluate salespeople, see Johnston and Marshall, *Churchill/Ford/Walker's Sales Force Management.*

credits

name index

M

Macale, Sherilynn, EN-3n55
MacDonnell, Rhiannon, EN-2n43
MacInnis, Deborah J., EN-30n11
Madden, Normandy, EN-14n38
Madden, Steve, 163–164
Mador, M., EN-20n51
Mahajan, Vijay, EN-4n57, EN-22n64
Maher, Kris, EN-3n39
Mahidhar, Vikram, EN-31n38
Mahoney, Sarah, EN-5n59
Makarem, Suzanne C., EN-24n35
Malhotra, Naresh K., EN-16n8
Malykhina, Elena, EN-12n10
Mamet, David, 609
Manchanda, Puneet, EN-21n22
Mangleburg, Tamara, EN-16n14
Mangold, John, 142
Manion, Michael T., EN-24n30
Mariampolski, Hy, EN-18n26
Markey, Rob, EN-4n10 (Ch3), EN-6n80,
    EN-6nn101–102, EN-6n110, EN-6n112
Markos, Ereni, EN-29n36
Markus, Hazel Rose, EN-11n50
Marquis, Christopher, EN-7n26
Marshall, Greg W., EN-33n9, EN-33n18,
    EN-34n33, EN-34n38, EN-34n42,
    EN-34n43, EN-34n45, EN-34n49
Marsicano, Mario, EN-20n43
Marta, Suzanne, EN-25n27
Marter, Heather, 53
Martin, Andrew, EN-7n8, EN-9n46
Martin, Kelly D., EN-11n50
Martin, Ricky, 621
Martins, Fernando, EN-15nn56–57
Marx, Patricia, EN-29n10,
    EN-29nn37–38
Maslow, A. H., EN-11n49
Maslow, Abraham, 190
Mattioli, Dana, EN-3n39, EN-23n89
Mattiolo, _, EN-23n90
Maul, Kimberly, EN-13n34
Maxwell, Sarah, EN-27n8
Mazar, Nina, EN-26n8
Mazerov, Michael, EN-26n41
McAdam, Lowell, 478
McAlister, Leigh, EN-2nn10–11
McCarthy, E. Jerome, EN-1n11
McCarthy, Melissa, 274
McCarthy, Michael, EN-3n27
McCracken, Harry, EN-1n21, EN-18n22
McDonald, Sean, EN-6n77, EN-6n108
McDougall, Dan, EN-7n19
McGinn, Dave, EN-12n81
McIntyre, Douglas A., EN-25n3
McKay, Betsy, EN-17n41
McKenzie, Richard B., EN-25n21
McQueary, Kristen, EN-17n11
McWilliams, Jeremiah, EN-14n14
Medvedev, Dmitry, 15
Meehan, Peter, EN-7n34

Mehta, Manish, 111
Mela, Carl F., EN-21n22
Melloy, John, EN-16n20
Menghia, Catrinel, 579
Menkes, Suzy, EN-8n17
Mentzer, John T., EN-3n17
Meredith, Geoffrey E., EN-8n15, EN-8n28
Merrilees, B., EN-20n51
Messer, Benjamin L., EN-18n44
Meyers-Levy, Joan, EN-30n11
Meyvis, Tom, EN-20n38
Miao, Fred, EN-28n13
Mickey Mouse, 554
Milkman, Katherine L., EN-2n34
Miller, Arthur, 609
Miller, Bennett, EN-25n10
Miller, Claire Cain, EN-11n44, EN-23n78
Miller, D., EN-20n51
Miller, George, 136
Miller, Kerry, EN-26n43
Missoni, Gregory, 328–329
Mitra, Sabyasachi, EN-10n17
Mittal, Banwari, EN-11n48, EN-11n54,
    EN-11n61, EN-12n70, EN-16n10,
    EN-16n15
Miyazaki, A. D., EN-16n29
Miyazaki, Anthony, EN-17n8, EN-25n9
Mizik, Natalie, EN-19n30
Monroe, Kent B., EN-1n23, EN-25n7,
    EN-25n9, EN-25n18, EN-25n21,
    EN-27n14
Montana, Hannah, 554
Montes Vazques, Marcos, EN-28n26
Moon, Mark, EN-28n7
Moore, Elizabeth S., EN-7n11, EN-19n18
Moore, J., EN-30n8
Moore, Kate, EN-34n47
Moorman, Christine, EN-30n11
Morales, Andrea C., EN-10n5
Moran, Chris, EN-12n77
Moreau, C. Page, EN-16n30
Morgan, Fred W., EN-24n25
Morgan, John, EN-26n51
Morgan, Neil A., EN-19n9, EN-19n30
Morhart, Felicitas M., EN-24n31
Morin, Sylvie, EN-11n63
Morran, Chris, EN-25n26
Morris, Sarah, EN-15n58
Morris, Tom, 124n
Morrison, Kara G., EN-19n31
Morrison, Toni, 357
Morvitz, Vicki G., EN-26n8
Moss, Rick, EN-3n43
Mothersbaugh, David L., EN-8n11
Mousouli, Vasiliki, EN-7n11
Ms. Brown, 551
Mudambi, Susan, EN-4n57
Mudambi, Susan M., EN-24n35
Mueller, M. P., EN-5nn21–22
Mueller, Rene Dentiste, EN-15n57
Muhammad, 245

Mulally, Alan, 253
Muller, Eitan, EN-21n21
Mulligan, Mark, EN-28n26
Munger, Jeanne, EN-34n49
Munshi, Neil, EN-33n57
Murnighan, J. Keith, EN-26n44,
    EN-26nn47–48
Murphy, Barry, EN-6n75
Murphy, Samantha, EN-30nn58–60
Muzellec, L., EN-20n51
Muzellec, Laurent, EN-20n51
Mycoskie, Blake, 122
Myers, James, EN-11n29

N

Nachiappan, S. P., EN-28n20
Nachtmann, Heather, EN-28n20
Nadal, Rafael, 8
Nagao, Kaori, EN-24n25
Nagle, Thomas T., EN-26n6
Nagpal, Anish, EN-11n52
Nairn, Agnes C., EN-31n12
Nakata, Cheryl, EN-23n19
Nakos, George, EN-14n41
Naverniouk, Igor, EN-31n12
Naylor, Rebecca Walker, EN-11n38
Needleman, Sarah, EN-18n28
Neff, Jack, EN-14n13, EN-14n18, EN-14n48,
    EN-32n31, EN-33n54
Neijens, Peter C., EN-33n56
Nel, Deon, EN-23n18
Nelson, Horatio, 576
Netemeyer, Richard G., EN-17n8
Newman, Andrew Adam, EN-10n79,
    EN-16n20, EN-19n12, EN-21n9,
    EN-25n32, EN-31nn46–47, EN-
    31n50, EN-31n52, EN-32n31
Newman, Bruce I., EN-16n10,
    EN-16n15
Newman, Jared, EN-22n46
Newman, Nell, EN-7n34
Newman, Paul, 127
Newton, Cam, 334
Ng, Sharon, EN-19n7
Nieman, Andrew Adam, EN-18n24
Nikolaeva, Ralitza, EN-21n24
Nitzan, Irit, EN-16n23
Noga, Tracy, EN-29n36
Nolgren, Stephen, EN-6n3
Novak, David, 581
Nudd, Tim, EN-30n10

O

Oakley, James L., EN-21n24
Obama, Barack, 15, 94, 256
Obama, Michelle, 542
Obermiller, Carl, EN-33n49
O'Brien, Keith, EN-21n16
O'Connell, Vanessa, EN-7n15, EN-25n31,
    EN-27n13, EN-28n18
O'Connor, Clare, EN-20n62

O'Connor, Mary Catherine, EN-30n52
O'Donnell, Jayne, EN-12n12, EN-24n50, EN-29n41
Ogg, Erica, EN-21n31
O'Leary, Noreen, EN-23n79
Oliver, Jamie, 518
Oliver, Jay, 567–569
Olsen, Ashley, 176
Olson, Carrie, 459
Olson, Elizabeth, EN-2nn39–40, EN-19n4, EN-19n5
Olson, Eric, 459
Olson, Jerry C., EN-10n6, EN-11n48, EN-11n54, EN-11n61, EN-12n70, EN-16n10, EN-16n15
O'Meara, Bethany, 630
Oppenheim, J. M., EN-8n43
Ostrow, Adam, EN-29n35
O'Sullivan, Arthur, EN-14n10
Ottman, Jacquelyn A., EN-9n55
Owens, Simon, EN-15n65
Oz, Mehmet, 357

P

Palmatier, Robert W., EN-2n32, EN-28n13
Palmer, Keke, 38
Panettiere, Hayden, 12
Parasuraman, A., 316n, 402n, EN-17n6, EN-17n9, EN-18n43, EN-23n18, EN-23n19, EN-24n45
Parekh, Rupal, EN-33n2
Park, Jongwon, EN-20n38
Parker, Alan, EN-30n6
Parker, R. Stephen, EN-34n47
Parker, Sarah Jessica, 176, 195
Parsons, Russel, EN-3n31
Passel, Jeffrey S., EN-9n38
Patton, Leslie, EN-2n54
Patton, Phil, EN-21n14
Paul, Pamela, EN-8n17
Pauly, Daniel, EN-6n2
Pauwels, Koen, EN-10n7, EN-21n13, EN-26n40
Payton, Susan, EN-4n7(Ch3), EN-27n11
Peachy, Kevin, EN-7n6
Peers, Martin, EN-9n63
Peloza, John, EN-32n29
Penenberg, Adam, EN-18n50
Penn, Mark, EN-18n48
Penz, Bernard, EN-28n25
Peres, Renana, EN-21n21
Perez, Sarah, EN-22n36
Perez, Steve, EN-14n10
Perot, Carolyn, EN-8n32
Perry, Katy, 578
Pessin, Jaime Levy, EN-1n6, EN-1n20
Peter, J. Paul, EN-10n6, EN-11n48, EN-11n54, EN-11n61, EN-12n70, EN-16n10, EN-16n15
Peteraf, Margaret A., EN-4n62

Petersen, A., EN-18n1
Petersen, J. Andrew, EN-2nn10–11, EN-18n1
Pettijohn, Charles E., EN-34n47
Petty, Ross D., EN-27n30
Pfeiffer, Markus, EN-32n13
Phelps, Glenn, EN-18n44
Pilon, Mary, EN-26n1
Pine, B. Joseph, EN-16n28
Pirovano, Tom, EN-9n37
Pitt, Brad, 427
Pitt, Leyland, EN-23n18
Pittman, Simon, EN-19n8
Plank, Kevin, 333
Podoshen, Jeffrey S., EN-24n35
Poggi, Jeanine, EN-16n9
Pogue, David, EN-23nn84–85, EN-23n92
Polamalu, Troy, 295
Pope, Barbara K., EN-26n40
Popick, Janine, EN-23n4
Porterfield, Amy, EN-5n58
Prabhu, Jaideep C., EN-21n22
Prasad, Naghi, EN-26n49
Price, Rob, EN-27n24, EN-29n36, EN-33n52
Pritzl, Rudolf, EN-12n65, EN-17n16
Puccinelli, Nancy, EN-29n36
Puck, Wolfgang, 517
Pujari, Devashish, EN-22n44
Pune, Jyoti Thottam, EN-22n60

Q

Qu, Riliang, EN-20n45
Quelch, John A., EN-19n7
Quinn, Laura S., EN-5n55
Quintos, Karen, 111
Quittner, Jeremy, EN-33nn29–30

R

Raghubir, Priya, EN-27n22, EN-29n36
Rainnie, Al, EN-24n30
Rajaratnam, Dan, EN-15n57
Raman, Sandhya, EN-29n35
Ramani, G., EN-18n1
Ramos Calamonte, José Antonio, EN-28n26
Rampell, Catherine, EN-10n73, EN-25n22
Rangaswamy, Arvind, EN-21n25
Rao, A. R., EN-26n37
Rao, Ram, EN-26n33
Rappaport, Alfred, EN-3n23
Ratchford, Brian, EN-26n40
Ravishanker, Nalini, EN-18n1
Ray, Rachael, 357
Ray, Ramon, EN-23n10
Raynor, Michael E., EN-21n23
Reda, Susan, EN-29n46
Reddy, Srinivas K., EN-20n40
Redman, Russell, EN-29n28
Reeves, Daniel, EN-26n49

Reeves, Randy, EN-26n40
Rego, Lopo L., EN-19n9, EN-19n30
Reibstein, David J., EN-2nn10–11
Reid, Leonard N., EN-32n38
Reidy, Chris, EN-6n4
Reinartz, Werner, EN-1n14, EN-18n1
Reingold, Jennifer, EN-17n20
Reinhardt, Uwe E., EN-27n33
Reisinger, Don, EN-21n18
Reitz, Stephanie, EN-12n17, EN-12n21
Reston, Ana Carolina, 558
Reynaud, Jasmine, 53
Reynolds, Christopher, EN-24n40
Richard, Joe, 325n
Richards, Jef I., EN-31n10, EN-32n44
Richards, Joe, EN-18n52, EN-18n53
Richtel, Matt, EN-8n24
Rideout, Victoria J., EN-7n11
Riley, Nicola, EN-20n45
Rinallo, Diego, EN-33n49
Rindfleish, Aric, EN-26n40
Rivera, Mariano, 450
Roan, Shari, EN-21n4
Roberts, Daniel, EN-19nn1–2
Roberts, Julia, 591
Rodgers, Everett M., 369n
Rodriguez, Alex, 12
Rodriguez, Mia, 142
Rodríguez-Escudero, Ana I., EN-22n44
Rogers, Ian, EN-16n27
Roggeveen, Anne L., EN-1n24, EN-23n19, EN-24n44, EN-24n45, EN-24nn46–47, EN-24n49, EN-25n7, EN-27n15
Roggio, Armando, EN-23n3
Rohter, Larry, EN-15n60
Roll, Oliver, EN-25n12
Romjin, Rebecca, 581
Rooney, Jennifer, EN-23n77
Roosevelt, Theodore, 129
Rose, Derrick, 30, 578
Rosen, Judith, EN-26n35
Rosenberg, Tina, EN-2nn45–46
Rosenbloom, Stephanie, EN-7n20
Rosencrance, L., EN-16n29
Rossum, Emmy, 84
Rotfeld, Herbert Jack, EN-32n42
Rubin, Courtney, EN-25n63
Rucker, Derek D., EN-10n27
Rudelius, William, EN-3n50, EN-4nn3–4(App2A)
Rush, Geoffrey, 192
Ryan, Tom, EN-5n47

S

Saad, Lydia, EN-12n73
Sabatté, Micheline, EN-31n38
Sabbatini, Roberto, EN-15nn56–57
Sack, Kevin, EN-25n30
Salter, Chuck, EN-3n40
Samaha, Stephen A., EN-2n32

company index

subject index